1,000,000 Books

are available to read at

Forgotten Books

www.ForgottenBooks.com

Read online
Download PDF
Purchase in print

ISBN 978-0-266-09643-6
PIBN 10947409

This book is a reproduction of an important historical work. Forgotten Books uses state-of-the-art technology to digitally reconstruct the work, preserving the original format whilst repairing imperfections present in the aged copy. In rare cases, an imperfection in the original, such as a blemish or missing page, may be replicated in our edition. We do, however, repair the vast majority of imperfections successfully; any imperfections that remain are intentionally left to preserve the state of such historical works.

Forgotten Books is a registered trademark of FB &c Ltd.
Copyright © 2018 FB &c Ltd.
FB &c Ltd, Dalton House, 60 Windsor Avenue, London, SW19 2RR.
Company number 08720141. Registered in England and Wales.

For support please visit www.forgottenbooks.com

1 MONTH OF FREE READING

at

www.ForgottenBooks.com

By purchasing this book you are eligible for one month membership to ForgottenBooks.com, giving you unlimited access to our entire collection of over 1,000,000 titles via our web site and mobile apps.

To claim your free month visit: www.forgottenbooks.com/free947409

* Offer is valid for 45 days from date of purchase. Terms and conditions apply.

English
Français
Deutsche
Italiano
Español
Português

www.forgottenbooks.com

Mythology Photography **Fiction** Fishing Christianity **Art** Cooking Essays Buddhism Freemasonry Medicine **Biology** Music **Ancient Egypt** Evolution Carpentry Physics Dance Geology **Mathematics** Fitness Shakespeare **Folklore** Yoga Marketing **Confidence** Immortality Biographies Poetry **Psychology** Witchcraft Electronics Chemistry History **Law** Accounting **Philosophy** Anthropology Alchemy Drama Quantum Mechanics Atheism Sexual Health **Ancient History Entrepreneurship** Languages Sport Paleontology Needlework Islam **Metaphysics** Investment Archaeology Parenting Statistics Criminology **Motivational**

Z
1037 Wisconsin.
W75 Dept. of
public in-

Southern Branch
of the
University of California
Los Angeles

Form L-1

Z
1037
W75

This book is DUE on the last date stamped below.

SOUTHERN BRANCH,
UNIVERSITY OF CALIFORNIA,
LIBRARY,
LOS ANGELES, CALIF.

THE LIBRARY
OF
THE UNIVERSITY
OF CALIFORNIA
LOS ANGELES

With the Compliments of

L. D. HARVEY,

State Superintendent.

Corner of High School Library, Sheboygan.   H. F. LEVERENZ, Superintendent.

LIST OF BOOKS

FOR

HIGH SCHOOL LIBRARIES

OF THE

STATE OF WISCONSIN.

ISSUED BY THE STATE SUPERINTENDENT,

L. D. Harvey

COMPILED, CLASSIFIED, AND ANNOTATED BY THE LIBRARIAN

ANNE H. McNEIL.

NOVEMBER, 1902.

MADISON
DEMOCRAT PRINTING COMPANY, STATE PRINTER
1902

N. B.—To secure prompt attention, all correspondence relating to library matters other than the ordering of books, should be addressed to the State Superintendent.

LIST OF BOOKS FOR HIGH SCHOOLS.

The following list contains what are believed to be the most representative and best books for High School libraries. Only such books have been placed on the list as are believed to be of interest and value to average high school pupils. The list is necessarily large so as to cover different interests, lines of reading, and courses of study, as well as to meet the local conditions which govern largely the selection of books. Books which are especially for older pupils or suitable especially for younger ones are indicated in the notes.

In general it is best to choose books that are certain to be within the capacity of the greater number of pupils. It is better to err on the side of selecting books that are too simple, than that of selecting those which will be of very little service because they are too difficult. Make the selection so as to cover as wide a range of subjects as possible and furnish books for all classes.

Books which are marked # should not be purchased until the reference library is of fairly good size. In some cases books so marked are expensive, and in others they are not so necessary to a working library as other books on the list.

ARRANGEMENT AND CLASSIFICATION OF BOOKS.

The books on this list have been arranged by subject and classified according to a simple scheme of classification taken from that prepared by C. A. Cutter. This scheme is the same that was used in the library section of the High School meetings, held during the winter of 1901 and 1902.

Schools that have not classified their libraries can do so very easily by labeling the books on the back and placing this classification on the label. The upper line of the classification refers to the subject of the book. The lower line is taken from the "Cutter decimal author table," a scheme which gives to each work its own exclusive book number, so contrived that the books stand on the shelves alphabeted by authors, under each subject.

AUTHOR AND TITLE CARD INDEX.

A complete *title card index* to the books in the library may be made by obtaining duplicate copies of this list, cutting out the entries, mounting them on catalog cards, and arranging the cards in alphabetical order by title.

An *author card index* may be made in the same manner by mounting another copy of these entries adding the author's name, inverted, on the top line of the card, and arranging the cards in alphabetical order by author.

These two indexes may be kept separately or arranged together in one alphabetical order by first lines.

GRADING.

The books have not been graded for each year, for what a pupil wants to read depends upon what he has read, what he is interested in, and the work the teacher does with him, rather than upon the number of years he has attended school.

NOTES ON BOOKS.

The notes on the books are made from the standpoint of the teacher, and to aid the teacher in directing the reading of the pupils. The educational and ethical values are pointed out, and the things which are apt to interest pupils are indicated.

ORDERING AND SHIPPING.

1. This list and the Township List constitute the High School list for 1902, and books selected for high schools in cities of the fourth class should not be selected from any other lists. Special

LIST OF BOOKS FOR HIGH SCHOOL LIBRARIES.

notice is called to that portion of the law which provides that all books purchased with the library funds *must* be selected from the list prepared by the State Superintendent. Though this list is intended primarily for High Schools coming under the township Library Law, all High Schools in the state will find it valuable.

2. Des Forges & Co., Milwaukee, Wis., will furnish the books this year, and will supply them at the prices given in the second column in this list. They will make no charges for boxing and cartage.

3. Make out all orders on regular order blanks which are furnished by the State Superintendent. The blanks furnished this year contain space for ordering books as second choice. Experience has shown that it is better not to make a second choice. *Order the books wanted and Des Forges & Co. will furnish them as ordered.* In case any books are shipped which are not ordered, it will be due to a mistake of the shipping clerk. Such books should be promptly returned to Des Forges & Co., at their expense, and their attention called to the error. They will correct the mistake promptly without further expense to the party ordering.

4. Give all directions for shipping *carefully and plainly;* the city for which the books are ordered, the line of railway, or by what express company shipment is to be made. Carelessness in these matters is sure to cause much trouble and unnecessary delay in getting books.

5. According to law the books may be purchased any time between the first days of May and September, but it is better to buy as early as possible so that classes about to be graduated may have the use of the books before leaving school, and it is desirable to have the books on hand at the beginning of the school year.

6. Charge freight, express, postage and exchange to the library fund.

7. Keep a duplicate of the order, and see that the books re-

ceived are those described in this list. *It is illegal to purchase with the library fund books or editions not included in these lists.*

8. Each superintendent should have this list of books on file in his own office and one in the school library.

9. Labels, order blanks, a blank book for keeping the clerk's record of the books, and blank loan record books for the use of librarians will be furnished by the State Superintendent upon application of the city or village clerk, or secretary of the school board.

School officers, town clerks, and teachers may procure single volumes or a few copies by adding ten per cent. of the list price (to cover postage) to the prices given in the second column.

In the preparation of this list, valuable assistance has been given by high school principals and by normal school and university professors, whose acquaintance with and experience in the use of reference books render their opinions valuable. Their cheerful response to requests for suggestions and criticisms is gratefully acknowledged.

L. D. HARVEY,
State Superintendent.

ABBREVIATIONS.

Anon.	Anonymous	o	octavo
arr.	arranged	pt.	part
Bost.	Boston	por.	portraits
bds.	boards	pseud.	pseudonym
capt.	captain	pub.	publisher
Chic.	Chicago.	Q	quarto
cl.	cloth	rev.	revised
col.	collection	S	16 mo.
co.	company	Ser.	series.
comp.	compiler.	S. A.	South America
c.	copyright	sq.	square
D	duodecimo	T	24 mo.
ed.	editor, edition.	trans.	translated, translator
enl.	enlarged	Tt	32 mo.
F	folio	U. S.	United States
Fe	48 mo.	v., vol.	volume.
il.	illustrated	[ ]	numbers inclosed refer to numbers in High School list of 1900.
jr.	junior		
lib.	library		
lit.	literature	——	to and including
N. Y.	New York	. . .	matter omitted.
N. A.	North America	#	books so marked should not be purchased by the smaller libraries.
n. d.	no date of publication		
obl.	oblong		

LIST OF BOOKS FOR HIGH SCHOOL LIBRARIES.

ETHICS, MYTHOLOGY AND FOLK-LORE.

	List price.	Price to schools.

B
A 14 pr

1. **Principles of logic.** Herbert Austin Aikins. N. Y., Henry Holt & Co., 1902. 489 p. D. cl.......... $1.50 $1.35

A good elementary reference book in logic for the use of teachers.

B
B 63 su

2. [704.] **Successward:** a young man's book for young men. Edward Bok. N. Y., Doubleday & McClure Co., 1899. 182 p. T. cl........................ .50   .33

Contents: A correct knowledge of himself; What, really, is success? The young man in business; His social life and amusements; In matters of dress; His religious life, etc.

B
B 87 a

3. **Age of chivalry.** Thomas Bulfinch. N. Y., Thomas Y. Crowell & Co., c1901. 329 p. D. cl............... .60   .40

These tales give excellent pictures of the manners and customs of the age of chivalry.

B
B 87 ag

4. **Age of fable: or, Beauties of mythology.** Thomas Bulfinch. N. Y., Thomas Y. Crowell & Co., n. d. 460 p. D. cl...................................... .60   .40

For reference: Stories of pagan mythology for the reader of English literature who wishes to comprehend the allusions so frequently made by public speakers, essayists and poets. Many pupils will enjoy these stories for library reading.

B
B 87 le

5. **Legends of Charlemagne: or, The romance of the Middle ages.** Thomas Bulfinch. N. Y., Thomas Y. Crowell & Co., c1901. 271 p. D. cl .... .60   .40

This volume will acquaint its readers with the subjects of the works of the great poets of Italy. Valuable for reference in the study of literature.

LIST OF BOOKS FOR HIGH SCHOOL LIBRARIES.

B
―――
F 54 my
                                  List Price to
                                price. schools.

6. [314.] **Myths and Myth Makers.** John Fiske. Bost., Houghton, Mifflin & Co., 1895. 251 p. il. D. cl. 2.00 1.28

    Explains the origin and gives something of the history and development of myths. This book may be used as a book of essays by the literature class.

B
―――
G 25 cl

7. **Classic myths in English literature.** Charles Mills Gayley, ed. Bost., Ginn & Co., 1902. 540 p. D. cl. 1.50 1.28

    Based chiefly on Bulfinch's "Age of Fable." A systematized presentation and interpretation of the myths that have most influenced English literature.

B
―――
G 93 ls

8. **Legends of Switzerland.** Helene A. Guerber. N. Y., Dodd, Mead & Co., 1899. 310 p. il. D. cl. ...... 1.50 .98

    These legends will enable the reader to gain a clearer insight into the life and thoughts of the Swiss people. An excellent book for library reading.

B
―――
G 93 lm

9. [317.] **Legends of the middle ages** narrated with special reference to literature and art. H. A. Guerber. N. Y., American Book Company, 1896. 340 p. il. D. cl. 1.50 1.28

    In the three foregoing volumes Miss Guerber has given us in a complete and entertaining way the most noted myths and legends.

B
―――
G 93 lr

10. **Legends of the Rhine.** Héléne A. Guerber. N. Y., A. S. Barnes & Co., c1895. 350 p. il. D. Ed. 4. cl. 1.50 1.35

    "This book is intended as a contribution to the study of Folklore, and as a Legendary Guide to the Rhine. The tales have been gathered from many sources, and while *all* the Rhine traditions are not recorded here. the principal ones have been given."—*Preface.*
    Excellent for library reading.

B
―――
G 93 mg

11. [315.] **Myths of Greece and Rome.** H. A. Guerber. N. Y., American Book Company, 1893. 428 p. il. D. cl. 1.50 1.28

	List price.	Price to schools.

B
G 93 mn

12. [316.] **Myths of Northern lands.** H. A. Guerber. N. Y., American Book Company, 1895. 319 p. il. D. cl. 1.50 1.28

In the three foregoing volumes the author has given in a complete and entertaining way the most noted myths and legends.

B
M 31 fe

13. [705.] **Few thoughts for a young man.** Horace Mann. Bost., Lee & Shepard. 91 p. T. cl........... .25 .18

Helpful suggestions for good living by a great man.

B
M 33 su

14. [703.] **Success: a book of ideals, helps, and examples for all desiring to make the most of life.** Orison Swett Marden. Boston, W. A. Wilde & Co., 1897. 347 p. il. D. cl. .... 1.25 .75

The book is filled with suggestive material, fresh living truths, inspiration, and encouragement.

B
M 92 on

15. [706.] **On the threshold.** Theodore T. Munger. Bost., Houghton, Mifflin & Co., 1898. 246 p. D. cl. .... 1.00 .65

Some of the main principles that enter into life as it is now opening before young men in this country. Some of the subjects are, purpose, friends, manners, thrift, self-reliance, health, reading, amusements, purity, and faith.

B
W 72 wh

16. [702.] **What shall our boys do for a living?** C. F. Wingate. N. Y., Doubleday & McClure Co., 1898. 287 p. D. cl. .... 1.00 .65

A practical and suggestive book.

LIST OF BOOKS FOR HIGH SCHOOL LIBRARIES. 11

CHURCH HISTORY.

D
———
F 53 re

List Price to
price. schools.

#17. **Reformation.** George P. Fisher. N. Y., Charles
Scribner's Sons, 1902. 620 p. D. cl............ 2.50 1.64

A brief account of the origin and nature, and the principal facts and characters of the Reformation.

Contents: Introduction: The general character of the reformation; Rise of the papal heirarchy and its decline through the centralization of nations; Special causes and omens of an ecclesiastical revolution prior to the sixteenth century; Luther and the German reformation to the diet of Augsburg, 1530; German reformation to the peace of Augsburg; Zwingle and the Swiss (German) reformation; Reformation in the Scandinavian kingdoms, in the Slavonic nations, and in Hungary; John Calvin and the Genevan reformation; Reformation in France; Reformation in the Netherlands; Reformation in England and Scotland; Reformation in Italy and Spain; the counter-reformation in the Roman Catholic church; Struggle of protestantism in the seventeenth century; Protestant theology; Constitution of the protestant churches and their relation to the civil authority; Relation of protestantism to culture and civilization.

BIOGRAPHY.

Grouping great events around the lives of great men who may become real persons to the pupils is one of the best ways to teach history. That a man lived and died at a certain time is not so important as what kind of a man he was, what he did, and what great events he took part in. The pupils are in the youth time of life, and the heroes who fire their imagination will often become their ideals of all that is noble and good.

E
———
Ad 1 ad

18. **Charles Francis Adams.** Charles Francis Adams, Jr.
Bost., Houghton, Mifflin & Co., 1900. 426 p. D.
(American Statesmen ser.) cl. .... 1.25 .82

A simple, direct narration, in detail, of the life of a man who lived during a critical period of the United States history.

Contents: Birth and education, 1 11; early life, 12 41; Massachusetts legislature, 42-49; "Boston whig," 50 80; Free-soil party, 81 91; ebb of the tide, 92-101; ante-bellum congress, 103-116; awakening, 117 146; proclamation of belligerency, 147 177; Seward's foreign war panacea, 178-199; treaty of Paris, 200 209;

12   LIST OF BOOKS FOR HIGH SCHOOL LIBRARIES.

                                                          List   Price to
                                                          price. schools.
Trent affair, 210-239; bout with the premier, 240-260; cotton famine, 261-277; crisis of recognition, 278-290; emancipation proclamation, 291-305; Alabama and the "Laird rams," 306-344; years of
fruition, 345-376; Geneva arbitration, 377-397; closing years,
398-402.

E
———
Ad 12 mo
  19. **John Adams.** John T. Morse, *Jr.* Bost., Houghton,
      Mifflin & Co., 1889. 337 p. D. (American states-
      men series.) cl................................ 1.25   .82
  Portions of the biography will be valuable for reference work
on the history of the Revolutionary period.
  Contents: Youth, 1-16; at the bar, 17-49; first congress, 50-81;
second session of congress, 82-103; independence, 104-129; after
independence, 130-146; first foreign mission, 147-155; second foreign mission, 156-197; treaty of peace, 198-240; vice-presidency,
241-264; presidency, 265-310; breaking up, 311-330.

E
———
Ad 13 mo
  20. **John Quincy Adams.** John T. Morse, *Jr.* Bost.,
      Houghton, Mifflin & Co., 1886. 315 p. D.
      (American Statesmen ser.) Ed. 11. cl......... 1.25   .82
  Contents: Youth and diplomacy, 1-101; secretary of state and
president, 102-225; house of representatives, 226-309.
  References: Impressment of American seamen, 43-46; treaty
of Ghent, 77-98; Monroe doctrine, 130-37; suppression of slave
trade, 136-40; slavery, 226-309; "Gag" rule, 251-52, 261-62, 306-
308.

E
———
Ad 14 ho
  21. **Samuel Adams.** James K. Hosmer. Bost., Hough-
      ton, Mifflin & Co., 1887. 442 p. D. (American
      Statesmen ser.) Ed. 5. cl. .... 1.25   .82
  An interesting account of the most important events in Mr.
Adam's career. Valuable for reference in studying the pre-revolutionary period.
  Contents: Youth and his surroundings, 1-20; pre-revolutionary
struggle, 21-32; writs of assistance, 33-45; Massachusetts assembly, 46-61; parliamentary representation and the Massachusetts
resolves, 62-77; stamp act before England, 78-89; true sentiments
of America, 90-108; arrival of the troops, 109-125; recall of Bernard, 126-144; non-importation agreements, 145-159; Sam Adams
regiments, 160-182; controversy as to royal instructions, 183-195;
committee of correspondence, 196-206; controversy as to parliamentary authority, 207-219; Hutchinson letters, 220-242; tea-
party, 243-256; Hutchinson and the tories, 257-288; preparations
for the first congress, 289-312; Lexington, 313-331; declaration of
independence, 332-350; character and service of Samuel Adams,
351-375; closing years, 376-417; town meeting today, 418-431.

E
Ag 1 ho
22. [265.] **Louis Agassiz,** his life and work. Charles
Frederick Holder. N. Y., G. P. Putnam's Sons,
1893. 327 p. il. D. (Leaders in science ser.)
cl. .... 1.50 .98

List price: 1.50 Price to schools: .98

The boy who is interested in science will enjoy this book.

E
Al 1 ch
23. [266.] **Louise M. Alcott:** life, letters and journals.
Ed. by E. D. Cheney. Bost., Little, Brown & Co.,
1898. D. cl. .... 1.50 .98

Will interest the pupils who have read her books.

E
Al 2 be
24. **Story of King Alfred.** Walter Besant. N. Y., D. Appleton & Co., 1901. 187 p. il. S. cl. (Lib. of
useful stories ser.) .... .35 .31

A short, well written life of King Alfred.
Contents: Author's design; Authorities; Genealogy of Alfred and his descendants; England in the ninth century; Childhood and education; Alfred's wars; Alfred in religion; Alfred as law-giver; Alfred as educator; Alfred as writer; Summary of the reign; Death of the king.

E
Al 2 hu
25. **Alfred the Great.** Thomas Hughes. Bost., Houghton,
Mifflin & Co., n. d. 324 p. D. cl. .... 1.00 .65

The life of a typical English king whose life and times are of most absorbing interest. The Saxon king is a true representative of the nation in contrast to Cæsar, so nearly his contemporary, whose aim was to weld together all nations and tribes in one lifeless empire under his own sceptre. Valuable for reference in history and literature and a good book for the biography class in library reading.

E
Al 5 h
26. [267.] **Ethan Allen:** the Robin Hood of Vermont.
Henry Hall. N. Y., D. Appleton & Co., 1892. 207
p. D. cl. .... 1.00 .65

A good biography of one of our heroes, whose life is apt to interest young people

E
B 13 ch

27. **Bacon.** Richard W. Church. N. Y., Harper & Bros., 1902. 214 p. (English men of letters series.) D. cl. .... .75 .49

E
B 44 r

28. [268.] **Thomas Hart Benton.** Theodore Roosevelt. Bost., Houghton, Mifflin & Co., 1889. 372 p. D. (American statesmen ser.) cl. .... 1.25 .82

Life of Benton, showing the part he took in public affairs.

E
B 54 l

29. [269.] **Prince Bismarck.** Charles Lowe. Bost., Little, Brown & Co., 1899. 245 p. por. D. cl. .... 1.00 .65

For older pupils.

E
B 54 po

30. **Conversations with Prince Bismarck.** Heinrich von Poschinger. English ed., *ed.* with an introduction by Sidney Whitman. N. Y., Harper & Bros., 1900. 299 p. por. D. cl. .... 1.50 .98

For reference in history.
Contents: Chancellor in the Franco-German war; Further conversations and interviews; Bismarck and his master; Bismarck on politics; Commerce and colonies; Bismarck and his fellow-workers; In lighter vein.

E
B 64 ab

31. **Daniel Boone: pioneer of Kentucky.** John S. C. Abbott. N. Y., Dodd, Mead & Co., c1900. 331 p. D. cl. .... .75 .67

The life of Boone is full of dramatic situations, and will appeal to the boy or girl who enjoys a story of adventure. An excellent book for library reading and for reference in the study of colonial history.
Contents: Discovery and settlement of America; Trials of the colonists; Louisiana, and its eventful history; Camp life beyond the Alleghanies; Indian warfare; Sufferings of the pioneers; Life in the wilderness; Captivity and flight; Victories and defeats; British allies; Kentucky as a state; Adventures romantic and perilous; New home in Missouri.

LIST OF BOOKS FOR HIGH SCHOOL LIBRARIES. 15

	List price.	Price to schools.

E
———
B 69 bo

32. **Goethe and Schiller:** their lives and works including a commentary on Goethe's Faust. Hjalmar H. Boyesen. N. Y., C: Scribner's Sons, 1901. 424 p. D. Ed. 9. cl. 2.00 1.30

Excellent for use of advanced German classes. The book contains many notes and observations on the works of both authors.

E
———
B 79 bo

33. [271.] **Phillips Brooks.** M. A. DeWolfe Howe. Bost., Small, Maynard & Co., 1899. 120 p. por. T. (Beacon biographies.) cl. .... .75 .67

E
———
B 81 ch

34. [272.] **John Brown.** Joseph Edgar Chamberlain. Bost., Small, Maynard & Co., 1899. 138 p. por. T. (Beacon biographies.) cl .... .75 .67

E
———
B 93 sh

35. **Robert Burns.** Principal Sharp. N. Y., Harper & Bros., 1900. 205 p. (English men of letters series.) D. cl. .... .75 .49

E
———
B 94 me

36. [273.] **Aaron Burr.** Henry Childs Merwin. Bost., Small, Maynard & Co., 1899. 150 p. por. T. (Beacon biographies.) cl. .... .75 .67

The Beacon biographies are short, well written and most interesting.

E
———
C 11 ab

37. **Julius Caesar.** Jacob Abbott. N. Y., Harper & Bros., 1901. 278 p. il. S. cl. .... .50 .33

This life of Cæsar will be interesting for the biography class in library reading.

Contents. Marius and Sylla, 13–34; Cæsar's early years, 35–57; advancement to the consulship, 58–81; Conquest of Gaul, 82–106; Pompey, 107–128; crossing the Rubicon, 129–153; battle of Pharsalia, 154–170; flight and death of Pompey, 171–190; Cæsar in Egypt, 193–212; Cæsar imperator, 213–234; conspiracy, 235–251; assassination, 255–278.

E
C 11 fo

　　　　　　　　　　　　　　　　　　　　　　　　List　Price to
　　　　　　　　　　　　　　　　　　　　　　　　price. schools.

38. [274.] **Julius Caesar**: and the foundation of the Roman
　　　imperial system. William Warde Fowler. N. Y.,
　　　G. P. Putnam's Sons, 1900. 389 p. il. maps. D.
　　　cl. (Heroes of the nations series.) ....　1.50　.98

　　"In this volume I have tried to meet the wishes of the publishers, by explaining to those who are comparatively unfamiliar with classical antiquity the place which Cæsar occupies in the history of the world. He was not the founder, much less was he the organizer of the Roman Empire; yet his life marks a great change in European history. I have tried to show (and have done my best to express on the title-page) what this change means, how it was in part the result of pre-existing tendencies, and was due in part to Cæsar's extraordinary force of will and intellect. . . .

　　The tendencies of the age, and the growth of Cæsar's character, are the two leading themes of the book; and I have endeavoured to treat these as far as possible by the help of contemporary evidence, and chiefly of Cæsar's own writings and those of Cicero."—*From Author's Preface.*

　　Contents: Birth, family and education; Boyhood during the civil war; Early life under the Sullan government; Quaestorship, and supremacy of Pompeius; Aedileship, and conspiracy of Catilina; Praetorship, and formation of triumvirate; Cæsar's first consulship; Defense of Transalpine Gaul; Defeat of the Germans; Conquest of Northwestern Gaul; Conference at Lucca, and campaign in Brittany; Invasions of Germany and Britain; Gallic rebellions; Pacification of Gaul and outbreak of civil war; Civil war in Italy and Spain; Dyrrhachium and Pharsalus; Cæsar's last wars; Caesar's use of absolute power.

E
C 11 fr

39. **Caesar**: a sketch. James Anthony Froude. N. Y.,
　　　C: Scribner's Sons, 1900. 550 p. map. D. cl.　1.50　.98

　　A book of great value to the student of Roman history. Froude evokes a strong plea in favor of Cæsar and in a few words draws one of the best short pictures of Cicero, leading his readers to despise Cicero's weak character. The author's point of view is about the same as Mommsen's.

　　References: The Gracchi, 23–34; Jugurtha, 35–40; Marius, 41–45; Cimbri and Teutons, 46–54; revolution from republic to empire; 24–550; Sylla, 66–98; Cataline conspiracy, 147–61; Druids, 216–19; Helvetii, 221–31; Pompey in Spain, 400–13; conspiracies against Cæsar, 493–514; character of Cicero, 528–31; character of Cæsar, 532–50.

E
C 12 ho

40. [275.] **John C. Calhoun**. Dr. Hermann von Holst.
　　　Bost., Houghton, Mifflin & Co., 1899. 374 p. D.
　　　cl. (American statesmen series.) ....　1.25　.82

　　The part played by Calhoun in the conflict between North and South puts him into the very first rank of the men who have acted

LIST OF BOOKS FOR HIGH SCHOOL LIBRARIES. 17

                  List Price to
                  price. schools.

on the political stage of the United States. From 1830 to the time of his death he was the very impersonation of the slavery question.

Contents: Youth; House of representatives; Secretary of war; Vice-president; Senate; Slavery; Under Van Buren; Texas; Oregon and the Mexican war.

E
―――
C 19 ni

41. **Thomas Carlyle.** John Nichol. N. Y., Harper & Bros., 1901. 257 p. (English men of letters series.) D. cl. .... .75 .49

E
―――
C 35 se

42. **Samuel De Champlain.** Henry Dwight Sedgwick, *Jr.* Bost., Houghton, Mifflin & Co., 1902. 126 p. (Riverside biographical series.) S. cl. .... .65 .58

 Mr. Sedgwick writes of the great French explorer and colonizer with keen understanding of French life and character, and with abundant knowledge of the whole period of Champlain's career. He has, consequently, painted this knight of France with rare vividness, making his adventures, his statesmanship, his daring, and his prudence as clear to us as the qualities of men of our time.

E
―――
C 39 wa

43. **Chaucer:** Adolphus William Ward. N. Y., Harper & Bros., 1901. 198 p. (English men of letters series.) D. cl. .... .75 .49

E
―――
C 42 ch

44. [280.] **Frederick Douglas.** Charles W. Chesnutt. Bost., Small, Maynard & Co., 1899. 141 p. por. T. (Beacon biographies.) cl. .... .75 .67

Brief and interesting.

E
―――
C 46 ph

45. **Story of Jesus Christ:** an interpretation. Elizabeth Stuart Phelps. Bost., Houghton, Mifflin & Co., 1901. 413 p. D. cl. .... 1.25 .82

 This remarkable book is not an ordinary biography, but—as one of its critics describes it—is the story of Jesus Christ told after the method of the novelist. It is not, therefore, fiction; rather is it a dramatic, passionate, enthusiastic setting forth of the facts and the spirit of the life of Jesus Christ with the imaginative truthfulness of a profound sympathy, and an uncommon literary power and grace.

B
―――
C 57 fr

46. **Mill boy of the slashes**: young folks' life of Henry Clay. John Frost. Bost., Lee & Shepard, c1887. 240 p. il. D. cl. .... 1.00 .65

"Mr. Clay's history is the history of the legislation of the United States; and we have labored so to present it, that our young readers may be introduced to a portion of the annals of their country, which is not usually embraced in brief and compendious narratives. His personal history, particularly that of his early years, is an incentive to labor and diligence; for what he accomplished, was won with less educational advantages than most of our young readers possess."—*Preface.*

B
―――
C 57 sc

47. [276.] **Life of Henry Clay.** Carl Schurz. Bost., Houghton, Mifflin & Co., 1888. 2 vols. 383; 424 p. D. (American statesmen series.) cl. each .... 1.25 .82

The public life of a man who played an important part in our national history "not, indeed, as an originator of ideas and systems, but as an arranger of measures, and as a leader of political forces."

B
―――
C 72 ad

48. **Christopher Columbus**: his life and his work. Charles Kendall Adams. N. Y., Dodd, Mead & Co., 1892. 261 p. por. D. cl. .... 1.00 .65

B
―――
C 72 se

49. [277.] **Story of Columbus.** Elizabeth Eggleston Seelye. Edward Eggleston, *ed.* N. Y., D. Appleton & Co., 1892. 303 p. il. D. cl. 1.75 1.12

For the younger pupils.

B
―――
C 78 ra

50. **Peter Cooper.** Rossiter W. Raymond. Bost., Houghton, Mifflin & Co., c1901. 109 p. (Riverside biographical series.) S. cl. .... .65 .58

Contents: Ancestry; Boyhood and youth; Business ventures; Inventions; Tom Thumb; Municipal affairs; Cooper Union for the advancement of science and art; National politics.

B
―――
C 88 ha

51. [278.] **Oliver Cromwell.** Frederick Harrison. N. Y., Macmillan Co., 1888. 228 p. D. (Twelve English statesmen series.) cl. .... .75 .50

A well written history of a strong character. For older pupils.

LIST OF BOOKS FOR HIGH SCHOOL LIBRARIES. 19

	List price.	Price to schools.

E
D 25 ho
52. [279.] **Charles Darwin:** his life and work. Charles Frederick Holder. N. Y., G. P. Putnam's Sons, 1891. 279 p. il. D. (Leaders in science series.) cl. .... 1.50 .98

An account of one of the greatest naturalists and his work. Will interest the boys.

E
D 39 bu
53. **Demosthenes.** Samuel H. Butcher. N. Y., D. Appleton & Co., 1897. 172 p. (Classical writers.) D. cl. .... .60 .40

Contents: Age of Demosthenes; His public life and speeches—early period; His public life and speeches—from the rise of Macedon to the fall of Olynthus; His public life and speeches—from the fall of Olynthus to the peace of Philocrates; His public life and speeches—from the peace of Philocrates to Chaeronea; His public life and speeches—from Chaeronea to his death; His private speeches; Demosthenes as a statesman and an orator; Table of the works of Demosthenes.

E
D 35 di
54. **My father as I recall him.** Mamie Dickens. N. Y., E. P. Dutton & Co., 1898. 149 p. il. S. cl. .... .50 .33

A short, well written biography of Dickens. Excellent for library reading and for the pupils in literature who are reading Dickens.

E
D 35 wa
55. **Dickens.** Adolphus William Ward. N. Y., Harper & Bros., 1901. 222 p. (English men of letters series.) D. cl. .... .75 .49

E
D 74 br
56. **Stephen Arnold Douglas.** William Garrott Brown. Bost., Houghton, Mifflin & Co., 1902. 141 p. (Riverside biographical series.) S. cl. .... .65 .58

The author of the "Life of Stephen A. Douglas" has attempted a somewhat more original task than has fallen to most of the writers in the "Riverside Biographical Series." No life of Douglas has been published since the civil war, and the three lives published about the time of his death were of the nature of campaign biographies. So, except for the references to Douglas in histories, no estimate of him has been made from the point of view of a later generation. The author has nevertheless endeavored to make the reader understand Douglas the man, and has not been content merely to try to fix his place in history.

LIST OF BOOKS FOR HIGH SCHOOL LIBRARIES.

	List price.	Price to schools.

D
―――
D 7S co
57. [281.] **Drake.** Julian Corbett. N. Y., Macmillan Co., D. (English men of action series.) cl. .... .75 .67

A most fascinating character to young people.

D
―――
D 7S to
58. **Drake: the Sea-king of Devon.** George M. Towle. Bost., Lee & Shepard, c1882. 274 p. il. (Young folks' heroes of history series.) D. cl. .... 1.00 .65

Drake's life is full of adventure and in spite of the piracies which were excused by his own time, is full of lessons of manly qualities and of great and often admirable deeds. A good book for library reading, will create an interest in history.

D
―――
D S4 sa
59. **Dryden.** George Saintsbury. N. Y., Harper & Bros., 1902. 192 p. (English men of letters series.) D. cl. .... .75 .49

E
―――
Em 3 ho
60. **Ralph Waldo Emerson.** Oliver Wendell Holmes. Bost., Houghton, Mifflin & Co., 1898. 441 p. por. (American men of letters series.) D. cl. ...... 1.25 .82

Valuable for reference for the literature class and a good book for library reading for the more advanced pupils.

E
―――
Er 1 fr
61. **Life and letters of Erasmus:** lectures delivered at Oxford 1893-4. James Anthony Froude. N. Y., C: Scribner's Sons, 1899. 433 p. D. cl. .... 1.50 .98

For reference in history.
The best description of the state of Europe in the age immediately preceding the Reformation is found in the correspondence of Erasmus.

E
―――
Eu 7 ma
62. **Euripides.** John P. Mahaffy. N. Y., D. Appleton & Co., 1879. 144 p. (Classical writers.) D. cl... .60 .40

Contents: His age and surroundings; Poet's life and studies; Survey of his works; His plots; Dramas of character and of situation—the cyclops; Special characters—heroines; Heroes, heralds, slaves; His lyric poetry—choral odes, monodies; Prologues, epilogues, lesser characteristics; History and fortunes of his works.

LIST OF BOOKS FOR HIGH SCHOOL LIBRARIES. 21

	List price.	Price to schools.
E F 24 ba 63. [282.] **David Glasgow Farragut.** James Barnes. Bost., Small, Maynard & Co., 1899. 132 p. por. T. (Beacon biographies.) cl.	.75	.67

Intensely interesting.

E F 85 f1
64. [283.] **Autobiography of Benjamin Franklin.** Bost., Houghton, Mifflin & Co., 1886. 238 p. D. (Riverside lit. series.). cl. .... .40 .34

E F 85 fo
#65. **Many-sided Franklin.** Paul Leicester Ford. N. Y., Century Co., 1899. 516 p. il. O. cl. 3.00 1.96

This is not a formal biography, but a series of papers in which Franklin is considered from various points of view. A feature of the book is its abundance of illustrations, reproductions of portraits, manuscripts, houses, and public buildings.

Contents: Family relations; Physique: theories and appetites; Education: Religion; Printer and publisher; Writer and journalist; Relations with the fair sex; Jack of all trades; Scientist; Humorist; Politician and diplomatist; Social life.

E F 95 kn
66. [284.] **Life of Robert Fulton and a history of steam navigation.** Thomas W. Knox. N. Y., G. P. Putnam's Sons, 1896. 507 p. il. D. cl. 1.75 1.15

Interesting to boys who are interested in machinery and boats.

E G 13 st
67. **Albert Gallatin.** John Austin Stevens. Bost., Houghton, Mifflin & Co., 1888. 419 p. D. (American statesmen series.) cl. .... 1.25 .82

From the peace following the Revolution to. the time of his death, Gallatin's influence either by direct or indirect counsel may be traced through the history of the United States. He belonged to the first rank of economists and statisticians and his maxims regarding the public debt became the fundamental principle of American finance.

Contents: Early life; Pennsylvania legislature; United States senate; Whiskey insurrection; Member of congress; Secretary of the treasury; In the cabinet; In diplomacy; Candidate for the vice-presidency; Society—literature—science.

LIST OF BOOKS FOR HIGH SCHOOL LIBRARIES.

                                                                                                                List Price to
     E
G 45 br   price. schools.

68. [285.] **William Ewart Gladstone.** James Bryce. N. Y., Century Co., 1898. 104 p. por. S. cl. ... 1.00 .65

    A short, concise, and interesting account of a great man.

E

G 45 sy

69. **Life of Gladstone**: a book for boys. N. B. Synge. N. Y., Thos. Nelson & Sons, 1899. 128 p. il. D. cl. .... .50 .33

    A short and interesting story of Gladstone's life. Suitable for biography class in library reading.

E

G 55 le

70. **Story of Goethe's life.** George Henry Lewes. Bost., Houghton, Mifflin & Co., 1898. 406 p. por. D. cl. .... 1.00 .65

    This book will be of special interest to the pupils studying German. It presents the main events of Goethe's career and indicates his leading characteristics. The advanced classes in library reading will enjoy reading selections from his life.

E

G 55 si

71. **Life of Johann Wolfgang Goethe.** James Sime. N. Y., C: Scribner's Sons, 1888. 232 p. O. cl. .. 1.00 .65

    A well written life of Goethe for the use of the German students. It will also be of interest to the advanced classes in library reading.

E

G 76 al

72. **Ulysses S. Grant.** Walter Allen. Bost., Houghton, Mifflin & Co., 1901. 153 p. (Riverside biographical series.) S. cl. .... .65 .58

    Contents: Our national military hero; His ancestry; Period of youth; His lifework appointed; Love and war; Years of dormant power; Summons of patriotism; From Springfield to Fort Donelson; Shiloh, Corinth, Iuka; Vicksburg; New responsibilities—Chattanooga; Lieutenant-general, commander of all the armies; Wilderness and Spottsylvania; From Spottsylvania to Richmond; In Washington among politicians; His first administration; His second administration; Tour of the world; Reverses of fortune—ill health; His last victory

LIST OF BOOKS FOR HIGH SCHOOL LIBRARIES. 23

	List price.	Price to schools.

E
———
G 76 ga
73. [286.] **Ulysses S. Grant: his life and character.** Hamlin Garland. N. Y., McClure, Phillips & Co., 1898. 524 p. il. O. cl. 2.50 1.60

Will be intensely interesting to older pupils.

E
———
G 76 gr
#74. [287.] **Personal memoirs of U. S. Grant.** N. Y., Charles L. Webster & Co., 1885. 2 vols. 584; 647 p. por. O. cl. 2.50 1.50

The charm in his great book is the simple, straightforward, and unassuming way in which a great hero tells of himself and the events in which he took part.

E
———
H 18 co
75. **Alexander Hamilton.** Charles A. Conant. Bost., Houghton, Mifflin & Co., 1901. 145 p. (Riverside biographical series.) S. cl. .... .65 .58

Contents: Youth and early services; Fight for the constitution; Establishing the public credit; Congress sustains Hamilton; Strengthening bonds of union; Foreign affairs and neutrality; Hamilton as a party leader; Hamilton's death and character.

E
———
H 18 lo
76. [288.] **Alexander Hamilton.** Henry Cabot Lodge. Bost., Houghton, Mifflin & Co., 1899. 317 p. D. (American statesmen series.) cl. .... 1.25 .82

A well written account of the work of one of our greatest statesmen. "Washington created or caused to be created the national entity; Hamilton did actually create the political entity."— *J. T. Morse, Jr.*

E
———
H 31 fi
77. [289.] **Nathaniel Hawthorne.** *Mrs.* James T. Fields. Bost., Small, Maynard & Co., 1899. 136 p. por. T. (Beacon biographies.) cl. .... .75 .67

Will interest pupils who have read his works.

E
———
H 31 ja
78. **Hawthorne.** Henry James, Jr. N. Y., Harper & Bros., 1901. 177 p. (English men of letters series.) D. cl. .... .75 .49

	List price.	Price to schools.

B
———
H 31 la

79. **Study of Hawthorne.** George Parsons Lathrop. Bost., Houghton, Mifflin & Co., 1899. 350 p. S. cl. .... 1.25   .82

A portrait of Hawthorne which will be of interest to the class in literature or library reading who have been reading his works.

B
———
H 38 be

80. **Prince Henry the navigator:** the hero of Portugal and of modern discovery, 1394-1460 A. D. Charles Raymond Beazley. N. Y., G. P. Putnam's Sons, 1901. 336 p. (Heroes of the nations series.) il. D. cl. .... 1.50   .98

A connected account from the originals of the expansion of Europe through geographical enterprise, from the conversion of the empire to the period of those discoveries which mark the transition from the Middle Ages to the modern world. A valuable book for reference in mediaeval history.

Contents: Greek and Arabic ideas of the world, as the chief inheritance of the Christian middle ages in geographical knowledge; Early Christian pilgrims; Vikings or Northmen; Crusades and land travel; Maritime exploration; Geographical science in Christendom from the first crusades; Portugal to 1400; Henry's position and designs at the time of the first voyages; Prince Henry and the capture of Ceuta; Henry's settlement at Sagres and first discoveries; Cape Bojador and the Azores; Henry's political life; From Bojador to Cape Verde; Armada of 1445; Voyages of 1446-8; Azores; Troubles of the regency and the fall of Don Pedro; Cadamostro; Voyages of Diego Gomez; Henry's last years and death; Results of Prince Henry's work.

E
———
H 39 ty

81. .[290.] **Patrick Henry.** Moses Coit Tyler. Bost., Houghton, Mifflin & Co., 1889. 398 p. D. (American statesmen series.) cl. .... 1.25   .82

Henry is usually one of the boys' heroes.

E
———
Ir 8 bo

82. **Washington Irving.** Henry W. Boynton. Bost., Houghton, Mifflin & Co., 1901. 116 p. (Riverside biographical series.) S. cl. .... .65   .50

Contents: Early years and surroundings; Man about town; Man of letters—first period; Man of letters—second period; Public character; Man himself.

E
—
Ir S wa
	List price.	Price to schools.

83. **Washington Irving.** Charles Dudley Warner. Bost., Houghton, Mifflin & Co., 1901. 304 p. (American men of letters series.) D. cl. .... 1.25 .82

Pupils should be encouraged to read portions of this book after they have made a study of the writings of Irving. A good book for library reading.

E
—
J 12 su

84. [291.] **Andrew Jackson.** William Graham Sumner. Bost., Houghton, Mifflin & Co., 1899. 503 p. (American statesmen series.) D. cl. .... 1.25 .82

Jackson's active political life was between 1800–1845 and his biography will be valuable to those studying the history of that period. Contains good reference material on the Banking system and on the Financial history of this period.

Contents: First forty-five years of Jackson's life; Creek war and the war with England; Jackson in Florida; Election of 1824; Adam's administration; "Relief" system of Kentucky; Internal history of Jackson's first administration; Public questions of Jackson's first administration; Campaign of 1832; Tariff, nullification, and the bank during Jackson's second administration; Speculation, distribution, currency legislation, and end of the bank of the United States; New spirit in various points of foreign and domestic policy; Election of 1836—End of Jackson's career.

E
—
J 34 ol

85. **Jeanne D'Arc:** her life and death. *Mrs.* Margaret Oliphant. N. Y., G. P. Putnam's Sons, 1899. 417 p. (Heroes of the nations series.) il. and maps. D. cl. .... 1.50 .98

An intensely interesting book. Should be used for reference in teaching French history, also for Library reading.

Contents: France in the fifteenth century; Domremy and Vaucouleurs; Before the king; Relief of Orleans; Campaign of the Loire; Coronation; Second period; Defeat and discouragement; Compiègne; Captive; Judges; Before the trial; Public examination; Examination in prison; Re-examination; Abjuration; Sacrifice; After.

E
—
J 35 do

#86. **Joseph Jefferson at home.** Nathan Haskell Dole. Bost., Estes and Lauriat, 1898. 110 p. il. O. cl. 1.50 .98

This monograph on Joseph Jefferson, the great American actor, and his home surroundings, includes a brief sketch of his life. The book is illustrated with sixteen full-page half-tones, from photographs of Mr. Jefferson's pictures and scenes in and around his famous summer home of "Crow's nest," near Buzzard's Bay.

Interesting for Biography class in Library Reading.

LIST OF BOOKS FOR HIGH SCHOOL LIBRARIES.

	List price.	Price to schools.

B
J 351 me
87. **Thomas Jefferson.** Henry Childs Merwin. Bost., Houghton. Mifflin & Co., c1901. 164 p. (Riverside biographical series.) S. cl. .... .65 .58

Contents: Youth and training; Virginia in Jefferson's day; Monticello and its household; Jefferson in the Revolution; Reform work in Virginia; Governor of Virginia; Envoy at Paris; Secretary of State; Two parties; President Jefferson; Second presidential term; Public man in private life.

B
J 351 mo
88. [293.] **Thomas Jefferson.** John T. Morse. Bost., Houghton, Mifflin & Co., 1886. 353 p. D. (American statesmen series.) cl. .... 1.25 .82

An interesting biography of a fascinating character.

B
J 63 bo
89. **Boswell's life of Johnson.** Mowbray Morris, ed. N. Y., Thomas Y. Crowell & Co., n. d. 609 p. por. D. cl. .... 1.25 .82

"Homer is not more decidedly the first of heroic poets, Shakespeare is not more decidedly the first of dramatists, Demosthenes is not more decidedly the first of orators, than Boswell is the first of biographers. He has no second. He has distanced all his competitors so decidedly that it is not worth while to place them."— *From editor's preface.*

Selections from this should be read by the classes in English literature.

B
J 72 ab
90. **Life of John Paul Jones.** John S. C. Abbott. N. Y., Dodd, Mead & Co., 1898. 359 p. D. cl. ... ... .75 .67

Good for Library reading.

Contents: Early life of John Paul Jones; Infant navy; Bearding the British lion; Captain Jones at Nantes and at Brest; Cruise of the Bon Homme Richard; Bon Homme Richard and the Serapis; Result of the victory; Commodore Jones at court; Mutiny of Landais; Return to America; War ended; Difficulties of diplomacy; Mission to Denmark; Russian campaign; Adventures in the Black sea; Retirement and death.

B
J 72 ha
91. **Paul Jones.** Hutchins Hapgood. Bost., Houghton, Mifflin & Co., 1901. 126 p. (Riverside biographical series.) S. cl. .... .65 .58

An unbiased, brief sketch.

Contents: Early voyages; Cruises of the Providence and the Alfred; Cruise of the Ranger; Efforts in France to secure a com-

rund: Fight with the Serapis; Diplomacy at the Texel; Society in Paris; Private ambition and public business; In the Russian service; Last days.

E
———
K 22 co

92. **Keats.** Sidney Colvin. N. Y., Harper & Bros., 1901. 229 p. (English men of letters series.) D. cl. .75 .49

E
———
L 32 ad

93. [294.] **Lucy Larcom:** life, letters and diary. Daniel Dulany Addison. Bost., Houghton, Mifflin & Co., 1895. 295 p. por. D. cl. .... 1.25 .82

Will interest the girls.

E
———
L 51 tr

94. [295.] **Robert E. Lee.** W. P. Trent. Bost., Small, Maynard & Co., 1899. 135 p. por. T. (Beacon biographies.) cl. .... .75 .67

E
———
L 56 ro

95. **Life of Gotthold Ephriam Lessing.** T. W. Rolleston. London, Walter Scott; N. Y., C: Scribner's Sons, 1889. 218 p. (Great writers series.) O. cl. ... 1.00 .75

An interesting biography for advanced German classes.

E
———
L 58 li

96. **Meriwether Lewis and William Clark.** William R. Lighton. Bost., Houghton, Mifflin & Co., 1901. 159 p. (Riverside biographical series.) S. cl... .65 .58

Contents: Characteristics; Expedition; Terms of the Commission; Start; With the Sioux; To the falls of the Missouri; Over the continental divide; Last stage of the westward journey; Winter on the coast; Homeward: in the mountains; Recrossing the divide; Home; After life.

E
———
L 63 ha

97. [297.] **Abraham Lincoln:** the man of the people. Norman Hapgood. N. Y., The Macmillan Co., 1900. 432 p. por. D. hf. leath...................... 2.00 1.28

An estimate of *the man*, by a writer who tells his story well. The personal history of one of our greatest heroes. The writer "has tried to select those incidents which are doubly true, because they are at once actual and significant, and this truth is as likely to inhere in the amusing as in the solemn."

28   LIST OF BOOKS FOR HIGH SCHOOL LIBRARIES.

E
———
L 63 mo
                  List Price to
                  price. schools.
98. [298.] **Abraham Lincoln.** John T. Morse. Bost., Houghton, Mifflin & Co., 1898. 2 vols., 387; 373 p. por. D. (American statesmen series.) cl. each 1.25 .82

 A well written biography of this great man—more especially from the political standpoint.

E
———
L 63 sc
99. [296.] **Abraham Lincoln.** Carl Schurz. Gettysburg speech and other papers. Abraham Lincoln. Bost., Houghton, Mifflin & Co., 1899. 98 p. por. D. (Riverside lit. series.) cl. .... .40 .34

E
———
L 63 ta
#100. [299.] **Life of Abraham Lincoln:** drawn from original sources and containing many speeches, letters and telegrams hitherto unpublished. Ida Tarbell. N. Y., McClure, Phillips & Co., 1900. 2 vols., 426; 459 p. il. pors. facsimiles. O. cl. 5.00 3.25

 The public life of Lincoln.

E
———
L 75 ca
101. **Livy.** William Wolfe Capes. N. Y., D. Appleton & Co., 1894. 119 p. (Classical writers.) S. cl. ... .60 .40

 A brief account of Livy's life and of the chief events which occurred during his life. Valuable for use of classical students and for the classes in Roman history.

E
———
L 95 h
102. [300.] **James Russell Lowell.** Edward Everett Hale, Jr. Bost., Small, Maynard & Co., 1899. 127 p. por. T. (Beacon biographies.) cl. .... .75 .67

 Pupils who have read Lowell's works will enjoy this book.

E
———
M 26 ga
104. **James Madison.** Sydney Howard Gay. Bost., Houghton, Mifflin & Co., 1889. 342 p. D. (American statesmen series.) cl. .... 1.25 .82

 Contents: Virginia Madisons, 1-15; Young Statesman, 16-28; In Congress, 29-46; In state assembly, 47-63; In Virginia legislature, 64-75; Public disturbances and anxieties, 76-87; Constitutional convention, 88-97; "Compromises," 98-114; Adoption of the

	List price.	Price to schools.

constitution, 115–127; First congress, 128–150; National finances—slavery, 151–171; Federalists and republicans, 172–192; French politics, 193–215; His latest years in congress, 216–233; At home, 234–251; Secretary of state, 252–263; Embargo, 264–282; Madison as president, 283–300; War with England, 301–320; Conclusion, 321–337.

E

M 26 go
105. [301.] **Dolly Madison.** Maud Wilder Goodwin. N. Y., C. Scribner's Sons, 1901. 287 p. (Women of colonial and revolutionary times.) D. cl. .... 1.25 .82

A charming sketch of the wife of President James Madison and of the social and domestic life of the epoch as it affected her. A good book for the advanced classes in Library reading.

E

M 33 fr
106. **Swamp fox:** young folks' life of *Gen.* Francis Marion. John Frost. Bost., Lee & Shepard, c1887. 208 p. il. D. cl. .... 1.00 .65

This story gives the principal and most interesting events in Marion's life, and incidentally gives a picture of the American revolution. An interesting and instructive book for the American history classes to read.

E

M 34 th
107. **Father Marquette.** Reuben Gold Thwaites. N. Y., D. Appleton & Co., 1902. 244 p. maps and il. D. cl. 1.20 1.08

Slight space has been given to the ancestry of Marquette or to his early years in France. The author's chief object has been to depict the great explorer's work in the western wilderness. Whenever practicable, "Jesuit Relations" and Marquette's own journals have been freely drawn upon. It has thus been sought to convey a picture of the conditions surrounding Marquette, delineated in large measure by himself and his contemporaries.

Contents: Laon and the Marquettes; Training of a man of action; Arrival in Canada; Two years of apprenticeship; Indians and the missions; Arrival at the Ottawa mission; Sault and its people; La Pointe mission; Lake Superior abandoned; Arrival at Mackinac; Strenuous life; Joliet arrives at Mackinac; Expedition starts; Arrival at De Pere; Mission of St. Francois Xavier; at the Mascouten village; Discovery of the Mississippi; Limit of the journey; Winter at St. Francois Xavier; Relief in death; Marquette's place in history.

LIST OF BOOKS FOR HIGH SCHOOL LIBRARIES.

B
————
A 35 ma
                    List Price to
                    price. schools.
108. **John Marshall.** Allan B. Magruder. Bost., Houghton, Mifflin & Co., c1885. 290 p. D. cl. .... 1.25 .82

  Contents: Youth; Military service; At the bar; In the state legislature; In the constitutional convention of Virginia; Return to the bar; French mission; In congress; In Mr. Adams's cabinet; Chief justice; Trial of Aaron Burr for high treason; "Life of Washington"; In the Virginia state convention; Opinions: personal traits; death.

B
————
M 35 th
109. **John Marshall.** James Bradley Thayer. Bost., Houghton, Mifflin & Co., 1901. 157 p. (Riverside biographical series.) S. cl. .... 1.25 .82

  Contents: His life before becoming Chief Justice: his personal characteristics; Arguments and speeches: life of Washington: relations with Jefferson; Beginnings of the Chief Justice's career: American constitutional law: Marbury v. Madison; Marshall's constitutional opinions; Working of our system of constitutional law; Letters of Marshall; Marshall as a citizen and neighbor; His last days.

B
————
A 42 we
\#110. **Cotton Mather: the Puritan priest.** Barrett Wendell. N. Y., Dodd, Mead & Co., c1891. 321 p. por. ("Makers of America.") D. cl. .... 1.00 .65

  The story of his career. Valuable for use in the study of Colonial history and Literature.

B
————
A 46 ar
111. **Lorenzo de' Medici: and Florence in the fifteenth century.** Edward Armstrong. N. Y., G. P. Putnam's Sons, 1902. 449 p. (Heroes of the nations series.) il. D. cl. .... 1.50 .98

  Lorenzo was the most typical citizen of Florence in the most interesting century of Italian history. This biography is written in a vivid, dramatic manner that will appeal to the interests of the pupils.

B
————
A 64 br
112. **Milton.** Stopford A. Brooke. N. Y., D. Appleton & Co., 1901. 167 p. (Classical writers.) D. cl. ... .60 .40

  A brief, well-written account of Milton's life and works.

		List	Price to
		price.	schools

E
———
M 64 pa

113. **Milton.** Mark Pattison. N. Y., Harper & Bros., 1902. 215 p. (English men of letters series.) D. cl. ... .75 .49

E
———
M 75 g

114. [302.] **James Monroe.** Daniel C. Gilman. Bost., Houghton, Mifflin & Co., 1889. 287 p. D. (American statesmen series.) cl. .... 1.25 .82

In his relations to public service during half a century.

E
———
M 76 se

115. **Montezuma and the conquest of Mexico.** Elizabeth Eggleston Seelye, *and* Edward Eggleston. N. Y., Dodd, Mead & Co., c1880. 385 p. D. cl. .... .75 .67

An interesting book for Library reading.

E
———
M 83 ro

116. **Gouverneur Morris.** Theodore Roosevelt. Bost., Houghton, Mifflin & Co., 1889. 370 p. D. (American statesmen series.) cl. .... 1.25 .82

Contents: His youth; Colonial New York; Outbreak of the Revolution: Morris in the provincial congress; Independence: forming the state constitution; In the continental congress; Finances: treaty of peace; Formation of the National constitution; First stay in France; Life in Paris; Mission to England; Return to Paris; Minister to France; Stay in Europe; Service in the United States Senate; Northern disunion movement among the federalists.

E
———
N 16 mo

117. [303.] **Napoleon, warrior and ruler,** and the military supremacy of revolutionary France. William O'Connor Morris. N. Y., G. P. Putnam's Sons, 1899. 433 p. il. D. (Heroes of the nations series.) cl. .... 1.50 .98

A popular account, good for reference in French history and for the advanced classes in Library reading.

E
———
N 16 se

118. **Short history of Napoleon the First.** John Robert Seeley. Bost., Little, Brown & Co., 1901. 328 p. por. D. cl. .... 1.50 .98

A brief, clear and concise life of Napoleon I. Good for reference work in French history and for advanced classes in Library reading.

LIST OF BOOKS FOR HIGH SCHOOL LIBRARIES.

| | List price. | Price to schools. |

E
Os 7 hi

119. **Margaret Fuller Ossoli.** Thomas Wentworth Higginson. Bost., Houghton, Mifflin & Co., 1898. 323 p. (American men of letters series.) D. Ed. 14. cl.   1.25   .82

For Literature and Library reading.

Contents: Introductory; Hereditary traits; Girlhood at Cambridge; Country life at Groton; Finding a friend; School-teaching in Boston and Providence; Suburban life at Jamaica Plain; Conversations in Boston; Literary club and its organ; Dial; Brook farm; Books published; Business life in New York; European travel; Marriage and motherhood; Letters between husband and wife; Closing scenes; Literary traits; Personal traits; Bibliographical appendix.

E
P 37 ho

120. **William Penn.** George Hodges. Bost., Houghton, Mifflin & Co., 1901. 140 p. (Riverside biographical series.) S. cl. 65   .58

Contents: Puritan boyhood: Wanstead church and Chigwell school; At Oxford: influence of Thomas Loe; In France and Ireland: The world and the other world; Penn becomes a quaker: persecution and controversy; Beginning of Penn's political life: holy experiment; Settlement of Pennsylvania: Penn's first visit to the province; At the Court of James the Second, and "in retirement;" Penn's second visit to the province: closing years.

The biographies in this series present in a few words the prominent characteristics of some of the leading Americans. They will be helpful adjuncts to the text-book study of American history.

E
P 44 ro

121. **Petrarch: the first modern scholar and man of letters.** James Harvey Robinson, *and* Henry Winchester Rolfe. N. Y., G. P. Putnam's Sons, 1898. 436 p. O. cl.... ....   1.50   .98

The purpose of this volume is historical. It views Petrarch not as a poet, nor even, as a many-sided man of genius, but as the mirror of his age. Few historical sources can rival his letters in value and interest.

E
P 53 ab

122. **King Philip.** Jacob Abbott. N. Y., Harper & Bros., 1901. 410 p. il. (Makers of history series.) S. cl. 50   .33

A good book for Library reading.

Contents: Landing of the Pilgrims; Massasoit; Clouds of war; Pequot war; Commencement of the reign of King Philip; Commencement of hostilities; Autumn and winter campaigns; Captivity of Mrs. Rowlandson; Indians victorious; Vicissitudes of war; Death of King Philip; Conclusion of the war.

LIST OF BOOKS FOR HIGH SCHOOL LIBRARIES. 33

	List price.	Price to schools.

E
P 68 ro
123. [304.] Pitt. Lord Rosebery. N. Y., Macmillan & Co., 1895. 301 p. D. (Twelve English statesmen series.) cl. .... .75 .50

For reference in English history and for advanced classes in Library reading.

E
P 68 to
124. **Pizarro:** his adventures and conquests. George M. Towle. Bost., Lee & Shepard, c1878. 327 p. il. (Young folks' heroes of history series.) D. cl.. 1.00 .65

A description of the travels and conquests of one of the most resolute and adventurous captains that any age has produced.

It will both entertain and instruct and should be read by the Biography class in Library reading.

Contents: Runaways; Pizarro a soldier; Pizarro in the new world; Golden land; Pizarro's departure; Pizarro's second venture; On the borders of Peru; Pizarro in Spain; Third expedition; Pizarro invades Peru; Inca's court and camp; Pizarro at Caxamalca; Atahualpa a prisoner; Inca's loom; Pizarro captures Cuzco; City of the kings; Siege of Cuzco; Alamagro's revolt; Thrilling adventures of Gonzalo; Death of Pizarro.

E
P 98 li
125. **Israel Putnam:** pioneer, ranger, and Major-General, 1718-1790. William Farrand Livingston. N. Y., G. P. Putnam's Sons, 1901. 442 p. il. D. cl. ... 1.50 .98

The writer has had access to some original sources of information relating to Israel Putnam which have never before been used in any formal presentation of his life. These documents include his official reports as a ranger or scout in the French and Indian war; the diary which he kept on his voyage to the south; his general orders in the Havana campaign and the American Revolution; and letters of his own life.

Contents: In old Salem village; Connecticut pioneer; Call to arms; Ranger; Guarding the forts; Savage warfare; Attack on Ticonderoga; Prisoner; Three more campaigns; Capture of Havana; Bradstreet's expedition; Honoured citizen; Military adventurer; Ardent patriot; War's alarms; Bold leader; Battle of Bunker Hill; Besieging Boston; Fortifying New York; Battle of Long Island; Forced retreat; At Philadelphia and Princeton; Command of the Hudson Highlands; In the recruiting service; Last years.

E
R 13 to
126. **Raleigh:** his exploits and voyages. George M. Towle. Bost., Lee & Shepart, c1881. 273 p. il. (Young folks' heroes of history series.) D. cl. .... 1.00 .65

Raleigh was famous in several fields of action—in the royal court of Elizabeth, on the battlefield and in the sturdy attempt to

	List price.	Price to schools.

make discoveries, and to settle English colonies in the new world. The narration of his life is of absorbing interest and should be read both by the History and Library reading classes.

D
———
R 89 ca
127. "Uncle Jerry." Life of General Jeremiah M. Rusk, stage driver, farmer, soldier, legislator, governor, cabinet officer. Henry Casson. With a chapter by Ex-President Benjamin Harrison. Madison, Junius W. Hill, 1895. 490 p. il. O. cl. 1.50 1.15

A plainly written story of the life of a plain man who was great, whose greatness was widely recognized and appreciated, and whose character, both private and public, affords an example well worthy of study and emulation.

This book will be of great interest to the parents of the pupils.

E
———
Sch 3 th
128. **Life and works of Friedrich Schiller.** Calvin Thomas. N. Y., Henry Holt & Co., 1902. 481 p. D. cl. ... 1.50 1.35

An attempt to reveal Schiller to us as he was and to help us to understand the national temperament to which he has endeared himself.

In discussing his plays Thomas has endeavored to deal with them in a large way, laying hold of each where it is most interesting. Questions of minute and technical scholarship have been avoided.

Contents: Parentage and schooling; Robbers; Stuttgart Medicus; Conspiracy of Fiesco at Genoa; Fugitive in hiding; Cabal and love; Theater poet in Mannheim; Boon of friendship; Don Carlos; Anchored in Thuringia; Historical writings; Dark days within and without; Aesthetic writings; Great triumvirate; Later poems; Wallenstein; Mary Stuart; Maid of Orleans; Bride of Messina; William Tell; End-un-finished plays and adaptations; Verdict of posterity.

E
———
Sco 3 hu
129. *Sir* Walter Scott. Richard H. Hutton. N. Y., Harper & Bros., 1902. 177 p. (English men of letters series.) D. cl. .... .75 .49

E
———
Se 8 lo
130. [305.] **William Henry Seward.** Thornton Kirkland Lothrop. Bost., Houghton, Mifflin & Co., 1898. 446 p. D. (American statesmen series.) cl. .... 1.25 .82

In his relation to national affairs.

E
———
Sh 1 ma
                                                                List Price to
                                                                price. schools.
#131. **William Shakespeare**: poet, dramatist, and man.
   Hamilton Wright Mabie. N. Y., Macmillan Co.,
   1901. 419 p. il. O. Ed. 3. cl., ... 2.00   1.80

   An excellent account of Shakespeare's life and works written from a literary standpoint. The classes who have studied the works of Shakespeare will enjoy reading the book.
   Contents: Forerunners of Shakespeare; Birth and breeding; Shakespeare's country; Marriage and London; London stage; Apprenticeship; First fruits; Poetic period; Sonnets; Historical plays; Comedies; Approach of tragedy; Earlier tragedies; Later tragedies; Ethical significance of the tragedies; Romances; Last years at Stratford.

E
———
Sh 3 sy
132. **Shelley.** John Addington Symonds. N. Y., Harper & Bros., 1901. 189 p. (English men of letters series.) D. cl. .... .75   .49

E
———
Sh 5 he
133. **Fighting Phil**: the life and military career of Philip Henry Sheridan. Rev. Philip Camp Headley. Bost., Lee & Shepard, 1899. 380 p. D. new ed. cl. .... 1.50   .98

   An interesting account of Sheridan's life suitable for Library reading classes.
   "An extended notice of the course of study and discipline in the Military Academy at West Point is given, and a brief history of the cavalry is added."—Preface.

E
———
So 7 ab
134. **Ferdinand De Soto.** John S. C. Abbott. N. Y., Dodd, Mead & Co., 1898. 351 p. D. cl. .... .75   .67

   This biography should be read by the pupils who are studying the early history of United States. An interesting book for Library reading.
   Contents: Childhood and youth; Spanish colony; Life at Darien; Demoniac reign; Invasion of Peru; Atrocities of Pizarro; Execution of the Inca, and embarrassments of De Soto; De Soto returns to Spain; Landing in Florida; March to Ochile; Conspiracy and its consequences; Winter quarters; Lost in the wilderness; Indian princess; Dreadful battle of Mobila; Days of darkness; Discovery of the Mississippi; Vagrant wanderings; Death of De Soto.

LIST OF BOOKS FOR HIGH SCHOOL LIBRARIES.

	List price.	Price to schools.

E
St 1 ab

135. **Miles Standish:** captain of the Pilgrims. John S. C. Abbott. N. Y., Dodd, Mead & Co., c1900. 372 p. map. D. cl. .... .75 .67

A vivid, dramatic description of the adventures of Miles Standish and the Pilgrim Fathers. Valuable for reference in History and for Library reading.

Contents: Pilgrims in Holland; Voyage; Exploring the coast; Landing; Life on shore; Indians; Exploring tours; Menaces of famine and war; Weymouth colonists; Sickness of Massasoit and end of the Weymouth colony; Domestic and foreign policy; Increase and growth of the settlements; Courtship of Miles Standish; Trading posts menaced; Removal to Duxbury; Standish monument.

E
T 22 se

136. **Tecumseh and the Shawnee prophet.** Elizabeth Eggleston Seelye, *and* Edward Eggleston. N. Y., Dodd, Mead & Co., c1878. 332 p. D. cl. .... .75 .67

A good picture of Indian life in early times. Tecumseh was a valuable ally of the English in the War of 1812 and portions of his life should be read by the History class when studying this period.

E
T 34 ho

137. **Theodoric the Goth:** the barbarian champion of civilization. Thomas Hodgkin. N. Y., G. P. Putnam's Sons, 1900. 442 p. (Heroes of the nations series.) il. and map. D. cl. .... 1.50 .98

Theodoric was one of the most striking figures in the history of the Early Middle Ages and his life will be of great interest to the pupils studying the history of Italy.

Contents: Theodoric's ancestors; Might of Attila; Theodoric's boyhood; Southward migration; Storm and stress; Italy under Odovacar; Conquest of Italy; Civilitas; Roman officials; Cassiodorus; Arian league; Anastasius; Rome and Ravenna; Boethius; Theodoric's tomb; Amalasuentha; Belisarius; Totila; Narses; Theodoric of Saga.

E
V 58 ne

138. **Vergil.** Henry Nettleship. N. Y., D. Appleton & Co., 1897. 106 p. (Classical writers.) S. cl... .60 .54

A brief sketch of the life of Vergil. Valuable for reference for the Classical students.

E

V 66 ho
#139. **Queen** Victoria, 1819-1901. Richard R. Holmes.
    N. Y., Longmans, Green & Co., 1901. 330 p. por.
    D. New ed. cl. 1.50 1.35

List price. Price to schools.

This biography was authorized by Queen Victoria and contains an accurate account of her childhood and youth. The narrative is brought down to the end of the queen's reign.

E

W 27 ha
#140. **George** Washington. Norman Hapgood. N. Y., Macmillan Co., 1901. 419 p. por. D. cl. 1.75 1.57

The author pays special attention to the human side of Washington and gives a condensed but complete picture of the man to whose simple idea of duty, unfailing tact and personal courage the United States owe their solid foundation. The man, the fighter, the planter, are shown with many little details of characterization that make the greatest man in history stand out as a private individual surrounded by his daily intimates, as well as his political association.

E

W 27 lo
141. [306.] **George** Washington. Henry Cabot Lodge. Bost., Houghton, Mifflin & Co., 1898. 2 vols., 341; 399 p. D. (American statesmen series.) cl. each .... 1.25 .82

A very interesting biography. The account of his public life is accurate, making the book an excellent one for reference in United States history.

E

W 27 sc
142. [307.] George Washington: an historical biography. Horace E. Scudder. Bost., Houghton, Mifflin & Co., 1886. 248 p. por. S. (Riverside lit. series.) cl. .... .40 .31

This short biography will be of interest to the younger pupils in Library reading. The treatment of his public life is not extended enough to make the book of much value for reference work in History.

E

W 27 wi
143. **George** Washington. Woodrow Wilson. N. Y., Harper & Bros., 1900. 333 p. il. D. cl.. .... 1.50 .98

An excellent account of Washington's life for the Biography class in Library reading.

E
W 271 wh

List price. / Price to schools.

144. **Martha Washington.** Anne Hollingsworth Wharton. N. Y., C: Scribner's Sons, 1899. 306 p. (Women of colonial and revolutionary times.) D. cl. ... 1.25 .82

An interesting picture of Mrs. Washington as she appeared in her own home, and in the official life that claimed so much of her time. Incidentally some glimpses of Washington as husband, host, and country gentleman are given.

E
W 39 ha

145. [308.] **Daniel Webster.** Norman Hapgood. Bost., Small, Maynard & Co., 1899. 119 p. por. T. (Beacon biographies.) cl. .... .75 .67

Brief and interesting.

E
W 39 lo

146. [309.] **Daniel Webster.** Henry Cabot Lodge. Bost., Houghton, Mifflin & Co., 1886. 372 p. D. (American statesmen series.) cl. .... 1.25 .82

A very interesting book, excellent for reference in United States History.

E
W 58 bu

147. **John Greenleaf Whittier.** Richard Burton. Bost., Small, Maynard & Co., 1901. 133 p. T. cl. (Beacon biographies.) .... .75 .67

A simple, attractive story of Whittier's life, with a bibliography.

E
W 73 ea

148. **Margaret Winthrop.** Alice Morse Earle. N. Y., C: Scribner's Sons, 1898. 341 p. (Women of Colonial and Revolutionary times.) D. cl. .... 1.25 .82

The heroine of this volume, the introductory one of a new and interesting series, was the third wife of the John Winthrop who played so important a part in the founding of New England. Her letters, of which the book is largely made up, and the occasional extracts from her husband's letters, afford a delightfully gossipy chronicle of the period in which they lived, especially during the time John Winthrop was Governor of Massachusetts. This new series aims "to present not only carefully studied portraits of the most distinguished women of Colonial and Revolutionary times, but to offer as a background for these portraits pictures of the domestic and social instead of the political and other public life of the people."

E
W 89 my

	List price.	Price to schools.
149. **Wordsworth.** Frederick W. H. Myers. N. Y., Harper & Bros., 1902. 182 p. (English men of letters series.) D. cl.	.75	.49

The biographies in the English men of letters series will be of especial value to the classes in Advanced Literature and Senior Library reading.

E
W 97 se

150. **John Wyclif**: last of the schoolmen and first of the English reformers. Lewis Sergeant. N. Y., G. P. Putnam's Sons, 1893. 377 p. (Heroes of the nations series.) il. D. cl. .... 1.50 .98

Contents: Character of Wyclif; Seething of Europe; Monks and friars; Wyclif and the schoolmen; Wyclif's early days; Wyclif as politician; Conference at Bruges; Wyclif and the national church; Persecution; Pope Gregory's bulls; Wyclif the evangelist; Decisive step; Condemned at Oxford; Wyclif's poor priests; Headless rebellion; Courtenay's triumph; Last stage; Work that lived; Chronology of events connected with Wyclif.

COLLECTIVE BIOGRAPHY.

Ec
B 63 f

151. **Famous European artists.** Sarah Knowles Bolton. N. Y., Thos. Y. Crowell & Co., c1890. 423 p. pors. D. cl. .... 1.50 .98

Contents: Michael Angelo; Leonardo da Vinci; Raphael of Urbino; Titian; Murillo; Rubens; Rembrandt; Sir Joshua Reynolds; Sir Edwin Landseer; Turner.

Ec
B 63 fm

152. **Famous leaders among men.** Sarah Knowles Bolton. N. Y., Thos. Y. Crowell & Co., c1894. 404 p. pors. D. cl. .... 1.50 .98

Contents: Napoleon Bonaparte; Horatio Nelson; John Bunyan; Thomas Arnold; Wendell Phillips; Henry Ward Beecher; Charles Kingsley; General William Tecumseh Sherman; Charles Haddon Spurgeon; Phillips Brooks.

Ec
B 63 fv

List price. Price to schools.

153. **Famous voyages and explorers.** Sarah Knowles Bolton. N. Y., Thos. Y. Crowell & Co., c1893. 509 p. pors. map. D. cl. .... 1.50 .98

Contents: Christopher Columbus; Marco Polo; Ferdinand Magellan; Sir Walter Raleigh; Sir John Franklin; Dr. Kane, C. H. Hall and others; David Livingstone; Matthew Galbraith Perry; General A. W. Greely and other Arctic explorers; Map of Arctic regions.

Ec
B 63 fw

154. **Famous leaders among women.** Sarah Knowles Bolton. N. Y., Thos. Y. Crowell & Co., c1895. 356 p. pors. D. cl. .... 1.50 .98

Contents: Madame de Maintenon; Catherine II of Russia; Madame le Brun; Dolly Madison; Catherine Booth; Lucy Stone; Lady Henry Somerset; Julia Ward Howe; Queen Victoria.

Ec
B 63 li

155. **Lives of poor boys who became famous.** Sarah K. Bolton. N. Y., Thos. Y. Crowell & Co., c1885. 367 p. pors. D. cl. .... 1.50 .98

Contents: George Peabody; Bayard Taylor; Captain James B. Eads; James Watt; Sir Josiah Mason; Bernard Palissy; Bertel Thorwaldsen; Wolfgang Mozart; Samuel Johnson; Oliver Goldsmith; Michael Faraday; Sir Henry Bessemer; Sir Titus Salt; Joseph Marie Jacquard; Horace Greeley; William Lloyd Garrison; Giuseppe Garibaldi; Jean Paul Richter; Leon Gambetta; David G. Farragut; Ezra Cornell; Lieut.-General Sheridan; Thomas Cole; Ole Bull; Meissonier; Geo. W. Childs; Dwight L. Moody; Abraham Lincoln.

An excellent series of books for Library reading.

Ec
B 63 su

156. **Successful women.** Sarah K. Bolton. Bost., Lothrop Pub. Co., c1888. 233 p. il. D. cl. .... 1.00 .65

Short interesting sketches.
Contents: Juliet Corson, 9-33; Mary Louise Booth, 34-50; Frances E. Willard, 51-71; Mrs. G. R. Alden ("Pansy"), 72-89; Mary Virginia Terhune ("Marion Harland"), 90-109; Margaret, 110-126; Ella Grant Campbell, 127-148; Rachel Littler Bodley, 149-174; Candace Wheeler, 175-197; Clara Barton, 198-222; Alice E. Freeman, 223-233.

	List price.	Price to schools.

Ec
B 79 gr

157. **Great men's sons:** who they were, what they did, and how they turned out, a glimpse at the sons of the world's mightiest men from Socrates to Napoleon. Elbridge S. Brooks. N. Y., G. P. Putnam's Sons, 1895. 303 p. il. D. cl. .... 1.50 .98

The seventeen great men whose sons are described are: Socrates, Alexander the great, Cicero, Marcus Aurelius, Constantine, Mahomet, Charlemagne, Alfred the Great, William the Conqueror, Saladin, Dante, Tamerlane, Columbus, Luther, Shakespeare, Cromwell, and Napoleon. Six of these sketches have appeared in Harper's Round Table.

Ec
B 791 dc

158. **Dames and daughters of colonial days.** Geraldine Brooks. N. Y., Thomas Y. Crowell & Co., c1900. 284 p. il. D. cl. .... 1.50 .98

The dames and daughters who are given place in this volume are: Anne Hutchinson of Bay Colony; Madame La Tour, of Acadia; Margaret Brent, of Maryland; Madam Sarah Knight, of Massachusetts and Connecticut; Eliza Lucas, of the Carolinas; Martha Washington, of Virginia; Abigail Adams, of Massachusetts; Betsy Schuyler, of New York, and Deborah Norris and Sally Wister, of Pennsylvania. All sections of the colonies and all phases of colonial life are thus represented.

A good book for Library reading.

Ec
B 791 dr

159. **Dames and daughters of the young Republic.** Geraldine Brooks. N. Y., Thomas Y. Crowell & Co., c1901. 287 p. il. D. cl. .... 1.50 .98

The sketches in this book are entertaining narratives of the lives of typical women of our Republic and are designed to show the varying types of character and conditions of society that governed life in America a century ago.

Contents: Dorothea P. Madison; Sarah Jay; Theodosia Burr; Elizabeth Patterson; Martha Jefferson; Rachel Jackson; Dorothy Hancock; Emily Marshall.

Ec
D 66 gr

160. [262.] **Great captains.** Theodore Ayrault Dodge. Bost., Houghton, Mifflin & Co., 1898. 219 p. maps. O. cl. 2.00 1.28

The great captains are Alexander, Hannibal, Caesar, Gustavus Adolphus, Frederick, and Napoleon. A very readable book.

Ec
E1 5 wo

List price.
Price to schools.

#161. **Women of the American Revolution.** Elizabeth F. Ellet. Phil., George W. Jacobs & Co., c1900. 2 vol. il. D. cl. 3.20 2.88

About one hundred biographical sketches of as many women, prominent in revolutionary history and society, with about forty portraits printed in two colors. This work was first published in the middle of the century, the material being collected while some men and women were still living who could recall the facts and figures of the statesmen and soldiers of the Revolutionary struggle, and there are many proofs that Mrs. Ellet availed herself of the opportunities afforded her to draw from original sources. An interesting book for Library reading.

Ec
F 46 ye

162. [263.] **Yesterdays with authors.** James T. Fields. Bost., Houghton, Mifflin & Co., 1890. 419 p. D. cl. 2.00 1.28

Interesting chats about eminent men and women whom Fields counted as his friends. "Some of them I have known intimately; several of them lived in other times; but they are all my friends and associates in a certain sense." Fields.

The leading ones are Thackeray, Hawthorne, Dickens, Wordsworth, Miss Mitford, and "Barry Cornwall."

Ec
G 65 am

163. **American leaders and heroes:** a preliminary textbook in United States history. Wilbur F. Gordy. N. Y., C: Scribner's Sons, 1901. 329 p. il. and maps. D. cl. .... .60 .50

The biographical element predominates in this book, but around the heroes and leaders are clustered typical and significant events in such a way as to give the basal facts of American history.

The book is elementary but will be very interesting for Library reading.

Ec
H 91 pr

#164. [264.] **Prisoners of the Tower of London.** Violet Brooks-Hunt. N. Y., E. P. Dutton & Co., 1899. 247 p. il. D. cl. 2.50 1.60

Brief and most interesting biographies of Richard II, Henry VI, Thomas More, Anne Boleyn, Thos. Cromwell, Lady Jane Grey, Walter Raleigh, and others who were prisoners in the Tower of London. A very readable book.

Ec
L 88 b 1
                                                                  List Price to
                                                                  price. schools.

165. **Beacon lights of history**; vol. I, Antiquity. John Lord. N. Y., Fords, Howard & Hulbert, c1883. 474 p. por. D. cl. 2.00 1.90

    Contents: Cyrus the Great; Socrates; Phidias; Julius Caesar; Cicero; Marcus Aurelius; Constantine the Great; Chrysostom; Saint Ambrose; Saint Augustine; Theodosius the Great; Leo the Great.

Ec
L 88 b 2
166. **Beacon lights of history**; vol. II, The Middle Ages. John Lord. N. Y., Fords, Howard & Hulbert, c1883. 478 p. D. cl. 2.00 1.90

    Contents: Mohammed; Charlemagne; Alfred the Great; Hildebrand; Saint Bernard; Saint Anselm; Thomas Aquinas; Thomas Becket; Feudal system; Crusades; William of Wykeham; John Wyclif.

Ec
L 88 b 3
167. **Beacon lights of history**; vol. III, Renaissance and reformation. John Lord. N. Y., Fords, Howard & Hulbert, c1884. 508 p. D. cl...   2.00 1.90

    Contents: Dante; Geoffrey Chaucer; Christopher Columbus; Savonarola; Michael Angelo; Martin Luther; Thomas Cranmer; Ignatius Loyola; John Calvin; Henry of Navarre; Lord Bacon; Galileo.

Ec
L 88 b 4
168. **Beacon lights of history**; vol IV, Warriors and statesmen. John Lord. N. Y., Fords, Howard & Hulbert, c1885. 495 p. D. cl. 2.00 1.90

    Contents: Gustavus Adolphus; Cardinal Richelieu; Oliver Cromwell; Louis XIV; Louis XV; Peter the Great; Frederick the Great; Edmund Burke; Mirabeau; Alexander Hamilton; Napoleon Bonaparte; Daniel Webster.

Ec
L 88 b 5
169. **Beacon lights of history**; vol. V, Great women. John Lord. N. Y., Fords, Howard & Hulbert, c1886. 522 p. D. cl. 2.00 1.90

    Contents: Cleopatra; Paula; Héloïse; Joan of Arc; Saint Theresa; Queen Elizabeth; Madame de Maintenon; Sarah, Duchess of Marlborough; Madame Récamier; Madame De Staël; Hannah More; George Eliot.

Ec
L 88 b 6   List   Price to
                                                                    price. schools.

170. **Beacon lights of history;** vol. VI, Modern European statesmen. John Lord. N. Y., Fords, Howard & Hulbert, c1891. 623 p. D. cl. 2.00   1.90

    Contents: Prince Metternich; Chateaubriand; George IV; Greek revolution; Louis Philippe; William IV; Sir Robert Peel; Cavour; Czar Nicholas; Louis Napoleon; Prince Bismarck; William Ewart Gladstone.

Ec
L 88 b 7

171. **Beacon lights of history,** vol. VII, American statesmen. John Lord. N. Y., Fords, Howard & Hulbert, c1894. 539 p. O. cl. 2.00   1.90

    Contents: Preliminary chapter; Benjamin Franklin; George Washington; John Adams; Thomas Jefferson; Andrew Jackson; Henry Clay; John C. Calhoun; Abraham Lincoln.

Ec
L 88 b 8

172. **Beacon lights of history;** vol. VIII, Nineteenth century writers. Also, The life of John Lord by Alex. S. Twombley. John Lord. N. Y., Fords, Howard & Hulbert, c1896. 292 + 326 pp. pors. and il. D. cl. 2.00   1.90

    Contents: Rousseau; Sir Walter Scott; Lord Byron; Thomas Carlyle; Lord Macaulay.

Ec
L 88 b 9

173. **Beacon lights of history;** First series, Jewish heroes and prophets. John Lord. N. Y., Fords Howard & Hulbert, c1888. 524 p. por. D. cl. 2.00   1.90

    Contents: Abraham; Joseph; Moses; Book of Job; Samuel; David; Solomon; Elijah; Isaiah; Jeremiah, Mordecai and Esther; Judas Maccabaeus; Saint Paul.

Ec
L 88 b 10

174. **Beacon lights of history;** First series, Old pagan civilizations. John Lord. N. Y., Fords, Howard & Hulbert, c1888. 607 p. O. cl. 2.00   1.90

    Contents: Ancient religions; Religions of India; Religion of the Greeks and Romans; Confucius; Ancient philosophy; Governments and laws; Literary genius; Fine arts; Ancient scientific knowledge; Material life of the ancients; Military art; Pagan society.

    This set of books is a series of biographies of the most eminent personages of history. The style is clear and vigorous and the facts.

given are accurate. An excellent reference series for High school teachers and pupils and for the general reader. Pupils will enjoy reading portions of this set for Library reading.

After Jan. 1, 1903, this set will be published in 15 volumes, and will be furnished at $27 per set instead of $19.

Ec

L 89 tw

175. **Two spies:** Nathan Hale and John André: including Anna Seward's monody on Major André. Benson J. Lossing. N. Y., D. Appleton & Co., 1901. 169 p. il. O. cl............................ 2.00 1.30

A brief account of the most important events in the life-career of these two notable spies.

Ec

Ol 3 ma

176. **Makers of Florence:** Dante Giotto, Savonarola, and their city. *Mrs.* Margaret W. Oliphant. N. Y., A. L. Burt, n. d. 436 p. il. D. cl............ 1.00 .50

The biographies in this volume touch upon and indicate many portions of the history of Florence and incidentally trace, to some extent, the struggle which was always going on. The vivid, dramatic style of the book makes it an excellent one for the use of the advanced classes in Library reading.
Contents: Dante; Arnolfo–Giotto; Ghiberti, Donatello, Brunelleschi; Agnolo; Fra Angelico; Sant Antonino; Girolamo Savonarola; Piagnoni painters; Michael Angelo.

Ec

Ol 3 mar

177. **Makers of modern Rome:** In four books, I, Honourable women not a few; II, The Popes who made the papacy; III, Lo Popolo and the tribune of the people; IV, The Popes who made the city. *Mrs.* Margaret W. Oliphant. N. Y., Macmillan Co., 1896. 618 p. il. D. cl.................. 3.00 1.96

An excellent book for Library reading.
Contents: Rome in the fourth century; Palace on the Aventine; Melania; Society of Marcella; Paula; Mother house; Gregory the Great; Monk Hildebrand; Pope Gregory VII; Innocent III; Rome in the fourteenth century; Deliverer; Buono Stato; Decline and fall; Soldiers of Fortune; End of the tragedy; Martin V—Eugenius IV—Nicolas V; Calixtus III Pius II—Paul II Sixtus IV; Julius II—Leo X

Ec
———
Ol 3 mav

　　　　　　　　　　　　　　　　　　　　　　　List　Price to
　　　　　　　　　　　　　　　　　　　　　　　price.　schools.

178. **Makers of Venice:** doges, conquerors, painters and men of letters. *Mrs. Margaret W. Oliphant.* N. Y., Macmillan Co., 1898. 410 p. il. D. cl...... 2.50　1.64

Contents: Orseoli; Micheli; Enrico Dandolo; Pietro Gradenigo; Doges disgraced; Travellers: Nicolo, Matteo, and Marco Polo; Popular hero; Soldiers of fortune—Carmagnola; Bartolommeo Colleoni; Three early masters; Second generation; Tintoretto; Guest of Venice; Historians; Aldus and the Aldines.

Ec
———
T 65 he

179. **Heroes and martyrs of invention.** *George M. Towle.* Bost., Lee & Shepard, c1890. 202 p. il. D. cl.　1.00　　.65

Contents: Early inventors, 7–22; Laurence Coster, the discoverer of type-printing, 23–32; John Gutenberg, the inventor of the printing-press, 33–42; Palissy the potter, 43–51; William Lee, the inventor of the stocking-frame, 52–61; Builders of the Eddystone, 62–70; Inventors of cotton-machinery: Kay, Hargreaves, Arkwright, 71–83; Inventors of cotton machinery: Crompton, Cartwright, Whitney, 84–102; James Watt, the inventor of the steam engine, 103–112; Montgolfiers and the balloon, 113–122; Humphrey Davy and the safety lamp, 123–131; James Nasmyth—steam hammer, 132–140; George Stephenson, the inventor of the railway locomotive, 141–150; Robert Stephenson, the great bridge builder, 151–159; Robert Fulton and the steamboat, 160–169; Struggles of Charles Goodyear, 170–179; Elias Howe and the sewing machine, 180–189; Iron and its workers, 190–202.

HISTORY.

THE PURPOSE OF HISTORICAL INSTRUCTION IN SCHOOLS.

It is now generally agreed that the utility of history as a high school study arises chiefly from the training which the subject affords to the judgment, and secondarily, from the training of the perception, imagination and memory. "To prepare the child for judgments in actual life the materials must resemble as nearly as possible the conditions of actual life. Such materials are found in history and found there in greater degree than in any other subject." The value of historical instruction in preparing students for good and intelligent citizenship is obvious. Aside from the body of information acquired, the weighing of evidence, the comparative study of political systems of other countries and of other times, and the formation of judgments upon men and measures, constitute a training most useful to the future citizen. Dr. Arnold expressed the utility of instruction in history, civics, and economics in the schools very well when he said: "It is clear that in whatever it is our duty to act, those matters also it is our duty to study." The teacher will find a fuller discussion of this subject in the *Report of the Committee of Seven,* and in Hinsdale's *How to Teach and Study History,* chapters i and iv. The importance given to the judgment in historical training should increase with the higher grades; and the judgment itself can best be exercised when the pupil's perception, imagination, and memory supply him with the necessary data. It is hardly necessary to say that by the imagination, in this case, is meant the power of the pupil to place himself in the attitude of the people of other times and of other countries.

It should not be the ideal of history teaching to furnish a bare outline of names and dates, a well proportioned set of pigeon holes to be filled up in after life. Such a process, however, attractive in theory, is not workable in fact; the names and dates come to have less than the value of algebraic symbols of unknown quantities. But it by no means follows that history can be taught without accurate knowledge of the most significant historical landmarks. These are means to an end, and should be so illuminated with concrete detail as to be held as vital elements rather than as a bare and dead weight on the memory. Institutions and men should be made real for the student by sufficient concrete and intelligible discussion of their essential characteristics. As a part of the training in judgment, and in the interest of mental economy, they should be taught to observe lines of causation, to distinguish between the enduring and the fleeting, between the essential and the non-essentials in history, and the important should be made clear, at whatever cost of time. To the objection that this mode of treating historical study as a training in judgment takes more time, the answer of the late Mary Sheldon Barnes is conclusive: "Good friend, it does; and it takes more time to solve a problem in arithmetic than to read its answer; and more time to read a play of Shakespeare than to read that Shakespeare was the greatest dramatist of all the ages; and more time finally to read the American constitution and the American newspaper, and make up your mind how to vote your own vote, than it does to be put into a 'block of five.' *But what is time for?*"

METHOD.

The books listed, which give bibliographies of works on historical method, render an extensive discussion of the subject here unnecessary. In general, it may be pointed out that the methods should be those which conduce to a training of the judgment. A text-book should, in most cases be used as a basis of work, and to give proportion, order, and definiteness to the instruction. Collateral material, used in additional reading, and in presentation of topical reports, is essential, and this involves a good library as much as modern science teaching involves a laboratory and apparatus. The moderate use of sources for illustration and for disciplinary work akin to laboratory practice is especially helpful in the later part of the course. It aids in training the student to extract the important elements out of his reading, develops the critical faculty, and gives the student some impression of the sort of materials out of which the textbook was made. Written work should be increasingly used in the later part of the course; the practice of keeping note books is to be commended.

History should be so taught as to make use of the studies of geography, (physiographic, economic, and political), literature, economics, civics, and similar subjects. All may be made mutually helpful. The use of pictures, of which there are now a multiplicity of cheap reprints, will aid in bringing the architecture, sculpture, and painting of past ages before the pupil; and these are important aids in understanding the culture of a period. Maps and atlases should be constantly used, including outline maps for constructive work. When the student is allowed to make something, whether a topical report or an illustrative map, his interest is aroused, and the subject takes on a definiteness that is well worth the time. Lantern slides make possible a large use of maps and pictures at comparatively slight expense.

ORIGINAL SOURCES.

Some attention should be paid to the use of original material in the teaching of history in the high school. To teach the History of Literature and text-book criticisms of authors without first having the pupils read the masterpieces of literature is acknowledged by nearly all present-day educators to be a faulty method and for the same reasons the teaching of history without giving any attention to the study of the documents upon which history is based is faulty.

The use of sources will show the pupil how the text book in

history has been prepared through the use of the writings that have been left to us and will call out his individuality; they will tend to make history a problem to him.

From reading the Satires of Juvenal the pupils will obtain a vivid picture of life and politics in Rome during the last half of the first century.

From reading the letters of Erasmus the pupils can make a fair estimate of his character, his attitude toward Luther, and toward the church. The text and the book of sources should supplement each other. The source book contains the material to be worked up into a narrative and the text contains the material which has been worked up into a narrative.

REFERENCE BOOKS FOR TEACHERS.

The teacher should have books which contain discussions of method, bibliographies, library lists, topics, etc. With them he will be able to suit his appliances and methods to the peculiar needs of the school.

BOOKS FOR PUPILS.

In selecting the books in history the aim has been to select a few good reference books and interesting books which the pupils will read.

Many of the books the teacher must read with the pupils and she must interest them in parts of the books which bear directly upon the history lesson by lists of references. So far as possible help the pupil to arrange his knowledge so that proper events and people, and events which grow out of each other are associated.

Manners and customs should be dwelt upon. The pupils should be required to make judgments upon the conditions of life, upon men and measures. Help them to admire bravery, courage, duty, perseverance and self-sacrifice.

GENERAL HISTORY.

(For books on Methods of teaching history, *see* EDUCATION.)

F
———
Ad 1 ma

                      List Price to
                      price. schools.

#180. **Manual of Historical literature**, comprising descriptions of the most important histories in English, French, and German, together with practical suggestions as to methods and courses of historical study for the use of students, general readers and collectors of books. Ed. 3 rev., enl. Charles Kendall Adams. N. Y., Harper & Bros., c1888. 720 p. O. cl. 2.50 1.64

 An excellent bibliography of history, including all of the best books published before 1888.

 "It has been my aim to furnish, as best as I could, such information about the most desirable books as the historical reader and student is likely to profit by; and, in the second to suggest the proper methods and order of using the materials so indicated. Each chapter consists of two parts; the first being devoted to descriptions of books, and the second to suggestions to students and readers as to the best order and method of using them.'—From the author's preface.

F
———
Al 5 hi

181. **History topics**: for the use of high schools and colleges. William Francis Allen. Bost., D. C. Heath & Co., 1897. 130 p. S. pa..................... .25 .17

 The first object of the topical method is to give prominence to the most important names and events of history, and concentrate the reading of the students upon certain selected ones of these.

 "Two sets of topics are here presented—the first for general dynastic and territorial history, the second for the history of the United States. The course of dynastic history is intended to occupy an entire year, and is for this purpose divided into thirty divisions, each of which may take up a week, while the rest of the school year may be devoted to reviews and examinations. The system is, however, very elastic, and the work may be compressed or expanded according to the amount of time at the disposal of the class. My way is, after going over a period in chronological order, to review by countries, so as to take up the same points of view. The course in American history consists of fifty daily lessons; but these again may be expanded or condensed at pleasure." Preface.

 Contents: Ancient history; Mediaeval history; Modern history; American history.

F
B 48 ch ·

#182. **Children of the Nations:** a study of colonization and its problems. Poultney Bigelow. N. Y., McClure, Phillips & Co., 1901. 365 p. O. cl. 2.50 2.25

List price. Price to schools.

This brief work is an attempt to explain the influence which the mother country exerts upon colonies, and which colonies in turn exert upon the mother country—for good or evil. It is largely the result of personal observation in parts of the world controlled by the great colonizing powers."—Preface.

This book will be especially valuable to the pupils collecting material for debates and orations.

Contents: How Spain commenced to colonize; First check to Spanish colonization; Development of South America; Relations of Spain with Cuba and Manila down to the end of the nineteenth century; Totter and tumble of Spain's colonial empire; Latter-day Cuba; Philippines in our time; Negro as an element in colonial expansion; Official German colonization; Colonial Portugal in our time; First years of Portuguese greatness; Colonial break-up of Portugal; Portugal in America; Evolution of the Boer; Dutch colonist of today; Boer at home; Scandinavian colonist; Some notes from the Danish West Indies in Santa Cruz; Chinaman as colonist; Old France in the new world; Spirit of France in the West Indies; West Indies two hundred years ago; Colonial France today; Spread of Russia; Beginnings of English colonization in America; When Americans were English; Why England lost her American colonies; Successful tropical republic in the West Indies; From my diary in British Guiana; West Indies today and tomorrow; Australasia; Can the white man and his wife flourish in the tropics; White invasion of China; Philosophy of colonization; American as a colonist.

F
C 84 gr

183. **Great battles of the world.** Stephen Crane. Phil., J. B. Lippincott Co., 1901. 278 p. D. cl. ...... 1.50 .98

The battles described in this volume were chosen by the author for their picturesque and theatrical qualities, as well as for their decisiveness. This is an excellent book for the Library reading class in History.

Contents: Battle of Bunker Hill; Vittoria; Siege of Plevna; Storming of Burkersdorf heights; Swede's campaign in Germany; Storming of Badajos; Brief campaign against New Orleans; Battle of Solferino.

F
F 53 ou

184. [322.] **Outlines of universal history.** T. P. Fisher. N. Y., American Book Company................. 2.40 2.05

A good general history for reference.

F
―――
F 64 st   List Price to
                                                       price. schools.
185. **Studies in European and American history.** Fred
   Morrow Fling, *and* Howard W. Caldwell. Chic.,
   Ainsworth & Co., 1897. 336 p. D. cl. .... 1.00   .80

   An introduction to the source study method in history. It will
enable teachers to see what the method means and how it may be
applied.
   Contents: Part I—Historical methods; Grecian period; Romans;
Middle Ages—period of transition; Middle Ages; Later Middle
Ages; Renaissance and reformation; Period of absolute monarchies; French Revolution; Nineteenth century.
   Part II—General principles and suggestions; Laboratory method;
Interpretation of the general spirit of American history; Interpretation of the colonial period; Study of early Virginia history;
Study of early Massachusetts history; Study of the early history
of the middle colonies; Interpretation of the Revolutionary era;
Interpretation of the period 1815–1830; Interpretation of the
period from 1830–1865.

F
―――
F 82 ge
186. **General sketch of history:** adapted for American students. Edward A. Freeman. N. Y., Henry Holt
   & Co., c1876. 400 p. maps. (Historical course
   for schools.) New, rev. ed., with chronological
   table, maps, and index. S. cl................ 1.10   .99

   A clear, simple and correct sketch of the history of Europe and
of the lands which have drawn their civilization from Europe.
   Contents: Origin of the nations; Greece and the Greek colonies; Roman commonwealth; Heathen empire; Early christian
empire; Roman empire in the east; Frankish empire; Saxon emperors; Franconian emperors; General view of the Middle Ages;
Swabian emperors; Decline of the empire; Greatness of Spain;
Greatness of France; Rise of Russia; French revolution; Reunion of Germany and Italy.

F
―――
H 33 hi
187. **Historical sources in schools:** report to the New England History Teachers' Association by a select
   committee, C. D. Hazen, E. D. Bourne, S. M.
   Dean, M. Farrand, and A. B. Hart. N. Y., Macmillan Co., 1902. 299 p. D. cl. .... .60 .54

   "The present volume has grown out of a report submitted by the
Committee on Historical Materials to the New England History
Teachers' Association at the April meeting in 1900. Believing that
a list of sources available for the study of history in the lower
schools, carefully compiled and critically estimated, would be of
direct value to teachers and students, we essayed the task of making such a list. We have endeavored to cover the various courses
ordinarily offered in the secondary schools, but we do not imagine

that our list is exhaustive or that our appreciations will be undisputed."—*Preface*.

The committee has thought it desirable to follow for its purposes the divisions of fields of history recommended by the Committee of Seven; that is, four courses of Ancient History, Mediaeval and Modern European History, English History, and American History, in the order named.

F

H 87 fl

#188. **Flags of the world:** their history, blazonry, and associations. Frederick Edward Hulme. N. Y., Frederick Warne & Co. n. d. 152 p. il. D. cl.   1.50 .93

A reliable reference book on the subject of flags.

F

M 99 ge

189. **General history for colleges and high schools.** Philip Van Ness Myers. Bost., Ginn & Co., 1901. 759 p. il. maps. D. cl. 1.50 1.28

This volume is based upon Myers' "Ancient History" and "Mediaeval and Modern History."

Contents: 1. Ancient history—Eastern nations; Grecian history; Roman history.

2. Mediaeval history—The Dark Ages; Age of Revival.

3. Modern history—Era of Protestant reformation; Era of Political revolution.

F

Sa 5 hi

189a. [323.] **History of the world,** from the earliest time to the year 1898. Edgar Sanderson. N. Y., D. Appleton & Co., 1898. 790 p. il. D. (Concise knowledge lib.) hf. leath. 2.00 1.28

Valuable for reference and an outline of the entire subject.

F

Sh 3 st

190. **Studies in general history.** Mary D. Sheldon. Bost., D. C. Heath & Co., 1900. 556 p. il. maps. D. cl. .... 1.12 .95

When properly used this book will be one of the most valuable text-books for secondary schools. It is designed to introduce the student to the sources of historical information and abounds with extracts from original authorities. The book is well supplied with maps, tables and illustrations.

"This book is not a history, but a collection of historical materials; it contains just the sort of things that historians must deal with when they want to describe or judge any period of history, and just the kind of things, moreover, which we Americans must constantly attend to and think about. In Greek history, it gives bare chronicles of deeds, pictures of buildings and statues, extracts from speeches, laws, poems; from these materials you must form your own judgment of the Greeks, discover their style of thinking, acting, living, feeling; you must, in short, imagine that you yourself are to write a Greek history, or that you are a Greek citizen, called upon to judge of the life about you. To help you in this, I have inserted in the midst of the material such questions and problems as the historian or citizen must always be asking himself, or rather must always be putting to the laws, events, poetry, and ruins which he studies, whether they belong to times and peoples far away or near at hand. In this way you can learn how to judge and interpret what you see before you in your own country, and help to make of America that which she may become—the strongest, noblest, finest nation in all the world."—*From Author's Preface.*

ANCIENT HISTORY.

F02
———
Al 5 an

191. **Ancient history for colleges and high schools.** William F. Allen, *and* Philip Van Ness Myers. Bost., Ginn & Co., 1899. 369 + 371 p. il. maps. D. cl. 1.50   1.28

    An excellent account of the development and advance of civilization, generally accurate in its statement of facts. It is well adapted to the class-room and to private reading.
    Contents: 1. Eastern nations and Greece; 2. Short history of the Roman people.

F02
———
An 2 st

192. [325.] **Story of extinct civilization of the East.** Robert E. Anderson. N. Y., D. Appleton & Co., 1899. 213 p. maps. S. (Lib. of useful stories.) cl. .... .40   .36

    A brief and interesting account of the civilizations of Chaldea, Babylonia, Egypt, Phoenicia, Judea, Arabia, and Persia.

F02
———
M 99 an

193. **Ancient history: for colleges and high schools.** Part I. Eastern nations and Greece. Philip Van Ness Myers. Bost., Ginn & Co., 1901. 369 p. 8 maps. il. D. cl. .... 1.00   .90

    The above is a revision and expansion of the corresponding part of Myers' "Outlines of Ancient History." Parts have been

	List price.	Price to schools.

entirely rewritten in the light of the most recent discoveries. Schools which purchase Allen & Myers' "Ancient history" (No. 191) should not purchase this volume as it is Part 1 of the above named book.

F02
―――
R 12 sta

194. [331.] **Story of Assyria** from the rise of the empire to the fall of Nineveh. Zenaide A. Ragozin. N. Y., G. P. Putnam's Sons, 1887. 450 p. il. D. (Story of the nations series.) cl. .... 1.50 .98

A very interesting account. A continuation of the story of Chaldea.

F02
―――
R 12 stc

195. [330.] **Story of Chaldea** from the earliest times to the rise of Assyria. Zenaide A. Ragozin. N. Y., G. P. Putnam's Sons, 1887. 381 p. il. D. (Story of the nations series.) cl. .... 1.50 .98

Very interesting. The book is a general introduction to the study of ancient history.

F02
―――
T 32 ma

196. **Manual of ancient history.** Mary Elsie Thalheimer. N. Y., American Bk. Co., c1900. 376 p. maps and il. O. cl. 1.60 1.36

An accurate reference book, giving briefly the conclusions reached by such modern scholars as Mommsen and Rawlinson. It is a book of facts rather than of opinions and contains some admirable maps and a few excellent illustrations.

Contents: Asiatic and African nations, from the dispersion at Babel to the rise of the Persian empire; Persian empire, from the rise of Cyrus to the fall of Darius; Grecian states and colonies, from their earliest period to the accession of Alexander the Great; History of the Macedonian empire, and the kingdoms formed from it, until their conquest by the Romans; History of Rome, from the earliest times to the fall of the western empire.

MODERN HISTORY.

F03
———
Ad 1 me

                List Price to
               price. schools.

197. **Medieval and modern history:** an outline of its development. George Burton Adams. N. Y., Macmillan Co., 1900. 474 p. il. and maps. O. cl.. 1.10 .99

 A very valuable feature of this book is the bibliography which follows the treatment of each period suggesting further reading which may be done.

 "In the preparation of the text I have endeavored to give especial emphasis to the different periods of history, and at the same time to make clear the continuous movement. If any fairly good conception can be gained from the study of history of the steady march of humanity up to its present level, one of its richest and most fruitful results has been secured, and it is a wish of mine, though one perhaps not easily realized, that the teacher should be able to make his class see in each lesson, or at least in each of the minor epochs of history, how the movement advances a stage in the given bit of time."—*From Author's Preface.*

 Contents: Roman world-state with its fall and its revival; Formation of the nations; Renaissance and reformation; Struggle of the nations for supremacy and expansion.

F03
———
D 93 hi

198. **History of modern times:** from the fall of Constantinople to the French Revolution. Victor Duruy. Translated and revised, with notes by Edwin A. Grosvenor. N. Y., Henry Holt & Co., 1894. 540 p. D. cl. 1.60 1.44

 No other single volume treats of this period in a more compact, accurate, and interesting manner.

 Contents: Revolution in the political order, or definitive ruin of the political institutions of the middle ages, and a new system of government; Consequences of the political revolution—First European wars; Revolution in interests, ideas, and creeds; Catholic restoration and the religious wars — preponderance of Spain; Ascendency of France under Louis XIII and Louis XIV; Eighteenth century—greatness of England, Russia, and Prussia; Preliminaries of the French revolution.

F03
———
T 32 ma

199. **Manual of mediaeval and modern history.** Mary Elsie Thalheimer. N. Y., American Bk. Co., n. d. 480 p. maps. O. cl. 1.60 1.36

 This, like the "Manual of Ancient History," is too dry for a text-book unless enlivened by the instruction of a live teacher. It is generally accurate, and is a good work of reference.

MEDIAEVAL HISTORY.

F04
Ad 1 ci

200. [349.] **Civilization during the middle ages**, especially in relation to modern civilization. George Burton Adams. N. Y., C: Scribner's Sons, 1899. 463 p. O. cl. 2.50 1.60

A most valuable book of reference. The bibliography is especially fine.

F04
C 47 be

201. **Beginning of the middle ages.** Richard William Church. N. Y., C: Scribner's Sons, 1900. 226 p. 3 maps. (Epochs of modern history series.) S. cl.
Same. N. Y., Longmans, Green & Co., 1900. 216 p. S. cl. .... 1.00 .65

This volume is an introduction to the series of "Epochs of Modern History." It is a general sketch, giving only a bare outline, while the remaining volumes of the series enter into detail, filling out this volume.

F04
D 93 hi

202. **History of the middle ages.** Victor Duruy. Translated from the twelfth edition by E. H. and M. D. Whitney; with notes and revisions by George Burton Adams. N. Y., Henry Holt & Co., 1891. 588 p. 13 maps. D. cl. 1.60 1.44

This gives a clear conception of the general life and growth of the race during the middle ages, and of the relation of the several lines of progress to one another.
Contents: Germanic invasion; Arab invasion; Carolingian empire, or the attempt to organize German and Christian Europe; Fall of the Carolingian empire—new barbarian invasions; Feudalism, or the history of the kingdoms formed from the Carolingian empire during the tenth and eleventh centuries; Struggle between the papacy and the empire; Crusades; Rivalry between France and England; Italy, Germany, and the other European states to the middle of the fifteenth century; Civilization in the last centuries of the middle ages.

F04
Em 3 in

203. [351.] **Introduction to the study of the middle ages.** (375-814.) Ephraim Emerton. Bost., Ginn & Co., 1894. 368 p. maps. D. cl. 1.12 1.01

An outline of the history of the middle ages. The bibliographies are good.

LIST OF BOOKS FOR HIGH SCHOOL LIBRARIES. 59

F04
Em 3 me
                                                            List   Price to
                                                            price. schools.
204. **Mediaeval Europe, 814–1300.** Ephriam Emerton.
    Bost., Ginn & Co., 1901. 607 p. 4 maps. D.
    cl. 1.50   1.28

 This book covers a period extending from the death of Charlemagne to about the middle of the thirteenth century.
 Contents: Bibliographical introduction; Formation of the European states; Roman papacy during the Carolingian period; Revival of the Roman empire on a German basis; Degradation and restoration of the papacy; Europe in the year 1000; Empire at its height; Parties in the great struggle; Conflict of the investiture; Hohenstaufen policy in Germany and Italy; Papal triumph over Frederick II; Crusades; Growth of the French monarchy; Intellectual life; Feudal institutions; Organization of the middle and lower classes; Ecclesiastical system.

F04
G 33 st
205. **Study of mediaeval history:** by the library method
    for high schools. M. S. Getchell. Bost., Ginn &
    Co., 1898. 73 p. D. cl. 50   .43

 Prepared for the use of the author's second-year classes in the Somerville English High School, Somerville, Mass. Not intended as an exhaustive study of mediaeval history, but as a practical work for the class-room. A list is given of the works cited, with author, title, publisher, and date of publication.

F04
G 94 ge
206. [352.] **General history of civilization in Europe.**
    Francois Pierre Guillaume Guizot, ed. by George
    Wells Knight. N. Y., D. Appleton & Co., 1896.
    403 p. D. cl. ....   1.50   .98

 The older student directed by the teacher will find much of interest in this book. The teacher will find it helpful to a better understanding of history.

F04
H 38 se
207. **Select historical documents of the Middle Ages.**
    Translated and edited by Ernest F. Henderson.
    London, George Bell & Sons (N. Y., Macmillan
    Co.), 1896. 177 p. D. (Bohn's libraries.) cl..   1.50   .98

 The documents chosen cover a period of nine hundred years of the world's history, and vary in length from one page to one hundred and twenty. Law, religion, politics, and general civilization are among the topics chosen for illustration.
 "I have tried first of all in this collection to choose the most comprehensive documents, i. e., those which were important not only for

| | List price. | Price to schools. |

the moment, but which, during long periods of time, were pointed to as conclusive. . . . And I have striven to give documents which will represent as far as possible the spirit of the time."— *Preface.*

F04

J 71 st

208. **Studies in European history:** civilization in the Middle ages. Guernsey Jones. Chic., Ainsworth & Co., 1900. 164 p. D. cl. .... 1.00 .80

The introduction to this book gives some very helpful suggestions on the Source study method of teaching history. The book itself is not a narrative like the ordinary school history, it contains the material to be worked up into a narrative.
Contents: Christian and pagan; Teutons and barbarians; Selections from the Koran; Chivalry and the mode of warfare; Feudalism; Monasticism; Jews of Angevin England; Rise of cities; Trades of Paris; Giraldus Cambrensis.

F04

M 99 mi

209. **Middle Ages.** Philip Van Ness Myers. Bost., Ginn & Co., 1902. 454 p. maps. D. cl. 1.25 1.06

A revision of the first half of "Mediaeval and Modern History." The narrative has been carefully revised, so that it embodies the latest positive results of late scholarly research. A valuable feature of the book is the brief bibliography appended to each chapter of the most important of the original sources and secondary works on the subject.

F04

Se 6 fr

210. [357.] **Franks,** from their origin as a confederacy to the establishment of the kingdom of France and the German Empire. Lewis Sergeant. N. Y., G. P. Putnam's Sons, 1898. 343 p. il. D. (Story of the nations series.) cl .... 1.50 .98

A most interesting period and one on which there is a scarcity of material.

F04

T 32 sh

211. **Short history of Mediaeval Europe.** Oliver J. Thatcher. N. Y., C: Scribner's Sons, 1900. 325 p. map. D. cl. 1.25 1.12

This is an abridgment of Thatcher and Schwill's "Europe in the Middle Age," and is intended for use as a text-book in high schools and for the general reader.
Contents: Europe, its peoples, and the Christian church; Migrations of the nations; Reaction of the empire against the Germans;

| | List price. | Price to schools. |

Franks; Dismemberment of the empire; Political history of France; Germany and its relation to Italy; England and the Norsemen; Normans in Italy; Feudalism; Growth of the papacy; Struggle between the papacy and the empire; Monasticism; Mohammed, Mohammedanism, and the Crusades; Development of the cities, more especially in France; Italy to the invasion of Charles VIII.; France, England; Lesser countries of Europe to 1500; Germany; Papacy; Italian Renaissance.

CRUSADES.

F05

Ar 2 cr

212. [354.] **Crusaders:** a story of the Latin Kingdom of Jerusalem. T. A. Archer, and C. L. Kingsford. N. Y., G. P. Putnam's Sons, 1895. il. map. D. (Story of the nations series.) cl. .... 1.50 .98

The history of the crusades, their causes and results, told in a readable way.

F05

C 83 cr

213. **Crusades.** George W. Cox. N. Y., C: Scribner's Sons, 1902. 228 p. maps. (Epochs of modern history series.) S. cl.
Same. N. Y., Longmans, Green & Co., 1901. 220 p. S. cl. .... 1.00 .65

For those who care to make a thorough study of the crusades, this book will be of little value, but as a high school reference book and for the general reader it is the best brief outline of the crusades.

F05

M 73 sh

214. [353.] **Short history of the crusades.** J. I. Mombert. N. Y., D. Appleton & Co., 1894. 301 p. S. cl.... 1.50 .98

A brief account of the leading events and personages in the crusades.

F05

R 38 ch

215. **Chronicles of the crusades:** contemporary narratives of the crusade of Richard Coeur de Lion. Richard of Devizes and Geoffrey de Vinsauf. Together with crusade of Saint Louis. Lord John de Joinville. London, George Bell & Sons (N. Y., Macmillan Co.), 1900. 562 p. D. (Bohn's libraries.) cl. 1.50 1.35

"The present volume comprises the three most interesting contemporary Chronicles of the Crusades which have been handed down

62   LIST OF BOOKS FOR HIGH SCHOOL LIBRARIES.

                                                                                                         List Price to
                                                                                                         price. schools.

to us; two of them recording very fully the romantic deeds of our lion-hearted Plantagenet; the third the chivalric career of the pious and exemplary Saint Louis of France.

Of the author of the first of these Chronicles, Richard of Devizes, nothing is known beyond what he himself informs us in his preface, by which it appears, that he was in early life a monk at St. Swithin's Priory at Winchester, and subsequently a Carthusian of Witham.

Other works have been ascribed to the same writer, but there is great uncertainty as to their authorship. His Chronicle is valuable because it connects affairs which were passing in England with the events which took place simultaneously in the Holy Land. . . .

The second work in this series is the History of the Expedition of Richard Coeur de Lion to the Holy Land, by Geoffrey de Vinsauf. . . .

Of all his works, the most important and intrinsically valuable is his History of the Third Crusade, under Richard the First of England and Philip Augustus of France. It is the only Chronicle written by an eye-witness, of those furious assaults which the army of Saladin made upon the Christians, and of the firmness with which the lion-hearted Richard withstood and repulsed them. If the reader takes the trouble of comparing Geoffrey's full and interesting account of the crusade with that of Richard of Devizes, he will perceive how much superior it is in every respect. Geoffrey lived to see the death of King Richard, and the accession of his brother John, and it is much to be lamented that he breaks off his history somewhat abruptly, just at the moment when the crusaders embark on board ship to leave the Holy Land, at the end of the year 1192. . . .

The third and last, and by no means the least interesting work in this volume, is Joinville's Memoirs of Saint Louis, the crusading king of France."—*Preface.*

EUROPE—HISTORY.

F30

Ad 1 eu

216. [324.] **European history:** an outline of its development. George Burton Adams. N. Y., Macmillan Co., 1899. 577 p. il. O. hf. leath.............. 1.40 1.26

A most valuable book for reference. The bibliographies are most excellent.

F30

F 99 hi

217. **History of modern Europe, 1792–1878.** Charles Alan Fyffe. N. Y., Henry Holt & Co., 1896. 1088 p. maps. D. cl. 2.75 2.47

The best narration that we have of the age of the revolution. It shows the fundamental characteristics of the revolutionary period, and Napoleon's connection with them.

Contents: France and Germany at the outbreak of the Revolutionary war; War, down to the treaties of Basle and the establish-

LIST OF BOOKS FOR HIGH SCHOOL LIBRARIES. 63

                                                           List Price to
                                                           price. schools.

ment of the Directory; Italian campaigns; treaty of Campo Formio; From the Congress of Rastadt to the establishment of the consulate; From Marengo to the rupture of the peace of Amiens; Empire, to the peace of Presburg; Death of Pitt, to the peace of Tilsit; Spain, to the fall of Saragossa; War of 1809; the Napoleonic empire—Spain, to the battle of Salamanca; Russian campaign, to the treaty of Kalisch; War of liberation, to the peace of Paris; Restoration; Progress of reaction; Mediterranean movements of 1820; Greece and eastern affairs; Movements of 1830; Spanish and eastern affairs; Europe before 1848; March revolution, 1848; Period of conflict, down to the establishment of the second French empire; Crimean war; Creation of the Italian kingdom; German ascendancy won by Prussia; War between France and Germany; Eastern affairs.

F30

H 27 ba

#218. **Balance of power, 1715–1789.** Arthur Hassall. N. Y., Macmillan Co., 1900. 433 p. maps. Period VI. (Periods of European history series.) D. cl.   1.60   1.44

    The volumes in the "Periods of European History" series are valuable for extended reference work but should not be purchased by the small High school libraries.

F30

J 55 st

219. [358.] **Story of the Normans.** Sarah Orne Jewett. N. Y., G. P. Putnam's Sons, 1887. 373 p. il. D. (Story of the nations series.) cl. ....   1.50   .98

    The story of the Normans chiefly in their relation to the conquest of England. One of the most interesting books in the series.

F30

J 62 eu

#220. **Europe in the sixteenth century, 1494–1598.** Arthur Henry Johnson, London, Rivingtons (N. Y., Macmillan Co.), 1900. 492 p. maps. Period IV. (Periods of European history series.) D. cl. ..   1.75   1.57

    The volumes in the "Periods of European History" series are valuable for extended reference work but should not be purchased by the small High school libraries.

F30

J 62 no

221. **Normans in Europe.** *Rev.* A. H. Johnson. N. Y., C: Scribner's Sons, 1901. 273 p. maps. (Epochs of modern history series.) S. cl.
    Same. N. Y., Longmans, Green & Co., 1899. 260 p. S. cl. ....   1.00   .65

    "The aim of this book is to present a connected view of these incursions, and to bring clearly before the reader the important fact,

		List price.	Price to schools.

that the Norman conquest was only the last of this long series of settlements and conquests."—*From Preface.*

Contents: Northmen in their home; Invasions of the Northmen; Settlements in Gaul; William Longsword; Capetian revolution; Richard the good and the Norman settlement in Italy; Richard III and Robert the magnificent; Earlier years of William in Normandy; Feudal system and monasticism; Review of English history; Later years of William in Normandy; Conquest of England; William's English policy; End of reign of William I; William Rufus; Henry I; Norman administration.

F30

Sch 9 hi

222. [359.] **History of Modern Europe.** Ferdinand Schwill. N. Y., C: Scribner's Sons, 1898. 434 p. maps. D. cl. 1.50 1.35

A general view of the subject for reference.

F30

Se 3 er

223. **Era of the Protestant Revolution.** Frederic Seebohm. Ed. 2 N. Y., C: Scribner's Sons, 1901. 250 p. maps. (Epochs of modern history series.) S. cl. Same. N. Y., Longmans, Green & Co., 1901. 236 p. S. cl. .... 1.00 .65

This is not one of the best of the series but is a concise and popular summary of events from the beginning of the seventeenth century to near the close.

F30

St 4 re

#224. **Revolutionary Europe.** 1789–1815. Henry Norse Stephens. London, Rivingtons (N. Y., Macmillan Co.), 1900. 423 p. maps. Period VII. (Periods of European history series.) D. cl. 1.40 1.26

The volumes in the "Periods of European History" series are valuable for extended reference work but should not be purchased by the small High school libraries.

F30

T 32 eu

225. **Europe in the Middle Age.** Oliver J. Thatcher *and* Ferdinand Schwill. N. Y., C: Scribner's Sons, 1901. 679 p. maps and charts. D. cl. 2.00 1.80

This book is intended as a text for the use of the freshman classes in college but will be very valuable for reference in the high school.

Contents: Europe, its peoples, and the christian church; Migrations of the nations; History of the new christian German

	List price.	Price to schools.

states; Reaction of the empire against the Germans; Franks; Dismemberment of the empire; Political history of France; Germany and its relation to Italy; England and the Norsemen; Normans in Italy; Feudalism; Growth of the papacy; Struggle between the papacy and the empire; Monasticism; Mohammed; Mohammedanism and the crusades; Development of the cities, more especially in France; Italy to the invasion of Charles VIII; France, England; Lesser countries of Europe to 1500; Germany; Papacy; Civilization of the Middle Age; Italian Renaissance.

F30
―――
T 32 ge
226. **General history of Europe, 350–1900.** Oliver J. Thatcher *and* Ferdinand Schwill. N. Y., C: Scribner's Sons, 1900. 613 p. maps. O. cl. 1.50   1.35

Two of the most helpful features of this book are the carefully selected list of books to be used as supplementary to the text which accompany each chapter and the special topics which conclude each chapter and are intended to suggest added work for study for the brighter and more active members of the class.

F30
―――
W 13 eu
#227. **Europe, 1598–1715.** Henry Offley Wakeman. N. Y., Macmillan Co., 1900. 392 p. maps. Period V. (Periods of European history series.) D. cl... 1.40   1.26

The volumes in the "Periods of European History" are valuable for extended reference work but should not be purchased by the small High school libraries.

GREECE—HISTORY.

F32
―――
B 38 ch
228. [346.] **Charicles;** or illustrations of the private life of the ancient Greeks. W. A. Becker. N. Y., Longmans, Green & Co., 1895. 512 p. il. D. cl. .. .. 1.25   .82

A short story portraying Greek life, with explanatory notes bringing out the facts of life. Valuable for work in history. Will also make real the life studied in the work in Greek.

F32
―――
B 43 tr
229. **Troy:** its legend, history and literature, with a sketch of the topography of the Troad in the light of recent investigation. Samuel G. W. Benjamin. N. Y., C: Scribner's Sons, 1901. 179 p. map. (Epochs of ancient history series.) S. cl....... 1.00   .65

In this book the attempt has been made to tell the Trojan story in the light of recent discoveries and explorations. The story is well

	List price.	Price to schools.

told but does not rest on a firm historical basis. It is probably as near the truth as any other account which we have.

Contents: Youth of Paris; Helen; Greeks at Aulis; Wrath of Achilles; Combat of Menelaus and Paris; Storming of the Greek camp; Death of Hector; Fall of Achilles; Sack of Troy; Origin of the legend; Homer; German criticism on Homer; English criticism of Homer; Historic evidences of the Trojan war; Site of Troy.

F32

B 65 hi

230. [341.] **History of Greece** for high schools and academies. George Willis Botsford. N. Y., Macmillan Co., 1899. 381 p. il. O. cl.... .... 1.10 .96

A valuable book for reference, with marginal references to original authors, and valuable bibliographies at the end of each chapter.

F32

C 47 pi

231. **Pictures from Greek life and story.** Rev. Alfred John Church. N. Y., G. P. Putnam's Sons, 1901. 320 p. il. D. cl. .... 1.25 .82

The title suggests the author's aim in this volume—to present a few picturesque scenes from Greek story. An excellent book for Library reading.

Contents: Statesman and poet; Famous marriage; Exiles of Phocaea; Battlefield of freedom; Three hundred; Wooden walls; Bow against spear; Spoilt by prosperity; Traitor or patriot? In the theater at Athens; Model aristocrat; Statesman and his friends; Great Plague of Athens; Colony; Holy island; Fate of Plataea; Fatal expedition; Last struggle; Eye of Greece; Lion's cub; Wisest of men; Willing prisoner; Cup of hemlock; One hero of Thebes.

F32

C 83 at

232. **Athenian empire.** George W. Cox. N. Y., C: Scribner's Sons, 1901. 257 p. 6 maps. (Epochs of ancient history series.) S. cl.
Same. N. Y., Longmans, Green & Co., 1897. 247 p. S. cl. .... 1.00 .65

Contents: Confederacy of Delos and the foundation of the Athenian empire; Beginnings of the struggle between Athens and Sparta; Peloponnesian war from the surprise of Plataea to the capture of Sphakteria; Peloponnesian war, from the surrender of the Spartans in Sphakteria to the massacre of Melos; Peloponnesian war; the Sicilian expedition; Peloponnesian (or Dekeleian) war, from the failure of the Sicilian expedition to the suppression of the oligarchy of the four hundred at Athens; Peloponnesian (Dekeleian or Ionian) war, from the battle of Kynossema to the surrender of Athens.

F32
C 83 ge

233. **General history of Greece:** from the earliest period to the death of Alexander the Great; with a sketch of the subsequent history to the present time. George W. Cox. N. Y., American Bk. Co., n. d. 709 p. maps. D. cl. .... .60 .54

List price. Price to schools.

One of the best of the smaller histories of Greece. The style is attractive, and the book is well supplied with maps and tables. The author attaches great importance to mythology as a key to the characteristics of early civilization.

Contents: Formation of Hellas; Struggle with Persia, and the growth of the Athenian empire; Empire of Athens; Struggle between Athens and Sparta; Empire of Sparta; Rise and culmination of the Macedonian power; Later fortunes of the Hellenic people.

F32
C 83 gr

234. **Greeks and the Persians.** *Rev.* George William Cox. N. Y., C: Scribner's Sons, 1902. 218 p. maps. (Epochs of ancient history series.) S. cl.
Same. N. Y., Longmans, Green & Co., 1900. 211 p. S. cl. .... 1.00 .65

This volume and the "Athenian empire" form a portion of the ground which is covered in Cox's History of Greece. Much of the history is presented from a different point of view but the descriptions of the most striking scenes and the most important actors in the great dramas are practically reproduced.

Contents: Origin and growth of Greek civilization; Settlements and government of the Greeks; Persian empire under Cyrus, Kambyses, and Dareios; History of Athens in the times of Solon, Peisistratos, and Kleisthenes; Ionic revolt; Invasion of Datis and Artaphernes Invasion and flight of Xerxes; Battles of Plataea and Mykale, and the formation of the Athenian confederacy.

F32
C 94 ri

235. **Rise of the Macedonian empire.** Arthur M. Curteis. N. Y., C: Scribner's Sons, 1900. 215 p. 8 maps. (Epochs of ancient history series.) S. cl.
Same. N. Y., Longmans, Green & Co., 1899. 207 p. S. cl. .... 1.00 .65

The best short history of Alexander that we have. It gives a clear and graphic picture of Macedonian power from its earliest development to the death of Alexander the Great. All unnecessary details are omitted.

Contents: Geography and inhabitants of Macedon; Kings of Macedon to the death of Amyntas II. father of Philip; Macedon and Hellas at Philip's accession; From the accession of Philip to his intervention in the sacred war; Peace of Philokrates: False legatio; Thermopylae in Philip's hands; From the peace of Philokrates to the battle of Chaironeia; From the battle of Chaironeia to the beginning of Alexander's Asiatic campaigns; Alexander in Asia Minor; From the siege of Halikarnassos to the battle of Issos; From the battle of Issos to the battle of Guagamela; From the battle of Guagamela to the sack of Persepolis; Death of Darius, reduction of Parthia: execution of Philotas and Permenion; Campaigns in Baktria and Sogdiana; From the Oxus to the Hyphasis; Return from the Hyphasis to Susa; Closing scenes.

F32
F 64 st

236. **Studies in European history: Greek and Roman civilization.** Fred Morrow Fling. Chic., Ainsworth & Co., 1900. 163 p. D. cl.............. 1.00 .80

This contains an introduction to the Source method of studying history. It is not a narrative like the ordinary school history but contains the material to be worked up into a narrative.

The text and book of sources should complement one another.

Contents: Homeric age; Athenian constitution; Spartan life; Alexander's methods of warfare; Achaean league; Roman constitution; Roman life of the first Punic war; Roman life of the Jugurthine period; Roman life under the empire; Roman law.

F32
G 17 ma

#237. [345.] **Manual of Greek antiquities.** Percy Gardner *and* Frank Byron Jevons. N. Y., C: Scribner's Sons, 1895. 736 p. il. D. cl. 4.00 3.60

A valuable and comprehensive book of reference for work in history.

Contents: The land and the people, the cities, the homes, dress, religion and religious ceremonies, philosophy, education, commerce, slavery, war, the theater, and constitutional and legal antiquities.

F32
G 93 li

238. [344.] **Life of the Greeks and Romans,** described from antique monuments. E. Guhl, *and* W. Koner, tr. by F. Hueffer. N. Y., D. Appleton & Co., 1898. 618 p. il. O. cl. 2.50 1.64

A valuable book of reference for older pupils, or for a large library.

F32
H 24 st

239. [342.] **Story of Greece.** James A. Harrison. N. Y., G. P. Putnam's Sons, 1889. 515 p. il. D. (Story of the nations series.) cl..................... 1.50 .98

"Whenever it was possible, the great and beautiful deeds, the fine stories, the narrations of admirable actions, the stirring and

| | List price. | Price to schools. |

illustrative anecdotes to be found in ancient writers, have been chosen to describe Greek life and civilization in preference to a dry chronicle of dates and events."—*The author.*

F32

M 83 hg

239a. [343.] **Historical tales: Greek.** Charles Morris. Phil., J. B. Lippincott Co., 1896. 366 p. il. D. cl. .... 1.00 .65

Short tales of the romantic events in Greek history for youngest pupils. Will serve to start an interest in Grecian history.

F32

M 99 hi

240. **History of Greece for colleges and high schools.** Philip Van Ness Myers. Bost., Ginn & Co., 1900. 577 p. il. 19 maps. D. cl............... 1.25 1.06

The author has aimed to give prominence to the permanent elements only of Greek history. Besides a list of books for further reading which is given after each chapter throughout the work, a short bibliography, classified by periods and subjects, is given at the end.

Contents: Hellas before the Persian wars; Persian wars; Persian wars to the beginning of the Peloponnesian war; Peloponnesian war; End of the Peloponnesian war to the conquest of Greece by the Romans; Greek art, culture, and social life.

F32

Om 1 hi

241. **History of Greece,** from the earliest times to the death of Alexander the Great. Charles W. C. Oman. N. Y., Longmans, Green & Co., 1901. 560 p. il. and maps. D. Ed. 7, rev. cl......... 1.50 .98

This book has been revised in the light of late original research. Valuable for reference.

F32

Sa 5 sp

242. **Spartan and Theban supremacies.** Charles Sankey. N. Y., C: Scribner's Sons, 1901. 231 p. 5 maps. (Epochs of ancient history series.) S. cl.
Same. N. Y., Longmans, Green & Co., 1898. 224 p. S. cl. .... 1.00 .65

"In treating this period, I have tried to bring out clearly the character of the leading men and the causes of the chief events; and I have omitted most of the infinitely small details with which Xenophon has filled the pages of his 'Hellenika.'"—*Author's Preface.*

Contents: Spartan supremacy; Athens under the thirty; Restoration of the Athenian democracy; Socrates; Ten thousand;

70　LIST OF BOOKS FOR HIGH SCHOOL LIBRARIES.

| | List price. | Price to schools. |

Sparta: her allies and subjects; Operations to Asia Minor; Corinthian war; Peace of Antalkidas; Suppression of Olynthos, and the liberation of Thebes; Rise of Thebes; Theban supremacy.

F32

W 14 li

243. **Little Arthur's history of Greece.** Arthur S. Walpole. N. Y., Thos. Y. Crowell & Co., c1901. 306 p. 11. D. cl. .... .60 　.40

An interesting story of the history of Greece; excellent for Library reading.

Contents: Greece and the Greeks; Trojan war; Manners and customs of the Spartans; Sparta conquers the Peloponnese; Age of the tyrants; Early history of Athens; Peisistratus and his sons; Athens; the reforms of Cleisthenes; Greeks of Asia and the Persians; Ionic revolt; First Persian invasion of Greece; Athens between the two invasions; Second invasion of Greece; Xerxes and Thermopylae; Battles of Artemisium, Salamis, and Himera; Battles of Plataea and Mycale; New walls of Athens and the Peiraeus; Fall of Pausanias: the confederacy of Delos; Latter day of Themistocles and Aristeides; Cimon leader of Athens; Rise of the Athenian empire; Pericles leader of Athens; Events which led to the Peloponnesian war; Peloponnesian war breaks out; Revolt of Lesbos: fate of Plataea; Phormio in the Corinthian gulf; Pylus and Sphacteria; Brasidas in Thrace; Alcibiades, the spoilt child of Athens; Athenian expedition to Sicily; Terrible fate of the Sicilian expedition; Uphill struggle of Athens; Government of the four hundred; War brought to an end; Thirty tyrants; Socrates; March of the ten thousand; Agesilaus, the lame king; Sparta's power: Pelopidas of Thebes; Thebes supreme in Greece; Philip of Macedon; Demosthenes, the Athenian orator; Alexander the Great; Alexander conquers Asia; Alexander the tyrant; Alexander's empire in pieces.

ROME—HISTORY.

F36

B 38 ga

244. [340.] **Galius:** or Roman scenes of the time of Augustus. W. A. Becker, tr. by Frederick Metcalfe. N. Y., Longmans, Green & Co., 1898. 535 p. D. cl. .... 1.25 　.82

A short story portraying the life of the Romans, with explanatory notes emphasizing the facts of life. Valuable for work in history.

LIST OF BOOKS FOR HIGH SCHOOL LIBRARIES. 71

	List price.	Price to schools.

F36
―――
B 39 gr
245. **Gracchi, Marius, and Sulla.** Augustus Henry Beesly. N. Y., C: Scribner's Sons, 1901. 217 p. maps. (Epochs of ancient history series.) S. cl. Same. N. Y., Longmans, Green & Co., 1899. 205 p. S. cl. .... 1.00 .65

The author has described admirably the social difficulties that led to the attempts of the Gracchi at reform. The meaning of the civil wars, and Sulla's triumph, are shown in a strong light.

Contents: Antecedents of the revolution; Tiberius Gracchus; Caius Gracchus; Jugurthine war; Cimbri and Teutones; Roman army; Saturninus and Drusus; Social war; Sulpicius; Marius and Cinna; First Mithridatic war; Sulla in Greece and Asia; Sulla in Italy; Personal rule and death of Sulla; Sulla's reactionary measures.

F36
―――
B 65 hi
246. **History of Rome:** for high schools and academies. George Willis Botsford. N. Y., Macmillan Co., 1902. 396 p. il. O. cl. .... 1.10 .99

"This book is similar in plan to the 'History of Greece'. It aims to present briefly the growth of Rome, the expansion and organization of her power, the development and decline of the imperial system, and the transformation of the ancient pagan empire of the Romans into the mediaeval Christian empire of the Germans. The narrative, accordingly, extends from the earliest times to Charlemagne. The treatment of the early constitution rests directly upon the sources, which uniformly represent the plebeians as citizens and the patricians as their leaders.

Emphasis is placed on the period of the emperors as the time during which Rome stamped her character upon the history of the world. Attention is directed not so much to the vices and intrigues of the imperial court as to the progress of mankind both in the capital and in the provinces. Wars are treated with reference to their influence on the current of history, and for the illustration of individual and national character."—*From the preface.*

Contents: People and the country; Beginning of Rome—The prehistoric age; Rome becomes supreme in Italy; Plebeians win their rights; Expansion of the Roman power; Growth of plutocracy; Revolution; Founding of the Imperial Government; Dyarchy to monarchy; Limited monarchy; Growth of absolute monarchy; Invasion of the Barbarians and the fall of the empire in the west; New German states and the Empire of Charlemagne; Private and social life of the Romans; Helps to the study of Roman history.

F36
―――
B 84 hi
247. **History of the Roman Republic:** abridged from the history by Prof. Mommsen. Clement Bryans *and* F. J. Hendy. N. Y., C: Scribner's Sons, 1901. 542 p. D. cl. 1.25 1.12

Mommsen is recognized as the prince of Roman historians but

	List price.	Price to schools.

his "History of Rome" is too large for the use of the ordinary High school. This abridgment is an excellent one.

Contents: Period anterior to the abolition of the monarchy; From the abolition of the monarchy in Rome to the Union of Italy; From the Union of Italy to the subjugation of Carthage and the Greek states; Revolution; Establishment of the military monarchy.

F36

B 84 ho

248. **Holy Roman Empire.** James Bryce. N. Y., Macmillan Co., 1902. 479 p. D. cl. .... 1.00 .50

A portrayal of the relations of Rome and Germany during the Middle Ages. This is a book which may well be the beginning of all systematic study of German history.

F36

B 95 hi

249. [334.] **History of the Roman empire** from its foundation to the death of Marcus Aurelius. J. B. Bury. N. Y., American Book Company, 1899. 638 p. il. D. (Student's series.) cl. 1.50 1.28

F36

C 17 ea

250. **Early empire:** from the assassination of Julius Caesar to that of Domitian. William Wolfe Capes. N. Y., C: Scribner's Sons, 1901. 240 p. maps. (Epochs of ancient history series.) S. cl.
Same. N. Y., Longmans, Green & Co., 1897. 230 p. S. cl. .... 1.00 .65

The author's style is spirited and graceful.
Contents: Augustus Tiberius; Caligula; Claudius; Nero; Galba; Otho; Vitellius; Vespasian; Titus; Domitian; Position of the emperor; Rights of Roman citizenship; Life in the provinces; State of trade; Growing depopulation of Italy and Greece; Frontiers and the army; Moral standard of the age; Revival of religious sentiment.

F36

C 17 ro

251. **Roman empire of the second century:** or, The age of the Antonines. William Wolfe Capes. N. Y., C: Scribner's Sons, 1901. 226 p. maps. (Epochs of ancient history series.) S. cl.
Same. N. Y., Longmans, Green & Co., 1897. 216 p. S. cl. .... 1.00 .65

This volume is fully as good as the earlier volume "The early empire". The chapters on the attitude of the empire towards the early Christians, on the characteristics of the state of religion, and on the administration forms of the imperial government are especially good.

Contents: Nerva; Trajan; Hadrian; Antoninus Pius; Marcus Aurelius Antonius; Attitude of the imperial government towards the Christians; Characteristics of the state religion, and of the rites imported from the east; Literary currents of the age; Administrative forms of the imperial government.

F36
C 47 ro
252. **Roman life in the days of Cicero.** Alfred J. Church. N. Y., Dodd, Mead & Co., n. d. 292 p. D. cl.. .75 .67

A sketch of the personality and career of Cicero. A very interesting book for Library reading.

"This book does not claim to be a life of Cicero or a history of the last days of the Roman Republic. Still less does it pretend to come into comparison with such a work as Bekker's *Gallus*, in which on a slender thread of narrative is hung a vast amount of facts relating to the social life of the Romans. I have tried to group round the central figure of Cicero various sketches of men and manners, and so to give my readers some idea of what life actually was in Rome, and the provinces of Rome, during the first six decades—to speak roughly—of the first century B. C."—*Preface.*

F36
G 35 hi
253. [335.] **History of the decline and fall of the Roman empire.** Edward Gibbon, abridged by William Smith. N. Y., American Book Company, 1899. 677 p. il. D. (Student's series.) cl. 1.25 1.08

F36
G 42 st
254. [336.] **Story of Rome** from the earliest times to the end of the republic. Arthur Gilman. N. Y., G. P. Putnam's Sons, 1888. 355 p. il. D. (Story of the nations series.) cl. .... 1.50 .98

The book is well written and events are given in their relations to each other and to general history.

"It is hoped to enter to some degree into the real life of the Roman people, to catch the true spirit of their actions, and to indicate the current of the national life."—*The author.*

F36
Ih 5 ea
255. **Early Rome:** from the foundation of the city to its destruction by the Gauls. William Ihne. N. Y., C: Scribner's Sons, 1902. 217 p. maps. (Epochs of ancient history series.) S. cl.
Same. N. Y., Longmans, Green & Co., 1895. 207 p. S. cl. .... 1.00 .65

The author of this volume is one of the most eminent German historians of Rome. He has given in readable form the results of

                                                              List   Price to
                                                              price. schools.
modern criticism and research on the earliest period of Roman history. All scientific references and notes have been excluded, yet no statement has been made which can not be substantiated by reference to the original authority.

Contents: Causes of the greatness of Rome; Sources of the history of Rome; Legends of the seven kings of Rome; Examination of the legends of the kings; Five phases of the history of Rome in the regal period; Religious institutions in the time of the kings; Character of the monarchy; Senate of the regal period; People in the regal period; Magistrates of the republic; Senate of the republic; Popular assemblies of the republic; Tribunes of the people; Agrarian law of Spurius Cassius; League with the Latins and Hernicans; Wars with the Volscians and Aequians; War with the Etruscans; Decemvirs and the laws of the twelve tables; Extension of plebeian rights; Foreign relations of Rome down to the conquest of Veii; Invasion of the Gauls.

F36

In 4 so

256. [339.] **Society in Rome under the Caesars.** William Ralph Inge. N. Y., C: Scribner's Sons, 1894. 276 p. D. cl. .... 1.25   .82

The manners and customs of the Romans at the time of their greatest power and civilization.

Contents: Religions, philosophy, morality, government, society, literature, art, grades of society, education, marriage, daily life, amusements, and luxury. Valuable reference book.

F36

M 54 ro

257. **Roman triumvirates.** Charles Merivale. N. Y., C: Scribner's Sons, 1901. 248 p. maps. (Epochs of ancient history series.) S. cl.
Same. N. Y., Longmans, Green & Co., 1899. 238 p. S. cl. .... 1.00   .65

The author begins by showing the strong reaction against Sulla, and the consequent rise of Pompey into power. He then passes in review the consulship of Cicero; the triumvirate of Caesar, Pompey and Crassus; the growth of Caesar's power; the rupture between Caesar and the Senate; Civil war; Death of Caesar; Establishment of the second triumvirate and the advancement of Octavius to the mastery of the State.

F36

M 81 ou

258. **Outlines of Roman history:** for the use of high schools and academies. William C. Morey. N. Y., American Book Company, c1901. 366 p. il. D. cl. .... 1.00   .85

An excellent short history of Rome. One good feature of the book is a classified list of the most valuable and available books in the English language upon Roman history.

F36
———
M S3 hr

259. [337.] **Historical tales:** Roman. Charles Morris. Phil., J. B. Lippincott Co., 1896. 340 p. il. D. cl. .... 1.00 .65

List Price to
price. schools.

Short stories of the romantic events in the history of Rome for youngest pupils. Interesting for Library reading.

F36
———
M 99 ro

260. **Rome: its rise and fall;** a text-book for high schools and colleges. Philip Van Ness Myers. Bost., Ginn & Co., 1901. 626 p. il. 19 maps. D. Ed. 2. cl. 1.25 1.06

"This book has been written in response to requests from many teachers that the author should expand his little text-book on Roman history into a more extended account of Roman affairs. Although the entire narrative has been laid on the lines drawn in the earlier book, still the present volume is practically a new work. The development of the Roman constitution during republican times has been traced carefully step by step; while special emphasis has been laid upon the causes that undermined the institutions of the republic, and which later brought about the fall of the empire. A somewhat larger space than usual has been given to the decay of paganism and to the rise and progress of Christianity in the empire. Three chapters at the end of the volume are devoted to an account of Roman civilization."

Contents: Rome as a kingdom; Rome as a republic; Rome as an empire; Architecture, literature, law, and social life; Romano-German or transition age.

F36
———
Se 4 hi

261. **History of the Roman people.** Charles Seignobos. Translation edited by William Fairley. N. Y., Henry Holt & Co., 1902. 528 p. il. 9 maps. D. cl. 1.25 1.12

The aim of the American editor has been to fit the French work to American class-room use. Some slight additions have been made. The original work was carried only through the reign of Theodosius. The period from that time to Charlemagne has been treated in four new chapters. Some omissions also have been made to bring the work into a certain compass. To each chapter has been appended a short list of sources in English. In the appendix is a list of sources..

Contents: Ancient populations of Italy; Kings of Rome; Abolition of royalty; Roman religion; Establishment of legal equality; Conquest of Italy; Roman army; First punic war; Second punic war; Conquest of the basin of the Mediterranean; Results of the conquest; Social and political transformation; Gracchi; Period of Marius and Sulla; Pompey; Caesar and the conquest of the Gauls; End of the republic; Empire; Literature arts and trade; Emperors of the Augustan family; Flavians; Antonines; Arts, letters, and social conditions; Christianity; Decline of the empire; Constantine and the Christian religion; Downfall of paganism; Barbarian invasion; Teutonic kingdoms; Eastern empire; Christianity and Mohammedanism; Charles the Great and the new empire.

	List price.	Price to schools.

F36
Sm 4 ro
262. **Rome and Carthage**: the Punic wars. Reginald Bosworth Smith. N. Y., C: Scribner's Sons, 1901. 298 p. 9 maps. (Epochs of ancient history series.) S. cl.
Same. N. Y., Longmans, Green & Co., 1901. 251 p. S. cl. .... 1.00 .65

This volume is an abbreviation of Smith's "Carthage and Carthaginians."

Contents: Carthage; Carthage and Rome; First Punic war—Messana and Agrigentum; First Roman fleet; Battles of Mylae and Ecnomus; Invasion of Africa: Regulus and Xanthippus; Hamilcar Barca and the siege of Lilybaeum; Hamilcar Barca and the mercenary war; Hamilcar Barca in Africa and Spain; Second Punic war—Passage of the Rhone and the Alps; Battles of Trebia and Trasimene; Hannibal overruns central Italy; Battle of Cannae: character of Hannibal; Revolt of Capua: Siege of Syracuse; Siege of Capua and Hannibal's march on Rome; Battle of the Metaurus; P. Cornelius Scipio; War in Africa: battle of Zama; Carthage at the mercy of Rome; Destruction of Carthage; Carthage as it is.

F36
Sm 6 sm
263. [333.] **Smaller History of Rome** from the earliest times to the establishment of the empire. *Sir* William Smith, rev. by A. H. J. Greenidge. N. Y., American Book Company, 1899. 371 p. il. D. (Student's series.) cl. .... .60 .53

F36
W 16 hl
#264. **History of Rome to the death of Caesar.** William Walsham How, *and* H. D. Leigh. N. Y., Longmans, Green & Co., 1898. 575 p. maps and il. D. cl. 2.00 1.80

A good text in Roman history. The more important and eventful wars and the history of the Roman army have been dwelt on at some length and an attempt has been made to describe clearly and briefly the development of the constitution.

FRANCE—HISTORY.

F39
Ad 1 gr

                                                                                                   List Price to
                                                                                                  price. schools.

265. **Growth of the French nation.** George Burton Adams. N. Y., Macmillan Co., 1902. 350 p. maps and il. D. cl. 1.25   1.12

This volume includes an account of the most important facts which show the growth of the nation from age to age.

Contents—Introduction; Gaul before the Franks; German conquest; Dynasty of the Merovingians; Carolingians and Charlemagne; Breaking up of Charlemagne's empire and the rise of the feudal system; First Capetians—feudal kings and the feudal system; Foundation of France and of the absolute monarchy; Steps toward absolutism; Hundred years' war; France begins to be a European power; Religious civil wars; France again a European power; Louis XIV; Eighteenth century; Causes of the French Revolution; Ten years of Revolution; Napoleon; France since 1815.

F39
B 64 st

266. [370.] **Story of modern France.** Andre le Bon. N. Y., G. P. Putnam's Sons. il. D. (Story of the nations series.) cl. .... 1.50   .98

An interesting account.

F39
C 86 fi

267. [371.] **First history of France.** Louise Creighton. N. Y., Longmans, Green & Co., 1893. 301 p. il. S. cl. .... 1.25   .82

Clearly and simply told for young readers.

F39
G 16 th

268. **Thirty years' war, 1618-1648.** Samuel Rawson Gardiner. N. Y., C: Scribner's Sons, 1901. 237 p. maps. (Epochs of modern history series.) S. cl.
Same. N. Y., Longmans, Green & Co., 1900. 233 p. S. cl. .... 1.00   .65

The account of the effects and results of the war are especially good, and as a brief sketch of a great conflict the book is without an equal.

Contents: Causes of the thirty years' war; Bohemian revolution; imperialist victories in Bohemia and the Palatinate; Mansfeld and Christian in North Germany; Interventon of the King of Denmark; Staalsund and Rochelle; Edict of restitution; Victories of Gustavus Adolphus; Death of Wallenstein and the treaty of Prague; Preponderance of France; End of the war.

F39
———
L 85 fr
269. **Frederick the Great and the seven years' war.** Frederick William Longman. N. Y., C: Scribner's Sons, 1900. 264 p. 2 maps. (Epochs of modern history series.) S. cl. .... 1.00 .65

<small>List price. Price to schools.</small>

This book is mainly intended for school use but will also be of interest to the general reader who wishes to read a short and interesting outline of the life of Frederick the Great and his times.

F39
———
L 95 ev
270. **Eve of the French Revolution.** Edward J. Lowell. Bost., Houghton, Mifflin & Co., 1892. 408 p. D. cl. 2.00 1.30

Contents: King and the administration; Louis XVI and his court; Clergy; Church and her adversaries; Church and Voltaire; Nobility; Army; Courts of law; Equality and liberty; Montesquieu; Paris; Provincial towns; Country; Taxation; Finance; "Encyclopaedia"; Helvetius, Holbach, and Chastellux; Rousseau's political writings; "La Nouvelle Héloise" and "Emile"; Pamphlets; Cahiers; Social and economical matters in the Cahiers; Conclusion.

F39
———
M 76 le
271. **Leading facts of French history.** David H. Montgomery. Bost., Ginn & Co., 1899. 295 p. + 29 p. maps. D. cl. (Leading facts of history series.) 1.12 .96

A very good text on French history, based mainly on the French history of Guizot, Rambaus, Martin, and Duruy.

F39
———
M 83 fr
272. **French Revolution and first empire:** an historical sketch. William O'Connor Morris. With an appendix upon the bibliography of the subject and a course of study by Hon. Andrew D. White. N. Y., C: Scribner's Sons, 1902. 306 p. maps. (Epochs of modern history series.) S. cl.
Same. N. Y., Longmans, Green & Co., 1900. 262 p. S. cl. .... 1.00 .65

Contents: State of France before the revolution; States-general and national assembly; Constitution of 1790-1; Legislative assembly; Convention, to the fall of the moderates; Reign of terror—war—fall of Robespierre; Thermidor—French conquests; Directory—Bonaparte: Egypt and the 18th Brumaire; Marengo, Lunéville, Amiens; Consulate, renewal of war; Empire to Tilsit; Empire to 1813; Fall of Napoleon; Hundred days and Waterloo,

F39
M 83 hf
273. [372.] **Historical tales: French.** Charles Morris. Phil., J. B. Lippincott Co., 1897. 322 p. il. D. cl. .... 1.00 .65

    Romantic events in French history for young readers.

F39
Sl 5 fr
274. **French Revolution and religious reform:** an account of ecclesiastical legislation and its influence on affairs in France from 1789-1804. William Milligan Sloane. N. Y., C: Scribner's Sons, 1901. 333 p. O. cl. 2.00 1.80

    The author has sought to outline the successive steps whereby the revolutionary governments sought the end so earnestly desired by the enlightened of all classes and to exhibit the retarding forces existing partly by foreign intervention, partly by the conservatism of the devout French who were adherents of the papacy, and partly by the fanaticism of unbelief.

    Contents: Introduction; Reform and revolution; Voltaire's indictment of ecclesiasticism; System of oppression; Attitude of the Prelacy; Ecclesiastical committee; Seizure and sale of ecclesiastical estates; Prelude to the civil constitution of the clergy; Civil constitution of the clergy; Climax of Jesuitry; Worship old and new; Carnival of irreligion; Glimpse of religious liberty; Ultramontane folly; Design and form of the concordat; Enforcement of the concordat.

F39
Yo 8 hi
275. [369.] **History of France.** Charlotte M. Yonge. N. Y., American Book Company. 122 p. S. (History primers.) flex. cl. .... .35 .31

    Brief outline of French history.

SPAIN—HISTORY.

F40
M 83 hs
276. [382.] **Historical tales: Spanish.** Charles Morris. Phil., J. B. Lippincott Co., 1899. 331 p. il. D. cl. .... 1.00 .65

    Romantic events in history of Spain for young readers.

F40
P 92 hi
#277. **History of the reign of Ferdinand and Isabella:** the catholic. William H. Prescott. *Ed. by* John Foster Kirk. 3 vols. Phil., J. B. Lippincott Co., c1876. pors. D. cl. each .... 1.50 .98

    The best description written of the important period of the con

	List price.	Price to schools.

solidation of Spain from a number of petty governments into what was practically one kingdom.

F40
Yo 8 st
278. **Story of the Christians and Moors of Spain.** Charlotte M. Yonge. N. Y., Macmillan Co., 1893. 299 p. S. (Golden treasury series.) cl. .... 1.00 .65

Contents: Goth and the Arab; Battle of Guadalete; Conquest; Limit to the Moslem; First Spanish Khalif; Pass of Roncesvalles; Little Christian states; Santiago, the patron of Spain; Count of the land of castles; Augustan age of Cordova; Loss of Compostella; Invincible Al Mansour; Fall of the Khalifate; Union of Castille and Leon; Ruy, mi Cid Campeador; Almoravides and their conquest; Don Alfonso, battle-fighter of Aragon; Broken chains of Navas de Tolosa; Conquests of San Fernando and Jayme el Conquistador; Cream of the west; Battle of Salado; Age of tyrants; Last bright days of Granada; Abencerrages and Zegris; Siege of Malaga; Last sigh of the Moor; Woe to the vanquished.

ENGLAND—HISTORY.

(Includes histories of Ireland and Scotland.)

F45
Al 5 to
279. **Topical outline of English history:** including references for literature for the use of classes in high schools and academies. Frederick J. Allen. Bost., D. C. Heath & Co., 1901. 71 p. D. bds.. .40 .34

This book is the result of practical teaching and will be very helpful to the teacher of English history. It covers the entire field, and aims to fill that place in its study which the laboratory manual fills in chemistry.

Contents: Old England; Feudal England; Modern England.

F45
B 76 hi
#280. **History of England.** *Rev.* James Franck Bright. Period I, Mediaeval monarchy from the departure of the Romans to Richard III, 449-1485; Period II, Personal monarchy, Henry VII to James II, 1485-1688; Period III, Constitutional monarchy, William and Mary to William IV, 1689-1837; Period IV, Growth of democracy, Victoria, 1837-1880. N. Y., Longmans, Green & Co., 1896-1901. 4 vols. maps. D. cl. 6.75 4.49

Excellent for reference,

F45
———
C 67 se

281. **Selections from the sources of English history:** being a supplement to text-books of English history, B. C. 55—A. D. 1832. Charles W. Colby. N. Y., Longmans, Green & Co., 1899. 325 p. D. cl. . . .   1.50   .98

List price.   Price to schools.

Care has been taken to keep both the passages and comments in the book within the compass of students sixteen years old.

Part I of "Historical sources in schools" (Macmillan Co.) will be helpful to the History teacher who is not familiar with the Source method.

F45
———
C 73 hi

282. [362.] **History of England.** Katharine Coman, *and* Elizabeth Kimball Kendall. N. Y., Macmillan Co., 1899. 507 p. il. D. cl. 1.25   1.05

"The physical environment afforded by the British Isles, the race traits of the peoples that have occupied the land, the methods by which they have wrought out industrial prosperity, the means by which they have attained self-government, all are essential to an adequate understanding of the growth of the English nation."

Most important sources of English history are indicated at the head of each chapter. The bibliographies are especially good.

F45
———
C 86 ag

283. **Age of Elizabeth.** Mandell Creighton. N. Y., C: Scribner's Sons, 1901. 244 p. maps. (Epochs of modern history series.) S. cl.
Same. N. Y., Longmans, Green & Co., 1899. 236 p. S. cl. . . . .   1.00   .65

A short, concise resume of the chief events in Queen Elizabeth's reign.

Contents: Religious settlement in Germany and England; France and Scotland; Spain and the Netherlands; Home government of Elizabeth; Conflict of catholicism and protestantism; League and the Armada; England after the Armada.

F45
———
C 86 ep

284. **Epochs of English history:** complete edition in one volume. *Rt. Rev.* Mandell Creighton. N. Y., Longmans, Green & Co., 1899. 748 p. 23 maps. S. Ed. 12. cl. 1.50   1.35

A good book for reference.

Contents: Early England; England a continental power; Rise of the people and growth of parliament; Tudors and the reformation; Struggle against absolute monarchy; Settlement of the constitution; England during the American and European wars; Modern England; Pedigrees.

F45
D 55 ch

	List price.	Price to schools.

285. **Child's history of England.** Charles Dickens. N. Y., American Book Co., n. d. 307 p. il. S. cl.... .60 .54

An attractive story of English history. Excellent for Library reading.

F45
G 12 ho

286. **Houses of Lancaster and York:** with the conquest and loss of France. James Gairdner. N. Y., C: Scribner's Sons, 1900. 262 p. 5 maps. (Epochs of modern history series.) S. cl.
Same. N. Y., Longmans, Green & Co., 1900. 252 p. S. cl. .... 1.00 .65

A short history of England during the turbulent century between the death of Edward III and the accession of Henry VII.

Contents: Preliminary; Richard II; Literature and science; Henry IV; Henry V; Council of Constance and the war in Bohemia; Henry VI; Edward IV; Edward V; Richard III; General view of European history; Conclusion.

F45
G 16 fi

287. **First two Stuarts and the Puritan Revolution, 1603-1660.** Samuel Rawson Gardiner. N. Y., C: Scribner's Sons, 1901. 222 p. maps. (Epochs of modern history series.) S. cl.
Same. N. Y., Longmans, Green & Co., 1899. 215 p. S. cl. .... 1.00 .65

This volume is a companion to the one on the "Thirty years' war" and it has therefore been unnecessary to break the course of the narrative by constant references to events passing on the Continent.—*Author's preface.*

Contents: Puritans and the house of commons; Spanish alliance; Ascendency of Buckingham; Personal government of Charles I; Reign of Thorough; Resistance in Scotland and England; Downfall of royalty; Commonwealth; Oliver's protectorate; End of the revolution.

F45
G 16 sc

288. **School atlas of English history.** Samuel Rawson Gardiner, ed. N. Y., Longmans, Green & Co., 1899. 88 + 23 p. maps. O. New ed. cl. 1.50 1.35

This atlas is a companion to "The Students' history of England" and should be in every school where English history is taught.

LIST OF BOOKS FOR HIGH SCHOOL LIBRARIES. 83

F45
———
G 16 st

                 List Price to
                 price. schools.

289. **Student's history of England:** from the earliest times to 1885. Samuel R. Gardiner. N. Y., Longmans, Green & Co., 1900. 1023 p. il. D. cl. 3.00 1.96

An excellent reference book on English history.

Contents: England before the Norman conquest; Norman and Angevin kings; Growth of the Parliamentary constitution; Lancaster, York, and Tudor; Renascence and the reformation; Puritan revolution; Political revolution; Rise of cabinet government; Fall of the whigs and the rise of the new toryism; Conflict with democracy; Growth of democracy.

F45
———
G 82 sh

290. [361.] **Short History of the English people.** John Richard Green. N. Y., American Book Company, 1899. 872 p. maps. O. cl. 1.20 1.03

One of the best books on the subject. It is essentially a history of the people; the incidents of constitutional, intellectual, and social development are given special attention.

F45
———
H 13 fa

291. **Fall of the Stuarts and western Europe:** from 1678 to 1697. *Rev.* Edward Hale. N. Y., C: Scribner's Sons, 1901. 248 p. maps. (Epochs of modern history series.) S. cl.
Same. N. Y., Longmans, Green & Co., 1898. 240 p. S. cl. .... 1.00 .65

An easy introduction to the study of this period.

Contents: Introductory; England and Scotland; Fourth and fifth parliaments of Charles—state trials; Scotland in 1680 and 1681; England and Scotland from 1682 until the death of Charles II, 1685; Lewis XIV and France to the revocation of the edict of Nantes, 1685; Accession of James II of England; Rebellions of Argyle and Monmouth; Foreign and domestic policy of James II; Ireland under James II; William, Lewis, and James, 1687-88; Revolution; Interregnum; First year of the reign of William and Mary; William III and Ireland; Pacification of Ireland and Scotland; War: 1691-1694; Death of Queen Mary—parliament until 1696; Various plots against William; New parliament—assassination plot—the progress of the war—peace; Literature and science in England and France in the latter part of the seventeenth century.

F45
———
H 27 ma

292. **Making of the British empire,** 1714-1832. Arthur Hassall. N. Y., C: Scribner's Sons, 1896. 149 p. S. cl. (Oxford Manuals of English history series.) .... .50 .45

"The 'Oxford Manuals', of which this is the first issue, are designed to occupy a place between general histories and 'epochs' or

	List price.	Price to schools.

'periods.' Six volumes are out, each part complete in itself, but as the volumes carefully fit on to each other, the whole will form together a single continuous history of England. All the volumes are written by resident members of the University of Oxford, actively engaged in teaching in the Final School of Modern History."

F45
H 53 en
293. **English history for Americans.** Thomas Wentworth Higginson, *and* Edward Channing. N. Y., Longmans, Green & Co., 1900. 334 p. il. maps. D. cl. 1.20 1.08

In this volume emphasis has been laid on events in English annals which have had the most direct influence on the history and institutions of United States regardless of their relative importance in England.

F45
H 97 ki
294. **King and baronage, 1135-1327.** William Holden Hutton. N. Y., C: Scribner's Sons, 1899. 117 p. S...cl. (Oxford Manuals of English history series.) .... .50 .45

F45
J 85 ch
295. [367.] **Child's history of Ireland.** Patrick Weston Joyce. N. Y., Longmans, Green & Co., 1897. 507 p. map. il. S. cl. .... 1.25 .82

F45
K 33 so
296. **Source-book of English history.** *Ed. by* Elizabeth Kimball Kendall. N. Y., Macmillan Co., 1900. 483 p. D. cl. ...., ... .80 .72

"Each year shows advance toward a general appreciation of the value and feasibility of source study by younger as well as by older students. It is no longer thought useless, or even dangerous, to place the original text in the hands of the boy or girl just beginning the study of history.

The definite gains from a moderate and carefully directed use of sources are manifold. First and foremost is the stronger sense of reality produced by coming in direct contact with the men who helped to make history, or with those who actually witnessed the events they describe. To the average school boy, historic personages are heroes or bores, as the case may be, but never men. To remedy this would be a long step toward success in the teaching of history, and here the value of the original letter or description is

	List price.	Price to schools.

at once apparent. . . . A deeper, a more lasting impression is secured by turning back to the original account. . . .

Still another advantage is the interest aroused through allowing the men of a bygone time to speak for themselves. The student feels that he is at the heart and beginning of things when he reads the story as told by the man who did the great deed, or at least by one who saw him do it. His interest is stimulated as it could not be by the careful account prepared in cold blood by the historian, a man of another age and of an alien temper. . . .

A certain judicial fairness of attitude toward men and events of the past is fostered by reading the original accounts with their marked personal stamp. Where each side has a chance to tell its own story, the student is led to weigh evidence, to consider probabilities. He is forced unconsciously to abandon his prejudices to see that right and wrong are often separated by a very narrow line, that the good are not all on one side, the bad all on the other."

F45

L 22 ma

297. [363.] **Manual of English history.** Edward M. Lancaster. N. Y., American Book Company, 1900. 334 p. map. il. D. cl. .... 1.00 .85

The essential facts of English history.

F45

L 32 hi

298. **History of England:** for the use of schools and academies. Josephus N. Larned. Bost., Houghton, Mifflin & Co., c1900. 675 p. maps and il. D. cl. 1.25 1.12

"A companion volume to Fiske's 'School history of the United States.'" It is an accurate and interesting representation of the leading events of English history, and gives special attention to the growth of the English constitution, and the territorial expansion of England into the British Empire. It also describes the social and industrial development of the nation. A special feature of the book is its surveys of general history. Beginning with the thirteenth century, these surveys present brief summaries of contemporaneous events that influenced English history."

F45

L 51 so

299. **Source-book of English history:** leading documents together with illustrative material from contemporary writers and a bibliography of sources. Guy Carleton Lee. N. Y., Henry Holt & Co., 1901. 609 p. D. cl. 2.00 1.80

"In editing this volume I have differed from the plan of selection adopted by Bishop Stubbs, in that I have included illustrative material not strictly documentary; and I have departed from the

| | List price. | Price to schools. |

method of Professor Hart—from whom I have borrowed the name, source-book—in that I have included the great constitutional and legal documents which furnish the framework of the history of national development. . . . The scope of this collection of sources is such as to make it available for use with any text-book upon English history. It extends from the first mention of Britain by ancient historians to the last great treaty with the Boers of South Africa."—*Preface.*

F45

M 11 hi

300. **History of Scotland:** adapted for American students. Margaret Macarthur. N. Y., Henry Holt & Co., c1874. 199 p. (Historical course for schools.) S. cl. .... .80 .72

Contents: Gaelic period; English period; Struggle for independence; Independent kingdom; Jameses; Reformation; Union of the crowns; After the Union.

F45

M 12 ep

301. **Epoch of reform,** 1830-1850. Justin McCarthy. N. Y., C: Scribner's Sons, 1899. 215 p. (Epochs of modern history series.) S. cl.
Same. N. Y., Longmans, Green & Co., 1898. 210 p. S. cl. .... 1.00 .65

"The object of this little book is to give a clear and concise account of the changes in our political system, from the introduction of Lord Grey's first Reform Bill to the death of Sir Robert Peel."—*Preface.*

F45

M 12 st

302. [366.] **Story of the people of England in the Nineteenth century.** Justin McCarthy. N. Y., G. P. Putnam's Sons, 1899. 2 vols., 1800-1835; 1832-1898. 280; 261 p. il. D. (Story of the nations series.) cl. each .... 1.50 .98

A description of the marvellous changes wrought by science and literature, by statesmen and philanthropists in the social life of England. Ought to be in every library.

F45

M 71 ea

303. **Early Tudors:** Henry VII; Henry VIII. Charles E. Moberly. N. Y., C: Scribner's Sons, 1900. 249 p. (Epochs of modern history series.) map. S. cl.
Same. N. Y., Longmans, Green & Co., 1901. 243 p. S. cl. .... 1.00 .65

F45

M 76 le

                    List Price to
                    price. schools.

304. **Leading facts of English history.** David H. Montgomery. Bost., Ginn & Co., 1901. 420 + 79 p. por. and maps. D. cl. .... 1.12 .96

  An excellent text on English history. The appendix gives a classified list of books for further reading.
  Contents: Britain before history begins; Relation of the geography of England to its history; Civilization which did not civilize: Roman Britain; Coming of the Saxons: Britain becomes England; Coming of the Normans; Angevins, or Plantagenets: Rise of the English Nation; Self-destruction of feudalism; Absolutism of the Crown, the Reformation, New learning; Stuart period; Divine right of kings vs. the Divine right of the people; American revolution, House of Commons the ruling power, Era of reform, Government by the people; General summary of English constitutional history.

F45

M 83 ag

305. **Age of Anne.** Edward E. Morris. N. Y., C: Scribner's Sons, 1901. 251 p. maps. (Epochs of modern history series.) S. cl.
  Same. N. Y., Longmans, Green & Co., 1898. 242 p. S. cl. .... 1.00 .65

  "This book is not a contribution to the general fund of historical knowledge. Those who before knew the history of its period will find here no new light. It is offered as an effort to assist in the teaching of history in schools. . . .
  History should be taught for the sake of its human interest. For this reason I have made it my first object to avoid being dull. I have been very biographical, taking care to introduce formally all new characters of importance as they come upon the stage."—*Author's Preface.*

F45

M 83 ea

306. **Early Hanoverians.** Edward E. Morris. N. Y., C: Scribner's Sons, 1900. 235 p. maps. (Epochs of modern history series.) S. cl.
  Same. N. Y., Longmans, Green & Co., 1899. 229 p. S. cl. .... 1.00 .65

  A continuation of the Epoch called "The Age of Anne."

F45

M 83 hi

307. [364.] **Historical tales:** English. Charles Morris. Phil., J. B. Lippincott Co., 1897. 336 p. il. D. cl. .... 1.00 .65

  The romantic events in English history for young readers.

		List price.	Price to schools.

F45
Om 1 e
308. **England and the Hundred Years' war, 1327-1485.** Charles William C. Oman. N. Y., C: Scribner's Sons, 1898. 168 p. S. cl. (Oxford manuals of English history series.) .... .50 .45

F45
Om 1 en
309. **England in the nineteenth century.** Charles W. Oman. N. Y., Longmans, Green & Co., 1900. 276 p. D. cl. .... 1.25 .82

Contents: Struggle with Bonaparte; From the fall of Bonaparte to the great reform bill; From the great reform bill to the Crimean war; Early Victorian England; From the Crimean war to the death of Lord Palmerston; Disraeli and Gladstone; Home rule question and imperialism; India and the colonies—Imperial federation; Conclusion.

F45
P 87 en
310. **England and the Reformation, 1485-1603.** George Wightman Powers. N. Y., C: Scribner's Sons, 1898. 143 p. S. cl. (Oxford manuals of English history series.) .... .50 .45

F45
R 54 ma
311. **Making of the English nation, 55-1135.** Charles Grant Robertson. N. Y., C: Scribner's Sons, 1900. 113 p. S. cl. (Oxford manuals of English history series.) .... .50 .45

F45
Se 3 ex
312. **Expansion of England: two courses of lectures.** *Sir* John Robert Seeley. Bost., Little, Brown & Co., 1901. 359 p. S. cl. 1.75 1.15

Contents: Tendency in English history; England in the eighteenth century; Empire; Old colonial system; Effect of the new world on the old; Commerce and war; Phases of expansion; Schism in Greater Britain; History and politics; Indian empire; How we conquered India; How we govern India; Mutual influence of England and India; Phases in the conquest of India; Internal and external dangers; Recapitulation.

F45
St 7 bu

313. [365.] **Building of the British empire:** the story of England's growth from Elizabeth to Victoria. Alfred Thomas Story. N. Y., G. P. Putnam's Sons, 1898. 2 vols., 1558-1688; 1689-1895. 391; 468 p. il. D. (Story of the nations series.) cl. each .... 1.50 .98

Interesting and valuable.

F45
St 9 ea

314. **Early Plantagenets.** William Stubbs. N. Y., C: Scribner's Sons, 1900. 300 p. maps. (Epochs of modern history series.) S. cl.
Same. N. Y., Longmans, Green & Co., 1898. 286 p. S. cl. .... 1.00 .65

One of the best of the series, presenting the course of events in England during the period in which parliamentary government was established.
Contents: Introduction; Stephen and Matilda; Early years of Henry II; Henry II and Thomas Becket; Latter years of Henry II; Richard Coeur de Lion; John; Henry III; Simon de Montfort; Edward I; Confirmation of the charters; Edward II.

F45
T 65 yo

315. **Young people's history of Ireland.** George Makepeace Towle. Bost., Lee & Shepard, 1890. 314 p. il. S. cl. .... 1.00 .65

A very interesting account of the history of the Irish people. Excellent for Library reading.
Contents: Irish legends; Ancient Irish; Saint Patrick; Christian Ireland; Early Irish kings; Invasion of the Danes; Condition of the Irish people; Invasion of the Normans; English settlement of Ireland; Norman knights; Bruces in Ireland; Richard the Second in Ireland; Condition of the Irish people; Irish parliament; Henry the Eighth and Ireland; Shane O'Neil; Ireland under Elizabeth; Revolt of Tyrone; Plantation of Ireland; Condition of the Irish people; Wentworth's iron rule; Ten years' rebellion; Cromwell's iron hand; Cromwell's settlement of Ireland; Orange and the green; Treaty of Limerick; Penal laws; Ireland prostrate; Condition of the Irish people; Irish patriots; Free parliament; Insurrection of ninety-eight; Union of the parliaments; Daniel O'Connell; Last three years' famine; Later revolts; Gladstone's Irish reforms; Land league; Gladstone proposes home rule.

F45
W 13 ki

316. **King and Parliament,** 1603-1714. G. H. Wakeling. N. Y., C: Scribner's Sons, 1896. 135 p. S. cl. (Oxford manuals of English history series.) .... .50 .45

F45
W 19 ed
317. **Edward III.** *Rev.* William Warburton. N. Y., C: Scribner's Sons, 1899. 293 p. (Epochs of modern history series.) maps. S. cl.
Same. N. Y., Longmans, Green & Co., 1897. 281 p. S. cl. .... 1.00 .65

F45
Yo 8 ca
#318. **Cameos from English history.** Charlotte M. Yonge. N. Y., Macmillan Co., 1887–1902. 9 vols. D. cl. each .... 1.25 .82

Contents: 1, From Rollo to Edward II; 2, Wars in France; 3, Wars of the roses; 4, Reformation times; 5, England and Spain; 6, Forty years of Stewart rule; 7, Rebellion and restoration; 8, End of the Stewarts; 9, Eighteenth century.

These books are intended for young people just beyond the elementary histories of England, and able to enter in some degree into the real spirit of events, and to be struck with characters and scenes presented in some relief.

"The endeavour has not been to chronicle facts, but to put together a series of pictures of persons and events, so as to arrest the attention and give some individuality and distinctness to the recollection, by gathering together details at the most memorable moments."—*Preface.*

Portions of these volumes will be interesting for Library reading.

HOLLAND—HISTORY.

F46
G 87 br
319. [380.] **Brave little Holland and what she taught us.** William Elliot Griffis. Bost., Houghton, Mifflin & Co., 1894. 252 p. S. (Riverside lib. for young people.) cl. .... .75 .48

An excellent, brief account of the chief events in Holland's history. Good for Library reading.

GERMANY—HISTORY.

F47
G 36 ge
320. [373.] **Germany, her people and their story.** Augusta Hale Gifford. Bost., Lothrop Pub. Co., 1899. 604 p. il. O. cl. 1.75 1.15

A popular history of the beginning, rise, development, and progress of the German Empire from Arminius to William II.

F47
———
G 73 st

                                                          List Price to
                                                         price. schools.

321. [375.] **Story of Germany.** Sabine Baring-Gould, *and* Arthur Gilman. N. Y., G. P. Putnam's Sons, 1887. 437 p. il. D. (Story of the nations series.) cl. .... 1.50 .98

   An interesting account of the leading events of German history. Will be interesting for Library reading.

F47
———
H 38 sh

#322. **Short history of Germany.** Ernest F. Henderson. In 2 vol.: Vol. 1, 9 A. D. to 1648 A. D.; vol. 2, 1648 A. D. to 1871 A. D. N. Y., Macmillan Co., 1902. O. cl. 4.00 3.60

   The narrative style of this history makes it interesting for general reading.

   Contents—Volume 1: Early Germans; Rise and fall of the Carolingians; Relations between church and state under the Saxon and Franconian emperors; Popes and the Hohenstaufens; Age of chivalry; Kings from different houses; Rulers of the House of Luxemburg; Teutonic order and the Hanseatic League; Era of the church councils; German life on the eve of the Reformation; Martin Luther and the Emperor Charles V; Friends and allies of the reformation; Anabaptism and Civil war; Emperor's wars and the protestant party in Germany; Charles V at war with the protestant princes; Roman Catholic reaction; beginning of the thirty years' war; Career of Wallenstein, the intervention of foreign powers, and the peace of Westphalia.

   Volume 2: Rise of the Prussian monarchy; Turkish campaigns, the aggressions of Louis XIV, and the Spanish succession war; Father of Frederick the Great; Wars of Frederick the Great; Frederick the Great in time of peace; French revolution, disruption of Germany, and the downfall of Prussia; Regeneration of Prussia and the war of liberation; Struggle for constitutional government and the Revolution of 1848; Reckoning with Austria; Reckoning with France and the attainment of German unity.

F47
———
L 58 hi

323. **History of Germany:** from the earliest times; founded on Dr. David Muller's "History of the German people." Charlton T. Lewis. N. Y., American Book Company, 1874. 799 p. maps and il. D. cl. 1.50 1.27

   The best brief history of Germany published.

   Contents: From the earliest ages to the great migration of nations; Great migrations and the fall of the western empire; Franks, Merovingians, and the family of Pepin; Charlemagne; Carlovingian emperors; Saxon emperors; Emperors of the house of Franconia; House of Hohenstaufen; German civilization under the Hohenstaufen emperors; To the death of Lewis the Bavarian;

| | List price. | Price to schools. |

From the accession of Charles IV to the death of Sigismund; From the accession of Albert II to the reformation; German civilization in the fourteenth and fifteenth centuries—cities and their leagues; German civilization—life of the people, plague and persecution, science and art; Beginning and early progress of the Reformation—Luther; Formation of the protestant churches, and the religious wars of Charles V; From the religious peace of Augsburg to the Edict of restitution; End of the thirty years' war—Peace of Westphalia—German civilization from Luther to the peace of Westphalia; Decline of the Hapsburg monarchy; Rise and rapid growth of Prussia; Frederick the Great, and his reign until the seven years' war; Seven years' war; From the peace of Hubertsburg to the French revolution; From the French revolution to the peace of Luneville; From the peace of Luneville to the peace of Tilsit; Napoleon's supremacy in Germany; Last years of French supremacy—Napoleon in Russia; New birth of German patriotism—war of freedom begins; Emancipation of Germany—Napoleon driven beyond the Rhine; Overthrow of Napoleon—Congress of Vienna; Period of the German confederation; War of 1866, and the North German confederation; War of 1870 to the surrender of Sedan; War with France—Capitulation of Paris—Peace of Frankfort; New German empire.

F47

M 83 hg

324. [376.] **Historical tales:** German. Charles Morris. Phil., J. B. Lippincott Co., 1895. 344 p. il. D. cl. .... 1.00 .65

Romantic events in history of Germany for young readers.

F47

Si 4 hi

325. **History of Germany:** adapted for American readers. James Sime. N. Y., Henry Holt & Co., c1874. 282 p. (Historical course for schools.) S. cl.. .80 .72

An interesting short outline of the history of Germany. Too brief to be satisfactory for extended reference work.

F47

T 21 hi

326. [374.] **History of Germany,** from the earliest times to the present day. Bayard Taylor. N. Y., D. Appleton & Co., 1899. 476 p. il. D. cl. ...... 1.50 .98

A clear, continuous narrative of leading events.

RUSSIA—HISTORY.

F54
M 81 st

	List price.	Price to schools.
327. [377.] **Story of Russia.** W. R. Morfil. N. Y., G. P. Putnam's Sons. 1890. 394 p. il. D. (Story of the nations series.) cl.	1.50	.98

An outline of Russian history giving the development of the country from the fifteenth century to the present empire.

F54
M 83 hr

328. **Historical tales:** Russian. Charles Morris. Phil.; J. B. Lippincott Co., 1902. 328 p. il. D. cl. .. 1.00 .65

Excellent for Library reading.

F54
N 66 ru

329. **Russia and the Russians.** Edmund Noble. Bost., Houghton, Mifflin & Co., 1901. 285 p. D. cl. .. 1.50 .98

Mr. Noble does not attempt to cover exhaustively the history of Russia, but to bring into prominence the great controlling processes of Russian development, and to present the story of Russia and the Russian people so as to make it intelligible to the reader.

Contents: Land and the people; Laying the foundations; How Russia became an autocracy; Peter the Great and "Europeanization"; Women reformers; Revolt of the "Decembrists"; Emancipation of the peasants; "Nihilism" and the revolutionary movement; Religious protest; Story of Russian expansion; Siberia and the exile system; Language and literature; Russian future.

ASIA—HISTORY.

F60
B 43 sp

330. [332.] **Story of Persia.** S. G. W. Benjamin. N. Y., G. P. Putnams Sons, 1887. 304 p. il. D. (Story of the nations series.) cl. .... 1.50 .98

A narrative of the most noteworthy characters and events of Persia. Will interest older pupils.

F60
D 74 ch

331. [385.] **China.** Robert K. Douglas. N. Y., G. P. Putnam's Sons, 1899. 456 p. il. D. (Story of the nations series.) cl. .... 1.50 .98

An interesting and readable history of China.

		List price.	Price to schools.

F60
M 83 hj
332. [386.] **Historical tales:** Japan and China. Charles Morris. Phil., J. B. Lippincott Co., 1898. 353 p. il. D. cl. .... 1.00 .65

Romantic events in history of Japan and China for young readers.

F60
M 96 sj
333. [383.] **Story of Japan.** D: Murray. N. Y., G. P. Putnam's Sons, 1894. il. maps. D. (Story of the nations series.) cl. .... 1.50 .98

An interesting history of Japan.

F60
R 19 st
334. [329.] **Story of Phoenicia.** George Rawlinson. N. Y., G. P. Putnam's Sons, 1890. 356 p. il. D. (Story of the nations series.) cl. .... 1.50 .98

The manners and customs of the people will interest pupils.

F60
Sm 9 cr
335. **Crisis in China.** George B. Smyth *and others.* N. Y., Harper & Bros., 1900. 271 p. il. D. cl. ...... 1.00 .65

A series of articles on the Chinese situation first published in the North American Review.
Contents: Causes of Anti-foreign feeling in China—G. B. Smyth; Powers and the partition of China—Rev. Gilbert Reid; Struggle for reform in China—Charles Johnston; Political possibilities in China—John Barrett; Gathering of the storm—Robert E. Lewis; Far eastern crisis—Archibald R. Colquhoun; Great Siberian railway—M. Mikhailoff; China and the powers—Rear-Admiral Lord Charles Beresford—Mutual helpfulness between China and the United States—His excellency Wu Ting-Fang—America's share in a partition of China—Demetrius C. Boulger; America's interests in China—Gen. James H. Wilson; American policy in China—Rt. Hon. Sir Charles W. Dilke.

F67
G 87 ja
336. [384.] **Japan in history, folk lore and art.** William Elliot Griffis. Bost., Houghton, Mifflin & Co., 1892. 230 p. S. (Riverside lib. for young people.) cl. .... .75 .48

The story of Japan of the past. Interesting for Library reading.

AFRICA—HISTORY.

	List price.	Price to schools.

F70
―――
B 84 im
337. **Impressions of South Africa.** Third edition, with a new prefatory chapter, and with the Transvaal conventions of 1881 and 1884. James Bryce. N. Y., The Century Co., 1900. 517 p. maps. O. cl. ... 3.50 ... 2.30

In addition to a series of chapters on the history and present condition of the colonies and republics of South Africa, the author describes the scenery and animal life of plain and mountain and valley, and the climatic conditions which afford so potently the country's development. The race problems involved in the rivalry of Dutch and English, and the numerical preponderance of blacks, are fully discussed, as being perhaps the most serious to be considered in connection with the progress of civilization and the probable effect of the discovery of gold upon the permanent welfare of the land.

F70
―――
C 47 lo
338. **London to Ladysmith via Pretoria.** Winston Spencer Churchill. N. Y., Longmans, Green & Co., 1900. 496 p. maps. D. cl. .... 1.50 .98

A personal record of the author's adventures and impressions during the first five months of the African war. It also gives a fairly good account of the operations conducted by General Buller for the relief of Ladysmith. A good book for Library reading.

F70
―――
D 77 gr
339. **Great Boer war.** Arthur Conan Doyle. N. Y., McClure, Phillips & Co., 1901. 478 p. 5 maps. D. cl. .... 1.50 .98

A work that will stand for years to come as a comprehensive history, presented with all the vividness of a picture and the rich imagination of an artist. Dr. Doyle secured his facts first hand. He served several months as a surgeon in South Africa during the war, and he has been enabled to see and describe events clearly and accurately.

Contents: Boer nations; Cause of quarrel; Negotiations; Eve of war; Talana hill; Elandslaagte and Rietfontein; Lombard's Kop and Nicholson's Nek; Lord Methuen's advance; Battle of Magersfontein; Battle of Stormberg; Battle of Colenso; Dark hour; Ladysmith; Colesberg operations; Spion Kop; Vaalkranz; Buller's final advance; Siege and relief of Kimberley; Paardeberg; Advance on Bloemfontein; Clearing of the southeast; Siege of Mafeking; March on Pretoria; Diamond hill—Rundle's operations; Lines of communication; Halt at Pretoria; End of the war; Some lessons on the war.

F70

H 55 oo

340. **Oom Paul's people.** Narrative of the British-Boer troubles in South Africa, with a history of the Boers, the country, and its institutions. Howard C. Hillegas. N. Y., D. Appleton & Co., 1900. 308 p. maps. por and il. D. cl. .... 1.50 .98

List price, 1.50. Price to schools, .98

The author is a New York newspaper man who spent nearly two years in South Africa enjoying special facilities at the hands of President Kruger and other Boer officials as well as from Sir Alfred Milner and other British representatives at Cape Colony. The book contains an important interview with Oom Paul and a special study of Cecil Rhodes. Mr. Hillegas blames stock-jobbers and politicians for all the trouble between the Boers and the English, and believes that war is the probable final outcome. One chapter is especially devoted to the American interests in South Africa, showing that, while British capital owns the vast gold mines, American brains operate them.

F70

M 38 li

341. [328.] **Life in Ancient Egypt and Assyria.** G. Maspero. N. Y., D. Appleton & Co., 1899. 376 p. il. D. cl. .... 1.50 .98

Life in its various phases in Egypt during the 14 c. B. C., and in Assyria 7 c. B. C. A most interesting book.

F70

R 19 st

342. [327.] **Story of ancient Egypt.** George Rawlinson, *and* Arthur Gilman. N. Y., G. P. Putnam's Sons, 1887. 408 p. il. D. (Story of the nations series.) cl. .... 1.50 .98

An interesting account of the life and events in ancient Egypt.

F70

St 2 af

#343. **Africa: its partition and its future.** Henry M. Stanley *and others.* With an introduction by Harry Thurston Peck. N. Y., Dodd, Mead & Co., 1898. 263 p. map. D. cl. .... 1.25 .82

The papers in this volume constitute a brief authoritative and lucid statement of the African situation as it is today. They describe with perfect clearness the possessions actually held by each of the rival powers; they define and explain the claims which have brought these powers into opposition; and they give an interesting forecast, from the point of view of each nation, of the manner in which the complicated problem is likely to be solved.

Contents: Introduction; Africa in the twentieth century; Partition of Africa; British empire in Africa; German empire in

                                                                                                  List Price to
                                                                                price. schools.
Africa; French empire in Africa; Independent Kongo state; England, the Sudan, and France; Future of Nigeria; Kingdom of Uganda; Abyssinia and its people; Republic of Liberia—its future; Commerce, railways, and telegraphs of Africa; Map of Africa.

F70
———
W 48 hi
344. [326.] **History of Egypt.** F. C. H. Wendel. N. Y., American Book Company, 1890. 159 p. maps. S. (History primers.) flex. cl. .... .35   .31
A brief account of the leading events in Egyptian history.

                                AMERICA—HISTORY.
F80
———
F 54 di
345. [404.] **Discovery of America,** with some account of ancient America and the Spanish conquest. John Fiske. Bost., Houghton, Mifflin & Co., 1892. 2 vols., 516; 631 p. il. D. cl. 4.00 2.60
A comprehensive account of the discovery of America. Older pupils will find much interesting reading and all can use the book for reference.

F81
———
G 87 ro
346. [407.] **Romance of American colonization:** how the foundation stones of our history were laid. William Elliot Griffis. Bost., W. A. Wilde & Co., 1898. 295 p. il. D. cl. .... 1.50   .85
Interesting for Library reading.

F81
———
H 53 yo
347. **Young folks' book of American explorers.** Thomas Wentworth Higginson. N. Y., Longmans, Green & Co., 1898. 367 p. il. D. cl. 1.20 1.08
"The explorers of various nations are represented in this book. There are Northmen, Italians, Englishmen, Frenchmen, Spaniards, and Dutchmen. Where the original narrative was in some foreign language, that translation has been chosen which gives most of the spirit of the original."—*Preface.*
Contents: Legends of the Northmen; Columbus and his companions; Cabot and Verrazzano; Strange voyages of Cabeza de Vaca; French in Canada; Adventures of De Soto; French in Florida; Sir Humphrey Gilbert; Lost colonies of Virginia; Unsuccessful New England settlements; Captain John Smith; Champlain on the war-path; Henry Hudson and the New Netherlands; Pilgrims at Plymouth; Massachusetts Bay colony.

98   LIST OF BOOKS FOR HIGH SCHOOL LIBRARIES.

F81
——————   List   Price to
P 23 co   price. schools.
348. Conspiracy of Pontiac; and the Indian war after the
    conquest of Canada. Francis Parkman. 2 vols.
    Bost., Little, Brown & Co., 1901. 367 + 384 pp.
    maps. D. Ed. 10, rev. cl. 3.00   1.96
   We have in this book a more vivid picture of Indian life and
warfare a hundred years ago than in any other. All of this series
of Parkman are written in a spirited, attractive style and are the
result of thorough research and study.
   Contents, Vol. 1: Introductory—Indian tribes east of the
Mississippi; France and England in America; French, English,
and the Indians; Collision of the rival colonies; Wilderness and
its tenants at the close of the French war; English take possession
of the western posts; Anger of the Indians—conspiracy; Indian
preparation; council at the river Ecorces; Detroit; Treachery of
Pontiac; Pontiac at the siege of Detroit; Rout of Cuyler's detach-
ment—fate of the forest garrisons; Indians continue to blockade
Detroit; Fight of bloody bridge; Michillimackinac; Massacre.
   Vol. 2: Frontier forts and settlements; War on the borders;
Battle of Bushy Run; Iroquois—ambuscade of the Devil's Hole;
Desolation of the frontiers; Indians raise the siege of Detroit;
Paxton men; Rioters march on Philadelphia; Bradstreet's army
on the lakes; Bouquet forces the Delawares and Shawanoes to sue
for peace; Illinois; Pontiac rallies the western tribes; Ruin of the
Indian cause; Death of Pontiac; Appendix.

F81
——————
P 23 la
349. [406.] **La Salle, and the discovery of the great west.**
    Francis Parkman. Bost., Little, Brown & Co.,
    1899. 483 p. maps. D. cl. .... 1.50   .98
   A very interesting and readable book.

F81
——————
P 23 mo
350. **Montcalm and Wolfe.** Francis Parkman. 2 vols.
    Bost., Little, Brown & Co., 1902. maps and pors.
    D. cl. 3.00   1.96
   A brilliant and scholarly account of the struggle between the
French and English in America.

F81
——————
P 23 pi
351. **Pioneers of France in the new world.** Francis Park-
    man. Bost., Little, Brown & Co., 1901. 473 p.
    maps and por. D. Rev. ed. cl. .... 1.50   .98
   This volume as well as the others in this series on the list are
excellent books for Library reading. The author has given a
graphic picture of the early French explorers of the continent.
   Contents—Part I: Huguenots in Florida—early Spanish adventure; Villegagnon; Jean Ribaut; Laudonnierre; Conspiracy;

		List price.	Price to schools.

Famine—war—succor; Menendez; Massacre of the heretics—Charles IX and Philip II; Dominique de Gourges.

Part 2: Champlain and his associates—early French adventure in North America; La Roche—Champlain—De Monts; Acadia occupied; Lescarbot and Champlain; Jesuits and their patroness; Jesuits in Acadia; La Saussaye—Argall; Ruin of French Acadia; Champlain at Quebec; Lake Champlain; War—trade—discovery; Impostor Vignau; Discovery of Lake Huron; Great war party; Hostile sects—rival interests; English at Quebec; Death of Champlain.

CANADA—HISTORY.

F82

B 66 st

352. [437.] **Story of Canada.** J. G. Bourinot. N. Y., G. P. Putnam's Sons, 1896. 463 p. map. il. D. (Story of the nations series.) cl. .... 1.50 .98

The events which have exercised the greatest influence on the national development of Canada. Customs and conditions of the people are given.

UNITED STATES HISTORY—GENERAL.

F83

Al 3 sp

#353. **Spanish-American war.** Russell A. Alger. N. Y., Harper & Bros., 1901. 466 p. maps. O. cl. ... 2.50 2.25

An important contribution to the history of the Spanish-American war, by the late President McKinley's much criticised Secretary of War, from March 5, 1897, to August 1, 1899. This history gives an inside view of many much discussed phases of the question, especially the conduct of the War Department during Secretary Alger's incumbency, the Miles-Alger controversy, the beef-supply investigation, etc.

This is not a full history of the war with Spain. It is a record of some of the prominent facts connected with the organization, equipment and movements of the army, together with the administration of the War department.

F83

An 2 hi

#354. [429.] **History of the last quarter-century in the United States, 1870–1895.** E. Benjamin Andrews. N. Y., C: Scribner's Sons, 1897. 2 vols. 390; 409 p. il. O. hf. leath. 6.00 3.90

Written in an interesting manner. Contains much not found in the usual text book. This book should only be purchased by the larger libraries.

F83

B 22 h

#355. **History of the formation of the constitution of the United States of America.** George Bancroft. N. Y., D. Appleton & Co., c1884. 495 p. O. cl. 2.50 1.64

List price. Price to schools.

A continuation of Bancroft's "History of the United States." Not so necessary for a High school library as the preceding volumes. An invaluable book to students of Constitutional history.

F83

B 22 hi

#356. **History of the United States of America: from the discovery of the continent.** George Bancroft. 6 vols. N. Y., D. Appleton & Co., c1882. O. cl. .. 15.00 9.84

An excellent reference book for the use of High school students. The author has a tendency to discursiveness, but a very full table of contents will enable the teacher to select such portions as he needs.

F83

B 72 am

357. **American fights and fighters:** stories of the first five wars of the United States from the war of the Revolution to the war of 1812. Cyrus Townsend Brady. N. Y., McClure, Phillips & Co., 1900. 326 p. il. O. cl. .... 1.50 .98

The main value of this book will be for use in Library reading. "This book is designed to call to the attention of those interested in our early struggles, some of the most remarkable of the great battles, heroic achievements and desperate undertakings through which we became a nation. No attempt has been made to cover all the events in the wars referred to. The author has chosen such as would serve to present a variety of incident, to illustrate the period and to exhibit the leaders and men."

F83

B 81 be

358. **Beneath old roof-trees.** Abram English Brown. Bost., Lee & Shepard, 1896. 343 p. il. D. cl..... 1.50 .98

A view of the opening of the Revolution. The author has, through ten years of reportorial work, come in touch with scores of New England people still living on old homesteads occupied by their parents or grandparents at the time of the alarm of April 19, 1775, and there he has heard the story of personal experience reported by the descendants of those who at their own doors or in the highway faced the army of the king. While delineating in his characteristic manner the story of Lexington and Concord, he has most happily shown the part taken by other towns in that memorable day's experience.

FS3

B 91 ci

List Price to
price. schools.

359. **Civil war and the constitution.** John W. Burgess.
N. Y., C: Scribner's Sons, 1901. 2 vols. D. cl.
(American history series.) 2.00 1.80

This period is illustrated in two distinct aspects, one, its military history, giving a condensed and succinct account of the campaigns and engagements of the war; and the other, its constitutional history, with discussions of the questions then or since mooted, concerning the constitutional phases of the movements of the period. The most valuable portion of this work is its constitutional history. The important subjects of Secession, Emancipation, the National powers of the government, and the war powers of the executive in their constitutional relations are scholarly and impartial.

Contents—Volume 1: Davis, Lincoln, and Douglas; Anti-slavery sentiment in the South between 1857 and 1860; Presidential election of 1860; Secession; Inauguration of Lincoln and the condition of the government he was called to administer; Attempt of the Southern Confederacy to negotiate with the government of the United States; Capture of Fort Sumter and the call to arms; Three months' war; Preparations for the three years' war; Military movements in the late summer and autumn of 1861; Mill Springs; Fort Henry, Donelson, Shiloh, Pea Ridge, and Island No. 10.

Volume 2: Capture of New Orleans; McClellan's campaign against Richmond; Pope's campaign in northeastern Virginia; Bragg's invasion of Kentucky; Emancipation; Antietam; Proclamation of emancipation and the downfall of McClellan; Fredericksburg; President's order executing the emancipation proclamation; Perryville—Murfreesborough campaign; Confederate attempts to regain the coasts of Virginia and North Carolina; Chancellorsville; Vicksburg and Port Hudson; Gettysburg; Chickamauga–Chattanooga campaign; Movements in northeastern Virginia in the autumn of 1863, and the Charleston expedition; Interpretation of the constitution under the stress of the military events of 1862 and 1863; Capture of Atlanta; Wilderness campaign and Early's dash for Washington; Sherman's march through Georgia, and Hood's march to Nashville; Last blows; International complications during the latter years of the civil war.

FS3

B 91 mi

360. [393.] **Middle period, 1817–1858.** John W. Burgess.
N. Y., C: Scribner's Sons, 1898. 544 p. maps. D.
(American hist. series.) cl.. .... 1.00 .90

The four volumes in this series, Fisher's "Colonial Era," Walker's "Making of the Nation," Sloane's "French War and the Revolution," and Burgess's "Middle Period," form a valuable, complete, and comprehensive history of the United States for reference. Political events have a prominent place; manners and customs, and phases of intellectual progress are brought out.

F83

B 91 re

361. **Reconstruction and the constitution.** 1866–1876. J. W. Burgess. N. Y., C: Scribner's Sons, 1902. 342 p. D. cl. (American history series.) .... 1.00 .90

List price. Price to schools.

An account of the processes employed for the rehabilitation of the insurrectionary states, from 1865–1872, referring, almost continuously, to the questions arising, as related to or affected by the constitution, so that the narrative deals with constitutional history in the proper sense. The author is impartial, both in praising and in blaming the leading actors of the Reconstruction period.

Contents: Theory of reconstruction; President Lincoln's views and acts in regard to reconstruction; President Johnson's plan of reconstruction and his proceedings in realization of it; Congressional plan of reconstruction; Execution of the reconstruction acts; Attempt to impeach the president; Reconstruction resumed; President Grant and reconstruction; "Carpet-bag" and negro domination in the southern states between 1868 and 1876; Presidential election of 1876 and its consequences; International relations of the United States between 1867 and 1877.

F83

C 12 am

362. **American territorial development:** source extracts. Howard W. Caldwell. Chic., Ainsworth & Co., 1900. 265 p. D. cl. .... .75 .60

Contents: Preface; Colonial claims; First national boundaries; Northwest territory; Acquisition of Louisiana; Purchase of Florida; Annexation of Texas; California and New Mexico; California and Oregon; Alaska and Hawaii; Porto Rico and the Philippines.

F83

C 12 gr

363. **Great American legislators:** source extracts. Howard W Caldwell. Chic., Ainsworth & Co., 1900. 247 p. D. cl................................. .75 .60

Contents: Albert Gallatin; John Quincy Adams; Henry Clay; Daniel Webster; John C. Calhoun; Stephen A. Douglas; William H. Seward; Salmon P. Chase; James G. Blaine.

F83

C 12 su

364. **Survey of American history:** source extracts. vol. 1. Howard W. Caldwell. Chic., Ainsworth & Co., 1900. 255 p. D. cl.......................... .65 .52

Contents: Founding of the colonies; Development of union among the colonies; Causes of the American Revolution; Steps in the formation of the United States constitution; Interpretation of the constitution, nationality; Slavery in the United States; Civil war and reconstruction; Study in American foreign relations and diplomacy; Study in economic history.

LIST OF BOOKS FOR HIGH SCHOOL LIBRARIES.

		List price.	Price to schools.

FS3
C 36 gu

365. [312.] **Guide to the study of American history.** Edward Channing, *and* Albert Bushnell Hart. Bost., Ginn & Co., 1898. 471 p. D. cl.................. 2.00   1.70

The book contains a discussion of the place of American history in the curriculum; methods, library lists for small and large libraries, and sets of topics and references are given.

FS3
C 36 st

366. [401.] **Students' history of the United States.** Edward Channing. N. Y., Macmillan Co., 1898. 615 p. il. O. hf. leath............................ 1.40   1.19

The constitutional, political, and industrial development of the United States, from earliest times to 1897. Many details of military history, descriptions of colonial life and manners, and customs of Red Men have been omitted. Valuable for reference.

FS3
C 65 bo

367. **Boys of '76:** a history of the battles of the Revolution. Charles Carleton Coffin. N. Y., Harper & Bros., 1902. 398 p. il. O. cl......................... 2.00   1.30

"In this volume an attempt has been made to give a concise, plain, and authentic narrative of the principal battles of the Revolution as witnessed by those who took part in them."—*Author's Preface.*
Excellent for Library reading.

F83
C 65 bu

368. **Building the nation:** events in the history of the United States from the Revolution to the beginning of the war between the states. Charles Carleton Coffin. N. Y., Harper & Bros., 1902. 485 p. il. O. cl. 2.00   1.30

Coffin's series on United States history are all interesting for the Library reading classes.

FS3
C 65 dr

369. **Drum-beat of the nation:** the first period of the war of the rebellion from its outbreak to the close of 1862. Charles Carleton Coffin. N. Y., Harper & Bros., 1898. 478 p. il. O. cl................. 2.00   1.30

	List price.	Price to schools.

F83
C 65 fr
370. **Freedom triumphant:** the fourth period of the war of the rebellion from September, 1864, to its close. Charles Carleton Coffin. N. Y., Harper & Bros., c1890. 506 p. il. O. cl. 2.00 1.30

The four books above form a complete history of the War of the Rebellion.

F83
C 65 ma
371. **Marching to victory:** the second period of the war of the Rebellion, including the year 1863. Charles Carleton Coffin. N. Y., Harper & Bros., 1899. 491 p. il. O. cl. 2.00 1.30

F83
C 65 re
372. **Redeeming the republic:** the third period of the war of the rebellion in the year 1864. Charles Carleton Coffin. N. Y., Harper & Bros., 1898. 478 p. il. O. cl. 2.00 1.30

F83
D 78 in
373. **Indian history for young folks.** Francis S. Drake, N. Y., Harper & Bros., c1884. 479 p. il. O. cl... 3.00 1.96

A very interesting account of Indian life in America, suitable for reference in the History class and for Library reading.

F83
D 92 es
374. **Essays on the Civil war and reconstruction and related topics.** William Archibald Dunning. N. Y., Macmillan Co., 1898. 376 p. D. cl. 2.00 1.30

Mr. Dunning takes up that interesting period in our history—the reconstruction of the South—and presents an admirable discussion of the problems which then presented themselves to the statesmen of the nation. An interesting chapter is added on American political philosophy.

Contents: Constitution of the United States in civil war; Constitution of the United States in reconstruction; Military government during reconstruction; Process of reconstruction; Impeachment and trial of President Johnson; Are the states equal under the constitution? American political philosophy.

F83
Eg 3 ho
375. [398.] **Household history of the United States and its people,** for young Americans. Edward Eggleston. N. Y., D. Appleton & Co., 1898. 396 p. il. O. cl. 2.50 1.64

Interesting and readable. The illustrations are particularly good.

FS3
El 7 si 1
                              List Price to
                            price. schools.

376. [421.] **Sidelights on American history.** Series 1, National period before the civil war. Henry W. Elson. N. Y., Macmillan Co., 1899. 398 p. D. cl. .75   .48

    A detailed account of some of the chief events in national life before the civil war.
    Contents: Declaration of Independence; Framing the constitution; Inauguration of Washington; Alien and sedition laws; Fulton and the steamboat; Lewis and Clarke expedition; Conspiracy of Aaron Burr; The Missouri compromise; The Monroe doctrine; Lafayette's visit; The Carolina affair; Campaign of 1840; Underground railroad; Kansas-Nebraska bill; Lincoln-Douglas debate; History of political parties; Relation of the states to the nation.

FS3
El 7 si 2

377. **Sidelights on American history.** Series 2' the Civil war and our own times. Henry W. Elson. N. Y., Macmillan Co., 1900. 410 p. S. cl. .... .75   .48

    Contents: Presidential election of 1860; Secession; Great leaders in congress during the war; Events leading up to the civil war; Battle of Gettysburg; Causes of Northern success; Reconstruction; Impeachment and trial of Andrew Jackson; Alabama claims; Liberal republican movement of 1872; Disputed presidential election of 1876; Garfield tragedy; Century of tariff legislation; Spanish war.

FS3
F 21 fa

378. [422.] **Famous adventures and prison escapes of the civil war.** N. Y., Century Co., 1898. 338 p. il. O. cl. .... 1.50   .98

    Intensely interesting. Boys will be especially interested.

FS3
F 53 co

379. [390.] **Colonial era.** George Park Fisher. N. Y., C: Scribner's Sons, 1898. 348 p. maps. D. (American history series.) cl. .... 1.00   .90

    See note for Burgess's "Middle Period."

FS3
F 54 am

380. **American Revolution.** John Fiske. Bost., Houghton, Mifflin & Co., 1901. 2 vols. maps. D. cl....... 4.00 2.60

    The lucid statement of the facts of the Revolution and the definement of character given to leaders in the field and on the

| | List price. | Price to schools. |

platform, make these two volumes indispensable to the student of American history.

The writer evidently prosecuted a work of love, tempered by a great purpose of analysis of military movement that lead steadily to independence.

Contents—Volume 1: Beginnings; Crisis; Continental congress; Independence; First blow at the center; Second blow at the center; Saratoga.

Volume 2: French alliance; Valley Forge; Monmouth and Newport; War on the frontier; War on the ocean; Year of disasters; Benedict Arnold; Yorktown.

F83
F 54 cr

381. [420.] **Critical period of American history, 1783–1789.** John Fiske. Bost., Houghton, Mifflin & Co., 1889. 368 p. D. cl................................... 2.00 1.30

A comprehensive account of the political history of the United States from the end of the Revolutionary war to the adoption of the constitution.

F83
F 54 hi

382. [399.] **History of the United States for schools.** John Fiske *and* Frank Alpine Hill. Bost., Houghton, Mifflin & Co., 1899. 573 p. il. D. hf. leath...... 1.00 .90

Valuable for reference. The grouping of facts so as to bring out the relation of cause and effect is especially good. References for collateral reading are given at the end of each chapter.

F83
F 54 mi

383. **Mississippi valley in the Civil war.** John Fiske. Bost., Houghton, Mifflin & Co., 1900. 368 p. maps. D. cl........ .... 2.00 1.30

A discriminating view of the salient features of the armies and their leaders who operated in the valley. Perusal of the volume inspires the reader with the theme, with the characters of the historic leaders, and with reverence for the author's care given to the leaders.

F83
F 54 wa

384. [419.] War of independence. John Fiske. Bost., Houghton, Mifflin & Co., 1899. 200 p. S. cl..... .75 .48

One of the best accounts for the younger pupils.

FS3
———
F 64 ma

#385. [433.] **Marching with Gomez:** a war correspondent's field note-book kept during four months with the Cuban army. Grover Flint. Bost., Houghton, Mifflin & Co., 1899. 294 p. il. D. cl............ 1.50 .98

 Graphic accounts of incidents in our late war. The author is a keen observer and the manners and customs of the Cubans are vividly portrayed.

List price. Price to schools.

FS3
———
F 93 ri

#386. **Rise of the republic of the United States.** Richard Frothingham. Bost., Little, Brown & Co., 1899. 640 p. O. Ed. 7. cl........................ 3.50 2.30

As a handbook for the study of our political life this book has no superior.

"I purpose in these pages to sketch the political history of the Rise of the Republic of the United States. I shall endeavor to frame a narrative of events, with their causes and relations, which derive interest and importance from their connection with the formation and direction of public opinion, the development of fundamental principles, and the embodiment of these principles into institutions and laws. I shall aim to show how the European emigrant, imbued with the spirit of a new civilization, organized self-governing communities, and to follow the stages of their growth into a union. I shall then trace the origin and rise of a sentiment of nationality, and the effort by which it became embodied in the Declaration of Independence, which was the first covenant of our country; and in the federal constitution, which is the supreme law of the land."—*From Introduction*.

Contents: Ideas of local self-government and of national union; Combination of local self-government and union in the New England confederacy; How aggression of the principle of local self-government led to revolution and intercolonial correspondence, and how a common peril occasioned a congress; Ideas of local self-government and of union for seventy years, and their combination in the plan adopted by the Albany convention; How the assertion by parliament of a right to tax the colonies by the stamp act evoked a sentiment of union, and occasioned a general congress; How the assertion by parliament, in the Townshend revenue acts, of absolute power over the colonies, was met by a constitutional opposition, and how an arbitrary royal order elicited action in a similar spirit by thirteen assemblies, in defence of their local self-government; How the patriots advanced from an embodiment of public opinion to a party organization, by forming committees of correspondence; How events developed the American union, and how the demand for a general congress was accompanied by pledges to abide by its decisions; How a general congress formed the association of the united colonies, and how support was pledged to the inhabitants of Massachusetts in resisting the alteration of their charter; When the popular leaders recognized the fact or revolution, and began to aim at independence, and how they met the question of sovereignty; How the people of the united colonies by the Declaration of Independence decreed their existence as a nation composed of free and independent states; How the people by ordaining the constitution of the United States instituted republican government.

F83

G 65 hi

387. **History of the United States for schools.** Wilbur F. Gordy. N. Y., C: Scribner's Sons, 1902. 482 p. il. and maps. O. New *ed.* cl.................. 1.00 .90

An excellent text in American history, including a careful account of our late war with Spain.

One very helpful feature of the book is a list of references for further reading appended to each chapter.

F83

G 65 pa

388. **Pathfinder in American history:** for the use of teachers, normal schools, and more mature pupils in grammar grades. Wilbur F. Gordy, *and* W. I. Twitchell. Bost., Lee & Shepard, c1893. 2 vol. in 1. D. cl. 1.20 1.08

This book covers a field hitherto unexplored in a systematic way. It will be of great value to the teacher of history and will also aid parents in the guidance of their children's reading.

Contents: Part 1. Educational value of the story; Where to begin; Use of pictures; Grouping topics; Grouping method illustrated; Manners and customs; Local history; Supplementary reading; Reading and the reading book; Patriotic poems; Geography and history; Language and history; Course of supplementary reading in United States history; Important anniversaries; Famous sayings of eminent men; Topics; History for primary grades; Preparatory work in history; List of reference books; Glimpse at the literature bearing upon American history; Few of our noted patriotic poems; Books to buy first.

Part 2. Few hints on conducting the recitation in history—Original inhabitants of America; Explorers and dscoverers; Colonization; Revolution; Republic before the civil war; Abraham Lincoln; Republc after the civil war.

F83

G 69 so

#389. **Soldier's story:** of his captivity at Andersonville, Belle Isle, and other rebel prisons. Warren Lee Goss. With an appendix containing the names of the Union soldiers who died at Andersonville, with the numbers of their graves, their rank, the companies and regiments to which they belonged, the dates of their decease, and the diseases of which they died. Bost., Lee & Shepard, c1866. 357 p. maps. O. cl. 2.50 1.64

The author depicts those scenes of prison life best fitted to con-

LIST OF BOOKS FOR HIGH SCHOOL LIBRARIES. 109

	List price.	Price to schools.

vey to the minds of general readers some of its characteristic phases, just as the prisoners saw it.

FS3
―――
G 87 ro
390. [430.] **Romance of conquest**: the story of American expansion through arms and diplomacy. William Elliot Griffis. Bost., W. A. Wilde Co., 1899. 312 p. il. D. cl................................. 1.50 .85

American expansion from earliest times to the close of the Spanish-American war.

FS3
―――
H 25 am
391. **American history leaflets**: colonial and constitutional. Albert Bushnell Hart *and* Edward Channing, *eds.* N. Y., A. Lovell & Co., 1892-1902. 33 Nos. D. pa. Each................................. .10 .09

These extracts from original documents are intended to facilitate the study of American history in the original documents. Each leaflet presents a single document, or a closely associated group of documents. They should be in the library of every progressive teacher of American history.

Contents: 1. Letters of Columbus to Luis de Sant Angel announcing his discovery, with extracts from his journal; 2. Ostend Manifesto, 1854; 3. Extracts from the Sagas describing the voyages to Vinland; 4. Extracts from official declarations of the United States embodying the Monroe doctrine, 1789-1891; 5. Documents illustrating the territorial development of the United States, 1763-1769; 6. Extracts from official papers relating to the Bering Sea controversy, 1790-1892; 7. Articles of Confederation of the United Colonies of New England, 1643-1684; 8. Exact text of the constitution of the United States *from the original manuscripts,* 1787-1870; 9. Documents describing the voyage of John Cabot in 1497; 10. Governor McDuffie's message on the slavery question, 1835; 11. Jefferson's proposed instructions to the Virginia delegates, 1774; and the original draft of the Declaration of Independence, 1776; 12. Ordinances of secession and other documents, 1860-1861; 13. Coronado's journey to New Mexico and the Great Plains, 1540-42; 14. Plans of union, 1696-1780; 15. Virginia and Kentucky resolutions, with the alien, sedition and other acts, 1798-1799; 16. Documents illustrating the territorial development of the United States, 1584-1774; 17. Documents relating to the Kansas-Nebraska act, 1854; 18. Lincoln's inaugural and first message to congress, 1861; 19. Extracts from the navigation acts, 1645-1696; 20. Exact text of the Articles of Confederation, with the Franklin and Dickinson drafts *from the original manuscripts,* 1776-1781; 21. Stamp act, 1765; 22. Documents illustrating state land claims and cessions, 1776-1802; 23. Extracts from the Dred Scott decision, 1857; 24. Documents relative to the bank controversy, 1829-1833;

25. Extracts from the Massachusetts body of liberties, 1641; 26. Extracts from Lincoln's state papers, Dec., 1861, to March, 1865; 27. Early history of Virginia. Extracts from John Smith's *True Relation*, etc.; 28. Proposals to amend the Articles of Confederation, 1780-1787; 29. Early history of Plymouth, extracts from Bradford and Mount; 30. Constitutional doctrines of Webster, Hayne, and Calhoun, 1828-1833; 31. Extracts from John Winthrop's history of New England; 32. Documents relating to territorial administration, 1778-1790; 33. James Otis and the writs of assistance.

F83

H 25 am 1

392. [396.] **American history told by contemporaries:** Vol. 1, Era of colonization, 1492-1689. Albert Bushnell Hart, ed. N. Y., Macmillan Co., 1898. 607 p. D. cl. 2.00 1.28

Contents: Practical introduction for teachers, libraries, and students; Discovery and early voyages; Conditions of colonization; Southern colonies; New England; Middle colonies.

F83

H 25 am 2

393. [396.] **American history told by contemporaries.** Vol. 2, Building of the republic, 1689-1783. Albert Bushnell Hart, ed. N. Y., Macmillan Co., 1899. 653 p. D. cl. 2.00 1.28

Contents: Practical introduction for teachers, pupils, students, and libraries; Separate colonies; Colonial government; Colonial life; Intercolonial; Causes of the revolution; Conditions of the revolution; Progress of the revolution.

F83

H 25 am 3

394. **American history told by contemporaries.** Vol. 3, National expansion, 1783-1845. Albert Bushnell Hart, Ed. N. Y., Macmillan Co., 1901. 668 p. D. cl. 2.00 1.30

Contents: Practical introduction for teachers, pupils, students, and libraries; United States in 1783; Confederation; Federal constitution; Federal supremacy; Jeffersonian supremacy; National consciousness; Social and political readjustment; Slavery and abolition.

F83

H 25 am 4

395. **American history told by contemporaries.** Vol. 4, Welding of the nation, 1845-1900. Albert Bushnell Hart, Ed. N. Y., Macmillan Co., 1901. 732 p. D. cl. 2.00 1.80

Contents: Practical introduction for teachers, libraries, and students; Expansion and slavery; Contest renewed; Causes of civil

LIST OF BOOKS FOR HIGH SCHOOL LIBRARIES. 111

	List price.	Price to schools.

war; Conditions of war; Progress of the war; Reconstruction; New United States; American problems.

The question of the availability and use of sources has been discussed in the report of the Committee of Seven in the "Study of history in schools"; in the report of the New England History Teachers' association on "The uses of sources"; in Hart's "Source-book of American History"; and in the introduction to each volume of the above series.

FS3

H 25 fo

296. [388.] **Formation of the Union, 1750-1829.** Albert Bushnell Hart. N. Y., Longmans, Green & Co., 1898. 278 p. maps. S. (Epochs of American history series.) cl. .... 1.25 .82

FS3

H 25 ep

397. **Epoch maps illustrating American history.** Albert Bushnell Hart. N. Y., Longmans, Green & Co., 1899. obl. S., flex. cl. .... .50 .45

These maps are enlarged reproductions of the ones prepared for the "Epochs of American History."

FS3

H 25 so

398. [395.] **Source-book of American history.** Albert Bushnell Hart. N. Y., Macmillan Co., 1899. 408 p. D. cl. .... .60 .54

A very helpful book in the history lesson. A brief series of illustrations of the leading events in United States history. These brief records may awaken an interest in the books from which they are taken.

FS3

H 37 ca

#399. [435.] **Cannon and camera.** John C. Hemment. N. Y., D. Appleton & Co., 1899. 282 p. il. D. cl... 2.00 1.30

The personal experiences of a photographer in Cuba during the war with Spain. Depicts stirring deeds by means of photographs and the pen.

FS3

H 53 la

400. **Larger history of the United States of America:** to the close of President Jackson's administration. Thomas Wentworth Higginson. N. Y., Harper & Bros., 1898. 470 p. il. O. cl..................... 2.50 1.64

An excellent narrative history for general readers.
Contents: First Americans; Visit of the Vikings; Spanish dis-

	List price.	Price to schools.

coverers; Old English seamen; French voyageurs; "An English nation'; Hundred years' war; Second generation of Englishmen in America; British yoke; Dawning of independence; Great declaration; Birth of a nation; Our country's cradle; Early American presidents; Second war for independence; Era of good feeling; Great western march; "Old Hickory."

F83
———
H 79 hl

401. **History of the Louisiana Purchase.** James K. Hosmer. N. Y., D. Appleton & Co., 1902. 223 p. il. and map. D. cl. 1.20   1.08

The story that Dr. Hosmer tells of the acquisition of the western empire included in the Louisiana purchase presents new and picturesque phases of a most important historical event of peculiar and timely interest, in view of the anniversary which comes next year. He pictures the vague and curious ideas of the Louisiana country held by most Americans one hundred years ago, and the objections to this form of expansion. He treats the changes in the ownership of the territory from France to Spain, and again to France, and he develops fully the purposes and acts of Jefferson and the American Commissioners in Paris. Of special importance from both the historical and personal points of view are the chapters which picture the leading part taken by Napoleon in bringing about the sale of Louisiana, and the relations between France and America, which are shown to possess a historical importance that has not been appreciated.

F83
———
J 64 hl

402. **High school history of the United States, with maps, plans and illustrations:** being a revision of the "History of the United States for schools." Alexander Johnston. *Rev.* and continued by Winthrop More Daniels; farther *rev.* and continued by William MacDonald. N. Y., Henry Holt & Co., 1901. 612 p. 60 maps. il. O. cl. 1.25   1.12

"The design of this book, then, is not simply to detail the events which make up the history of the United States, but to group those events which seem likely to shed light on the responsibilities of the citizen to the present or future, and to give the student the light in connection with the event. In this process the effort has been made, with caution and with a studied simplicity of language, to interest the pupil in the wonderful development of the United States and the difficult economic problems which have grown out of it."—*Preface.*

LIST OF BOOKS FOR HIGH SCHOOL LIBRARIES. 113

	List price.	Price to schools.

FS3
———
L 49 am
403. **American Revolution, 1763-1783:** being the chapters and passages relating to America from the author's history of England in the eighteenth century; arranged and edited with historical and bibliographical notes by James Albert Woodburn. William Edward Hartpole Lecky. N. Y., D. Appleton & Co., c1898. 518 p. D. cl. .... 1.25 .82

"This volume is intended, then, to supply the need of an extensive text-book upon a well-defined and important period of our history.

Under the guidance of American teachers, American students should be greatly benefited by the study of the struggles of the Revolution as presented by a fair and judicial English historian.

A classified bibliography and some historical notes have been included in the volume for the use of students. These, and the footnotes of Mr. Lecky, give full references to the 'sources.'" *Preface.*

FS3
———
L 82 wa
404. [431.] **War with Spain.** Henry Cabot Lodge. N. Y., Harper & Bros., 1899. 276 p. il. O. cl. 2.50 1.64

A complete account of the war based upon the official reports of the military and naval operations.

FS3
———
M 11 sc
405. **Select charters:** and other documents illustrative of American history, 1606-1775. William MacDonald, *ed.* N. Y., Macmillan Co., 1899. 401 p. O. cl. 2.00 1.80

"The present work forms a companion volume to my "Select Documents illustrative of the History of the United States, 1776-1861", and follows, in the main, the general method and arrangement of the earlier work. The aim has been to bring together, in a form suitable for class-room use, the chief constitutional and legal documents of the American colonial period commonly dwelt upon in systematic general courses of instruction. The list will be found to contain, among other pieces, the significant portions of the most important colonial charters, grants, and frames of government, and the acts of Parliament most directly affecting the American colonies."

FS3
———
M 11 sd
406. **Select documents illustrative of the history of the United States:** 1776-1861, with notes. William MacDonald, *ed.* N. Y., Macmillan Co., 1901. 465 p. O. cl. 2.25 2.02

"The present volume covers the period from 1776 to 1861—from the adoption of the Declaration of Independence to the eve of the

	List price.	Price to schools.

Civil War. None of the documents given are "new" or "rare", but many of them have not hitherto been very accessible, save to students fortunate enough to have at hand large libraries. I have aimed to include the important documents which a systematic course of instruction, making some pretension to thoroughness, would be likely to dwell upon, while excluding everything an acquaintance with which could be demanded only of those students devoting especial attention to the subject."—*Preface.*

F83

M 22 hi

407. [400.] **History of the American nation.** Andrew C. McLaughlin. N. Y., D. Appleton & Co., 1899. 587 p. il. D. (Twentieth century series.) cl....... 1.40 1.19

For reference. Especially good for political facts, and questions of government and administration. Short lists of references throughout the book.

F83

M 221 hi

#408. **History of the people of the United States, from the Revolution to the Civil war:** John Bach McMaster. N. Y., D. Appleton & Co., 1901. 5 vols. maps. O. cl. 12.50 8.20

An excellent reference work on the period which it covers.
This book should not be purchased until the school has a good working library of more elementary and less expensive reference books.

F83

M 221 sc

409. [397.] **School history of the United States.** John Bach McMaster. N. Y., American Book Company, 1897. 480 +-31 p. il. D. hf. leath............. 1.00 .85

Valuable for reference. Especially good on industrial development.

F83

M 76 st

410. **Student's American history.** David H. Montgomery. Bost., Ginn & Co., 1900. 548 + 60 p. maps. D. cl........ .... 1.40 1.19

An admirable history. The author has shown excellent judgment in the selection of topics, and in the emphasis bestowed upon salient facts and principles. The style is lucid and all parts of the book are readily comprehended by the average second year high school student.

LIST OF BOOKS FOR HIGH SCHOOL LIBRARIES. 115

	List price.	Price to schools.

FS3
———
M 83 ha
411. **Historical tales: American.** Charles Morris. Phil., J. B. Lippincott Co., 1902. 319 p. il. D. cl...... 1.00 .65

Excellent for Library reading class in history.
Contents: Vineland and the Vikings; Frobisher and the northwest passage; Champlain and the Iroquois; Sir William Phips and the silver-ship; Story of the Regicides; How the charter was saved; How Franklin came to Philadelphia; Perils of the wilderness; Some adventures of Major Putnam; Gallant defence; Daniel Boone, the pioneer of Kentucky; Paul Revere's ride; Green Mountain boys; British at New York; Quakeress patriot; Siege of Fort Schuyler; On the track of a traitor; Marion, the swamp-fox; Fate of the Philadelphia; Victim of a traitor; How the electric telegraph was invented; Monitor and the Merrimac; Stealing a locomotive; Escape from Libby prison; Sinking of the Albemarle.

FS3
———
Ol 1 ol
412. **Old South leaflets.** 5 vols. Bost., Directors of the Old South Work, 1902. D. cl. each 1.50 1.12

This set consists of one hundred twenty-five leaflets which can be purchased separately or in the edition here listed. They are reprints of documents, speeches, etc., and are of great value to both teachers and students in history.

FS3
———
R 27 pr
413. **Problems of expansion: as considered in papers and addresses.** Whitelaw Reid. N. Y., Century Co., 1900. 294 p. D. cl.......................... 1.50 .98

Contents: Territory with which we are threatened; Was it too good a treaty; Purport of the treaty; Duties of peace; Open door; Some consequences of the treaty of Paris; Our new duties; Later aspects of our new duties; Continental union; Our new interests; "Unofficial instruction"; Appendices: Power to acquire and govern territory, Tariff in United States territory, Resolutions of congress as to Cuba, Protocol of Washington, Peace of Paris.

FS3
———
R 34 hi
#414. **History of the United States from the compromise of 1850: 1850–1864.** James Ford Rhodes. N. Y., Macmillan Co., 1902. 4 vols. O. cl. 10.00 6.56

One of the best reference books on the period which it covers. The language is clear, simple, and not beyond the understanding of High school pupils.

LIST OF BOOKS FOR HIGH SCHOOL LIBRARIES.

| | List price. | Price to schools. |

FS3
R 67 ro

415. [434.] **Rough riders.** Theodore Roosevelt. N. Y., C: Scribner's Sons, 1899. 298 p. il. O. cl........ .50 .33

Every boy will enjoy this book which contains accounts of some of the most dramatic events in our late war.

FS3
Sch 6 hi

416. [394.] **History of the United States of America, under the constitution.** James Schouler. N. Y., Dodd, Mead & Co., 1894. 6 vols. O. cl................ 13.50 9.00

A valuable comprehensive history of the United States for reference. It should be in all the larger libraries.

FS3
Scu 4 hi

417. [402.] **History of the United States of America, with an introduction narrating the discovery and settlement of North America.** Horace E. Scudder. N. Y., Butler, Sheldon & Co., 1897. 520 p. il. D.... 1.00 .85

General view of the subject for reference.

FS3
Sl 5 fr

418. [392.] **French war and the revolution.** William Mulligan Sloane. N. Y., C: Scribner's Sons, 1898. 413 p. maps. D. (American history series.) cl..... 1.00 .90

See note for Burgess's "Middle Period".

FS3
So 4 bo

419. **Boys of 1812: and other naval heroes.** James Russell Soley. Bost., Dana Estes & Co., c1888. 338 p. il. O. bds.......... .... 1.50 .98

Valuable for supplementary reading in History and for Library reading.

FS3
So 4 sa

420. **Sailor boys of '61.** James Russell Soley. Bost., Dana Estes & Co., c1887. 381 p. il. O. bds.......... 1.50 .98

This book gives a vivid, dramatic picture of the part the navy played in the Civil war. It will be interesting to the class in United States history and for Library reading.

Contents: Outbreak of the Civil war; Defence of the Chesapeake; Sounds of North Carolina; Du Pont and the battle of Port

LIST OF BOOKS FOR HIGH SCHOOL LIBRARIES. 117

                                                                           List Price to
                                                                        price. schools.
Royal; Gunboat flotilla on the western rivers; Battle of New Orleans; Twelve months' struggle at Vicksburg; Attacks upon Charleston; Red river; Blockade; Semmes and the confederate cruisers; Cushing and the "Albemarle"; Battle of Mobile Bay; Fort Fisher.

F83

Sp 3 ou

421. [432.] Our navy in the war with Spain. John R.
     Spears. N. Y., C: Scribner's Sons, 1898. 406 p.
     il. D. cl.. 2.00 1.30

An interesting account of operations of our navy in the late war. For young readers.

F83

St 6 bu

422. Buccaneers and pirates of our coasts. Frank R.
     Stockton. N. Y., Macmillan Co., 1898. 325 p. il.
     map. D. cl....................................... 1.50   .98

Stories taken from the lives of sea-robbers, pirates, and buccaneers who have a world-wide reputation. Beginning with "Some masters in piracy", under which title are included Columbus and Sir Francis Drake, the writer goes through the annals of the many heroes of the sea, ending with Captain Kidd. The romance and cruelties belonging to these stories are vividly presented, with much of the author's quaint humor.

F83

T 39 co

#423. Constitutional history of the American people.
     Francis Newton Thorpe. N. Y., Harper & Bros.,
     1898. 2 vols. maps. O. cl.................... 5.00 3.25

This is a history of the evolution of government in this country, and it recalls the changes in the ideas and opinions which the American people have held respecting the principles, the organization, and the administration of their civil institutions. It deals with the nation as a great constituency engaged in working out a political system. The process has been one of individual and social amelioration, through many struggles, among which the chief are those for the extension of the suffrage; for the equitable apportionment of representation; for the abolition of discriminations on account of race; for the organization of systems of free schools; for the separation of the state from questionable practices, and for the establishment of government directly upon the will of the people. Nine maps illustrate the changes in population and in the political division of the country from 1776 to 1850. An exhaustive index and an analytical table of contents, by chapters, add to the usefulness of the work.

This book should not be purchased until the school has a good working library of more elementary books.

Contents—Volume 1: State; Form of democracy in the eighteenth century; Organization of government in the states; Transi-

| | List price. | Price to schools. |

tion to independent states; Constitutional elements; First struggle for sovereignty; Political estate at the opening of the nineteenth century; First migration west; From the Alleghanies to the Mississippi; Federal relations—Missouri; Beyond the Mississippi; People without a country; Democracy in a gulf state, 1845—Louisiana; Basis of representation; Elements of discord in the commonwealth.

Volume 2: Democracy in a border state, 1849—Kentucky; Changes in the judicial system; Exclusion of clergymen from civil office; Legislative apportionment; Rights of property; Free states and slave states contrasted; Democracy in a northern state, 1850—Michigan; Creation and regulation of corporations; Rights and privileges of citizens; Democracy in a western state, 1850—California; California and the Union; Dictates of free labor; Half-century of constitutional changes; Corporations, finance, local government and education; Courts, people, social and civil progress.

F83

T 39 hi

424. **History of the American people.** Francis Newton Thorpe. Chic., A. C. McClurg & Co., 1901. 627 p. map. O. cl...................... .... 1.50   1.35

The publishers claim that this work fills a gap in our literature which the late Moses Coit Tyler pointed out—"the need for a one volume history of our country which is at once exact in scholarship and readable as literature." It covers the period from the discovery of America to the present time.

F83

T 42 co

425. [387.] **Colonies, 1492-1750.** Reuben Gold Thwaites. N. Y., Longmans, Green & Co., 1898. 301 p. maps. S. (Epochs of American history series.) cl..... 1.25   .82

F83

W 15 ma

426. [391.] **Making of the nation, 1783-1817.** Francis A. Walker. N. Y., C: Scribner's Sons, 1898. 332 p. maps. D. (American history series.) cl........ 1.00   .90

See note for Burgess's "Middle Period".

F83

W 69 di

427. [389.] **Division and reunion, 1829-1889.** Woodrow Wilson. N. Y., Longmans, Green & Co., 1899. 326 p. maps. S. (Epochs of American history series.) cl........................... .... 1.25   .82

The books in this series form a concise and complete account of United States history.

UNITED STATES HISTORY.

(Colonial History and History of separate sections of the United States.)

FS31
———
Ar 1 st

	List price.	Price to schools.

#428. **Story of the Pilgrim fathers, 1606-1623 A. D.;** as told by themselves, their friends, and their enemies. Edited from the original texts. Edward Arber, *ed.* Bost., Houghton, Mifflin & Co., 1897. 634 p. maps and por. D. cl.................. 2.00   1.30

A source book.

"What has been here attempted has been to select those facts which are material to the Story, and which are also absolutely, or morally, certain; to explode whatever myths we may happen to have met with; and to give exact references for everything that is adduced. In one sense, it has been a resetting of old material; in another, the production of new facts. Our great desire has been, that there should be nothing in this Volume that the Reader may be hereafter compelled to unlearn; but that he may feel sure that, in respect to all its contents, that he is standing upon the solid rock of truth."—*From Preface.*

FS31
———
B 72 co

429. **Colonial fights and fighters;** stories of exploration, adventure, and battle on the American continent prior to the war of the Revolution. Cyrus Townsend Brady. N. Y., McClure, Phillips & Co., 1901. 341 p. il. O. cl...................... 1.20   1.08

Supplements "American fights and fighters", being a collection of short stories dealing with the early Colonial wars, the French and Indian war, the buccaneers, explorers, etc.
Suitable for Library reading.

FS31
———
D 78 bo

#430. **Book of New England legends and folk lore;** in prose and poetry. Samuel Adams Drake. Bost., Little, Brown & Co., 1901. New *Rev. ed.* 477 p. il. O. cl.......... .... 2.50   1.64

A collection, for the most part, of historical legends which will be of interest to the classes in United States colonial history and in Library reading. They give many vivid pictures of colonial life.

FS31
———
D 78 m

431. **Making of New England, 1580-1643.** Samuel Adams Drake. N. Y., C: Scribner's Sons, 1900. 251 p. il. D. bds................ .... 1.50   .98

"This little book is intended to meet, so far as it may, the want of brief, compact, and handy manuals of the beginnings of our

	List price.	Price to schools.

country. It aims to occupy a place between the larger and the lesser histories,—to so condense, or eliminate from, the exhaustive narrative as to give it greater vitality, or so extend and elucidate what the school history too often leaves obscure for want of space as to supply the deficiency. To enhance the interest of this story, emphasis has been given to everything that went to make up the home life of the pioneer settlers or relates to their various avocations."—*Preface.*

A good book to use as supplementary to the text in history, also interesting for the Library reading class in History.

F831

D 78 ma

432. **Making of the Ohio valley states, 1660-1837.** Samuel Adams Drake. N. Y., C: Scribner's Sons, 1894. 269 p. il. D. cl.................................. 1.50 .98

A very interesting description of the conquest of and advance into the West; suitable for use in History and Library reading.

F831

Ea 7 ch

433. [414.] **Child life in colonial days.** Alice Morse Earle. N. Y., Macmillan Co., 1899. 418 p. il. D. cl.. 2.50 1.64

One of the most interesting books on the list for Library reading.

F831

Ea 7 co

434. **Colonial days in old New York.** Alice Morse Earle. N. Y., C: Scribner's Sons, 1901. 312 p. D. cl... 1.25 .82

An intensely interesting account of colonial life in New York. The Library reading classes will enjoy reading it, also the United States history class.

Contents: Life of a day; Education and child-life; Wooing and wedding; Town life; Dutch town homes; Dutch farmhouses; Dutch larder; Dutch vrouws; Colonial wardrobe; Holidays; Amusements and sports; Crimes and punishments; Church and Sunday in old New York; "End of his days."

F831

Ea 7 cos

#435. [417.] **Costume of colonial times.** Alice Morse Earle. N. Y., C: Scribner's Sons, 1894. 264 p. D. cl. .... 1.25 .82

Very interesting for general reading.

F831
Ea 7 cu

	List price.	Price to schools.

436. [410.] **Customs and fashions in old New England.** Alice Morse Earle. N. Y., C: Scribner's Sons, 1898. 387 p. D. cl............................ 1.25 .82

  Intensely interesting account of child life, courtship and marriage customs, domestic service house interiors, table plenishings, supplies of the larder, old colonial drinks and drinkers, travel, taverns, holidays, sports, books, dress, funeral and burial customs in Colonial New England.

F831
Ea 7 ho

437. [416.] **Home life in colonial days.** Alice Morse Earle. N. Y., Macmillan Co., 1899. 470 p. il. D. cl...... 2.50 1.64

  Domestic life in the colonies. Very interesting and will prove helpful in teaching history. The illustrations are unusually good.

F831
Ea 7 sa

438. [411.] **Sabbath in Puritan New England.** Alice Morse Earle. N. Y., C: Scribner's Sons, 1898. 335 p. D. cl.. 1.25 .82

  Very readable and interesting.

F831
Eg 3 be

439. [403.] **Beginners of a nation;** a history of the source and rise of the earliest English settlements in America with special reference to the life and character of the people. Edward Eggleston. N. Y., D. Appleton & Co., 1899. 377 p. il. O. cl.... 1.50 .98

  The character of the age in which the English colonies were begun, the traits of the colonists, and the social, political, intellectual, and religious forces that promoted emigration are portrayed.

F831
Eg 3 tr

440. **Transit of civilization from England to America in the seventeenth century.** Edward Eggleston. N. Y., D. Appleton & Co., 1901. 344 p. O. cl...... 1.50 .98

  In this volume the historian captures the literary, scientific, and other influences which were brought to this country from Europe in the early years of our history. He divides his subject into six chapters: Mental outfit of the early colonists; Digression concerning medical notions at the period of settlement; Mother English, folk-speech, folk-lore, and literature; Weights and measures of conduct; The tradition of education; Land and labor in the early colonies.

F831

F 54 be

441. [409.] **Beginnings of New England** or the Puritan theocracy in its relations to civil and religious liberty. John Fiske. Bost., Houghton, Mifflin & Co., 1890. 296 p. map. D. cl...................... 2.00   1.30

    List Price to price. schools.

Excellent for reference and good for advanced classes in Library reading.

F831

F 54 du

442. [412.] **Dutch and Quaker colonies in America.** John Fiske. Bost., Houghton, Mifflin & Co., 1899. 2 vols. 294; 400 p. D. cl...................... 4.00   2.60

Excellent for reference.

F831

F 54 ne

443. **New France and New England.** John Fiske. Bost., Houghton, Mifflin & Co., 1902. 378 p. maps. O. cl.......... .... 1.65   1.48

This volume deals with the rise and fall of New France, and the development of the English colonies as influenced by the prolonged struggle with these dangerous and troublesome neighbors. It completes the story of the settlement and development of the colonies up to the point where Mr. Fiske's "American Revolution" has already taken up the narrative, and therefore gives a final unity to the sequence of remarkable volumes which he has devoted to American history.

Contents: From Cartier to Champlain; Beginnings of Quebec; Lords of Acadia—later history of Champlain; Wilderness and empire; Witchcraft in Salem village; Great awakening; Norridgewock and Louisburg; Beginnings of the great war; Crown Point, Fort William Henry, and Ticonderoga; Louisburg, Fort Duquesne, and the fall of Quebec.

F831

F 54 ol

444. [413.] **Old Virginia and her neighbors.** John Fiske. Bost., Houghton, Mifflin & Co., 1898. 2 vols. 318; 421 p. D. cl............................ 4.00   2.60

For older pupils.

F831

F 77 st

445. **Story of the soldier.** George A. Forsyth. N. Y., D. Appleton & Co., 1900. 389 p. D. cl........... 1.50   .98

In telling the story of the soldiers the author has practically outlined the whole history of the regular soldier of the United States army. An excellent book for Library reading.

FS31
G 63 co

| | List price. | Price to schools. |

446. [415.] **Colonial cavalier or southern life before the revolution.** Maud Wilder Goodwin. Bost., Little, Brown & Co., 1897. 316 p. il. D. cl. 2.00 1.30

Interesting description of life in the south.

FS31
G 87 pi

447. [408.] **Pilgrims in their three homes, England, Holland, and America.** William Elliot Griffis. Bost., Houghton, Mifflin & Co., 1898. 296 p. il. S. (Riverside library for young people.) cl. ...... .75 .48

Will give the pupils a good idea of the early history of New England.

FS31
G 88 st

448. **Story of the Indian.** George Bird Grinnell. N. Y., D. Appleton & Co., 1898. 270 p. il. D. cl. (Story of the west series.) .... 1.50 .98

"There is no word simpler and more elastic than the word story to describe the plan of the series, and although we shall deal with the realities of history, the humbler term seems more broadly significant. These books are intended to be stories of human interest, not categories of facts."

"Mr. Grinnell takes us directly to the camp fire and the council. He shows us the Indian as a man subject to like passions and infirmities with ourselves. He shows us how the Indian wooed and fought, how he hunted and prayed, how he ate and slept—in short, we are admitted to the real life of the red man, and as we learn to know him we discard two familiar images; the red man of the would-be philanthropic sentimentalist, and the raw-head-and-bloody-bones figure that has whooped through so many pages of fiction."

F831
H 59 ol

#449. **Old northwest: the beginnings of our colonial system.** Burke A. Hinsdale. Bost., Silver, Burdett & Co., 1899. 430 p. map. O. cl. 1.75 1.57

A very excellent reference book on Colonial history. Too advanced for beginning classes in United States history.

Contents: North America in outline; First division of North America; French discover and colonize the northwest; England wrests the northwest from France—the first treaty of Paris; Thirteen colonies as constituted by the royal charters; Western land policy of the British government from 1763 to 1775; Northwest in the revolution; United States wrest the northwest from England—the second treaty of Paris; Northwestern land-claims; Northwestern cessions; Land ordinance of 1785; Ordinance of 1787; Territory of the United States northwest of the river Ohio; Admission of the northwestern states to the Union; Slavery in the northwest; Connecticut western reserve; Northwestern progress.

F831

H 79 sh

450. **Short history of the Mississippi valley.** James K. Hosmer. Bost., Houghton, Mifflin & Co., 1901. 230 p. il. D. cl. 1.20   1.08

After sketching the vastness and fitness of the Mississippi valley for a great history, Mr. Hosmer tells of the coming into it of the Spaniards, the French, and the English; and describes the conflicts and the changes of control until the Americans were masters. The narrative includes brilliant individual actors, Coronado, La Salle, Boone, G. R. Clarke, Jackson, Farragut, and Grant.

F831

H 81 st

451. [633.] **Story of the cowboy.** E. Hough. N. Y., D. Appleton & Co., 1898. 349 p. il. D. (Story of the west series.) cl. .... 1.50   .98

The books in the "Story of the West" series contain fine descriptions of some of our leading industries, from which many facts can be gained for illustration in the study of economics. They will also be helpful in geography and history.

F831

H 88 ho

452. **How New England was made.** Frances A. Humphrey. Bost., Lothrop Pub. Co., c1890. 267 p. il. O. cl.   1.25   .82

An elementary but exceedingly interesting account of colonial life in New England.

F831

In 4 so

453. **Southern sidelights:** a picture of social and economic life in the south a generation before the war. Edward Ingle. N. Y., Thomas Y. Crowell & Co., c1896. 373 p. (Library of economics and politics series.) D. cl. 1.75   1.17

"To outline a picture of social and economic life in the South during the generation before the war is the purpose of this work."

After defining what he means by the term "Southern", Mr. Ingle takes up in turn the following topics: 1, Traits of the people; 2, Where cotton was ruler; 3, Phases of industry; 4, Trade and commerce; 5, The educational situation; 6, Literary aspirations; 7,

	List price.	Price to schools.

Plans for progress; 8, The peculiar institution, and 9, The crisis. The material upon which the volume is based was gathered from contemporary magazine and newspaper articles, public documents, private letters, etc.

F831
L 82 sh

#454. **Short history of the English colonies in America.** Henry Cabot Lodge. N. Y., Harper & Bros., 1881. 560 p. O. cl. 3.00 1.96

Very good for reference in colonial history, especially good on colonial government.

F831
P 14 ol

455. **Old South: essays social and political.** Thomas Nelson Page. N. Y., C: Scribner's Sons, 1900. 344 p. D. cl. .... 1.25 .82

"These essays are given to the public in the hope that they may serve to help awaken inquiry into the true history of the Southern people and may aid in dispelling the misapprehension under which the Old South has lain so long."—*Preface.*

Contents: Old South; Authorship in the south before the war; Glimpses of life in colonial Virginia; Social life in old Virginia before the war; Two old colonial places; Old Virginia lawyer; Want of a history of the southern people; Negro question.

F831
P 87 hi

#456. **Historic towns of the western states.** Lyman P. Powell, *ed.* N. Y., G. P. Putnam's Sons, 1901. 702 p. il. O. cl. 3.00 2.70

The history of twenty-two western cities. The history given of the Mormons in Salt Lake City and the references to the Mound Builders in the history of Marietta, Cincinnati, Vincennes, and Des Moines are special features of this volume. The introduction gives a summary of the titanic struggle for settlement in North America made respectively by Spain, France, and England.

A good book for library reading.

F831
R 67 wi

#457. **Winning of the west.** Theodore Roosevelt. N. Y., G. P. Putnam's Sons, 1901. 4 vols. maps. O. cl. 10.00 6.50

An excellent reference book. This set should be purchased only by the larger libraries.

Contents—Vol. 1: Spread of the English-speaking peoples; French of the Ohio valley, 1763–1775; Appalachian confederacies, 1765–1775; Algonquins of the northwest, 1769–1774; Backwoods-

    List Price to
    price. schools.
men of the Alleghanies, 1769-1774; Boone and the long hunters,
and their hunting in No-Man's-land, 1769-1774; Sevier, Robertson,
and the Watauga commonwealth, 1769-1774; Lord Dunmore's war,
1774; Battle of the Great Kanawha, and Logan's speech, 1774;
Boone and the settlement of Kentucky, 1775; Current of the revolution—the southern backwoodsmen overwhelm the Cherokees, 1776;
Growth and civil organization of Kentucky, 1776.
Vol. 2: War in the northwest, 1777-1778; Clark's conquest of
the Illinois, 1778; Clark's campaign against Vincennes, 1779; Continuance of the struggle in Kentucky and the northwest, 1779-
1781; Moravian massacre, 1779-1782; Administration of the conquered French settlements, 1779-1783; Kentucky until the end of
the revolution, 1782-1783; Holston settlements, 1777-1779; King's
mountain. 1780; Holston settlements to the end of the revolution,
1781-1783; Robertson founds the Cumberland settlement, 1779-
1780; Cumberland settlements to the close of the revolution, 1781-
1783; What the westerners had done during the revolution.
Vol. 3: Inrush of settlers, 1784-1787; Indian wars, 1784-1787;
Navigation of the Mississippi, separatist movements and Spanish
intrigues, 1784-1788; State of Franklin, 1784-1788; Kentucky's
struggle for statehood, 1784-1790; Northwest territory, Ohio,
1787-1790; War in the northwest, 1787-1790; Southwest territory; Tennessee, 1788-1890.
Vol. 4: St. Clair's defeat, 1791; Mad Anthony Wayne, and the
fight of the fallen timbers, 1792-1795; Tennessee becomes a state,
1791-1796; Intrigues and land speculations—the treaties of Jay
and Pinckney, 1793-1797; Men of the western waters, 1798-1802;
Purchase of Louisiana, and Burr's conspiracy, 1803-1807; Explorers of the far west, 1804-1807.

F831
Scu 7 me
458. [418.] **Men and manners in America one hundred
    years ago.** *Ed.* by Horace E. Scudder. N. Y.,
    C: Scribner's Sons, 1891. 320 p. D. cl. .... 1.25   .82

    For reference.

F831
Sh 6 stm
459. [635.] **Story of the mine,** as illustrated by the Great
    Comstock lode of Nevada. Charles Howard
    Shinn. N. Y., D. Appleton & Co., 1898. 272 p.
    il. D. (Story of the west series.) cl. .... 1.50 .98

F831
W 23 str
460. [634.] **Story of the railroad.** Cy Warman. N. Y.,
    D. Appleton & Co., 1898. 280 p. il. D. (Story
    of the west series.) cl. .... 1.50   .98

F831

W 72 we

List price. Price to schools.

#461. **Westward movement:** the colonies and the republic west of the Alleghanies, 1763-1798. Justin Winsor. Bost., Houghton, Mifflin & Co., 1899. 595 p. maps and il. O. cl. 4.00   2.60

An excellent reference book. This should only be purchased by schools that already have a fair working library in United States history.

Contents: Introductory survey; Property line; Louisiana, Florida, and the Illinois country; Kentucky region; Quebec bill and the Dunmore war; South of the Ohio; Fortunes of the Mississippi; George Rogers Clark, arbiter and suppliant; Sinister purposes of France; Year of suspense; East and west; Peace; Insecurity of the northwest; Northwest occupied; Southwest insecure; Spanish question; Uncertainties in the southwest; Conditions of 1790; Harmar's and St. Clair's campaigns; Northwest tribes at last defeated; Jay's treaty and the territorial integrity of the northwest secured; Wayne's treaty and the new northwest; Unrest of the southwest; Pinckney's treaty and the Kentucky intrigue; United States completed.

UNITED STATES HISTORY.

(History of separate states.)

F832

B 27 or

#462. [424.] **Oregon:** the struggle for possession. William Barrows. Bost., Houghton, Mifflin & Co., 1896. 363 p. map. D. (American commonwealth series.) cl. .... 1.25   .82

The story of the struggle of the nations for Oregon and the final treaty.

F832

C 23 mi

463. [426.] **Missouri:** a bone of contention. Lucien Carr. Bost., Houghton, Mifflin & Co., 1896. 377 p. map. D. (American commonwealth series.) cl. ...... 1.25   .82

The Missouri compromise was the pivot on which slavery swung. This volume is a complete history of slavery.

F832

C 77 vi

464. [428.] **Virginia:** a history of the people. John Esten Cooke. Bost., Houghton, Mifflin & Co., 1894. 523 p. map. D. (American commonwealth series.) cl. .... 1.25   .82

Virginia shaped the development of the life of the south and to the understanding of that life a good history of Virginia is necessary. Older pupils will enjoy this book and portions may be read

FS32
H 12 bl

List price. / Price to schools.

465. **Blockaded family.** Parthenia Antoinette Hague. Bost., Houghton, Mifflin & Co., 1899. 176 p. D. cl. .... 1.00 .65

This volume gives an excellent picture of life in Southern Alabama during the Civil war and should be read by every member of the American history class when studying the Civil war. It gives a true picture of the hardships which the Southern people underwent and the devices which they had to resort to to obtain substitutes for the articles of food and clothing which they were accustomed to have.

F832
H 37 st

466. **Story of Manhattan.** Charles Hemstreet. N. Y., C: Scribner's Sons, 1901. 249 p. il. D. cl. ...... 1.00 .90

An accurate and interesting history of New York City. Suitable for Library reading. The illustrations are largely from old prints and wood engravings.

F832
Ir 8 hi

467. **History of New York:** from the beginning of the world to the end of the Dutch dynasty. * * * being the only authentic history of the times that ever hath been or ever will be published. Washington Irving. (Diedrich Knickerbocker, *pseud.*) Rev. ed. N. Y., G. P. Putnam's Sons, 1897. 528 p. S. cl. .... 1.00 .50

A concise history of the city of New York.

"The main object of my work, in fact, had a bearing wide from the sober aim of history; but one which, I trust, will meet with some indulgence from poetic minds. It was to embody the traditions of our city in an amusing form; to illustrate its local humors, customs, and peculiarities; to clothe home scenes and places and familiar names with those imaginative and whimsical associations so seldom met with in our new country, but which live like charms and spells about the cities of the old world, binding the heart of the native inhabitant to his home."—*From Author's preface.*

F832
J 64 co

#468. [423.] **Connecticut:** a study of a commonwealth-democracy. Alexander Johnston. Bost., Houghton, Mifflin & Co., 1895. 409 p. map. D. (American commonwealth series.) cl. .... 1.25 .82

The first conscious and deliberate effort on this continent to establish the democratic principles in control of government was the settlement of Connecticut. Democratic state government as adopted by Connecticut has influenced the general development of state systems in this country.

F832

L 52 le

469. **Leading events of Wisconsin history:** the story of the State. Henry Legler. Milwaukee, Sentinel Co., 1898. 322 p. il. O. cl. .... .75   .55

    List Price to
    price. schools.

    The chapters of this book were originally written for newspaper publication. Beginning with the travels and adventures of the early explorers and settlers and continuing through the later period, the narrative has been told, as nearly as circumstances would permit, in the words of actual participants.
    References: Building of the mounds in Wisconsin, p. 14-17.; Red men of Wisconsin, p. 22-28; Legendary lore of Wisconsin; Indians, p. 29-37; Jesuits in Wisconsin, p. 62-77; La Salle, p. 78-79; Fur-traders, p. 118-21, 152-56; Black Hawk's war, p. 172-80; Rescue of Joshua Glover, a runaway slave, p. 226-29; Strange story of a spurious prince, p. 235-41; Civil war, p. 244-79.

F832

P 23 or

470. [425.] **Oregon trail:** sketches of prairie and Rocky-mountain life. Francis Parkman. Bost., Little, Brown & Co., 1896. 381 p. il. D. cl. .... 1.50   .65

    Intensely interesting for younger pupils.

F832

R 81 ca

471. [427.] **California,** from the conquest in 1846 to the second vigilance committee in San Francisco: a study of American character. Josiah Royce. Bost., Houghton, Mifflin & Co., 1896. 513 p. maps. D. (American commonwealth series.) cl. .... 1.25   .82

    The growth of a state out of the chaotic elements gathered in California during the "Golden days." Story of the exciting period of Californian history, 1846-1856.

F832

T 42 st

472. **Story of Wisconsin.** Reuben Gold Thwaites. Bost., Lothrop Publishing Co., c1891. 389 p. il. O. cl. 1.50   .98

    The teacher should interest pupils in the history of their own state. Selections from this volume read to the pupils in connection with the national events studied in the history class, and also in connection with the geography of Wisconsin will do much toward fostering this interest.
    References: Mound-builders, 14-19; explorations, 19-35, 61-88; discovery of the Mississippi, 36-60; Joliet, 56-59, 61-63; La Salle, 63-68; Perrot, 71-76; Pierre le Sueur, 80; under British rule, 89;

		List price.	Price to schools.

Indians, 92–93, 122, 134, 155–159, 163–192; conspiracy of Pontiac, 96; life of the settlers, 98–105; events of the War of 1812, 135–148; lead mining, 161–163; Black Hawk War, 180–192; territorial days, 193–229; becomes a state, 230–246; Fugitive Slave Act, 247–254; Wisconsin in Civil War, 270–329; since the war, 330–367.

MEXICO—HISTORY.

F95

H 13 st

473. [439.] **Story of Mexico.** Susan Hale. N. Y., G. P. Putnam's Sons, 1889. 428 p. il. D. (Story of the nations series.) cl. .... 1.50 .98

F95

P 92 hi

474. [438.] **History of the Conquests of Mexico.** William H. Prescott, *ed. by* John Foster Kirk. Phil., J. B. Lippincott Co. 3 vols. 77; 463; 522 p. D. (Popular ed.) cl. 3.00 1.50

WEST INDIES—HISTORY.

F96

F 54 we

475. [436.] **West Indies:** a history of the islands of the West Indian archipelago, together with an account of their physical characteristics, natural resources and present condition. Amos Kidder Fiske. N. Y., G. P. Putnam's Sons, 1899. 414 p. il. D. (Story of nations series.) cl. .... 1.50 .98

SOUTH AMERICA—HISTORY.

F98

P 92 hi

476. [440.] **History of the conquest of Peru.** William H. Prescott, *ed. by* John Foster Kirk. Phil., J. B. Lippincott Co. 2 vols. 510; 530 p. D. (Popular ed.) cl. 2.00 1.00

TRAVEL AND DESCRIPTION.

In reading these books the aim should be to see the places and people described so far as possible. Travel in imagination and see how the people live, what they do for a living, how they amuse themselves, their food, clothing, etc. Descriptions of natural scenery, vegetation and animals, great cities, and famous buildings, should be carefully read.

GENERAL BOOKS.

G

Ad 1 te

477. **Text-book of commercial geography.** Cyrus C. Adams. N. Y., D. Appleton & Co., 1901. 505 p. il. D. cl. (Twentieth century text books.) 1.30   1.17

(List price. / Price to schools.)

An excellent text-book.

"The author has endeavored to limit the contents of this text-book of Commercial Geography to those dominating features of commerce and industry that should be most strongly impressed upon the student. The facts of commerce are treated as the effect of conditions that determine the quality and the quantity of trade. The effort is made throughout the book to connect cause and effect; to trace the great and small streams of commerce, and also to show the causes that give them direction and volume. Geographic and many other controlling influences, such as inventions, governmental aids or impediments, and the improvement of products, industrial processes, and means of transportation, are therefore made prominent.

Each product is treated in the chapter relating to the commerce of that country in which the production or manufacture of the commodity is specially prominent."—*Preface.*

G

C 44 sm

478. **Smaller commercial geography.** George G. Chisholm. N. Y., Longmans, Green & Co., 1900. 208 p. D. New ed. cl. .... .90   .81

An abridgment of Adams' "Handbook of Commercial geography."

G

J 15 st

479. [538.] **Story of geographical discovery:** how the world became known. Joseph Jacobs. N. Y., D. Appleton & Co., 1899. 200 p. maps. S. (Lib. of useful stories.) cl. .... .40   .32

Will be of interest in the history and in the geography classes.

G
M 59 hi

	List price.	Price to schools.

480. Hints to teachers and students on the choice of geographical books for reference and reading, with classified lists: prepared at the request of the Geographical Association. Hugh Robert Mill. N. Y., Longmans, Green & Co., 1897. 142 p. D. cl. .... 1.25 .82

"The object of this little volume is to place before teachers and students a selection of the best available books on Geography as an educational subject, and on different parts of the world. An effort has been made to include all cheap editions of recognized authorities; and in order to guide the reading of those to whom a good library is available, a selection of more expensive works, and of books now out of print, has been added."—*Preface.*
Valuable for reference for teachers.

G
M 59 in

481. [537.] **International geography.** By seventy authors. Edited by H. R. Mill. N. Y., D. Appleton & Co., 1900. 1088 p. il. O. cl. 3.50 2.30

A fine book for general reference. General principles of geography are discussed and the main facts in the geography of various countries are given.

VOYAGES AND TRAVELS AROUND THE WORLD.

G12
B 12 fo

482. **Foot-prints of travel:** or, Journeyings in many lands. Maturin M. Ballou. Bost., Ginn & Co., 1901. 472 p. il. and por. D. cl. .... .60 .51

Much valuable information as well as pleasure will be derived from reading this book.

G12
B 87 cr

483. [593.] **Cruise of the Cachalot round the world after sperm whales.** Frank T. Bullen. N. Y., D. Appleton & Co., 1899. 379 p. map. il. D. cl. .. 1.50 .98

A book which will prove intensely interesting to boys who are interested in the sea.

G12
B 87 id

484. [594.] **Idylls of the sea.** Frank T. Bullen. N. Y., D. Appleton & Co., 1899. 266 p. D. cl. .... 1.25 .82

Brief sketches of the sea. Certain sea animals are well described.

LIST OF BOOKS FOR HIGH SCHOOL LIBRARIES. 133

G12

C 68 am

485. **American girl's trip to the Orient and around the world.** Christine Colibran. Chic., Rand, McNally & Co., c1900. 176 p. il. D. cl. ....   List price. 1.25   Price to schools. .82

An entertaining account of trip around the world.

G12

C 82 so

486. [441.] **A social departure.** Mrs. Everard Cotes. N. Y., D. Appleton & Co., 1893. 417 p. il. D. cl.   1.75   1.15

Interesting and amusing incidents in a journey around the world by two women. Reads like a novel. A good book to start an interest in books of travel.

G12

D 19 tw

487. **Two years before the mast.** Richard H. Dana, *jr.* Bost., Houghton, Mifflin & Co., c1895. 470 p. D. cl. ....   1.00   .65

A narrative of life as a sailor and of sea adventure. The author of this book, Dana, an undergraduate at Harvard, was troubled with a weakness of the eyes and was compelled to give up his work. He shipped as a common sailor and made a trip by water to California. His account of what he saw and experienced makes a vivid, dramatic picture.

G12

Sw 3 on

488. [442.] **One way round the world.** Delight Sweetser. Indianapolis, Bowen-Merrill Co., c1898. 270 p. il. D. Ed. 4. cl. ....   1.25   .82

A journey from San Francisco to Japan, with a short stoppage at the Hawaiian Islands, and afterward to China, India, and Egypt, is here described, with many amusing incidents of travel.

ARCTIC REGIONS.

G14

P 31 my

489. **My Arctic journal: a year among ice-fields and Eskimos.** Josephine Diebitsch-Peary: with an account of the great white journey across Greenland by Robert E. Peary. N. Y., The Contemporary Pub. Co., 1897. 240 p. il. map. O. cl..   2.00   1.30

The simple narrative of a year spent by a refined woman in the Arctic regions.

"In reading the pages of this narrative it should be remembered that within sixty miles of where Kane and his little party endured such untold sufferings, within eighty miles of where Greely's men one by one starved to death, and within less than fifty miles of where Hayes and his party and one portion of the "polaris" party underwent their Arctic trials and tribulations, this woman lived for a year in safety and comfort."

Contents: Northward bound; In the Melville Bay pack; Establishing ourselves; Hunts and explorations; Boat journeys and preparations for winter; Winter upon us; Eskimo visitors; Arctic festivities; New year; Sunshine and storm; Sledge journey into Inglefield Gulf; Off for the inland ice; Weary days of waiting; My camping experience in Tooktoo valley; "Oomiaksoak Tigalay!" (The ship has come!) Return of the explorers; Boat journey into Inglefield gulf; Farewell to Greenland; Greenland revisited; Great white journey.

OCEANS AND ISLANDS.

G15

B 21 tr

490. **Travels under the southern cross:** being a second edition of "Under the southern cross, or travels in Australia, Tasmania, New Zealand, Samoa, and other Pacific Islands." Maturin M. Ballou. Bost., Houghton, Mifflin & Co., 1899. 405 p. D. Ed. 8. cl. .... 1.50 .98

Excellent for Library reading.

G15

B 22 ne

491. [493.] **New Pacific.** Hubert Howe Bancroft. N. Y., Bancroft Co., 1900. 538 p. map. O. cl. 2.50 1.64

Not only a valuable book of reference, but a very readable book. The resources, climate, history and romance, and present condition of the islands and shores of the Pacific Ocean.

G15

B 87 lo

492. [497.] **Log of a sea-waif,** being recollections of the first few years of my sea life. Frank T. Bullen. N. Y., D. Appleton & Co., 1899. 370 p. il. D. cl. 1.50 .98

Excellent portrayal of life on the sea. Descriptions of voyages to Havana, Jamaica, Bombay, and Melbourne. "I have written nothing but the truth and in most cases, I have given the real names of ships and individuals."

G15

D 73 be

493. [459.] **Bermuda:** an idyl of the summer lands. Julia C. R. Dorr. N. Y., C: Scribner's Sons, 1899. 148 p. map. S. cl. .... 1.25 .82

Beautiful descriptions of a beautiful place.

LIST OF BOOKS FOR HIGH SCHOOL LIBRARIES.

G15
H 53 ja

              List Price to
              price. schools.

494. [498.] **Java the pearl of the East.** S. J. Higginson. N. Y., Houghton, Mifflin & Co., 1897. 204 p. map. S cl. .... .75 .48

"The object of this little volume is to give the young people of this country, in as concise and complete a manner as possible, some trustworthy information in regard to the people, the weather, and the resources of the island of Java, together with a brief outline of its history."—*Author's preface.*

G15
Sci 2 ja

495. [499.] **Java the garden of the east.** Eliza Ruhamah Scidmore. N. Y., Century Co., 1898. 339 p. il. D. bds. .... 1.50 .98

An account of Java for older pupils.

G15
St 4 in

496. **In the south seas.** Robert Louis Stevenson. N. Y., C: Scribner's Sons, 1900. 370 p. map. D. cl. 1.50 .98

This volume is made up of selections from interesting sketches contributed to periodicals by Mr. Stevenson, narrating his experiences and observations in the Marquesas, Paumotus and Gilbert islands in the course of two cruises on the yacht "Casco" (1888) and the schooner "Equator" (1889).

G15
St 4 ye

497. [496.] **Yesterdays in the Philippines.** Joseph Earle Stevens. N. Y., C: Scribner's Sons, 1899. 232 p. map. il. D. cl. .... 1.50 .98

A most fascinating account of life in the Philippines.

G15
St 6 so

498. [495.] **South-sea idyls.** Charles Warren Stoddard. N. Y., C: Scribner's Sons, 1899. 339 p. D. cl. 1.50 .98

Description of people and places in Sandwich Islands.

HAWAII.

G161
Yo 8 re
499. [494.] **Real Hawaii:** its history and present condition. Lucien Young. N. Y., Doubleday & McClure Co., 1899. 371 p. il. D. cl. ....   1.50   .98

    A record of facts based upon personal observation and investigation.

EUROPE.

G30
D 85 la
500. [470.] **Land of the long night.** Paul Du Chaillu. N. Y., C: Scribner's Sons, 1899. 266 p. il. D. cl.   2.00   1.30

    Bright and entertaining experiences of a traveler in the far North.
    For younger pupils.

G30
H 83 on
501. [466.] **One year abroad.** Blanche Willis Howard. Bost., Houghton, Mifflin & Co., 1877. 247 p. T. cl. ....   1.25   .82

    Charming descriptions of important places in Europe. For younger pupils.

G30
J 12 bi
502. **Bits of travel.** Helen Hunt Jackson. (H. H., *pseud.*) Bost., Little, Brown & Co., 1898. 304 p. por. T. cl. ....   1.25   .82

    Vivid, dramatic pictures of life in Germany and Italy.
    Contents: German landlady; Valley of Gastein; Ampezzo Pass and the House of the Star of Gold; May-day in Albano; Afternoon in Memoriam, in Salzburg; Returned veterans' feet, in Salzburg; Morning in the Etruscan museum in the Vatican; Albano days; Sunday morning in Venice; Convent of San Lazarro, in Venice; Encyclicals of a traveller.

G30
J 12 gl
503. [467.] **·Glimpses of three coasts.** Helen Hunt Jackson. (H. H.) Bost., Little, Brown & Co., 1888. 418 p. D. cl. ....   1.50   .98

    Descriptions of California, Oregon, Scotland, England, Norway, Denmark, and Germany, written in Mrs. Jackson's charming style.

G30

K 58 ro

504. [465.] **Roundabout rambles in Northern Europe.** Charles F. King. Bost., Lee & Shepard, 1898. 353 p. il. D. cl. .... 1.25 .80

List price. Price to schools.

A fine account of travel in Europe for younger students.

G30

L 86 ou

505. **Outre-Mer: a pilgrimage beyond the sea.** Henry Wadsworth Longfellow. Bost., Houghton, Mifflin & Co., c1866. Rev. ed. 364 p. S. cl. .... 1.50 .98

Enough of the story element enters into the tales in this book to make it exceedingly interesting for Library reading. Students should read this or some other of Longfellow's prose works in their study of American literature.

G30

Sm 5 we

506. [476.] **Well-worn roads of Spain, Holland, and Italy.** F. Hopkinson Smith. Bost., Houghton, Mifflin & Co., 1899. 186 p. il. D. cl. .... 1.25 .82

"These sketches are the record of some idle days spent in rambling about odd places, and into quaint nooks, and along well-worn roads of travel."
Impressions of an artist.

GREECE.

G 32

H 78 mo

507. **Modern Athens.** George Horton. N. Y., C: Scribner's Sons, 1901. 91 p. il. O. cl. 1.25 1.12

A graphic description, richly illustrated, of modern Athens. Its streets, its picturesque people, its houses, theatres, etc., are all depicted by one who lived there many years while in the diplomatic service.

ITALY.

G35

B 34 It

509. [480.] **Italians of today.** René Bazin, tr. by William Marchant. N. Y., Henry Holt & Co., 1897. 247 p. D. cl. 1.25 1.12

Clear and concise account of Italy and her people.

G35

D 56 at

510. **At home in Italy.** *Mrs.* E. Dickinson (Rice) Bianciardi. Bost., Houghton, Mifflin & Co., 1884. 300 p. D. cl. .... 1.25 .82

List price. Price to schools.

Interesting for Library reading.
Contents: Italy as a residence; City of the winds; Mountain excursion in the province of Siena; Summer days in Perugia; Italian watering-place; Week in northern Italy; April day on the Consuma Pass; Florentine family in the fifteenth century; Camaldoli; Vallombrosa.

G35

H 31 pa

511. **Passages from the French and Italian note-books.** Nathaniel Hawthorne. Bost., Houghton, Mifflin & Co., c1899. 573 p. D. cl. 2.00 1.30

The main portion of these journals is devoted to Italy. The daily experiences of the author's Italian sojourn are set down just as they presented themselves to him at the time. Portions of these note-books should be read by the Literature classes in their study of Hawthorne.

G35

H 83 ve

512. [478.] **Venetian life.** W. D. Howells. Bost., Houghton, Mifflin & Co., 1885. 2 vols. 279; 287 p. S. (Riverside Aldine series.) cl. 2.00 1.30

Most beautiful descriptions of a beautiful city.

G35

Sm 5 go

513. [477.] **Gondola days.** Francis Hopkinson Smith. Bost., Houghton, Mifflin & Co., 1902. 205 p. il. D. cl. .... 1.50 .98

The contents indicate the points of view and the objects in Venice which most attract Mr. Hopkinson Smith; Arrival; Gondola days; Along the Riva; Piazza of San Marco; In an old garden; Among the fishermen; Gondola race; Some Venetian cafes; On the hotel steps; Open air markets; On rainy days; Legacies of the past; Life in streets; Night in Venice. The text is the same as that of 'Venice of today", published as a subscription-book by the Henry T. Thomas Company.

The artist has given us "the Venice of light and life, of sea, and sky, and melody". Most beautiful and graphic descriptions of Venice as an artist sees it.

SWITZERLAND.

G38
———
St 7 sw

List Price to
price. schools.

514. **Swiss life in town and country.** Alfred Thomas
Story. N. Y., G. P. Putnam's Sons, 1902. 282 p.
(Our European neighbors series.) il. D. cl. ..   1.20   1.08

Contents: Switzerland and the Swiss; Struggle with nature; Sovereignty of the people; Gemeinden and the Landsgemeinden; Public education; Philanthropic work; National industry; Culture of the vine; Life and work in the Alps; Cantonal life and character; Swiss women and Swiss homes; Swiss children; Military system; Workingmen's societies and co-operation; Religious life and influences; Popular fetes and festivals; Literature and the press; Types and characters.

FRANCE.

G39
———
St 4 tr

515. **Travels with a donkey in the Cevennes.** Robert
Louis Stevenson. N. Y., C: Scribner's Sons, 1901.
209 p. D. cl. ....   1.00   .65

"The author sees everything with the eye of a philosopher. He has a steady flow of humor that is as apparently spontaneous as a mountain brook, and he views a landscape or a human figure, not only as a tourist seeking subjects for a book, but as an artist to whom the slightest line or tint carries a definite impression."

SPAIN.

G40
———
M 86 la

516. **Lazy tours in Spain and elsewhere.** Louise Chandler
Moulton. Bost., Little, Brown & Co., 1898. 377
p. O. Ed. 5. cl. ....   1.50   .98

Contents: Lazy tour in Spain; In southern Italy; In and about Rome; Florence the fair; Paris and pictures; Rambles in Switzerland; Certain French cures; How they cure themselves in Germany; At Wiesbaden and after; An English "cure" and a glimpse of Yorkshire.

G40
———
St 6 sp

517. **Spanish cities:** with glimpses of Gibraltar and Tangier. Charles Augustus Stoddard. N. Y., C:
Scribner's Sons, 1895. 228 p. il. D. cl. ......   1.50   .98

Descriptions of some of Spain's most beautiful cities. A good book for the Travel class in Library reading.

ENGLAND.

(Including Ireland and Scotland.)

G45
B 46 ea

List Price to
price. schools.

#518. **East London.** Walter Besant. Illustrated by Phil May, Joseph Pennell, and L. Raven-Hill. N. Y., Century Co., 1901. 364 p. il. O. cl. 3.50 2.30

East London is that part of Greater London given over mostly to the very poor and is a city in itself. "It is my task", the author says, "to lay before my readers some of the aspects of this city which may redeem it from the charges of monotony and unloveliness." This he does with many charming illustrations in chapters entitled: "What East London is", "The city of the many crafts", "The pool and the riverside", "Factory girl", "Key of the street", "The alien", "The houseless", "The submerged", "The memories of the past". "On sports and pastimes", "The helping hand".
Too expensive a book for the small libraries.

G45
D 29 ou

519. [469.] **Our English cousins.** Richard Harding Davis. N. Y., Harper & Bros., 1899. 228 p. il. D. cl. 1.25 .82

Intensely interesting descriptions of life in England. Graphic pictures of life at Oxford, London in the season, and the west and east ends of London.

G45
H 31 ou

520. **Our old home and English note-books.** Nathaniel Hawthorne. Bost., Houghton, Mifflin & Co., c1898. 2 vols. D. cl. 2.00 1.30

These volumes will be of interest to the American Literature class and the Travel class in Library reading.
Contents: Volume 1—Introductory note; Dedication; To a friend; Consular experiences; Leamington Spa; About Warwick; Recollections of a gifted woman; Lichfield and Uttoxeter; Pilgrimage to Old Boston; Near Oxford; Some of the haunts of Burns; London suburb; Up the Thames; Outside glimpses of English poverty; Civic banquets; Passages from the English note-books of Nathaniel Hawthorne.

G45
J 62 is

521. **Isle of shamrock.** Clifton Johnson. N. Y., Macmillan Co., 1902. 258 p. il. D. cl. 2.00 1.80

Mr. Johnson depicts the rustic life of Ireland in many localities, from the beautiful Lakes of Killarney in the south to the wild

| | List price. | Price to schools. |

crags of the Giant's Causeway on the north coast. He visited not only the pleasanter sections such as "The golden vale" of Limerick, but the forbidding boglands of Connemara and Donegal. He describes the homes and ways of farm folk and the peasantry, the country schools, the beggars, the peculiar superstitions, etc. Illustrated from photographs made by the author.

G45
———
W 58 en
522. [468.] **England without and within.** Richard Grant
    White. Bost., Houghton, Mifflin & Co., 1896.
    601 p. D. cl. 2.00   1.30

    A very complete description of English life.

G45
———
W 73 ol
523. **Old shrines and ivy.** William Winter. N. Y., Macmillan Co., 1901. 296 p. T. cl. .... .75   .49

    "The shrines upon which these offerings of homage are laid are shrines of history and shrines of literature. It has been the author's design, alike in description and commentary, and whether depicting scenes of travel or celebrating achievements of genius, to carry through his books the thread of Shakespearean interest."—*Preface.*

    Contents: 1—Shrines of history—Storied Southampton; Pageantry and relics; Shakespeare church; Stratford chronicle; From London to Dover; Beauties of France; Ely and its cathedral; From Edinburgh to Inverness; Field of Culloden; Storm-bound in Iona.

    II—Shrines of literature—Forest of Arden: As you like it; Fairy land: A midsummer night's dream; Will o' the wisp: Love's labour's lost; Shakespeare's shrew; Mad world: Antony and Cleopatra; Sheridan and the school for scandal; Farquhar and the inconstant; Longfellow; Thought on Cooper's novels; Man of letters: John R. G. Hassard.

                        HOLLAND.
G46
———
Am 5 ho
524. **Holland and its people.** Edmondo de Amicis. *Trans.*
    by Caroline Tilton. N. Y., G. P. Putnam's Sons,
    c1880. 484 p. il. map. D. cl. 2.00   1.30

    An extremely interesting and well written description of a trip through Holland. The illustrations are very fine. Excellent for Library reading.

G46

H 81 du

List price. Price to schools.

525. **Dutch life in town and country.** P. M. Hough. N. Y., G. P. Putnam's Sons, 1902. 291 p. il. (Our European neighbors series.) D. cl. 1.20 1.08

Describes the social life of Holland; its national characteristics; court and society; the professional classes; the position of women; The workman of the towns; rural customs and national amusements; and gives an insight to the political and religious life and thought of the Dutch, with reflections on the art and literature of the country.

G46

M 48 ho

526. **Holland and the Hollanders.** David S. Meldrum. N. Y., Dodd, Mead & Co., 1900. 405 p. il. O. cl. 2.00 1.30

An admirable book describing the natural, political and social features of Holland and its sturdy inhabitants. The main feature of the book is its pictures, of which there are eighty, many of them reproductions of well-known specimens of Dutch and Flemish art.

Contents: Impressions of Holland today; How Holland is governed; Fight with the waters; How Holland is educated; 'S Hertogenbosch and the southern provinces; Utrecht, and the East; Groningen and the North; Amsterdam and the Holland provinces; Middelburg and the Islands of Zeeland.

GERMANY.

G47

B 17 se

527. **Seen in Germany.** Ray Stannard Baker. N. Y., McClure, Phillips & Co., 1901. 317 p. il. O. cl. 2.00 1.80

It was during a recent visit to Germany which Mr. Baker, accompanied by George Varian, the artist, made in the interests of this work that these things were "seen". Furnished with credentials which afforded him unusual opportunities, this popular magazine writer employed his rare faculty as a gatherer of interesting facts in an intimate study of the German workingman at home and in the shop, the soldier on and off duty, the typical German scientist, the industries and schools—in fact, all sides of German life.

Contents: Common things seen in Germany; Kaiser; German private soldier; view of the German workingman; German professor; Typical scientific institution; How the Germans created a new industry; German venture in practical philanthropy; How the Germans build ships; Some new educational ideas in Germany; Glimpse of German student life; New Germany.

G47
—
D 32 ge

List price. Price to schools.

528. **German life in town and country.** William Harbutt Dawson. N. Y., G. P. Putnam's Sons, 1902. 323 p. il. (Our European neighbors series.) D. cl.   1.20   1.08

Chapters on: What is the German's Fatherland? Social divisions; "Arbeiter"; Rural life and labor; Military service; Public education; Religious life and thought; Woman and the home; Pleasures and pastimes; Berliner; Political life; Local government; Newspaper and its readers.

G47
—
N 82 in

529. [475.] **In and around Berlin.** Minerva Brace Norton. Chic., A. C. McClurg & Co., 1889. 268 p   S. cl.   1.00   .50

Very interesting account of family and social life, education, churches, museums, streets, parks, palaces, and public buildings, of the Germans in Berlin.

NORWAY.

G48
—
N 51 no

530. [474.] **Norway summer.** Laura D. Nichols. Bost., Little, Brown & Co., 1898. 178 p. il. D. cl..   1.25   .82

Descriptions of life and places in Norway.

RUSSIA.

G54
—
H 21 ru

531. **Russian rambles.** Isabel F. Hapgood. Bost., Houghton, Mifflin & Co., c1895. 369 p. D. cl. ....   1.50   .98

Few Americans are more familiar with Russia than Miss Hapgood is, both through a long residence there and study of its literature. Her judgments, based upon keen observation of its social and political conditions, differ from those of many other writers; she found much to praise and admire.
Contents: Passports, police, and postoffice in Russia; Névsky Prospekt; My experience with the Russian censor; Bargaining in Russia; Experiences; Russian summer resort; Stroll in Moscow with Count Tolstoy; Count Tolstoy at home; Russian holy city; Journey on the Volga; Russian Kumys cure; Moscow memoirs; Nizbni Novgorod fair and the Volga.

	List price.	Price to schools.

G54
P 1S ru
532. **Russian life in town and country.** Francis H. E. Palmer. N. Y., G. P. Putnam's Sons, 1902. 320 p. (Our European neighbors series.) il. D. cl. ..   1.20   1.08

Contents: Russia behind the veil; The landed proprietor's home; Country life in summer; Strada; The peasant in serfage; The country priest; Life on a large estate; Peasant characteristics; Rural self-government; A country town; Jewish town life; The Jewish trader; The "Odnodvortsy;" The orthodox church and the clergy; Religious thought and ritual; The Russian dissenters; Life in winter; Town society; The urban working classes; Industrial co-operative associations; Education and the army; Index.

All the volumes in this series are extremely interesting and well adapted to the needs of the "Travel" classes in Library reading.

G54
P 94 ru
533. **Russian journey.** Edna Dean Proctor. Bost., Houghton, Mifflin & Co., 1900. 320 p. il. D. Rev. ed. cl. ....   1.25   .82

Very interesting sketches of life in Russia.

G54
St 6 ac
534. [471.] **Across Russia from the Baltic to the Danube.** Charles Augustus Stoddard. N. Y., C: Scribner's Sons, 1899. 253 p. il. D. cl. ....   1.50   .98

Entertaining descriptions of Russia and her people, particularly in the great cities of St. Petersburg, Moscow, Novgorod, and Buda-Pesth. Amusements, schools and libraries, art and science, religious sects, and peculiar customs, are some of the subjects discussed.

TURKEY.

G59
C 85 co
535. [479.] **Constantinople.** F. Marion Crawford. N. Y., C: Scribner's Sons, 1895. 79 p. il. O. cl. ...   1.50   .98

Vivid descriptions of the life of Constantinople.

ASIA.

G60
Al 5 ac
                                                                List Price to
                                                               price. schools.

536. **Across Asia on a bicycle:** the journey of two American students from Constantinople to Peking. Thomas Gaskell Allen, Jr., and W. L. Sachtleben. N. Y., Century Co., 1897. 234 p. il. D. cl. ....   1.50   .98

"This volume is made up of a series of sketches describing the most interesting part of a bicycle journey around the world."— *From Preface.*

During the author's travels he took more than twenty-five hundred photographs, many of the best of which have been reproduced in this volume.

Contents: Beyond the Bosporus; Ascent of Mount Ararat; Through Persia to Samarkand; Journey from Samarkand to Kuldja; Over the Gobi desert and through the western gate of the great wall; Interview with the prime minister of China.

G60
B 13 ja
537. **Japanese interior.** Alice Mabel Bacon. Bost., Houghton, Mifflin & Co., c1893. 272 p. D. cl. ..   1.25   .82

The author of this book was a teacher in a Japanese school for the girls of the nobility. This naturally brought her into close contact with the most refined and cultivated Japanese women.

G60
B 13 ja
538. [484.] **Japanese girls and women.** Alice Mabel Bacon. Bost., Houghton, Mifflin & Co., 1897. 333 p. S. cl. 75   .48

Manners and customs of Japan.

G60
B 53 un
539. [482.] **Unbeaten tracks in Japan.** Isabella L. Bird. N. Y., G. P. Putnam's Sons. D. (Popular ed.) cl. 2.50   1.60

One of the best books on Japan.

G60
C 71 ov
#540. **Overland to China.** Archibald R. Colquhon. N. Y., Harper & Bros., 1900. 465 p. il. maps. O. cl.   3.00   1.96

The present work is the result of such fresh observations, and an attempt to interest the general reader and give him an idea of the ground by presenting, without elaboration, a series of im-

	List price.	Price to schools.

pressions of the conditions, physical and political, under which the Trans-Siberian railway will shortly become an accomplished fact. Much of the information is drawn from original sources, and the whole is connected by a thread of the writer's personal experiences.

Contents: Siberia: the conquest; Occupation; Industries and products; Great Trans-Siberian–Manchurian railway; Peking: past and present; Manchuria; Eastern Mongolia; Yangstze valley; Southwest China; Tongking; Conclusions.

G60

G 74 fi

541. [473.] **Five thousand miles in a sledge:** a midwinter journey across Siberia. Lionel F. Gowing. N. Y., D. Appleton & Co., 1891. 257 p. map. il. D. cl. .... 1.50 .98

Personal experiences and a record of a journey across Siberia during midwinter. A very interesting book.

G60

H 35 gl

*542. **Glimpses of unfamiliar Japan.** Lafcadio Hearn. 2 vols. Bost., Houghton, Mifflin & Co., 1901. O. cl. 4.00 2.60

Contents: Volume 1. My first day in the Orient; Writing of Kobodaishi; Jizo; Pilgrimage to Enoshima; At the market of the dead; Bon-Odori; Chief city of the province of the gods; Kitzuki; most ancient shrine in Japan; In the cave of the children's ghosts; At Mionoskei; Notes on Kitzuki; At Hinomisaki; Shinju; Yaegaki. Jinja; Kitsune.

Volume 2. In a Japanese garden; Household shrine; Of women's hair; From the diary of an English teacher; Two strange festivals; By the Japanese sea; Of a dancing-girl; From Hoki to Oki; Of souls; Of ghosts and goblins; Japanese smile; Savonara.

G60

K 14 en

543. [485.] **Enchanted India.** *Prince* Bojidar Karageorgevitch. N. Y., Harper & Bros., 1899. 305 p. por. D. cl. 1.75 1.15

Most beautiful description of the scenery of India.

G60

K 36 te

544. [472.] **Tent life in Siberia.** George Kennan. N. Y., G. P. Putnam's Sons, 1870. map. 425 p. D. cl. 1.25 .82

A narrative of two years' life in northeastern Siberia, giving a clear idea of inhabitants, scenery, customs, and general features of the country.

G60

R 13 al

545. **Alone in China,** and other stories. Julian Ralph. N. Y., Harper & Bros., 1900. 282 p. il. D. cl. ...   List price. 2.00   Price to schools. 1.30

    A very interesting description of life in China. The author went to China and spent all his time among the Chinese, denying himself entirely of the hospitality of the white men and women in the treaty ports. In this book he has described his most interesting experiences and in the form of tales and romances has narrated what he saw and learned of the surroundings and customs of the people in districts where they have not been affected by foreign influences.

G60

R 18 ja

#546. [483.] **Japan in transition.** Stafford Ransome. N. Y., Harper & Bros., 1899. 261 p. il. O. cl. ..   3.00   1.96

    A comparative study of the progress, policy, and methods of the Japanese since their war with China. The book deals with the changes going on in Japan today. Some of the leading subjects discussed are: popular misconceptions of Japan, traveling and accommodation, the studying of the foreigner, present day education, commercial integrity and international business relations, and modern industries. The school statistics will interest the teacher.

G60

Sci 2 ch

547. **China: the long-lived empire.** Eliza Ruhamah Scidmore. N. Y., Century Co., 1900. 466 p. il. O. cl. 2.50   1.64

    Miss Scidmore's knowledge of China is due to the fact that she has visited it seven times within the past fifteen years. Several of her eight and twenty chapters are devoted to the capital, Peking; one to the foreign missions; one each to the cities of Tientsin, Canton, and Shanghai, and two to the Great Wall. "The Decadence of the Manchus," the alien ruling family, is the subject of another chapter, while the Dowager Empress, "Tsze Hsi and the Great," is treated of at equal length. An amusing account is given of the Tsung-li Yamun, the group of old men that is nominally responsible for the empire's foreign policy.

G60

Sh 7 qu

548. [486.] **Quaint corners of ancient empires, Southern India, Burma, and Manila.** Michael Meyers Shoemaker. N. Y., G. P. Putnam's Sons, 1899. 212 p. il. D. cl. 2.25   1.48

    An account of unusual places in India, Burma, and Manila.

G60
Sm 5 ch
                                           List Price to
                                           price. schools.

549. [481.] **Chinese characteristics.** Arthur H. Smith. Chic., Revell & Co., 1894. il. O. cl. 2.00 1.30

Complete account of Chinese manners and customs.

AFRICA.

G70

B 13 ou

550. **Our houseboat on the Nile.** Lee Bacon. (*Mrs.* Henry Bacon.) Bost., Houghton, Mifflin & Co., 1901. 286 p. il. O. cl. 1.75 1.57

Mrs. Henry Bacon tells the story of a voyage of several weeks on the Nile in a dahabéah, in the late fall of 1899 and the early part of 1900. The voyage began about six miles above Assouan and extended some two hundred miles, returning then to the starting-point. The whole trip was between the first and second cataracts. Mrs. Bacon describes the difficulties of hiring and fitting the boat; the character of the crew; daily life on board; the sights along the shores; explorations of old temples; excursions into the desert; and the natives as she saw them.

G70

B 48 wh

551. **White man's Africa.** Poultney Bigelow. N. Y., Harper & Bros., 1900. 271 p. il. O. cl. 2.50 1.64

An excellent book on South Africa.

Contents: Jameson's raid; President Kruger; Portuguese progress in South Africa; President of the Orange Free State; Last of a great black nation; At the cape of Good Hope; White man's black man; Dutch feeling toward England; Natal—colonial paradise; British and Boer government.

G70

D 84 tr

553. [490.] **Tropical Africa.** Henry Drummond. N. Y., C: Scribner's Sons, 1897. 228 p. maps. il. D. cl. .... 1.00 .65

A small book of travel, with the larger features of the country lightly sketched and just enough narrative to add to the interest. The people and their customs are described and the difficulties in civilizing Africa discussed.

G70

M 36 ho

554. [491.] **Home life on an ostrich farm.** Annie Martin. N. Y., D. Appleton & Co., 1898. 288 p. D. cl. .. 1.25 .82

Most interesting accounts of ostriches and other animals, as well as descriptions of life in South Africa.

		List price.	Price to schools.

G70
P 37 pr

555. [487.] **Present-day Egypt.** Frederic Courtland Penfield. N. Y., Century Co., 1899. 372 p. il. O. cl. 2.50 1.64

Graphic descriptions of life in Cairo and Alexandria. "Aiming at being a discursive budget of information and comment, social, political, economical, and administrative, the volume presents a series of faithful pictures of the Egypt'which is interesting to the winter visitor, health seekers, and general reader desirous of learning something of contemporary conditions in the oldest country in the world."—*Author's Preface.*
Valuable material for work in geography.

G70
St 3 eg

556. [488.] **Egypt in 1898.** G. W. Steevens. N. Y., Dodd, Mead & Co., 1899. 283 p. il. D. cl. .... 1.50 .98

Pen sketches of places and people by an observing traveler.

G70
W 24 my

557. [489.] **My winter on the Nile.** Charles Dudley Warner. Bost., Houghton, Mifflin & Co., 1889. 496 p. D. cl. 2.00 1.30

Experiences and observations of a charming writer. Graphic descriptions of life on the Nile.

AMERICA.

G80
F 75 tr

558. **Tropical America.** Isaac N. Ford. N. Y., C: Scribner's Sons, 1893. 409 p. il. O. cl. 2.00 1.30

Contents: Voyage to Rio; Rio's three glorious days; Petropolis without an emperor; New era in Brazil; Entrance of the plate; Across the Argentine; Heart of the Andes; Chili and its civil war; Rainless coast; Lima in carnival week; Guayaquil and the Isthmus; Cartagena and Caracas; Jamaica and the Bahamas; Last Spanish stronghold; Circuit of Mexican towns; Future of Mexico; Mosquito reservation; Up the San Juan; Glimpses of Central America; Our continent.

G81
D 74 ac

559. **Across Greenland's ice-fields:** the adventures of Nansen and Peary on the great ice-cap. M. Douglas. N. Y., Thos. Nelson & Sons, 1897. 217 p. il. D. cl. .... .80 .53

"The author has selected those heart-stirring narratives for her theme which relate the difficulties and perils attendant on the

	List price.	Price to schools.

exploration of the Inland Ice of Greenland. Miss Douglas conducts her readers over those trackless wastes of snow and ice, in the footsteps of Norden-skiold, of Nansen, and of Peary; and certainly those who begin the journey with her will, in continuing it to the end, derive no small amount of pleasure and instruction."—*Clements R. Markham.*

UNITED STATES.

GS3

C 44 ye

560. [451.] **Yellowstone National Park:** historical and descriptive. Hiram Martin Chittenden. Cin., O., Robert Clarke Co., 1895. 397 p. il. pors. maps. O. cl. 1.50   1.13

A description of one of the most interesting places in the world.

GS3

C 96 bo

561. [452.] **"Boots and Saddles:"** or life in Dakota with General Custer. Elizabeth B. Custer. N. Y., Harper & Bros., 1885. 312 p. por. map. D. cl.   1.50   .98

An excellent picture of Custer is given in both this and the following volume.

GS3

C 96 fo

562. **Following the guidon.** Elizabeth B. Custer. N. Y., Harper & Bros., 1899. 341 p. il. D. cl. ......   1.50   .98

The story of a summer's camp on Big Creek, Kansas, by United States cavalry, with General Custer at the head.

Contents: March into the Indian territory; General Custer's letters describing the march; White scouts; Battle of the Washita; Indian trails, councils, and captives; In camp on Big Creek; Indian prisoners; Corral of the captives; Pets of the camp; Slow mule-race; Tales of soldiers' devotion and drollery; Wild Bill as a magistrate; Home of the buffalo; First women to hunt buffaloes; Hunting records; Army house-keeping; Necessity the mother of invention; "Garryowen" leads the hunt; Army promotions; Flood on Big Creek; Rattlesnakes as neighbors; Dandy.

GS3

C 96 te

563. [453.] **Tenting on the plains;** or General Custer in Kansas and Texas. Elizabeth B. Custer. N. Y., Harper & Bros., 1895. 403 p. il. D. cl. .... 1.50   .98

Life in military posts and on the plains in Dakota is described in these two books. The boys will find this book especially interesting.

G83

D 29 we

564. [448.] **West from a car-window.** Richard Harding Davis. N. Y., Harper & Bros., 1892. 243 p. il. D. cl. .... 1.25 .82

List Price to
price. schools.

Entertaining descriptions of life in the western part of United States.

G83

D 51 th

565. [456.] **Through the gold fields of Alaska.** Henry De Windt. N. Y., Harper & Bros., 1898. 314 p. por. map. il. O. cl. 2.50 1.64

An interesting account of life in the gold fields.

G83

In 6 gr

566. [455.] **Great Salt Lake trail.** *Colonel* Henry Inman *and Colonel* William F. Cody. N. Y., Macmillan Co., 1898. 529 p. por. il. O. cl. .... 1.50 .48

Of the historic trails crossing the great plains none has a more stirring story than that known as the Salt Lake trail. Over this historical highway the Mormons made their toilsome way. Over this route also were made those world-renowned expeditions by Fremont, Stansbury, and others to the heart of the Rocky mountains. Over this same route the overland stage lumbered along, long before the building of a railroad was believed to be possible. This book deals with the era of the trapper, the scout, the savage, and the passage of emigrants to the gold fields of California, and with the adventures which marked the long and weary march. A book of intense interest.

G83

In 6 ol

567. [454.] **Old Santa Fé trail:** the story of a great highway. *Colonel* Henry Inman. N. Y., Macmillan Co., 1899. 493 p. por. il. O. cl. .... 1.50 .48

"When the famous highway was established across the great plains, the only method of travel was by the slow freight caravan drawn by patient oxen, or the lumbering stage-coach with its complement of four or six mules. There was ever to be feared an attack by the Cheyennes, Comanches, and Kiowas."—*W. F. Cody.*

The story is told by one who took part in the adventures related. A very interesting book.

G83

J 12 bi

568. **Bits of travel at home.** Helen Hunt Jackson. (H. H., *pseud.*) Bost., Little, Brown & Co., 1898. 413 p. T. cl. 1.25 82

This volume is fully as interesting as the author's "Bits of Travel." It is a series of sketches of trips in California, New England and Colorado.

GS3
L 97 so
569. [444.] **Some strange corners of our country:** the wonderland of the southwest. Charles F. Lummis. N. Y., Century Co., 1898. 270 p. D. cl. ...   List price. 1.50   Price to schools. .98

A most interesting book of travel, containing good descriptions of the Grand canon of the Colorado, the Great American Desert, the Pueblo cities of Moqui, and the Natural Bridge in Virginia. Also descriptions of the manners and customs of the Pueblos and the Navajo Indians.

GS3
L 97 tr
570. [446.] **Tramp across the continent.** Charles F. Lummis. N. Y., C: Scribner's Sons, 1898. 270 p. D. cl. .... 1.25   .82

A truthful record of some of the experiences and impressions of a tramp across the continent—"the diary of a man who got outside the fences of civilization, and was glad of it. It is a simple story of joy on legs." Some of the subjects touched upon in the book are: in and out among the Rockies; the land of the adobe; across the Rio Grande; territorial types; western Arizona; the great American desert.

GS3
R 13 di
571. [443.] **Dixie:** or southern scenes and sketches. Julian Ralph. N. Y., Harper & Bros., 1896. 412 p. il. O. cl. 2.50   1.64

Graphic descriptions of the people and life of the south. These papers show the resources and development of the south, and will be found most valuable in work in Geography.
Contents: New Orleans, 44–90; along Bayou Teche, 91–120; sunny Mississippi, 122–159; Florida, 160–205; industrial region of northern Alabama, Tennessee, and Georgia, 206–298; mountain life, 299–336; Washington, 337–387; St. Louis, 388–411.

GS3
R 13 ou
572. [447.] **Our great West:** a story of the present conditions and future possibilities of the new commonwealths and capitals of the United States. Julian Ralph. N. Y., Harper & Bros., 1893. 478 p. O. cl. 2.50   1.64

In a part "of each chapter I have tried to point out the future possibilities of these imperial reaches of plains and mountain country—and of the cities that distinguish them—between the Great Lakes and the Pacific coast." There is no better description of life in our western cities.

G83
___
R 2S po

                   List Price to
                   price. schools.

573. [450.] **Pony tracks.** Frederic Remington. N. Y., Harper & Bros., 1899. 269 p. il. O. Half cl. ... 1.75 1.15

 Sketches of pioneer life in the west. Will interest every boy.

G83
___
R 67 ra

*574. [449.] **Ranch life and the hunting-trail.** Theodore Roosevelt. N. Y., Century Co., 1897. 186 p. il. Q. cl. 2.50 1.64

 Graphic pen pictures of life and hunting in our western country. The illustrations by Remington add much to the book.

G83
___
W 15 la

575. [445.] **Land of the Pueblos.** Susan E. Wallace. N. Y., John B. Alden, 1888. 285 p. il. D. cl. ... .75 .50

 Very interesting. Younger pupils will enjoy it.

UNITED STATES.

(Separate Sections of Country.)

G831
___
B 21 ne

576. **New Eldorado:** a summer journey to Alaska. Maturin M. Ballou. Bost., Houghton, Mifflin & Co., 1899. 355 p. D. Ed. 11. cl. .... 1.50 .98

 An interesting description of a trip from St. Paul west through Yellowstone Park to Alaska.
 References: St. Paul, 2–3; Badlands, 10–11; Yellowstone Park, 14–56; Montana, 58–68; Washington, 69–81; Seals and sea islands, 151–72; Eskimo, 179–80, 219–21; Muir glacier, 281–83.

G831
___
F 45 ou

577. **Our western archipelago.** Henry M. Field. N. Y., C: Scribner's Sons, 1896. 250 p. il. O. Ed. 2. cl. 2.00 1.30

 An interesting story of travel in our own country.
 Contents: Longest railroad in the world; On the north shore of Lake Superior; In Rupert's land—the Hudson Bay company; Banff and the Rocky Mountain park; How we kept the Fourth of July; Riding on the cow-catcher; Glacier of the Selkirks; To Vancouver and Victoria; Alaska; Glaciers; Muir glacier; Nature and

man farther north; Sitka and the government; Schools and missions; Story of Metlakahatla; Puget sound—Seattle and Tacoma; State of Washington; City of Portland; Homeward bound—the strikes; Montana—vigilantes; Yellowstone park; Geysers; Lake and the river; Canon of the Yellowstone.

G831
H 83 ni
578. **Niagara book.** William Dean Howells, *and others.* N. Y., Doubleday, Page & Co., 1901. 353 p. il. maps. O. New rev. ed. cl. .... 1.50   .98

Portions of this book will be very interesting for Library reading.
Contents: What to see; Dramatic incidents; Historic Niagara; Geology of Niagara Falls; Flora and fauna of Niagara Falls; Utilization of Niagara's power; First authentic mention of Niagara falls; Niagara, first and last; As it rushes by; Famous visitors at Niagara Falls; Buffalo and the Pan American exposition.

G831
J 62 ne
579. **New England country.** Clifton Johnson. Bost., Lee & Shepard, 1896. 121 p. il. O. cl. .... 1.25   .82

A realistic story of life in New England. One of the most interesting books of description and travel on the list. One of the chief features of the book is its abundance of fine illustrations.
Contents: Old times on a New England farm; New England of today; New England as the traveler sees it; Camping among the New England hills.

G831
T 21 to
580. **Touring Alaska and the Yellowstone.** Charles M. Taylor, *jr.* Phil., George W. Jacobs & Co., c1901. 388 p. il. D. cl. 1.60 1.44

Mr. Taylor made an extended tour through these interesting regions, and from his well-filled note-books and ever-ready camera we have here a delightful and interesting publication, one which not only entertains but instructs as well.
Contents: From Montreal to the Rocky mountains; Among the giants; From the mountains to the sea; In Alaskan waters; Through the archipelago to Wrangel; Juneau and the famous Treadwell mine; Over the White Pass to Lake Bennett; Glacier Bay; Muir glacier and Killisnoo; Capital of Alaska; Yellowstone Park; Geysers and hot springs; In the Upper Geyser basin; Yellowstone lake and the Grand Canon.

LIST OF BOOKS FOR HIGH SCHOOL LIBRARIES. 155

	List price.	Price to schools.

GS31
———
T 42 do

581. **Down historic waterways:** six hundred miles of canoeing upon Illinois and Wisconsin rivers. Reuben Gold Thwaites. Chic., A. C. McClurg & Co., 1902. 300 p. il. D. Ed. 2. cl. 1.20 1.08

    The description of the author's canoe voyages upon Illinois and Wisconsin waters are told in a manner which will hold the interest of every boy and girl who reads them. He is a true lover of nature and his writing inspires the same feeling in his readers.

GS31
———
T 63 fo

582. **Footing it in Franconia.** Bradford Torrey. Bost., Houghton, Mifflin & Co., 1901. 251 p. D. cl. ... 1.10 .99

    Mr. Torrey describes the vacation doings of some enthusiastic nature-lovers in the beautiful valley-and-mountain Franconia country. It has to do with nature as these happy people saw and enjoyed it. There is much in the book about birds and plants, edible berries, fine prospects, and the like. One of its chief attractions is its sunny, out-of-doors quality,—its atmosphere. It is a record of happy days, and its humor and enthusiasm are delightful.

    Contents: Autumn; Spring; Day in June; Berry-time felicities; Red leaf days; American skylarks; Quiet morning; In the Landaff valley; Visit to Mount Agassiz.

GS31
———
W 24 on

583. **On horseback:** a tour in Virginia, North Carolina and Tennessee, with notes of travel in Mexico and California. Charles Dudley Warner. Bost., Houghton, Mifflin & Co., 1899. 331 p. D. cl. ... 1.25 .82

    This book gives an excellent picture of the Southern country and incidentally of Southern life.

GS31
———
W 24 st

584. **Studies in the south and west:** with comments on Canada. Charles Dudley Warner. N. Y., Harper & Bros., 1899. 484 p. D. bds. 1.75 1.15

    Contents: Impressions of the south in 1885; Society in the new south; New Orleans; Voudoo dance; Acadian land; South revisited in 1887; Far and fair country; Economic and social topics Minnesota and Wisconsin; Chicago; Three capitals—Springfield, Indianapolis, Columbus; Cincinnati and Louisville; Memphis and Little Rock; St. Louis and Kansas City; Kentucky; Comments on Canada.

CALIFORNIA.

GS32
―――
M 89 mo
　　　　　　　　　　　　　　　　　　　　　　　List　Price to
　　　　　　　　　　　　　　　　　　　　　　price. schools.
585. **Mountains of California.** John Muir. N. Y., Century
　　　Co., 1901. 381 p. il. D. cl. .... 1.50　.98

　　This book contains many good descriptions of California scenery. Portions of it will be valuable for use in the Geology class.

　　Contents: Sierra Nevada; Glaciers; Snow; Near view of the High Sierra; Passes; Glacier lakes; Glacier meadows; Forests; Douglas squirrel; Wind-storm in the forests; River floods; Sierra thunder storms; Water-ouzel; Wild sheep; In the Sierra foothills; Bee-pastures.

MEXICO.

G95
―――
L 97 aw
586. [460.] **Awakening of a Nation:** Mexico of today.
　　　Charles F. Lummis. N. Y., Harper & Bros., 1902.
　　　179 p. il. map. O. cl. .... 2.50　1.64

　　An excellent picture of life in Mexico at the present time.

　　Contents: Awakening of a nation; Astir in the north; Among the old bonanzas; Surface gold; Heart of the nation; New wine in old bottles; Cheap money; Unfamiliar page; Clubs not trumps; Man; Ladder; Some outdoor activities; Glimpses of the west coast; Borrowed from the enemy; Spanish-American face.

G95
―――
Sm 5 wh
587. [461.] **White umbrella in Mexico.** Francis Hopkinson Smith. Bost., Houghton, Mifflin & Co., 1899.
　　　227 p. il. D. bds. .... 1.50　.98

　　A pretty picture of life in Mexico. The author calls it a land of white sunshine redolent with flowers; a land of gay costumes, crumbling churches, and old convents; a land of kindly greetings, of extreme courtesy, of open, broad hospitality.

　　Contents: Introduction; Morning in Guanajuato; After dark in Silao; Opals of Queretaro; Some peons at Aguas Calientes; Old chair in the sacristy at Zacatecas; City's streets; On the Paseo; Palm Sunday in Puebla de los Angeles; Day in Toluca; To Morelia with moon; Patzcuaro and the lake; Tzintzuntzan and the Titian.

CUBA AND PUERTO RICO.

G96
―――
B 21 du
588. **Due south:** or Cuba past and present. Maturin M.
　　　Ballou. Bost., Houghton, Mifflin & Co., 1898. 316
　　　p. D. Ed. 10. cl. . ... 1.50　.98

　　One of the most interesting books out on life in Cuba. It was written before the late war in Cuba, so gives nothing on that subject.

G96

D 19 to

589. **To Cuba and back:** a vacation voyage. Richard Henry Dana. Bost., Houghton, Mifflin & Co., c1887. 288 p. D. cl. .... 1.25 .82

List price. Price to schools.

This volume gives an excellent picture of life and conditions in Cuba.

G96

D 61 pu

#590. **Puerto Rico:** its conditions and possibilities. William Dinwiddie. N. Y., Harper & Bros., 1899. 294 p. il. O. cl. 2.50 1.64

A presentation of the industrial, commercial, political, and social conditions existing in Puerto Rico today, with a mass of facts, figures, and comparisons of past institutions with present. Intended primarily to give all who are personally interested in the future development of the island a comprehensive grasp of the administrative problems which confront us, and of the outlook for Americans in industrial enterprises. Mr. Dinwiddie sets forth in a clear and serviceable way the present state of coffee, tobacco, sugar, and fruit culture, with valuable statements as to the expense and best methods of conducting such plantations. He also gives a full discussion of the opportunities offered to American capitalists in railroads, tram-ways, ice-plants, cattle-raising, dairy-farming, and manufacturing.

Portions of this book will be excellent for Library reading.

G96

H 55 cu

591. [458.] **Cuba and Puerto Rico,** with the other islands of the West Indies. Robert T. Hill. N. Y., Century Co., 1899. 447 p. map. il. O. cl. 3.00 1.96

It is a complete account of these islands from the economic standpoint. Their topography, climate, flora, products, industries, cities, people, and political conditions. Particularly fine on commerce, resources, and transportation.

G96

Ob 2 pu

592. [457.] **Puerto Rico and its resources.** Frederick A. Ober. N. Y., D. Appleton & Co., 1899. 282 p. maps. il. D. cl. .... 1.50 .98

Brief and interesting account of Puerto Rico.

696
P 39 to
#593. **To-morrow in Cuba.** Charles M. Pepper. N. Y., Harper & Bros., 1899. 362 p. O. cl. 2.00 1.30

A work that will be invaluable to every one of that large number of Americans who are eager for sound information on the present conditions and future prospects of Cuba. This volume should be purchased by the large libraries only.

Contents: Prologue to autonomy; Western invasion; Campos and Weyler; Wooing the lost colony; Epilogue to autonomy; Transition to local home rule; Provinces as a federal framework; Race or color; Spanish colony; Immigration and colonization; Sugar and tobacco—other products; Trade and taxation—railways and internal development; Religion as a withered branch; Cuban priests the living branch; Manners and morals; American military control; Political aptitudes; Today.

SOUTH AMERICA.

G98
An 2 br
594. [463.] **Brazil:** its conditions and prospects. C. C. Andrews. N. Y., D. Appleton & Co., 1893. 352 p. D. cl. .... 1.50 .98

Material for geography and economics.

G98
B 21 eq
595. **Equatorial America:** an interesting description of a visit to St. Thomas, Martinique, Barbadoes, and the principal capitals of South America, containing much information that will be of value to supplement the text in geography. Maturin M. Ballou. Bost., Houghton. Mifflin & Co., 1900. 371 p. D. cl. .... 1.50 .98

G98
C 65 so
#596. **South America:** social, industrial, and political. Frank G. Carpenter. Akron, Ohio. Saalfield Pub. Co., 1901. 625 p. il. Q. cl. 3.00 2.40

"The present volume is the outcome of a journalistic expedition to South America in search of information for the American business man and the general reader. . . . The work is more a study of the commercial and social life of the cities, and a description of how the people live and work in the country, than a diary of travel and adventure. It describes the chief industries, notes the characteristic features of the inhabitants, discusses the resources and possibilities of the various countries, and incidentally points out the chances for the investment of American capital and the increase of American trade.

These matters, however, are discussed from the standpoint of human interest and for the average reader, the aim being to give a plain, simple narrative, conveying the information about South America most desired at the present time."

Portions of the book will be very interesting for Library reading.

G98

D 25 jo

597. [462.] **Journal of researches** into the natural history and geology of the countries visited during the voyage of H. M. S. Beagle round the world, under the command of Captain Fitz Roy, R. N. Charles Darwin. N. Y., T. Nelson & Sons, 1896. 615 p. il. D. cl. 2.00 1.00

Cape Verd Islands, Rio de Janerio, Buenos Ayres, Patagonia, Tierre del Fuego, Straits of Magellan, Chili, Peru, Tahiti, New Zealand, Australia and Mauritius, as seen by a scientist. A pupil interested in natural science will enjoy this book.

G98

D 29 th

598. [464.] **Three Gringos in Venezuela and Central America.** Richard Harding Davis. N. Y., Harper & Bros., 1896. 282 p. il. D. cl.............. 1.50 .98

Bright and entertaining descriptions of people and places.

SOCIAL SCIENCES.

(Includes Economics, Labor, Commerce, Banking, Taxation, and Public Finance.)

POLITICAL ECONOMY.

The study of political economy will be chiefly useful to pupils in a high school as an introduction to the serious and thoughtful consideration of the practical affairs of life. Its purpose is not so much to present a body of knowledge as to form a habit of and give a basis for estimating economic values and results. To many persons the statement that values originate in labor, and that wealth represents services performed, comes at first as a great novelty. The full realization of the truth and of its bearing on various ways of money getting current in society, comes not from memorizing the text, but from an abundance of illustrations brought out in the class-room, with the usual accompanying comment and criticism. Possibly no other study in the course so urgently demands the conversational method of conducting a recitation, and can so ill endure the verbal memorizing of text-books.

Pupils who have studied the conditions affecting the production of wealth, including the division of labor, the consequent frequent separation of the capitalist from the laborer and the growth of combinations on each side, should be better able to read intelligently the current discussions of the "labor problem" in leading journals and magazines. If they are led to read such discussions of important questions and to subject the articles to the test of measurement by the principles stated and accepted previously, there may be less satisfaction with dogmatic statements, but there should result a wider interest in human affairs and current news, with a broader toleration of divergent views. Established facts and accepted theories may be made intelligible by copious illustrations. Teachers may make clear what facts and principles are involved in the settlement of any controverted subject, but should avoid all fruitless discussion. Pupils must learn what taxes are, what kinds are known, what arguments are advanced to support them, how their imposition or removal may affect industries; but all debates having personal or political tendencies are unfortunate. There is no place in a public school for partisanship or propagandism.

The books given in this list will be of assistance to the teacher in preparing his class work and some of them may be used by the pupils under the careful guidance of the teacher for reference.

II
———
At 5 di
                List Price to
                price. schools.

599. [627.] Distribution of products; or the mechanism and the metaphysics of exchange. Edward Atkinson. N. Y., G. P. Putnam's Sons, 1892. 365 p. D. cl. .... 1.50   .96

 A comprehensive treatise on the subjects of rate of wages, banks and banking, the railway, the farmer and the public.

II
———
B 67 ec
600. [626.] **Economics for the people.** R. Rogers Bowker. N. Y., Harper & Bros., 1893. S. cl.............. .75   .48

 A popular exposition of the subject for the general reader.

II
———
B 87 es
601. **Essays on the monetary history of the United States.** Charles J. Bullock. N. Y., Macmillan Co., 1900. 292 p. D. cl. 1.25   1.12

 Contents: Three centuries of cheap money in the United States; Paper currency of North Carolina; Paper currency of New Hampshire; Bibliography.

II
———
D 49 ec
602. [625.] **Economics.** Edward Thomas Devine. N. Y., Macmillan Co., 1898. 404 p. S. cl. ....1.00   .85

 A short, concise, and interesting exposition of the general subject of economics and terms in general use. For the beginner.

11

H

El 9 mo

		List price.	Price to schools.
603. Monopolies and trusts. Richard T. Ely. N. Y., Macmillan Co., 1902. 284 p. (The Citizen's Library series.) D. cl.		1.25	1.12

For use of teacher of political economy and for debaters.

A small part of a large work, "The Distribution of Wealth," which Professor Ely has been at work upon during the past seven years.

Contents: The idea of monopoly; Classification and causes of monopolies; Law of monopoly price; Limits of monopoly and the permanency of competition; Concentration of production and trusts; Evils and remedies.

H

El 9 ou

604. **Outlines of economics.** Richard T. Ely. N. Y., Macmillan Co., 1901. 432 p. (The Citizen's Library series.) D. cl. 1.25   1.12

An excellent book for reference, if used with guidance of teacher.

H

G 29 p

605. **Progress and poverty:** an inquiry into the cause of industrial depressions and of increase of want with increase of wealth, the remedy. Henry George. N. Y., Doubleday, Page & Co., 1902. 568 p. D. New ed. cl. .... 1.00   .65

This book gives in substance Henry George's theory of the land question. Portions of it are more fascinating than a romance. No previous knowledge of economic literature is necessary to the understanding of the arguments he makes or the passing of judgment upon its conclusions.

Contents: Introductory; Wages and capital; Population and subsistence; Laws of distribution; Effect of material progress upon the distribution of wealth; Problem solved; Remedy; Justice of the remedy; Application of the remedy; Effects of the remedy; Law of human progress; Conclusion.

H

G 29 pr

606. **Protection or free trade:** an examination of the tariff question with especial regard to the interests of labor. Henry George. N. Y., Doubleday & McClure, 1897. 359 p. D. cl .... 1.00   .65

This book contains excellent material for debaters.

"In this book I have endeavored to determine whether protection or free trade better accords with the interests of labor, and to bring to a common conclusion on this subject those who really desire to raise wages.

I have not only gone over the ground generally traversed, and examined the arguments commonly used, but, carrying the inquiry further than the controversialists on either side have yet ventured to go, I have sought to discover why protection retains such popular strength in spite of all exposures of its fallacies; to trace the connection between the tariff question and those still more important social questions, now rapidly becoming the "burning questions" of our times; and to show to what radical measures the principle of free trade logically leads."—*Preface.*

Contents: Introductory: Clearing ground; Of method; Protection as a universal need; Protective unit; Trade; Production and producers; Tariffs for revenue; Tariffs for protection; Encouragement of industry; Home market and home trade; Exports and imports; Confusions arising from the use of money; Do high wages necessitate protection? Of advantages and disadvantages as reasons for protection; Development of manufactures; Protection and producers; Effect of protection on American industry; Protection and wages; Abolition of protection; Inadequacy of the free-trade argument; Real weakness of free trade; Real strength of protection; Paradox; Robber that takes all that is left; True free trade; Lion in the way; Free trade and socialism; Practical politics; Conclusion.

H

G 42 pr

607. **Profit sharing between employer and employee:** a study in the evolution of the wages system. Nicholas Paine Gilman. Bost., Houghton, Mifflin & Co., 1900. 460 p. D. cl.................. 1.75 1.15

A standard work for the use of the teacher of political economy. "A great contribution to economic literature. * * The clear recital of the facts relating to various experiments in different countries, together with the argument, stamps the work as the very best that has appeared in the English language, while it is far more complete in its general construction than any that has appeared in any language."

H

G 45 to

608. [629.] **Tools and the man.** Washington Gladden. Bost., Houghton, Mifflin & Co., 1893. 308 p. D. cl. .... 1.25 .82

Property and industry under the Christian law.

H

G 95 ou

609. **Outlines of political science.** George Gunton, *and* Hayes Robbins. N. Y., D. Appleton & Co., 1901. 228 p. D. cl. .... .75 .67

"The present volume has been written with the special view of making clear and obvious, to young citizens especially, the funda-

164 LIST OF BOOKS FOR HIGH SCHOOL LIBRARIES.

| | List price. | Price to schools. |

mental principles of government and the lines of practical action which government may and ought to undertake. While careful to avoid any special pleading or bias, it does not hesitate to suggest such broad lines of helpful constructive policy as seem most thoroughly justified by experience and reason."

It is especially adapted for study clubs, literary and debating societies and high schools.

H

J 42 tr

610. **Trust problem.** Jeremiah Whipple Jenks. N. Y., McClure, Phillips & Co., 1901. 341 p. maps. S. cl. .... 1.00 .90

This book gives briefly a good statement of present industrial conditions as related to industrial combinations in their various forms. It discusses the probable future development of these combinations, their effect upon competition and upon the permanent supply of their products at reasonable prices. Remedies for evils resulting from combination are suggested.

The book should be read by all interested in the problem of modern industrial development and organization.

H

L 36 el

611. [623.] **Elements of political economy.** J. Laurence Laughlin. N. Y., American Book Company, 1898. 363 p. il. D. cl............ 1.20 1.02

The elementary principles of political economy are presented in plain and simple form. Fundamental principles are emphasized.

H

L 77 la

612. **Labor copartnership.** Henry Demarest Lloyd. N. Y., Harper & Bros., 1899. 351 p. D. cl. .... 1.00 .65

Notes of a visit to co-operative workshops, factories and farms in Great Britain and Ireland, in which employer, employe, and consumer share in ownership, management and results.

H

L 77 we

613. **Wealth against commonwealth.** Henry Demarest Lloyd. N. Y., Harper & Bros., 1902. 563 p. O. cl. 1.00 .65

One of the strongest books in economics that has appeared since Henry George's "Progress and Poverty;" it is a comprehensive and striking statement of the concentration of capital and power in trusts, monopolies, and other combinations and is as absorbing and exciting in its intensity of interest as a romance of real life. Edward Everett Hale called it the "Uncle Tom's Cabin" of the present crisis.

		List price.	Price to schools.

H
———
M 59 pr

#614. **Principles of political economy**: with some of their applications to social philosophy. John Stuart Mill. N. Y., Longmans, Green & Co., 1898. 591 p. People's *ed*. D. cl. .... 1.25 .82

A standard reference book in economics for the use of teachers.

H
———
P 27 po

615. **Political economy**: for American youth, written from an American standpoint. Jacob Harris Patton. N. Y., A. Lovell & Co., c1892. 297 p. D. cl... 1.00 .90

Treats the facts and principles of the subject in a simple, yet satisfactory, manner. The discussions are within easy grasp of high school students.

H
———
St 5 ha

616. **Handbook to the labor law of the United States.** F. Jessup Stimson. ("J. S. of Dale", *pseud*.) N. Y., C: Scribner's Sons, 1896. 385 p. D. cl 1.50 1.35

Sets forth as it exists in the United States today, that law of labor disputes and the regulation of industrial affairs and protection of employees which has had its greatest development in the last few years. While the work is sufficiently full and accurate to serve as a legal text-book, the author's chief object has been to make it a clear and trustworthy guide for laboring men and their several organizations throughout the United States.

Contents: Labor contract; Statutes regulating the employment contracts; Political protection and legal privileges of laborers; Profit-sharing, co-operation, and laborers' stock; State regulation of factories, mines, etc.; Other legal rights and liabilities of master; Trades union; Strikes and boycotts; Equity process and injunctions—the anti-trust law and the interstate commerce law; Remedies by arbitration.

H
———
W 15 fi

617. [624.] **First lessons in political economy.** Francis A. Walker. N. Y., Henry Holt & Co., 1893. 323 p. (American Science series.) D. cl. .... 1.00 .90

A simple, clear and direct presentation of the subject not surpassed by any other like contribution to economic literature.

"This book has been prepared for use in High Schools and Academies. . . . In preparing a text-book for students in the period of life indicated, I have not thought it necessary to make the work childish. It is no 'Primer of Political Economy' which is here offered; but a substantial course of study in this vitally important subject."—*Preface*.

	List price.	Price to schools.

II
———
W 15 po

#618. **Political economy.** Francis A. Walker. N. Y., Henry Holt & Co., 1888. 537 p. (American science series—advanced course.) Ed. 3, rev. enl. O. cl. 2.00 1.80

    The best introduction to the most modern point of view as to economical questions. This is an excellent reference book for the use of the teacher of Political economy but should be purchased only by the larger libraries.
    Contents: Character and logical method of political economy; Production; Exchange; Distribution; Consumption; Some applications of economic principles.

H
———
W 58 mo

619. **Money and banking:** illustrated by American history. Horace White. Bost., Ginn & Co., 1896. 488 p. il. D. cl. 1.50 1.28

    Begins with the first settlement at Jamestown, and traces the course of the tobacco currency of Virginia and Maryland, the commodity currencies of New England, New York, and South Carolina, the introduction of Spanish coins and the different valuations of the same in the different colonies, and the final establishment of the money of account of the United States. The subjects of coinage, of legal tender, and of the gold standard are treated in both their local and their general aspects, and a chapter is given to the Brussels Monetary Conference. The subject of representative money is divided into two parts, viz.: fiat money and banknotes, Colonial bills of credit, continental money, greenbacks, treasury notes, and silver dollars are separately treated. The course of banking development forms the concluding part.

II
———
W 93 in

620. [628.] **Industrial evolution of United States.** Carroll D. Wright. N. Y., C: Scribner's Sons, 1895. 362 p. map. il. D. cl. 1.25 1.12

    An account of the development of American industries from colonial times to 1895. The illustrations add much to the value of the book. An interesting and readable book.

	List price.	Price to schools.

I
B 64 in
#623. **In darkest England**: and the way out. General William Booth. N. Y., Funk & Wagnalls Co., 1890. 285 + 31 pp. O. cl .... 1.00 .65

A suggested social scheme for the betterment of the condition of England's "submerged tenth". It gives a vivid picture of the sufferings and hardships of the poorer classes.

I
C 11 ne
624. **Negro question.** George W. Cable. N. Y., C: Scribner's Sons, 1898. 173 p. D. cl................. .75 .49

This book should be in every High school library. The question discussed is whether a certain seven millions of the people, one-ninth of the whole, dwelling in and natives to the Southern States of the Union, and by law an undifferentiated part of the Nation, have or have not the same full measure of the American citizen's rights that they would have were they entirely of European instead of wholly or partly African descent."

Contents: 1. Negro question—Have colored Americans in the South the same rights as Americans of foreign birth?

2. Color discrimination, Inconsistencies.

3. Answer to negro question—Social basis of slavery still exists; Enfranchisement a cause of apprehension; Freedmen loyal to government; Distinction between civil and social equality; Responsibility of southern white men; Material development in the South.

4. National aid to southern schools; What shall the negro do? Simpler southern question; What makes the color line? Southern struggle for pure government—First necessity; Does the negro want pure government? Supposing the negro unsuppressed; Policy of pure government first; Industrial new south; Reign of the one-party idea; Inventions of despair; More excellent way.

I
F 67 tr
625. [619.] **Tramping with tramps.** Josiah Flynt. N. Y., Century Co., 1899. 398 p. il. D. cl............ 1.50 .98

Studies and sketches of a vagabond life. Pictures of the tramp world with references to causes and occasional suggestions of remedies.

I
G 29 so
626. **Social problems.** Henry George. N. Y., Doubleday, McClure & Co., 1898. 342 p. D. cl............ 1.00 .65

This is written in the same interesting style as "Progress and poverty" and reads like a novel. This is an excellent book for Library reading.

Contents: Increasing importance of social questions; Political dangers; Coming increase of social pressure; Two opposing tenden-

SOCIOLOGY.

In reading these books the aim should be to get actual conditions of life, standards, and social forces that are at work. Out of this reading there should grow a deepening consciousness of human relationship and obligation. Many illustrations may be drawn from history, fiction, and the actual life around the pupil. Some of the books have been selected because they portray conditions of life and the social forces which are at work. The reading of these books will enable the pupil to see more clearly the conditions existing about him.

	List price.	Price to schools.

I
———
Ad 2 de

621. **Democracy and social ethics.** Jane Addams. N. Y., Macmillan Co., 1902. 281 p. (Citizen's Library series.) D. cl. 1.25 1.12

    An interesting book for general reading made up of lectures originally delivered in college and university extension centres. The titles are: Charitable effort; Filial relations; Household adjustment; Industrial amelioration; Educational method; Political reform.

I
———
Am 3 a

#622. **America's race problem:** Addresses at the annual meeting of the American Academy of Political and Social Science, Philadelphia, April twelfth and thirteenth, 1901. McClure, Phillips & Co., 1901. 187 p. O. cl............................... 1.50 1.35

    Contents: Races of the Pacific—Natives of Hawaii, a study of Polynesian charm, T. M. Coan; Races of the Philippines, tagals, *Rev.* C. C. Pierce; Semi-civilized tribes of the Philippine islands, *Rev.* O. C. Miller; Causes of race superiority, E. A. Ross; Race problem at the South—Introductory remarks by *Col.* H. A. Herbert; Relation of the whites to the negroes, G. T. Winston; Relation of the negroes to the whites in the South, *Prof.* W. E. Burghardt Du Bois; Races of the West Indies, Our Relation to the people of Cuba and Porto Rico, *Hon.* O. H. Platt; Spanish population of Cuba and Porto Rico, C. M. Pepper; Report of the Academy Committee on Meetings.

LIST OF BOOKS FOR HIGH SCHOOL LIBRARIES. 169

                                                       List Price to
                                                       price. schools.

cies; March of concentration; Wrong in existing social conditions; Is it the best of all possible worlds? That we all might be rich; First principles; Rights of man; Dumping garbage; Over-production; Unemployed labor; Effects of machinery; Slavery and slavery; Public debts and indirect taxation; Functions of government; What we must do; Great reform; American farmer; City and country; Conclusion.

I

G 36 el

627. **Elements of sociology:** a text-book for colleges and schools. Franklin Henry Giddings. N. Y., Macmillan Co., 1901. 353 p. D. cl. .... 1.10 .99

Sociology as set forth in this volume is nothing more or less than an elementary description of society in clear and simple terms.

Contents: Population and society; Where aggregations of people are formed; How aggregations of people are formed; Composition and the unity of a social population; Practical activities of society; Socialization; Cooperation; Social pleasure; Social nature; Classes of socii; Preeminent social class; Social mind: modes of like-mindedness; Sympathetic like-mindedness and impulsive social action; Formal like-mindedness: tradition and conformity; Rational like-mindedness: public opinion and social values; Social organization; Component societies; Constituent societies; Character and efficiency of organization; Early history of society; Tribal society; Civilization; Progress; Democracy; Theory of society.

I

H 83 pr

628. **Prisoners of Russia:** a personal study of convict life in Sakhalin and Siberia. Benjamin Howard. N. Y., D. Appleton & Co., 1902. 389 p. il.D. cl.. 1.40 1.26

An intensely interesting account of prison life in Siberia. Excellent for Library reading.

Dr. Benjamin Howard was born in Chesham, Bucks, England, March 21, 1836. He became interested in the prison systems of the world in 1859; and began his investigations of prison life in 1888. The present work is founded on a personal study of prison life and his experience while confined in a Russian prison, and on observations made during a visit to the convict Island Sakhalin.

I

J 62 wo

629. **Woman and the republic:** a survey of the woman-suffrage movement in the United States and a discussion of the claims and arguments of its foremost advocates. Helen Kendrick Johnson. N. Y., D. Appleton & Co., 1897. 327 p. D. cl...... 1.50 .98

Valuable for use of debaters.

"Largely a reply to Dr. Putnam-Jacbobi's "Common sense applied to woman's suffrage" and "The history of woman's suffrage",

	List price.	Price to schools.

by Elizabeth Cady Stanton and others. Mrs. Johnson gives the opposite side of the question, with many new and old arguments, supported by carefully gathered facts and figures. Her conclusions are that woman's suffrage is not the offspring of democracy, but has received its warmest support under monarchical or even despotic governments; that the advance women have made in the professions and the changes for the better brought about in their condition under the laws are to be credited to the broadening of thought, not to the suffrage agitation; that woman, through her sex, is unfitted for political life; that the suffrage would tend to disintegrate the home; that women would lack the physical power to defend a vote, or to carry out the laws she might enact."

I
———
R 44 ch
630. [616.] **Children of the poor.** Jacob A. Riis. N. Y., C: Scribner's Sons, 1892. 300 p. il. D. bds... 1.25 1.12

I
———
R 44 ho
631. [615.] **How the other half lives:** studies among the tenements of New York. Jacob A. Riis. N. Y., C: Scribner's Sons, 1899. 304 p. il. D. bds.... 1.25 1.12

The two books above are as interesting as a romance and will open up to the students a side of life with which few of them are familiar. Excellent for Library reading.

I
———
R 44 ma
632. **Making of an American.** Jacob A. Riis. N. Y., The Macmillan Co., 1901. 443 p. il. O. cl.......... 2.00 1.30

The papers which form this autobiography were originally published in The Outlook, two appeared in The Century, and one in The Churchman. Mr. Riis was born in Denmark in 1849 and came to this country about thirty years ago. He struggled with poverty, and has spent his life making an intelligent study of the condition of the poor and the causes which produce poverty. Under Mayor Strong's administration he did much faithful work in New York City. The book is lavishly illustrated.
Excellent for Library reading.

I
———
R 44 te
633. [617.] **Ten years' war:** an account of the battle with the slums in New York. Jacob A. Riis. Bost., Houghton, Mifflin & Co., 1900. 267 p. por. D. cl. 1.50 .98

A true picture of life in the slums.

LIST OF BOOKS FOR HIGH SCHOOL LIBRARIES. 171

                                                                             List Price to
I

Sm 1 in   price. schools.

634. [613.] **Introduction to the study of society.** Albion W. Small, *and* George E. Vincent. N. Y., American Book Company, 1894. 384 p. D. cl........ 1.80 1.53

    A general treatise on sociology and a guide to its study. The subjects for investigation will be found especially helpful.

    Contents: Origin and scope of sociology; the natural history of a society; social anatomy; social physiology and pathology; social psychology.

I

T 41 tu

635. **Tuskegee:** its story and its work, with an introduction by Booker T. Washington. Max Bennett Thrasher. Bost., Small, Maynard & Co., 1901. 215 p. il. D. cl............................ 1.00 .65

    "In this volume Mr. Max Bennett Thrasher, a Boston newspaper and magazine writer who has spent much time during the last five years travelling in the South, has told the story of the school in a very interesting way. He has shown how Mr. Washington's early life was a preparation for his work. He has given a history of the Institute from its foundation, explained the practical methods by which it gives industrial training, and then he has gone on to show some of the results which the institution has accomplished. The human element is carried through the whole so thoroughly that one reads the book for entertainment as well as for instruction."

I

W 24 am

#636. **American charities:** a study in philanthropy and economics. Amos G. Warner. N. Y., Thos. Y. Crowell & Co., c1894. 430 p. maps. (Library of Economics and Politics series.) D. cl......... 1.75 1.15

    "The writer is Professor of Economics and Social Science in the Leland Stanford Jr. University. He recognizes heredity, environment, social conditions, intoxicants, selfishness, sickness, all inextricably interwoven as some of the innumerable causes of pauperism. He traces the origin of philanthropy among heathen nations. He analyzes proposed methods of relief, and shows by carefully prepared tables what influences tend toward deepening degradation and what tend toward elevating and improving the poor. His tone is optimistic and wholesome. The practical suggestions would save millions of dollars. A full bibliography, showing how wide is the author's reading, covers eleven pages. His facts are made serviceable by a remarkably well-made index."

    This volume is excellent for reference but should be purchased by the larger libraries only.

I
―――
W 27 up
637. **Up from slavery:** an autobiography. Booker T. Washington. N. Y., Doubleday, Page & Co., 1901. 330 p. por. D. cl. 1.50 1.35

This volume is the outgrowth of a series of articles dealing with the incidents in Mr. Washington's life, which were published consecutively in the Outlook. It tells of his life from the days when he was a little slave, until the present when he fills the principal's chair at Tuskegee, an educational institution founded by himself, for the betterment of his own people.

I
―――
W 85 po
638. [618.] **Poor in great cities;** their problems and what is doing to solve them. Robert A. Woods, and others. N. Y., C: Scribner's Sons, 1895. 400 p. il. O. cl. 3.00 1.96

Most interesting studies.

I
―――
W 93 ou
639. [614.] **Outline of practical sociology.** Carroll D. Wright. N. Y., Longmans, Green & Co., 1899. 431 p. D. (American citizen series.) cl........ 2.00 1.30

An interesting hand-book on the subject of sociology for reference. The bibliographies are good.

Contents: Basis of practical sociology: units of organization, social and political; questions of population, immigration, urban and rural population, special problems of city life; questions of the family; the labor system; social well being; defence of society; remedies.

I
―――
W 97 da
640. **Day with a tramp and other days.** Walter A. Wyckoff. N. Y., C: Scribner's Sons, 1901. 191 p. D. cl. .... 1.00 .90

The five narratives comprised under this title, like those published in the series of "The workers", east and west, are drawn from notes taken by Mr. Wyckoff during an expedition made by him ten years ago. Their titles are: A day with a tramp; With Iowa farmers; Section hand on the Union Pacific Railway; "Burro-puncher"; Incidents of the slums.

I
―――
W 97 w
641. [630.] **Workers:** an experiment in reality: the East. Walter A. Wyckoff. N. Y., C: Scribner's Sons, 1899. 270 p. il. D. cl. .... 1.25 .82

LIST OF BOOKS FOR HIGH SCHOOL LIBRARIES. 173

	List price.	Price to schools.

I
———
W 97 wo
642. [631.] **Workers:** an experiment in reality in the West. Walter A. Wyckoff. N. Y., C: Scribner's Sons, 1899. 378 p. il. D. cl. .... 1.50   .98

A study of labor from the personal experiences of the author.

EDUCATION.

Books for the teacher and the classes in Pedagogy.

When possible, teacher and pupils must read these together. The value of reading will be greatly enhanced by observations on teaching in lower grades and in the high school. Several of the books listed will be helpful to the grade teachers. A careful study of these books should be made in the teachers' meetings.

PSYCHOLOGY.

The study of psychology in the high schools must necessarily be elementary and will be successful in so far only as it is simple and direct. No effort should be made to teach a system of philosophy or to engage in metaphysical disputation. The end will be reached if the pupil is taught what the mind can do and how it does it. A simple scheme of the mental faculties should be presented and the pupil should learn the office of each and the order in which it is developed. Definitions of mental powers and processes should be given, so far as possible, in simple, unequivocal English. When it is found necessary to use a foreign term, its meaning and the necessity for its use should be clearly shown, and the pupil should be required to use it in his recitations until the term acquires the force and distinctness of a native idiom. The teacher should remember that mental methods can be defined and illustrated only by appeals to individual experience, and that facts and theories are worthless to the student until he finds them there. Fundamental processes, such as perception and consciousness, should be clearly realized by each pupil, but no effort should be made to explain their source.

The influence of the emotions and the will in determining character and conduct may be explained and illustrated. The mind is the instrument through whose activity all accretions of knowledge come. The study of its powers, modes of action and limitations is noble in itself and ought to be rich in results. The examination of the sequence in the unfolding of its powers furnishes the guide lines for student and teacher. The habit of sober and accurate thought which this study necessitates is the prerequisite of wise action. To impart the power of fixing the attention, of holding the mind steadily to the subject in hand is preeminently the province of psychological study, and is the highest outcome of intellectual training.

THEORY AND ART OF TEACHING.

Sec. 496a of the Wisconsin Statutes authorizes the state superintendent "to prepare a course or courses of study suitable to be pursued in the free high school," and specifically states that: "Each free high school shall offer at least a twelve weeks' course of instruction each year in the theory and art of teaching; in the organization, management, and course of study of ungraded schools; and in the duties of citizens in the organization and administration of local systems. Such course of instruction shall be open to all students in this school." Provision must be made for this study in each course excepting courses in manual training. It should be understood by teachers and members of school boards that this is not a study which is of value to those pupils only who expect to teach in the schools of the state. The pupils in the public schools will soon be in positions where they will be responsible for the development and maintenance of those schools. The work in Theory and Art of Teaching may be so broadened as to include a consideration of the proper organization of the public schools, the necessity for an intelligent interest in their welfare, and in what is necessary to secure that welfare.

This subject if properly taught, may afford as valuable a training for citizenship as any in the course; it is also of high value as a disciplinary study.

The best text book for use in the study of pedagogy is the Manual of the Course of Study for Common Schools issued by the state superintendent. It should be made the basis of the work in this subject. As an aid to the study of the Manual a good reference library should be provided, containing texts on school management, pedagogy, courses of study, etc.

Ik
———
Ad 1 he

                        List Price to
                        price. schools.

643. [653.] **Herbartian psychology applied to education.** John Adams. Bost., D. C. Heath &. Co., 1898. 284 p. D. (Heath's pedagogical lib.) cl....... 1.00   .90

    A series of essays applying the psychology of Herbart to education.

Ik
———
Ad 5 mo

644. [673.] **Moral instruction of children.** Felix Adler. N. Y., D. Appleton & Co., 1898. 278 p. D. (International ed. series.) cl.................... 1.50   .98

    An interesting and instructive book.

Ik
———
B 19 el

645. [650.] **E₁ementary psychology and education.** Joseph Baldwin. D. Appleton & Co., 1899. 299 p. D. (International ed. series.) cl.................. 1.50   .96

    Valuable for reference.

Ik
———
B 19 sc

646. **School management and school methods.** Joseph Baldwin. N. Y., D. Appleton & Co., 1897. 395 p. D. (International education series.) cl.......... 1.50   .98

    Contents: Public improvement through better educational conditions; Pupil improvement through better educational facilities;

                                                         List   Price to
                                                         price. schools.
Pupil improvement through educative school of government; Pupil
improvement through educative class management and class work;
Pupil improvement through better school and college organization
and correlation; Pupil improvement through efficient methods of
teaching.

Ik

B 26 st
647. **Studies in historical method.** Mary Sheldon Barnes.
   Bost., D. C. Heath & Co., 1899. 144 p. (Heath's
   pedagogical library.) D. cl. .... 1.12   .95

   For the use of the teacher in the secondary school who wishes to specialize in history.
   Contents: As to the intent of this book; Part I—Method as determined by the nature of history; Content of history; Sources of history; Study of contemporary history; Study of local history; Special study on ballads as historical material; Relation of travel to historical study; Tools of history; Relation of adjunct subjects to history; Principles of method deducted from preceding studies.
   Part II—Method as determined by the historic sense; Historic sense among primitive peoples; Historic sense among children; Special study on the historic memory of children; Special study on children's sense of historical time; Principles of method deduced from Part II.
   Part III—Method as determined by the aim of historical study; Special study on the making of patriots; Special study on the philosophy of history; Part IV—Practical application of principles of method to history in the high school; Part V—Descriptive and select bibliography of works on method.

Ik

B 43 te
648. **Teaching of Latin and Greek in the secondary school.** Charles E. Bennett, *and* George P. Bristol. N. Y.. Longmans, Green & Co., 1901. 336 p. (American Teachers series.) D. cl.... 1.50   .98

   Contents: Part I, Teaching of Latin in the secondary school; Historical position of the study of Latin in modern education; Justification of Latin as an instrument of secondary education; Beginning work; What authors are to be read in the secondary school, and in what sequence? Conduct of the secondary work in Latin; Latin composition; Latin prosody; Some miscellaneous points; Preparation of the teacher.
   Part II, Teaching of Greek in the secondary school; Aim of Greek study in the high school; Pronunciation; Beginning work; Xenophon and other prose writers—the Greek; Homer, Greek composition; Geography and history; Mythology and art.
   The "American teachers series," of which this is the first volume, will review the principal subjects of the secondary school curriculum. The purpose is to discuss the educational value of each subject, the reasons for including it in the curriculum, the

LIST OF BOOKS FOR HIGH SCHOOL LIBRARIES.

                                                                                  List Price to
                                                                                  price. schools.

selection and arrangement of materials in the course, the essential features of class instruction and the various helps which are available for teachers' use. The editor of the series claims no more for the books than "merely contributions to the professional knowledge necessary in secondary education."

Ik

B 62 le
649. **Letters to a mother:** on the philosophy of Froebel. Susan E. Blow. N. Y., D. Appleton & Co., 1899. 311 p. (International Education series.) D. cl. 1.50   .98

"The philosophy of Froebel is here explained in language addressed to the general public. The author takes up the most important doctrines one after the other as they were developed in the *Mutter und Kose Lieder*, and shows their equivalents in the different systems of thought that prevail. In some cases these systems are in harmony with Froebel, and in other cases there is profound disagreement."

Ik

B 62 sy
650. **Symbolic education:** a commentary on Froebel's "Mother Play." Susan E. Blow. N. Y., D. Appleton & Co., 1901. 251 p. (International Education series.) D. cl. .... 1.50   .98

This book is intended primarily for Kindergarten teachers but it will be of interest and value to every live teacher.
Contents: Atomism; Development: Childhood of the race; Symbolism of childhood; Meaning of play; Old Lady Gairfowl; Pattern experiences; Vortical education.

Ik

B 63 se
652. [661.] **Secondary school systems of Germany.** Frederick E. Bolton. N. Y., D. Appleton & Co., 1900. 398 p. D. (International Education series.) cl. .... 1.50   .98

An interesting and readable book. Valuable for reference.

Ik

B 64 ed
#653. [660.] **Education in the United States:** its history from the earliest settlements. Richard G. Boone. N. Y., D. Appleton & Co., 1901. 410 p. (International Education series.) D. cl. .... 1.50   .98

Contents: Earliest American schools; Colonial colleges; Colonial school systems; Elementary education; Academies and colleges; Centralizing tendencies; Preparation of teachers; Recent colleges; Professions; Technological education; Education of unfortunates

12

and criminal classes; Supplementary institutions; Learned societies and libraries; General government and education; Compulsory school attendance; Gradation of schools; Education in the south; Higher education of women; Conclusion.

Ik

B 66 te

654. **Teaching of history and civics in the elementary and the secondary school.** Henry E. Bourne. N. Y., Longmans, Green & Co., 1902. 385 p. (American Teachers' series.) D. cl. .... 1.50 .98

"It is the aim of this book to aid teachers of history, and especially those who have not had special training in historical work, better to comprehend the nature of the subject. Until they have considered the development of history as a way of portraying the experience of mankind, and know something of the methods by which it seeks to reach the sure basis of fact, and until they have seriously studied the problems of historical instruction, they can not feel a large interest in the subject, and consequently cannot inspire their pupils with such an interest. The first part of this book has been written to set them on the way toward a better comprehension of those aspects of history. The second part offers a review of the general field, which may guide those who require such help intelligently to study its many phases. . . .

In the bibliography prefixed to each chapter and in the notes will be found the names of the books chiefly consulted, or useful in a farther study of the subject."—*Preface.*

Part I—Study and teaching of history: Meaning of history; Foundations of historical scholarship; History in French and German schools; History in American schools; Value of history; Aim in teaching civics; Programme for history; School and the library; Facts of most worth; Methods of teaching history; Source method.

Part II—Course of study: Ancient history; Greek history; Roman history; Mediaeval history; Expansion of Europe; the founding of America; European history since 1560; History of the United States; Course of study in the elementary school; Teaching of civics.

Ik

B 67 fr

655. [676.] **Froebel, and education through self-activity.** H. Courthope Bowen. N. Y., C: Scribner's Sons, 1897. 209 p. D. (Great Educators series.) cl... 1.00 .90

Ik

B 82 in

656. [659.] **Introduction to the history of educational theories.** Oscar Browning. N. Y., Harper & Bros., 1882. 199 p. S. (Educational Library series.) cl. .... .50 .33

A brief history of education.

LIST OF BOOKS FOR HIGH SCHOOL LIBRARIES. 179

Ik
───
B 97 me
657. [664.] **Meaning of education and other essays and addresses.** Nicholas Murray Butler. N. Y., Macmillan Co., 1898. 230 p. D. cl. .... 1.00 .65

 Interesting and valuable essays on the meaning of education in its broad sense.
 Contents: Meaning of education; What knowledge is of most worth? Is there a new education? Democracy and education; The American college and the American university; The function of the secondary school; The reform of secondary education in the United States.

Ik
───
C 35 ch
#658. **Child: a study in the evolution of man.** Alexander Francis Chamberlain. N. Y., C: Scribner's Sons, 1902. 498 p. il. (Contemporary science series.) D. cl. 1.50 1.35

 A study of the child in the light of the literature of evolution, and an attempt to record, and, if possible interpret some of the most interesting and important phenomena of human beginnings in the individual and in the race.

Ik
───
C 73 hi
#659. **History of pedagogy.** Gabriel Compayré. Translated, with an introduction, notes, and an index by W. H. Payne. Bost., D. C. Heath & Co., 1901. 598 p. (Heath's pedagogical library.) D. cl... 1.75 1.57

 For reference.

Ik
───
C 73 le
660. **Lectures on pedagogy:** theoretical and practical. Gabriel Compayré. Translated with an introduction, notes, and an appendix by W. H. Payne. Bost., D. C. Heath & Co., 1898. 491 p. (Heath's pedagogical library.) D. cl. 1.75 1.57

 An elementary manual of teaching well adapted to the needs of teachers.
 Contents: Part I—Theoretical pedagogy; Education in general; Physical education; Intellectual education; Education of the senses; Culture of the attention; Culture of the memory; Culture of the imagination; Faculties of reflection, judgment, abstraction, reasoning; Culture of the feelings; Moral education; Will, liberty, and habit; Higher sentiments: Aesthetic education, religious education; Part II—Practical pedagogy; Methods in general; Reading and writing; Object-lessons; Study of the Mother-Tongue;

Teaching of history; Teaching of geography; Teaching of the sciences; Morals and civic instruction; Drawing—music—singing; Other exercises of the school; Rewards and punishments; Discipline in general; Appendix—Doctrine of memory; Analysis and synthesis; Problem of primary reading; Value of subjects.

	List price.	Price to schools.

[Ik

C 73 st

661. [310.] **Study of History in schools:** report to the American historical association. Committee of Seven, Andrew C. McLaughlin, Chm. N. Y., Macmillan Co., 1899. 267 p. D. cl.................. .50 .44

A very suggestive book to the teacher of history. It should be in every library.

Ik

C 81 am

662. **American at Oxford.** John Corbin. Bost., Houghton, Mifflin & Co., 1902. 325 p. il. D. cl. .... 1.00 .90

Mr. Corbin is a Harvard man who has resided at Oxford, and has seen much of English life. He covers in his narrative the whole range of college activities, outdoor and indoor life, athletics and clubs, examinations and amusements, the university and the outside world. He deals lightly with the history of Oxford, its past and its influence on English life, and in the light of this history and study, touches on the problems which now concern the American university, the social and athletic problem, the administrative and educational, and the large question of the service of the University to the country.

Students will enjoy reading this book. The language is simple and the subject matter extremely interesting.

Ik

D 28 ar

#663. **Aristotle:** and ancient educational ideals. Thomas Davidson. N. Y., C: Scribner's Sons, 1901. 256 p. (Great Educators series.) D. cl............... 1.00 .90

There is no English book that covers the field of Greek education as well as "Aristotle".

The book touches upon the whole subject of ancient pedagogy, the course of education being traced up to Aristotle,—and down from him through the decline of ancient civilization.

Ik

D 28 ed

664. **Education of the Greek people:** and its influence on civilization. Thomas Davidson. N. Y., D. Appleton & Co., 1900. 229 p. (International education series.) D. cl. 1.50 1.00

"This work is not intended for scholars or specialists, but for that large body of teachers throughout the country who are trying

	List price.	Price to schools.

to do their duty, but are suffering from that want of enthusiasm which necessarily comes from being unable clearly to see the end and purpose of their labors, or to invest any end with sublime import. I have sought to show them that the end of their work is the redemption of humanity, an essential part of that process by which it is being gradually elevated to moral freedom, and to suggest to them the direction in which they ought to turn their chief efforts."—*Preface.*

Ik
———
D 2S hi

#665. **History of education.** Thomas Davidson. N. Y., C: Scribner's Sons, 1901. 292 p. D. cl. .... 1.00 .90

Contents: Savage, barbarian, and civic education; Introductory; Rise of intelligence; Savage education; Barbarian education; Civic education; Human education; Supernatural beginnings of humanism; Hellenistic education; Christian "catechetical school" of Alexandria; Patristic education; Muslin education; Mediaeval education; Period of Charles the Great; Scholasticism and Mysticism; Mediaeval universities; Renaissance, reformation, and counter-reformation; Modern education; Fifteenth, sixteenth, and seventeenth centuries; Eighteenth century; Nineteenth century; Outlook; Bibliography.

Ik
———
D 51 sc

666. **School and society;** three lectures; supplemented by a statement of the University elementary school. John Dewey. (Chicago.) N. Y., McClure, Phillips & Co., 1900. 129 p. il. D. cl. .... 1.00 .65

A book which should be read by every teacher.
Contents: School and social progress; School and the life of the child; Waste in education; Three years of the university elementary school.

Ik
———
D 84 he

667. **Helps for ambitious girls.** William Drysdale. N. Y., Thomas Y. Crowell & Co., c1900. 505 p. D. cl. . 1.50 .98

A most sensible book for girls to read whether they are in school, college, workshop, office, or the wife or mother of a home. The author believes that nature has planned a work for every girl and that it is her first duty to find that work, never losing sight, however, of home and its refining influences. He discusses the different professions, trades, and other occupations in which women are found employed today, pointing out the advantages and disadvantages of each as related to the girl and her future.

An important part of the work is the practical information in almost every subject about where to turn. The requirements for admission to leading colleges for girls are shown at length; the

	List price.	Price to schools.

courses of study for expectant teachers in the public schools; full information from the largest hospitals on the necessary steps for becoming a trained nurse; courses of study necessary for the woman lawyer, doctor, preacher, dentist, and so through the whole list. These practical parts of the book, girls who desire to become self-supporting will find invaluable.

Ik

El 5 me

668. **Methods of teaching modern languages**: papers on the value and on methods of modern language instruction. A. Marshall Elliott, *and others*. Bost., D. C. Heath & Co., 1901. 217 p. (Heath's pedagogical library.) D. cl.................... .90 .76

Contents: Modern languages as a college discipline; Observations upon method in the teaching of modern languages; Reading in modern language study; Natural method; Notes on the teaching of French; Practical and psychological tests of modern language study; Collegiate instruction in the romance languages; How to use modern languages as a means of mental discipline; Teaching of French and German in our public high schools; Aim and scope of the study of modern languages and methods of teaching them; Natural method explained; "Reader" the center of modern language teaching; On the use of foreign language in the class-room; Common sense in teaching modern languages; Recommendations in the "Report of the Committee of Ten".

Ik

F 31 sc

669. [685.] **School inspection.** D. R. Fearon. N. Y., Macmillan Co., 1883. 93 p. D. cl.................. 1.50 .98

Two valuable books for superintendents and supervising principals.

Ik

F 55 le

670. [665.] **Lectures on teaching.** James G. Fitch. N. Y., Macmillan Co., 1881. 436 p. D. cl............. 1.00 .85

A good book.

Ik

F 74 bo

671. **Boy problem**: a study in social pedagogy. Second ed., rev. and enl. William Byron Forbush, with introduction by G. Stanley Hall. Bost., Pilgrim Press, c1901. 194 p. D. Ed. 2, rev., enl. cl. .. .75 .67

This book should be read by every teacher both in the grades and High school. Though the author does not attempt to solve the boy problem, he accomplishes the aim which he evidently had in view

LIST OF BOOKS FOR HIGH SCHOOL LIBRARIES. 183

                                                    List Price to
                                                  price. schools.

of impressing his readers with the gravity of the problem and interesting them in taking some active steps toward a solution of it. He says: "The solution of the problem may be sought from three sources: from a study of boy life, from a study of the ways in which children spontaneously organize socially, and from a study of the ways adults organize for the benefit of boys."—*Preface*.

  Contents: Boy-life; By-laws of boy life; Ways in which boys spontaneously organize socially; Social organizations formed for boys by adults; Some suggestions as to how to help boys; Boy problem in the church; Directory of social organizations for boys; List of books and pamphlets about work with boys; Reading course on the boy problem.

Ik
———
G 18 ne
672. [670.] **New manual of method.** A. H. Garlick. N. Y., Longmans, Green & Co., 1897. 378 p. il. D. cl. 1.20 1.08

For reference.

Ik
———
H 15 ps
673. [651.] **Psychology and psychic culture.** R. P. Halleck. N. Y., American Book Company, 1896. 368 p. D. cl. 1.25 1.07

Brief outline of the subject. A clear statement of principles.

Ik
———
II 17 mi
674. [682.] **Mind and hand:** manual training the chief factor in education. Charles H. Ham. N. Y., American Book Company, 1900. 464 p. il. D. cl.... 1.25 1.08

A very complete discussion of manual training.

Ik
———
II 19 ed
675. **Educational aims and educational values.** Paul H. Hanus. N. Y., Macmillan Co., 1900. 211 p. D. cl. .... 1.00 .65

"The book consists of a series of essays on contemporary educational problems. In the first five chapters the attempt is made to formulate the aims of elementary and secondary education, and to describe the scope and methods of an education that meets the demands of modern life, both in its provisions for the development of the individual and in its training for social service. The remaining chapters deal with the professional training of the college-bred teacher, and with the services of John Amos Comenius

	List price.	Price to schools.

who, in the seventeenth century, advocated nineteenth-century educational reforms."

Contents: Educational aims and educational values; Recent tendency in secondary education examined; Attempted improvements in the course of study; What should the modern secondary school aim to accomplish? Secondary education as a unifying force in American life; Preparation of the high school teacher of mathematics; Study of education at Harvard University; Permanent influence of John Amos Comenius.

Ik

H 59 ar

676. **Art of study**: a manual for teachers and students of the science and art of teaching. Burke A. Hinsdale. N. Y., American Bk. Co., c1900. 266 p. D. cl. 1.00   90

"The ultimate object of this book is to place the Art of Study as a tool or instrument in the hands of pupils and students in schools. But as this object can be reached only by way of the teachers, the books is primarily addressed to them, and to students of the science and the art of teaching." Preface.

Contents: Learning and teaching; Study and its relations to learning and teaching; Art of study defined; Neglect of the art of study; Is knowledge or mental development the end of teaching?; First stage of instruction in the art of study; Child's first contact with the book; Study—recitation; Study—lesson; Attacking the lesson; Recitation—lesson; Attention: its nature, kinds, and value; Passive attention: interest; Cultivation of passive attention; Active attention: will; Cultivation of active attention; Thoroughness; Relations of feeling to study and learning; Methods of learning; Methods of teaching; Formal teaching of the art of study; Teaching as a mode of learning.

Ik

H 59 h

677. [675.] **Horace Mann, and the common school revival in the United States.** B. A. Hinsdale. N. Y., C: Scribner's Sons, 1898. 326 p. D. (Great educators series.) cl. .... 1.00   .90

Ik

H 59 ho

678. [311.] **How to study and teach history**, with particular reference to the history of the United States. B. A. Hinsdale. N. Y., D. Appleton & Co., 1898. 365 p. D. (International educational series.) cl. 1.50   .98

The teacher will find this book very helpful and suggestive. The uses of history, the criteria for the choice of facts, the necessity for the organization of facts, sources of information, the necessary qualifications of the teacher are given.

The grouping and relating of facts are illustrated by some important chapters in American history.

Ik
H 59 te

List price. Price to schools.

679. [681.] **Teaching the language-arts—speech, reading, composition.** B. A. Hinsdale. N. Y., D. Appleton & Co., 1896. 205 p. D. (International educational series.) cl. .... 1.00 .65

Treats of the use and growth of language, its grammatical and logical structure, its mastery in speaking, reading, and writing; its place in the cultivation of the powers of thought, and the significance of philology among the sciences.

Ik
H 83 sy

#680. **Systematic science teaching: a manual of inductive elementary work for all instructors.** Edward Gardiner Howe. N. Y., D. Appleton & Co., 1900. 336 p. il. (International education series.) D. cl. .... 1.50 .98

An excellent manual of instruction in Natural science for the elementary schools.

Ik
H 87 di

681. **Dickens as an educator.** James L. Hughes. N. Y., D. Appleton & Co., 1901. 319 p. (International education series.) D. cl. 1.50 1.00

Mr. Hughes considers Charles Dickens the greatest educational reformer that England has produced. He claims he has done more than any one else to secure for the child a considerate treatment of his tender age. His book aims to prove that he was the great apostle of the "new education", and to bring into connected form, under appropriate headings, the educational principles advocated through his novels and other writings. Seventeen chapters gather together extracts under the headings: The place of Dickens among educators; Infant gardens; The overthrow of coercion; The doctrine of child depravity; Cramming; Free childhood; Individuality; Child study and child nature, etc.

Ik
J 23 ta

682. [649.] **Talks to teachers on psychology: and to students on some of life's ideals.** William James. N. Y., Henry Holt & Co., 1899. 301 p. O. cl... 1.50 1.35

One of the most practical and helpful books for the teacher. It is readable and interesting.

Ik
K 67 eu

#683. **European schools:** or, What I saw in the schools of Germany, France, Austria, and Switzerland. Louis Richard Klemm. N. Y., D. Appleton & Co., 1896. 426 p. il. (International education series.) D. cl. 2.00   1.30

List price. Price to schools.

"The author of this book went to Europe with the intention of seeing what was worth reading. Schools inferior to the average American school he avoided. He strove, during a journey of ten months, to see the best that Europe could offer him, and in this volume he thinks he has pictured the best results, described the most advanced methods, and given a great number of valuable hints that will be serviceable to teachers who have not sunk back into that detestable state of self-sufficiency and satisfaction which is the arch-foe of progress."—*From preface.*

Ik
L 12 pr

684. **Primer of psychology.** George Trumbull Ladd. N. Y., C: Scribner's Sons, 1898. 224 p. D. cl.....   1.00   .90

A narrative in plain, simple English of the more obvious facts and principles known to modern scientific psychology for high school pupils and general readers.

Ik
L 26 ap

685. [652.] **Apperception:** a monograph on psychology and pedagogy. *Dr.* Karl Lange, *ed.* by Charles De Garmo. Bost., D. C. Heath & Co., 1894. 279 p. D. (Heath's pedagogical lib.) cl...............   1.00   .90

The nature, conditions, and significance of apperception, and its application to pedagogy.

Ik
M 11 me

686. **Method in history,** for teachers and students. William H. Mace. Bost., Ginn & Co., 1901. 311 p. D. cl. ....   1.00   .85

An excellent book for the use of the History teacher. "The aim has not been to discuss devices and external manipulations in teaching history; the term 'method' is not even intended to suggest diagrams, chronological charts, or expedients of like nature. But something far more fundamental has been the aim; the determining factors in method and not the determined. . . .

It is the prevailing custom among teachers in secondary and primary schools to look upon the subject they teach as contributing very little to the method of its teaching. The result is to lower the subject—and, worst of all, the work of teaching—in the estimation of the teacher. The subject stands as so much simple and

	List price.	Price to schools.

easy matter upon which no special preparation for the recitation is needed. The work ceases to be interesting and sinks into mere drudgery. College graduates, as a rule, take the same low view of work in these schools. They feel that the branches taught even in the best secondary schools present no problem worthy of their metal. There is a problem here worthy of their best endeavors and one that challenges, in point of difficulty, their strongest and keenest powers. They generally do not know where to look for it; it is a pedagogical, and not an academical problem. This work is written with the confident hope that such a problem will be perceived in the domain of history teaching in the primary and secordary schools."—*From preface.*

Ik
―――
M 22 ap

687. [663.] **Applied psychology:** introd. to the principles and the practice of education. James A. McLellan. Bost., Small, Maynard & Co., 1892. D. cl. . 1.00   .80

One of the best books on this subject.

Ik
―――
M 27 ol

688. [347.] **Old Greek education.** J. P. Mahaffy. N. Y., Harper & Bros., 1882. 144 p. S. (Education lib.) cl.... 75   .64

A clear and simple account of the practice and theory of Greek education. Valuable in the history of education.

Ik
―――
M 75 bi

689. **Bibliography of education.** Will S. Monroe. N. Y., D. Appleton & Co., 1897. 202 p. (International education series.) D. cl. 2.00   1.30

This book will be of value to the teacher who wishes a complete reference list of the best books on education. It will be of no use whatever to High school students and should not be purchased by the smaller libraries.

"A valuable classed bibliography of works relating to education to be found in the English language, except in the matter of works of reference. It includes the titles of 3,200 books and pamphlets, grouped under twenty-two different classes, which are again broken into sections and subsections. The leading headings are: Works of reference; History and theory of education; Principles and practice of teaching; Methods of instruction; School administration; Kindergarten; Education of colored children; Of defective children; Professional education; Manual training; Philosophy; Psychology; Moral education; Physical education and school hygiene; Education of women; Self-culture and home education; Sociological aspects of education; School systems; Educational conferences and exhibits; American reports; Educational journals."

	List price.	Price to schools.

Ik
———
M 82 ps

690. **Psychology for teachers.** Conway Lloyd Morgan, with a preface by Henry W. Jameson. N. Y., C: Scribner's Sons, 1901. 240 p. D. cl........... 1.00 .90

This volume was written to meet the requirements of those who are preparing themselves for the profession of teaching. It is a practical book, dealing with the problems of school life in a manner which will develop interest and arouse enthusiasm.

Ik
———
M 83 ve

691. **Ventilation and warming of school buildings.** Gilbert B. Morrison. N. Y., D. Appleton & Co., 1900. 181 p. il. (International education series.) D. cl. .... 1.00 .65

Contents: Needed information; Effects of breathing impure air; Air; Examination of the air; Amount of air required; General principles of ventilation; Natural ventilation; Inlets; Regulating the drafts of openings—the wind; Ventilation by windows; Artificial ventilation; Movement of the air by mechanical means; Air-propellers; Can the plenum movement be afforded? Cost of ventilation; Warming; Methods of warming; Steam heating; Ideal plan for warming and ventilating.

Ik
———
Op 5 de

692. **Development of the child.** Nathan Oppenheim. N. Y., Macmillan Co., 1898. 296 p. D. cl.......... 1.25 1.12

Contents: Introductory; Facts in the comparative development of the child; Comparative importance of heredity and environment; Place of the primary school in the development of the child; Place of religion in the development of the child; Value of the child as a witness in suits at law; Development of the child-criminal; Child's development as a factor in producing the genius or the defective; Institutional life in the development of the child; Profession of maternity. Author is attending physician to the children's department of Mt. Sinai Hospital Dispensary.

Ik
———
P 16 hi

693. **History of education:** Franklin V. N. Painter. N. Y., D. Appleton & Co., 1901. 343 p. (International series.) D. cl....................... 1.50 .98

"I have endeavored to present clearly the leading characteristics of each period, and the labors and distinctive principles of prominent educators. Considerable prominence has been given to Comenius, Pestalozzi, Froebel, and other educational reformers, who laid the foundations of the scientific methods now coming into general use. In support or illustration of various statements, recognized authorities have been permitted to speak freely."—*Preface.*

LIST OF BOOKS FOR HIGH SCHOOL LIBRARIES.

		List price.	Price to schools.
Ik P 22 no	694. [667.] **Notes of talks on teaching.** Francis W. Parker, reported by Lelia E. Partridge. N. Y., E. L. Kellogg & Co. 182 p. S. cl............	1.00	.85

Interesting talks which will be found helpful in the classes in theory and art.

Ik P 58 sc	695. [684.] **School supervision.** Josiah L. Pickard. N. Y., D. Appleton & Co., 1901. 183 p. (International education series.) D. cl...................	1.00	.65

Contents: Introductory; Historical sketch of supervision of schools in the United States; Character of school supervision; State supervision; County superintendency; City supervision; City superintendent of schools; City superintendent's relation to pupils; Superintendent's relation to teachers; Gradation and course of study; Promotions and examinations; Relation of superintendent to parents and patrons; Relation of superintendent to the physical training of pupils; Relation of superintendent to moral training; Relation of superintendent to government and discipline of pupils; Relation of superintendent to the board of education; Relation of the superintendent to agencies for improvement of teachers; Relation of public schools to morality and religion; What shall we do with our boys?

Ik P 92 me	696. **Mental development in the child.** William T. Preyer. Translated from the German by H. W. Brown. N. Y., D. Appleton & Co., 1901. 176 p. (International education series.) D. cl........	1.00	.65

An excellent book for Kindergartners and mothers.

Ik Qu 4 es	697. [658.] **Essays on educational reformers.** Robert Herbert Quick. N. Y., D. Appleton & Co., 1899. 568 p. D. (International education series.) cl..	1.50	.98

One of the best histories of education.

Ik R 29 rf	698. [669.] **Report of the committee of fifteen.** N. Y., American Book Company, 1894................	.30	.27

These two reports are on the subjects of study and the methods of instruction in secondary schools, including public high schools, private academies, and schools preparing students for college.

	List price.	Price to schools.

Ik
R 29 rt
C99. [688.] **Report of the committee of ten.** N. Y., American Book Company, 1892........................ .30 .27

Ik
R 29 rtw
700. **Report of the committee of twelve** of the modern language association of America: with an introduction by the chairman Calvin Thomas. Bost., D. C. Heath & Co., 1901. 99 p. S. cl.......... .16 .14

"The problem of the Modern Language Committee was, then, to suggest to the secondary teacher what should be taught and how it should be taught, and to do this in such a way as to leave to the schools a large measure of liberty in the management of details. But the *what* and the *how* were inextricably bound up with the *why*, since the teacher's theory as to the purpose for which a modern language is studied will inevitably exert a determining influence upon the character and method of the instruction. It was first necessary, therefore, to take a definite position with regard to the educational value of the modern languages.'

Ik
R 76 em
701. **Emile:** or, treatise of education. Rosseau, *trans.* by W. H. Payne. N. Y., D. Appleton & Co., 1901. 355 p. (International education series.) D. cl 1.50 .98

One of the greatest educational classics. Rousseau was the great leader in social and political reform and from his "Emile" our later great writers on education have caught their inspiration.

Instead of writing a formal treatise on education, he gives us in moving pictures a sort of panorama of a human life from infancy up to maturity. Every teacher should read this book and Plato's "Republic".

Ik
Se 1 id
702. **Ideal school:** or, looking forward. Preston W. Search. N. Y., D. Appleton & Co., 1901. 357 p. (International education series.) D. cl......... 1.20 1.08

Although many of the ideas presented in this book seem beyond practical application, the author claims that there is scarcely a feature of the book not supported by something tested and proven. Its main value to the teacher will be as a source of inspiration.

Contents: Proposition stated—introductory queries; Losses of the school; Fundamentals in planning a school; School plant; Scope of the school; Course of study; Individual variations; Illustrative methods; Applicability to different grades of instruction; Child's opportunity traced through the school; Function of the teacher; Re-enforcement of evolution; Municipal difficulties and organization; Something for the physicians to think about; Ethical basis of the school; Conclusion.

	List price.	Price to schools.

Ik
———
Se 3 hi
703. [657.] **History of education.** Levi Seeley. N. Y., American Book Company, 1899. 343 p. D. cl..   1.25   1.07

    A clear and concise account of the history of education. The outlines, references to literature, and the bibliography are good.

Ik
———
Sm 5 te
704. **Teaching of chemistry and physics in the secondary school.** Alexander Smith, *and* Edwin H. Hall. N. Y., Longmans, Green & Co., 1902. 377 p. (American teachers' series.) O. cl.............   1.50   .98

    An excellent reference book on methods, for the use of the teacher in Chemistry and Physics.

    Contents: Introduction; Chemistry in the curriculum; Introduction of the subject; Introduction in the laboratory; Instruction in the class-room; Some constituents of the course; Laboratory, equipment and illustrative material; Teacher, his preparation and development; Whether to be a teacher of physics; Preparation for teaching; Teacher as student, observer, and writer; Problems of laboratory practice; School text-books of physics; Discovery, verification, or inquiry? Technique of laboratory management; Lectures and recitations; Physics in primary and grammar schools; Physics in various kinds of secondary schools; On the presentation of dynamics; Plan and equipment of a laboratory; Physics teaching in other countries.

Ik
———
Sp 3 ed
705. [662.] **Education:** intellectual, moral and physical. Herbert Spencer. N. Y., D. Appleton & Co. 283 p. D. cl......................................   1.25   .82

    A broad and masterly exposition of the general principles of education.

Ik
———
Su 5 st
706. [654.] **Studies of childhood.** James Sully. N. Y., D. Appleton & Co., 1898. 527 p. O. cl.............   2.50   1.60

    Certain aspects of children's minds which have come to the notice of the writer. Interesting and helpful, and will prove very suggestive to the student interested in child study.

Ik
———
Su 5 te
707. **Teacher's handbook of psychology:** on the basis of "Outlines of psychology." James Sully. N. Y., D. Appleton & Co., 1900. 590 p. D. Ed. 4, enl. cl. 2.00   1.30

    A clear, systematic treatise well adapted to the use of teachers.

Ik

T 21 st

                                                                                               List Price to
                                                                                              price. schools.

708. **Study of the child:** a brief treatise on the psychology of the child, with suggestions for teachers, students, and parents. Albert R. Taylor. N. Y., D. Appleton & Co., 1899. 215 p. (International education series.) D. cl. ....   1.25   .82

"The principal aim of this book has been to bring the subject within the comprehension of the average teacher and parent. Technical terms and scientific formulae have been avoided as much as possible. The desire to announce new principles has been wholly subservient to that of wishing to serve my fellow-workers by assisting them to a closer relationship with the child."—*Preface.*

Contents: Chapters on the senses; Consciousness and apperception; Attention; Symbolism; Language; Muscular or motor control; Feelings; Will and its functions; Intellect and its functions; Self, habit, and character; Children's instincts and plays; Manners and morals; Normals and abnormals; Stages of growth, fatigue point, etc. Bibliography.

Ik

T 59 ph

709. **Philosophy of school management.** Arnold Tompkins. Bost., Ginn & Co., 1901. 222 p. D. cl....   .75   .64

This book discusses the subject of school management from the kindergarten to the university. It should be in every teacher's library and in the larger school libraries.

Ik

T 67 ps

710. [655.] **Psychology of childhood.** Frederick Tracy. Bost., D. C. Heath & Co., 1896. 170 p. D. (Heath's pedagogical lib.) cl..................   .90   .80

The results of the systematic study of children.

Ik

Uf 3 in

711. [671.] **Introduction to the pedagogy of Herbart.** Christian Ufer, *tr.* by J. C. Zinser, ed. by Charles De Garmo. Bost., D. C. Heath & Co., 1896. 123 p. D. (Heath's ped. lib.) cl..................   .90   .81

For the advanced pupils.

Ik

W 24 st

712. [656.] **Study of children and their school training.** Francis Warner. N. Y., Macmillan Co., 1898. 264 p. il. D. cl. ....   1.00   .85

Child study from the standpoint of a physician. The principles used in biological study and natural history are applied to child study.

LIST OF BOOKS FOR HIGH SCHOOL LIBRARIES. 193

	List price.	Price to schools.

lk
W 58 el
713. [666.] **Elements of pedagogy.** Emerson E. White. N. Y., American Book Company, 1886. 336 p. D. cl. .... 1.00 .85

Clear statements and concise discussion on the elements of psychology, the principles of teaching, and methods in teaching. For beginners in the subject.

lk
W 58 sc
714. [683.] **School management.** Emerson E. White. N. Y., American Book Company, 1894. 320 p. D. cl. .... 1.00 .85

Clear statements of principles and their application to school work. The book contains many concrete illustrations, and these will appeal to the young teacher.

lk
W 63 ch
715. [672.] **Children's rights:** a book of nursery logic. Kate Douglas Wiggin. Bost., Houghton, Mifflin & Co., 1898. 236 p. D. cl.................... 1.00 .65

Charming and valuable essays on rights of the child, his plays and playthings, and his reading. The relation of the kindergarten to social reform is also discussed. Younger pupils will enjoy.

lk
W 63 fg
716. [678.] **Froebel's gifts.** Kate Douglas Wiggin, *and* Nora Archibald Smith. Bost., Houghton, Mifflin & Co., 1895. 202 p. D. (Republic of childhood series.) cl. .... 1.00 .65

lk
W 63 fo
717. [677.] **Froebel's occupations.** Kate Douglas Wiggin *and* Nora Archibald Smith. Bost., Houghton, Mifflin & Co., 1897. 313 p. D. (Republic of childhood series.) cl. .... 1.00 .65

lk
W 63 kl
718. [679.] **Kindergarten principles and practice.** Kate Douglas Wiggin *and* Nora Archibald Smith. Bost., Houghton, Mifflin & Co., 1898. 205 p. D. (Republic of childhood series.) cl................. 1.00 .65

These four books on the principles of the kindergarten and its workings will be of value in the study of psychology and the methods of teaching. Popular treatises for the general reader.

		List price.	Price to schools.

Ik
W 71 pl

719. **Place of the story in early education: and other essays.** Sara E. Wiltse. Bost., Ginn & Co., 1892. 132 p. D. cl. .... .50 .43

For kindergarten and primary teachers.
Contents: Place of the story in early education; Study of children; Children's habits; Learning to use money; Sound-blindness; Study of adolescense; Mental imagery of boys.

Ik
W 73 gr

720. **Great American educators with chapters on American education.** Albert Edward Winship. N. Y., Werner School Bk. Co., c1900. 252 p. il. D. cl. (Four Great American series.).................. .50 .33

Brief elementary biographies of some of the leading American educators, and a sketch of the history of public school education in America. The presentation is simple enough to be of interest to High school pupils.
Contents: Horace Mann; Mary Lyon; David P. Page; Henry Barnard; John Dudley Philbrick; Newton Bateman; Edward A. Sheldon; James P. Wickersham; Founders and benefactors of American colleges; Historical sketch of American education.

CIVICS AND GOVERNMENT.

Provision is made by statute for the teaching of the Constitution of the United States and of Wisconsin in the public schools.

A knowledge of the fundamental laws of the land is indispensable to every citizen, and with this end in view the constitutions should be taught, the more important clauses being memorized. The error, however, should not be made of treating the subject in a meaningless, routine manner, for every section and every clause possesses a life which more or less affects our every-day existence. Let the teacher make the branch a practical one, losing no opportunity of bringing out its full meaning by the application of current history or local events. In this way an interest will be excited, and more than all, the great object in the teaching of civil government will be more nearly attained, viz., to create law-abiding citizens. The young people must early learn the duties of the citizen and the individual responsibility of that citizen toward maintaining a stable government for the nation.

It will be well to deal with the different forms of governments, as administered in the county, town, village, city, and school districts. These governments come within the immediate knowledge of the children or their parents, and a study of details will be found profitable. It will be well also to take up the subject of elections. The present system of voting, known as the "Australian" method, may be illustrated by securing samples of the ballot. The method of nominations through primary caucuses is important.

If there is a literary society in connection with the school, much assistance can be given to the subject of civil government by providing for debates upon important national questions, for moot courts, and mock legislative deliberations. Every opportunity to visit the state legislature, the county board of supervisors, the town meeting, and other assemblages of governmental character, should be improved. Throughout the entire work on this subject an attempt should be made to have pupils realize the essentials of good citizenship. A knowledge of constitutions and of the details of governmental activities may make more intelligent citizens, but it does not necessarily make better ones.

J
―――
Al 7 am

                 List Price to
                 price. schools.

721. [646.] **Among the law-makers.** Edmund Alton.
  N. Y., C: Scribner's Sons, 1896. 308 p. il. D. cl. 1.50 .98

 Various phases of congressional life, showing characteristics of the respective Houses.

J
―――
B 79 ho

722. [643.] **How the republic is governed.** Noah Brooks.
  N. Y., C: Scribner's Sons, 1898. 169 p. S. cl.. .75 .67

 A brief, concise, and clear statement of how our government is carried on.

J
B 79 sh

723. [647.] **Short studies in party politics.** Noah Brooks. N. Y., C: Scribner's Sons, 1895. 205 p. il. D. cl. .... 1.25 .82

Some first things in politics, the passing of the whigs, when slavery went out of politics, the party platforms of sixty years, are some of the subjects discussed in this valuable little book.

J
B 84 am

724. [641.] **American commonwealth.** James Bryce. N. Y., Macmillan Co., 1898. 547 p. D. Abridged ed. cl. 1.75 1.57

An excellent book filled with much valuable information. Will be useful as a reference book for older pupils.

J
C 67 mu

725. **Municipal government: as illustrated by the charter, finances, and public charities of New York.** Bird S. Coler. N. Y., D. Appleton & Co., 1900. 200 p. D. cl. .... 1.00 .65

A statement of conditions that exist in New York city, with reports of progress. Details are presented of errors in the charter, changes that should be made, with facts showing how public charity has been abused. Other chapters relate to income and expenses; water supply; transportation; city development; Church in politics; Political machines. Mr. Coler is Comptroller of New York city.

J
C 76 am

#726. **American political history: to the death of Lincoln; popularly told.** Viola A. Conklin. N. Y., Henry Holt & Co., 1901. 435 p. D. cl. 1.50 1.35

A course of lectures on the political history of United States for general reading. Good for reference in United States History.

J
C 76 ci

727. **City government in the United States: with a chapter on the greater New York charter of 1897.** Alfred R. Conkling. N. Y., D. Appleton & Co., 1899. 245 p. D. Ed. 4, rev. cl. .... 1.00 .65

A clear presentation of the question of city government.
Contents: Government of American cities; Mayor; Boards of aldermen; Public parks; Fire department; Police department;

LIST OF BOOKS FOR HIGH SCHOOL LIBRARIES. 197

                    List Price to
                    price. schools.
Police courts; Excise; Water, gas and electricity; Streets; Street-cleaning; Street pavements; Public works; Charitable institutions; Public schools and trade schools; Finance and taxation; Municipalization; Elections; Remedies; Greater New York charter.

J
———
C 94 un
 728. [648.] **United States and foreign powers.** William E.
   Curtis. N. Y., C: Scribner's Sons, 1899. 314 p.
   il. D. cl. 1.25 1.08

 A simple narrative of the principal incidents in our diplomatic history in a form that will enable them to be properly understood by those not versed in international law.

J
———
F 54 am
 #729. **American political ideas:** viewed from the standpoint of universal history; three lectures delivered at the Royal Institution of Great Britain in May, 1880. John Fiske. N. Y., Harper & Bros., 1901. 158 p. D. cl. .... 1.00 .65

 An endeavor to illustrate some of the fundamental ideas of American politics by setting forth their relations to the general history of mankind.
 "The government of the United States is not the result of special creation, but of evolution. As the town-meetings of New England are lineally descended from the village assemblies of the early Aryans; as our huge federal union was long ago foreshadowed in the little leagues of Greek cities and Swiss cantons, so the great political problems which we are (thus far successfully) solving is the very same problem upon which all civilized peoples have been working ever since civilization began."—*Preface*.
 Contents: Town-meeting; Federal union; "Manifest destiny."

J
———
F 54 ci
 730. [640.] **Civil government in the United States.** John
   Fiske. Bost., Houghton, Mifflin & Co., 1890. 360
   p. D. cl. .... 1.00 .90

 A study of our government from the historical standpoint. Political institutions are explained, their origin given, and processes through which they have acquired their present shape indicated.

J
———
G 65 hi
 #731. **History of political parties in the United States.**
   John P. Gordy. N. Y., Henry Holt & Co., 1900.
   4 vol. Ed 2, rev. D. cl. each 1.75 1.57

 An excellent reference book.

| | List | Price to |
| | price. | schools. |

J

H 18 fe

#732. **Federalist and other constitutional papers.** Hamilton, Jay, Madison, and other statesmen of their time. *Ed.* by E. H. Scott. Chic., Albert, Scott & Co., 1894. 945 p. O. cl. 2.50   2.25

Valuable for reference in United States history. This volume should only be purchased by the largest libraries.

J

H 24 th

733. [645.] **This country of ours.** Benjamin Harrison. N. Y., C: Scribner's Sons, 1901. 360 p. D. cl.   1.50   .98

"This book is a modest attempt to give my readers a view of the machinery of our national government in motion, and some instruction as to the relations and uses of its several parts. . . Its purpose is to give a better knowledge of things that have been too near and familiar to be well known."—*Preface.*

Contents: Constitution; Congress; President; State department; Treasury department; Departments of war and justice; Post-office department; Navy department; Departments of the interior and of agriculture; Independent boards and commissions; Judiciary; Constitution of the United States.

J

H 25 fo

734. **Foundations of American foreign policy: with a working bibliography.** Albert Bushnell Hart. N. Y., Macmillan Co., 1901. 307 p. D. cl. 1.50   1.35

This book does not claim to be a history of American diplomacy, it simply gives a history of some phases of our foreign relations.

Contents: United States as a world power; Experience of the United States in foreign military expeditions; Boundary controversies and commissions; Century of Cuban diplomacy; Brother Jonathan's colonies; What the founders of the union thought concerning territorial problems; Monroe doctrine and the doctrine of permanent interest; Working bibliography of American diplomacy.

J

H 25 pr

735. **Practical essays on American government.** Albert Bushnell Hart. N. Y., Longmans, Green & Co., 1894. 311 p. D. cl. ....   1.50   .98

Contents: Speaker as premier; Exercise of the suffrage; Election of a president; Do the people wish civil service reform? Chilean controversy; a study in American diplomacy; Colonial town meeting; Colonial shire; Rise of American cities; Biography of a river and harbor bill; Public land policy of the United States; Why the South was defeated in the civil war.

LIST OF BOOKS FOR HIGH SCHOOL LIBRARIES.

	List price.	Price to schools.

J

H 59 am

736. [639.] **American government;** national and state. B. A. Hinsdale. N. Y., Werner School Book Co., 1898. 494 p. D. cl. 1.25 1.12

A comprehensive view of the origin and growth of the American government and our state system; a careful study of the constitution of the U. S.

J

J 23 go

737. **Government in state and nation.** James A. James, and A. H. Sanford. N. Y., C: Scribner's Sons, 1901. 383 p. O. cl. .... 1.00 .90

The subject matter presented partially represents the plan pursued by the authors as teachers of civil government for a number of years in secondary schools. A study of the actual methods by which the affairs of government are conducted gives constant interest to the work, and consequently the practical side has been emphasized. Many problems besides those presented in the supplementary questions may be worked out from the official reports. The appendix contains an excellent list of reference books on government.

Contents: Town and county government; State governments; City government; Elections and party government; Public finances; Judicial trials; Charitable and penal institutions; Educational systems; Exercise of the police power; Labor legislation; Steps leading to union; Constitutional convention; Organization of the legislative department; Powers and duties of the separate houses; Procedure in congress; National finances; Power of congress over commerce; Money of the United States; Other general powers of congress; Powers denied the United States and the several states; Executive department; Election of a president; Powers and duties of the president; Cabinet and the executive departments; Judiciary; Relations between the states, and between the federal government and the states; Territories and public lands; Amendments to the constitution; Miscellaneous provisions; Relations of states and nation; Some features of international law and arbitration; Constitution of the United States of America; Key to periodical literature; Reference books.

J

J 64 hi

738. [638.] **History of American politics.** Alexander Johnston. N. Y., Henry Holt & Co., 1890. 355 p. S. cl. .... .80 .72

A very good handbook for general readers.

J
M 11 po

	List price.	Price to schools.

#739. **Political parties in the United States, 1846-1861.** Jesse Macy. N. Y., Macmillan Co., 1900. 333 p. (Citizen's library of economics, politics and sociology.) D. cl. 1.25 1.12

A study of the American party system.

Contents: Origin and nature of the modern political party; Origin of the American party system; Party issues; Spoils system and party organization; Ante-bellum vs. present politics; Science and politics; Slavery as a party issue; Causes of the civil war; Last Whig administration; Great Whig failure; Fugitive slave law; Importance of the American party system; Rise of the republican party; War in Kansas; Campaign of 1856; Dred Scott decision; Free Soil victory in the territories under the leadership of Douglas; Abraham Lincoln as a typical democrat; Republican party revived; John Brown at Harper's Ferry; Campaign of 1860; Drifting into war.

J
M 22 wi

740. **With the fathers:** studies in the history of the United States. John Bach McMaster. N. Y., D. Appleton & Co., 1899. 334 p. D. cl. .... 1.50 .98

A series of essays.

Contents: Monroe doctrine; Third-term tradition; Political depravity of the fathers; Riotous career of the Know-Nothings; Framers and the framing of the constitution; Washington's inauguration; Century of constitutional interpretation; Century's struggle for silver; Is sound finance possible under popular government? Franklin in France; How the British left New York; Struggle for territory; Four centuries of progress.

J
M 29 jo

#741. **Journal of the Constitutional Convention.** James Madison. *Ed.* by E. H. Scott. Chic., Scott, Foresman & Co., 1898. 805 p. O. cl. 2.50 2.25

Valuable for reference in an extended study of United States history and government. This volume should only be purchased by the largest libraries.

J
P 18 ne

742. **New parliamentary manual:** a guide for deliberative bodies, and a text-book for high schools and colleges. Edmond Palmer. N. Y., Hinds & Noble, ©1901. 276 p. T. cl. .... .75 .50

Contents: Parliamentary questions answered at a glance; Nature and authority of parliamentary law; Assemblies and their organization; Introduction and consideration of business; Disposal of business; Incidental questions that may grow out of preceding motions; Privileged questions; Consideration anew of business already disposed of; Conduct of business within committee and upon committee's report; Vote and voting; Duties of officers; Miscellaneous matters.

J
R 27 wo
‡743. **World politics at the end of the nineteenth century:** as influenced by the oriental situation. Paul S. Reinsch. N. Y., Macmillan Co., 1902. 366 p. map. (Citizen's library series.) D. cl. 1.25 1.12

"The plan of the book is as follows: the first part is an introduction, and gives a general view of the forces at work, covering the various elements of intellectual and economic life that influence modern politics. The second part treats of what the author considers the true center of interest in present international politics—namely: the Chinese question; the consequences of the Chinese situation on European politics are traced in part third. The part devoted to German imperial politics presents the well-considered policy of a great empire, while in the last part some considerations upon the position of the United States as a world-power are given. The whole material of the book is focussed upon the Chinese problem. The documents and works upon which the author bases his conclusions are cited at the end of each part. Author is assistant professor of political science in the University of Wisconsin."

A book for the use of the teacher in politics and government.

Contents: National imperialism; Opening of China; Consequences of the opening of China in world politics; German imperial politics; Some considerations on the position of the United States as a factor in oriental politics.

J
W 68 ri
744. [644.] **Rights and duties of American citizenship.** Westel Woodbury Willoughby. N. Y., American Book Company, 1898. 236 p. D. cl. .... 1.00 .85

Practical information as to the rights and duties of American citizenship. The book is divided into two parts. The first is devoted to a general introduction to the practical science, the second to a description of civil government in the United States.

J
W 69 st
745. [642.] **State:** elements of historical and practical politics. Woodrow Wilson. Bost., D. C. Heath & Co., 1899. 656 p. O. cl. 2.00 1.80

A general study of the subject of government. Valuable for reference both in history and civics.

202 LIST OF BOOKS FOR HIGH SCHOOL LIBRARIES.

	List price.	Price to schools.

J
Yo 8 go
746. **Government class book:** a manual of instruction in the principles of constitutional government and law. Andrew W. Young. Thoroughly rev., 1894, by S. S. Clark. Wisconsin ed., with supplement: Wisconsin—its state and local government with the constitution as amended, by A. J. Hutton. N. Y., Maynard, Merrill & Co., 1900. 380 p. D. cl. .... 1.05 .95

"The aim of this book, in supplying a manifest want, is to present, in such form as to be used chiefly as a text-book for schools, a broad and comprehensive view of the principles of government and law in the United States."—*Preface.*

LEGISLATION, LAW, WOMEN.

K
As 3 bu
747. [708.] **Business girl in every phase of her life.** Ruth Ashmore. N. Y., Doubleday & McClure Co., 1898. 177 p. T. cl. .... .50 .33

Helpful and good advice for girls.

K
B 89 es
748. **Essentials of business law.** Francis M. Burdick. N. Y., D. Appleton & Co., 1902. 285 p. (Twentieth century text-books.) D. cl. 1.25 1.12

A concise treatment of those principles of law which the ordinary individual is liable to meet with in his daily contact with the world. A strong book for the commercial department, and one needed for reference in connection with the study of civics in any high school.

K
C 15 wo
749. [632.] **Women wage-earners:** their past, their present, and their future. Helen Campbell. Bost., Little, Brown & Co., 1893. 313 p. D. cl. ..... 1.00 .85

Interesting and valuable.

K
C 71 ge
750. **General principles of constitutional law in the United States of America.** Thomas M. Cooley. Ed. 3, by Andrew C. McLaughlin. Bost., Little, Brown & Co., 1898. 423 p. D. cl. 2.50 2.25

"This manual has been prepared for the use of students in law schools and other institutions of learning. The design has been

                                                             List Price to
                                                             price. schools.
to present succinctly the general principles of constitutional law,
whether they pertain to the federal system, or to the state system,
or to both."—*Preface.*

This will be of value in the High school for reference only.

Contents: Constitution of the United States; Rise of the American union; Definitions and general principles; Distribution of the powers of government; Powers of congress; Powers of the federal executive; Judicial department of the federal government; Checks and balances in government; Government of the territories; Admission of new states; Constitutional rules of state comity; Guaranty of republican government to the states; Amendments to the constitution; Civil rights and their guaranties; Political privileges and their protections; Protections to persons accused of crime; Protections to contracts and property; Municipal corporations; Formation and construction of state constitutions.

K
———
D 66 wh
751. [707.] **What women can earn:** occupations of women
     and their compensation. Grace Hoadley Dodge.
     N. Y., F. A. Stokes Co., 1899. 354 p. D. cl. ... 1.00   .65

Essays on all the leading trades and professions and facts as to compensation in each.

K
———
H 24 we
752. [709.] **Well-bred girl in society.** *Mrs.* Burton Harrison. N. Y., Doubleday & McClure Co., 1898. 213
     p. por. T. cl. 50   .33

Good sound advice for girls on dress and ornaments, her behavior in public places, and the small courtesies of her social life.

SCIENCE.

GENERAL SUGGESTIONS ON SCIENCE TEACHING.

Science in the high school is designed primarily for the purpose of getting simple information from text books and by observing phenomena; later the purpose is toward classification, so as to lead pupils toward possible inductions, and to confidence in themselves that shall in turn profoundly stimulate their activities. The discipline gained by having (a) a definite aim, (b) a definite method to accomplish this aim, (c) the power of careful and accurate observation, (d) the ability to reach correct conclusions, is important. The extremes of these purposes are found: (1) In the instruction which attempts to teach mere text-book, without the assistance of a suitable laboratory or sufficient apparatus. This is manifestly a most serious mistake, and no instructor should attempt the teaching of a scientific subject unless the school has a proper room or place to carry on experimental work and can provide itself with a suitable amount of apparatus to make the subject practical. (2) In those schools in which the pure laboratory method is followed. Here the text-book is abandoned and pupils are set at work to rediscover all the laws and reaffirm too many of the principles that have concerned the scientists of past ages. It is unfortunate that in many high schools the teaching force is inadequate to give careful supervision to laboratory work, for without efficient supervision such work is likely to be worse than useless. Whatever laboratory work is done should be under the close supervision of a competent instructor. The high school laboratory is no place for a pupil teacher.

The instructor in science should undertake to strike the golden mean between these extremes. The text-book is a valuable adjunct to the study of science and its utility should be fully appreciated. Each subject under consideration should first be thoroughly studied in the text to gain all the possible knowledge concerning the details which have been worked out by others; with this knowledge as a basis the teacher should direct experiments which are intended to confirm the statements of the text,—returning to the text after the experimental work has been performed, with a view of clinching the principles under consideration.

Economy in experiment is a feature of science teaching which the instructor must study with care. Schools may waste time in permitting the pupils to spend days in proving phenomena that are already familiar,—as that heat expands and cold contracts. One or two experiments, supplemented by the common-sense which most American children possess, is sufficient to demonstrate the truth of the law. Every science teacher should plan the entire work for the period of its continuance, before he begins his teaching, blocking out the amount of time which he can allow to each phase of the study. As he proceeds, he should keep strictly within the limits established. The simple principles should be passed over somewhat rapidly, allowing more time for the demonstration of the more difficult problems.

So far as possible the pupils themselves should do the actual experimental work. They should handle the material. The instructor will find, however, that some independent supplementary experiments and illustrations will be profitable.

Too much importance cannot be attached to drawings in connection with all laboratory work. It is not necessary that the pupil be an artist in order to outline in the note book a representation of the apparatus or material used. The instructor should see that each drawing, though not artistic, is accurate in outline and details.

Physics and botany furnish the best opportunities for thorough science teaching. They are practical subjects, having an intimate relation to our every-day life. Providing a suitable laboratory and sufficient apparatus as aids, is no great burden for school districts. Physiology and physical geography are likewise practical subjects. No special laboratory is required, however; the apparatus used in physics and botany can be employed in these branches.

Psychology is worthy of students' attention, and pedagogy, though chiefly beneficial to the prospective teacher, gives information which every intelligent citizen should possess.

SUGGESTIONS.

The field of original investigation is beyond the high school student; it belongs to the college post-graduate.

Experiments for display and entertainment are appropriate for evening shows, but are not productive of the best results for the student of science.

Laboratories should be provided with suitable tables and blackboards. They should be well lighted and provided with means for darkening the windows.

The pupils can, under the direction of the teacher, make much simple but useful apparatus outside of school hours. The caution here is, however, to employ the pupils as students of science, not as carpenters and blacksmiths.

REFERENCE BOOKS.

The aim has been to select a few good reference books, and books in the various divisions of science which are written in such a way as to interest the pupils.

When possible, all reading in these books should be accompanied by observation and experimentation. Teacher and pupils must read many of them together.

GENERAL SCIENCE.

	List price.	Price to schools.

L
———
B 85 fa
753. [500.] **Fairy-land of science.** Arabella B. Buckley. N. Y., D. Appleton & Co., 1899. 252 p. il. D. cl.   1.50   .98

The original volume has been extended, and notices of the latest scientific discoveries added. Will interest younger pupils.

L
———
G 79 na
754. **Nature's miracles:** familiar talks on science. Vol. I, World-building and life, earth, air, and water; Vol. II, Energy and vibration, energy, sound, heat, light, explosives; Vol. III, Electricity and magnetism. Elisha Gray. N. Y., Fords, Howard & Hulbert, ℗1900. 3 vols. S. cl. set 1.80   1.35

Three very interesting volumes: suitable as references to the general texts used by secondary pupils. They are excellent supplementary books. The mode of treatment of each volume is exceptionally strong.

L
———
J 13 na
755. **Nature study:** for the common schools. Wilbur S. Jackman. N. Y., Henry Holt & Co., 1894. 448 p. Ed. 2, *rev.* D. cl. 1.20   1.08

"In the preparation of this book it has been the aim to furnish a guide for teachers in the common schools who wish their pupils to pursue an adequate and symmetrical course in Natural Science."—*Preface.*

PHYSICS.

The first element of success in teaching physics is to *interest* the members of the class in the subject. It is a comparatively easy matter to accomplish this end, owing to the fact that this branch deals with matters of every-day observation, such as light, heat, sound, motion, electricity, etc. Owing to this fact, illustrations in every department of physics may be drawn from daily experiences. Moreover, many of the principles of physics can be readily demonstrated so that students may see the beauties which exist in the phenomena of nature. When their interest is thoroughly aroused, even the obscure parts of the subject acquire a new meaning through their connection with the parts which are more easily understood.

A demonstration of a principle in physics fixes it in the student's mind so that in recalling an experiment which he has seen he will not fail to grasp the principle which that experiment illustrates. No other science lends itself to exhibitition more easily than physics, and there are few of its principles which cannot be illustrated before a class. In all cases it should be pointed out that the law of nature operates whenever the operator supplies the necessary conditions, and it is the object of the experiment, and, indeed, the object of the study of physics to observe and to study the laws of the universe.

The teacher should remember that the pupil is not likely to grasp a subject at first presentation, and that it must be approached from many sides and with many illustrations. Even then a student does not fully comprehend the subject till he himself has dealt with it, and therefore it is desirable that students not only repeat the experiments shown by the instructor, but that others be devised, tending to make clearer the principle. This should be done by the class in small sections, if the class be large, and not during the hour of recitation. Whatever subjects are studied, the experiments which the students themselves perform should not be undertaken in the laboratory until after the corresponding subjects have been studied in some good text-book and thoroughly discussed and illustrated in class. In other words, the laboratory practice in any department of physics should follow and not precede the work of the text. Moreover, there should not be assigned to the student in the laboratory any experiment which does not illustrate some important scientific principle. The students should record all results and conclusions in a neatly kept notebook, which the teacher shoud read and correct.

The following plan of note-book may be suggestive:

I. *Aim.*—What is the object of the experiment; what do you expect to prove or determine?

II. *Method.*—Give briefly the details of the apparatus and the preparation made to perform the experiment.

III. *Observation.*—As a result of your experiment, note carefully what you see.

IV. *Conclusion.*—As a result of your observations, what conclusions do you reach?

A certain amount of equipment and apparatus is required for the experimental part of the instruction. While much of this must be purchased outright, much more may be extemporized by the ingenuity of the instructor and the students. In choosing the apparatus for a school whose appropriations must remain small, such pieces should be selected as are capable of being used for a variety of purposes.

Lh
———
Ad 1 pb

List Price to
price. schools.

756. **Physical laboratory manual**: for secondary schools and colleges. Charles F. Adams. Chic., Werner School Book Co., c1896. 183 p. il. D. cl. 75   .68

This book is an excellent manual for High school students. It is a book that will stimulate thought and endeavor. The experiments are few and well selected. Valuable and explicit directions to students are given.

		List	Price to
		price.	schools.

Lh

Am 3 th

757. [536.] **Theory of physics.** Joseph S. Ames. N. Y., American Book Company, 1897. 513 p. il. O. cl. 1.60   1.36

Especial prominence is given to mechanics. This book is a good reference book for the use of the teacher but is too advanced for the average High school student.

Lh

At 5 el

758. [529.] **Electricity for everybody:** its nature and uses explained. Philip Atkinson. N. Y., Century Co., 1899. 266 p. il. D. cl. ....   1.50   .98

This volume is devoted entirely to the subject of electricity and its uses. An excellent book for reference. All electrical apparatus of modern design and use are given and described.

Contents: Nature of electricity and electric transmission; Static electricity; Electric batteries; Magnetism; Dynamos; Electric motors; Electric lighting; Heat and electricity; Telegraph and telephone; Röntgen X-Rays.

Lh

At 5 na

759. **Natural philosophy:** for general readers, and young people. Edmund Atkinson. 9th ed., carefully *rev.* by A. W. Reinold. N. Y., Longmans, Green & Co., 1900. 752 p. il. D. cl. 2.50   1.64

This is a valuable reference book on scientific literature. The physical phenomena are clearly and concisely explained in familiar language. It is a book well suited for direct teaching purposes; and contains many excellent diagrams. The work has been recently and carefully revised.

Lh

Av 3 fi

760. **First lessons in physical science:** for use in grammar schools. Elroy M. Avery, *and* Charles P. Sinnott. N. Y., Sheldon & Co., c1897. 160 p. il. D. cl..   .60   .54

Suitable for elementary work. Excellent for use in the eighth grade. The special features of the book are, the experiments may be performed with very simple and inexpensive apparatus; they are illustrative of fundamental principles; they are interesting to the pupils because they are new to them; while most of them are qualitative, and, therefore, better adapted to the abilities and uses of the pupils, enough of them are quantitative to furnish needed training in that line.

	List price.	Price to schools.

Lh
Av 3 sc

761. **School physics:** a new text-book for high schools and academies. Elroy M. Avery. N. Y., Sheldon & Co., c1895. 608 p. il. D. cl. 1.25 1.12

A good text, containing many practical illustrations and experiments. It is well and interestingly written, and has given excellent satisfaction wherever used.

Lh
B 24 ph

762. **Physics:** advanced course. George F. Barker. N. Y., Henry Holt & Co., 1893. 902 p. il. Ed. 4, rev. O. cl. 3.50 3.15

A very good reference book for High school teachers and pupils. A splendid supplement to an elementary text. This book is well recommended by those who have used it.

Lh
B 24 ro

#763. **Röentgen rays:** memoirs by Röentgen, Stokes and J. J. Thomson. George F. Barker, ed. N. Y., American Book Company, 1899. 76 p. (Harper's scientific memoirs.) O. cl. .... .60 .51

This little book is one of the most exhaustive treatises on the subject. The most important researches are here given. The book is good authority.

Lh
C 19 ph

764. **Physics for high school students.** Henry S. Carhart, *and* Horatio N. Chute. Bost., Allyn & Bacon, 1902. 433 p. il. D. cl. 1.25 1.12

A distinctively new book: with a new order in the arrangement of sub-divisions. No laboratory exercises are given in this book. The author believes in separate class room and laboratory books.

Lh
C 47 ph

765. **Physical laboratory manual:** for schools and colleges. Horatio N. Chute. Bost., D. C. Heath & Co., 1902. 218 p. il. D. cl. .... .80 .68

This manual is well adapted for students of secondary schools. The work is largely quantitative in character; and is judiciously distributed over the several divisions of physics.

The author has taken special pains to select problems that could be solved by aid of simple and inexpensive apparatus.

Lh
C 54 pr

	List price.	Price to schools.

766. [535.] **Practical methods in microscopy.** Charles H. Clark. Bost., D. C. Heath & Co., 1896. 261 p. il. D. cl. 1.60   1.44

This book gives in simple and concise language, detailed directions for many processes that the student must learn in order to make practical use of the microscope. For reference.

Lh
C 64 wo

767. [527.] **Wonders of modern mechanism:** a resumé of recent progress in mechanical, physical and engineering science. Charles Henry Cochrane. Phil., J. B. Lippincott Co., 1896. il. O. cl. .... 1.50   .93

The book contains in popular language the results obtained within recent years by engineering and mechanical science.

Lh
C 77 ph

768. **Physics:** the student's manual for the study room and laboratory. LeRoy C. Cooley. N. Y., American Book Company, c1897. 448 p. il. D. cl. ... 1.00   .85

This book contains a plain, logical and very accurate outline of the various phases of physics. The amount of descriptive material on the purely illustrative work is limited. The prominent feature of this book is the amount of material for systematic quantitative study. The work is clear and concise.

Lh
C 86 el

769. **Elements of physics:** for use in high schools. Henry Crew. N. Y., Macmillan Co., 1899. 347 p. il. D. cl. .... 1.10   .99

This volume is intended for use in connection with a course of laboratory instruction. An excellent elementary book.

Lh
D 68 te

770. [533.] **Telephone:** an account of the phenomena of electricity, magnetism, and sound, as involved in its action; with directions for making a speaking telephone. Amos Emerson Dolbear. Bost., Lee & Shepard, c1877. il. T. cl. .... .50   .33

A very interesting, plain, and intelligible volume on the phenomena of electricity, magnetism, and sound. A valuable reference and a good supplement to these subjects as given in the regular text-books in physics.

Lh
———
G 12 pr

List Price to
price. schools.

771. **Principles of physics.** Alfred P. Gage. Bost., Ginn
& Co., 1901. 638 p. il. D. cl. 1.30   1.10

A splendid work for reference for the teacher. A good text for mature students in High schools, well equipped.

"The work contains two courses—one which is termed a *High school course*, and the other *an advanced course*. The former is printed in larger type; the latter comprises the former and additional matter printed in smaller type, which is *indented* about one-fourth of an inch at the left margin of the page. The former embraces a full course for those High schools and academies which are able to do a fairly good work. While the advanced course does not aspire to meet the requirements of a technical scientific course in the higher institutions, yet it is believed that, supplemented by lectures, as all text-books should be in the higher institutions, it may meet the requirements of the so-called *classical courses* in many colleges."—*Preface.*

Lh
———
H 14 te

772. **Text-book of physics:** largely experimental. Including the Harvard college "Descriptive List of Elementary Exercises in Physics." Edwin H. Hall, *and* Joseph Y. Bergen. N. Y., Henry Holt & Co., 1899. 596 p. il. *rev.* and *enl.* D. cl. 1.25   1.12

This book is a text-book and laboratory manual combined. The work is based on the requirements in elementary experimental physics for admission to Harvard college and the Lawrence Scientific school.

Lh
———
H 38 el

773. **Elements of physics.** C. Hanford Henderson, *and* John F. Woodhull. N. Y., D. Appleton & Co., 1901. 112 p. (Twentieth century text-books.) il. D. cl. .... 1.10   .99

A book well adapted to the age and attainments of High school pupils. Intensely interesting to students. Introduces the humanistic element. Laboratory work has been excluded, the authors preferring to devote a whole volume to this part of the study, which is published under the title of "Physical Experiments."

Lh
———
H 65 br

774. **Brief course in general physics:** experimental and applied. George A. Hoadley. N. Y., American Book Company., c1900. 463 p. il. D. cl. 1.20   1.02

A practical book. The subjects are presented in a logical manner. The book contains many questions and problems on the appli-

| | List price. | Price to schools. |

cation of stated laws. The numerical answers to these problems are given in the back of the book. Especial stress is put upon the subject of mechanical principles.

Lh

H 73 st
#775. **Steam engine.** George C. V. Holmes. N. Y., Longmans, Green & Co., 1900. 528 p. il. S. Ed. 11. cl. 2.00 1.30

An elementary, yet very complete and satisfactory treatise on the steam engine. An excellent supplement to regular text-books of Physics. Subject matter easy to understand.

Contents: Introduction; Nature of heat: the mode of measuring it, its effects on gases and water; Theoretically perfect heat engines; Connection between the size of an engine, the evaporative power of the boiler, and the external work which it can do; Mechanics of the steam engine; Mechanism and details of steam engines; Valves and valve gears; Indicators and indicator diagrams; Fuel—combustion—generation of steam boilers and their fittings; Condensation and condensers; On some of the principal causes of loss of efficiency in steam engines, and the methods employed for reducing the loss—super-heating—steam jacketing—compounding.

Lh

H 77 ex
776. [525.] **Experimental science.** George M. Hopkins. N. Y., Munn & Co., 1898. 914 p. il. O. cl. 5.00 3.75

A collection of experiments and descriptions of mechanical devices illustrating the principles of Physics. Most of the apparatus described can be constructed by anyone having ordinary mechanical skill and the simple devices for physical demonstration can be easily made. One of the best books on the subject.

Lh

H 77 pr
777. **Preparatory physics:** a short course in the laboratory. William J. Hopkins. N. Y., Longmans, Green & Co., 1894. 147 p. il. O. cl. .... 1.25 .82

This manual is intended primarily as a preparation for advanced work in general physics. The author does not attempt to cover the whole ground of physics. The subject of Mechanics has been selected for fullest treatment. Comparatively simple apparatus is required.

Contents: Physical measurement; Discussion of observations upon related quantities—plotting curves; Instruction for notebooks; Mensuration; Composition of forces; Parallel forces; Center of gravity; Levers and pulleys; Breaking strength of a wire; Deflection of beams; Trusses; Inclined plane—friction—work and energy; Composition of motions—velocity—acceleration; Pendulum; Fluid pressure; Density; Specific gravity; Gases—barometer—pumps; Heat; Sound—vibrations of strings; Light—photometry: reflection and refraction; Magnetism; Appendix.

Lh

H 77 te

778. **Telephone lines and their properties.** William J. Hopkins. N. Y., Longmans, Green & Co., 1901. 307 p. il. D. cl. .... 1.50 .98

    The book gives a very full and complete treatment of the subject. It contains an account of the latest developments of the telephone; and gives an outline of the methods of design and construction. It also contains many diagrams and half-tone reproductions of photographs.

    Contents: Design and construction of city lines; Underground work; Long distance lines; Wire; Insulators; Exchanges; Switchboards; Propagation of energy; Telephone current; Measurement; Properties of city lines; Interferences from outside sources; Properties of metallic circuits; Cables; "Composite" working and wireless telephony.

Lh

Il 3 fl

779. [528.] **Flame, electricity, and the camera:** man's progress from the first kindling of fire to the wireless telegraph and the photography of color. George Iles. N. Y., Doubleday & McClure Co., 1900. 398 p. il. O. cl. 2.00 1.80

    The chief uses of fire, electricity, and photography, bringing the narrative of discovery and invention to the close of 1899.
    A fascinating book.

Lh

J 12 el

780. **Elementary book on electricity and magnetism and their applications:** a text-book for manual training schools and high schools, and a manual for artisans, apprentices, and home readers. Dugald C. Jackson, *and* John Price Jackson. N. Y., Macmillan Co., 1902. 482 p. il. D. cl. 1.40 1.26

    A very good elementary text-book; it is also interesting to all readers who have a taste for sciences.
    This book is full of inspiration. The order is from the simple to the complex. It is built upon the common experiences of pupils.

Lh

M 45 th

781. **Theory of heat.** James Clerk Maxwell. With corrections and additions by Lord Rayleigh. N. Y., Longmans, Green & Co., 1897. 348 p il. S. cl. 1.50 .98

    A standard book for reference.

	List price.	Price to schools

Lh
M 46 ae
782. [531.] **A. B. C. of electricity.** W. H. Meadowcroft. N. Y., American Technical Book Co., 1896. il. D. cl. .... .50 .35

Lh
M 46 ax
783. [532.] **A. B. C. of the X-ray.** W. H Meadowcroft. N. Y., American Technical Book Co., 1896. il. D. cl. .... .75 .55

The elements of electricity.

Lh
M 92 st
784. [530.] **Story of electricity.** John Munro. N. Y., D. Appleton & Co., 1896. 187 p. il. S. (Library of useful stories.) cl. .... .40 .32

A small and interesting book giving a brief exposition of the subject and descriptions of inventions.

Lh
N 51 ou
785. **Outlines of physics: an elementary text-book.** Edward L. Nichols. N. Y., Macmillan Co., 1898. 452 p. il. D. cl. 1.40 1.26

This book is built up on the laboratory method and the experiments are largely quantitative. The experiments are well selected and calculated to illustrate all of the important principles of physics. This book is adapted to schools having only moderate equipment.

Lh
Sh 1 ph
786. **Physics by experiment: an elementary text-book for the use of schools.** Edward R. Shaw. N. Y., Maynard, Merrill & Co., 1901. 328 p. il. D. cl. 1.05 .95

A book suitable for elementary work, excellent for eighth grade students. It appeals to the student and teacher interested in manual training for pupils of this age.

"This book is intended to lead pupils to acquire, by means of experiments, an elementary knowledge of physics. It seeks to bring directly under the pupil's observation the reality itself, thus training him to observe for himself, to reason for himself, to rely upon himself, and to test the accuracy of his inferences and observations by new experiments, and by the comparison of his work with the work of others."—*Preface.*

		List price.	Price to schools.

Lh
Sm 6 ea

787. **Easy experiments in physics.** Preston Smith. N. Y., Morse Co., 1901. 217 p. (New century series.) il. D. cl. .... .60 .54

This volume is intended for use in the intermediate and grammar grades. The experiments are quautitative. The book is a preparation for scientific work in the high school.

Lh
St 4 le

788. **Lessons in elementary physics.** Balfour Stewart. N. Y., Macmillan Co., 1895. 475 p. maps and il. *New* and *enl. ed.* S. cl. .... 1.10 .99

An excellent book for reference, subjects well arranged. The work is elementary, yet very complete.

By the careful arrangement of topics the student is continually reminded of the importance of subject.

Lh
T 37 el

789. **Elementary lessons in electricity and magnetism.** Silvanus P. Thompson. N. Y., Macmillan Co., 1901. 638 p. il. D. *New ed. rev.* cl. 1.40 1.26

One of the best books on this subject. It treats of every part of the phenomena of electricity and magnetism and is a book that can be easily understood by any general reader of moderate intelligence as well as by High school pupils.

Lh
T 37 li

790. **Light, visible and invisible:** a series of lectures delivered at the Royal Institution of Great Britain at Christmas, 1896. Silvanus P. Thompson. N. Y., Macmillan Co., 1897. 294 p. il. D. cl. .... 1.50 .98

The language used is simple and can be easily understood by the average High school pupil and general reader.

Lh
T 42 el

791. **Elementary physics:** for secondary schools. Charles Burton Thwing. Bost., B. H. Sanborn & Co., 1900. 371 p. il. D. cl. 1.20 1.08

A good book: modern, scientifically accurate, and well adapted to schools having the usual equipment of apparatus. Not too difficult nor too profuse for high school pupils.

Lh
———
T 75 wh

	List price.	Price to schools.

792. **What is electricity?** John Trowbridge. N. Y., D. Appleton & Co., 1896. 315 p. il. (International scientific series.) D. cl. .... 1.50 .98

A popular treatise. It points out the present direction of investigation. Technical, yet interesting.

Contents: Standpoint of physicists; Measurements in electricity; Magnetism; Electric current; Flow of electricity in the earth; Voltaic cell; Galvanometer; Dynamo machine; Sources of electric power; Transformations of energy; Alternating currents; Transmission of power by electricity; Self-induction; Leyden jar; Step-up transformers; Lighting; Wave motion; Electric waves; Electro-magnetic theory of light and the ether; X rays; Sun; What is electricity?

Lh
———
T 83 el

793. **Electricity in modern life.** G. W. de Tunzelmann. N. Y., C: Scribner's Sons, 1896. 272 p. il. (Contemporary science series.) D. cl. 1.50 1.35

This book is intended for general reading for those who have no previous knowledge of electricity. There are many and excellent skeleton diagrams of apparatus to be found in it. A very interesting volume.

Contents: What we know about electricity; What we know about magnetism; Mutual actions between magnets and conductors traversed by electric currents; Force, work, and power; Sources of electricity; Magnetic fields; Electrical measurement; Magneto and dynamo electric machines; Story of the telegraph; Overland telegraphs; Submarine telegraphs; Telephone; Telephone exchange system; Distribution and storage of electrical energy; Electric lighting; Electro-motors and their uses; Electro-metallurgy; Electricity in warfare; Medical electricity; Miscellaneous applications of electricity.

Lh
———
W 59 co

#794. **Course of experiments in physical measurement.** In four parts, complete in one volume for the use of teachers and students. Harold Whiting. Bost., D. C. Heath & Co., 1897. 1226 p. il. O. cl. 3.75 3.19

A volume for use by teachers and an excellent work for reference.

Purely experimental. Not too difficult for advanced students. This should not be purchased by schools until they have a fair working library of more elementary books.

CHEMISTRY.

Lo
―――
C 54 el

                                                                                         List Price to
                                                                                        price. schools.

795. **Elementary chemistry.** F. W. Clark, *and* L. M. Dennis. N. Y., American Book Company, c1902. 340 p. il. D. cl. .... 1.10   .94

    This book is well adapted to the needs of pupils of secondary schools. It is sufficiently full for those students to whom chemistry is only one factor in their education. It also serves as a good foundation for subsequent higher study for those who desire an advanced course in chemical science.

Lo
―――
C 54 la

796. **Laboratory manual: to accompany Clark and Dennis's elementary chemistry.** L. M. Dennis, *and* F. W. Clark. N. Y., American Book Company, c1902. 254 p. il. D. cl. .... .50   .42

    This manual is well adapted to aid and stimulate the development of pupils. Numerous illustrations are given of the apparatus actually to be used by the students. The experiments are largely quantitative and are based upon the requirements for college entrance examinations.

Lo
―――
F 22 co

797. **Course of six lectures on the chemical history of a candle: to which is added a lecture on platinum.** Michael Faraday. Edited by William Crookes. N. Y., Harper & Bros., 1899. 223 p. il. S. cl. .. .75   .49

    A course of six lectures. Well arranged and admirably planned to supplement a regular text book in chemistry on the subject of the Candle Flame.
    The work is scientifically accurate and intensely interesting.

Lo
―――
F 98 el

798. **Elementary chemistry, inorganic and organic: alternative course.** William S. Furneaux. N. Y., Longmans, Green & Co., 1900. 182 p. il. D. Ed. 8. cl. .... .80   .72

    A chemistry of Common Things—an elementary text for young students. A very interesting and practical book. Students enjoy reading it.

Lo
H 46 es

List Price to
price. schools.

799. **Essentials of chemistry: for secondary schools.** John C. Hessler, *and* Albert L. Smith. Bost., B. H. Sanborn & Co., c1902. 96 p. il. D. cl. .... 1.20· 1.08

An excellent text book, in three divisions: (1) the text proper; (2) the laboratory exercises; (3) the hand book. The text and the laboratory exercises are in one volume.

This book is planned to meet the limitations of secondary schools, both as to equipment and time given to the subject. The experiments are chiefly qualitative.

Lo
J 64 ch

800. [523.] **Chemistry of common life.** James F. W. Johnston. N. Y., D. Appleton & Co., 1879. 592 p. il. D. cl. 2.00 1.30

A popular exposition touching the daily life of man.

Lo
N 48 el

801. **Elementary inorganic chemistry.** G. S. Newth. N. Y., Longmans, Green & Co., 1902. 288 p. il. D. cl. .... .90 .81

A modern and up to date book, so planned and arranged as to lead pupils to *observe* and *think* for themselves. It is highly commended by those who have used it.

Lo
R 28 in

802. **Introduction to the study of chemistry.** Ira Remsen. N. Y., Henry Holt & Co., 1902. 460 p. il. (American science series—briefer course.) Ed. 6, rev., enl. D. cl. 1.12 1.91

This book has been recently revised by the author after years of experience. It is well arranged, very accurate, and up to date.

It is a book which is highly commended by teachers. The experiments have been carefully selected.

Lo
R 39 ch

803. **Chemistry of cooking and cleaning: a manual for housekeepers.** Ellen H. Richards, *and* S. Maria Elliott. Bost., Home Science Pub. Co., 1897. 158 p. Ed. 2, rev. S. cl. .... 1.00 .80

An interesting and very practical little volume for use in the home. It is a book that girls will enjoy. It answers the questions "How"? and "Why"? that are continually arising in the home.

Contents: Matter and its composition; Elementary chemistry; Starches, sugars, fats, their preparation as food; Nitrogenous con-

| | List price. | Price to schools. |

stituents; Flavors and condiments—diet; Dust; Dust mixtures (Grease and dust); Stains, spots, tarnish; Laundry; Chemicals for household use; Books of reference.

Lo
———
T 39 ou
#804. [521.] **Outlines of industrial chemistry:** a text-book for students. Frank Hall Thorp. N. Y., Macmillan Co., 1899. 541 p. D. cl. 3.50   3.15

For reference.

Lo
———
W 67 ch
805. [522.] **Chemistry of cookery.** W. Mattieu Williams. N. Y., D. Appleton & Co., 1899. 328 p. il. D. cl. .... 1.50   .98

A simple and readable account of this subject.

Lo
———
W 67 el
806. **Elements of chemistry.** Rufus P. Williams. Bost., Ginn & Co., 1901. 412 p. il. D. cl. .... 1.10   .94

In this book the subject matter has been accurately and clearly stated. It is a text that will interest the pupils and make the subject of chemistry fascinating.
One of the most satisfactory high school texts in use.

Lo
———
W 96 el
#807. **Elements of modern chemistry.** Charles Adolphe Wurtz. Ed. 6, rev., enl. by W. H. Greene, *and* H. F. Keller. Phil., J. B. Lippincott Co., 1900. 808 p. il. D. cl. 2.00   1.30

A valuable reference book, very complete, yet concise and exact. Excellent illustrations and experiments.

ASTRONOMY.

Lr
B 21 ea

#808. **Earth's beginning.** *Sir* Robert Stawell Ball. N. Y., D. Appleton & Co.,1902. 384 p. il. D. cl. ....   List price 1.80   Price to schools 1.62

A popular narrative of the evolution of the Earth, the planets and the sun from the fire-mist. The narration is made up of a series of lectures which were delivered to an audience of young people.

Contents: The problem stated; The fire-mist; Nebulæ—apparent and real; The heat of the sun; How the sun's heat is maintained; The history of the sun; The earth's beginning; Earthquakes and volcanoes; Spiral and planetary nebulæ; The unerring guide; Evolution of the solar system; Unity of material in the heavens and the earth; Objections to the nebular theory; The beginning of the nebula, etc.

Lr
B 21 st

809. **Starland:** being talks with young people about the wonders of the heavens. *Sir* Robert Stawell Ball. New, rev. ed. Bost., Ginn & Co., 1902. 402 p. il. D. cl. .... 1.00   .85

This is an excellent book for the Library reading class in Science.

Contents: Sun; Moon; Inner planets; Giant planets; Comets and shooting stars; Stars; How to name the stars.

Lr
B 34 pi

810. [514.] **Pith of astronomy.** Samuel G. Bayne. N. Y., Harper & Bros., 1898. 122 p. il. S. cl. ...... 1.00   .65

The latest facts and figures as developed by the giant telescopes. The book is written in a simple and concise way for those who know but little of astronomy, and will undoubtedly interest the students in that subject.

Lr
C 35 st

811. [520.] **Story of eclipses simply told for general readers.** George F. Chambers. N. Y., D. Appleton & Co., 1900. 222 p. il. S. (Library of useful stories.) cl. .... .40   .32

The subject is treated from the historical, as well as a scientific standpoint. Will interest older pupils.

| | List price. | Price to schools. |

Lr

C 73 te

812. **Text-book of astronomy.** George C. Comstock. N. Y., D. Appleton & Co., 1901. 391 p. il. D. (Twentieth century text-books.) cl. 1.30 1.17

An excellent reference book for high schools. Excellent for reference in Physical geography. It is not a compendium of astronomy or an outline course of popular reading in that science. It has been prepared as a text-book, and the author has purposely omitted from it much matter interesting as well as important to a complete view of the science, and has endeavored to concentrate attention upon those parts of the subject that possess special educational value.

Contents: Different kinds of measurement; Stars and their diurnal motion; Fixed and wandering stars; Celestial mechanics; Earth as a planet; Measurement of time; Eclipses; Instruments and the principles involved in their use; Moon; Sun; Planets; Comets and meteors; Fixed stars; Stars and nebulæ; Growth and decay.

Lr

H 71 el

813. **Elementary astronomy:** a beginner's text-book. Edward S. Holden. N. Y., Henry Holt & Co., 1899. 446 p. il. (American science series—elementary course.) D. cl. 1.20 1.08

This book is addressed especially to pupils who are studying Astronomy for the first time. Every High school library should contain at least one elementary reference book on the subject.

Lr

H 71 fa

814. [519.] **Family of the sun;** conversations with a child. Edward S. Holden. N. Y., D. Appleton & Co., 1899. 252 p. il. D. (Home reading books.) cl. .50 .45

This volume deals descriptively with the planets that form the family of the sun—with their appearances in the telescope, and the main conclusions that can be drawn from these appearances. The relation of the solar system to distant stellar systems is considered. The unity, as well as the variety of the solar system is exhibited. The book is for the younger pupils.

Lr

P 83 st

815. **Stars in song and legend.** Jermain G. Porter. Bost., Ginn & Co., 1901. 129 p. il. D. cl. .... .50 .43

The author has attempted in this book to present to his readers the legendary lore of the heavens, and by numerous poetical quotations, to show the close relation of the stars to the best and highest in literature. An interesting book for Library reading.

| | List price. | Price to schools. |

Lr
P 94 os
816. [517.] **Other suns than ours.** Richard A. Proctor. N. Y., Longmans, Green & Co., 1896. 419 p. il. D. (Silver lib.) cl. .... 1.25 .82

Lr
P 94 ow
817. [518.] **Other worlds than ours.** Richard A. Proctor. N. Y., Longmans, Green & Co., 1899. 318 p. il. D. (Silver lib.) cl. .... 1.25 .50

Two volumes covering the subject of astronomy, which will interest older pupils. Good books for reference.

Lr
Se 6 as
818. [515.] **Astronomy with an opera-glass.** Garrett P. Serviss. N. Y., D. Appleton & Co., 1895. 154 p. il. O. cl. .... 1.58 .98

"The author has endeavored to encourage the study of the heavenly bodies by pointing out some of the interesting and marvelous phenomena of the universe that are visible with little or no assistance from optical instruments, and indicating means of becoming acquainted with the constellations and the planets."

Lr
Sh 2 as
819. **Astronomy; for schools and general readers.** Isaac Sharpless, *and* George Morris Philips. Phil., J. B. Lippincott Co., c1892. 315 p. il. D. cl. .... 1.00 .65

A simple presentation of the subject of astronomy. An original feature of the work is the directions given for observations with the naked eye and with small telescopes.

Lr
T 56 ne
820. [516.] **New astronomy for beginners.** D. P. Todd. N. Y., American Book Company, 1898. 480 p. por. il. D. cl. 1.30 1.15

Of special value for reference. Shows how to study by observation, with simple instruments.

NATURAL HISTORY.

M

A1 5 fl
821. [512.] **Flashlights on nature.** Grant Allen. N. Y., Doubleday & McClure Co., 1898. 312 p. il. D. bds. .... 1.50 .98

List Price to price. schools.

Some of the unusual things in science are presented in this book. Contents: Cows that ants milk; plants that melt ice; a beast of prey (a spider); a woodland tragedy; marriage among the clovers; those horrid earwigs; the first paper-maker (wasp); abiding cities (ants); a frozen world; British bloodsuckers (mosquitoes); a very intelligent plant (gorse); foreign invasion of England (Prussian fly). An intensely interesting book.

M

G 35 ey
822. [503.] **Eye spy:** afield with nature among flowers and animate things. William Hamilton Gibson. N. Y., Harper & Bros., 1898. 264 p. il. O. cl. ... 2.50 1.64

M

G 35 my
823. [502.] **My studio neighbors.** William Hamilton Gibson. N. Y., Harper & Bros., 1898. 245 p. il. O. cl. 2.50 1.64

M

G 35 sh
824. [504.] **Sharp eyes.** William Hamilton Gibson. N. Y., Harper & Bros., 1898. 322 p. il. O. cl. 2.50 1.64

A rambler's observations during the four seasons.

These three books, well written and beautifully illustrated, will interest the pupils in nature and stimulate observation. Younger pupils will enjoy.

M

In 4 bo
825. [556.] **Book of the ocean.** Ernest Ingersoll. N. Y., Century Co., 1898. 279 p. il. O. cl. .... 1.50 .98

A very interesting book about the ocean, the life in the ocean, and some of the stirring events which have taken place on the ocean. For younger pupils.

M

H 66 na
826. **Nature study and life.** Clifton F. Hodge. Bost., Ginn & Co., 1902. 514 p. il. D. cl. 1.50 1.28

"For this book I have no hesitation in predicting a most wholesome, widespread, and immediate influence upon primary and gram-

15

mar school grades of education in this country. No one has gone so far toward solving the burning question of nature teaching, and to every instructor in these subjects this volume will be not only instructive but inspiring. Unlike the authors of most of the many nature-study manuals now current, Professor Hodge has been for some years the head of a University Department, is a specialist in two or more of the fields of biology, and has made original contributions of value to the sum of human knowledge. His mind thus moves with independence, authority, and unusual command of the resources in the field here treated.

This work is opportune because it stimulates spontaneous out-of-door interests. It is with abundant reason that we find now on every hand a growing fear of the effects of excessive confinement, sedentary attitudes, and institutionalizing influences in the school. Such work as is here described must tend to salutary progress in the direction of health."

Contents: Point of view; Values of nature study; Children's animals and pets; Plan for insect study; Insects of the household; Lessons with plants; Elementary botany; Garden-studies—home and school gardens; Nature-study property of children; Propagation of plants; Insects of the garden; Beneficial insects—honeybee; Insectivorous animals—common toad; Common frogs and salamanders; Common birds; Bird census and food chart; Practical domestication of our wild birds; Taming and feeding birds; Elementary forestry; Aquaria—their construction and management; Miscellaneous animals; Flowerless plants; Grade plan.

M

W 58 bo

827. **Boys' and girls' Pliny:** being parts of Pliny's "Natural History" edited for boys and girls, with an introduction. John S. White. N. Y., G. P. Putnam's Sons, 1885. 326 p. il. O. cl. 2.00 1.30

Contents: Dedication; Account of the world and the elements; Man, his birth and organization; Nature of terrestrial animals; Domestic animals; Natural history of fishes; Natural history of birds; Various kinds of insects; Natural history of metals; Conclusion.

GEOLOGY.

Mc

B 76 te

828. **Text-book of geology.** Albert Perry Brigham. N. Y., D. Appleton & Co., 1901. 10 + 477 p. il. O. (Twentieth century text-books.) cl. 1.40 1.26

An elementary treatise for secondary schools. The three parts are devoted to: Dynamical geology; Structural geology; and Historical geology.

Mc
———
D 19 ge
                List Price to
                price. schools.
829. **Geological story briefly told.** James D. Dana. N. Y., American Book Company, c1895. 302 p. il. D. Rev. ed. cl. .... 1.15 .98

  One of the best elementary books published on the subject of geology.

  Contents: Geology; Part I, Rocks or what the earth is made of—Minerals; Kinds of rocks; Structure of rocks; Part II, Geological causes and effect—Making of rocks; Making of valleys; Making of mountains and attendant effects.; Part III, Historical geology—Archaean time; Paleozoic time; Mesozoic time; Cenozoic time; Observations on geological history.

Mc
———
D 19 mi
830. [561.] **Minerals and how to study them:** a book for beginners in mineralogy. E. Salisbury Dana. N. Y., J. Wiley & Sons, 1895. 380 p. il. D. cl. .. 1.50 1.28

  Presents the subject in a clear and simple form. For reference.

Mc
———
D 19 re
831. [540.] **Revised text-book of geology.** James D. Dana, ed. by William North Rice. N. Y., American Book Company, 1897. 482 p. il. D. cl. 1.40 1.19

  An excellent book for reference.

Mc
———
D 29 el
832. **Elementary physical geography.** William Morris Davis. Bost., Ginn & Co., 1902. 401 p. il. and maps. D. cl. 1.25 1.06

  An excellent elementary text in physical geography, pronounced by many teachers who have made practical use of it one of the few best texts. The plan of the book is to give the problems of Physical geography a rational treatment. The ideas of cause and of consequence, one preceding, the other following, the physiographic fact, have therefore been held constantly in mind by the author. Well illustrated.

  Contents: Earth as a globe; Atmosphere; Ocean; Lands; Plains and plateaus; Mountains; Volcanoes; Rivers and valleys; Deserts and glaciers; Shore lines; Distribution of plants, animals, and man.

Mc
———
D 84 le
833. **Lessons in physical geography.** Charles R. Dryer. N. Y., American Book Co., c1901. 430 p. il. D. cl. 1.20 1.02

  No attempt is made to discuss all the physical features of the earth, or those of any special region. The best type forms are se-

| | List price. | Price to schools. |

lected and treated with sufficient fullness to give a clear and definite picture. From a study of the type general laws are developed, and the student is thus provided with a key for the solution of geographical problems wherever they may arise. Written with a view to the needs of the teacher as well as those of the student. Bibliography (9p.) Well illustrated.

Contents: Planet earth; Land; Sea; Atmosphere; Life.

Mc
―――
G 27 ea

834. [550.] **Earth sculpture or the origin of land-forms.** James Geikie. N. Y., G. P. Putnam's Sons, 1898. 397 p. il. O. (Science series.) cl. 2.00 1.30

A general account of the origin of surface features, and the development of land forms. Well written and interesting.

Mc
―――
G 83 co

835. [637.] **Coal and the coal mines.** Homer Greene. Bost., Houghton, Mifflin & Co., 1892. 246 p. il. S. cl. .... .75 .48

This book contains an excellent description of the industry, coal-mining. Will be helpful in economics, geography, and science.

Mc
―――
H 36 ea

836. **Earth and its story: a first book of geology.** Angelo Heilprin. N. Y., Silver, Burdett & Co., 1898. 267 p. il. D. cl. .... 1.00 .90

"An excellent elementary text book on geology and valuable for supplementary reading in study of Physical Geography. Entertaining as well as instructive. Deals in an interesting manner with structure of earth's surface and changes which are continually taking place in it. Profusely Illustrated by remarkably fine reproductions from photographs."—Prof. Burgess, Univ. of Wisconsin.

Mc
―――
H 87 vo

#837. **Volcanoes: past and present.** Edward Hull. N. Y., C: Scribner's Sons, 1892. 270 p. il. (Contemporary science series.) D. cl. .... 1.50 .98

A standard reference book.

Contents: Introduction; European volcanoes; Dormant or moribund volcanoes of other parts of the world; Tertiary volcanic districts of the British Isles; Pre-tertiary volcanic rocks; Special volcanic and seismic phenomena; Volcanic and seismic problems; Brief account of the principal varieties of volcanic rocks.

LIST OF BOOKS FOR HIGH SCHOOL LIBRARIES. 229

Mc
H 97 st
                   List Price to
                   price. schools.
838. **Story of the hills:** a book about mountains for general readers. *Rev.* H. N. Hutchinson. N. Y., Macmillan Co., 1895. 357 p. il. D. cl. .... 1.50 .98

 The author has interpreted in simple language the story of the hills as it is written in the rocks of which they are made. A very interesting presentation of the subject. An excellent book for Library reading.
 Contents: Mountains and men; Uses of mountains; Sunshine and storm on the mountains; Mountain plants and animals; How the materials were brought together; How the mountains were upheaved; How the mountains were carved out; Volcanic mountains; Mountain architecture; Ages of mountains and other questions.

Mc
J 88 vo
#839. **Volcanoes:** what they are and what they teach. John W. Judd. N. Y., D. Appleton & Co., 1895. 381 p. il. (International scientific series.) D. cl. 2.00 1.30

 Good for reference in physical geography.
 Contents: Introductory—Nature of the enquiry; Nature of volcanic action; Products of volcanic action; Distribution of the materials ejected from volcanic vents; Internal structure of volcanic mountains; Various structures built up around volcanic vents; Succession of operations taking place at volcanic centres; Distribution of volcanoes upon the surface of the globe; Volcanic action at different periods of the earth's history; Part played by volcanoes in the economy of nature; What volcanoes teach us concerning the nature of the earth's interior; Attempts which have been made to explain the causes of volcanic action.

Mc
L 49 co
840. [541.] **Compend of geology.** Jos. LeConte. N. Y., American Book Company, 1898. 426 p. D. cl... 1.20 1.02

 An excellent general work for the beginner.

Mc
L 49 el
#841. **Elements of geology:** a text-book for colleges, and for the general reader. Joseph Le Conte. N. Y., D. Appleton & Co., 1901. 670 p. il. O. Ed. 4, rev., enl. cl. 4.00 2.60

 An excellent reference book for the use of the teacher of geology in the High school.

230 LIST OF BOOKS FOR HIGH SCHOOL LIBRARIES.

	List price.	Price to schools.

Mc
―――
M 36 st
842. [560.] **Story of a piece of coal:** what it is, whence it comes, and whither it goes. Edward A. Martin. N. Y., D. Appleton & Co., 1898. 169 p. il. S. (Lib. of useful stories.) cl................ .40 .32

A clear, concise, and complete account of coal, and its uses.

Mc
―――
Sco 3 in
843. **Introduction to geology.** William B. Scott. N. Y., Macmillan Co., 1902. 573 p. il. O. cl......... 1.90 1.71

An excellent book for reference work.

"The book is intended to serve as an introduction to the science of Geology, both for students who desire to pursue the subject exhaustively, and also for the much larger class of those who wish merely to obtain an outline of the methods and principal results of the science."—*Preface.*

Contents: Dynamical geology; Structural geology; Physiographical geology; Historical geology.

Mc
―――
Se 3 st
844. [544.] **Story of the earth in past ages.** H. G. Seeley. N. Y., D. Appleton & Co., 1895. 186 p. il. S. (Lib. of useful stories.) cl.................. .40 .32

A brief and interesting account of the earth from the standpoint of geology.

Mc
―――
Sh 1 fi
845. **First book in geology:** designed for the use of beginners. Nathaniel Southgate Shaler. Bost., D. C. Heath & Co., 1899. 255 p. il. D. bds... .45 .39

For use in High schools and in eighth grades. This will be a good book for the Science section in Library reading.

Contents: Pebbles, sand, and clay; Making of rocks; Work of water and air; Depths of the earth; Irregularities of the earth; Origin of valleys and lakes; Movements of the earth's surface; Place of animated things in the world; Sketch of the earth's organic life; Nature and teaching of fossils; Origin of organic life; Brief account of the succession of events on the earth's surface; Crystalline rocks.

Mc
―――
T 17 el
846. [545.] **Elementary geology.** Ralph Stockman Tarr. N. Y., Macmillan & Co., 1897. 499 p. O. hf. leath. 1.40 1.26

A fine reference book.

LIST OF BOOKS FOR HIGH SCHOOL LIBRARIES. 231

	List	Price to
Mc V 28 de	price.	schools.

847. **Desert:** further studies in natural appearances. John C. Van Dyke. N. Y., C: Scribner's Sons, 1901. 233 p. D. cl. 1.25 1.12

The author of "Nature for its own sake" and "Art for art's sake" has been studying during the past two years the great Colorado-Mojave desert. He gives not only a complete picture of the desert, but a chronicle of the aesthetic and moral sensations awakened in this unique environment.

The book is an artist's description of natural phenomena and will be very interesting reading for the Library reading class in Science.

Contents: Approach; Make of the desert; Bottom of the bowl; Silent river; Light, air, and color; Desert sky and clouds; Illusions; Cactus and grease wood; Desert animals; Winged life; Mesas and foot-hills; Mountain barriers.

PHYSICAL GEOGRAPHY AND PHYSIOGRAPHY.

This is a branch of study that involves the elements of all the sciences. It is therefore necessary for the instructor before he begins the subject to ascertain what knowledge the pupils have of botany, physics, geology, astronomy, chemistry, etc. If they have had training in nature work and elementary science in the grades, the study of physical geography may not be found difficult.

In some instances it will be found necessary for the instructor to revert to some of the elementary principles of the sciences involved.

The aim of the teacher in physical geography should be to have the pupil acquire a knowledge of the relation of earth to man, which must necessarily involve a thorough study of the immediate environment of man.

After establishing a definite aim for each recitation, the teacher should carefully ascertain what things the pupil must know in order to realize this aim; what of these things *are now known*, and proceed accordingly with the instruction, teaching what remains to be known.

As text-books differ in the subject-matter treated, it is recommended that the study of physical geography shall include the following general considerations, consuming the time allotted to the subject in the high school:

1. The earth as a planet and its relation to the solar system.
2. A brief geological history of the earth with special reference to Wisconsin and the United States.
3. The land distribution and the relief of its various divisions,— volcanoes and earthquakes.
4. The water distribution, continental drainage, erosion, waves, tides, ocean currents, glaciers, and geysers.
5. The atmospheric movements and their causes, with a careful study of climate and its causes.

(If time permits, the following subjects may be pursued:)

6. The human race as distributed.
7. The animals and plants as distributed.
8. The economic products, including variety of soil, distribution and use of coal, ores, building stone, and natural gas.

The practical side of the subject should not be neglected. The rivers, creeks, lakes, hills, valleys, railroad-cuts, storms, the sky, day and night,—all furnish an opportunity for personal observation. The laboratory will probably furnish apparatus for demonstration.

Mg
—
Ar 2 st

	List price.	Price to schools.

848. [558.] **Story of the earth's atmosphere.** Douglas Archibald. N. Y., D. Appleton & Co., 1898. 194 p. il. S. (Lib. of useful stories.) cl............ .40   .32

This book is a brief account of the origin and heat of the atmosphere, its nature, composition, temperature, and general circulation. There are chapters on dew, fog and clouds, rain, snow and hail, cyclones, whirlwinds, water-spouts, tornadoes, etc.

Mg
—
B 64 ic

849. [555.] **Ice-work present and past.** T. G. Bonney. N. Y., D. Appleton & Co., 1896. 295 p. il. D. (International scientific series, no. 84.) cl...... 1.50   .98

Most interesting topics are: Glaciers past and present; Arctic and Ant-arctic ice-sheets; lake basins and their relation to glaciers;

ice work in various parts of the world; possible causes of glacial epoch; glacial deposits and general principles of interpretation.

Mg
B 64 vo

850. [549.] **Volcanoes:** their structure and significance. T. G. Bonney. N. Y., G. P. Putnam's Sons, 1899. 332 p. il. O. (Science series.) cl............ 2.00 1.30

"In writing this book I have endeavored to lead the reader through the discussions of varied phenomena of volcanic action in the present and in the past towards ascertaining by inference the cause or causes of eruptions.
Contents: Life history of volcanoes; the products of volcanoes; dissection of volcanoes; geological history of volcanoes; distribution of volcanoes; theories of volcanoes.

Mg
D 29 el

851. **Elementary meteorology.** William Morris Davis. Bost., Ginn & Co., 1899. 355 p. il. O. cl. 2.50 2.12

A valuable reference book for teachers and students of physical geography. This treatise is accurate, systematic, and complete.

Mg
D 66 re

852. **Reader in physical geography for beginners.** Richard Elwood Dodge. N. Y., Longmans, Green & Co., 1900. 237 p. il. D. cl. .... .70 .63

A very suggestive book bringing together the more important principles of Physical Geography in a form that can be used by beginners in the subject.
References: Centers of industry, 28-35; Agriculture, 36-40; Lumbering, 43-46; Erosion, 65-80, 101-4, 125-27; Volcanoes, 154-64; Mountains, 144-53; Weather, 171-75; Soils, 198-205; Commerce, 33-36; Tides, 111-13; Glaciers, 121-36; Climate, 171-197.

Mg
G 37 in

853. **Introduction to physical geography.** Grove Karl Gilbert, *and* Albert Perry Brigham. N. Y., D. Appleton & Co., 1902. 380 p. il. (Twentieth century text-book.) D. cl. 1.25 1.12

"The authors have striven to adapt this book to the earlier stages of the High school course. To this end the statements are simple, technical terms are sparingly used, and when employed they are promptly defined. Thus approached, physical geography may well serve to introduce young students to the spirit and method of science. The aim of this volume as set forth will explain the omis-

234   LIST OF BOOKS FOR HIGH SCHOOL LIBRARIES.

                                                             List Price to
                                                           price. schools.
sion of a few of the more difficult conceptions of land physiography which appear in some school texts.'—*Preface*.

The illustrations are closely correlated with the text and are a feature of the book which deserve special commendation.

Contents: Earth, Earth and the sun; Rivers; Weathering and soils; Wind work; Glaciers; Plains; Mountains and plateaus; Volcanoes; Atmosphere; Winds, storms and climate; Earth's magnetism; Ocean; Meeting of the land and sea; Life; Earth and man.

Mg
———
H 23 ab

854. [559.] **About the weather.** Mark W. Harrington. N. Y., D. Appleton & Co., 1899. 246 p. il. D. (Appleton's home reading books.) cl. .... .65 .58

A good elementary book for reference.

Mg
———
H 81 el

855. **Elements of physical geography:** for the use of schools, academies, and colleges. Edwin J. Houston. Philadelphia, Eldredge & Brother, 1901. 399 p. maps and il. O. ro. 1.25 1.12

This is a complete revision of the old Houston Physical geography. Its mechanical features have been greatly improved, especially in reducing the size to an octavo; the print is clear and the cuts will be found valuable additions to the text matter. A good elementary text.

Mg
———
H 98 ph

856. [543.] **Physiography:** an introduction to the study of nature. T. H. Huxley. N. Y., D. Appleton & Co., 1895. 384 p. map. il. D. cl. 2.50 1.64

A broad view of the general subject of physiography. Good for reference.

Mg
———
P 87 ph

857. [542.] **Physiography of the United States.** J. W. Powell and seven others. N. Y., American Book Company, 1897. 345 p. il. Q. cl. 2.50 2.10

One of the best books on the list. Will interest older pupils. Contents: Physiographic processes; physiographic features; physiographic regions of the United States; present and extinct lakes of Nevada; beaches and tidal marshes of the Atlantic coast; the northern Appalachians; Niagara Falls and their history; Mount Shasta a typical volcano; physical geography of southern New England; the southern Appalachians.

	List price.	Price to schools.

Mg
R 24 el
858. **Elementary physical geography:** an outline of physiography. Jacques W. Redway. N. Y., C: Scribner's Sons, 1901. 383 p. il. and maps. O. cl... 1.25 1.12

"In scope this book contains all the principles recommended by the Committee of Fifteen, and such other features as have suggested themselves to the author. It is designed to be used in the junior grades of the High school, and in Normal schools. The arrangement of the subjects is logical, but the teacher may readily organize a course of study in the subject without reference to the present arrangement.

Mg
R 91 gl
859. [554.] **Glaciers of North America.** Israel Cook Russell. Bost., Ginn & Co., 1897. 210 p. il. O. cl. 1.75 1.50

Older pupils will find very interesting.

Mg
R 91 la
860. [551.] **Lakes of North America.** Israel Cook Russell. Bost., Ginn & Co., 1895. 125 p. il. O. cl. 1.50 1.28

Lakes, like mountains and rivers, have life histories which exhibit varying stages from youth through maturity to old age. The tracing of the life histories of lakes, and the recognition of the numerous agencies that vary their lives, and lead to their death, gives to this branch of physiography one of its principal charms. The history of the lakes of North America is considered in their origin, movements of waters, changes they produce in the topography of their shores, their relations to climate, their geological functions, and their connection with plant and animal life. A very readable book.

Mg
R 91 ri
861. [552.] **Rivers of North America.** Israel Cook Russell. N. Y., G. P. Putnam's Sons, 1898. 327 p. il. O. (Science series.) cl. 2.00 1.30

A reading lesson for the students of geography and geology. Rivers and their work are treated of in this book in a most interesting way. "When once the idea is grasped that each and every one of the elements in a landscape has a history which can be read, and that the end is not yet, but still other transformations are to come, a desire is awakened for more knowledge concerning especially the work of streams, to which so many of the changes that have been made on the earth's surface, are due."

		List price.	Price to schools.

Mg
R 91 vo
862. [548.] **Volcanoes of North America.** Israel Cook Russell. N. Y., Macmillan Co., 1897. 346 p. O. cl. 4.00   2.60

Complete account of the subject for reference.

Mg
Sh 1 as
863. [547.] **Aspects of the earth.** Nathaniel Southgate Shaler. N. Y., C: Scribner's Sons, 1896. 344 p. il. O. cl.. 2.50   1.30

A well written and readable book. The greater part of the several books have already been printed in Scribner's magazine.
Contents: Stability of the earth; volcanoes; caverns and cavern life; rivers and valleys; instability of the atmosphere; forests of America; origin and nature of soils.

Mg
Sh 1 ou
864. [546.] **Outlines of the earth's history: a popular study in physiography.** Nathaniel Southgate Shaler. N. Y., D. Appleton & Co., 1898. 417 p. il. D. cl. 1.75   1.15

The object of this book is to provide the beginner in the study of the earth's history with a general account of those actions which can be readily understood, and which will afford a clear understanding as to the nature of the processes which have made this and other celestial spheres. It has been the writer's purpose to select those series of facts which serve to show the continuous operations of energy so that the reader might be helped to a clearer conception of the nature of this sphere than he can obtain from the ordinary text books.

Mg
T 17 el
865. [539.] **Elementary physical geography.** Ralph S. Tarr. N. Y., Macmillan Co., 1897. 488 p. il. D. half leath............................. 1.40   1.26

A good book of reference.

Mg
T 97 fo
866. [553.] **Forms of water in clouds and rivers, ice and glaciers.** John Tyndall. N. Y., D. Appleton & Co., 1897. 196 p. il. D. (International scientific series.) cl. .... 1.50   .98

One of the best books on the subject. Especially good on glaciers.

LIST OF BOOKS FOR HIGH SCHOOL LIBRARIES.   237

Mg
———
W 14 el
867. [557.] **Elementary** meteorology. Frank Waldo. N. Y., American Book Company, 1896. 373 p. il. D. cl. 1.50 1.28

    List Price to
    price. schools.

    This is a brief outline of the subject of meteorology for reference. Conditions of atmosphere and their probable explanations, and atmospheric movements, are discussed.

BIOLOGY.

Mv
———
C 62 pr
868. [566.] **Primer of evolution.** Edward Clodd. N. Y., Longmans, Green & Co., 1895. 186 p. il. S. cl. .75 .50

    The subject of evoluton in a nutshell. Brief, concise, and clear.

Mv
———
C 76 st
869. [565.] **Story of germ life.** H. W. Conn. N. Y., D. Appleton & Co., 1898. 199 p. il. S. (Lib. of useful stories.) cl. .... .40 .32

    A brief outline of the subject of bacteria, and their importance in the world, not only in causing disease, but as agents in other natural phenomena. Will open up a new field of interest to the pupils.

Mv
———
D 25 or
#870. **Origin of species by means of natural selection:** or the preservation of favored races in the struggle for life, with additions and corrections from sixth and last English edition. Charles Darwin. N. Y., D. Appleton & Co., 1902. 2 vol. in 1. O. cl..... 2.00 .50

    For reference for the teacher and advanced students in Biology.
    The author believes that Natural Selection has been the most important means of modification of the species and has made an effort in th's volume to give his readers a clear insight into the means of modification and co-adaptation.
    Contents: Introduction; Variation under domestication; Variation under nature; Struggle for existence; Natural selection; or, the survival of the fittest; Laws of variation; Difficulties of the theory; Miscellaneous objections to the theory of natural selection; instinct.

Mv

D 84 as

List Price to
price. schools.

871. **Lowell lectures on the ascent of man.** Henry Drummond. N. Y., James Pott & Co., 1902. 346 p. D. Ed. 12. cl. .... 1.00 .65

In these pages an attempt is made to tell in a plain way a few of the things which science is now seeing with regard to the Ascent of Man.

What science has to say about himself is of transcendent interest to man, and the practical bearings of this theme are coming to be more vital than any on the field of knowledge.

Contents: Evolution in general; Missing factor in current theories; Why was evolution the method chosen; Evolution and sociology; Ascent of the body; Scaffolding left in the body; Arrest of the body; Dawn of mind; Evolution of language; Struggle for life; Struggle for the life of others; Evolution of a mother; Evolution of a father; Involution.

Mv

F 54 ex

872. [568.] **Excursions of an evolutionist.** John Fiske. Bost., Houghton, Mifflin & Co., 1891. 379 p. D. cl. 2.00 1.30

For older pupils. Suitable for use in the advanced literature class as a book of essays.

Mv

J 76 fo

#873. [567.] **Foot-notes to evolution:** a series of popular addresses on the evolution of life; with supplementary essays by Edwin Grant Conklin, Frank Mace McFarland, and James Perrin Smith. David Starr Jordan. N. Y., D. Appleton & Co., 1898. 392 p. il. D. cl. 1.75 1.15

Excellent for reference for the teacher.

Contents: Kinship of life; Evolution: what it is and what it is not; Elements of organic evolution; Factors of evolution from the standpoint of embryology; Heredity of Richard Roe; Physical basis of heredity; Distribution of species; Latitude and vertebrae; Evolution of fossil cephalopoda; Evolution of the mind; Degeneration; Hereditary inefficiency; Woman of evolution and the woman of pessimism; Stability of truth; Struggle for realities.

Mv

M 82 li

874. **Life and love.** Margaret Warner Morley. Chic., A. C. McClurg & Co., 1899. 214 p. il. D. cl...... 1.25 .82

This is a book which should be read by every High school girl and boy. The author has handled the delicate topic of the development of life in a clean and fearless manner.

Contents: Introduction; First parents; Spirogyra; Division of labor; Fish life; Crustaceans; Metamorphosis of insects; Repro-

                                                              List   Price to
                                                              price. schools.
duction of insects: Flowers and insects; Plant life; Bird life;
Skin changes; Periodic activity; Mammal; Variability and inheritance; Nutrition and reproducton; Value of sexual reproduction; Individuality; Male and female; Maturity; Human life; Man and the community; Conclusion.

Mv

M 82 so
875. **Song of life.** Margaret Warner Morley. Chic., A. C.
    McClurg & Co., 1902. 155 p. il. D. cl......... 1.25   .82

Something of flower life, of fish life, of frogs and of birds, and of human life, form the subjects of this book. The author has a keen insight into Nature's secrets and has the ability to impart this secret to others in a graceful, simple manner.

This book is intended for the children of the grammar grades but contains much that will interest and instruct High school boys and girls.

Mv

P 64 la
876. [563.] **Laboratory guide for an elementary course in general biology.** J. H. Pillsbury. Bost., Silver, Burdett & Co., 1895. 176 p. D. cl. 60   .54

"A simple guide to a logical series of elementary studies of typical living organisms, of such nature as shall enable both teacher and student to accomplish the most desirable results." For reference.

Mv

W 69 in
877. [562.] **Introduction to general biology.** Edmund B.
    Wilson *and* W. T. Sedgwick. N. Y., Holt & Co.,
    1895. 231 p. O. (American science series.) cl. 1.75 1.58

For reference.

BOTANY.

The aim that should be insisted upon in the teaching of botany in the high school is purely a pedagogical one, namely, to make of the student to just the extent of the botany studied, a more perfect, more powerful man or woman. When the course is completed, the teacher should be able to recognize something definite and positive as having been accomplished in each of the following points:

The development of originality and independence of thought.

The ability to see the relation between cause and effect.

The faculty to observe closely, and to see a thing in all its parts and bearings.

Training of the hand to express exactly and neatly, either by words or by drawings, what the eye sees and the mind conceives.

Fixed habits of patient, unremitting inquiry.

The *practical* question for the teacher of botany is simply this: What to select for his pupils to study and how to set them about it.

The first thing that should be done is to work out the conditions of plant life and economy, as illustrated by typical, closely related flowering plants. One might say to a class beginning the study of botany: "We are to investigate during the course upon which we are now starting, the question of *Getting on in the world from the standpoint of a plant*" (as, for example, a geranium in full flower placed before pupils). "We want to find out by very careful study and experiment the conditions,— the elements of *success in life,* considered solely from the point of view of the plants." Obviously this constitutes a *problem,* and a problem just as definite as a problem in algebra, or a question concerning the success of any man or nation. By thus stating a problem that can be clearly comprehended at the outset, little time will be lost; there will be no rambling or vagueness, and all the attention and energy of the student can be directed at once to the solution of the problem.

In dealing with this problem of *how does the plant succeed in life,* one should begin where the life of the plant begins—with the seed—and from that point trace its life-history step by step through its development into the adult plant, to the point where the seeds are once more formed, thus completing the cycle of life. Of course, in all the phases and stages of this study of a life history, it is not necessary or desirable for the teacher to confine himself to the same plant or the same species of plants even. It is sufficient that any plants or parts of plants be used that are representatives of a common class.

This work should be done at *first hand;* the student should have in his own hands the plant or its parts under consideration, and should have, moreover, tools and means with which to work. Keep prominent by constant emphasis through the material and work in hand, the great law of *utility,* or *adaptation of structure to purpose.* Lay stress upon the *life* relations of the plant to its environments of soil, air, light, and moisture, and upon the mutual relations and interdependence of the parts of a plant.

In the study of each phase of this life-problem there should be introduced, *just so far as time will permit,* other more or less closely related forms, including the fern and some others of the cryptograms, in order to illustrate the differences arising in different plants to adapt them more perfectly to their peculiar environments; to enable them to win more successfully in *their* struggle for a place in the world. At the same time, if this very important *comparative work* is properly developed by the teacher, it will become apparent to the pupil that there is a singleness, a oneness in essential structures and devices that unifies and simplifies the whole conception of plants. Accurate drawings and descriptions of things studied should be insisted upon, the drawings to be done on good paper with hard lead pencil, and the notes written in ink on the same paper. Moreover, the drawings and notes should be completed at the time the study is made, and should *never be copied.* Such a plan will eventually lead to accurate work done at first trial; while if the student is permitted to make rough sketches and hurried descripscriptions at the time he is studying the plant, to be "written up" afterwards, he will be encouraged to do careless, superficial observation, and inaccurate work.

Perhaps the most satisfactory note book is one made from heavy paper, which can be obtained from any printing office, cut to a convenient size, and punched for binding in some convenient manner,—the back of an old book or heavy manila cardboard making a good binder. The best pencil for the drawings is a Faber "6 H." Good simple microscopes with hand-rests can be had for $1.25 each. Enough should be provided by the school, together with dissecting knife and pair of needles, to furnish each student with a set. Most of the work of this course requires no use of a compound microscope; but at times, in order to fully carry out the scheme, its need is imperative, and every high school should be supplied with enough to make it possible for students to personally study the microscopic structure of the things, an understanding of which is necessary to the full solution of the problem they are investigating.

If microscopes cannot be provided, then the teacher must substitute drawings on the blackboard, to be discussed and interpreted by the class together.

If the time of the teacher is so occupied that it is impossible to devote a period distinct from the recitation period to laboratory work every day, it will be found the best plan to alternate the laboratory work with the recitation. Less ground can be covered in that way, but in a much more satisfactory manner than if the students are left to work by themselves. In many cases the ground which the teacher attempts to cover is *far too much;* and the result is a superficial view that breeds a contempt for the study. Be content to do a little thoroughly.

The plan outlined will not only secure the culture for the

student, but will result in giving him the fullest information, the *greatest familiarity* with the plant world about him; for there is no limit,—except the limit set by time—to the *amount of comparative* study that may be done. But a comparative study of plants implies a clearly defined point of departure,— " a *type thoroughly* mastered on which to base comparisons; and with *that* accomplished each new plant that is introduced will be alive with meaning based upon its relationships, and these meanings will all fit together to form a perfect whole, instead of being a mass of dead, disconnected facts, or unrelated, unorganized items of information.

For the use of the teacher, the following text and reference books will be found helpful:

N

Al 5 co

List price. Price to schools.

#878. [587.] **Colours of flowers as illustrated in the British flora.** Grant Allen. N. Y., Macmillan Co., 1891. 119 p. il. D. (Nature ser.) cl. .... 1.00 .65

Some facts for use in evolution of plant life.

N

At 5 el

879. [580.] **Elementary botany.** G. F. Atkinson. N. Y., Henry Holt & Co., 1898. 444 p. il. D. cl. 1.25 1.13

For reference. The method is first to study some of the life processes of plants, especially those which illustrate the fundamental principles of nutrition, assimilation, growth, and irritability. Plants are selected from several of the great groups to show that processes are fundamentally the same.

N

B 15 bo

880. **Botany: an elementary text for schools.** Liberty H. Bailey. N. Y., Macmillan Co., 1900. 355 p. il. D. cl. .... 1.10 .99

A very good elementary text for the use of High school pupils.
"There are four general subjects in this book: the nature of the plant itself; the relation of the plant to its surroundings; histological studies; determination of the kinds of plants.
Each of the subjects is practically distinct, so that the teacher may begin where he will."— *Preface.*

	List price.	Price to schools.

N
B 15 le
881. [575.] **Lessons with plants.** L. H. Bailey. N. Y., Macmillan & Co., 1898. 491 p. il. D. cl. ..... 1.10 .98

A good book of reference for beginners. Teachers will find the introduction very suggestive.

N
B 26 pl
882. [578.] **Plant life:** considered with special reference to form and function. Charles Reid Barnes. N. Y., Henry Holt & Co., 1898. 428 p. il. D. cl... 1.12 1.00

An outline of botany from the standpoint of form and function. A good book of reference and for use in the laboratory. "Plant life" is an attempt to exhibit the variety and progressive complexity of the vegetable body; to discuss the more important functions; to explain the unity of plan in both structure and action of the reproductive organs; and finally to give an outline of the more striking ways in which plants adapt themselves to the world about them.

N
B 45 fo
884. **Foundations of botany.** Joseph Y. Bergen. Bost., Ginn & Co., 1902. 257 p. il. D. cl. 1.20 1.02

A good book. It gives the latest method of teaching botany, and contains sufficient standard descriptive matter and outlines for laboratory work to prepare for any college that demands botany as an entrance requirement. The book is liberally illustrated and contains a complete key to the flora of the central and northeastern states.

N
B 45 ha
885. **Handbook for the use of teachers:** to accompany Bergen's Foundations of botany. Joseph Y. Bergen. Bost., Ginn & Co., 1901. 64 p. il. D. cl. .30 .25

A valuable aid to the teacher of botany, intended primarily to accompany the author's Foundations of botany, but may be used with other texts. It contains direction for conducting laboratory work, experimentation, and sets of questions.

N
B 59 na
886. [585.] **Nature's Garden:** an aid to knowledge of our wild flowers and their insect visitors. Neltje Blanchan. N. Y., Doubleday, Page & Co., 1900. 415 p. il. O. cl. 3.00 2.25

"Over five hundred flowers in this book have been classified according to color, because it is believed that the novice, with no knowledge of botany whatever, can most readily identify the specimen found afield by this method, which has the added advantage of being the simple one adopted by the higher insects. Technicalities have been avoided wherever possible."

Most beautiful plates.

N

C 54 la
887. [574.] **Laboratory manual in practical botany.** Charles H. Clark. N. Y., American Book Co., 1898. 271 p. il. D. cl. .... .96 .84

A general view of the subject such as will lay the foundation upon which more advanced work may be built.

N

C 83 pl
888. **Plants: a text-book of botany.** John M. Coulter. N. Y., D. Appleton & Co., 1902. 348 p. (Twentieth Century Text-books.). il. D. cl. 1.80 1.62

This is one of the few good books in botany which every High school library should be supplied with if it is not used in the school as a text. It is comprehensive in its scope, dealing with types which represent all forms of plant life. The cuts and photographs add much to the value of the book. It gives a thoroughly scientific treatment of the subject of botany.

N

D 25 in
889. [584.] **Insectiverous plants.** Charles Darwin. N. Y., D. Appleton & Co., 1897. 462 p. D. cl. 2.00 1.30

Darwin's books are intensely interesting to older pupils, though younger pupils will find portions interesting.

N

D 25 mo
890. [583.] **Movements and habits of climbing plants.** Charles Darwin. N. Y., D. Appleton & Co., 1897. 208 p. il D. cl. .... 1.25 .82

N

D 25 po
#891. [582.] **Power of movement in plants.** Charles Darwin, *and* Francis Darwin. N. Y., D. Appleton & Co., 1898. 592 p. il. D. cl. 2.00 1.30

N
G 56 fi
#892. [586.] **Field, forest and wayside flowers,** with chapters on grasses, sedges and ferns. Maud E. Going. (E. M. Hardinge.) N. Y., Baker & Taylor Co., 1899. 411 p. il. O. cl.................. 1.50 1.13

List price. Price to schools.

"Untechnical studies for unlearned lovers of nature."

N
H 21 wi
893. **With the wild flowers:** from pussy-willow to thistle-down. E. M. Hardinge (Maud Going, *pseud.*) N. Y., Baker & Taylor Co., c1901. 271 p. il. D. Rev. ed. cl..................................... 1.00 .65

An interesting book on flowers for general reading.

N
K 24 ou
894. **Our native trees and how to identify them.** Harriet L. Keeler. N. Y., C: Scribner's Sons, 1900. 533 p. il. D. cl............................... 2.00 1.80

"The trees described in this volume are those indigenous to the region extending from the Atlantic Ocean to the Rocky Mountains and from Canada to the northern boundaries of the southern states; together with a few well-known and naturalized foreign trees such as the Horse-chestnut, Lombardy poplar, Ailanthus and Sycamore maple."—*Preface.*

Contents: Genera and species; Illustrations; Guide to the trees; Descriptions of the trees; Form and structure of roots, stems, leaves, flowers, and fruit; Tree stem or trunk; Species and genus; Glossary of botanical names; Index of Latin names; Index of common names.

N
L 48 ou
895. **Outlines of botany:** for the high school laboratory and classroom (based on Gray's "Lessons in botany"). Robert Greenleaf Leavitt. N. Y., American Book Co., 1901. 272 p. il. O. cl........................ 1.00 .85

"This book offers (1) a series of laboratory exercises in the morphology and physiology of phanerogams, (2) directions for a practicable study of typical cryptogams, representing the chief groups from the lowest to the highest, and (3) a substantial body of information regarding the forms, activities, and relationships of plants and supplementing the laboratory studies.

The practical exercises and experiments have been so chosen that schools with compound microscopes and expensive laboratory apparatus may have ample opportunity to employ to advantage their superior equipment. On the other hand, the needs of less fortunate schools, which possess as yet only simple microscopes and very limited apparatus, have been constantly borne in mind. Even when the cryptogams and certain anatomical features of the phanerogams are to be dealt with, much may be accomplished with the hand lens, and, when applicable at all, it is in an elementary course usually a better aid to clear comprehension of objects examined than the compound microscope. Furthermore, the experiments covering the fundamental principles of plant physiology have been so far as possible arranged in such a manner as to require only simple appliances."— *Preface.*

N
———
L 93 gu

#896. [589.] **Guide to the trees.** Alice Lounsberry. N. Y., Frederick A. Stokes Co., 1900. 313 p. il. D. cl.   2.50   2.25

The leading points of recognition in connection with about two hundred trees are concisely given. The illustrations are especially fine and helpful.

N
———
M 11 na

897. [576.] **Nature and work of plants:** introduction to the study of botany. D. T. Macdougal. N. Y., Macmillan Co., 1900. 218 p. D. cl................   .80   .66

A good reference book.

N
———
M 42 f

898. **Familiar features of the roadside:** the flowers, shrubs, birds, and insects. Ferdinand Schuyler Mathews. N. Y., D. Appleton & Co., 1897. 269 p. il. D. cl. 1.75   1.15

Contents: Early wild flowers, catkins, and spring peepers; Early flowering shrubs; Shrubs belonging to the rose family— cherries, brambles, etc.; Woodland road—shrubs and flowers belonging to the heath family; Meadow singers; Little songsters—yellowbird, sparrows, and phoebe bird; Birds with unmusical voices; Birds of brilliant feathers—humming bird, jay, bluebird, tanager, oriole, etc.; Woodland singers—thrushes, vireo, and peabody bird; In leafy June—green leaves and a few beetles and butterflies; Tall midsummer weeds—members of the composite family; Bees which we pass by; Nature's color on mountain, meadow, and woodland; Golden-rod and asters; Autumn flowers, squirrels, and autumn colors.

N
———
M 42 fa

899. **Familiar flowers of field and garden.** Ferdinand Schuyler Mathews. N. Y., D. Appleton & Co., 1901. 308 p. il. D. New ed. cl. 1.40   1.26

Good for general reference.

N
M 42 fam
900. **Familiar trees and their leaves.** Ferdinand Schuyler Mathews. N. Y., D. Appleton & Co., 1901. 320 p. il. O. cl. 1.75 1.57

List price. Price to schools.

For reference. One of the features of this book deserving special commendation is its illustrations, over two hundred in number.

N
P 25 ac
901. **According to season:** talks about the flowers in the order of their appearance in the woods and fields. Frances Theodore Parsons. New, enl. ed. with thirty-two plates in color by Elsie Louise Shaw. N. Y., C: Scribner's Sons, 1902. 197 p. il. O. cl. 1.75 1.57

Interesting for the Library reading class in Science.
Contents: Introductory; Winter; Early glimpses; Spring in the city; Spring holiday; May notes; "Leafy month of June"; Long Island Meadow; Midsummer; Early August; Golden-rod and aster; Autumn.

N
Sa 7 co
902. [588.] **Corn plants:** their uses and ways of life. Frederick Leroy Sargent. Bost., Houghton, Mifflin & Co., 1899. 106 p. il. D. cl.................... .75 .50

Information regarding a few of the most important plants in the world. Intimate relations with our daily lives are pointed out and only such features are dwelt upon as may be readily observed. Important material for geography.

N
Se 2 la
903. **Laboratory practice for beginners in botany.** William A. Setchel. N. Y., Macmillan Co., 1897. 14 + 199 p. 16°. cl. .... .90 .81

N
W 93 fl
#904. **Flowers and ferns in their haunts.** Mabel Osgood Wright. N. Y., Macmillan Co., 1901. 358 p. il. O. cl. 2.50 1.64

A beautiful story of Nature, excellent for Library reading.
The illustrations are fine, the full page plates being engraved directly from the photographs.
Contents: Coming of spring; Along the waterways; Escaped from gardens; Silent woods; Some humble orchids; Poisonous plants; Fantasies of ferns; Flowers of the sun; Composite family; Wayfarers; Drapery of vines; Aftermath.

ZOOLOGY.

O
―――
Ar 6 se

                                                                                                                        List Price to
                                                                                                                        price. schools.

*905. **Sea-beach at ebb-tide:** a guide to the study of the seaweeds and the lower animal life found between tide-marks. Augusta Foote Arnold. N. Y., Century Co., 1901. 490 p. il. O. cl.............. 2.40 2.16

    A guide for the amateur collector and student of the organisms, both animal and vegetable, which are found upon North American beaches. Many invertebrates and some of the more notable varieties of seaweeds are described, and each individual is given its proper place in the latest classification. The book is not technical and yet is scientific enough to furnish a good foundation for wider technical knowledge. The author gives careful directions with regard to collecting—telling what to look for and where to find it, what methods and tools to use in securing specimens, and how to preserve them.

    This book should only be purchased by the largest High school libraries. Valuable for extended reference work.

O
―――
B 14 ro

906. [609.] **Romance of the insect world.** L. N. Badenoch. N. Y., Macmillan Co., 1898. 341 p. il. D. cl... 1.25 .82

    An interesting account of insect life in general.
    Contents: Metamorphoses, food, hermit homes, social homes, and defences of insects.

O
―――
B 21 up

907. [612.] **Up and down the brooks.** Mary E. Bamford. Bost., Houghton, Mifflin & Co., 1890. 222 p. il. S. (Riverside library for young people.) cl .... .75 .48

    Insect life in the brooks.

O
―――
B 29 sa

908. **Story of the amphibians and the reptiles.** James Newton Baskett, *and* Raymond L. Ditmars. N. Y., D. Appleton & Co., 1902. 217 p. (Appleton's home reading books.) D. cl. .... .60 .54

    Effort is made to familiarize the young reader with the anatomical structure and habits of many forms of amphibians and reptiles.

O
―――
B 29 sf

909. [608.] **Story of the fishes.** James Newton Baskett. N. Y., D. Appleton & Co., 1899. 297 p. il. D. (Appleton's home reading books.) cl .... .65 .58

    An unusually interesting book for young readers.

	List price.	Price to schools.

O
———
B 85 li
910. **Life and her children:** glimpses of animal life from the amoeba to the insects. Arabella B. Buckley. N. Y., D. Appleton & Co., 1897. 312 p. il. D. cl.   1.50   .98

"The main object of this book is to acquaint young people with the structure and habits of the lower forms of life; and to do this in a more systematic way than is usual in ordinary works on Natural History, and more simply than in text-books on Zoology."—*Preface.*

Portions of this book will be interesting reading for the Library reading class in Science.

O
———
C 73 in
911. [610.] **Insect life.** John Henry Comstock. N. Y., D. Appleton & Co., 1898. 349 p. il. D. cl............   1.50   .98

General study of insect life. A good book for reference.

O
———
D 55 mo
912. **Moths and butterflies.** Mary C. Dickerson. Bost., Ginn & Co., 1901. 344 p. il. O. cl............   2.50   2.12

The author is head of the department of biology and nature study in the Rhode Island Normal School, Providence, R. I. The book is entirely untechnical in its treatment of the subject. It will identify by means of photographs from life forty common forms, in caterpillar, chrysalis, or cocoon, and adult stages. It makes clear the external structure adapting the creature to its life; it describes and illustrates the changes in form from caterpillar to chrysalis, from chrysalis to butterfly.

Portions of this book will be of great interest to the Library reading class in science.

O
———
G 18 ap
913. **Apes and monkeys:** their life and language. R. L. Garner. *Introd.* by Edward Everett Hale. Bost., Ginn & Co., 1900. 297 p. il. D. cl............   2.00   1.28

"This volume is the natural product of many years devoted by the author to studying the speech and habits of monkeys. That naturally led him up to the study of the great apes. The matter contained in this work is chiefly a record of the tabulated facts gleaned from his special field of research. The aim in view is to convey to the casual reader a more correct idea than now prevails concerning the physical, mental, and social habits of apes and monkeys and to prepare him for a wider appreciation of animals in general.

Believing that a more perfect knowledge of these animals will bring man into closer fellowship and deeper sympathy with nature, and with an abiding trust that it will widen the bounds of humanity and cause man to realize that he and they are but common links in the great chain of life."—*From the author's preface.*

The story is written in a vivid, dramatic manner that will interest boys and girls. A good book for Library reading.

O
―――
G 35 bl

914. **Blossom hosts and insect guests;** how the heath family, the bluets, the figworts, the orchids and similar wild flowers welcome the bee, the fly, the wasp, the moth and other faithful insects. William Hamilton Gibson. *Ed.* by Eleanor E. Davie. N. Y., Newson & Co., 1901. 197 p. il. D. cl..... .80 .72

A compilation of all Mr. Gibson ever contributed, either in the way of text or illustration, to the subject of the fertilization of flowers. First the theory of cross-fertilization is clearly explained and the history of the subject traced out step by step. Twenty-five flowers are then carefully analyzed and the method of their fertilization shown.

O
―――
H 44 ge

915. **General principles of zoology.** Richard Hertwig. Translated by George W. Field. N. Y., Henry Holt & Co., 1897. 226 p. il. O. cl............ 1.60 1.44

A most valuable reference work for students and teacher. It contains fascinating accounts of the historic development of the different phases of this subject in addition to a complete and systematic exposition of the entire science. The chapter on organology and embryology are particularly interesting. It may be used to supplement the study of physiology.

O
―――
H 52 st

916. [595.] **Story of life in the seas.** Sydney J. Hickson. N. Y., D. Appleton & Co., 1898. 170 p. il. S. cl. .40 .27

A sketch of the most important lines of scientific investigation in ocean fauna.

O
―――
H 83 in

#917. **insect book:** a popular account of the bees, wasps, ants, grasshoppers, flies and other North American insects exclusive of the butterflies, moths and beetles, with full life histories, tables and bibliographies. Leland O. Howard. N. Y., Doubleday, Page & Co., 1901. 429 p. il. Q. cl. 3.00 1.70

"A popular description by the foremost authority in this country of Bees, Wasps, Ants, Grasshoppers, Flies and other North American

	List price.	Price to schools.

insects. This book has full-life histories, giving an intimate account of the most wonderful facts in that insect world all around us, which is so completely unknown, even to scientists. There is today almost nothing that covers authoritatively, yet popularly, this vast field, so that the present volume has special importance. With the 300 text cuts and the 16 colored and 32 black and white pages made direct from the insects tnemselves, the subject is abundantly as well as beautifully pictured."

This volume should only be purchased by the largest libraries.

O

In 4 wi

918. [591.] **Wild neighbors**: out-door studies in the United States. Ernest Ingersoll. N. Y., Macmillan Co., 1897. 301 p. il. D. cl...................... 1.50 .98

Life and habits of our leading wild animals. For younger readers.

O

J 76 an

919. **Animals**: a text-book of zoology. David Starr Jordan, and Vernon L. Kellogg, and Harold Heath. N. Y., D. Appleton & Co., 1902. 258 p. il. (Twentieth Century Text-books.) D. cl. 1.80 1.62

In two parts. Part I deals with animal life with special reference to animal ecology—that is, the relations of animals to their surroundings and their responsive adaptation to these surroundings. Part II treats of animal forms, dealing mostly with morphology. Types of life from the lowest to the highest are dealt with. The book will be found valuable for reference in the subjects of zoology, physical geography, and Nature study.

O

K 29 el

920. **Elementary zoology.** Vernon L. Kellogg. N. Y., Henry Holt & Co., 1902. 484 p. il. D. cl...... 1.20 1.08

Divided into three parts. Part 1 is an introduction to an elementary knowledge of animal structure, function, and development. It consists of practical exercises in the laboratory, each followed by a recitation in which the significance of the facts already observed is pointed out. Part 2 is devoted to a consideration of the principal branches of the animal kingdom: it deals with systematic zoology. Part 3 is devoted to a necessarily brief consideration of certain of the more conspicuous and interesting features of animal ecology. It has in it the suggestion for much interesting field-work.

O

L 64 st

921. **Story of animal life.** B. Lindsay. N. Y., D. Appleton & Co., 1902. 196 p. il. (Library of useful stories.) S. cl. .... .35 .31

A brief study of the distinctive forms of animal life as they are seen under a microscope and as they are affected by scientific experiment and modern research. Describes also the methods and appliances of zoologists and includes a classification of specimens of the animal kingdom and an index.

A good book for the student who wishes to make a brief review of the subject of zoology.

O

L 85 be

922. **Beasts of the field.** William J. Long. Bost., Ginn & Co., 1901. 332 p. il. D. cl...................... 1.75   1.17

The two books "Beasts of the field" and "Fowls of the air" include many of the sketches given in Long's previous books, "Ways of wood folk," "Wilderness ways," and "Secrets of the woods." They contain enough new material to give a wide range of acquaintance with the wood folk. The beautiful illustrations in these books will attract the attention of the pupil and lead him to read the stories.

O

M 26 li

923. **Life of the bee.** Maurice Maeterlinck. *Translated* by Alfred Sutro. N. Y., Dodd, Mead & Co., 1902. 426 p. D. cl................................. 1.40   1.26

Deals with the life of the bee, treated in Maeterlinck's own peculiar vein. The book is by no means technical; passages of the higher lyrical beauty abound, while reflections, analogies and poetical digressions are not wanting. Excellent for Library reading.

Contents: On the threshold of the hive; Swarm; Foundation of the city; Life of the bee; Young queens; Nuptial flight; Massacre of the males; Progress of the race; Appendix.

O

N 28 el

924. **Elementary lessons in zoology:** a guide in studying animal life and structure in field and laboratory. James G. Needham. N. Y., American Bk. Co., c1896. 310 p. il. D. cl. .... .90   .76

A good book to supplement the laboratory work in zoology. Treated from the scientific standpoint, it deals with animal life in the interior of this continent making it a practical book for those who do not have access to the sea shore specimens.

O

Or 28 co

925. **Comparative zoology:** structural and systematic, for use in schools and colleges. James Orton. New rev. ed. by Charles Wright Dodge. N. Y., American Bk. Co., c1894. 434 p. il. O. cl............ 1.80   1.53

A good work. It shows in a clear, systematic way the variations and development of organs and their functions from the simplest to

254 LIST OF BOOKS FOR HIGH SCHOOL LIBRARIES.

                List Price to
                price. schools.

the most complex states. This is followed by brief, systematic classification and description of animals.

Well adapted by style and illustrations for High school work.

O
——
P 12 zo
926. Zoology. Alpheus S. Packard. N. Y., Henry Holt & Co., 1899. 364 p. il. Ed. 7, rev. (American science series—briefer course.) D. cl. 1.12 1.01

A standard text book giving a good classification of animals, and treating the different forms of animal life in a manner which will commend itself to the student.

O
——
R 54 ki
927. **Kindred of the wild:** a book of animal life. Charles G. D. Roberts. Illustrated by Charles Livingston Bull. Bost., L. C. Page & Co., 1902. 374 p. il. O. cl. 1.75 1.57

Stories about wild animals, entitled: The moonlight trails; The lord of the air; Wild motherhood; The homesickness of Kebouka; Savory meats; The boy of Hushwing; A treason of nature; The haunter of the pine gloom; The watchers of the camp-fire; When twilight falls on the stump lots; The king of the Mamozekel; In panoply of spears. Also an essay on "The animal story."
Excellent for Library reading.

O
——
Scu 4 ev
#928. [611.] **Every-day butterflies.** Samuel Hubbard Scudder. Bost., Houghton, Mifflin & Co., 1899. 391 p. il. D. cl. 2.00 1.30

Lives of our commonest butterflies. A good book of reference.

O
——
Sh 1 wi
929. **Wild life near home.** Dallas Lore Sharp. N. Y., Century Co., 1901. 357 p. il. O. cl. 2.00 1.30

A very attractive book made up of a series of stories of wild life. The illustrations are fine. Good for Library reading.

Contents: In persimmon time; Birds' winter beds; Some snug winter beds; Bird of the dark; Pine-tree swift; In the October moon; Feathered neighbors; "Mus rattin'"; Study in bird morals; Rabbit roads; Brick-top; Second crops; Wood-pussies; From river-ooze to tree-top; Buzzards' banquet; Up Herring run.

O
T 37 li

                                                                    List Price to
                                                                    price. schools.

930. **Lives of the hunted:** containing a true account of the doings of five quadrupeds and three birds and, in elucidation of the same, over 200 drawings. Ernest Seton-Thompson. N. Y., C: Scribner's Sons, 1901. 360 p. il. O. cl.................. 1.75 1.57

"In my previous books I have tried to emphasize our kinship with the animals by showing that in them we can find the virtues most admired in man. Lobo stands for dignity and love-constancy; Silverspot, for sagacity; Redruff, for obedience. In this volume, Majesty, Grace, the power of Wisdom, the sweet uses of adversity, and the two-edged sorrows of rebellion are similarly set forth. The material of the accounts is true. The chief liberty taken is in ascribing to one animal the adventures of several."—*From the author's preface.*

These stories may be read and told to the children of the lower and middle forms.

The animal stories embraced under this title are: Krag, the Kootenay ram; A street troubadour, being the adventures of a cock sparrow; Johnny Bear; The Mother Teal and the overland route; Chink, the development of a pup; the Kangaroo rat; Tito, the story of a coyote that learned how; Why the chickadee goes crazy once a year. A handsomely gotten up book of narrow pages, decorated margins, etc.

O
T 38 st

931. [590.] **Study of animal life.** J. Arthur Thomson. N. Y., C: Scribner's Sons, 1896. 375 p. il. D. (University series.) cl. 1.50 1.35

Animal life in general. A good book of reference and portions will be found very readable by older students.

Contents: Everyday life of animals, forms of animal life, and evolution of animal life.

BIRDS.

Pe

Ap 2 bi

#932. [599.] **Birds of the United States east of the Rocky mountains.** Austin C. Apgar. N. Y., American Book Company, 1898. 415 p. il. D. cl........ 2.00 1.70

A good book of general reference in observing and identifying birds.

Pe

B 59 b

933. [596.] **Bird neighbors..** Neltje Blanchan. N. Y., Doubleday & McClure Co., 1897. 234 p. il. O. cl. 2.00 1.30

One of the best books for young readers. Excellent descriptions of appearance and habits of 150 common birds.

		List price.	Price to schools.

Pe
B 59 bi
934. [597.] **Birds that hunt and are hunted.** Neltje Blanchan. N. Y., Doubleday & McClure Co., 1898. 359 p. il. O. cl 2.00 1.30

Describes appearance and habits of 170 birds of prey, game birds, and waterfowls. Illustrations are especially fine.

Pe
B 63 fr
935. [606.] **From Blomidon to Smoky,** and other papers. Frank Bolles. Bost., Houghton, Mifflin & Co., 1894. 278 p. D. cl. .... 1.25 .82

General observations on birds which will interest the students in nature study, and will stimulate observation.

Pe
C 36 bi
936. [598.] **Bird-life:** a guide to the study of our common birds. Frank M. Chapman. N. Y., D. Appleton & Co., 1899. 269 + 88 p. il. D. (Teacher's edition.) cl. 2.00 1.30

For those who desire a general knowledge of bird-life. "Portraits, names, and addresses of upward of one hundred birds of North America, with such information concerning their comings and goings as will lead to their being found at home."
Valuable for use in identifying birds.

Pe
D 87 bi
#937. **Bird homes:** the nests, eggs and breeding habits of the land birds breeding in the eastern United States; with hints on the rearing and photographing of young birds. A. Radclyffe Dugmore. N. Y., Doubleday & McClure Co., 1900. 183 p. il. Q. cl. 2.00 1.80

This is a popular and intimate account of the nests, eggs and breeding habits of the land birds that nest in the Eastern United States. It is the first time that this subject has been adequately treated for the general reader, and the book is a revelation of bird "personality" in many ways. Particularly notable are the illustrations (in color, and black and white), all of which were made directly from the nests and birds by the author. The notes on bird photography and on the rearing of young birds give information not attainable elsewhere and of great interest to nature-lovers and students.

	List price.	Price to schools.

Pe
―――
Ec 5 bi

938. **Bird book.** Fannie Hardy Eckstrom. Bost., D. C. Heath & Co., 1901. 281 p. il. D. cl. .... .60 .51

The arrangement of the book has two ends in view: to adapt the study to the school year, and to present it so that when the pupil begins field work he shall be able to do it with some general idea of what is worth observing: Divided into four parts: 1. Waterbirds in their homes; 2. Structure and comparison; 3. Problems in bird life; 4. Some common land-birds.

Portions of this book will be of interest to Library reading class in science.

Pe   1
―――
G 76 ou

939. **Our common birds and how to know them.** John B. Grant. N. Y., C: Scribner's Sons, 1901. 224 p. il. obl. T. cl. 1.50 1.35

An excellent and inexpensive reference book giving a description of ninety common birds. Plates of sixty-four birds, an introductory chapter on "How to know our common birds," and a "Bird calendar" will be of great assistance to those interested in the study of birds.

Pe
―――
J 27 am

940. **Among the water-fowl: observation, adventure, photography.** A popular narrative account of the water-fowl as found in the northern and middle states and lower Canada, east of the Rocky mountains. Herbert K. Job. N. Y., Doubleday, Page & Co., 1902. 224 p. il. O. cl 1.35 1.21

Mr. Job has for years made a special study of the gulls and waterfowl whose life histories are the least known of our wild birds. His photographs (generally made with a string over a hundred yards long attached to the camera) are marvels of intimate bird picturing. Many prominent members of the American Ornithological Union have declared them unequaled, and Mr. Job's pen is almost as ready as his camera. At sea, in the far north, and in the swamps of Dakota where they breed, he has studied these gulls, ducks and geese to such good purpose that his entertaining narrative contains much of real new information.

Contents—Part 1: "The submerged tenth" relates to grebes and loons. Part 2: "Modern cliff-dwellers" to gannets, guillemots, auks, puffins, kittiwakes, etc. Part 3. "Ocean wanderers" to shearwaters, gaegers or skuas, petrals, phalarope. Part 4: "The white-winged fleet" to grills and terns. Part 5: "Wild fowl of wild fowl" to ducks and geese.

Excellent for Library reading.

Pe

K 52 in

941. [603.] **In bird land.** Leander S. Keyser. Chic., A. C. McClurg & Co., 1894. 269 p. D. cl............ 1.25 .82

Pe

L 85 fo

942. **Fowls of the air.** William J. Long. Bost., Ginn & Co., 1901. 310 p. il. D. cl. 1.75 1.17

See Long's "Beasts of the field" for note.

Pe

M 55 ab

943. [600.] **A-birding on a bronco.** Florence A. Merriam. Bost., Houghton, Mifflin & Co., 1896. 226 p. il. D. cl. .... 1.25 .82

Pe

M 55 bi

944. [607.] **Birds of village and field: a book for beginners.** Florence A. Merriam. Bost., Houghton, Mifflin & Co., 1898. 406 p. il. D. cl. 2.00 1.30

A fine book for beginners.

Pe

M 61 bi

945. [601.] **Bird-lover in the west.** Olive Thorne Miller. Bost., Houghton, Mifflin & Co., 1894. 278 p. D. cl. .... 1.25 .82

Pe

M 61 up

946. [602.] **Upon the tree-tops.** Olive Thorne Miller. Bost., Houghton, Mifflin & Co., 1897. 245 p. il. D. cl..... .... 1.25 .82

The two books above will furnish interesting material for the Library reading class and for the class in literature that are studying essays.

Pe

W 93 ci

947. **Citizen Bird:** scenes from bird-life in plain English for beginners: l. by L: Agassiz Fuertes. Mabel Osgood Wright, *and* Elliott Coues. N. Y., Macmillan Co., c1897. 14 + 430 p. D. cl............ 1.50 1.35

The first volume of the *Heart of nature series* which derives its title from the old man who played such a delightful part in Miss

Wright's "Story of Tommy Anne and the three hearts." The scene is the orchard farm, the time from spring to autumn, the characters are Dr. Roy Hunter, a naturalist; Olive, the doctor's daughter; Nat and Dodo, his nephew and niece; Rap, a country boy; Mammy Bun, an old colored nurse, and Olaf, an old fisherman. Everything to be known about birds is taught by Dr. Hunter by conversations according to the inductive method. The joint author's name is guarantee of accuracy, and Miss Wright has the genius of pleasing children.

ANTHROPOLOGY.

Pw
———
C 62 st

948. [570.] **Story of "primitive" man.** Edward Clodd. N. Y., D. Appleton & Co., 1897. 190 p. il. S. (Lib. useful stories.) cl........................ .40 .32

Brief and interesting account of man's place in earth's life-history, and in earth's time-history. Will open a new field to students.

Pw
———
H 11 st

949. [571.] **Study of man.** Alfred C. Haddon. N. Y., G. P. Putnam's Sons, 1898. 410 p. il. O. (Science series.) cl. 2.00 1.30

The book is for the general reader who will find much of interest in it. Some of the most interesting subjects touched upon are: Measurements, hair and eye color in anthropology, the evolution of the cart, toys, and games.

Pw
———
St 2 so

950. [569.] **Some first steps in human progress.** F: Starr. Meadville, Pa., Flood and Vincent, 1895. 305 p. il. D. (Chautauqua reading circle lit.) cl...... 1.00 .88

The first steps in human progress in fire making, food getting, basket making, hunting, cultivation of plants, etc.

PHYSIOLOGY.

The work in physiology should cover, in a general way, the work outlined in any good text-book. The study should be made as objective as possible, special emphasis being given to diagraming organs and systems at the time they are studied, and suggested experiments made when possible. Too much attention should not be given to details, but the fundamentals should be thoroughly taught.

The work should give to the student a clear idea of the living body, the divisions of bodies into organic and inorganic, into plants and animals, of what is meant by the structure of a body, anatomy, physiology, hygiene, cell tissue, membrane, gland, muscle, tendon, blood vessel, nerve, lymphatic, bone, and joint. There should also be a clear notion of the kinds of work done in the human body and of the systems by which it is accomplished.

Q
———
B 77 ph

List price. Price to schools.

951. **Physiology**: by the laboratory method for secondary schools. William J. Brinckley. Chic., Ainsworth & Co., 1902. 504 p. il. O. cl.............. 1.25 1.00

A most admirable work for teacher and students. It may be used in connection with any purely descriptive text book. The directions for experimental study are clear and explicit, and the experiments outlined will furnish a sound foundation for the comprehension of the description and functions of the different organs. The appendix contains valuable information relative to histological methods, ferments, diseases, accidents, etc.

Q
———
H 15 ki

952. **Kirke's Hand-book of physiology.** William Dobinson Halliburton. Phil., P. Blakiston's Son & Co., 1901. 388 p. il. O. Ed. 17. cl.............. 3.00 2.70

A good reference work for the teacher. It is used in many medical colleges as the basis of study on this subject.

	List price.	Price to schools.

Q
J 38 sy
953. **Syllabus of human physiology:** for high schools, normal schools, and colleges. John I. Jegi. Milwaukee, S. Y. Gillan & Co., 1901. 264 p. il. O. cl. .... 1.00 .80

An excellent summary of the essential points of this subject. It contains ample references to additional information and to discussions in larger texts. The syllabus may be used by teachers and students as a guide to the study of this subject.

Q
M 36 hu
#954. **Human body:** its structure and activities and the conditions of its healthy working. Henry Newell Martin. N. Y., Henry Holt & Co., 1898. 685 p. il. (American science series—advanced course.) Eighth ed., rev. O. cl. 2.50 2.25

A standard text for colleges and a valuable reference for High school classes. The style is lucid and the text is accurate and complete. The illustrations are excellent.

Q
N 47 sc
955. **School hygiene:** or, the laws of health in relation to school life. Arthur Newsholme. Bost., D. C. Heath & Co., 1901. 143 p. (Heath's pedagogical library.) D. cl. .... .75 .67

For reference for the teacher.

Contents: Site of school; Construction of school buildings; School furniture; Lighting of school-rooms; General principles of ventilation; Natural ventilation; Ventilation and warming; Drainage arrangements; Mental exercise; Excessive mental exercise; Age and sex in relation to school work; Muscular exercise and recreation; Rest and sleep; Children's diet; Children's dress; Baths and bathing; Eyesight in relation to school life; Communicable diseases in schools; School accidents.

Q
P 84 ha
956. **Handbook of school-gymnastics of the Swedish system:** with one hundred consecutive tables of exercises and an appendix of classified lists of movements. Baron Nils Posse. Bost., Lee & Shepard, 1902. 193 p. il. New rev. ed. T. cl. .75 .68

A handbook for the use of the teacher of gymnastics.

Q
P 84 sp
#957. **Special kinesiology of educational gymnastics.** Baron Nils Posse. Bost., Lee & Shepard, 1901. 380 p. il. O. cl. 3.00 2.00

A treatise on the mechanics, effects and classification of special

| | List price. | Price to schools. |

exercises. The subject matter of the book describes the Swedish system of education gymnastics. For use of teachers of gymnastics.

Q
———
P 93 ha

958. **Handbook of sanitation:** a manual of theoretical and practical sanitation. George M. Price. N. Y., John Wiley & Sons, 1901. 317 p. il. D. cl... 1.50 1.28

Treats among other subjects pertaining to sanitation the following: The proper ventilation and heating of public and private buildings; pure water; construction of sewers and house drainage pipes; Chapters are also introduced touching upon sanitary practice, sanitary inspection, and sanitary law. School house architects, teachers, and members of school boards will find the book not only helpful but almost a necessity when they are considering the sanitary features of schools. Written from a hygienic standpoint. (This book may be classified under S with the other books on Sanitation.)

Q
———
St 3 gy

#959. **Gymnastics:** a text-book of the German–American system of gymnastics. William A. Stecher. Bost., Lee & Shepard, c1896. 348 p. il. O. cl. 3.00 2.00

A series of twenty-six lessons, by sixteen of the best-known teachers of German–American gymnastics in this country; on tactics, free exercises (calisthenics), wand exercises, club-swinging, dumb-bell exercises, ring exercises, games, etc., high-jumping and pole-vaulting, spear-throwing, etc.

R
———
Q 4 pu

960. [621.] **Public health problems.** John F. J. Sykes. N. Y., C: Scribner's Sons, 1899. 370 p. il. D. cl. .... 1.25 .82

Will prove interesting if read with the teacher and accompanied by observation.

USEFUL ARTS AND INDUSTRIES.

(Including Mining, Agriculture, and Domestic Economy.)

	List Price to
	price. schools.

R
―――
B 15 ga

961. [734.] **Garden-making.** L. H Bailey. N. Y., Macmillan Co., 1899. 417 p. il. S. (Garden craft series.) cl. .... 1.00 .65

A very suggestive book on garden making. Sections I, II, and III will be especially valuable in improving the school grounds.

R
―――
B 15 pr

962. **Principles of agriculture.** a text-book for schools and rural societies. Liberty H. Bailey, *ed.* N. Y., Macmillan Co., 1902. 300 p. il. (Rural science series.) S. cl. .... 1.25 .82

One of the best texts on the subject. Teachers of botany will be glad to have this book in the reference library as many of the principles of agriculture can be correlated with the study of botany.

R
―――
B 17 bo

963. [526.] **Boy's book of inventions.** Ray Stannard Baker. N. Y., Doubleday & McClure Co., 1899. 354 p. il. O. cl. 2.00 1.30

The very latest scientific inventions. Will interest every boy. Submarine boats, liquid air, wireless telegraphy, automobile, x-ray photography, tailless kites, story of the phonograph, modern sky scrapers, and aerial navigation are some of the topics considered. One of the best books on the list.

R
―――
B 83 no

964. [622.] **North American forests and forestry;** their relations to the national life of the American people. Ernest Bruncken. N. Y., G. P. Putnam's Sons, 1900. 265 p. O. cl. 2.00 1.30

Forestry from the economic standpoint.

R
―――
C 15 ho

965. [731.] **Household economics.** *Mrs.* Helen Campbell. N. Y., G. P. Putnam's Sons. 1897. 286 p. D. cl. 1.50 .98

Treats of various subjects relating to household economy. Especially interesting topics are house decoration, furnishing, household industries, and food and its preparation. Good bibliographies on each subject.

R
C 61 pr

	List price.	Price to schools.

966. **Practical forestry:** for beginners in forestry, agricultural students, woodland owners, and others desiring a general knowledge of the nature of the art. John Gifford. N. Y., D. Appleton & Co., 1902. 284 p. il. D. cl. 1.20 1.08

"The author has endeavored to include those parts of the science and art of forestry which are of interest and importance to the general reader and beginner. It has been his endeavor also to make this book as practical as possible."—*Preface.*

Contents: Meaning of forest and forestry, and other introductory notes; Wood-lots on farms, forest estates, and the relation of silviculture to the kindred arts of agriculture, horticulture and landscape gardening; Forest canopy, forest floor, and wood-mass; Forest as an agent in modifying the surface of the earth and in checking the destructive forces of nature; Geographical distribution of forests; Formation of forests; Tending of forests; Forest industries and products; Forest trees and products of the tropics; Principal federal and state reservations; List of fifty American forest trees, twenty-five conifers and twenty-five hardwoods.

R
Ew 5 ar

967. **Art of cookery:** a manual for homes and schools. Emma P. Ewing. Indianapolis, Bowen-Merrill Co., c1899. 377 p. D. cl. 1.75 1.15

For reference for schools having cooking departments.

"A great need exists in our homes and schools for more intelligent instruction in regard to the preparation of food. This book was written to supply that need. In it the principles underlying the art of cookery are clearly explained."—*Preface.*

Contents: Marketing; Food materials; Methods of cooking; Mixing; Seasoning; Serving and garnishing.

R
G 55 pr

968. [738.] **Principles of plant culture.** E. S. Goff. Madison, E. S. Goff, 1899. 287 p. il. D. cl. .... 1.10 .85

For students who have had no previous instruction in botany.

R
H 21 sc

969. **School needlework:** a course of study in sewing designed for use in schools. Olive C. Hapgood. Bost., Ginn & Co., 1893. 162 p. il. D. bds. ... .50 .43

This book is the result of practical experience in the school-room and should be in the library of every school that has classes in Sewing.

Contents: General suggestions; Plain sewing; Ornamental stitches; Drafting, cutting, and making garments; Index.

LIST OF BOOKS FOR HIGH SCHOOL LIBRARIES.

	List price.	Price to schools.

R
―――
H 89 am

970. [733.] **Amateur's practical garden-book:** containing the simplest directions for the growing of the commonest things about the house and garden. C. E. Hunn, *and* L. H. Bailey: N. Y., Macmillan Co., 1900. 250 p. il. D. cl. .... 1.00 .65

The contents are arranged alphabetically, making the book very convenient for reference.

R
―――
J 23 pr

971. [735.] **Practical agriculture.** Charles C. James. *ed.* by John Craig. N. Y., D. Appleton & Co., 1899. 203 p. il. D. cl. .... .80 .65

An exposition of the principles of the science of agriculture and their application to the art of agriculture. A good text book for the study of agriculture in our public schools.

R
―――
L 63 bo

972. **Boston school kitchen text-book:** lessons in cooking for the use of classes in public and industrial schools. *Mrs.* Mary J. Lincoln. Bost., Little, Brown & Co., 1899. 237 p. D. cl. .... 1.00 .65

"In the preparation of this book the aim has not been to furnish a complete cook-book, or to cater to the widely prevalent desire for new receipts and elaborate dishes; but rather to prepare such a study of food and explanation of general principles in connection with practical lessons in plain cooking as should be adapted to the use of classes in public and industrial schools."—*Preface.*

R
―――
M 45 la

973. [737.] **Landscape gardening as applied to home decoration.** Samuel T. Maynard. N. Y., John Wiley & Sons, 1899. 338 p. il. D. cl. 1.50 1.12

A complete, practical, and helpful treatise on gardening, especially valuable for the home and the school yard.

R
―――
R 39 ai

*974. **Air, water and food from a sanitary standpoint.** Ellen H. Richards, *and* Alpheus G. Woodman. N. Y., John Wiley & Sons, 1900. 226 p. il. O. cl. 2.00 1.70

Deals largely with the chemistry of air, water, and food as related to human life. The science teacher will find this book good for reference in the subjects of physiology, physics, and physical geography, and for determining the wholesomeness of atmosphere and water for school purposes.

	List price.	Price to schools.

R
―――
R 39 cf
975. **Cost of food: a study in dietaries.** Ellen H. Richards. N. Y., John Wiley & Sons, 1901. 158 p. D. cl. .... 1.00 .85

If some of the practical suggestions in this book relative to foods and dietaries were taught in our public schools in place of much of the present day material on anatomy of bones, histology of tissues, etc., we might look for more healthy bodies in our children. This will be found a valuable reference work in Physiology.

R
―――
R 39 cl
976. **Cost of living: as modified by sanitary science.** Ellen H. Richards. N. Y., John Wiley & Sons, 1901. 127 p. D. cl. .... 1.00 .85

Relates mostly to the cost of keeping house. A good book for the home.

Contents: Standards of living; Service of sanitary science in increasing productive life; Household expenditure—division between departments according to ideals; House-rent or value and furnishing; Operating expenses: fuel, light, wages; Food; Clothing in relation to health; Emotional and intellectual life; Organization of the household.

R
―――
R 39 fo
977. **Food materials and their adulterations.** Ellen H. Richards. Bost., Home Science Pub. Co., 1898. 183 p. New ed. D. cl. .... 1.00 .80

Contains interesting information on quality of food supply, methods of adulteration, and tests for discovering them. A good book for the cooking class.

R
―――
R 39 ru
978. **Rumford kitchen leaflets.** Ellen H. Richards, *and others*. Bost., Home Science Pub. Co., 1899. 173 p. S. cl. 1.50 1.35

Valuable for reference in schools having a Cooking department.

Contents: Count Rumford and his work for humanity; Rumfordiana; King palate; Comparative nutrition; External digestion; Water and air as food; Chemistry of proteid foods; Digestibility of proteid foods; Proteids in our daily fare; Chemistry of fats and carbohydrates; Digestion and nutritive value of the carbohydrates; Place of fats in nutrition; Food of school children and young students; Prophylactic and therapeutic value of food; Some suggestions about nourishment in acute disease; Good food for little money; Story of the New England kitchen; Public kitchens in relation to the workingman and the average housewife; Public kitchens in relation to school-lunches and to restaurants; Food of institutions.

LIST OF BOOKS FOR HIGH SCHOOL LIBRARIES. 267

	List price.	Price to schools.

R

W 67 el

979. **Elements of the theory and practice of cookery:** a text-book of household science for use in schools. Mary E. Williams, *and* Katharine Rolston Fisher. N. Y., Macmillan Co., 1901. 347 p. il. D. cl. .   1.00   .88

    This book will be of value to all interested in the better preparation of home-makers for their duties. It furnishes much excellent material which may be given to pupils by the teacher in talks and in simple experiments, showing the reasons for doing or not doing many things now done without reasons in every home.

    The book contains many practical lessons for girls which they may be interested in applying in their own homes.

    Section 4 on "Cleanliness and Cleaning" and the chapters on "Fuel Foods" and "Tissue-building Foods" should be read by every mother in the district. These chapters also give excellent matter to supplement the school work in physiology.

R

W 69 ha

980. [732.] **Handbook of domestic science and household arts,** for use in elementary schools. *Ed.* by Lucy L. W. Wilson. N. Y., Macmillan Co., 1900. 407 p. il. D. cl. ....   1.00   .65

    Will interest the pupils in the various operations of daily life and at same time teach them how to perform well many duties in the home. The care and beautifying of the home, cooking, washing, cleaning, mending and sewing are discussed by experts.

R

W 73 pr

981. [736.] **Principles of agriculture for common schools.** I. O. Winslow. N. Y., American Book Company, 1891. 152 p. il. D. cl. 60   .51

    Clear and simple statements of the natural laws and principles which underlie the subject of agriculture.

ENGINEERING AND BUILDING.

(Includes Arts of transportation, Roads, Railroads, Sanitation.)

	List price.	Price to schools.

S
B 17 mu
982. **Municipal engineering and sanitation.** Moses Nelson Baker. N. Y., Macmillan Co., 1902. 317 p. (Citizen's library series.) D. cl. 1.25   1.12

Contains good material for compositions and debates.

"This volume is intended for that large and rapidly growing class of persons who, either as officials or as citizens, are striving to improve municipal conditions. It is designed to be a review of the whole field of municipal engineering and sanitation, rather than an exhaustive study of one or a few branches of the subject. The most vital points, however, under each class of activities and interests have been dwelt upon, the underlying principles stated, and, in many instances, details from actual practice given."—*Preface.*

Contents: Introduction; Ways and means of communication; Municipal supplies; Collection and disposal of wastes; Protection of life, health, and property; Administration, finance, and public policy.

S
B 94 sc
983. **School sanitation and decoration.** Severance Burrage, *and* Henry Turner Bailey. Bost., D. C. Heath & Co., c1899. 224 p. il. D. cl. 1.50   1.10

A study of health and beauty in their relations to the public schools. The illustrations include reproductions of great masterpieces, plans and elevations of school buildings, specimens of artistic work by pupils, and many suggestive diagrams. The book contains much that will be helpful to teachers and school officers who have become interested in the subject of the sanitation and decoration of schools.

Contents: Location of schools, 1-7; Construction and requirements of school buildings, 8-32; Principles of ventilation, heating, and lighting, 33-59; Sanitary problems of the schoolhouse, 60-72; School furniture, 73-82; The schoolroom, 83-93; Schoolroom decoration, 94-121; Old country schoolroom, 122-27; School children, 127-145; Influence of school life upon the eye, 146-58; School authorities and patrons, 159-67; Beauty in school work, 168-84; Classified list of works of art for schoolroom decorations, 213-19.

S
G 69 be
984. **Bench work in wood:** a course of study and practice designed for the use of schools and colleges. W. F. M. Goss. Bost., Ginn & Co., 1902. 161 p. il. D. cl. .... .70   .60

This book is in three parts. Part I contains the essential facts concerning common bench tools for wood; it describes their action, explains their adjustments, and shows how they may be kept in order.

LIST OF BOOKS FOR HIGH SCHOOL LIBRARIES. 269

	List price.	Price to schools.

Part II presents a course of practice by which ability to use the tools may be acquired; and Part III discusses such forms and adaptations of joints as will meet the requirements of ordinary construction.

A very helpful book for Manual training classes.

S
―――
R 56 im

985. **Improvement of towns and cities:** or the practical basis of civic aesthetics. Charles Mulford Robinson. N. Y., G. P. Putnam's Sons, 1901. 309 p. D. cl. 1.25 1.12

Not only discusses the subjects of improvement of town and cities, but reviews the whole broad field of modern effort, picks out the salient points, states the best that has been done along every line, and encourages future effort by showing the progress attainable because somewhere attained.

Contents: Site of the city; Street plan; Elementary construction; Suppression and depression; Advertisement problem; Making utilities beautiful; Tree's importance; Possibilities of gardening; Parks and drives; "Squares" and playgrounds; Architectural development; Architectural obligations; Function and placing of sculpture; Popular education in art; Work of individuals and societies; Work of officials; Conclusion.

S
―――
Sh 1 am

986. [620.] **American highways:** a popular account of their condition and the means by which they may be bettered. Nathaniel Southgate Shaler. N. Y., Century Co., 1896. 293 p. D. cl. .... 1.50 .98

Refers mainly to rural highways.

S
―――
W 23 st

#987. **Street-cleaning:** and the disposal of a city's wastes: methods and results and the effect upon public health, public morals, and municipal prosperity. George E. Waring, *Jr.* N. Y., Doubleday & McClure Co., 1899. 230 p. il. D. cl. 1.25 1.12

This volume will furnish excellent material for debates and compositions.

During recent years Colonel Waring has revolutionized the cleaning of a great city. What this means is indicated by the statement that in New York the death rate has decreased from 26.78 per thousand inhabitants to 21.52, for which the clean streets are entitled to their own large share. It is interesting to know that in the near future Colonel Waring estimates that the revenue derived from the city's waste will pay half the expenses of the work. The book will be found of great value to all students of municipal questions and is the only one published devoted to Street Cleaning in the larger sense. It includes also the author's studies of foreign cities. It is frank, outspoken, and of the utmost practical value.

Contents: History; Conditions under recent administrations; Effect of political control as shown by the condition of the department at the beginning of the present administration; Reorganization of the force; Street-sweeping; Carting; Final disposition of garbage; Final disposition of street-sweeping and ashes; Final disposition of paper and rubbish; Stock and plant; Removal of snow; Street-railroads and pavements in New York; Street-cleaning in Europe: report of observations made in the summer of 1896; Juvenile street-cleaning leagues; Conclusion; Appendix.

T
—
W 65 sc

988. [636.] **Story of the cotton plant.** F. Wilkinson. N. Y., D. Appleton & Co., 1899. 272 p. il. T. (Library of useful stories.) cl. .... .40 .32

ATHLETIC AND RECREATIVE ARTS.

Some of these books ought to be in every library. They are sure to interest the majority of the pupils and many a boy or girl who does not care to read may be led to read them through the interest in play or out-of-door life, and from this reading they may be led to other reading.

V
—
Am 3 am

989. [718.] **American game fishes;** their habits, habitat, and peculiarities; how, when, and where to angle for them. By various writers. Chic., Rand, McNally & Co., 1892. 582 p. il. D. cl. .... 1.50 .98

Intensely interesting.

V
—
B 38 am

990.[714.] **American boy's book of sport.** D. C. Beard. N. Y., C: Scribner's Sons, 1896. 496 p. il. D. cl. 2.50 1.64

In this book boys will find directions for many games.

V
—
B 92 he

991. [730.] **Hermann the magician:** his life, his secrets. H. J. Burlingame. Chic., Laird & Lee, 1897. 298 p. il. O. cl. .... 1.00 .65

Fifty of the great magician's most noted tricks are explained and directions given for their performance.

		List price.	Price to schools.

V / C 15 am
992. [715.] **American girl's home book of work and play.** Helen Campbell. N. Y., G. P. Putnam's Sons, 1896. 431 p. il. D. cl. 1.75 1.15

Girls will find this a helpful book.

V / C 15 fo
993. [726.] **Football.** Walter Camp, *and* Lorin F. Deland. Bost., Houghton, Mifflin & Co., 1896. 425 p. il. O. cl. 2.00 1.30

History of the game, explanation of the game, directions for playing, and values of the game are given.

V / C 36 st
994. [698.] **Story of the Rhine-gold.** Anna Alice Chapin. N. Y., Harper & Bros., 1899. 138 p. il. D. cl. 1.25 .82

V / D 17 ho
995. [727.] **How to swim.** *Captain* Davis Dalton. N. Y., G. P. Putnam's Sons, 1899. 133 p. il. D. cl. .. 1.00 .65

Directions for the proper way of swimming.

V / F 57 st
996. [697.] **Stories of famous songs.** Sarah J. A. Fitz Gerald. Phil., J. B. Lippincott Co., 1898. 426 p. O. cl. 2.00 1.30

A very interesting book.

V / F 86 ca
997. [721.] **Canoe cruising and camping.** Perry D. Frazer. N. Y., Forest & Stream Pub. Co., 1897. 87 p. il. S. cl. .... 1.00 .75

Contains many hints and suggestions for the camper.

V / G 35 ca
998. [719.] **Camp life in the woods and the tricks of trapping and trap making.** William Hamilton Gibson. N. Y., Harper & Bros., 1899. 300 p. il. S. cl.. 1.00 .65

Boys will like this book.

V

G 88 tr

                                                                                   List Price to
                                                                                    price. schools.

999. **Trail and camp-fire:** the book of the Boone and Crockett club. George Bird Grinnell, *and* Theodore Roosevelt, *eds*. N. Y., Forest and Stream Pub. Co., 1897. 353 p. il. O. cl. 2.50 2.00

    Contents: The Labrador peninsula, by A. P. Low; Cherry, by L. S. Thompson; An African shooting trip, by W. Lord Smith; Sintamaskin, by C. Grant La Farge; Wolves and wolf nature, by G. Bird Grinnell; On the little Missouri by Theodore Roosevelt; Bear traits; Adirondack deer law, by W. Cary Sanger; Newfoundland caribou hunt, by Clay Arthur Pierce; Origin of the New York Zoological Society, by Madison Grant. "Books on big game" is a bibliographical article; it is followed by a list of books, written by members of the Boone and Crockett club, on hunting, exploration, natural history, etc.
    Interesting for Library reading.

V

G 93 s

1000. [700.] **Stories of famous operas.** H. A. Guerber. N. Y., Dodd, Mead & Co., 1899. 258 p. il. D. cl. 1.50 .98

V

G 93 st

1001. [699.] **Stories of the Wagner Operas.** H. A. Guerber. N. Y., Dodd, Mead & Co., 1899. 191 p. il. D. cl. .... 1.50 .98

    The stories are well told in the foregoing books and will be of interest to the Library reading classes.

V

H 38 st

1002. [696.] **Story of music.** W. J. Henderson. N. Y., Longmans, Green & Co., 1898. 212 p. S. cl. .. 1.25 .82

    The historical development of modern music.

V

H 77 ma

#1003. [729.] **Magic stage illusions and scientific diversions,** including trick photography. A. A. Hopkins. N. Y., Munn & Co., 1897. 566 p. il. O. cl. 2.50 1.87

    An attractive book for boys.

V

K 96 ro

1004. [723.] **Ropes, their knots and splices.** C. P. Kunhardt. N. Y., Forest and Stream Pub. Co., 1893. 48 p. il. S. cl. .... .50 .38

    Every boy will find this a fascinating book.

LIST OF BOOKS FOR HIGH SCHOOL LIBRARIES.

                                                                                    List Price to
V

M 45 sp   price. schools.

#1005. [716.] **Sport with gun and rod in American woods and waters.** *Ed.* by Alfred M. Mayer. N. Y., Century Co., 1883. 892 p. il. Q. cl. 5.00   3.25

    A fascinating book. One the boys will go to again and again.

V

P 21 wo

1006. **Woman's book of sports:** a practical guide to physical development and outdoor recreation. J. Parmly Paret. N. Y., D. Appleton & Co., 1901. 167 p. il. D. cl........................ 1.00   .90

    Contents: Introduction; A rudimentary lesson in golf; Lawn-tennis for beginners; How to sail a cat-boat; The useful art of swimming; The use and abuse of bicycling; Basketball for young women; Physical exercise and development; Men's sports from a woman's viewpoint—football, baseball, yacht-racing, rowing, athletics.

V

R 63 hu

1007. [710.] **Hunting.** Archibald Rogers, and six others. N. Y., C: Scribner's Sons, 1896. 327 p. il. D. (Out of door library.) cl. .... 1.50   .98

V

R 67 hu

1008. **Hunting in many lands:** the book of the Boone and Crockett club. Theodore Roosevelt, *and* George Bird Grinnell, *eds.* N. Y., Forest and Stream Pub. Co., 1895. 447 p. O. cl. 2.50   2.00

    The first volume published by the Boone and Crockett club, under the title "American big-game hunting," confined itself, as its title implied, to sport on this continent. In the second volume a number of sketches are included, written by members who have hunted big game in other lands, such as China, Tibet, Africa, etc.

    Boys who like out-door life and sports will enjoy this book and "Trail and camp-fire" by the same authors.

V

R 67 wi

#1009. [717.] **Wilderness hunter:** an account of the big game of the United States and its chase with horse, hound, and rifle. Theodore Roosevelt. G. P. Putnam's Sons, 1893. il. O. cl. .... .50   .33

    Every boy will like this book.

		List price.	Price to schools.
V Sa 7 at 1010. [712.]	**Athletic sports.** D. A. Sargent and seven others. N. Y., C: Scribner's Sons, 1897. 318 p. il. D. (Out of door library.) cl.	1.50	.98
V Sh 6 ca 1011. [720.]	**Camping and camp outfits.** G. O. Shields. Chic., Rand, McNally & Co., 1890. 169 p. il. D. cl.	1.25	.82

Contains practical points on how to dress for hunting, or other camping trips; what to provide in the way of bedding, tents, eatables, cooking-utensils, and all kinds of camp equipage; how to select camping-grounds; how to build camps, or shelters of various kinds; how to build camp-fires, and on many other topics in connection with the subject of outdoor life.

V Sm 5 mu 1012. [695.]	**Music: how it came to be what it is.** Hannah Smith. N. Y., C: Scribner's Sons, 1899. 254 p. il. D. cl.	1.25	1.12

A brief account of the progressive steps in the development of music as an art.

V Sm 6 st 1013. [701.]	**Stories of great national songs.** *Colonel* Nicholas Smith. Mil., Young Churchman Co., 1899. 238 p. il. D. cl.	1.25	1.00

Tells how our great national songs came to be written.

V St 4 ca 1014. [722.]	**Canoe and boat building.** W. P. Stephens. N. Y., Forest and Stream Pub. Co., 1898. 263 p. il. D. cl.	2.00	1.50

A practical book for the assistance of those who wish to build canoes.

V T 67 tr 1015. [724.]	**Track athletics in detail.** N. Y., Harper & Bros., 1896. 147 p. il. O. ("Harper's round table" library.) cl.	1.25	.82

A description of track and field sports for the young athlete who cannot secure personal training and instruction.

Contents: Track events, field events, and bicycling.

		List	Price to
V		price.	schools.
W 17 co			

#1016. **Complete angler:** or The contemplative man's recreation. Izaak Walton, *and* Charles Cotton. *Ed.* by John Major. Phil., J. B. Lippincott Co., 1899. 445 p. il. D. cl. 2.00 1.30

A dissertation on the delights of fishing, written from the literary standpoint. It will be of interest to the classes in English literature.

V
———
W 63 ho

1017. [725.] **How to play golf.** H. G. Wigham. Chic., H. S. Stone, 1898. 335 p. il. D. cl. .... 1.50 .96

Directions and rules for playing the game.

V
———
W 69 mo

1018. [713.] **Mountain climbing.** Edward L. Wilson, and six others. N. Y., C: Scribner's Sons, 1897. 358 p. il. D. (Out of door library.) cl. ....1.50 .98

The chapters in these books have appeared at different times in Scribner's magazine. They will fascinate the boys.

V
———
Ya 1 an

1019. [711.] **Angling.** Leroy M. Yale, and six others. N. Y., C: Scribner's Sons, 1896. 305 p. il. D. (Out of door library.) cl. .... 1.50 .98

V10
———
G 91 e

1020. [270.] **Edwin Booth.** Recollections by his daughter Edwina Booth Grossman. N. Y., Century Co., 1894. 292 p. il. O. cl. 3.00 1.90

The life and letters of an interesting and great artist.

V10
———
J 35 a

#1021. [292.] **Autobiography of Joseph Jefferson.** N. Y., Century Co., 1897. 509 p. il. O. cl. 4.00 2.50

The story of a great man's life most delightfully told by himself.

FINE ARTS.

W
―――
Ad 1 am

              List Price to
              price. schools.

1022. [728.] **Amateur photography:** a practical guide for the beginner. W. I. Lincoln Adams. N. Y., Baker & Taylor Co., 1899. 135 p. il. O. cl. ... 1.00 .75

 One of the best books on the subject.

W
―――
B 41 el

#1023. **Elementary history of art:** architecture, sculpture, painting. - *Mrs.* Arthur Bell. (N. D'Anvers, *pseud.*) N. Y., C: Scribner's Sons, 1900. 323 p. il. O. cl. 3.75 2.45

 A good reference book.

W
―――
B 81 fi

1024. **Fine arts.** Gerald Baldwin Brown. N. Y., C: Scribner's Sons, 1901. 321 p. il. (University series.) D. cl. .... 1.00 .90

 A good exposition of the principles underlying aesthetics, of the criteria in judging works of art, and of the historic development of architecture, sculpture, and painting.

 Contents: Beginnings of art; Festival, in its relation to the form and spirit of classical art; Mediaeval Florence and her painters; Some elements of effect in the arts of form; Work of art as significant; Work of art as beautiful; Architectural beauty in relation to construction; Conventions of sculpture; Painting old and new.

W
―――
Em 3 ho

1025. [692.] **How to enjoy pictures.** Mabel S. Emery. Bost., Prang Educational Co., 1898. 290 p. il. O. cl. 1.50 1.10

 A guide to the appreciation of more than fifty famous paintings.

W
―――
G 17 ha

#1026. **Handbook of Greek sculpture.** Ernest Arthur Gardner. N. Y., Macmillan Co., 1897. 553 p. il. (Handbooks of archaeology and antiquities.) D. cl. 2.50 2.25

 A good reference work. This should only be purchased by the larger libraries.

W
G 63 hi

#1027. **History of art**: for classes, art students, and tourists in Europe. William Henry Goodyear. Ed. 14, rev., enl. N. Y., A. S. Barnes & Co., c1896. 394 p. il. O. cl..... ....   2.80   2.52

List Price to
price. schools.

An excellent reference book on art, containing a brief survey of the history of Architecture, Sculpture, Painting, and Music.

W
G 91 be

1028. |573.] **Beginnings of art.** Ernst Grosse. N. Y., D. Appleton & Co., 1897. 327 p. il. D. (Anthropological series.) cl. 1.75   1.15

Very interesting account of personal decoration, ornamentation, drawing, dancing, poetry, and music among primitive peoples. Read with the teacher a new field of interests will be opened for students.

W
H 25 hi

#1029. **History of American art.** Sadakichi Hartmann. Bost., L. C. Page & Co., 1902. 2 vols. il. (Art lovers' series.) D. cl. 4.00   2.60

A standard treatise on this subject. The illustrations and descriptions are in themselves works of art. The volumes contain interesting information relating to American history and may be used to supplement instruction in this subject. This set should be purchased only by the larger libraries.

Contents—Vol. 1. American art before 1828; Our landscape-painters; The old school; The new school. Vol. 2: American sculpture; The graphic arts; American art in Europe; Latest phases. The illustrations are reproductions of the works of representative artists and sculptors such as West, Tryon, La Farge, Whistler, St. Gaudens, Sargent, and others.

W
H 85 wo

1030. **World's painters and their pictures.** Deristhe L. Hoyt. Bost., Ginn & Co., 1899. 272 p. il. D. cl. 1.25   1.96

A handbook for young students and general readers, which defines the art of painting and other questions in historic art. Some of the subjects discussed are: Ancient painting—Egyptian, Greek, Roman; Beginning of modern Christian painting; Italian painting—Florentine, or Tuscan schools, Gothic, early Renaissance, and high Renaissance periods; with other issues of Italian, Dutch, German, Flemish, English, and American art, etc.

W
H 93 tu
1031. **Tuscan sculpture of the fifteenth century:** a collection of sixteen pictures reproducing works by Donatello, the Della Robbia, Mino Da Fiesole, and others, with introduction and interpretation. Estelle M. Hurll. Bost., Houghton, Mifflin & Co., 1902. 97 p. il. (Riverside Art series.) O. cl. .75 .67

W
H 93 va
1032. **Van Dyck:** a collection of fifteen pictures and a portrait of the painter with introduction and interpretation. Estelle M. Hurll. Bost., Houghton, Mifflin & Co., 1902. 92 p. il. (Riverside art series.) O. cl. .... .75 .67

The previous volumes in this series are now on the 1902 "Township List."
The whole series will furnish interesting material for the Library reading class in Art.

W
L 35 ma
1033. **Manual of wood carving.** Charles G. Leland. Rev. by John J. Holtzapffel. N. Y., C: Scribner's Sons, 1897. 162 p. il. O. bds. 1.75 1.15

A good book for schools having a course in Manual training.

W
M 34 te
1034. [694.] **Text-book of the history of sculpture.** Allan Marquand, *and* Arthur L. Frothingham. N. Y., Longmans, Green & Co., 1896. 293 p. il. D. (College histories of art.) cl. .... 1.50 .98

For reference only.

W
St 7 st
1035. [534.] **Story of photography.** Alfred T. Story. N. Y., D. Appleton & Co., 1898. 169 p. il. S. (Library of useful stories.) cl. .... .40 .32

A scientific and historical account of photography.

W
T 79 sh
1036. [693.] **Short history of architecture.** Arthur Lyman Tuckerman. N. Y., C: Scribner's Sons, 1897. 168 p. il. O. cl. .... 1.50 .98

For reference only.

W
———
V 28 ar

List price. Price to schools.

1037. [686.] **Art for art's sake.** John C. Van Dyke. N. Y., C: Scribner's Sons, 1899. 249 p. il. D. cl. ...   1.50   .98

Essays on painting, color, light and shade, perspective, values, textures and surfaces, and brush work, which older pupils will find interesting.

W
———
V 28 te

1038. [687.] **Text-book of the history of painting.** John C. Van Dyke. N. Y., Longmans, Green & Co., 1898. 289 p. il. D. (College histories of art.) cl. ..   1.50   .98

Main facts in the history of painting. Good book for reference.

W
———
W 57 sc

#1039. **School architecture: a general treatise for the use of architects and others.** Edmund March Wheelwright. Bost., Rogers & Manson, 1901. 324 p. il. Q. cl. 5.00   4.50

A very useful volume for preliminary study where the building of a schoolhouse becomes necessary. The plans and specifications will prove very helpful. The chapter on heating, ventilation and sanitation deserves close study on the part of every principal and school officer.

ENGLISH LANGUAGE.

X
———
B 31 ta

1040. [680.] **Talks on writing English.** Arlo Bates. Bost., Houghton, Mifflin & Co., 1901. 259 p. D. cl. ..   1.50   .98

Made up from material used in a course of lectures given in the Lowell Free Classes as supplementary to the author's previous "Talks on writing English." The book takes up many of the more delicate matters of composition, which would have been out of place in the earlier course, such as "Little foxes," the faults which spoil writing; Composition and revision; Participles and gerunds; Parallel construction; The topic sentence; Paragraphs; The point of view; Figures; Exposition; Description; Narration; Dialogue; Punctuation; Letter-writing, etc.

For reference for the teacher of English.

X
———
C 12 fo

1041. **Forms of discourse: with an introductory chapter on style.** William B. Cairns. Bost., Ginn & Co., 1898. 356 p. D. cl. ....   1.15   .98

"This work is an attempt to present the subject of 'literary invention in a form suited to the needs of pupils in high schools and

	List price.	Price to schools.

colleges. It has been prepared because the author was unable to find, in the many excellent text-books on formal rhetoric, any adequate discussion of this subject that he could use with his own classes. The authors of many recent text-books have assumed that the study of rhetoric is the study of style, and nothing more. If they have treated the forms of discourse at all, they have done so by way of literary analysis, and not in a manner that will prove helpful to young writers."—*Preface.*

X

C 54 s

1042. **Study of English and American poets:** a laboratory method. J. Scott Clark. N. Y., C: Scribner's Sons, 1900. 859 p. O. cl. 2.00 1.80

A complementary volume to the author's "Study of English prose writers," published in 1898. The method here offered consists in determining the particular and distinctive features of a writer's style (using the term style in its widest sense), in sustaining this analysis by a very wide concensus of critical opinion, in illustrating the particular characteristics of each writer by carefully selected extracts from his works, and in then requiring the pupil to find, in the works of the writer, parallel illustrations. Biographical outlines precede each author discussed and a bibliography.
Valuable for reference for the teacher.

X

C 54 st

1043. **Study of English prose writers:** a laboratory method. J. Scott Cark. N. Y., C: Scribner's Sons, 1900. 879 p. D. cl. 2.00 1.80

Valuable for reference for the teacher of English. The method used in this book consists in determining the particular and distinctive features of a writer's style (using the term *style* in its wide sense), in sustaining that analysis by a very wide concensus of critical opinion, in illustrating the particular characteristics of each writer by voluminous and carefully selected extracts from his works, and in then requiring the pupil to find in the works of the writer parallel illustrations.—*Preface.*

Contents: Bacon; Milton; Bunyan; Addison; Steele; Defoe; Swift; Goldsmith; Samuel Johnson; Burke; Lamb; Scott; De Quincey; Macaulay; Thackeray; John Henry Newman; Matthew Arnold; Carlyle; Eliot; Dickens; Ruskin; Irving; Hawthorne; Emerson; Lowell; Holmes.

X

D 98 st

1044. **Story-teller's art.** Charity Dye. Bost., Ginn & Co., 1899. 90 p. D. cl. .... .50 .43

A guide to the elementary study of fiction, intended for high schools and academies. This book will be helpful to both teachers and pupils in the study of Literature.

Contents: To the teacher; To the student; Materials; Setting; Plot; Study of incident; Character study; Method; Purpose; Com-

                                                         List   Price to
                                                         price. schools.
ment; Exercises illustrating the development of power in the study
of fiction; Word about realism; Some books suitable for study in
secondary schools; Some good books and stories that every person
should know; References upon the study of fiction.

X
―――
G 16 fo
1045. **Forms of prose literature.** J: Hays-Gardiner. N.
       Y., C: Scribner's Sons, 1901. 498 p. D. cl. ... 1.50   1.35
   Contains many valuable suggestions for the teacher of composition.

X
―――
M 47 ar
1046. **Art of writing English:** a manual for students with
       chapters on paraphrasing, essay-writing, précis-
       writing, punctuation, and other matters. John M.
       D. Meiklejohn. N. Y., D. Appleton & Co., 1900.
       334 p. D. cl. .... 1.50   .98
   Good as a reference book for class in English.

                              ORATORY.

                       (Composition and delivery.)

Xx
―――
Al 2 ar
1047. **Art of debate.** Raymond MacDonald Alden. N. Y.,
       Henry Holt & Co., 1900. 279 p. D. cl. .... 1.00   .90
   In the literary society and in the rhetorical work of the high
school, the debate is gaining prominence as the best means for
developing the expressive powers of the pupils. The free discussion of questions of state and nation, especially during political
campaigns, calls not only for a mastery of the facts concerning
them, but also for ability to present them in a logical manner and
with the greatest effectiveness. This book will be found a good
helper in promoting these ends. It treats of: 1, Nature of debate;
2, Subjects of debate; 3, Preliminary work; 4, Burden of proof;
5, Methods of proof; 6, Methods of refutation; 7, Structure and
style; 8, The spoken debate; 9, Sample arguments; briefs; and
suggestive questions for debate.

Xx
―――
B 79 br
1048. [739.] **Briefs for debate on current, political, eco-
       nomic, and social topics.** Ed. by W. Du Bois
       Brookings, *and* Ralph Curtis Ringwalt. N. Y.,
       Longmans, Green & Co., 1897. 213 p. D. cl. .. 1.25   1.12
   Material and suggestions with valuable references for debates.

	List price.	Price to schools.

Xx
C 54 ar

1049. **Art of reading aloud**: a text-book for class instruction in practical elocution. J. Scott Clark. N. Y., Henry Holt & Co., 1892. 159 p. S. cl. .... .60 .54

A little book which takes up the study of "A Christmas carol" with the one object of reading it expressively. The marginal references in the main text to the principles of good reading in the first part of the book are helpful. High school teachers will find this book an aid in teaching the subject of expressive reading.

Xx
C 54 pr

1050. **Practical public speaking**: a text-book for colleges and secondary schools. Solomon H. Clark, *and* Frederick M. Blanchard. N. Y., C: Scribner's Sons, 1901. 301 p. D. cl. .... 1.00 .90

A helpful book for the teacher of English. Will also be found interesting to members of high school literary societies who are anxious to master the art of public speaking. This is not a book on voice culture or gesture. It deals directly and clearly with those essential qualities of speech which are necessary for good public speaking. Many examples of oratory are given illustrative of the special phases of the subject emphasized by the author such as: "The call to arms"; Patrick Henry; America's Duty to Greece, Henry Clay; Gettysburg speech, Lincoln; Reply to Hayne, Webster; Spartacus to the gladiators.

Xx
C 84 pr

1051. **Pros and cons**: complete debates, important questions fully discussed in the affirmative and the negative. A. H. Craig. N. Y., Hinds & Noble. c1897. 461 p. D. cl. 1.50 1.15

The debating society will want this book. It tells how to organize a society, gives rules governing debates, fully discusses in the affirmative and negative twenty questions, outlines six others, furnishes two hundred fifty selected topics for debate, and gives sample addresses for salutatories, valedictories, and for other occasions.

Xx
L 51 pr

1052. [741.] **Principles of public speaking**. Guy Carleton Lee. N. Y., G. P. Putnam's Sons, 1900. 465 p. il. D. cl. 1.75 1.15

A practical exposition of the art of public speaking.

	List price.	Price to schools.

Xx
M 43 re
1053. [740.] References for literary workers: with introduction to topics and questions for debate. Henry Matson. Chic., A. C. McClurg & Co., 1892. O. cl. 3.00 1.96

Valuable outlines and references for essays and debates. This volume and Brookins and Ringwalt's "Briefs for debate" should be in every library.

Xx
R 47 mo
1054. [742.] Modern American oratory: seven representative orations, with notes and an essay on the theory of oratory. Ralph Curtis Ringwalt. N. Y., Henry Holt & Co., 1898. 334 p. D. cl. .... 1.00 .90

Treats of the oration only; what oratory is; the different kinds; analysis of the oration with reference to its preparation; examples of orations by Schurz, Black, Phillips, Depew, Curtis, Grady, and Beecher are given. A good manual for students of oratory and one which will furnish excellent material for classes in argumentation and oral expression.

Xx
So 8 st
1055. **Steps to oratory:** a school speaker. F. Townsend Southwick. N. Y., American Book Company, c1900. 464 p. D. cl. .... 1.00 .85

"This collection includes representative selections from the best literature, arranged and condensed for effective use in school declamation.

Part First gives a sufficient outline of the technique to guide the student, but presupposes some knowledge and training on the part of the teacher, and Part Second consists entirely of selections, arranged as closely as practicable on a historical plan, but interspersed with examples of colloquial and humorous styles."

GERMAN LANGUAGE.

X47
H 37 ge
1056. **German orthography and phonology:** a treatise with a word-list. George Hempl. Bost., Ginn & Co., 1898. 298 p. D. cl. 2.00 1.70

A helpful reference book for the teachers of German.

"This book aims to be a systematic and practical treatise on subjects pertaining to the writing, printing, and uttering of Modern German. These subjects have received various degrees of attention from scholars. In the case of those that had already been fully treated, for example, Spelling & Phonetics, it was my chief

	List price.	Price to schools.

business to select and arrange the most important elements; on the other hand, in treating neglected subjects like Accent and the Development of German Letter-forms, I felt myself warranted in presenting more or less fully such contributions as I had to make."—*Preface*.

Contents: Orthography—Alphabet; Spelling; Division of words; Use of capitals; Punctuation.

Phonology—Phonetics; German speech-sounds; Pronunciation; Accent—Nature of accent; Pitch; Stress; Sentence-stress; Word-stress; Word-list and index.

X47
―――
T 36 pr

1057. Practical German grammar. Ed. 3, rev. Calvin Thomas. N. Y., Henry Holt & Co., 1901. 463 p. D. cl. 1.12   1.01

X47
―――
T 71 sh

1058. Short historical grammar of the German language: translated and adapted from Professor Behaghel's "Deutsche Sprache." Emil Trechmann. N. Y., Macmillan & Co., 1899. 194 p. S. cl. .... 1.00   .90

"This little book is published in the hope that it may be of some use to those who are entering upon the study of the history of the German language. It is a translation, slightly altered and adapted for English students, of Dr. Otto Behaghel's book of the same name (Die deutsche Sprache), which forms one of a series of little volumes intended to popularize science and knowledge in all its departments (Das Wissen der Gegenwart). The author is well known as one of the most diligent researchers in the field of Old German and Teutonic philology and literature, and his book is the only one hitherto published which attempts to give in small compass and in popular form the results of recent studies in that sphere."—*Preface*.

This book will be helpful to the teacher of German.

LITERATURE.

The study of literature is not the study of the history of literature with the occasional poem or fragment of prose thrown in. To stuff the mind with the biographies of authors, and to memorize the list of books they have written is not to study literature. Instead of reading about authors and studying a text-book on literature, the student must come into direct contact with the literature and read for himself. The practice in teaching literature has been to take a few pieces of literature and to spend much time in analyzing each one. The meaning of every word is studied and its derivation traced, figures are pointed out and named, historical facts verified, accuracy of scientific facts tested, every allusion traced until in this process of vivisection the real life has been lost. Great pieces of literature have lived not because they furnish fine fields for mental gymnastics, but because they reveal the deepest, the truest, the most beautiful, the best in life. Literature is an expression of the soul of humanity, of the whole range of human experiences, and the study of literature should consist in the interpretation of the experiences, the thoughts, the feelings, and the aspirations of the race. Dr. J. W. Stearns says: "Interpretation should consist in such things as the artistic presentation of character types, the setting forth of the play of circumstances in moulding character, the unfolding of the consequences of actions and the might of destiny, the manifestations of the spiritual meaning of material things revealing the charm of beauty in things common, touching into life the springs of noble emotions in us, filling us with a sense of the deeper meanings of life, and enlarging our sympathies."

AIMS IN TEACHING LITERATURE.

The aims in teaching literature should be to inculcate a love and desire for reading, resulting in the formation of the habit of reading; to interpret life; to give power and information; to uplift by giving new ideals and inspirations; and to cultivate a taste for good reading. The pupil ought to be taught how to read, how to handle a book, how to use an index, how to read to a topic, and how to read by skipping.

LITERARY MERIT.

Judgments in literary merit can only be formed after wide reading and many comparisons. As the student makes these comparisons he is building up his conception of style. Is the author clear in his statements? What of his skill in narration and illustration? Are his descriptions vivid? How does he interpret nature? Are his men and women real flesh and blood? How does this composition compare with others of the same kind? With others by the same author?

WHAT TO READ.

"If literature be the life of the people, it should also prepare for that kind of life in which the child is forced to live, immediately after passing out of school. While there may be room for discussion as to the style in which thought should be expressed, it is beyond dispute that the clearest writers, those who use the language to express unmistakably what they mean, those who deal with subjects that are nearest to the daily life of the people themselves, ought to become a part of the mental furnishing of each high school pupil."--J. M. Greenwood.

Lists of novels, essayists, and poets in the library should be made out, from which pupils may select what they wish to read. At least six novels should be read, each by a different author, part of them portraying life and part of them character. The students should read enough poetry by six different poets and essays by six different essayists to get a fair idea of their way of writing, as well as to get the uplift and power which come from reading. It is best to have all in the class reading novels, poetry, or essays at the same time,— though after the first two or three pieces of literature read together to show how to study, it is best to have students read different works of literature in any one line. The library law providing for libraries in the schools now extends to high schools in cities of the fourth class, so that schools ought to have books to carry on this work. Teachers will find the notes on the books in this list especially valuable in teaching literature and directing literary readings.

PLACE OF HISTORY OF LITERATURE,—BIOGRAPHY AND LITERARY CRITICISM.

History of literature: A short course in history of literature, —taking the history in great epochs,—these epochs based upon the kind of literature produced,—may be of value in the study of literature. The history should serve as a frame-work to keep the reading organized and to help the student to get some idea of the entirety of literature. In the study of the history of literature some of the most typical pieces of literature might be read in a cursory way. It will scarcely be best to attempt anything before the period of Shakespeare.

The history of literature should come in the last term's work in literature.

Place of biography: When the student becomes so filled with the writings of any author that his personality becomes of interest then the biography may be read with profit. But the biography of an author should always be approached through his writing. In the literary production the writer has given us the best of himself.

Place of the text-book and literary criticism: After the student has read and made his judgments it is well to compare these judgments with those of critics, as found in his text-book, periodicals, and essays in criticism. The text-book should always be an *aid* in the work, not an *end*. When the study of literature is confined to the memorizing of the facts found in a text-book, the text-book is harmful. The text-book shows the scope of the subject, is a suggestive index for study, shows where things may be found, and brings together in compact form judgments on authors in their writings.

College entrance requirements: Essays, poetry, and fiction indicated as college entrance requirements, should fall in their proper place with other compositions of the same kind,—reserving those intended for more intensive study till the last part of the course.

THE RECITATION.

In beginning the work in any form of literature it is well to take one book or piece of literature, and for teachers and pupils to work together until the pupils gain some insight into the right way of reading.

For fiction is suggested: Ivanhoe—a picture of past life. Silas Marner—a study of character development. Rise of Silas Lapham—a study of American life, a novel of theme and a novel of character study.

For poetry is suggested: Vision of Sir Launfal, Lady of the Lake, The Princess, or a similar long poem which furnishes sufficient variety to cover work outlined under poetry.

For essays is suggested: Hunting of the Deer, or any short essay from pupils' readers.

Then let the pupil select from a given list of books such as he will like to read,—the teacher guiding the choice through the pupils' interests. In his study and recitations he should follow the models, studied with the teacher.

The work in reading and in class should be definite and clear. The student's judgments should be based upon facts he can point out. It is not enough that he says the music is smooth and flowing—he must recite or read the portions he considers "smooth and flowing" and tell what makes them so. If he call a poem imaginative he must prove his statement by selecting the imaginative portions.

The judgments should be *his own* and based upon *his own reading*.

As the student progresses the study of literature may become more and more intensive but it should never degenerate into parsing and analyzing.

The value of the study of literature will be greatly enhanced by the constant memorizing of such portions of literature as have appealed to the student in his reading, and certain recitations should be devoted to the reciting of memory gems.

Remember, that in all this work the teacher must know as far as possible what is in the pupil's mind—for the pupil can only understand and feel by the assistance of what he has already experienced, felt, and learned. He can only assimilate new ideas by means of his present ones. Every new relation of the idea helps to correct, clear, and extend the meaning, and instead of trying to get the whole meaning in its one relation it is often better to read on, getting at truth in different relations and deepening and enriching experience at the same time.

It is impossible for a student at any one time of his life to comprehend the whole of a piece of literature, no matter how much time is spent in studying it.

LITERARY READINGS.

Special Aims:
    a. To learn how to read and to utilize that knowledge in practice.
    b. To extend student's knowledge of books and to develop a taste for and a love of good literature.
    c. Through his reading to put the student in touch with life around him by making him interested in what people of the world are interested in.

NATURE OF THE READING—CURSORY.

Scudder says, "There can be no manner of question that between the ages of six and sixteen a large part of the best literature of the world may be read." Which means that in the grades as well as in the high school this cursory reading must be carried on. Cursory reading does not mean skimming through a book and throwing it aside with no further thought—*it means rapid reading to get the pith and point—which implies skill in the right way of reading and in the use of books.* Says John Burroughs, "The way they teach literature in the schools and colleges is calculated to kill any love for it. It seems to me I would lose my love of Shakespeare if I had to dissect him, and find out the meaning of every word and expression. I want to ride buoyantly over the waves. I want to feel the wind and the motion—not talk about them. If I had to teach literature, I hardly know myself how I would do it. You can't by bearing on—you can't by mere intellectual force on a book show its charm. It appeals to the emotions. You have got to approach it in a different way. You must be fluid. All I should hope to do would be to give the student the key to the best literature. We would read books together. We would read good books and we would read poor books. I would say, 'well, we won't talk; we will read and see. Here is a poor book—don't you see? It's overdrawn—'t isn't delicate!' I would get at books in their sentiment and general character, not in their details. If you tear it all in to bits, you haven't the thing itself any more."

LINES OF READING.

Literary reading should include all lines of reading. So far as possible the pupils should be guided in their choice of reading through their interests. Lists of books which are in the library should be made out in the various lines of reading from which the pupils may select the books they wish to read. It is not necessary that all the pupils in a class read the same book, or books on the same subject. Nor is it necessary that a pupil read a book from cover to cover. Many times only a portion of a book will appeal to a pupil—or be of value to him. This is especially so in science books, books of poetry, and books where a part meets some interest started in the regular school work; as, a part of a book of history which relates to a topic in the history lesson.

GUIDING A PUPIL IN HIS CHOICE OF READING THROUGH HIS INTERESTS.

The teacher cannot guide the pupils' reading unless she makes a careful study of their interests and needs. She must lead them from the interests of today to higher and wider interests and utilize at every step interests gained in other lines of work. She must take advantage of interests closely related to old interests, or those naturally growing out of old interests; interests created by pupils' environment, as Indian relics in Wisconsin; interests in current events coming to his notice; as, a circus in town, the Spanish-American War, the celebration of Washington's Birthday, etc., etc.; interests created by another's interests; as reading a book because another says it is good. Make the pupil's present interest the basis which shall determine his present line of reading. If he is interested in fiction only, then give him a list of fiction from which he may select a book to read. By questioning, by directing his attention, or arousing his curiosity, he may be made interested in some character, place, fact, or event in the book, and this interest may be made the basis for future reading. Thus a pupil reading Ivanhoe may be led to read English history by arousing an interest in Richard, the Lion-Hearted. Again, a pupil who has read a story of Holland may be led to read a book of travel in Holland, because of interest aroused in the manners and customs of that country. If the pupils' present interest is in history, science, or other lines of work, a similar plan may be pursued. The work will have to be largely individual.

THE WAY TO GUIDE THE PUPIL IN HIS READING.

The teacher should have clearly in mind the way to read the different kinds of literature as outlined in this list, under the topic "Literature." By questioning, by directing attention to what is essential, and by directing discussions, lead the pupils into the right way of reading. Remember that the work is new to the pupils and do not expect too much at first. Suppose the class has been reading fiction portraying life. The teacher can not expect them to cover all the points in the outline. He may ask for a single point—as descriptions of characters in the book which may be considered as types. The student may be asked to be able to report on homes and surroundings, and amusements for the next recitation. Successive topics may be taken up with the same books or others until the pupil has a fairly good idea of what he is expected to get out of the novel of life. After considerable practice he will be able to discuss all the points in a single book.

THE RECITATION.

For convenience the classes should be divided into groups— the smaller, the better; each group meeting the teacher twice a week for forty or forty-five minutes to report.

The recitations should consist of reports of what has been read, and these reports should be oral. The recitation ought to be an exchange of impressions and feelings, a talking over of what has been found enjoyable, good, beautiful, and helpful. The pupil makes his report as a contribution to the whole and stands ready to answer questions by his class-mates and teachers; to discuss with them what he has found; and to compare his judgments with theirs. Thus all take part in the recitation and attention is secured. The reports should not be too much in detail and should follow in general the plan of reading outlined in *Literature*. It is not necessary that the students in any one group read and report on the same book or on different books in the same subject.

UTILIZE THE MATERIAL GAINED IN THIS READING IN OTHER LINES OF WORK.

In the geography class the descriptions found in fiction and in books of travel may be used to advantage to help the pupils see the places studied. In the history class descriptions of life from historical fiction will help the pupil to vizualize history and to get the spirit of the times. Biography will make history real, besides giving to the pupil ideals of character and action. In the class in science the student may be led to read the books of science which will broaden and make more interesting his study of science.

Suppose the pupils are studying the topic in history "Results of the Norman Conquest in English History." There is no book that will give them a better idea of life in England at that time than Scott's "Ivanhoe." Under the topic "Character of the Saxons and Normans"—ask those pupils who have read Ivanhoe to describe the characters of Athelstane, Rowena, and Cedric, as types of Saxons; and the Norman nobles Beouf, Fitzurse, de Bracy, Bois-Guilbert, as types of Norman character. Results in language will be shown in the conversation between Gurth and Wamba. Results in literature will be shown in the French verses and Anglo-Saxon ballads. Condition in religion will be shown by the conditions of the church and the intolerance of all classes as portrayed in the novel, etc., etc.

By calling for these topics the pupils may be led to read portions of the book more carefully, and with a young or inexperienced class it may be well to refer to the novel by pages under each topic. Not all of the literary reading is for the purpose of supplementary school work. Care should be taken not to make the work a drudgery, but a delight.

RECORDS.

A careful record of what pupils read should be kept. It is a good plan to have pupils when they have read a book write on a sheet of paper the title of the book, the author, date of reading, and things in the book which they have liked best. The following form has been found practical:

Name of Pupil — Class.

Title.	Author.	When read.	Remarks.
Prince and Pauper.	D. Clemens......	Jan. 1, 1900.	A very interesting story about two boys who change places.
Ivanhoe...........	Sir Walter Scott	Jan. 20, 1900..	Fine book. Tells about Richard the Lion Hearted, also about knights in England long ago.
Nobility of Labor..	Thomas Carlyle..	Feb. 4, 1900..	Shows that all labor is honorable, be it high or low, with head or hand.

If these sheets are carefully kept they will show what a student has read during his four years in the high school. Many times "the remarks" are a key to the pupil's interests and tell what he has gained from his reading.

HISTORIES OF LITERATURE.

Y
―――
Ar 6 ma
#1059. **Manual of English literature:** historical and critical, with an appendix on English metres. Thomas Arnold. N. Y., Longmans, Green & Co., 1899. 662 p. Ed. 9, rev. O. cl. 2.00 1.80

    A good book of reference. Too extended a treatment of the subject for use as anything but a reference book.

Y
―――
B 31 ta
1060. [6.] **Talks on the study of literature.** Arlo Bates. Bost., Houghton, Mifflin & Co., 1898. 260 p. D. cl. .... 1.50 .98

    For the teacher. Many of the essays will be enjoyed by the older pupils. Can be used in essay reading.

Y
―――
B 39 st
1061. **Studies in American letters.** Henry A. Beers. Phil., George W. Jacobs & Co., c1895. 291 p. il. D. cl. 1.00 .90

    A short sketch of American literature valuable as a guide-book. A reading course is appended to the chapters on each period suggesting some of the works of the most important authors of those periods, which should be read.

                                                                         List Price to
                                                                       price. schools.

Y
———
B 65 ha
1062. [1.] **Handbook of universal literature.** Anne C. Lynch Botta. Bost., Houghton, Mifflin & Co., 1898. 575 p. D. cl. 2.00 1.30

    A general survey of literature which will prove helpful in finding an author's place and what he has written.
    For reference only.

Y
———
B 78 sh
1063. **Short history of American literature:** designed primarily for use in schools and colleges. Walter C. Bronson. Bost., D. C. Heath & Co., 1900. 374 p. S. cl. .... .80   .72

    The literature has been presented in its relation to the larger life of the nation, and to the literatures of England and the continent of Europe, for only so can American literature be completely understood and its significance perceived. The greater writers have the larger amount of space given them, although the minor authors have not been neglected. The appendix contains nearly forty pages of extracts from not easily accessible colonial newspapers and magazines, a bibliography of colonial and revolutionary literature (13 p.), a reference list of books and articles, and index.

Y
———
B 79 en
1064. **English literature.** Stopford A. Brooke. With chapters on English literature (1832–1892) and on American literature by George R. Carpenter. N. Y., Macmillan Co., 1902. 358 p. S. cl. .... .90   .81

    One of the best short surveys of English literature.

Y
———
B 95 li
1065. **Literary landmarks.** Mary E. Burt. Bost., Houghton, Mifflin & Co., 1899. 173 p. il. D. cl. ..... .75   .49

    "A guide to good reading for young people, and teachers' assistant, with a carefully selected list of seven hundred books."
    Contents: Theories of children's reading; Reading which does not deal with totals—epigrammatic literature; Works of the creative imagination; Scientific and geographical reading, books of travel; History and biography; Utilitarian literature, books of reference, miscellaneous; List of books referred to in the preceding pages; Additional list of books.

Y

F 53 ge

                    List Price to
                    price. schools.

1066. [5.] **General survey of American literature.** Mary Fisher. Chic., A. C. McClurg & Co., 1899. 391 p. D. cl. .... 1.50   .98

 Essays in criticism which older pupils may enjoy. For comparison.

Y

F 75 ne

#1067. **New England primer:** a reprint of the earliest known edition, with many facsimiles and reproductions, and an historical introduction. Paul Leicester Ford, *ed.* N. Y., Dodd, Mead & Co., 1899. 78 p. il. D. bds. .... 1.50   .98

 This little volume is a specimen of the earliest New England literature. It shows the stern Puritan mood with absolute faithfulness, and will be of interest to the classes in Colonial history and American literature. The introduction gives an excellent history of its origin and development.

Y

G 69 sh

1068. **Short history of modern English literature.** Edmund Gosse. N. Y., D. Appleton & Co., 1900. 416 p. D. cl. .... 1.50   .98

 For reference only.

 The main aim in the volume has been to show the movement of English literature and to survey the process of its growth.

 Contents: Age of Chaucer; Close of the Middle Ages; Age of Elizabeth; Decline; Age of Dryden; Age of Anne; Age of Johnson; Age of Wordsworth; Age of Byron; Early Victorian age; Age of Tennyson; Epilogue; Biographical list; Bibliographical note.

Y

G. 95 ha

1069. **Handbook of poetics:** for students of English verse. Francis B. Gummere. Bost., Ginn & Co., 1898. 250 p. D. cl. .... 1.00   .85

 A concise, systematic statement of the principles of poetry. This book will be helpful to the teacher of Literature.

 Contents: I. Subject-matter—Epic, Lyric and dramatic poetry; II. Style; III. Metre.

Y

H 33 le

1070. **Lectures on the literature of the age of Elizabeth:** and characters of Shakespeare's plays. William Hazlitt. London, George Bell and Sons (N. Y., Macmillan Co.), 1901. 268 + 247 pp. D. (Bohn's libraries.) cl. .... 1.00   .90

 Good for extended reference work and for the use of the Literature teacher.

Y
———
H 51 ho

                                                                                                                                        List Price to
                                                                                                                                       price. schools.

1071. **How to study literature**: a guide to the intensive study of literary masterpieces. Benjamin A. Heydrick. N. Y., Hinds & Noble, c1902. 118 p. S. cl. .... .75 .67

"The aim of this manual is to facilitate the systematic, careful, and appreciative study of literature as literature. It concentrates attention upon the text itself, not upon editorial explanation or comment. It furnishes means by which the student may ascertain for himself the chief characteristics of the book studied. It acquaints him with the fundamental principles of literary construction, and asks him to decide for himself how far these principles have been observed. Not to present ready-made opinions for his acceptance, but to teach him to see for himself and to judge for himself is the aim throughout.

Each book is treated as a type, a representative of a class, so that the study of a few books may open the way to the appreciation of many.

Outlines are given for the study of six literary types: in poetry, the epic, lyric, and drama; in prose, fiction, the essay, and the oration."—*Preface*.

Y
———
H 66 gu

1072. [3.] **Guide to the study of nineteenth century authors.** Louise Manning Hodgkins. Bost., D. C. Heath & Co., 1898. 101 + 56 p. D. cl. .... .60 .52

Will help the teacher in making selections in various lines.

Y
———
M 23 in

1073. **Introductory lessons in English literature**: for high schools and academies. I. C. McNeill, *and* S. A. Lynch. N. Y., American Book Company, c1901. 376 p. D. cl. .... 1.00 .85

This volume contains selections from representative American and British authors for critical study. Helpful notes and suggestions are added to each selection.

Y
———
M 43 as

1074. [11.] **Aspects of fiction and other ventures in criticism.** Brander Matthews. N. Y., Harper & Bros., 1896. 234 p. D. cl. .... 1.50 .98

Will prove helpful to the teacher and will interest older pupils. Can also be used in essay reading.

Y
———
M 43 in
1075. [4.] **Introduction to the study of American literature.** Brander Matthews. N. Y., American Book Company, 1896. 256 p. il. D. cl. .... 1.00   .85

    A brief and concise account of American writers and judgments on their writings. An attempt has been made to show how each of these authors influenced his time and how he in turn was influenced by it. Students may compare their judgments on what they read with these.

Y
———
M 69 am
1076. [247.] **American lands and letters.** Donald G. Mitchell. 2 vols. N. Y., C: Scribner's Sons, 1898. il. O. cl. each 2.50   1.60

    Delightful reading. Older pupils will enjoy portions when already interested in an author through his writings.

Y
———
M 69 en
1077. [248-251.] **English lands, letters, and kings:** 1. From Celt to Tudor; 2. From Elizabeth to Anne; 3. Queen Anne to the Georges; 4. The latter Georges to Victoria. Donald G. Mitchell. N. Y., C: Scribner's Sons, 1897-1898. 4 vols. D. cl. each .... 1.50   .98

    "I shall reckon my commentary only so far forth good as it may familiarize the average reader with the salient characteristics of the writers brought under notice, and shall put those writers into such a swathing of historic and geographic environments as shall keep them better in mind."

    Delightful reading which the teachers will find very helpful. Let pupils compare their judgments on their reading with these.

Y
———
M 77 hi
1078. **History of English literature.** William Vaughn Moody, *and* Robert Morss Lovett. N. Y., C: Scribner's Sons, 1902. 433 p. D. cl. 1.25   1.12

    "An attempt has here been made to present the history of English literature from the earliest times to our own day, in a historical scheme simple enough to be apprehended by young students, yet accurate and substantial enough to serve as a permanent basis for study, however far the subject is pursued. But within the limits of this formal scheme, the fact has been held constantly in mind that literature, being the vital and fluid thing it is, must be taught, if at all, more by suggestion, and by stimulation of the student's own instinctive mental life, than by dogmatic assertion."—*Preface.*

    Emphasis has been placed upon the chief authors of each era and many minor writers who are given unnecessary space in some texts are omitted. An excellent working bibliography for further reading is given.

Y
———
N 43 am
1079. **American literature.** Alphonso G. Newcomer. Chic., Scott, Foresman & Co., 1901. 364 p. pors. D. cl. .... 1.00 .90

 A brief but excellent resume of American literature. The appendix contains a classified list of late and contemporary writers and a bibliography suggesting added books for reading and study.

Y
———
On 1 hi
#1080. **History of American verse 1610-1897.** James L. Onderdonk. Chic., A. C. McClurg & Co., 1901. 395 p. O. cl. .... 1.25 .82

 Contents: Voices from the wilderness; Puritan muse; Literature in the middle colonies; Hints of nationalism; Freneau and the Connecticut choir; Delia Cruscan echoes; Birth of the artistic spirit; "The Knickerbocker school"; Poets of sentiment and passion; Poets of nature and American life; Idyllic and lyric poets; Humor and satire; Idealism and realism; Aftermath.

Y
———
P 16 hi
1081. **History of English literature.** Franklin Verzelius Newton Painter. Bost., Sibley & Ducker, c1899. 697 p. il. D. cl. 1.40 1.26

 For reference.

 This book presents a survey of the whole field of English literature. It gives considerable attention to the historical and social conditions that largely determined the character of the literature of each era. The authors of importance have been treated at length while a list of the less important writers, together with their principal works is prefixed to each period.

 Unusual prominence has been given to the nineteenth century writers.

Y
———
R 39 am
#1082. **American literature, 1607-1885.** Charles F. Richardson. N. Y., G. P. Putnam's Sons, 1899. 2 vol. in 1. O. cl. 3.00 1.96

 An excellent reference book for use of teacher of literature.
 This book should only be purchased by the larger libraries.
 Contents: Part I—Perspective of American literature; Race elements in American literature; New environment of the Saxon mind; Early descriptive and historical writers; Theologians of the seventeenth and eighteenth centuries; Benjamin Franklin; Political literature; Washington Irving; Religion and philosophy in later years; Ralph Waldo Emerson; Essayists; Historians; Borderlands of American literature.

 Part II—Early verse-making in America; Dawn of imagination; Henry Wadsworth Longfellow; Edgar Allan Poe; Emerson as poet;

Poets of freedom and culture: Whittier, Lowell and Holmes; Tones and tendencies of American verse; Belated beginnings of fiction; James Fenimore Cooper; Nathaniel Hawthorne; Lesser novelists; Later movements in American fiction.

                        List Price to
                      price. schools.

Y

Sa 2 sh

#1083. **Short history of English literature.** George Saintsbury. N. Y., Macmillan Co., 1898. 819 p. D. cl. 1.50 1.35
    For reference.

Y

St 3 na

1084. [8.] **Nature and elements of poetry.** Edmund Clarence Stedman. Bost., Houghton, Mifflin & Co., 1898. 338 p. D. cl. .... 1.50 .98

    A discussion of the essentials of poetry. One of the most valuable books for the teacher.

Y

St 3 po

1085. [10.] **Poets of America.** Edmund Clarence Stedman. Bost., Houghton, Mifflin & Co., 1899. 516 p. D. cl. 2.25 1.50

Y

St 3 vi

1086. [9.] **Victorian poets.** Edmund Clarence Stedman. Bost., Houghton, Mifflin & Co., 1898. 521 p. D. cl. 2.25 1.50

    These three foregoing volumes ought to be in every library, for every teacher of literature will find them invaluable. The criticisms are from the right standpoint, and portions of many of them can be read to pupils for them to compare with their own judgments on what they have read.

Y

T 13 hi

#1087. **History of English literature.** Hippolyte A. Taine. Abridged from the translation of H. Van Laun, and edited with chronological table, notes, and index by John Fiske. N. Y., Henry Holt & Co., c1872. 502 p. D. cl. 1.40 1.26
    A good reference book for the use of the teacher.

Y

T 16 to.

1088. **Topical notes on American authors.** Lucy Tappan. N. Y., Silver, Burdett & Co., 1898. 334 p. D. cl. 1.00 .90

    "These notes were gathered during several years' teaching in the department of literature. The general plan of treatment is

| | List price. | Price to schools. |

as follows: (1) Short selections from works, (2) list of reference books and magazines, (3) topical outlines of life, (4) appellations, (5) notes on writings, (6) miscellaneous notes.

This is an excellent book for reference for the advanced students in literature.

Y
———
W 24 re
1089. [7.] **Relation of literature to life.** Charles Dudley Warner. N. Y., Harper & Bros., 1898. 320 p. D. cl. .... 1.50 .98

The principles brought out in this book ought to form the basis of the work in literature. For the teacher in preparing her work.

Y
———
W 46 de
1090. [2.] **Development of English literature and language.** Alfred H. Welsh. Chic., Scott, Foresman & Co., 1896. 506; 560 p. O. (University ed., two vol. in one.) cl. 3.00 2.50

For the use of the teacher. Some of the judgments on writings may be read to or by the pupils after they have made their judgments on what they have read.

Y
———
W 48 li
#1091. **Literary history of America.** Barrett Wendell. N. Y., C: Scribner's Sons, 1901. 574 p. O. cl. .. 3.00 1.96

An extended reference work, for the use of the teacher of literature. This book should only be purchased by the larger libraries.

COLLECTIONS.

Yc
———
B 31 en
1092. **English history told by English poets: a reader for school use.** Katharine Lee Bates, *and* Katharine Coman, *comps.* N. Y., Macmillan Co., 1902. 452 p. D. cl. .... .60 .54

"Poets are spirited historians; they enlist imagination and sympathy in the cause of the fading past. They turn the task of memory to pastime. They are not always accurate, but neither are more sedate chroniclers. The dulness of a record was never yet proof of its veracity.

The London populace of Elizabethan times learned English history from the stage. The reigns of the Plantagenets, the Wars

	List price.	Price to schools.

of the Roses, and the reigns of the Tudors were set forth in a long series of chronicle plays and historical dramas. In these, as in the lyrics and ballads that more commonly express the Stuart reigns, the tendency is to concentrate attention on royal and noble personages rather than on the life of the nation as a whole. It is a stately and a tragic story as the poets tell it,—too stately and too tragic to give an altogether just impression of the growth of a great people; but it furnishes the dramatic outline to which a fuller knowledge may easily relate itself. . . .

The present book illustrates, by carefully chosen selections from English poetry, the history of England from Queen Boadicea to Queen Victoria. Notes introductory to the selections carry on a connected account of principal events and make manifest the historic bearing of each poem. Further notes, at the end of the book, explain allusions and difficulties in the text, and also set the poets right in flagrant cases of misreporting."—*Preface.*

Yc
―――
B 41 st

1093. **Standard elocutionist:** principles and exercises, followed by a copious selection of extracts in prose and poetry classified and adapted for reading and recitation. David Charles Bell, *and* Alexander Melville Bell. N. Y., Funk & Wagnalls Co., 1901. 600 p. D. cl. .... 1.50 .98

A comprehensive book on the subject of elocution. It deals with voice culture, gestures and contains a large number of selections for elocutionary work.

Yc
―――
C 23 be

1094. [745.] **Beacon lights of patriotism;** or, Historic incentives to virtue and good citizenship. Henry B. Carrington. N. Y., Silver, Burdett & Co., 1895. 443 p. D. cl. .... .80 .72

For declamations.

Yc
―――
C 84 pi

1095. **Pieces for prize speaking contests:** a collection of over one hundred pieces which have taken prizes in Prize Speaking Contests. A. H. Craig, *and* Binney Gunnison, *comps.* N. Y., Hinds & Noble, c1899. 418 p. D. cl. 1.25 1.00

It contains one hundred of the best selections for prize speaking. Will be found valuable for those schools connected with the declamatory leagues of the state.

Yc
C 91 ch

	List price.	Price to schools.

1096. **Choice readings for public and private entertainments:** and for the use of schools, colleges and public readers with elocutionary advice. Robert McLean Cumnock. Chic., A. C. McClurg & Co., 1901. 602 p. D. cl. .... 1.50 .98

A well known compilation of good selections, with suggestions on how to speak correctly and effectively; by a master of the art of elocution. Each chapter deals with a special phase of the subject, giving carefully selected examples to illustrate the same.

Yc
F 95 ch

1097. **Choice readings:** from standard and popular authors embracing a complete classification of selections, a comprehensive diagram of the principles of vocal expression, and indexes to the choicest readings from Shakespeare, the Bible, and the hymnbooks. Robert I. Fulton, and Thomas C. Trueblood, *comps.* Bost., Ginn & Co., 1902. 710 p. D. cl. 1.50 1.28

A classified compilation of selections illustrative of the different modes of life. Will be helpful to the teacher of English, and to the pupils in the literary society.

Yc
G 29 fr

1098. **From Chaucer to Arnold:** types of literary art in prose and verse; an introduction to English literature with preface and notes. Andrew J. George. N. Y., Macmillan Co., 1898. 676 p. por. D. cl. 1.00 .65

This volume contains selections from the representative authors from the time of Chaucer to the Nineteenth century. An excellent collection for the small libraries.

Yc
L 58 in

1099. **Introduction to the study of literature for the use of secondary and graded schools.** Edwin Herbert Lewis. N. Y., Macmillan Co., 1900. 409 p. D. cl. .... 1.10 .99

A collection of selections from the works of the best American and English authors. The author emphasizes the fact that little time should be spent on biographical and analytic notes till after the student has read and enjoyed the literature itself.

304 LIST OF BOOKS FOR HIGH SCHOOL LIBRARIES.

                                                List Price to
Yc / M 12 li   price. schools.

1100. [744.] **Lincoln literary collection.** J. P. McCaskey. N. Y., American Book Company, 1897. 576 p. D. cl. .... 1.00 .85

    More than six hundred selections in prose and poetry for declamations.

Yc / M 69 sc

1101. **School and college speaker.** Wilmot Brookings Mitchell. N. Y., Henry Holt & Co., 1901. 358 p. D. cl. .... 1.00 .90

    Designed for the use of classes in public speaking in colleges and secondary schools. Gives instruction in the essentials of elocution, and furnishes declamations adapted to school and college boys and girls. Will be suggestive to the teacher of expression in arranging for contests among the older pupils.

Yc / P 17 go

1102. **Golden treasury of the best songs and lyrical poems in the English language.** Francis Turner Palgrave. N. Y., Thomas Y. Crowell & Co., n. d. 354 p. D. (Astor edition.) cl. .... .60 .40

    This collection includes all the best original Lyrical pieces and songs in our language, by writers not living.

Yc / P 19 st

1103. **Standard English poems:** Spenser to Tennyson. Henry S. Pancoast, *ed.* N. Y., Henry Holt & Co., 1902. 749 p. S. cl. 1.50 1.35

    An excellent but less extended collection of selections from English literature than Ward's "English poets."

Yc / So 8 ho

1104. **How to recite:** a school speaker. F. Townsend Southwick. N. Y., American Bk. Co., c1900. 464 p. D. cl. .... 1.00 .85

    A collection of selections from the best literature with a sufficient outline of the technique to guide the student.

LIST OF BOOKS FOR HIGH SCHOOL LIBRARIES.

		List price.	Price to schools.
Yc / St 3 am	1105. **American anthology, 1787-1900**: selections illustrating the editor's critical review of American poetry in the nineteenth century. Edmund Clarence Stedman, ed. Bost., Houghton, Mifflin & Co., 1901. 878 p. O. cl.	3.00	1.96

This contains the choicest and most typical examples of the poetry of America and together with the author's "Victorian Anthology" should be in every school library.

Yc / St 3 vi	1106. **Victorian anthology, 1837-1895**: selections illustrating the editor's critical review of British poetry in the reign of Victoria. Edmund Clarence Stedman, ed. Bost., Houghton, Mifflin & Co., c1895. 744 p. O. cl.	2.50	1.64

Designed, as the title-page implies, to supplement Stedman's "Victorian poets" by choice and typical examples of the work discussed in that review; it is a very truthful exhibit of the course of song during the last sixty years, as shown by the poets of Great Britain in the best of their shorter productions. The selections are not given chronologically, but first in three divisions of the reign, and secondly in classes of poets. There are indexes of authors, first lines and titles, brief biographies of the poets quoted; and a fine frontispiece portrait of Queen Victoria.

This volume should be in every school library.

Yc / T 72 co	1107. **Colonial prose and poetry: 1607-1775.** William P. Trent, *and* Benjamin W. Wells, eds. N. Y., Thos. Y. Crowell & Co., 1901. 3 vols. S. cl. set	2.25	1.47

This series illustrate the literature of the American colonies and aim to show the development of national culture and ideals. The only other collection of this kind is Stedman and Hutchinson's "Library of American literature", which is far too extended and expensive for the average High school library.

Every library should contain this set of Trent's for use in the study of American Literature and History.

Contents: Vol. 1—Selections from Captain John Smith; Colonel Norwood; William Bradford; Mourt's relation; Thomas Morton; Francis Higginson; John Winthrop; Bay Psalm Book; John Underhill; John Mason; John Cotton; Roger Williams; Thomas Hooker; Thomas Shepard; Nathaniel Ward; Anne Bradstreet.

Vol. 2—Selections from Edward Johnson; John Eliot; Michael Wigglesworth; John Josselyn; Daniel Gookin; Thomas Wheeler; Peter Folger; William Penn; Daniel Denton; George Alsop; Bacon's Rebellion; William Hubbard; Mary Rowlandson; Urian Oakes; Increase Mather; Cotton Mather; Samuel Sewall; Sarah Kemble Knight; Robert Beverly.

Vol. 3—Selections from John Wise; Hugh Jones; William Byrd;

New England primer; Benjamin Colman and the Turells; John Seccomb; Patrick Tailfer; Thomas Prince; William Douglass; William Stith; Jonathan Edwards; Benjamin Franklin; Mather Byles; Joseph Green; John Osborn; Thomas Hutchinson; John Barnard; Benjamin Church; Thomas Godfrey and Nathaniel Evans; Jonathan Boucher; John Woodman; Philip Vickers Fithian.

	List price.	Price to schools.

Yc
―――
W 21 en

1108. **English poets:** selections with critical introduction by various writers and a general introduction by Matthew Arnold. Thomas Humphrey Ward, *ed.* N. Y., Macmillan Co., 1901-1902. 4 vols. D. cl. 5.00   3.28

This collection should be in every school library. It contains selections from the works of all the leading English authors from the age of Chaucer to that of Tennyson, together with biographical notes.

Yc
―――
W 24 bo

1109. [743.] **Book of eloquence:** a collection of extracts in prose and verse from the most famous orators and poets. Charles Dudley Warner. Bost., Lee & Shepard. 452 p. D. cl..................... 1.00   .65

Selections suitable for declamations.

DRAMA.

Yd
―――
B 41 re

#1110. **Reader's Shakespeare:** his dramatic works condensed, connected, and emphasized for school, college, parlor, and platform. David Charles Bell. N. Y., Funk & Wagnalls Co., 1895-7. 3 vols. D. cl. each .... 1.50   .98

Abridged editions of Shakespeare's plays. Each play is preceded by a brief narrative, historical and literary. These volumes will be good for use in the class in expression.

Yd
―――
D 75 in

1111. **Introduction to Shakespeare.** Edward Dowden. N. Y., C: Scribner's Sons, 1901. 136 p. por. D. cl.   .75   .67

An excellent, brief handbook on Shakespeare's life and work.

Yd
―――
D 87 ki

1112. [748.] **King's jester,** and other short plays for small stages. Caro Atherton Dugan. Bost., Houghton, Mifflin & Co., 1899. 364 p. D. cl.............. 1.50   .98

Little plays for closing exercises.

	List price.	Price to schools.

Yd
———
H S3 mo

1113. [747.] **Mouse-trap:** a farce. W. D. Howells. N. Y., Harper & Bros., 1894. il T. (Black and white series.) cl. ...... .50 .33

For school entertainments.

Yd
———
H S3 sl

1114. **Sleeping-car and other farces.** William D. Howells. Bost., Houghton, Mifflin & Co., 1899. 212 p. D. cl. .... 1.00 .65

Short farces suitable for use by the class in expression.
Contents: Parlor-car; Sleeping-car; Register; Elevator.

Yd
———
H 86 sh

1115. **Shakespeare:** his life, art, and characters, with an historical sketch of the origin and growth of the drama in England. *Rev.* Henry Norman Hudson. Bost., Ginn & Co., 1900. 2 vols. Ed. 4, rev. D. cl. 4.00 3.40

These volumes should be in every High school library for use in reference work in the study of English dramatic literature.
Contents: Life of Shakespeare; Origin and growth of the drama in England; Shakespeare's contemporaries; Shakespeare's art; Shakespeare's characters.

Yd
———
H 87 sh

1116. **Shakespeare:** in tale and verse. Lois Grosvenor Hufford. N. Y., Macmillan Co., 1902. 445 p. D. cl. .... 1.00 .90

An interesting book for Library reading.
"The author has endeavored to tell the stories from Shakespeare's point of view; to interpret sympathetically and truthfully the motives of the dramas and of the characters; to omit unessential details; and to select for quoting, passages that are notable for strength and beauty, and those that have especial significance in revealing character."

Yd
———
J 23 da

1117. **Daisy Miller:** a comedy in three acts. Henry James. Bost., Houghton, Mifflin & Co., 1899. 189 p. D. cl. .... 1.25 .82

Yd
———
J 23 sh

#1118. **Shakespeare's heroines.** *Mrs.* Anna B. Jameson. N. Y., E. P. Dutton & Co., 1901. 379 p. il. D. cl. 2.50 1.64

Excellent for reference for Shakespeare class.
Contents: Characters of intellect—Portia, Isabella, Beatrice,

Rosalind; Characters of passion and imagination—Juliet, Helena, Perdita, Viola, Ophelia, Miranda; Characters of the affections—Hermione, Desdemona, Imogen, Cordelia; Historical characters—Cleopatra, Octavia, Volumnia, Constance, Elinor of Guienne, Blanche of Castile, Lady Percy, Portia, Margaret of Anjou, Katherine of Arragon, Lady Macbeth.

                List Price to
                price. schools.

Yd
———
J 73 ev
1119. [189.] **Every man in his humour.** Ben. Johnson. ed. by Henry B. Wheatley. N. Y., Longmans, Green & Co., 1891. 209 p. S. (London series of English classics.) cl. .... .75 .63

  The old dramas may be of interest to the pupils. Let them compare them with those of Shakespeare which they have read.

Yd
———
M 31 sp
1120. **Specimens of the Pre-Shaksperean drama:** with an introduction, notes, and a glossary. John Matthews Manly. Bost., Ginn & Co., 1900. 2 vols. (Athenaeum Press series.) D. cl. each.. 1.25 1.06

  The purpose of these volumes is to help the student to follow the fortunes of the modern drama through its strange and interesting nonage, to come into sympathy with the aims and methods of the known and nameless artists whose work is here presented, and to form some conception of the vast amount of dramatic activity and the widespread dramatic interest which made possible the career of Shakespeare.
  Valuable for reference in the study of English dramatic literature.

Yd
———
M 34 do
1121. [188.] **Dr. Faustus.** Christopher Marlowe, intr. by Wilhelm Wagner. N. Y., Longmans, Green & Co., 1892. 140 p. S. (London series of English classics.) cl. .... .60 .50

  The story of a man who sold himself to Lucifer and Mephistophilis for the privilege of indulging his propensities freely for a certain length of time, at the end of which he was to consign both his body and soul to Lucifer.

Yd
———
Sh 1 dh
1122. [192.] **Dramas.** Shakespeare. Hudson edition, ed. by Henry Hudson. Bost., Ginn & Co., sq. T. cl. .45 .38

  One play in each volume. History and sources of the play, and character estimates given. Notes on text at the bottom of the pages.

	List price.	Price to schools.

Yd

Sh 1 dr

1123. [190.] **Dramas.** Shakespeare. *Ed.* by William J. Rolfe. N. Y., American Book Company, 1899. il. S. cl. per vol.............................. .56 .48

Each volume contains one play. The history of the play, the sources of the plot, and critical comments on the play, are given. Copious notes on the text are given in the back of the book.

Yd

Sh 1 dt

1124. [191.] **Dramas.** Shakespeare. Temple edition. N. Y., Macmillan Co. il. T. cl. each............. .45 .30

One play in each volume. A fine edition of Shakespeare with few notes at close of book.

Yd

Sh 5 ri

1125. **Rivals.** Richard Brinsley Sheridan. N. Y., Dodd, Mead & Co., 1901. 184 p. il. D. cl............ 1.25 .82

The illustrations in this volume will be very suggestive to students who are planning to present this as a class play.

ESSAYS.

Essays and prose compositions reveal the thought of mankind.

The special aims:

    a. To get the author's thought.

    b. To think with the author by seeing relations.

    c. To knit the knowledge gained to what is already known.

To get the author's idea: The first step is to get the general idea of the composition, then the parts upon which the general idea is based. If description,—the things which go to make up the picture; if narrative,—the events which form the narration; if argumentative,—the points on which the author has based his argument, etc.

To think with the author: In seeing the relation of these parts to each other and to the general idea,—discriminating, comparing, judging,—the pupil is thinking with the author.

To knit new knowledge to the old: The student has been using the knowledge he already has to interpret the new knowledge, but he ought consciously to bring up what he already knows on the subject, gained through experience or previous reading. For instance, he has just read Carlyle's idea of a great man; he compares with Emerson's idea as gained in previous reading,— also with Lowell's idea. These ideas together with his own knowledge and his experience of great men constitute his body of knowledge of great men, which he will use in gaining new knowledge on the subject which new knowledge will in turn be compared with the old.

Ye
———
Ab 2 no

                    List Price to
                    price. schools.

1126. [252.] **Notes of the night,** and other outdoor sketches. Charles Conrad Abbott. N. Y., Century Co., 1896. 231 p. D. cl.......................... 1.50 .98

 Essays by a lover of nature for a lover of nature.

Ye
———
Ad 2 sp

1127. [220.] **Spectator.** Joseph Addison. *Ed.* by Alex. Charles Ewald. N. Y., Frederick Warne & Co., 1891. 469 p. D. ("Chandos classics.") cl. .... 1.00 .67

 Essays selected from the "Spectator."

Ye
———
B 72 wo

1128. **Woman and the higher education.** Anna C. Brackett, *ed.* N. Y., Harper & Bros., 1893. 214 p. S. cl. .... 1.00 .65

 A series of essays which will be of interest to the girls of the school and suggestive to the debaters.
 Contents: General introduction, Mrs. Blanche Wilder Bellamy; Preface, Miss Anna C. Brackett; Plan for improving female education, Mrs. Emma Willard, 1819; Female education, Mrs. Emma C. Embury, 1831; Collegiate education of girls, Prof. Maria Mitchell, Vassar college, 1880; New knock at the old door, Mrs. Lucia Gilbert Runkle, 1883; Review of the higher education of women, Mrs. Alice Freeman Palmer, 1889; Teaching of history in academies and colleges, Prof. Lucy M. Salmon, Vassar college, 1890; Private schools for girls, Miss Anna C. Brackett.

		List price.	Price to schools.

Ye
―――
B 87 sa

1129. **Sack of shakings:** shakings are odds and ends of rope and canvas accumulated during a voyage. They were formerly the perquisites of the Chief Mate. Frank T. Bullen. N. Y., McClure, Phillips & Co., 1901. 389 p. D. cl.................... 1.50 .98

Essays and sketches that appeared in the Spectator. Some of the subjects are: The orphan; Porpoise myth; Cats on board ship; Old East Indiaman; Floor of the sea; Shakespeare and the sea; Skipper of the "Amulet;" Sociable fish; Alligators and mahogany; Battleship of today; Nat's monkey; Big game at sea, etc. The writer explains that "shakings are odds and ends of rope and canvas accumulated during a voyage. They were formerly the perquisites of the chief mate."

Ye
―――
B 94 bi

1130. [511.] **Birds and bees.** John Burroughs. Bost., Houghton, Mifflin & Co. 96 p. D. (Riverside literary series.) cl. .... .40 .34

Ye
―――
B 94 fr

1131. [507.] **Fresh fields.** John Burroughs. Bost., Houghton, Mifflin & Co., 1897. 241 p. S. cl.......... 1.50 .82

Ye
―――
B 94 lo

1132. [510.] **Locusts and wild honey.** John Burroughs. Bost., Houghton, Mifflin & Co. 253 p. S. cl.... 1.50 .82

Ye
―――
B 94 pe

1133. [506.] **Pepacton.** John Burroughs. Bost., Houghton. Mifflin & Co., 1897. 241 p. S. cl........... 1.50 .82

Ye
―――
B 94 si

1134. [508.] **Signs and seasons.** John Burroughs. Bost., Houghton, Mifflin & Co. 289 p. S. cl.......... 1.50 .82

Ye
―――
B 94 wa

1135. [505.] **Wake-robin.** John Burroughs. Bost., Houghton, Mifflin & Co., 1896. 233 p. S. cl.......... 1.50 .82

Ye
―――
B 94 wi

1136. [509.] **Winter sunshine.** John Burroughs. Bost., Houghton, Mifflin & Co., 255 p. S. cl.......... 1.50 .82

In the foregoing books will be found the observations of a sci-

	List price.	Price to schools.

entist, who takes his readers with him and points out the interesting and enjoyable things to be seen. There is just enough of the personal to make Burroughs a favorite with young readers. These essays may be used to interest pupils in essay reading and will also be interesting for the students in the Library reading class in Science.

Ye

C 19 he

1137. [223.] **Heroes, hero-worship, and the heroic in history.** Thomas Carlyle. N. Y., C: Scribner's Sons, 1897. 235 p. S. cl .... 1.25 .50

This is the period when children are interested in the heroic. Properly brought to them this will become one of their favorite books.

Ye

C 59 ho

1138. **How to tell a story, and other essays.** Samuel L. Clemens. (Mark Twain, *pseud.*) N. Y., Harper & Bros., 1902. 233 p. D. cl .... 1.50 .98

Contents: How to tell a story; In defence of Harriet Shelley; Fenimore Cooper's literary offences; Travelling with a reformer; Private history of the "jumping frog" story; Mental telegraphy again; What Paul Bourget thinks of us; Little note to M. Paul Bourget.

Ye

C 85 no

1139. [259.] **Novel: what it is.** F. Marion Crawford. N. Y., Macmillan Co., 1896. 108 p. T. (Miniature series.) cl .... .75 .48

Concise and interesting.

Ye

C 94 fr 1

1140. [257.] **From the easy chair.** George William Curtis. N. Y., Harper & Bros., 1894. 232 p. por. T. cl. 1.00 .65

Ye

C 94 fr 2

1141. [258.] **Other essays from the easy chair.** George William Curtis. N. Y., Harper & Bros., 1892. 229 p. por. T. cl .... 1.00 .65

Two volumes of delightful short essays on various interesting subjects. For the beginner in essay reading.

	List price.	Price to schools.

Ye
C 94 fr 3

1142. **From the easy chair.** Third series. George William Curtis. N. Y., Harper & Bros., 1894. 232 p. S. cl.. 1.00 .65

Contents: Hawthorne and Brook Farm; Beecher in his pulpit after the death of Lincoln; Killing deer; Autumn days; From Como to Milan during the war of 1848; Herbert Spencer on the Yankee; Honor; Joseph Wesley Harper; Review of Union troops, 1865; April, 1865; Washington in 1867; Reception to the Japanese Ambassadors at the White House; Maid and the wit; Departure of the Great Eastern; Church street; Historic buildings; Boston Music hall; Public benefactors; Mr. Tibbins's New Year's call; New England Sabbath; Reunion of Anti-slavery veterans, 1884; Reform charity; Bicycle riding for children; Dead bird upon Cyrilla's hat an encouragement of "Slarter"; Cheapening his name; Clergymen's salaries.

Ye
Em 3 co

1143. [229.] **Conduct of life.** Ralph Waldo Emerson. Bost., Houghton, Mifflin & Co., 1898. 256 p. S. (Little classics ed.) cl........................... 1.25 .82

Ye
Em 3 es

1144. [228.] **Essays.** Ralph Waldo Emerson. Bost., Houghton, Mifflin & Co., 1883. Two volumes in one. 343; 270 p. D. (Cambridge classics.) cl.. 1.00 .50

Ye
Em 3 re

1145. **Representative men, nature, addresses and lectures.** Ralph Waldo Emerson. Bost., Houghton, Mifflin & Co., c1883. 2 vol. in 1. D. cl............... 1.00 .65

Contents: Part I—Uses of great men; Plato; or, the philosopher; Plato—new readings; Swedenborg; or, the Mystic; Montaigne; or, the skeptic; Shakespeare; or, the poet; Napoleon; or, the man of the world; Goethe; or, the writer.

Part II—Nature; American scholar; Address to senior class in Divinity college, Cambridge, 1838; Literary ethics; Method of nature; Man the reformer; Lecture on the times; Conservative; Transcendentalist; Young American.

Ye
G 69 cr

1146. **Critical kit-kats.** Edmund Gosse. N. Y., Dodd, Mead & Co., 1900. 302 p. D. cl................ 1.50 .98

The author has tried to produce in this volume a combination of criticism with biography,—life illustrated by the work, the work relieved by the life.

Contents: Sonnets from the Portuguese; Keats in 1894;

	List price.	Price to schools.

Thomas Lovell Beddoes; Edward FitzGerald; Walt Whitman; Count Lyof Tolstoi; Christina Rossetti; Lord De Tabley; Toru Dutt; M. José-Maria de Heredia; Walter Pater; Robert Louis Stevenson.

Ye
—
H 24 ch

1147. **Choice of books.** Frederic Harrison. N. Y., Macmillan Co., 1893. 163 p. T. cl.................. .75 .49

This little volume is the result of wide reading and research and suggests what we should read in the region of pure literature.

Ye
—
H 53 ar

1148. **Army life in a black regiment.** Thomas Wentworth Higginson. Bost., Houghton, Mifflin & Co., 1900. 413 p. D. New ed. cl...................... 2.00 1.30

This series of essays give an excellent picture of the negro as a soldier. They bring out admirable traits of negro character which we are very apt to overlook.

Contents: Introductory; Camp diary; Up the St. Mary's; Up the St. John's; Out on picket; Night in the water; Up the Edisto; Baby of the Regiment; Negro spirituals; Life at Camp Shaw; Florida again? The negro as a soldier; Conclusion; Fourteen years after; Appendix—Roster of soldiers; First black soldiers; General Saxton's instructions; Cowpen's anniversary, 1881.

Ye
—
H 53 ch

1149. **Cheerful yesterdays.** Thomas Wentworth Higginson. Bost., Houghton, Mifflin & Co., 1900. 374 p. D. cl. 2.00 1.30

Autobiographic chapters describe Colonel Higginson's boyhood in Cambridge, his years and associates in Harvard College, the period of the Transcendental movement, the observations and experiences which made him a reformer, the storm and stress of the time when the Fugitive Slave Law excited the country, the development of literature and his own literary work in the fifties; the stirring episode of the Kansas conflicts and the daring and doom of John Brown, and the Civil War, with a very modest account of his share in it. Later chapters describe literary London and Paris twenty years ago, and some of the notable persons he met in those capitals; and the book concludes with a paper "On the outskirts of public life."

Ye
—
H 53 c

1150. [253.] **Concerning all of us.** Thomas Wentworth Higginson. N. Y., Harper & Bros., 1893. 210 p. por. T. cl...... .... 1.00 .65

Short essays on various interesting topics.

	List price.	Price to schools.

Ye
───
H 53 co

1151. **Contemporaries.** Thomas Wentworth Higginson. Bost., Houghton, Mifflin & Co., 1900. 379 p. D. cl. 2.00 1.30

Biographical sketches of Emerson, Alcott, Theodore Parker, Whittier, Walt Whitman, Sidney Lanier, Mrs. Hawthorne, Lydia Marea Child, Helen Jackson (H. H.), John Holmes; Thaddeus W. Harris, W. Lloyd Garrison, Wendell Phillips, C. Sumner, Ulysses S. Grant, etc. Also papers entitled A visit to John Brown's household in 1859, Dr. Howe's anti-slavery career, The eccentricities of reformers, and The road to England.

Ye
───
H 53 ou

1152. **Outdoor studies, poems.** Thomas Wentworth Higginson. Bost., Houghton, Mifflin & Co., 1900. 407 p. D. cl. 2.00 1.30

Contents: Outdoor studies—Saints, and their bodies; Procession of the flowers; April days; Water-lilies; Summer afternoon; Life of birds; Snow; Footpaths; Shadow; Search for the Pleiades; Fayal and the Portuguese: Poems—Prelude; Trumpeter; Sonnet to duty; Jar of rose-leaves; Sub pondere crescit; Playmate hours; Baby sorceress; Heirs of time; Sixty and six: or, a fountain of youth; "Since Cleopatra died"; Soul of a butterfly; Decoration; "Snowing of the pines"; Lesson of the leaves; Vestis Angelica; To my shadow; Two voyages; Sea-gulls at Fresh pond; Dying house; Song of days; Treasure in Heaven; Beneath the violets; "The knock alphabet"; Reed immortal; Dame Craigie; Gifts; Dwelling-places; To the memory of H. H.; Venus multiformis; To John Greenleaf Whittier; Waiting for the bugle; Astra Castra; Memorial ode; Serenade by the sea; Frozen cascade; Things I miss; Egyptian banquet; American stonehenge; Horizon line; Fairy coursers; Rabiah's defence; Baltimore oriole; Sleeping-car; Nemesis; Mab's ponies; Mono of La Trappe; Ode to a butterfly; Two lessons; Crossed swords; Outdoor kindergarten; Dirge; Madonna Di San Sisto; Poems from "Thalatta"; February hush; June; Hymns; Sappho's ode to Aphrodite; Forward; Nature's cradle song; Sonnets from Camoens.

Ye
───
H 53 pr

1153. **Procession of the flowers, and kindred papers.** Thomas Wentworth Higginson. N. Y., Longmans, Green & Co., 1897. 178 p. D. cl. .... 1.25 .82

Contents: Procession of the flowers; April days; Water-lilies; My Out-door study; Life of birds; Moonglade.

All of Higginson's essays are admirably adapted for use in the Literature classes of the High school. They are within the understanding of the people and are exceedingly interesting.

	List price.	Price to schools.

Ye
———
H 73 au
1154. [235.] **Autocrat of the breakfast-table.** Oliver Wendell Holmes. Bost., Houghton, Mifflin & Co., 1895. 321 p. por. D. (Riverside school lib.) cl. .... .60 .52

Delightful talks on various subjects. Good for the class reading essays.

Ye
———
H 83 li
#1155. **Literary friends and acquaintance:** a personal retrospect of American authorship. William Dean Howells. N. Y., Harper & Bros., 1901. 288 p. por. il. O. cl.. 2.50 1.64

Emerson, Lowell, Hawthorne, Julia Ward Howe, Bayard Taylor, Celia Thaxter, Stedman, Holmes, were all friends of Mr. Howells, and he writes of each, and of others as well, as no other living person could.

Contents: My first visit to New England; First impressions of literary New York; Roundabout to Boston; Literary Boston as I knew it; Oliver Wendell Holmes; The White Mr. Longfellow; Studies of Lowell; Cambridge neighbors.

Ye
———
Ir 8 re
1156. [216.] **Representative essays.** Washington Irving and eleven others. N. Y., G. P. Putnam's Sons, 1899. 395 p. D. cl.. 1.25 .82

A selection of the best essays by Irving, Lamb, DeQuincy, Emerson, Arnold, Morley, Carlyle, Macaulay, Froude, Freeman, and Gladstone.

Ye
———
Ir 8 sk
1157. [232.] **Sketch book.** Washington Irving. N. Y., G. P. Putnam's Sons, 1895. 544 p. D. (Student's ed.) cl.. 1.00 .50

The text of this volume is that of the complete edition published in 1848, which was revised by Irving himself. The edition is well bound, and the notes are few.

Ye
———
J 35 fi
1158. **Field and hedgerow:** being the last essays of Richard Jefferies. Collected by his widow. Richard Jefferies. N. Y., Longmans, Green & Co., 1900. 331 p. por. D. cl.. 1.25 .82

Contents: Hours of spring; Nature and books; July grass; Winds of Heaven; Country Sunday; Country-side: Sussex; Swallow-time; Buckhurst Park; House-martins; Among the nuts;

	List price.	Price to schools.

Walks in the wheat-fields; Just before winter; Locality and nature; Country places; Field words and ways; Cottage ideas; April gossip; Some April insects; Time of year; Mixed days of May and December; Makers of summer; Steam on country roads; Field sports season; Under the acorns; Downs; Forest; Beauty in the country; Summer in Somerset; English deer-park; My old village; My chaffinch.

Ye
———
J 35 op
1159. **Open air.** Richard Jefferies. N. Y., Harper & Bros., 1901. 270 p. S. cl............................ .25 .17

Contents: Saint Guido; Golden-brown; Wild flowers; Sunny Brighton; Pine wood; Nature on the roof; One of the new voters; Modern Thames; Single-barrel gun; Haunt of the hare; Bathing season; Under the acorns; Downs; Forest; Beauty in the country; Out of doors in February; Haunts of the lapwing; Outside London; On the London roads; Red roofs of London; Wet night in London.

Ye
———
L 16 es
1160. [222.] **Essays of Elia.** C: Lamb. N. Y., Macmillan Co., 1897. por. T. (Temple classics.) cl....... .50 .42

Ye
———
L 78 en
1161. [219.] **English Essays.** Intr. by J. H. Lobban. N. Y., C: Scribner's Sons, 1896. 257 p. D. cl...... 1.50 .98

Representative essays by Bacon, Cowley, DeFoe, Steele, Addison, Swift, Fielding, Pope, Cowper, Walpole, Johnson, Goldsmith, Hunt, Hazlitt, and Lamb.

Ye
———
L 95 am
#1162. [226.] **Among my books.** James Russell Lowell. Bost., Houghton, Mifflin & Co., 1898. 2 vols. 380; 327 p. D. cl............................... 4.00 2.40

Delightful literary essays which older pupils may be made interested in.

Ye
———
L 95 fi
1163. [227.] **Fireside travels.** James Russell Lowell. Bost., Houghton, Mifflin & Co., 1888. 282 p. S. (Riverside Aldine series.) cl..................... 1.00 .65

318   LIST OF BOOKS FOR HIGH SCHOOL LIBRARIES.

Ye
———
L 95 my
                    List Price to
                    price. schools.
1164. **My study windows.** James Russell Lowell. Bost.,
  Houghton, Mifflin & Co., c1899. 433 p. D. cl.... 2.00 1.30
  Contents: My garden acquaintance; Good word for winter; On a certain condescension in foreigners; Great public character; Carlyle; Abraham Lincoln; Life and letters of James Gates Percival; Thoreau; Swinburne's tragedies; Chaucer; Library of old authors; Emerson, the lecturer; Pope.

Ye
———
M 11 bo
1165. [242.] **Books and culture.** Hamilton Wright Mabie.
  N. Y., Dodd, Mead & Co., 1899. 279 p. S. cl......1.25 .82
  The foregoing books by Mabie are delightful and thoughtful essays on a variety of subjects. Older pupils will enjoy.

Ye
———
M 11 cr
1166. [221.] **Critical and historical essays.** T. B. Macaulay. N. Y., Longmans, Green & Co. D. (Students' ed.) cl. 1.75 1.15
  For single essays by Macaulay, see classics.

Ye
———
M 11 en
1167. [240.] **Essays on nature and culture.** Hamilton Wright Mabie. N. Y., Dodd, Mead & Co., 1899. 326 p. por. S. cl............................. 1.25 .82

Ye
———
M 11 ew
1168. [241.] **Essays on work and culture.** Hamilton Wright Mabie. N. Y., Dodd, Mead & Co., 1899. 247 p. S. cl............................. 1.25 .82

Ye
———
M 11 my
1169. [238.] **My study fire.** Hamilton Wright Mabie. N. Y., Dodd, Mead & Co., 1897. 204 p. S. cl...... 1.25 .82
  Contents: Fire lighted; Nature and childhood; Answer of life; Failings of genius; Christmas eve; New Year's eve; Scholar's dream; Flame of driftwood; Dream worlds; Text from Sidney; Artist talks; Escaping from bondage; Some old scholars; Dull days; Universal biography; Secret of genius; Books and things; Rare nature; Cuckoo strikes twelve; Glimpse of spring; Primeval mood; Method of genius; Hint from the season; Bed of embers; Day out of doors; Beside the Isis; Word for idleness; "The bliss of solitude"; Mystery of atmosphere; New hearth; Idyl of wandering; Open window.

Ye
M 11 mys
                                                    List   Price to
                                                    price. schools.
1170. **My study fire.** Second series. Hamilton Wright
   Mabie. N. Y., Dodd, Mead & Co., 1901. 280 p.
   S. cl. ....   1.25   .82

Contents: Book and the reader; Reader's secret; Poetry of flame; Finalties of expression; Enjoying one's mind; Neglected gift; Concerning culture; Magic of talk; Work and art; Joy in life; Real and the sham; Lightness of touch; Poet's corner; Joy of the moment; Lowell letters; Tyranny of books; Spell of style; Speech as literature; Poet of aspiration; Reading public; Sanity and art; Manner and man; Outing of the soul; Power which liberates; Unconscious artist; Law of obedience; Struggle in art; Passion for perfection; Criticism as an interpreter; Educational quality of criticism; Plato's dialogues as literature; Power of the novel; Concerning originality; By the way.

Ye
M 11 sh
1171. [239.] **Short studies in literature.** Hamilton Wright
   Mabie. N. Y., Dodd, Mead & Co., 1898. 203 p.
   S. cl. ....   1.25   .82

Ye
M 43 pe
1172. [260.] **Pen and ink;** papers on subjects of more or
   less importance. Brander Matthews. N. Y.,
   Longmans, Green & Co., 1894. 229 p. D. cl...   1.00   .65

Short essays on various literary subjects.

Ye
M 69 dr
1173. [254.] **Dream life:** a fable of the seasons. Donald G.
   Mitchell. N. Y., C: Scribner's Sons, 1892. 282 p.
   D. cl. ....   1.25   .50

A book of reveries. The pupils will enjoy portions of this volume.

Ye
R 29 bo
1174. [246.] **Books and men.** Agnes Repplier. Bost.,
   Houghton, Mifflin & Co., 1898. 224 p. D. cl...   1.25   .82

Miss Repplier is an interesting and brilliant writer.

Ye
R 29 es
1175. [245.] **Essays in idleness.** Agnes Repplier. Bost.,
   Houghton, Mifflin & Co., 1896. 224 p. D. cl...   1.25   .82

Ye

R 29 esm

	List price.	Price to schools.

1176. **Essays in miniature.** Agnes Repplier. Bost., Houghton, Mifflin & Co., c1895. 237 p. D. cl.......... 1.25 .82

Contents: Our friends, the books; Trials of a publisher; Oppression of notes; Conversation in novels; Short defence of villains; By-way in fiction; Comedy of the Custom House; Mr. Wilde's *Intentions;* Humors of gastronomy; Children in fiction; Three famous old maids; Charm of the familiar; Old world pets; Battle of the babies; Novel of incident; Ghosts.

Ye

R 29 fi

1177. **Fireside sphinx.** Agnes Repplier. Bost., Houghton, Mifflin & Co., 1901. 305 p. il. D. cl.......... 2.00 1.80

Miss Repplier is an authority and an enthusiast on cats, and here traces their history from their first appearance on the Nile down to the present time in chapters entitled: The cat of antiquity; Dark ages; Persecution; Renaissance; Cat of Albion; Cat in art; Cat triumphant; Some cats of France; The cat today.

Ye

R 29 in

1178. [243.] **In the dozy hours and other papers.** Agnes Repplier. Bost., Houghton, Mifflin & Co., 1895. 235 p. D. cl................................ 1.25 .82

Ye

R 29 po

1179. [244.] **Points of view.** Agnes Repplier. Bost., Houghton, Mifflin & Co., 1896. 289 p. D. cl.......... 1.25 .82

Ye

R 29 va

1180. **Varia.** Agnes Repplier. Bost., Houghton, Mifflin & Co., 1898. 232 p. D. cl...................... 1.25 .82

Essays full of good sense and delicate humor, under the titles: The eternal feminine; Deathless diary; Guides, a protest; Little Pharisees in fiction; Fete de Gayant; Cakes and ale; Old wine and new; Royal road of fiction; From the reader's standpoint (the latter was first issued in the North American Review under the title "The contentiousness of modern novel-writers").

Ye

R 67 am

1181. [256.] **American ideals and other essays social and political.** Theodore Roosevelt. N. Y., G. P. Putnam's Sons, 1897. 354 p. D. cl.............. 1.00 .65

Essays on questions of the day. A good book.

Contents: American ideals; True Americanism; Manly virtues and practical politics; The college graduate and public life; Ma-

	List price.	Price to schools.

chine politics in New York city; Six years of civil service reform; Administering the New York police force; How not to help our poorer brothers; Washington's forgotten maxims; National life and character.

Ye

R 67 st

1182. **Strenuous life: essays and addresses.** Theodore Roosevelt. N. Y., Century Co., 1902. 332 p. por. D. cl. .... 1.50 .98

Contents: Strenuous life; Expansion and peace; Latitude and longitude among reformers; Fellow-feeling as a political factor; Civic helpfulness; Character and success; Eighth and ninth commandments in politics; Best and the good; Promise and performance; American boy; Military preparedness and unpreparedness; Admiral Dewey; Grant; Two Americas; Manhood and statehood; Brotherhood and the heroic virtues; National duties; Labor question; Christian citizenship.

Ye

R 89 se

1183. [224.] **Sesame and lilies.** John Ruskin. Chic., McClurg & Co., 1899. 237 p. D. cl. .... 1.00 .50

Ye

Si 6 tu

1184. [261.] **Turrets, towers, and temples;** the great buildings of the world, as seen and described by famous writers. Ed. and tr. by Esther Singleton. N. Y., Dodd, Mead & Co., 1898. 317 p. il. D. cl. 2.00 1.28

The descriptions are selected from great works in literature. Among the writers are Ruskin, Thackeray, Gautier, Ebers, Dickens, Victor Hugo, DeAmicis, Amelia B. Edwards.

Ye

T 39 ex

1185. [231.] **Excursions.** Henry D. Thoreau. Bost., Houghton, Mifflin & Co., 1888. 319 p. D. cl. .... 1.50 .98

These essays will interest the boy interested in the life of nature around him. A winter, Succession of forest trees, Walking, Autumnal tints, Wild apples, are especially good.

Ye

T 39 wa

1186. [230.] **Walden.** Henry D. Thoreau. Bost., Houghton, Mifflin & Co., 1889. 2 vols. 514 p. S. (Riverside Aldine series.) cl. each .... 1.00 .65

Observations and thoughts on nature by Thoreau when he lived alone in the woods on the shores of Walden pond, in Concord, Mass.

Ye
T 36 b

List price. Price to schools.

1187. [605.] **Birds in the bush.** Bradford Torrey. Bost., Houghton, Mifflin & Co., 1898. 298 p. D. cl.... 1.25 .82

The two books above will furnish material for the Library reading class in Science and for the Essay class in Literature.

Ye
T 63 fl

1188. **Florida sketch-book.** Bradford Torrey. Bost., Houghton, Mifflin & Co., 1895. 242 p. D. cl.... 1.25 .82

Contents: In the flat-woods; Beside the marsh; On the beach at Daytona; Along the Hillsborough; Morning at the old sugar mill; On the upper St. John's; On the St. Augustine road; Ornithology on a cotton plantation; Florida shrine; Walks about Tallahassee.

Ye
T 63 fo

1189. **Foot-path way.** Bradford Torrey. Bost., Houghton, Mifflin & Co., 1900. 245 p. D. cl. .... 1.25 .82

Contents: June in Franconia; December out-of-doors; Dyer's hollow; Five days on Mount Mansfield; Widow and twins; Male ruby-throat; Robin roosts; Passing of the birds; Great blue heron; Flowers and folks; In praise of the Weymouth pine.

Ye
T 63 ra

1190. **Rambler's lease.** Bradford Torrey. Bost., Houghton, Mifflin & Co., 1899. 222 p. D. cl.......... 1.25 .82

Contents: My real estate; Woodland intimate; An old road; Confessions of a bird's-nest hunter; Green mountain corn-field; Behind the eye; November chronicle; New England winter; Mountain-side ramble; Pitch-pine meditation; Esoteric peripateticism; Butterfly psychology; Bashful drummers.

Ye
T 63 sp

1191. [604.] **Spring notes from Tennessee.** Bradford Torrey. Bost., Houghton, Mifflin & Co., 1896. 223 p. D. cl. .... 1.25 .82

Ye
T 63 wo

1192. **World of green hills:** observations of nature and human nature in the blueridge. Bradford Torrey. Bost., Houghton, Mifflin & Co., 1898. 285 p. D. cl. .... 1.25 .82

Contents: North Carolina—Day's drive in three states; in quest of ravens; Mountain pond; Birds, flowers, and people; Virginia—Nook in the Alleghanies; At natural bridge.

	List price.	Price to schools

Ye
V 28 li
1193. **Little rivers.** Henry Van Dyke. N. Y., C: Scribner's Sons, 1901.. 277 p. S. cl.................. 2.00 1.30

   Contents: Prelude; Little rivers; Leaf of spearmint; Ampersand; Handful of heather; Ristigouche from a horse yacht; Alpenrosen and goat's milk; Au large; Trout-fishing in the Traun; At the sign of the Balsam-bough; Song after sundown.

Ye
V 28 na
1194. [255.] **Nature for its own sake.** John C. Van Dyke. N. Y., C: Scribner's Sons, 1898. 292 p. D. cl.... 1.50 .98

   By nature the author means "lights, skies, clouds, waters, lands, foliage—the great elements that reveal form and color in landscape, the component parts of the earth—beauty about us."
   The books will point out to the reader much of the beauty which is all around us.

Ye
W 24 ah
1195. [237.] **A-hunting of the deer, and other essays.** Charles Dudley Warner. Bost., Houghton, Mifflin & Co., 1895. 321 p. D. (Riverside literature series.) cl. .... 1.25 .20

   Delightful and interesting.

Ye
W 24 as
1196. **As we were saying.** Charles Dudley Warner. With illustrations by Harry W. McVicker and others. N. Y., Harper & Bros., 1891. 219 p. il. S. bds. 1.00 .65

   Contents: Rose and chrysanthemum; Red bonnet; Loss in civilization; Social screaming; Does refinement kill individuality? Directoire gown; Mystery of the sex; Clothes of fiction; Broad A; Chewing gum; Women in congress; Shall women propose? Frocks and the stage; Altruism; Social clearing-house; Dinner-table talk; Naturalization; Art of governing; Love of display; Value of the commonplace; Burden of Christmas; Responsibility of writers; Cap and gown; Tendency of the age; Locoed novelist.

Ye
W 24 my
1197. [236.] **My summer in a garden.** Charles Dudley Warner. Bost., Houghton, Mifflin & Co., 1896. 194 p. S. (Riverside Aldine series.) cl........ 1.00 .65

   Delightful book for beginners in essay reading.

FICTION.

Hamilton Mabie says:—"The novel is contemporaneous with a new and deepening consciousness of human relationship and obligation. Today we feel more distinctly than ever before the pervasive influence of other lives upon our lives. We are weighted down as never before by a sense of our incalculable obligations to our fellows. We no longer think of ourselves as alone, but always in the thick of relationships of every kind and quality,—in the solitude of our own souls we are conscious of the whole conscious, suffering world about us."

Fiction: Fiction portrays life on the social side as no other form of literature does. Social conditions, standards, forces, and conventions are revealed, and the problem of the individual life is worked out with full recognition of countless social influences.

Special aims in studying fiction:—
    a. To enjoy the story.
    b. To picture life portrayed.
    c. To judge character portrayed.
    d. To trace character development.

NOVELS PORTRAYING LIFE.

"By sympathetic insight into life of the most diverse aspects and under the most diverse conditions it (the novel) quickens our appreciation of the life each of us can see around him, makes us more tolerant of the differences of taste and character in our neighbor, more awake to the humor and purpose of this existence of ours. In a word, the novel gives us humanity."

To picture the life portrayed study the things which go to make up the life of any community—descriptions of the environment, characters as types, appearance and dress, food, homes, and surroundings, amusements, religion, occupations, education, and language.

Much of the material found in novels portraying life, can be used in geography.

NOVELS PORTRAYING CHARACTER, CHARACTER DEVELOPMENT, AND LESSONS IN RIGHT DOING.

Character is revealed through description and analysis by the author, by conversation, by the feeling, and attitude of characters toward each other. Judgments upon individual character and upon lines of action should be formed from a study of the foregoing points. Conditions, standards, and forces which influence the character for good or evil should be considered. In tracing character development, trace the changes which take place in the character, and study the conditions, ideals, and forces surrounding the character which bring about the changes.

HISTORICAL NOVELS.

Historical fiction makes history real for it reveals not only the life but the spirit of the times. Properly read it helps the pupil to see and feel history. Manners and customs, that is characters as types, homes, surroundings, food, clothing, ways of travel, amusements, occupations, mode of warfare, language, religion, etc., etc., as touched upon in the story should be noted. The historical events upon which the story is based should be read. The teacher should help the pupils to form high ideals of life and character, and encourage them to admire the good, the true, the noble.

GOOD STORIES.

Let the pupils read some books simply for the joy of reading. The story of adventure will always interest the pupil and in selecting these care has been taken that they are not sensational and not such as will lead him to poorer literature.

Above all, give the pupils healthy, simple and pure love stories. They are bound to read them, and unless they can get them from the library, they will get them elsewhere and most likely they will not be the best kind.

	List price.	Price to schools.

Yf
———
Al 2 ma

1198. [108.] **Marjorie Daw and other stories.** Thomas Bailey Aldrich. Bost., Houghton, Mifflin & Co., 1897. 287 p. S. (Riverside Aldine series.) cl..   1.00   .65

Interesting short stories.

Yf
———
Al 5 fl

1199. **Flute and violin:** and other Kentucky tales and romances. James Lane Allen. N. Y., Macmillan Co., 1900. 308 p. D. cl......................   1.50   .98

Contents: Flute and violin; King Solomon of Kentucky; Two gentlemen of Kentucky; White cowl; Sister Dolorosa; Posthumous fame.

Yf
———
Al 5 ke

1200. [114.] **Kentucky cardinal.** New ed. James Lane Allen. N. Y., Macmillan & Co., 1899. 138 p. il. S. cl. ....   1.00   .65

A pretty story filled with many beautiful bits of descriptions of Nature.

Yf
———
Au 7 pr

1201. **Pride and prejudice.** Jane Austen. N. Y., Thomas Y. Crowell & Co., n. d. 328 p. D. cl...........   .60   .40

An interesting romance of the life of two sisters. Good for Library reading.

Yf
———
Aus 7 st

1202. [165.] **Standish of Standish;** a story of the Pilgrims. Jane Goodwin Austin. Bost., Houghton, Mifflin & Co., 1889. D. cl........................   1.25   .82

An interesting story of Colonial time filled with pictures of life and customs.

Yf
———
Aus 7 be

1203. **Betty Alden:** the first-born daughter of the pilgrims. Jane G. Austin. Bost., Houghton, Mifflin & Co., 1891. 384 p. D. cl........................   1.25   .82

This story depicts the life of the Pilgrims in early New England and gives an excellent picture of Myles Standish and his family. Excellent for pupils to read in connection with the study of New England history.

Yf

B 23 ha
1204. [88.] **Half back:** a story of school, foot-ball and golf. Ralph Henry Barbour. N. Y., D. Appleton & Co., 1899. 267 p. il. D. cl.................. 1.50 .85
 A good story for the younger boys.

              List Price to
              price. schools.

Yf

B 24 ir
1205. [79.] **Irish idylls.** Jane Barlow. N. Y., Dodd, Mead & Co., 1898. 317 p. D. cl..................... 1.25 .65
 Fascinating stories sympathetically portraying life in Ireland. The pictures are faithful transcripts of nature and life amid the boglands of western Ireland.

Yf

B 26 dr
1206. [153.] **Drake and his yeomen.** James Barnes. N. Y., Macmillan Co., 1899. 415 p. il. D. cl...... 2.00 1.28
 "A true accounting of the character and adventures of Sir Francis Drake." An intensely interesting book filled with adventure.

Yf

B 26 fo
1207. [178.] **For king or country.** James Barnes. N. Y., Harper & Bros., 1898. 269 p. il. D. cl........ 1.50 .98
 No boy can read this volume without acquiring a strong impression of the suffering, sacrifice, and daring in the war for American independence.

Yf

B 26 lo
1208. [181.] **Loyal traitor:** James Barnes. N. Y., Harper & Bros., 1899. 306 p. il. D. cl................ 1.50 .98
 A thrilling story of the war of 1812.

Yf

B 26 pr
1209. [85.] **Princetonian.** James Barnes. N. Y., G. P. Putnam's Sons, 1898. 431 p. il. D. cl........ 1.25 .82
 A good story. Portrays life in Princeton College.

Yf

B 27 li
1210. **Little minister.** James M. Barrie. N. Y., Thomas Y. Crowell & Co., c1891. 311 p. il. D. cl...... .60 .40
Same. N. Y., H. M. Caldwell Co. 454 p. c1898. il. O. cl. .... 1.00 .60
 A pretty story of Scotch life. The principal characters are

	List price.	Price to schools.

Garvin Dishart, the Auld Licht minister and Babbie, his gypsy sweet-heart.
The edition published by the Caldwell Co. contains excellent illustrations.

Yf
B 27 se
1211. [55.] **Sentimental Tommy; a story of his boyhood.** J. M. Barrie. N. Y., C: Scribner's Sons, 1899. 478 p. il. D. cl.................... 1.50 .98

A story portraying the character of a very imaginative child. The lives of Tommy and his sister, Elspeth, in the slums of London and in Thrums, are described with a wealth of humor, of pathos, and with wonderful insight into character.

Yf
B 27 to
1212. **Tommy and Grizel.** James M. Barrie. N. Y., C: Scribner's Sons, 1900. 509 p. D. cl............ 1.50 .98

A sequel to the author's "Sentimental Tommy".

Yf
B 27 wh
1213. **When a man's single.** James M. Barrie. N. Y., A. L. Burt. n. d. 326 p. D. cl.................. 1.00 .40

A pretty story of Scotch life suitable for Library reading.

Yf
B 27 wi
1214. [78.] **Window in Thrums.** J. M. Barrie. N. Y., Dodd, Mead & Co., 1896. 292 p. il. D. cl...... 2.00 .82

From her window Jess looks out upon the brae and the life and history of little Thrums as it came to her are told. The petty strife and gossip of these people, their pinching poverty, their disappointments, and their triumphs are all told. Here is the whole range of human experience.

Yf
B 28 pi
1215. **Pine knot: a story of Kentucky life.** William E. Barton. N. Y., D. Appleton & Co., 1900. 360 p. D. cl. 1.50 .98

A story of Kentucky life before and during the Civil war. The early customs and manners of the mountaineers are carefully pictured.

Yf
B 41 du
1216. **Duke of Stockbridge.** Edward Bellamy. N. Y., Silver, Burdett & Co., 1900. 371 p. O. cl........ 1.50 1.20

This romance incidentally gives an excellent description of Shay's rebellion.

	List price.	Price to schools.

Yf
B 41 lo
1217. [96.] **Looking backward, 2000 — 1887.** Edward Bellamy. Bost., Houghton, Mifflin & Co., 1890. 337 p. D. cl. .... 1.00 .65
A story showing the working out of a system of socialism.

Yf
B 43 ma
1218. [154.] **Master sky-lark:** a story of Shakespeare's time. John Bennett. N. Y., Century Co., 1898. 380 p. il. D. cl. .... 1.50 .98
A good story of the time of Queen Elizabeth. Shakespeare and Ben Jonson appear in the story.

Yf
B 46 all
1219. **All sorts and conditions of men:** an impossible story. Walter Besant. N. Y., Harper & Bros., 1902. 412 p. il. D. cl.................................... 1.25 .82
The story of a young heiress who, under an assumed name, goes to live at White Chapel, London, among the people who are employed in a large brewery left by her grandfather. The story is an improbable one but it gives a good picture of life among the working-classes of East London.

Yf
B 46 ch
1220. **Children of Gibeon.** Walter Besant. N. Y., Harper & Bros., 1900. 447 p. D. cl................ 1.25 .82
A sociological novel. Depicts the life of the working-classes of London in a vivid, dramatic manner.

Yf
B 56 lo
1221. [157.] **Lorna Doone:** a romance of Exmoor. R. D. Blackmore. N. Y., Harper & Bros., 1898. 576 p. il. D. cl. .... 1.00 .50
"Any son of Exmoor, chancing on this volume cannot fail to bring to mind the nurse-tales of his childhood, the savage deeds of the outlaw Doones in the depth of Bayworthy Forest, the beauty of the hapless maid brought up in the midst of them, the plain John Ridd's Herculean power, and the exploits of Tom Faggus". The book contains many remarkably graphic descriptions of Devonshire scenery. Time of James II in England.

Yf
B 72 fo
1222. [179.] **For love of country.** Cyrus Townsend Brady. N. Y., C.: Scribner's Sons, 1899. 354 p. D. cl... 1.25 .82
A story of land and sea in the days of the revolution.

Yf
B 81 he
  List Price to
  price. schools.
1223. **Her sixteenth year.** Helen Dawes Brown. Bost., Houghton, Mifflin & Co., 1901. 191 p. D. cl... 1.00 .90

This is a continuation of the story "Little Miss Phoebe Gay" by the same author. It is a clean, pretty story of the life of a young girl and will be of interest to the girls in the Fiction section of Library reading.

Yf
B 81 me
1224. [61.] **Meadow-grass: tales of New England life.** Alice Brown. Bost., Houghton, Mifflin & Co., 1899. 315 p. D. cl.............. 1.50 .98

Portrays village life in New England.

Yf
B 81 ra
1225. [103.] **Rab and his friends.** John Brown. Bost., Houghton, Mifflin & Co., 299 p. D. (Riverside school library series.) cl................... .60 .51

Stories of a dog and his friends.

Yf
B 87 la
1226. **Last days of Pompeii.** Sir Edward G. Bulwer-Lytton (Lord Lytton). N. Y., Thomas Y. Crowell & Co., n. d. 422 p. D. cl......................... .60 .40

An historical novel telling the story of events preceding the great eruption of Vesuvius in 79 A. D., when Pompeii and Herculaneum were destroyed.

Yf
B 87 las
1227. **Last of the barons.** *Sir* Edward G. Bulwer-Lytton. (Lord Lytton) N. Y., Thomas Y. Crowell & Co., n. d. 600 p. D. cl........................... .60 .40

The scene of the story is in England at the time of the "War of Roses". The aim has been to illustrate the actual history of the period, and to bring into a fuller display than History has, the characters of the principal personages of the time; the motives by which they were actuated; the state of parties; the condition of the people; and the great social interests which were involved in what, regarded imperfectly, appear but the feuds of rival factions.

The hero is Richard Neville, earl of Warwick, whose downfall is the main point of the story.

Pupils will gain a better idea of this important age, characterized by the decline of the feudal system, and immediately preceding the great change in society which is usually dated from the accession of Henry VII by reading this book than he will get from wading through a vast mass of chronicles.

		List price.	Price to schools.

Yf
———
B 88 lo

1228. [110.] **Love in old cloathes, and other stories.** H. Cuyler Bunner. N. Y., C: Scribner's Sons, 1896. 217 p. D. cl.. 1.50 .98

Collection of interesting short stories, good for Library reading.

Yf
———
B 88 pi

1229. **Pilgrim's progress from this world to that which is to come:** delivered under the similitude of a dream. John Bunyan. N. Y., Thomas Y. Crowell & Co., n. d. 371 p. il. D. cl................. .60 .40

This is supposed to be a dream, and to allegorize the life of a Christian from his conversion to his death. Its value in a school library is as an example of seventeenth century literature.

Yf
———
B 93 lo

1230. [54.] **Louisiana.** Frances Hodgson Burnett. N. Y., C: Scribner's Sons, 1899. 163 p. D. cl........ 1.25 .82

A good story for girls containing a noble lesson. Life in the mountains of North Carolina is portrayed.

Yf
———
C 11 bo

1231. [51.] **Bonaventure: a prose pastoral of Acadian Louisiana.** George W. Cable. N. Y., C: Scribner's Sons, 1898. 314 p. D. cl............... 1.25 .82

A character study. The character of the school-master, Bonaventure, is most delicately and most beautifully portrayed.
Contents: Carancro, 1-72; Grande Pointe, 73-141; Au Large, 142-314.

Yf
———
C 28 da

1232. [159.] **Days of Jeanne D'Arc.** Mary Hartwell Catherwood. N. Y., Century Co., 1897. 278 p. il. D. cl. .... 1.50 .98

Life and times of Joan of Arc. "Mrs. Catherwood has made a close study of the life and times of the Maid of Doremy. Her Jeanne is no military maid, but a timid, loving, tender child—a child devout and single-minded, and possessed with the passionate devotion of her sex and carried forward by love of country."

Yf
———
C 28 la

1233. **Lady of Fort St. John.** Mary Hartwell Catherwood. Bost., Houghton, Mifflin & Co., 1900. 284 p. S. cl. .... 1.25 .82

The scene of the story is laid in Nova Scotia which then in-

| | List price. | Price to schools. |

cluded not only Arcadia, but also about two-thirds of Maine, during the time that Louis XIII was king of France.

Yf
C 28 ma
1234. [125.] **Mackinac and lake stories.** Mary Hartwell Catherwood. N. Y., Harper & Bros., 1900. 222 p. il. D. cl...... .... 1.50.. .96

Short stories of life and scenes on the islands of the Great Lakes.

Yf
C 28 st
1235. **Story of Tonty.** Mary Hartwell Catherwood. Chic., A. C. McClurg & Co., 1901. 225 p. il. Ed. 6 with new introduction by the author. D. cl........ 1.25 .82

This story gives a fine picture of La Salle and his life. The friendship existing between him and his friend Henri de Tonty is told and brings out a side of La Salle's character which we do not find depicted in history.

Contents: Montreal beaver fair; Fort Frontenac; Fort St. Louis of the Illinois.

Yf
C 33 do
1236. [97.] **Ingenious gentleman, Don Quixote, of La Mancha.** Miguel de Cervantes. Clifton Johnson, ed. N. Y., Macmillan Co., 1899. 398 p. il. S. cl. .75 .50

The original story of Don Quixote has been brought down to readable proportions without excluding any really essential incident or detail, and at the same time make the text clean and wholesome. Yet in no instance has anything vital been sacrificed. Except for omissions the original text is practically unchanged. A satire on chivalry.

Yf
C 43 un
1237. [180.] **Unknown patriot: a story of the secret service.** Frank Samuel Child. Bost., Houghton, Mifflin & Co., 1899. 396 p. il. D. cl............. 1.50 .98

A good historical study of revolutionary times.

Yf
C 45 ba
1238. [65.] **Bayou folk.** Kate Chopin. Bost., Houghton, ton, Mifflin & Co., 1895. 313 p. S. cl.......... 1.25 .82

Stories portraying Creole life and character.

Yf
C 47 cr
                                        List Price to
                                        price. schools.

1239. **Crisis.** Winston Churchill. N. Y., Macmillan Co., 1901. 522 p. il. D. cl...................... 1.50 .96

    This book should be read by every child who is studying United States history. It will give to them a new and vivid picture of Lincoln. It also gives pictures of the typical Northern and Southern soldier and of life in the South at the time of the Civil war.

    The text and reference books in history lack in point of vivid and dramatic interest and should be supplemented by books like the "Crisis".

    "A vivid picture of the events leading up to our Civil War, particularly as seen in St. Louis. Colonel Carvel and his daughter Virginia, descendants of 'Richard Carvel', are the central characters. They represent the rich, refined southerners, believing in state rights. Contrasting is Stephen Brice, a Boston lawyer, called 'a black republican', who is a rival of a Confederate officer for Virginia's hand. Lincoln, Douglas, Sherman, Grant and other men, who afterwards became famous are brought in."

Yf
C 47 ri

1240. [174.] **Richard Carvel.** Winston Churchill. N. Y., Macmillan Co., 1899. 538 p. il. D. cl.......... 1.50 .98

    An historical novel of colonial times in Maryland. The scene shifts to London. Fox, Garrick, and Lord Baltimore are introduced as well as leading men in Maryland.

Yf
C 59 co

1241. [98.] **Connecticut yankee in King Arthur's court.** Mark Twain. (pseud.) N. Y., Harper & Bros. 1899. 433 p. il. D. cl...................... 1.75 1.15

    "It is not pretended that these laws and customs existed in England in the sixth century; no, it is only pretended that inasmuch as they existed in the English and other civilizations of far later times, it is safe to conclude that it is no libel upon the sixth century to suppose them to have been in practice in that day also." *Author's preface.*

    One of the best stories.

Yf
C 65 da

1242. **Daughters of the Revolution and their times, 1769–1776:** a historical romance. Charles Carleton Coffin. Bost., Houghton, Mifflin & Co., 1895. 387 p. il. D. cl................ 1.50 .98

    This historical story opens in the Province of New Hampshire in 1769, immediately after the repeal of the Stamp Act. The period was characterized by enthusiasm and devotion among the women as well as the men, and the sacrifices and sufferings of the col-

	List price.	Price to schools.

onists are graphically described. A thread of fiction holds the facts together. The extravagance and folly of the society surrounding the court of George III is contrasted with the stern puritanism of the colonists. The author has carefully consulted newspapers, almanacs, diaries, genealogies and family histories. Illustrated with portraits and photographs of historic houses and places.

Yf

C 77 pi

1243. **Pilot:** a tale of the sea. James Fenimore Cooper. N. Y., G. P. Putnam's Sons, n. d. 443 p. (Mohawk edition.) O. cl. .... 1.25 .50

The author's aim in writing the "Pilot" was to present a true picture of sea-life.

Yf

C 78 de

1244. [39.] **Deerslayer:** or, The first warpath. James Fenimore Cooper. N. Y., G. P. Putnam's Sons, 1897. (Mohawk ed.) O. cl. .... 1.25 .50

Deerslayer is the nickname of the hero of the story. He is a model, uncivilized man, honorable, truthful, brave, and pure of heart. He is introduced in five of Cooper's novels.

Yf

C 78 la

1245. [40.] **Last of the Mohicans:** or, A narrative of 1757. James Fenimore Cooper. N. Y., G. P. Putnam's Sons, 1897. (Mohawk ed.) O. cl. .... 1.25 .50

The story is so called from the nickname of Uncas, son of the chief of the Mohicans, one of the characters.

Yf

C 78 pa

1246. [41.] **Pathfinder:** or, The inland sea. James Fenimore Cooper. N. Y., G. P. Putnam's Sons, 1897. (Mohawk ed.) O. cl. .... 1.25 .50

Yf

C 78 pi

1247. [42.] **Pioneers:** or, The sources of the Susquehanna. James Fenimore Cooper. N. Y., G. P. Putnam's Sons, 1897. O. cl. (Mohawk ed.) .... 1.25 .50

All of the foregoing are Indian stories. Cooper in presenting Indian life and character has dwelt on the best traits of the picture, and his best characters are cast in a noble mould.

		List price.	Price to schools.

Yf
C 78 sp

1248. [43.] **Spy**. James Fenimore Cooper. N. Y., G. P. Putnam's Sons, 1897. O. cl. (Mohawk ed.) ... 1.25 .50

    A story of the American Revolution. General Washington appears in the story.

Yf
C 82 am

1249. [75.] **American girl in London.** *Mrs.* Sara Jeannette Duncan Cotes. N. Y., D. Appleton & Co., 1891. il. D. cl. .... 1.50 .98

    Interest in this book may lead to the reading of books of travel.

Yf
C 82 cr

1250. **Crow's nest.** *Mrs.* Everard Cotes. (Sara Jeannette Duncan.) N. Y., Dodd, Mead & Co., 1901. 243 p. D. cl. .... 1.25 .82

    This is a delightful account of a summer spent "on the other side of the latch." The locality is a mountain top of the Himalayas, known as Simla, the summer headquarters of the government of India.

    The garden, in which most of the action takes place, is perched, like a crow's nest, on a ledge or shelf projecting from the mountain side, a situation which afforded unusual opportunities, perplexities, satisfactions and rewards.

Yf
C 82 th

1251. **Those delightful Americans.** *Mrs.* Everard Cotes. (Sara Jeannette Duncan.) N. Y., D. Appleton & Co., 1902. 353 p. D. cl. .... 1.50 .98

    Mrs. Cotes novel is a new "social departure," wherein English travelers sketch a summer of lively experiences in the United States. The author gives a fresh and witty picture of America and Americans as seen through English eyes. The impressions of New York and of country-house life are noted with a humor and vivacity and occasional naïve self-betrayals on the part of the visiting strangers that are constantly entertaining.

Yf
C 83 sp

1252. [156.] **Splendid spur:** being memoirs of the adventures of Mr. John Marvel, a servant of his late Majesty, King Charles I, in the years 1642-43: written by himself. Arthur T. Quiller-Couch, *ed.* N. Y., C: Scribner's Sons, 1898. 328 p. S. cl.. 1.25 .82

    A good story of adventure in England.

Yf
C 85 ma

List price. Price to schools.

1253. **Marietta: a maid of Venice.** Francis Marion Crawford. N. Y., Macmillan Co., 1901. 458 p. D. cl.   1.50   .98

A story, dealing with the fortunes of a certain Zorzi, who was a Dalmatian and glass-worker in Venice at a time when Venetian law made it a criminal offense for a foreigner to learn the jealously guarded art of glass making. Zorzi's audacity, however, did not stop at this, but he dared to love the daughter of his master, Beroviero, one of the master workers in the glass guild and the richest manufacturer on the Island of Murano.

This story gives an excellent picture of early Venetian life.

Yf
C 85 ro

1254. [80.] **Roman singer.** Francis Marion Crawford. N. Y., Macmillan & Co., 1884. 378 p. D. cl. ..   1.50   .98

Life in Italy graphically portrayed.

Yf
C 87 st

1255. **Stickit minister's wooing.** Samuel Rutherford Crockett. N. Y., Doubleday & McClure Co., 1900. 368 p. O. cl. ....   1.50   .98

Short stories depicting Scotch life.

Yf
D 29 ga

1256. [116.] **Gallegher, and other stories.** Richard Harding Davis. N. Y., C: Scribner's Sons, 1899. 236 p. D. cl. ....   1.00   .65

Bright, wholesome stories for young people.

Yf
D 29 so

1257. [118.] **Soldiers of fortune.** Richard Harding Davis. N. Y., C: Scribner's Sons, 1899. 364 p. il. D. cl. .... 1.50   .98

An interesting story. The scene of the plot is laid partly in a South American republic where a revolution is one of the leading incidents in the story.

Yf
D 29 va

1258. [117.] **Van Bibber and others.** Richard Harding Davis. N. Y., Harper & Bros., 1892. il. D. cl.   1.00   .65

Interesting short stories, good for Library reading.

Yf
D 49 fr

1259. [176.] **From kingdom to colony.** Mary Devereux. Bost., Little, Brown & Co., 1900. 382 p. il. D. cl. .... 1.50 .98

A charming story of Marblehead in the early days of the revolution.

Yf
D 55 ba

1260. **Barnaby Rudge;** Master Humphrey's clock, and The mystery of Edwin Drood. Charles Dickens. With an introduction by Edwin Percy Whipple. Bost., Houghton, Mifflin & Co., c1894. 2 vols. il. O. cl. each ..... 1.50 .50

The story of the Gordon riots in London in 1780. Barnaby, a half-witted boy of twenty-three whose companion was a large raven, named Grip, became mixed up with the rioters and was condemned to death, but was reprieved and lived the rest of his life with his mother in a cottage and garden near the Maypole.

Yf
D 55 bl

1261. **Bleak house.** Charles Dickens. With an introduction by Edwin Percy Whipple. Bost., Houghton, Mifflin & Co., c1894. 2 vols. il. New. ed. O. cl. each .... 1.50 .50

The main story is the interminable law-suit of Jarndyce vs. Jarndyce. The story is named from Bleak House at Broadstairs, on the coast of Kent, Dickens' summer home.

Yf
D 55 ch

1262. [58.] **Christmas carol, and the cricket on the hearth.** Charles Dickens. Bost., Houghton, Mifflin & Co., 1893. 118; 112 p. D. (Riverside school library.) cl. .... .50 .43

A good story teaching a Christmas lesson.

Yf
D 55 da

1263. [48.] **David Copperfield:** the personal history of David Copperfield. Charles Dickens. With an introduction by Edwin Percy Whipple. Bost., Houghton, Mifflin & Co., c1894. 2 vols. il. O. cl. each .... 1.50 .50

The David of this story is Dickens himself, and Micawber is Dickens's father. According to the tale, David's mother was a nursery governess in a family where Mr. Copperfield visited. At

	List price.	Price to schools.

the death of Mr. Copperfield, the widow married Edward Murdstone, a hard, tyrannical man, who made the home of David a dread and terror to the boy. Dickens preferred this story to all his others, and in it depicted many scenes of his own life.

Yf

D 55 ni

1264. [50.] **Life and adventures of Nicholas Nickleby.** Charles Dickens. With an introduction by Edwin Percy Whipple. Bost., Houghton, Mifflin & Co., c1894. 2 vols. il. O. cl. each .... 1.50 .50

The hero of this story, Nicholas, son of a poor country gentleman, becomes an usher in Mr. Squeers's school at Dotheboys Hall, Yorkshire, but leaves in disgust at the treatment by Squeers and his wife of half-witted boy Smike. Smike runs away and follows him, and remains with him until death. Other characters are Mrs. Nickelby, Nicholas's mother, who tells long stories with no connection; Kate Nickelby, his sister; and Ralph Nickelby, his uncle, and father of Smike, a hard, grasping money-broker.

Shows abuses in English school system. Mr. Squeers is a famous school master.

Yf

D 55 ol

1265. [47.] **Old curiosity shop.** Charles Dickens. With an introduction by Edwin Percy Whipple. Bost., Houghton, Mifflin & Co., c1894. 573 p. il. New ed. O. cl. .... 1.50 .50

An old man, having run through his fortune, opened a curiosity shop in order to earn a living, and brought up his grand-daughter, Little Nell. Deluded by the hope of making a fortune by gambling, he lost everything and went out into the world, with the child, a beggar. Their wanderings and adventures are recounted.

Yf

D 55 pi

1266. [46.] **Pickwick papers:** the posthumous papers of the Pickwick club. Charles Dickens. With an introduction by Edwin Percy Whipple. Bost., Houghton, Mifflin & Co., c1894. 2 vols. il. O. cl. .... 1.50 .50

The adventures of Samuel Pickwick, the chief character and chairman of the club, and several other members, in their travels to investigate the Hampstead ponds.

Yf

D 55 ta

1267. [49.] **Tale of two cities.** Charles Dickens. With an introduction by Edwin Percy Whipple. Bost., Houghton, Mifflin & Co., c1894. 373 p. il. O. cl. 1.50 .50

The two cities are London and Paris during the Revolution of 1789.

	List price.	Price to schools.

Yf

D 64 hu

1268. [155.] **Hugh Gwyeth:** a roundhead cavalier. Beulah Marie Dix. N. Y., Macmillan Co., 1899. 376 p. il. D. cl. .... 1.50 .98

A story of the times of Charles I, of England, whose nephew appears in the story. The hero, whose father is a royalist, is brought up in his Puritan grandfather's household. His fortunes in the wars of Charles I are portrayed.

Yf

D 64 so

1269. [164.] **Soldier Rigdale;** how he sailed in the "Mayflower," and how he served Miles Standish. Beulah Marie Dix. N. Y., Macmillan Co., 1899. 323 p. il. D. cl. .... 1.50 .98

An interesting story of Plymouth colony. For the younger pupils.

Yf

D 77 re

1270. [173.] **Refugees:** a tale of two continents. A. Conan Doyle. N. Y., Harper & Bros., 1893. 366 p. il. D. cl. 1.75 1.15

A story of the life of a French Huguenot family both in France and in the New World in colonial days. Their trials and persecutions in France and their hardships in the new world are vividly portrayed.

Yf

D 77 wh

1271. [145.] **White company.** A. Conan Doyle. N. Y., Harper & Bros., 1895. 435 p. il. D. cl. ...... 1.75 .50

The story of the achievements of a body of English archers, called the White Company, that went into Spain with the Black Prince in the fourteenth century to aid Pedro the Cruel against his brother, Henry of Trastaman.

Yf

D 89 th

1272. **Three musketeers.** Alexandre Dumas. Bost., Little, Brown & Co., 1900. 418 p. D. cl. .... 1.25 .82

The scene is in France in the time of Richelieu. The three musketeers, Athos, Porthos, and Aramis, are comrades in the army. D'Artagan is another of the principal characters. He is a young Gascon, who goes to Paris to seek his fortune, and after many adventures, dies upon the battle-field.

		List price.	Price to schools.

Yf
D 91 fo
1273. **Folks from Dixie.** Paul Laurence Dunbar. With illustrations by E. W. Kemble. N. Y., Dodd, Mead & Co., 1899. 263 p. il. D. cl. .... 1.25 .82

A collection of short stories depicting Southern negro life. The author is a full-blooded negro of slave parentage.

Yf
D 92 ge
1274. [182.] **General Nelson's scout.** Byron A. Dunn. Chic., A. C. McClurg & Co., 1898. 320 p. il. D. cl. .... 1.25 .82

Historical story of the first year of the civil war.

Yf
D 92 on
1275. [183.] **On General Thomas's staff.** Byron A. Dunn. Chic., A. C. McClurg & Co., 1899. 379 p. il. D. cl. .... 1.25 .82

An historical story of the civil war from the siege of Corinth to the battle of Missionary Ridge.

Yf
Eb 3 eg
1276. [139.] **Egyptian princess.** Georg Ebers, *tr.* by Eleanor Grove. N. Y., D. Appleton & Co., 1891. 368 p. D. cl. .... 1.00 .50

An historical story portraying the manners and customs of the Greeks, Persians, and Egyptians during the sixth century before Christ.

Yf
Eb 3 ua
1277. [140.] **Uarda: a romance of ancient Egypt.** Georg Ebers, *tr.* by Clara Bell. N. Y., D. Appleton & Co. 1896. 320 p. D. cl. .... 1.00 .50

An interesting story portraying the religious, public, and private life of the ancient Egyptians during the reign of Rameses II.

Yf
Eg 3 so
1278. [184.] **Southern soldier stories.** George Cary Eggleston. N. Y., Macmillan Co., 1898. 251 p. il. D. cl. .... 1.50 .98

Stories portraying the life and character of southern soldiers in the civil war. Shows the pupils the other side of the civil war.

Yf

El 4 ad

1279. **Adam Bede.** George Eliot, *pseud.* (*Mrs.* Mary Ann Evans (Lewes) Cross.) N. Y., Thomas Y. Crowell & Co., n. d. 482 p. D. cl. .... .60 .40

An excellent novel. Adam is a young carpenter, who loves Hetty Sorrell, a pretty dairy-maid, but finally marries another girl. Mrs. Poyser, another of the principal characters, is a hard-working woman, who makes many shrewd observations that have become proverbial.

Yf

El 4 da

1280. **Daniel Deronda.** George Eliot, *pseud.* (*Mrs.* Mary Ann Evans (Lewes) Cross.) N. Y., Thomas Y. Crowell & Co., n. d. 729 p. D. cl. .... .60 .40

The hero is a Hebrew, who devotes his life to an attempt to restore the Jewish nation to its former political position.

Yf

El 4 ro

1281. **Romola.** George Eliot, *pseud.* (*Mrs.* Mary Ann Evans (Lewes) Cross.) N. Y., Thomas Y. Crowell & Co., n. d. 530 p. il. D. cl. .... .60 .40

The scene is in Florence, Italy, in the latter part of the eighteenth century. Romola, the heroine whose marriage proves a failure, sacrifices herself in devotion to the people during the plague.

Yf

El 4 si

1282. [52.] **Silas Marner.** George Eliot. N. Y., American Book Company, 1894. 208 p. D. cl. .... .30 .27

A book which will interest the oldest pupils in the school. It is a story of village life in England, and teaches one of the most valuable lessons in life, the "influence of pure, natural, human relations."

Yf

Er 2 co

1283. **Conscript: a story of the French war of 1813.** Emile Erckmann, *and* Alex. Chatrain. Translated from the French. N. Y., C: Scribner's Sons, 1900. 330 p. il. D. cl. .... 1.25 .82

One of the most impressive statements of the darker side of the national pursuit of military glory that has ever been made.

The first part of the book is taken up with a vivid and pathetic account of the passage of the *grande armée* through Alsace on its way to Moscow and the Beresina, of the anxious waiting for news of the battles that succeeded, of the first suspicions of disaster and their overwhelming confirmation, of the final rout and awful straggling retreat and return of the great expedition, and its demoralized and harassed entry within the national frontiers once more. The second and major portion narrates the rude surprise of the continuation of warfare and the still more fatal campaign which opened so dubiously with Lutzen and Bautzen, and culminated so disastrously in Leipsic and the capitulation of Paris.

	List price.	Price to schools.

Yf

Er 2 in

1284. **Invasion of France in 1814:** comprising the night-march of the Russian army past Phalsbourg. Emile Erckmann, *and* Alex. Chatrain. Translated from the French, with a memoir of the authors. N. Y., C: Scribner's Sons, 1871. 369 p. il. D. cl. .... 1.25 .82

This historical novel gives a vivid, dramatic account of the event in history which its title suggests.

Yf

Er 2 wa

1285. **Waterloo:** a sequel to the Conscript of 1813. Emile Erckmann, *and* Alex. Chatrain. Translated from the French. N. Y., C: Scribner's Sons, 1900. 368 p. il. D. cl. .... 1.25 .82

The narration of the story of the campaign of Waterloo by a private soldier. It presents an interesting picture of the state of affairs after the first Bourbon restoration and shows how gradually but surely the stupidity of the new régime paved the way for that return to power of Napoleon which seems so dramatically sudden and unexpected to a superficial view of the events of the time.

Yf

F 45 ho

1286. **Holy cross and other tales.** Eugene Field. N. Y., C: Scribner's Sons, 1901. 293 p. D. cl. ...... 1.25 .82

Contents: Holy cross; Rose and the thrush; Pagan seal-wife; Flail, trask, and bisland; Touch in the heart; Daniel and the devil; Methuselah; Félice and Petit-Poulain; River; Franz Abt; Mistress Merciless; Platonic bassoon; Hawaiian folk tales; Lute Baker and his wife Em; Joel's talk with Santa Claus; Lonesome little shoe.

Yf

F 45 ho

1287. **House:** an épisode in the lives of Reuben Baker, astronomer, and his wife Alice. Eugene Field. N. Y., C: Scribner's Sons, 1900. 268 p. D. cl.. 1.25 .82

LIST OF BOOKS FOR HIGH SCHOOL LIBRARIES.

	List price.	Price to schools.

Yf
F 45 li

1288. **Little book of profitable tales.** Eugene Field. N. Y., C: Scribners Sons, 1901. 286 p. D. cl. ...   1.25   .82

A collection of some of Field's most beautiful short stories.
Contents: First Christmas tree; Symbol and the saint; Coming of the prince; Mouse and the moonbeam; Divell's Chrystmasse; Mountain and the sea; Robin and the violet; Oak-tree and the ivy; Margaret: a pearl; Springtime; Rodolph and his king; Hampshire hills; Ezra's Thanksgivin' out west; Ludwig and Eloise; Fido's little friends; The old man; Bill, the lokil editor; Little yaller baby; The "cyclopeedy;" Dock Stebbins; Fairies of Pesth.

Yf
F 45 se

1289. **Second book of tales.** Eugene Field. N. Y., C: Scribner's Sons, 1900. 314 p. S. cl. ....   1.25   .82

Contents: Humin natur' on the Han'bul 'nd St. Jo.; Mother in Paradise; Mr. and Mrs. Blossom; Death and the soldier; 'Jinin' farms; Angel and the flowers; Child's letter; Singer mother; Two wives; Wooing of Miss Woppit; Talisman; George's birthday; Sweet-one-darling and the dream fairies; Sweet-one-darling and the moon-garden; Samuel Cowles and his horse Royal; Werewolf; Marvelous invention; Story of Xanthippe; Baked beans and culture; Mlle. Prud'homme's book; Demand for condensed music; Learning and literature; "Die Waikure" und der Boomerangelungen; Works of Sappho.

Yf
F 61 ha

1290. [87.] **Harvard episodes.** C. M. Flandrau. Bost., Copeland & Day, 1897. 339 p. D. cl. ....   1.25   .50

College life in Harvard.

Yf
F 72 le

1291. [69.] **Led-horse claim: a romance of a mining camp.** Mary Hallock Foote. Bost., Houghton, Mifflin & Co., 1883. D. cl. ....   1.25   .82

Life in a mining camp.

Yf
F 75 ho

1292. [94.] **Honorable Peter Stirling and what people thought of him.** Paul Leicester Ford. N. Y., Henry Holt & Co., 1899. 417 p. D. cl. ....   1.50   .98

A story of a "political boss" showing the political leader at his best.

Yf
———
F 75 ja   List   Price to
                                                                 price.   schools.

1293. [177.] **Janice Meredith:** a story of the American
  Revolution. Paul Leicester Ford. N. Y., Dodd,
  Mead & Co., 1899. 536 p. il. D. cl. .... 1.50 . .98

  A charming story of the war in the years 1774 and 1775 to the surrender at Yorktown. The historical setting of the story is fairly accurate, and the life is well depicted.

Yf
———
F 88 st

1294. [68.] **Stories of a western town.** Alice French.
  N. Y., C: Scribner's Sons, 1897. 243 p. il. D.
  cl. .... 1.25   .82

  Simple stories of the life of a people in a western town. "The Besetment of Kurt Lieders," "Tommy and Thomas," and "Harry Larsing" are the best.

Yf
———
F 95 ac

1295. [91.] **Across the campus:** a story of college life.
  Caroline M. Fuller. N. Y., C: Scribner's Sons,
  1899. 441 p. D. cl. .... 1.50   .98

  Story of life in a girl's college. Will interest younger pupils.

Yf
———
F 95 pr

1296. [64.] **Pratt portraits sketched in a New England
  suburb.** Anna Fuller. N. Y., G. P. Putnam's
  Sons, 1899. 325 p. il. D. cl. .... 1.50   .95

  Delightful bits of New England life. Good character sketches.

Yf
———
G 18 ma

1297. [119.] **Main-travelled roads.** Hamlin Garland. N.
  Y., Macmillan Co., 1899. 299 p. D. cl. .... 1.50   .98

  Scenes of many of the stories are laid in Wisconsin.

Yf
———
G 21 cr

1298. [124.] **Cranford.** *Mrs.* Gaskell. N. Y., Longmans,
  Green & Co., 1896. 316 p. il. D. cl. .... 1.00   .50

  A pleasing story of life in an English village. Cranford is in possession of the Amazons; all the holders of houses above a certain rent, are women.

	List price.	Price to schools.

Yf
G 42 ba

1299. **Back to the soil:** or, From tenement house to farm colony; a circular solution of an angular problem. Bradley Gilman. Bost., L. C. Page & Co., 1901. 242 p. D. cl. .... 1.25 .82

"This book," the preface says, "aims at setting forth the hopeful possibilities of country life, in contrast with the forlorn and desperate actualities of the crowded life of our larger cities. It depicts, in fiction form, the concrete conditions under which country life should be undertaken, and it points out many of the resources and opportunities of the country, which thus far have been overlooked."

Yf
G 61 co

1300. [89.] **College girls.** Abbe Carter Goodloe. N. Y., C: Scribner's Sons, 1899. 288 p. il. D. cl. ... 1.25 .82

Good stories portraying life in Wellesley college.

Yf
G 63 he

1301. [168.] **Head of a hundred:** being an account of certain passages in the life of Humphrey Huntoon, Esq., some time an officer in the Colony of Virginia. Ed. by Maud Wilder Goodwin. Bost., Little, Brown & Co., 1897. 225 p. il. D. (Romances of Colonial Virginia, no. 1.) cl. .... 1.25 .82

Life in the colony of Virginia.

Yf
G 63 wh

1302. [170.] **White Aprons:** a romance of Bacon's rebellion: Virginia, 1676. Maud Wilder Goodwin. Bost., Little, Brown & Co., 1899. 339 p. D. cl. 1.25 .82

A love story. The leading events are based upon the struggle between tyranny and popular rights which took place in Virginia, known as Bacon's Rebellion.

Yf
G 64 pr

#1303. **Princess's story book,** being historical stories collected out of English romantic literature in illustration of the reigns of English monarchs from the conquest to Queen Victoria. Ed. by George Laurence Gomme. N. Y., Longmans, Green & Co., 1901. 443 p. il. .D. cl. 2.00 1.30

These stories will be useful as specimens of English literature and will also be valuable to the classes in English history.

Contents: Harold: with the queen and princesses before the battle Lord Lytton; William I: Princesses in the lighting line—

	List price.	Price to schools.

Sir W. Napier; Henry II: king or priest—W. Miller; Richard I: In camp and tent—Sir Walter Scott; Edward I: At Falkirk—Jane Porter; Edward II: Queen and king—Froissart; Edward III: Battle of Poictiers—Froissart; Richard II: Wooing of a princess—Froissart; Henry VI: Struggle for crown or duty—Lord Lytton; Edward IV: Discrowned queen—Sir Walter Scott; Henry VII: Message of fate—Mary W. Shelley; Henry VIII: Dishonoured queen—W. H. Ainsworth; Mary: Princess Elizabeth sent to the Tower—W. H. Ainsworth; Elizabeth: Men who fought for queen and country—Charles Kingsley; James I: How the good king tried to mend a bad business—Sir Walter Scott; Charles I: King, queen, and parliament—Horace Smith; Commonwealth: fight for the king—Sir Walter Scott; Charles II: At the fire of London—W. H. Ainsworth; Anne: At the court of the queen—W. H. Ainsworth; George I: Border raid in the prince's name—Sir Walter Scott; George II: for country or for king—Fenimore Cooper; George: "Brittannia rules the waves"—Samuel Lover; Victoria: "For whom was the Queen sent?"—Lord Beaconsfield.

Yf

G 65 sk

1304. [70.] **Sky pilot:** a tale of the foot hills. Ralph Connor (*pseud.*) N. Y., and Chic., Fleming H. Revell Co., 1899. 300 p. D. cl. .... 1.25 .82

A story of western life portraying life of the cowboys. Fine descriptions of mountain scenery.

Yf

G 69 je

1305. **Jed:** a boy's adventures in the army of '61-'65; a story of battle and prison, of peril and escape. Warren Lee Goss. N. Y., Thomas Y. Crowell & Co., c1889. 404 p. il. D. cl. .... 1.50 .98

"In this story the author has aimed to furnish true pictures of scenes in the great civil war, and not to produce sensational effects. The incidents of the book are real ones, drawn in part from the writer's personal experiences and observations, as a soldier of the Union, during that war. He is also indebted to many comrades for reminiscences of battle and prison life. The perilous escape of Jed and Dick from Andersonville down the Flint and Apalachicola rivers; to the Gulf of Mexico, is in substance the narrative of a comrade whom the writer knew at Andersonville, and afterwards met when the war closed. The descriptions of the prison are especially truthful, for in them the author briefly tells what he himself saw.

"There is not a description of battle or camp scene in the book that is not as faithful to the reality as the author can make it, and he believes that these sketches will be recognized as true by the veterans of the war who may chance to read them."—*Preface.*

	List price.	Price to schools.

Yf

G 76 re

1306. [163.] **Reds of the Midi:** an episode of the French Revolution: tr. from Provencal by Catherine A. Janvier. Felix Gras. N. Y., D. Appleton & Co., 1896. 366 p. por. S. cl. .... 1.50 .98

In the feelings of a single peasant Gras has given us an epitome of the motive power of the French Revolution.

Yf

H 13 ab

1307. [107.] **Abbe Constantin.** Ludovic Halévy. N. Y., T. Y. Crowell & Co., 1899. 166 p. il. D. (Copley series.) cl. .... 1.00 .50

A pretty little love story.

Yf

H 13 ma

1308. [60.] **Man without a country.** Edward E. Hale. Bost., Little, Brown & Co., 1899. 59 p. D. cl. .. .50 .30

One of the best lessons in patriotism ever taught.

Yf

H 25 lu

1309. **Luck of Roaring Camp, and other stories.** Bret Harte. Bost., Houghton, Mifflin & Co., c1899. 279 p. S. cl. .... 1.25 .82

Bret Harte's stories depict traits of character of the rougher class of western people that we are apt to overlook in forming our estimate of them. They show us the love, sympathy and good fellowship that exist among these people and tend to make us more charitable in forming our estimates of them. The class in American literature should read selected stories from this volume in their study of the nineteenth century writers.

Contents: Luck of Roaring Camp; Mliss; Outcasts of Poker Flat; Miggles; Tennessee's partner; Idyl of Red Gulch; How Santa Claus came to Simpson's Bar; Fool of Five Forks; Romance of Mandrono Hollow; Princess Bob and her friends.

Yf

H 31 ho

1310. [45.] **House of the seven gables.** Nathaniel Hawthorne. N. Y., Houghton, Mifflin & Co., 1896. D. (Riverside edition.) cl. 2.00 1.28

A story of retribution and a study in heredity.

Yf

H 31 ma

List price. Price to schools.

1311. [44.] **Marble faun:** or, The romance of Monte Beni. Nathaniel Hawthorne. N. Y., Houghton, Mifflin & Co., 1896. (Riverside edition.) cl. 2.00   1.28

Some of the older students will enjoy this romance. It contains many fine descriptions of Italian scenery, and works of art.

Yf

H 31 mo

1312. **Mosses from an old manse.** Nathaniel Hawthorne. Bost., Houghton, Mifflin & Co., c1882. 559 p. D. (Riverside edition.) cl. 2.00   1.28

A collection of sketches written by the author at the Manse, Concord, Massachusetts, after his marriage, in 1842.

Contents: Introductory note; Old manse; Birthmark; Select party; Young Goodman Brown; Rappaccini's daughter; Mrs. Bullfrog; Fire worship; Buds and bird voices; Monsieur du Miroir; Hall of fantasy; Celestial railroad; Procession of life; Feathertop: a moralized legend; New Adam and Eve; Egotism: or, the bosom serpent; Christmas banquet; Drowne's wooden image; Intelligence office; Roger Malvin's burial; P.'s correspondence; Earth's holocaust; Passages from a relinquished work; Sketches from memory; Old apple dealer; Artist of the beautiful; Virtuoso's collection.

Yf

H 31 sn

1313. **Snow image and other twice-told tales.** Nathaniel Hawthorne. N. Y., Thos. Y. Crowell & Co., c1899. 253 p. S. cl. .... .60   .40

"The short stories of Nathaniel Hawthorne may be described as black-and-white work leading up to the great canvasses which best display his power: *The Scarlet Letter* and the other full-length novels. Most of them belong to the Salem days when Hawthorne, a lonely recluse, was impelled to body forth his imaginings and, looking into his own heart, expressed in terms of humanity as he then knew it, the symbolic significances of the eternal spirit of man. The qualities of the tales are derived from his prime characteristics as a young man, conditioned by the somewhat bleak environment in which they were produced. For this very reason these stories are, after all, as typical as anything he ever did and well-nigh as interesting; while they may not show us Hawthorne in his master years nor illustrate the rich maturity of a great artist, they do have the impress of his essential features; they are Hawthornesque to the core."—*Preface.*

Contents: Snow-image: a childish miracle; Great stone face; Main-street; Ethan Brand; Bell's biography; Sylph Etherege; Canterbury Pilgrims; Old news; Man of adamant: an apologue; Devil in manuscript; John Inglefield's Thanksgiving; Old Ticonderoga: picture of the past; Wives of the dead; Little daffydowndilly; Major Molineux.

LIST OF BOOKS FOR HIGH SCHOOL LIBRARIES. 349

	List price.	Price to schools.

Yf
H 55 st

1314. [71.] **Stories of the railroad.** John A. Hill. N. Y., Doubleday & McClure Co., 1899. 297 p. il. D. cl. .... 1.50 .98

Interesting stories dealing with railroad life. For the boy who does not care to read but is interested in railroads.

Yf
H 83 on

1315. [112.] **One summer.** Blanche W. Howard. Bost., Houghton, Mifflin & Co., 1899. D. cl. .... 1.25 .82

A pretty love story, interesting for Library reading.

Yf
H 83 ri

1316. [56.] **Rise of Silas Lapham.** William D. Howells. Bost., Houghton, Mifflin & Co., 1884. 515 p. D. cl. .... 1.50 .98

A character study portraying the character of a typical American —Silas Lapham. The book is essentially American, and deals with a problem which every young man must solve.

Yf
H 85 ba

1317. **Barbara's heritage,** or, Young Americans among the old Italian masters. Deristhe L. Hoyt. Bost., W. A. Wilde Co., c1899. 358 p. il. D. cl. ..... 1.50 .85

The story of an American woman and her son and daughter who take a trip to Italy. They are accompanied by two young girls.

Their personal experiences and the history of the art treasures they study together, with the illustrations, make a book full of valuable information.

Yf
H 87 to

1318. [83.] **Tom Brown at Oxford.** Thomas Hughes. N. Y., Macmillan & Co. 546 p. il. D. cl. .... 1.50 .50

Life in an English college.

Yf
Ir 8 al

1319. [234.] **Alhambra.** Washington Irving, ed. by Arthur Marvin. N. Y., G. P. Putnam's Sons, 1899. 523 p. il. D. (Students' edition.) cl. .. .. 1.00 .50

A volume of legends and narratives. Complete edition which was revised by Irving himself. A very good edition, well bound, print clear, and not too many notes.

350 LIST OF BOOKS FOR HIGH SCHOOL LIBRARIES.

| | List price. | Price to schools. |

Yf
―――
Ir 8 st

1320. [126.] **Stories and legends from Washington Irving.** N. Y., G. P. Putnam's Sons, 1896. 312 p. il. D. cl. .... 1.50 .95

Good selections from Irving which may lead to the reading of his works.

Yf
―――
Ir 8 ta

1321. [233.] **Tales of a traveller.** Washington Irving, ed. by William Lyon Phelps. N. Y., G. P. Putnam's Sons, 1895. 558 p. (Students' edition.) cl. .... 1.00 .50

Yf
―――
J 12 ra

1322. [95.] **Ramona:** a story. Helen Hunt Jackson. Bost., Little, Brown & Co., 1899. 490 p. D. cl.. 1.50 .98

The Indian question from the standpoint of the Indian. True pictures of southern California.

Yf
―――
J 47 th

1323. [100.] **Three men in a boat** (to say nothing of the dog). Jerome K. Jerome. N. Y., Henry Holt & Co., 1890. 293 p. il. D. cl. .... 1.25 .50

A charming book, delightfully written and full of humor.

Yf
―――
J 45 co

1324. [63.] **Country doctor.** Sarah Orne Jewett. Bost., Houghton, Mifflin & Co., 1884. D. cl. .... 1.25 .82

Some of the best pictures of New England village life. "Their bare external life, their moral courage, their eccentric tempers, and ironical humor are set forth with infinite sympathy, skill, and variety."

Yf
―――
J 55 c

1325. **Country by-ways.** Sarah Orne Jewett. Bost., Houghton, Mifflin & Co., 1899. 249 p. S. cl. .. 1.25 .82

A collection of short stories.
Contents: River driftwood; Andrew's fortune; An October ride; From a mournful villager; An autumn holiday; A winter drive; Good luck: A girl's story; Miss Becky's pilgrimage.

LIST OF BOOKS FOR HIGH SCHOOL LIBRARIES. 351

	List price.	Price to schools.

Yf
———
J 55 co

1326. **Country of the pointed firs.** Sarah Orne Jewett. Bost., Houghton, Mifflin & Co., 1896. 213 p. D. cl. .... 1.25 .82

A pretty story of life in a New England village. Interesting for Library reading.

Yf
———
J 55 ta

1327. **Tales of New England.** Sarah Orne Jewett. Bost., Houghton, Mifflin & Co., 1896. 276 p. D. cl. .. 1.00 .65

As an interpreter of New England life the author has won a high place. Of the many phases of this life she has chosen the one which has quiet and tenderness, patience and self-reliance, behind its limitations, its joys and its sorrows. She feels keenly both the pathos and humor of life.
Contents: Introduction; Miss Tempy's watchers; Dulham ladies; Only son; Marsh rosemary; White heron; Law Lane; Lost lover; Courting of Sister Wisby.

Yf
———
J 62 to

1328. [167.] **To have and to hold.** Mary Johnston. Bost., Houghton, Mifflin & Co., 1900. 403 p. il. D. cl. 1.50 .98

An historical story of the early days in the colony of Virginia. Vivid and dramatic portrayal of life and an intensely interesting story.

Yf
———
J 63 hi

1329. **History of Rasselas, Prince of Abyssinia.** Samuel Johnson. Edited with introduction and notes by Oliver Farrar Emerson. N. Y., Henry Holt & Co., 1895. 179 p. S. cl. .... .50 .45

The story of an Abyssinian prince who, with his brothers and sisters, is confined in a beautiful valley until he shall be called to rule over his ancestral dominions.
This should be read by the class in English literature.

Yf
———
K 61 he

1330. [148.] **Hereward, the wake.** Charles Kingsley. N. Y., Macmillan Co., 1893. 246 p. il. S. (Macmillan's school library.) cl. .... .50 .41

A story of life in England in the earliest times. Hereward is a noted English patriot who heads an insurrection against the Normans. He burns the Abby of Peterborough and fortifies his camp in the Isle of Ely, where he is besieged by William the Conqueror.

Yf

K 61 hy

1331. [143.] **Hypatia:** or, New foes with an old face. Charles Kingsley. N. Y., G. P. Putnam's Sons, 1897. 401 p. D. cl. .... 1.00 .50

The story of Hypatia, the daughter of Theon, a mathematician in Egypt. Her beauty and learning aroused the jealousy of the Archbishop of Alexandria, who stirred up his friends against her. She was seized by a band of fanatical monks and torn to pieces. A true picture of life in the fifth century.

Yf

K 61 we

1332. **Westward Ho!** or, The voyages and adventures of Sir Amys Leigh, knight of Burrough, in the county of Devon, in the reign of her most glorious majesty Queen Elizabeth. Charles Kingsley. N. Y., Macmillan Co., 1900. 591 p. D. cl. .... .50 .45

A story of adventure in the reign of Queen Elizabeth, the scenes being laid in Southwestern England and in America.

Yf

K 62 ca

1333. [81.] **"Captains courageous":** a story of the Grand Banks. Rudyard Kipling. N. Y., Century Co., 1899. 323 p. il. D. cl. .... 1.50 .98

A story of the Gloucester fishing fleets. The life aboard a sloop in the fishing season off the Banks of Newfoundland is vividly portrayed. The story teaches a lesson in self-effort and self-reliance.

Yf

K 62 da

1334. [105.] **Day's work.** Rudyard Kipling. N. Y., Doubleday & McClure Co., 1898. 431 p. O. cl. ..... 1.50 .98

Stories in which Kipling makes the inanimate things live and tell their own stories.

Yf

L 51 qu

1335. [113.] **Quaker girl of Nantucket.** Mary Catherine Lee. Bost., Houghton, Mifflin & Co., 1889. D. cl. .... 1.25 .82

An entertaining story that will be of interest to the Library reading class in Fiction.

	List price.	Price to schools.

Yf
L 86 hy

1336. **Hyperion and Kavanagh.** Henry Wadsworth Longfellow. Bost., Houghton, Mifflin & Co., 1886. 417 p. D. cl. (Cambridge classics.) .... 1.00 .65

 The hero of Hyperion, Paul Flemming, was heart-broken at the loss of a dear friend and traveled abroad to assuage his grief, spending a winter at Heidelberg. He has a love affair but is separated from the girl by pride, and they never meet again. The story is interwoven with charming translations from German poetry.

Yf
L 92 ab

1337. [57.] **Abandoned claim.** Flora Haines Loughead. Bost., Houghton, Mifflin & Co., 1899. 330 p. S. cl. .... 1.25 .82

 A story of some young people who "take up" an abandoned claim in California. The account of their efforts and success is very interesting. Teaches self-reliance.

Yf
L 96 ca

1338. [146.] **Captain of the Janizaries.** James M. Ludlow. N. Y., Harper & Bros., 1898. 404 p. S. cl. ..... 1.50 .98

 An intensely interesting and dramatic story of the fall of Constantinople.

Yf
L 97 en

1339. [73.] **Enchanted burro:** stories of New Mexico and South America. Charles F. Lummis. Chic., Way & Williams, 1897. 277 p. il. D. cl. .... 1.50 .50

 Stories and sketches of the Southwest, teaching bravery, courage, and self-reliance.

Yf
L 97 ne

1340. [74.] **New Mexico David.** Charles F. Lummis. N. Y., C: Scribner's Sons, 1891. 217 p. D. cl. .... 1.25 .82

 A collection of most interesting short stories of life in New Mexico, Peru, and Bolivia.

Yf
M 29 wh

1341. [151.] **When knighthood was in flower:** or the love story of Charles Brandon and Mary Tudor, the king's sister, and happenings in the reign of King

	List price.	Price to schools.

Henry VIII; rewritten and rendered into modern English from Sir Edwin Caskoden's memoirs. Charles Major. (Edwin Caskoden, *pseud.*) Indianapolis, Ind., Bowen-Merrill Co., 1898. 249 p. D. cl. .... 1.50 .98

The love story of Charles Brandon and the Princess Mary Tudor, sister of Henry VIII. A fine portrayal of the character of Mary Tudor.

Yf

M 69 hu

1342. [175.] **Hugh Wynne, free Quaker.** S. Weir Mitchell. N. Y., Century Co., 1897. 2 vols. 306; 261 p. por. il. D. cl. .... 2.00 .98

Social life in Philadelphia during and before the Revolutionary war is graphically pictured as well as exciting scenes of the war itself. Among the characters in the story are Washington, Franklin, Benedict Arnold, and Maj. André. One of the best historical stories.

Yf

M 81 ut

1343. **Utopia.** *Sir* Thomas More. Translated into English by Raphe Robynson. N. Y., Cassell & Co., 1899. 183 p. S. cl. .... .20 .15

A political romance. Utopia is an imaginary island where everything is perfect,—the laws, the politics, the morals, etc. The author, by contrast, shows the evils of existing laws. This story will be of interest to the classes in English literature, as a specimen of the literature of the sixteenth century.

Yf

M 94 in

1344. [66.] **In the Tennessee mountains.** Charles Egbert Craddock. Bost., Houghton, Mifflin & Co., 1899. 322 p. S. cl. .... 1.25 .82

Stories portraying life in the Tennessee mountains. The descriptions of scenery are exceptionally good.

Yf

M 94 pr

1345. **Prophet of the Great Smoky Mountains.** Mary N. Murfree. (Charles Egbert Craddock, *pseud.*) Bost., Houghton, Mifflin & Co., c1885. 308 p. D. cl. .... 1.25 .82

A romance which gives a vivid picture of life in the Tennessee mountains.

		List price.	Price to schools.

Yf
Ol 3 bo

1346. [101.] **Bob, son of battle.** Alfred Ollivant. N. Y., Doubleday & McClure Co., 1899. 356 p. D. cl. 1.50 1.35

The interesting story of a shepherd dog. Life of shepherds of extreme north of England depicted. A good character study.

Yf
P 14 In.

1347. [186.] **In ole Virginia:** or, Marse Chan and other stories. Thomas Nelson Page. N. Y., C: Scribner's Sons, 1899. 230 p. D. cl. .... 1.25 .82

Beautiful stories of life in the south since the war. Marse Chan is a classic.

Yf
P 14 ma

1348. **Marse Chan.** Thomas Nelson Page. N. Y., C: Scribner's Sons, 1900. 53 p. il. O. cl. .... 1.00 .65

A tale of life in old Virginia. This story is included in a collection of short stories "In Ole Virginia" which is on the list so that libraries which purchase the collection should not duplicate by purchasing this.

Yf
P 14 ol

1349. **Old gentleman of the Black Stock.** Thomas Nelson Page. N. Y., C: Scribner's Sons, 1901. 170 p. il. D. cl. .... 1.50 .98

A charming story of Southern life. Will be interesting for Library reading.

Yf
P 14 re

1350. [185]. **Red Rock:** a chronicle of reconstruction. Thomas Nelson Page. N. Y., C: Scribner's Sons, 1898. 584 p. il. D. cl. .... 1.50 .98

Reconstruction in the south after the civil war. Pictures southern life. Good character sketches.

Yf
P 14 sa

1351. [59.] **Santa Claus's partner.** Thomas Nelson Page. N. Y., C: Scribner's Sons, 1899. 177 p. il. D. cl. .... 1.50 .98

A most delightful story teaching the joy of giving.

Yf
P 22 pi

List price. Price to schools.

1352. [67.] **Pierre and his people:** tales of the far north. Gilbert Parker. N. Y., Macmillan & Co., 1899. 318 p. D. cl. .... 1.25   .82

Graphic portrayals of typical characters.

Yf
P 75 ta

1353. **Tales:** with an introduction by Hamilton Wright Mabie. Edgar Allan Poe. N. Y., Century Co., 1901. 499 p. por. D. cl. 1.25 1.12

The introduction gives an excellent estimate of Poe and his works.
Contents: Gold-bug; Descent into the Maelstrom; MS. found in a bottle; Murders in the Rue Morgue; Mystery of Marie Rôget; Purloined letter; Fall of the House of Usher; William Wilson; Man of the crowd; Black cat; Telltale heart; Assignation; Masque of the red death; Cask of Amontillado; Pit and the pendulum.

Yf
P 83 sc

1354. **Scottish chiefs.** Jane Porter. Rev. and cor. with a new retrospective introduction, notes, etc. N. Y., Thomas Y. Crowell & Co., n. d. 2 vol. in 1. il. D. cl. 60   .40

Robert Burns and William Wallace are the heroes of this story. The scene is laid in Scotland.

Yf
P 83 th

1355. **Thaddeus of Warsaw:** a tale founded on Polish heroism. Jane Porter. N. Y., A. L. Burt, n. d. 461 p. D. cl. .... 1.00   .40

The story of a Polish exile. The description of the scenes and occurrences in Poland are very accurate.

Yf
R 22 cl

1356. [147.] **Cloister and the hearth.** Charles Reade. N. Y., T. Y. Crowell & Co., 1898. 679 p. il. O. cl. 1.50   .50

A story of the period immediately preceding the reformation in Holland, Burgundy, and Rome. The invention of printing is touched upon. The hero of the story is Gerard, the father of Erasmus.

| | List price. | Price to schools. |

Yf
R 39 ge

1357. **Geoffrey Strong.** Laura E. Richards. Bost., Dana Estes & Co., c1901. 217 p. il. S. cl. .... .75 .49

A story of a New England sea-board village. Geoffrey Strong is a clever young doctor who boards in the house of two exclusive maiden ladies. To them comes a young girl who is the heroine of Geoffrey's love story. The sketches of rural types are amusing and lifelike.
A pretty story for Library reading.

Yf
R 54 he

1358. **Heart of the ancient wood.** Charles G. D. Roberts. N. Y., Silver, Burdett & Co., c1900. 276 p. il. D. cl. .... 1.50 .98

A realistic romance of the folk of the forest and a pioneer's daughter whose home is in the depths of the ancient wood. The wild beasts of the wood become her friends and she learns to care more for them than for the human kind.
"The book stands alone—it is like no other. The talking beasts of the wondrous Jungle tales are fabulous. The thinking wild animals Mr. Seton-Thompson has known are character studies. But in 'The Heart of the Ancient Wood' there is a problem drama. The imagination is subtler than in the adventures of Mowgli; the reportorial correctness is as unimpeachable as in the biography of Wahb; and in addition there is the fact of a master novelist turning to the unfathomed sympathies and dramatic possibilities of the relation of the human to the animal as seriously and as analytically as Mr. Howells turns to his familiar people."—*The Criterion.*

Yf
Sa 2 pa

1359. [123.] **Paul and Virginia.** J. H. Bernardin de Saint-Pierre, *tr.* by Melville B. Anderson. Chic., A. C. McClurg & Co., 1895. 218 p. D. cl. ...... 1.50 .50

A beautiful story, the scene of which is laid in the island of Mauritius. Paul and Virginia, the children of neighbors, are playmates from childhood. The story is the subject of plays and operas in several languages.

Yf
Sa 5 co

1360. [84.] **Cornell stories.** James Gardner Sanderson. N. Y., C: Scribner's Sons, 1899. 251 p. D. cl... 1.00 .65

Fine college stories showing best side of fraternity life. The story "Little Tyler" is a classic.

Yf
Sco 3 an	List price.	Price to schools.

1362. **Anne of Gierstein: or, The maiden of the mist.** *Sir* Walter Scott. N. Y., Macmillan Co., 1894. 482 p. il. (Dryburgh edition.) O. cl. .... 1.25 .82

A novel based on the conquest of Charles the Bad, duke of Burgundy, by the Swiss at Nancy. The Secret Tribunal of Westphalia was in full power at the time.

Yf
Sco 3 ant

1363. **Antiquary.** *Sir* Walter Scott. London, Adam and Charles Black; N. Y., Macmillan Co., 1893. 431 p. il. (Dryburgh edition.) O. cl. .... 1.25 .82

This story is named after one of its characters, Jonathan Oldbuck, who is interested in antiquities. The Antiquary meets William Lovel in Edinburgh, and invites him to Monk-bairn. Lovel there meets Sir Arthur Wardour and his daughter, and later marries the daughter. He turns out to be the son of the Earl of Glenallaw. The story is of the time of George III.

Yf
Sco 3 bl

1364. **Black dwarf and A legend of Montrose.** *Sir* Walter Scott. London, Adam and Charles Black; N. Y., Macmillan Co., 1893. 382 p. il. (Dryburgh edition.) O. cl. .... 1.25 .82

The scene of "The Black dwarf" is laid in Scotland, in the reign of Queen Anne.

The heroine of the story is Isabella Vere, daughter of Richard Vere who was at the head of the Jacobite conspiracy.

The plot of the "Legend of Montrose" consists of a battle between the Royalists and Parliamentarians, in the reign of Charles I. Dugald Dalgerty, a soldier, is one of Scott's best characters.

Yf
Sco 3 br

1365. **Bride of Lammermoor.** *Sir* Walter Scott. London, Adam and Charles Black; N. Y., Macmillan Co., 1893. 330 p. il. (Dryburgh edition.) O. cl. ... 1.25 .82

One of Scott's most finished novels, presenting a unity of plot from beginning to end. It is the subject of several plays and operas. The time is during the reign of William III.

Yf
Sco 3 co

1366. **Count Robert of Paris.** *Sir* Walter Scott. N. Y., Macmillan Co, 1894. 400 p. il. (Dryburgh ed.) O. cl. .... 1.25 .82

Count Robert is a French crusader, who was with Godfrey de Bouillon at the siege of Constantinople. The time of the novel is

| | List price. | Price to schools. |

the reign of Rufus. This was written after Scott's health began to fail and does not come up to the standard of "Ivanhoe" and "Quentin Durward."

Yf

Sco 3 fa

1367. **Fair maid of Perth: or, St. Valentine's day.** *Sir* Walter Scott. N. Y., Macmillan Co., 1894. 467 p. il. (Dryburgh ed.) O. cl...................... 1.25 .82

The scene is at Perth, Scotland, during the time of Henry IV of England and Robert III of Scotland. A description of the famous Battle of the Clans, in which the chosen representatives of two quarrelsome Highland clans fight out their feud on the North Inch, in the presence of the king and his court.

Yf

Sco 3 fo

1368. **Fortunes of Nigel.** *Sir* Walter Scott. London, Adam and Charles Black (N. Y., Macmillan Co.) 1898. 478 p. il. (Dryburgh ed.) O. cl........ 1.25 .82

A masterly sketch of the character of James I. The account of Alsatia is wholly unrivalled.

Yf

Sco 3 he

1369. [36.] **Heart of Midlothian.** *Sir* Walter Scott. London, Adam and Charles Black. N. Y., Macmillan Co., 1893. 576 p. il. (Dryburgh ed.) O. cl.... 1.25 .50

This story is so-called from the name of the old jail or tolbooth of Edinburgh, taken down in 1817. The time is during the reign of George II, and the novel opens with a description of the Porteous riots.

Yf

Sco 3 ke

1370. [34.] **Kenilworth.** *Sir* Walter Scott. London, Adam and Charles Black, N. Y., Macmillan Co., 1893. 473 p. il. (Dryburgh ed.) O. cl........ 1.25 .50

The scene of this story is in England, during the reign of Elizabeth. The pictures given of the queen and of country life are excellent ones. The tale is about the infidelity of the Earl of Leicester, and the tragical fate of his wife, Amy Robsart.

Yf

Sco 3 ol

1371. **Old mortality.** *Sir* Walter Scott. London, Adam and Charles Black, N. Y., Macmillan Co., 1893. 441 p. il. (Dryburgh ed.) O. cl.............. 1.25 .82

The scene of this novel was laid in Scotland, during the rising of the Covenanters in 1679-90, in the reigns of Charles II, James

	List price.	Price to schools.

II, and William and Mary. The two classes of characters, the brave, dissolute cavaliers, and the determined, oppressed Covenanters, are well delineated. One of the best of Scott's novels.

Yf
———
Sco 3 qu

1372. [35.] **Quentin Durward.** *Sir* Walter Scott. London, Adam and Charles Black, N. Y., Macmillan Co., 1894. 461 p. il. (Dryburgh ed.) O. cl. ...... 1.25 .50

A story of French history during the reign of Louis XI in France and Edward IV in England. The delineations of Louis XI and Charles the Bold, of Burgundy, are excellent. Several other well-known historic personages are introduced in the story.

Yf
———
Sco 3 ro

1373. **Rob Roy.** *Sir* Walter Scott. London, Adam and Charles Black, N. Y., Macmillan Co., 1893. 423 p. il. (Dryburgh ed.) O. cl...................... 1.25 .82

The scene is in the Highlands of Scotland during the rebellion of 1715. Rob Roy is Robert McGregor, chief of the McGregor clan. He became an outlaw and was known as "Robin Hood of Scotland." The pictures of Scotch scenery given are excellent.

Yf
———
Sco 3 ta

1374. [33.] **Talisman.** *Sir* Walter Scott. London, Adam and Charles Black; N. Y., Macmillan Co., 1894. 433 p. il. (Dryburgh ed.) O. cl. .... 1.25 .50

The scene is laid in the Holy Land in about 1193, during the truce of the Saracens, which preceded the abandonment of the crusade led by Richard I, Coeur de Lion. The story of Richard I, Coeur de Lion, being cured of a fever in the Holy Land, by the soldan. The Talisman is the pebble belonging to Saladin, the soldan of the Saracens, which had the power of curing a fever.

Yf
———
Sch 9 wa

1375. [90.] **Vassar studies.** Julia Augusta Schwartz. N. Y., G. P. Putnam's Sons, 1899. 290 p. D. cl.... 1.25 .82

Interesting stories portraying life in Vassar college.

Yf
———
Sco 3 iv

1376. [32.] **Ivanhoe: a romance.** *Sir* Walter Scott. London, Adam and Charles Black, N. Y., Macmillan Co., 1893. 472 p. il. (Dryburgh ed.) O. cl.... 1.25 .50

The scene is laid in England in the reign of Richard I. We are introduced to Robin Hood in Sherwood forest, banquets in Saxon

	List price.	Price to schools.

halls, tournaments, and are enabled to contrast the rude Saxon life with the chivalric life of the Normans. The story is a working out of the results of the Norman Conquest.

Yf

Se 1 hi

1377. **History of the Lady Betty Stair.** Molly Elliot Seawell. N. Y., C: Scribner's Sons, 1899. 144 p. D. cl. .... 1.25 .82

The story of a simple, daring, spirited Scotch girl, who lived during the time of the Napoleonic wars. She became a Sister of Mercy and followed the army courageously through many battles.

Yf

Se 1 ma

1378. [115.] **Maid Marion, and other stories.** Molly Elliot Seawell. N. Y., D. Appleton & Co., 1891. S. cl. .... 1.00 .65

Pretty, short love stories.

Yf

Se 1 vi

1379. [171.] **Virginia Cavalier.** Molly Elliott Seawell. N. Y., Harper & Bros., 1899. 349 p. il. D. cl...... 1.50 .98

George Washington as a Virginia gentleman. Will interest young readers.

Yf

Sm 5 to

1380. [93.] **Tom Grogan.** Francis Hopkinson Smith. Bost., Houghton, Mifflin & Co., 1899. 247 p. il. D. cl. 1.50 .98

This very good story deals with the Labor Union. Tom Grogan is a woman contractor who continues her husband's business after his death.

Yf

St 4 bl

1381. [150.] **Black Arrow: a tale of the two roses.** Robert Louis Stevenson. N. Y., C: Scribner's Sons, 1898. 322 p. il. D. cl............................... 1.25 .82

A good story of adventure at the time of the wars in England between the houses of York and Lancaster.

Yf
St 4 ki
                                                                                     List Price to
                                                                                     price. schools.

1382. [121.] **Kidnapped**, being memoirs of the adventures of David Balfour, in the year 1751. Robert Louis Stevenson. N. Y., C: Scribner's Sons, 1899. 324 p. il. D. cl.................................... 1.50 .50

An interesting story of the adventures of a Scottish youth who is kidnapped and cast away on a desert island, and of his sufferings at the hands of his uncle. It is continued in "David Balfour."

Yf
St 4 tr

1383. [120.] **Treasure island.** Robert Louis Stevenson. N. Y., C: Scribner's Sons, 1899. il. D.......... 1.00 .50

An exciting story of the Spanish Main, dealing with a mysterious island, pirates, and buried treasure.

Yf
St 5 ki

1384. [166.] **King Noanett**: a story of old Virginia and the Massachusetts Bay. F. J. Stimson. N. Y., C: Scribner's Sons, 1899. 327 p. il. D. cl........ 1.00 .50

A good story filled with thrilling adventures.

Yf
Eb 3 em

1385. **Emperor.** Georg Ebers. Translated from the German by Mrs. C. H. Storrs. N. Y., A. L. Burt, n. d. 388 p. por. D. cl. .... 1.00 .40

The scene is laid in ancient Egypt during the time of Roman dominion, and the early upspringing of Christianity. The author devoted years of study to the infancy of Christianity, especially in Egypt.

Yf
St 6 ru

1386. [99.] **Rudder Grange.** Frank R. Stockton. N. Y., C: Scribner's Sons, 1898. 292 p. D. cl........ 1.25 .82

One of the most charming of Stockton's stories.

Yf
St 6 st

1387. [109.] **Story-teller's pack.** Frank R. Stockton. N. Y., C: Scribner's Sons, 1897. 380 p. il D. cl.. 1.50 .98

A good collection of short stories for Library reading.

		List price.	Price to schools.

Yf
St 7 dr

1388. **Dred: a tale of the great dismal swamp.** Harriet Beecher Stowe. Bost., Houghton, Mifflin & Co. c1884. 607 p. (Cambridge classics series.) O. cl. .... 1.50 .98

    Dred is a runaway negro slave living in the Dismal Swamp. This book and "Uncle Tom's Cabin" should be read by the classes in United States history.

Yf
St 7 un

1389. **Uncle Tom's cabin;** or, life among the lowly. With an introductory account of the work by the author, fifteen illustrations from designs by E. W. Kemble, and a portrait of the author. Harriet Beecher Stowe. Bost., Houghton, Mifflin & Co., 1900. 500 p. il. and por. D. cl..................... .60 .54

    A story of slave life in the South before the civil war. The scene is chiefly in Kentucky and Louisiana.

Yf
St 71 sa

1390. [137.] **Stories by American authors.** N. Y., C: Scribner's Sons, 1896. 10 vols. por. S. cl. each ... .75 .50

    Ten volumes of the best short stories by leading American authors.

Yf
St 71 se

#1391. [127-136.] **Stories by English authors.** N. Y., C: Scribner's Sons, 1896. 10 vols. S. cl. each .. .75 .49

    The foregoing ten volumes contain short stories by leading English authors portraying life in America, England, France, Germany, Ireland, Italy, London, Scotland, the Orient, and on the sea.

Yf
Sw 5 gu

1392. **Gulliver's travels.** Dean Swift. Chic., Rand, McNally & Co., n. d. 353 p. il. D. cl............ 1.00 .65

    Gulliver was first a surgeon, then a sea-captain of several ships. He gets wrecked on the coast of Lilliput, a country of pygmies, and subsequently makes three other voyages. These voyages are satires on the court, ministry and policy of George I; on William IV; and on the false philosophers and quack pretenders to science.

Yf
T 32 he

1393. [37.] **Henry Esmond.** William Makepeace Thackeray. Bost., Houghton, Mifflin & Co. il. O. cl. 1.50 .50

    A story of Queen Anne's reign, giving an excellent picture of the manners and customs of the period.

LIST OF BOOKS FOR HIGH SCHOOL LIBRARIES.

	List price.	Price to schools.

Yf
———
T 32 vi

1394. [38.] **Virginians:** a tale of the last century. William Makepeace Thackeray. Introductory note setting forth the history of the work. Bost., Houghton, Mifflin & Co., 1886. 2 vols. il. O. cl .... 1.50 .50

This story is a sequel to "Henry Esmond," containing the history of some of its characters. The scene is in Virginia in the eighteenth century.

Yf
———
T 37 bi

1395. [104.] **Biography of a grizzly;** with 75 drawings. Ernest Seton Thompson. N. Y., Century Co., 1900. sq. D. cl............................... 1.50 .98

The story of a grizzly bear told with wonderful insight and sympathy.

Yf
———
T 67 fi

1396. [122.] **Final war.** Louis Tracy. N. Y., G. P. Putnam's Sons, 1896. 464 p. il. D. cl............ 1.50 .98

Imaginative description of a war of the world in 1898, of England and America against the other powers. The chief characters are many of the leading people in the political world. The descriptions of the battles are vivid and the narration is interesting.

Yf
———
V 65 ic

1397. [82.] **Iceland fisherman.** L: Marie Julien Viaud, *tr.* by A. F. deKoven. Chic., A. C. McClurg & Co., 1893. D. cl .... 1.00 .65

A beautiful story. Life of the fishermen graphically described.

Yf
———
W 15 be

1398. [142.] **Ben-hur:** a tale of the Christ. Lew Wallace. N. Y., Harper & Bros., 1899. 560 p. S. cl...... 1.50 .98

An interesting story containing many graphic descriptions of Roman and Hebrew life and of Roman rule in Jerusalem during the times of Christ.

Yf
———
W 15 fa

1399. [187.] **Fair God;** or, the last of the 'Tzins: a tale of the conquest of Mexico. Lew Wallace. Bost., Houghton, Mifflin & Co., 1899. 586 p. D. cl.... 1.50 .98

A very interesting story filled with graphic descriptions.

	List price.	Price to schools.

Yf
W 23 ex

1400. [72.] **Express messenger, and other tales of the rail.** Cy Warman. N. Y., C: Scribner's Sons, 1897. 238 p. D. cl. .... 1.25 .82

Boys are usually interested in railroad life. This is a book for boys who are not much interested in reading.

Yf
W 23 sn

1401. [92.] **Snow on the headlight: a story of the great Burlington strike.** Cy Warman. N. Y., D. Appleton & Co., 1899. 249 p. D. cl.................. 1.25 .82

An impartial view of both sides of a great railroad strike.

Yf
W 29 st

1402. [138.] **Story of Ab.** Stanley Waterloo. N. Y., Doubleday & McClure Co., 1897. 351 p. D. cl.. 1.50 .98

An interesting tale of the time of the cave men. Many new interests may be started in the reading of this novel.

Yf
W 33 be

1403. [77.] **Beside the bonnie brier bush.** Ian Maclaren. (pseud.) N. Y., Dodd, Mead & Co., 1897. 327 p. D. cl. .... 1.25 .50

Stories portraying the home life and character of the Scotch people. Doctor MacLure is one of the characters which will live in literature.

Yf
W 33 da

1404. **Days of Auld Lang Syne.** John Watson. (Ian Maclaren, *pseud.*) N. Y., Dodd, Mead & Co., 1895. 366 p. D. cl. 2.00 1.30

Short stories which give interesting pictures of life in Scotland. Contents: Triumph in diplomacy; For conscience sake; Manifest judgment; Drumsheugh's love story; Past redemption; Good news from a far country; Jamie; Servant lass; Milton's conversion; Oor lang hame.

Yf
W 52 da

1405. [53.] **David Harum: a story of American life.** E: Noyes Wescott. N. Y., D. Appleton & Co., 1898. 392 p. D. cl. .... 1.50 .98

One of the best character studies.

	List price.	Price to schools.

Yf
W 54 ge

1406. [161.] **Gentleman of France**; being the memoirs of Gaston de Bonne, Sieur de Marsac. Stanley J. Weyman. N. Y., Longmans, Green & Co., 1899. 412 p. D. cl. .... 1.25 .82

A story of adventure in France in the latter part of the sixteenth century.

Yf
W 63 ca

1407. [111.] **Cathedral courtship and Penelope's English experience.** Kate Douglas Wiggin. Bost., Houghton, Mifflin & Co., 1895. 164 p. il. D. cl. ...... 1.00 .65

An interesting story for Library reading. The story is mostly one of travel with a thread of romance running through it.

Yf
W 63 di

1408. **Diary of a goose girl.** Kate Douglas Wiggin. Bost., Houghton, Mifflin & Co., 1902. 117 p. il. D. cl. 1.00 .65

A pretty American girl, "very tired of people," runs away from her friends and from a too ardent suitor and takes up life anew on an English goose farm as a paying guest, and becomes interested in assisting in the care of the geese. Her experience is amusingly told, and information, based upon keen observation, is given of the hens, ducks and geese that she plays attendant to.

Interesting for Library reading.

Yf
W 63 p

1409. **Penelope's Irish experiences.** Kate Douglas Wiggin. Bost., Houghton, Mifflin & Co., 1901. 329 p. D. cl. .... 1.25 .82

"The experiences in Ireland of Penelope, Francesca, and Salemina,—the same fun-loving trio of unconventional travelers who made such amusing excursions through England and Scotland. The quality of the books defies definition. It is all spontaneous fun, innocent mischief, and pure sentiment,—elusive in definition, but most certain in entertainment. The three friends visit picturesque localities and out of the way places, every turn of the road making its contribution to their joyous progress. The narrative is mostly of travel and sight-seeing, but there is also a sprightly romance in which Salemina falls a victim to an Irish lover."

Yf
W 63 pe

1410. [76.] **Penelope's Progress:** being such extracts from the commonplace book of Penelope Hamilton as relate to her experiences in Scotland. Kate Douglas Wiggin. Bost., Houghton, Mifflin & Co., 1899. 268 p. S. cl. .... 1.25 .82

Delightful descriptions of places and people in Scotland,

	List price.	Price to schools.

Yf
W 65 ne

1411. [62.] **New England nun.** Mary E. Wilkins. N. Y., Harper & Bros., 1891. D. cl.................. 1.25 .82
Miss Wilkins portrays the hard side of New England life.

Yf
W 67 pr

1412. [86.] **Princeton stories.** Jesse Lynch Williams. N. Y., C: Scribner's Sons, 1899. 319 p. D. cl...... 1.00 .65
Bright, interesting stories of college life.

Yf
W 75 di

1413. [102.] **Diomed; the life, travels and observations of a dog.** John Sergeant Wise. N. Y., Macmillan & Co., 1899. 330 p. il. D. cl................... 2.00 1.28
The story of a hunting dog who loved loyally, fought valiantly, and filled the place assigned him in Nature to the best of his ability.

Yf
W 76 re

1414. **Red men and white.** Owen Wister. N. Y., Harper & Bros., 1901. 280 p. il. D. cl............... 1.50 .98
"These eight stories are made up from our Western Frontier as it was in a past as near as yesterday and almost as by-gone as the Revolution ; so swiftly do we proceed. They belong to each other in a kinship of life and manners, and a little through the nearer tie of having here and there a character in common. They are about Indians and soldiers and events west of the Missouri. In certain ones the incidents, and even some of the names, are left unchanged from their original reality."—*Preface.*
Contents: Little Big Horn medicine ; Specimen Jones ; Serenade at Siskiyou ; General's bluff ; Salvation gap ; Second Missouri compromise ; La Tinaja Bonita ; Pilgrim on the Gila.

Yf
Yo 8 la

1415. **Lances of Lynwood.** Charlotte M. Yonge. N. Y., Macmillan Co., 1900. 264 p. il. D. cl........ 1.25 .82
The scene is laid in France during the time of Edward III. The story describes the expedition of Edward the Black Prince in aid of Pedro the Cruel of Spain.

Yf
Yo 8 li

1416. [158.] **Little Duke Richard, the fearless.** Charlotte M. Yonge. N. Y., Macmillan & Co., 1898. 223 p. il. D. cl...................................... 1.25 .82
Historical novel dealing with childhood of William, the Norman. Younger pupils will enjoy it.

Yf
Yo 8 pr
                                                              List   Price to
                                                              price. schools.
1417. **Prince and the page.** Charlotte M. Yonge. N. Y.,
    Macmillan Co., 1901. 259 p. il. D. cl........ 1.25   .82

   A story of the last crusades.

Yf
Yo 8 un
1418. **Unknown to history:** a story of the captivity of Mary
    of Scotland. Charlotte M. Yonge. N. Y., Mac-
    millan Co., 1901. 589 p. D. cl................ 1.25   .82

   This story is founded on historical facts which may be found in Strickland's Life of Mary Queen of Scots.

Yf
Za 1 th
1419. **"They that walk in darkness:"** Ghetto tragedies.
    Israel Zangwill. N. Y., Macmillan Co., 1899. 486
    p. D. cl. .... 1.50   .98

   These stories all have a basis in real life and will be interesting and instructive to the classes in Sociology and Library reading. They picture the dark side of life and are full of pathos.

   Contents: "They that walk in darkness"; Transitional; Noah's ark; Land of promise; To die in Jersualem; Bethulah; Keeper of conscience; Satan Makatrig; Diary of a Meshumad; Incurable; Sabbath-breaker.

FICTION.

The following Fiction list is classified according to the contents of the book—all the novels portraying life are grouped together, all sociological novels together, etc. For notes on the books see the preceding Fiction list.

HISTORICAL NOVELS.

Ancient times.

1226. **Bulwer Lytton,** *Sir* **E. G.** Last days of Pompeii.
1276. **Ebers, Georg.** Egyptian princess.
1385. **Ebers, Georg.** Emperor.
1277. **Ebers, Georg.** Uarda.
1331. **Kingsley, Charles.** Hypatia.
1398. **Wallace, Lew.** Ben-Hur.
1402. **Waterloo, Stanley.** Story of Ab.

Middle Ages.

1271. **Doyle A. C.** White company.
1338. **Ludlow, J. M.** Captain of the Janizaries.
1356. **Reade, Charles.** Cloister and the hearth.
1374. **Scott,** *Sir* **Walter.** Talisman.

French life.

1232. **Catherwood, M. H.** Days of Jeanne D'Arc.
1272. **Dumas, Alexandre.** Three musketeers.
1283. **Erckmann, Emile** *and* **Chatrain, Alex.** Conscript.
1284. **Erckmann, Emile** *and* **Chatrain, Alex.** Invasion of France in 1814.
1285. **Erckmann, Emile** *and* **Chatrain, Alex.** Waterloo.
1306. **Gras, Felix.** Reds of the Midi.
1362. **Scott,** *Sir* **Walter.** Anne of Geirstein.
1366. **Scott,** *Sir* **Walter.** Count Robert of Paris.
1372. **Scott,** *Sir* **Walter.** Quentin Durward.
1377. **Seawell, M. E.** History of the Lady Betty Stair.
1406. **Weymann, S. J.** Gentleman of France.
1415. **Yonge, C. M.** Lances of Lynwood.
1416. **Yonge, C. M.** Little Duke Richard, the fearless.

English and Scotch life.

1206. Barnes, James. Drake and his yeomen.
1218. Bennett, John. Master sky-lark.
1221. Blackmore, R. D. Lorna Doone.
1227. Bulwer-Lytton, *Sir* E. G. Last of the barons.
1252. Couch, A. T. Q. Splendid spur.
1260. Dickens, Charles. Barnaby Rudge.
1267. Dickens, Charles. Tale of two cities.
1268. Dix, B. M. Hugh Gwyeth.
1303. Gomme, G. L. Princess's story book.
1330. Kingsley, Charles. Hereward, the wake.
1332. Kingsley, Charles. Westward Ho!
1341. Major, Charles. When knighthood was in flower.
1364. Scott, *Sir* Walter. Black dwarf and Legend of Montrose.
1367. Scott, *Sir* Walter. Fair maid of Perth.
1368. Scott, *Sir* Walter. Fortunes of Nigel.
1369. Scott, *Sir* Walter. Heart of Midlothian.
1370. Scott, *Sir* Walter. Kenilworth.
1371. Scott, *Sir* Walter. Old mortality.
1373. Scott, *Sir* Walter. Rob Roy.
1376. Scott, *Sir* Walter. Ivanhoe.
1381. Stevenson, R. L. Black arrow.
1392. Swift, Dean. Gulliver's travels.
1393. Thackeray, W. M. Henry Esmond.
1417. Yonge, C. M. Prince and the page.
1418. Yonge, C. M. Unknown to history.

United States.

Period of discovery and colonial times.

1202. Austin, J. G. Standish of Standish.
1203. Austin, J. G. Betty Alden.
1233. Catherwood, M. H. Lady of Fort St. John.
1235. Catherwood, M. H. Story of Tonty.
1240. Churchill, Winston. Richard Carvel.
1242. Coffin, C. C. Daughters of the Revolution and their times.
1269. Dix, B. M. Soldier Rigdale.
1270. Doyle, A. C. Refugees.
1301. Goodwin, M. W. Head of a hundred.
1302. Goodwin, M. W. White aprons.
1328. Johnston, Mary. To have and to hold.
1379. Seawell, M. E. Virginia cavalier.
1384. Stimson, F. J. King Noanett.
1394. Thackeray, W. M. Virginians.

Revolutionary times.

1207. Barnes, James. For king or country.
1216. Bellamy, Edward. Duke of Stockbridge.
1222. Brady, C. T. For love of country.
1237. Child, F. S. Unknown patriot.
1248. Cooper, J. F. Spy.
1259. Devereux, Mary. From kingdom to colony.
1293. Ford, P. L. Janice Meredith.
1342. Mitchell, S. W. Hugh Wyne, free Quaker.

War of 1812.

1208. Barnes, James. Loyal traitor.

Civil War.

1239. Churchill, Winston. Crisis.
1274. Dunn, B. A. General Nelson's scout.
1275. Dunn, B. A. On General Thomas's staff.
1278. Eggleston, G. C. Southern soldier stories.
1305. Goss, W. L. Jed.
1347. Page, T. N. In ole Virginia.
1348. Page, T. N. Marse Chan.
1350. Page, T. N. Red rock.
1388. Stowe, H. B. Dred.
1389. Stowe, H. B. Uncle Tom's cabin.

Indian life.

1244. Cooper, J. F. Deerslayer.
1245. Cooper, J. F. Last of the Mohicans.
1246. Cooper, J. F. Pathfinder.
1247. Cooper, J. F. Pioneers.
1322. Jackson, H. H. Ramona.
1414. Wister, Owen. Red men and white.

Mexico.

1399. Wallace, Lew. Fair God.

NOVELS PORTRAYING CHARACTER, CHARACTER DEVELOPMENT, AND LESSONS IN RIGHT DOING.

1211. **Barrie, J. M.** Sentimental Tommy.
1212. **Barrie, J. M.** Tommy and Grizel.
1230. **Burnett, F. H.** Louisiana.
1231. **Cable, G. W.** Bonaventure.
1262. **Dickens, Charles.** Christmas carol, and The cricket on the hearth.
1263. **Dickens, Charles.** David Copperfield.
1265. **Dickens, Charles.** Old curiosity shop.
1279. **Eliot, George.** Adam Bede.
1280. **Eliot, George.** Daniel Deronda.
1281. **Eliot, George.** Romola.
1282. **Eliot, George.** Silas Marner.
1308. **Hale, E. E.** Man without a country.
1229. **Bunyan, John.** Pilgrim's progress.
1309. **Harte, Bret.** Luck of roaring camp.
1310. **Hawthorne, Nathaniel.** House of the seven gables.
1316. **Howells, W. D.** Rise of Silas Lapham.
1329. **Johnson, Samuel.** History of Rasselas, Prince of Abyssinia.
1337. **Loughead, F. H.** Abandoned claim.
1351. **Page, T. N.** Santa Claus's partner.
1405. **Wescott, E. N.** David Harum.

NOVELS PORTRAYING LIFE.

1205. **Barlow, Jane.** Irish idylls.
1210. **Barrie, J. M.** Little minister.
1213. **Barrie, J. M.** When a man's single.
1214. **Barrie, J. M.** Window in Thrums.
1215. **Barton, W. E.** Pine knot.
1224. **Brown, Alice.** Meadow-grass.
1238. **Chopin, Kate.** Bayou folk.
1243. **Cooper, J. F.** Pilot.
1249. **Cotes, *Mrs.* Everard.** American girl in London.
1250. **Cotes, *Mrs.* Everard.** Crow's-nest.
1251. **Cotes, *Mrs.* Everard.** Those delightful Americans.
1253. **Crawford, F. M.** Marietta.
1254. **Crawford, F. M.** Roman singer.
1255. **Crockett, S. R.** Stickit minister's wooing.
1261. **Dickens, Charles.** Bleak house.
1266. **Dickens, Charles.** Pickwick papers.
1273. **Dunbar, P. L.** Folks from Dixie.

1291. Foote, M. H. Led-horse claim.
1294. French, Alice. Stories of a western town.
1296. Fuller, Anna. Pratt portraits sketched in a New England suburb.
1298. Gaskell, *Mrs.* E. C. Cranford.
1304. Gordon, C. W. Sky pilot.
1309. Harte, Bret. Luck of roaring camp and other stories.
1311. Hawthorne, Nathaniel. Marble faun.
1314. Hill, John. Stories of the railroad.
1317. Hoyt, D. L. Barbara's heritage.
1324. Jewett, S. O. Country doctor.
1326. Jewett, S. O. Country of the pointed firs.
1327. Jewett, S. O. Tales of New England.
1333. Kipling, Rudyard. "Captains courageous."
1336. Longfellow, H. W. Hyperion and Kavanagh.
1339. Lummis, C. F. Enchanted burro.
1340. Lummis, C. F. New Mexico David.
1344. Murfree, M. N. In the Tennessee mountains.
1345. Murfree, M. N. Prophet of the Great Smoky Mountains.
1349. Page, T. N. Old gentleman of the Black Stock.
1352. Parker, Gilbert. Pierre and his people.
1354. Porter, Jane. Scottish chiefs.
1355. Porter, Jane. Thaddeus of Warsaw.
1357. Richards, L. E. Geoffrey Strong.
1363. Scott, *Sir* Walter. Antiquary.
1365. Scott, *Sir* Walter. Bride of Lammermoor.
1397. Viaud, L. M. J. Iceland fisherman.
1400. Warman, Cy. Express messenger and other tales of the rail.
1403. Watson, John. Beside the bonnie brier bush.
1404. Watson, John. Days of auld lang syne.
1407. Wiggin, K. D. Cathedral courtship and Penelope's English experience.
1409. Wiggin, K. D. Penelope's Irish experiences.
1410. Wiggin, K. D. Penelope's progress.
1411. Wilkins, M. E. New England nun.

SOCIOLOGICAL NOVELS.

1217. Bellamy, Edward. Looking backward, 2000–1887.
1219. Besant, Walter. All sorts and conditions of men.
1220. Besant, Walter. Children of Gibeon.
1292. Ford, P. L. Honorable Peter Stirling.
1299. Gilman, Bradley. Back to the soil.
1322. Jackson, H. H. Ramona.
1343. More, *Sir* Thomas. Utopia.

1380. **Smith, F. H.** Tom Grogan.
1396. **Tracy, Louis.** Final war.
1401. **Warman, Cy.** Snow on the headlight.
1419. **Zangwill, Israel.** "They that walk in darkness."

STORIES PORTRAYING SCHOOL AND COLLEGE LIFE.

1204. **Barbour, R. H.** Half back.
1209. **Barnes, James.** Princetonian.
1264. **Dickens, Charles.** Life and adventures of Nicholas Nickleby.
1290. **Flandrau, C. M.** Harvard episodes.
1295. **Fuller, C. M.** Across the campus.
1300. **Goodloe, A. C.** College girls.
1318. **Hughes, Thomas.** Tom Brown at Oxford.
1360. **Sanderson, J. G.** Cornell stories.
1375. **Schwartz, J. A.** Vassar studies.
1412. **Williams, J. L.** Princeton stories.

NATURE STORIES.

1200. **Allen, J. L.** Kentucky cardinal.
1358. **Roberts, C. G. D.** Heart of the ancient wood.

ROMANCES AND COLLECTIONS OF SHORT STORIES.

1198. **Aldrich, T. B.** Marjorie Daw and other stories.
1199. **Allen, J. L.** Flute and violin.
1201. **Austen, Jane.** Pride and prejudice.
1223. **Brown, H. D.** Her sixteenth year.
1228. **Bunner, H. C.** Love in old cloathes and other stories.
1234. **Catherwood, M. H.** Mackinac and lake stories.
1256. **Davis, R. H.** Gallegher, and other stories.
1257. **Davis, R. H.** Soldiers of fortune.
1258. **Davis, R. H.** Van Bibber and others.
1286. **Field, Eugene.** Holy cross.
1287. **Field, Eugene.** House.
1288. **Field, Eugene.** Little book of profitable tales.
1289. **Field, Eugene.** Second book of tales.
1297. **Garland, Hamlin.** Main-travelled roads.
1307. **Halévy, Ludovic.** Abbe Constantin.
1312. **Hawthorne, Nathaniel.** Mosses from an old manse.
1313. **Hawthorne, Nathaniel.** Snow image and other twice-told tales.
1315. **Howard, B. W.** One summer.
1319. **Irving Washington.** Alhambra.
1320. **Irving, Washington.** Stories and legends from Washington Irving.

LIST OF BOOKS FOR HIGH SCHOOL LIBRARIES. 375

1321. **Irving, Washington.** Tales of a traveller.
1325. **Jewett, S. O.** Country by-ways.
1334. **Kipfing, Rudyard.** Day's work.
1335. **Lee, M. C.** Quaker girl of Nantucket.
1353. **Poe, Edgar.** Tales.
1359. **Saint-Pierre, Jacques Henri Bernardin de.** Paul and Virginia.
1378. **Seawell, M. E.** Maid Marion, and other stories.
1382. **Stevenson, R. L.** Kidnapped.
1383. **Stevenson, R. L.** Treasure island.
1387. **Stockton, F. R.** Story-teller's pack.
1390. Stories by American authors.
1391. Stories by English authors.
1408. **Wiggin, K. D.** Diary of a goose girl.

STORIES OF ANIMALS.

1225. **Brown, John.** Rab and his friends.
1346. **Ollivant, Alfred.** Bob, son of battle.
1395. **Thompson, Ernest-Seton.** Biography of a grizzly.
1413. **Wise, J. S.** Diomed.

HUMOROUS FICTION.

1241. **Clemens, S. L.** Connecticut yankee in King Arthur's court.
1236. **Cervantes, Saavedra Miguel de.** Ingenious gentleman, Don Quixote of La Mancha.
1323. **Jerome, J. K.** Three men in a boat.
1386. **Stockton, F. R.** Rudder Grange.

LEGENDS AND FOLK-LITERATURE.
(Books written from a literary standpoint.)

Yl
———
C 83 po
1420. [318.] **Popular romances of the middle ages.** *Sir* George W. Cox *and* Eustace Hinton Jones. N. Y., Henry Holt & Co., 1886. 514 p. D. cl...... 2.25 1.50
Interesting and brings to the pupil many tales referred to in his general reading.

Yl
———
G 88 pu
1421. **Punishment of the stingy;** and other Indian stories. George Bird Grinnell. N. Y., Harper & Bros. 1901. 235. p. il. (Portrait collection of short stories.) O. cl. 1.50 1.35
Indian folk-lore tales. The author has written these stories just as he received them from the lips of aged Indian historians.

	List price.	Price to schools.

"As the Indians have no written characters, memorable events are retained only in the minds of the people, and are handed down by the elders to their children, and by these again transmitted to their children, so passing from generation to generation. Until recent years, one of the sacred duties of certain elders of the tribes was the handing down of these histories to their successors. As they repeated them, they impressed upon the hearer the importance of remembering the stories precisely as told, and of telling them again exactly as he had received them; neither adding nor taking away any thing. Thus early taught his duty, each listener strove to perform it, and to impress on those whom he in turn instructed a similar obligation."—*Preface.*

Contents: Stories and the story-tellers; Bluejay stories; Punishment of the stingy; Bluejay, the imitator; Bluejay visits the ghosts; Girl who was the ring; First corn; Star boy; Grizzly bear's medicine; First medicine lodge; Thunder maker and cold maker; Blindness of Pi-wap-ok; Ragged head; Nothing child; Shield quiver's wife; Beaver stick; Little friend coyote.

Yl

L 27 bf

1422. **Boy's Froissart:** being Sir John Froissart's Chronicles of adventure, battle and custom in England, France, Spain, etc. Edited for boys with an introduction by Sidney Lanier. N. Y., C: Scribner's Sons, 1901. 422 p. il. O. cl.................... 2.00 1.30

Froissart's Chronicle is, in a certain sense, a sort of continuation of Malory's novel. Malory's book gives a picture of knighthood in the twelfth and thirteenth centuries, while Froissart's is a picture of knighthood in the fourteenth century.

Froissart gives us real events occurring in definite localities while Malory's King Arthur is unhistorical.

Yl

L 27 bk

1423. **Boy's King Arthur:** being Sir Thomas Malory's history of King Arthur and his Knights of the Round Table. Edited for boys with an introduction by Sidney Lanier. N. Y., C: Scribner's Sons, 1901. 403 p. il. D. cl.................... 2.00 1.30

The introduction gives a short history of the sources of the cycle of Arthurian romances which will be helpful to the student of English literature. These romances should be read by the classes in English literature and English history. It gives a picture of knighthood in the twelfth and thirteenth centuries. The only changes from Malory's King Arthur are a modernization of the spelling and a cutting out of some parts of the story.

Y1

M S3 ki

List price. Price to schools.

1424. **King Arthur and the Knights of the round table.** Charles Morris. Phil., J. B. Lippincott Co., 1900. 767 p. il. D. cl. .... 1.50 .98

A modernized version of the "Morte d' Arthur." The original version of this by Malory is also on the list but it is not easy or attractive reading. This volume will be of more interest to the Library reading classes while the original version will perhaps be more valuable for use by the advanced classes in Literature.

Y1

R 12 fr

1425. [319.] **Frithjof, the viking of Norway, and Roland the paladin of France.** Zenaide A. Ragozin. N. Y., G. P. Putnam's Sons, 1899. 295 p. il. D. (Tales of the heroic ages.) cl .... 1.50 .98

Y1

R 12 si

1426. [320.] **Siegfried, the hero of the North, and Beowulf, the hero of the Anglo-Saxons.** Zenaide A. Ragozin. N. Y., G. P. Putnam's Sons, 1898. 332 p. il. D. (Tales of the heroic ages.) cl .... 1.50 .98

The two foregoing books contain tales of the heroic ages for young readers. Very well written.

Y1

Sk 3 my

1427. [321.] **Myths and legends of our own land.** C. M. Skinner. Phil., J. B. Lippincott & Co., 1896. 2 vols., 317; 335 p. il. D. cl 3.00 1.96

Legends of the various portions of the United States charmingly told.

Y1

St 8 ie

#1428. **Le Morte d'Arthur:** *Sir* Thomas Malory's book of King Arthur and of his noble knights of the round table; text of Caxton edited, with an introduction. *Sir* Edward Strachey. N. Y., Macmillan Co., 1901. 509 p. D. cl 1.75 1.15

A compilation of the Arthurian legends. The influence of Sir Thomas Malory's book upon English literature, and English life, upon our thoughts, morals, and manners, has been great and important, hence the students of English literature should not neglect to read at least some selections from this, our first great work of English prose. The legends furnish a series of vivid pictures of knight-errantry.

See also Lanier's "Boy's King Arthur."

POETRY.

Poetry portrays the emotional side of life. It breathes the joys, hopes, fears, sorrows, strivings, and aspirations of humanity. It gives us the divine fire of genius, teaches us the love of the beautiful, swings us into the world of imagination, and encourages us to do and to be. A poem is a work of art to be admired, and enjoyed, and felt. Music, beauty, imagination, passion, insight, inspiration, and faith are the essential characteristics of poetry and these are what should be studied.

Music: Read the poetry to the pupils so as to bring out the music and let them read it that way. They will soon find that music is varied, sometimes smooth and flowing; again, rough and broken; sometimes light and quick, again heavy and slow moving. Analyzing a number of poems by a single poet they will find that there is a sameness about his way of singing; that Tennyson's music is varied, polished and exquisite; that Bryant's music is deep, full, and resounding; that Riley's is dainty and light. Comparisons of different poets will lead to a better understanding of each one.

Beauty: Ask the pupils to select the beautiful pictures and read them to the class. Ask them to see these pictures as they are read, and encourage them to admire. Let them gather together the beautiful pictures painted by the poets and compare, and they will find that Scott's pictures are highly colored; that Tennyson gives us exquisite landscapes and beautiful pen portraits; that Byron paints nature in her grandeur; that Lowell's pictures are full of life and beauty. A careful study of how these pictures are painted will bring out that some are in detail, some in broad strokes, some clearly outlined and some only suggested.

Passion, inspiration, insight, truth and faith: Call for the passages the pupils like best and nearly always they will select those expressing passion, inspiration, insight, truth, and faith. Because they select them, be sure they appreciate them to some degree. As they read more and more, they will come to recognize, name, and understand these characteristics, and to see that they differ in different poets. Do not expect learned discussions. Get them to give themselves up to these influences. They will read Shelley and Milton and exercise their imaginations. They will learn that some poets look deep into the human heart and see beyond the symbol, the essence, and that is insight. They will learn to look for the poet's faith in God and humanity.

Yp
―――
Al 2

                                                                                                 List Price to
                                                                                                price. schools.

1429. **Poems.** Thomas Bailey Aldrich. Bost., Houghton, Mifflin & Co., c1885. 422 p. il. D. cl.......... 1.50   .98

Yp
―――
Are 6 lo

1430. **Lotus and jewel:** containing "In an Indian temple," "A casket of gems," "A queen's revenge," with other poems. Edwin Arnold. Bost., Little, Brown & Co., 1899. 263 p. D. cl. .... 1.00   .65

Yp
―――
Arm 6 se

1431. **Selected poems.** Matthew Arnold. N. Y., Macmillan Co., 1900. 235 p. (Golden treasury series.) S. cl. .... 1.00   .90

    Contents: Sonnets; Question; Requiescat; Youth and calm; Memory—picture; Youth's agitations; World's triumphs; Stagirius; To a gipsy child by the sea-shore; Sohrab and Rustum; Tristram and Iseult; Saint Brandan; Neckan; Forsaken merman; Sonnets; Switzerland; Strayed reveller; Cadmus and Harmonia; Apollo Musagetes; Urania; Euphrosyne; Calais sands; Dover beach; Progress; Revolutions; Self-dependence; Morality; Summer night; Lines written in Kensington Gardens; Scholar-gipsy; Thyrsis; Memorial verses; Stanzas from Carnac; Southern night; Rugby chapel; Future; Notes.

Yp
―――
Arm 6 so

1432. [209.] **Sohrab and Rustum:** an episode. Matthew Arnold, intr. by Merwin Marie Snell. Chic., Werner School Book Co., 1896. 123 p. D. cl... .50   .45

Yp
―――
B 31 ba

1433. [212.] **Ballad book.** Ed. by Katharine Lee Bates. Chic., Sibley & Ducker, 1890. 230 p. S. cl. ... .50   .44

    These rough, frank, spirited old poems are almost always favorites with children.

Yp

B 45 be
1434. **Beowulf:** An Anglo-Saxon poem, and the fight at Finnsburg. Translated by James M. Garnett. Bost., Ginn & Co., 1900. 110 p. Fourth ed. D. cl. .... 1.00 .85

List price. Price to schools.

The introduction gives a short outline of the history of the Beowulf poem. This book will be of interest to the students in advanced English literature.

Yp

B 72
#1435. **Poetical works of Thomas Gray:** English and Latin, edited with an introduction, life, notes, and a bibliography. John Bradshaw. London, George Bell & Son, N. Y., Macmillan Co., 1901. 319 p. S. Aldine ed. cl. .... .40 .36

Yp

B 82
1436. [202.] **Poems.** *Mrs.* E. B. Browning. N. Y., T. Y. Crowell & Co., D. (Standard library series.) cl. .... 1.00 .65

Yp

B 82 l
1437. **Complete poetic and dramatic works.** Robert Browning. Bost., Houghton, Mifflin & Co., c1895. 1,033 p. por. (Cambridge ed.) O. cl. 3.00 1.96

Yp

B 84
1438. [199.] **Poetical works of William Cullen Bryant.** N. Y., D. Appleton & Co., 1897. 362 p. il. D. (Household ed.) cl. .... 1.50 .98

Yp

B 93
1439. [198.] **Complete poetical works of Robert Burns.** Bost., Houghton, Mifflin & Co., 1897. 397 p. por. O. (Cambridge ed.) cl. 2.00 1.30

Yp

B 94 so
1440. **Songs of nature.** *Ed.* by John Burroughs. N. Y., McClure, Phillips & Co., 1901. 359 p. D. cl.... 1.50 .98

A collection of the best poems in English literature which have nature as their inspiration.

LIST OF BOOKS FOR HIGH SCHOOL LIBRARIES.

	List price.	Price to schools.

Yp
B 99 ch
1441. [208.] **Childe Harold's pilgrimage.** Lord Byron. Ed. by William J. Rolfe. Bost., Houghton, Mifflin & Co., 1898. 288 p. il. S. cl. .... .75 .64

Yp
C 19 ci
1442. **City ballads.** Will Carleton. N. Y., Harper & Bros., 1900. 164 p. D. New ed. from new plates. cl. 2.00 1.30

Yp
C 19 fa
1443. **Farm ballads.** Will Carleton. New ed. from new plates. N. Y., Harper & Bros., 1901. 147 p. il. D. cl. 2.00 1.30

Contents: Betsey and I are out; How Betsey and I made up; Gone with a handsomer man; Johnny Rich; Out of the old house; Over the hill to the poor-house; Over the hill from the poor-house; Uncle Sammy; Tom was goin' for a poet; Goin' home today; Out o' the fire; New church organ; Editor's guests; House where we were wed; Reunited; How Jamie came home; Clang of the yankee reaper; "Why should they kill my baby"? Old man meditates; Apple-blossoms; Apples growing; Christmas-tree; Autumn days; Fading flower; Picnic Sam; One and two; Death-doomed; Up the line; Forward! Ship-builder; How we kept the day; Our army of the dead; "Mending the old flag".

Yp
C 25
1444. **Poetical works.** Alice *and* Phoebe Cary. Bost., Houghton, Mifflin & Co., c1882. 341 p. il. D. cl. .... 1.50 .98

Yp
C 39 ca
1445. **Canterbury tales.** Geoffrey Chaucer. From the text and with the notes and glossary of Thomas Tyrwhitt condensed and arranged under the text. N. Y., D. Appleton & Co., 1897. 585 p. New ed. S. cl. .... 1.00 .65

Yp
C 67
1446. [204.] **Poetical works of Samuel Taylor Coleridge.** ed. by Derwent and Sara Coleridge. N. Y., D. Appleton & Co., 1887. 388 p. por. D. (Household edition.) cl. .... 1.50 .98

Yp

D 91 l

1447. **Lyrics of lowly life.** Paul Laurence Dunbar. Introduction by W. D. Howells. N. Y., Dodd, Mead & Co., 1902. 208 p. por. S. cl. .... 1.25   .82

 Mr. Dunbar is a negro, born of negroes who were slaves, and in whom there was no admixture of white blood. He was an elevator-boy before and after he began to write poems. Knowing these facts it seems almost a miracle that he should have produced this volume. Mr. Howells thinks the most original poems in the collection are those written in the negro dialect and believes them a distinctly new contribution to our literature. Of the whole volume he says, "He has at least produced something that, however we may critically disagree about it, we cannot well refuse to enjoy; in more than one piece he has produced a work of art."

Yp

D 91 ly

1448. **Lyrics of the hearthside.** Paul Laurence Dunbar. N. Y., Dodd, Mead & Co., 1902. 227 p. por. S. cl. .... 1.25   .82

 A pretty volume of verse, which includes dialect poems, uniform with the author's "Lyrics of lowly life."

Yp

Eg 3 am

1449. [214.] **American war ballads and lyrics.** Ed. by George Cary Eggleston. N. Y., G. P. Putnam's Sons, 1889. Two volumes in one. 226; 278 pp. il. S. cl. .... 1.50   .98

 It is the poetry of strength and manly self reliance.

Yp

Em 3

1450. **Complete poetical works.** Ralph Waldo Emerson. Bost., Houghton, Mifflin & Co., c1895. 315 p. por. D. (Household edition.) cl. .... 1.50   .98

Yp

F 45 li

1451. **Little book of western verse.** Eugene Field. N. Y., C: Scribner's Sons, 1901. 202 p. D. cl. ...... 1.25   .82

 Contents: Casey's table d'hote; Our lady of the mine; Conversazzhyony; Prof. Vere de Blaw; Marthy's younkit; Old English lullaby; "Lollyby, lolly, lollyby"; Orkney lullaby; Lullaby: by the sea; Cornish lullaby; Norse lullaby; Sicilian lullaby; Japanese lullaby; Little croodlin-doo; Dutch lullaby; Child and mother; Mediaeval eventide song; Christmas treasures; Christmas hymn; Chrystmasse of olde.

LIST OF BOOKS FOR HIGH SCHOOL LIBRARIES. 383

		List price.	Price to schools.

Yp
―――
F 45 lo
1452. **Love-songs of childhood.** Eugene Field. N. Y., C: Scribner's Sons, 1901. 111 p. S. cl. .... 1.00 .65

 Contents: Rock-a-by lady; "Booh"! Garden and cradle; Night wind; Kissing time; Jest 'fore Christmas; Beard and baby; Dinkey-bird; Drum; Dead babe; Happy household; So, so, rock-a-by so! Song of Luddy-dud; Duel; Good-children street; Delectable ballad of the Waller lot; Stork; Bottle tree; Googly-goo; Bench-legged Fyce; Little Miss Brag; Humming top; Lady Button-eyes; Ride to Bumpville; Brook; Picnic-time; Shuffle-shoon and Amber-locks; Shut-eye train; Little-oh-dear; Fly-away horse; Swing high and swing low; When I was a boy; At play; Valentine; Little All-aloney; Seein' things; Cunnin' little thing; Doll's wooing; Inscription for my little son's silver plate; Fisherman Jim's kids; "Fiddle-dee-dee"; Over the hills and far away.

Yp
―――
F 45 se
1453. **Second book of verse.** Eugene Field. N. Y., C: Scribner's Sons, 1901. 260 p. D. cl. .... 1.25 .82

 Contents: Father's way; To my mother; Korner's battle prayer; Gosling stew; Catullus to Lesbia; John Smith; St. Martin's lane; Singing in God's-Acre; Dear old London; Corsican lullaby (Folk-song); Clink of the ice; Bells of Notre Dame; Lover's lane, St. Jo; Crumpets and tea; Imitation of Dr. Watts; Intrymintry; Modjesky as Cameel; Telling the bees; Tea-gown; Doctors; Barbara; Café Molineau; Holly and ivy; The Boltons, 22; Dibdin's ghost; Hawthorne children; Bottle and the bird; An eclogue from Virgil; Pittypat and tipplytoe; Ashes on the slide; Lost Cupid of Moschus; Christmas Eve; Carlsbad; Sugar-plum tree; Red; Jewish lullaby; At Cheyenne; Naughty doll; Pneumogastric nerve; Teeny-weeny; Telka; Plaint of a Missouri 'coon; Armenian lullaby; Partridge; Corinthian hall; Red, red west; Three kings of Cologne; Ipswich; Bill's tenor and my bass; Fiducit (from the German); "St. Jo Gazette"; In Amsterdam: To the passing saint; Fisherman's feast; Nightfall in Dordrecht (Slumber song); Onion tart; Grandma's bombazine; Rare roast beef; Gander-father's gift; Old times, old friends, old love; Our whippings; Bion's song of Eros; Mr. Billings of Louisville; Poet and king; Lydia Die; Lizzie; Little Homer's slate; Always right; "Trot, my good steed"; Providence and the dog; Gettin' on; Schnellest Zug; Bethlehem-town; Peace of Christmas-time; Doings of Delsarte; Buttercup, poppy, forget-me-not.

 These two books contain many of Field's most beautiful poems and should be in every library.

Yp
―――
G 37 fo
1454. [215.] **"For the country."** Richard Watson Gilder. N. Y., Century Co., 1897. 69 p. D. cl. .... 1.00 .65

 A little collection of patriotic poems.
 Contents: Washington at Trenton; The spirit of Abraham Lin-

	List price.	Price to schools.

coln; The burial of Grant; The dead comrade; Sheridan; Sherman; Memorial Day; The North to the South; Lowell; Failure and success.

Yp
―――
H 73

1455. [194.] **Complete poetical works of Oliver Wendell Holmes.** Bost., Houghton, Mifflin & Co., 1895. 352 p. por. O. (Cambridge edition.) cl. 2.00   1.30

Yp
―――
In 4

1456. [201.] **Poems.** Jean Ingelow. N. Y., T. Y. Crowell & Co. D. (Standard library series.) cl. ...... 1.00   .65

A book of poems which will be interesting to the girls.

Yp
―――
K 22

1457. **Complete poetical works and letters.** John Keats. Bost., Houghton, Mifflin & Co., 1899. 473 p. por. O. (Cambridge edition.) cl. 2.00   1.30

Yp
―――
K 62 de

1458. **Departmental ditties and ballads and barrack-room ballads.** Rudyard Kipling. N. Y., Doubleday & McClure Co., 1899. 217 p. O. cl. .... 1.50   .98

Yp
―――
L 26 vi

1459. **Vision of Piers the plowman: an English poem of the fourteenth century.** William Langland. Done into modern prose with an introduction by Kate M. Warren. N. Y., Macmillan Co., 1899. 143 p. Ed. 2, rev. D. cl. 90   .81

"This book has been prepared for an audience of general readers. It naturally does not aim at appealing to the circle who read the poem in the original; nor has there been any attempt to adapt it to the requirements of those students who look upon English literature as a subject for examination to be 'got up' from 'set books'. My rendering is not a line-for-line translation. But it has been prepared for an increasing number of readers who, without being scholars in Early English, are yet sufficiently interested in our early literature to wish to read Piers the Plowman for themselves, either as pure literature, or in order to find the social history in it. In connection with the teaching of English literature in schools, and with lectures of different kinds under the University Extension system, I hope the book may also be of use."—*Preface.*

		List price.	Price to schools.

Yp
L 27 bp

1460. **Boy's Percy:** being old ballads of war, adventure and love, from Bishop Thomas Percy's "Reliques of ancient English poetry"; together with an appendix containing two ballads from the original Percy folio Ms. Edited for boys with an introduction by Sidney Lanier. N. Y., C: Scribner's Sons, 1898. 441 p. il. D. cl. 2.00 1.30

Each ballad is given here exactly as it stands in the original except that the spelling has been modernized and some parts cut out. These thoughts and forms of the old English harpers and singers will give the students a more vivid picture of the early heroic souls that loved harp and song. Students of early English history should read these ballads.

Yp
L 32

1461. **Complete poetical works.** Lucy Larcom. Bost., Houghton, Mifflin & Co., c1884. 325 p. por. (Household edition.) D. cl. .... 1.50 .98

Yp
L 86

1462. [195.] **Complete poetical works of Henry Wadsworth Longfellow.** Bost., Houghton, Mifflin & Co., 1893. 689 p. por. O. (Cambridge edition.) cl. 2.00 1.30

Yp
L 95

1463. [193.] **Complete poetical works of James Russell Lowell.** Bost., Houghton, Mifflin & Co., 1896. 492 p. por. O. (Cambridge edition.) cl. 2.00 1.30

Yp
M 11 la

1464. [213.] **Lays of ancient Rome,** together with Ivry, The Armada, A radical war song, The battle of Moncontour, Songs of the civil war. Lord Macaulay. N. Y., G. P. Putnam's Sons. 237 p. il. T. cl. .50 .35

Stirring poems.

Yp
M 64

1465. [205.] **Poetical works of John Milton.** Intr. by David Masson. N. Y., Macmillan & Co., 1887. 625 p. D. (Globe edition.) cl. 1.75 1.15

Yp
M 64 pa

1466. [206.] **Paradise lost.** John Milton. Bost., Houghton, Mifflin & Co., 1898. 409 p. S. (Riverside classics series.) cl. .... 1.00 .80

Yp
R 29 bo

1467. [211.] **Book of famous verse.** Sel. by Agnes Repplier. Bost., Houghton, Mifflin & Co., 1894. 244 p. S. (Riverside library for young people.) cl. 1.25 .48
A collection of best poems for young people.

Yp
R 44 af

1468. **Afterwhiles.** James Whitcomb Riley. Indianapolis, Bowen-Merrill Co., c1898. 196 p. D. cl. .... 1.25 .82

Contents: Proem; Herr Weiser; Beautiful city; Lockerbie street; Das Krist Kindel; Anselmo; Home-made fairy tale; South wind and the sun; Lost kiss; Sphinx; If I knew what poets know; Ike Walton's prayer; Rough sketch; Our kind of a man; Harper; Old Aunt Mary's; Illileo; King; Bride; Dead lover; Song; When Bessie died; Shower; Life-lesson: Scrawl; Away; Who bides his time; From the headboard of a grave in Paraguay; Laughter holding both his sides; Fame; Ripest peach; Fruit-peace; Their sweet sorrow; John McKeen; Out of Nazareth; September dark; We to sigh instead of sing; Blossoms on the trees; Last night—and this; Discouraging model; Back from a two-years' sentence; Wandering jew; Becalmed; To Santa Claus; Where the children used to play; Glimpse of Pan; Pan; Dusk; June; Silence; Sleep; Her hair; Dearth; Voice from the farm; Serenade; Art and love; Longfellow; Indiana; Time; Grant—at rest—August 8, 1885; Old-fashioned roses; Griggsby's station; Knee-deep in June; When the hearse comes back; Canary at the farm; Liz-town humorist; Kingry's mill; Joney; Like his mother used to make; Train-misser; Granny; Old October; Jim; To Robert Burns; New Year's time at Willard's; Town karnteel; Regardin' Terry hut; Leedle Dutch baby; Down on Wriggle Crick; When de folks is gone; Little town o' Tailholt; Little orphant Annie.

Yp
R 44 ar

1469. **Armazindy.** James Whitcomb Riley. Indianapolis, Bowen-Merrill Co., 1895. 167 p. D. cl. .... 1.25 .82

Contents: Armazindy; Blind girl; Dreamer, say; Empty glove; For this Christmas; Good-bye; He and I; How did you rest, last night? Little David; Little red ribbon; Muskingum valley; My bride that is to be; My Henry; Natural perversities; Noon lull; Old school-chum; Old-timer; Old trundle bed; Our own; Out of the hitherwhere; Poor man's wealth; Rabbit in the Cross-ties; Ring-worm Frank; Serenade—to Nora; Silent victors; Song I never sing; This dear child-hearted woman; Three singing friends; To a poet-critic; To Edgar Wilson Nye; Up and down old Brandywine; We defer things; What redress; When Lide married him; When Maimie married; Windy day; Writin' back to the home-folks; Make-believe and child-play; Albumania; Barefoot boy; Charms—for corns; Circus-parade; Dolores; Envoy; Eros; Few of the bird-family; Folks at Lonesomeville; Frog; Great explorer; Home-made riddles; Idyl of the king; Jargon-jingle; King of the OO-rinktum-jing; Leonainie; Little dog-woggle; Little mock-man; Lovely child; My Mary; Orlie Wilde; Ponchus Pilut; School-boy's favorite; Slumber-song; Summer-time and winter-time; Three jolly hunters; Through sleepy-land; To a jilted swain; To remove freckles; Toy penny-dog; Trestle and the buck-saw; Twiggs and Tudens; Twintorette; Voices; When I do mock; Yellow-bird; Youthful patriot.

Yp
R 44 gr

	List price.	Price to schools.
1470. **Green fields and running brooks.** James Whitcomb Riley. Indianapolis, Bowen–Merrill Co., c1892. 224 p. D. cl.	1.25	.82

Contents: Proem; Artemus of Michigan; As my uncle used to say; At Utter Loaf; August; Autumn; Bedouin; Being his mother; Blind; Blossoms on the trees; By any other name; By her white bed; Chant of the cross-bearing child; Country pathway; Cup of tea; Curse of the wandering foot; Cyclone; Dan Paine; Dawn, noon and dewfall; Discouraging model; Ditty of no tone; Don Piatt of Mac-o-chee; Dot leedle boy; Dream of Autumn; Elizabeth; Envoy; Farmer Whipple—bachelor; Full harvest; Glimpse of Pan; Go, winter; Her beautiful eyes; Hereafter; His mother's way; His vigil; Home at night; Home-going; Hoodoo; Hoosier folk-child; How John quit the farm; Iron horse; Iry and Billy and Jo; Jack the giant-killer; Jap Miller; John Alden and Percilly; John Brown; John McKeen; Judith; June at Woodruff; Just to be good; Last night—and this; Let us forget; Little fat doctor; Longfellow; Lounger; Monument for the soldiers; Mr. What's-His-Name; My friend; Nessmuk; North and South; Old retired sea captain; Old winters on the farm; Old Year and the new; On the banks o' Deer Crick; Out of Nazareth; Passing of a heart; Plaint human; Quarrel; Quiet lodger; Reach your hand to me; Right here at home; Rival; Rivals: or the showman's ruse; Robert Burns Wilson; Rose; September dark; Shoemaker; Singer; Sister Jones's confession; Sleep; Some scattering remarks of Bub's; Song of long ago; Southern singer; Suspense; Thanksgiving; Their sweet sorrow; Them flowers; To an importunate ghost; To hear her sing; Tom Van Arden; To the serenader; Tugg Martin; Twins; Wandering jew; Watches of the night; Water color; We to sigh instead of sing; What Chris'mas fetched the Wigginses; When age comes on; Where-away; While the musician played; Wife-blessed; Wraith of summertime.

Yp
R 44 ho

1471. **Home-folks.** James Whitcomb Riley. Indianapolis, Bowen–Merrill Co., c1900. 166 p. D. cl.	1.25	.82

Contents: As created; At Crown hill; At his wintry tent; At

	List price.	Price to schools.

sea; Ballad with a serious conclusion; Ballade of the coming rain; Bed; Cassauder; Christ; Christmas along the wires; Edge of the wind; Emerson; Enduring; Equity? Eugene Field; Feel in the Christmas-air; From Delphi to Camden; Green grass of old Ireland; Henry W. Grady; Hired man's faith in children; His love of home; Home-ag'in; Home-folks; Home-voyage; Hymn exultant; Idiot; In the evening; Let something good be said; Lincoln; Loving cup; Mister Hop-toad; Moonshiner's serenade; Mother sainted; Mr. Foley's Christmas; My dancin' days is over; Name of Old Glory; Naturalist; Noblest service; Old guitar; O life! O beyond! On a fly-leaf; On a youthful portrait of Stevenson; One with a song; Onward trail; Oscar C. McCulloch; Our boyhood haunts; Our queer old world; Peace-hymn of the Republic; Red riding hood; Rhymes of Ironquill; Say something to me; Sermon of the rose; Short'nin' bread song; Silent singer; Smitten purist; Song of the road; Them old cheery words; To Robert Louis Stevenson; To the judge; To "Uncle Remus"; Traveling man; Uncle Sidney's logic; What the wind said; Whittier; Wholly unscholastic opinion; Your height is ours.

Yp

R 44 ne
1472. [207.] **Neghborly poems and dialect sketches.** James Whitcomb Riley. Indianapolis, Bowen-Merrill Co., 1899. 215 p. il. D. cl. .... 1.25   .82

Yp

R 44 pi
1473. **Pipes o' Pan at Zekesbury.** James Whitcomb Riley. Indianapolis, Bowen-Merrill Co., c1888. 203 p. D. cl. .... 1.25   .82

Contents: At Zekesbury; Down around the river; Kneeling with Herrick; Romancin'; Has she forgotten; A' old played-out song; Lost path; Little tiny kickshaw; His mother; Kissing the rod; How it happened; Babyhood; Days gone by; Mrs. Miller; Tree-toad; Worn-out pencil; Stepmother; Rain; Legend glorified; Whur mother is; Old man's nursery rhyme; Three dead friends; In Bohemia; In the dark; Wet-weather talk; Where shall we land; Champion checker-player of Ameriky; An old sweetheart; Marthy Ellen; Moon-drowned; Long afore he knowed; Dear hands; This man Jones; To my good master; When the green gits back; At broad ripple; When old Jack died; Doc Sifers; At noon—and midnight; Wild Irishman; When my dreams come true; A dos't o' blues; Bat; Way it wuz; Drum; Tom Johnson's quit; Lullaby; In the south; Old home by the mill; Leave-taking; Wait for the morning; When June is here; Gilded roll.

Yp

R 44 sk
1474. **Sketches in prose:** and occasional verse. James Whitcomb Riley. Indianapolis, Bowen-Merrill Co., c1900. 259 p. D. cl. .... 1.25   .82

Contents: God bless us every one; Jamesy; Bells jangled; An

LIST OF BOOKS FOR HIGH SCHOOL LIBRARIES.   389

                                                                           List Price to
                                                                          price. schools.
adjustable lunatic; Tod; Fame; Remarkable man; Nest-egg; Tale of a spider; Elf-child; Where is Mary Alice Smith? Ban; Eccentric Mr. Clark; "Boy from Zeeny"; Old man.

Yp
———
Sco 3

1475. [200.] **Poetical works of** *Sir* **Walter Scott.** Memoir by Francis Turner Palgrave. N. Y., Macmillan Co., 1881. 559 p. D. (Globe edition.) cl. 1.75 1.15

Yp
———
Sh 4

1476. **Complete poetical works.** Percy Bysshe Shelley. Bost., Houghton, Mifflin & Co., 1901. 651 p. por. O. (Cambridge edition.) cl. 2.00 1.30

Yp
———
Sh 4 pr

1477. [26.] **Prometheus unbound.** Percy Bysshe Shelley, ed. by Vida D. Scudder. Bost., D. C. Heath & Co., 1897. 169 p. D. (Heath's English classics series.) cl. .... .60 .54

A lyrical drama.

Yp
———
T 18 je

#1478. **Jerusalem delivered.** Torquato Tasso. Translated into English Spenserian verse, with a life of the author, by J. H. Wiffin. N. Y., D. Appleton & Co., 1898. 624 p. il. S. Ed. 3. cl. .... 1.00 .65

An epic poem in twenty books. The story of the deliverance of Jerusalem from the unbelievers by the Crusaders under Godfrey de Bouillon. When the Christian army reach Jerusalem, they find it can not be taken without the aid of Rinaldo, who has withdrawn from the army, because Godfrey had cited him for the death of Grinaldo. He is brought back from the enchanted island of Armida, and on his return Jerusalem is captured, the Christians making a triumphant entrance into the city.

The advanced classes in Literature should read selections from this; Homer's "Iliad" and "Odyssey"; and Milton's "Paradise lost" in their study of the epic.

Yp
———
T 26

1479. [197.] **Poetic and dramatic works of Lord Alfred Tennyson.** Bost., Houghton, Mifflin & Co., 1898. 887 p. por. O. (Cambridge edition.) cl. 2.00 1.30

Yp
W 59 ch

                                                              List Price to
                                                              price. schools.

#1480. **Christ of Cynewulf:** a poem in three parts, the Advent, the Ascension, and the Last Judgment. Translated into English prose by Charles Huntington Whitman. Bost., Ginn & Co., 1900. 62 p. D. cl. .... .40 .34

This will be of interest to the English literature class as a specimen of Early English literature.

Yp
W 61

1481. [196.] **Complete poetical works of John Greenleaf Whittier.** Bost., Houghton, Mifflin & Co., 1894. 542 p. por. O. (Cambridge edition.) cl· 2.00 1.30

Yp
W 89

1482. [203.] **Poems.** William Wordsworth. N. Y., T. Y. Crowell & Co. D. (Standard library series.) cl. .... 1.00 .65

SPEECHES, ORATIONS.

Ys
Ad 1 re

1483. **Representative British orations:** with introductions and explanatory notes. Charles Kendall Adams, ed. with an additional volume edited by John Alden. N. Y., G. P. Putnam's Sons, 1887–1900. 4 vols. D. cl. 5.00 3.25

The orators included are, Vol. 1, Eliot; Pym; Chatham; Mansfield; Burke; Vol. 2, Pitt; Fox; Mackintosh; Erskine; Vol. 3, Canning; Macaulay; Cobden; Bright; Beaconsfield; Gladstone; Vol. 4, O'Connell; Palmerston; Lowe; Chamberlain; Rosebery.

Ys
F 91 ne

1484. **New Century speaker:** for school and college. Henry Allyn Frink. Bost., Ginn & Co., 1899. 341 p. D. cl. .... 1.00 .85

An excellent representative collection of extracts from leading American orators. A good book for use of the students in expression.

Ys
G 79 gr
                                                                                    List Price to
                                                                                    price. schools.

1485. [218.] **Great words from great Americans**...N. Y., G. P. Putnam's Sons, 1898. 195 p. il. D. (Citizen's edition.) cl. .... 1.50   .98

    Includes the Declaration of Independence, the constitution of the United States. Washington's inaugural and farewell addresses, Lincoln's inaugural, farewell, and Gettysburg addresses.

Ys
J 64 am
1486. [217.] **American orations**: studies in American political history. Ed. by Alexander Johnston, re-ed. by James Albert Woodburn. N. Y., G. P. Putnam's Sons, 1899. 4 vols. 405; 433; 416; 481 pp. D. cl. 5.00   3.25

    From the colonial period to the present time, selected as specimens of eloquence, and with special reference to their value in throwing light upon the more important epochs and issues of American history. Will serve as models to those engaging in oratorical contests.

Ys
W 12 mo
1487. **Modern political orations.** Leopold Wagner. N. Y., Henry Holt & Co., 1896. 344 p. D. cl. .... 1.00   .90

    Noted examples of British political oratory of Victoria's reign. Contains the speech of Lord Brougham on negro emancipation, Daniel O'Connell on repeal of the Union, Bulwer on the Crimean war, Isaac Butt on home rule, Joseph Cowen on the foreign policy of England, Lord Randolph Churchill on the Egyptian crisis, Chas. S. Parnell on the Coercion Bill, the Right Honorable John Morley on home rule, Richard Cobden on the corn laws, etc.

WIT AND HUMOR.

Yw
B 22 co
1488. **Coffee and repartee.** John Kendrick Bangs. N. Y., Harper & Bros., 1901. 123 p. il. T. bds. (Harper's black and white series.) .... .50   .33

    This little volume records the conversations at the table of a boarding-house. It is light, humorous and artistically written.

Many publishers issue selections from standard literature known as "English classics."

The following are well bound and sold at reasonable prices: Longmans, Green & Co., Longman's English classics; Houghton, Mifflin & Co., Riverside Literature Series; American Book Company, Eclectic English Classics; Macmillan & Co., Temple Classics; Sibley & Ducker, The Student's Series of English Classics; D. C. Heath & Co., Heath's English Classics; Silver, Burdett & Co., Studies in English Classics; Ginn & Co., Standard English Classics; Ainsworth & Co., Lakeside Classics; Globe School Book Co., English Classics. See publishers' lists.

CLASSICAL LITERATURE.

The greater part of the translations of Classical literature which follow have been placed on the list for the use of the schools that use the source method in the teaching of history.

Yo 2
Q 2 Il
	List price.	Price to schools.
1489. [15.] **Illustrated history of ancient literature;** oriental and classical. John D. Quackenbos. N. Y., American Book Company, 1899. 435 p. maps. il. D. cl.	1.20	1.05

A general survey of ancient literature for reference only.

GREEK LITERATURE.

Y 32 (t)
Ae 8 dr
1490. [22.] **Dramas. Aeschylus.** Tr. by Anna Swanwick. N. Y., Macmillan Co. D. cl. 1.50 1.30

Aeschylus was the father of Greek tragic drama and the greatest of the Greek tragic poets.

Y 32 (t)
Ae 8 pr
1491. [25.] **Prometheus bound. Aeschylus.** Tr. by Paul Elmer More. Bost., Houghton, Mifflin & Co., 1899. 110 p. D. cl. .... .75 .50

Prometheus, bound to the rocks by the order of Zeus for his benevolence to man, resists all efforts to subdue his will and pur-

	List price.	Price to schools.

pose, bids defiance to the father of the gods, and disappears in an appalling tempest.

Y 32 (t)

Ae S tr

1492. **Tragedies of Aeschylus:** New translation, with a biographical essay, and an appendix of rhymed choral odes, translated by Edward Hayes Plumptre. N. Y., George Routledge & Sons, n. d. 378 p. S. cl. .... 1.50 .98

Aeschylus was the first of the three great tragic poets of Athens. His tragedies will be of interest and value to the students of Ancient history.

Y 32 (t)

Ar 4 co

#1493. **Comedies of Aristophanes:** a new and literal translation from the revised text of Dindorf, with notes and extracts from the best metrical versions by William James Hickie. Aristophanes. London, George Bell & Sons (N. Y., Macmillan Co.), 1900, 2 vols. D. (Bohn's libraries.) cl. each 1.50 1.35

The Comedies of Aristophanes reflect the opinions of the opposition party in Athens during the time of the Peloponnesian war. They give good pictures of the social and private life of the time.

"Aristophanes was the greatest of the Greek comic poets. His comedies unite elements which meet nowhere in literature. There is a play of fancy as extravagant as in a modern burlesque, a humor as delicate, a literary satire as keen, as the most exquisite wit could offer to the most subtle appreciation. There are lyric strains of a wild woodland sweetness hardly to be matched save in Shakespeare."—*Jebb, Greek literature.*

Y 32 (t)

Ar 4 on

#1494. **On the Athenian constitution.** Aristotle. Translated with introduction and notes by Frederick G. Kenyon. London, George Bell & Sons (N. Y., Macmillan Co.), 1901. 126 p. S. cl. .... 1.10 .99

This volume contains many new facts on the early development of the constitution, and is very valuable for reference in the study of the early history of Athens.

Y 32

C 17 fr

1495. **From Homer to Theocritus:** a manual of Greek literature. Edward Capps. N. Y., C: Scribner's Sons, 1901. 476 p. il. D. cl. 1.50 1.35

Presents a concise but complete survey of the Greek literature of the classical period, extended so as to include the two branches

394 LIST OF BOOKS FOR HIGH SCHOOL LIBRARIES.

                                                  List Price to
                                                  price. schools.
of poetry, the new comedy and the idyll, which were brought to
perfection after the overthrow of Greek liberty by Alexander. Selections from representative English translations are quoted in connection with the principal authors.

Y 32 (t)

D 39 or

1496. [27.] **Oration on the crown. Demosthenes.** N. Y., Macmillan Co. D. cl. .... .50 .44

    The author was the greatest of Greek orators.

Y 32 (t)

Ep 4 di

#1497. **Discourses of Epictetus:** with the Encheiridion and fragments. Epictetus. Translated, with notes, a life of Epictetus, and a view of his philosophy by George Long. London, George Bell & Sons (N. Y., Macmillan Co.), 1890. 452 p. D. (Bohn's libraries.) cl. 1.50 1.35

    One of the best sources in Roman stoicism. Epictetus was a Greek slave in Rome and became a Stoic.

Y 32 (t)

Eu 7 tr

1498. [21.] **Tragedies. Euripides.** Tr. by E. P. Coleridge. N. Y., Macmillan Co. 2 vols. D. cl. each 1.50 1.30

    The author was a celebrated Athenian tragic poet.

Y 32 (t)

Eu 7 th

1499. **Three dramas of Euripides.** William Cranston Lawton, *trans*. Bost., Houghton, Mifflin & Co., 1900. 261 p. D. cl. .... 1.50 .98

    Of value in the study of Greek history for the picture of Greek life which they give.

Y 32 (t)

F 82 hi

1499a. **History of ancient Greek literature.** Harold N. Fowler. N. Y., D. Appleton & Co., 1902. 501 p. il. (Twentieth century text-books.) D. cl. 1.40 1.26

    Intended primarily for use in secondary schools and colleges; interesting also to the general reading public. The greater part of the book is taken up with the history of Greek literature before the Alexandrian period. A summary account of Alexandrine and

LIST OF BOOKS FOR HIGH SCHOOL LIBRARIES. 395

	List price.	Price to schools.

Graeco-Roman literature is included; also an account of some of the Christian writers.

"The pupil in the secondary school may not always have the time to pay any attention to the less important Greek authors. It may therefore be in many instances desirable to stop the classroom use of the book at the end of the Attic period, adding only enough from the later parts to make the pupils acquainted with Theocritus, Callimachus, Appollonius Rhodius (especially if the pupils have read or are to read Virgil), Polybius, Plutarch, and Lucian. In the case of immature pupils, it may be well to omit the chapter on the Homeric Question, and even the chapters on the early prose writers."—*Preface.*

Y 32 (t)

H 43 he

#1500. **Herodotus.** *Rev.* Henry Cary, *trans.* London, George Bell & Sons (N. Y., Macmillan Co.), 1901. 613 p. D. (Bohn's libraries.) cl. .... 1.00 .90

This history presents a vivid dramatic picture of the old world, giving the manners and customs, traditions, and geographical features of the countries, as well as historical events. His work is not entirely accurate but is intensely interesting, and should be in every school where the source method of teaching history is used.

Y 32 (t)

H 75 ilb

1501. [29.] Iliad. **Homer.** Tr. by William Cullen Bryant. Bost., Houghton, Mifflin & Co., 1898. Two volumes in one. 332; 355 pp. D. (Student's edition.) cl. .... 1.00 .90

Poetical translation of Homer.

Y 32 (t)

H 75 ill

1502. [30.] Iliad. **Homer.** Tr. by Andrew Lang, Walter Leaf, *and* Ernest Myers. N. Y., Macmillan & Co., 1883. 518 p. D. cl. (School edition.) 1.50 1.30

The best prose translation of Homer.

Y 32 (t)

H 75 odb

1503. [28.] **Odyssey. Homer.** Tr. by William Cullen Bryant. Bost., Houghton, Mifflin & Co. Two volumes in one. 272; 256 pp. D. (Student's edition.) cl. .... 1.00 .90

The best poetical translation.

Y 32 (t)

H 75 odbu

1504. [31.] **Odyssey. Homer.** Tr. by S. H. Butcher, and A. Lang. N. Y., Macmillan & Co., 1888. 428 p. D. cl. 1.50 1.30

List price. Price to schools.

The best prose translation.

Y 32

J 34 gr

1505. [19.] **Greek literature.** R. C. Jebb. N. Y., American Book Company. 176 p. S. (Literary primers.) cl. .... .35 .31

A brief outline of writers and writings for reference.

Y 32 (t)

L 96 se

#1506. **Selections.** Lucian (Lucianus Samosatensis). Translated by Emily James Smith. N. Y., American Book Company, 1892. 287 p. D. cl. 1.25 1.07

Lucian wrote in the time of the Antonines. He depicted the weaknesses of the Greek Gods and heroes.

Y 32 (t)

L 99 or

1507. **Orations of Lysias.** Literally translated. N. Y., Hinds & Noble, c1898. 168 p. (Handy literal translations.) S. cl. .... .50 .45

The language of Lysias is simple and his orations are excellent illustrations of phases of life in Athens during his time. He was one of the greatest Athenian orators during the period of Spartan supremacy.

Y 32 (t)

P 76 hi

#1508. **Histories of Polybius**: translated from the text of F. Hultsch. Evelyn S. Shuckburgh. N. Y., Macmillan Co., 1889. 2 vols. D. cl. 6.00 5.40

Polybius was the best qualified historian of ancient times, being noted for his breadth of view and his fairness. His purpose was to trace the growth of Roman power, throughout the Mediterranean world, and to include the events in Greece during the Roman conquest.

Too expensive a set to be purchased by small libraries.

Y 32 (t)

So 6 an

1509. [24.] **Antigone. Sophocles.** Tr. by George Herbert Palmer. Bost., Houghton, Mifflin & Co., 1899. 100 p. D. cl. .... .75 .50

	List price.	Price to schools.

Y 32 (t)
So 6 tr

1510. [20.] **Tragedies of Sophocles.** Tr. by E. H. Plumptre. Bost., D. C. Heath & Co., 1900. 502 p. D. cl. .... 1.00   .87

The author was one of the three great tragic poets of Greece.

Y 32 (t)
T 42 hi

#1511. **History of the Peloponnesian war.** Thucydides. Literally translated by *Rev.* Henry Dale. London, George Bell & Sons (N. Y., Macmillan Co.), 1896. 2 vols. D. (Bohn's libraries.) cl. each .... 1.00   .80

The author lived during the Peloponnesian War. His work begins with a brief sketch of the history of Greece from the early tribal period. It is well written and follows the chronological order.

His work is considered accurate, and together with Herodotus and Homer should be in every school where history is taught by the source method.

Y 32 (t)
Xe 2 cy·

#1512. **Cyropaedia: or, Institution of Cyrus and the Hellenics.** Xenophon. Translated by *Rev.* J. S. Watson, and *Rev.* Henry Dale. London, George Bell & Sons (N. Y., Macmillan Co.), 1898. 579 p. D. (Bohn's libraries.) cl. .... .60   .54

The history of Greece during the period of Spartan supremacy and the contest with Thebes.

The other works of the author valuable for reference work are "The Anabasis, or Retreat of the ten thousand", and "Memorabilia of Socrates".

LATIN LITERATURE.

Y 35 (t)
D 23 di

1513. **Divine comedy.** Dante Alighieri. Translated by Henry Wadsworth Longfellow. Bost., Houghton, Mifflin & Co., c1895. 760 p. O. cl. 2.50   1.64

This is one of the greatest poems and it has had a wonderful influence on the literature of all lands. It is divided into three parts: Inferno, Purgatorio, and Paradiso. Dante gave full poetical expression to the Mediaeval thoughts. "He immortalized the centuries behind him, and inaugurated the new age."

Y 35 (t)
———
L 76 hi

#1514. **History of Rome.** Titus Livius. Literally translated by D. Spillan. London, George Bell & Sons (N. Y., Macmillan Co.), 1899-1901. 4 vols. D. (Bohn's libraries.) cl. 4.00   3.45

List price. Price to schools.

Livy, one of the greatest of Roman historians, lived during the early days of the empire. His work is valuable for its literary excellence, and as an example of the way in which the Romans regarded their own history. This should only be purchased by the larger libraries.

Y 35 (t)
———
M 23 ro

#1515. **Roman history of Ammianus Marcellinus:** during the reigns of the Emperors Constantius, Julian, Jovianus, Valentinian, and Valens. Translated by C. D. Yonge. London, George Bell & Sons (N. Y., Macmillan Co.), 1894. 646 p. D. (Bohn's libraries.) cl. 2.25   2.02

Ammianus is a contemporary source of great value. His history covers a period of 282 years, from the accession of Nerva, 96 A. D. to the death of Valens, 378 A. D.

It contains interesting and instructive descriptions of the manners and customs of the time.

Y 35 (t)
———
P 71 le

#1516. **Letters of Caius Plinius Caecilius Secundus.** Pliny (the younger). Melmoth's translation, revised by Rev. F. C. T. Bosanquet. London, George Bell & Sons (N. Y., Macmillan Co.), 1901. 415 p. D. (Bohn's libraries.) cl. 1.50   1.35

Pliny's letters are valuable for the picture they give of the events and opinions of the Augustan Age. The letters between Trojan and Pliny, when Pliny was governor, gave the attitude toward the Christians at that time.

Y 35 (t)
———
T 11 an

#1517. **Works of Tacitus: the annals.** Tacitus. Oxford translation, revised with notes. London, George Bell & Sons (N. Y., Macmillan Co.), 1900. 464 p. D. (Bohn's libraries.) cl. each .... 1.00   .90

Tacitus wrote at the time of the Emperor Trajan. His writing is of value because of the picturesqueness of his style. His other works are Agricola, Germania, and his History.

Y 36 (t)
———
C 11co

1518. [17.] **Commentaries.** Caesar. Translation. N. Y., Macmillan Co. D. cl. .... 1.00   .85

LIST OF BOOKS FOR HIGH SCHOOL LIBRARIES. 399

Y 36 (t)

C 48 de

	List price.	Price to schools.

1519. **De Amicitia.** Marcus Tullius Cicero. Translated from the Latin by Benjamin E. Smith. N. Y., Century Co., 1901. 173 p. T. leath. ....   1.00   .65

    An essay on friendship.

Y 36 (t)

J 98 sa

1520. **Satires of Juvenal:** literally translated with explanatory notes. *Rev.* Lewis Evans. N. Y., Hinds & Noble, n. d. 198 p. (Handy literal translations.) S. cl. 50   .40

    These Satires give a vivid picture of life and politics in Rome during the last half of the first century. Juvenal was the greatest satirist of Roman literature.

Y 36 (t)

M 35 th

1521. **Thoughts of the Emperor Marcus Aurelius Antonius.** George Long, *trans.* N. Y., G. P. Putnam's Sons, n. d. 315 p. T. flex. leath. ....   1.00   .50

    A most valuable account of the inner life of the most famous Stoic.

Y 36 (t)

Se 5 tr

1522. [18.] **Two tragedies of Seneca;** Medea and The daughters of Troy. Tr. by Ella Isabel Harris. Bost., Houghton, Mifflin & Co., 1899. 96 p. D. cl   .75   .50

    Seneca was one of the most famous Roman Stoic philosophers.

Y 36 (t)

V 81 ae

1523. [16.] **Aeneid of Virgil.** Tr. by Christopher Pearse Cranch. Bost., Houghton, Mifflin & Co., 1897. 388 p. D. cl. ....   1.00   .90

FRENCH LITERATURE.

Y 39
D 75 hi

List Price to price. schools.

#1524. **History of French literature.** Edward Dowden. N. Y., D. Appleton & Co., 1901. 444 p. D. cl. .. 1.50 .98

An excellent short sketch of French literature. Valuable for reference only.

Y 39
M 43 fr

#1525. **French dramatists of the 19th century.** Brander Matthews. N. Y., C: Scribner's Sons, 1901. 321 p. D. Ed. 3. cl. 1.25 1.12

For reference. This volume should not be purchased by the smaller libraries.

Contents: Romantic movement; Victor Hugo; Alexandre Dumas; Eugène Scribe; Emile Augier; Alexandre Dumas *fils;* Victorien Sardou; Octave Feuillet; Eugène Labiche; Meilhac and Halévy; Emile Zola and the present tendencies of French drama; Ten years' retrospect: 1881–1891; End of the century: 1891–1900.

GERMAN LITERATURE.

Y 47
Am 2 ma

1526. **Märchen.** Hans Christian Andersen. Edited with notes and vocabulary by O. B. Super. Bost., D. C. Heath & Co., 1901. 247 p. (Heath's modern language series.) D. cl. .... .70 .60

Andersen's tales are easy, and interesting reading for students who have had at least one year of German.

Y 47 (t)
G 55 wi

1527. **Wilhelm Meister's apprenticeship and travels:** from the German of Goethe. Thomas Carlyle, *tr.* Bost., Houghton, Mifflin & Co., n. d. 2 vols. 397 + 388 pp. D. cl. 3.00 1.96

Y 47
F 84 hi

#1528. **History of German literature:** as determined by social forces (in English). Kuno Francke. N. Y., Henry Holt & Co., 1901. 595 p. O. Ed. 4 of "Social forces in German literature." cl. 2.50 2.25

An excellent book for the teacher of German. This volume should only be purchased by the larger libraries.

Contents: Epochs of German culture; Period of the migrations; Growth of mediaeval hierarchy and feudalism; Height of

	List price.	Price to schools.

chivalric culture; Rise of the middle classes; Era of the Reformation; Struggle against absolutism and the beginnings of modern life; Age of Frederick the Great and the height of enlightenment; Age of the Revolution and the climax of individualism; Era of national reconstruction and the growth of the collectivistic deal; Epilogue—Richard Wagner—contemporary drama.

Y 47

F 89 do

1529. **Doktor Luther: eine Schilderung.** Gustav Freytag. Edited, with introduction and notes, by Frank P. Goodrich. Bost., Ginn & Co., 1899. 177 p. D. cl. .... .60 .51

For advanced classes.

Y 47

G 55 eg

1530. **Egmont.** Johann Wolfgang von Goethe. Together with Schiller's Essays, "Des Grafen Lamoral von Egmont leben und Tod," and "Uber Egmont, Trauerspiel von Goethe." Edited, with introduction and notes by Max Winkler. Bost., Ginn & Co., 1899. 276 p. (International modern language series.) D. cl. .... .90 .76

For advanced classes.

Y 47

G 55 fa

1531. **Faust: a tragedy.** Johann Wolfgang von Goethe. Translated in the original metres, by Bayard Taylor. Bost., Houghton, Mifflin & Co., c1898. 2 vol. in one. O. cl. 2.50 1.64

Y 47

G 55 he

1532. **Hermann und Dorothea.** Johann Wolfgang von Goethe. Edited with an introduction and notes by Waterman T. Hewett. Bost., D. C. Heath & Co., 1901. 243 p. (Heath's modern language series.) D. cl. .... .75 .68

For advanced classes.

Y 47

G 55 ip

1533. **Iphigenie auf Tauris.** Johann Wolfgang von Goethe. With introduction and notes by Charles A. Eggert. N. Y., Macmillan Co., 1901. 180 p. S. cl. .... .60 .54

For advanced reading.

This, of all the dramas of Goethe, holds the first place, as a

	List price.	Price to schools.

school study, for advanced classes. It is a poem of rare and exquisite beauty of thought and expression.

Y 47
G 55 to
1534. **Torquato Tasso.** Johann Wolfgang von Goethe. Edited for the use of students by Calvin Thomas. Bost., D. C. Heath & Co., 1900. 181 p. (Heath's German series.) D. cl. .... .75 .67

For advanced students.

Y 47
G 69 ou
1535. **Outlines of German literature** (in English). Joseph Gostwick, *and* Robert Harrison. N. Y., Henry Holt & Co., n. d. 588 p. D. cl. 2.00 1.80

The German language is now taught in all our best High schools and Colleges, as well as at Universities and it is quite important that students should know something of the history of German literature. This book covers in outline the periods from 380 A. D. to 1870. It is correct and thorough. A very necessary book for the teacher of German and excellent for reference for students in advanced German class.

Y 47
H 29 ta
1536. **Tales.** Wilhelm Hauff. With introduction, notes and vocabulary by Charles B. Goold. Bost., Ginn & Co., 1897. 200 p. (International modern language series.) D. cl. .... .70 .59

For advanced students.

Y 47
H 36 p
1537. **Poems.** Heinrich Heine. Edited, with notes by Horatio Stevens White. Bost., D. C. Heath & Co., 1900. 220 p. (Heath's Modern Language Series.) D. cl. .... .75 .67

For advanced classes.

Y 47
H 36 pr
1538. **Heine's prose**: with introduction and notes by Albert R. Faust. Heinrich Heine. N. Y., Macmillan Co., 1899. 341 p. map and por. S. cl. .... .60 .54

For advanced classes.

LIST OF BOOKS FOR HIGH SCHOOL LIBRARIES. 403

Y 47
H 79 sh
                  List Price to
                 price. schools.

1539. Short history of German. literature (in English.) James K. Hosmer. N. Y., C: Scribner's Sons, 1901. 605 p. Rev. ed. D. cl. 2.00 1.30

  "In the present sketch of the history of German literature, the writer confines himself to one field, "Die schöne Literatur,"—*Belles-Lettres,* Polite literature. . . . The authors mentioned are comparatively few in number. Attention is concentrated upon "epoch-making" men and books, the effort being made to consider these with care. What is of subordinate importance has not been neglected; but the attempt has been made in every case to proportion the amount of light thrown to the significance of the figure which was to receive it."—*Preface.*

  Contents: Beginnings; Nibelungen Lied; Gudrun; Minnesingers; Development of prose; Mastersingers; Luther in literature; Thirty years' war; Lessing; Klopstock, Wieland, and Herder; Göethe, the man; Göethe, the poet; Schiller; Romantic school; Heinrich Heine; Modern era; German style; Appendix.

Y 47
L 56 em
1540. Emilia Galotti: ein Trauerspiel in fünf Augügen. Gotthold Ephraim Lessing. With introduction and explanatory notes by Max Poll. Bost., Ginn & Co., 1902. 131 p. (International Modern Language Series.) D. cl........................ 60 .51
  Same. Edited by Max Winkler. Bost., D. C. Heath & Co., 1902. 128 p. (Heath's modern language series.) D. cl. .... 60 .51

For advanced classes.
  One of Lessing's greatest works and one from which modern German tragedy takes its rise. The language is not very difficult.

Y 47
L 56 mi
1541. Minna von Barnhelm oder Das Soldatengluck: Lustspiel in fünf Aufzügen. Gotthold Ephraim Lessing. Edited with introduction and notes by Sylvester Primer. Rev. ed. Bost., D. C. Heath & Co., 1902. 218 p. (Heath's modern language series.) D. cl .... .60 .51
  Same. Edited by M. B. Lambert. N. Y., Amer. Bk. Co., 1897. 159 p. D. bds..................... .50 .42

For advanced classes.

Y 47 (t)
L 97 se
1542. Selections from the table-talk of Martin Luther. Martin Luther. Translated by *Capt.* Henry Bell. N. Y., Cassell & Co., 1899. 192 p. (Cassell's National library, new series.) T. cl........... .20 .15

  This shows the character and philosophy of Luther, and is

404   LIST OF BOOKS FOR HIGH SCHOOL LIBRARIES.

               List Price to
              price. schools.
written in a simple, clear style that is within the understanding of High school pupils. It should be used to supplement the textbook study on the Reformation.

Y 47
M 88 de
1543. **Deutsche Gedichte:** for high schools. Hermann Mueller. Bost., Ginn & Co., 1899. 71 p. (International modern language series.) D. cl........ .40 .34

 A selection of popular German poems for sight reading and memorizing.

Y 47
P 91 jo
1544. **Journalistic German:** Selections from current German periodicals. August Prehn, ed. N. Y., American Bk. Co., c1900. 208 p. D. cl.......... .50 .42

 The aim of this volume is to provide reading material on the doings and events of modern times, presenting the great facts of invention, discovery, commerce, and industry. This will be good reading for the students in the Commercial course who have had two years German.

Y 47
R 72 wa
1545. **Waldheimat.** Petri Kettenfeier Rosegger. With introduction and explanatory notes by Laurence Fossler. Bost., Ginn & Co., 1896. 103 p. (International modern language series.) D. cl....... .50 .43

 Selections from the "Waldheimat." This can be read by students who have had two years' German.

Y 47
Sch 2 ek
1546. **Ekkehard:** eine Geschichten aus dem zehnten Jahrhundert. Joseph Victor von Scheffel. Abbreviated and edited with English notes by Carla Wenckebach. Bost., D. C. Heath & Co., 1901. 235 p. (Heath's modern language series.) D. cl. .... .70 .63

 One of the masterpieces of German prose. It presents many interesting phases of German life and thought and is one of the best German historical novels.
 For advanced students.

LIST OF BOOKS FOR HIGH SCHOOL LIBRARIES. 405

Y 47 (t)
Sch 2 hi

List price. Price to schools.

#1547. **History of German literature.** W. Scherer. Tr. by *Mrs.* F. C. Connybeare. F. Max Muller, ed. N. Y., C: Scribner's Sons, 1901. 2 vols. D. cl........ 3.50 2.30

A history of German literature from the earliest times to the death of Goethe.

Y 47
Sch 3 gu

1548. **Gustav Adolf in Deutschland, 1630–1632:** from Schiller's History of the Thirty Years' War. Johann Christoph von Schiller. With notes and vocabulary by Wilhelm Bernhardt. N. Y., American Bk. Co., c1894. 143 p. D. bds.................... .45 .38

The volume presents the story of the most interesting part of the Thirty Years' War, the "Swedish Period."
For advanced students.

Y 47
Sch 3 ju

1549. **Jungfrau von Orleans.** J. C. F. Schiller. With introduction and notes by Willard Humphreys. N. Y., Macmillan Co., 1900. 259 p. map and por. S. cl. .... .60 .54

For advanced classes.

Y 47
Sch 3 ma

1550. **Maria Stuart:.** Ein Trauerspiel. Johann Christoph Schiller. Edited with German comments, notes, and questions by Margarethe Müller *and* Carla Wenckebach. Bost., Ginn & Co., 1901. 262 p. D. cl. .... .90 .76

For advanced classes.

Y 47 (t)
Sch 3 wa

1551. **Wallenstein and Wilhelm Tell.** Friedrich Schiller. Translated by S. T. Coleridge, J. Churchill, *and Sir* Theodore Martin. London, George Bell & Sons, N. Y., Macmillan Co., 1901. 420 p. (Bohn's libraries.) D. cl. .... 1.00 .85

Y 47
Sch 3 wi

1552. **Wilhelm Tell:** Johann F. von Schiller. With introduction, notes and a vocabulary by W. H. Carruth. N. Y., Macmillan Co., 1902. 317 p. S. cl. .50 .45

For advanced classes. Accepted as the best classic play for young students.

Y 47
St 4 ge
1553. **Geschichten vom Rhein.** Menco Stern. N. Y., American Bk. Co., c1899. 318 p. D. cl......... .85 .72

These stories were written fourteen years ago, and have been used in the manuscript form in many intermediate and advanced classes as a reader, and as material for conversation and composition. Though different in subject and character they form a complete unit, the stories beginning at the sources of the Rhine and following continuously the course of the river to its mouth. Through them the author has acquainted his students with many geographical, historical, and literary facts, and awakened in them an interest, and oftentimes a love, for German traditions and customs.

Y 47
St 4 ges
1554. **Geschichten von deutschen Stadten.** Menco Stern. N. Y., American Bk. Co., c1902. 420 p. D. cl.. 1.25 1.07

Short stories which in tone and contents portray the local color, and conduct the students systematically through the German empire. Can be read by students who have had about two years of German.

Y 47
St 6 un
1555. **Unter dem Christbaum.** Five Christmas stories. Helene Stökl. With grammatical and explanatory notes by Dr. Wilhelm Bernhardt. Bost., D. C. Heath & Co., 1898. 168 p. (Heath's modern language series.) D. cl. .... .60 .54

For middle classes.

Y 60 (t)
M 72 sp
1556. **Speeches and table-talk of the prophet Mohammad:** chosen and translated, with introduction and notes. Stanley Lane-Poole. N. Y., Macmillan & Co., 1882. 196 p. S. (Golden treasury series.) cl. .... 1.00 .65

"The aim of this volume is to present all that is most enduring and memorable in the public orations and private sayings of Mohammed in such form that the general reader may be tempted to learn a little of what a great man was and what made him great." A large part of the book consists of chapters from the Koran, presenting the religious and ethical teachings of the prophet. It also contains sayings of Mohammed which were said in a private unofficial way to his circle of intimate friends. This is the most usable book of source material concerning Mohammedanism.

LIST OF BOOKS FOR HIGH SCHOOL LIBRARIES. 407

BOOK ARTS.

Z
―――
B 19 bo
                  List Price to
                 price. schools.

1557. [14.] **Book-lover:** a guide to the best reading. James Baldwin. Chic., A. C. McClurg & Co., 1898. 222 p. S. cl .... 1.00 .90

Some very suggestive thoughts on reading and the value of reading.

Z
―――
H 67 be

1558. [572.] **Beginnings of writing.** Walter James Hoffman. Int. by Frederick Starr. N. Y., D. Appleton & Co., 1895. 209 p. il. D. (Anthropological series.) cl. 1.75 1.15

An account of the beginning and early development of the art of writing. Leading chapters are: Pictographs on stone; pictographs on material other than stone; interpretation of pictographs; symbols, gesture signs, and attitudes; mnemonic signs; growth of conventional signs.

Z
―――
K 83 ma

1559. [13.] **Mastery of books:** hints on reading and the use of libraries. Harry Lyman Koopman. N. Y., American Book Company, 1896. 214 p. D. cl.. .90 .78

Valuable hints for the teacher. Older pupils will enjoy portions. Can be used in essay reading.

Z
―――
M 86 fo

1560. [12.] **Four years of novel reading:** an account of an experiment in popularizing the study of fiction. Ed. by Richard G. Moulton. Bost., D. C. Heath & Co., 1896. 100 p. D. cl....................... .50 .42

Shows the value of fiction reading and by illustration shows how to read fiction. A very suggestive book.

Z
―――
P 38 il

1561. [691.] **Illustration of books.** Joseph Pennell. N. Y., Century Co., 1898. 166 p. D. cl.............. 1.00 .65

The various methods of making and reproducing drawings for book and newspaper illustration.

408   LIST OF BOOKS FOR HIGH SCHOOL LIBRARIES.

Z
                                                                                                  List Price to
R 19 st   price. schools.

1562. **Story of books.** Gertrude Burford Rawlings. N. Y., D. Appleton & Co., 1901. 160 p. il. (Library of useful stories.) S. cl. .... .35 .31

Contents: Introductory: Preservation of literature; Books and libraries in classical times; Books in mediaeval times; Libraries in mediaeval times; Beginning of printing; Who invented movable types? Gutenberg and the Mentz press; Early printing; Early printing in Italy, England, Scotland, Ireland; Book binding; How a modern book is produced.

Interesting for Library reading.

BIBLIOGRAPHIES.

Zw

N 55 gu

1563. **Guide to the best historical novels and tales.** Jonathan Nield. N. Y., G. P. Putnam's Sons, 1902. 122 p. O. cl. 1.75 1.57

This volume will be helpful to the teacher of History. The author has suggested books of historical fiction which depict the life and events during each period of history, beginning with the Pre-Christian era up to, and including the nineteenth century.

GENERAL REFERENCE WORKS

A

Ad 1 jo

1564. [754.] **Johnson's universal cyclopaedia.** Charles K. Adams, ed. New ed. N. Y., D. Appleton & Co., 1900. 12 vols. il. maps plans. Q. cl........ 72.00 47.50

Every large library should have this encyclopaedia for reference. It is up to date and excellent in every respect and the publishers have made such a large reduction from the retail price that all schools should take advantage of it.

REFERENCE WORKS ON SPECIAL SUBJECTS.

Af

B 75 hi

#1565. **Historic note-book:** with an appendix of battles. Ebenezer Cobham Brewer. Phil., J. B. Lippincott Co., 1901. 997 p. D. hf. leath............... 3.50 2.30

This book is purely historical and explains with the greatest brevity, allusions to historical events, acts of parliament, treaties, and customs, terms and phrases, made in books, speeches, and familiar conversation.

LIST OF BOOKS FOR HIGH SCHOOL LIBRARIES. 409

Af
―――
B 97 lo

	List price.	Price to schools.

#1566. **Longmans' atlas of ancient geography.** Ed. by *Rev.* George Butler. N. Y., Longmans, Green & Co., 1899. 28 + 20 p. maps. Q. New ed. cl...... 2.00 1.80

The maps in this book were selected with a view of facilitating the study of ancient geography in connection with history. Particular attention has been paid to those maps which illustrate classical authors. In studying the history of any great campaign, such as Caesar's Gallic wars, a good general knowledge of the geography of the country can be obtained by studying these maps.

Af
―――
L 11 hi

1567. **Historical atlas, 3800 B. C. to 1886 A. D.** Robert H. Labberton. N. Y., Silver, Burdett & Co., 1891. Ed. 15. O. bds. 64 maps. 1.25 1.12

Contents: Maps on History of the East; Greek history; Roman history; Mediaeval history; Modern history; American history.

Af
―――
L 32 hi

1568. [755.] **History for ready reference:** from the best historians, biographers and specialists; their own words in a complete system of history for all uses, extending to all countries and subjects, and representing for both readers and students the better and newer literature of history in the English language, with numerous historical maps from original studies and drawings by Alan C. Reiley. Josephus N. Larned. Rev., enl. ed. Springfield, C. A. Nichols Co., 1901. 6 vols. Q. cl. 30.00 27.00

This is the most complete reference history published and should be in the library of every school that has a sufficient fund to purchase it.

Af 83
―――
H 23 ha

#1569. **Harper's encyclopaedia of United States history:** from 458 A. D. to 1902. Based upon the plan of Benson John Lossing, with special contributions covering every phase of American history and development by eminent authorities, including John Fiske, Wm. R. Harper, Albert Bushnell Hart, William T. Harris, Woodrow Wilson, Moses Coit Tyler, and others with a preface on the study of American history by Woodrow Wilson, and with original documents, portraits, maps, etc. N. Y., Harper & Bros., 1902. 10 vols. il. O. cl...... 35.00 33.25

An excellent, up-to-date reference history.

410 LIST OF BOOKS FOR HIGH SCHOOL LIBRARIES.

	List price.	Price to schools.
Ag C 44 lo 1570. Longmans' new school atlas. Ed. by Geo. G. Chisholm, *and* C. H. Leete. N. Y., Longmans, Green & Co., 1901. 32 p. Maps. Q. New ed. cl.....	1.50	1.35

"In the preparation of the present Atlas for use in schools three things have been aimed at, as of chief importance: first, the adequate representation of the physical features; second, the careful and somewhat exclusive selection of names; third, the facilitating of comparison as to size between the countries and regions included in the different maps. In order that the Atlas may also be used as a work of reference, a great many more names have been included in the index than are named on the maps."
An excellent geographical atlas.

Ag
T 85 ha
1571. [757.] **Handbook of Wisconsin, its history and geography.** Comp. by Lura J. *and* J. M. Turner. Burlington, Wis., J. M. Turner, 1898. 266 p. il. Q. cl. 3.75 1.00

This book contains much valuable information concerning Wisconsin that cannot be found in any other volume.

Ah
L 15 cy
#1572. **Cyclopaedia of political science, political economy, and of the political history of the United States.** John J. Lalor, ed. N. Y., Maynard, Merrill & Co., 1899. 3 vols. Q. cloth. 5.00 4.50

"In no country in the world is the necessity of the study of political science and political economy greater than in the United States, in which every citizen is, directly or indirectly,—through the medium of his vote—a legislator; and yet, in no great country, perhaps, has the study of politics as a science been so utterly neglected. Our experience as a people during the last decade has demonstrated how very important it is to lay before the great body of readers reliable works to which they may refer, when occasion requires, for the principles by which all great national questions are solved. The people of the United States for the past ten years, to go no farther back in their history, have been, so to speak, one great debating club, discussing such questions as the resumption of specie payments, contraction of the currency, inflation of the currency, money, paper money, the nature and cure of commercial depressions, the demonetization of silver, banks, savings banks, bi-metallism, the relations of capital and labor, the right of employment, socialism, communism, strikes, railroad policy, civil service, civil service reform, etc. . . .

Other questions equally important are springing up every year, both in the national and state legislatures, questions relating to interest, the hours of labor, taxation, temperance, etc. These and kindred questions are, or may very easily become, questions of prac-

| | List price. | Price to schools. |

tical politics, or of political economy as applied to politics. In the present work these and similar subjects can be found discussed, from the standpoint of the statesman and legislator, by the best minds of the age, each under its proper title and in alphabetical order."

This book wil be very helpful to the classes in History, Economics, and Government and contains much material that will be helpful to the debating societies and to students preparing orations and theses.

Aik
―――
B 97 ed

#1573. **Education in the United States:** a series of monographs prepared for the United States exhibit at the Paris exposition 1900. Nicholas Murray Butler, ed. 2 vols. N. Y., J. B. Lyon Company, 1900. 977 + 469 pp. maps and il. O. cl. 3.50   3.15

"The present work passes in review many tendencies in American education. It describes the organization and influence of each type of formal school; it takes note of the more informal and popular organizations for popular education and instruction; it discusses the educational problems raised by the existence of special classes and of special needs, and sets forth how the United States has set about solving these problems. It may truly be said to be a cross-section view of education in the United States in 1900."

Contents—Vol. 1: Introduction, by Nicholas Murray Butler; Educational organization and administration, by Andrew Sloan Draper; Kindergarten education, by Susan E. Blow; Elementary education, by W. T. Harris; Secondary education, by Elmer Ellsworth Brown; American college, by A. F. West; American university, by E. D. Perry; Education of women, by M. Carey Thomas; Training of teachers, by B. A. Hinsdale; School architecture and hygiene, by G. B. Morrison. Vol. 2: Professional education, by Ja. R. Parsons; Scientific, technical, and engineering education, by T. C. Mendenhall; Agricultural education, by C. W. Dabney; Commercial education, by Edmund J. James; Art and industrial education, by I. Edwards Clarke; Education of defectives, by E. E. Allen; Summer schools and university extension, by Herbert B. Adams; Scientific societies and associations, by Ja. McKeen Cattell; Education of the negro, by Booker T. Washington; Education of the Indian, by W. N. Hailmann.

Ax
―――
B 75 di

1574. **Dictionary of phrase and fable:** giving the derivation, source, or origin of common phrases, allusions, and words that have a tale to tell. Ebenezer Cobham Brewer. Phil., J. B. Lippincott Co., 1902. 1440 p. D. hf. leath. New ed., rev., enl. ...... 1.50   .98

The object of this book is to explain the meaning of words and expressions in which an allusion is made to some fable, custom, or character, more or less familiarly known.

Ax
C 84 en   List   Price to
                                                                   price. schools.
1575. [756.] **English synonyms explained in alphabetical
    order with copious illustrations, examples drawn
    from the best writers.** George Crabb. N. Y.,
    Harper & Bros. 856 p. D. cl..................   1.25   .82

Ax
So 8 dl
1576. **Dictionary of English synonyms and synonymous or
    parallel expressions:** designed as a practical guide
    to aptness and variety of phraseology. Richard
    Soule. New ed. rev., and enl. by George H. Howi-
    son. Bost., Little, Brown & Co., 1902. 488 p.
    O. cl. 2.00   1.30

The aim of this book has been to present at a single glance the words or modes of speech which denote the same object, or which express the same general idea, with only slight shades of difference. There has been no attempt at elaborate discussion of the nice distinctions that obtain between words apparently synonymous; but hints of such distinctions have been given whenever it was practicable to give them briefly in a parenthetical remark.

No high school library can be considered complete without a dictionary of synonyms. One often finds it necessary, for the sake of emphasis, to repeat the same idea, and, to avoid monotony, a variety of expression is required. This book will be found helpful in this direction. Again, when one is at a loss for a word or an expression which will suit a particular turn of thought, or mood of the mind, this dictionary will be found of great assistance.

Ax 36
L 58 el
1577. **Elementary Latin dictionary.** Charlton T. Lewis.
    N. Y., American Bk. Co., c1890. 952 p. D. cl...   2.00   1.70

An abridgment of Lewis's "Latin dictionary for schools." Every school having a Latin course should have either this edition or the larger unabridged one for reference.

Ax 47
Sch 5 fl
#1578. **Flügel-Schmidt-Tanger's Dictionary of the English
    and German languages, for home and school;** with
    special reference to Dr. Felix Flügel's "Universal
    English-German and German-English dictionary."
    In 2 pts.: pt. 1, English-German; pt. 2, German-
    English. Immanuel Schmidt *and* Gustav Tanger,
    eds. N. Y., Lemcke & Buechner, 1901. 968 +
    1006 pp. Q. hf. 2 mor......................   4.50   3.25

This is an excellent German dictionary for the schools that can afford it. The German-English volume will be sold separately to those who cannot afford both volumes.

LIST OF BOOKS FOR HIGH SCHOOL LIBRARIES. 413

Ax 47

W 61 co

                                                                        List Price to
price. schools.

1579. **Compendious German and English dictionary:** with notation of correspondences and brief etymologies. William Dwight Whitney. Assisted by August Hjalmar Edgren. N. Y., Henry Holt & Co., c1887. 538 + 362 p. O. cl. 1.50 1.35

Excellent for the smaller libraries.

Ay

Al 5 po

1580. **Poetical quotations from Chaucer to Tennyson:** with copious indexes. Samuel Austin Allibone. Phil., J. B. Lippicott Co., 1902. 788 p. O. cl......... 2.50 1.64

Ay

Al 5 pr

1581. **Prose quotations from Socrates to Macaulay:** with indexes. Samuel Austin Allibone. Phil., J. B. Lippincott Co., 1901. 764 p. O. cl............. 2.50 1.64

One often hears or reads a poetical or prose quotation and desires to know its source. These books supply one with this information. There is a complete index to subjects, first lines and authors.

The quotations in the body of the book are arranged under subjects which makes the book helpful to one wanting quotations to illustrate some particular point which he may have in mind.

Ay

B 28 fa

#1582. **Familiar quotations:** a collection of passages, phrases, and proverbs traced to their sources in ancient and modern literature. John Bartlett. Bost., Little, Brown & Co., 1900. 1158 p. O. Ed. 9. cl. 3.00 1.96

Familiar quotations in this volume are arranged under author's names. The book has an author and a general subject index.

Ay

B 75 re

#1583. **Reader's handbook:** of famous names in fiction, allusions, references, proverbs, plots, stories, and poems. Ebenezer Cobham Brewer. Phil., J. B. Lippincott Co., 1902. 1243 p. D. hf. leath. New ed. 3.50 2.30

"The object of this Handbook is to supply readers and speakers with a lucid but very brief account of such names as are used in allusions and references, whether by poets or prose writers,—to

                                                                                List Price to
                                                                            price. schools.

furnish those who consult it with the plot of popular dramas, the story of epic poems, and the outline of well-known tales.

"It gives in a few lines the story of Homer's Iliad and Odyssey, of Virgil's Aeneid, Lucan's Pharsalia, and the Thebaid of Statius; of Dante's Divine Comedy, Ariosto's Orlando Furioso, and Tasso's Jerusalem delivered; of Milton's Paradise lost and Paradise regained; of Thompson's Seasons; of Ossian's Tales, the Nibelungen Lied of the German minnesingers, the Romance of the Rose, the Lusiad of Camoens, the Loves of Theagenes and Charicleia by Heliodorus (fourth century), with the several story poems of Chaucer, Gower, Piers Plowman, Hawes, Spenser, Drayton, Phineas Fletcher, Prior, Goldsmith, Campbell, Southey, Byron, Scott, Moore, Tennyson, Longfellow, and so on. Far from limiting its scope to poets, the Handbook tells, with similar brevity, the stories of our national fairy tales and romances, such novels as those by Charles Dickens, Vanity Fair by Thackeray, the Rasselas by Johnson, Gulliver's Travels by Swift, the Sentimental Journey by Sterne, Don Quixote and Gil Blas, Telemachus by Fenelon, and Undine by De la Motte Fouque. Great pains have been taken with the Arthurian stories, whether from Sir T. Malory's collection or from the *Mabinogion,* because Tennyson has brought them to the front in his Idylls of the King, and the number of dramatic plots sketched out is many hundreds.

"Another striking and interesting feature of the book is the revelation of the source from which dramatists and romancers have derived their stories, and the strange repetitions of historic incidents."

Two appendices are added. The first contains the name, birthplace, dates of birth and death, and a pretty full list of works (first editions, dated) of our principal authors."

"Appendix II contains the names and dates of the ancient Greek and Latin plays, with those of the best-known translations and imitations; the names and dates of those French and German dramas which have been adapted to the English stage, or have been borrowed from our own dramatists; and the titles, names, and dates of some thousands of British plays."

A valuable reference book for the High school library.

Ay

B 84 ne
#1584. **New library of poetry and song.** William Cullen Bryant, ed., with his review of poets and poetry from the time of Chaucer. Revised and enlarged with recent authors, and containing a dictionary of poetical quotations. N. Y., Fords, Howard & Hulbert, c1900. 1100 p. pors and il. O. cl...... 3.00 2.00

    A well known, standard compilation of the best in poetry and song, including a dictionary of poetical quotations. Many manuscript and autograph fac-similes of authors are given, and frequent illustrations make it an attractive volume. The book has recently been thoroughly revised and is up-to-date. This volume should only be purchased by the largest libraries.

LIST OF BOOKS FOR HIGH SCHOOL LIBRARIES.

		List price.	Price to schools.

Ay
―
C 35 yo

1585. **Young folks' cyclopaedia of literature and art.** John Denison Champlin. N. Y., Henry Holt & Co., 1901. 604 p. il. O. cl. 2.50 1.60

A brief account of the acknowledged masterpieces in literature and in art. In literature the great works in all languages, some popular works, many juvenile books, the principal characters in fiction and in poetry, the pen-names of prominent writers, such popular names of persons and places as have found their way into literature, and many familiar short poems and hymns are described. In architecture are described the most important cathedrals, temples, castles, monuments, and other important structures, accompanied usually with suitable illustrations; in sculpture, the principal statues of the world, especially those that have come down to us from antiquity, also with illustrations; in painting, the great masterpieces of the European galleries, with outline illustrations from noted French etchings; and in music, the popular operas, symphonies, and other great musical works, and many familiar songs.

This is a new volume in the series of Young Folks Cyclopaedias. The previous volumes are on the Township list.

Ay
―
H 85 cy

1586. **Cyclopedia of practical quotations:** English, Latin, and modern foreign languages. New ed., rev., enl. J. K. Hoyt. N. Y., Funk & Wagnalls Company, 1896. 1178 p. O. cl.......................... 6.00 5.40

Possibly the most complete book of quotations in print, if accessibility be considered. Besides the regular list of quotations arranged alphabetically according to subjects, there is a topical index with cross references, and an extensive "key-word" concordance to English quotations which enables one to find almost any poetical or prose reference. Besides these features, there is a list of proverbs and well known sayings, quotations from the Latin and modern foreign languages (with translations), Latin and French mottoes, a concordance to Latin and modern foreign quotations, and a list of noted authors and pages whereon quoted.

Ay
―
W 56 ex

1587. **Explanatory and pronouncing dictionary of the noted names of fiction.** William A. Wheeler. Bost., Houghton, Mifflin & Co., 1898. 440 p. D. cl.... 2.00 1.30

This is really a pronouncing encyclopaedia of names found in fiction. Rules are given for pronunciation of foreign words. There is also an index of the real names of persons, places, etc., whose nicknames, pseudonyms, or popular appellations, are given in the preceding dictionary. This book should only be purchased by the largest libraries.

		List price.	Price to schools.
Ay 32 Sm 6 di #158S. Dictionary of Greek and Roman antiquities. William Smith, Ed. 3. carefully rev. by Charles Anthon. N. Y., Harper & Bros., c1843. 1124 p. il. Q. sh.		4.25	3.62

A guide to a knowledge of Greek and Roman antiquities. Will be found of great assistance to classical students dealing with the modern and ancient languages, and likewise to students of English literature.

PERIODICALS.

Every school should take two or three periodicals. Some of the magazines listed contain much material that will be of service in the preparation of lessons.

Atlantic	$4.00	$3.50
Boston cooking school magazine	1.00	.90
Cassier's magazine	3.00	2.70
Century	4.00	3.75
Country life	3.00	1.75
Harper	4.00	3.50
Harper's weekly	4.00	3.50
McClure	1.00	.90
Outlook	3.00	2.80
Review of reviews	2.50	2.25
Scribner	3.00	2.85
World's work	3.00	1.75

See also Periodicals listed in the 1902 "List of books for Township libraries."

Doubleday, Page & Co. have made a great reduction on the price of both the magazines listed that are published by them, "World's work" and "Country life." "World's work" is one of the best magazines on current events published, and should be in every high school library in the state.

AUTHOR AND TITLE INDEX.

782.	A. B. C. of electricity	W. H. Meadowcroft
783.	A. B. C of the X-ray	W. H. Meadowcroft
36.	Aaron Burr	H. C. Merwin
1337.	Abandoned claim	F. H. Loughead
1307.	Abbe Constantin	Ludovic Halévy
1126.	Abbott, Charles Conrad	Notes of the night
	Abbott, Evelyn, ed	See Heroes of the Nation series
37.	Abbott, Jacob.	Julius Caesar
122.	Abbott, Jacob	King Philip
31.	Abbott, John S. C	Daniel Boone
134.	Abbott, John S. C	Ferdinand De Soto
90.	Abbott, John S. C	Life of John Paul Jones
135.	Abbott, John S. C	Miles Standish
943.	A-birding on a bronco	F. A. Merriam
854.	About the weather	M. W. Harrington
97.	Abraham Lincoln	Norman Hapgood
98.	Abraham Lincoln	J. T. Morse
99.	Abraham Lincoln	Carl Schurz
901.	According to season	F. T. Parsons
536.	Across Asia on a bicycle	T. G. Allen, jr., and W. L. Sachtleben
559.	Across Greenland's ice-fields	M. Douglas
534.	Across Russia from the Baltic to the Danube	C. A. Stoddard
1295.	Across the campus	C. M. Fuller
1279.	Adam Bede	George Eliot
18.	Adams Charles Francis, jr	Charles Francis Adams
756.	Adams, Charles Francis	Physical laboratory manual
477.	Adams, Cyrus C	Text-book of commercial geography
48.	Adams, Charles Kendall	Christopher Columbus
180.	Adams, Charles Kendall	Manual of historical literature
1564.	Adams, Charles Kendall, ed	Johnson's Universal cyclopaedia
1483.	Adams, Charles Kendall, ed	Representative British orations
200.	Adams, George Burton	Civilization during the middle ages
216.	Adams, George Burton	European history
265.	Adams, George Burton	Growth of the French nation
197.	Adams, George Burton	Medieval and modern history
643.	Adams, John	Herbartian psychology applied to education
1022.	Adams W. I. Lincoln	Amateur photography
621.	Adams, Jane.	Democracy and social ethics
92.	Addison, Daniel Dulany	Lucy Larcom; life, letters, and diary
1127.	Addison, Joseph	Spectator
611.	Adler Felix	Moral instruction of children
1523.	Aeneid. Cranch, trans	Virgil

27

1490.	Aeschylus. Swanvick, *trans.*	Dramas
1491.	Aeschylus. More, *trans.*	Prometheus bound
1492.	Aeschylus. Plumptre, *trans.*	Tragedies
343.	Africa	H. M. Stanley *and others*
1468.	Afterwhiles	J. W. Riley
305.	Age of Anne	E. E. Morris
3.	Age of chivalry	Thomas Bulfinch
283.	Age of Elizabeth	Mandell Creighton
4.	Age of fable	Thomas Bulfinch
1195.	A-hunting of the deer, and other essays	C. D. Warner
1.	Aikins, Herbert Austin	Principles of logic
974.	Air, water and food from a sanitary standpoint...E. H. Richards, *and* A. G. Woodman	
67.	Albert Gallatin	J. A. Stevens
1483.	Alden, John, *ed.*	Representative British orations, v. 4
1047.	Alden, Raymond MacDonald	Art of debate
1197.	Aldrich, Thomas Bailey	Marjorie Daw and other stories
1429.	Aldrich, Thoms Bailey	Poems
75.	Alexander Hamilton	C. A. Conant
76.	Alexander Hamilton	H. C. Lodge
25.	Alfred the Great	Thomas Hughes
353.	Alger, Russell A.	Spanish-American war
1319.	Alhambra	Washington Irving
1219.	All sorts and conditions of men	Walter Besant
279.	Allen, Frederick J.	Topical outline of English history
878.	Allen, Grant. Colours of flowers as illustrated in the British flora
821.	Allen, Grant	Flashlights on nature
1199.	Allen, James Lane	Flute and violin
1200.	Allen, James Lane	Kentucky cardinal
536.	Allen, Thomas Gaskell, *jr., and* Sachtleben, W. L.........Across Asia on a bicycle
72.	Allen, Walter	Ulysses S. Grant
181.	Allen, William Francis	History topics
191.	Allen, William Francis, *and* Myers, Philip Van Ness.........Ancient history
1580.	Allibone, Samuel Austin...........Poetical quotations from Chaucer to Tennyson
1581.	Allibone, Samuel Austin...........Prose quotations from Socrates to Macaulay
545.	Alone in China, and other stories	Julian Ralph
721.	Alton, Edmund	Among the law-makers
1022.	Amateur photography	W. I. L. Adams
970.	Amateur's practical garden-book..C. E. Hunn, *and* L. H. Bailey
1105.	American anthology, 1787-1900	E. C. Stedman, *ed.*
662.	American at Oxford	John Corbin
990.	American boy's book of sport	D. C. Beard
636.	American charities	A. G. Warner
	American citizen series.	
	Wright, C. D. Outline of practical sociology.	
724.	American commonwealth	James Bryce
	American commonwealth series, *ed.*......... by H. E. Scudder	
	Barrows, William. Oregon.	
	Carr, Lucien. Missouri.	
	Cooke, J. E. Virginia.	
	Johnston, Alexander. Connecticut.	
	Royce, Josiah. California.	

357.	American fights and fighters	C. T. Brady
939.	American game fishes.	
1249.	American girl in London	*Mrs.* Everard Cotes
992.	American girl's home book of work and play	Helen Campbell
485.	American girl's trip to the Orient and around the world	Christine Collbran
736.	American government	B. A. Hinsdale
986.	American highways	N. S. Shaler
391.	American history leaflets: colonial and constitutional	A. B. Hart, *and* Edward Channing, *eds.*

American history series.
    Burgess, J. W. Civil war and the constitution.
    Burgess, J. W. Middle period, 1817–1858.
    Burgess, J. W. Reconstruction and the constitution, 1866–1876.
    Fisher, G. P. Colonial era.
    Sloane, W. M. French war and the revolution.
    Walker, F. A. Making of the nation.

392.	American history told by contemporaries: Vol. 1. Era of colonization, 1492–1689	A. B. Hart, *ed.*
393.	American history told by contemporaries: Vol. II:: Building of the republic, 1689–1783	A. B. Hart, *ed.*
394.	American history told by contemporaries: vol. III: National expansion, 1783–1845	A. B. Hart, *ed.*
395.	American history told by contemporaries: Vol IV: Welding of the nation, 1845–1900	A. B. Hart, *ed.*
1181.	American ideals and other essays	Theodore Roosevelt
1076.	American lands and letters	D. G. Mitchell
163.	American leaders and heroes	W. F. Gordy
1079.	American literature	A. G. Newcomber
1082.	American literature, 1607–1885	C. F. Richardson

American men of energy series.
    Audubon, Lucy. John James Audubon.
    Brooks, Noah. Henry Knox.
    Livingston, W. F. Israel Putnam.
    Robins, Edward. Benjamin Franklin.

American men of letters series; *ed.* by Charles Dudley Warner.
    Higginson, T. W. Margaret Fuller Ossoli.
    Holmes, O. W. Ralph Waldo Emerson.
    Warner, C. D. Washington Irving.

1486.	American orations	Alexander Johnston, *ed.*
726.	American political history	V. A. Conklin
729.	American political ideas	John Fiske
380.	American Revolution	John Fiske
403.	American Revolution, 1763–1783	W. E. H. Lecky

American science series.
    Barker, G. F. Physics.
    Holden, E. S. Elementary astronomy.
    Martin, H. N. Human body.
    Packard, A. S. Zoology.
    Remsen, Ira. Introduction to the study of chemistry.
    Walker, F. A. First lessons in political economy.
    Walker, F. A. Political economy (advanced course).
    Wilson, E. B., and Sedgwick, W. T. Introduction to general biology.

American statesmen series; *ed.* by John T. Morse, *jr.*
    Adams, C. F., *jr.* Charles Francis Adams.
    Gay, S. H. James Madison.
    Gilman, D. C. James Monroe.
    Holst. *Dr.* H. von John C. Calhoun.
    Hosmer, J. K. Samuel Adams.
    Lodge, H. C. Alexander Hamilton.
    Lodge, H. C. Daniel Webster.
    Lodge, H. C. George Washington.
    Lothrop, T. K. William Henry Seward.
    Magruder, A. B. John Marshall.
    Morse, J. T. *jr.* Abraham Lincoln.
    Morse, J. T. John Adams.
    Morse, J. T. John Quincy Adams.
    Morse, J. T. Thomas Jefferson.
    Roosevelt, Theodore. Gouverneur Morris.
    Roosevelt, Theodore. Thomas Hart Benton.
    Schurz, Carl. Life of Henry Clay.
    Stevens, J. A. Albert Gallatin.
    Sumner, W. M. Andrew Jackson.
    Tyler, M. C. Patrick Henry.

American teachers series: *ed.* by James E. Russell.
    Bennett, C. E., *and* Bristol, G. P. Teaching of Latin and Greek.
    Bourne, H. E. Teaching of history and civics.
    Smith, Alexander, *and* Hall, E. H. Teaching of chemistry and physics.

362.	American territorial development	H. W. Caldwell
1449.	American war ballads and lyrics	G. C. Eggleston, *ed.*
622.	America's race problem.	
757.	Ames, Joseph S.	Theory of physics
524.	Amicis, Edmondo de	Holland and its people
1162.	Among my books	J. R. Lowell
721.	Among the law-makers	Edmund Alton
940.	Among the water-fowl	H. K. Job
191.	Ancient history	W. F. Allen *and* P. N. Myers
1526.	Andersen, Hans Christian	Märchen

Anderson, Melville B., *trans. See* Saint-Pierre, J. H. B. de,
    Paul and Virginia

192.	**Anderson, Robert E.**	
	Story of extinct civilization of the East	
84.	Andrew Jackson	W. G. Sumner
594.	**Andrews, C. C.**	Brazil
354.	**Andrews, Elisha Benjamin**	
	History of the last quarter-century in the United States	
1019.	Angling	L. M. Yale *and others*
919.	Animals	D. S. Jordan, *and* V. L. Kellogg, *and* Harold Heath
1362.	Anne of Geierstein	*Sir* Walter Scott

Anthropological series.
    Grosse, Ernst. Beginnings of art.
    Hoffman, W. J. Beginnings of writing.

1509.	Antigone. Palmer, *trans.*	Sophocles
1363.	Antiquary	*Sir* Walter Scott
913.	Apes and monkeys	H. L. Garner
932.	**Apgar, Austin C.**	
	Birds of the United States east of the Rocky mountains	

AUTHOR AND TITLE INDEX. 421

685. Apperception ....Karl Lange
Appleton's home reading books series.
    Baskett, J. N. Story of the fishes.
    Harrington, M. W. About the weather.
    Holden, E. S. Family of the sun.
Appleton's life histories series.
    Thwaites, R. G. Father Marquette.
687. Applied psychology ....J. A. McLellan
428. Arber, Edward, *ed.* ....Story of the Pilgrim fathers
212. Archer, T. A. ....Crusaders
848. Archibald, Douglas ....Story of the earth's atmosphere
1493. Aristophanes. Hickie, *trans.* ....Comedies
1494. Aristotle. Kenyon, *trans.* ....On the Athenian constitution
663. Aristotle ....Thomas Davidson
1469. Armazindy ....J. W. Riley
111. Armstrong, Edward ....Lorenzo de' Medici
1148. Army life in a black regiment ....T. W. Higginson
905. Arnold, Augusta Foote ....Sea-beach at ebb-tide
1430. Arnold, Edwin ....Lotus and jewel
1431. Arnold, Matthew ....Selected poems
1432. Arnold, Matthew ....Sohrab and Rustum
1059. Arnold, Thomas ....Manual of English literature
1037. Art for art's sake ....J. C. Van Dyke
967. Art of cookery ....E. P. Ewing
1047. Art of debate ....R. M. Alden
1049. Art of reading aloud ....J. S. Clark
676. Art of study ....B. A. Hinsdale
1046. Art of writing English ....J. M. D. Meiklejohn
1196. As we were saying ....C. D. Warner
871. Ascent of man ....Henry Drummond
747. Ashmore, Ruth ......Business girl in every phase of her life
1074. Aspects of fiction and other ventures in criticism ....
    ....Brander Matthews
863. Aspects of the earth ....N. S. Shaler
819. Astronomy ....Isaac Sharpless, *and* G. M. Philips
818. Astronomy with an opera-glass ....G. P. Serviss
510. At home in Italy ....*Mrs.* E. D. (Rice) Bianciardi
232. Athenian empire ....G. W. Cox
1010. Athletic sports ....D. A. Sargent, *and others*
759. Atkinson, Edmund ....Natural philosophy
599. Atkinson, Edward ....Distribution of products
879. Atkinson, G. F. ....Elementary botany
758. Atkinson, Philip ....Electricity for everybody
1201. Austen, Jane ....Pride and prejudice
1203. Austin, Jane G. ....Betty Alden
1202. Austin, Jane G. ....Standish of Standish
64. Autobiography of Benjamin Franklin.
1021. Autobiography of Joseph Jefferson.
1154. Autocrat of the breakfast-table ....O. W. Holmes
760. Avery, Elroy M., *and* Sinnott, C. P.
    ....First lessons in physical science
761. Avery, Elroy M. ....School physics
586. Awakening of a Nation ....C. F. Lummis

1299. Back to the soil ....Bradley Gilman
538. Bacon, Alice Mabel ....Japanese girls and women
537. Bacon, Alice Mabel ....Japanese interior
550. Bacon, Lee (*Mrs.* Henry Bacon) ....Our houseboat on the Nile
27. Bacon ....R. W. Church
906. Badenoch, L. N. ....Romance of the insect world
Bailey, Henry Turner, *jt. author. See* Burrage, Severance.
880. Bailey, Liberty H. ....Botany
961. Bailey, Liberty H. ....Garden-making
881. Bailey, Liberty H. ....Lessons with plants
962. Bailey, Liberty H., *ed.* ....Principles of agriculture
Bailey, L. H., *jt. author. See* Hunn, C. E.
982. Baker, Moses Nelson ....Municipal engineering and sanitation
963. Baker, Ray Stannard ....Boy's book of inventions
527. Baker, Ray Stannard ....Seen in Germany
218. Balance of power ....Arthur Hassall
1557. Baldwin, James ....Book-lover
645. Baldwin, Joseph ...... Elementary psychology and education
646. Baldwin, Joseph ......School management and school methods
808. Ball, *Sir* Robert Stawell ....Earth's beginning
809. Ball, *Sir* Robert Stawell ....Starland
1433. Ballad-book ....K. L. Bates, *ed.*
588. Ballou, Maturin M. ....Due south
595. Ballou, Maturin M. ....Equatorial America
482. Ballou, Maturin M. ....Foot-prints of travel
576. Ballou, Maturin M. ....New Eldorado
490. Ballou, Maturin M. ....Travels under the southern cross
907. Bamford, Mary E...................Up and down the brooks
355. Bancroft, George ....History of the formation of
................the constitution of the United States
356. Bancroft, George' ....History of the United States
491. Bancroft, Hubert Howe ....New Pacific
1488. Bangs, John Kendrick ....Coffee and repartee
1317. Barbara's heritage ....D. L. Hoyt
1204. Barbour, Ralph Henry ....Half back
Baring-Gould, Sabine. *See* Gould, Sabine Baring-.
762. Barker, George F. ....Physics
763. Barker, George F., *ed.* ....Röntgen rays
1205. Barlow, Jane ....Irish idylls
1260. Barnaby Rudge ....Charles Dickens
882. Barnes, Charles Reid ....Plant life
63. Barnes, James ....David Glasgow Farragut
1206. Barnes, James ....Drake and his yeomen
1207. Barnes, James ....For king or country
1208. Barnes, James ....Loyal traitor
1209. Barnes, James ....Princetonian
647. Barnes, Mary Sheldon ....Studies in historical method
1210. Barrie, James M. ....Little minister
1211. Barrie, James M. ....Sentimental Tommy
1212. Barrie, James M. ....Tommy and Grizel
1213. Barrie, James M. ....When a man's single
1214. Barrie, James M. ....Window in Thrums
1582. Bartlett, John ....Familiar quotations
1215. Barton, William E. ....Pine knot
909. Baskett, James Newton ....Story of the fishes

AUTHOR AND TITLE INDEX. 423

908. Baskett, James Newton, *and* Ritmars, R. L. ....
................Story of the amphibians and the reptiles
462. Barrows, William ....Oregon
1060. Bates, Arlo ....Talks on the study of literature
1040. Bates, Arlo ....Talks on writing English
1433. Bates, Katherine Lee, *ed.* ....Ballad-book
1092. Bates, Katherine Lee, *and* Coman, Katharine, *comps.* ....
................English history as told by English poets
810. Bayne, Samuel G. ....Pith of astronomy
1238. Bayou folk ....Kate Chopin
509. Bazin, René ....Italians of today
Beacon biographical series; *ed.* by M. A. De Wolfe Howe.
 Barnes, James. David Glasgow Farragut.
 Burton, Richard. John Greenleaf Whittier.
 Chamberlain, J. E. John Brown.
 Chestnutt, C. W. Frederick Douglas.
 Fields, *Mrs.* J. T. Nathaniel Hawthorne.
 Hale, E. E., *jr.* James Russell Lowell.
 Hapgood, Norman. Daniel Webster.
 Howe, M. A. D. Phillips Brooks.
 Merwin, H. C. Aaron Burr.
 Trent, W. P. Robert E. Lee.

165-174. Beacon lights of history ....John Lord
1094. Beacon lights of patriotism ....H. B. Carrington
990. Beard, D. C. ....American boy's book of sport
922. Beasts of the field ....W. J. Long
80. Beazley, Charles Raymond ....Prince Henry the navigator
228. Becker, W. A. ....Charicles
244. Becker, W. A. ....Gallus
1061. Beers, Henry A. ....Studies in American letters
245. Beesley, Augustus Henry ....Gracchi, Marius, and Sulla
439. Beginners of a nation ....Edward Eggleston
201. Beginning of the middle ages ....R. W. Church
1028. Beginnings of art ....Ernst Grosse
441. Beginnings of New England ....John Fiske
1558. Beginnings of writing ....W. J. Hoffman
Bell, Alexander Melville, *jt. author. See* Bell, David Charles.
1023. Bell, *Mrs.* Arthur ....Elementary history of art
Bell, Clara, *trans. See* Ebers, Georg. Uarda
1110. Bell, David Charles ....Reader's Shakespeare
1093. Bell, David Charles, *and* Bell, A. M. .....Standard elocutionist
Bell, *Capt.* Henry, *trans. See* Luther, Martin.
..........Selections from the table-talk of Martin Luther
Bell, *Mrs.* Nancy R. E. M. *See* Bell, *Mrs.* Arthur.
1216. Bellamy, Edward ....Duke of Stockbridge
1217. Bellamy, Edward ....Looking backward
1398. Ben-Hur ....Lew Wallace
984. Bench work in wood ....W. F. M. Goss
358. Beneath old roof-trees ....A. E. Brown
330. Benjamin, S. G. W. ....Story of Persia
229. Benjamin, S. G. W. ....Troy
648. Bennett, Charles E., *and* Bristol, G. P. ....
................Teaching of Latin and Greek
1218. Bennett, John ....Master sky-lark
1434. Beowulf ....J. M. Garnett, *trans.*

884.	Bergen, Joseph Y.	Foundations of botany
885.	Bergen, Joseph Y.	Handbook for the use of teachers
	Bergen, Joseph Y., *jt. author. See* Hall, Edwin H.	
493.	Bermuda	J. C. R. Dorr
1219.	Besant, Walter	All sorts and conditions of men
1220.	Besant, Walter	Children of Gibeon
518.	Besant, Walter	East London
24.	Besant, Walter	Story of King Alfred
1403.	Beside the bonnie brier bush	John Watson
1203.	Betty Alden	J. G. Austin
510.	Bianciardi, *Mrs.* E. Dickinson (Rice)	At home in Italy
689.	Bibliography of education	W. S. Monroe
182.	Bigelow, Poultney	Children of the Nations
551.	Bigelow, Poultney	White man's Africa
1395.	Biography of a grizzly	Ernest Seton-Thompson
539.	Bird, Isabella L.	Unbeaten tracks in Japan
938.	Bird book	F. H. Eckstorm
937.	Bird homes	A. R. Dugmore
936.	Bird-life	F. M. Chapman
945.	Bird-lover in the west	*Mrs.* H. M. Miller
933.	Bird neighbors	Neltje Blanchan
1130.	Birds and bees	John Burroughs
1187.	Birds in the bush	Bradford Torrey
932.	Birds of the United States east of the Rocky mountains ..... A. C. Apgar	
944.	Birds of village and field	F. A. Merriam
934.	Birds that hunt and are hunted	Neltje Blanchan
502.	Bits of travel	H. H. Jackson
568.	Bits of travel at home	H. H. Jackson
1381.	Black arrow	R. L. Stevenson
1384.	Black dwarf and Legend of Montrose	*Sir* Walter Scott
1221.	Blackmore, Richard Doddridge	Lorna Doone
933.	Blanchan, Neltje	Bird neighbors
934.	Blanchan, Neltje	Birds that hunt and are hunted
886.	Blanchan, Neltje	Nature's garden
	Blanchard, Frederick M., *jt. author. See* Clark, Solomon H.	
1261.	Bleak house	Charles Dickens
465.	Blockaded family	P. A. Hague
914.	Blossom hosts and insect guests	W. H. Gibson
649.	Blow, Susan E.	Letters to a mother
650.	Blow, Susan E.	Symbolic education
1346.	Bob, son of battle	Alfred Ollivant
2.	Bok, Edward	Successward
935.	Bolles, Frank	From Blomidon to Smoky
652.	Bolton, Frederick E.	Secondary school systems of Germany
151.	Bolton, Sarah Knowles	Famous European artists
152.	Bolton, Sarah Knowles	Famous leaders among men
154.	Bolton, Sarah Knowles	Famous leaders among women
153.	Bolton, Sarah Knowles	Famous voyagers and explorers
155.	Bolton, Sarah Knowles	Lives of poor boys who became famous
156.	Bolton, Sarah Knowles	Successful women
	Bon, Andre Le. *See* Le Bon, Andre.	
1231.	Bonaventure	G. W. Cable
849.	Bonney, T. G.	Ice-work present and past
850.	Bonney, T. G.	Volcanoes

AUTHOR AND TITLE INDEX.

1557. Book-lover ....James Baldwin
1100. Book of eloquence ....C. D. Warner
1467. Book of famous verse ....Agnes Repplier, *comp.*
450. Book of New England legends and folk-lore.......S. A. Drake
825. Book of the ocean ....Ernest Ingersoll
1165. Books and culture ....H. W. Mabie
1174. Books and men ....Agnes Repplier
653. Boone, Richard G. ....Education in the United States
623. Booth, *Gen.* William ....In darkest England
561. Boots and saddles ....E. B. Custer
972. Boston school kitchen text-book ....*Mrs.* M. J. Lincoln
89. Boswell, James ....Life of Samuel Johnson
880. Botany ....L. H. Bailey
230. Botsford, George Willis ....History of Greece
246. Botsford, George Willis ....History of Rome
1062. Botta, Anne C. Lynch ....Handbook of universal literature
352. Bourinot, J. G. ....Story of Canada
654. Bourne, Henry E. ....Teaching of history and civics
655. Bowen, H. Courthope ....
  ....Fröebel, and education through self-activity
600. Bowker, Richard Rogers ....Economics for the people
671. Boy problem ....W. B. Forbush
32. Boyesen, Hjalmar H. ....Goethe and Schiller
82. Boynton, Henry W. ....Washington Irving
827. Boys' and girls' Pliny ....J. S. White
963. Boy's book of inventions ....R. S. Baker
1422. Boy's Froissart .... Sidney Lanier, *ed.*
1423. Boy's King Arthur ....Sidney Lanier
419. Boys of 1812 ....J. R. Soley
367. Boys of '76 ....C. C. Coffin
1460. Boy's Percy ....Sidney Lanier, *ed.*
1128. Brackett, Anna C., *ed.* ......Woman and the higher education
357. Brady, Cyrus Townsend ....American fights and fighters
429. Brady, Cyrus Townsend ....Colonial fights and fighters
1222. Brady, Cyrus Townsend ....,....For love of country
319. Brave little Holland ....W. E. Griffis
594. Brazil ....C. C. Andrews
1574. Brewer, Ebenezer Cobham ....Dictionary of phrase and fable
1565. Brewer, Ebenezer Cobham ....Historic notebook
1583. Brewer, Ebenezer Cobham ....
  ....Reader's handbook of famous names in fiction
1365. Bride of Lammermoor ....*Sir* Walter Scott
774. Brief course in general physics ....G. A. Hoadley
1048. Briefs for debate ......W. D. B. Brookings, *and* R. C. Ringwalt
828. Brigham, Albert Perry ....Text-book of geology
   Brigham, Albert Perry, *jt. author.* *See* Gilbert, Karl Grove.
280. Bright, *Rev.* James Franck ....History of England
951. Brinckley, William J. ....Physiology
   Bristol, George P., *jt. author.* *See* Bennett, Charles E.
1063. Bronson, Walter C. ......Short history of American literature
1064. Brooke, Stopford A. ....English literature
112. Brooke, Stopford A. ....Milton
1048. Brookings, W. Du Bois ....Briefs for debate
157. Brooks, Elbridge S. ....Great men's sons
158. Brooks, Geraldine ......Dames and daughters of colonial days
159. Brooks, Geraldine ....
  ....Dames and daughters of the young Republic

722.	Brooks, Noah	How the Republic is governed
723.	Brooks, Noah	Short studies in party politics
	Brooks-Hunt, Violet. See Hunt, Violet Brooks-.	
358.	Brown, Abram English	Beneath old roof-trees
1224.	Brown, Alice	Meadow-grass
1024.	Brown, Gerald Baldwin	Fine arts
1223.	Brown, Helen Dawes	Her sixteenth year
1225.	Brown, John	Rab and his friends
56.	Brown, William Garrett	Stephen Arnold Douglas
1436.	Browning, Mrs. Elizabeth Barrett	Poems
656.	Browning, Oscar ... Introduction to the history of educational theories	
1437.	Browning, Robert	Complete poetic and dramatic works
964.	Bruncken, Ernest	North American forests and forestry
247.	Bryans, Clement, and Hendy, F. J. R. ... History of the Roman republic	
1438.	Bryant, William Cullen	Poetical works
	Bryant, William Cullen, trans. See Homer. Iliad.	
1584.	Bryant, William Cullen, ed.	New library of poetry and song
724.	Bryce, James	American commonwealth
248.	Bryce, James	Holy Roman empire
337.	Bryce, James	Impressions of South Africa
68.	Bryce, James	William Ewart Gladstone
422.	Buccaneers and pirates of our coasts	F. R. Stockton
753.	Buckley, Arabella B.	Fairy-land of science
910.	Buckley, Arabella B.	Life and her children
3.	Bulfinch, Thomas	Age of chivalry
4.	Bulfinch, Thomas	Age of fable
5.	Bulfinch, Thomas	Legends of Charlemagne
313.	Building of the British empire	A. T. Story
368.	Building the nation	C. C. Coffin
483.	Bullen, Frank T. ... Cruise of the Cachalot round the world after sperm whales	
484.	Bullen, Frank T.	Idylls of the sea
492.	Bullen, Frank T.	Log of a sea-waif
1129.	Bullen, Frank T.	Sack of shakings
601.	Bullock, Charles J. ... Essays on the monetary history of the United States	
1226.	Bulwer-Lytton, Sir Edward G.	Last days of Pompeii
1227.	Bulwer-Lytton, Sir Edward G.	Last of the barons
1228.	Bunner, H. Cuyler	Love in old cloathes
1229.	Bunyan, John	Pilgrim's Progress
748.	Burdick, Francis M.	Essentials of business law
359.	Burgess, John W.	Civil war and the constitution
360.	Burgess, John W.	Middle period, 1817-1858
361.	Burgess, John W.	Reconstruction and the constitution
991.	Burlingame, H. J.	Hermann, the magician
1230.	Burnett, Frances Hodgson	Louisiana
1439.	Burns, Robert	Complete poetical works
983.	Burrage, Severance, and Bailey, H. T. ... School sanitation and decoration	
1130.	Burroughs, John	Birds and bees
1131.	Burroughs, John	Fresh fields
1132.	Burroughs, John	Locusts and wild honey
1133.	Burroughs, John	Pepacton
1134.	Burroughs, John	Signs and seasons

AUTHOR AND TITLE INDEX.

1135.	Burroughs, John	Wake-robin
1136.	Burroughs, John	Winter sunshine
1440.	Burroughs, John, ed.	Songs of nature
1065.	Burt, Mary E.	Literary landmarks
147.	Burton, Richard	John Greenleaf Whittier
249.	Bury, J. B.	History of the Roman empire
747.	Business girl in every phase of her life	Ruth Ashmore
53.	Butcher, Samuel H.	Demosthenes
	Butcher, Samuel H., *trans*. *See* Homer. Odyssey.	
1566.	Butler, *Rev*. George, *ed*.	Longman's atlas of ancient geography
657.	Butler, Nicholas Murray	Meaning of education
1573.	Butler, Nicholas Murray, *ed*.	Education in the United States
1441.	Byron, Lord	Childe Harold's pilgrimage
1231.	Cable, George W.	Bonaventure
624.	Cable, George W.	Negro question
1518.	Caesar	Commentaries
39.	Caesar	J. A. Froude
1041.	Cairns, William B.	Forms of discourse
362.	Caldwell, Howard W.	American territorial development
363.	Caldwell, Howard W.	Great American legislators
364.	Caldwell, Howard W.	Survey of American history
	Caldwell, Howard W., *jt. author*. *See* Fling, Fred Morrow.	
471.	California	Josiah Royce
318.	Cameos from English history	C. M. Yonge
993.	Camp, Walter	Football
998.	Camp life in the woods	W. H. Gibson
992.	Campbell, *Mrs*. Helen	American girl's home book of work and play
965.	Campbell, *Mrs*. Helen	Household economics
749.	Campbell, *Mrs*. Helen	Women wage-earners
1011.	Camping and camp outfits	G. O. Shields
399.	Cannon and camera	J. C. Hemment
1014.	Canoe and boat building	W. P. Stephens
997.	Canoe cruising and camping	P. D. Frazer
1445.	Canterbury tales	Geoffrey Chaucer
250.	Capes, William Wolfe	Early empire
101.	Capes, William Wolfe	Livy
251.	Capes, William Wolfe	Roman empire of the second century
1495.	Capps, Edward	From Homer to Theocritus
1338.	Captain of the Janizaries	J. M. Ludlow
1333.	Captains courageous	Rudyard Kipling
764.	Carhart, Henry S., *and* Chute, H. N.	Physics
1442.	Carleton, Will	City ballads
1443.	Carleton, Will	Farm ballads
1137.	Carlyle, Thomas	Heroes, hero-worship and the heroic in history
	Carlyle, Thomas, *trans*. *See* Goethe, Johann Wolfgang. William Meister's apprenticeship.	
596.	Carpenter, Frank G.	South America
463.	Carr, Lucien	Missouri
1094.	Carrington, Henry B.	Beacon lights of patriotism
1444.	Cary, Alice *and* Phoebe	Poetical works
	Cary, *Rev*. Henry, *trans*. *See* Herodotus. History.	

	Cary, Phoebe, *jt. author. See* Cary, Alice.	
	Caskoden, Edwin, *pseud. See* Major, Charles.	
127.	Casson, Henry	
	..................."Uncle Jerry": Life of Jeremiah M. Rusk	
1407.	Cathedral courtship and Penelope's English experience........	
	....K. D. Wiggin	
1232.	Catherwood, Mary Hartwell ....Days of Jeanne D'Arc	
1233.	Catherwood, Mary Hartwell ....Lady of Fort St. John	
1234.	Catherwood, Mary Hartwell ....Mackinac and lake stories	
1235.	Catherwood, Mary Hartwell ....Story of Tonty	
1236.	Cervantes, Saavedra Miguel de...........Ingenious gentleman	
	Chailiu, Paul Belloni du. .*See* Du Chaillu, Paul Belloni.	
658.	Chamberlain, Alexander Francis	
	...............Child: a study in the evolution of man	
34.	Chamberlain, Joseph Edgar ....John Brown	
811.	Chambers, George F. ....Story of eclipses simply told	
1585.	Champlin, John Denison.....................................	
	.... Young folks' cyclopaedia of literature and art	
365.	Channing, Edward	
	..................Guide to the study of American history	
366.	Channing, Edward, ... Students' history of the United States	
	Channing, Edward, *jt. author. See* Higginson, Thomas Wentworth.	
	Channing, Edward, *jt. editor. See* Hart, Albert Bushnell.	
994.	Chapin, Anna Alice ....Story of the Rhine-gold	
936.	Chapman, Frank M..................................Bird-life	
228.	Charicles ....W. A. Becker	
18.	Charles Francis Adams ....C. F. Adams, *jr.*	
52.	Charles Darwin ....C. F. Holder	
	Chatrain, Alexander, *jt. author. See* Erckmann, Emile.	
1445.	Chaucer, Geoffrey ....Canterbury tales	
43.	Chaucer ....A. W. Ward	
1149.	Cheerful yesterdays ....T. W. Higginson	
797.	Chemical history of a candle ....Michael Faraday	
800.	Chemistry of common life ....J. F. W. Johnston	
805.	Chemistry of cookery ....W. M. Williams	
803.	Chemistry of cooking and cleaning............................	
	..........................E. H. Richards *and* S. M. Elliott	
23.	Cheney, E. D., *ed.* ....Louise M. Alcott	
44.	Chestnutt, Charles W. ....Frederick Douglas	
1237.	Child, Frank Samuel ....Unknown patriot	
658.	Child: a study in the evolution of man ....A. F. Chamberlain	
433.	Child life in colonial days ....A. M. Earle	
1441.	Childe Harold's pilgrimage ....Lord Byron	
1220.	Children of Gibeon ....Walter Besant	
182.	Children of the Nations ....Poultney Bigelow	
630.	Children of the poor ....J. A. Riis	
715.	Children's rights ....K. D. Wiggin	
285.	Child's history of England ....Charles Dickens	
295.	Child's history of Ireland ....P. W. Joyce	
331.	China ....R. K. Douglas	
547.	China ....E. R. Scidmore	
549.	Chinese characteristics ....A. H. Smith	
478.	Chisholm, George G. ....Smaller commercial geography	
1570.	Chisholm, George G., *and* Leete, C. H., *eds.*	
	............................Longman's new school atlas	

560.	Chittenden, Hiram M.	Yellowstone National Park
1147.	Choice of books	Frederic Harrison
1097.	Choice readings ..... R. I. Fulton *and* T. C. Trueblood, *comps.*	
1096.	Choice readings for public and private entertainments	
		R. M. Cumnock
1238.	Chopin, Kate	Bayou folk
1480.	Christ of Cynewulf	C. H. Whitman, *trans.*
1262.	Christmas carol and The cricket on the hearth	
		Charles Dickens
48.	Christopher Columbus	C. K. Adams
215.	Chronicles of the crusades	
	Richard de Vizes, *and* Geoffrey de Vinsauf, *and* Lord John de Joinville.	
231.	Church, *Rev.* Alfred John	Pictures from Greek life and story
252.	Church, Alfred J.	Roman life in the days of Cicero
27.	Church, Richard W.	Bacon
201.	Church, Richard W.	Beginning of the middle ages
	Churchill, James, *and* Coleridge, S. T., *trans. See* Schiller, Freidrich. Wallenstein.	
1239.	Churchill, Winston S.	Crisis
338.	Churchill, Winston S.	London to Ladysmith via Pretoria
1240.	Churchill, Winston S	Richard Carvel
1138.	Clemens, Samuel L	How to tell a story
868.	Clodd, Edward	Primer of evolution
948.	Clodd, Edward	Story of "primitive" man
1356.	Cloister and the hearth	Charles Reade
835.	Coal and the coal mines	Homer Greene
767.	Cochrane, Charles Henry	Wonders of modern mechanism
	Cody, *Col.* William F., *jt. author. See* Inman, *Col.* Henry.	
1488.	Coffee and repartee	J. K. Bangs
367.	Coffin, Charles Carleton	Boys of '76
368.	Coffin, Charles Carleton	Building the nation
1242.	Coffin, Charles Carleton	
		Daughters of the Revolution and their times
369.	Coffin, Charles Carleton	Drum-beat of the nation
765.	Chute, Horatio N.	Physical laboratory manual
	Chute, Horatio N., *jt. author. See* Carhart, Henry S.	
1519.	Cicero, Marcus Tullius. Smith, *trans.*	De Amicitia
947.	Citizen bird	M. O. Wright, *and* Elliott Coues
	Citizen's library series; *ed.* by R. T. Ely.	

Addams, Jane. Democracy and social ethics.
Baker, M. N. Municipal engineering and sanitation.
Bullock, C. J. Essays on the monetary history of the United States.
Ely, R. T. Monopolies and trusts.
Ely, R. T. Outlines of economics.
Macy, Jesse. Political parties in the United States.
Reinsch, P. S. World politics.

1442.	City ballads	Will Carleton
727.	City government in the United States	A. R. Conkling
730.	Civil government in the United States	John Fiske
359.	Civil war and the constitution	J. W. Burgess
200.	Civilization during the middle ages	G. B. Adams
887.	Clark, Charles H.	Laboratory manual in practical botany
766.	Clark, Charles H.	Practical methods in microscopy
	Clark, F. W., *jt. author. See* Dennis, L. M.	

795.	Clark, F. W., *and* Dennis, L. M.	Elementary chemistry
1049.	Clark, J. Scott	Art of reading aloud
1042.	Clark, J. Scott	Study of English and American poets
1043.	Clark, J. Scott	Study of English prose writers
1050.	Clark, Solomon H., *and* Blanchard, F. M. Practical public speaking	
7.	Classic myths in English literature.	C. M. Gayley, *ed.*

Classical writers; *ed.* by J. R. Green.
    Brooke, S. A. Milton.
    Butcher, S. A. Demosthenes.
    Capes, W. W. Livy.
    Mahaffy, J. P. Euripides.
    Nettleship, Henry. Virgil.

1241.	Clemens, Samuel L.	Connecticut yankee in King Arthur's court
370.	Coffin, Charles Carleton	Freedom triumphant
371.	Coffin, Charles Carleton	Marching to victory
372.	Coffin, Charles Carleton	Redeeming the republic
281.	Colby, Charles W.	Selections from the sources of English history
725.	Coler, Bird S.	Municipal government

Coleridge, E. P., *trans. See* Euripides. Tragedies.
Coleridge, Sara, *jt. author. See* Coleridge, Derwent.

1446.	Coleridge, Samuel Taylor	Poetical works

Coleridge, Samuel T., *jt. trans. See* Churchill, James.

485.	Collbran, Christine	American girl's trip to the Orient and around the world
1300.	College girls	A. C. Goodloe

College histories of art series
    Marquand, Allan, *and* Frothingham, A. L. Text-book of the history of sculpture.
    Van Dyke, J. C. Text-book of the history of painting

446.	Colonial cavalier	M. W. Goodwin
434.	Colonial days in old New York	A. M. Earle
379.	Colonial era	G. P. Fisher
429.	Colonial fights and fighters	C. T. Brady
1107.	Colonial prose and poetry	W. P. Trent *and* B. W. Wells, *eds.*
425.	Colonies	R. G. Thwaites
878.	Colours of flowers	Grant Allen
540.	Colquhon, Archibald R.	Overland to China
92.	Colvin, Sidney	Keats
282.	Coman, Katherine	History of England

Coman, Katherine, *jt. comp. See* Bates, Katherine Lee.

1493.	Comedies. Hickie, *trans.*	Aristophanes
1518.	Commentaries	Caesar
698.	Committee of Fifteen	Report of committee of fifteen
661.	Committee of Seven	Study of history in schools
639.	Committee of Ten	Report of the committee of Ten
700.	Committee of Twelve	Report of the committee of twelve
925.	Comparative zoology	James Orton
659.	Compayré, Gabriel. Payne, *trans.*	History of pedagogy
660.	Compayré, Gabriel. Payne, *trans.*	Lectures on pedagogy
840.	Compend of geology	Joseph LeConte
1579.	Compendius German and English dictionary	W. D. Whitney
1016.	Complete angler	Isaac Walton, *and* Charles Cotton

1437. Complete poetic and dramatic works ....Robert Browning
1439. Complete poetical works ....Robert Burns
1450. Complete poetical works ....R. W. Emerson
1455. Complete poetical works ....O. W. Holmes
1457. Complete poetical works and letters ....John Keats
1461. Complete poetical works ....Lucy Larcom
1462. Complete poetical works ....H. W. Longfellow
1463. Complete poetical works ....J. R. Lowell
1476. Complete poetical works ....P. B. Shelley
1481. Complete poetical works ....J. G. Whittier
812. Comstock, George C. ....Text-book of astronomy
911. Comstock, John Henry ....Insect life
75. Conant, Charles A. ....Alexander Hamilton
1150. Concerning all of us ....T. W. Higginson
1143. Conduct of life ....R. W. Emerson
726. Conklin, Viola A. ....American political history
727. Conkling, Alfred R. ......City government in the United States
869. Conn, H. W. ....Story of germ life
468. Connecticut ....Alexander Johnston
1241. Connecticut yankee in King Arthur's court ......S. L. Clemens
Connor, Ralph, *pseud. See* **Gordon, C. W.**
Connybeare, *Mrs.* F. C., *trans. See* Scherer, W. History of German literature.
1283. Conscript ....Emile Erckmann, *and* Alex. Chatrain
348. Conspiracy of Pontiac ....Francis Parkman
535. Constantinople ....F. M. Crawford
423. Constitutional history of the American people......F. N. Thorpe
1151. Contemporaries ....T. W. Higginson
Contemporary science series; *ed.* by Havelock Ellis.
Chamberlain, A. F. Child: a study in the evolution of man.
Hull, Edward. Volcanoes.
Tunzelmann, C. W. de Electricity in modern life.
20. Conversations with Prince Bismarck...Heinrich von Poschinger
464. Cooke, John Esten ....Virginia
768. Cooley, Leroy C. ....Physics
750. Cooley, Thomas M. ....
General principles of constitutional law in the United States
1244. Cooper, James Fenimore ....Deerslayer
1245. Cooper, James Fenimore ....Last of the Mohicans
1246. Cooper, James Fenimore ....Pathfinder
1243. Cooper, James Fenimore .... Pilot
1247. Cooper, James Fenimore .... Pioneers
1248. Cooper, James Fenimore .... Spy
57. Corbett, Julian ....Drake
622. Corbin, John ....Americans at Oxford
902. Corn plants ....F. L. Sargent
1360. Cornell stories ....J. G. Sanderson
975. Cost of food ....E. H. Richards
976. Cost of living ....E. H. Richards
135. Costume of colonial times ....A. M. Earle
1249. Cotes, *Mrs.* Everard ....American girl in London
1250. Cotes, *Mrs.* Everard ....Crow's-nest
486. Cotes, *Mrs.* Everard ....Social departure
1251. Cotes, *Mrs.* Everard .... Those delightful Americans
Cotton, Charles, *jt. author. See* **Walton, Izaak.**
110. Cotton, Mather ....Barrett Wendell

LIST OF BOOKS FOR HIGH SCHOOL LIBRARIES.

1252. Couch, Arthur T. Quiller, ed. ....Splendid spur
Coues, Elliott, jt. author. See Wright, Mabel Osgood.
888. Coulter, John M. ....Plants
1366. Count Robert of Paris ....Sir Walter Scott
1325. Country by-ways ....S. O. Jewett
1324. Country doctor ....S. O. Jewett
1326. Country of the pointed firs ....S. O. Jewett
794. Course of experiments in physical measurement..............
....Harold Whiting
232. Cox, George W. ....Athenian empire
213. Cox, George W. ....Crusades
233. Cox, George W. ....General history of Greece
234. Cox, Rev. George William, ...Greeks and the Persians
Cox, Rev. G. W., and Sankey, Charles, eds. ....
..................See Epochs of ancient history series
1420. Cox, Sir George W., and Jones, E. H. ....
....................Popular romances of the Middle ages
1575. Crabb, George ....English synonyms
Craddock, Charles Egbert, pseud. See Murfree, Mary N.
1051. Craig, A. H. ....Pros and cons
1095. Craig, A. H., and Gunnison, Binney, comps. ....
.....................Pieces for prize speaking contests
Craig, John, ed. See James, Charles C. ....
.................................Practical agriculture
Cranch, Christopher Pearse, trans. See Virgil ....Aeneid
183. Crane, Stephen ....Great battles of the world
1298. Cranford ....Mrs. E. C. Gaskell
535. Crawford, Francis Marion ....Constantinople
1253. Crawford, Francis Marion ....Marietta
1139. Crawford, Francis Marion ....Novel
1254. Crawford, Francis Marion ....Roman singer
207. Creighton, Louise ....First history of France
283. Creighton, Mandell ....Age of Elizabeth
284. Creighton, Mandell ....Epochs of English history
769. Crew, Henry ....Elements of physics
1239. Crisis ....W. S. Churchill
335. Crisis in China ....G. B. Smyth, and others
1166. Critical and historical essays ....T. B. Macaulay
1146. Critical kit-kats ....Edmund Gosse
381. Critical period of American history ....John Fiske
1255. Crockett, Samuel Rutherford ....Stickit minister's wooing
Cross, Mrs. Mary Ann Evans (Lewes). See Eliot, George, pseud.
1250. Crow's-nest ....Mrs. Everard Cotes
483. Cruise of the Cachalot round the world after sperm whales
....F. T. Bullen
212. Crusaders ....T. A. Archer, and C. L. Kingsford
213. Crusades ....G. W. Cox
591. Cuba and Puerto Rico ....R. T. Hill
1096. Cumnock, Robert McLean ....
.....Choice readings for public and private entertainments
235. Curteis, Arthur M. ....Rise of the Macedonian empire
1140. Curtis, George William ....From the easy chair
1142. Curtis, George William .....From the easy chair; third series
1141. Curtis, George William ......Other essays from the easy chair
728. Curtis, William E. ....United States and foreign powers
561. Custer, Elizabeth B. ....Boots and saddles

AUTHOR AND TITLE INDEX. 433

562.	Custer, Elizabeth B.	....................Following the guidon
563.	Custer, Elizabeth B.	....................Tenting on the plains
436.	Customs and fashions in old New England	.........A. M. Earle
1572.	Cyclopaedia of political science, political economy, and of the political history of the United States	.........J. J. Lalor, ed.
1586.	Cyclopedia of practical quotations	.................J. K. Hoyt
1480.	Cynewulf. Whitman, trans.	......................Christ
1512.	Cyropaedia. Watson & Dale, trans.	.................Xenophon

1117.	Daisy Miller	................................Henry James
	Dale, Rev. Henry, trans. See Thucydides	....
	................................History of the Peloponnesian war	
	Dale, Rev. Henry, jt. trans. See Watson, Rev. J. S.	
995.	Dalton, Davis	................................How to swim
158.	Dames and daughters of colonial days	.......Geraldine Brooks
159.	Dames and daughters of the young republic	...Geraldine Brooks
830.	Dana, E. Salisbury	...........Minerals and how to study them
829.	Dana, James D.	.................Geological story briefly told
831.	Dana, James D.	.................Revised text-book of geology
589.	Dana, Richard Henry, jr.	.................To Cuba and back
487.	Dana, Richard Henry, jr.	.........Two years before the mast
31.	Daniel Boone	................................J. S. C. Abbott
1280.	Daniel Deronda	..............................George Eliot
145.	Daniel Webster	....Norman Hapgood
146.	Daniel Webster	................................H. C. Lodge
1513.	Dante, Alighieri. Longfellow, trans.	...........Divine comedy
	D'Anvers, D., pseud. See Bell, Mrs. Arthur.	
889.	Darwin, Charles	....Insectivorous plants
597.	Darwin, Charles	.......................Journal of researches
890.	Darwin, Charles	.....Movements and habits of climbing plants
870.	Darwin, Charles	................................Origin of species
891.	Darwin, Charles	...............Power of movement in plants
	Darwin, Francis, jt. author. See Darwin, Charles.	
1242.	Daughters of the Revolution and their times	......C. C. Coffin
1263.	David Copperfield	..........................Charles Dickens
63.	David Glasgow Farragut	.......................James Barnes
1405.	David Harum	..............................E. N. Westcott
663.	Davidson, Thomas	....Aristotle
664.	Davidson, Thomas	...........Education of the Greek people
665.	Davidson, Thomas	....................History of education
	Davie, Eleanor E., ed. See Gibson, William Hamilton	....
	................................Blossom hosts and insect guests	
1256.	Davis, Richard Harding	.........Gallegher, and other stories
519.	Davis, Richard Harding	.................Our English cousins
1257.	Davis, Richard Harding	... .Soldiers of fortune
598.	Davis, Richard Harding	....
	.........Three Gringos in Venezuela and Central America	
1258.	Davis, Richard Harding	..............Van Bibber and others
564.	Davis, Richard Harding	.............West from a car-window
851.	Davis, William Morris	....Elementary meteorology
832.	Davis, William Morris	........Elementary physical geography
528.	Dawson, William Harbutt	....German life in town and country
640.	Day with a tramp and other days	..............W. A. Wyckoff
1404.	Days of auld lang syne	........................John Watson

28

1232.	Days of Jeanne D'Arc	M. H. Catherwood
1334.	Day's work	Rudyard Kipling
	De Amicis, Edmondo. *See* Amicis, Edmondo de.	
1519.	De Amicitia. Smith, *trans.*	M. T. Cicero
	De Cervantes, Saavedra Miguel. *See* Cervantes, Saavedra Miguel de.	
1244.	Deerslayer	J. F. Cooper
	De Garmo, *ed. See* Ufer, Christian.................Introduction to the pedagogy of Herbart	
	De Koven, A. F., *trans. See* Viaud, L. Marie Julien...............Iceland fisherman	
	Deland, Lorin F., *jt. author. See* Camp, Walter.	
621.	Democracy and social ethics	Jane Addams
1496.	Demosthenes	Oration on the crown
53.	Demosthenes	S. H. Butcher
	Dennis, L. M., *jt. author. See* Clark, F. W.	
796.	Dennis, L. M., *and* Clark, F. W.	Laboratory manual
1458.	Departmental ditties and ballads	Rudyard Kipling
	De Saint-Pierre, Jacques Henri Bernardin. *See* Saint-Pierre, Jacques Henri Bernardin de.	
847.	Desert	J. C. Van Dyke
1543.	Deutsche Gedichte	Hermann Mueller
1090.	Development of English literature and language	A. H. Welsh
692.	Development of the child	Nathan Oppenheim
1259.	Devereux, Mary	From kingdom to colony
602.	Devine, Edward Thomas	Economics
666.	Dewey, John	School and society
565.	De Windt, Henry	Through the gold fields of Alaska
1408.	Diary of a goose girl	K. D. Wiggin
1260.	Dickens, Charles	Barnaby Rudge
1261.	Dickens, Charles	Bleak house
285.	Dickens, Charles	Child's history of England
1262.	Dickens, Charles	Christmas carol and the cricket on the hearth
1263.	Dickens, Charles	David Copperfield
1264.	Dickens, Charles	Life and adventures of Nicholas Nickleby
1265.	Dickens, Charles	Old curiosity shop
1266.	Dickens, Charles	Pickwick papers
1267.	Dickens, Charles	Tale of two cities
55.	Dickens	A. W. Ward
681.	Dickens as an educator	J. L. Hughes
54.	Dickens, Mamie	My father as I recall him
912.	Dickerson, Mary C.	Moths and butterflies
1576.	Dictionary of English synonyms	Richard Soule
1588.	Dictionary of Greek and Roman antiquities	William Smith, *ed.*
1574.	Dictionary of phrase and fable	E. C. Brewer
590.	Dinwiddie, William	Puerto Rico
1413.	Diomed	J. S. Wise
1497.	Discourses of Epictetus. Long, *trans.*	Epictetus
345.	Discovery of America	John Fiske
599.	Distribution of products	Edward Atkinson
	Ditmars, Raymond L., *jt. author. See* Baskett, James Newton.	
1513.	Divine comedy	Dante
427.	Division and reunion	Woodrow Wilson
1268.	Dix, Beulah Marie	Hugh Gwyeth

AUTHOR AND TITLE INDEX. 435

1269.	Dix, Beulah Marie	Soldier Rigdale
571.	Dixie	Julian Ralph
1121.	Dr. Faustus	Christopher Marlowe
751.	Dodge, Grace Hoadley	What women can earn
852.	Dodge, Richard Elwood	Reader in physical geography
160.	Dodge, Theodore Ayrault	Great captains
1529.	Doktor Luther	Gustav Freytag
770.	Dolbear, Amos Emerson	Telephone
86.	Dole, Nathan Haskell	Joseph Jefferson at home
105.	Dolly Madison	M. W. Goodwin
493.	Dorr, Julia C. R.	Bermuda
559.	Douglas, M.	Across Greenland's ice-fields
331.	Douglas, Robert K.	China
1524.	Dowden, Edward	History of French literature
1111.	Dowden, Edward	Introduction to Shakespeare
581.	Down historic waterways	R. G. Thwaites
339.	Doyle, Arthur Conan,	Great Boer war
1270.	Doyle, Arthur Conan	Refugees
1271.	Doyle, Arthur Conan	White company
373.	Drake, Francis S.	Indian history for young folks
430.	Drake, Samuel Adams	Book of New England legends and folklore
431.	Drake, Samuel Adams	Making of New England
432.	Drake, Samuel Adams	Making of the Ohio valley states
57.	Drake	Julian Corbett
58.	Drake	G. M. Towle
1206.	Drake and his yeomen	James Barnes
1490.	Dramas. Swanwick, *trans.*	Aeschylus
1499.	Dramas. Lawton, *trans.*	Euripides
1122.	Dramas. *Hudson* ed.	William Shakespeare
1123.	Dramas. *Rolfe* ed.	William Shakespeare
1124.	Dramas. *Temple* ed.	William Shakespeare
1173.	Dream life	D. G. Mitchell
1388.	Dred	H. B. Stowe
369.	Drum-beat of the nation	C. C. Coffin
871.	Drummond, Henry	Lowell lectures on the ascent of man
553.	Drummond, Henry	Tropical Africa
59.	Dryden	George Saintsbury
833.	Dryer, Charles R.	Lessons in physical geography
667.	Drysdale, William	Helps for ambitious girls
500.	Du Chaillu, Paul	Land of the long night
588.	Due south	M. M. Ballou
1112.	Dugan, Caro Atherton	King's jester
937.	Dugmore, A. Radclyffe	Bird homes
1216.	Duke of Stockbridge	Edward Bellamy
1272.	Dumas, Alexandre	Three musketeers
1273.	Dunbar, Paul Laurence	Folks from Dixie
1147.	Dunbar, Paul Laurence	Lyrics of lowly life
1448.	Dunbar, Paul Laurence	Lyrics of the hearthside
	Duncan, Sara Jeannette. *See* Cotes, *Mrs.* Everard.	
1274.	Dunn, Byron A.	General Nelson's scout
1275.	Dunn, Byron A.	On General Thomas's staff
374.	Dunning, William Archibald	Essays on the Civil war and reconstruction
202.	Duruy, Victor	History of the Middle ages
198.	Duruy, Victor	History of modern times
442.	Dutch and Quaker colonies in America	John Fiske

525.	Dutch life in town and country	P. M. Hough
1044.	Dye, Charity	Story-teller's art

433.	Earle, Alice Morse	Child life in colonial days
434.	Earle, Alice Morse	Colonial days in old New York
435.	Earle, Alice Morse	Costume of colonial times
436.	Earle, Alice Morse .... Customs and fashions in old New England	
437.	Earle, Alice Morse	Home life in colonial days
148.	Earle, Alice Morse	Margaret Winthrop
438.	Earle, Alice Morse	Sabbath in Puritan New England
250.	Early empire	W. W. Capes
306.	Early Hanoverians	E. M. Morris
314.	Early Plantagenets	William Stubbs
255.	Early Rome	William Ihne
303.	Early Tudors	C. E. Moberly
836.	Earth and its story	Angelo Heilprin
834.	Earth sculpture or the origin of land-forms	James Geikie
808.	Earth's beginning	*Sir* R. S. Ball
518.	East London	Walter Besant
193.	Eastern nations and Greece	P. V. Myers
787.	Easy experiments in physics	Preston Smith
1276.	Ebers, Georg. Grove, *trans.*	Egyptian princess
1385.	Ebers, Georg. Storrs, *trans.*	Emperor
1277.	Ebers, Georg. Bell, *trans.*	Uarda
938.	Eckstorm, Fannie Hardy	Bird book
600.	Economics for the people	R. R. Bowker
602.	Economics	E. T. Devine
653.	Education in the United States	R. G. Boone
1573.	Education in the United States	N. M. Butler, *ed.*
705.	Education	Herbert Spencer
664.	Education of the Greek people	Thomas Davidson
675.	Educational aims and educational values	P. H. Hanus
	Educational library series.	
	Browning, Oscar. Introduction to the history of educational theories.	
317.	Edward III	*Rev.* William Warburton
1020.	Edwin Booth	E. B. Grossman
439.	Eggleston, Edward	Beginners of a nation
375.	Eggleston, Edward .... Household history of the United States and its people	
440.	Eggleston, Edward .... Transit of civilization from England to America	
	Eggleston, Edward, *ed. See* Seelye, Elizabeth Eggleston .... Story of Columbus	
	Eggleston, Edward, *jt. author. See* Seelye, Elizabeth Eggleston.	
1278.	Eggleston, George Cary	Southern soldier stories
1449.	Eggleston, George Cary, *ed.* .... American war ballads and lyrics	
1530.	Egmont	J. W. V. Goethe
556.	Egypt in 1898	G. W. Steevens
1276.	Egyptian pirncess. Grove, *trans.*	Georg Ebers
1546.	Ekkehard	J. V. von Scheffel
758.	Electricity for everybody	Philip Atkinson

AUTHOR AND TITLE INDEX. 437

793.	Electricity in modern life	G. W. de Tunzelmann
813.	Elementary astronomy	E. S. Holden
780.	Elementary book on electricity and magnetism	D. C. Jackson, and J. P. Jackson
879.	Elementary botany	G. F. Atkinson
795.	Elementary chemistry	F. W. Clark, and L. M. Dennis
798.	Elementary chemistry	W. S. Furneaux
846.	Elementary geology	R. S. Tarr
1023.	Elementary history of art	Mrs. Arthur Bell
801.	Elementary inorganic chemistry	G. S. Newth
1577.	Elementary Latin dictionary	C. T. Lewis
789.	Elementary lessons in electricity and magnetism	S. P. Thompson
924.	Elementary lessons in zoology	J. G. Needham
851.	Elementary meteorology	W. M. Davis
867.	Elementary meteorology	Frank Waldo
832.	Elementary physical geography	W. M. Davis
858.	Elementary physical geography	J. W. Redway
835.	Elementary physical geography	R. S. Tarr
791.	Elementary physics	C. B. Thwing
645.	Elementary psychology and education	Joseph Baldwin
920.	Elementary zoology	V. L. Kellogg
806.	Elements of chemistry	R. P. Williams
841.	Elements of geology	Joseph Le Conte
807.	Elements of modern chemistry	C. A. Wurtz
713.	Elements of pedagogy	E. E. White
855.	Elements of physical geography	E. J. Houston
769.	Elements of physics	Henry Crew
773.	Elements of physics	C. H. Henderson, and J. F. Woodhull
611.	Elements of political economy	J. L. Laughlin
627.	Elements of sociology	F. H. Giddings
973.	Elements of the theory and practice of cookery	M. E. Williams, and K.H. Fisher
161.	Ellet, Elizabeth F.	Women of the American Revolution
1279.	Eliot, George	Adam Bede
1280.	Eliot, George	Daniel Deronda
1281.	Eliot, George	Romola
1282.	Eliot, George	Silas Marner
	Elliott, S. Maria, jt. author. See Richards, Ellen H.	
668.	Elliott, A. Marshall, and others	Methods of teaching modern languages
376.	Elson, Henry W.	Sidelights on American history, series 1
377.	Elson, Henry W.	Sidelights on American history, series 2
603.	Ely, Richard T.	Monopolies and trusts
604.	Ely, Richard T.	Outlines of economics
	Ely, Richard T., ed. ...See Citizen's library of economics, politics, and sociology	
1450.	Emerson, Ralph Waldo	Complete poetical works
1143.	Emerson, Ralph Waldo	Conduct of life
1144.	Emerson, Ralph Waldo	Essays
1145.	Emerson, Ralph Waldo	Representative men
203.	Emerton, Ephraim	Introduction to the study of the Middle ages
204.	Emerton, Ephraim	Mediaeval Europe
1025.	Emery, Mabel S.	How to enjoy pictures
701.	Emile. Payne, trans.	Rosseau

1540.	Emilia Galotti	G. E. Lessing
1385.	Emperor. Storrs, *trans.*	Georg Ebers
1339.	Enchanted burro	C. F. Lummis
543.	Enchanted India	Prince Bojidar Karageorgevitch
308.	England and the Hundred years' war	C. W. C. Oman
310.	England and the Reformation	G. W. Powers
309.	England in the nineteenth century	C. W. C. Oman
522.	England without and within	R. G. White
1161.	English essays	J. H. Lobban
293.	English history for Americans	T. W. Higginson, *and* Edward Channing
1092.	English history told by English poets	K. L. Bates, *and* Katharine Coman, *comps.*
1077.	English lands, letters, and kings	D. G. Mitchell
1064.	English literature	S. A. Brooke

English men of action series.
Corbett, Julian. Drake.

English men of letters series; *ed.* by John Morley.
Church, R. W. Bacon.
Colvin, Sidney. Keats.
Hutton, R. H. *Sir* Walter Scott.
James, Henry, *jr.* Hawthorne.
Myers, F. W. H. Wordsworth.
Nichol, John. Thomas Carlyle.
Pattison, Mark. Milton.
Saintsbury, George. Dryden.
Shairp, Principal. Robert Burns.
Symonds, J. A. Shelley.
Ward, A. W. Chaucer.
Ward, A. W. Dickens.

1108.	English poets	T. H. Ward, *ed.*
1575.	English synonyms	George Crabb
1497.	**Epictetus.** Long, *trans.*	Discourses
397.	Epoch maps illustrating American history	A. B. Hart
301.	Epoch of reform	Justin McCarthy

Epochs of American history series; *ed.* by A. B. Hart.
Hart, A. B. Formation of the Union.
Thwaites, R. G. Colonies.
Wilson, Woodrow. Division and reunion.

Epochs of ancient history series; *ed.* by G. W. Cox, *and* Charles Sankey.
Benjamin, S. G. W. Troy.
Beesly, A. H. Gracchi, Marius, and Sulla.
Capes, W. W. Early empire.
Capes, W. W. Roman empire of the second century.
Cox, G. W. Athenian empire.
Cox, G. W. Greeks and the Persians.
Curteis, A. M. Rise of the Macedonian empire.
Ihne, William. Early Rome.
Merivale, Charles. Roman triumvirates.
Sankey, Charles. Spartan and Theban supremacies.
Smith, R. B. Rome and Carthage.

284.	Epochs of English history	Mandell Creighton

Epochs of modern history series; *ed.* by E. E. Morris.
   Church, R. W. Beginning of the middle ages.
   Cox, G. W. Crusades.
   Creighton, Mandell. Age of Elizabeth.
   Gairdner, James. Houses of Lancaster and York.
   Gardiner, S. R. First two Stuarts and the Puritan Revolution.
   Gardiner, S. R. Thirty years' war.
   Hale, *Rev.* Edward. Fall of the Stuarts and western Europe.
   Johnson, *Rev.* A. H. Normans in Europe.
   Longman, F. W. Frederick the Great and the seven years' war.
   McCarthy, Justin. Epoch of reform.
   Moberly, C. E. Early Tudors.
   Morris, E. E. Age of Anne.
   Morris, E. E. Early Hanoverians.
   Morris, W. O. French Revolution and first empire.
   Seebohm, Frederic. Era of the Protestant Revolution.
   Stubbs, William. Early Plantagenets.
   Warburton, *Rev.* William. Edward III.

595.	Equatorial America	M. M. Ballou.
223.	Era of the Protestant Revolution	Frederic Seebohm
1283.	Erckmann, Emile, *and* Chatrain, Alexander.	Conscript
1284.	Erckmann, Emile, *and* Chatrain, Alexander	Invasion of France
1285.	Erckmann, Emile, *and* Chatrain, Alexander	Waterloo
1144.	Essays	R. W. Emerson
1175.	Essays in idleness	Agnes Repplier
1176.	Essays in miniature	Agnes Repplier
1160.	Essays of Elia	C: Lamb
1167.	Essays on nature and culture	H. W. Mabie
374.	Essays on the Civil war and reconstruction	W. A. Dunning
697.	Essays on educational reformers	R. H. Quick
601.	Essays on the monetary history of the United States	C. J. Bullock
1168.	Essays on work and culture	H. W. Mabie
748.	Essentials of business law	F. M. Burdick
799.	Essentials of chemistry	J. C. Hessler *and* Smith, A. L.
26.	Ethan Allen	Henry Hall
1499.	Euripides. Lawton, *trans.*	Three dramas
1498.	Euripides. Coleridge, *trans.*	Tragedies
62.	Euripides	J. P. Mahaffy
227.	Europe, 1598–1715	H. O. Wakeman
225.	Europe in the Middle Age. O. J. Thatcher, *and* Ferdinand Schwill
220.	Europe in the sixteenth century	A. H. Johnson
216.	European history	G. B. Adams
683.	European schools	L. R. Klemm
	Evans, *Rev.* Lewis, *trans. See* Juvenal. Satires.
270.	Eve of the French Revolution	E. J. Lowell
928.	Every-day butterflies	S. H. Scudder
1119.	Every man in his humour	Ben Jonson
	Ewald, Alexander Charles, *ed. See* Addison, Joseph. Spectator.
967.	Ewing, Emma P.	Art of cookery
1185.	Excursions	H. D. Thoreau
872.	Excursions of an evolutionist	John Fiske
312.	Expansion of England	*Sir* J. R. Seeley
776.	Experimental science	G. M. Hopkins

1587. Explanatory and pronouncing dictionary of noted names of fiction .... W. A. Wheeler
1400. Express messenger .... Cy Warman
822. Eye spy .... W. H. Gibson

1399. Fair God .... Lew Wallace
1367. Fair maid of Perth .... *Sir* Walter Scott
753. Fairy-land of science .... A. B. Buckley
291. Fall of the Stuarts and western Europe ..... *Rev.* Edward Hale
898. Familiar features of the roadside .... F. S. Mathews
899. Familiar flowers of field and garden .... F. S. Mathews
1582. Familiar quotations .... John Bartlett
900. Familiar trees and their leaves .... F. S. Mathews
814. Family of the sun .... E. S. Holden
378. **Famous** adventures and prison escapes of the civil war........
151. Famous European artists .... S. K. Bolton
152. Famous leaders among men .... S. K. Bolton
154. Famous leaders among women .... S. K. Bolton
153. Famous voyagers and explorers .... S. K. Bolton
797. **Faraday, Michael** .... Chemical history of a candle
1443. Farm ballads .... Will Carleton
107. Father Marquette .... R. G. Thwaites
1531. Faust .... J. W. von Goethe
669. **Fearon, D. R.** .... School inspection
732. Federalist and other constitutional papers .... Hamilton, *and others*
134. Ferdinand De Soto .... J. S. C. Abbott
13. Few thoughts for a young man .... Horace Mann
1158. Field and hedgerow .... Richard Jefferies
1286. **Field, Eugene** .... Holy cross
1287. **Field, Eugene** .... House
1288. **Field, Eugene** .... Little book of profitable tales
1451. **Field, Eugene** .... Little book of western verse
1452. **Field, Eugene** .... Love-songs of childhood
1289. **Field, Eugene** .... Second book of tales
1453. **Field, Eugene** .... Second book of verse
892. Field, forest and wayside flowers .... E. M. Hardinge
Field, George W., *trans.* *See* Hertwig, Richard. General principles of zoology.
577. **Field, Henry M.** .... Our western archipelago
162. **Fields, James T.** .... Yesterdays with authors
77. **Fields,** *Mrs.* **James T.** .... Nathaniel Hawthorne
133. Fighting Phil .... *Rev.* P. C. Headley
1396. Final war .... Louis Tracy
1024. Fine arts .... G. B. Brown
1177. Fireside sphinx .... Agnes Repplier
1163. Fireside travels .... J. R. Lowell
845. First book in geology .... N. S. Shaler
267. First history of France .... Louise Creighton
760. First lessons in physical science .... E. M. Avery, *and* C. P. Sinnott
617. First lessons in political economy .... F. A. Walker
287. First two Stuarts and the Puritan Revolution .... S. R. Gardiner
379. **Fisher, George Park** .... Colonial era

17.	Fisher, George Park.................	Reformation
	Fisher, Katharine Rolston, *jt. author.* *See* Williams, Mary E.	
1066.	Fisher, Mary..........	General survey of American literature
184.	Fisher, T. P...............	Outlines of universal history
475.	Fiske, Amos Kidder.......................	West Indies
729.	Fiske, John...........................	American political ideas
380.	Fiske, John...........................	American Revolution
441.	Fiske, John......................	Beginnings of New England
730.	Fiske, John...........	Civil government in the United States
381.	Fiske, John...............	Critical period of American history
345.	Fiske, John.........................	Discovery of America
442.	Fiske, John............	Dutch and Quaker colonies in America
872.	Fiske, John...................	Excursions of an evolutionist
382.	Fiske, John.................	History of the United States
383.	Fiske, John................	Mississippi valley in the Civil war
6.	Fiske, John......................	Myths and myth makers
443.	Fiske, John..................	New France and New England
444.	Fiske, John...............	Old Virginia and her neighbors
384.	Fiske, John...........................	War of independence
	Fiske, John, *ed.* *See* Taine, H. A. History of English literature.	
670.	Fitch, James G.........................	Lectures on teaching
996.	Fitz Gerald, Sarah J. A.	Stories of famous songs
541.	Five thousand miles in a sledge.................	L. F. Gowing
188.	Flags of the world	F. E. Hulme
779.	Flame, electricity, and the camera................	George Iles
1290.	Flandrau, C. M.....................	Harvard episodes
821.	Flashlights on nature	Grant Allen
236.	Fling, Fred Morrow...............	Studies in European history
185.	Fling, Fred Morrow, *and* Caldwell, H. W.....................	
	....	Studies in European and American history
385.	Flint, Grover	Marching with Gomez
1183.	Florida sketch-book	Bradford Torrey
904.	Flowers and ferns in their haunts	M. O. Wright
1578.	Flügel-Schmidt–Tanger's dictionary of the English and German	
	languages. .... Immanuel Schmidt, *and* Gustav Tanger, *eds.*	
1199.	Flute and violin	J. L. Allen
625.	Flynt, Josiah	Tramping with tramps
1273.	Folks from Dixie	P. L. Dunbar
562.	Following the guidon	E. B. Custer
977.	Food materials and their adulterations..........	E. H. Richards
993.	Football	Walter Camp, *and* L. F. Deland
1291.	Foote, Mary Hallock	Led-horse claim
582.	Footing it in Franconia.....................	Bradford Torrey
873.	Foot-notes to evolution	D. S. Jordan
1189.	Foot-path way	Bradford Torrey
489.	Foot-prints of travel...........................	M. M. Ballou
1207.	For king or country	James Barnes
1222.	For love of country	C. T. Brady
1454.	For the country	R. W. Gilder
671.	Forbush, William Byron........................	Boy problem
558.	Ford, Isaac N.............................	Tropical America
1292.	Ford, Paul Leicester	Honorable Peter Stirling
1293.	Ford, Paul Leicester	Janice Meredith
65.	Ford, Paul Leicester	Many-sided Franklin
1067.	Ford, Paul Leicester, *ed*...............	New England primer
396.	Formation of the Union	A. B. Hart

442 LIST OF BOOKS FOR HIGH SCHOOL LIBRARIES.

1041.	Forms of discourse ....W. B. Cairns
1045.	Forms of prose literature ....J. H. Gardiner
866.	Forms of water in clouds and rivers, ice and glaciers.......... John Tyndall
445	Forsyth, George A. ....Story of the soldier
1368.	Fortunes of Nigel ....*Sir* Walter Scott
734.	Foundations of American foreign policy............A. B. Hart
884.	Foundations of botany ....J. Y. Bergen
	Four Great Americans series; *ed.* by James Baldwin.
	Winship, A. E. Great American educators.
1560.	Four years of novel reading ....R. G. Moulton, *ed.*
1499a.	**Fowler, Harold N.**.......... History of ancient Greek literature
38.	**Fowler, William Warde** ....Julius Caesar
942.	Fowls of the air ....W. J. Long
1528.	**Francke, Kuno** ....History of German literature
64.	**Franklin, Benjamin** ....Autobiography
210.	Franks ....Lewis Sergeant
997.	**Frazer, Perry D.**.................Canoe cruising and camping
44.	Frederick Douglas ....C. W. Chestnutt
269.	Frederick the Great and the seven years' war................ ....F. W. Longman
370.	Freedom triumphant ....C. C. Coffin
186.	**Freeman, Edward A.**..............General sketch of history
	Freeman, Edward A., *ed.* See **Historical course for schools.**
1294.	**French, Alice** ....Stories of a western town
1525.	French dramatists of the 19th century......Brander Matthews
272.	French Revolution and the first empire..........W. O. Morris
274.	French Revolution and religious reform........W. M. Sloane
418.	French war and the revolution.................W. M. Sloane
1131.	Fresh fields ....John Burroughs
1529.	**Freytag, Gustav**............................ Doktor Luther
1484.	**Frink, Henry Allyn**....................New century speaker
1425.	Frithjof, the viking of Norway..................Z. A. Ragozin
655.	Froebel, and education through self-activity ......H. C. Bowen
716.	Froebel's gifts ....K. D. Wiggin, *and* N. A. Smith
717.	Froebel's occupations ....K. D. Wiggin, *and* N. A. Smith
935.	From Blomidon to Smoky......................Frank Bolles
1098.	From Chaucer to Arnold........................A. J. George
1495.	From Homer to Theocritus....................Edward Capps
1259.	From kingdom to colony.....................Mary Devereux
1140.	From the easy chair.................. .... G. W. Curtis
1142.	From the easy chair, third series...............G. W. Curtis
46.	**Frost, John**................ ....Mill boy of the slashes
106.	**Frost, John** ....Swamp fox
	Frothingham, Arthur L., *jt. author.* See **Marquand, Allan.**
386.	**Frothingham, Richard** ....Rise of the republic of the United States
39.	**Froude, James Anthony**............ .... Caesar
61.	**Froude, James Anthony**..........Life and letters of Erasmus
1296.	**Fuller Anna**..Pratt portraits sketched in a New England suburb
1295.	**Fuller, Caroline M.**................. ....Across the campus
1097.	**Fulton, Robert I.,** *and* **Trueblood, Thomas C.,** *comps.*.......... ....Choice readings
798.	**Furneaux, William S.**...................Elementary chemistry
217.	**Fyffe, Charles Alan**..................History of modern Europe

771.	Gage, Alfred P	Principles of physics
286.	Gairdner, James	Houses of Lancaster and York
1256.	Gallegher, and other stories	R. H. Davis
244.	Gallus. Metcalfe, *trans.*	W. A. Becker
961.	Garden-making	L. H. Bailey
1045.	Gardiner, J. Hays	Forms of prose literature
287.	Gardiner, Samuel Rawson	
		First two Stuarts and the Puritan Revolution
289.	Gardiner, Samuel Rawson	Student's history of England
268.	Gardiner, Samuel Rawson	Thirty years' war
288.	Gardiner, Samuel Rawson, *ed.*	School atlas of English history
1026.	Gardner, Ernest Arthur	Handbook of Greek sculpture
237.	Gardner, Percy, *and* Jevons, F. B	
		Manual of Greek antiquities
1297.	Garland, Hamlin	Main-travelled roads
73.	Garland, Hamlin	Ulysses S. Grant
672.	Garlick, A. H	New manual of method
913.	Garner, R. L	Apes and monkeys
1434.	Garnett, James M., *trans.*	Beowulf
1298.	Gaskell, *Mrs.* Elizabeth C	Cranford
104.	Gay, Sydney Howard	James Madison
7.	Gayley, Charles Mills, *ed.*	
		Classic myths in English literature
834.	Geikie, James	Earth sculpture or the origin of land-forms
189.	General history	P. V. Myers
206.	General history of civilization in Europe	F. P. G. Guizot
226.	General history of Europe	
		O. J. Thatcher, *and* Ferdinand Schwill
233.	General history of Greece	G. W. Cox
1274.	General Nelson's scout	B. A. Dunn
750.	General principles of constitutional law	T. M. Cooley
915.	General principles of zoology. Field, *trans.*	Richard Hertwig
186.	General sketch of history	E. A. Freeman
1066.	General survey of American literature	Mary Fisher
1406.	Gentleman of France	S. J. Weyman
1351.	Geoffrey Strong	L. E. Richards
829.	Geological story briefly told	J. D. Dana
1098.	George, Andrew J	From Chaucer to Arnold
605.	George, Henry	Progress and poverty
606.	George, Henry	Protection or free trade
626.	George, Henry	Social problems
140.	George Washington	Norman Hapgood
141.	George Washington	H. C. Lodge
142.	George Washington	H. E. Scudder
143.	George Washington	Woodrow Wilson
528.	German life in town and country	W. H. Dawson
1056.	German orthography and phonology	George Hempl
320.	Germany, her people and their story	A. H. Gifford
1553.	Geschichten vom Rhein	Menco Stern
1554.	Geschichten von deutschen Städten	Menco Stern
205.	Getchell, M. S	Study of mediaeval history
99.	Gettysburg speech and other papers	
		Abraham Lincoln. *In* (99) Carl Schurz's Lincoln
253.	Gibbon, Edward	
		History of the decline and fall of the Roman empire
911.	Gibson, William Hamilton	Blossom hosts and insect guests

998.	Gibson, William Hamilton	Camp life in the woods
822.	Gibson, William Hamilton	Eye spy
823.	Gibson, William Hamilton	My studio neighbors
824.	Gibson, William Hamilton	Sharp eyes
627.	Giddings, Franklin Henry	Elements of sociology
320.	Gifford, Augusta Hale	Germany, her people and their story
966.	Gifford, John	Practical forestry
853.	Gilbert, Karl Grove, *and* Brigham, Albert Perry	Introduction to physical geography
1454.	Gilder, Richard Watson	For the country
254.	Gilman, Arthur	Story of Rome
	Gilman, Arthur, *jt. author. See* Rawlinson, George.	
	Gilman, Arthur, *jt. author. See* Gould, Sabine Baring-.	
1299.	Gilman, Bradley	Back to the soil
114.	Gilman, Daniel C	James Monroe
607.	Gilman, Nicholas Paine	Profit sharing between employer and employee
859.	Glaciers of North America	I. C. Russell
608.	Gladden, Washington	Tools and the man
503.	Glimpses of three coasts	H. H. Jackson
542.	Glimpses of unfamiliar Japan	Lafcadio Hearn
1530.	Goethe, Johann Wolfgang von, *and* Schiller, J. F. Egmont: with Schiller's "Des Grafen Lamoral von Egmont Leben und Tod," and "Uber Egmont, Trauerspiel von Goethe."	
1531.	Goethe, Johann Wolfgang von	Faust
1532.	Goethe, Johann Wolfgang von	Hermann und Dorothea
1533.	Goethe, Johann Wolfgang von	Iphigenie auf Tauris
1534.	Goethe, Johann Wolfgang von	Torquato Tasso
1527.	Goethe, Johann Wolfgang von	Wilhelm Meister's apprenticeship
32.	Goethe and Schiller	H. H. Boyesen
968.	Goff, E. S.	Principles of plant culture
	Going, Maud E., *pseud. See* Hardinge, E. M.	
1102.	Golden treasury	F. T. Palgrave
	Golden treasury series. Arnold, Matthew. Selected poems. Lane-Poole, Stanley. Speeches and table-talk of the prophet Mohammad. Yonge, C. M. Story of the Christians and Moors.	
1303.	Gomme, George Laurence, *ed.*	Princess's story book
513.	Gondola days	F. H. Smith
1300.	Goodloe, Abbie Carter	College girls
446.	Goodwin, Maud Wilder	Colonial cavalier
105.	Goodwin, Maud Wilder	Dolly Madison
1301.	Goodwin, Maud Wilder	Head of a hundred
1302.	Goodwin, Maud Wilder	White aprons
1027.	Goodyear, William Henry	History of art
1304.	Gordon C. W.	Sky pilot
731.	Gordy, John P.	History of political parties in the United States
163.	Gordy, Wilbur F.	American leaders and heroes
387.	Gordy, Wilbur F.	History of the United States
388.	Gordy, Wilbur F., *and* Twitchell, W. I.	Pathfinder in American history
984.	Goss, W. F. M.	Bench work in wood

AUTHOR AND TITLE INDEX. 445

1305.	Goss, Warren Lee	Jed
389.	Goss, Warren Lee	Soldier's story
1146.	Gosse, Edmund	Critical kit-kats
1068.	Gosse, Edmund	Short history of modern English literature
1535.	Gostwick, Joseph, *and* Harrison, Robert	
		Outlines of German literature
321.	Gould, Sabine Baring-	Story of Germany
116.	Gouverneur Morris	Theodore Roosevelt
746.	Government class book	A. W. Young
737.	Government in state and nation	
		J. A. James, *and* A. H. Sanford
541.	Gowing, Lionel F.	Five thousand miles in a sledge
245.	Gracchi, Marius, and Sulla	A. H. Beesly
939.	Grant, John B.	Our common birds and how to know them
74.	Grant, Ulysses S.	Personal memoirs
1306.	Gras, Felix	Reds of the Midi
754.	Gray, Elisha	Nature's miracles
1435.	Gray, Thomas	Poetical works
720.	Great American educators	A. E. Winship
363.	Great American legislators	H. W. Caldwell
183.	Great battles of the world	Stephen Crane
339.	Great Boer war	A. C. Doyle
160.	Great captains	T. A. Dodge

Great educators series: *ed.* by N. M. Butler.
   Bowen, H. C. Froebel.
   Davidson, Thomas. Aristotle.
   Hinsdale, B. A. Horace Mann.

157.	Great men's sons	E. S. Brooks
566.	Great Salt Lake trail	*Col.* Henry Inman, *and Col.* W. F. Cody
1485.	Great words from great Americans.	

"Great Writers" series; *ed.* by E. S. Robertson.
   Rolleston, T. W. Life of Gotthold Ephraim Lessing.
   Sime, James. Life of Johann Wolfgang Goethe.

1505.	Greek literature	R. C. Jebb
234.	Greeks and the Persians	*Rev.* G. W. Cox
1470.	Green fields and running brooks	J. W. Riley
290.	Green, John Richard	Short history of the English people
	Green, John Richard, *ed.* *See* Classical writers series.	
825.	Greene, Homer	Coal and the coal mines
319.	Griffis, William Elliot	Brave little Holland
336.	Griffis, William Elliot	Japan in history
447.	Griffis, William Elliot	Pilgrims in their three homes
346.	Griffis, William Elliot	Romance of American colonization
390.	Griffis, William Elliot	Romance of conquest
1421.	Grinnell, George Bird	Punishment of the stingy
448.	Grinnell, George Bird	Story of the Indian
999.	Grinnell, George Bird, *and* Roosevelt, Theodore, *eds.*	
		Trail and campfire
	Grinnell, George Bird, *jt. author. See* Roosevelt, Theodore.	
1028.	Grosse, Ernst	Beginnings of art
1020.	Grossman, Edwina Booth	Edwin Booth
	Grove, Eleanor, *trans. See* Ebers, Georg	Egyptian princess
265.	Growth of the French nation	G. B. Adams
8.	Guerber, Helene A.	Legends of Switzerland
9.	Guerber, Helene A.	Legends of the Middle ages

LIST OF BOOKS FOR HIGH SCHOOL LIBRARIES.

10.	Guerber, Helene A.	Legends of the Rhine
11.	Guerber, Helene A.	Myths of Greece and Rome
12.	Guerber, Helene A.	Myths of northern lands
1000.	Guerber, Helene A.	Stories of famous operas
1001.	Guerber, Helene A.	Stories of the Wagner operas
238.	Guhl, E., *and* Koner, W.	Life of the Greeks and Romans
1563.	Guide to the best historical novels	Jonathan Nield
365.	Guide to the study of American history	Edward Channing, *and* A. B. Hart
1072.	Guide to the study of nineteenth century authors	L. M. Hodgkins
896.	Guide to the trees	Alice Lounsberry
206.	Guizot, Francois P. T.	General history of civilization in Europe
1392.	Gulliver's travels	Dean Swift
1069.	Gummere, Francis B.	Handbook of poetics
	Gunnison, Binney, *jt. comp. See* Craig, A. H.	
609.	Gunton, George, *and* Robbins, Hayes	Outlines of political science
1548.	Gustav Adolf in Deutschland	J. C. Schiller
959.	Gymnastics	W. A. Stecher
	H. H., *pseud. See* Jackson, Helen Hunt.	
949.	Haddon, Alfred C.	Study of man
465.	Hague, Parthenia Antoinette	Blockaded family
291.	Hale, *Rev.* Edward E.	Fall of the Stuarts and western Europe
102.	Hale, Edward Everett, *jr.*	James Russell Lowell
1308.	Hale, Edward E.	Man without a country
473.	Hale, Susan	Story of Mexico
1307.	Halévy, Ludovic	Abbe Constantin
1204.	Half back	R. H. Barbour
772.	Hall, Edwin H., *and* Bergen, J. Y.	Text-book of physics
	Hall, Edwin H., *jt. author. See* Smith, Alexander.	
26.	Hall, Henry	Ethan Allen
673.	Halleck, R. P.	Psychology and psychic culture
952.	Halliburton, William Dobinson	Kirke's handbook of physiology
674.	Ham, Charles H.	Mind and hand
732.	Hamilton, Alexander, *and others*	Federalist and other constitutional papers
885.	Handbook for use of teachers	J. Y. Bergen
980.	Handbook of domestic science	L. L. W. Wilson, *ed.*
1026.	Handbook of Greek sculpture	E. A. Gardner
1069.	Handbook of poetics	F. B. Gummere
958.	Handbook of sanitation	G. M. Price
956.	Handbook of school-gymnastics of the Swedish system	B. N. Posse
1062.	Handbook of universal literature	A. C. Lynch
1571.	Handbook of Wisconsin	L. J. *and* J. M. Turner, *comps.*
616.	Handbook to the labor law of the United States	F. J. Stimson
	Handbooks of archaeology and antiquity.	
	Gardner, E. A. Handbook of Greek sculpture.	
675.	Hanus, Paul H.	Educational aims and educational values
91.	Hapgood, Hutchins	Paul Jones
531.	Hapgood, Isabel F.	Russian rambles
97.	Hapgood, Norman	Abraham Lincoln
145.	Hapgood, Norman	Daniel Webster

140.	Hapgood, Norman	George Washington
969.	Hapgood, Olive C.	School needlework
892.	Hardinge, E. M.	Field, forest and wayside flowers
893.	Hardinge, E. M.	With the wild flowers
1569.	Harper's encyclopaedia of United States history.	

Harper's scientific memoirs; ed. by J. S. Ames.
    Barker, G. F., ed. Roentgen rays.

854.	Harrington, Mark W.	About the weather

Harris, Ella Isabel, trans. See Seneca .... Two tragedies of Seneca

Harris, W. T., ed. See International education series.

733.	Harrison, Benjamin	This country of ours
752.	Harrison, Mrs. Constance Cary ("Mrs. Burton Harrison")	Well-bred girl in society
1147.	Harrison, Frederic	Choice of books
51.	Harrison, Frederic	Oliver Cromwell
239.	Harrison, James A.	Story of Greece

Harrison, Robert, jt. author. See Gostwick, Joseph.

396.	Hart, Albert Bushnell	Formation of the Union
734.	Hart, Albert Bushnell	Foundations of American foreign policy
735.	Hart, Albert Bushnell	Practical essays on American government
392.	Hart, Albert Bushnell, ed.	Era of colonization
393.	Hart, Albert Bushnell, ed.	Building of the republic
394.	Hart, Albert Bushnell, ed.	National expansion
395.	Hart, Albert Bushnell, ed.	Welding of the nation
397.	Hart, Albert Bushnell, ed.	Epoch maps illustrating American history
398.	Hart, Albert Bushnell, ed.	Source-book of American history
391.	Hart, Albert Bushnell, and Channing, Edward, eds.	American history leaflets: colonial and constitutional

Hart, Albert Bushnell, jt. editor. See Channing, Edward.

1309.	Harte, Bret	Luck of roaring camp
1029.	Hartmann, Sadakichi	History of American art
1290.	Harvard episodes	C. M. Flandrau
218.	Hassall, Arthur	Balance of power
292.	Hassall, Arthur	Making of the British empire
1536.	Hauff, Wilhelm	Tales
1310.	Hawthorne, Nathaniel	House of the seven gables
1311.	Hawthorne, Nathaniel	Marble faun
1312.	Hawthorne, Nathaniel	Mosses from an old manse
520.	Hawthorne, Nathaniel	Our old home and English note-books
511.	Hawthorne, Nathaniel	Passages from the French and Italian note-books
1313.	Hawthorne, Nathaniel	Snow image and other twice-told tales
78.	Hawthorne	Henry James, jr.
187.	Hazen, C. D., and others	Historical sources in schools
1070.	Hazlitt, William	Lectures on the literature of the age of Elizabeth
1301.	Head of a hundred	M. W. Goodwin, ed.
133.	Headley, Rev. Philip Camp	Fighting Phil
512.	Hearn, Lafcadio	Glimpses of unfamiliar Japan
1369.	Heart of Midlothian	Sir Walter Scott

1358. Heart of the ancient wood ....C. G. D. Roberts
Heath, Harold, *jt. author.* *See* Jordan, David Starr.
Heath's German series.
    Goethe, Johann Wolfgang von. Torquato Tasso.
Heath's modern language series.
    Andersen, Hans Christian. Märchen.
    Goethe, Johann Wolfgang. Hermann und Dorothea.
    Heine, Heinrich. Poems.
    Lessing, Gotthold Ephraim. Emilia Galotti.
    Lessing, Gotthold Ephraim. Minna von Barnhelm oder Das Soldatenglück.
    Scheffel, Joseph Victor von. Ekkehard.
    Stökl; Helene. Unter dem Christbaum.
Heath's pedagogical library series.
    Adams, John. Herbartian psychology applied to education.
    Barnes, Mary Sheldon. Studies in historical method.
    Compayré, Gabriel. History of pedagogy.
    Compayré, Gabriel. Lectures on pedagogy.
    Elliott, A. Marshall, *and others*. Methods of teaching modern languages.
    Lange, *Dr.* Karl. Apperception.
    Newsholme, Arthur. School hygiene.
    Tracy, Frederick. Psychology of childhood.

836. Heilprin, Angelo ....Earth and its story
1538. Heine, Heinrich ....Heine's prose
1537. Heine, Heinrich ....Poems
1538. Heine's prose ....Heinrich Heine
667. Helps for ambitious girls ....William Drysdale
399. Hemment, John C. ....Cannon and camera
1056. Hempl, George ....German orthography and phonology
466. Hemstreet, Charles ....Story of Manhattan
773. Henderson, C. Hanford *and* Woodhull, J. F. ....
    ....Elements of physics
322. Henderson, Ernest F. ....Short history of Germany
207. Henderson, Ernest F., *trans.* ....
    ....Select historical documents of the Middle ages
1002. Henderson, W. J. ....Story of music
Hendy, F. J. R., *jt. author.* *See* Bryans, Clement.
1393. Henry Esmond ....W. M. Thackeray
1223. Her sixteenth year ....H. D. Brown
643. Herbartian psychology applied to education ......John Adams
1330. Hereward, the wake ....Charles Kingsley
991. Hermann the magician ....H. J. Burlingame
1532. Hermann und Dorothea ....J. W. Goethe
1500. Herodotus. Cary, *trans.* ....History
179. Heroes and martyrs of invention ....G. M. Towle
1137. Heroes, hero-worship and the heroic in history ....
    ....Thomas Carlyle
Heroes of the nations series; *ed.* by Evelyn Abbott.
    Armstrong, Edward. Lorenzo de' Medici.
    Beazley, C. R. Prince Henry the navigator.
    Fowler, W. W. Julius Caesar.
    Hodgkin, Thomas. Theodoric the Goth.
    Oliphant, *Mrs.* Margaret. Jeanne D'Arc.
    Sergeant, Lewis. John Wyclif.
    Morris, W. O. Napoleon, warrior and ruler.

915.	Hertwig Richard. Field, *trans.*	General principles of zoology
799.	Hessler, John C., *and* Smith, A. L.	Essentials of chemistry
1071.	Heydrick, Benjamin A.	How to study literature
	Hickie, William James, *trans. See* Aristophanes	Comedies
916.	Hickson, Sydney J.	Story of life in the seas
402.	High school history of the United States	Alexander Johnston
494.	Higginson, S. J.	Java the pearl of the East
1148.	Higginson, Thomas Wentworth	Army life in a black regiment
1149.	Higginson, Thomas Wentworth	Cheerful yesterdays
1150.	Higginson, Thomas Wentworth	Concerning all of us
1151.	Higginson, Thomas Wentworth	Contemporaries
400.	Higginson, Thomas Wentworth	Larger history of the United States
119.	Higginson, Thomas Wentworth	Margaret Fuller Ossoli
1152.	Higginson, Thomas Wentworth	Outdoor studies, poems
1153.	Higginson, Thomas Wentworth	Procession of the flowers
347.	Higginson, Thomas Wentworth	Young folks' book of American explorers
293.	Higginson, Thomas Wentworth, *and* Channing, Edward	English history for Americans
	Hill, Frank Alpine, *jt. author. See* Fiske, John.	
1314.	Hill, John A.	Stories of the railroad
591.	Hill, Robert T.	Cuba and Puerto Rico
340.	Hillegas, Howard C.	Oom Paul's people
736.	Hinsdale, B. A.	American government
676.	Hinsdale, B. A.	Art of study
677.	Hinsdale, B. A.	Horace Mann
678.	Hinsdale, B. A.	How to study and teach history
449.	Hinsdale, B. A.	Old Northwest
679.	Hinsdale, B. A.	Teaching the language-arts
480.	Hints to teachers and students on the choice of geographical books for reference and reading	H. R. Mill
1565.	Historic note-book	E. C. Brewer
456.	Historic towns of the western states	L. P. Powell, *ed.*
1567.	Historical atlas	R. H. Labberton
	Historical course for schools; *ed.* by E. A. Freeman.	
	Freeman, E. A. General sketch of history.	
	Macarthur, Margaret. History of Scotland.	
187.	Historical sources in schools	C. D. Hazen, *and others*
411.	Historical tales: American	Charles Morris
307.	Historical tales: English	Charles Morris
273.	Historical tales: French	Charles Morris
324.	Historical tales: German	Charles Morris
239a.	Historical tales: Greek	Charles Morris
332.	Historical tales: Japan and China	Charles Morris
259.	Historical tales: Roman	Charles Morris
328.	Historical tales: Russian	Charles Morris
276.	Historical tales: Spanish	Charles Morris
1508.	Histories. Shuckburg, *trans.*	Polybius
1568.	History for ready reference	J. N. Larned
1029.	History of American art	Sadakichi Hartmann
738.	History of American politics	Alexander Johnston
1080.	History of American verse	J. L. Onderdonk

1499a.	History of ancient Greek literature	H. N. Fowler
1027.	History of art	W. H. Goodyear
665.	History of education	Thomas Davidson
693.	History of education	F. V. N. Painter
703.	History of education	Levi Seeley
344.	History of Egypt	F. C. H. Wendel
280.	History of England	Rev. J. F. Bright
282.	History of England	Katharine Coman and E. K. Kendall
298.	History of England	J. N. Larned
1078.	History of English literature	W. V. Moody, and R. M. Lovett
1081.	History of English literature	F. V. N. Painter
1087.	History of English literature	H. A. Taine
275.	History of France	C. M. Yonge
1524.	History of French literature	Edward Dowden
1528.	History of German literature	Kuno Francke
1547.	History of German literature	W. Scherer
323.	History of Germany	C. T. Lewis
325.	History of Germany	James Sime
326.	History of Germany	Bayard Taylor
230.	History of Greece	G. W. Botsford
240.	History of Greece	P. V. Myers
241.	History of Greece	C. W. C. Oman
217.	History of modern Europe	C. A. Fyffe
222.	History of modern Europe	Ferdinand Schwill
198.	History of modern times	Victor Duruy
467.	History of New York	Washington Irving
659.	History of pedagogy	Gabriel Compayré
731.	History of political parties in the United States	J. P. Gordy
1329.	History of Rasselas	Samuel Johnson
246.	History of Rome	G. W. Botsford
1514.	History of Rome	Titus Livius
264.	History of Rome	W. W. How, and H. D. Leigh
300.	History of Scotland	Margaret Macarthur
407.	History of the American nation	A. C. McLaughlin
424.	History of the American people	F. N. Thorpe
476.	History of the conquest of Peru	W. H. Prescott
474.	History of the conquests of Mexico	W. H. Prescott
253.	History of the decline and fall of the Roman empire	Edward Gibbon
355.	History of the formation of the constitution of the United States	George Bancroft
1377.	History of the Lady Betty Stair	M. E. Seawell
354.	History of the last quarter century in the United States	E. B. Andrews
401.	History of the Louisiana purchase	J. K. Hosmer
202.	History of the Middle ages	Victor Duruy
1511.	History of the Peloponnesian war	Thucydides
408.	History of the people of the United States	J. B. McMaster
277.	History of the reign of Ferdinand and Isabella	W. H. Prescott
249.	History of the Roman empire	J. B. Bury
261.	History of the Roman people	Charles Seignobos
247.	History of the Roman republic	Clement Bryans, and F. J. R. Hendy
356.	History of the United States	George Bancroft
382.	History of the United States	John Fiske and F. A. Hill
387.	History of the United States	W. F. Gordy

AUTHOR AND TITLE INDEX. 451

417.	History of the United States	H. E. Scudder
416.	History of the United States	James Schouler
414.	History of the United States	J. F. Rhodes
189a.	History of the world	Edgar Sanderson
	History primers series; ed. by J. R. Green.	
	Wendel, F. C. H. History of Egypt.	
	Yonge, C. M. History of France.	
181.	History topics	W. F. Allen
	Hitchcock, Ripley, ed. See Story of the West series.	
774.	Hoadley, George A.	Brief course in general physics
826.	Hodge, Clifton H.	Nature study and life
120.	Hodges, George	William Penn
137.	Hodgkin, Thomas	Theodoric the Goth
1072.	Hodgkins, Louise Manning	
	Guide to the study of nineteenth century authors	
1558.	Hoffman, Walter James	Beginnings of writing
52.	Holder, Charles F.	Charles Darwin
22.	Holder, Charles F.	Louis Agassiz
524.	Holland and its people	Edmondo de Amicis
526.	Holland and the Hollanders	D. S. Meldrum
775.	Holmes, George C. V.	Steam engine
1154.	Holmes, Oliver Wendell	Autocrat of the breakfast-table
1455.	Holmes, Oliver Wendell	Complete poetical works
60.	Holmes, Oliver Wendell	Ralph Waldo Emerson
139.	Holmes, Richard R.	Queen Victoria
40.	Holst, Dr. H. von	John C. Calhoun
	Holtzapffel, John J., revisor. See Leland, Charles G.	
1286.	Holy cross	Eugene Field
248.	Holy Roman empire	James Bryce
1471.	Home-folks	J. W. Riley
437.	Home life in colonial days	A. M. Earle
554.	Home life on an ostrich farm	Annie Martin
1501.	Homer. Bryant, trans.	Iliad
1502.	Homer. Lang, Leaf, and Myers, trans.	Iliad
1503.	Homer. Bryant, trans.	Odyssey
1504.	Homer. Butcher and Lang, trans.	Odyssey
1292.	Honorable Peter Stirling	P. L. Ford
813.	Holden, Edward S.	Elementary astronomy
814.	Holden, Edward S.	Family of the sun
1003.	Hopkins, A. A.	
	Magic stage illusions and scientific diversions	
776.	Hopkins, George M.	Experimental science
777.	Hopkins, William J.	Preparatory physics
778.	Hopkins, William J.	Telephone lines and their properties
677.	Horace Mann	B. A. Hinsdale
507.	Horton, George	Modern Athens
401.	Hosmer, James K.	History of the Louisiana purchase
21.	Hosmer, James K.	Samuel Adams
1539.	Hosmer, James K.	Short history of German literature
450.	Hosmer, James K.	
	Short history of the Mississippi valley	
451.	Hough, E.	Story of the cowboy
525.	Hough, P. M.	Dutch life in town and country
1287.	House	Eugene Field
1310.	House of the seven gables	Nathaniel Hawthorne
965.	Household economics	Mrs. Helen Campbell
375.	Household history of the United States	Edward Eggleston

286.	Houses of Lancaster and York	James Gairdner
855.	Houston, Edwin J.	Elements of physical geography
452.	How New England was made	F. A. Humphrey
631.	How the other half lives	J. A. Riis
722.	How the republic is governed	Noah Brooks
1025.	How to enjoy pictures	M. S. Emery
1017.	How to play golf	H. G. Wigham
1104.	How to recite	F. T. Southwick
678.	How to study and teach history	B. A. Hinsdale
1071.	How to study literature	B. A. Heydrick
995.	How to swim	Capt. Davis Dalton
1138.	How to tell a story	S. L. Clemens
264.	How, William Walsham, and Leigh, H. D.	History of Rome
628.	Howard, Benjamin	Prisoners of Russia
1315.	Howard, Blanche W.	One summer
501.	Howard, Blanche W.	One year abroad
917.	Howard, Leland O.	Insect book
680.	Howe, Edward Gardiner	Systematic science teaching
33.	Howe, M. A. DeWolfe	Phillips Brooks
1155.	Howells, William Dean	Literary friends and acquaintance
1113.	Howells, William Dean	Mouse-trap
1316.	Howells, William Dean	Rise of Silas Lapham
1114.	Howells, William Dean	Sleeping-car and other farces
512.	Howells, William Dean	Venetian life
578.	Howells, William Dean, and others	Niagara book
1317.	Hoyt, Deristhe L.	Barbara's heritage
1030.	Hoyt, Deristhe L.	World's painters and their pictures
1586.	Hoyt, J. K.	Cyclopaedia of practical quotations
1115.	Hudson, Rev. Henry Norman	Shakespeare
	Hudson, Rev. Henry Norman, ed. See Shakespeare, William	Dramas
	Hueffer, F., trans. See Guhl, E.	Life of the Greeks and Romans
1116.	Hufford, Lois Grosvenor	Shakespeare
1268.	Hugh Gwyeth	B. M. Dix
1342.	Hugh Wynne, free Quaker	S. W. Mitchell
681.	Hughes, James L.	Dickens as an educator
25.	Hughes, Thomas	Alfred the Great
1318.	Hughes, Thomas	Tom Brown at Oxford
837.	Hull, Edward	Volcanoes
188.	Hulme, Frederick Edward	Flags of the world
954.	Human body	H. N. Martin
452.	Humphrey, Frances A.	How New England was made
970.	Hunn, C. E.	Amateur's practical garden-book
164.	Hunt, Violet Brooks-	Prisoners of the tower of London
1007.	Hunting	Archibald Rogers and others
1003.	Hunting in many lands	Theodore Roosevelt and G. B. Grinnell, eds.
1031.	Hurll, Estelle M.	Tuscan sculpture
1032.	Hurll, Estelle M.	Van Dyck
838.	Hutchinson, Rev. H. N.	Story of the hills
129.	Hutton, Richard H.	Sir Walter Scott
294.	Hutton, William Holden	King and baronage
856.	Huxley, T. H	Physiography
1331.	Hypatia	Charles Kingsley
1336.	Hyperion and Kavanagh	H. W. Longfellow
1397.	Iceland fisherman. DeKoven, trans.	L. M. J. Viaud

AUTHOR AND TITLE INDEX.   453

849.	Ice-work present and past	T. G. Bonney
702.	Ideal school	P. W. Search
484.	Idylls of the sea	F. T. Bullen
255.	Ihne, William	Early Rome
779.	Iles, George	Flame, electricity, and the camera
1501.	Iliad. Bryant, *trans.*	Homer
1502.	Iliad. Lang, Leaf *and* Myers. *trans.*	Homer
1489.	Illustrated history of ancient literature	J. D. Quackenbos
1561.	Illustration of books	Joseph Pennell
337.	Impressions of South Africa	James Bryce
985.	Improvement of towns and cities	C. M. Robinson
529.	In and around Berlin	M. B. Norton
491.	In bird land	L. S. Keyser
623.	In darkest England	*Gen.* William Booth
1347.	In ole Virginia	T. N. Page
1178.	In the dozy hours and other papers	Agnes Repplier
496.	In the south seas	R. L. Stevenson
1344.	In the Tennessee mountains	M. N. Murfree
373.	Indian history for young folks	F. S. Drake
620.	Industrial evolution of United States	C. D. Wright
256.	Inge, William Ralph	Society in Rome under the Caesars
1456.	Ingelow, Jean	Poems
1236.	Ingenious gentleman	Saavedra Miguel de Cervantes
825.	Ingersoll, Ernest	Book of the ocean
918.	Ingersoll, Ernest	Wild neighbors
453.	Ingle, Edward	Southern sidelights
566.	Inman, Henry	Great Salt Lake trail
567.	Inman, Henry	Old Santa Fé trail
917.	Insect book	L. O. Howard
911.	Insect life	J. H. Comstock
889.	Insectiverous plants	Charles Darwin

International educational series; *ed.* by W. T. Harris.
    Adler, Felix. Moral instruction of children.
    Baldwin, Joseph. Elementary psychology and education.
    Baldwin, Joseph. School management and school methods.
    Blow, S. E. Letters to a mother.
    Blow, S. E. Symbolic education.
    Bolton, F. E. Secondary school systems of Germany.
    Boone, R. G. Education in the United States.
    Davidson, Thomas. Education of the Greek people.
    Hinsdale, B. A. How to study and teach history.
    Hinsdale, B. A. Teaching the language arts.
    Howe, E. G. Systematic science teaching.
    Hughes, J. L. Dickens as an educator.
    Klemm, L. R. European schools.
    Monroe, W. S. Bibliography of education.
    Morrison, G. B. Ventilation and warming of school buildings.
    Painter, F. V. N. History of education.
    Payne, W. H. Rosseau's Emile.
    Pickard, J. L. School supervision.
    Preyer, W. T. Mental development in the child.
    Quick, R. H. Essays on educational reformers.
    Search, P. W. Ideal school.
    Taylor, A. R. Study of the child.

481.	International geography	H. R. Mill, *ed.*

International modern language series.
   Goethe, J. W. Egmont, with Schiller's essays.
   Hauff, Wilhelm, Tales.
   Lessing, G. E. Emilia Galotti.
   Mueller, Hermann. Deutsche Gedichte.
   Rosegger, P. K. Waldheimat.

International scientific series.
   Bonney, T. G. Ice-work present and past.
   Judd, J. W. Volcanoes.
   Trowbridge, John. What is electricity?
   Tyndall, John. Forms of water in clouds and rivers.

877.	Introduction to general biology	E. B. Wilson *and* W. T. Sedgwick
843.	Introduction to geology	W. G. Scott
853.	Introduction to physical geography	G. K. Gilbert *and* A. P. Brigham
1111.	Introduction to Shakespeare	Edward Dowden
656.	Introduction to the history of educational theories	Oscar Browning
711.	Introduction to the pedagogy of Herbart. Zinzer, *trans.*	Christian Ufer
1075.	Introduction to the study of American literature	Brander Matthews
802.	Introduction to the study of chemistry	Ira Remsen
1099.	Introduction to the study of literature	E. H. Lewis
634.	Introduction to the study of society	A. W. Small *and* G. E. Vincent
203.	Introduction to the study of the middle ages	Ephraim Emerton
1073.	Introductory lessons in English literature	I. C. McNeill *and* S. A. Lynch
1284.	Invasion of France in 1814	Emile Erckmann *and* Alex. Chatrain
1533.	Iphigenie auf Tauris	J. W. Goethe
1205.	Irish idylls	Jane Barlow
1319.	Irving, Washington	Alhambra
467.	Irving, Washington	History of New York
1157.	Irving, Washington	Sketch book
1320.	Irving, Washington	Stories and legends
1321.	Irving, Washington	Tales of a traveller
1156.	Irving, Washington, *and others*	Representative essays
521.	Isle of the shamrock	Clifton Johnson
125.	Israel Putnam	W. F. Livingston
509.	Italians of today. Marchmant, *trans.*	René Bazin
1376.	Ivanhoe	*Sir* Walter Scott
	"J. S. of Dale," *pseud. See* Stimson, F. Jessup.	
755.	Jackman, Wilbur S.	Nature study
780.	Jackson, Dugald C. *and* Jackson, J. P. Elementary book on electricity and magnetism	
502.	Jackson, Helen H.	Bits of travel
568.	Jackson, Helen H.	Bits of travel at home
503.	Jackson, Helen H.	Glimpses of three coasts
1322.	Jackson, Helen H.	Ramona
	Jackson, John Price, *jt. author. See* Jackson, Dugald C.	
479.	Jacobs, Joseph	Story of geographical discovery
971.	James, Charles C.	Practical agriculture
1117.	James, Henry, *jr.*	Daisy Miller

AUTHOR AND TITLE INDEX. 455

78.	James, Henry, *jr*	Hawthorne
737.	James, James A., *and* Sanford, A. H.	
		Government in state and nation
682.	James, William	Talks to teachers on psychology
102.	James Russell Lowell	E. E. Hale, *jr.*
104.	James Madison	S. H. Gay
114.	James Monroe	D. C. Gilman
1118.	Jameson, *Mrs.* Anna B.	Shakespeare's heroines
1293.	Janice Meredith	P. L. Ford
	Janvier, Catherine A., *trans.* *See* Gras, Felix. Reds of the Midi.	
336.	Japan in history	W. E. Griffis
546.	Japan in transition	Stafford Ransome
538.	Japanese girls and women	A. M. Bacon
537.	Japanese interior	A. M. Bacon
495.	Java the garden of the East	E. R. Scidmore
494.	Java the pearl of the East	S. J. Higginson
85.	Jeanne D'Arc	*Mrs.* Margaret Oliphant
1505.	Jebb, R. C.	Greek literature
1305.	Jed	W. L. Goss
1158.	Jefferies, Richard	Field and hedgerow
1159.	Jefferies, Richard	Open air
1021.	Jefferson, Joseph	Autobiography
953.	Jegi, John I.	Syllabus of human physiology
610.	Jenks, Jeremiah Whipple	Trust problem
1323.	Jerome, Jerome K.	Three men in a boat
1478.	Jerusalem delivered	Torquato Tasso
	Jevons, Frank Byron, *jt. author.* *See* Gardner, Percy.	
1325.	Jewett, Sarah Orne	Country by-ways
1324.	Jewett, Sarah Orne	Country doctor
1326.	Jewett, Sarah Orne	Country of the pointed firs
219.	Jewett, Sarah Orne	Story of the Normans
1327.	Jewett, Sarah Orne	Tales of New England
940.	Job, Herbert K.	Among the water-fowl
19.	John Adams	J. T. Morse, *jr.*
20.	John Quincy Adams	J. T. Morse, *jr.*
34.	John Brown	J. E. Chamberlain
40.	John C. Calhoun	*Dr.* H. Von Holst
108.	John Marshall	A. B. Magruder
109.	John Marshall	J. B. Thayer
147.	John Greenleaf Whittier	Richard Burton
150.	John Wyclif	Lewis Sergeant
220.	Johnson, *Rev.* Arthur Henry	Europe in the sixteenth century
221.	Johnson, *Rev.* Arthur Henry	Normans in Europe
521.	Johnson, Clifton	Isle of the shamrock
579.	Johnson, Clifton	New England country
	Johnson, Clifton, *ed.* *See* De Cervantes, Saavedra Miguel. Ingenious gentleman.	
629.	Johnson, Helen Kendrick	Woman and the republic
1329.	Johnson, Samuel	History of Rasselas
1564.	Johnson's Universal cyclopedia	C. K. Adams, *ed.*
468.	Johnston, Alexander	Connecticut
402.	Johnston, Alexander	
		High school history of the United States
738.	Johnston, Alexander	History of American politics
1486.	Johnston, Alexander, *ed.*	American orations

800.	Johnston, James F. W..............	Chemistry of common life
1328.	Johnston, Mary	To have and to hold
215.	Joinville, *Lord* John de	Chronicles of the crusades
	Jones, Eustace Hinton, *jt. author*. *See* Cox, *Sir* George W.	
208.	Jones, Guernsey	Studies in European history
1119.	Jonson, Ben	Every man in his humour
873.	Jordan, David Starr	Foot-notes to evolution
919.	Jordan, David Starr, *and* Kellogg, V. L., *and* Heath, Harold...	
	....	Animals
86.	Joseph Jefferson at home ....:.............	N. H. Dole
597.	Journal of researches	Charles Darwin
741.	Journal of the Constitutional Convention.......	James Madison
1544.	Journalistic German	August Prehn, *ed.*
295.	Joyce, Patrick Weston	Child's history of Ireland
839.	Judd, John W................	Volcanoes
37.	Julius Caesar	Jacob Abbott
38.	Julius Caesar	W. W. Fowler
1549.	Jungfrau von Orleans	J. C. F. von Schiller
1520.	Juvenal. Evans, *trans.*	Satires
543.	Karageorgevitch, Bojidar	Enchanted India
1336.	Kavanagh..H. W. Longfellow. *In* (1336) Longfellow's Hyperion	
1457.	Keats, John	Complete poetical works and letters
92.	Keats.........	Sidney Colvin
894.	Keeler, Harriet L....	Our native trees and how to identify them
920.	Kellogg, Vernon L.........	Elementary zoology
	Kellogg, Vernon L., *jt. author*. *See* Jordan, David Starr.	
296.	Kendall, Elizabeth Kimball, *ed*.............	
	....	Source book of English history
	Kendall, Elizabeth Kimball, *jt. author*. *See* Coman, Katharine.	
1370.	Kenilworth	*Sir* Walter Scott
544.	Kennan, George	Tent life in Siberia
1200.	Kentucky Cardinal	J. L. Allen
	Kenyon, Frederick G., *trans*. *See* Aristotle. .On the Athenian constitution.	
941.	Keyser, Leander S...........	In bird land
1382.	Kidnapped	R. L. Stevenson
718.	Kindergarten principles and practice ....:................	
	....	K. D. Wiggin *and* N. A. Smith
927.	Kindred of the wild	C. G. D. Roberts
504.	King, Charles F........	Roundabout rambles in northern Europe
294.	King and baronage	W. H. Hutton
316.	King and parliament	G. H. Wakeling
1424.	King Arthur	Charles Morris
1384.	King Noanett	F. J. Stimson
122.	King Philip	Jacob Abbott
1112.	King's jester	C. A. Dugan
	Kingsford, C. L., *jt. author*. *See* Archer, T. A.	
1330.	Kingsley, Charles...............	Hereward, the wake
1331.	Kingsley, Charles............................	Hypatia
1332.	Kingsley, Charles..............................	Westward Ho!
1333.	Kipling, Rudyard	Captains courageous
1334.	Kipling, Rudyard...........................	Day's work
1458.	Kipling, Rudyard...........	Departmental ditties and ballads
952.	Kirke's handbook of physiology :...........	W. D. Halliburton
683.	Klemm, Louis Richard	European schools
	Knickerbocker, Diedrich, *pseud*. *See* Irving, Washington.	

AUTHOR AND TITLE INDEX. 457

66. Knox, Thomas W............... ....
..Life of Robert Fulton and a history of steam navigation
Koner, W., *jt. author.* See Guhl, E.
1559. Koopman, Harry Lyman................. ..Mastery of books
1004. Kunhardt, C. P.................Ropes, their knots and splices
349. La Salle, and the discovery of the great west..Francis Parkman
1567. Labberton, Robert H............ ....Historical atlas
612. Labor copartnership ....H. D. Lloyd
876. Laboratory guide for an elementary course in general biology...
....J. H. Pillsbury
796. Laboratory manual ....L. M. Dennis, *and* F. W. Clark
887. Laboratory manual in practical botany............C. H. Clark
903. Laboratory practice for beginners in botany......W. A. Setchel
684. Ladd, George Trumbull ....Primer of psychology
1233. Lady of Fort St. John.......................M. H. Catherwood
860. Lakes of North America ....I. C. Russell
1572. Lalor, John J., *ed.* ....Cyclopedia of political science
1100. Lamb, Charles ....Essays of Elia
297. Lancaster, Edward M................Manual of English history
1415. Lances of Lynwood ....C. M. Yonge
500. Land of the long night ....Paul Du Chaillu
575. Land of the Pueblos .... S. E. Wallace
973. Landscape gardening as applied to home decoration...........
.... S. T. Maynard
Lane-Poole, Stanley, *trans.* See Mohammad. Speeches and table-talk.
Lang, Andrew, *trans.* See Homer, Iliad.
Lang, Andrew, *jt. trans.* See Butcher, Samuel H.
685. Lange, *Dr.* Karl ....Apperception
1459. Langland, William ....Vision of Piers the plowman
1422. Lanier, Sidney, *ed.* ....Boy's Froissart
1423. Lanier, Sidney, *ed.* ....Boy's King Arthur
1460. Lanier, Sidney, *ed.*.......................... .....Boy's Percy
1461. Larcom, Lucy ....Complete poetical works
400. Larger history of the United States............T. W. Higginson
1568. Larned, Josephus N............. History for ready reference
298. Larned, Josephus N................. .... History of England
1226. Last days of Pompeii ....*Sir* E. G. Bulwer-Lytton
1227. Last of the barons .... *Sir* E. G. Bulwer-Lytton
1245. Last of the Mohicans ....J. F. Cooper
79. Lathrop, George Parsons ....Study of Hawthorne
611. Laughlin, James Laurence ......Elements of political economy
Lawton, William Cranston, *trans.* See Euripides. Dramas.
1464. Lays of ancient Rome ....T. B. Macaulay
516. Lazy tours in Spain and elsewhere ....L. C. Moulton
266. Le Bon, Andre........... ....Story of modern France
840. Le Conte, Joseph ....Compend of geology
841. Le Conte, Joseph ....Elements of geology
1128. Le Morte d'Arthur ....*Sir* Edward Strachey
Leaders in science series.
    Guillemard, F. Life and work of Alex. Humboldt.
    Holder, C. F. Charles Darwin.
    Holder, C. F. Life and work of Louis Agassiz.
469. Leading events of Wisconsin history. ....Henry Legler
304. Leading facts of English history ....D. H. Montgomery

458   LIST OF BOOKS FOR HIGH SCHOOL LIBRARIES:

271. Leading facts of French history ....D. H. Montgomery
      Leading facts of history series.
         Montgomery, D. H. Leading facts of English history.
         Montgomery, D. H. Leading facts of French history.
         Montgomery. D. H. Student's American history.

      Leaf, Walter, jt. trans. See **Lang, Andrew.**
895. Leavitt, Robert Greenleaf ....Outlines of botany
403. Lecky, William Edward Hartpole ....American Revolution
660. Lectures on pedagogy ....Gabriel Compayré
670. Lectures on teaching ....J. G. Fitch
1070. Lectures on the literature of the age of Elizabeth ....
         ....William Hazlitt
1291. Led-horse claim ....M. H. Foote
1052. Lee, Guy Carleton ....Principles of public speaking
299. Lee, Guy Carleton .... Source-book of English history
1335. Lee, Mary Catherine ....Quaker girl of Nantucket
      Leete, C. H., jt. editor. See **Chisholm, George G.**
5.   Legends of Charlemagne ....Thomas Bullfinch
8.   Legends of Switzerland ....H. A. Guerber
9.   Legends of the Middle ages ....H. A. Guerber
10.   Legends of the Rhine ....H. A. Guerber
469. Legler Henry, ...Leading events of Wisconsin history
      Leigh, H. D., jt. author. See **How, William Walsham.**
1033. Leland, Charles G ....Manual of wood carving
1540. Lessing, Gotthold Ephraim ....Emilia Galotti
1541. Lessing, Gotthold Ephraim ....Minna von Barnhelm
788. Lessons in elementary physics ....Balfour Stewart
833. Lessons in physical geography ....C. R. Dryer
881. Lessons with plants ....L. H. Bailey
1516. Letters of Caius Plinius Caecilius Secundus .....C. C. S. Pliny
649. Letters to a mother ....S. E. Blow
70.   Lewes, George Henry ....Story of Goethe's life
1577. Lewis, Charlton T. ....Elementary Latin dictionary
323. Lewis, Charlton T. ....History of Germany
1099. Lewis, Edwin Herbert ....
         ....Introduction to the study of literature
      Library of economics and politics series; ed. by R. T. Ely.
         Ingle, Edward. Southern sidelights.
         Warner, A. G. American charities.

      Library of useful stories series.
         Anderson, R. E. Story of extinct civilization of the east.
         Archibald, Douglas. Story of the earth's atmosphere.
         Chambers, G. F. Story of eclipses simply told.
         Clodd, Edward. Story of primitive man.
         Conn, H. W. Story of germ life.
         Jacobs, Joseph. Story of geographical discovery.
         Lindsay, B. Story of animal life.
         Martin, E. A. Story of a piece of coal.
         Munro, John. Story of electricity.
         Rawlings, G. B. Story of books.
         Seeley, H. G. Story of the earth in past ages.
         Story, A. T. Story of photography.
         Wilkinson, F. Story of the cotton plant.

910. Life and her children ....A. B. Buckley
61.   Life and letters of Erasmus ....J. A. Froude

874.	Life and love	M. W. Morley
128.	Life and works of Friedrich Schiller	Calvin Thomas
341.	Life in ancient Egypt and Assyria	G. Maspero
100.	Life of Abraham Lincoln	Ida Tarbell
69.	Life of Gladstone	M. B. Synge
95.	Life of Gotthold Ephraim Lessing	T. W. Rolleston
47.	Life of Henry Clay	Carl Schurz
71.	Life of Johann Wolfgang Goethe	James Sime
90.	Life of John Paul Jones	J. S. C. Abbott
66.	Life of Robert Fulton and a history of steam navigation	T. W. Knox
89.	Life of Samuel Johnson	James Boswell
923.	Life of the bee	Maurice Maeterlinck
238.	Life of the Greeks and Romans. Hueffer, *trans.*	E. Guhl, *and* W. Koner
790.	Light, visible and invisible	S. P. Thompson
96.	Lighton, William R.	Meriwether Lewis and William Clark
99.	Lincoln, Abraham	Gettysburg speech and other papers
	In (99) Carl Schurz's Lincoln.	
972.	Lincoln, *Mrs.* Mary J.	Boston school kitchen text-book
1100.	Lincoln literary collection	J. P. McCaskey
921.	Lindsay, B.	Story of animal life
1155.	Literary friends and acquaintance	W. D. Howells
1091.	Literary history of America	Barrett Wendell
1065.	Literary landmarks	M. E. Burt
243.	Little Arthur's history of Greece	A. S. Walpole
1288.	Little book of profitable tales	Eugene Field
1451.	Little book of western verse	Eugene Field
1416.	Little Duke Richard the fearless	C. M. Yonge
1210.	Little minister	J. M. Barrie
1193.	Little rivers	Henry Van Dyke
155.	Lives of poor boys who became famous	S. K. Bolton
930.	Lives of the hunted	Ernest Seton-Thompson
125.	Livingston, William Farrand	Israel Putnam
1514.	Livius, Titus	History of Rome
101.	Livy	W. W. Capes
612.	Lloyd, Henry Demarest	Labor copartnership
613.	Lloyd, Henry Demarest	Wealth against commonwealth
1161.	Lobban, J. H., *and others*	English essays
1132.	Locusts and wild honey	John Burroughs
76.	Lodge, Henry Cabot	Alexander Hamilton
146.	Lodge, Henry Cabot	Daniel Webster
141.	Lodge, Henry Cabot	George Washington
454.	Lodge, Henry Cabot	Short history of the English colonies in America
404.	Lodge, Henry Cabot	War with Spain
492.	Log of a sea-waif	F. T. Bullen
338.	London to Ladysmith via Pretoria	W. S. Churchill
	Long, George, *trans. See* Epictetus	Discourses
	Long, George *trans. See* Antonius, Marcus Aurelius.	Thoughts
922.	Long, William J.	Beasts of the field
942.	Long, William J.	Fowls of the air
1462.	Longfellow, Henry Wadsworth	Complete poetical works
1336.	Longfellow, Henry Wadsworth	Hyperion and Kavanagh
505.	Longfellow, Henry Wadsworth	Outre-Mer

	Longfellow, Henry Wadsworth, *trans.* See Dante ....
	....Divine comedy
269.	Longman, Frederick William ....
	............Frederick the Great and the seven years' war
1566.	Longmans' atlas of ancient geography ....
	....*Rev.* George Butler, *ed.*
1570.	Longmans' new school atlas ....
	....................G. C. Chisholm, *and* C. H. Leete, *eds.*
1217.	Looking backward ....Edward Bellamy
165–174.	Lord, John ....Beacon lights of history
111.	Lorenzo de'Medici ....Edward Armstrong
1221.	Lorna Doone ....R. D. Blackmore
175.	Lossing, Benson J. ....Two spies
130.	Lothrop, Thornton Kirkland ....William Henry Seward
1430.	Lotus and jewel ....Edwin Arnold
1337.	Loughead, Flora Haines ....Abandoned claim
22.	Louis Agassiz ....C. F. Holder
1230.	Louisiana ....F. H. Burnett
23.	Louise M. Alcott ....E. D. Cheney, *ed.*
896.	Lounsberry, Alice ....Guide to the trees
1228.	Love in old cloathes ....H. C. Bunner
1452.	Love-songs of childhood ....Eugene Field
	Lovett, Robert Morss, *jt. author.* See Moody, William Vaughn.
29.	Lowe, Charles ....Prince Bismarck
270.	Lowell, Edward J. ....Eve of the French revolution
1162.	Lowell, James Russell ....Among my books
1463.	Lowell, James Russell ....Complete poetical works
1163.	Lowell, James Russell ....Fireside travels
1164.	Lowell, James Russell ....My study windows
1208.	Loyal traitor ....James Barnes
1506.	Lucian (Lucianus Samosatensis). Smith, *trans.* ...Selections
1309.	Luck of roaring camp ....Bret Harte
93.	Lucy Larcom ....D. D. Addison
1338.	Ludlow, James M. ....Captain of the Janizaries
586.	Lummis, Charles F. ....Awakening of a nation
1339.	Lummis, Charles F. ....Enchanted burro
1340.	Lummis, Charles F. ....New Mexico David
569.	Lummis, Charles F. .....Some strange corners of our country
570.	Lummis, Charles F. ....Tramp across the continent
1542.	Luther, Martin. Bell, *trans.* ....
	..........Selections from the table-talk of Martin Luther
	Lynch, S. A., *jt. author.* See McNeill, I. C.
1447.	Lyrics of lowly life ....P. L. Dunbar
1448.	Lyrics of the hearthside ....P. L. Dunbar
1507.	Lysias ....Orations
	Lytton, Lord. Sec Bulwer-Lytton, *Sir* Edward G.
1165.	Mabie, Hamilton Wright ....Books and culture
1167.	Mabie, Hamilton Wright ....Essays on nature and culture
1168.	Mabie, Hamilton Wright ....Essays on work and culture
1169.	Mabie, Hamilton Wright ....My study fire
1170.	Mabie, Hamilton Wright ....My study fire. Second series
1171.	Mabie, Hamilton Wright ....Short studies in literature
131.	Mabie, Hamilton Wright ....William Shakespeare
300.	Macarthur, Margaret ....History of Scotland
1166.	Macaulay, T. Babington ....Critical and historical essays
1464.	Macaulay, T. Babington ....Lays of ancient Rome

301.	McCarthy, Justin	Epoch of reform
302.	McCarthy, Justin	
	Story of the people of England in the Nineteenth century	
1100.	McCaskey, J. P.	Lincoln literary collection
405.	MacDonald, William, *ed.*	Select charters
406.	MacDonald, William, *ed.*	Select documents
	MacDonald, William, *revisor. See* Johnston, Alexander	
		High school history of the United States
897.	Macdougal, D. T.	Nature and work of plants
686.	Mace, William H.	Method in history
1234.	Mackinac and lake stories	M. H. Catherwood
	Maclaren, Ian, *pseud. See* Watson, John.	
407.	McLaughlin, Andrew C.	History of the American nation
	McLaughlin, Andrew C., *chairman. See* Committee of Seven.	
687.	McLellan, James A.	Applied psychology
408.	McMaster, John Bach	
		History of the people of the United State
409.	McMaster, John Bach	School history of the United States
740.	McMaster, John Bach	With the fathers
1073.	McNeill, I. C., *and* Lynch, S. A.	
		Introductory lessons in English literature
739.	Macy, Jesse	Political parties in the United States
741.	Madison, James	Journal of the Constitutional Convention
923.	Maeterlinck, Maurice. Sutro, *trans.*	Life of the bee
1003.	Magic stage illusions and scientific diversions	A. A. Hopkins
108.	Magruder, Allan B.	John Marshall
62.	Mahaffy, John P.	Euripides
688.	Mahaffy, John P.	Old Greek education
1378.	Maid Marion and other stories	M. E. Seawell
1297.	Main-travelled roads	Hamlin Garland
1341.	Major, Charles	When knighthood was in flower
	Makers of America series.	
	Wendell, Barrett. Colton Mather.	
176.	Makers of Florence	*Mrs.* Margaret Oliphant
177.	Makers of modern Rome	*Mrs.* Margaret Oliphant
178.	Makers of Venice	*Mrs.* Margaret Oliphant
632.	Making of an American	J. A. Riis
431.	Making of New England	S. A. Drake
292.	Making of the British empire	Arthur Hassall
311.	Making of the English nation	C. G. Robertson
426.	Making of the nation	F. A. Walker
432.	Making of the Ohio valley states	S. A. Drake
1308.	Man without a country	E. E. Hale
1120.	Manly, John Matthews	
		Specimens of Pre-Shakespearean drama
13.	Mann, Horace	Few thoughts for a young man
196.	Manual of ancient history	M. E. Thalheimer
207.	Manual of English history	E. M. Lancaster
1059.	Manual of English literature	Thomas Arnold
237.	Manual of Greek antiquities	Percy Gardner *and* F. B. Jevons
180.	Manual of historical literature	C. K. Adams
199.	Manual of mediaeval and modern history	M. E. Thalheimer
1033.	Manual of wood carving	C. G. Leland
65.	Many-sided Franklin	P. L. Ford
1311.	Marble faun	Nathaniel Hawthorne
1515.	Marcellinus, Ammianus	Roman history
	Marchant, William, *trans. See* Bazin, René	Italians of today

1526.	Märchen	H. C. Andersen
371.	Marching to victory	C. C. Coffin
385.	Marching with Gomez	Grover Flint
1521.	Marcus, Aurelius Antonius. Long, *trans.*	Thoughts
14.	Marden, Orison Swett	Success
119.	Margaret Fuller Ossoli	T. W. Higginson
148.	Margaret Winthrop	A. M. Earle
1550.	Maria Stuart	J. C. Schiller
1253.	Marietta	F. M. Crawford
1198.	Marjorie Daw and other stories	T. B. Aldrich
1121.	Marlowe, Christopher	Dr. Faustus
1034.	Marquand, Allan	Text-book of the history of sculpture
1348.	Marse Chan	T. N. Page
144.	Martha Washington	A. H. Wharton
554.	Martin, Annie	Home life on an ostrich farm
842.	Martin, Edward A.	Story of a piece of coal
954.	Martin, Henry Newell	Human body
	Martin, *Sir* Theodore, *trans.* *See* Schiller, Friedrich . . . . Wilhelm Tell	
	Marvin, Arthur, *ed.* *See* Irving, Washington	Alhambra
341.	Maspero, Gaston	Life in ancient Egypt and Assyria
1260.	Master Humphrey's clock	Charles Dickens
	In his (1260) Barnaby Rudge.	
1218.	Master sky-lark	John Bennett
1559.	Mastery of books	H. L. Koopman
898.	Mathews, Ferdinand Schuyler . . . . Familiar features of the roadside	
899.	Mathews, Ferdinand Schuyler . . . . Familiar flowers of field and garden	
900.	Mathews, Ferdinand Schuyler . . . . Familiar trees and their leaves.	
1053.	Matson, Henry	
	References for literary workers: with introduction to topics . . . . and questions for debate	
1074.	Matthews, Brander . . . . Aspects of fiction and other ventures in criticism	
1525.	Matthews, Brander . . . . French dramatists of the nineteenth century	
1075.	Matthews, Brander . . . . Introduction to the study of American literature	
1172.	Matthews, Brander	Pen and ink
781.	Maxwell, James Clerk	Theory of heat
1005.	Mayer, Alfred M., *ed.*	Sport with gun and rod
973.	Maynard, Samuel T. . . . . Landscape gardening as applied to home decoration	
782.	Meadowcroft, W. H.	A. B. C. of electricity
783.	Meadowcroft, W. H.	A. B. C. of the X-ray
1224.	Meadow-grass	Alice Brown
657.	Meaning of education	N. M. Butler
197.	Mediaeval and modern history	G. B. Adams
204.	Mediaeval Europe	Ephraim Emerton
1046.	Meiklejohn, John M. D.	Art of writing English
526.	Meldrum, David B.	Holland and the Hollanders
458.	Men and manners in America	H. E. Scudder, *ed.*
696.	Mental development in the child	W. T. Preyer
257.	Merivale, Charles	Roman triumvirates
96.	Meriwether Lewis and William Clark	W. R. Lighton

943.	Merriam, Florence A.	A-birding on a bronco
944.	Merriam, Florence A.	Birds of village and field
36.	Merwin, Henry Childs	Aaron Burr
87.	Merwin, Henry Childs	Thomas Jefferson
	Metcalfe, Frederick, *trans.* See Becker, W. A.	Gallus
686.	Method in history	W. H. Mace
668.	Methods of teaching modern languages	
		A. M. Elliott, *and others*
209.	Middle Ages	P. V. Myers
360.	Middle period	J. W. Burgess
135.	Miles Standish	J. S. C. Abbott
480.	Mill, Hugh Robert	
	Hints to teachers and students on the choice of geographical books for reference	
481.	Mill, Hugh Robert, *ed.*	International geography
614.	Mill, John Stuart	Principles of political economy
46.	Mill boy of the slashes	John Frost
945.	Miller, *Mrs.* Harriet Mann	Bird-lover in the west
946.	Miller, *Mrs.* Harriet Mann	Upon the tree-tops
	Miller, Olive Thorne, *pseud.* See Miller, *Mrs.* Harriet Mann.	
1466.	Milton, John	Paradise lost
1465.	Milton, John	Poetical works
112.	Milton	S. A. Brooke
113.	Milton	Mark Pattison
674.	Mind and hand	C. H. Ham
830.	Minerals and how to study them	E. S. Dana
1541.	Minna von Barnhelm oder Das Soldatenglück	
		G. E. Lessing
383.	Mississippi valley in the Civil war	John Fiske
463.	Missouri	Lucien Carr
1076.	Mitchell, Donald Grant	American lands and letters
1173.	Mitchell, Donald Grant	Dream life
1077.	Mitchell, Donald Grant	English lands, letters and kings
1342.	Mitchell, Silas Weir	Hugh Wynne, free Quaker
1101.	Mitchell, Wilmot Brookings	School and college speaker
303.	Moberly, Charles E.	Early Tudors
1054.	Modern American oratory	R. C. Ringwalt
507.	Modern Athens	George Horton
1487.	Modern political orations	Leopold Wagner
1556.	Mohammad. Lane–Poole, *trans.*	Speeches and table-talk
214.	Mombert, J. I.	Short history of the crusades
	Mommsen, *Dr.* Theodor	
	History of the Roman republic, abridged ed. *See* Bryans *and* Hendy's History of the Roman republic.	
619.	Money and banking	Horace White
603.	Monopolies and trusts	R. T. Ely
689.	Monroe, Will S.	Bibliography of education
350.	Montcalm and Wolfe	Francis Parkman
115.	Montezuma and the conquest of Mexico	
		E. E. Seelye, *and* Edward Eggleston
304.	Montgomery, David H.	Leading facts of English history
271.	Montgomery, David H.	Leading facts of French history
410.	Montgomery, David H.	Student's American history
1078.	Moody, William Vaughn, *and* Lovett, Robert Morss	
		History of English literature
641.	Moral instruction of children	Felix Adler
	More, Paul Elmer, *trans.* See Aeschylus	Prometheus bound

1343.	More, Sir Thomas. Robynson, trans.		Utopia
258.	Morey, William C.		Outlines of Roman history
327.	Morfill, W. R.		Story of Russia
690.	Morgan, Conway Lloyd		Psychology for teachers
874.	Morley, Margaret Warner		Life and love
875.	Morley, Margaret Warner		Song of life
	Morley, John, ed. See English men of letters series.		
411.	Morris, Charles		Historical tales: American
307.	Morris, Charles		Historical tales: English
273.	Morris, Charles		Historical tales: French
324.	Morris, Charles		Historical tales: German
239a.	Morris, Charles		Historical tales: Greek
332.	Morris, Charles		Historical tales: Japan and China
259.	Morris, Charles		Historical tales: Roman
328.	Morris, Charles		Historical tales: Russian
276.	Morris, Charles		Historical tales: Spanish
1424.	Morris, Charles		
	King Arthur and the Knights of the round table		
305.	Morris, Edward E.		Age of Anne
306.	Morris, Edward E.		Early Hanoverians
	Morris, Edward E., ed. See Epochs of modern history series.		
89.	Morris, Mowbray, ed. See Boswell		Life of Johnson
272.	Morris, William O'Connor		
	French Revolution and first empire		
117.	Morris, William O'Connor		Napoleon, warrior and ruler
691.	Morrison, Gilbert B.		
	Ventilation and warming of school buildings		
98.	Morse, John T.		Abraham Lincoln
19.	Morse, John T., jr.		John Adams
20.	Morse, John T., jr.		John Quincy Adams
88.	Morse, John T.		Thomas Jefferson
	Morse, John T., jr., ed. See American statesmen series.		
1012.	Mosses from an old manse		Nathaniel Hawthorne
912.	Moths and butterflies		M. C. Dickerson
516.	Moulton, Louise Chandler		
	Lazy tours in Spain and elsewhere		
1560.	Moulton, Richard G., ed.		Four years of novel reading
1018.	Mountain climbing		E. L. Wilson
585.	Mountains of California		John Muir
1113.	Mouse-trap		W. D. Howells
890.	Movements and habits of climbing plants		Charles Darwin
1543.	Mueller, Hermann		Deutsche Gedichte
585.	Muir, John		Mountains of California
	Muller, Frederick Max, ed. See Scherer, W.		
	History of German literature		
15.	Munger, Theodore T.		On the threshold
982.	Municipal engineering and sanitation		M. N. Baker
725.	Municipal government		B. S. Coler
784.	Munro, John		Story of electricity
1344.	Murfree, Mary N.		In the Tennessee mountains
1345.	Murfree, Mary N.		Prophet of the Great Smoky mountains
333.	Murray, David		Story of Japan
1012.	Music		Hannah Smith
489.	My Arctic journal		J. D. Peary
54.	My father as I recall him		Mamie Dickens
823.	My studio neighbors		W. H. Gibson
1169.	My study fire		H. W. Mabie

1170.	My study fire. Second series	H. W. Mabie
1164.	My study windows	J. R. Lowell
1197.	My summer in a garden	C. D. Warner
557.	My winter on the Nile	C. D. Warner
	Myers, Ernst, *jt. trans. See* Lang, Andrew.	
149.	Myers, Frederick W. H.	Wordsworth
193.	Myers, Philip Van Ness	Ancient history
189.	Myers, Philip Van Ness	General history
240.	Myers, Philip Van Ness	History of Greece
209.	Myers, Philip Van Ness	Middle ages
260.	Myers, Philip Van Ness	Rome
	Myers, Philip Van Ness, *jt. author. See* Allen, William F.	
1260.	Mystery of Edwin Drood	Charles Dickens
	In his (1260) Barnaby Rudge.	
1427.	Myths and legends of our own land	C. M. Skinner
6.	Myths and myth makers	John Fiske
11.	Myths of Greece and Rome	H. A. Guerber
12.	Myths of Northern lands	H. A. Guerber
117.	Napoleon, warrior and ruler	W. O. Morris
77.	Nathaniel Hawthorne	Mrs. J. T. Fields
759.	Natural philosophy	Edmund Atkinson
1084.	Nature and elements of poetry	E. C. Stedman
897.	Nature and work of plants	D. T. Macdougal
1194.	Nature for its own sake	J. C. Van Dyke
755.	Nature study	W. S. Jackman
826.	Nature study and life	C. H. Hodge
886.	Nature's garden	Neltje Blanchan
754.	Nature's miracles	Elisha Gray
924.	Needham, James G.	Elementary lessons in zoology
1472.	Neghborly poems and dialect sketches	J. W. Riley
624.	Negro question	G. W. Cable
138.	Nettleship, Henry	Vergil
820.	New astronomy for beginners	D. P. Todd
1484.	New century speaker	H. A. Frink
576.	New Eldorado	M. M. Ballou
579.	New England country	Clifton Johnson
1411.	New England nun	M. E. Wilkins
1067.	New England primer	P. L. Ford, *ed.*
443.	New France and New England	John Fiske
1584.	New library of poetry and song	W. C. Bryant, *ed.*
672.	New manual of method	A. H. Garlick
1340.	New Mexico David	C. F. Lummis
491.	New Pacific	H. H. Bancroft
742.	New parliamentary manual	Edmund Palmer
1079.	Newcomer, Alphonso G.	American literature
955.	Newsholme, Arthur	School hygiene
801.	Newth, G. S.	Elementary inorganic chemistry
578.	Niagara book	W. D. Howells, *and others*
41.	Nichol, John	Thomas Carlyle
1264.	Nicholas Nickleby	Charles Dickens
785.	Nichols, Edward L.	Outlines of physics
530.	Nichols, Laura D.	Norway summer
1563.	Nield, Jonathan	Guide to the best historical novels
329.	Noble, Edmund	Russia and the Russians
221.	Normans in Europe	*Rev.* A. H. Johnson
964.	North American forests and forestry	Ernest Bruncken
529.	Norton, Minerva Brace	In and around Berlin

30

LIST OF BOOKS FOR HIGH SCHOOL LIBRARIES.

530.	Norway summer	L. D. Nichols
694.	Notes of talks on teaching	F. W. Parker
1126.	Notes of the night	C. C. Abbott
1139.	Novel	F. M. Crawford
592.	Ober, Frederick A.	Puerto Rico and its resources
1503.	Odyssey. Bryant, trans.	Homer
1504.	Odyssey. Butcher and Lang, trans.	Homer
1265.	Old curiosity shop	Charles Dickens
1349.	Old gentleman of the Black Stock	T. N. Page
688.	Old Greek education	J. P. Mahaffy
1371.	Old mortality	Sir Walter Scott
449.	Old northwest	B. A. Hinsdale
567.	Old Santa Fé trail	Col. Henry Inman
523.	Old shrines and ivy	William Winter
455.	Old South	T. N. Page
412.	Old South leaflets	Directors of Old South work
444.	Old Virginia and her neighbors	John Fiske
85.	Oliphant, Mrs. Margaret W.	Jeanne D'Arc
176.	Oliphant, Mrs. Margaret W.	Makers of Florence
177.	Oliphant, Mrs. Margaret W.	Makers of modern Rome
178.	Oliphant, Mrs. Margaret W.	Makers of Venice
51.	Oliver Cromwell	Frederick Harrison
1346.	Ollivant, Alfred	Bob, son of battle
308.	Oman, Charles W. C.	England and the Hundred Years' war
309.	Oman, Charles W. C.	England in the nineteenth century
241.	Oman, Charles W. C.	History of Greece
	Oman, Charles W. C., ed. See Oxford Manuals of English history series.	
1275.	On General Thomas's staff	B. A. Dunn
583.	On horseback	C. D. Warner
1494.	On the Athenian constitution. Kenyon, trans.	Aristotle
15.	On the threshold	T. T. Munger
1080.	Onderdonk, James L.	History of American verse
1315.	One summer	B. W. Howard
488.	One way round the world	Delight Sweetser
501.	One year abroad	B. W. Howard
340.	Oom Paul's people	H. C. Hillegas
1159.	Open air	Richard Jefferies
692.	Oppenheim, Nathan	Development of the child
1496.	Oration on the crown	Demosthenes
1507.	Orations	Lysias
462.	Oregon	William Barrows
470.	Oregon trail	Francis Parkman
870.	Origin of species	Charles Darwin
925.	Orton, James	Comparative zoology
1141.	Other essays from the easy chair	G. W. Curtis
816.	Other suns than ours	R. A. Proctor
817.	Other worlds than ours	R. A. Proctor
939.	Our common birds and how to know them	J. B. Grant
519.	Our English cousins	R. H. Davis
	Our European neighbours series; ed. by W. H. Dawson	
	Dawson, W. H. German life in town and country.	
	Hough, P. M. Dutch life in town and country.	
	Palmer, F. H. E. Russian life in town and country.	
	Story, A. T. Swiss life in town and country.	

AUTHOR AND TITLE INDEX.

572.	Our great west	Julian Ralph
550.	Our houseboat on the Nile	Lee Bacon (*Mrs.* Henry Bacon)
894.	Our native trees and how to identify them	H. L. Keeler
421.	Our navy in the war with Spain	J. R. Spears
520.	Our old home and English note-books	Nathaniel Hawthorne
577.	Our western archipelago	H. M. Field
1152.	Outdoor studies, poems	T. W. Higginson
639.	Outline of practical sociology	C. D. Wright
895.	Outlines of botany	R. G. Leavitt
604.	Outlines of economics	R. T. Ely
1535.	Outlines of German literature	Joseph Gostwick *and* Robert Harrison
804.	Outlines of industrial chemistry	F. H. Thorp
785.	Outlines of physics	E. L. Nichols
609.	Outlines of political science	George Gunton *and* Hayes Robbins
258.	Outlines of Roman history	W. C. Morey
864.	Outlines of the earth's history	N. S. Shaler
184.	Outlines of universal history	T. P. Fisher
505.	Outre-Mer	H. W. Longfellow
540.	Overland to China	A. R. Colquhon

Oxford manuals of English history series; *ed.* by C. W. C. Oman.
   Hassall, Arthur. Making of the British Empire.
   Hutton, W. H. King and baronage.
   Oman, C. W. C. England and the Hundred Years' war
   Powers, G. W. England and the Reformation.
   Robertson, C. G. Making of the English nation.
   Wakeling, G. H. King and Parliament.

926.	Packard, Alpheus S.	Zoology
1347.	Page, Thomas Nelson	In ole Virginia
1348.	Page, Thomas Nelson	Marse Chan
1349.	Page, Thomas Nelson	Old gentleman of the Black Stock
455.	Page, Thomas Nelson	Old South
1350.	Page, Thomas Nelson	Red Rock
1351.	Page, Thomas Nelson	Santa Claus's partner
692.	Painter, Franklin V. N.	History of education
1031.	Painter, Franklin V. N.	History of English literature
1102.	Palgrave, Francis Turner	

Golden treasury of the best songs and lyrical poems in the English language.

742.	Palmer, Edmond	New parliamentary manual
532.	Palmer, Francis H. E.	Russian life in town and country
	Palmer, George Herbert, *trans. See* Sophocles	Antigone
1103.	Pancoast, Henry S., *ed.*	Standard English poems
1466.	Paradise lost	John Milton
1006.	Paret, J. Parmly	Woman's book of sports
694.	Parker, Francis W.	Notes of talks on teaching
1352.	Parker, Gilbert	Pierre and his people
348.	Parkman, Francis	Conspiracy of Pontiac
349.	Parkman, Francis	La Salle and the discovery of the great west
350.	Parkman, Francis	Montcalm and Wolfe
470.	Parkman, Francis	Oregon trail
351.	Parkman, Francis	Pioneers of France in the new world
901.	Parsons, Frances Theodora	According to season
	Partridge, Lelia E., *jt. author. See* Parker, Francis W.	

511.	Passages from the French and Italian note-books............................	Nathaniel Hawthorne
1246.	Pathfinder	J. F. Cooper
388.	Pathfinder in American history...........................	W. F. Gordy, *and* W. I. Twitchell
81.	Patrick Henry	M. C. Tyler
113.	**Pattison, Mark**	Milton
615.	Patton, Jacob Harris.............................	Political economy
1359.	Paul and Virginia. Anderson, *trans*..............................	J. H. B. de Saint Pierre
91.	Paul Jones	Hutchins Hapgood
	Payne, William H., *trans*. *See* Rousseau. Emile.	
	Payne, William H., *trans*. *See* Compayré, Gabriel. Lectures on pedagogy.	
	Payne, William H., *trans*. *See* Compayré, Gabriel. History of pedagogy.	
489.	**Peary, Josephine Diebitsch–**..................	My Arctic journal
1172.	Pen and ink	Brander Matthews
1409.	Penelope's Irish experience.............................	K. D. Wiggin
1410.	Penelope's progress	K. D. Wiggin
555.	**Penfield, Frederic Courtland**	Present-day Egypt
1561.	**Pennell, Joseph**	Illustration of books
1133.	Pepacton	John Burroughs
593.	**Pepper, Charles M.**	Tomorrow in Cuba
	Periods of European history series; *ed.* by Arthur Hassall.	
	Hassall, Arthur. Balance of power.	
	Johnson, A. H. Europe in the sixteenth century.	
	Stephens, H. M. Revolutionary Europe.	
	Wakeman, H. O. Europe.	
74.	Personal memoirs	U. S. Grant
50.	Peter Cooper	R. W. Raymond
121.	Petrarch .... J. H. Robinson, *and* H. W. Rolfe	
45.	**Phelps, Elizabeth Stuart**	Story of Jesus Christ
	Phelps, William Lyon, *ed*. *See* Irving, Washington. Tales of a traveller	
	Philips, George Morris, *jt. author. See* Sharpless, Isaac.	
33.	**Phillips, Brooks**	M. A. D. Howe
709.	Philosophy of school management	Arnold Tompkins
762.	Physics—advanced course	G. F. Barker
768.	Physics	L. C. Cooley
786.	Physics by experiment	E. R. Shaw
764.	Physics for high school students .... H. S. Carhart *and* H. N. Chute	
756.	Physical laboratory manual	C. F. Adams
765.	Physical laboratory manual	H. N. Chute
856.	Physiography	T. H. Huxley
857.	Physiography of the United States.....	J. W. Powell *and others*
951.	Physiology	W. J. Brinckley
695.	**Pickard, Josiah L.**	School supervision
1266.	Pickwick papers	Charles Dickens
231.	Pictures from Greek life and story..........	Rev. A. J. Church
1095.	Pieces for prize speaking contests............................. A. H. Craig *and* Binney Gunnison, *comps*.	
1352.	Pierre and his people	Gilbert Parker
447.	Pilgrims in their three homes, England, Holland and America.............................	W. E. Griffis

AUTHOR AND TITLE INDEX. 469

1229.	Pilgrim's progress	John Bunyan
876.	Pillsbury, J. H.	
	Laboratory guide for an elementary course in general biology	
1243.	Pilot	J. F. Cooper
1215.	Pine knot	W. E. Barton
1247.	Pioneers	J. F. Cooper
351.	Pioneers of France in the new world	Francis Parkman
1473.	Pipes O' Pan at Zekesbury	J. W. Riley
810.	Pith of astronomy	S. G. Bayne
123.	Pitt	Lord Rosebery
124.	Pizarro	G. M. Towle
719.	Place of the story in early education	S. E. Wiltse
882.	Plant life	C. R. Barnes
888.	Plants	J. M. Coulter
1516.	Pliny, Caius Caecilius Secundus. Melmoth, *trans.*	
		Letters of Pliny
	Plumptre, Edward H., *trans. See* Aeschylus. Tragedies.	
	Plumptre, Edward H., *trans. See* Sophocles. Tragedies.	
1353.	Poe, Edgar Allan	Tales
1429.	Poems	T. B. Aldrich
1436.	Poems	*Mrs.* E. B. Browning
1537.	Poems	Heinrich Heine
1456.	Poems	Jean Ingelow
1482.	Poems	William Wordsworth
1479.	Poetic and dramatic works	Alfred Tennyson
1580.	Poetical quotations from Chaucer to Tennyson	S. A. Allibone
1438.	Poetical works	W. C. Bryant
1444.	Poetical works	Alice *and* Phoebe Cary
1446.	Poetical works	Samuel Taylor Coleridge
1435.	Poetical works	Thomas Gray
1465.	Poetical works	John Milton
1475.	Poetical works	*Sir* Walter Scott
1085.	Poets of America	E. C. Stedman
1179.	Points of view	Agnes Repplier
615.	Political economy	J. H. Patton
618.	Political economy—advanced course	F. A. Walker
739.	Political parties in the United States	Jesse Macy
1508.	Polybius. Shuckburgh, *trans.*	Histories
573.	Pony tracks	Frederic Remington
638.	Poor in great cities	R. A. Woods, *and others*
1420.	Popular romances of the middle ages	
		G. W. Cox *and* E. H. Jones
1354.	Porter, Jane	Scottish chiefs
1355.	Porter, Jane	Thaddeus of Warsaw
815.	Porter, Jermain G.	Stars in song and legend
30.	Poschinger, Heinrich von	Conversations with Prince Bismarck
956.	Posse, Baron Nils	
		Handbook of school-gymnastics of the Swedish system
957.	Posse, Baron Nils	
		Special kinesiology of educational gymnastics
857.	Powell, J. W., *and others*	Physiography of the United States
456.	Powell, Lyman P., *ed.*	Historic towns of the western states
891.	Power of movement in plants	
		Charles Darwin *and* Francis Darwin
310.	Powers, George Wightman	England and the Reformation
971.	Practical agriculture	C. C. James
735.	Practical essays on American government	A. B. Hart

966.	Practical forestry	John Clifford
1057.	Practical German grammar	Calvin Thomas
766.	Practical methods in microscopy	C. H. Clark
1050.	Practical public speaking	S. H. Clark, and F. M. Blanchard
1296.	Pratt portraits sketched in a New England suburb	Anna Fuller
1544.	Prehn, August, ed.	Journalistic German
777.	Preparatory physics	W. J. Hopkins
476.	Prescott, William H	History of the conquest of Peru
474.	Prescott, William H	History of the conquests of Mexico
277.	Prescott, William H	History of the reign of Ferdinand and Isabella
555.	Present-day Egypt	F. C. Penfield
696.	Preyer, William T	Mental development in the child
958.	Price, George M	Handbook of sanitation
1201.	Pride and prejudice	Jane Austen
868.	Primer of evolution	Edward Clodd
684.	Primer of psychology	G. T. Ladd
1417.	Prince and the page	C. M. Yonge
29.	Prince Bismarck	Charles Lowe
80.	Prince Henry the navigator	C. R. Beasley
1303.	Princess's story book	G. L. Gomme, ed.
1412.	Princeton stories	J. L. Williams
1209.	Princetonian	James Barnes
962.	Principles of agriculture	L. H. Bailey, ed.
981.	Principles of agriculture for common schools	I. O. Winslow
1.	Principles of logic	H. A. Aikins
771.	Principles of physics	A. P. Gage
968.	Principles of plant culture	E. S. Goff
614.	Principles of political economy	J. S. Mill
1052.	Principles of public speaking	G. C. Lee
628.	Prisoners of Russia	Benjamin Howard
164.	Prisoners of the Tower of London	Violet Brooks-Hunt
413.	Problems of expansion	Whitelaw Reid
1153.	Procession of the flowers	T. W. Higginson
533.	Proctor, Edna Dean	Russian journey
816.	Proctor, Richard A	Other suns than ours
817.	Proctor, Richard A	Other worlds than ours
607.	Profit sharing between employer and employee	N. P. Gilman
605.	Progress and poverty	Henry George
1491.	Prometheus bound. More, trans.	Aeschylus
1477.	Prometheus unbound	P. B. Shelley
1345.	Prophet of the Great Smoky Mountains	M. N. Murfree
1051.	Pros and cons	A. H. Craig
1581.	Prose quotations from Socrates to Macaulay	S. A. Allibone
606.	Protection or free trade	Henry George
673.	Psychology and psychic culture	R. P. Halleck
690.	Psychology for teachers	C. L. Morgan
710.	Psychology of childhood	Frederick Tracy
960.	Public health problems	J. F. J. Sykes
590.	Puerto Rico	William Dinwiddie
592.	Puerto Rico and its resources	F. A. Ober
1421.	Punishment of the stingy	G. B. Grinnell
1489.	Quackenbos, John D	Illustrated history of ancient literature
548.	Quaint corners of ancient empires	M. M. Shoemaker
1335.	Quaker girl of Nantucket	M. C. Lee

AUTHOR AND TITLE INDEX. 471

139.	Queen Victoria	R. R. Holmes
1372.	Quentin Durward	*Sir* Walter Scott
697.	Quick, Robert Herbert	Essays on educational reformers
1225.	Rab and his friends	John Brown
1425.	Ragozin, Zenaide A	Frithjof, the viking of Norway
1426.	Ragozin, Zenaide A	Siegfried, the hero of the North
194.	Ragozin, Zenaide A	Story of Assyria
195.	Ragozin, Zenaide A	Story of Chaldea
128.	Raleigh	G. M. Towle
545.	Ralph, Julian	Alone in China and other stories
571.	Ralph, Julian	Dixie
572.	Ralph, Julian	Our great west
60.	Ralph Waldo Emerson	O. W. Holmes
1190.	Rambler's lease	Bradford Torrey
1322.	Ramona	H. H. Jackson
574.	Ranch life and the hunting trail	Theodore Roosevelt
546.	Ransome, Stafford	Japan in transition
1562.	Rawlings, Gertrude Burford	Story of books
334.	Rawlinson, George	Story of Phoenicia
342.	Rawlinson, George, *and* Gilman, Arthur	Story of ancient Egypt
50.	Raymond, Rossiter W	Peter Cooper
1356.	Reade, Charles	Cloister and the hearth
852.	Reader in physical geography for beginners	R. E. Dodge
1583.	Reader's handbook	E. C. Brewer
1110.	Reader's Shakespeare	D. C. Bell
499.	Real Hawaii	Lucien Young
361.	Reconstruction and the constitution	J. W. Burgess
1414.	Red men and white	Owen Wister
1350.	Red rock	T. N. Page
372.	Redeeming the republic	C. C. Coffin
1306.	Reds of the Midi. Janvier, *trans.*	Felix Gras
858.	Redway, Jacques W	Elementary physical geography
1053.	References for literary workers	Henry Matson
17.	Reformation	G. P. Fisher
1270.	Refugees	A. C. Doyle
413.	Reid, Whitelaw	Problems of expansion
743.	Reinsch Paul S	World politics
1039.	Relation of literature to life	C. D. Warner
573.	Remington, Frederic	Pony tracks
802.	Remsen, Ira	Introduction to the study of chemistry
661.	Report of the committee of seven on the study of history in schools	Committee of Seven
699.	Report of the committee of ten	Committee of Ten
700.	Report of the committee of twelve	Committee of Twelve
698.	Report of the committee of fifteen	Committee of Fifteen
1467.	Repplier, Agnes, *comp.*	Book of famous verse
1174.	Repplier, Agnes	Books and men
1175.	Repplier, Agnes	Essays in idleness
1176.	Repplier, Agnes	Essays in miniature
1177.	Repplier, Agnes	Fireside sphinx
1178.	Repplier, Agnes	In the dozy hours and other papers
1179.	Repplier, Agnes	Points of view
1180.	Repplier, Agnes	Varia
1183.	Representative British orations	C. K. Adams, *ed.*
1156.	Representative essays	Washington Irving, *and others*
1145.	Representative men	R. W. Emerson

Republic of childhood series.
    Wiggin, K. D., *and* Smith, N. A. Froebel's gifts.
    Wiggin, K. D., *and* Smith, N. A. Froebel's occupations.
    Wiggin, K. D., *and* Smith, N. A. Kindergarten principles and practices.
831. Revised text-book of geology .... J. D. Dana
224. Revolutionary Europe .... H. M. Stevens
414. Rhodes, James Ford .... History of the United States
Rice, William North, *ed. See* Dana, James D. ....
.... Revised text-book of geology
1240. Richard Carvel .... W. S. Churchill
215. Richard de Devizes *and* Geoffrey de Vinsauf..................
.... Chronicles of the Crusades
975. Richards, Ellen H........................... Cost of food
976. Richards, Ellen H........................... Cost of living
977. Richards, Ellen H...... Food materials and their adulterations
803. Richards, Ellen H., *and* Elliott, S. M. ....
.... Chemistry of cooking and cleaning
974. Richards, Ellen H., *and* Woodman, A. G. ....
.... Air, water and food from a sanitary standpoint
978. Richards, Ellen H., *and others* .... Rumford kitchen leaflets
1357. Richards, Laura E. .... Geoffrey Strong
1082. Richardson, Charles F. .... American literature
744. Rights and duties of American citizenship ... W. W. Willoughby
630. Riis, Jacob A. .... Children of the poor
631. Riis, Jacob A. .... How the other half lives
632. Riis, Jacob A. .... Making of an American
633. Riis, Jacob A. .... Ten years' war
1468. Riley, James Whitcomb ....Afterwhiles
1469. Riley, James Whitcomb ....Armazindy
1470. Riley, James Whitcomb ......Green fields and running brooks
1471. Riley, James Whitcomb ....Home-folks
1472. Riley, James Whitcomb ....
.... Neghborly poems and dialect sketches
1473. Riley, James Whitcomb ....Pipes o' Pan at Zekesbury
1474. Riley, James Whitcomb .:...............Sketches in prose
1052. Ringwalt, Ralph Curtis .... Modern American oratory
1316. Rise of Silas Lapham .... W. D. Howells
235. Rise of the Macedonian empire .... A. M. Curteis
386. Rise of the republic of the United States ....
.... Richard Frothingham
1125. Rivals .... R. B. Sheridan
861. Rivers of North America .... I. C. Russell
Riverside Art series; *ed.* by Estelle M. Hurll.
    Hurll, E. M. Tuscan sculpture.
    Hurll, E. M. Van Dyck.
    For other books in this series, *See* 1902 Township list.
Riverside biographical series.
    Allen, Walter. Ulysses S. Grant.
    Boynton, H. W. Washington Irving.
    Brown, W. G. Stephen Arnold Douglas.
    Conant, C. A. Alexander Hamilton.
    Hapgood, Hutchins. Paul Jones.
    Hodges, George. William Penn.
    Lighton, W. R. Meriwether Lewis and William Clark.
    Merwin, H. C. Thomas Jefferson.
    Raymond, R. W. Peter Cooper.
    Sedgwick, H. D., *jr.* Samuel De Champlain.
    Thayer, J. B. John Marshall.

1373.	Rob Roy	Sir Walter Scott
35.	Robert Burns	Principal Shairp
94.	Robert E. Lee	W. P. Trent
1358.	Roberts, Charles G. D.	Heart of the ancient wood
927.	Roberts, Charles G. D.	Kindred of the wild
311.	Robertson, Charles Grant	Making of the English nation
	Robertson, Eric S., *ed.* *See* "Great Writers" series.	
	Robbins, Hayes, *jt. author.* *See* Gunton, George.	
985.	Robinson, Charles Mulford	Improvement of towns and cities
121.	Robinson, James Harvey, *and* Rolfe, H. W.	Petrarch
	Robynson, Raphe, *trans.* *See* More, *Sir* Thomas	Utopia
1007.	Rogers, Archibald, *and others*	Hunting
	Rolfe, Henry W., *jt. author.* *See* Robinson, James Harvey.	
	Rolfe, William J., *ed.* *See* Byron, Lord	Childe Harold's pilgrimage
	Rolfe, William J., *ed.* *See* Shakespeare, William	Dramas
95.	Rolleston, T. W.	Life of Gotthold Ephraim Lessing
251.	Roman empire of the second century	W. W. Capes
1515.	Roman history	Ammianus Marcellinus
252.	Roman life in the days of Cicero	A. J. Church
1254.	Roman singer	F. M. Crawford
257.	Roman triumvirates	Charles Merivale
346.	Romance of American colonization	W. E. Griffis
330.	Romance of conquest	W. E. Griffis
906.	Romance of the insect world	L. N. Badenoch
262.	Rome and Carthage	R. B. Smith
260.	Rome	P. V. Myers
1281.	Romola	George Eliot
763.	Röntgen rays	G. F. Barker, *ed.*
1181.	Roosevelt, Theodore	American ideals
116.	Roosevelt, Theodore	Gouverneur Morris
574.	Roosevelt, Theodore	Ranch life and the hunting-trail
415.	Roosevelt, Theodore	Rough riders
1182.	Roosevelt, Theodore	Strenuous life
28.	Roosevelt, Theodore	Thomas Hart Benton
1009.	Roosevelt, Theodore	Wilderness hunter
457.	Roosevelt, Theodore	Winning of the west
1008.	Roosevelt, Theodore, *and* Grinnell, G. B.	Hunting in many lands
	Roosevelt, Theodore, *jt. editor.* *See* Grinnell, George Bird.	
1004.	Ropes, their knots and splices	C. P. Kunhardt
123.	Rosebery, *Lord*	Pitt
1545.	Rosegger, Petri Kettenfeier	Waldheimat
415.	Rough riders	Theodore Roosevelt
504.	Roundabout rambles in Northern Europe	C. F. King
761.	Rousseau, Payne, *trans.*	Emile
471.	Royce, Josiah	California
1386.	Rudder Grange	F. R. Stockton
973.	Rumford kitchen leaflets	E. H. Richards, *and others*
	Rural science series; *ed.* by L. H. Bailey.	
	Bailey, L. H., *ed.* Principles of agriculture.	
1183.	Ruskin, John	Sesame and lilies
859.	Russell, Israel Cook	Glaciers of North America
860.	Russell, Israel Cook	Lakes of North America
861.	Russell, Israel Cook	Rivers of North America
862.	Russell, Israel Cook	Volcanoes of North America

329.	Russia and the Russians	Edmund Noble
533.	Russian journey	E. D. Proctor
532.	Russian life in town and country	F. H. E. Palmer
531.	Russian rambles	I. F. Hapgood
438.	Sabbath in Puritan New England	A. M. Earle
	Sachtleben, William Lewis, *jt. author.* See **Allen, Thomas Gaskell,** *jr.*	
1129.	Sack of shakings	F. T. Bullen
420.	Sailor boys of '61	J. R. Soley
1359.	Saint-Pierre, Jacques Henri de. Anderson, *trans.* Paul and Virginia	
59.	Saintsbury, George	Dryden
1083.	Saintsbury, George ....Short history of English literature	
21.	Samuel Adams	J. K. Hosmer
42.	Samuel De Champlain	H. D. Sedgwick, *jr.*
189a.	Sanderson, Edgar	History of the world
1360.	Sanderson, James Gardner	Cornell stories
	Sanford, A. H., *jt. author.* See **James, James A.**	
242.	Sankey, Charles ....Spartan and Theban supremacies	
	Sankey, Charles, *jt. editor.* See **Cox, Rev. George W.**	
1351.	Santa Claus's partner	T. N. Page
1010.	Sargent, D. A., *and others*	Athletic sports
902.	Sargent, Frederick Leroy	Corn plants
1520.	Satires. Evans, *trans.*	Juvenal
1546.	Scheffel, Joseph Victor von	Ekkehard
1547.	Scherer, W.	History of German literature
1548.	Schiller, Johann Christoph ......Gustav Adolf in Deutschland	
1550.	Schiller, Johann Christoph	Maria Stuart
1549.	Schiller, Johann Christoph	Jungfrau von Orleans
1551.	Schiller, Johann Christoph. Coleridge, Churchill, *and* Martin, *trans.*	Wallenstein and Wilhelm Tell
1552.	Schiller, Johann Christoph	Wilhelm Tell
1578.	Schmidt, Immanuel, *and* Tanger, Gustav, *eds.* Flügel-Schmidt-Tanger's dictionary of the English and German languages	
1101.	School and college speaker	W. B. Mitchell
666.	School and society	John Dewey
1039.	School architecture	E. M. Wheelwright
288.	School atlas of English history	S. R. Gardiner, *ed.*
409.	School history of the United States	J. B. McMaster
955.	School hygiene	Arthur Newsholme
669.	School inspection	D. R. Fearon
714.	School management	E. E. White
646.	School management and school method	Joseph Baldwin
969.	School needlework	O. C. Hapgood
761.	School physics	E. M. Avery
983.	School sanitation and decoration ...... Severance Burrage *and* H. T. Bailey	
695.	School supervision	J. L. Pickard
416.	Schouler, James .... History of the United States	
99.	Schurz, Carl	Abraham Lincoln
47.	Schurz, Carl	Life of Henry Clay
1375.	Schwartz, Julia Augusta	Vassar studies
222.	Schwill, Ferdinand	History of modern Europe
	Schwill, Ferdinand, *jt. author.* See **Thatcher, Oliver J.**	
547.	Scidmore, Eliza Ruhamah	China

AUTHOR AND TITLE INDEX. 475

495. Scidmore, Eliza Ruhamah ....Java the garden of the East
Science series; *ed.* by J. M. Cattell *and* F. E. Beddard.
    Bonney, T. G. Volcanoes.
    Geikie, James. Earth sculpture.
    Haddon, A. C. Study of man.
    Russell, I. C. Rivers of North America.
    Scott, E. H. *ed.* *See* Hamilton, Alexander, *and others* ....
    .... Federalist and other constitutional papers
    Scott, E. H. *ed.* *See* Madison, James ....
    .... Journal of the Constitutional Convention
1362. Scott, *Sir* Walter .... Anne of Geierstein
1363. Scott, *Sir* Walter ....Antiquary
1364. Scott, *Sir* Walter ....Black dwarf and Legend of Montrose
1365. Scott, *Sir* Walter .... Bride of Lammermoor
1366. Scott, *Sir* Walter .... Count Robert of Paris
1367. Scott, *Sir* Walter .... Fair maid of Perth
1368. Scott, *Sir* Walter .... Fortunes of Nigel
1369. Scott, *Sir* Walter .... Heart of Midlothian
1376. Scott, *Sir* Walter ....Ivanhoe
1370. Scott, *Sir* Walter ....Kenilworth
1371. Scott, *Sir* Walter ....Old mortality
1475. Scott, *Sir* Walter ....Poetical works
1372. Scott, *Sir* Walter ....Quentin Durward
1373. Scott, *Sir* Walter ....Rob Roy
1374. Scott, *Sir* Walter ....Talisman
843. Scott, William B. .... Introduction to geology
1354. Scottish chiefs .... Jane Porter
142. Scudder, Horace E. .... George Washington
417. Scudder, Horace E. .... History of the United States
458. Scudder, Horace E. ....
    .....Men and manners in America one hundred years ago
928. Scudder, Samuel Hubbard ....Every-day butterflies
    Scudder, Vida D., *ed.* *See* Shelley, Percy Bysshe ....
    ....Prometheus unbound
905. Sea-beach at ebb-tide .... A. F. Arnold
702. Search, Preston W. .... Ideal school
1377. Seawell, Molly Elliott .... History of the Lady Betty Stair
1378. Seawell, Molly Elliott .... Maid Marion and other stories
1379. Seawell, Molly Elliott ....Virginia cavalier
1289. Second book of tales .... Eugene Field
1453. Second book of verse .... Eugene Field
652. Secondary school systems of Germany .... F. E. Bolton
42. Sedgwick, Henry Dwight *jr.* .... Samuel De Champlain
    Sedgwick, W. T., *jt. author.* *See* Wilson, Edmund B.
223. Seebohm, Frederic .... Era of the Protestant Revolution
844. Seeley, H. G. .... Story of the earth in past ages
312. Seeley, *Sir* John Robert .... Expansion of England
118. Seeley, John Robert ...... Short history of Napoleon the First
703. Seeley, Levi .... History of education
49. Seelye, Elizabeth Eggleston .... Story of Columbus
115. Seelye, Elizabeth Eggleston, *and* Eggleston, Edward ....
    .... Montezuma and the conquest of Mexico
136. Seelye, Elizabeth Eggleston, *and* Eggleston, Edward .. ..
    .... Tecumseh and the Shawnee prophet
527. Seen in Germany .... R. S. Baker

261.	Seignobos, Charles	History of the Roman people
405.	Select charters	William MacDonald, ed.
406.	Select documents	William MacDonald, ed.
207.	Select historical documents of the Middle Ages .... E. F. Henderson, trans.	
1431.	Selected poems	Matthew Arnold
1506.	Selections. Smith, trans.	Lucian (Lucianus Samosatensis)
281.	Selections from the sources of English history	C. W. Colby
1542.	Selections from the table-talk of Martin Luther	Martin Luther
1522.	Seneca. Harris, trans.	Tragedies
1211.	Sentimental Tommy	J. M. Barrie
210.	Sergeant, Lewis	Franks
150.	Sergeant, Lewis	John Wyclif
818.	Serviss, Garrett P.	Astronomy with an opera-glass
1183.	Sesame and lilies	John Ruskin
903.	Setchel, William A. .... Laboratory practice for beginners in botany	
	Seton-Thompson, Ernest. *See* Thompson, Ernest Seton-.	
35.	Shairp, Principal	Robert Burns
1122.	Shakespeare, William	Dramas. Hudson ed.
1123.	Shakespeare, William	Dramas. Rolfe ed.
1124.	Shakespeare, William	Dramas. Temple ed.
1115.	Shakespeare: life, art, and characters	Rev. H. N. Hudson
1116.	Shakespeare: in tale and verse	L. G. Hufford
1118.	Shakespeare's heroines	Mrs. A. B. Jameson
983.	Shaler, Nathaniel Southgate	American highways
863.	Shaler, Nathaniel Southgate	Aspects of the earth
845.	Shaler, Nathaniel Southgate	First book in geology
864.	Shaler, Nathaniel Southgate	Outlines of the earth's history
929.	Sharp, Dallas Lore	Wild life near home
824.	Sharp eyes	W. H. Gibson
819.	Sharpless, Isaac, *and* Philips, G. M.	Astronomy
786.	Shaw, Edward R.	Physics by experiment
190.	Shelton, Mary D.	Studies in general history
1476.	Shelley, Percy Bysshe	Complete poetical works
1477.	Shelley, Percy Bysshe	Prometheus unbound
132.	Shelley	J. A. Symonds
1125.	Sheridan, Richard Brinsley	Rivals
1011.	Shields, G. O.	Camping and camp outfits
459.	Shinn, Charles Howard	Story of the mine
548.	Shoemaker, Michael Meyers	Quaint corners of ancient empires
1058.	Short historical grammar of the German language	Emil Trechmann
1063.	Short history of American literature	W. C. Bronson
1036.	Short history of architecture	A. L. Tuckerman
1083.	Short history of English literature	George Saintsbury
1539.	Short history of German literature	J. K. Hosmer
322.	Short history of Germany	E. F. Henderson
211.	Short history of mediaeval Europe	O. J. Thatcher
1068.	Short history of modern English literature	Edmund Gosse
118.	Short history of Napoleon the First	J. R. Seeley
214.	Short history of the crusades	J. I. Mombert
454.	Short history of the English colonies in America	H. C. Lodge

290.	Short history of the English people	J. R. Green
450.	Short history of the Mississippi valley	J. K. Hosmer
1171.	Short studies in literature	H. W. Mabie
723.	Short studies in party politics	Noah Brooks
	Shuckburgh, Evelyn S., *trans.* See Polybius	Histories
376.	Sidelights on American history. Series 1	H. W. Elson
377.	Sidelights on American history. Series 2	H. W. Elson
1426.	Siegfried, the hero of the North	Z. A. Ragozin
1134.	Signs and seasons	John Burroughs
1282.	Silas Marner	George Eliot
325.	Sime, James	History of Germany
71.	Sime, James	Life of Johann Wolfgang Goethe
1184.	Singleton, Esther, *ed.*	Turrets, towers, and temples
	Sinnott, Charles P., *jt. author.* See Avery, Elroy M.	
1157.	Sketch book	Washington Irving
1474.	Sketches in prose	J. W. Riley
1427.	Skinner, C. M.	Myths and legends of our own land
1304.	Sky pilot	C. W. Gordon
1114.	Sleeping-car and other farces	W. D. Howells
274.	Sloane, William Mulligan	French Revolution and religious reform
418.	Sloane, William Mulligan	French war and the revolution
634.	Small, Albion W.	Introduction to the study of society
478.	Smaller commercial geography	G. G. Chisholm
263.	Smaller history of Rome	Sir William Smith
	Smith, Albert L., *jt. author.* See Hessler, John C.	
704.	Smith, Alexander, *and* Hall, E. H.	Teaching of chemistry and physics
549.	Smith, Arthur H.	Chinese characteristics
	Smith, Benjamin E., *trans.* See Cicero, Marcus Tullius	De Amicitia
	Smith, Emily James, *trans.* See Lucian (Lucianus Samosatensis)	Selections
513.	Smith, Francis Hopkinson	Gondola days
1380.	Smith, Francis Hopkinson	Tom Grogan
506.	Smith, Francis Hopkinson	Well-worn roads of Spain, Holland, and Italy
587.	Smith, Francis Hopkinson	White umbrella in Mexico
1012.	Smith, Hannah	Music
1013.	Smith, *Col.* Nicholas	Stories of great national songs
	Smith, Nora Archibald, *jt. author.* See Wiggin, Kate Douglas.	
787.	Smith, Preston	Easy experiments in physics
262.	Smith, Reginald Bosworth	Rome and Carthage
263.	Smith, *Sir* William	Smaller history of Rome
1588.	Smith, *Sir* William, *ed.*	Dictionary of Greek and Roman antiquities
335.	Smyth, George B., *and others*	Crisis in China
1313.	Snow image and other twice-told tales	Nathaniel Hawthorne
1401.	Snow on the headlight	Cy Warman
486.	Social departure	*Mrs.* Everard Cotes
626.	Social problems	Henry George
256.	Society in Rome under the Caesars	W. R. Inge
1432.	Sohrab and Rustum	Matthew Arnold
1269.	Soldier Rigdale	B. M. Dix
1257.	Soldiers of fortune	R. H. Davis

478 LIST OF BOOKS FOR HIGH SCHOOL LIBRARIES.

389.	Soldier's story	W. L. Goss
419.	Soley, James Russell	Boys of 1812
420.	Soley, James Russell	Sailor boys of '61
950.	Some first steps in human progress	F. Starr
569.	Some strange corners of our country	C. F. Lummis
875.	Song of life	M. W. Morley
1440.	Songs of nature	John Burroughs, ed.
1509.	Sophocles. Palmer, *trans.*	Antigone
1510.	Sophocles. Plumptre, *trans.*	Tragedies
1576.	Soule, Richard	Dictionary of English synonyms
398.	Source-book of American history	A. B. Hart
296.	Source-book of English history	E. K. Kendall, ed.
299.	Source-book of English history	G. C. Lee
596.	South America: social, industrial, and political	F. G. Carpenter
453.	Southern sidelights	Edward Ingle
1278.	Southern soldier stories	G. C. Eggleston
498.	South-sea idyls	G. W. Stoddard
1104.	Southwick, F. Townsend	How to recite
1055.	Southwick, F. Townsend	Steps to oratory
353.	Spanish-American war	Russell Alger
517.	Spanish cities	C. A. Stoddard
242.	Spartan and Theban supremacies	Charles Sankey
421.	Spears, John R.	Our navy in the war with Spain
957.	Special kinesiology of educational gymnastics	B. N. Posse
1120.	Specimens of Pre-Shakesperean drama	J. M. Manly
1127.	Spectator	Joseph Addison
1556.	Speeches and table-talk of Mohammad	Stanley Lane-Poole
705.	Spencer, Herbert	Education
	Spillan, D., *trans. See* Livius, Titus	History of Rome
1252.	Splendid spur	A. T. Q. Couch, ed.
1005.	Sport with gun and rod	A. M. Mayer, ed.
1191.	Spring notes from Tennessee	Bradford Torrey
1248.	Spy	J. F. Cooper
1093.	Standard elocutionist	D. C. Bell *and* A. M. Bell
1103.	Standard English poems	H. S. Pancoast, ed.
1202.	Standish of Standish	J. G. Austin
343.	Stanley, Henry M., *and others*	Africa
809.	Starland	*Sir* R. S. Ball
950.	Starr, F.	Some first steps in human progress
815.	Stars in song and legend	J. G. Porter
745.	State	Woodrow Wilson
775.	Steam engine	G. C. V. Holmes
959.	Stecher, William A.	Gymnastics
1085.	Stedman, Edmund Clarence	Poets of America
1084.	Stedman, Edmund Clarence	Nature and elements of poetry
1086.	Stedman, Edmund Clarence	Victorian poets
1105.	Stedman, Edmund Clarence, *ed.*	American anthology
1106.	Stedman, Edmund Clarence, *ed.*	Victorian anthology
556.	Steevens, G. W.	Egypt in 1898
56.	Stephen Arnold Douglas	W. G. Brown
224.	Stephens, Henry Morse	Revolutionary Europe
1014.	Stephens, W. P.	Canoe and boat building
1055.	Steps to oratory	F. T. Southwick
1553.	Stern, Menco	Geschichten vom Rhein
1554.	Stern, Menco	Geschichten von deutschen Städten

AUTHOR AND TITLE INDEX. 479

67.	Stevens, John Austin	Albert Gallatin
497.	Stevens, Joseph Earle	Yesterdays in the Philippines
1381.	Stevenson, Robert Louis	Black arrow
496.	Stevenson, Robert Louis	In the south seas
1382.	Stevenson, Robert Louis	Kidnapped
515.	Stevenson, Robert Louis	Travels with a donkey in the Cevennes
1383.	Stevenson, Robert Louis	Treasure island
788.	Stewart, Balfour	Lessons in elementary physics
1255.	Stickit minister's wooing	S. R. Crockett
616.	Stimson, F. Jessup	Handbook to the labor law of the United States
1384.	Stimson, F. Jessup	King Noanett
422.	Stockton, Frank R.	Buccaneers and pirates of our coasts
1386.	Stockton, Frank R.	Rudder Grange
1387.	Stockton, Frank R.	Story-teller's pack
534.	Stoddard, Charles Augustus	Across Russia from the Baltic to the Danube
517.	Stoddard, Charles Augustus	Spanish cities
498.	Stoddard, Charles Warren	South-sea idyls
1555.	Stöckl, Helene	Unter dem Christbaum
1320.	Stories and legends	Washington Irving
1390.	Stories by American authors	
1391.	Stories by English authors	
1294.	Stories of a western town	Alice French
1000.	Stories of famous operas	H. A. Guerber
996.	Stories of famous songs	S. J. A. Fitz Gerald
1013.	Stories of great national songs	*Col.* Nicholas Smith
1314.	Stories of the railroad	J. A. Hill
1001.	Stories of the Wagner operas	H. A. Guerber
	Storrs, *Mrs.* C. H., *trans. See* Ebers, Georg. Emperor.	
313.	Story, Alfred Thomas	Building of the British empire
1035.	Story, Alfred Thomas	Story of photography
514.	Story, Alfred Thomas	Swiss life in town and country
842.	Story of a piece of coal	E. A. Martin
1402.	Story of Ab	Stanley Waterloo
342.	Story of ancient Egypt	George Rawlinson *and* Arthur Gilman
921.	Story of animal life	B. Lindsay
194.	Story of Assyria	Z. A. Ragozin
1562.	Story of books	G. B. Rawlings
352.	Story of Canada	J. G. Bourinot
195.	Story of Chaldea	Z. A. Ragozin
49.	Story of Columbus	E. E. Seelye
811.	Story of eclipses simply told for general readers	G. F. Chambers
784.	Story of electricity	John Munro
192.	Story of extinct civilization of the East	R. E. Anderson
479.	Story of geographical discovery	Joseph Jacobs
869.	Story of germ life	H. W. Conn
321.	Story of Germany	Sabine Baring-Gould *and* Arthur Gilman
70.	Story of Goethe's life	G. H. Lewes
239.	Story of Greece	J. A. Harrison
333.	Story of Japan	D. Murray
45.	Story of Jesus Christ	E. S. Phelps
21.	Story of King Alfred	Walter Besant

916.	Story of life in the seas	S. J. Hickson
466.	Story of Manhattan	Charles Hemstreet
473.	Story of Mexico	Susan Hale
266.	Story of modern France	Andre le Bon
1002.	Story of music	W. J. Henderson
330.	Story of Persia	S. G. W. Benjamin
334.	Story of Phoenicia	George Rawlinson
1035.	Story of photography	A. T. Story
948.	Story of primitive man	Edward Clodd
254.	Story of Rome	Arthur Gilman
327.	Story of Russia	W. R. Morfill
908.	Story of the amphibians and the reptiles .... J. N. Baskett and D. L. Ditmars	
278.	Story of the Christians and Moors	C. M. Yonge
988.	Story of the cotton plant	F. Wilkinson
451.	Story of the cowboy	E. Hough
844.	Story of the earth in past ages	H. G. Seeley
848.	Story of the earth's atmosphere	Douglas Archibald
909.	Story of the fishes	J. N. Baskett
838.	Story of the hills	Rev. H. N. Hutchinson
448.	Story of the Indian	G. B. Grinnell
459.	Story of the mine	C. H. Shinn

  Story of the nations series.
   Benjamin, S. G. W. Story of Persia.
   Bourinot, J. G. Story of Canada.
   Douglas, R. K. China.
   Fiske, A. K. West Indies.
   Gilman, Arthur. Story of Rome.
   Gould, Sabine Baring–and Gilman, Arthur. Story of Germany.
   Hale, Susan. Story of Mexico.
   Harrison, J. A. Story of Greece.
   Jewett, S. O. Story of the Normans.
   Le Bon, Andre. Story of modern France.
   McCarthy, Justin. Story of the people of England in the nineteenth century.
   Morfill, W. R. Story of Russia.
   Murray, D. Story of Japan.
   Ragozin, Z. A. Story of Assyria.
   Ragozin, Z. A. Story of Chaldea.
   Rawlinson, George. Story of Phoenicia.
   Rawlinson, George and Gilman, Arthur. Story of ancient Egypt.
   Sergeant, Lewis. Franks.
   Story, A. T. Building of the British empire.

219.	Story of the Normans	S. O. Jewett
302.	Story of the people of England in the Nineteenth century	Justin McCarthy
428.	Story of the Pilgrim fathers	Edward Arber, ed.
460.	Story of the railroad	Cy Warman
994.	Story of the Rhine-gold	A. A. Chapin
445.	Story of the soldier	G. A. Forsyth

  Story of the west series; ed. by Ripley Hitchcock.
   Grinnell, G. B. Story of the Indian.
   Hough, E. Story of the cowboy.
   Shinn, C. W. Story of the mine.
   Warman, Cy. Story of the railroad.

1235.	Story of Tonty	M. H. Catherwood
472.	Story of Wisconsin	R. G. Thwaites
1044.	Story-teller's art	Charity Dye
1387.	Story-teller's pack	F. R. Stockton
1388.	Stowe, Harriet Beecher	Dred
1389.	Stowe, Harriet Beecher	Uncle Tom's cabin
1428.	Strachey, *Sir* Edward	Le Morte d'Arthur
987.	Street-cleaning	G. E. Waring, *jr.*
1182.	Strenuous life	Theodore Roosevelt
314.	Stubbs, William	Early Plantagenets
410.	Student's American history	D. H. Montgomery
289.	Student's history of England	S. R. Gardiner
366.	Student's history of the United States	Edward Channing

Student's series.
    Bury, J. B. History of the Roman empire.
    Gibbon, Edward. History of the decline and fall of the Roman empire.
    Smith, *Sir* William. Smaller history of Rome.

1061.	Studies in American letters	H. A. Beers
185.	Studies in European and American history	F. M. Fling *and* H. W. Caldwell
208.	Studies in European history	Guernsey Jones
236.	Studies in European history	F. M. Fling
190.	Studies in general history	M. D. Sheldon
647.	Studies in historical method	M. S. Barnes
584.	Studies in the south and west	C. D. Warner
706.	Studies of childhood	James Sully
931.	Study of animal life	J. A. Thompson
712.	Study of children and their school training	Francis Warner
1042.	Study of English and American poets	J. S. Clark
1043.	Study of English prose writers	J. S. Clark
79.	Study of Hawthorne	G. P. Lathrop
661.	Study of history in schools	Committee of Seven
949.	Study of man	A. C. Haddon
205.	Study of mediaeval history	M. S. Getchell
708.	Study of the child	A. R. Taylor
14.	Success	O. S. Marden
156.	Successful women	S. K. Bolton
2.	Successward	Edward Bok
706.	Sully, James	Studies of childhood
707.	Sully, James	Teacher's handbook of psychology
84.	Sumner, William Graham	Andrew Jackson
364.	Survey of American history	H. W. Caldwell

    Sutro, Alfred, *trans.* See Maeterlinck, Maurice. Life of the bee.

106.	Swamp fox	John Frost

    Swanwick, Anna, *trans.* See Aeschylus. Dramas.

488.	Sweetser, Delight	One way round the world
1392.	Swift, Dean	Gulliver's travels
514.	Swiss life in town and country	A. T. Story
960.	Sykes, John F. J	Public health problems
953.	Syllabus of human physiology	J. I. Jegi
650.	Symbolic education	S. E. Blow
132.	Symonds, John Addington	Shelley
69.	Synge, M. B.	Life of Gladstone
680.	Systematic science teaching	E. G. Howe
1517.	Tacitus	works: annals

1087.	Taine, Hippolyte A. Van Laun, *trans.* ....History of English literature
1267.	Tale of two cities ....Charles Dickens
1353.	Tales ....E. A. Poe
1536.	Tales ....Wilhelm Hauff
1321.	Tales of a traveller ....Washington Irving
1327.	Tales of New England ....S. O. Jewett
	Tales of the heroic ages series.
	Ragozin, Z. A. Frithjof, the viking of Norfay.
	Ragozin, Z. A. Siegfried, the hero of the north.
1374.	Talisman ....Sir Walter Scott
1060.	Talks on the study of literature ....Arlo Bates
1040.	Talks on writing English ....Arlo Bates
682.	Talks to teachers on psychology............William James
	Tanger, Gustav, *jt. editor*. *See* Schmidt, Immanuel.
1088.	Tappan, Lucy ....Topical notes on American authors
100.	Tarbell, Ida ....Life of Abraham Lincoln
846.	Tarr, Ralph Stockman......................Elementary geology
865.	Tarr, Ralph Stockman ....Elementary physical geography
1478.	Tasso, Torquato. Wiffin, *trans.* ....Jerusalem delivered
708.	Taylor, Albert R.............................Study of the child
326.	Taylor, Bayard............................History of Germany
	Taylor, Bayard, *trans*. *See* Goethe, Johann Wolfgang von. Faust.
580.	Taylor, Charles M., *jr*..Touring Alaska and the Yellowstone
707.	Teacher's handbook of psychology ....James Sully
704.	Teaching of chemistry and physics ....Alexander Smith *and* E. H. Hall
654.	Teaching of history and civics ....H. E. Bourne
648.	Teaching of Latin and Greek ....C. E. Bennett *and* G. P. Bristol
679.	Teaching the language-arts ....B. A. Hinsdale
136.	Tecumseh and the Shawnee prophet ....E. E. Seelye *and* Edward Eggleston
770.	Telephone ....A. E. Dolbear
778.	Telephone lines and their properties ....W. J. Hopkins
633.	Ten years' war ....J. A. Riis
544.	Tent life in Siberia ....George Kennan
1479.	Tennyson, Alfred ....Poetic and dramatic works
563.	Tenting on the plains ....E. B. Custer
812.	Text-book of astronomy ....G. C. Comstock
477.	Text-book of commercial geography ....C. C. Adams
828.	Text-book of geology ....A. P. Brigham
772.	Text-book of physics ....E. H. Hall *and* J. Y. Bergen
1038.	Text-book of the history of painting ....J. C. Van Dyke
1034.	Text-book of the history of sculpture ....Allan Marquand *and* A. L. Frothingham
1393.	Thackeray, William Makepeace.............. Henry Esmond
1394.	Thackeray, William Makepeace................... Virginians
1355.	Thaddeus of Warsaw.........................Jane Porter
196.	Thalheimer, Mary Elsie ....Manual of ancient history
199.	Thalheimer, Mary Elsie..Manual of mediaeval and modern history
211.	Thatcher, Oliver J. ....Short history of mediaeval Europe
225.	Thatcher, Oliver J., *and* Schwill, Ferdinand ....

AUTHOR AND TITLE INDEX 483

	..................................Europe in the Middle Age
226.	Thatcher, Oliver J., *and* Schwill, Ferdinand ....
	..............................General history of Europe
109.	Thayer, James Bradley......................John Marshall
137.	Theodoric the Goth ....Thomas Hodgkin
781.	Theory of heat ....J. C. Maxwell
757.	Theory of physics ....J. S. Ames
1419.	They that walk in darkness ....Israel Zangwill
268.	Thirty years' war ....S. R. Gardiner
733.	This country of ours ....Benjamin Harrison
128.	Thomas, Calvin..........Life and works of Friedrich Schiller
1057.	Thomas, Calvin ....Practical German grammar
28.	Thomas Hart Benton ....Theodore Roosevelt
41.	Thomas Carlyle ....John Nichol
87.	Thomas Jefferson ....H. C. Merwin
88.	Thomas Jefferson ....J. T. Morse
1395.	Thompson, Ernest Seton–.............Biography of a grizzly
930.	Thompson, Ernest Seton–...............Lives of the hunted
789.	Thompson, Silvanus P..
	.........Elementary lessons in electricity and magnetism
790.	Thompson, Silvanus P............Light, visible and invisible
931.	Thomson, J. Arthur ....Study of animal life
1185.	Thoreau, Henry D...............................Excursions
1186.	Thoreau, Henry D..................................Walden
804.	Thorp, Frank Hall ....Outlines of industrial chemistry
423.	Thorpe, Francis Newton ....
	..........Constitutional history of the American people
424.	Thorpe, Francis Newton.......History of the American people
1251.	Those delightful Americans ....*Mrs.* Everard Cotes
1521.	Thoughts. Long, *trans.* ....Marcus Aurelius Antoninus
635.	Thrasher, Max Bennett ....Tuskegee
598.	Three Gringos in Venezuela and Central America...R. H. Davis
1323.	Three men in a boat ....J. K. Jerome
1272.	Three musketeers ....Alexandre Dumas
565.	Through the gold fields of Alaska ....Henry De Windt
1511.	Thucydides. Dale, *trans.* .....History of the Peloponnesian war
425.	Thwaites, Reuben Gold.............................Colonies
581.	Thwaites, Reuben Gold.............Down historic waterways
107.	Thwaites, Reuben Gold.................Father Marquette
472.	Thwaites, Reuben Gold...............Story of Wisconsin
791.	Thwing, Charles Burton ....Elementary physics
589.	To Cuba and back..............................R. H. Dana
1328.	To have and to hold............................Mary Johnston
820.	Todd, D. P. ....New astronomy for beginners
1318.	Tom Brown at Oxford ....Thomas Hughes
1380.	Tom Grogan ....F. H. Smith
1212.	Tommy and Grizel ....J. M. Barrie
593.	Tomorrow in Cuba ....C. M. Pepper
709.	Tompkins, Arnold.........Philosophy of school management
608.	Tools and the man.....................Washington Gladden
1088.	Topical notes on American authors ....Lucy Tappan
279.	Topical outline of English history ....F. J. Allen
1534.	Torquato Tasso ....J. W. Goethe
1187.	Torrey, Bradford.........................Birds in the bush
1188.	Torrey, Bradford.........................Florida sketch-book

582.	Torrey, Bradford	Footing it in Franconia
1189.	Torrey, Bradford	Foot-path way
1190.	Torrey, Bradford	Rambler's lease
1191.	Torrey. Bradford	Spring notes from Tennessee
1192.	Torrey, Bradford	World of green hills
580.	Touring Alaska and the Yellowstone	C. M. Taylor, *jr.*
58.	Towle, George M	Drake
179.	Towle, George M	Heroes and martyrs of invention
124.	Towle, George M	Pizarro
126.	Towle, George M	Raleigh
315.	Towle, George M	Young people's history of Ireland
1015.	Track athletics in detail	
710.	Tracy, Frederick	Psychology of childhood
1396.	Tracy, Louis	Final war
1492.	Tragedies. Plumptre, *trans.*	Aeschylus
1498.	Tragedies. Coleridge, *trans.*	Euripides
1510.	Tragedies. Plumptre, *trans.*	Sophocles
999.	Trail and camp-fire G. B. Grinnell *and* Theodore Roosevelt, *eds.*	
570.	Tramp across the continent	C. F. Lummis
625.	Tramping with tramps	Josiah Flynt
440.	Transit of civilization from England to America in the seventeenth century	Edward Eggleston
490.	Travels under the southern cross	M. M. Ballou
515.	Travels with a donkey in the Cevennes	R. L. Stevenson
1383.	Treasure island	R. L. Stevenson
1058.	Trechmann, Emil Short historical grammar of the German language	
94.	Trent, W. P.	Robert E. Lee
1107.	Trent, William P., *and* Wells, B. W., *eds.* Colonial prose and poetry	
553.	Tropical Africa	Henry Drummond
558.	Tropical America	I. N. Ford
792.	Trowbridge, John	What is electricity?
229.	Troy	S. G. W. Benjamin
	Trueblood, Thomas C., *jt. author. See* Fulton, Robert I.	
610.	Trust problem	J. W. Jenks
1036.	Tuckerman, Arthur L	Short history of architecture
793.	Tunzelmann, G. W. de	Electricity in modern life
1571.	Turner, Lura J., *and* Turner, J. M.	Handbook of Wisconsin
1184.	Turrets, towers and temples	Esther Singleton, *ed.*
1031.	Tuscan sculpture	E. M. Hurll
635.	Tuskegee	M. B. Thrasher
	Twain, Mark, *pseud. See* Clemens, Samuel Langhorne.	

Twelve English statesmen series.
    Harrison, Frederick. Oliver Cromwell.
    Rosebery, Lord. Pitt.

Twentieth century series.
    McLaughlin, A. C. History of the American nation.

Twentieth century text-book series; *ed.* by A. F. Nightingale.
    Adams, C. C. Text-book of commercial geography.
    Brigham, A. P. Text-book of geology.
    Burdick, F. M. Essentials of business law.
    Comstock, G. C. Text-book of astronomy.
    Coulter, J. M. Plants.
    Fowler, H. N. History of ancient Greek literature.

AUTHOR AND TITLE INDEX.   485

Gilbert, G. K., *and* Brigham, A. P. Introduction to physical geography.
Henderson, C. H., *and* Woodhull, J. F. Elements of physics.
Jordan, D. S., *and* Kellogg, V. L., *and* Heath, Harold. Animals.

Twitchell, W. I., *jt. author. See* **Gordy, Wilbur F.**

175.	Two spies	B. J. Lossing
1522.	Two tragedies: Medea and the daughters of Troy. Harris, *trans.*	Seneca
487.	Two years before the mast	R. H. Dana, *jr.*
81.	**Tyler, Moses Coit**	Patrick Henry
866.	**Tyndall, John**	
	Forms of water in clouds and rivers, ice and glaciers	
1277.	Uarda. Bell, *trans.*	Georg Ebers
711.	**Ufer, Christian.** Zinzer, *trans.*	
	Introduction to the pedagogy of Herbart	
72.	Ulysses S. Grant	Walter Allen
73.	Ulysses S. Grant	Hamlin Garland
539.	Unbeaten tracks in Japan	I. L. Bird
127.	"Uncle Jerry": Life of *Gen.* Jeremiah M. Rusk	Henry Casson
1389.	Uncle Tom's cabin	H. B. Stowe
728.	United States and foreign powers	W. E. Curtis
	University extension manuals; *ed.* by William Knight. Brown, C. B. Fine arts. Thomson, J. A. Study of animal life.	
1237.	Unknown patriot	F. S. Child
1418.	Unknown to history	C. M. Yonge
1555.	Unter dem Christbaum	Helene Stökl
907.	Up and down the brooks	M. E. Bamford
637.	Up from slavery	B. T. Washington
946.	Upon the tree-tops	Mrs. H. M. Miller
1343.	Utopia	*Sir* Thomas More
1258.	Van Bibber and others	R. H. Davis
1032.	Van Dyck, Anthony	E. M. Hurll
1193.	**Van Dyke, Henry**	Little rivers
1037.	**Van Dyke, John C.**	Art for art's sake
847.	**Van Dyke, John C.**	Desert
1194.	**Van Dyke, John C.**	Nature for its own sake
1038.	**Van Dyke, John C.**	Text-book of the history of painting
1180.	Varia	Agnes Repplier
1375.	Vassar studies	J. A. Schwartz
512.	Venetian life	W. D. Howells
691.	Ventilation and warming of school buildings	G. B. Morrison
138.	Vergil	Henry Nettleship
1397.	**Viaud, L. Marie Julien.** DeKoven, *trans.*	Iceland fisherman
1106.	Victorian anthology	E. C. Stedman, *ed.*
	Vincent, George E., *jt. author. See* **Small, Albion W.**	
	Vinsauf, Geoffrey de, *jt. author. See* **Richard de Devizes.**	
1523.	Virgil. Cranch, *trans.*	Aeneid
464.	Virginia	J. E. Cooke
1379.	Virginia cavalier	M. E. Seawell
1394.	Virginians	W. M. Thackeray
1086.	Victorian poets	E. C. Stedman
1459.	Vision of Piers the plowman	William Langland
850.	Volcanoes: their structure and significance	T. G. Bonney
837.	Volcanoes: past and present	Edward Hull

839.	Volcanoes: what they are and what they teach	J. W. Judd
862.	Volcanoes of North America	I. C. Russell
	Von. *For* names beginning with this prefix *see* the latter part of the name.	
1487.	Wagner, Leopold	Modern political orations
316.	Wakeling, G. H.	King and Parliament
227.	Wakeman, Henry Offley	Europe
1135.	Wake-robin	John Burroughs
1186.	Walden	H. D. Thoreau
1545.	Waldheimat	P. K. Rosegger
867.	Waldo, Frank	Elementary meteorology
617.	Walker, Francis A.	First lessons in political economy
426.	Walker, Francis A.	Making of the nation
618.	Walker, Francis A.	Political economy—advanced course
1398.	Wallace, Lew	Ben-Hur
1393.	Wallace, Lew	Fair God
575.	Wallace, Susan E.	Land of the Pueblos
1551.	Wallenstein and Wilhelm Tell	Friedrich Schiller
243.	Walpole, Arthur S.	Little Arthur's history of Greece
129.	Walter Scott	R. H. Hutton
1016.	Walton, Izaak, *and* Cotton, Charles	Complete angler
384.	War of independence	John Fiske
404.	War with Spain	H. C. Lodge
317.	Warburton, *Rev.* William	Edward III
43.	Ward, Adolphus William	Chaucer
55.	Ward, Adolphus William	Dickens
1108.	Ward, Thomas Humphrey, *ed.*	English poets
987.	Waring, George E., *jr.*	Street-cleaning
1400.	Warman, Cy.	Express messenger
1401.	Warman, Cy.	Snow on the headlight
460.	Warman, Cy.	Story of the railroad
636.	Warner, Amos G.	American charities
1195.	Warner, Charles Dudley	A-hunting of the deer
1196.	Warner, Charles Dudley	As we were saying
1109.	Warner, Charles Dudley	Book of eloquence
1197.	Warner, Charles Dudley	My summer in a garden
557.	Warner, Charles Dudley	My winter on the Nile
583.	Warner, Charles Dudley	On horseback
1089.	Warner, Charles Dudley	Relation of literature to life
584.	Warner, Charles Dudley	Studies in the South and West
83.	Warner, Charles Dudley	Washington Irving
	Warner, Charles Dudley, *ed. See* American men of letters series.	
712.	Warner, Francis	Study of children and their school training
637.	Washington, Booker T.	Up from slavery
82.	Washington Irving	H. W. Boynton
83.	Washington Irving	C. D. Warner
1285.	Waterloo	Emile Erckman *and* Alex. Chatrain
1402.	Waterloo, Stanley	Story of Ab
1403.	Watson, John	Beside the bonnie brier bush
1404.	Watson, John	Days of auld lang syne
	Watson, *Rev.* J. S., *trans. See* Xenophon	Cyropaedia
613.	Wealth against commonwealth	H. D. Lloyd
752.	Well-bred girl in society	Mrs. C. C. Harrison (*"Mrs.* Burton Harrison")
	Wells, Benjamin W., *jt. author. See* Trent, William P.	

506.	Well-worn roads of Spain, Holland, and Italy .....F. H. Smith
1090.	Welsh, Alfred H. ....
	...........Development of English literature and language
110.	Wendell, Barrett ....Cotton Mather
1091.	Wendell, Barrett ....Literary history of America
344.	Wendel, F. C. H. ....History of Egypt
564.	West from a car-window ....R. H. Davis
475.	West Indies ....A. K. Fiske
1405.	Westcott, Edward Noyes ....David Harum
1332.	Westward Ho ....Charles Kingsley
461.	Westward movement ....Justin Winsor
1406.	Weyman, Stanley J. ....Gentleman of France
144.	Wharton, Anne Hollingsworth ....Martha Washington
792.	What is electricity? ....John Trowbridge
16.	What shall our boys do for a living? ....C. F. Wingate
751.	What women can earn ....G. H. Dodge
	Wheatley, Henry B., ed. See Jonson, Ben ....
	..............................Every man in his humour
1587.	Wheeler, William A. ....Explanatory
	and pronouncing dictionary of the noted names of fiction
1039.	Wheelwright, Edmund March ....School architecture
1213.	When a man's single ....J. M. Barrie
1341.	When knighthood was in flower ....Charles Major
713.	White, Emerson E. ....Elements of pedagogy
714.	White, Emerson E. ....School management
619.	White, Horace ....Money and banking
827.	White, John S. ....Boys' and girls' Pliny
522.	White, Richard Grant ....England without and within
1302.	White aprons ....M. W. Goodwin
1271.	White company ....A. C. Doyle
551.	White man's Africa ....Poultney Bigelow
587.	White umbrella in Mexico ....F. H. Smith
794.	Whiting, Harold ....
	..........Course of experiments in physical measurement
	Whitman, Charles Huntington, trans. See Cynewulf ...Christ
	Whitman, Sidney, ed. See Poschinger, Heinrich von ....
	....Conversations with Bismarck
	Whitney, E. H., and M. D., trans. See Duruy, Victor ....
	..........................History of the Middle Ages
1579.	Whitney, William Dwight ....
	.............Compendious German and English dictionary
1481.	Whittier, John Greenleaf ....Complete poetical works
	Witfin, J. H., trans. See Tasso, Torquato ....
	....Jerusalem delivered
1407.	Wiggin, Kate Douglas ....
	.....Cathedral courtship and Penelope's English experience
715.	Wiggin, Kate Douglas ....Children's rights
1408.	Wiggin, Kate Douglas ....Diary of a goose girl
1409.	Wiggin, Kate Douglas ....Penelope's Irish experiences
1410.	Wiggin, Kate Douglas ....Penelope's progress
716.	Wiggin, Kate Douglas, and Smith, N. A. .. ...Froebel's gifts
717.	Wiggin, Kate Douglas, and Smith, N. A. ....
	....Froebel's occupations
718.	Wiggin, Kate Douglas, and Smith, N. A. ....
	....................Kindergarten principles and practice
1017.	Wigham, H. G. ....How to play golf

488 LIST OF BOOKS FOR HIGH SCHOOL LIBRARIES.

929.	Wild life near home	D. L. Sharp
918.	Wild neighbors	Ernest Ingersoll
1009.	Wilderness hunter	Theodore Roosevelt
1527.	Wilhelm Meister's apprenticeship. Carlyle. *trans.*	J. W. Goethe
1551.	Wilhelm Tell	Friedrich Schiller
	See his (1551) Wallenstein and Wilhelm Tell.	
1552.	Wilhelm Tell	J. C. F. von Schiller
1411.	Wilkins, Mary E.	New England nun
988.	Wilkinson, F.	Story of the cotton plant
68.	William Ewart Gladstone	James Bryce
130.	William Henry Seward	T. K. Lothrop
120.	William Penn	George Hodges
131.	William Shakespeare	H. W. Mabie
1412.	Williams, Jesse Lynch	Princeton stories
979.	Williams, Mary E., *and* Fisher, K. R.	
	Elements of the theory and practice of cookery	
806.	Williams, Rufus P.	Elements of chemistry
805.	Williams, W. Mattieu	Chemistry of cookery
744.	Willoughby, Westel W.	
	Rights and duties of American citizenship	
877.	Wilson, Edmund B., *and* Sedgwick, W. T.	
	Introduction to general biology	
1018.	Wilson, Edward L.	Mountain climbing
980.	Wilson, Lucy L. W., *ed.*	
	Handbook of domestic science and household arts	
427.	Wilson, Woodrow	Division and reunion
143.	Wilson, Woodrow	George Washington
745.	Wilson, Woodrow	State
719.	Wiltse, Sara E.	Place of the story in early education
1214.	Window in Thrums	J. M. Barrie
16.	Wingate, C. F.	What shall our boys do for a living?
457.	Winning of the west	Theodore Roosevelt
720.	Winship, Albert Edward	Great American educators
981.	Winslow, I. O.	Principles of agriculture for common schools
461.	Winsor, Justin	Westward movement
523.	Winter, William	Old shrines and ivy
1136.	Winter sunshine	John Burroughs
1413.	Wise, John Sergeant	Diomed
1414.	Wister, Owen	Red men and white
740.	With the fathers	J. B. McMaster
893.	With the wild flowers	E. M. Hardinge
1128.	Woman and the higher education	A. C. Brackett, *ed.*
629.	Woman and the republic	H. K. Johnson
1006.	Woman's book of sports	J. P. Paret
	Women of colonial and revolutionary times.	
	Earle, A. M. Margaret Winthrop.	
	Goodwin, M. W. Dolly Madison.	
	Wharton, A. H. Martha Washington.	
161.	Women of the American Revolution	E. F. Ellet
749.	Women wage-earners	*Mrs.* Helen Campbell
767.	Wonders of modern mechanism	C. H. Cochrane
	Woodhull, John F., *jt. author. See* Henderson, C. Hanford.	
	Woodman, Alpheus G., *jt. author. See* Richards, Ellen H.	
638.	Woods, Robert A., *and others*	Poor in great cities
1482.	Wordsworth, William	Poems

149.	Wordsworth	F. W. H. Myers
641.	Workers: the East	W. A. Wyckoff
642.	Workers: the West	W. A. Wyckoff
1192.	World of green hills	Bradford Torrey
743.	World politics	P. S. Reinsch
1030.	World's painters and their pictures	D. L. Hoyt
1517.	Works: the annals	Tacitus
620.	Wright, Carroll D.	Industrial evolution of United States
639.	Wright, Carroll D.	Outline of practical sociology
904.	Wright, Mabel Osgood	Flowers and ferns in their haunts
947.	Wright, Mabel Osgood, *and* Coues, Elliott	Citizen Bird
807.	Wurtz, Charles Adolphe	Elements of modern chemistry
640.	Wyckoff, Walter A.	Day with a tramp
641.	Wyckoff, Walter A.	Workers: the East
642.	Wyckoff, Walter A.	Workers: the West
1512.	Xenophon. Watson *and* Dale. *trans.*	Cyropaedia
1019.	Yale, Leroy M., *and others*	Angling
560.	Yellowstone National Park	H. M. Chittenden
497.	Yesterdays in the Philippines	J. E. Stevens
162.	Yesterdays with authors	J. T. Fields
318.	Yonge, Charlotte M.	Cameos from English history
275.	Yonge, Charlotte M.	History of France
1415.	Yonge, Charlotte M.	Lances of Lynwood
1416.	Yonge, Charlotte M.	Little Duke Richard, the fearless
1417.	Yonge, Charlotte M.	Prince and the page
278.	Yonge, Charlotte M.	Story of the Christians and Moors
1418.	Yonge, Charlotte M.	Unknown to history
	Yonge, C. D., *trans. See* Marcellinus, Ammianus	Roman history
746.	Young, Andrew W.	Government class book
499.	Young, Lucian	Real Hawaii
347.	Young folks' book of American explorers	T. W. Higginson
1585.	Young folks' cyclopaedia of literature and art	J. D. Champlin
	Young folks' heroes of history series.	
	Towle, G. M. Drake.	
	Towle, G. M. Pizarro.	
	Towle G. M. Raleigh.	
315.	Young people's history of Ireland	G. M. Towle
1419.	Zangwill, Israel	"They that walk in darkness"
	Zinzer, *trans. See* Ufer, Christian	Introduction to the pedagogy of Herbart
926.	Zoology	A. S. Packard

Fifth grade room in Lincoln school, Appleton, showing simple wall decorations.
LOUISE IRVING, Teacher.

LIST OF BOOKS

FOR

TOWNSHIP LIBRARIES

OF THE

STATE OF WISCONSIN.

Issued by the State Superintendent.

MAY, 1902.

MADISON
DEMOCRAT PRINTING COMPANY, STATE PRINTER
1902

*This list was prepared by Anne H. McNeil, Library Clerk,
under the direction of the State Superintendent.*

N. B.—To secure prompt attention, all correspondence relating to library matters should be addressed to the State Superintendent.

Township, Village, and City Library Law.

Attention is called to the fact that the legislature of 1899 extended the provisions of the township library law to include incorporated villages and cities of the fourth class.

It also modified the law relating to the funds from towns having joint districts. (See section below.) The time for purchasing books is now from May first to September first.

Special notice is called to that portion of the law which provides that all books purchased with the funds hereby provided for, *must be selected from the list prepared by the state superintendent.*

Funds for library and duties of treasurer—Section 486a. The treasurer of every town, incorporated village, or city of the fourth class in this state, shall withhold annually from the apportionment received from the school fund or other income for the school district or districts, the schoolhouse or schoolhouses of which are located in his town, village or city, an amount equal to ten cents per capita for each person of school age residing therein, for the purchase of library books as hereinafter provided.

In case of joint districts—In case of joint districts between one or more towns, a town or towns and an incorporated village or city, the treasurer or treasurers of the town or towns, shall transmit to the treasurer of the town, village or city in which the schoolhouse or houses may be located, on or before the first day of June of each year, an amount equal to ten cents per capita for each person of school age residing in that part of the joint district in his town at the time of the last annual school census.

Books how and when purchased—2. Between the first days of May and September of each year, the town, village, or city clerk except that in cities having a board of education such board of education or a majority thereof, shall act in place of the city clerk, shall, with the assistance and advice of the county or city superintendent of schools, as the case may be, expend all such money in the purchase of books selected from the list prepared by the state superintendent, for the use of the several school districts from which money has been so withheld, said books to be distributed among said districts, in proportion to the amount of money withheld from each.

Lists of books to be prepared—3. The state superintendent shall prepare, as often as he shall deem necessary, lists of books suitable for school district libraries, and furnish copies of such list to each town, village or city clerk, or secretary of the board of education, and to each county or city superintendent, from which lists the above designated officers shall select and purchase books for use in such school libraries.

Duties of town, village, city clerks, or secretaries of boards of education—4. Each town, village or city clerk, or secretary of the board of education, shall keep a record of the books so purchased and distributed in a book provided for that purpose. For such services properly performed, each clerk or secretary shall be allowed two dollars per day for each day actually and necessarily devoted thereto, such sum to be paid out of the town, village or city treasury.

Suspension of law—Section 2. The state superintendent shall have authority to suspend the operation of this act in any school district, town, village or city which shall maintain a free public library by giving due notice of such suspension to the clerk of such school district, town, village or city.

Librarian and records—Section 486b. Unless the school district shall at the annual meeting elect some other person librarian, the clerk shall act as librarian and receive and have the care and custody of the books so distributed to the district, and shall loan them to teachers, pupils and other residents of the district in accordance with the regulations prescribed by the state superintendent. The clerk shall keep a record of the books received from the town clerk in a book furnished by the state superintendent through the town clerk; but during the time school is in session the library shall be placed in the schoolhouse, and the teacher shall act as librarian under the supervision of the clerk or of the librarian elected at the annual meeting. The state superintendent shall furnish to each town clerk suitable record books for his use and the use of the several clerks in his town.

Farm institute bulletins—Section 486c. The superintendent of agricultural institutes shall deposit with the state superintendent a sufficient number of copies of the bulletins of such institutes to supply every public school library with one copy of each edition thereof, which bulletins the state superintendent shall send to the various town clerks, who shall distribute them to such libraries in their respective towns, from which they shall be loaned in like manner and under the same regulations prescribed for the loaning of books therein.

To treasurers of towns, villages, and cities of the fourth class—Section 486a of the statutes of 1898, as amended by chapter 272 of the laws of 1899, requires that you shall withhold each year from the apportionment received from the school fund or other income, *for the school district or districts the schoolhouse or schoolhouses of which are located in your town, village, or city,* ten cents for each person between the ages of four and twenty years residing therein, for the purchase of library books for such districts.

If there are no joint districts in the town, it will be evident that the sum to be withheld amounts to ten cents for each child of school age residing within the town. If there are joint districts, and the schoolhouses of these districts are located in your town, village or city, you must withhold from the school funds apportioned to you, ten cents for each child of school age residing in that part of the joint school district lying outside your town in addition to the amount withheld for the districts lying wholly within your town, village, or city. If in any joint district the schoolhouse is not located in your town, you should not withhold any money for that portion of the district lying in your town to be paid to the town clerk; but should set aside ten cents for each child of school age residing in this portion of the district in your town, village, or city to be paid to the treasurer of the town, village, or city in which the other part of the district lies on or before June 1.

All money required for library purposes under the law, should be set apart immediately after the school fund income has been apportioned and paid to you for your town, village, or city, and on and after May 1, that portion of it which is to be used by town, village, or city clerks, boards of education in cities, or secretaries of boards of school directors in towns having the township system of school organization, should be subject to their order. That portion which is to be paid to treasurers of other towns, cities or villages on account of joint school districts should at the same time report to these officers, although the law gives until June 1, for this payment. If it is paid over promptly May 1, there need be no excuse for delay in ordering the books.

Many complaints have been made during the past year, by town treasurers, that they have not received the sums due them from the town treasurers of other towns in which there were parts of joint districts, and town clerks have complained that they have never received the full amounts due, for this reason. If the full amount is withheld as required in each case, then the entire sum will be available at once, for the purchase of books, and any town treasurer neglecting to pay over such sums as may be due on account of the joint districts, the schoolhouses of which are located in other towns, will render himself liable, as will every other officer not complying with the provisions of law, to a fine of five hundred dollars, or one year's imprisonment, as provided by section 4549–4550 of the Wisconsin statutes.

Illustration showing how to determine amount to be withheld in case of joint districts.

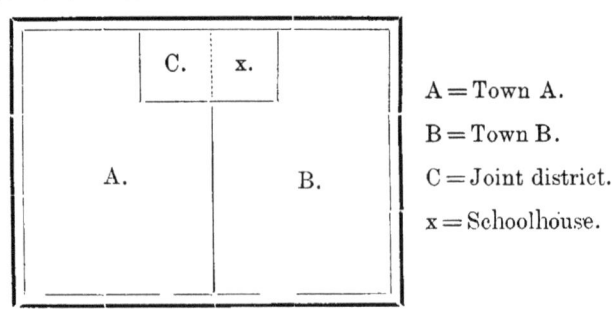

A = Town A.
B = Town B.
C = Joint district.
x = Schoolhouse.

Suppose there are sixteen children of school age in the part of joint district in Town A. Suppose there are forty children of school age in the part of joint district in Town B, where schoolhouse is located. Treasurer of Town B sets aside $5.60 ($1.60 + $4.00), for joint district. Treasurer of Town A should immediately transmit to Treasurer of Town B, $1.60. This $1.60 should be taken from the portion of the school fund income which the town treasurer of Town A apportions to the treasurer of the joint district. Treasurer of Town A withholds no money for the sixteen children in that part of the joint district in Town A, to be used by the town clerk, as that amount has already been transmitted to the Treasurer of Town B, and will be used by the clerk of that town in the purchase of books for the district.

To clerks of towns, villages, boards of education of cities of the fourth class, and secretaries of boards of school directors in towns having the township system of school organization—By section 486a, Statutes of 1898, as amended by chapter 272 of the laws of 1899, you are required to purchase, between the first days of May and September of each year, books for the schools in your town, village or city, selected from the list prepared by the state superintendent, to the amount of the full sum which the treasurer of your town, village or city is required to withhold for that purpose. These books are to be distributed among the several districts in proportion to the amount of money withheld from each. It is your duty under the law to keep a record of books so purchased and distributed, in a book provided by the state superintendent for that purpose, and for such services properly performed, you are entitled to two dollars per day, for each day actually and necessarily devoted thereto, such sum to be paid out of the town, village or city treasury, and not from the amount withheld by the town treasurer for the purchase of books. These books should be distributed by you to the clerks of the several districts, unless you have been notified that some other person than the clerk has been elected at the annual meeting as librarian.

It is made the duty of the state superintendent to prepare lists of books for the use of the officers required by law to purchase books for the libraries, from which these officers, with such assistance and advice as they may get from the county or city superintendent of schools, as the case may be, shall select the books to be purchased. It is illegal to purchase with the money withheld by the town treasurer, any other books than those given in the list. It is the duty of the town treasurer to withhold this money and have it subject to the order of the officers whose duty it is to purchase the books, on May 1st. Before that day the new library list will be issued, from which the books must be selected. As on May 1st the money is available for the purchase of books, the proper officers should at once make up their orders and secure the books at the earliest possible date, and at once distribute them, so that they may be available for use before the school year closes. If books are ordered early, the orders can be more promptly filled than later in the season, for the reason that in many cases the dealer is unable to secure books, because the editions have become exhausted, and thus is delayed in filling orders. The firm selected by the state superintendent to furnish the books at prices quoted, is responsible for filling orders exactly as made. If for any reason books are not in stock when the order is placed, you may rest assured that the order will be filled as soon as the lacking books can be secured, without additional expense to you.

Failure to comply with the requirements of the law renders every officer so failing liable to a fine of five hundred dollars, or one year's imprisonment, as provided in sections 4549–4550 of the Wisconsin statutes.

L. D. HARVEY,
State Superintendent.

To those Charged by Law with the Selection and Purchase of Books.

1. The following list contains what are believed to be the choicest books for school libraries. In making selection for purchases it is well to consider the needs of each individual district. The law directs that the county superintendent shall assist the town clerk in making the selections. County superintendents should make it a point to get the advice of the teachers and profit by their experience with books and children. In general it is best to choose books that are certain to be within the capacity of the greater number of children. *It is better to err on the side of selecting books that are too simple than that of selecting those which will be of little service because they are too difficult.* Make the selection so as to cover as wide a range of subjects as possible and furnish books for all grades. As soon as this list is received the order should be prepared and sent in to the firm that is to supply the books.

At the beginning of the year, the dealer has the full list in stock. His contract is for one year only and it is to his advantage to close out the stock before the end of the year. If the books are ordered late he is not likely to have them in stock and they must be ordered from the publishers, thus causing delay and unnecessary trouble.

2. Leading topics in many of the books have been paged. See "References." Not only will these indicate the contents of the books to the town clerks and the county superintendents, but the teachers will find them helpful in using the books in school and in finding material on various subjects in which the children should be interested.

NOTES ON BOOKS.

3. The notes on the books are made from the standpoint of the teacher, and to aid the teacher in directing the reading of the pupils. The educational and ethical values are pointed out and the things which will interest pupils are indicated.

GRADING.

4. It is very difficult to grade books to suit all schools. What a child wants to read depends upon what he has read, what he is interested in, and the work the teacher does with him in the line of reading, rather than upon the number of years he has attended school. Many books of the upper form ought to be read to children of the lower form by the teacher. Parts of books directly in the line of children's interests can be read by the children, when the entire book would be out of the question.

SUBJECT INDEX.

5. A new feature of this year's list is a subject index. The arrangement of this index is an alphabetical one, and under each subject are grouped the references to books upon the list containing material on that subject. Each reference is made to the List number, Author and Title of a book and when only a portion of a book bears upon a topic, reference is also made to the pages of the books on which the topic is treated.

The intention has not been to make an exhaustive index to all the material in all of the books upon the List. The purpose is rather to make a suggestive list of references to books containing material valuable for supplementary work.

If no references are found under a specific subject, it does not necessarily mean that there are no books upon the list containing material on that subject. For example, very few references are given on the subjects "Plants" and "Seeds," but more material on these topics will be found in books referenced under the general heading "Botany."

The references to books on United States history have been made by period—United States History—Discovery and Colonial; Revolution; War of 1812, etc. Reference is made first to all books of history and biography on each period and following this a list of Historical fiction on each period is given.

This index will be very helpful to the teacher searching for material to supplement the regular work in text-books and will also be suggestive to the teacher of Library Reading.

The growing teacher will study the interests of her pupils and try to lead them from one line of reading to another which suggests itself to her because of some interest which she finds the boy or girl has in some subject related to the one upon which he is reading, for example—the pupil reading Butterworth's story, "In the days of Audubon," may become interested in the subject of Birds and wish to read more about them. The teacher can immediately turn to this index and find a list of books upon the subject of "Birds" from which she can make her selection of a book to meet the interest of the pupil. The reading of this book may so interest him in outdoor life that he will enjoy reading a book which will give him descriptions of other things in nature besides birds. In the index under the subject "Nature study," the teacher will find a list of books from which selections may be made. Through the book selected he may be led to read some beautiful nature poems or a book of travel containing descriptions of nature—the index again suggesting books of travel and poems. The index will help the teacher in preparing a list of new books which she desires to have purchased for her school. If she finds very little supplementary material in her library along some certain line, the index will suggest other books upon the Township List that contain the desired material.

AUTHOR AND TITLE INDEX.

6. The Author and Title indexes have been combined, and are arranged in one alphabetical list.

DUPLICATES.

7. It is not advisable to purchase duplicates of books for districts when the amount of money available for library purposes is small.

TO TEACHERS.

8. Teachers should encourage the reading of library books by the adults in the district as well as by the pupils in the school.

ORDERING AND SHIPPING OF BOOKS.

9. This list is the list for 1902. No books should be ordered from any other list.

The following are the numbers of the books which have been added to the list this year: 2' 3, 4, 5, 7, 8, 9, 21, 22, 23, 26, 27, 31, 32, 34, 35, 36, 37, 45, 50, 51, 52, 54, 59, 64, 66, 67, 68, 72, 76, 81, 82, 83, 87, 89, 99, 100, 101, 102, 104, 112, 114, 120, 121, 122, 126, 139, 145, 146, 147, 148, 149, 150, 151, 154, 155, 159, 162, 163, 164, 166, 169, 170, 173, 177, 181, 189, 190, 192, 196, 202, 205, 210, 213, 216, 221, 233, 237, 238, 239, 246, 249, 251, 260, 261, 270, 272, 273, 276, 285, 292, 296, 298, 300, 308, 311, 313, 316, 321, 322, 324, 325, 326, 337, 339, 340, 342, 344, 350, 354, 355, 357a, 359, 365, 366, 369, 371, 372, 374, 375, 380, 393, 395, 397, 398, 401, 403, 411, 420, 424, 428, 430, 431, 436, 441, 442, 450, 454, 461, 468, 474, 476, 482, 483, 485, 486, 494, 509, 510, 514, 519, 531, 532, 533, 536, 539, 540, 541, 549, 556, 560, 561, 562, 563, 566, 570, 577, 578, 590, 598, 601, 602, 604, 606, 607, 615, 619, 622, 624, 626, 627, 628, 629, 630, 634, 635, 646, 652, 654, 658, 666, 667, 668, 674, 675, 676, 701, 712, 713, 715, 716, 723, 724, 729, 734, 739, 745, 746, 751, 752, 755, 762, 771, 773.

10. Send in all orders on regular order blanks which are furnished by the state superintendent. The blanks furnished this year contain space for ordering books as second choice. Experience has shown that it is better *not* to make a second choice. Order from the list the books wanted, and Des Forges & Co. will furnish them as ordered. In case any books are shipped which are not ordered, it will be due to a mistake of the shipping clerk. Such books should be promptly returned to Des Forges & Co. at their expense and their attention called to the error. They will correct the mistake promptly without further expense to the party ordering.

INSTRUCTIONS TO SCHOOL OFFICERS.

11. Give all directions for shipping *carefully and plainly;* the postoffice address, including the county, the town, village or city for which the books are ordered, and the name of the station to which the books are to be shipped. Also state on what line of railway or by what express company shipment is to be made. Carelessness in these matters is sure to cause much trouble and unnecessary delay in getting books.

12. Examine the record book carefully to avoid purchasing for districts duplicates of books that have already been purchased, and which it is not desirable to duplicate.

13. Charge freight, express, postage and exchange to the library fund. Charge the per diem for delivering books to the general fund of the town.

14. Keep a duplicate of your order and see that the books received are those described in this list. *It is illegal to purchase with the library fund books or editions not included in this list. The town clerk who orders other books or editions renders himself liable for a violation of law.*

15. This list should be kept on file in the town clerk's office, the county superintendent's office, and in the district school library.

16. The record of the books in each library should be kept by author and title as well as by list number, as the removal of old books and insertion of new ones each year make it necessary to change the numbers of the books when a new list is published.

17. Labels, order blanks, a blank book for keeping the town clerk's record of the books sent to the district, and blank loan record books for the use of district librarians will be furnished by the state superintendent upon application of the town clerks.

18. Des Forges & Co., Milwaukee, Wis., will furnish the books this year, and will supply them at the prices given in the second column in these lists. They will make no charges for boxing and cartage.

School officers, town clerks, and teachers may procure single volumes or a few copies by adding 10 per cent. of the list price to the prices given in the second column.

In payment for books send money order or draft. Do not send town orders on the treasurer as it costs Des Forges & Co. seventy cents or one dollar to collect them.

L. D. HARVEY,
State Superintendent.

ABBREVIATIONS.

Anon.	anonymous.	o	octavo
arr.	arranged	pt.	part
Bost.	Boston	por.	portraits
bds.	boards	pseud.	pseudonym
capt.	captain	pub.	publisher
Chic.	Chicago.	Q	quarto
cl.	cloth	rev.	revised
col.	collection	S	16 mo.
co.	company	Ser.	series.
comp.	compiler.	S. A.	South America
c.	copyright	sq.	square
D	duodecimo	T	24 mo.
ed.	editor, edition.	trans.	translated, translator
enl.	enlarged	Tt	32 mo.
F	folio	U. S.	United States
Fe	48 mo.	v., vol.	volume.
il.	illustrated	( )	numbers inclosed refer to numbers in Township list of 1899, and 1900.
jr.	junior		
lib.	library		
lit.	literature	[ ]	numbers inclosed refer to numbers in Township list of 1901.
N. Y.	New York		
N. A.	North America		
n. d.	no date of publication	——	to and including
obl.	oblong	. . .	matter omitted.

PRIMARY FORM OR GRADES.

PICTURE BOOKS FOR THE YOUNGEST CHILDREN.

Children enjoy looking at pictures. Not only is their love of the beautiful cultivated but many things are learned from good pictures. Their value in connection with history, geography, and nature study can not be over-estimated. Through pictures the surrounding text becomes of interest and thus they form an incentive to the children to learn to read.

Serviceable picture books may be made at small expense by pasting pictures from magazines, illustrated papers, etc., on sheets of paper cambric, and then stitching these sheets together.

	List price.	Price to districts.
1. [11.] **Book of ships.** N. Y., E. P. Dutton & Co., il. obl. O. Linen. bds.	75	.45

Every boy will like this book. By means of fascinating pictures it shows something of the development in ship building from the days of Alfred to the present time.

| 2. **Happy playtimes.** N. Y., E. P. Dutton & Co. (n. d.) il. Q. cl. | 1.50 | .88 |

The greatest value of this book is as a picture book. The illustrations of children at play are excellent. Interesting little stories are told about each picture.

| 3. **Little people's scrap book.** N. Y., E. P. Dutton & Co. (n. d.) il. F. bds. | 1.50 | .88 |

| 4. **Mother Goose.** *Ed.* and *il.* by W. W. Denslow. N. Y., McClure, Phillips & Co., 1901. 94 p. il. O. bda. | 1.50 | .90 |

A beautifully illustrated edition.

| 5. **Our doggies.** N. Y., E. P. Dutton & Co. (n. d.) il. F. pap. | .50 | .30 |

	List price.	Price to districts.

6. [7.] **Our farmyard.** N. Y., E. P. Dutton & Co. il. Q. Mounted on linen. bds. .... .50 .25

7. **Pets' picture farm.** N. Y., E. P. Dutton & Co. (n. d.) il. Q. bds. .... 1.50 .88

Excellent illustrations of fowls and domestic animals. A good book for the youngest children.

8. **Pictures for little people.** N. Y., E. P. Dutton & Co., (n. d.) 36 p. il. sq. Q. bds. .... 1.25 .75

Colored illustrations.

FIRST BOOKS FOR CHILDREN'S READING.

Books containing short selections which children can read for themselves. The print is large, the illustrations are good, the selections are short, and of such a nature as to interest the child.

9. **Arnold primer.** Sarah Louise Arnold. N. Y., Silver, Burdett & Co., c1901. 128 p. il. D. cl. .... .30 .27

10. [14.] (555.) **Baldwin primer.** May Kirk. N. Y., American Book Co., 1899. 128 p. il. sq. D. cl. .30 .26

11. [31.] (565.) **Child life:** a first reader. Etta Austin Blaisdell, *and* Mary Frances Blaisdell. N. Y., The Macmillan Co., 1899. 127 p. il. D. cl. .... .25 .22

12. [32.] (566.) **Child life in tale and fable:** a second reader. Etta Austin Blaisdell, *and* Mary Frances Blaisdell. N. Y., The Macmillan Co., 1899. 159 p. il. D. cl. .... .35 .31

13. [25.] **Choice literature:** Bk. Two, for primary grades. *Comp.* by Sherman Williams. N. Y., Butler, Sheldon & Co., 1900. 160 p. D. cl. .... .30 .26

14. [35.] (569.) **Fairy tale and fable:** second year. John G. Thompson *and* Thomas E. Thompson. N. Y., Morse Co., 1899. 164 p. il. D. (New Century readers.) cl. .... .40 .32

	List price.	Price to districts.

15. [21.] (558.) **First book: pictures—rhymes—stories.** Geo. I. Aldrich *and* Alexander Forbes. N. Y., Butler, Sheldon & Co., 1899. 132 p. il. D. (Progressive course in reading.) cl............ .20 .17

16. [22.] (559.) **Second book: pictures—rhymes—stories.** George I. Aldrich *and* Alexander Forbes. N. Y., Butler, Sheldon & Co., 1899. 176 p. il. D. (Progressive course in reading.) cl............... .30 .25

17. [23.] (560.) **Third book: stories—studies—rhymes—riddles.** George I. Aldrich and Alexander Forbes. N. Y., Butler, Sheldon & Co., 1900. 272 p. il. D. (Progressive course in reading.) cl............ .40 .34

18. [33.] (567.) **First reader.** Lottie E. Jones *and* S. W. Black. Chicago, Eaton & Co., 1897. 97 p. il. D. (New Era ser.) cl. .... .15 .13

19. [34.] (568.) **Second reader.** Lottie E. Jones *and* S. W. Black. Chicago, Eaton & Co. 1897. 160 p. il. D. (New Era ser.) cl. .... .25 .22

20. [38a.] **Folklore stories and proverbs.** Sara E. Wiltse. Bost., Ginn & Co., 1901. 81 p. il. D. cl....... .30 .27

21. **Little-folk tales: a first reader.** Mary L. Gilman, *and* Isabella Austin *and* S. Lilian Blaisdell. N. Y., Globe School Book Co., c1901. 168 p. il. D. (Hawthorne readers.) cl. .... .24 .21

22. **Story land: a** second reader. Mary F. Hall, *and* Mary L. Gilman. N. Y., Globe School Book Co., c1901. 224 p. il. D. (Hawthorne readers.) cl.. .36 .30

23. **From many lands: a third reader.** Florence Holbrook, *and* Mary F. Hall. N. Y., Globe School Book Co., c1901. 288 p. il. D. (Hawthorne readers.) cl. .... .48 .40

24. [36.] **Graded literature readers.** First book. Harry Pratt Judson *and* Ida C. Bender, *eds.* N. Y., Maynard, Merrill, & Co., 1899. 128 p. il. D. cl,.... .25 .22

25. [37.] **Graded literature readers.** Second book. Harry Pratt Judson, *and* Ida C. Bender, *eds.* N. Y., Maynard, Merrill, & Co., 1900. 192 p. il. D. cl..... .40 .35

	List price.	Price to districts.

26. **Hiawatha primer.** Florence Holbrook. Bost., Houghton, Mifflin & Co., c1898. 139 p. il. D. cl...... .40 .35

27. **Holton primer.** M. Adelaide Holton. Chic., Rand, McNally & Co., c1901. 111 p. il. D. (Lights to literature series.) cl. .... .25 .22

28. [26.] (562.) **Lights to literature:** book one: a first reader. H. Avis Perdue *and* Florence E. La Victoire. Chicago, Rand, McNally & Co., 1898. 119 p. il. D. cl. .... .25 .22

29. [27.] (563.) **Lights to literature:** book two: a second reader. Sarah E. Sprague. Chicago, Rand, McNally & Co., 1898. 156 p. il. D. cl............ .36 .32

30. [28.] (564.) **Lights to literature:** book three. A. E. Lane. Chicago, Rand, McNally & Co., 1898. 303 p. il. D. cl. .... .48 .43

31. **New Century second reader.** H. Avis Perdue, *and* Florence E. La Victoire. Chic., Rand, McNally & Co., c1899. 160 p. il. D. cl................... .25 .22

The story of child life in other lands. The stories present in a vivid and attractive way the home life, appearance, folk-stories, and myths of Indian, Eskimo, Chinese, Japanese, Norwegian, Dutch and German children.
References: Indian children, 9–33; Eskimo children, 38–51; Chinese children, 52–76; Japanese children, 77–96; Children of Norway, 102–17; Children of Holland, 118–38; German children, 138–46.

32. **New Century third reader.** H. S. Tibbits. Chic., Rand, McNally & Co., c1901. 159 p. il. D. cl......... .35 .32

33. [13.] **New education readers;** a synthetic and phonic word method. A. J. Demarest, *and* William M. Van Sickle. Bk. 1. N. Y., American Book Company, 1900. 144 p. il. D. cl.................. .35 .30

34. **New education readers:** a synthetic and phonic word method. A. J. Demarest, *and* William M. Van Sickle. Bk. 2. N. Y., American Book Co., c1900. 144 p. il. D. cl................................ .35 .31

LIST OF BOOKS FOR TOWNSHIP LIBRARIES.

	List price.	Price to districts.

35. **New education readers:** a synthetic and phonic word method. A. J. Demarest, *and* William Van Sickle. Bk. 3. N. Y., American Book Co., c1901. 160 p. il. D. cl. .... .40 .34

36. **Oriole stories.** M. A. L. Lane. Bost., Ginn & Co., 1900. 86 p. il. D. cl. .... .28 .25

37. **Old friends in new dresses:** supplementary first reader. Ed. 2 rev. Wm. F. Sell *and* John G. Nageler. Milwaukee, S. Y. Gillan & Co., 1900. 63 p. D, bds. .... .15 .13

37a. [12.] **Our little book for little folks.** *Arr.* by W. E. Crosby. N. Y., American Book Company, 1896. 106 p. il. D. cl. .... .30 .25

38. [15.] **School reading by grades:** first year. James Baldwin. N. Y., American Book Company, 1897. 128 p. il. D. cl. .... .25 .21

39. [16.] (556.) **School reading by grades:** second year James Baldwin. N. Y., American Book Co., 1897. 160 p. il. D. cl. .... .35 .30

40. [17.] (557.) **School reading by grades:** third year. James Baldwin. N. Y., American Book Co., 1897. 208 p. il. D. cl. .... .40 .33

41. [24.] (561.) **Sight reader.** Primary teachers. N. Y., Butler, Sheldon & Co., 1898. 80 p. il. D. bds. .15 .13

42. [19.] **Story reader.** Alfred E. Logie *and* Clara H. Uecke. N. Y., American Book Company, 1901. 128 p. il. D. cl. .... .30 .27

43. [30.] **Taylor school readers.** First reader. Frances Lillian Taylor. N. Y., Werner School Book Co., 1900. 128 p. il. D. cl. .... .30 .26

44. [38.] **Wheeler's graded readers:** a primer. Gail Calmerton, *and* William H. Wheeler. Chic., W. H. Wheeler & Co., 1900. 128 p. il. D. cl. .... .30 .26

22   LIST OF BOOKS FOR TOWNSHIP LIBRARIES.

NURSERY RHYMES AND JINGES.

The teacher should read or recite these rhymes to the children until they become perfectly familiar, and should encourage the children to memorize. Children enjoy the music.

	List price.	Price to districts.
45. Book of nursery rhymes: being Mother Goose's Melodies arranged in the order of attractiveness and interest. Charles Welsh. Bʳst., D. C. Heath & Co., 1901. 169 p. il. D. ci....................	.30	.27

"Rhymes and jingles not only fall naturally into the four great divisions of mother play, mother stories, child play, and child stories, but there is a logical order in which each section may be advantageously presented to the child.

An attempt has been made to arrange the rhymes and jingles in this collection so as to follow the child's growing intellectual powers by beginning each division with the more simple and concrete rhymes, jingles, and stories, and gradually advancing to those which contain more complex and abstract ideas.'—From Author's preface.

Contents: Mother play—Rhymes personal to the child. Mother stories—Animals and their doings; other children, and other people in relation to the child; days and nights, weeks and months and years; time and the weather. Child play—Plays, games, riddles, counting-out rhymes. Child stories and child play—Stories, proverbs, paradoxes, experience rhymes, rhyming alphabets.

(The binding of the books in the series of Heath's home and school classics, deserves especial commendation.)

| 46. [41.] Chinese Mother Goose rhymes. Isaac Taylor Headland. N. Y., Fleming H. Revell Co., 1900. 157 p. il. O. bds. .... | 1.00 | .60 |

A charming book of rhymes translated from the Chinese and illustrated with photographs of Chinese child life. The middle form children will enjoy the pictures and learn many things concerning the life of Chinese children.

| 47. [42.] Goops and how to be them: a manual of manners for polite infants, inculcating many juvenile virtues both by precept and example. Gelett Burgess. N. Y., F. A. Stokes Co., 1900. il. sq. O. | 1.50 | .85 |

Cleanliness, generosity, honesty, and tidiness as well as other important things are taught in delightful rhymes.

LIST OF BOOKS FOR TOWNSHIP LIBRARIES. 23

	List price.	Price to districts.
48. [44.] (18.) **Heart of oak books.** 1st bk. *Ed.* by Charles Eliot Norton. Bost., D. C. Heath & Co., 1897. 100 p. D. cl.	.25	.22

A collection of nursery rhymes and jingles for the youngest children.

49. [45.] (541.) **Jingle book.** Carolyn Wells. N. Y., Macmillan Co., 1899. 124 p. il. D. cl.......... 1.00 .65

Merry jingles for merry children.

50. **Jumbles and other nonsense verses,** with drawings by L. L. Brooks. Edward Lear. N. Y., Frederick Warne & Co., (n. d.) 72 p. il. O. bds......... 1.25 .75

This book and the "Pelican chorus" include all of Lear's "Nonsense songs."

51. **Kids of many colors.** Grace Duffie Boylan, *and* Ike Morgan. Chic., Jamieson–Higgins Co., c1901. 156 p. il. O. cl. .... 1.50 .75

Descriptive verses and lullabies, with colored pictures of the children of many nations at play. This book should not be a first choice where the amount of money available for purchase of books is small.

52. **Memoirs of Simple Simon.** D. B. Keeler. N. Y., R. H. Russell, 1901. il. Q. bds. .... 1.50 .90

Contains many funny pictures. This should not be a first choice where the amount of money available for the purchase of books is small.

53. [43.] **Moon Babies.** Verses by G. Orr Clark. N. Y., R. H. Russell, 1900. 48 p. il. obl. O. bds..... 1.50 .90

Charming verses about Chinese children, most beautifully illustrated.

54. **Mother Goose jingles.** N. Y., E. P. Dutton & Co., (n. d.) 184 p. il. O. bds..................... 1.50 .88

An excellent collection of rhymes. Contains several fine illustrations in color.

LIST OF BOOKS FOR TOWNSHIP LIBRARIES.

	List price.	Price to districts.

55. [40.] (19.) **Nursery rhyme book.** Andrew Lang, *ed.* N. Y., Frederick Warne & Co., 1898. 288 p. il. O. cl. 2.00   1.18

One of the best collections of nursery rhymes and jingles. It is arranged into historical tales, literal tales, proverbs, songs, riddles, charms and lullabies, gaffers and gammers, games, jingles, natural history stories, and accumulative stories. A fine preface on the value of these rhymes. The children should be encouraged to memorize them.

56. [47.] **Pelican chorus and other nonsense verses.** Edward Lear. N. Y., Frederick Warne & Co., 1900. sq. O. Art linen .... 1.25   .75

Nonsense rhymes and pictures.

57. [39.] (17.) **Verse and prose for beginners;** selected from English and American literature. Horace E. Scudder. Bost., Houghton, Mifflin & Co., 1893. 98 p. D. cl. .... .25   .22

This collection includes many nursery rhymes and jingles with which the children are already familiar. Many of the selections the child can read for himself. Teachers will find the preface very suggestive.

58. [46.] **When life is young;** a collection of verse for boys and girls. Mary Mapes Dodge. N. Y., Century Co., 1894. 255 p. il. D. cl..... .... 1.25   .75

A collection of poems and jingles for the youngest children. There is a good deal of wholesome fun in this book.

59. **Yankee Doodle Gander,** a Jingo Jingle book. Oscar Hunt von Gottschalk. N. Y., R. H. Russell, 1901. il. Q. bds. .... 1.50   .90

A nonsense book with illustrations in color.

FICTION.

Some of these books the children can read for themselves but many the teacher will have to read to the children. Children never tire of hearing over and over the story that they like best, and many times after hearing a story they will wish to read it for themselves. Besides the pleasure which the children get from the reading, the concrete lessons in good living, and the inspiration from the story, many stories furnish valuable material for the history and the geography lesson. See Manual of the Elementary Course of Study. *Geography and History—Primary and Middle Forms.* The telling of the story by the children, talking over with the teacher what they have enjoyed and found good, telling how the children in these books lived, what they did at school, in their games, and at home, will give the children practice in language. See Manual, *Language—Primary Form.*

	List price.	Price to districts.
60. [72.] (40.) **Adventures of a brownie, as told to my child.** *Mrs.* Dinah M. Craik. Bost., Educational Pub. Co., 159 p. il. D. cl.	.40	.28

A little book for little children about those queer little people, the brownies.

61. [614.] **April baby's book of tunes.** Author of Elizabeth and her German Garden. N. Y., Macmillan Co., 1900. 75 p. sq. D. cl. 1.50 1.15

A charming bit of child life and mother love.

62. [64.] (581.) **Arabella and Araminta stories.** Gertrude Smith. Bost., Copeland & Day, 1897. 103 p. O. cl. .... 1.00 .65

Events in the lives of two little girls aged four. "Sometimes Arabella was naughty when Araminta was good, and sometimes Araminta was naughty when Arabella was good." The print is clear and large, the stories bright and entertaining. Children of this form can read for themselves.

	List price.	Price to districts.
63. [70.] (32.) **Bed-time stories.** Louise Chandler Moulton. Bost., Little, Brown & Co., 1898. 239 p. il. D. cl.	1.25	.75

A number of attractive little stories about children, each one teaching a truth in good living, without preaching. A book for the teacher to read to children.

64. **Big outdoors.** Clara G. Froelich. Wausau, Wis., Van Vechten & Ellis, c1899. 74 p. D. bds.	.50	.40

A collection of delightful little nature stories that may be read and told to the youngest children.
Contents: What Isabelle saw; When the days' asleep; Bright eyes; Rose fairy; Wonder bird; Four little neighbors; What love will do; A tra la la song.

65. [73.] (41.) **Bird's Christmas carol.** Kate Douglas Wiggin. Bost., Houghton, Mifflin & Co., 1894. 66 p. il. D. bds.	.50	.30

The story of an invalid girl whose sweet benevolent character was a blessing to her home. In the tenderest and most effective way, Carol Bird's life teaches the beauty of love and devotion in the household. The children will enjoy the humorous descriptions of the Ruggles family.

66. **Boston collection of kindergarten stories:** written and collected by Boston kindergarten teachers. Bost., J. L. Hammett Co., 1898. 124 p. D. cl.	.60	.48

An excellent collection of stories for use in the primary school and kindergarten. Many of these stories should be told by the teacher to the children.
Contents: Dora, the little girl of the lighthouse; Naughty little gold finger; Amy Stuart; How the sparrows were fed; The honest woodman; The three bears; The little rooster; The man on the chimney; The lion and the mouse; The three gold fishes; The sunbeams; Chickadees; Thanksgiving story; The fairy in the mirror; What the winds bring; Story of the morning-glory seed; April; Helix, the snail; What a bird thought; The lost lamb; The bramble-bushes and the lamb; The swallow's nest; The hare and the tortoise; Story of a cowslip; Courtesy in birds; Diamonds and toads; Little water drops; The lost knife; North wind and the sun; Spring; Story of a bean; The echo; Ten peas in a pod; Not a busy bee; What Robin saw; The ugly duckling; The bunch of keys; The discontented weather-cock; Wise old Dobbin; The woodpecker; The birdie that tried; Story of an acorn; The hen-hawk; Taming the pig; Five peas in one pod; Little lammie; Story of buzzy; The surgeon bird; Annie's new shoes; Bennie's sunshine; A lesson of faith; Mrs. Vespa; The star and the lily; Over in the meadow; The johnny-cake; The little fir-tree; Thumbling; Selected; The fox and the grapes; The ant and the dove; The dog and his shadow; The lark and her young ones.

LIST OF BOOKS FOR TOWNSHIP LIBRARIES.

	List price.	Price to districts.
67. **Captain Fritz:** his friends and adventures. Emily Huntington Miller. N. Y., E. P. Dutton & Co., 1887. 128 p. il. D. cl..........................	1.50	.90

The story of a dog's life told by himself.

68. **Child stories and rhymes for little people of nursery and kindergarten.** Emilie Poulsson. Bost., Lothrop Pub. Co., c1898. 89 p. il. O. cl............ 1.25   .75

A charming book of short stories and pleasing rhymes designed for the youngest children written by one of America's most successful kindergartners.

69. [82.] (584.) **Counterpane-fairy.** Katherine Pyle. N. Y., E. P. Dutton & Co., 1899. 191 p. il. D. cl... 1.25   .75

Dainty fairy tales.

70. [84.] **Echo-maid and other stories.** Alicia Aspinwall. N. Y., E. P. Dutton & Co., 1897. 192 p. il. D. cl. .... 1.50   .88

Interesting and helpful stories for youngest readers.

71. [81.] **Eyes and no eyes and other stories.** Dr. Aiken, and others. Bost., D. C. Heath & Co., 1900. 66 p. il. D. cl. .... .25   .20

Stories for youngest children.

72. **Four-footed folk.** Raymond Fuller Ayers. N. Y., R. H. Russell, 1901. 148 p. il. O. bds............ 1.25   .80

A collection of stories and legends of animals. This book should not be a first choice where the amount of money available for the purchase of books is small.

Contents: Mr. Wildcat and Mr. Owl go hunting; Why the elephant fears the mouse; Why Mr. Fox and Mr. Rabbit don't speak; How Mr. Weasel came to pop; Why the frogs sing at night; Mr. Fox feeds his children; Why Mr. Turtle emigrated; Why Mr. Hog roots in the ground; Why Mr. Crow is black; Mr. Greyhound loses his shoes; Vanity of Mr. Ram; How Miss Hen lost her teeth; Why bears sleep all winter; Mr. Beaver has a narrow escape; Mr. Groundhog's goose box; Why horseshoes are lucky; Why Mr. Tiger has stripes on his back; Why cats dislike the water; A thief in animal land; Why bears walk on all fours.

	List price.	Price to districts.
73. [86.] **Hal o' the fells.** Beatrice De Burgh. N. Y., E. P. Dutton & Co. 64 p. il. S. cl.	.25	.15

Story of a courageous little boy.

74. [67.] **In the chimney corner.** G. Manville Fenn, *and others*. N. Y., E. P. Dutton & Co., 1900. 143 p. il. sq. O. bds.	2.00	1.08

75. [74.] (42.) **Jolly good times;** or, Child life on the farm. Mary P. W. Smith. Bost., Little, Brown & Co., 1898. 277 p. il. D. cl.	1.25	.75

A very pretty picture of the life of country children. It is a charming little story, too, for boys and girls who live in cities and know nothing about what fine times their country cousins have.— *St. Louis Republican.*

76. **Jumping kangaroo and the apple-butter cat.** John W. Harrington. N. Y., McClure, Phillips & Co., 1900. 130 p. il. O. bds.	1.00	.60

A book of animal stories for children. The animals are endowed with speech, play practical jokes on each other, and have many funny experiences.

This book should not be a first choice where the amount of funds available for the purchase of books is small.

77. [61.] (26.) **Letters from a cat;** published by her mistress for the benefit of all cats and the amusement of little children. Helen Hunt Jackson. Bost., Little, Brown & Co., 1898. 89 p. il. D. cl.	1.25	.75

Delightful letters which older children can read for themselves.

78. [75.] (44.) **Little Jarvis.** Molly Elliot Seawell. N. Y., D. Appleton & Co., 1894. 64 p. il. D. cl.	1.00	.55

The story of a boy who was midshipman on the Constellation and who sacrificed his life in his devotion to duty.

"As his life was without fear, so was his death without reproach." The child's interest in the Constellation may be used to start an interest in our history.

79. [60.] **Little lame prince and his traveling cloak.** Dinah M. Craik. N. Y., Gilbert H. McKibbin, 1900. il. D. (Manhattan young people's ser.) cl.	.40	.32

A new edition of this delightful story.

	List price.	Price to districts.

80. [76.] (46.) **Little Miss Phoebe Gay.** Helen Dawes Brown. Bost., Houghton, Mifflin & Co. 139 p. il. D. cl. .... 1.00 .60

It is full of the fancies and experiences of a typically bright, lovable little girl. Tho' written for little girls many older girls will enjoy the book very much.

81. **Lonesomest doll.** Abbie Farwell Brown. Bost., Houghton, Mifflin & Co., 1901. 76 p. il. D. bds. .85 .77

A story of two small girls, one a princess, the other a porter's child. The princess had a doll quite too splendid for every-day use,—it was therefore locked up and was the lonesomest doll in the kingdom. The porter's child, using her father's keys, got into the treasure-room where the doll was. The princess found her way thither and the doll made the children friends.

82. **Marjorie and her papa:** how they wrote a story and made pictures for·it. Robert Howe Fletcher. N. Y., Century Co., 1900. 66 p. il. O. bds........ 1.00 .60

A simple and pretty story of a little girl.

83. **My friend Jim:** a story of real boys and for them. Martha James. Bost., Lee & Shepard, 1901. 212 p. il. D. cl. .... 1.00 .60

The story of a little city boy who spends a summer in the country. It shows the influence that a bright, honest, healthy boy can exert over his companions and draws an attractive picture of country life.

84. [48.] (21.) **New baby world;** stories, rhymes, and pictures for little folks. Compiled from St. Nicholas by Mary Mapes Dodge. N. Y., Century Co., 1897. 200 p. O. cl...................... 1.50 .88

Some of the old favorites from earlier editions, but for the most part, the present volume is made up of new material from recent volumes of the St. Nicholas. This book is for the youngest children.

86. [83.] (585.) **Prince Uno:** Uncle Frank's visit to fairy-land. N. Y., Doubleday, Page & Co., 1897. 241 p. il. D. cl. .... 1.25 .75

Most interesting fairy stories delightfully told. Children of middle form will be interested in them.

			List price.	Price to districts.

87. **Rabbit's ransome and other stories.** Clara Vawter. Indianapolis, Bowen-Merrill Co., 1902. (To be published in May.) il. D. cl.................... 1.25 .75

This book is put on the list because of its artistic value, as well as on account of its value as an excellent collection of stories and rhymes.

The teacher should aim to cultivate in the children a love of the beautiful, and books like Seton-Thompson's "Lives of the hunted," Long's "Beasts of the field," Riley's "Child-rhymes," and Vawter's "Rabbit's ransome" will do much to aid in accomplishing this aim.

88. [65.] **Roggie and Reggie stories.** Gertrude Smith. N. Y., Harper & Bros., 1900. 95 p. il. sq. O. cl. 1.50 .90

A story filled with the doings of two little boys.

89. **Rosamund tales:** sixteen short stories intended for children; il. by the author. Cuyler Reynolds. Bost., L. C. Page & Co., 1901. 284 p. O. cl..... 1.50 .90

These stories are intended for children between the ages of four and ten or twelve years. The words are simple and can be understood by very young readers.

The book consists of sixteen short stories of a little boy's life at home and in the country and touches upon a wide range of topics in nature study. The happiest side of farm life for children is shown. Contains several excellent illustrations.

Contents: The lost child; Old black Joe; At the circus; The child monkey; Only a rabbit; Taming pets; On the farm; Making a garden; In the woods; Blowing bubbles; The lost coin; The bear hunt; The lost lamb; The fishing-pool; Taming a squirrel; Snow forts.

90. [77.] (49.) **Seraph, the little violiniste.** *Mrs.* C. V. Jamison. Bost., W. A. Wilde & Co., 300 p. il. D. cl. .... 1.50 .85

The scene of the story is the French quarter of New Orleans, and charming bits of color add to its attractiveness.—*The Boston Journal.*

Fine descriptions: River and levee, 31, 32, 203-205; scene in garden, 16-17, 229-230; making of paper flowers, 23, 108-109; poorer classes,—Marc, the water rat, 33, 35-41, 43.

91. [71.] (39.) **Seven little people.** Horace E. Scudder. Bost., Houghton, Mifflin & Co., 1891. 240 p. D. cl. .... 1.00 .60

The stories are simply stories and nothing more. That Mr. Scudder wrote them is sufficient warrant that they possess high literary merit and are popular with the children.

	List price.	Price to districts.

92. [85.] (587.) **Short stories for short people.** Alicia Aspinwall. N. Y., E. P. Dutton, 1897. 254 p. il. O. cl. ...... 1.50 .88

Stories for young readers.

93. [69.] (577.) **Sleepy-time stories.** Maud Ballington Booth. N. Y., G. P. Putnam's Sons, 1899. 177 p. il. D. cl. ...... 1.50 .90

Beautiful stories by one who loves and understands children. The illustrations are very beautiful.

94. [57.] (22.) **Stories for children.** *Mrs.* Charles A. Lane. N. Y., American Book Company, 1895. 104 p. il. D. cl. ...... .25 .22

A collection of stories and poems about things children are interested in. Children in first reader can read this book for themselves. A good supplementary reader.

95. [62.] (30.) **Stories for kindergartens and primary schools.** Sarah E. Wiltse. Bost., Ginn & Co., 1890. 80 p. il. D. cl. ...... .35 .27

These stories have been told to children, and none has been put in this volume until judged and approved by the small critics.— *From the authors preface.*
Many of these stories the children can read for themselves.

96. [63.] (31.) **Story hour.** Kate Douglas Wiggin, *and* Nora A. Smith. Bost., Houghton, Mifflin & Co., 1896. 185 p. il. D. cl. ...... 1.00 .60

The introduction on story telling will prove helpful to teachers. These little stories are to be told to the youngest children.
The stories are about: Orioles, 29-37; a drop of water, 52-58; a fly, 96-100; the maple leaf and the violet, 133-138; the forest, 146-155; a frog, 170-178; the story of Christmas, 101-106; story of first Thanksgiving, 107-114; little George Washington, 115-122; great George Washington, 123-132; Froebel's birthday, 179-185.

97. [68.] **Sunny days.** L. T. Meade, *and others.* N. Y., E. P. Dutton & Co., 1900. 73 p. il. sq. O. bds. 1.25 .70

These three volumes contain pictures, stories and verses for little folks. Children of middle form will read for themselves.

LIST OF BOOKS FOR TOWNSHIP LIBRARIES.

	List price.	Price to districts.
98. [78.] (51.) **Sweet William.** Margaret Bouvet. Chic., A. C. McClurg & Co., 1895. 209 p. il. O. cl....	1.25	.75

A story of two cousins, the children of a Duke of Normandy and his brother. The scenes are of the chivalric age, and the story gives a clear picture of the castles, sports, and customs of Normandy during the age of feudalism. The characters of the children are beautifully drawn and are full of sweetness and love.

References: Falcon and chase, 89; description of castle, 13–14, 130; tournament, 151–152, 156–175; royal life, 186–187.

| 99. **Through the farmyard gate:** rhymes and stories for little children at home and in kindergarten. Emilie Poulsson. Bost., Lothrop Publishing Co., c1896. il. O. cl. .... | 1.25 | .75 |

"Made up of stories and rhymes for little children at home and in the kindergarten, especially about the pets and animals with whom the little folks become acquainted through the farmyard gate. Lummux the lamb, Midget the puppy, Barney the donkey, Lady Jane the cow, and Fritz the "big doggie," are all delightful friends, while Trottino and Lapino, the wonderful rabbits, are better than the best fairy story folks. This book is also delightfully illustrated."

| 100. **Tommy's adventures.** Emily Paret Atwater. Phil., George W. Jacobs & Co., c1900. 110 p. D. cl... | .40 | .32 |

The story of a dissatisfied boy who on his way home from school falls asleep in the woods. In his dreams he in turn becomes an ant, bee, butterfly, cricket, and spider. On awakening he decides that none of these creatures are any happier than he is in his school boy life.

| 101. **Tommy Toddles.** Albert Lee. N. Y., Harper & Bros., 1898. 192 p. il. D. cl....................... | 1.25 | .78 |

A very humorous story of a little boy. The teacher ought to read this book to the school. Some of the fun may be beyond the pupil, but books with good pure fun for children are so rare this book is put on the list with the hope that it may help some to appreciate humor.

| 102. [79.] (52.) **When Molly was six.** Eliza Orne White. Bost., Houghton, Mifflin & Co., 1898. 133 p. il. D. cl. .... | 1.00 | .60 |

One of the most charming of children's books. It is a year's record of Molly's life with a chapter for every month of the year.

FAIRY STORIES, FOLK STORIES, MYTHS AND LEGENDS.

Myths, fables, fairy stories, and folklore form an inseparable part of art and literature, and unlock the best in each. Not only are they interesting as stories, but many myths may start an interest in history, in nature, and in beautiful pictures. Here again is valuable material for the language lesson. Manual, *Language—Primary Form.*

	List price.	Price to districts.
103. [88.] (576.) **Book of legends told over again.** Horace E. Scudder. Bost., Houghton, Mifflin & Co., 1899. 64 p. S. cl.	.50	.32

Some of the best legends for young children, which they can read for themselves.

| 104. **Child stories from the masters.** Maud Menefee. Chic., Rand, McNally & Co., 1901. 102 p. il. D. cl. | .30 | .27 |

The material for these stories has been taken from the great world artists,—Browning, Dante, Goethe, and Wagner. They are based on the suggestion of some verse or motive, and are told in a pretty, simple way that can be understood by the youngest child. These stories of the great masters will introduce the child to the world of poetry and music and may awaken an interest in the child, which will lead him as he grows older to read such books as "Siegfried and Beowulf" and "The Wagner story book."

They may also suggest to teachers how they may make use of the great store of art and poetry. The illustrations are excellent copies in color of beautiful paintings.

Contents: Pippa; Mignon; Siegfried; A fish and a butterfly; How Margaret led Faust through the perfect world; Beatrice; Parsival; Angelus; Friedrich and his child-garden; Holy night; Saul and David.

| 105. [95.] (59.) **Choice literature;** series intended to create and foster a taste for good reading. *Comp.* and *arr.* by Sherman Williams. Bk. 1, for primary grades. N. Y., Butler, Sheldon & Co., 1898. 144 p. D. cl. | .22 | .20 |

This book is made in the belief that many of the old rhymes and tales such as are herein contained, "Children's Classics," if I may term them so, are, or should be, the birthright of every child—*Author's "To the Reader."* Excellent supplementary reading.

	List price.	Price to districts.
106. [93.] (57.) **Classic stories for little ones.** Adapted from the tales of Andersen, Grimm Brothers, and others, by *Mrs. Lida Brown McMurry.* Bloomington, Public School Pub. Co., 1897. 143 p. il. S. cl.	.40	.30

Second grade children may read these stories for themselves.

An explanation of the function of fairy stories in a child's education and the method of using these stories is given in the teachers' and mothers' edition.

| 107. [87.] (53.) **Fables and folk stories.** *Ed.* by Horace E. Scudder. Bost., Houghton, Mifflin & Co., 1890. 200 p. D. (Riverside lit. ser.) cl. | .40 | .32 |

A collection of the most famous folk stories. These stories rightfully belong to the early period of childhood and may be told or read to children too young to read for themselves.

| 108. [91.] (55.) **Fairy stories and fables.** *Ed.* by James Baldwin. N. Y., American Book Company, 1896. 176 p. il. D. cl. | .35 | .31 |

One of the best collections of fairy stories for children because of its excellent English.

| 109. [92.] (56.) **Hans Andersen's stories.** Bost., Houghton, Mifflin & Co., 1891. 205 p. D. (Riverside lit. ser.) cl. | .40 | .32 |

It is idle at this day to dwell upon the charms of the greatest child-poet in all literature. We need only say that from the first glimmer of the poetic fancy of childhood—and who can say how early that appears—until the last spark of child-like freshness and sympathy is extinguished, there is no age which may not derive delight from the exquisite purity, and sympathy that overlie great depths of meaning in these quaint stories.—*New York Christian Union.*

| 110. [89.] (54.) **Heart of oak books.** 2d bk. *Ed.* by Charles Eliot Norton. Bost., D. C. Heath & Co., 1897. 206 p. D. cl. | .35 | .31 |

A collection of fables and nursery tales. This book will prove valuable in the language lessons. See Manual, *Language—Primary Form.*

The teacher will find the preface very helpful.

	List price.	Price to districts.

111. [94.] (58.) **King of the Golden River.** John Ruskin. Bost., Houghton, Mifflin & Co., 1898. 98 p. D. (Riverside lit. ser.) cl. .... .25 .22

A story in which the youngest brother in a family wins the prize lost by the elders through avarice and wickedness. This story ought to be read to the children of the primary form. The children in the middle form can read it.

112. **Mopsa the fairy.** Jean Ingelow. N. Y., T. Y. Crowell & Co., c1901. 228 p. il. S. cl. .... .60 .30

The story of a little boy's adventures in Fairyland. This will be a very dainty little story to read to the children of the lower form.

113. [99.] (64.) **Nature myths and stories for little ones.** Flora J. Cook. Chic., A. Flanagan & Co., 1895. 102 p. D. cl. .... .35 .26

Children of second and third grades can read. The preface is very suggestive.
Reference: Flower stories, 9-12, 13-15; insects, 16-17, 18; 19-23; birds, 24-25, 26-28, 29-30; clouds, 36-48, 54-55; sun myths, 39-42, 48-53, 83-88; animals, 43-47, 59-60, 77-78, 79-82, 89-90, 91; trees, 56-58, 61-65, 66-70, 71-73, 74-76.

114. **New wonderland:** being the first account ever presented of the Beautiful Valley, and the wonderful adventures of its inhabitants. Pictures by Frank Verbeck. L. Frank Baum. Indianapolis, Bowen-Merrill Co., 1900. 190 p. il. Q. bds. .... 1.50 .98

"A laugh book for children of all ages."
This book should not be a first choice where the amount of money available for the purchase of books is small.

115. [96.] (60.) **Old Greek stories.** Ed. by James Baldwin. N. Y., American Book Company, 1895. 208 p. il. D. cl. .... .45 .38

Perhaps no other stories have ever been told so often or listened to with so much pleasure as the classic tales of ancient Greece. * * * They have become so incorporated into our language and thought, and so interwoven with our literature that we could not do away with them now if we would. They are a portion of our heri-

	List price.	Price to districts.

tage from the distant past, and they form perhaps as important a part of our intellectual life as they did that of the people among whom they originated.—*From the author's preface.*

These stories should be read and told to the children until they are familiar with them. Third grade children can read them and the book is an excellent supplementary reader for that grade. They furnish excellent material for language lessons. See Manual, *Language—Primary Form.*

116. [98.] (62.) **'Round the year in myth and song.** Florence Holbrook, *ed.* N. Y., American Book Company, 1897. 200 p. il. D. cl................... .60 .51

Myths and poems for the various seasons of the year. The book is most beautifully illustrated. A very valuable book as a basis for language work. The teacher may train herself to be a good story teller by memorizing such stories as these which are short, well told, and in most excellent English. Children of middle form will read.

117. [97.] (61.) **Story of Ulysses.** Adapted from the Odyssey of Homer by Agnes Spofford Cook. Bloomington, Public School Pub. Co., 1897. 153 p. D. cl. .50 .38

118. [100.] (68.) **Uncle Remus:** his songs and his sayings. Joel Chandler Harris. New ed. with new preface and revisions. N. Y., D. Appleton & Co., 1900. 265 p. il. D. cl. 2.00 1.28

The stories are full of quaint plantation dialect, droll humor, and sly wisdom. Tho' the book can be read by children of the middle form, many of the stories ought to be read to the children of the primary form. The Tar Baby is a universal favorite with little folks. The fun in many of the stories will appeal to the oldest children as well as to the youngest.

119. [90.] **Wonderful chair and the tales it told.** Frances Browne. Pts. I *and* II. Bost., D. C. Heath & Co., 1900. 192 p. il. D. cl....................... .30 .27

Fairy stories well told.

HISTORY AND BIOGRAPHY.

In this form much valuable work may be done in preparation for the formal study of history. Certain of our great heroes may be made real personages to the children and an interest created in what they have done. How the people, especially children, of other times have lived is the best kind of history. See Manual, *History—Primary and Middle Forms.*

The teacher and children ought to read most of these books together. Reproducing these stories will help in language. See Manual, *Language—Primary Form.*

	List price.	Price to districts.
120. America's story for America's children. Bk. 1. Beginner's book. Mara L. Pratt. Bost., D. C. Heath & Co., 1901. 132 p. il. D. cl..............	.35	.31

This book may be used as a supplementary reader in the third grade.
Contents: Northmen, 1–7; Olaf and Snorri, 8–22; Columbus, 23–36; Leaping wolf, 53–67; Little Pueblo prince, 67–82; Virginia Dare, 83–88; Betty Alden, 89–100; Hans and Katrina, 101–107; Boston boys, 108–15; Army of two, 116–20; Boy in gray, 121–26; Boy in blue, 127–32.

121. America's story for America's children. Bk. 2. Exploration and Discovery, A. D. 1000 to 1609. Mara L. Pratt. Bost., D. C. Heath & Co., 1901. 152 p. il. D. cl.	.40	.35

Stories of the discoverers and explorers from Leif Ericson to Henry Hudson. An interesting supplementary reader for the fourth and fifth grades.
References: Coming of Norsemen, 1–10; Columbus, 17–32; Ponce de Leon, 33–37; Balboa, 38–50; Cortez and the Aztecs, 51–67; Cartier, 68–76; De Soto, 77–83; Coronado, 84–101; Cabrillo, 102–14; Spanish monks, 115–26; Drake, 127–36; Hudson, 137–43.

122. Child of Urbino: Raphael. Louise de la Ramé. Bost., Educational Pub. Co., c1900. 64 p. il. D. cl....	.30	.23

The story of Raphael's early life and his first success in his work as an artist. A beautiful little story written in an artistic manner.

	List price.	Price to districts.

123. [104.] (73.) **Fifty famous stories retold.** James Baldwin. N. Y., American Book Company, 1896. 172 p. il. D. cl............................. .35 .31

Many of these stories present interesting incidents in the lives of heroes such as King Alfred, King Canute, Sir Walter Raleigh, Napoleon, Julius Caesar, George Washington, and others, and will prove valuable in starting an interest in history. The child reads the story about the good and wise King Alfred and is interested to know what else he did and why he was called good and wise. See Manual of the Course of Study, *History.* Some of the stories teach courage, bravery, loyalty, gratitude, and kindness to others. The language is most excellent. The book furnishes good material for reproduction exercises in language. See Manual, *Language—Primary Form.*

124. [109.] (77.) **First book in American history;** with especial reference to the lives and deeds of great Americans. Edward Eggleston. N. Y., American Book Company, 1899. 203 p. il. D. cl......... .60 .51

This book will interest the children because it is about heroes of our country and their great deeds. The personal element in history appeals to children, and stories like these form the best preparation for the formal study of history.

Some of the leading men are: John Cabot, Chap. 4; John Smith, Chap. 5, 6, 7; Indians, pp. 9–16; Henry Hudson, Chap. 9; Miles Standish, Chap. 10; Wm. Penn, Chap. 11; King Philip, Chap. 12; Roger Bacon, Chap. 15; Franklin, Chap. 16, 17; George Washington, Chap. 28–31; Daniel Boone, Chap. 23. *Great events:* Discovery of America, Chap 2, p. 7–12; discovery by Cabots, Chap. 4; discovery by Hudson, Chap 4; Captain Smith's attempts to settle N. E., Chap. 6; famine at Jamestown, Chap. 9; Bacon's rebellion, Chap. 14; French war, Chap. 19; Revolutionary war, Chap. 19; invention of telegraph, Chap. 27–28; Civil war, Chap. 31.

125. [105.] (590.) **First steps in the history of our country.** William A. Mowry *and* Arthur May Mowry. N. Y., Silver, Burdette & Co., 1899. 315 p. S. cl. .60 .54

A history for young children in which a few characters are made prominent and leading events grouped about these persons.

126. **Four American inventors.** Robert Fulton; Eli Whitney; Samuel F. B. Morse; Thomas A. Edison: a book for young Americans. Frances M. Perry. N. Y., Werner School Book Co., c1901. 260 p. il. por. D. cl. .... .50 .42

An account of our American heroes who have won the gratitude of the whole world by their wonderful and useful inventions. These stories bring the young reader into close touch with the marvelous lives of those great men.

References: Robert Fulton, 11–69; Eli Whitney, 73–130; Samuel F. B. Morse, 133–201; Thomas A. Edison, 205–260.

LIST OF BOOKS FOR TOWNSHIP LIBRARIES.

	List price.	Price to districts.

127. [113.] (81.) **Four American naval heroes.** Mabel Beebe. N. Y., Werner School Book Co., 1899. 254 p. il. D. cl. .... .50 .42

Brief biographies of Paul Jones, Oliver Perry, Admiral Farragut, and Admiral Dewey for young children. Younger pupils of middle form will enjoy reading them.

128. [114.] (82.) **Four American patriots.** Alma Holman Burton. N. Y., Werner School Book Co., 1898. 254 p. il. D. cl. .... .50 .42

Brief biographies of Henry, Hamilton, Jackson, and Grant. Younger children of middle form will enjoy these biographies.

129. [112.] (80.) **Four great Americans.** James Baldwin. N. Y., Werner School Book Co., 1897. 246 p. il. D. cl. .... .50 .42

Biographies for readers of the second or third grades. The four great Americans are Franklin, Washington, Webster, Lincoln.

130. [106.] (74.) **Grandfather's chair:** true stories from New England history, 1620–1692. Nathaniel Hawthorne. Bost., Houghton, Mifflin & Co., 1883. D. (Riverside lit. ser.) cl. .... .50 .40

Stories of the history of New England. The children will follow with interest the varying fortunes of the old chair, and will get a great deal of historical information in the guise of the tales related to a number of boys and girls by the benignant grandfather.
References: The Puritans, Chap. 2; Roger Williams, 20-21; early colonial government, 27, 28, 50, 51; the Pinetree shilling, Chap. 6; the Quakers, Chap. 7; John Eliot and work with Indians, Chaps. 8, 9, 10, 12; French and English war, Part II, 21, 22; Siege of Quebec, Part II, 63, 64, 65; Boston massacre, Part III, 21-34; Continental congress, Part III, 45, 48.

131. [102.] (70.) **Old stories of the east.** James Baldwin. N. Y., American Book Company, 1896. 215 p. il. D. cl. .... .45 .38

"In the present volume it has been the aim of the author to retell these stories from a literary standpoint, and in exactly the same manner as he would retell other stories pertaining to the infancy of the human race." The stories are beautifully and dramatically told.

	List price.	Price to districts.

132. [108.] (76.) **Stories of American life and adventure.** Edward Eggleston. N. Y., American Book Company, 1895. 214 p. il. D. cl.................... .50 .43

The author announces three purposes of the volume, (1) to make school reading pleasant by supplying matter simple and direct in style, (2) to cultivate an interest in narratives of fact by selecting chiefly incidents full of action, (3) but principally to make the reader acquainted with American life and manners in other times. Such stories filled with adventures of frontier life, daring feats, and personal encounters with savages and wild beasts are intensely interesting to the children. Their personal character makes real the personages in history and the sketches of the homes, the food, the dress, the manners, and the schools, make real the life of the early times. Third grade children can read.

133. [107.] (75.) **Stories of great Americans for little Americans.** Edward Eggleston. N. Y., American Book Company, 1895. 159 p. il. D. cl......... .40 .34

The author in telling these stories has seized upon one of the strongest interests in this period of the child's school life—his interests in the doings of other boys and girls—and episodes in the boyhood of Franklin, Washington, Boone, Washington Irving, Audubon, Daniel Webster, Longfellow, Horace Greeley will create an interest in the leading figures in the history of our country.

It will surely serve to excite an early interest in our national history by giving some of the great personages of that history a place among the heroes that impress the susceptible imagination of a child.—*Author's preface.*

See Manual, *History—Primary and Middle Forms.*

134. [111.] (591.) **Stories of Indian chieftains.** Mary Hall Husted. Bloomington, Ill., Public School Pub. Co., 1900. 141 p. il. D. cl..................... .50 .38

A companion volume to "Stories of Indian children" by the same author. This volume shows the conflict between the Indian and white man both in war and in peace. It begins with the discovery of America by Columbus and closes with a picture of Indian life of today.

135. [110.] (79.) **Stories of Indian children.** Mary Hall Husted. Bloomington, Public School Pub. Co., 1898. 137 p. il. D. cl........................ .50 .38

Depicts Indian child life in such a way that little children will be interested and can read for themselves.

References: Home of Indian, 7–11; the little papoose, 12–21; boy's games, 22–26; little girls' games and work, 27–34; how they move, 37–39; the warrior, 40–45; the hunter, 45–48; stories they tell, 56–134.

	List price.	Price to districts.

136. [115.] (83.) **Story of Lincoln.** Frances Cravens. Bloomington, Public School Pub. Co., 1898. 117 p. il. S. cl. .... .35 .27

Biography of Lincoln written for young children.

137. [103.] (71.) **Story of the chosen people.** H. A. Guerber. N. Y., American Book Company, 1896. 240 p. il. D. cl. .... .60 .50

The author in the preface says, "I have found that, when told to young children, these historical narratives prove a source of much interest, and that the elementary knowledge then obtained remains so clear and vivid that even when they are grown up, and able to enter into the subject more thoroughly, the impression of the story as first heard is the one which is most permanent."

The historical value of these stories cannot be overestimated. See Manual, *History—Primary and Middle Forms.*

138. [101.] (69.) **Ten boys who lived on the road from long ago to now.** Jane Andrews. Bost., Ginn & Co., 1885. 240 p. il. D. cl..................... .50 .41

A vivid description of the world's progress from the earliest times to the present time. Children of this grade are interested in stories of other children and this interest is used to start an interest in history, for each story is about a boy whose life is typical of the life of his times. Special prominence should be given to the manners and customs. Try to make children see the life. Many of the stories teach moral truths.

GEOGRAPHY.

How people live, what they do for a living, what they do to amuse themselves, their homes, their food, their clothing, ways of travel, is geography. If these facts are grouped about children of the cold countries, of the hot countries, of the mountains, of the plains, the pupils of this form are sure to be interested and a good foundation for the formal study of geography is being laid. Some of the best material for this work is found in fiction. The teacher will find much which she can read to these children in the books of the other forms. See Manual, *Geography—Primary and Middle Forms.*

	List price.	Price to districts.
139. **Around the world:** Geographical readers. Primary, Book I. Stella W. Carroll. *Ed.* by Clarence F. Carroll. N. Y., Morse Co., 1901. 160 p. il. D. cl. (New century series. First book.)	.40	.32

A reader on the Eskimo, Indians, Arabs, Dutch, Chinese, and Japanese depicting their manners and customs.

| 140. [126.] (596.) **Around the world:** Geographical readers. Book 2. Stella W. Carroll *and* Harriet Jerome, *Ed.* by Clarence F. Carroll. N. Y., Morse Co., 1898. 232 p. il. D. (New Century ser. Second book.) cl. .... | .50 | .41 |

Short description of places in Alaska, Mexico, Norway, Sweden, and Switzerland which the older children of Primary form can read for themselves.

| 141. [124.] (595.) **Big people and little people of other lands.** Edward R. Shaw. N. Y., American Book Co., 1900. 128 p. il. D. cl. .... | .30 | .27 |

In this form the child's interest in other peoples is in their physical appearance, their dress, their ways of living, their customs, their manners. This book is written from the standpoint of the child's interest. Children can read for themselves.

LIST OF BOOKS FOR TOWNSHIP LIBRARIES. 43

	List price.	Price to districts.
141a. [127.] **Boys of other countries.** Bayard Taylor. New ed. N. Y., G. P. Putnam's Sons, 1901. 166 p. il. D. cl.	1.25	.80

Valuable stories for use in geography. Description of boy life in Sweden, Africa, Iceland, Germany and Russia.

Pupils of the middle form will enjoy reading this book and teachers will find it an attractive book to read to the lower form pupils.

| 142. [123.] (94a.) **Geographical nature studies for primary work in home geography.** Frank Owen Payne. N. Y., American Book Company, 1898. 144 p. il. D. bds. | .25 | .22 |

The two foregoing books ought to be made the basis for oral lessons in primary geography. (See Manual of Course of Study, Geography.) They will prove helpful to the teacher and the child will be interested to read for himself about the things he has heard of in the geography lesson. The teacher will find the preface of each book very helpful.

| 143. [122.] (94.) **Home geography.** C. C. Long. N. Y., American Book Company, 1894. 142 p. il. D. bds. | .25 | .22 |

| 144. [125.] (95.) **Little folks of other lands.** Fannie P. Chaplin, *and* Mrs. F. A. Humphrey. Bost., Lothrop Pub. Co., 1882. 203 p. il. D. cl. | .40 | .33 |

Little folks never tire of listening to stories of children of foreign countries. Their dress, tools, habits, and surroundings are interestingly set forth in this volume. These stories will start an interest in geography.

References: The Arabian child, 7–16; the Lapland baby, 26–32; the poor boy of Turkey, 31–38; the little Arctic girl, 39–47; the Egyptian boy and girl, 50–58; little Statian child, 59–63; Malay baby, 66–69; Holland girl and boy, 74–81; Scotch lassie, 90–107; English child, 19–25; 128–142; Norwegian boy and girl, 147–161.

| 145. **Little people of the snow.** Mary Muller. Chic., A. Flanagan Co., c1900. 109 p. il. D. cl. | .35 | .28 |

A story of the lives of Eskimo children.

References: Climate, 5–8; Dress, 10–13; Home, 17–21; Eskimo dogs, 22–31; Games, 32–50; Work of children, 51–58; Seal hunting, 59–66; Eskimo stories, 85–104.

	List price.	Price to districts.

146. **Lolami, the little cliff-dweller.** Clara Kern Bayliss. Bloomington, Public School Publishing Co., 1901. 188 p. il. S. bds............................ .50 .38

The story of Lolami, the little Cliff-dweller, touches an ancient order of things belonging to our own country. The lives and customs of the cliff-dwellers of New Mexico and Arizona, their houses, and the topography of the country in which they lived are all pictured in connection with the little Lolami's life of courage and perseverance.

147. **Longmans' pictorial geographical readers.** Bk. 1. N. Y., Longmans, Green & Co., 1901. 160 p. il. D. cl. .... .36 .33

Suggestive to the teacher who is teaching beginning geography. This book will make an excellent supplementary reader for the third grade.
References: Shadows, 29-33; Clocks, 35-48; Points of compass, 48-54; Magnet, 61-70; Compass, 70-79; Plans of class room, school grounds, and city, 92-107; Maps, 111-122; Weather signals, 123-25; Schools in other lands, 130-39; Steam, 139-47; Water, 147-150; Frost, 150-53; Pictures of snowflakes, 152.

148. **Our little Brown cousin.** Mary Hazelton Wade. Bost., L. C. Page & Co., 1901. 54 p. il. D. (Little cousin series.) cl. .... .60 .36

149. **Our little Indian cousin.** Mary Hazelton Wade. Bost., L. C. Page & Co., 1901. 83 p. il. D. (Little cousin series.) cl. .... .60 .36

150. **Our little Japanese cousin.** Mary Hazelton Wade. Bost., L. C. Page & Co., 1901. 66 p. il. D. (Little cousin series.) cl. .... .60 .36

151. **Our little Russian cousin.** Mary Hazelton Wade. Bost., L. C. Page & Co., 1901. 79 p. il. D. (Little cousin series.) cl. .... .60 .36

The books of this series are the most interesting and delightful accounts possible of child-life in other lands, filled with quaint sayings, doings and adventures. The "Little Japanese Cousin," with her toys in her wide sleeve and her tiny bag of paper handkerchiefs; the "Little Brown Cousin," in whose home the leaves of the breadfruit-tree serve for plates and the halves of the cocoanut shells for cups; the "Little Indian Cousin," who lives the free life of the forest, and the "Little Russian Cousin," who dwells by the wintry Neva, are truly fascinating characters to the little cousins who will read about them.

LIST OF BOOKS FOR TOWNSHIP LIBRARIES. 45

| | List price. | Price to districts. |

152. [128.] (96.) **Seven little sisters who live on the round ball that floats in the air.** Jane Andrews. N. Y., Ginn & Co., 1890. 142 p. S. cl.................. .50 .41

I think that the mere reading of this book, read over and over as children always read a book they like, will give to the young readers a more vivid impression of the shape of the earth, of the distribution of nations over it and of the essential brotherhood of man, than the study of most text books. The "Seven Little Sisters" is a story book, and a book of real intellectual value at the same time.—*T. W. Higginson.*

A vivid description of the child life, manners and customs, climate and scenery, of the principal countries of the globe.

References: Hindoo child, 31-34; Esquimaux child, 35-47; Arabian child, 48-66; Swiss child, 67-79; Chinese child, 80-93; African child, 94-107; German baby, 108-136.

153. [129.] (47.) **Seven little sisters prove their sisterhood.** Jane Andrews. N. Y., Ginn & Co., 1890. 162 p. S. .... .50 .41

Gives more about Pen-se and Agoonack. These children represent widely different nationalities and in the stories about them the author conveys important information about the homes, customs, and peculiarities of the parents of these curious little folks. May be used to start an interest in geography.

154. **Snow baby, a true story with true pictures.** Josephine Diebitsch Peary. N. Y., F. A. Stokes & Co., 1901. 84 p. il. sq. Q. cl..................... 1.20 1.08

"The story of little Marie Peary, the daughter of Peary the Arctic explorer, who was born near the North Pole. Her mother tells her unique story, in a charmingly simple style for young readers. It reads like a fairy tale, and is fully illustrated with reproductions of photographs of the Arctic regions."

This book ought to be in every school library. It is artistically gotten up and gives an excellent picture of life among the Eskimos.

155. **Stories of country life.** Sarah Powers Bradish. N. Y., American Book Co., c1901. 170 p. il. D. (Eclectic school reading ser..) cl.............. .40 .34

These stories are recollections of a childhood spent on a farm. They will interest children in country life and will give to the children in the cities a true picture of life on the farm.

"The stories of animals are true stories of actual occurrences."

References: Kinds of sugar, 5-13; Wheat, 14-17, 147-70; Chipmunks, 18-19; Blacksmithing, 20-25; Birds, 30-34; 65-67; 131-33; Lumbering, 35-49; Nails, 53-55; Flax, 58-61; Haying, 72-77; Harvesting, 82-85; Thrashing, 86-91; Corn husking, 92-95; Coal, 96-130; Iron, 134-43; Steel, 144-46.

SCIENCE.

As a rule children will not read these books for themselves. Teacher and pupil must read together such portions as have become of interest through observation, or by the teachers telling of the facts. The child's senses are most active at this period, and it is by means of his senses he is laying the foundation of his future knowledge. The teacher should aim to make the child see quickly and accurately the things around him; that is, train his observation.

All reading in science should be accompanied by observations. The teacher can get valuable material for use in the nature lesson from the science books in the other forms. See Manual, *Nature lessons, Primary and Middle Forms.*

The results of the child's observations, and what he has learned, may be told in the language lesson. See Manual, *Language—Primary Form.*

	List price.	Price to districts.
156. [118.] (592.) **Among the farmyard people.** Clara Dillingham Pierson. N. Y., E. P. Dutton & Co., 1899. 245 p. il. D. cl	1.25	.75

Delightful nature stories for the youngest readers, about the domestic animals. The book belongs to the set, Among the Forest People, and Among the Meadow People, by the same author. The author says,—"I want to introduce the farmyard people to you, and to have you call upon them and become better acquainted as soon as you can. Some of them are working for us, and we surely should know them. Perhaps, too, some of us are working for them, since that is the way in this delightful world of ours, and one of the happiest parts of life is helping and being helped."

| 157. [116.] (88.) **Among the forest people.** Clara Dillingham Pierson. N. Y., E. P. Dutton & Co., 1898. 219 p. il. D. cl | 1.25 | .75 |

Delightful stories about the animals of the forest, to be told or read to the youngest children. They will interest the children in the life about them. Starting with these stories the teacher may lead the pupils to observe and thus lay a good foundation for later work in science.

	List price.	Price to districts.

158. [117.] (89.) **Among the meadow people.** Clara Dillingham Pierson. N. Y., E. P. Dutton & Co., 1897. 127 p. il. D. cl. .... 1.25 .75

Stories of nature for the youngest readers. The author says, "Many of these stories of field life were written for the little ones of my kindergarten, and they gave so much pleasure and aroused such a new interest in the 'meadow people' that it seemed wise to collect and add to the original number and send them out to a larger circle of boys and girls." The value of these stories told to the children is that they will arouse an interest in, and a love for nature. The wise teacher will set them to seeing for themselves, and follow up this interest with some of the more scientific reading as found in "Our shy neighbors," or "Histories of American insects."

159. **Among the pond people.** Clara Dillingham Pierson. N. Y., E. P. Dutton & Co., c1901. 210 p. il. D. cl. .... 1.25 .75

A book about the people who live in the ponds: Frogs, minnows, water spiders, tad-poles, snapping turtles, eels, muskrats and others. This series of books treating of the forest, meadow, farmyard, and pond people ought to be in every school library. They will arouse the children's interest in the creatures about them and develop their powers of observation. These stories will interest the youngest children in school if read or told to them by the teacher.

160. [121.] (594.) **Bee people.** Margaret Warner Morley. Chicago, A. C. McClurg & Co., 1900. 177 p. il. D. cl. .... 1.25 .75

The life of a bee for little people. Middle form children will read.

161. [120.] (593.) **Buz-buz: his twelve adventures.** Charles Stuart Pratt. Bost., Lothrop Publishing Co., 1898. 102 p. il. D. cl. .... .75 .45

Twelve adventures of a house fly which will interest the youngest readers. The print is large and the illustrations are good.

162. **History of the robins.** Sarah Trimmer. *Ed. by* Edward Everett Hale. Bost., D. C. Heath & Co., 1901. 90 p. il. D. cl. .... .20 .18

This story is about the English robin redbreast which is very different from our American bird of the same name. It will do much to interest the children in birds and will teach them a lesson of kindness.

The teacher may make the reading of this the introduction to the study of birds with the younger children.

	List price.	Price to districts.
163. **Jingle book of birds.** Edward B. Clark. Chic., A. W. Mumford, 1901. 36 p. il. Q. bds..............	.60	.33

Rhymes and jingles about birds containing illustrations in color of several of our common birds.

164. [268.] (220.) **Leaves and flowers,** *or* Plant studies for young readers. Mary A. Spear. Bost., D. C. Heath & Co., 1900. 103 p. il. D. bds................	.25	.22

Simple lessons on leaves and flowers. This should be read to the children by the teacher in connection with observation lessons.

165. [119.] **Stories of my four friends.** Jane Andrews. Bost., Ginn & Co., 1901. 100 p. il. S. cl.......	.45	.41

Prepared for publication by Jane Andrew's sister.

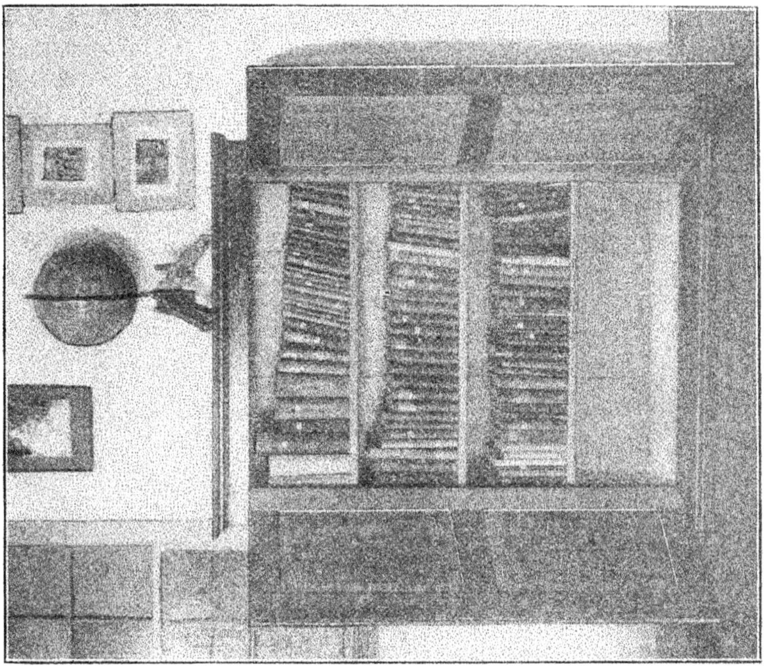

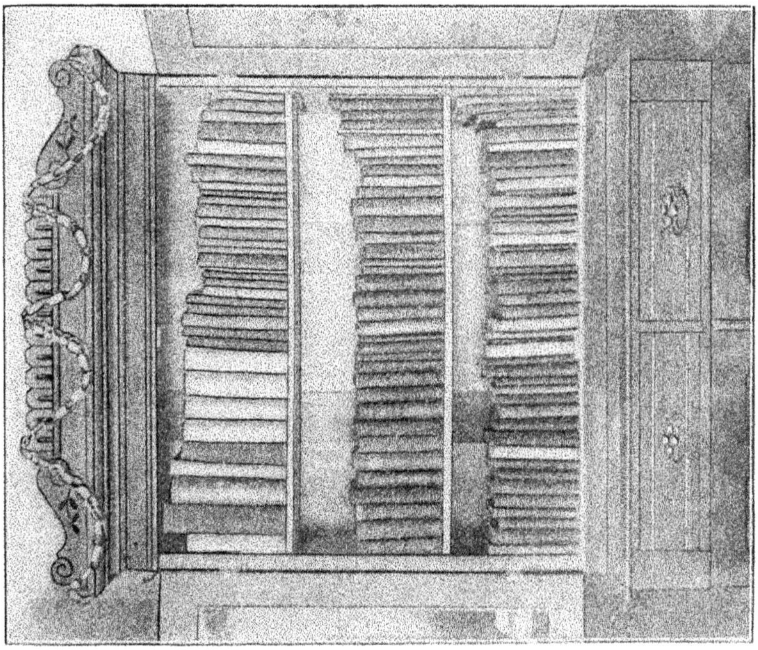

MIDDLE FORM OR INTERMEDIATE GRADES.

FICTION.

The children should read these books through for the pleasure the story gives them. At the same time the teacher should emphasize high ideals of character, and of action. Not by preaching but by questions and discussions with the pupils which shall call out from them the characters they like best—the lines of action they think good. Certain qualities of fine characters may be noted. The result of actions good and bad discussed.

The stories which portray life are invaluable in the work in geography. The descriptions of places, homes, dress, food, amusements, occupations, religions and religious ceremonies, schools, transportation, should be noted. In no geographies are there more graphic and truer descriptions than in much of our fiction. See Manual, *Geography—Primary and Middle Forms*. Fiction dealing as it does with characters which appeal to the child makes real the life of a country more than any other form of literature. If the child reads to the geography class good things he has found in his reading which are on the subject and which are interesting, he is getting the best kind of practice in reading. See Manual, *Reading—Middle Form*. And if the child tells what he has found accurately, well arranged in thought, and so as to interest his classmates, he can have no better practice in language. See Manual, *Language—Middle Form*.

	List price.	Price to districts.
166. Adventures of Joel Pepper. Margaret Sidney. Mrs. H. M. Lothrop. Bost., Lothrop Pub. Co., 1900. 461 p. il. D. cl.	1.50	.88

Continues the story of the Pepper family, especially Joel's adventures and pranks.

LIST OF BOOKS FOR TOWNSHIP LIBRARIES.

	List price.	Price to districts.

167. [131.] (98.) **Alice's adventures in Wonderland.** Lewis Carroll (Charles Dodgson). N. Y., Macmillan Co., 1888. 192 p. il. D. cl. .... 1.00 .65

One of the best children's books.

168. [185.] **Aunt Hannah and Seth.** James Otis (J. O. Kaler). N. Y., Thomas Y. Crowell & Co., 1900. 109 p. il. D. ,bds. .... .50 .30

A story of a little newsboy who finds friends and a home in the country.

169. **Bears of Blue River.** Charles Major. N. Y., Doubleday & McClure Co., 1901. 277 p. il. D. cl. 1.50 1.12

"No kind of tale has a firmer or more lasting grip upon the minds of both young and old than the 'bear story.' It would be hard to find a boy who has not shivered with breathless and delicious terror over the adventures of some hero with a 'big bear.' Balser Brent, the youthful hero of the tale, lives in Indiana during the early '20's, when that state was a frontier wilderness and the woods were full of bear, catamount and other varmints. Sol Balser's life did not lack excitement, and the narrative of his adventures from the time he could hardly hold up his father's big gun makes the most irresistible sort of reading. The many illustrations by A. B. Frost and Mrs. Mary Baker-Baker help to give reality to the stirring scenes of the story."

170. **Bernardo and Laurette.** Marguerite Bouvet. Chic., A. C. McClurg & Co., 1901. 217 p. il. D. cl... 1.00 .90

A story of two little people of the Alps.

171. [164.] (101.) **Beautiful Joe.** Marshall Saunders. Barnes & Co., 1898. 304 p. il. S. cl. .... .25 .22

The story of a dog as told by himself. This is one of the children's favorites. It teaches kindness to animals and shows the influence of love and care upon dumb animals.

172. [163.] (123.) **Black Beauty; his grooms and companions.** Anna Sewell. Chic., University Pub. Co. 245 p. il. D. cl. .... .40 .30

Beyond doubt the best book published to cultivate a spirit of kindness to the horse. The personality of Black Beauty is so strongly presented that the reader follows the intelligent creature's varied fortunes with as much interest, if not greater, than if he were human. One of the most popular books among children.

	List price.	Price to districts.

173. **Boy I knew, four dogs, and some more dogs.** Laurence Hutton. N. Y., Harper & Bros., 1901. 116 p. il. O. cl. .... 1.25 .78

This interesting story of the boy and the four dogs is a *true* story and as such will appeal to many children who upon hearing or reading a story, ask, "Is it true?" Children will enjoy hearing it read.

174. [146.] (604.) **Cable story book:** selections for school reading. George W. Cable. *Ed.* by Mary E. Burt. N. Y., C. Scribner's Sons, 1899. 176 p. il. D. (Scribner ser. of school reading.) cl. .... .60 .50

Charming stories from the writings of George W. Cable suitable for children, and portraying the life of the south. In editing the volume no changes have been made in the text except with Mr. Cable's approval. Too much can not be said in praise of these writings of Cable. The south ceases to be a "place on the map" and the child gets in close contact with what is vital in her life. 'To read Cable is to live in the South, to bask in its sunshine, eat of its figs and pomegranates, and dream its dreams. No other writer has so recorded its pulse-beats."—*Editor's preface.*

Contents: Children's New Orleans, 1-25; The story of Bras-Coupe, 26-65; Jean ah Poquelin, 66-105; New Orleans before the capture, 106-123; Gregory's Island, 124-159; Story of the author's life, 160-176.

175. [148.] (599.) **Camp and trail:** a story of the Maine woods. Isabel Hornibrook. Bost., Lothrop Pub. Co., 1897. il. D. cl. .... 1.50 .88

Adventures in camp and on the trail among the woods and lakes of Northern Maine. An unusually good book on this subject.

176. [155.] (118.) **Captain January.** Laura E. Richards. N. Y., Dana Estes & Co., 1898. il. D. cl........ .50 .30

The story of a child who lived in a lighthouse on the coast of Maine. The story depicts life in a lighthouse and teaches a wonderful lesson in loyalty.

177. **Child's Don Quixote:** being the adventures of Don Quixote retold for young people by Calvin Dill Wilson. Saavedra M. de Cervantes. N. Y., T. Y. Crowell & Co., c1901. 251 p. il. S. cl.......... .60 .30

The style of Don Quixote as told by Cervantes is not simple enough to be within the understanding of children. The tale has

LIST OF BOOKS FOR TOWNSHIP LIBRARIES. 53

	List price.	Price to districts.

been retold in a simple and shorter manner and will give the children much pleasure and introduce to them the famous characters, Don Quixote and Sancho Panza.

This story will create an interest in knights and their manner of life and may lead to the reading later on of Baldwin's "Story of Roland;" Frost's "Knights of the Round table" and "The Court of King Arthur;" and Wilson's "Story of the Cid."

The teacher should have the children read stories of some of the great heroes of our own country and compare their lives and characters and the brave deeds done by them with the lives, characters and brave deeds of the knights of olden times.

178. [183.] **Christmas angel.** Katherine Pyle. Bost., Little, Brown & Co., 1900. 136 p. il. D. cl..... 1.25 .75

A pretty and imaginative story for the youngest children. Older children in this form will enjoy reading for themselves.

179. [167.] (126.) **Christmas every day, and other stories.** W. D. Howells. N. Y., Harper & Bros., 1893. 150 p. il. D. cl. .... 1.25 .80

Ought to be read to children of primary form.

180. [174.] (145.) **Chuck Purdy.** W. O. Stoddard. Bost., Lothrop Pub. Co., 1891. 318 p. il. D. cl........ 1.25 .70

A wholesome, breezy story, rich in suggestions to teachers as to the treatment of boys who study hard but learn slowly, and stimulating to the boys themselves.

181. **Citizen Dan of the Junior Republic.** Ida T. Thurston. Bost., A. I. Bradley & Co., 1901. 307 p. il. D. cl. 1.25 .70

This is the story of a colony of boys living in a settlement similar to the George Junior Republic.

It will teach lessons of thrift, honesty, kindness, and truthfulness.

182. [170.] (141.) **Dab Kinzer:** a story of a growing boy. W. O. Stoddard. N. Y., C. Scribner's Sons, 1896. 321 p. D. cl. .... 1.00 .65

Every page is full of life and every instance related touches some phase of a boy's interests. The next best thing to going on fishing, boating or crabbing excursions is to read these lively descriptions of Dab's experiences on the Long Island shore in company with his active companions. Descriptions of 'long shore life on the coast of Long Island.

References: 'Long shore farm, 3, 7, 21, 38-40, 131-134 ; fishing, 71-74, 290-299 ; crab fishing, 46-58 ; 67-75 ; sailing, 91-123 ;156-158, 175-191 ; a New England academy, 248, 251, 260-266, 279-281.

54   LIST OF BOOKS FOR TOWNSHIP LIBRARIES.

	List price.	Price to districts.

183. [184.] **Divided skates.** Evelyn Raymond. N. Y., Thomas Y. Crowell & Co., 1900. 127 p. il. D. bds. .... .50 .30

A story about a newsboy, teaching generosity and helpfulness.

184. [180.] (610.) **Dozen from Lakerim.** Rupert Hughes. N. Y., Century Co., 1899. 223 p. il. D. cl...... 1.50 .85

A story of preparatory school life, especially games and out of door life.

185. [188.] **Ednah and her brothers.** Eliza Orne White. Bost., Houghton, Mifflin & Co., 1900. 143 p. il. D. cl. .... 1.00 .60

A well written and entertaining account of the doings of the children of an artist in their father's studio in the country, and in New York City.

186. [147.] (605.) **Eugene Field book:** verses, stories, and letters for school reading. *Ed.* by Mary E. Burt. N. Y., C. Scribner's Sons, 1899. 134 p. il. D. (Scribner's ser. of school reading.) cl........... .60 .50

These selections from Field's writings have been made upon a basis furnished by the interests of the children themselves. The selections the children like and which appeal most directly to them, will be found in this book.

187. [145.] (602.) **Fanciful tales.** Frank R. Stockton. N. Y., C. Scribner's Sons, 1899. 135 p. il. D. (Scribner's ser. of school reading.) cl............... .60 .50

The introduction by Miss Burt, is a strong plea for reading of such character. This book is a general favorite with the children. These stories are also for primary form.
  Contents: Old pipes and the dryad, 1-31; Beeman of Orn, 32-51; Clocks of Rondaine, 52-80; The griffin and the Minor Canon, 81-107; The Christmas truants, 108-130.

188. [161.] (121.) **Five little Peppers, and how they grew.** Margaret Sidney (*Mrs.* H. M. Lothrop). Bost., Lothrop Pub. Co., 1881. 410 p. il. D. cl....... 1.50 .85

A good story for children. The moral tone is good and wholesome, and many lessons of love, helpfulness and unselfishness **are** taught by the Pepper children.

LIST OF BOOKS FOR TOWNSHIP LIBRARIES. 55

	List price.	Price to districts.

189. **Four on a farm.** Mary P. Wells Smith. Bost., Little, Brown & Co., 1901. 309 p. il. D. cl............ 1.20 1.08

This is another of the "Jolly Good times" series of books and tells of the children's experiences at "Hilltop."
It will teach children to appreciate the joy and beauty of country life and the happiness to be derived from helping one another.

190. **Frigate's namesake.** Alice Balch Abbot. N. Y., Century Co., 1901. 204 p. il. D. cl............... 1.00 .90

The story of a little girl named after the frigate *Essex*. Her love and admiration for the United States navy bring in stories about the navy and unusual experiences of which she is the heroine.

191. **Hans Brinker,** or, The silver skates: a story of life in Holland. Mary Mapes Dodge. New Amsterdam ed. N. Y., C. Scribner's Sons, 1901. 393 p. il. D. cl. .... 1.50 .96

The story of Hans Brinker includes much of the story of Holland,—of its history, life, and the characteristics of its people. The descriptions of Dutch life and customs are very accurate, making the book invaluable to the geography class while studying Holland.
It teaches a lesson of courage and nobility of character.
Geographical references: Dutch art, 92-94, 209, 222; Amsterdam, 84-96; Canals, 11-14, 98, 156-62; Climate, 105-106, 169-70; 251-52; 349-50; Characteristics of the people, 16-17, 104-105, 154, 156-58; Dykes, 6-9, 10-11, 21-24, 111, 150-54; Dunes, 16, 145; Dress, 31, 46, 143-44, 156, 350-351; Dutch cities, 12-13, 61-62, 132-46; Dutch homes and buildings, 107-108, 213-16, 217-26; Food, 174, 218; Famous Dutchmen, 17-18, 62-65, 111-12, 142-44, 200; St. Nicholas eve, 47, 55-59, 73-83; Hotels, 173-197, 232; Iceboating, 161-62, 168-71; Leyden, 205-12; Manners and customs, 132-33, 143, 242-45; Occupations of the people, 25-26, 54-55, 87-88; Skating, 2-6, 31-35, 44, 66, 97, 349-69; Story of the siege of Haarlem, 202-204; Tulip mania, 99-102; The Hague, 231-41; Windmills, 16, 18.

192. **Heidi:** a little Swiss girl's city and mountain life. Frau Johanna Spyri. *Tr.* by Helen B. Dole. Bost., Ginn & Co., 1900. 363 p. il. S. cl.............. .40 .34

The experiences of a little German girl in the Alps. The picture is so vividly drawn that one will forget for the moment that he is not reading a chapter from real life.
This is an excellent book to have the children read while they are studying the geography of Switzerland and may lead to the reading of the chapters on Switzerland in Carpenter's "Europe;" Shaw's "Big people;" and Jane Andrew's "Little mountain maiden" in her "Seven little sisters."

56 LIST OF BOOKS FOR TOWNSHIP LIBRARIES.

	List price.	Price to districts.
193. [181.] (614.) **Hoosier school-boy.** Edward Eggleston. N. Y., C. Scribner's Sons, 1899. 130 p. il. D. (Scribner's ser. of school reading.) cl.	.60	.50
194. [160.] (138.) **Jack and Jill.** Louisa M. Alcott. Bost., Little, Brown & Co., 1899. 325 p. il. D. cl.	1.50	.88

Child life in a New England village.

195. [156.] (120.) **Jack Hall.** Robert Grant. N. Y., C. Scribner's Sons, 1898. 394 p. il. D. cl.	1.25	.82

A capital story for boys. The experience and adventures of a live boy are portrayed and it is a thoroughly healthful, manly and earnest story and one that is calculated to keep the boy who reads it to the unconscious ideals of good character.

196. **Jack Morgan: a boy of 1812.** William O. Stoddard. Bost., Lothrop Pub. Co., c1901. 353 p. il. D. cl.	1.25	.75

This is a tale of the war of 1812. Jack Morgan, a manly frontier boy, and a stout son of the border, is the central figure of this stirring story which deals with the war on land and water, along Lake Erie, between American soldiers, sailors, and frontiersmen, on one side and the British and Indians on the other. It describes General Harrison's defence of Fort Meigs and Major Croghan's brilliant repulse of the British at Fort Stephenson, Perry's wonderful victory on Lake Erie and Harrison's triumph over Proctor and Tecumseh at the battle of the Thames. In all these historic events Jack Morgan bears a prominent part, along with his father, the farmer-frontiersman, his brave and loving mother, John Waller, a typical scout, Pohig, Perry's Indian follower, and other men and women of the frontier, the army and the fleet. The story is full of Indians, soldiers and sailors, adventure, fighting and courage, and is a splendid boy's story of action thrown against a notable historical background.

197. [178.] (608.) **Jack, the young ranchman: or, A boy's adventures in the Rockies.** George Bird Grinnell. N. Y., Frederick A. Stokes & Co., 1899. 304 p. il. D. cl.	1.25	.70

A narrative of the actual occurrences in the life of a youth who spent several seasons on a ranch in the West, in the days when the cattle business was at its best, and before the extermination of the buffalo and the wild Indian. Belongs also to upper form.

198. [132.] **Josey and the chipmunk.** Sydney Reid. N. Y., Century Co., 1900. 301 p. il. D. bds.	1.50	.88

An imaginative story for the children who like fairy stories.

	List price.	Price to districts.

199. [166.] (125.) **Juan and Juanita.** Frances Countenay Baylor (*Mrs. Frances Baylor Barnum*). Bost., Houghton, Mifflin & Co., 1896. 276 p. il. O. cl. 1.50 .90

An interesting story of two Mexican children who were captured by the Indians. The portrayal of Indian and Mexican life is very graphic.

References for geography: Mexican home, 14-20; weaving of blankets, 21-23; description of Indians, 31-32; description of Northern Texas, 40; mountain scenery, 126-128; mirage, 130-131; Indian customs, 29-33, 51, 102, 34; animal life, 69-70, 76-78, 206, 113-115, 200.

200. [142.] (112.) **Jungle book.** Rudyard Kipling. N. Y., Century Co., 1898. 303 p. il. D. cl............ 1.50 .96

201. [143.] (113.) **Second jungle book.** Rudyard Kipling. N. Y., Century Co., 1897. 324 p. il. D. cl....... 1.50 .96

The animal life of the jungle is portrayed in these stories. No stories have ever been written which make the child realize more keenly his relationship to the animal world.

202. **Junior cup.** Allen French. N. Y., Century Co., 1901. 246 p. il. D. cl. 1.20 1.08

A very attractive story of boy life at school.

203. [179.] (609.) **Lakerim athletic club.** Rupert Hughes. N. Y., Century Co., 1898. 286 p. il. D. cl...... 1.50 .85

A spirited story of boy life.

204. [150.] (110.) **Left behind.** James Otis (J. O. Kaler) N. Y., Harper & Bros., 1897. 205 p. il. S. cl... .60 .40

A story of two little gamins setting to work to make honestly a living and a home.

205. **Lem: a New England village boy:** his adventures and his mishaps. Noah Brooks. N. Y., C: Scribner's Sons, 1901. 301 p. il. D. cl............. 1.00 .90

A faithful portrayal of boy life in a New England village fifty or sixty years ago. The story is full of adventure and will appeal to the interests of boys.

LIST OF BOOKS FOR TOWNSHIP LIBRARIES.

	List price.	Price to districts.

206. [140.] (109.) **Life and adventures of Robinson Crusoe.** Daniel DeFoe. *Ed.* by Kate Stephens. N. Y., American Book Company, 1896. 246 p. il. D. cl.   .50   .43

The story has been divided into short chapters, long sentences are split up into shorter ones, antiquated expressions are either explained in foot notes or replaced by their modern equivalents.

207. [134.] (100.) **Little Daffydowndilly, and other stories.** Nathaniel Hawthorne. Bost., Houghton, Mifflin & Co., 1887. 82 p. il. D. (Riverside lit. ser.) cl.   .15   .12

Some very good stories in Hawthorne's inimitable English. Ought to be read to the children. The biographical stories are about the childhood of Benjamin West, Newton, Samuel Johnson, Cromwell, Franklin, and Queen Christina.

208. [157.] (135.) **Little men.** Louisa M. Alcott. Bost., Little, Brown & Co., 1898. 376 p. il. S. cl.....   1.50   .88

209. [158.] (136.) **Little women;** or, Meg, Jo, Beth and Amy. Louisa M. Alcott. Bost., Little, Brown & Co. 532 p. il. S. cl. ....   1.50   .88

Two of the best children's books ever written. Portrayals of child life, natural, wholesome and inspiring.

210. **Maggie McLanehan.** Gulielma Zollinger. Chic., A. C. McClurg & Co., 1901. 319 p. il. D. cl..........   1.00   .90

The heroine is a courageous young Irish girl, thrown on her own resources at an early age, the story describing her successful efforts to earn a living for herself and her little cousin.

211. [153.] (133.) **Mr. Stubbs's brother;** a sequel to Toby Tyler. James Otis (J. O. Kaler). N. Y., Harper & Bros., 1898. 283 p. il. S. cl................   .60   .42

The pupils who enjoyed Toby Tyler will like this book.

212. [176.] (606.) **Nelly's silver mine:** a story of Colorado life. Helen Hunt Jackson. Boston, Little, Brown & Co., 1900. 379 p. S. cl.....................   1.50   .88

A charming story of a little girl, whose good will, patience and truth will inspire the children.

	List price.	Price to districts.

213. **Old ballads in prose.** Eva March Tappan. Bost., Houghton, Mifflin & Co., 1901. 228 p. il. D. cl.   1.10   .99

Miss Tappan gives modern versions in prose of old ballads formerly sung by minstrels. These include Willie Wallace, King John and the Abbot, How Robin Hood served the King, and The King and the Miller of Mansfield. The selection of ballads seems judicious, and the experiment of putting them in fresh and familiar language is successful. The book is primarily intended for children, but older persons will enjoy reading it.

214. [138.] (106.) **Play days;** stories for children. Sarah Orne Jewett. Bost., Houghton, Mifflin & Co., 1889. 213 p. S. cl. ....   1.50   .90

Entertaining stories of child life.

215. [177.] (607.) **Purpose and success.** Bost., Perry Mason & Co., 1900. 256 p. il. D. (Companion ser.) cl. 50   .40

Interesting stories by prominent writers filled with concrete lessons in right doing.

216. **Pussy Meow:** the autobiography of a cat. S. Louise Patteson. *Introd.* by Sarah K. Bolton. Phil., George W. Jacobs & Co., c1901. 237 p. il. D. cl.   .60   .48

"In *Pussy Meow* we have the latest contribution to the literature devoted to dumb animals of which 'Black Beauty,' and 'Beautiful Joe' are notable examples.

This little book is written—as its name indicates—in behalf of the cat, and seeks to do for that often much abused little creature what those two named books have done for the horse and the dog. And inasmuch as the cat is so entirely helpless to defend herself the need for such an appeal is even greater in her case than in that of either the horse or the dog. The book is written in a spirit of sympathy that makes the story a touching one without being sentimental. More cruelty to animals comes from thoughtlessness and indifference than through real malice and in the trials and tribulations of *Pussy Meow* this truth is forcibly brought out. The author also weaves much useful information as to the care of the cat in the telling of *Pussy's* story."

217. [171.] (142.) **Quartet.** W. O. Stoddard. N. Y., C. Scribner's Sons, 1890. 332 p. D. cl. ....   1.00   .65

This is a sequel to Dab Kinzer and tells the story of the life of Dab and his friends in the Grantley Academy.

	List price.	Price to districts.

218. [190.] **Road to nowhere.** Livingston B. Morse. N. Y., Harper & Bros., 1900. 236 p. il. D. cl. ....   1.50   .90

An imaginative story for imaginative children.

219. [175.] (598.) **St. Nicholas Christmas book.** N. Y., Century Co., 1899. 218 p. il. O. cl. ....   1.50   .88

Verse and prose on the subject of Christmas by various authors selected from the best published in the St. Nicholas magazine. Some of the stories can be read in primary form.

220. [149.] (111.) **Solomon Crow's Christmas pockets.** Ruth McEnery Stuart. N. Y., Harper & Bros., 1898. 201 p. il. D. cl. ....   1.25   .80

Most delightful stories portraying negro life. Ought to be read to children of the primary form.

221. **Spectacle man: a story of the missing bridge.** Mary F. Leonard. Bost., W. A. Wilde Company, 1901. 266 p. il. D. cl. ....   1.00   .60

The scene of this story is laid in Louisville, Kentucky, and is full of picturesque scenes characteristic of that part of the country. The story is about a little girl. Children of the Upper Form will enjoy reading it.

222. [137.] (105.) **Stories and poems for children.** Celia Thaxter. Bost., Houghton, Mifflin & Co., 1896. 257 p. D. (Riverside school lib.) cl. 60   .48

223. [162.] (613.) **Stories Polly Pepper told to the five little Peppers in the little brown house.** Margaret Sidney (*Mrs.* H. M. Lothrop). Bost., Lothrop Pub. Co., 1899. 469 p. il. D. cl. ....   1.50   .85

To the children who learned to know and to love the Pepper family this volume will be especially delightful. Ought to be read to primary form.

224. [136.] (102.) **Story of a bad boy.** Thomas Bailey Aldrich. Bost., Houghton, Mifflin & Co., 1897. 261 p. il. D. (Riverside school lib.) cl. 70   .60

A New England boy's autobiography frankly and humorously told.

LIST OF BOOKS FOR TOWNSHIP LIBRARIES.

	List price.	Price to districts.

225. [173.] (144.) **Success against odds.** W. O. Stoddard. N. Y., D. Appleton & Co., 1898. il. D. cl...... 1.50 .85

A story of a boy whose pluck and energy helps a whole family. The book is filled with the life on the coast of Long Island. References: 'Long shore sand farm, 34-36, 130-136, 265; fishing, 161-165.

226. [151.] (131.) **Tim and Tip.** James Otis (J. O. Kaler). N. Y., Harper & Bros., 1885. 179 p. il. S. cl... .60 .40

The adventures of a boy and a dog. The child who is fond of a dog will like this story.

227. [152.] (132.) **Toby Tyler;** or, ten weeks with the circus. James Otis (J. O. Kaler). N. Y., Harper & Bros., 1898. 265 p. il. D. cl................. .60 .40

The explanatory title might possibly suggest that this would not be the best sort of a story for young folks, but it is really one of the books that appeal strongly to the feelings, kindle right sympathies, and broaden the reader's interest in humble humanity. Toby is a most lovable little fellow, and Mr. Stubbs is inimitable. Older people will enjoy the book as well as boys and girls.

228. [159.] (137.) **Under the lilacs.** Louisa M. Alcott. Bost., Little, Brown & Co., 1890. 305 p. il. S. cl...... .... 1.50 .88

229. [130.] (97.) **Water babies;** a fairy tale for a land baby. Charles Kingsley. New ed. N. Y., Macmillan Co. 310 p. il. D. cl.................. .50 .38

A beautiful story for children about a chimney sweep called Tom and the inhabitants of water.

230. [139.] (108.) **Widow O'Callaghan's boys.** Gulielma Zollinger. Chic., A. C. McClurg & Co., 1898. 297 p. il. D. cl. .... 1.25 .75

The story of seven boys who learned that the little duty close at hand is often the most difficult and the noblest. The children will enjoy the story. The teacher will find in it some of the soundest pedagogy ever put into a story.

231. [144.] (600.) **Will Shakespeare's little lad.** Imogen Clark. N. Y., C. Scribner's Sons, 1897. 306 p. il. D. cl. .... 1.50 .96

A charming little story of Shakespeare's little lad, containing a beautiful lesson in truth.

	List price.	Price to districts.

232. [172.] (143.) **Winter fun.** W. O. Stoddard. N. Y., C. Scribner's Sons, 1897. 273 p. D. cl............ 1.00 .65

A story that has the spirit and freshness of winter air. The boys especially feel a sympathetic interest in such lively accounts of rabbit hunts, trapping, snow-ball battles, deer-stalking in the snow, and sports of similar nature.

HISTORICAL FICTION.

Historical fiction makes history real, for it reveals not only the life but the spirit of the times. If properly read it helps the child to visualize—to see history. Manners and customs,— that is, homes, surroundings, food, clothing, ways of travel, amusements, occupations, mode of warfare, language, religion, etc., etc.,—as touched upon in the story should be noted and grouped, and their characteristics dwelt upon, the historical event upon which the story is based read or told to the children.

The teacher should help the child to form high ideals of life and character, and encourage the child to admire the good, the true, and the noble.

	List price.	Price to districts.

233. **Among the camps**, or, young people's stories of the war. Thomas Nelson Page. N. Y., C: Scribner's Sons, 1892. 163 p. il. O. cl. .... 1.50 .98

"Children's stories of the Civil War among confederate camps. Tells of a brave little boy's courageous deed. "Kittykin, and the part she played in the war," is an amusing story about a cat. "Nancy Pansy," a story of a brave little girl and her doll. Jack and Jake," a story of a boy and his slave."

Children will enjoy this book because it is the story of the life and adventures of other boys and girls. By means of this interest the teacher may create a new interest in the story of the Civil war and lead some of the children to desire to learn more about the war which they will find in Blaisdell's "Stories of the civil war;" Brook's "Abraham Lincoln" and other books upon the Township list.

234. [197.] (151). **Big brother.** George Cary Eggleston. N. Y., G. P. Putnam's Sons, 1898. 182 p. il. D. cl. .... 1.25 .75

A story of Creek Indian war.

	List price.	Price to districts.

235. [207.] (617.) **Cadet Standish of the St. Louis:** a story of our naval campaign in Cuban waters. William Drysdale. Bost., W. A. Wilde & Co., 1899. 354 p. il. D. cl. .... 1.50 .85

A good story of a boy who goes to Cuba on a mission in the government's secret service during our late war. Will do for upper form also.

236. [198.] **Childhood of Ji-shib', the Ojibwa.** Albert Ernest Jenks. Madison, American Thresherman Co., 1900. 130 p. il. D. cl..................... 1.00 .60

An Indian story filled with the spirit of Indian life, which will appeal to every child.

237. **Docas, the Indian boy of Santa Clara.** Genevra Sisson Snedden. Bost., D. C. Heath & Co., 1899. 150 p. il. D. cl. .... .35 .32

Stories of Indian childhood, life, and customs.

238. **Flower of the wilderness.** Almira G. Plympton. Bost., Little, Brown & Co., 1899. 260 p. il. D. cl. .... 1.50 .90

Colonial life in Massachusetts is the subject of this story. The tale is founded on a mystery in the history of a little colonial girl. The book incidentally gives much information about the plant life of New England.

This is an excellent book to read to the school for opening exercises and may serve as a source of several new lines of interests.

Some children will be interested in reading more books on Colonial and Indian life and others in reading more about the Plant and Bird Life in New England.

239. **Gordon highlander.** E. Everett-Green. N. Y., Thomas Nelson & Sons, 1901. 272 p. D. cl............ 1.00 .50

The story of a young boy whose father was a captain in the English army. The children will get much valuable information about the Boer war in South Africa by reading this book.

240. [191.] (622.) **Havelock the Dane:** a legend of Old Grimsby and Lincoln. Charles W. Whistler. N. Y., Thomas Nelson and Sons, 1900. 393 p. il. D. cl. .... 1.25 .63

An old legend fascinatingly told. Children of the upper form will read.

	List price.	Price to districts.

241. [200.] (623.) **In Colonial times: the adventures of Ann, the bound girl of Samuel Wales, of Braintree, in the province of Massachusetts Bay.** Mary E. Wilkins. Bost., Lothrop Pub. Co., 1899. 115 p. il. D. cl. .... .50 .27

Presents a new phase of Colonial life. The documents in the case are given. Upper form will enjoy.

242. [192.] (148.) **In the brave days of old.** Ruth Hall. Bost., Houghton, Mifflin & Co., 1898. 334 p. il. D. cl. .... 1.50 .90

The adventures of two English boys who followed Henry Hudson to America.

243. [194.] **King Robert's page.** G. Manville Fenn. N. Y., E. P. Dutton & Co., 72 p. il. D. bds....... .75 .45

A charming story of a brave little boy who became the King's page and sword bearer.

244. [199.] (43.) **Little girl of long ago.** Eliza Orne White. Bost., Houghton, Mifflin & Co., 1898. 151 p. il. D. cl. .... 1.00 .60

A story of a little girl who lived long ago in Boston. Her companions, games, her playthings, her pleasure trips, her work, and her home are all described. Compare with the life of a little girl of today.

245. [195.] (149.) **Little Smoke.** W. O. Stoddard. N. Y., D. Appleton & Co., 1898. 295 p. il. D. cl....... 1.50 .85

An exciting story of the adventures of a boy who was captured by the Sioux Indians and lived with Sitting Bull's band. A valuable book in connection with history. The illustrations depict many curious weapons, utensils, and articles of dress, used by the Indians.

246. **Margot: the Court shoemaker's child.** Millicent E. Mann. Chic., A. C. McClurg & Co., 1901. 231 p. il. D. cl. .... 1.00 .90

Margot's father, who is shoemaker to the Court of France in the reign of Louis xiv., is a Huguenot; and when the times of persecution come, little Margot is hurried out of France. She escapes to America, and has many strange adventures in the wilderness.

	List price.	Price to districts.

247. [193.] (625.) **Micah Clarke**; a tale of Monmouth's rebellion. A. Conan Doyle. N. Y., Longmans, Green & Co., 1894. 217 p. il. D. (Longmans' supplementary readers.) cl. .... .50 .40

This stirring story has been adapted for school use.

248. [202.] **Noank's log**; a privateer of the Revolution. W. O. Stoddard. Bost., Lothrop Pub. Co., 1900. 337 p. il. D. cl. .... 1.25 .75

Story of life on an American cruiser during the Revolutionary war.

249 **Otto of the silver hand.** Howard Pyle. N. Y., C: Scribner's Sons, 1901. 170 p. il. O. cl........ 2.00 1.28

The story of a little boy who lived during the Middle Ages.

250. [206.] (155.) **Two little confederates.** Thomas Nelson Page. N. Y., C: Scribner's Sons. 1891. 156 p. il. O. cl. .... 1.50 .98

A story of home life on a plantation in Virginia during the Rebellion. The interest centers about two boys who had many stirring adventures.

References: Plantation and surroundings, 1-3, 31, 35, 37; mode of travel, 1, 10-11; poor whites, 31-34, 38; negro peculiarities, 25-28, 54-57, 60-64; the beginning of the war, 5-6; confederate army, 9; feeding the soldiers, 9-17, 19, 47; description of camp, 11-18; conscript officers, 30-34, 43; deserters, 30-34; 44, 111-115.

FAIRY STORIES, FOLK STORIES, MYTHS, AND LEGENDS.

Many of the children in this form still enjoy fairy stories, myths, and legends. They are valuable as a means of training the imagination; and because they form an indispensable part of art and literature, familiarity with them will unlock much in art and literature which otherwise the child will pass by because it is too much of a task to "look it up." Here is good material for work in language. Manual, *Language—Middle Form.*

	Price List price.	Price to districts.
251. **Asgard stories:** tales from Norse mythology. Mary H. Foster *and* Mabel H. Cummings. N. Y., Silver, Burdett & Co., c1901. 110 p. il. D. cl.	.36	.33

"This charming little book is devoted to tales from Norse mythology. The stories are told clearly and interestingly, as befits the understanding of children. The authors have had much experience with children, for whom these stories are written, and fully understand their needs for literature of this class. The illustrations are excellent and the book will prove very attractive to young people."

252. [212.] **At the back of the north wind.** George MacDonald. N. Y., George Routledge & Sons. 378 p. il. D. cl.	1.00	.38

Delightful stories. Upper form children will also enjoy them.

253. [223.] (631.) **Court of King Arthur:** stories from the land of the round table. William Henry Frost. N. Y., C: Scribner's Sons, 1899. 302 p. il. D. cl.	1.50	.96

Well told stories of the land of King Arthur. Children who read and enjoyed "Knights of the Round Table" by the same author, will enjoy these stories.

254. [214.] (627.) **Danish fairy and folk tales:** a collection of popular stories and fairy tales. From the Danish of Svend Grundtvig, E. T. Kristensen, Ingvor Bodesen, and L. Budde. *Ed.* by J. Christian Bay. N. Y., Harper & Bros., 1899. 293 p. il. cl.	1.50	.85

"The folk tales of the Danes are prominently illustrative of the ways and habits of this nation. Interwoven as they are with the

	List price.	Price to districts.

best and brightest thoughts, hopes and aspirations of 'the plain people'—the rural population—they cannot but represent essential features of popular belief and aspiration." *Editor's preface.* Good material for stories to be told to lower form.

255. [211.] (162.) **German household tales.** J. L. K. *and* W. K. Grimm. Bost., Houghton, Mifflin & Co., 1897. 241 p. D. cl. .... .40 .32

The best of these fairy stories.

256. [209.] **Grey fairy book.** Andrew Lang, *ed.* N. Y., Longmans, Green & Co., 1900. 387 p. il. D. cl. 2.00 1.25

A collection of fairy stories from many countries.

257. [222.] (171.) **Knights of the Round Table.** William Henry Frost. N. Y., C. Scribner's Sons, 1898. 281 p. il. D. cl. .... 1.50 .96

Stories of King Arthur and his knights told in a most fascinating way. The older pupils in this form can read the book and children of the upper form will enjoy it.

258. [215.] (163.) **Little Mr. Thimblefinger.** Joel Chandler Harris. Bost., Houghton, Mifflin & Co., 1895. 230 p. il. O. cl. 2.00 1.20

The story of the experiences of two Southern children Buster John and Sweetest Susan and their negro nurse Drusilla in Mr. Thimblefinger's queer country.

259. [216.] (164.) **Mr. Rabbit at home;** a sequel to little Mr. Thimblefinger. Joel Chandler Harris. Bost., Houghton, Mifflin & Co., 1895. 304 p. il. O. cl. 2.00 1.20

Buster John, Sweetest Susan, and Drusilla of the "Little Mr. Thimblefinger" stories make a second visit to Mr. Thimblefinger's queer country and hear from Mr. Rabbit and Mrs. Meadows a number of odd stories about "Where the thunder lives," "The jumping-off place," "The blue hen's chickens," "The cow with the golden horns," and other strange animals.

The last two books are collections of negro folk-stories filled with quaint humor, wisdom and negro life. Most children are delighted with these books. Many of the stories ought to be read to children of the primary form.

	List price.	Price to districts.

260. **Aaron in the wildwoods.** Joel Chandler Harris. Bost., Houghton, Mifflin & Co., 1897. 270 p. il. O. cl. 2.00 1.20

This story carries the young reader back to the early days of Aaron's career, when he was a fugitive in the wildwoods and before Buster John and Sweetest Susan were born. It completes the personal history of Aaron and gives incidentally a description of night life on a Southern plantation. A chapter on "The secrets of the swamps" written from the point of view of the negro, is woven into the narrative.

261. **Story of Aaron** (so named): the son of Ben Ali. Joel Chandler Harris. Bost., Houghton, Mifflin & Co., 1897. 198 p. il. O. cl................. 2.00 1.20

The children of the "Thimble-finger" stories had been told by Mr. Thimblefinger that there was a man named Aaron in the Abercrombie place who knew the language of animals. They make themselves known to him and then follow curious stories told by the horse, the dog, the white pig, and others, oddly interwoven with the family history.

262. [220.] (630.) **Odysseus: the hero of Ithaca,** adapted from the Third Book of the Primary Schools of Athens, Greece. Mary E. Burt *and* Zenaide Alexeieona Ragozin. N. Y., C: Scribner's Sons, 1898. 223 p. D. (Scribner's ser. of school reading.) cl. .60 .50

Stories from Homer's Odysseus. The volume is divided into three parts, the first of which gives a short resume of the war against Troy and the destruction of that city; the second, the wanderings of Odysseus till his arrival in Ithaca; the third, his arrival.

263. [213.] (626a.) **Old Norse Stories.** Sarah Powers Bradish. N. Y., American Book Company, 1900. 240 p. il. D. cl. ...... .45 .40

The most popular of these stories told in such a way as to be very attractive to young readers.

264. [210.] (157.) **Stories from the Arabian nights.** *Ed. by* M. Clarke. N. Y., American Book Company, 1897. 271 p. D. cl. .... .60 .51

The best stories from the Arabian Nights.

265. [218.] (168.) **Stories of long ago.** Grace H. Kupfer. Bost., D. C. Heath & Co., 1897. 177 p. il. D. cl. .35 .31

Some of the most pleasing stories from Greek and Roman mythology. Following many of the stories are poems of our greatest authors on the same subjects. The book is most beautifully illustrated with reproductions of famous paintings and sculptures.

LIST OF BOOKS FOR TOWNSHIP LIBRARIES.

	List price.	Price to districts.

266. [221.] (170.) **Story of Aeneas.** M. Clarke. N. Y., American Book Company, 1898. 203 p. il. D. cl.   .45   .40

The story of the Aeneid told for young readers. Beautiful illustrations.

267. [219.] (169.) **Story of Troy.** M. Clarke. N. Y., American Book Company, 1898. 251 p. il. D. cl.....   .60   .51

Story of the Iliad told in a very interesting way for young readers. The book is most beautifully illustrated.

268. [225.] (628.) **Tales of Languedoc.** Samuel Jaques Brun. N. Y., Macmillan Co., 1899. 240 p. il. D. cl. ......   1.50   .96

Most imaginative folk stories of the south of France told with directness and a dramatic quality which is unusual. The main lessons conveyed by these fireside tales are those elementary ones which appeal so forcibly to a child's sense of justice. Stories ought to be told or read to primary form.

269. [217.] (167.) **Tanglewood tales.** Nathaniel Hawthorne. Bost., Houghton, Mifflin & Co., 1883. 222 p. il. D. (Riverside Lit. ser.) cl...............   .40   .32

Hawthorne's excellent English makes these stories of particular value to children. The older children can read for themselves.

270. **Violet fairy book.** *Ed. by* Andrew Lang. N. Y., Longmans, Green & Co., 1901. 388 p. il. D. cl.....   1.60   1.44

The stories in this book are translations of the popular traditional tales of other countries. Many of these were originally told long before reading and writing were invented. Some of the most interesting are from the Scandinavian and Roumanian.

BIOGRAPHY.

Grouping great events around great men who may become real persons to children is one of the best ways of teaching history. That the man lived and died at a certain time is not so important as what kind of a man he was, what he did, and what great events he took part in. Aim to make some of the great personages real by dwelling upon some of those personal anecdotes which are of interest to the child. Make these leading figures in history so familiar to the child that they become the centers around which much of his knowledge of history may be grouped. The child is in the susceptible stage in which the heroes who have fired his imagination will often become his ideals of all that is noble and good and he will desire to share their experiences and aspirations. See Manual, *History—Primary and Middle Forms.*

	List price.	Price to districts.
271. [224.] (172.) **Wagner story book.** William Henry Frost. N. Y., C: Scribner's Sons. 1898. 245 p. il. D. cl.	1.50	.96

The stories of Wagner's famous operas most fascinatingly told. Pupils of the upper form will enjoy these stories.
References: Nibelungen lied, 3–94; Lohengrin, 97–114; Tannhauser, 194–212; Parzifal, 216–239.

272. **American boys' life of William McKinley.** Edward Stratemeyer. Bost., Lee & Shepard, 1901. 316 p. il. D. cl.	1.25	.75

Here is told the whole story of McKinley's boyhood days, his life at school and at college, his work as a school teacher, his glorious career in the army, his struggles to obtain a footing as a lawyer, his efforts as a Congressman, and lastly his prosperous career as our President. There are many side lights on the work of the White House during the war with Spain, and in China, all told in a style particularly adapted to boys and young men.

273. **Boy general:** story of the life of Major-General George A. Custer. Elizabeth B. Custer. *Ed.* by Mary E. Burt. N. Y., C: Scribner's Sons, 1901. 204 p. il. D. cl.	.60	.54

This is a condensed survey of the life of Custer, as told by his wife, in "Tenting on the plains," "Following the Guidon,"

	List price.	Price to districts.

and "Boots and Saddles." It summarizes his public services, from the reorganization of Texas after the Civil War and the suppression of the intended Mexican Invasion, to the pioneer work of himself and his brave soldiers in opening up the Northwest.

Its pages are full of examples of self-control; self-sacrifice, fortitude, kindliness, patriotism, and temperance.

274. [234.] (197.) **Boy life of Napoleon.** Eugenie Foa. Tr. from the French by E. S. Brooks. Bost., Lothrop Pub. Co., 1895. 251 p. il. O. cl...... 1.25   .70

The story of Napoleon's boyhood vividly told.

275. [233.] (203.) **Children's life of Abraham Lincoln.** M. Louise Putnam. Chic., A. C. McClurg & Co., 1898. 290 p. il. D. cl. .... 1.25   .75

One of the best accounts of the life of Lincoln for children.

276. **Decatur and Somers.** Molly Elliott Seawell. N. Y., D. Appleton & Co., 1894. 169 p. il. D. cl...... 1.00   .55

A most interesting story of two young naval heroes. The story is full of action and will certainly interest the boys. Life aboard a naval ship, the trip to the Mediterranean, the capture of the Tripolitan pirates, the capture of the Philadelphia and its recapture, and the assaults on Tripoli are most graphically described.

277. [226.] (632.) **Discoverers and explorers.** Edward R. Shaw. N. Y., American Book Company, 1900. 120 p. il. D. cl. .... .35   .31

Interesting events in the lives of those heroes whose adventures and daring exploits always appeal to children. The heroes are Marco Polo, Columbus da Gama, Cabot, Ponce de Leon, Balboa, Magellan, Cortes, Pizarro, De Soto, Drake, and Hudson.

278. [228.] **Four American pioneers:** Daniel Boone, George Rogers Clark, David Crockett, Kit Carson: a book for young Americans. Frances M. Perry, and Katherine Beebe. N. Y., Werner School Book Co., 1900. 255 p. il. D. (Four great American ser.) cl. .... .50   .42

Will interest older children.

	List price.	Price to districts.

279. [236.] (636.) **Four American poets.** Sherwin Cody. N. Y., Werner School Book Co., 1899. 254 p. D. cl. ...... .50 .42

The children may become interested in the lives of these poets through their poems. The poets are Bryant, Longfellow, Whittier, and Holmes.

280. [225.] (205.) **Fridtjof Nansen.** Jacob B. Bull. Bost., D. C. Heath & Co., 1898. 132 p. D. cl. .... .30 .27

A very interesting account of the life and adventures of Nansen. This book will prove very valuable used in connection with the geography of the cold countries.
References: Nansen's home, 1; his boyhood, 2–18; the Greenland expedition, 35–72; the Polar expedition, 73–132.

281. [220.] (201.) **Lafayette.** Alma Holman Burton. N. Y., Werner School Book Co., 1898. 85 p. il. S. cl. ...... .35 .30

A brief account of the life of Lafayette for children.

282. [203.] (154.) **Paul Jones.** Molly Elliot Seawell. N. Y., D. Appleton & Co., 1893. 166 p. il. D. cl... 1.00 .55

A spirited story of one of our greatest naval heroes and his daring deeds during the Revolution. The story is filled with the adventures of Jones as he cruises in British waters.

283. [205.] **Reuben James:** a hero of the forecastle. Cyrus Townsend Brady. N. Y., D. Appleton & Co., 1900. 158 p. il. D. .... 1.00 .55

The story of a common sailor whose bravery and devotion to duty will be an inspiration.

284. [231.] **Story of Captain Meriwether Lewis and Captain William Clark; for young readers.** Nellie F. Kingsley. N. Y., Werner School Book Co., 1900. 128 p. il. S. (Baldwin's biog. booklets.) cl.... .25 .22

Will create an interest in history and lead children from stories of pure adventure to history.

	List price.	Price to districts.

285. **Talks about Authors and their work.** Ella Reeve Ware. Chic., A. Flanagan Co., c1899. 230 p. il. D. cl. .... .60 .45

Simple sketches of the lives of well known authors.
References: Nathaniel Hawthorne, 52–61; Lewis Agassiz, 62–70; Henry Wadsworth Longfellow, 71–86; John Greenleaf Whittier, 87–99; Charles Dickens, 101–115; Harriet Beecher Stowe, 117–25; Charles Kingsley, 126–31; Edward Eggleston, 132–39; William Dean Howells, 141–47; Frances Willard, 149–51; Edward Everett Hale, 153–58; Bjornstjerne Bjornson, 159–62; Louisa Alcott, 163–72; Samuel Clemens, 173–81; Wolfgang Mozart, 9–12; Felix Mendelssohn, 13–16; Robert Burns, 17–25; Washington Irving, 26–36; Jacob L. Grimm and W. K. Grimm, 37–40; Hans Christian Andersen, 41–51; Frances Hodgson Burnett, 182–89; Joel Chandler Harris, 190–97; Eugene Field, 199–202; Robert Louis Stevenson, 203–10; James Whitcomb Riley, 211–18; Rudyard Kipling, 219–30.

286. [229.] (202.) **True story of Benjamin Franklin.** E. S. Brooks, Bost., Lothrop Pub. Co., 1898. 250 p. O. cl. .... 1.50 .85

287. [227.] (198.) **True story of Christopher Columbus.** E. S. Brooks. Bost., Lothrop Pub. Co., 1892. 187 p. il. O. cl. .... 1.50 .85

The biography of Columbus written in a simple, straightforward, earnest way, that will appeal to young readers.

288. [232.] (204.) **True story of U. S. Grant.** E. S. Brooks. Bost., Lothrop Pub. Co., 1897. 234 p. il. O. cl. .... 1.50 .85

A vivid and dramatic account of this hero's life.

289. [204.] (620.) **With Perry on Lake Erie:** a tale of 1812. James Otis (J. O. Kaler). Bost., W. A. Wilde Co., 1899. 307 p. il. D. cl.............. 1.50 .85

The deeds of Commodore Perry related from the standpoint of the younger brother who shared his triumphs.

HISTORY.

These books will be found valuable in connection with the work in history. Many of the books the child will not read himself, nor from cover to cover. The teacher must read with him and interest him in parts of books which bear directly upon the topic in history. When the pupil is interested, he will read. See Manual, *History—Primary and Middle Forms.*

So far as possible help the child to arrange his knowledge so that proper events and people, and events which grow out of each other, are associated. Help the child to admire all lessons in bravery, courage, loyalty, steadfastness to purpose, truth, devotion to duty, perseverance, and self-sacrifice.

As in fiction, whenever manners and customs are portrayed, they should be studied. See "Historical Fiction."

	List price.	Price to districts.
290. [243.] (188.) **American Indians.** Frederick Starr. Bost., D. C. Heath & Co., 1899. 277 p. il. D. cl.	.45	.40

A very interesting and clear account of the various tribes of American Indians. Though written for children, older readers will find it interesting. The topical arrangement of the book is fine, and the illustrations are good. See table of contents.

References: General facts about Indians: Houses, 7; dress, 14; child-life, 22; their stories, 31; war, 39; hunting and fishing, 46; the campfire, 53; sign language, 60; picture writing, 65; totem posts, 195; money, 73; medicine men, 80; dances and ceremonials, 85-92, 155-160, 168-174; burial and graves, 92.

Special facts about Indians: The mound builders, 98; various tribes in U. S., 108-155; Pueblos, 161; cliff dwellers, 175; Indians of California, 201; the Aztecs, 208; the Mayas, 215.

291. [251.] **American inventions and inventors.** William A. Mowry *and* Arthur May Mowry. N. Y., Silver, Burdett & Co., 1900. 298 p. il. D. cl..........	.65	.60

Historical as well as biographical, showing the progress of inventions.

	Price
List	to dis-
price.	tricts.

292. **American leaders and heroes**: a preliminary textbook in United States history. Wilbur F. Gordy. N. Y., C: Scribner's Sons, 1901. 329 p. il. D. cl. .60 .50

A historical reader which makes prominent personal traits in the characters of American heroes and leaders. It narrates incidents in the lives of those men in a vivid, dramatic manner.

References: Roger Williams, 81-91; Puritans, 81-91; William Penn, 92-102; Quakers, 92-102; Christopher Columbus, 1-21; Hernando DeSoto, 22-30; Sir Walter Raleigh, 31-34; John Smith, 42-54; Nathaniel Bacon, 55-63; Miles Standish, 64-80; Pilgrims, 64-80; Benjamin Franklin, 175-188; Nathaniel Greene, 210-221; Francis Marion, 217-21; Daniel Boone, 222-33; Thomas Jefferson, 243-45; Louisiana purchase, 241-44; Robert Fulton, 246-52; Andrew Jackson, 253-63; Cavelier de LaSalle, 103-15; George Washington, 117-35, 189-210; James Wolfe, 136-45; Patrick Henry, 146-55; Samuel Adams, 156-64; Paul Revere, 165-74; Boston Tea party, 156-64; Fanueil hall, 159-60; Robert Fulton and the steamboat, 246-52; William McKinley, 317-19; Massasoit, 75-76; Tobacco, 56-58; Daniel Webster, 265-72; Samuel Finley Breese Morse and the electric telegraph, 273-81; Abraham Lincoln, 282-301; Ulysses S. Grant, 302-13; Spanish-American war, 314-26.

293. [247.] (192.) **Boys of '76**; a history of the Revolution. Charles Carleton Coffin. N. Y., Harper & Bros., 1876. 388 p. il. O. cl. 2.00 1.25

In this volume the story of the sufferings and contests, the victories and defeats, the patriotism and self-denial, of the heroes in the struggle for American independence are told so vividly and appreciatively that the reader's pride is kindled in the deeds of bravery and the wonderful achievement of our forefathers. No one who reads these stirring pages will under-rate the importance of that conflict, and such perusal must quicken to an enthusiastic love of liberty and the rights of man.

294. [250.] (193.) **Century book of the American Revolution.** E. S. Brooks. N. Y., Century Co., 1897. 248 p. il. O. cl. .... 1.50 .90

The book is profusely illustrated. The information is given in the conversation of these young people who talk over what happened at the various places they visit.

References: Lexington, 17-34; Concord, 35-54; Bunker Hill, 55-72; New York (Washington's retreat), 73-94; along the Delaware, 95-114; the Schuylkill and thereabouts, 115-138; up the Hudson, 139-158; with Burgoyne, 159-174; Savannah, 174-192; Camden and King's Mountain, 193-210; in the region of Cowpens, 211-228; Yorktown, 229-248.

295. [252.] (185.) **Children's stories of American progress.** Henrietta Christian Wright. N. Y., C: Scribner's Sons, 1898. 333 p. il. D. cl......... 1.25 .80

Almost every notable occurrence in the gradual development of our country is woven into an attractive story for young people.

References: Life on the frontier, 1 40, 268 278; Daniel Boone,

	List price.	Price to districts.

12-40; Barbary pirates, 41-54; purchase of Louisiana, 55-85; expedition of Lewis & Clarke, 86-103; Robert Fulton and the first steamboat, 104-120; battle of Tippecanoe, 121-129; War of 1812, 130-144; purchase of Florida, 145-158; slavery, 159-178; story of the railroad, 179-198; Indian troubles, 199-208; story of the telegraph, 209-228; annexation of Texas, 229-247; Mexican War, 248-267; discovery of gold, 279-298; Civil war, 299-333.

296. **Elementary history of the United States.** Allen C. Thomas. Bost., D. C. Heath & Co., 1901. 346 p. il. maps. D. cl. .... .60 .52

This book contains sketches of the representative makers of the Union and is written in an attractive and interesting manner. To illustrate some of the most important phases of national growth, the difficulties and dangers of exploration, the risks and hardships of settlement, the independence and patriotism of the colonists, the development of the people in politics and government and in social life, and the progress of invention and its effect upon national development.

References: Christopher Columbus, 7-25; Explorers, 7-66; Pilgrims, 67-84; Puritans, 85-91; King Philip's war, 95-101; William Penn, 123-32; Benjamin Franklin, 150-67; French and Indian War, 168-86; George Washington, 168-86; U. S. History, Revolution, 187-218; Daniel Boone, 219-31; Thomas Jefferson, 232-40; Lewis and Clark, 241-47; Inventors: John Fitch, Robert Fulton, Eli Whitney, and others, 253-64; 277-89; War of 1812, 265-76; Abraham Lincoln, 306-17; Civil war, 318-28.

297. [245.] (186.) **How New England was made.** Frances A. Humphrey. Bost., Lothrop Pub. Co., 1890. 267 p. il. O. cl. .... 1.25 .70

The younger children can read this book for themselves. The type is large and the story clearly told.

298. **Massasoit: a romantic story of the Indians of New England.** Alma Holman. N. Y., Morse Co., 1897. 273 p. il. D. cl.............................. .67 .57

The story of Massasoit and his kinsmen is typical of the life of the Indian in colonial times.

References: Pilgrims, 88-112; Thanksgiving, 107-12; Thomas Morton: Merrymount, 128-32; Puritans, 133-36; Pequot war, 137-50; King Philip's war, 193-205; Pirates of New England, 244-52; French and Indian wars, 253-61.

299. [246.] (191.) **Pioneer history stories of the Mississippi valley.** Charles McMurry. Bloomington, Public School Pub. Co., 1995. 173 p. D. Cl..... .50 .38

References: La Salle, 9-32; Geo. R. Clarke, 33-49; Lincoln, 50-59; Joliet and Marquette, 60-68; Hennepin, 69-77; the Sioux massacre, 78-90; Daniel Boone, 91-102; Robertson, 103-135; Lewis and Clarke, 136-148; Fremont, 149-162; De Soto, 163-173.

	List price.	Price to districts.

300. **Primary history of the United States.** John Bach McMaster. N. Y., American Book Co., c1901. 254 p. il. D. cl. .... .60 .51

An interesting narrative of important events in United States history.
References: Colonial history, p. 7–120; French and Indian war, p. 103–107; Revolutionary war, p. 120–50; Building the West, p. 161–73; Slavery, p. 174–82; 190–95, 215–19; Civil war, p. 193–213; Spanish-American war, p. 238–42.

301. [242.] (184.) **Short history of the United States.** Horace E. Scudder. N. Y., Butler, Sheldon & Co., 1890. 286 p. il. D. cl. .... .60 .50

Our history given in a form to excite an interest in the continuous growth of the nation.

302. [239.] (175.) **Story of Caesar.** M. Clarke. N. Y., American Book Company, 1898. 173 p. il. D. cl. .... .45 .40

A most interesting account of the life of Caesar and a vivid picture of the military life of Rome at that time.

303. [237.] (173.) **Stories of Greek gods, heroes, and men.** Caroline H. Harding *and* Samuel B. Harding. Chic., Scott, Foresman & Co., 1897. 195 p. il. D. cl. .... .50 .43

A beautiful little book, beautifully illustrated, with the stories of the Greek gods and heroes well told.
Stories are divided into: Stories of the gods, 3–84; stories of the heroes, 85–128; stories from Greek history, 129–195.

304. [241.] (182.) **Story of our country.** Alma Holman Burton. N. Y., Werner School Book Co., 1896. 238 p. il. D. cl. .... .60 .50

A well written history which the younger children can read.

305. [248.] **Stories of the American Revolution.** Everett T. Tomlinson. Bost., Thos. R. Shewell & Co., 1897. Part I. 164 p. il. S. cl................ .30 .27

306. [249.] **Stories of the American Revolution.** Everett T. Tomlinson. Bost., Thos. R. Shewell & Co., 1898. Part II. 193 p. il. S. cl................ .30 .27

The foundation of these stories is historically true. They portray the incidents of homelife, the struggles of the women and children, the bravery and the heroism of those who never went to the battle-field as well as the life of the soldier.

	List price.	Price to districts.

307. [253.] (639.) **Stories of the Badger state.** Reuben G. Thwaites. N. Y., American Book Company, 1900. 255 p. il. D. cl. .... .60 .51

Stories of the leading events in the history of Wisconsin. Will interest young readers.

308. **Stories of the Civil War**: adapted for supplementary reading. Albert F. Blaisdell. Bost., Lee and Shepard, c1890. 244 p. il. S. bds............. .30 .27

A series of pictures of life during the late war which will interest the children and excite in their minds a desire to know more of the noble deeds of our fore-fathers. The teacher may suggest this book to read to the child who has read and enjoyed Page's "Two little confederates".
References: Fort Sumter, 11-22; the Monitor and the Merrimac, 42-46; Abraham Lincoln, 54-61; Sheridan's ride, 82-88; destruction of the Albemarle, 93-98; Gettysburg, 99-108; Kearsarge and Alabama, 124-128; Sherman's march to the sea, 138-145; Andersonville prison, 158-163, 178-181; Lee's surrender, 187-192; Memorial day, 237-244.

309. [238.] (174.) **Story of the Greeks.** H. A. Guerber. N. Y., American Book Company, 1896. 288 p. il. D. cl. .... .60 .51

These stories give a clear idea of the most important events of Grecian history. They are also filled with lessons of perseverance, courage, patriotism, and virtue.

310. [240.] **Strange peoples.** Frederick Starr. Bost., D. C. Heath & Co., 186 p. il. D. cl................ .40 .35

A series of sketches which read in connection with the geography lesson will make it real and interesting. Some of the material can be used in the Primary Form.

311. **Wigwam stories told by North American Indians.** *Comp.* by Mary Catherine Judd. Bost., Ginn & Co., 1901. 276 p. il. D. cl. .... .75 .65

These stories, told by and about the Indians, have been gathered from various sources. They show, among other interesting facts, that the love of the beautiful, and also of the humorous, dwells in the heart of the wild Indian. The book contains many fine illustrations which will be invaluable to the history class.
Contents: Sketches of various tribes of North American Indians; Traditions and myths; Stories recently told of Hiawatha and other heroes.

GEOGRAPHY.

In using the following books for work in geography the aim should be to make the children see the places and people described so far as possible as they would were they actually traveling. Pictures will prove very valuable in this work. As in primary form, how people live, what they do for a living, how they amuse themselves, their food, clothing, ways of travel, etc., etc., must be studied. Descriptions of natural scenery, vegetables, and animals, the great cities, famous buildings, should be carefully read and reproduced in the geography class. The books are carefully referenced so the teacher may select such portions to read to, or to be read by, the children, as bear directly on the lesson in geography. See Manual, *Geography—Primary and Middle Forms.*

	List price.	Price to districts.
312. [284.] **Alice's visit to the Hawaiian islands.** Mary H. Krout. N. Y., American Book Company, 1900. 208 p. il. D. cl.	.45	.40

The travels of a little girl in the Hawaiian Islands and what she saw there. Valuable material for work in geography.
References: Honolulu, 18–49; 111–122; 135–156; 172–180; Hilo, 55–83; sugar plantation, 93–89; Maui, 90–103; Kanai, 103–111; Molokai, 156–172; ostrich farm, 186–191; Hawaiian schools, 191–197; Chinese schools, 197–202.

| 313. **Around the world:** Geographical readers. Book 3. Stella W. Carroll *and* Estelle M. Hart. *Ed.* by Clarence F. Carroll. N. Y., Morse Co., 1901. 268 p. il. D. cl. | .60 | .50 |

Much information of value not found in the text book of geography is given in this book. It is a home geography for the fifth grade, treating of social, industrial, and commercial interests of all sections of the United States and possessions.
The illustrations are excellent, and represent the life, industries and varied natural features of our country.
References: Lumbering, 20–22; Niagara Falls, 23–27; Hunting in the Maine woods, 28–38; Indians of North America, 39–42, 150–52; Washington (D. C.), 47–53; Iron 53–56; Coal, 56–59; Oil, 60–62; Great Lakes, 63–73; Copper mines, 75; Wheat fields, 76–81; Stock yards, 81–85; Zinc mining in Missouri, 86–88; California, 89–119; Cave and cliffdwellers, 119–21; Ostrich, 101–103; Alaska, 122–31; Seal fisheries, 131–32; Gold mining, 133–39; Salmon fish-

LIST OF BOOKS FOR TOWNSHIP LIBRARIES.

	List price.	Price to districts.

cries, 142–43; Yellowstone Park, 144–46; Great Salt Lake, 147–49; Southern states of U. S., 153–69; Turpentine, 156–59; Cotton, 159-66; New England states, 170–214; Sugar making, 198–201; Cheese factory, 201–203; Ice crop, 212–14; Cuba, 215–22; Porto Rico, 223–27; Hawaiian islands, 228–40; Philippine islands, 241–266.

314. [274.] (227.) **Asia.** Frank G. Carpenter. N. Y., American Book Company, 1897. 304 p. il. D. cl. .... .60 .51

A vivid portrayal of life in Asia as it is today. Though written for children the adult will find it interesting. One of the best books on the list.

References: Japan: The island, 15–23; Tokio, 24–32; home life, 33–42; emperor, 43–49; child life, 49–58; farms, 59–68; commerce and industries, 69–75.

Corea, 76–82.

Siberia and the Trans-Siberia R. R., 93–101.

China, 102–110; Pekin, 111–119; emperor, 120–127; great wall, 128–133; boats and boat people, 134–142; farms and farming, 143–153; curious customs, 154–161.

Siam, 162–178; Singapore and the Malays, 179–185.

Burma, 185–199.

India, 202–208; farms and farming, 209–216; stores and trades, 217–224; wild animals, 225–233; Benares, 234–240; native states, 241–248; Himalaya Mountains, 249–256.

Tibet, 257–264;
Persia, 265–272;
Arabia, 272–281;
Palestine, 282–289;
Turkey, 290–296;
Russia, 297–304.

315. [272.] (223.) **By land and sea.** Bost., Perry Mason & Co., 1895. 256 p. il. O. cl. .... .50 .40

Good descriptions of places of interest in Europe, the American tropics, the Orient, and the life of the ocean.

References: London, 3–5; Westminister Abbey, 6–11; Holland, 12–15; Belgium, 16–21; Paris, 23–26; Spain, 27–32; Venice, 33–36; Mt. Vesuvius, 37–41; Alpine village, 42–46; Moselle River, 47–52; Sweden, 53–59; Norway, 61–64; Quito, 67–72; Lima, 73–76; Venezuela, 77–81; Bolivia, 82–86; Brazil, 87–91; South American games, 92–96; a growing mountain, 97–101; Mexico, 102–112; Bahamas, 113–123; trip to Santo Domingo, 124–128; China, 132–140; Corea, 141–145; Japan, 147–159; Siam, 161–165; E. India, 166–182; Egypt, 183–187; ice-bergs, 195–199; gulf-stream, 201–206; kuro siwo, 207–209; trade winds, 210–213; mariner's compass, 214–219; Minot's ledge light, 220–224; buoys, 225–230; pilot-boat, 231–236; South Shoal light-ship, 237–243; ocean observatory, 244–248; U. S. life-saving service, 249–256.

316. **Child-life in Japan and Japanese child stories.** *Mrs.* M. Chaplin Ayrton. *Ed.* by William Elliot Griffis. Bost., D. C. Heath & Co., 1901. 70 p. il. D. cl.. .20 .18

"Many years ago Mrs. M. Chaplin Ayrton published a large and costly book on Child Life in Japan. Mrs. Ayrton was a grad-

	List price.	Price to districts.

uate of Edinburgh University and had obtained the degrees of Bachelor of Letters and Bachelor of Science, besides studying medicine in Paris. Her little daughter was born in Japan and had a native nurse. The home life of Japan and the pictures and stories that amused the children in the "Land of the Rising Sun" appealed to Mrs. Ayrton especially for her own child's sake. During her residence in Japan, she was always a keen and enthusiastic student of the country and its people. She translated some of the Japanese tales and the rest of her book is composed of her own studies, picturing with true and sympathetic pen the quaint life of old Japan. Dr. W. E. Griffis, who was active in introducing our public school system into Japan and whose own writings on things Japanese are considered authoritative, has made an interesting compilation from Mrs. Ayrton's book, retaining the best parts and reproducing all of the pictures, which were drawn and engraved by Japanese artists." The result is a little book of much interest and value.

317. [285.] (238.) **Great American Industries.** Vol. 1. Minerals. W. F. Rocheleau. Chic., A. Flanagan, 1896. 192 p. il. D. cl. .... .50 .30

A book which will prove of value in the teaching of geography. It treats of the minerals, how they are obtained, and how prepared for use.

References: Coal, 7–44; petroleum, 45–68; natural gas, 69–74; iron and steel, 75–112; marble, 113–134; granite, 135–155; slate, 152–162; gold and silver, 163–192.

318. [286.] (239.) **Great American industries.** Vol. 2. Products of the soil. W. F. Rocheleau. Chic., A. Flanagan & Co., 1898. 178 p. il. D. cl.... .50 .30

Books on industries are very difficult to find and yet there is no line of geography so valuable and so interesting to pupils.

References: Lumber, 7–50; sugar, 51–88; cotton, 89–123; cereals, 124–178.

319. [287.] **Great American industries.** Vol. 3. Manufactures. W. F. Rocheleau. Chic., A. Flanagan Co., 1900. 236 p. il. D. cl.................... .50 .30

Valuable for work in geography.

References: Motors, 7–36; glass, 37–74; leather, 75–80; boots and shoes, 81–99; dressed meat, 100–125; pins and needles, 127–132; lead pencils, 132–136; pens, 136–140; paper, 141–159; printing, 160–192; newspapers, 193–221; books, 222–236.

320. [273.] (224.) **Guyot geographical reader and primer.** Mary H. S. Pratt. N. Y., American Book Company, 1898. 282 p. il. D. cl.................... .60 .51

A very interesting and valuable book for the classes in geography.

References: North America: Upper Mississippi, 26–32; Lower Mississippi, 33–37; Hudson, 27–46; Erie canal and Great Lakes,

	List price.	Price to districts.

46-50; St. Lawrence, 52-56; Lake Champlain and the Adirondacks, 56-58; New England, 59-63; Rocky Mountain country, 63-66; Sierra Nevada, 66-70; California, 70-74; Northwest, 75-77; Canada, 78-82; Southern States, 82-85; West Indies, 86-88.

South America: Amazon, 89-93; Silvas, 93-97; Andes, 97-102; Llanos, 102-104; La Plata, 105-108; Atlantic Ocean, 108-112. Other countries: England, 113-119; Scotland and Ireland, 119-122; France, 122-130; Netherlands, 131-133; Denmark, Sweden, and Norway, 133-134; Spain, 135-140; Italy, 140-145; Switzerland, 145-150; Germany, 150-153; Turkey in Europe, 155-157; Greece, 157; Russia, 158-159; Sahara, 160-163; Egypt, 163-166; Turkey in Asia, 167-168; Arabia, 169; Persia, 170; Indies, 171-172; China, 173-176; Middle Asia, 176-179; Australia, 180-182; Pacific Ocean, 182-183.

321. **Home geography and the earth as a whole.** Ralph S. Tarr, *and* Frank M. McMurry. N. Y., Macmillan Co., 1901. 279 p. il. D. cl. (Tarr & McMurray's geographies: first book) .... .60   .54

Teachers in the lower form will find in this book much material that will be suggestive and helpful to them in the teaching of home geography.

References: Geography, soil, 1-9; Hills, 10-16; Mountains, 17-27; Valleys, 28-38; Rivers, 39-52; Lakes, 53-61; Ocean, 62-70; Air, 71-80; Commerce, 81-91; Government, p. 92-101; Maps, 102-10; Earth, 111-36; United States, 141-87; Alaska, 188-89; South America, 199-206; Europe, 207-29; Asia, 230-41; Africa, 242-48; Australia, 249-55; Geography-Bibliography, 256-61.

322. **North America: with an especially full treatment of the United States and its dependencies.** Ralph S. Tarr, *and* Frank M. McMurry. N. Y., Macmillan Co., 1901. 469 p. il. maps. D. cl. (Tarr & McMurry's geographies: second book.) .75   .68

The series of which this is the second book will furnish an excellent source of reference material to use to supplement the outline given in the general text book in geography.

The accounts given in the average text of the leading industries of a country are short and inadequate. In these books they are discussed more in detail in connection with the sections of a country in which they are most prominent.

One very excellent feature of these books is a selected list of references in the back of each volume suggesting further readings in geography and travel, that may be carried on to supplement the study of the text. These reference lists will be of great value to the teacher.

References: United States, 121-349; North America (in general), 1-120; Alaska, 323-30; Cuba and Porto Rico, 330-36; Hawaiian islands, 336-40; Philippine islands, 341-49; Mexico, 378-88; Central America, 389-92; West Indies, 393-98; Bermudas, 399-400; Canada, 351-371; Newfoundland, 351-71.

LIST OF BOOKS FOR TOWNSHIP LIBRARIES. 83

                                                                              Price
                                                                           List to dis-
                                                                          price. tricts.

323. [169.] (140.) **Land of pluck.** Mary Mapes Dodge. N. Y., Century Co., 1894. 313 p. D. cl............ 1.50 .88

    The first part is devoted to stories and sketches of Holland, which portray the life most vividly. Valuable in geography.

324. **Little journeys to Alaska and Canada,** for Intermediate and Upper Grades. Marian M. George. Chic., A. Flanagan Co., c1901. 80+94 p. il. D. (Library of Travel.) cl.................... .50 .36

    References: Location and history of Alaska, Part I, 4-11; Climate, 11-12; Sitka, 20-25; Alaskan Indians, 25-36; 44-45; Mission schools, 36-42; Juneau, 42-44; Klondike region, 49-52; Muir glacier, 52-55; Salmon fishing, 57-61; Seal-hunting, 61-65; Eskimos, 69-80; Canada, Part 2, 5-93.

325. **Little journeys to Cuba and Puerto Rico,** for Intermediate and Upper Grades. Marian M. George. Chic., A. Flanagan Co., c1900. 80+79 p. il. D. (Library of Travel). cl....................... .50 .36

    References on Cuba: Location and history of Cuba, Part I, 5-7, 8-10; Climate, 7-8; Havana, 11-15; Cuban homes, 15-20; Manners and customs, 20-26; Education, 27-28; Religion, 28-30; Amusements, 30-31; Child life, 32-36; Modes of transportation, 36-38; Animal life, 55-65; Sugar making, 67-69; Coffee, 69-71; Tobacco, 72-73.
    References on Puerto Rico: Location and history, Part 2, 3-7; Homes, 23-27; Child life, 31-33; Education, 33-34; Animal life, 64-67; Plant life, 68-76.

326. **Little journeys to Hawaii and the Philippine Islands,** for Intermediate and Upper Grades. Marian M. George. Chic., A. Flanagan Co., c1900. 88+88 p. il. D. (Library of Travel.) cl.............. .50 .36

    References to Hawaii: Lcation and history, Part I, 3-21, 34-48; Honolulu, 21-31; Occupations, manners and customs, 48-51; Child life, 53-56; Modes of transportation, 58-59; Father Damien, 61-63; Volcano of Kilauea, 68-70; Animal life, 74-76; Plant life, 77-86.
    References to Philippines: History and location, Part 2, 3-19; International date line, 21-22; Manila, 28-46; Schools, 46-49; Homes, 50-51; Animal life, 80-83; Plant life, 83-86.

327. [275.] (226.) **Little people of Asia.** Olive Thorne Miller. (*Mrs.* Harriet Mann Miller.) N. Y. E. P. Dutton & Co., 1896. 405 p. il. O. cl......... 2.50 1.45

    A vivid account of the dress, homes, surroundings, games and schools of the children of Asia.
    References: Turkish life, 16-59; Syrian life, 60-97; Persian life, 98-116; Hindu life, 130-188; Tibetan life, 189-201; Tartar life, 203-222; Siamese life, 223-261; Siberian life, 262-280; Eskimo life, 280-295; Chinese life, 301-359; Japanese life 360-405.

	Price
List	to dis-
price.	tricts.

328. [276a.] (229.) **Lost in the jungle.** Paul Du Chaillu.
N. Y., Harper & Bros., 1869. 260 p. il. D. cl.   1.00   .58

Most interesting accounts of adventures in Africa. The natives, animal and vegetable life are described. Boys are especially fond of these books.

329. [278.] (235.) **Our country: East.** Bost., Perry Mason & Co., 1898. 256 p. il. O. cl...........   .50   .40

Descriptions of interesting places and industries in the eastern and southern parts of the U. S. by various good writers.
References: Harnessing Niagara, 3-8; St. Clair tunnel, 9-15; winter-fishing on Saginaw Bay, 16-19; dog-sledges in Michigan, 20-23; Ishpeming dog race, 24-27; Wisconsin skate-sail, 28-30; trip to Lake Superior, 31-34; hop-picking in Central N. Y., 35-57; charcoal burners, 38-40; Natural gas, 41-45; oil-country crater, 46-49; mound builders, 50-56; Mammoth cave, 57-64; New Orleans, 67-72; Galveston, 73-76; lights of the Florida reefs, 86-90; Florida everglades, 96-100; a tree that builds islands, 101-105; pine-apples, 106-110; the purseweb spider, 111-116; a southern village, 121-122; St. Augustine, 123-128; the Capitol, Washington, D. C., 131-135; Mount Vernon, 137-140; Washington's birthplace, 141-143; on the Caroline banks, 149-153; Georgia Crackers, 154-159; peanuts, 160-164; Chesapeake oysters, 165-169; statue of Liberty, 179-181; Brooklyn bridge, 183-186; Grant monument, 187-189; elevated railroads, 190-192; Plymouth Rock, 193-199; Provincetown, 200-204; Newport, 211-213; Boston market, 219-224; maple-sugar camp, 225-228; a N. H. fish-farm, 229-232; among the pines, 233-237; winter harvest, 238-243; moose-calling, 244-250; fox-hunting in N. E., 251-256.

330. [279.] (236.) **Our country: West.** Bost., Perry Mason & Co., 1897. 256 p. il. O. cl...........   .50   .40

Fine descriptions of our western country by various writers.
References: Alaska, 3-11, 21-52; salmon fishing, 17-20; sea lions, 53-56; sea-otter, 57-64; Bighorn canon, 67-72; hunting elk, 73-77; Yellowstone park, 78-85; Rocky Mountain burros, 86-89; Chinese railway laborers, 90-95; some Rocky Mountain animals, 96-101; digging up a fossil monster, 106-111; petrified tree, 112-116; Holy Cross and Twin Lakes, 117-120; Pike's Peak, 121-128; big trees of California, 132-133; the Sierras, 135-142; California raisin-making, 143-147; Death Valley, 149-152; Nevada, 153-156; Pyramid Lake, 157-160; Grand canon, 161-166; cave-dwellers of Arizona, 167-172; the oldest American houses, 178-182; New Mexico, 183-188; adobe, 189-192; prairie schooner, 195-196; prairies signs, 197-202; pioneer life in Dakota, 203-207; coyote, 209-211; boy-life on the prairie, 212-216; ranch life, 217-221; cowboys, 222-227; great cattle-trails, 228-232; language of cattle-brands, 233-235; water cactus, 249-251.

… | List price. | Price to districts. |

331. [280.] (231.) **Picturesque geographical reader.** 2d Bk. This continent of ours. Charles F. King. Bost., Lee & Shepard, 1891. 315 p. il. D. cl... | .72 | .58 |

References: Cold countries, 1-20; mountains, 21-45, 80-89; Yellowstone park, 46-57; central plain, 59-72; Mississippi river, 98-108; Columbia and grand cañon, 109-119; Great Lakes, 129-139; Canada, 140-200; Mexico, 252-286; West Indies, 288-305; the atmosphere, 73-97; climate, 120-128.

332. [281.] (232.) **Picturesque geographical reader.** 3d Bk. The land we live in. Charles F. King. Bost., Lee & Shepard, 1892. 227 p. il. D. cl... .56 .46

The third book of this series is devoted to the New England and Middle States, and the fourth to the Middle, Central and Southern States.

333. [282.] (233.) **Picturesque geographical readers.** 4th Bk. The land we live in. Charles F. King. Bost., Lee & Shepard, 1893. 235 p. il. D. cl... .56 .46

References: South to Florida, 1-16; New Orleans, 17-30; Mississippi river, 31-42; St. Louis, 43-50; Pittsburg and iron, 51-60; oil fields, 61-69; coal mines, 71-86; American schools, 87-105; along the shore of New England, 106-119; among lighthouses, 106-138; Chicago, 138-148; domestic commerce, 159-172; railroads, 173-196; Indian reservations, 197-208.

334. [277.] (644.) **South America.** Frank G. Carpenter. N. Y., American Book Company, 1899. 352 p. il. D. cl. .... .60 .51

An interesting account of life in South America. Not only is the life graphically described but the great industries have received special attention. Most of the descriptions were written on the ground and a large number of pictures are from photographs made by the author. The volume is a fit companion for North America and Asia by the same author. Every library ought to own a set of Carpenter geographical readers.
References: Isthmus of Panama, 16-29; Republic of Columbia, 29-38; land of the Equator, 38-50; great desert, 50-58; Lima, 58-66; the Andes, 67-72; Peru, 72-86; Batavia, 87-100; Chile, 100-167; Argentina and Patagonia, 167-200; Uruguay, 201-217; Paraguay, 218-241; Brazil, 243-327; Venezuela, 327-342; The Guianas, 342-350.

335. [276.] (228.) **Wild life under the equator.** Paul Du Chaillu. N. Y., Harper & Bros., 1868. 231 p. il. D. cl. .... 1.00 .58

		List price.	Price to districts.
336.	[283.] (234.) **World and its people.** Bk. 3. Our own country. Minna C. Smith. Bost., Silver, Burdett & Co., 1892. 217 p. il. D. cl..........	.50	.45

An interesting account of the geography of the United States which younger children in this form can read for themselves.

| 337. | **World and its people.** Book 10. South American Republics. W. Fisher Markwick, *and* William A. Smith. N. Y., Silver, Burdett & Co., c1901. 348 p. il. D. cl. .... | .60 | .54 |

References: Columbus, 1–12; General features, 16–25; Colombia, 31–56; Venezuela, 56–94; Ecuador, 95–117; Peru, 117–153; Bolivia, 154–173; Brazil, 173–220; Amazon valley, 200–213; Argentine Republic, 227–72; Paraguay, 272–86; Uruguay, 286–300; Chile, 301–27; Guiana, 327–34.

SCIENCE.

All reading in these books should be accompanied by observations. Teacher and pupils must read many of the books together and the reading must be accompanied by observation. Do not expect the children to read from cover to cover. They will read only such portions are they are interested in. Aim to make the child quick to see, accurate in his observations, accurate and logical in his statements. See Manual, *Nature lessons—Primary and Middle Forms.*

Many books of the primary form may be used by children of this form.

Here is good material for language work. See Manual, *Language—Middle Form.*

	List price.	Price to districts.
338. [258.] (209.) **Animal story book.** *Ed.* by Andrew Lang. N. Y., Longmans, Green & Co., 1896. 400 p. il. D. cl.	2.00	1.25

A collection of stories which will please children interested in animals.

339. **Fowls of the air.** William J. Long. Bost., Ginn & Co., 1901. 310 p. il. D. cl.	1.75	1.17

340. **Beasts of the field.** William J. Long. Bost., Ginn & Co., 1901. 332 p. il. D. cl.	1.75	1.17

The two books "Beasts of the field" and "Fowls of the air" include many of the sketches given in Long's previous books, "Ways of wood folk," "Wilderness ways," and "Secrets of the woods." They contain enough new material to give a wide range of acquaintance with the wood folk. The beautiful illustrations in these books will attract the attention of the child and lead him to read the stories.

Schools should make a selection between these two sets of books and not purchase both unless the library is large enough to make the purchase of duplicates advisable. This set is the more expensive because of the beautiful illustrations.

LIST OF BOOKS FOR TOWNSHIP LIBRARIES.

	List price.	Price to districts.
341. [266.] (218.) **Buz; or, The life and adventures of a honey bee.** Maurice Noel. N. Y., Henry Holt & Co., 1892. 134 p. il. D. cl........................	1.00	.65

Life of the bee told in story form. The younger children in upper form will enjoy it.

342. **Everyday birds: elementary studies.** Bradford Torrey. Bost., Houghton, Mifflin & Co., 1901. 106 p. il. D. cl.	1.00	.65

"Everyday Birds' is a collection of sketches of a number of well-known birds, some biographical, and others general, in character. The volume is an interesting bird-study book, written in a manner to interest children and older people in birds and bird-life. The illustrations include twelve colored plates from Audubon—the first considerable reproduction of the colored drawings from the "Birds" of that author. Mr. Torrey combines entire scientific accuracy with much literary charm, and readers of all ages will find it delightfully interesting."

Contents: Two little kings, 1-6; Chickadee, 7-9; Brown creeper, 10-14; Brown thrasher, 15-18; Butcher-bird, 19-21; Scarlet tanager, 22-25; Song sparrow, 26-29; Field sparrow and the chipper, 30-34; Some April sparrows, 35-39; Rose-breasted grossbeak, 40-42; Blue jay, 43-46; King bird, 47-50; Hummingbird, 51-55; Chimney swift, 56-58; Nighthawk and whip-poor-will, 59-63; Flicker, 64-67; Bittern, 68-81; Birds for everybody, 82-86; Winter pensioners, 87-92; Watching the procession, 93-98; Southward bound, 99-105.

343. [262.] **First book of birds.** Olive Thorne Miller. (*Mrs.* Harriet Mann Miller.) School ed. Bost., Houghton, Mifflin & Co., 1900. il sq. D. cl...	.60	.50

A book of birds which will interest young children in the ways and habits of birds, and stimulate them to habits of observation. It is one of the best of its kind in the market. To add to the interest, the birds are studied from the standpoint of the child, and the book deals with the things he is sure to be interested in. For instance, the bird's language is discussed, what he eats, where he sleeps, his education, how he changes his clothes, etc., etc. Material will be valuable in primary form.

344. **Flowers and their friends.** Margaret Warner Morley. Bost., Ginn & Co., 1901. 255 p. il. D. cl..	.50	.42

A collection of interesting stories about flowers. Observation of the flowers by teacher and pupils should accompany the reading of these stories.

Contents: Morning-glory stories; Stories about the geranium family; Hyacinth stories; Stories about all sorts of things.

LIST OF BOOKS FOR TOWNSHIP LIBRARIES. 89

	Price
List	to dis-
price.	tricts.

345. [267.] (219.) **Glimpses at the plant world.** Fannie D. Bergen. Bost., Ginn & Co., 1891. 156 p. il. S. cl. .... .50 .41

    Descriptions of a number of common plants.
    References: Plant cells, Chap. 2; mould, Chap. 3; toadstools, Chap. 4; some other flowerless plants, Chap. 5; sea plants, Chaps. 7 and 8; ferns, Chaps. 10 and 11; cacti, Chap. 12; flax, Chap. 13; parts of a flower, Chap. 15; how seeds are perfected, Chap. 16; how pollen is carried, Chap. 17; some pollen carriers, Chap. 18; how seeds travel, Chaps. 24-27.

346. [265.] (643.) **Insect world:** a reading book of entomology. Clarence Moores Weed. N. Y., D. Appleton & Co., 1899. 210 p. il. D. (Appleton's home reading books.) cl. .... .60 .50

    A series of articles especially adapted to interest and instruct young people in the habits and life-histories of insects. Must be read with the teacher and accompanied by observations. Will be of value in upper form.
    References: Dragon fly, 1-2, 45-53; transformation of insects, 2-6; what is an insect, 7-11; small size of insects, 19-22; internal structures of insects, 23-37; the May fly, 37-45; white ants, 54-61; insects of the fields, 67-69; true bugs, 77-79; poplar-leaf gall-louse, 85-91; caterpillars, 92-98; butterflies, 99-106; habits of cut-worms, 125-132; moths, 136-142; mosquitoes, 154-160; house flies, 161-166; beetles, 167-173; meal worms, 174-176; fire-fly, 184; bees and flowers, 188-191; insects and flowers, 192-194; the honey bee, 200-207.

347. [264.] (217.) **Little brothers of the air.** Olive Thorne Miller. (*Mrs.* Harriet Mann Miller.) Bost., Houghton, Mifflin & Co., 1898. 271 p. D. cl.... 1.25 .78

    A very interesting account of birds for young people. Valuable because arousing in children a love for birds. See index of book.

348. [260.] (207.) **Little folks in feathers and fur.** Olive Thorne Miller. (*Mrs.* Harriet Mann Miller.) N. Y., E. P. Dutton & Co., 1891. 368 p. il. O. cl... 2.50 1.45

    A collection of sketches, telling what is interesting for anyone to know, about a few of the millions of creatures on our globe. It was written for the little people, but will not be without interest to any one who is curious about the ways of our little neighbors, and who does not already know too much about them.— *From the Preface.*

	List price.	Price to districts.

349. [257.] (641.) **Lobo, Rag, and Vixen, and pictures.** Ernest Seton Thompson. N. Y., C: Scribner's Sons, 1899. 147 p. il. D. (Scribner's ser. of school reading.) cl. .... .60 .50

The personal histories of Lobo, Redruff, Raggylug, and Vixen.—Selections suitable for young children from Thompson's "Wild animals I have known," one of the best collections of animal stories ever written. These stories are intensely interesting, and will surely awaken an interest in, and love for animal life.

350. **Mr. Chupes and Miss Jenny:** the life story of two robins. Effie Bignell. N. Y., Baker & Taylor Co., c1901. 250 p. il. D. cl..................... 1.00 .65

A charming account of the history of two robins in captivity who became at first the involuntary companions of people, and whose affection for their benefactress made them unwilling to leave her for a life of freedom. The story has been told by a bird lover in a fascinating manner and shows the keenest love and sympathy for bird life. It is a true robin history and shows the character and temperament of the robin.

The book is worth reading as a study of bird life and as a pleasing story.

"No sweeter, more sympathetic story of animal life has ever been written than that which is contained in this little book. Rudyard Kipling and Seton-Thompson have opened up for us a new literature, in which animals play the principal parts. This little story of Mrs. Bignell's is a worthy companion of the master pieces of those famous authors." Dr. David Murray.

351. [269.] **Mother Nature's children.** Allen Walton Gould. Bost., Ginn & Co., 1900. 261 p. il. D. cl. .... .60 .50

A book that aims to help the young to see the spirit rather than the form of nature.

352. [263.] (215.) **Our feathered friends.** Elizabeth Grinnell *and* Joseph Grinnell. Bost., D. C. Heath & Co., 1898. 144 p. il. D. cl....:................,.. .30 .27

A very interesting book on birds which the younger children can read.

References: Mocking bird, 2–10; crow black bird, 11; turkey buzzard, 15; linnet, 30; humming birds, 35; blue jays, 38; woodpeckers, 42; king bird, 51; English sparrow, 55; song sparrow, 64; Baltimore oriole, 75; owl, 77–86; barn swallow, 87; cat bird, 94; brown thrush, 95; robin, 108; whip-poor-will, 121; meadow lark, 135; phoebe bird, 124.

LIST OF BOOKS FOR TOWNSHIP LIBRARIES. 91

	List price.	Price to districts.

353. [255.] (206.) **Outdoor studies.** James G. Needham. N. Y., American Book Company, 1898. 90 p. il. D. cl. .... .40 .34

This book is for children who have observed some and are interested in things around them, as it calls for closer observation than the books indicated in the primary list. Children of upper form will enjoy the book.
References: Chipmunks, Chap. 2; galls, Chap. 3; goldenrod and its visitors, Chap. 4; crows, Chap. 5; dragon flies, Chap. 6; ant lions, Chap. 8.

354. **Second book of birds:** Bird families. Olive Thorne Miller. Bost., Houghton, Mifflin & Co., 1901. 209 p. il. D. cl. .... 1.00 .90

"This book is intended to stimulate interest in the study of bird life among young people. It considers the many families of North American birds, excluding game birds, explaining clearly and succinctly why these birds are thus grouped and how the families may be distinguished. The most prominent and interesting members of the several families are chosen to represent them, and personal accounts of these, their habits and customs and anecdotes concerning them, are given. The book has been made comprehensive by selecting in a family an Eastern, a Western, and a Southern bird; or one bird to represent the family in cases where that bird is common to all sections. The book is thus made useful in all parts of the United States, and, being profusely illustrated, is pictorially interesting as well as descriptively valuable in a study of the bird families of North America. Illustrated with twenty-four full-page pictures, eight of which are drawn in color by Louis Agassiz Fuertes."
Contents: What is a bird family? 1-4; Thrush family, 5-13; Kinglet and gnatcatcher family, 14-17; Nuthatch and chickadee family, 18-26; Creeper family, 27-29; Cave-dwelling family, 30-41; Dipper family, 42-45; Wagtail family, 46-48; Warbler family, 49-54; Vireo family, 55-58; Shrike family, 59-62; Waxwing family, 63-66; Swallow family, 69-74; Tanager family, 75-79; Sparrow and finch family, 80-85; Grosbeaks, 86-89; Crossbills, 91-93; Blackbirds, 94-99; Meadow starlings, 100-101; Orioles, 104-109; Crow-blackbirds, 110-116; Crows, 117-130; Larks, 131-134; Flycatching family, 135-142; Hummingbirds, 143-149; Swift family, 150-154; Goatsucker family, 155-159; Woodpeckers, 160-169; Kingfishers, 170-173; Cuckoos, 174-177; Owls, 178-186; Hawk and eagle family, 188-193; Scavenger family 194-196.

355. **Secrets of the woods.** William J. Long. Bost., Ginn & Co., 1901. 184 p. il. D. (Wood Folk ser., Book three.) cl. .... .50 .42

Stories of the wild creatures of the fields and woods. The third in the series of which "Ways of wood folk" and "Wilderness ways" were the first and second volumes.
References: Wood mouse, p. 3-22; Otter, p. 27-53; King fisher, p. 54-72; Squirrel, p. 73-102; Partridge, p. 103-127; Deer, p. 128-184.

	List price.	Price to districts.

356. [256.] (214.) **Short stories of our shy neighbors.** Mrs. M. A. B. Kelly. N. Y., American Book Company, 1896. 214 p. il. D. cl.................... .50 .43

Nature studies, treating of the form, structure, color, and habits of the most familiar animals the child is apt to meet in every day life. This book can be made most valuable if supplemented by careful observation. It will train the child's observation besides creating an interest in his surroundings. Teachers will find the book very helpful as it points out what to observe.

The material gathered by observation may be used with profit in the language lessons. See Manual, Par. 60.

References: Fox and dog, 203-205; chipmunk, 200-201; squirrels, 202-205, 211-214; weasel, 205-207; hare, 207-209; muskrat, 209-211; mice, 92-98; wood mice, 198-200; robin, 79-84; phoebe bird, 22-30; brown thrasher, 56-61; chicken hawks, 122-129; blue birds and blue jay, 158-164; chickadee, 182-185; nut hatch, 185-187; woodpeckers, 187-189, 192-193; wrens, 190-191, 194-196; grouse, 196-198; frogs, 41-50; toads, 108-111; crayfish, 67-71; moths, 7-14, 36-40, 61-67, 76-79; butterflies, 15-22, 51-56; flies, 84-91; grasshoppers, 98-102; bees, 142-155; crickets, 103-108; dragon flies, 155-158; ants, 114-122; squash bug, 131-135; beetles, 135-139; spiders, 168-180; snails, 164-167; tent caterpillar, 30-35; water bugs, 72-76.

357. [254.] (640.) **Stories of animal life.** Charles Frederick Holder. N. Y., American Book Company, 1899. 261 p. il. S. cl........................ .60 .51

Stories of animal life derived mainly from the personal experience of the author. Interesting, striking, and unusual phases of animal life are presented. Some of the older children in primary form will be able to read this book.

References: The bear's story, 7-11; the fox, 33-39; pelicans, 39-45; the greyhound, 46-57; games of animals, 66-73; a whale, 73-77; a humming bird, 78-86; elephants, 96-108, 123-133; baby birds, 108-115; jelly fish, 133-139; dragon flies, 147-153; animal mimics, 153-159; a dog's trip around the world, 160-167; how animals talk, 178-188; home of a fish, 194-202; sword fish, 208-217; fishes out of water, 239-247; birds of the ocean, 247-255.

357a. **Summer of Saturdays:** an account of familiar acquaintances in field, forest and stream, as interpreted by a boy enthusiast. Chester W. Smith. Milwaukee, S. Y. Gillan & Co., c1900. 175 p. D. cl. .... .65 .56

An interesting story for Library Reading.

358. [261.] (213.) **Talks about animals.** Bost., Perry Mason & Co., 1895. 256 p. il. O. cl............. .50 .40

Interesting talks about animals by some of our best writers.

References: Lobsters and lobstering, 3-6; mackerel and cod, 7-15; swordfish, 17-20; Scotch herring fishery, 21-24; sardines,

	List price.	Price to districts.

25-28; catching sharks, 29-33; sturgeon, 35-38; whale, 39-44; fiddlers and hermits, 45-51; seal, 53-56; where sponges grow, 57-64; bird life, 67-73; oriole, 74-78; crow, 79-85; robin, 86-91; red-headed woodpecker, 93-96; carrier-pigeon, 97-102; partridge, 103-109; ostrich-farming, 110-115; ruby-throated humming-bird, 117-121; owls, 122-128; spider, 131-136; bee-keeping, 137-143; silk-worms, 145-149; frogs and toads, 151-153; chameleon lizards, 155-159; newt, 160-164; bats, 165-169; flying squirrel, 170-173; chipmunk, 174-176; prairie-dog, 177-181; gophers, 182-185; mantis, 187-192; elephant, 195-202; wild animal farm, 203-209; crocodiles and alligators, 211-216; some Australian animals, 217-220; muskrat, 221-225; beaver, 226-230; monkey, 231-239; Indian snakes and tigers, 240-248; wolverine, 249-256.

359. **Ten common trees.** Susan Stokes. N. Y., American Book Co., 1901. 108 p. il. D. (Eclectic school readings ser.) cl. .... .40 .34

Simple stories about trees.
References: Willow, p. 7-15; Elm, p. 16-24; Apple tree, p. 25-36; Horse-chestnut, p. 37-46; Birch tree, p. 47-54; Oak, p. 55-66; Chestnut trees, p. 67-71; Walnut trees, p. 72-79; Cone bearers, p. 80-93; Red maple, p. 94-104; Forests and their preservation, p. 105-108.

360. [270.] **Ways of wood folk.** William J. Long. Bost., Ginn & Co., 1899. 205 p. il. D. cl............. .50 .42

Records of personal observation in the woods and fields.

361. [259.] **Wilderness ways.** William J. Long. Bost., Ginn & Co., 1901. 154 p. il. D. cl. .45 .40

"These sketches are studies of animals, pure and simple—not animals with human motives and imaginations.'—*Author's preface.*

362. [262a.] **Woodpeckers.** Fannie Hardy Eckstorm. Bost., Houghton, Mifflin & Co., 1901. 131 p. il. D. cl. .... 1.00 .65

A complete and interesting account. Upper form pupils will enjoy.

COLLECTIONS.

	List price.	Price to districts.

363. [288.] (241.) **Choice literature.** Bk. 1. For intermediate grades. *Comp.* and *arr.* by Sherman Williams. N. Y., Butler, Sheldon & Co., 1898. 189 p. D. cl. .... .28 .25

364. [289.] (242.) **Choice literature.** Bk. 2. For intermediate grades. *Comp.* and *arr.* by Sherman Williams. N. Y., Butler, Sheldon & Co., 1898. 256 p. D. cl. .... .35 .32

The selections in these books are from the best in literature. Not only are the selections from the longer pieces of literature the best possible, but they are such as will certainly create an interest in the works from which they are taken. Fine books for supplementary reading.

365. **Cumnock's school speaker:** rhetorical recitations for boys and girls. *Comp.* by Robert McLean Cumnock. Chic., A. C. McClurg & Co., 1899. 303 p. D. cl. .... .75 .45

"One marked feature of this collection is the high character of the pieces and their good speaking qualities. There is no 'trashy' matter in the entire book; all of the selections are fresh and inspiring, worthy to be committed to memory."—*Boston Journal of Education.*

366. **School speaker and reader.** *Ed.* by William DeWitt Hyde. Bost., Ginn & Co., 1901. 474 p. D. cl... .80 .67

A good collection of selections for rhetoricals.

mary room, graded school at Athens, Marathon County, showing simple interior decorations. KATHRYN MAYNES, Teacher.

Reading room and library in High School building, Plymouth, Wis. OTTO GAFFRON, Principal.

UPPER FORM OR GRAMMAR GRADE.

FICTION.

No form of literature portrays life and character as fiction does. If the novel portrays life the aim should be to get a clear idea of the various things which go to make up the life of a people, occupations, amusements, etc., etc. (See "Fiction," middle form.) In the novel of character and character development the characters should be judged as characters in real life are, by what they do, what they think, what they love and hate, what their aspirations are, what they say, how other characters feel toward them, what people say of them. Actions should be judged by their results on the actor, and how they affect the happiness, well being, and conduct of others. If it is a novel of character development, in what ways has the character changed? What has brought about these changes?

Though the work in this form is essentially the same as in the other forms (see "Fiction," lower and middle forms), the pupils are better able to judge and reason and should be required to be more definite, and to form independent and more extended judgments. They should be asked for comparisons, and generalizations. Thus,—Compare the Saxons and Normans as portrayed in the novel, Ivanhoe. Compare the life of children in New England as portrayed in Three Little Daughters of the Revolution, and in the Diary of Anna Green Winslow. Compare characters of Meg, Beth and Jo as portrayed in Little Women.

In Captain January, the little girl sacrificed much because of her loyalty to the old lighthouse keeper who had saved her life and cared for her. The results of that action showed it is noble to be loyal.

In story of Sonny Sahib, Sonny would not betray the Maharajah to the English even at the risk of losing his own life because the Maharajah had saved his life and befriended him. The results showed the nobility of loyalty.

In Little Jarvis, Jarvis gave his life on account of his loyalty to duty.

After reading these stories the pupils readily make the generalization—it is noble to be loyal. Again, in the novel Silas Marner, each time that Silas Marner selfishly loves and gives his whole energy to what is ignoble he becomes like the thing he loves. It is not until he loves a little child unselfishly that he begins to grow to be a good man. The generalization from that novel is, "If a man loves that which is noble it will make him noble. If his affection is centered on an ignoble thing, it will make him ignoble."

An opportunity for the children to express their thoughts on what they are interested in is the best kind of language teaching.

	List price.	Price to districts.
367. [339.] (658.) **Adventures of a freshman.** Jesse Lynch Williams. N. Y., C: Scribner's Sons, 1899. 201 p. il. D. cl.	1.25	.82

An interesting account of a boy's freshman year in college.

| 368. [319.] **Almost as good as a boy.** Amanda M. Douglas. Bost., Lee & Shepard, 1900. 375 p. il. D. cl. | 1.25 | .75 |

A good story for girls. Teaches self-reliance.

| 369. **Barbara's heritage, or, young Americans among the old Italian masters.** Deristhe L. Hoyt. Bost., W. A. Wilde Co., c1899. 358 p. il. D. cl. | 1.50 | .85 |

The story of an American woman and her son and daughter who take a trip to Italy. They are accompanied by two young girls.

Their personal experiences and the history of the art treasures they study together, with the illustrations, make a book full of valuable information.

		Price
	List	to dis-
	price.	tricts.

370. [293.] (249.) **Boyhood in Norway.** Hjalmar H. Boyesen. N. Y., Chas. Scribner's Sons, 1898. 243 p. il. D. cl. .... 1.25   .82

Stories of boy-life in the land of the midnight sun. Fine descriptions of Norway, 15–16, 34, 39, 43, 119.

371. **Boy's life at school: Cuore:** the diary of a school boy. Edmondo de Amicis. *Tr.* by Oscar Durante. Chic., Henneberry Co., c1901. 357 p. il. D. cl. 1.00   .40

An Italian school boy kept a diary of what he saw, felt, and thought in and out of school for a year. At the end of the year his father wrote this book from the boy's diary, preserving as far as possible the words of his son. It is intensely interesting, and will inspire the children reading it to live nobler lives.

372. **Boys of Fairport.** Noah Brooks. N. Y., C: Scribner's Sons, 1899. 266 p. il. D. cl. .... 1.25   .82

A story of boy life recounting their adventures on the baseball field and in other sports.

This book was originally published with the title of "The Fairport nine." but has been revised and several new chapters have been added.

373. [317.] (266.) **Cadet days.** *Capt.* Charles King. N. Y., Harper & Bros., 1894. 293 p. il. D. cl. .... 1.25   .80

A story of West Point.

374. **Camp venture:** a story of the Virginia mountains. George Cary Eggleston. Bost., Lothrop Pub. Co., c1901. 401 p. il. D. cl. .... 1.50   .88

"A party of boy friends, residing in a hill town of south-western Virginia, undertake a contract to supply to a new railroad company a certain amount of logs for railroad ties, to be cut on the property of the mother of two of the boys, on one of the "high mountains" of Virginia. They spend the winter at this work, building their log home on the mountain top, and calling it Camp Venture. The boys are all strong, sturdy, and reliable young fellows, who know what they are about. They have, as companion, a young doctor who joins them for his health, and is a boy with them, sharing their labors, their dangers, and their successes. These dangers, especially from the Moonshiners of the mountains, form a prominent part of the tale; and their experiences with them, and with the revenue officers and soldiers who invade the mountain region about Camp Venture, are full of exciting interest. How the boys succeed in spite of privations and discouragements, how they fill their contract and come upon greater and unexpected success, is capitally told by Mr. Eggleston in his very interesting story of pluck and effort."

	List price.	Price to districts.

375. **Captain of the crew.** Ralph Henry Barbour. N. Y., D. Appleton & Co., 1901. 279 p. il. D. cl..... 1.20 1.08

"In this as in the two preceding volumes of the series,—"The Half-Back" and "For the honor of the school"—an attempt is made to show that athletics rightly indulged in is beneficial to the average boy and is an aid rather than a detriment to study. In it, a plea is made for honesty and simplicity in sports." *From the Introduction.*

This series of books contain many interesting anecdotes of school life and the boys in the story are typical American boys, just such as we find in our schools today. Boys will enjoy these stories because they deal with phases of life with which they are familiar and in which they are interested.

376. [295.] (646.) **Cattle ranch to college:** the true tale of a boy's adventures in the far west. Russell Doubleday. N. Y., Doubleday, Page & Co., 1899. 347 p. il. D. cl. .... 1.50 .90

A true account of the amusements, trials, work, and play of a boy in the West twenty-five years ago. Much valuable material for work in geography.

377. [330.] (283.) **Christmas carol,** *and* **The Cricket on the Hearth.** Charles Dickens. Bost., Houghton, Mifflin & Co., 1893. 118, 112 p. D. cl......... .60 .50

378. [351.] **Chronicles of Sir John Froissart,** condensed for young readers, *by* Adam Singleton. N. Y., D. Appleton & Co., 1900. 235 p. D. (Appleton's home reading books.) cl. .... .75 .60

These old stories of the fourteenth century ought to be made familiar to the children. They are well selected and well told.

379. [329.] (282.) **City boys in the woods.** Henry P. Wells. N. Y., Harper & Bros., 1889. 277 p. il. O. cl. 2.50 1.50

A trapping venture in Maine.

380. **Crisis.** Winston Churchill. N. Y., Macmillan Co., 1901. 522 p. il. D. cl. .... 1.50 .96

This book should be read by every child who is studying United States history. It will give to them a new and vivid picture of Lincoln. It also gives pictures of the typical Northern and Southern soldier and of life in the South at the time of the Civil war.

The text and reference books in history lack in point of vivid and dramatic interest and should be supplemented by books like the "Crisis."

"A vivid picture of the events leading up to our Civil War, particularly as seen in St. Louis. Colonel Carvel and his daughter Virginia, descendants of "Richard Carvel," are the central characters. They represent the rich, refined southerners, believing in state rights. Contrasting is Stephen Brice, a Boston lawyer, called "a black republican," who is a rival of a Confederate officer for Virginia's hand. Lincoln, Douglas, Sherman, Grant and other men, who afterward became famous are brought in."

	List price.	Price to districts.
381. [300.] (253.) **Crowded out o' Crofield.** W. O. Stoddard. N. Y., D. Appleton & Co., 1895. 261 p. il. D. cl.	1.50	.85

A good wholesome boy's story the reading of which will stimulate manliness and self-dependence.

382. [337.] (291.) **Deerslayer.** James Fenimore Cooper. N. Y., T. Y. Crowell & Co. 472 p. D. cl.	.60	.40
383. [327a.] **Dog-watches at sea.** Stanton H. King. Boston, Houghton, Mifflin & Co., 1901. 299 p. il. D. cl. (Riverside lit. ser.)	1.50	.90

One of the best sea stories.

384. [294.] (252.) **Donald and Dorothy.** Mary Mapes Dodge. N. Y., Century Co., 1898. 355 p. il. D. cl.	1.50	.88

An interesting story of a boy and his sister.

385. [323.] (267.) **Down the ravine.** Charles Egbert Craddock (Mary Noailles Murfree). Bost., Houghton, Mifflin & Co., 1897. 196 p. il. D. cl.	1.00	.60

Portrays life in the Tennessee mountains. Most beautiful descriptions of mountain scenery.

386. [313.] (261.) **Eight cousins.** Louisa M. Alcott. Bost., Little, Brown & Co., 1898. 291 p. il. S. cl.	1.50	.88

	List price.	Price to districts.

387. [332.] (286.) **Enchanted burro**: stories of New Mexico and South America. Charles F. Lummis. N. Y., Doubleday, Page & Co., 1897. 277 p. il. D. cl.   1.50   .88

A collection of most interesting short stories portraying life in New Mexico, Peru, and Bolivia.

388. [304.] (254.) **Five little Peppers grown up.** Margaret Sidney. (*Mrs.* H. M. Lothrop.) Bost., Lothrop Pub. Co., 1892. 537 p. il. D. cl. ....   1.50   .88

A sequel to Five Little Peppers Midway.

389. [299.] **For the honor of the school.** Ralph Henry Barbour. N. Y., D. Appleton & Co., 1900. 253 p. il. D. cl. ....   1.50   .85

A good story of school life and interscholastic sport.

390. [346.] **Gold-seeking on the Dalton trail.** Arthur R. Thompson. Bost., Little, Brown & Co., 1900. 352 p. il. D. cl. ....   1.50   .85

A timely story recording the experiences of two New England boys who accompanied their father and uncle on a trip into the Northwest gold regions, journeying along the Dalton trail toward the Klondike. Filled with hunting episodes.

391. [334.] (288.) **Gray champion, and other stories and - sketches.** Nathaniel Hawthorne. Bost., Houghton, Mifflin & Co., 1889. 278 p. S. (Riverside Aldine ser.) cl. ....   1.00   .65

392. [298.] (650.) **Half-back.** Ralph Henry Barbour. N. Y., D. Appleton & Co., 1899. 267 p. il. D. cl..   1.50   .85

A breezy wholesome story of football, and golf. The hero's life is portrayed at a preparatory school and, later, at college.

393. **Heart of the ancient wood.** Charles G. D. Roberts. N. Y., Silver, Burdett & Co., c1900. 276 p. il. D. cl. 1.50   1.08

A realistic romance of the folk of the forest and a pioneer's daughter whose home is in the depths of the ancient wood. The wild beasts of the wood become her friends and she learns to care more for them than for the human kind.

"The book stands alone—it is like no other. The talking beasts of the wondrous Jungle tales are fabulous. The thinking wild

animals Mr. Seton-Thompson has known are character-studies. But in "The Heart of the Ancient Wood" there is a problem drama. The imagination is subtler than in the adventures of Mowgli; the reportorial correctness is as unimpeachable as in the biography of Wahb; and in addition there is the fact of a master novelist turning to the unfathomed sympathies and dramatic possibilities of the relation of the human to the animal as seriously and as analytically as Mr. Howells turns to his familiar people."
—*The Criterion.*

394. [314.] (263.) **His level best and other stories.** Edward E. Hale. Bost., Little, Brown & Co., 1898. 293 p. S. cl. .... 1.50 .90

A collection of short stories.

395. **In the days of Audubon: a tale of the "protector of birds."** Hezekiah Butterworth. N. Y., D. Appleton & Co., 1901. 236 p. il. D. cl. 1.20 1.08

This story of Audubon's life and of his struggles in the pioneer days of the west is told in a vivid, dramatic manner that will appeal to the sympathies of children. Children who are interested in this story may be led to read some of the books about birds given in this list.

The story is intended to encourage the formation of societies for the protection of birds and the appendix gives suggestions on how to form Audubon societies and how to study the habits of birds.

An excellent book for all school libraries.

396. [347.] **Jack among the Indians.** George Bird Grinnell. N. Y., F. A. Stokes Co., 1900. 301. p. il. D. cl. .... 1.25 .70

A boy's summer on the buffalo plains.

397. **Lady Lee and other animal stories,** with an introductory memoir of the author by Francis F. Browne, editor of the "Dial." Hermon Lee Ensign. Chic., A. C. McClurg & Co., 1901. 256 p. il. O. cl. .. 2.00 1.34

This volume of stories gives the views which Mr. Ensign took of the duties of a human being to the dumb animals who are dependent on him and who cannot express in words their needs. During his life the author devoted himself actively to the cause of humanity toward domestic animals.

The reading of such sketches as "Lady Lee" and "My friend the elephant" will inspire one to do all within his power toward the protection of animals against ill-treatment.

The book contains many admirable illustrations and children will be intensely interested in it.

It is an excellent book for the teacher to read to the school and will lead to the reading of other books on the same and related subjects—Sarah Bolton's "Our devoted friend, the dog;" Patteson's "Pussy meow;" Roberts' "Heart of the ancient wood;" Holder's "Stories of animal life;" Long's "Beasts of the field;" and Thompson's "Lives of the hunted."

398. **Larry Hudson's ambition.** James Otis. (J. O. Kaler.) Bost., L. C. Page & Co., 1901. 261 p. il. D. cl. 1.25 .75

The story gives an attractive picture of life on a farm as contrasted with city life. Larry Hudson is a bootblack. Deacon Doak and his family on a visit to New York from the country, are befriended by the boy, and take him back home with them, giving him a chance to realize his ambition.

399. [322.] **Last of the flatboats;** a story of the Mississippi and its interesting family of rivers. George Cary Eggleston. Bost., Lothrop Pub. Co., 1900. 382 p. il. D. cl. .... 1.50 .85

The experiences of some boys who take a trip down the Mississippi in a flatboat.

400. [340.] (659.) **Life savers:** a story of the United States life-saving service. James Otis (J. O. Kaler). N. Y., E. P. Dutton & Co., 1899. 327 p. il. D. cl. .... 1.50 .85

A graphic portrayal of American life-saving service. Older children in middle form will enjoy.

401. **Little book of profitable tales.** Eugene Field. N. Y., C: Scribner's Sons, 1901. 286 p. D. cl......... 1.25 .82

A collection of some of Field's most beautiful short stories.
Contents: First Christmas tree; Symbol and the saint; Coming of the prince; Mouse and the moonbeam; Divell's Chrystmasse; Mountain and the sea; Robin and the violet; Oak-tree and the ivy; Margaret: a pearl; Springtime; Rodolph and his king; Hampshire hills; Ezra's Thanksgivin' out west; Ludwig and Eloise; Fido's little friends; The old man; Bill, the lokil editor; Little yaller baby; The "cyclopeedy;" Dock Stebbins; Fairies of l'esth.

402. [343.] **Little Colonel's house party.** Annie Fellows-Johnston. Bost., L. C. Page & Co., 1901. 264 p. il. D. cl. .... 1.00 .65

A delightful story of three girls. The story is filled with inspiration.

	List price.	Price to districts.

403. **Lorna Doone**: a romance of Exmoor. R. D. Blackmore. N. Y., Harper & Bros., 1898. 576 p. il. D. cl. .... 1.00 .45

An intensely interesting story portraying the life and deeds of the outlaw Doones of Bagworthy forest during the reign of James II in England. The descriptions of Devonshire scenery and of the people are excellent.

404. [311.] **Middle five**; Indian boys at school. Francis La Flesche. Bost., Small, Maynard & Co., 1900. 277 p. il. S. cl. .... 1.25 .75

Sketches of the life, studies, and amusements of boys in an Indian mission school, written by one of them. A good book for the teacher to read.

405. [331.] (285.) **New Mexico David.** Charles F. Lummis. N. Y., C: Scribner's Sons, 1891. 217 p. il. D. cl. .... 1.25 .80

Stories and sketches of the Southwest, teaching bravery, courage, and self-reliance.

406. [341.] (664.) **Nurnberg Stove.** Louise de la Ramé. N. Y., Maynard, Merrill & Co., 1895. 73 p. S. (Maynard's Eng. Classic ser., No. 151.) bds..... .20 .18

407. [312.] (260.) **Old-fashioned girl.** Louisa M. Alcott. Bost., Little, Brown & Co., 1898. 378 p. il. S. cl. 1.50 .88

408. [305.] (656.) **Phronsie Pepper**: the youngest of the "five little Peppers." Margaret Sidney. *Mrs. H. M. Lothrop.* Bost., Lothrop Pub. Co., 1897. 437 p. il. D. cl. .... 1.50 .85

The last book of that charming series, "Five Little Peppers." Older girls of middle form can read.

409. [338.] (292.) **Pilgrim's progress.** John Bunyan. Bost., Houghton, Mifflin & Co., 1896. 195 p. D. cl..... .40 .32

410. [335.] (289.) **Pilot.** James Fenimore Cooper. N. Y., American Book Company, 1898. 271 p. D. bds. .... .40 .34

An edition of Cooper's Pilot adapted to the needs of pupils in the upper form.

	List price.	Price to districts.

411. **Pine Ridge plantation,** *or,* The trials and successes of a young cotton planter. William Drysdale. N. Y., Thomas Y. Crowell & Co., c1901. 320 p. il. D. cl. ...... 1.50 .85

The story of an ambitious boy who went south and acquired a small "cotton-patch" of his own. By his industry and strict attention to business he slowly added to his small "patch" until it became a prosperous plantation. An excellent picture of southern life on a typical cotton plantation.

412. [326.] (276.) **Polly Oliver's problem.** Kate Douglas Wiggin. Bost., Houghton, Mifflin & Co., 1896. 212 p. il. D. cl. ...... .60 .50

A very interesting story for girls.

413. [333.] (287.) **Rab and his friends.** John Brown. Bost., Houghton, Mifflin & Co. [n. d.] 299 p. D. cl. ...... .60 .50

Stories of a dog and his friends.

414. [296.] (648.) **Santa Claus's partner.** Thomas Nelson Page. N. Y., C: Scribner's Sons, 1899. 177 p. il. D. cl. ...... 1.50 .96

A charming Christmas story, teaching the joy of giving.

415. [350.] **Stories and legends.** Washington Irving. N. Y., G. P. Putnam's Sons, 1896. 312 p. il. D. (Knickerbocker ser.) cl. ...... 1.25 .75

"These stories are, like all that Irving wrote, excellent examples of good English style, the narrative being simple, graphic, and picturesque." Contains: Dolph Heyliger, Legend of the Stormship, Kidd, the pirate, Rip Van Winkle, Legend of Sleepy Hollow, Philip of Pokanokio, and others.

416. [309.] (256.) **Stories for boys.** Richard Harding Davis. N. Y., Chas. Scribner's Sons, 1893. 204 p. il. D. cl. ...... 1.00 .65

A collection of very good stories for boys. The "Reporter who made himself King" is one of the best.

	List price.	Price to districts.

417. [349.] **Stories from the classic literature of many nations.** Bertha Palmer, *ed.* N. Y., Macmillan Co., 1898. 297 p. D. cl.......................... 1.25 .80

Interesting stories from many countries and with which children ought to become familiar. Ought to be told to children of lower grades.

418. [328.] (284.) **Story of Ab.** Stanley Waterloo. N. Y., Doubleday, Page & Co., 1897. 351 p. D. cl..... 1.50 .88

An interesting tale of the time of the cave men. Will arouse new interests.

419. [306.] (255.) **Story of Babette.** Ruth McEnery Stuart. N. Y., Harper & Bros., 1898. 209 p. il. D. cl. .... 1.50 .90

The story of a little Creole girl. Fine descriptions of life in New Orleans.

420. **Story of Little Nell.** Charles Dickens. *Ed.* by Jane Gordon. N. Y., American Book Company, c1901. 357 p. D. (Eclectic school readings.) cl....... .50 .43

An abridged version of "The old curiosity shop"; the narrative geing confined solely to the pathetic adventure of "little Nell."

421. [342.] (50.) **Story of Patsy.** Kate Douglas Wiggin. Bost., Houghton, Mifflin & Co., 1897. 68 p. il. D. bds. .... .60 .36

I have read Patsy from cover to cover. It is a book of that high order of writing which I call the second gospel of St. John—like Kingsley's Water Babies and Mrs. Ewing's Story of a Short Life. Its pathos is very deep. It is the true spirit of the Kindergarten, the most Christian part of our school system. The good that may be done by the kindergartens among the poor cannot be told adequately except by such stories.—*Dr. W. T. Harris U. S. Commissioner of Education.*

Portrayal of life in slum district of San Francisco and the Silver St. kindergarten. A book for children and older people.

422. [315.] (264.) **Story of Sonny Sahib.** Sara Janette Duncan Cotes. N. Y., D. Appleton & Co., 1896. 111 p. il. D. cl. .... 1.00 .65

Portrays life in India and teaches a beautiful lesson in loyalty. Children in middle form will enjoy.

	List price.	Price to districts.

423. [321.] **Swiss family Robinson.** Jean Rudolph Wyss. *Trans.* by W. H. G. Kingston. N. Y., E. P. Dutton & Co. il. sq. O. cl. 2.50   1.10

Middle form will read also.

424. **Summer in a cañon: a California story.** Kate Douglas Wiggin. Bost., Houghton, Mifflin & Co., 1895. 272 p. il. cl. .... 1.25   .75

A good description of camp life in a cañon in California. Some very good descriptions of scenery in southern California on pages 5, 19-22, 32-33, 41, 59-61; Mexicans, 37-38.

425. [325.] (275.) **Timothy's quest.** Kate Douglas Wiggin. Bost., Houghton, Mifflin & Co., 1898. 201 p. D. cl. .... 1.00   .60

The story of a little boy who starts out in quest of a mother for little Gay and himself. The story teaches generosity and manliness.

426. [292.] (246.) **Tom Brown's school days.** Thomas Hughes. Bost., Houghton, Mifflin & Co., 1895. 364 p. D. (Riverside lit. ser.) cl.............. .50   .38

A vivid portrayal of school life. The book is filled with concrete lessons in good living for the pupils, and the teacher will find much sound pedagogy in it.

427. [291.] **Treasure island.** Robert L. Stevenson. *New ed.* with the original il. by Walter Paget. N. Y., C: Scribner's Sons, 1900. 388 p. D. cl.......... 1.25   .70

One of the best stories of adventure for older pupils.

428. **Treasury club:** a story of the Treasury Department, illustrating how important a factor is money in our national life. William Drysdale. Bost., W. A. Wilde Co., 1900. 330 p. il. D. cl.......... 1.50   .85

The first volume in a new series entitled "The United States government series." It gives very fully the workings of the Treasury department in all its branches and the accuracy of this information has been attested to by a former United States Treasurer, Hon. D. N. Morgan. It will aid children to a better understanding of how the financial business of our country is transacted.

The story of Len Gray shows what a boy may accomplish by being persevering, ambitious, and industrious.

	List price.	Price to districts.

429. [348.] (652.) **Under the cactus flag**: a story of life in Mexico. Nora Archibald Smith. Bost., Houghton, Mifflin & Co., 1899. 218 p. il. D. cl....... 1.25 .75

The experiences of a young girl who goes to Mexico to teach school. The life of the Mexicans is portrayed in a charming way. Undoubtedly this book will prove as popular in the upper form as Juan and Juanita in the middle form. Good material for work in geography.

430. **Young consul**: a story of the Department of State. William Drysdale. Bost., W. A. Wilde Co., c1901. 356 p. il. D. cl. .... 1.50 .85

This is the second volume of the "United States Government Series," and is a story of the State Department. Through the influence of official friends, and by hard work on his own part, the young hero of the story wins an appointment as vice consul to Marseilles, France. By this means the reader is introduced to the various workings of the State Department, and the statistics and facts which necessarily must be introduced are treated in such a way that they lend interest to the story rather than detract from it.

431. **Young supercargo**: a story of the merchant marine. William Drysdale. Bost., W. A. Wilde Co., c1898. 352 p. il. D. (Brain and brawn ser.) cl. ...... 1.50 .85

The story of a young boy who is determined to make his way in life. It abounds in incidents and adventure. Children may be led to read an interesting book of travel after reading the story of the voyages and travels of this boy.

HISTORICAL FICTION.

See also "Historical Fiction," Middle Form, and "Fiction," Upper Form.

All of the material gathered in this reading should be read in the history class. References on the topic under discussion placed upon the blackboard, will prove very helpful to the pupils in the history lesson and will not only make the history lesson more interesting but may interest the pupils in reading good books. See Manual, *History—Upper Form*.

	List price.	Price to districts.
432. [366.] **Anneke:** a little dame of New Netherlands. Elizabeth W. Champney. N. Y., Dodd, Mead & Co., 1900. 313 p. il. D. cl.	1.50	.88

Life in the New York colonies.

433. [392.] **Between Boer and Briton:** or two boys' adventures in South Africa. Edward Stratemeyer. Bost., Lee & Shepard, 1900. 354 p. il. D. cl....	1.25	.75

An interesting story of the Boer war.

434. [388.] (325.) **Boy emigrants.** Noah Brooks. N. Y., C: Scribner's Sons, 1898. 309 p. il. D. cl.....	1.25	.82

A story of the eventful history of the early overland travelers to California.

435. [369.] (307.) **Boys of old Monmouth.** Everett T. Tomlinson. Bost., Houghton, Mifflin & Co., 1898. 427 p. il. D. cl.	1.50	.90

A story of Washington's campaign in New Jersey in 1778.

436. **Boy of the first empire.** Elbridge S. Brooks. N. Y., Century Co., 1901. 320 p. il. D. cl.	1.50	.90

A brave French boy, whose father had been guillotined, makes his way into Napoleon's presence and warns him of a desperate plot against his life. The Emperor, in return for his loyalty

	List price.	Price to districts.

takes him into his service, making him page at court. He becomes a special favorite of Napoleon and is sent on many secret errands. The most important incidents in the history of the first Empire are brought out in a way that will be pleasing to young readers.

437. [385.] (671.) **Cleared for action:** a story of the Spanish-American war of 1898. Willis Boyd Allen. N. Y., E. P. Dutton & Co., 1900. 346 p. il. D. cl. .... 1.50 .88

A sequel to "Navy Blue." A practical application of the lessons learned at the U. S. naval academy at Annapolis.

438. [376.] **Daughter of freedom:** a story of the latter period of the war for independence. Amy E. Blanchard. Bost., W. A. Wilde Co., 1900. 312 p. D. cl. .... 1.50 .85

A story for girls.

439. [362.] (668.) **Drake and his yeomen.** James Barnes. N. Y., The Macmillan Co., 1899. 415 p. il. D. cl. 2.00 1.28

An intensely interesting account of the character and adventures of Sir Francis Drake, as told by Sir Matthew Maunsell, his friend and follower. For older pupils in the upper form.

440. [375.] (314.) **For King or country.** James Barnes. N. Y., Harper & Bros., 1898. 269 p. il. D. cl... 1.50 .90

No boy can read this volume without acquiring a strong impression of the suffering, sacrifice, and daring in the war for American independence.

441. **Godson of Lafayette.** Being the story of young Joe Harvey, and how he found the way to duty in the days of Webster and Jackson and the conspiracy of that American adventurer, Eleazer Williams, sometimes called "The False Dauphin." Eldridge S. Brooks. Bost., W. A. Wilde Co., c1900. 333 p. il. D. cl. .... 1.50 .85

"The story of the disloyalty and strategy of Rev. Eleazer Williams, who was possessed with the belief that he was the lost Dauphin of France, son of Louis XVI, and in line for the throne. The hero is for the time influenced by the "false Dauphin," and follows his fortunes, in his schemes of Empire—that is, the uniting of the Indians of America into one great Confederacy, which should dominate and control the west."—*From Publisher's Weekly.*

	List price.	Price to districts.

442. **Golden arrow:** a story of Roger Williams's day. Ruth Hall. Bost., Houghton, Mifflin & Co., 1901. 316 p. D. cl. 1.25 1.12

" 'The Golden Arrow' is a tale of the American Colonies between 1635 and 1660. The young hero, Richard Markham, helps defend Anne Hutchinson against persecution, fights Indians at Wethersfield, aids in rescuing Anne Hutchinson's daughter from savages, goes to England, where he sees Charles I., and serves James II., then a boy. Returning to America he joins Roger Williams in Rhode Island, and later helps in the defense of the Quakers against persecution in Boston."

443. [390.] **Graysons:** a story of Abraham Lincoln. Edward Eggleston. N. Y., Century Co., 1900. 362 p. il. D. cl. .... 1.50 .96

Older pupils will find this story most interesting.

444. [355.] (298.) **Hereward, the Wake.** Charles Kingsley. N. Y., Macmillan Co., 1893. 256 p. il. S. cl. .... .50 .42

A story of life in the earliest times in England.

445. [389.] **Hero in homespun:** a tale of the loyal South. William E. Barton. N. Y., D. Appleton Co., 1897. 393 p. il. D. cl. .... 1.00 .65

A story of the crude life of the mountaineers of Tennessee during the civil war.

446. [363.] (666.) **Hugh Gwyeth:** a roundhead cavalier. Beulah Marie Dix. N. Y., Macmillan Co., 1899. 376 p. il. D. cl. .... 1.50 .96

The hero was the son of a royalist father and the grandson of a stern Puritan Roundhead. He joined the followers of Charles I. Prince Rupert, the nephew of Charles I., appears in the story, which is historically correct.

447. [367.] **Hugh Wynne, free quaker:** sometime Brevet Lieutenant Colonel on the staff of His Excellency General Washington. S. Weir Mitchell. *New ed.* N. Y., Century Co., 1900. 567 p. il. D. cl...... 1.50 .96

A new edition of one of the greatest of our American historical novels.

	List price.	Price to districts.

448. [370.] **In hostile red**: a romance of the Monmouth campaign. J. A. Altsheler. N. Y., Doubleday, Page & Co., 1900. 340 p. D. cl. .... 1.50 .88

Story of two young American officers who go into Philadelphia disguised as two British officers. The time is during the Revolutionary war. Character of General Howe is well portrayed.

449. [356.] **In the days of Alfred, the great.** Eva March Tappan. Bost., Lee & Shepard, 1900. 296 p. il. D. cl. .... 1.00 .58

A life of Alfred, the great, told in story form.

450. **In the days of William the Conqueror.** Eva March Tappan. Bost., Lee & Shepard, 1901. 298 p. il. D. cl. .... 1.00 .60

Tells the story of William the Conqueror in the same style and with the same historical accuracy as the author's "In the days of Alfred the Great."

451. [368.] **In the hands of the red coats**: a tale of the Jersey Ship and the Jersey shore in the days of the Revolution. Everett T. Tomlinson. Bost., Houghton, Mifflin & Co., 1900. 370 p. il. D. cl. 1.50 .90

The story portrays the experiences and sufferings of some of the hardy and humble patriots of the Revolutionary period.

452. [360.] (299.) **In the Wars of the Roses.** E. Everett-Green. N. Y., T. Nelson & Sons, 1897. 256 p. D. cl. .... 1.00 .48

A good story portraying life in England during the wars of the Roses.

453. [359.] (297.) **Ivanhoe.** *Sir* Walter Scott. N. Y., American Book Company, 1892. 484 p. D. bds. .50 .40

A fine portrayal of life in England during the reign of Richard the Lion-Hearted, showing the results of the Norman conquest.

References: Saxon homes and surroundings, 433, 436, 27, 67, 28, 31, 59, 62; Norman castles, 205, 210, 279, 219, 227; Jew's home, 116, 268; language, 8-19, 22, 39, 50, 104; ways of travel, 13, 14, 34, 26, 44, 163, 166, 118, 189-193; dress, 73, 407, 78, 14, 15, 38, 220, 77, 30, 91, 99, 7, 146, 195, 167, 170, 48, 76, 79, 380; amusements, 44, 73, 145, 36, 42, 452; feudalism, 154, 239, 263, 281, 290, 299-304; character of Saxons, 23, 25, 34, 103, 157, 188, 81, 194, 221, 223, 270, 155, 47, 46; character of Normans, 20, 80, 322, 345, 154, 73, 407, 429, 78, 86, 100, 160, 23, 36, 43, 52.

LIST OF BOOKS FOR TOWNSHIP LIBRARIES. 113

	List price.	Price to districts.
454. Last of the Mohicans: a narrative of 1757. James Fenimore Cooper. N. Y., Globe School Book Co., c1900. 446 p. il. D. (English classics—star ser.) cl.	.48	.40

One of the best of Cooper's novels, depicting frontier life in New York at the time of the French and Indian war. It may be made the starting point of several lines of reading.

Some children may be interested in reading more about Montcalm and the French and Indian war; some, in the Colonial history of New York and still others in knowing more about the Indians of North America.

| 455. [386.] (674.) Loyal hearts and true. Ruth Ogden. N. Y., Frederick A. Stokes Co., 1899. 352 p. il. D. cl. | 1.50 | .78 |

The story of some children who lived in a Navy Yard. Our late war with Spain furnishes some of the most interesting instances.

| 456. [378.] (313.) Loyal traitor. James Barnes. N. Y., Harper & Bros, 1899. 306 p. il. D. cl. | 1.50 | .90 |

A thrilling story of the War of 1812.

| 457. [391.] (304.) Man without a country. Edward E. Hale. Bost., Little, Brown & Co., 1899. 59 p. D. cl. | .50 | .28 |

One of the best lessons in patriotism ever taught.

| 458. [354.] (295.) Men of iron. Howard Pyle. N. Y., Harper & Bros., 1898. 328 p. il. O. cl. | 2.00 | 1.20 |

A picture of chivalry in England during the time of Henry IV.

| 459. [357.] (296.) Merry Adventures of Robin Hood. Howard Pyle. N. Y., Charles Scribner's Sons, 1897. 296 p. il. O. cl. | 3.00 | 1.90 |

You who so plod amid serious things that you feel it a shame to give yourself up even for a few short moments to mirth and joyousness in the land of Fancy; you, who think that life hath nought to do with innocent laughter that can harm no one; these pages are not for you; clap to the leaves and go no farther than this, for I tell you plainly that if you go farther, you will be scandalized by seeing good, sober folks of real history so frisk and caper in gay colors and motley, that you would not know them but for the names tagged to them.—*From the Author to the Reader.*

| | List price. | Price to districts. |

460. [387.] (670.) **Navy blue:** a story of cadet life in the United States naval academy at Annapolis. Willis Boyd Allen. N. Y., E. P. Dutton & Co., 1899. 341 p. il. D. cl. .... 1.50 .88

The boys will be interested in this book.

461. **Prairie schooner:** a story of the Black Hawk war. William E. Barton. Bost., W. A. Wilde Co., c1900. 382 p. il. D. cl. .... 1.50 .85

The "Prairie Schooner" is the name given to the white-covered wagons used by the early settlers in making their journey to their new homes on the western frontier. It is introduced to us in this story just as it is nearing the end of its long journey from New York to the tiny village of Chicago. The story gives an excellent picture of the Middle west before and during the Black Hawk war.

462. [361.] (300.) **Prince and pauper.** Mark Twain (Samuel Clemens). N. Y., Harper & Bros., 1898. 309 p. il. O. cl. 1.75 1.15

Two boys, one the future Edward VI of England and a peasant change places for a time. The story portrays life in England in the 16th century.

References: London in time of Henry VIII, 3–6, 10–11; life in the slums, 20–25; 147–170; London Bridge, 82–84; life and ceremonies at court, 48–61, 75–81, 107–114, 122–126, 138–142; punishment of criminals, 127–137; coronation ceremonies, 259–274.

463. [377.] (312.) **Rock of the lion.** Molly Elliot Seawell. N. Y., Harper & Bros., 1898. il. D. cl.......... 1.50 .88

A story depicting naval life.

464. [367a.] **Soldier of Virginia.** Burton E. Stevenson. Bost., Houghton, Mifflin & Co., 1901. 325 p. il. D. cl. .... 1.50 .95

A tale of Colonel Washington and Braddock's defeat.

465. [365.] (667.) **Soldier Rigdale:** how he sailed in the "Mayflower," and how he served Miles Standish. Beulah Marie Dix. N. Y., Macmillan Co., 1899. 323 p. il. D. cl. .... 1.50 .96

The story of a boy who came to America in the Mayflower. Child life in the Plymouth colony is well portrayed. A good story to read to the middle form. Some of the older children can read for themselves.

LIST OF BOOKS FOR TOWNSHIP LIBRARIES. 115

	List price.	Price to districts.

466. [374.] (321.) **Son of the Revolution.** E. S. Brooks. Bost., W. A. Wilde & Co., 1898. 301 p. il. D. cl. 1.50 .85

The story of young Tom Edwards, adventurer, and how he labored for liberty and fought it out with his conscience in the days of Burr's conspiracy.

467. [384.] (672.) **Story of old Fort Loudon.** Charles Egbert Craddock (Mary Noailles Murfree). N. Y., The Macmillan Co., 1899. 409 p. il. D. cl. 1.50 .96

A good pioneer story.

468. **Story of the Cid for young people.** Calvin Dill Wilson. Bost., Lee & Shepard, 1901. 313 p. il. D. cl. .... 1.25 .75

The story of Rodrigo Diaz, one of Spain's greatest soldiers, who fought in the long and fierce struggles between the Christians and the Mahometans. The poets and minstrels have mingled a good many legends with the facts of his life and the story is told here with all its romance. It will give to the children vivid pictures of a great hero with whom few of them are now familiar and will create a new interest in the history of and life in Spain. This book may lead to the reading of the chapters on Spain in Carpenter's "Europe;" Coe's "Modern Europe"; Knox's "Boy Travellers in Southern Europe," and Tarr and McMurry's "Europe and other continents."

469. [364.] (665.) **Tales of an old chateau.** Marguerite Bouvet. Chicago, A. C. McClurg & Co., 1899. 236 p. il. S. cl. .... 1.25 .75

Most beautiful stories, being the youthful experiences of an aristocratic old French lady during the French revolution, told to her grandchildren. A dainty little volume which will appeal to every girl.

470. [372.] (309.) **Three colonial boys.** Everett T. Tomlinson. Bost., W. A. Wilde & Co., 1895. 368 p. il. O. cl. .... 1.50 .85

A story of the exciting times of '76.

471. [352.] (293.) **Three Greek children.** Alfred J. Church. N. Y., G. P. Putnam's Sons, 1895. 205 p. D. cl. .... 1.25 .75

The home life of Greek children is skillfully depicted.

	List price.	Price to districts.

472. [373.] (310.) **Three young continentals.** Everett T. Tomlinson. Bost., W. A. Wilde & Co., 1896. 364 p. il. O. cl. .... 1.50 .85

A story of the American Revolution.

473. [371.] (308.) **Washington's young aids.** Everett T. Tomlinson. Bost., W. A. Wilde & Co., 1897. 391 p. il. O. cl. .... 1.50 .85

The messengers Gen. Washington sent to Gen. Lee, the retreat and advance of the patriot forces, the life in the prison houses of New York, the raids of the pine robbers, the tempting of the Hessians, the end of Fagan and his band, are all taken from the records, and there is nothing in the story which might not have occurred in the struggle.—*From the author's preface.*

474. **With Porter in the Essex.** James Otis (J. O. Kaler). Bost., W. A. Wilde Co., c1901. 344 p. il. D. (Great Admiral ser.) cl. .... 1.50 .85

A graphic account of Commodore Porter's famous voyage around Cape Horn during the war of 1812, when he wrought such havoc to British shipping interests, and only lowered his colors when overpowered by a vastly superior force.

475. [383.] **With Preble at Tripoli.** James Otis (J. O. Kaler). Bost., W. A. Wilde Co., 1900. 349 p. il. D. cl. .... 1.50 .85

A story of "Old Ironsides" and the Tripolitan war. A good story of adventure filled with some of the most fascinating achievements of the American navy.

476. **With Washington in the west,** or a soldier boy's battles in the wilderness. Edward Stratemeyer. Bost., Lee & Shepard, 1901. 302 p. il. D. cl... 1.25 .75

The hero of this story is David Morris, a young boy who becomes acquainted with Washington and goes on a surveying trip with him. At the time of the wars between the French and English in America he joins the "Virginia rangers," who are under Washington's command. The historical portions of the story are reasonably correct and the story is an attractive one for boys.

478. [382.] (318.) **Yankee ships and Yankee sailors.** James Barnes. N. Y., Macmillan Co. 281 p. il. D. cl. .... 1.50 .96

We can draw accurate conclusions as to what kind of men these fine old fellows were; how they looked, how they spoke and acted. Their deeds are a part of the nation's record, and their ships exist now in the shape of a few old hulls.—*Author's preface.*

MYTHS AND LEGENDS.

	List price.	Price to districts.

479. [394.] (327.) **Heroes of Asgard.** A. Keary *and* E. Keary. N. Y., Macmillan Co., 1893. 232 p. il. D. cl. .... .50 .42

Stories from Scandinavian mythology very interestingly written. They should be told to children of lower grades.

480. [393.] **Norse stories retold from the Eddas.** Hamilton Wright Mabie. *New ed.* N. Y., Dodd, Mead & Co., 1900. 250 p. S. cl..................... 1.25 .75

A new edition of these old stories told in a delightful way.

481. [396.] **Siegfried and Beowulf.** Zenaide A. Ragozin. N. Y., G. P. Putnam's Sons, 1898. 332 p. il. D. cl. .... 1.50 .90

Stories of Siegfried, the hero of the North, and Beowulf, the Anglo-Saxon.

482. **Stories from Homer.** Alfred J. Church. N. Y., T. Y. Crowell & Co., c1901. 252 p. il. S. cl......... .60 .30

A good book to suggest to children who enjoyed reading Clarke's "Story of Troy" in the middle form, and who are interested in knowing more about Troy.

483. **Stories from Virgil.** Alfred J. Church. N. Y., T. Y. Crowell & Co., c1901. 212 p. il. S. cl......... .60 .30

Stories from the "Aeneid" of Virgil. The children who become interested in these stories may later on be led to read a translation of the Aeneid.

484. [353.] **Story of Roland.** James Baldwin. N. Y., C: Scribner's Sons, 1901. 415 p. il. D. (Heroes of the olden time.) cl. .... 1.50 .96

This story introduces some of the most pleasing of the poems and legends of France. Roland, the nephew of the Charlemagne of romance is unknown to history, but he is a typical knight, the greatest hero of the Middle ages.

	List price.	Price to districts.

485. **Story of Siegfried.** James Baldwin. N. Y., C: Scribner's Sons, 1901. 306 p. il. D. (Heroes of the olden time.) cl. .... 1.50 .96

"Children should become familiar with the myths of our Northern ancestors because they are what our forefathers once believed. There are many things in them that are beautiful and true and that will lead us to have a better understanding and appreciation of the thoughts and feelings of our old Northern ancestors."

486. **Story of the golden age.** James Baldwin. N. Y., C: Scribner's Sons, 1901. 286 p. il. D. (Heroes of the olden time.) cl. .... 1.50 .96

A story weaving into one continuous narrative the legends which relate to the causes of the Trojan war. The child who becomes interested in this story will later on enjoy reading a translation of Homer's Odyssey as the hero of this story is also the hero of the Odyssey.

487. [395.] (328.) **Story of the Rhinegold.** Anna Alice Chapin. N. Y., Harper & Bros., 1899. 138 p., il. D. cl. .... 1.25 .78

Stories from Wagner's operas.

BIOGRAPHY.

See also "Biography," Middle Form.

	List price.	Price to districts.

488. [413.] **Abraham Lincoln:** his youth and early manhood with a brief account of his later life. Noah Brooks. N. Y., G. P. Putnam's Sons, 1901. *New ed.* 204 p. il. D. (Knickerbocker Lit. Ser.) cl.   .90   .81

This biography shows how Lincoln's early training shaped and developed his character, and how his humble life fitted him for his work in later life. It was written by a personal friend of Lincoln and gives a lifelike picture of the man as many men knew him. Portions should be read by the history class in connection with the study of the topics of slavery and the Civil war.

References: Boyhood and early manhood, p. 1–89; Missouri compromise, p. 91–94, 108; Kansas struggle, p. 98–102; Ordinance of 1787, p. 91; Lincoln–Douglas debate, p. 103–16; S. A. Douglas, p. 72–73, 92–97, 103–105, 109–18; 127–47; U. S. Grant, p. 76, 179–81; 188–93; Dred Scott decision, p. 108–109, 144; Mason & Slidell, p. 152–55; Emancipation proclamation, p. 160, 162–64; Civil war, p. 90–200.

489. [414.] (391.) **Abraham Lincoln.** Charles Carleton Coffin. N. Y., Harper & Bros., 1892. 542 p. il. O. cl. 2.00   1.20

For older pupils.

490. [407.] (384.) **Autobiography of Benjamin Franklin.** Bost., Houghton, Mifflin & Co., 1886. 238 p. D. (Riverside lit. ser.) cl. .... .40   .32

Every library ought to have this book on its shelves. Not only does the book give a vivid picture of the life of the times, but it is filled with the prudence, honesty, and wisdom of one of our greatest men.

491. [400.] (376.) **Book of American explorers.** Thomas Wentworth Higginson, *ed.* N. Y., Longmans, Green & Co., 1877. 367 p. il. D. cl. 1.20   1.05

The original narratives so far as possible are given in this volume.

	Price
List	to dis-
price.	tricts.

492. [397.] (371.) **Boys' and girls' Plutarch.** *Ed. by* John
S. White. G. P. Putnam's Sons, 1893. 468 p. O.
cl. 1.75   1.05

A very good edition of Plutarch's Lives edited for boys and girls.
References: Theseus, 3-27; Romulus, 28-47; Lycurgus, 49-72; Solon, 73-87; Themistocles, 88-105; Camillus, 106-135; Pericles, 136-167; Demosthenes, 168-189; Cicero, 190-228; Alcibiades, 233-259; Coriolanus, 260-287; Aristides, 288-305; Cimon, 306-325; Pompey, 326-369; Archimedes, 370-374; Cleopatra, 375-379; a Roman triumph, 388-392; Alexander, 420-444.

477, 493. [420.] (397.) **Captains of industry.** James Parton. Bost., Houghton, Mifflin & Co., 1891-96. 2 v. 399; 393 p. D. cl. per vol................ .60   .50

Leaders in the world of industry. All the narrations teach the same lesson—that patience and perseverance with good habits may accomplish anything aimed at.
References: Vol. 1. Elihu Burritt, 27-35; Peter Fanueil, 65-78; Israel Putnam, 96-103; George Flower, 104-116; Peter H. Burnett, 126-132; Gerrit Smith, 133-139; Richard Cobden, 195-205; Henry Bessemer, 206-211; John Bright, 212-223; Horace Greeley, 254-263; James Gordon Bennett, 264-273; three John Walters, 274-287; William B. Astor, 307-312; Peter Cooper, 313-331; Christopher Wren, 363-371; Moses Montefiore, 379-384.
Vol. 2: Captain Meriwether Lewis, 51-59; Joel Barlow, 67-73; Andrew Jackson, 98-110; Gabriel D. Fahrenheit, 144-54; Joliet, 192-99; George Peabody, 208-15; Elizabeth Fry, 344-52.

494. **Century book of famous Americans.** Elbridge S. Brooks. N. Y., Century Co., c1896. 251 p. il. O. cl. .... 1.50   .90

An interesting account of the pilgrimage of a party of young people to historic homes.
References: Fanuell hall, 3-5, 11; Alexander Hamilton, 54-63; Benjamin Franklin, 68-76; Declaration of Independence, 76-77; Patrick Henry, 94-101; Thomas Jefferson, 125-32; John C. Calhoun, 140-44; Henry Clay, 145-55; Andrew Jackson, 162-72.

495. [379.] (315.) **Commodore Bainbridge.** James Barnes. N. Y., D. Appleton & Co., 1897. 168 p. il. D. cl. 1.00   .55

An account of one of the heroic naval officers who rendered conspicuous service to our country in the wars of 1803 and 1812.

496. [403.] (378.) **De Soto and his men in the land of Florida.** Grace King. N. Y., Macmillan & Co., 1898. 326 p. il. D. cl. .... 1.50   .96

A fascinating biography of De Soto.

	List price.	Price to districts.

497. [411.] (388.) **Diary of Anna Green Winslow.** *Ed.* by Alice Morse Earle. 4th ed. Bost., Houghton, Mifflin & Co., 1896. 121 p. D. cl.............. 1.25 .80

Diary of a Boston school girl of 1771. It is a fine historical picture of the domestic life of the time.

498. [417.] (394.) **Famous American statesmen.** Sarah K. Bolton. N. Y., T. Y. Crowell & Co., 1888. 399 p. D. cl. .... 1.50 .85

Short and interesting biographies of the following: George Washington, 1-37; Benjamin Franklin, 38-66; Thomas Jefferson, 67-98; Alexander Hamilton, 99-132; Andrew Jackson, 133-176; Daniel Webster, 177-229; Henry Clay, 230-267; Charles Sumner, 268-306; U. S. Grant, 307-360; James A. Garfield, 361-399.

499. [408.] (385.) **George Washington.** Horace E. Scudder. Bost., Houghton, Mifflin & Co., 1889. 248 p. S. (Riverside lib. for young people.) cl........ .75 .45

Mr. Scudder has presented just what the boys need—a clear, correct, plain narrative of life that is its own rich ornament. The simple story is eloquent, and will hold the attention of many youth from seven to seventy. With full appreciation of his character, and with patriotic spirit, the author follows the young Virginian from his humble home to his throne in the hearts of the American people.—*Public Opinion.*

References: Virginia Plantation, 14-20; boyhood and school days, 21-36; Ohio Company, 52-59; Indians, 73-79; Braddock's defeat, 80-94; the Continental Congress, 131-143; Revolutionary War, 144-202; Valley Forge, 170-177; Conway Cabal, 178-186; President of the U. S., 219-241.

500. [416.] (393.) **Girls who became famous.** Sarah K. Bolton. N. Y., T. Y. Crowell & Co., 1886. 347 p. D. cl. .... 1.50 .85

Short and interesting sketches of the lives of the following women: Harriet Beecher Stowe, 1-17; Helen Hunt Jackson, 18-32; Lucretia Mott, 33-49; Mary A. Livermore, 50-67; Margaret Fuller Ossoli, 68-86; Maria Mitchell, 87-103; Louisa M. Alcott, 104-121; Mary Lyon, 122-140; Harriet G. Hosmer, 141-157; Madame de Stael, 158-179; Rosa Bonheur, 180-193; Elizabeth Barrett Browning, 194-212; George Eliot, 213-239; Elizabeth Fry, 240-260; Elizabeth Thompson Butler, 261-277; Florence Nightingale, 278-299; Lady Brassey, 300-319; Baroness Burdett-Coutts, 320-330; Jean Ingelow, 331-347.

501. [381.] (317.) **Hero of Erie.** James Barnes. N. Y., D. Appleton & Co., 1898. 167 p. il. D. cl...... 1.00 .55

The hero of Erie is Oliver Perry. A book filled with inspiration and interest for the members of the history class.

| | List price. | Price to districts. |

502. [424.] (675.) **Hero of Manila:** Dewey on the Mississippi and the Pacific. Rossiter Johnson. N. Y., D. Appleton & Co., 1899. 152 p. il. D. cl....... 1.00 .55

A biography of Dewey which will be very interesting to young readers.

503. [410.] (387.) **Hero tales from American history.** Henry Cabot Lodge, *and* Theodore Roosevelt. N. Y., Century Co., 1898. 385 p. il. D. cl........ 1.50 .95

Most fascinating stories of the heroes of our country.
References: George Washington, 1–15; Daniel Boone, 19–28; George Rogers Clark, 31–41; battle of Trenton, 45–55; battle of Bennington, 59–67; Stony Point, 81–89; Gouverneur Morris, 93–99; cruise of the "Wasp," 117–126; battle of New Orleans, 139–147; John Quincy Adams, 151–159; Francis Parkman, 163–170; the Alamo, 173–181; Hampton Roads, 185–195; Gettysburg, 227–236; Vicksburg campaign, 239–248; Abraham Lincoln, 325–335.

504. [422.] (399.) **Heroes and martyrs of invention.** G. M. Towle. Bost., Lee & Shepard, 1892. 202 p. il. D. cl. .... 1.00 .45

Sketches of the life and work of some of our greatest inventors.
References: Archimedes, 7–14; Coster, and the invention of the type-printing, 23–32; Gutenberg and the printing press, 33–42; Palissy the potter, 43–51; William Lee, inventor of the stocking-frame, 52–61; Eddystone lighthouse, 62–70; Richard Arkwright, 75–83; Eli Whitney, 93–102; James Watt, and the steam engine, 103–112; Montgolfiers, and the balloon, 113–122; Humphrey Davy, and the safety lamp, 123–131; James Nasmyth, and the steam hammer, 132–140; George Stephenson, and the railway locomotive, 141–150; Robert Stephenson, the bridge builder, 151–159; Robert Fulton, and the steamboat, 160–169; Charles Goodyear, 170–179; Elias Howe, and the sewing machine, 180–189; iron and its workers, 190–202.

505. [406.] **Heroes of our Revolution.** T. W. Hall. N. Y., F. A. Stokes Co., 1900. 317 p. il. D. cl......... 1.25 .67

Well told biographies of the leading heroes of the Revolutionary war.

506. [404.] (382.) **Heroes of the middle West.** Mary Hartwell Catherwood. Bost., Ginn & Co., 1898. 141 p. il. D. cl. .... .50 .41

References: Father Jacques Marquette and Louis Joliet, 1–18; Indians, 10–15, 23–31, 35–39, 49, 80–82; explorations of the Mississippi, 17–43, 45–70, 71–101; La Salle and explorations of the N. W., 45–70; Pontiac, 117–141.

	List price.	Price to districts.

507. [415.] **Historic Americans.** Elbridge S. Brooks. N. Y., Thomas Y. Crowell & Company, 1899. 384 p. il. D. cl. .... 1.50 .85

Pen pictures of some pivotal event, chief characteristic or impulse, which led these leading historic Americans along the way of patriotism.

508. [398.] (373.) **Historic girls.** Elbridge S. Brooks. N. Y., G. P. Putnam's Sons, 1887. 225 p. il. O. cl. 1.50 .90

"This volume seeks to tell for the girls and boys of today, the stories of some of their sisters of long ago,—girls who by eminent position or valient deeds became historic even before they had passed the charming season of girlhood."
References: Zenobia, 1-21; Helena (mother of Constantine), 22-44; Pulcheria (of Constantinople), 45-60; Clotilda (first queen of France), 61-78; Woo of Hwango-ho (Empress of China), 79-97; Edith of Scotland, 98-113; Jacquelin of Holland, 114-133; Catrina of Venice, 134-152; Theresa of Avila, 153-173; Elizabeth of Tudor (Queen Elizabeth), 174-191; Christina of Sweden, 192-207; Ma-ta-oka of Pow-ha-tan (Pocahontas), 208-225.

509. **How they succeeded:** life stories of successful men told by themselves. Orison Swett Marden. Bost., Lothrop Pub. Co., c1901. 365 p. il. D. cl...... 1.50 .90

"The fact that these stories are concrete examples taken from real life makes them far more effective than that which is culled from fancy.
They are intended to show that energy, character and ambition will succeed in the world, and that in this land, where all men are born equal and have an equal chance in life, there is no good reason for failure and discouragement."
References: Marshall Field, 19-29; Alexander G. Bell, 30-43; Helen Gould, 44-64; Philip D. Armour, 65-86; Mary E. Procter, 87-95; Jacob Gould Schurman, 96-104; John Wanamaker, 105-28; Lillian Nordica, 149-70; William Dean Howells, 171-84; John D. Rockefeller, 185-208; Mrs. Julia Ward Howe, 209-19; Thomas A. Edison, 220-40; Gen. Lew Wallace, 241-52; Andrew Carnegie, 253-75; Amelia E. Barr, 304-313; Theodore Thomas, 314-26; John B. Herreshoff, 276-303; John Burroughs, 327-40; Herbert H. Vreeland, 341-56; James Whitcomb Riley, 357-65.

510. **Lincoln in story:** Life of the Martyr-President told in authenticated anecdotes. *Ed.* by Silas G. Pratt. N. Y., D. Appleton & Co., 1901. 224 p. il. D. cl. .75 .67

"A biography in story form, illustrating the salient points of Lincoln's career. The scattered anecdotes—each revealing some quality of his great character—have been gathered and arranged chronologically with a connecting warp."

LIST OF BOOKS FOR TOWNSHIP LIBRARIES.

	List price.	Price to districts.

511. [419.] (396.) **Men of business.** W. O. Stoddard. N. Y., C: Scribner's Sons, 1897. 317 p. il. D. cl.   1.50   .96

These biographies of successful business men contain invaluable lessons for the young people in our state.
References: John Jacob Astor, 9-30; Cornelius Vanderbilt, 31-52; Charles Louis Tiffany, 53-74; John Roach, 75-93; Levi Parsons Morton, 98-110; Edwin Denison Morgan, 111-130; Cyrus West Field, 131-160; Chauncey Mitchell Depew, 161-181; Alexander Turney Stewart, 182-196; Philip Danforth Armour, 197-211; Horace Brigham Claflin, 212-228; Marshall Owen Roberts, 229-245; George Mortimer Pullman, 246-263; Peter Cooper, 264-280; Marshall Field, 281-294; Leland Stanford, 295-317.

512. [380.] (316.) **Midshipman Farragut.** James Barnes. D. Appleton & Co., 1898. 151 p. il. D. cl......   1.00   .55

A story of the boyhood of Admiral Farragut. The characters, with one exception, are historical, and but one or two small incidents are imaginary.

513. [405.] (383.) **New exploits of Myles Standish.** Henry Johnson. N. Y., D. Appleton & Co., 1897. 276 p. D. cl. 1.50   80

Interesting biography of Myles Standish, depicting the life of his time.

514. **Poor boy's chances.** John Habberton. Phil., Henry Altemus Co., c1900. 280 p. il. D. cl............   .50   .35

An interesting account of the lives of poor boys who have become successful men.
Contents: Benjamin Franklin; George Washington; Alexander Hamilton; Stephen Girard; John Jacob Astor; Eli Whitney; Andrew Jackson; Henry Clay; Peter Cooper; Horace Mann; "Commodore" Vanderbilt; Abraham Lincoln; Alexander H. Stephens; General Grant; Stonewall Jackson; George Peabody; President Garfield; Jay Gould; "Buffalo" Bill; "Wizard" Edison.

515. [421.] (398.) **Poor boys who became famous.** Sarah K. Bolton. N. Y., T. Y. Crowell & Co., 1885. 367 p. D. cl. ....   1.50   .85

Interesting sketches of the lives of the following famous men: George Peabody, 1-12; Bayard Taylor, 13-25; James B. Eads, 26-32; James Watt, 33-45; Josiah Mason, 46-53; Bernard Palissy, 54-64; Bertel Thorwaldsen, 65-71; Mozart, 72-82; Samuel Johnson, 83-89; Oliver Goldsmith, 90-95; Michael Faraday, 96-111; Henry Bessemer, 112-123; Titus Salt, 124-129; Joseph Marie Jacquard, 130-137; Horace Greeley, 138-155; William Lloyd Garrison, 156-171; Guiseppe Garibaldi, 172-186; Jean Paul Richter, 187-203; Leon Gambetta, 204-218; David Glasgow Farragut, 219-237; Ezra Cornell, 238-250; Lieutenant-General Sheridan, 251-269; Thomas Cole, 270-283; Ole Bull, 284-302; Meissonier, 303-312; George W. Childs, 313-322; Dwight L. Moody, 323-341; Abraham Lincoln, 342-367.

516. [418.] (395.) **Statesmen.** Noah Brooks. N. Y., C: Scribner's Sons, 1898. 347 p. il. D. cl......... 1.50 .96

Short biographies of eminent statesmen.
References: Henry Clay, 9-38; Daniel Webster, 39-68; John C. Calhoun, 69-90; Thomas H. Benton, 91-118; William H. Seward, 119-142; Salmon P. Chase, 143-174; Abraham Lincoln, 175-222; Charles Sumner, 223-254; Samuel J. Tilden, 255-280; James G. Blaine, 281-312; James A. Garfield, 313-332; Grover Cleveland, 333-347.

517. [402.] (377.) **Story of Columbus.** Elizabeth Eggleston Seelye. N. Y., D. Appleton & Co., 1892. 303 p. il. D. cl. 1.75 1.10

Most interesting biography of Columbus.

518. [399.] (375.) **Story of Marco Polo.** Noah Brooks. N. Y., Century Co., 1898. 247 p. il. D. cl...... 1.50 .88

An interesting and entertaining account of the travels of Marco Polo which reads like a romance. Many selections are given from the original narrative.

519. **Story of Washington.** Elizabeth Eggleston Seelye. *Ed. by* Edward Eggleston. N. Y., D. Appleton & Co., 1893. 382 p. il. D. cl..................... 1.75 1.10

This account of Washington, while giving careful attention to his military and administrative acts, emphasizes the personality of them and gives many interesting personal anecdotes of his life.
References: Early life, p. 1-44; French and Indian wars, p. 45-100; Revolutionary war, p. 101-326; Benedict Arnold, p. 270-82; Washington as president, p. 327-355.

520. [423.] **Turning points in successful careers.** William M. Thayer. N. Y., Thomas Y. Crowell & Co., 1895. 410 p. il. D. cl. .... 1.50 .85

"There is a tide in the affairs of men, which, taken at the flood, leads on to fortune."—Shakespeare.

	List price.	Price to districts.

521. [412.] (676.) **Twelve naval captains.** Molly Elliot Seawell. N. Y., C: Scribner's Sons, 1899. 233 p. il. D. (Scribner's ser. of school reading.) cl... .60 .50

Brief accounts of the lives of Paul Jones, Richard Dale, Thomas Truxtun William Bainbridge, Edward Preble, Stephen Decatur, Richard Somers, Isaac Hull, Charles Stewart, Oliver Hazard Perry, Thomas Macdonough, James Lawrence.

522. [401.] **World's discoverers:** the story of bold voyagers by brave navigators during a thousand years. William Henry Johnson. Bost., Little, Brown & Co., 1900. 416 p. il. D. cl.................... 1.50 .90

The book includes voyages of discovery made with a view to finding a sea-route to the Indies.
References: Marco Polo, 3-13; Early discoveries of the Portuguese, 14-17; Columbus, 18-92; Vasco da Gama, 93-118; Magellan, 119-176; Verrazano, 177-188; Earliest seekers of a Northwest passage, 189-227; Sea Kings of Elizabeth's time, 228; Dutch explorers, 272-348; Northwest passage discovered, 349-364; Nordenskiold's voyage, 364-416.

523. [425.] **Ye mariners of England.** Herbert Hayens. N. Y., T. Nelson & Sons, 1901. .... 2.00 .98

A boy's book of the English navy.

HISTORY.

See also "History," Middle Form.
The references ought to be used with the history lesson.
See directions for using references.
See Manual, *History—Upper Form.*

	List price.	Price to districts.
524. [439.] (343.) **Border wars of New England.** Samuel Adams Drake. N. Y., C: Scribner's Sons, 1897. 305 p. il. maps. D. cl......................	1.50	.96

References: King William's War, 9-138; Queen Anne's War, 141-294.

525. [433.] **Boys' book of explorations.** Tudor Jenks. N. Y., Doubleday, Page & Co., 1900. 441 p. il. D. cl. 2.00 1.20

True stories of the heroes of travel and discovery on Africa, Australia, and the Americas, from the dark ages to the "wonderful century." These subjects will prove intensely interesting to boys.

526. [431.] (338.) **Brave little Holland.** William Elliot Griffis. Bost., Houghton, Mifflin & Co., 1894. 252 p. S. (Riverside library for young people.) cl. .... .75 .45

A book which tells of the brave struggle of Holland with the sea, and with Spain for her independance.
References: A general view of Holland, 1-11; the country, 12-18; how a dam became a city, 19-25; the first inhabitants, 26-63; feudal system, 64-78; the Dutch crusaders, 79-86; results of the crusades, 87-98; how a mud-hole became a garden, 110-121; intellectual movements, 122-130; Erasmus, 131-138; the struggle for independence, 140-178; Pilgrims in Leyden, 192-200; Pilgrims in America, 201-219.

527. [448.] (355.) **Building the nation; events in the history of the United States from the Revolution to the war between the States.** Charles Carleton Coffin. N. Y., Harper & Bros., 1882. 485 p. il. O. cl. 2.00 1.20

An account of the principal events in the United States between the time of the adoption of the Constitution to the election

	List price.	Price to districts.

of Abraham Lincoln to the presidency. There are many clear and accurate charts.

References: Social life, 78–112; progress of inventions, 63–78, 425–440; religion and morals, 251–282; education, 63–78; literature and science, 450–460; growth of slavery, 282–291, 387–425.

528. [457.] (196.) **Century book for young Americans.** E. S. Brooks. N. Y., Century Co., 1894. 249 p. il. O. cl. .... 1.50 .90

A very interesting way to find out about our government at Washington. There are some very good descriptions of the city of Washington and public buildings.

References: The government before the constitution, 1–16; the first years under the constitution, 17–30; the president, home and duties, 33–49; the cabinet, 51–62; the senate, 62–75; the house, 77–89; the supreme court, 91–102; departments, 107–152; the office holder, 161–176; our flags, 177–189; state government, 191–201; the citizen, 203; scenery, 235–249.

Geographical: White House, 38; Mt. Vernon, 103–105; Arlington Heights, 154–155; Washington, the city, 219–234; America's wonderful scenery, 235–249.

529. [438.] **Century book of the American colonies.** Elbridge S. Brooks. N. Y., Century Co., 1900. 233 p. il. sq. O. cl. .... 1.50 .90

Visits to places made famous by our colonial history.

530. [437.] (677.) **Child life in colonial days.** Alice Morse Earle. N. Y., Macmillan Co., 1899. 418 p. il. D. cl. 2.50 1.60

A book which will prove of great value in the history classes in upper form. In lower forms the children are always interested in the doings of other children, and taking this book as a basis, the teacher can arouse an interest in history, and do much in preparation for the formal study of history.

References: Babyhood, 1–33; children's dress, 34–62; school life, 63–116; school books, 117–149; penmanship and letters, 150–162; diaries and commonplace books, 163–175; manners, 211–226; religious thought and training, 227–247; story and picture books, 264–304; work, 305–341; games, 342–360; toys, 361–373.

531. **Colonies, 1492–1750.** Reuben Gold Thwaites. N. Y., Longmans, Green & Co., 1898. 301 p. maps. S. (Epochs of American history ser.) cl.......... 1.25 .80

532. **Formation of the Union, 1750–1829.** Albert Bushnell Hart. N. Y., Longmans, Green & Co., 1898. 278 p. maps. S. (Epochs of American history ser.) cl. 1.25 .80

	List price.	Price to districts.

533. **Division and reunion, 1829–1889.** Woodrow Wilson. N. Y., Longmans, Green & Co., 1899. 326 p. maps. S. (Epochs of American history ser.) cl.   1.25   .80

The three books above give a concise and complete survey of American history from the discovery of America to the present time and are valuable to use as supplementary to the text book.

534. [443.] **Conquest of the Old Northwest and its settlement by Americans.** James Baldwin. N. Y., American Book Company, 1901. 272 p. il. D. cl. .... .60 .51

Baldwin is one of the children's favorite authors and these two books are written in his usual interestingy way. They present a subject which ought to interest every child in Wisconsin.

535. [442.] **Discovery of the Old Northwest and its settlement by the French.** James Baldwin. N. Y., American Book Company, 1901. 272 p. il. D. cl. .60 .51

536. **First across the continent: the story of the exploring expedition of Lewis and Clark in 1803-4-5.** Noah Brooks. N. Y., C: Scribner's Sons, 1901. 365 p. il. map. O. cl. 1.50 1.35

Lewis and Clarke were the first white men to cross the continent of America, the first to explore the valleys of the Upper Missouri, the Yellowstone and the Columbia and its tributaries. This compilation, as fully as possible in the explorers' own words, has been made with the special view of interesting young readers, although adults will find it a thrilling and accurate history.

537. [447.] (354.) **Grandmother's story of Bunker Hill Battle, and other verse and prose.** Oliver Wendell Holmes. Bost., Houghton, Mifflin & Co., 1891. 96; 93 p. D. (Riverside school library.) cl. .60 .50

538. [434.] (339.) **History of the United States and its people, for the use of the schools.** Edward Eggleston. N. Y., American Book Company, 1888. 398 p. O. cl. 1.05 .90

A clear, concise, interesting, and well arranged history of the U. S. for children. Particular attention is given to manners and customs. The illustrations are unusually good, and add greatly to the interest and value of the book, making history visible,

	List price.	Price to districts.

539. **History of the United States for Junior classes.** Francis Newton Thorpe. Phil., Eldridge & Brother, 1901. 301 p. il. maps. D. cl......... .80 .72

A simple, clear, and forceful narrative of the history of our country. The book is well illustrated and contains thirty-five maps.

540. **Leading events of Wisconsin history: the story of the State.** Henry Legler. Milwaukee, Sentinel Co., 1898. 322 p. il. O. cl.................... .75 .55

"The chapters of this book were originally written for newspaper publication. Beginning with the travels and adventures of the early explorers and settlers and continuing through the later period, the narrative has been told, as nearly as circumstances would permit, in the words of actual participants."

References: Building of the mounds in Wisconsin, p. 14–17; Red men of Wisconsin, p. 22–28; Legendary lore of Wisconsin Indians, p. 29–37; Jesuits in Wisconsin, p. 62–77; La Salle, p. 78–79; Fur-traders, p. 118–21, p. 152–56; Black Hawk's war, p. 172–80; Rescue of Joshua Glover, a runaway slave, p. 226–29; Strange story of a spurious prince, p. 235–41; Civil war, p. 244–79.

541. **Making of New England, 1580–1643.** Samuel Adams Drake. N. Y., C: Scribner's Sons, 1900. 251 p. il. D. cl.................................... 1.50 .96

A narrative of the periods of discovery, exploration, and settlement of New England from the earliest beginnings to the time when the colonists established a secure foothold. Emphasis has been given to every thing that went to make up the home life of the colonists. This book should be read by the children in connection with the text book in studying the colonial history of New England.

References: Pilgrims, 67–103; Plymouth Rock, 80–87; Morton of Merry-mount, 115–119; Indian traits, 142–48, 184–86; Puritans, 149–60; Pequot war, 203–13; Harvard college, 214–16; First printing press, 216–18.

542. [444.] (347.) **Making of the great West, 1512–1883.** Samuel Adams Drake. N. Y., C: Scribner's Sons, 1896. 339 p. il. D. cl. .... 1.50 .96

The most interesting and most important facts in the Spanish, French, and English discoveries in America, the explorations, settlements and acquisition of territory beyond the Mississippi river, the growth and development of our great West, are well told.

	List price.	Price to districts.

543. [440.] (344.) **Making of Virginia and the middle colonies.** Samuel Adams Drake. N. Y., C: Scribner's Sons, 1893. 228 p. il. D. cl......... 1.50 .96

References: Voyages of Sir Humphrey Gilbert and Sir Walter Raleigh, 1-14; first colony at Roanoke, 15-22; second colony at Roanoke, 24-29; Virginia Indians, manners and customs, 30-31, 40-42; beginnings of Jamestown, 31-40; Capt. John Smith, and struggles of the colonists, 42-54; prosperity, 54-65; the massacre, 64-65; founding of Maryland, the Calverts, 66-76; Puritans, in Maryland, 81-82; treaties with the Iroquois, 86-89; the Iroquois, country and nations, 90-101; the Iroquois, manners and customs, 101-107; voyage of Hudson, 110-116; beginnings of New York, 117-123; Dutch rule in New York, 123-145; Long Island, 146-157; Albany, 158-160; settlement of New Jersey, 161-176; Founding of Delaware, 177-87; Penn, and the founding of Pennsylvania, 188-195; Philadelphia, 195-207; founding of the commonwealth of Pennsylvania, 207-215..

544. [453.] (680.) **Marching with Gomez:** a war correspondent's field note-book kept during four months with the Cuban army. Grover Flint. Bost., Houghton, Mifflin & Co., 1899. 294 p. map il. D. cl............................... 1.50 .96

A graphic account of incidents in our late war. The author is a keen observer, and manners and customs of the Cubans are vividly portrayed.

545. [436.] (342.) **Old times in the colonies.** Charles Carleton Coffin. N. Y., Harper & Bros., 1898. 460 p. il. O. cl. 2.00 1.20

Portrays life in the colonies. The book will prove valuable in making history real.

546. [456.] (370.) **Our country's flag.** Edward S. Holden. N. Y., D. Appleton & Co., 1898. 165 p. il. D. cl. .80 .65

A brief history of our own flag and the flags of foreign nations. The meaning of the flag is brought out in such a way as to give every boy and girl who reads the book a deeper love and veneration for our flag, the symbol of liberty and union.

547. [452.] (679.) **Our navy in the war with Spain.** John Spears. N. Y., C: Scribner's Sons, 1898. 406 p. il. D. cl. 2.00 1.28

A very good account of the part our navy took in the late war with Spain.

	List price.	Price to districts.

548. [432.] **Red true story book.** *Ed.* by Andrew Lang. N. Y., Longmans, Green & Co., 1897. 165 p. il. D. cl. .... .50 .41

Among the stories in this book are "Life and death of Joan of Arc," "The Burke and Wills exploring expedition," "How Marbot crossed the Danube," "The Conquest of Peru."

549. **Short history of the American Revolution.** Everett Tomlinson. N. Y., Doubleday, Page & Co., 1901. 419 p. il. D. cl. 2.00 1.80

"In this volume the author has tried to meet the demand for a clear, stirring and impartial one-volume history of the long struggle which resulted in American Independence. Mr. Tomlinson is an adept at the kind of writing that grips the essential interest of his subject, and for readers, either young or old, who wish to understand this crucial period of American history nothing could be better than this unenvolved, straightforward narrative. The 50 full page illustrations from old engravings, add greatly to its value."

550. [450.] (358.) **Smoked Yank.** Melvin Grigsby. *New and rev. ed.* Melvin Grigsby, 1899. 238 p. il. O. cl. .... .75 .60

There were some objectionable features in the first edition of this book, which are eliminated in this. It gives the experience of a Wisconsin man in the war for the Union, and will give the pupil some idea of the terrible cost of that war, in hardship and suffering.

551. [451.] (678.) **Story of our war with Spain.** Elbridge S. Brooks. Bost., Lothrop Pub. Co., 1899. 349 p. il. O. cl. .... 1.50 .85

A concise account of our war with Spain for young people. There is no discussion of methods or an elaborate plan of campaign, but simply a bird's eye view of the war from its beginning to its close. Older children in the middle form will read.

552. [445.] (348.) **Story of the great Republic.** H. A. Guerber. N. Y., American Book Company, 1899. 348 p. D. cl. .... .65 .56

A companion volume to the story of the Thirteen Colonies.

LIST OF BOOKS FOR TOWNSHIP LIBRARIES. 133

                                                            Price
                                                     List to dis-
                                                     price. tricts.

553. [441.] (345.) **Story of the Indian.** George Bird Grinnell. N. Y., D. Appleton & Co., 1898. 270 p. il. D. cl. .... 1.50 .96

    The volume gives a general view of Indian life.
    References: Home life, 1–15; amusements, 16–29; manners and customs, 30–47; occupations, 48–86; as warriors, 87–142; implements, 143–162; religion, 202–223; the coming of the white man, 224–239.

554. [454.] **Story of a soldier.** George A. Forsyth. N. Y., D. Appleton & Co., 1900. 389 p. il. D. cl...... 1.50 .96

    The life and work of the American soldier on the frontier.

555. [435.] (341.) **Story of the thirteen colonies.** H. A. Guerber. N. Y., American Book Company, 1898. 342 p. il. D. cl. .... .65 .56

    The main facts in our early history simply and vividly told. Read in connection with the history lesson these stories will add greatly to the interest.
    References: Indians, manners and customs, 13–20; mound builders, 20–23; Northmen, 24–30; Columbus, 36–59; explorations, 62–73; Huguenots, 73–76; introduction of slavery, 80; English expeditions, 81–86; Capt. John Smith's adventures, 87–97; Hudson, 102–105; Mayflower, 105–109; Plymouth Rock, 109–113; first Thanksgiving, 113–118; beginning of Boston, 122–125; John Eliot and Roger Williams, 126–134; Quakers, 134–136; King Philip's War, 138–142; beginning of New York, 142–146; William Penn, 147–152; Bacon's rebellion, 157–160; Charter Oak, 166–170; witchcraft, 170–173; explorations of Mississippi, 174–183; King William's War, 183–187; Queen Anne's War, 187–191; Washington, 191–199, 323; Franklin, 199–205; Braddock's defeat, 206–210; Wolfe at Quebec, 210–14; trouble with England, 214–32; War of Revolution, 233–323.

556. **Story of Wisconsin.** Reuben Gold Thwaites. Bost., Lothrop Publishing Co., c1891. 389 p. il. O. cl. 1.50 .85

    The teacher should interest the child in the history of his own state. Selections from this volume read to the pupils in connection with the national events studied in the history class, and also in connection with the geography of Wisconsin will do much toward fostering this interest.
    References: Mound-builders, 14–19; explorations, 19–35, 61–88; discovery of the Mississippi, 36–60; Joliet, 56–59, 61–63; La Salle, 63–68; Perrot, 71–76; Pierre le Sueur, 80; under British rule, 89; Indians, 92–93, 122, 134, 155–159, 163–192; conspiracy of Pontiac, 96; life of the settlers, 98–105; events of the War of 1812, 135–148; lead mining, 161–163; Black Hawk War, 180–192; territorial days, 193–229; becomes a state, 230–246; Fugitive Slave Act, 247–251; Wisconsin in Civil War, 270–329; since the war, 330–367.

	List price.	Price to districts.

557. [455.] **Thrilling days in army life.** George A. Forsyth. N. Y., Harper & Bros., 1900. 196 p. il. D. cl. .... 1.50 .96

Intensely interesting accounts of army life on the frontier, and in the civil war.

558. [446.] (349.) **War of Independence.** John Fiske. Bost., Houghton, Mifflin & Co., 1894. 200 p. maps. D. (Riverside lit. ser.) cl. .... .40 .32

A brief account of the War of Independence which has the charm of all of Fiske's historical writings. It will be found a valuable aid in the history class.

559. [449.] (357.) **Young folks' history of the War for the Union.** John D. Champlin, *jr.* N. Y., Henry Holt & Co., 1881. 593 p. il. O. cl. 2.50 1.60

This is a full and complete history of the war. The references call attention to a few of the principal events and heroes of that war.
References: Slavery, 17-31; John Brown's raid, 29; Secession 32-49; Lincoln, 32, 50-52, 63, 68, 242, 270, 315, 317, 349, 478, 505, 515, 541-542, 544; Sumter, 50-62; Harper's Ferry, 28, 69, 78, 282; Bull Run, 92-104; Ulysses S. Grant, 117, 123, 172, 210-213, 305-309, 341, 380, 433-468, 535, 538; Merrimac and Monitor, 231-239; Gettysburg, 354-371; Lee's surrender, 533-540.

560. **Child's history of Ireland.** Patrick Weston Joyce. N. Y., Longmans, Green & Co., 1897. 507 p. map. il. S. cl. .... 1.25 .80

A simple and instructive story of the history of Ireland.

561. **England's story; a history for Grammar and High Schools.** Eva March Tappan. Bost., Houghton, Mifflin & Co., c1901. 370 p. il. D. cl. .... .85 .77

The story of England told in a simple, interesting manner.

562. **Stories from English history.** Louise Creighton. N. Y., Longmans, Green & Co., 1898. 312 p. il. S. cl. .... 1.25 .80

Stories based on historical facts. They will serve to awaken an interest in English history.

LIST OF BOOKS FOR TOWNSHIP LIBRARIES. 135

| | List price. | Price to districts. |

563. **Stories from English history**: from B. C. 55 to A. D. 1901. Henry P. Warren, *Ed.* Bost., D. C. Heath & Co., 1901. 482 p. il. D. cl.................. .80 .70

Prepared with the object of interesting boys and girls in English history by stories of some of its great events and some of its great men.

References: King Alfred, p. 26–41; Norman conquest, p. 47–61; Crusades, p. 81–88; Hundred years war, p. 121—37; Joan of Arc, p. 133–37; Wars of the Roses, p. 147–55; William Caxton, p. 156–65; U. S. History, Discovery and colonial, p. 171–87; Reformation, p. 188–98; Sir Thomas More, p. 199–205; Queen Elizabeth, p. 214–21; Mary Queen of Scots, p. 222–28; Spanish Armada, p. 234–41; William Shakespeare, p. 248–54; Pilgrims, p. 255–57; Oliver Cromwell, p. 280–81; John Milton, p. 297–301; Crimean war, p. 423–26; Queen Victoria, p. 455–63.

564. [430.] (336.) **Story of the English.** H. A. Guerber. N. Y., American Book Company, 1898. 356 p. il. D. cl. .... .65 .56

Our history and institutions are so closely connected with those of England, it is desirable that the pupils should be familiar with the leading events of English history. The prominent characters, salient events, manners and customs of English life are so depicted in this volume as to rouse enthusiasm, stimulate further reading, and lead to a better understanding of our own history.

References: Druids, 13–17; Britons, 17–21, 24–26; Caesar in Britain, 21–23; Roman walls, 26–28; Anglo-Saxons, 31–34, 36–38; King Arthur, 34–36; Danes, 42–56; monasteries, 57–58; King Canute, 63–67; Battle of Hastings, 73–76; Norman Conquests, 76–79; arms and armour, 88–90; Thomas a Becket, 90–105; Richard Coeur de Lion, 105–117; Magna Charta, 119–124; Battle of Crecy, 152–155; age of chivalry, 159–161; Battle of Poitiers, 162–166; War of Roses, 187–195; Elizabeth, 217–250; Mary, Queen of Scots, 238–243; Spanish Armada, 244–246; gunpowder piot, 254–257; Cromwell, 264–275; loss of the 13 colonies, 305–308; Waterloo, 314–317; Victoria, 320–338.

565. [428.] (331.) **Story of Japan.** R. Van Bergen. N. Y., American Book Company, 1897. 294 p. il. D. cl. .... 1.00 .85

A brief and interesting history of Japan with many characteristic stories which illustrate the manners and customs of the people.

566. **Storied West Indies.** Frederick A. Ober. N. Y., D. Appleton & Co., 1900. 291 p. il. D. (Appleton's home reading books.) cl. .... .75 .65

This book gives the results of twenty years of travel and investigation by the author in the West Indies.

Contents: San Salvador; Columbus and Cuba; The search for Cipango; An Indian paradise; Fruits of the first voyage; The cannibal Caribs; First forts and settlements; The last Caciques; Destruction of the Indians; A city of sad memories; More about Santo Domingo; Buccaneers and treasure seekers; Conquest of Haiti; Black kings and emperors; Santiago and Havana; Jamaica and the maroons; Puerto Rico and the Virgin Isles; In the volcanic chain; Historic battlefields; Barbadoes, Tobago, and Trinidad.

567. [427.] **Stories of ancient peoples.** Emma J. Arnold. N. Y., American Book Company, 1901. 240 p. il. D. cl. .... .60 .43

A series of sketches of the manners and customs of the Egyptians, Babylonians, the Hittites, the Pheonicians, the Hebrews, the Medes, the Persians, the Hindus, and the Chinese, written in such a way as to interest young people and to arouse an interest in early history.

568. [429.] (332.) **Story of the Romans.** H. A. Guerber. N. Y., American Book Company, 1896. 288 p. il. D. cl. .... .60 .51

An interesting story of Rome, in which the main facts are simply and directly told for young readers. Many of the picturesque and mythical tales which form an important part of classical history, literature, and art are given. Older children of middle form will be interested in this book.

References: Aeneas, 11-22; founding of Rome, 25-27; Horatii and Curiatii, 39-42; lictors, 49; oracle of Delphi, 60-62; a Roman triumph, 69-72; patricians and plebians; 81-86; invasion of the Gauls, 104-106; ancient ships, 121-124; first Punic war, 124-128; Hannibal, 128-132; Archimedes, 133-137; destruction of Carthage, 139-142; Roman amusements, 142-145; Roman gladiators, 167-170; Pompey, 170-172; Caesar, 176-187; Antony and Cleopatra, 192-197; Augustan age, 197-203; Nero, 218-227; Pompeii and Herculaneum, 231-234; Marcus Aurelius Antonius, 248-251; invasion of the Goth, 262-264; Zenobia, 264-266.

569. [426.] **Wonder stories from Herodotus.** Retold by G. H. Boden, *and* W. Barrington D'Almeida. N. Y., Harper & Bros., 1900.. 163 p. il. D. cl......... 2.50 1.50

Interesting stories from Herodotus, delightfully told.

GEOGRAPHY AND TRAVEL.

See also "Geography," Middle Form.

References to those books on the various topics in geography ought to be placed upon the board for the lesson in geography. Remember the best geography is found in good books of travel and in fiction.

	List price.	Price to districts.
570. **Arctic Alaska and Siberia**, or, eight months with the Arctic whalemen. Herbert L. Aldrich. Chic., Rand, McNally & Co., 1889. 234 p. il. D. cl...	1.00	.65

A picture of life among the Arctic whalers described by one who made the cruise. The writer narrates in a vivid, dramatic manner his experiences on a whaling expedition and depicts the life of the Eskimos—their manners and customs, homes, games, and sports, modes of transportation, occupations, dress food and superstitions. The typical experiences of Arctic whalers in this region that is so full of inconceivable dangers and risks are told in a vivid, picturesque manner that will please the boy or girl who enjoys a story of adventure.

Contents: Icing in Behring sea; Among the Siberian Eskimo; Along the shores of Nakoorukland; Whaling; From Point Barrow, home; The Nakooruks; Some typical experiences.

571. [497.] (440.) **Book of the ocean.** Ernest Ingersoll. N. Y., Century Co., 1898. 279 p. il. O. cl......	1.50	.90

A very interesting book about the ocean, the life in the ocean, and some of the stirring events which have taken place on the ocean. Portions can be read in intermediate grades.

References: The ocean, 1-9; the bottom of the ocean, 9-13; ingredients found in sea water, 13-15; waves and their work, 15-16; tides, 17-20; ocean currents and their work, 20-26; the building and rigging of ships, 27-38; early voyages and explorations, 39-76; voyages of discovery to north pole, 77-105; famous warships, 107-122; some famous battles, 122-133; warships since the Revolution, 138-154; merchant vessels, 155-165; steamship routes, 165-170; robbers of the sea, 171-186; yachting and pleasure boating, 187-200; dangers of the sea, 202-210; for guidance and help of sailors, 211-227; our life saving service, 227-230; fishing and marine industries, 231-248; the plants of the sea and their uses, 249-258; animal life in the sea, 259-274.

	List price.	Price to districts.

572. [509.] (458.) **Boy travellers in Central Europe.** Thomas W. Knox. N. Y., Harper & Bros., 1893. 532 p. il. O. cl. 2.00 1.20

References: Havre, 1-50; Trouville, 50-68; Rouen, 70-79; Paris, 82-240; Geneva, 258-293; Castle of Chillon, 313-322; Switzerland and the glaciers, 324-368; the Rhine, 369-375; Zurich, 379-385; Tyrol, 399-422; Munich, 433-458; Salzburg, 459-475; Vienna, 480-522; Buda-Pesth, 523-532.

573. [508.] (457.) **Boy travellers in Northern Europe.** Thomas W. Knox. N. Y., Harper & Bros., 1892. 531 p. O. cl. 2.00 1.20

References: Holland: Manners and customs, 19-42, 132-133, 151-152; Erasmus, 35; canals and dykes, 43-46, 98-102; farm buildings and farm life, 48-53; Delft and its ware, 54-58; interesting historical facts, 59-67, 82-89, 106-108, 122-125; voyage on a canal, scenery, etc., 68-71; The Hague, 72-74; government, 74-76; education, 76, 138; Dutch art, 38-40, 78-82, 110, 120-122, 134-136; fisheries, 93-98; Leyden, 108-112; Haarlem, 113-117; invention of printing, 116-119; industries, 125-126, 136-137, 141, 149.

Germany: Krupp manufacturing works, 155-159; Cologne, 160-162; Drachenfels, 166-171; interesting historical facts, 172, 178-180, 222-246, 258-260, 379-383, 391-394; mediaeval furniture, 174-176; Rhine scenery and legends, 176-186; Gutenberg, 187-190; Wiesbaden, 191-210; Frankfort; Goethe, the Rothchilds, the cathedral, 210-223; Martin Luther, 222-246; Goethe and Schiller, 238-246; Wagner and his music, 260-265; German army, 268-274; Berlin and its neighborhood, 275-305; German art, 342-347; German manners and customs, 348-364, 396-398; Hamburg and neighborhood, 365-375; German navy, 375-379; Lubeck, 384-390.

Denmark: Copenhagen, 399; Hans C. Andersen, 406; Danish art, 413-416; interesting historical facts, 424-430; industries, 432, 444; manners and customs, 434-442.

Norway: Christiana, 450; exports, 451, 468; manners and customs, 466, 469; industries, 467-471, 481-482, 489, 502; traveling by post, 474-482; school system, 483; government, 484, 486-488; interesting historical facts, 484-485; northernmost town of Europe, 490-494; midnight sun, 494-499; Lapps, manners and customs, 500; Bergen, 502-506.

Sweden: Gotha canal and Stockholm, 508-523; interesting historical facts, 515-516, 518; manners and customs, 521-523; Upsala, 524; universities, 524; industries, 530.

574. [505.] (451.) **Boy travellers in South America.** Thomas W. Knox. N. Y., Harper & Bros., 1885. 510 p. il. O. cl. 2.00 1.20

Adventures of two youths in a journey through Ecuador, Peru, Bolivia, Paraguay, Argentine Republic, and Chili, with descriptions of voyages upon the Amazon and La Plata rivers.

		Price
	List price.	to districts.

575. [510.] (459.) **Boy travellers in Southern Europe.** Thomas W. Knox. N. Y., Harper & Bros., 544 p. il. O. cl. 2.00 1.20

References: Venice, 1–60; Verona, 61–77; Lake Como, 99–105; Milan, 109–118; Genoa, 119–150; Spezia, 160–161; Carrara marbles, 161–163; Pisa, 163–171; Florence, 173–232; Rome, 255–315; Naples, 315–349; Vesuvius, 350–362; Pompeii, 363–374; the Italian army, 384–400; Malta, 407–436; the Riviera, 443–463; Monaco, 477–491; Spain, 501–544.

576. [511.] (461.) **Boy travellers in the far East.** Pt. 1. Adventures of two youths in a journey to Japan and China. Thomas W. Knox. N. Y., Harper & Bros., 1879. 421 p. il. map. O. cl............. 2.00 1.20

References: Japan: Yohohama, 79–100; Tokio, 109–155; Enoshima, 169–182; Fusiyama, 183–214; hari-kari, 215–226; amusements, 227–238; 262–265; Japanese art, 239–253, 295–300; Japanese women, 254–261.
China: Shanghai, 319–327; Pekin, 352–376; Great Wall, 377–387; Hongkong, 400–404; Canton, 405–421.

577. **Europe.** Frank G. Carpenter. N. Y., American Book Company, 1902. 456 p. il. maps. D. cl....... .70 .60

The fourth book in the "Carpenter geographical reader" series. This and the "Tarr and McMurry" set ought to be in every school library.
References: Across the Atlantic, 9–14; Southern Ireland, 15–24; Central and Northern Ireland, 25–31; Glasgow and the Clyde, 32–39; The Scottish Highlands—Edinburgh, 40–47; Rural England, 48–54; Manufacturing England, 55–65; London—the commercial center of the world, 66–75; How England is governed—a visit to Parliament, 76–84; Rural France, 85–94; Commercial and manufacturing France, 95–105; Paris—the most beautiful city of the world, 106–116; How France is governed, 117–124; Belgium—the busiest workshop of Europe, 125–132; A country below the sea, 133–143; In the Dutch cities—Amsterdam, Rotterdam, and the Hague, 144–155; The land of the Danes, 156–162; Where the sun shines at midnight, 163–175; Travels in Norway and Sweden, 176–185; In the German empire, 186–194; The seaports of Germany, 195–202; Berlin, 203–214; The Emperor—how Germany is governed, 215–222; Rural and manufacturing Germany, 223–233; Up the Rhine to Switzerland, 234–248; Switzerland—the Alps, 249–259; The Swiss people and how they are governed, 260–270; The Upper Danube—from Ulm to Vienna, 271–279; In the capital of Austria-Hungary, 280–292; Hungary and the Hungarians, 293–300; On the lower Danube from Budapest to the Black Sea, 301–310; In Odessa—general view of Russia, 311–319; The Russian peasants—a nation of villages, 320–329; In St. Petersburg, 330–339; Moscow—commercial and manufacturing Russia, 340–350; Down the Volga to the Caspian sea, 351–360; In Constantinople, 361–370; Among the Mohammedans, 371–380; In modern Greece, 381–391; Venice, 392–401; Northern Italy, 402–410; Rome, the capital of Italy, 411–416; Naples and Mount Vesuvius, 417–427; Rural Spain, 428–435; In the cities of Spain, 436–444; The kingdom of Portugal, 445–452.

	List price.	Price to districts.

578. **Europe and other continents**: with review of North America. Ralph S. Tarr, *and* Frank M. McMurry. N. Y., Macmillan Co., 1901. 574 p. il. maps D. cl. (Tarr & McMurry's geographies: third book.) .... .75 .68

The series of which this is the third book will furnish an excellent source of reference material to use to supplement the outline given in the general text book in geography. The accounts given in the average text of the leading industries of a country are short and inadequate. In these books they are discussed more in detail in connection with the sections of a country in which they are most prominent.

One very excellent feature of the books is a selected list of references in the back of each volume suggesting further readings in geography and travel that may be carried on in connection with the study of the text.

These reference lists will be of great value to the teacher.

References: South America, p. 96-148; Europe, p. 149-352; Cuba, p. 353-414; Africa, p. 415-60; Australia, p. 461-85; United States, p. 487-516, 523-41; North America, p. 487-522.

579. [501.] **Greater America**; the latest acquired insular possession. Bost., Perry Mason & Co., 1900. 189 p. il. D. cl. .... .50 .40

References: Porto Rico, 3-66; Manila, 67-130; Hawaii, 131-189.

580. [502.] **Hawaii and its people**: the land of the rainbow and palm. Alexander S. Twombly. N. Y., Silver, Burdett & Co., 1900. 384 p. il. D. cl. (World and its people. Bk. 9.) .... .68 .62

Valuable in the work in geography.

581. [504.] (450.) **In and out of Central America**, and other sketches and studies of travel. Frank Vincent. 4th ed. N. Y., D. Appleton & Co., 1896. 246 p. il. maps. D. cl..................... 2.00 1.25

Valuable for work in geography.

References: Central America: size and population, 2-3; history, 4; manners and customs, 5-6; inhabitants, 6-7; industries, 7-8; government, 9-10.

Costa Rica: Punta Arenas, 12-17; dress of natives, 14-15, 23, 31; productions, 18, 34-35; San Jose, 20-36; manners and customs, 32-33.

Nicaragua: Manners and customs, 52-54, 65-66; Granada, 58-61; Leon, 62-68.

Honduras: Tegucigalpa, 77-87; manners and customs, 82-88.

Salvador: San Salvador, 94-105; earthquakes and volcanoes, 107, 109-110; manners and customs, 103.

LIST OF BOOKS FOR TOWNSHIP LIBRARIES. 141

	Price
List	to dis-
price.	tricts.

Guatemala: San Jose, 110-138; University of Guatemala, 133-136; manners and customs, 136-137.
Cambodita: History, 152-153; productions, 154; Buddhist temple, 154-175.
Antilles: Martinique, 184-185; Guadeloupe, 186-188; dress, 192-193.
Burmah: Government, 202-204; Mandalay, 204; court life and customs, 205-208.
Dom Pedro, 213-225; white elephants, 226-246.

582. [512.] (462.) **Japanese girls and women.** Alice Mabel Bacon. Bost., Houghton, Mifflin & Co., 1897. 333 p. S. (Riverside lib. for young people.) cl..... .75 .45

A very interesting account of life in Japan. The book ought to be read to the pupils in connection with the study of geography. The older pupils will enjoy reading for themselves.

References: Empress, 154-159, 167; court lady, 153-154; Japanese mother, 99-100; 129-130; dancing girls, 286-287; servant, 320-323; peasants, 230-231, 235, 260-261; children, 2-9, 17, 20, 22-24; children's amusements, 25-33; dress, all classes, 6, 7, 14-16, 61-62, 126-128; 146, 188-189, 190-192, 243-244; dress, lower classes, 126-128; buildings of interest, 249, 251-253, 280; modes of travel, 26, 70, 92, 268, 272, 320-321; manners and customs, 126-127, 202, 204-205, 252-253, 264-269, 315-317; funeral customs, 131-132; marriage, 19-20, 57-72, 74; amusements, 38, 44-46, 63-64, 136-137, 145, 165-166, 270-277, 287-288; theaters, 33, 99, 293-294; holidays, 25; occupations of women, 23-24, 82, 95-96, 126-127, 158, 161-166; 226, 236-238, 245-249. 280-285; religion, 240-241; education, 37-48, 79, 162-163, 308-309; music, 41-42; language, 40-41, 179; flowers, 295-297.

583. [507.] (688.) **Land of the long night.** Paul du Chaillu. N. Y., C: Scribner's Sons, 1899. 266 p. il. D. cl. 2.00 1.30

"The Land of the Long Night is a land of darkness, of snow, of wind, and at times of intense cold. We shall sleep on the snow in bags made of reindeer skins, follow the nomadic Laplander and his reindeer, live with him, and sleep in his Kata, or tent. We shall hunt wolves, bears, and different kinds of foxes and other animals, and sail and fish on the stormy Arctic seas." The introduction.

For upper form, though older children of middle form will read. The book is very interesting.

References: The journey, 1-28, 244-266; the long night, 73-76; the return of the sun, 109-111; cold and wind storms, 173-182; travel, 60-72, 92-98, 106-108, 155; in mountains, 183-189; dogs, 90-92; reindeer, 92-98, 104-105, 138-140; wolves, 112-128; 136-137; foxes, 160-164; bears, 165-169; Finlander's home, 43-47; Laplander's dress, 31-35, 147; Lapp hospitality, 75; Lapp tent, 80-84; food, 83-84, 89-90; baby's cradle, 86-87; shoes, 48-55, 129-135; bathing, 56-59, 143-144; washing clothes, 145; at sea, 190-204; life of fishermen, 205-218; Hammerfest, 227-231; Lapp hamlet, 232-240.

	Price List to dis- price. tricts.

584. [499.] (443.) **North America.** Frank G. Carpenter. N. Y., American Book Company, 1898. 352 p. il. maps. D. cl. .... .60 .51

A journey through the most characteristic parts of North America. The greater part of the journey is taken in the United States. The chief cities are visited, the sources of our national wealth are dwelt upon, the great belts of productions are visited, and processes of preparing raw material for markets watched. The great natural wonders of our country are vividly described.

References: General view, 9-14; City of Washington, 14-44; Baltimore and oyster beds, 45-75; New York and some of its wonders, 57-65, 73-75; our foreign commerce, 65-73; commerce and manufactures in New England, 76-90; Boston, 91-99; Virginia, 99-103; tobacco, 104-108; cotton, 109-118; among the ice fields, 119-124; Savannah, 125; turpentine, 126-150; Florida, 130-135; Mississippi River jetties, and traffic, 135-138, 150-159; New Orleans, 138-143; sugar plantations, 143-150; corn belt, 159-164; wheat farm, 164-171; the Great Lakes, 172-179, 190-195; iron regions, 179-181; copper, 182-183; lumber regions, 184-190; Niagara Falls, 195-202; oil regions, 203-218; Pittsburg and iron works, 218-225; Chicago, 225-234; Pike's Peak, 235-236; grand cañon of Colorado, 238-239; gold and gold mines, 240-248; silver mine, 248-255; Salt Lake City and Great Salt Lake, 259-264; Southern California, 264-274; San Francisco, 274-278; Pacific northwest, 278-284; Yellowstone Park, 284-289; Indian reservations, 290-298; Alaska, 298-306; British America, 306-327; Mexico, 327-345; Central America, 345-352.

585. [506.] (454.) **Personally conducted.** Frank R. Stockton. N. Y., C: Scribner's Sons, 1889. 240 p. il. O. cl. 2.00 1.25

The reader is personally conducted by Stockton to the various interesting places in Europe.

References: Avignon, 7-19; Genoa, 20-38; Pisa, 40-44; Rome, 45-80; Naples, 81-89; Capri, 90-99; Florence, 100-105; Venice, 106-118; Mont Blanc, 120-137; Paris, 138-157; London, 158-180; England, 181-200; Holland, 201-208; Cologne, 210-212; the Rhine, 212-218; Brussels, 218-221; Antwerp, 222-225.

586. [498.] **Sailing alone around the world.** Captain Joshua Slocum. N. Y., Century Co., 1900. 294 p. il. D. cl. 2.00 1.30

Boys who are interested in boats and sailing will read this book.

587. [503.] (449.) **Winter in Central America and Mexico.** Helen J. Sanborn. Bost., Lee & Shepard, 1887. 321 p. D. cl. ....:....... 1.50 .95

Valuable in geography.

References: The Mississippi and the gulf, 12-18; British Honduras, 21-24; Guatemala, 25-185; Indians, 27-30, 44-46, 63-83,

93; bull fight, 122-133; government, 154-158; coffee plantations, 162-169; character and customs of the people, 170-182; Isthmus of Panama, 196-206.
Mexico: 221-321; Vera Cruz, 225-232; city of Mexico, 248-304.

588. [496.] **Wonders of nature as seen and described by famous writers.** Esther Singleton, *ed.* N. Y., Dodd, Mead & Co., 1900. 366 p. il. D. cl...... 2.00   1.20

Descriptions of the grand, the curious, and the awe-inspiring in nature, from our best writers. Valuable for work in geography.

589. [500.] (447.) **World and its people.** Bk. 4. Our American neighbors. Fanny E. Coe. N. Y., Silver, Burdett & Co., 1897. 328 p. il. D. cl...... .60   .54

References: Canada, 13-148; fisheries of Newfoundland, and life of the fisherman, 15-25; New Brunswick, 25-35; industries, 26, 28-29, 32, 33, 86; Nova Scotia, 33-35; exports, 33; tides, 33-35; Montreal, 35-49; amusements, 49-67; through the Great Lakes, 68-83; St. Lawrence, 83-93; government, 86-88; Quebec, 93-108; French-Canadian farm life, 108-120; lumberman's life, 120-131; Canadian prairie, 131-134, 139-143; Winnipeg, 134-136; life of Indian trapper, 137-139; British Columbia, 143-148; Indians of Vancouver Island, 148.

Mexico: 151-193: manners and customs, 156-157, 165, 173, 179-181, 190; ranch life, 157-158, 160-161; mines, 158-160, 163-164; city of Mexico, 166-181; industries, 181-185, 190-191.

Central America: 197-215; industries, 201, 206, 213, 214; manners and customs, 202-203, 211-213.

South America: 219-324; Brazil, 222-249; Paraguay, 249-254; Uruguay, 254-257; animals, 227-228; industries, 230, 233-234, 237-239, 253, 263, 275, 279, 307; Argentine Republic, 257-268; manners and customs, 236-237, 239, 245-247, 250-251, 253, 259-263, 280, 285, 296, 306-307, 311, 320; Chili, 274-287; Peru 287-299; Bolivia, 300-303; Ecuador, 303-307; Colombia, 308-313; Venezuela, 313-320; Guiana, 320-324.

590. **World and its people:** Bk. 5. Modern Europe. Fanny E. Coe. N. Y., Silver, Burdett & Co., 1898. 403 p. il. D. cl............................. .60   .54

References: Bird's eye view of Europe, 13-18; England, 18-59; Scotland, 59-78; Ireland, 78-91; Norway and Sweden, 92-119; Denmark, 119-132; Holland, 133-154; Belgium, 154-167; Germany, 167-197, 213-225; Austria, 202-212; Switzerland, 225-249; France, 249-278; Spain, 278-299; Italy, 299-334; Greece, 335-349; Turkey, 350-357; Servia, 357-359; Russia, 359-398.

591. [513.] (464.) **World and its people.** Bk. 6. Life in Asia. Mary Cate Smith. N. Y., Silver, Burdett & Co., 1897. 328 p. il. map. D. cl............ .60   .54

References: India, 18-105; Ceylon, 105-114; Indo-China, 115-131; China, 131-181; Japan, 181-232; Korea, 232-252; Persia, 253-269; Turkestan, 270-286; Palestine, 287-324.

592. [514.] (465.) **World and its people.** Bk. 7. Views in Africa. Ann B. Badlam. N. Y., Silver, Burdett & Co., 1897. 544 p. il. D. cl.................. .70 .63

References: The "Dark Continent," 13-97; Congo River, 102-114; Congo Free State, 114-117; lake region, 117-156; mountain life, 156-162; soil, 162-166; minerals, 166-180; South Africa, 180-276; western Africa, 277-283; climate, 306-310; vegetation, 311-321; animals, 322-383, 393-401; equatorial Africa, 388-392; people, 402-451; Morocco, 451-469; Algiers, 470-484; Tunis, 484-488; Tripoli, 488-496; Egypt, 500-544.

593. [515.] (471.) **World and its people.** Bk. 8. Australia, and the islands of the sea. Eva M. C. Kellogg. N. Y., Silver, Burdett & Co., 1898. 448 p. il D. cl. .... .68 .61

References: Australia, 13-73; Tasmania, 74-81; New Zealand, 82-94; Greenland, 94-111; Iceland, 112-122; Nova Zembla, 150, 158; Newfoundland, 160-170; Bermudas, 172-186; West Indies, 187-206; Haiti, 207-212; Jamaica, 213-219; Porto Rico, 220-225; Trinidad, 226-232; Cape Verde Islands, 242-247; Azores, 248-254; Canary Islands, 255-265; Isles of Wight and Man, 273-281; Sardinia, 288-298; Sicily, 299-312; Crete, 319-329; Malay Archipelago, 350-359; Sumatra and Java, 360-369; Philippine Islands, 378-382; Samoan Islands, 403-418; Hawaiian Islands, 418-430; Islands of S. America, 431-437.

CIVICS.

594. [459.] (401.) **American citizen.** Charles F. Dole. Bost., D. C. Heath & Co., 1891. 320 p. D. cl.... .80 .67

The book not only states the facts about our government, but illustrates some of the moral principles which underlie the life of civilized man.

595. [462.] (404.) **Among the law makers.** Edmund Alton. N. Y., C: Scribner's Sons, 1896. 308 p. D. cl..... .... 1.50 .95

By means of the full illustration and entertaining description, the reader of this book can get a very good picture of transactions and scenes in our national legislature. The book is largely a personal reminiscence of a former congressional page.

	Price
List	to dis-
price.	tricts.

596. [460.] (402.) **Civics for young Americans.** William M. Giffin. Lovell & Co., 1892. 132 p. il. D. cl. .50 .45

Our constitution, together with simple explanations of leading facts for children.

597. [458.] **True citizen: how to become one.** W. F. Markwick, *and* W. A. Smith. N. Y., American Book Company, 1900. 259 p. D. (Eclectic school readings.) cl. .... .60 .51

Citizenship from the moral and ethical standpoint. Lessons in right living are given in such a way, with anecdote and incident, as to interest and hold attention.

598. **Uncle Sam abroad.** J. E. Conner. Chic., Rand, McNally & Co., c1900. 238 p. il. D. cl........... 1.25 .82

Instructive chapters on our consular and diplomatic service entitled: The state department; Consular service—officers; Consular service—duties; Diplomatic service; Uncle Sam and expansion. In an appendix are given lists of our present diplomatic and Consular officers and their present stations.

599. [461.] (403.) **Young American.** Henry Pratt Judson. Bost., Maynard, Merrill & Co., 1897. 244 p. il. D. cl. .... .60 .52

An outline of our system of government clearly told. The younger children may be interested in portions through the history lesson. The books includes a number of patriotic writings in prose and poetry, suitable for general exercises.

References: Patriotism, 11-21; laws and their makers, 36-42; our government, 42-47; how the U. S. became independent, 63-72; Revolutionary War, 72-94; the constitution and federal government, 94-104; American home-rule, 109-118; congress, 119-125; administration of general government of U. S., 126-166; administration in the states, 167-179; trial by jury, 181-194; taxation, 195-201.

SCIENCE.

Observation and reading must go hand in hand. Aim to make the pupil alive to his surroundings, quick to see, accurate in his observations, and logical and accurate in his statements. See Manual, *Nature lessons—Upper Form.*

	List price.	Price to districts.
600. [494.] (687.) **About the weather.** Mark W. Harrington. N. Y., D. Appleton & Co., 1899. 246 p. il. D. (Appleton's home reading books.) cl........	.65	.55

A knowledge of the laws underlying the science of the weather is not only interesting, but of the greatest possible utility. Few fields of scientific investigation offer more interesting and valuable results in teaching close and discriminating observation of nature. The teacher will find this book very suggestive and helpful in the work in the middle form.

References: Pressure of air, 33-47; the winds, 48-59; temperature and humidity of the air, 66-72; dew, fog, cloud, rain, and snow, 73-98; general storms, 99-109; the cyclone, 110-135; tornadoes, 156-165; storms of ice, sleet, ball now, and hail, 166-173; thunder storms, 174-179; lightning and thunder, 180-186; local influences on weather, 194-202; weather predictions, 203-222.

601. **Animals in action:** studies and stories of beasts, birds and reptiles; their habits, their homes and their peculiarities. *Comp.* by Elbridge S. Brooks. Bost., Lothrop Pub. Co., 1901. 360 p. il. O. cl.	1.50	.88

"The most of the illustrated books about animals picture them in repose, or as seen in captivity. The chief feature of the illustrations in this book is that the artist who has drawn the most of them, the noted German animal artist Specht, studied his subjects in their own haunts and homes, and has presented them in action and the fierce struggle for life rather than in the enforced listlessness of captivity. The nature of wild animals being wild, the drawings by Specht naturally lean toward personal conflict and the rivalries of the jungle, the desert, and the forest; but he is true to nature, and correct in presentation. The text accompanying the illustrations is most of it adapted from the German of Brahm, the best living authoritiy on natural history."

Contents: Golden eagle in his nest, 1-5; Fight between two golden eagles, 6-9; Gorilla fighting with a leopard. 10-13; Coralling the zebra, 14-17; Otter and the wild goose, 18-21; Partridge and the mouse weasel, 22-25; Fur seals fighting for a mate, 26-29; A mail carrier of the desert, 30-32; Black-backed jackal gnus, 33-36; Marsh hen and pike, 37-40; Blackcocks fighting, 41-44; Aurochs, or European bison, 45-48; Crocodiles in battle, 49-52;

Apteryx and the dingo, 53-56; Anaconda fishing, p. 57-60; Sea-elephants, 61-64; Life beneath the sea, 65-68; Condor and the Llama, 69-72; Giant salamander, 73-76; Hunting with the Chetah, 77-80; Climbing kangaroo, 81-82; Striped adder and the frog, 82-85; The walrus, 86-89; The water moccasin, 90-92; The great turtle, 93-96; An Esquimau in battle with a polar bear, 97-100; The swan and the fox, 101-102; Hunting the tiger with elephants, 102-108; Saved, 109-112; The shrike, 113-116; Black gelada, 117-120; Eagle hawk and chameck, 121-124; The yak, 125-130; Sea eagle, 131-132; Dolphin and his guests, 132-134; Oryx and the painted hyena, or hunting dog, 135-140; African ostrich, 141-142; Grizzly bear attacked by a buffalo, 142-144; A diver defending himself against sharks, 145-150; Wood owl, 151-152; Albatroses and sea gulls, 152-154; Desert lynx, 155-158; Ocelot and night monkey, 159-160; "Who stops to choose waits to lose," 160-162; Hamster and polecat, 163-166; The spectral Tarsier hunting Drosera, 167-170; The Aoudad, 171-172; Sparrow owl catches a squirrel, 172-176; The hyena and the zebra, 177-180; The opossum and the earth squirrel, or chipmunk, 181-184; Fighting sea-lions, 185-186; Mother bear bathing her cubs, 186-190; Tiger with a booty, 191-192; Giraffes at a lagoon, 192-197; The Fossa, 198-200; Ant-bears in a quarrel, 201-202; A prairie scene in winter, 202-207; Wart hogs, 208-211; The saiga, or antelope of the Steppes, 212-215; Ocelot capturing a flamingo, 216-218; The orang-outang, 219-220; Suricate and the great shrew mouse, 220-225; Bearded vulture and common griffin in combat, 226-229; The peacock Argus, 230-233; The tapir, 234-237; Octopus and the lobster, 238-241; California bighorn, 242-245; A vanishing animal, 246-249; Bezoar and lynx, 250-253; Frigate bird, 254-257; Mongoos and Cobra de Capello, 258-261; The Cougar, or puma, 262-264; The crocodile and the pelican, 265-268; Egyptian asp capturing a jerboa, or jumping mouse, 269-274; Marabou in battle with hyenas, 275-276; Sperm whale and polar fox, 276-279; Elk in battle with wolves, 280-282; Dingo and duckbill, 283-286; The ibex, 287-289; The narwhal, 291-294; Buffalo attacked by lions, 295-296; John Dory and the octopus 296-301; A family of chimpanzees, 302-304; Fighting kangaroos, 305-306; A whale attached by grampi, 306-310; a battle between deer, 311-312; Wapiti deer on a Rocky Mountain range, 312-317; A duel in an Indian jungle, 318-320; Wandering reindeer, 321-326; Dogs pursuing a wild boar, 327-328; Tyras pouncing upon a pampas deer, 328-330; An elk at bay, 331-332; Kite, or glede, and saker, 332-336; Monitor and Egyptian goose, 337-338; Tree panther and tree snake, 338-343; The leopard meets his match, 344-346; A battle between giants, 347-350; A beaver colony, 351-355; Quarrelsome storks, 356-358; The cat and the donkey, or a safe port, 359-360; Types of dogs, 360.

602. **Apes and monkeys:** their life and language. R. L. Garner. *Introd.* by Edward Everett Hale. Bost., Ginn & Co., 1900. 297 p. il. D. cl. 2.00 1.28

"This volume is the natural product of many years devoted by the author to studying the speech and habits of monkeys. That naturally led him up to the study of the great apes. The matter contained in this work is chiefly a record of the tabulated facts gleaned from his special field of research. The aim in view is to convey to the casual reader a more correct idea than now prevails concerning the physical, mental, and social habits of apes and monkeys and to prepare him for a wider appreciation of animals in general.

Believing that a more perfect knowledge of these animals will bring man into closer fellowship and deeper sympathy with nature, and with an abiding trust that it will widen the bounds of humanity and cause man to realize that he and they are but common links in the one great chain of life." From the Author's preface.

The story is written in a vivid, dramatic manner that will interest the boys and girls of the upper form. A good book for Library Reading.

	List price.	Price to districts.
603. [464.] **Biography of a Grizzly.** Ernest Seton-Thompson. N. Y., Century Co., 1900. sq. D. cl........	1.50	.96

Intensely interesting. All grades will enjoy this story.

604. **Bird day: how to prepare for it.** Charles A. Babcock. N. Y., Silver, Burdett & Co., c1901. 95 p. il. D. cl....................................	.50	.45

Contains many good suggestions on "How to study the birds" and on the Observation of Bird Day.

Contents: History of the movement for "Bird day"; The value of birds; The destruction of birds; Plan of study; Further suggestions; Directions for written work; Programs for bird day; The poets and the birds; Objects and results of Bird day; Some representative birds.

605. [480.] (429.) **Birds and bees:** Sharp eyes. John Burroughs. Bost., Houghton, Mifflin & Co., 1887. 88; 96 p. D. (Riverside lit. ser.) cl..............	.40	.32

"To read John Burroughs is to live in the woods, and fields, and to associate intimately with all their timid inhabitants."—Mary E. Burt.

606. **Birds of lakeside and prairie.** Edward B. Clark. Chic., A. W. Mumford, 1901. 150 p. il. D. cl..	1.00	.55

An interesting and instructive book on birds. An excellent book for Library Reading.

Contents: Birds of a smoky city; Songsters of the Skokie; Through the Lost River valley; In Southern Hoosier hills; In winter fields; on the trail of Pokagon; Some odd bits of bird life; In God's Acre; Where the black tern builds; Comedy and tragedy; Spring on the Kankakee; "From haunts of coot and hern"; Reaches of the prairie; G. N. Shrike, Butcher.

	List price.	Price to districts.

607. **Birds of song and story.** Elizabeth *and* Joseph Grinnell. Chic., A. W. Mumford, 1901. 150 p. il. D. cl. .... 1.00 .55

Contains several excellent colored plates of our common birds. References: Robin, 17–28; Mocking bird, 29–35; Cat-bird, 36–39; Hermit-thrush, 40–44; Grosbeaks, 45–52; Orioles, 53–60; Canary bird, 61–72; Sparrows, 73–82; Summer yellowbird, 83–93; Bluebird, 94–100; Tanagers, 101–106; Meadow-lark, 107–14; Skylark, 115–20; Bobolink, 121–29; Nesting-time, 130–43.

608. [477.] (423.) **Birds of village and field.** Florence A. Merriam. Bost., Houghton, Mifflin & Co., 1898. 406 p. il. D. cl. 2.00 1.28

A very good book for beginners to use in the study of birds. The suggestions as to how to observe birds, the key to birds, and the illustrations, are especially fine.

609. [476.] **Bird studies with a camera.** Frank M. Chapman. N. Y., D. Appleton & Co., 1900. 218 p. il. D. cl. 1.75 1.08

"It is sincerely hoped that these studies may increase the interest in the study of birds in nature, and at the same time furnish a more profitable and delightful outlet for the hunting instinct than is afforded by the shotgun or rifle,"—The author.

610. [493.] (683.) **Boy's book of inventions: stories of the wonders of modern science.** Ray Stannard Baker. N. Y., McClure, Phillips & Co., 1899. 354 p. il. D. cl. 2.00 1.20

Contains fine descriptions of our latest inventions. Sub-marine boats, liquid air, wireless telegraphy, auto-mobile, x-ray photography, the phonograph, and modern sky scrapers, are the leading subjects. One of the best books.

611. [472.] (413.) **Curious homes and their tenants.** James Carter Beard. N. Y., D. Appleton & Co., 1897. 275 p. il. D. cl. .... .65 .52

The book treats of many queer homes that certain tribes of human beings, monkeys, lemurs, ants, birds, fish, and other animals, build for themselves. The homes are divided into homes in the earth, in the rocks, in the trees, in the grass, in the snow, in the water, and portable houses.

	List price.	Price to districts.

612. [473.] (414.) **Eye spy.** William Hamilton Gibson. N. Y., Harper & Bros., 1898. 264 p. il. O. cl... 2.50   1.55

Among flowers and animate things.
References: The floundering beetle, 1-10; fox fire, 7-23; figwort, 24-33; oak galls, 34-43; green pansies, 44-52; tumble-bug, 53-63; horse-hair snakes, 64-71; beetle, 83-90; paper wasp, 91-103; spider's span, 104-111; ballooning spiders, 112-121; lace wing fly, 122, 129; perfumed beetle, 130-135; musbrooms, 136-144; cocoons, 145-153; nettle-leaf tent-builders, 154-162; the dandelion burglar, 170-174; house-fly, 178-184; tendrils, 185-194; grasshopper, 195-201; riddles in flowers, 202-212; clover, 213-220; barberries, 221-229; locust, 246-256.

613. [495.] (682.) **Fairy-land of science.** Arabella B. Buckley. N. Y., D. Appleton & Co., 1899. 252 p. il. D. cl. ......   1.50   .40

The original volume, "Fairy-land of science," has been considerably extended so as to include the latest scientific discoveries. The work has been largely re-illustrated. It is a very readable book.

614. [492.] (433.) **First lessons in physical science.** Elroy M. Avery *and* Charles P. Sinnott. N. Y., Butler, Sheldon & Co., 1897. 160 p. il. D. cl.........   .60   .51

A book filled with experiments in physics which may be performed with very simple and inexpensive apparatus. Many of the experiments with explanations and discussions in general exercises will create in the school an interest in physical science.

615. **First studies of plant life.** George Francis Atkinson. Bost., Ginn & Co., 1901. 266 p. il. D. cl   .60   .50

The object of this book is to interest children in the life and work of the plants. The topics outlined should be presented by the teacher and the book should serve as a source of reference material for the children.
Contents: Growth and parts of plants; Work of plants; Behavior of plants; Life stories of plants; Battles of plants in the world.

616. [471.] (411.) **Flashlights on nature.** Grant Allen. N. Y., Doubleday, Page & Co., 1898. 312 p. il. D. cl. .....   1.50   .88

A most interesting book for teacher and pupil to read together. Facts of life around us not generally known.

	List price.	Price to districts.

617. [469.] (408.) **Four-footed Americans and their kin.** Mabel Osgood Wright. N. Y., Macmillan Co., 1898. 432 p. il. D. cl. 1.50   1.20

A story of four children who spent the winter at the farm of Dr. Hunter, a naturalist. The book tells what they did and how they became acquainted with the animals described. The older children in the middle form can read this book. The illustrations and diagrams are especially fine.

References: The woodchuck, Chap. 5; the bison, Chap. 10; hares, Chap. 11; otter, skunk, weasel, raccoon, mink, sable, Chap. 13; foxes, Chap. 14; wolves, Chap. 15; puma, wild cat, Chap. 16; bears, Chap. 17; musk ox and polar bear, Chap. 19; walrus, sea lion, seal, Chap. 20; elk, Amer. deer, moose, Chap. 22; whales, porpoises, Chap. 23; rats and mice, Chap. 24; squirrels, chipmunks, Chap. 25; beaver, Chap. 26; moles, bats, Chap. 28.

618. [470.] (409.) **Four-handed folk.** Olive Thorne Miller. (*Mrs.* Harriet Mann Miller.) Bost., Houghton, Mifflin & Co., 1897. 201 p. il. S. (Riverside lib. for young people.) cl.................. 1.25   .50

A very interesting account of monkeys.

619. **Home studies in nature.** Mary Treat. N. Y., American Book Co., c1885. 243 p. il. D. cl.......... .90   .78

Very interesting talks on Birds, Insects and Plants. A good book for Library Reading.

Contents: Our familiar birds; Birds of Florida; Our winter birds; Do birds improve as architects; Habits of insects; Plants that consume animals; Flowering plants.

620. [490.] (435.) **In brook and bayou.** Clara Kern Bayliss. N. Y., D. Appleton & Co., 1897. 180 p. D. cl. .... .60   .48

A simple treatise on the microscopic forms of life. Teacher and pupil ought to read this book together.

621. [479.] (428.) **In nesting time.** Olive Thorne Miller. (*Mrs.* Harriet Mann Miller.) Bost. Houghton, Mifflin & Co., 1898. 275 p. D. cl............... 1.25   .78

A most fascinating account of the birds of the South. For the older pupils in this form.

	Price
List price.	to districts.

622. **Ivory king:** popular history of the elephant and its allies. Charles Frederick Holder. N. Y., C: Scribner's Sons, 1897. 330 p. il. D. (Marvels of animal life series.) cl. 1.75 1.10

An interesting book treating of the animal in all its relations to man; in war, pageantry, games and sports, as a faithful laborer and servant, comrade and friend. An excellent book for Library Reading.

623. [484.] (417.) **Life histories of American insects.** Clarence Moores Weed. N. Y., Macmillan Co., 1897. 272 p. il. D. cl. .... 1.50 .96

The life histories of a few of the common American insects are told in an interesting and non-technical way. The book is most beautifully illustrated. Since these insects are common, the reading should be accompanied by observations. Teachers may use in lower grades by telling facts to the children.
References: Water bugs, 4-10; beetle, 11-41; cricket, 45-51; walking stick, 60-64; locust, 67-73; grasshopper, 77-81; army worm, 85-96; moth, 99-102; apple leaf insects, 103-134; butterfly, 137-144; sand wasp, 146-165; hornet, 168-178; plant lice, 209-247; spiders, 250-270.

624. **Lives of the hunted:** containing a true account of the doings of five quadrupeds and three birds and, in elucidation of the same, over 200 drawings. Ernest Seton-Thompson. N. Y., C: Scribner's Sons, 1901. 360 p. il. O. cl.................. 1.75 1.58

"In my previous books I have tried to emphasize our kinship with the animals by showing that in them we can find the virtues most admired in man. Lobo stands for dignity and love-constancy; Silverspot, for sagacity; Redruff, for obedience. In this volume, Majesty, Grace, the power of Wisdom, the sweet uses of adversity, and the two-edged sorrows of rebellion are similarly set forth. The material of the accounts is true. The chief liberty taken, is in ascribing to one animal the adventures of several."— From the Author's preface.
These stories may be read and told to the children of the lower and middle forms.
The animal stories embraced under this title are: Krag, the Kootenay ram; A street troubadour, being the adventures of a cock sparrow; Johnny Bear; The Mother Teal and the overland route; Chink, the development of a pup; The Kangaroo rat; Tito, the story of a coyote that learned how; Why the chickadee goes crazy once a year. A handsomely gotten up book of narrow pages, decorated margins, etc.

	List price.	Price to districts.

625. [474.] (415.) **My studio neighbors.** William Hamilton Gibson. N. Y., Harper & Bros., 1898. 245 p. il. O. cl. 2.50 1.55

References: The hornet, 3–19; the cuckoo, 23–52; the cicindela, 57–84; the cicada, 87–101; fertilization of flowers, 105–148; insect picnic, 151–167; a few native orchids, 171–224; the milkweed, 227–237.

626. **Nature biographies:** the lives of some everyday butterflies: moths: grasshoppers and flies. Clarence Moores Weed. N. Y., Doubleday, Page & Co., 1901. 164 p. il. O. cl. 1.50 1.35

"This volume by a well known professor of entomology, is a sort of personal acquaintance with the lives of the more common butterflies, moths, grasshoppers, flies, and so on; the fascinating details of which make the reader want to go out and study these everyday marvels for himself. Many photographic illustrations help to give reality and charm to the author's descriptions."

Contents: The making of a Butterfly; The Viceroy Butterfly; The American Tent Caterpillar; A Rural Imposter; A Devastator of Forests; Studies of Walking Sticks; The Antiopa or Mourning Cloak Butterfly; Locust Mummies; Catching Butterflies with a Camera; An Insect Potter; The Camera and the Entomologist; Studies of Insect Parasites; A Parasite of Colonial Caterpillars; A Parasite of Butterfly Eggs; A Moth that Failed; Insects in Winter.—I. The Egg, Aphid Eggs on Willow Bark. II. The Larva. III. Cocoons and Chrysalids. IV. The Adults.

627. **Neighbours of field, wood and stream:** or, through the year with Nature's children. Morton Grinnell. N. Y., F. A. Stokes Co., c1901. 285 p. il. D. cl. 1.30 1.17

A book of country life and manners, in which the characters instead of being men and women are the wild creatures of the fields, swamps and forests of our country. The book is divided into twenty-four chapters, two for each month, thus taking the reader through the cycle of the seasons. The natural history is accurate, its facts being given entertainingly. For the book's purpose the birds, animals and plants are given human intelligence and speech. The illustrations are from the author's specimens placed with their natural surroundings.

628. **Our bird friends.** Richard Kearton. N. Y., Cassell & Co., 1900. 215 p. il. D. cl. .:.................. 1.50 .95

A brief presentation of the facts of natural history which are most likely to interest young readers and set them to observing and inquiring for themselves.

154 LIST OF BOOKS FOR TOWNSHIP LIBRARIES.

	List price.	Price to districts.

629. **Our common birds and how to know them.** John B. Grant. N. Y., C: Scribner's Sons, 1901. 224 p. il. obl. T. cl. 1.50 1.35

An excellent and inexpensive reference book giving a description of ninety common birds. Plates of sixty-four birds, an introductory chapter on "How to know our common birds", and a "Bird calendar" will be of great assistance to those interested in the study of birds.

630. **Our devoted friend, the dog.** Sarah Knowles Bolton. Bost., L. C. Page & Co., 1902. 444 p. il. O. cl.. 1.50 .90

Stories showing the devotion, bravery, and intelligence of dogs. This book cannot fail to cultivate a spirit of kindness to animals.

631. [482.] (431.) **Pepacton.** John Burroughs. Bost., Houghton, Mifflin & Co., 1897. 241 p. S. cl..... 1.25 .75

The quiet enthusiasm of the author's essays begets enthusiasm in the reader. A book for pupil and teacher to read together.

632. [487.] (420.) **Plant world.** *Comp. and ed.* by Frank Vincent. N. Y., D. Appleton & Co., 1897. 228 p. il. D. cl. .... .60 .48

Contains descriptions of many unusual plants as well as some of the more common ones.

633. [485.] (418.) **Plants and their children.** *Mrs.* William Starr Dana (*Mrs.* Frances T. Parsons.) N. Y., American Book Company, 1896. 272 p. il. D. cl. .... .65 .56

The subjects are so arranged as to begin with the opening of the school year and to follow it to its close. It is not necessary for the child to read the book from cover to cover. It is better to let him read such portions as may be supplemented by specimens and observations. The teacher may tell these facts to lower grades in connection with nature lessons.
References: Fruits and seeds, Pt. 1; young plants, Pt. 2; roots and stems, Pt. 3; buds, Pt. 4; leaves, Pt. 5; flowers, Pt. 6.

634. **Reader in physical geography for beginners.** Richard Elwood Dodge. N. Y., Longmans, Green & Co., 1900. 237 p. il. D. cl.................... .70 .63

A very suggestive book bringing together the more important principles of Physical Geography in a form that can be used by

	Price
List	to dis-
price.	tricts.

beginners in the subject. This book contains much material that will be helpful to the upper form geography classes and to the classes in Agriculture.

References: Centers of industry, 28-35; Agriculture, 36-40; Lumbering, 43-46; Erosion, 65-80, 101-4, 125-27; Volcanoes, 154-64; Mountains, 144-53; Weather, 171-75; Soils, 198-205; Commerce, 33-36; Tides, 111-13; Glaciers, 121-36; Climate, 171-197.

635. **Seed dispersal.** William J. Beal. Bost., Ginn & Co., 1898. 87 p. il. D. cl. .... .35 .31

A helpful book for teachers.
References: Plants spread by means of roots, 4-11; Plants multiply by means of stems, 12-17; Water transportation of plants, 18-29; Seeds transported by wind, 30-56; Plants that shoot off their spores of seeds, 57-60; Plants that are carried by animals, 61-79; Dispersal of seeds and plants by man, 80-83; Some reasons for plant migration, 84-87; List of references on seed dispersal, 89.

636. [489.] (422.) **Seed travellers.** Clarence Moores Weed. Bost., Ginn & Co., 1898. 53 p. il. D. cl........ 25 ..22

Studies of the methods of dispersal of various common seeds. The teacher can use the material in this book in the lower forms.
References: The wind as a seed distributer, 1-28; the birds as distributers, 29-44; seeds dispersed by spines and hooks, 45-53.

637. [475.] (416.) **Sharp eyes.** William Hamilton Gibson. N. Y., Harper & Bros., 1898. 322 p. il. O. cl... 2.50 1.55

A rambler's observations during the four seasons.
The last three books ought to be in every library in Wisconsin. The books are works of art. The text is most interesting and the material is presented in such a way that the reading is bound to stimulate observation.

638. [468.] **Squirrels and other fur-bearers.** John Burroughs. Bost., Houghton, Mifflin & Co., 1900. 149 p. il. D. cl. .... 1.00 .65

Observations by one of our most delightful writers. Children will find them very interesting, especially if read with the teacher.
References: Squirrels, 1-14; chipmunk, 15-31; woodchuck, 32-37; rabbit, 38-42; muskrat, 43-47; skunk, 47-52; fox, 53-71; weasel, 72-89; mink, 90-93; raccoon, 94-97; porcupine, 98-105; opossum, 106-110; wild mice, 111-124.

	List price.	Price to districts.

639. [483.] (685.) **Story of the fishes.** James Newton Baskett. N. Y., D. Appleton & Co., 1899. 297 p. il. D. (Appleton's home reading books.) cl.... .75 .63

An intensely interesting account of fishes. Reading with the teacher, the children of the middle form will enjoy this book.

640. [486.] (419.) **Story of the plants.** Grant Allen. N. Y., D. Appleton & Co., 1898. 213 p. il. D. cl... .35 .30

A short account of the principal phenomena of plant life. References: How plants eat, 33-52; how plants drink, 53-72; the wind as a carrier, 124-134; what plants do for their young, 149-160; the stem and the branches, 161-181; biographies of some plants, 182-201; past history of plants, 203-213.

641. [478.] (427.) **Upon the tree-tops.** Olive Thorne Miller. (*Mrs.* Harriet Mann Miller.) Bost., Houghton, Mifflin & Co., 1898. 245 p. il. D. cl. 1.25 .78

Interesting observations of birds.

642. [481.] (430.) **Wake-robin.** John Burroughs. Bost., Houghton, Mifflin & Co., 1896. 233 p. il. S. cl. 1.25 .65

John Burroughs brings his readers into such close and loving contact with Nature, that they learn to love her and understand her secrets.

643. [463.] (405.) **Wild animals I have known.** Ernest Seton-Thompson. N. Y., C: Scribner's Sons, 1898. 358 p. il. O. cl. 2.00 1.30

This book is most beautifully illustrated, and is put on the list because of its artistic value as well as on account of the interesting and true stories of animals. "Such a collection of histories naturally suggest a common thought—a moral it would have been called in the last century. No doubt each different mind will find a moral to its taste, but I hope some will herein find emphasized a moral as old as Scripture—we and the beasts are kin."—*From Author's Preface.*

No more entertaining stories of wild animals have ever been written. Deeper than the mere story lies a truth which links man to the brute and appeals to that sense of kinship in the brotherhood of all living things created.—*From "The Bookman."*

644. [466.] (406.) **Wild neighbors;** outdoor studies in the U. S. Ernest Ingersoll. N. Y., Macmillan Co., 1897. 301 p. il. D. cl. .... 1.50 .95

The wild animals of the U. S. most fascinatingly described. References: Gray squirrels, 1-32; puma, 33-60; the service of tails, 61-98; coyote, 99-118; the badger and his kin, 119-156; animal training, 156-185; the porcupine, 186-208; the skunk, 209-250; woodchuck, and ground-hog, 251-271; raccoon, 272-297.

LIST OF BOOKS FOR TOWNSHIP LIBRARIES. 157

	Price
List	to dis-
price.	tricts.

645. [465.] **World of the great forest.** Paul du Chaillu. N. Y., C: Scribner's Sons, 1900. 323 p. il. O. cl. 2.00 1.30

How animals, birds, reptiles, insects, talk, think, work, and live. All grades will enjoy.

ART.

646. **Landseer:** a collection of fifteen pictures and a portrait of the painter with introduction and interpretation. Estelle M. Hurll. Bost., Houghton, Mifflin & Co., 1901. 93 p. il. por. O. cl. (Riverside art ser.) .... .50 .42

647. [519.] (692.) **Michelangelo:** a collection of pictures and a portrait of the painter with an introduction and interpretation. Estelle M. Hurll. Bost., Houghton, Mifflin & Co., 1899. 94 p. il. por. D. (Riverside art ser.), cl. .... .50 .42

648. [521.] **Jean Francois Millet:** a collection of fifteen pictures and a portrait of the painter with introduction and interpretation. Estelle M. Hurll. Bost., Houghton, Mifflin & Co., 1900. 96 p. il. por. D. .... .50 .42

649. [518.] (691.) **Raphael:** a collection of fifteen pictures and a portrait of the painter, with introduction and interpretation. Estelle M. Hurl. Bost., Houghton, Mifflin & Co., 1899. 92 p. il. por. D. (Riverside art ser.), cl. .... .50 .42

650. [517.] (690.) **Rembrandt:** a collection of pictures and a portrait of the painter with introduction and interpretation. Estelle M. Hurll. Bost., Houghton, Mifflin & Co., 1899. 96 p. il. por. D. (Riverside art ser.), cl. .... .50 .42

651. [520.] **Sir Joshua Reynolds:** a collection of fifteen pictures and a portrait of the painter with introduction and interpretation. Estelle M. Hurll. Bost., Houghton, Mifflin & Co., 1900. 94 p. il. por. D. (Riverside art ser.) cl.............. .50 .42

	List price.	Price to districts.

652. **Titian:** a collection of fifteen pictures and a portrait of the painter with introduction and interpretation. Estelle M. Hurll. Bost., Houghton, Mifflin & Co., 1901. 93 p. il. por. O. cl. (Riverside art ser.) .... .50 .42

653. [522.] **Greek sculpture.** Estelle M. Hurll. Bost., Houghton, Mifflin & Co., 1901. 97 p. il. D. cl.. .50 .42

654. **Correggio:** a collection of fifteen pictures and a supposed portrait of the painter, with introduction and interpretation. Estelle M. Hurll. Bost., Houghton, Mifflin & Co., 1901. 94 p. il. O. cl. (Riverside art series.) .... .50 .42

The object of this series of books is to awaken an interest in and cultivate a love for the best in art. Each book contains pictures which are representative of the work of a famous painter and the text is an interpretation of those pictures.

Every school library ought to have at least two or three of these books. The interpretations are writtten in a simple, attractive manner that will interest the children.

655. [523.] (693.) **Story of music and musicians for young readers.** Lucy C. Lillie. N. Y., Harper & Brothers, 1899. 245 p. por. S. bds............ 1.00 .38

The simple story of an art which many children are interested in. Short and interesting biographies of the great musicians.

DRAMA.

	List price.	Price to districts.
656. [559.] (520.) **As you like it.** William Shakespeare. Bost., Houghton, Mifflin & Co., 1897. D. (Riverside lit. ser.) cl.	.25	.21
657. [560.] (521.) **Julius Caesar.** William Shakespeare. Bost., Houghton, Mifflin & Co., 1897. D. (Riverside lit. ser.) cl.	.25	.21
658. **Macbeth.** William Shakespeare. N. Y., Globe School Book Co., 1900. 144 p. il. D. (English Classics —star ser.) cl.	.32	.27
659. [558.] (519.) **Merchant of Venice.** William Shakespeare. Bost., Houghton, Mifflin & Co., 1897. D. (Riverside lit. ser.) cl.	.25	.21

ESSAYS.

660. [562.] (483.) **A-hunting of the deer, and other essays.** Charles Dudley Warner. Bost., Houghton, Mifflin & Co., 1888. 85 p. D. (Riverside lit. ser.) cl... .25 .21

Many of these essays are humorous and as such will delight the children. There are many fine descriptions.

661. [561.] (481.) **Sketch book.** Washington Irving. Bost., Houghton, Mifflin & Co., 1897. 206 p. D. (Riverside school lib.) cl. .60 .50

See also Essays of John Burroughs, William H. Gibson, and Olive T. Miller in Science, Upper Form.

COLLECTIONS.

	List price.	Price to districts.

662, 663. [563, 564.] (473, 474.) **Choice literature.** Bks. 1 and 2. For grammar grades. *Comp. and arr.* by Sherman Williams. N. Y., Butler, Sheldon & Co., 1898. 336, 506 p. D. cl.
Bk. 1 .... .40 .34
Bk. 2 .... .50 .43

Exceptionally fine selections from the very best in literature. The selections from the larger works of literature are sure to create an interest in those works, the teacher must meet that interest so far as possible by giving the pupil the complete work.

664. [565.] (475.) **Lincoln literary collection.** *Comp.* by J. P. McCaskey. N. Y., American Book Company, 1897. 576 p. D. cl. .... 1.00 .85

Selections from the best literature for memorizing. The book is well indexed. There are selections for Arbor Day, Bird Day, Christmas, Memorial Day, and patriotic songs. Teachers will find these selections very helpful for general and public exercises.

665. [566.] (479.) **Patriotic citizenship.** Thomas J. Morgan. N. Y., American Book Company, 1895. 368 p. il. D. cl. .... 1.00 .85

Selections on patriotic subjects.
References: Patriotism, 15-34; the flag, 37-50; discovery of America, 53-72; the colonists, 75-100; the Revolution, 103-124; the nation, 127-164; Civil War, 167-188; the Negroes, 191-206; civil liberty, 209-236; religious liberty, 239-254; population and immigration, 257-270; citizenship, 273-300; labor, 303-314; capital, 317-326; perpetuity of the republic, 329-344; constitution of the U. S., 345-358; Declaration of Independence, 359-362.

666, 667, 668. **Speaker's garland and literary bouquet.** Combining 100 choice selections, Nos. 25—36, embracing new and standard productions of oratory, sentiment, eloquence, pathos, wit, humor and amateur plays. Phineas Garrett, *Ed.* Phil., P. Garrett & Co., 1899. Vol. 7, 8, 9. D. cl. per vol. 2.00 1.28

This series of books contain many good selections for rhetorical work. One of the three volumes contains sufficient material of this class for the smaller schools.

Schoolhouse in district No. 9, town of Tilden, Chippewa County.

Schoolhouse in district No. 7, town of Eagle Point, Chippewa County.

POETRY.

As a rule poetry will not be read by the children unless the teacher creates a love for poetry by reading it to them. Often they cannot call the words readily enough to get the swing of the music which is one of the greatest charms of poetry for children. In selecting poetry to be read to the pupils follow their present interests and awaken new ones. Children are always interested in a story and there are many fine narrative poems. The story may form a starting point for creating an interest in poetry. Interests created by the various holidays, the seasons, and observations of nature may be deepened by beautiful poems. Help the child to see the beautiful pictures in poetry and to compare them with the real pictures so far as possible. Thus after a beautiful sunset a beautiful description of a sunset by a poet will interest the children. Let them see how nearly the poet's description pictures the sunset they saw. At the same time that they are gaining a love for poetry a love for nature may be created.

Encourage the pupils to memorize the bits of poetry which they like best.

No work in the schoolroom is productive of better results in forming a taste for good reading, creating a love for the beautiful, and developing permanent and ennobling interests.

LIST OF BOOKS FOR TOWNSHIP LIBRARIES. 163

	List price.	Price to districts.
669. [552.] (510.) **Ballad book.** *Ed.* by Katherine Lee Bates. Bost., Sibley & Ducker, 1890. 229 p. S. cl.	.50	.42

These rough, frank, spirited old poems are almost always favorites with children.

| 670. [551.] (699.) **Boy's Browning.** Robert Browning. Dana Estes & Co., 1899. 96 p. il. S. cl. ...... | 50 | ..30 |

The best of Browning's poems of action and incident selected for boys.

| 671. [525.] (491.) **Poetical works.** William Cullen Bryant. *Household ed.* N. Y., D. Appleton & Co., 1897. 362 p. il. por. O. cl. ...... | 1.50 | .85 |

References: Poems of nature: Inscription for the entrance to a wood, 24; Winter piece, 29; West wind, 53; Walk at sunset, 37; Rivulet, 50; March, 53; Summer wind, 57; Autumn woods, 68; November, 70; To a cloud, 72; Forest hymn, 79; June, 83; Firmament, 86; October, 99; Earth, 160; Hunter of the prairie, 165; Hymn of the sea, 203; Song of the sower, 244.
   Flowers: Yellow violet, 23; Death of the flowers, 92.
   Birds: To a water-fowl, 26; Robert of Lincoln, 229; Return of the birds, 310.
   Trees: Planting of the apple tree, 222; Among the trees, 321; Forest hymns, 79.
   Poems of life. Journey of life, 137; Life, 174; Flood of years, 344.
   Poems of death: Thanatopsis, 21; Hymn to death, 39.
   Story of poems: Rizpah, 47; Indian story, 54; Monument mountain, 63; Damsel of Peru, 100; Hunter's vision, 176; Sella, 268; Little people of the snow, 297.
   Patriotism and historical poems: The ages, 11; Italy, 253; Seventy-six, 166; Not yet, 262; Our country's call, 263; Death of Lincoln, 316; Death of slavery, 317.
   Ballads: Song of Marion's men, 134; Song for New-Year's eve, 234.

| 672. [548.] (515.) **American war ballads and lyrics.** *Ed.* by George Cary Eggleston. 2 v. in 1. N. Y., G. P. Putnam's Sons, 1889. 278 p. il. S. cl. ...... | 1.50 | .90 |

A collection of songs and ballads of the colonial wars, the Revolution, the war of 1812-15, the war with Mexico, and the Civil War. "It is the poetry of strength and manly self-reliance. It is inspired from beginning to end by a high and unfaltering faith in the truth of the doctrines of human liberty that underlie our entire history and constitute the vital principle of our institutions."

	List price.	Price to districts.

673. [549.] (698.) **Boy's book of battle lyrics.** Thomas Dunn English. N. Y., Harper & Bros., 1885. 168 p. il. O. cl. 2.00 1.20

A collection of verses illustrating some notable events in the history of the United States from the colonial period to the outbreak of the civil war.

674. **Little book of western verse.** Eugene Field. N. Y., C: Scribner's Sons, 1901. 202 p. D. cl......... 1.25 .82

675. **Second book of verse.** Eugene Field. N. Y., C: Scribner's Sons, 1901. 260 p. D. cl............ 1.25 .82

These two books contain many of Field's most beautiful poems and should be in every library.

676. **Love-songs of childhood.** Eugene Field. N. Y., C: Scribner's Sons, 1901. 111 p. S. cl. .... 1.00 .67

This is a collection of Field's best poems for primary form children, but the middle form children will also enjoy reading them.

677. [537.] (501.) **Lullaby-land.** Eugene Field. N. Y., C: Scribner's Sons, 1894. 229 p. il. D. cl......... 1.50 .96

A most beautiful edition of Field's songs of childhood. The illustrations are unusually good.

678. [542.] (506.) **Blue poetry book.** *Ed.* by Andrew Lang. (New ed. for use in schools.) N. Y., Longmans, Green & Co., 1896. 263 p. S. cl..... .60 .50

All children like a story. Out of this interest may be created an interest in poetry by use of narrative, or story poems. The majority of poems in this collection are narrative poems of the best kind.
Selections which may be used for Arbor or Bird days: A Boy's song, 2; I remember, I remember, 3; To daffodils, 60; To the cuckoo, 75; to a waterfowl, 117; The skylark, 130; To a skylark, 134; The nightingale, 137; Spring, 139; The recollection, 103.
Evening poems: Night, 4; Evening, 79; Il penseroso, 98; The day is done, 126; The sleeper, 137.
To the sea: Sea dirge, 51.
Winter: Winter, 64.
Morning: L'allegro, 94; Morning, 115.
The story poems are not paged.

	Price
List price.	Price to districts.

679. [538.] (502.) **Childhood songs.** Lucy Larcom. Bost., Houghton, Mifflin & Co., 1898. 202 p. il. D. cl.   1.00   .60

Dainty, pretty poems for children. The nature poems are especially good.

680. [524.] (490.) **Complete poetical works.** Henry Wadsworth Longfellow. *Cambridge ed.* Bost., Houghton, Mifflin & Co., 1893. 689 p. Por. O. cl....   2.00   1.20

References: Voices of the night: Hymn to the night, 2; Psalm of life, 2; Footsteps of angels, 4; the beleagured city, 5; Midnight mass for the dying year, 6; The bridge, 63; Curfew, 69; Night, 348; The evening star, 69; Twilight, 105; Sundown, 353.

Nature poems: An April day, 7; Autumn, 8, 69; Woods in winter, 8; Sunrise on the hills, 9; Rain in summer, 59; The evening star, 69; Autumn, 69; Flower-de-luce, 287; Palingenesis, 287; The four lakes of Madison, 351; Snow flakes, 202; The bridge of cloud, 288; The brook and the wave, 296; Nature, 318; The harvest moon, 320; The poet's calendar, 349; The brook, 593.

Story poems: The wreck of the Hesperus, 13; The belfry of Bruges, 54; Nuremberg, 57; Evangeline, 70; The song of Hiawatha, 113; The courtship of Miles Standish, 164; The hanging of the crane, 308; Skeleton in armor, 11; Pegasus in pound, 110; The emperor's bird's-nest, 189; The discoverer of the North cape, 198; Tales of a wayside inn, 204; The revenge of Rain-in-the-face, 336; Leap of Roushan Beg, 338.

Poems on slavery, 20-23.

Drama: The Spanish student, 23; Christus, 361; the golden legend, 408; Michael Angelo, 537.

Ballads and songs: The village blacksmith, 14; It is not always May, 15; The rainy day, 16; God's acre, 16; Maidenhood, 18; Excelsior, 19; The day is done, 64; The old clock on the stairs, 67; The arrow and the song, 68; Auf wiedersehen, 354; To river Charles, 16; The secret of the sea, 104; The builders, 108; Day break, 199; A day of sunshine, 202; Something left undone, 203; Sleep, 317; The windmill, 347; Song of the bell, 612.

Holiday poems: Christmas bells, 289; The three kings, 339; Thanksgiving, 645; A Christmas carol, 628; Decoration Day, 359; The dead, 610.

Poems of persons: The fiftieth birthday of Agassiz, 199; Hawthorne, 289; Chaucer, 315; Shakespeare, 315; Milton, 315; Charles Sumner, 324; Robert Burns, 345; President Garfield, 357.

Poems of places: Venice, 318; To the river Rhine, 320; Boston, 321; Lake of Como, 325.

Poems on children: Children, 200; The children's hour, 201; The children's comrade, 352.

Poems of the sea: The building of the ship, 99; Seaweed, 103; The secret of the sea, 104; The lighthouse, 106; The sound of the sea, 316; A summer day by the sea, 316; The tides, 317; The tide rises, the tide falls, 347; The city and the sea, 356; The sea hath its pearls, 615.

681. [543.] (507.) **Courtship of Miles Standish.** Henry Wadsworth Longfellow. Bost., Houghton, Mifflin & Co., 1886. 90 p. D. (Riverside lit. ser.) cl...   .25   .21

	List price.	Price to districts.
682. [544.] (508.) **Song of Hiawatha.** Henry Wadsworth Longfellow. Bost., Houghton, Mifflin & Co., 1898. 193 p. D. (Riverside lit. ser.) cl...............	.40	.32

Though Longfellow's complete works are on the list, this poem is such a favorite with children, it is thought best to duplicate.

| 683. [553.] (513.) **Poetry of the seasons.** *Comp.* by Mary I. Lovejoy. N. Y., Silver, Burdett & Co., 1898. 336 p. il. D. cl. .... | .60 | .52 |

Some of the best nature poems for the various seasons.

| 684. [550.] (516.) **Lays of ancient Rome.** T. B. Macaulay. N. Y., G. P. Putnam's sons. (World's classics.) cl. .... | .50 | .32 |

| 685. [545.] (696.) **Songs of the tree-top and meadow.** *Arr.* by Lida Brown McMurry *and* Agnes Spofford Cook. Bloomington, Ill., Public School Pub. Co., 1899. 192 p. il. T. cl. .... | .60 | .45 |

A good collection of poems suitable for youngest children.

| 686. [547.] (697.) **Poems of American patriotism.** Chosen by Brander Matthews. N. Y., C: Scribner's Sons, 1899. 279 p. D. (Scribner's ser. of school reading.) cl. .... | .60 | .50 |

A collection of old favorites, well arranged. Brief notes have been prefixed to many of the poems, making plain the occasion of their origin, and removing any chance of obscurity of allusion. Suitable for middle and upper forms.

| 687. [546.] (695.) **Our country in poem and prose.** *Arr.* by Eleanor A. Persons. N. Y., American Book Company, 1899. 204 p. il. D. (Eclectic school reading ser.) cl. .... | .50 | .43 |

The selections are arranged for collateral and supplementary reading. Much of the material in the book will prove of value in making the history lesson interesting and entertaining.

| 688. [536.] (694.) **Prose and verse for children.** Katherine Pyle. N. Y., American Book Company, 1899. 168 p. D. cl. .... | .40 | .34 |

Imaginative selections which will please the children since they deal mainly with the things of childhood.

	List price.	Price to districts.

689. [526.] (492.) **Complete poetical works.** James Russell Lowell. *Cambridge ed.* Bost., Houghton, Mifflin & Co., 1896. 492 p. Por. O. cl......... 2.00   1.20

References: Story poems: A legend of Brittany, 28; Prometheus, 30; A Chippewa legend, 53; The vision of Sir Launfal, 106; A fable for critics, 113; The courtin,' 219; Rhoecus, 46; Singing leaves, 293.

Patriotic and historical poems: Columbus, 55; Bigelow papers, 181; Poems of the war, 334; The Fatherland, 14; The present crisis, 67; Freedom, 97; Under the old elm, 364; Ode for the fourth of July, 370; Stanzas of freedom, 55.

Nature poems: Under the willows, 286; The first snow-fall, 292; The Nomades, 301; Summer storm, 7; The fountain, 11; Song (The violet), 17; To a pine tree, 62; The Indian summer reverie, 68; The oak, 76; The birch tree, 79; To the dandelion, 83.

Poems of the sea: The sirens, 2; Pictures from Appledore, 303.

Poems of life: The parting of the ways, 298; The falcon, 48; A glance behind the curtain, 49; To the future, 64; Above and below, 78; the changeling, 89.

Ballads: Auf wiedersehen, 308; The fountain of youth, 316; The beggar, 5; The rose, 16.

Holidays: A Christmas carol, 403; A New Year's greeting, 410.

Poems of persons: Wendell Phillips, 24; Kossuth, 100; Garrison, 102; Hood, 105; Agassiz, 374; Holmes, 381; Whittier, 3-6.

690. [541.] (505.) **Book of famous verse.** *Sel.* by Agnes Repplier. Bost., Houghton, Mifflin & Co., 1894. 244 p. S. (Riverside lib. for young people.) cl.   .75   .45

Some of the best children's poems in literature.

691. [531.] (497.) **Child-rhymes.** James Whitcomb Riley. Indianapolis, Bowen-Merrill Co., 1899. 188 p. il. D. cl....... .... 1.25   .75

A beautiful edition of the best of Riley's poems for children.

692. [532.] (498.) **Child world.** James Whitcomb Riley. Indianapolis, Bowen-Merrill Co., 1897. 209 p. il. D. cl....... .... 1.25   .75

One of the best of Riley's books of poetry. Humorous, looks at things from the child's standpoint. A good book for child study since child life is portrayed with a master hand.

693. [533.] (499.) **Neghborly poems.** James Whitcomb Riley. Indianapolis, Bowen-Merrill Co., 1899. 215 p. il. D. cl............................. 1.25   .75

Poems of country life filled with the beauty of nature which may help the country child to see some of the beauty around him.

	List price.	Price to districts.

694. [530.] (496.) **Boy's book of rhyme.** Clinton Scollard. Bost., Small, Maynard & Co., 1896. 53 p. D. cl.   1.00   .60

As the title indicates, these poems are essentially for boys—but many girls will find them good. The poems are about boyish games, favorite birds and flowers, and the various seasons dear to a boy's heart.

The teacher will find some very good material for closing exercises, the holidays, Bird and Arbor days, and to read to the children at the general exercises in the morning.

695. [557.] (518.) **Lady of the lake.** *Sir* Walter Scott. N. Y., American Book Company, 1897. D. (Eclectic English classics.) cl. 30   .26

Boys will like the stirring music and martial sound of Scott's poetry.

696. [556.] (517.) **Marmion.** *Sir* Walter Scott. N. Y., American Book Company, 1892. 247 p. Por. D. (Eclectic English classics.) cl. 40   .34

697. [529.] (495.) **Little-folk lyrics.** Frank Dempster Sherman. Bost., Houghton, Mifflin & Co., 1897. 140 p. il. D. cl. ....   1.50   .85

This is one of the best volumes of poems for children. The book is artistically bound and illustrated. Though written for little folks, children of all grades enjoy it. It is filled with nature poems of the most beautiful kind. The teacher will find in this book some of the best material for Arbor and Bird days, and general exercises at close of school.

698. [534.] **Child's garden of verses.** Robert Louis Stevenson. With an *introd.* by Lloyd Osborne. N. Y., C: Scribner's Sons, 1901. 76 p. il. D. cl...   .60   .50

These poems show the perfect faith, purity and simplicity of the child mind. Many of the poems are for the youngest children.

"The child of the "Child's Garden" was Stevenson himself. The plays were his plays; the dreams were his dreams; the fears and fantasies were all his own."—*From the Introduction.*

699. [527.] (493.) **Poetic and dramatic works.** Alfred Tennyson. *Cambridge ed.* Bost., Houghton, Mifflin & Co., 1898. 887 p. O. cl..................   2.00   1.20

References: Story poems: The lady of Shalott, 27; The miller's daughter, 35; The May queen, 47; Dora, 72; Locksley Hall, 90; The day-dream, 96; St. Agnes' eve, 100; Lady Clare, 105; The

LIST OF BOOKS FOR TOWNSHIP LIBRARIES. 169

Price
List to dis-
price. tricts.

princess, 115; Maud, 19S; The brook, 217; Enoch Arden, 227; Sea-dreams, 252; The grandmother, 258; The defense of Lucknow, 470; Locksley Hall sixty years after, 517; The gardner's daughter, 68.

Poems of life: The two voices, 30.

Poems of death: In memoriam, 162; Nothing will die, 3; All things will die, 4.

Holiday poems: The death of the old year, 58.

Nature poems: Early spring, 513; The progress of spring, 548; The snowdrop, 556; The owl, 9; The throstle, 556; The blackbird, 58; The flower, 264; Flower in the crannied wall, 274; Spring, 279; Winter, 279; Early spring, 513.

Legends: A dream of fair women, 53; Morte d'Arthur, 64; Sir Galahad, 101; Idylls of the king, 302.

Ballads and songs: The first quarrel, 452; Rizpah, 454; In the children's hospital, 468; Break, break, break, 115; The beggar maid, 110; The owl, 9; Choric song, 51; Sweet and low, 128; The splendor falls on castle walls, 134; Home they brought her warrior dead, 145.

Patriotism and historical poems: The charge of the Light Brigade, 226.

Dramatic poems: Harold, 622; Queen Mary, 557; Becket, 659.

700. [535.] **Listening child**; a selection from the stores of English verse, made for the youngest readers and hearers; with an introductory note by T. W. Higginson. Lucy W. Thatcher. School ed. N. Y., Macmillan Co., 1900. 408 p. D. cl.............. .50 .45

Fine collection of poetry from the best authors.

701. **Among flowers and trees with the poets.** *Comp. and arr.* by Minnie Curtis Wait *and* Merton Channing Leonard. Bost., Lee & Shepard, 1901. 415 p. il. O. cl. .... 1.50 .88

A companion volume to "Through the year with birds and poets" published last year. The choicest poems in English, descriptive of the floral kingdom are arranged according to alphabetical order of plants described by the poets. In six parts: Flowers—in general; Flowers—specified; Trees and shrubs, in general and specified; Flowerless plants; National flowers, illustrated with fifteen plates.

702. [528.] (464.) **Complete poetical works.** John Greenleaf Whittier. *Cambridge ed.* Bost., Houghton, Mifflin & Co., 1894. 542 p. Por. O. cl........ 2.00 1.20

References: Story poems: The Vaudois teacher, 3; The Norsemen, 9; The cypress-tree of Ceylon, 14; Kathleen, 37; The chapel of the hermits, 39; Maud Muller, 47; Skipper Ireson's ride, 55; Cobbler Keezar's vision, 77; Miriam, 93; The sisters, 100; Marguerite, 101; The Pennsylvania pilgrim, 103; King Volmer and Elsie, 112; The witch of Wenham, 117; King Solomon and the ants,

	List price.	Price to districts.

120; The bay of seven islands, 127; The brown dwarf of Rügen, 138; The tent on the beach, 243.

Poems of persons: Tauler, 44; Conductor Bradley, 117; Benedicite, 188; Kossuth, 189; To Charles Sumner, 196; Burns, 196; Brown of Ossawatomie, 201; Bryant on his birthday, 203; Garibaldi, 204; Lydia Maria Child, 205; The singer, 206; Sumner, 208; Thiers, 210; Fitz-Greene Halleck, 211; Bayard Taylor, 212; Our autocrat, 213; The poet and the children, 215; A welcome to Lowell, 216.

Patriotism and historical poems: The Norsemen, 9; St. John, 12; The exiles, 14; Cassandra Southwick, 18; The angels of Buena Vista, 35; the truce of Piscataqua, 74; The king's missive, 124; Lexington, 232; Yorktown, 302;/ The slaves of Martinique, 305; Barbara Frietchie, 342; Our country, 383.

Nature poems: The fountain, 7; The sycamores, 56; Among the hills, 83; The robin, 102; How the robin came, 136; The frost spirit, 141; The Merrimac, 141; A dream of summer, 143; The lakeside, 144; Autumn thoughts, 144; April, 145; Summer by the lakeside, 147; Flowers in white, 148; The Mayflower, 149; The last walk in autumn, 150; The first flowers, 153; The palm-tree, 155; The river path, 155; The pressed gentian, 159; The trailing arbutus, 164; A summer pilgrimage, 165; A day, 168; A song of the harvest, 219; For an autumn festival, 220; June on the Merrimac, 226; The worship of nature, 261; Snow-bound, 398.

Poems of life: Questions of life, 432; Trust, 434; My trust, 411; The answer, 441; The two angels, 455.

Poems for children: At school-close, 234; Hymn of the children, 235; The barefoot boy, 396; In school-days, 407; Red Riding-hood, 408.

Anti-slavery poems: Touissant L'Ouverture, 262; The slave-ships, 265; Expostulation, 267; The Yankee girl, 269; The hunters of men, 270; Stanzas for the times, 271; A summons, 273; The moral warfare, 275; The farewell, 278; The new year, 281; The Christian slave, 288; The branded hand, 296; Thy will be done, 333; Laus deo, 345.

Holiday poems: A Christmas carmen, 453.

703. [540.] (504.) **Once upon a time.** Mary E. Wilkins. Bost., Lothrop Pub. Co., 1897. 187 p. il. D. cl.. 1.00 .60

A collection of child-verses. Many for the youngest children and some for the oldest.

704. [554.] **Through the year with birds and poets.** *Comp.* by Sarah Williams. Bost., Lee & Shepard, 1900. 323 p. il. D. cl. 2.00 1.15

Most beautiful nature poems from the best literature. Fine material for Arbor Day and nature study.

MISCELLANEOUS.

                                                                         Price
                                                                    List to dis-
                                                                  price. tricts.

705. [576.] (705.) **American big-game hunting.** *Ed.* by Theodore Roosevelt *and* George Bird Grinnell. N. Y., Forest and Stream Pub. Co., 1893. 345 p. il. D. 2.50 1.65

A book which will interest boys.

706. [567.] (484.) **American girls' handy book.** Lina *and* Adelia B. Beard. N. Y., C: Scribner's Sons, 1890. 474 p. il. D. cl. 2.00 1.30

A vast amount of information on decorations, amusements, painting, drawing, gift-making, and scores of other subjects that girls are generally desirous of knowing.

707. [568.] (707.) **American girls' home book of work and play.** Helen Campbell. N. Y., G. P. Putnam's Sons, 1896. 431 p. il. D. cl................... 1.75 1.10

The girls will find this a valuable guide to work and play. Some of the leading subjects are rainy day games, forfeits, parlor plays, charades, Hallowe'en games, lawn tennis, boating, doll's dressmaking, Christmas gifts, care of birds, candy making, and cooking.

708. [585.] (710.) **Business girl, in every phase of her life.** Ruth Ashmore (*Mrs.* Isabel A. Mallon). N. Y., Doubleday, Page & Co., 1898. 176 p. T. cl..... .50 .30

Some very good and helpful advice for girls.

709. [569.] (486.) **Boys' book of sports and outdoor life.** *Ed.* by Maurice Thompson. N. Y., Century Co., 1886. 352 p. il. O. cl....................... 2.00 1.20

Chapters on the use of guns, fishing, archery, boats and boating, camps and campers, swimming, the camera, and ice-boating, which will interest the boys and give them many suggestions for their own sports.

	List price.	Price to districts.

710. [573.] (709.) **Boy's workshop.** A boy and his friends. Bost., Lothrop Co., 1884. 221 p. il. D. cl....... 1.00 .55

Nearly every boy at some period of his life wants to "make things." This little book will give him much valuable information in regard to the making of things he likes to make, and if wisely encouraged by parents and teachers, he may develop mechanical ingenuity which will be of great value to him in after life.

711. [577.] (706.) **Camping and camp outfits.** G. O. Shields. Chicago, Rand, McNally & Co., 1890. 169 p. il. D. cl. .... 1.25 .75

A manual of instruction for young and old sportsmen. This book contains points on how to dress for hunting, fishing or other camping trips; what to provide in way of bedding, tents, eatables, and cooking utensils; how to select camping grounds; how to build camps, or shelters of various kinds; how to build camp fires; and many other topics in connection with the subject of outdoor life.

712. **Careers of danger and daring.** Cleveland Moffett. N. Y., Century Co., 1901. 419 p. il O. cl.......... 1.80 1.62

The dangers that one must face who becomes a steeple-climber, a deep-sea diver, a bridge-builder, a pilot, a fireman, a locomotive engineer, etc., are told with much vividness of phrase and picturesqueness of illustration.
References: Steeple-climbing, 3–39; Diving, 40–86; Ballooning, 87–129; Pilots, 130–72; Bridge-builders, 172–208; Firemen, 209–54; Acrobats, 255–92; Animal tamer, 293–347; Dynamite workers, 348–376; Engineers, 377–419.

713. **Elements of the theory and practice of cookery:** a text-book of household science for use in schools. Mary E. Williams *and* Katharine Rolston Fisher. N. Y., Macmillan Co., 1901. 347 p. il. D. cl.... 1.00 .88

This book will be of value to all interested in the better preparation of home-makers for their duties. It furnishes much excellent material which may be given to pupils by the teacher in talks and in simple experiments, showing the reasons for doing or not doing many things now done without reasons in every home.
The book contains many practical lessons for girls which they may be interested in applying in their own homes.
Section 4 on "Cleanliness and Cleaning" and the chapters on "Fuel Foods" and "Tissue-building Foods" should be read by every mother in the district. These chapters also give excellent matter to supplement the school work in physiology.

714. [516.] (689.) **Fighting a fire.** Charles T. Hill. N. Y., Century Co., 1897. 246 p. il. D. cl............. 1.50 .88

An interesting account of the workings of the New York fire department. Every pupil will be interested in the personal observations of the author, and he will learn much of how fires are extinguished in our large cities.

| | List price. | Price to districts. |

715. **Hour of opportunity.** Orison Swett Marden *and* Abner Bayley. N. Y., T. Y. Crowell & Co., c1900. 54 p. il. D. cl............................... .50 .30

This book relates the beginning of the careers of some of our most successful men and women of today. It contains many suggestions valuable to boys and girls.

716. **How to make baskets.** Mary White. With a chapter on "What the basket means to the Indian," by Neltje Blanchan. N. Y., Doubleday, Page & Co., 1901. 194 p. il. D. cl....................... 1.00 .90

"The great interest in Indian baskets has drawn new attention to the art of basket-making, with the result that basketry has found immediate favor, not only in schools and training classes, but as a most attractive pastime and means of occupation among grown people as well. This little manual is the only guide to the work. Miss White describes in detail the few necessary implements and materials, and then tells how to weave, first the simpler forms, next the more difficult patterns, and finally the complicated and beautiful work for which the Indians were once famous, but which is now rapidly becoming a lost art."

Contents: Materials, Tools, Preparation, Weaving; Raffia, and Some of its Uses; Mats and Their Borders; The Simplest Baskets; Covers; Handles; Work Baskets; Candy Baskets; Scrap Baskets; Bird's Nests; Oval Baskets; The Finishing Touch; How to Cane Chairs; Some Indian Stitches; What the Basket Means to the Indian.

717. [571.] **Jack of all trades.** D. C. Beard. N. Y., C: Scribner's Sons, 1900. 295 p. il. D. cl......... 2.00 1.30

New ideas for occupying play hours indoors and out.

Contents: Treetop club houses, hunting without a gun, backyard zoo, pigeon lofts, backyard work shop, a Daniel Boone cabin, a house boat, a toboggan slide, and numerous indoor amusements.

To the best of the author's knowledge and belief there is not a thing described in this book which has not been proved practical.

718. [570.] **Outdoor handy book for play-ground, field, and forest.** Daniel C. Beard. (*New ed.*) N. Y., C: Scribner's Sons, 1900. 496 p. il. D. cl........ 2.00 1.30

A new edition of "American boy's book of sport," one of the best books on the list.

719. [587.] **Robert's primer of parliamentary law.** Joseph Thomas Robert. N. Y., Doubleday, Page & Co., 1900. 264 p. S. cl. .... .75 .45

Societies and clubs will find this book very helpful.

	List price.	Price to districts.

720. [586.] (711.) **Successward: a young man's book for young men.** Edward Bok. N. Y., Doubleday, Page & Co., 1899. 182 p. T. cl. .... .50 .30

Some very good suggestions for boys.

721. [572.] **Woodworking for beginners.** Charles G. Wheeler. N. Y., G. P. Putnam's Sons, 1900. 550 p. il. D. cl. 3.50 2.10

Suggestions and directions for the making of many things from wood.

721a. **John Nagle's philosophy.** *Comp.* by Sidney T. Pratt. Manitowoc, (Wis.) The Pilot. 1902. cl......... 1.50 .98

This book contains the addresses made by John Nagle to the Farmers' Institutes of Wisconsin.

Mr. Nagle wrote to make life purer and sweeter. He understood the besetting traps laid to snare the young from paths of rectitude, hence, in no uncertain language did he show his solicitude for them. —*From the Compiler's Preface.*

AMATEUR PLAYS.

722. [580.] **Fairy tale plays and how to act them.** *Mrs.* Hugh Bell. N. Y., Longmans, Green & Co., 1899. 366 p. il. D. cl. .... 1.50 .95

The most familiar fairy tales arranged to be acted by boys and girls.

723. **"Little men play,"** a two-act, forty-five minute play. *Adapted by* Elizabeth Lincoln Gould from Louisa May Alcott's famous story "Little men," with pictures by R. B. Birch. Bost., Little, Brown & Co., c1900. 103 p. il. D. bds.................. .50 .30

724. **"Little women play,"** a two-act, forty-five minute play. *Adapted by* Elibabeth Lincoln Gould from Louisa May Alcott's famous story "Little women," with pictures by R. B. Birch. Bost., Little, Brown & Co., c1900. 101 p. il. D. bds. .... .50 .30

Interesting plays for school entertainments. After reading Louisa Alcott's 'Little men" and "Little women" the children will enjoy reading these plays. A comparison of the plays with the stories noting the similarities and differences will afford an excellent elementa— exercise in the study of literature.

LIST OF BOOKS FOR TOWNSHIP LIBRARIES. 175

| | List price. | Price to districts. |

725. [578.] **St. Nicholas book of plays and operettas.** N. Y., Century Co., 1900. 231 p. il. D. cl.......... 1.00 .65

These plays and operettas were published originally in "St. Nicholas." They will be found very valuable for entertainments and closing exercises.

726. [581.] **Wild animal play for children,** with alternate reading for very young children. Ernest Seton-Thompson. N. Y., Doubleday, Page & Co., 1900. 79 p. il. D. cl. .... .50 .30

Plays based upon the stories told in 'Wild Animals I Have Known."

ENCYCLOPAEDIAS.

727. [582.] (488.) **Young folks' cyclopedia of common things.** John D. Champlin, *jr. 2d ed., rev. and enl.* N. Y., Henry Holt & Co., 1893. 850 p. il. O. cl. 2.50 1.60

728. [584.] (702.) **Young folks' cyclopedia of games and sports.** John D. Champlin *and* Arthur E. Bostwick. N. Y., Henry Holt & Co., 1899. 784 p. il. O. cl. 2.50 1.60

A compendium of recreations of all kinds.

729. **Young folks' cyclopedia of literature and art.** John Denison Champlin. N. Y., Henry Holt & Co., 1901. 604 p. il. O. cl........................ 2.50 1.60

Although the scope of the earlier volumes of this series is quite comprehensive, including in the first volume physics, mechanics, and physiology, and in the second geography, biography, and history, it has been suggested by teachers and critics that the aesthetic side of cyclopaedic literature has been in a measure neglected. To fill this suggested want and to help to round out the series into a complete cyclopaedia, the "Young folk's cyclopaedia of literature and art" has been prepared. Its aim is to give a brief account of the acknowledged masterpieces in literature and in art, the latter term being understood to include architecture, sculpture, painting and music.

730. [583.] (489.) **Young folks' cyclopedia of persons and places.** John D. Champlin, *jr. 2d ed., rev.* N. Y., Henry Holt & Co., 1893. 936 p. il. O. cl....... 2.50 1.60

Teachers should train pupils to use the indexes. There is only one article on the Mississippi river, but a reference to the index shows that six other articles contain something of interest on the Mississippi river.

SONG BOOKS.

	List price.	Price to districts.

731. [590.] (525.) **Children's songs and how to sing them.** Wm. L. Tomlins. Chic., Lyon & Healy, 1894. 126 p. O. cl. .... .30 .25

Most beautiful songs for children.

732. [599.] (701.) **Choice songs.** H. O. R. Siefert. N. Y., Butler, Sheldon & Co., 1899. 158 p. sq. O. cl.   .40 .35

Beautiful songs for all times and seasons, expressly adapted for school use. Many old favorites so arranged as to make the songs easy to sing, without sacrificing the beauties of original harmony.

733. [589.] **Earth, sky and air in song.** Book 1. W. H. Neidlinger. N. Y., American Book Company, 1900. 127 p. il. sq. O. .... .75 .65

Beautiful songs of nature for youngest children.

734. **Earth, sky and air in song.** Book 2. W. H. Neidlinger. N. Y., American Book Co., c1900. 160 p. il. O. cl. .... .80 .70

Songs of nature, containing many fine illustrations.

735. [597.] **Favorite songs and hymns.** J. P. McCaskey, *ed.* N. Y., American Book Company, 1899. 400 p. O. cl. .... .80 .68

A fine collection of songs.

736. [596.] (530.) **Franklin Square song collection, Nos. 1 to 8.** *Comp.* by J. P. McCaskey. N. Y., American Book Company, 1897. O. cl. each........ .60 .52

Collections of favorite songs.

737. [591.] (526.) **Gems of school song.** *Ed.* by Carl Betz. N. Y., American Book Company, 1896. 190 p. O. cl. .... .70 .60

A very fine collection of songs for all times and seasons.

LIST OF BOOKS FOR TOWNSHIP LIBRARIES. 177

	List price.	Price to districts.

738. [595.] **Music reader for rural and village schools.** A. J. Gantvoort. N. Y., American Book Company. bds. ...... .40 .34

739. **St. Nicholas songs.** Waldo S. Pratt, *ed.* N. Y., Century Co., c1885. 190 p. il. Q. bds. ...... 1.25 .75

A collection of songs that originally appeared in the "St. Nicholas." Includes many lullabies and mother's songs. This book is too expensive to be purchased by schools where the amount of money available for library purposes is small.

740, 741. [593, 594.] **Short course in music.** Bks. 1, 2. Frederick H. Ripley *and* Thomas Tapper. N. Y., American Book Company, 1898. 144, 175 p. D. cl.
Bk. 1 ...... .35 .30
Bk. 2 ...... .40 .35

A course in music especially prepared for the rural schools. There are a large number of suitable songs.

742. [598.] (700.) **Songs of all lands.** W. S. B. Matthews. N. Y., American Book Company, 1899. 157 p. sq. O. bds. ...... .50 .43

Taking as a foundation the patriotic and typical folk songs of American life the national songs of all the leading countries are included in this excellent collection. Fine material for general exercises.

743. [592.] (527.) **Songs of life and nature.** Eleanor Smith. Chic., Scott, Foresman & Co., 1898. 208 p. Q. cl. ...... .75 .65

A collection of beautiful songs for older pupils.

744. [588.] (524.) **Songs of the child-world.** Music by Jessie L. Gaynor. Chicago, John Church Co., 1897. 121 p. Q. cl. ...... 1.25 .75

Some of the most beautiful songs ever written for children.

178 LIST OF BOOKS FOR TOWNSHIP LIBRARIES.

BOOKS FOR THE TEACHER.

Every teacher ought to read some of the good books in the line of her profession. The following books will prove very helpful to the earnest teacher. Read in connection with the Manual they will prove invaluable.

	List price.	Price to districts.
745. **As the twig is bent:** a story for mothers and teachers. Susan Chenery. Bost., Houghton, Mifflin & Co., 1901. 164 p. D. cl.	1.00	.90

This is called "a story for mothers and teachers." It is a book upon theoretical discipline, with practical illustrations that in many cases bear the test of genuine experience. For the most part, the practical side very considerably balances against the theoretical, and mothers or teachers reading the book will find many a helpful suggestion right to the point. The book bears directly upon the influence of discipline, and the methods suggested are to bring that influence about. That is, of course, the first principle in directing the life of a child, whether at home or in school. The book is written from a high standard, with an understanding of little children, and in a familiar style, as if the author sat down to talk things over with you. It is attractive and helpful.

| 746. **Beckonings from little hands.** Patterson Du Bois. Phil., Dodd, Mead & Co., 1898. 166 p. il. D. Fourth Edition. cl. | .75 | .45 |

This book was written by a mother and relates her actual experience with her four little ones. It should be read by every kindergartner and primary teacher and will be of value to all who are making a study of children from either a scientific or humanitarian point of view. Its purpose is both to awaken sympathy and to inform. It pleads for justice to children by exhibiting some phases of the strength and the weakness of child nature.

| 747. [603.] **Biography of a baby.** Milicent W. Shinn. Bost., Houghton, Mifflin & Co., 1900. 247 p. D. cl. | 1.50 | .90 |

Carefully observed facts handled in a scientific spirit about the first year of a normal girl baby's life.

LIST OF BOOKS FOR TOWNSHIP LIBRARIES. 179

	List price.	Price to districts.

748. [604.] (533.) **Elements of pedagogics.** J. N. Patrick. Becktold & Co., 1894. 224 p. D. cl............. 1.00 .67

The book is intended for those who have not already studied pedagogy. It states clearly, concisely, and simply the well-established principles of correct methods of instruction.

749. [601.] (532.) **Elements of pedagogy.** Emerson E. White. N. Y., American Book Company, 1886. 336 p. D. cl. .... 1.00 .85

Teachers will find this book very helpful studied in connection with the Manual.

References: Elements of psychology, 21-96; principles of teaching, 97-132; methods of teaching, 133-218; reading, 219-242; language, 243-254; grammar, 255-269; geography, 279-294; arithmetic, 294-312; moral training, 312-330.

750. [605.] (534.) **First school year.** Katherine Beebe. N. Y., Werner Co., 1895. 147 p. S. cl........... .75 .60

A very suggestive and helpful book.

References: Games, 5-18; science work, 31-42; holidays, 43-56; trades, industries, 68; self-expression in the school room, 79-93; literature for children, 94-109; growth in school life, 120-133.

751. **First years in handicraft.** Walter J. Kenyon. N. Y., Baker & Taylor Co., c1901. 124 p. il. D. cl.... 1.00 .65

"This is a primary book and solves the manual-training problem for primary children." It tells how to make many pretty and useful things out of paper, cardboard, and similar materials at a small cost. Scissors, ruler, and paste are the only necessary tools. The book contains over one hundred cuts and the text describes these cuts and gives directions to the teacher for the guidance of the children.

A suggestive book to mothers.

752. **Plans for busy work.** *Ed.* by Sarah Louise Arnold. N. Y., Silver, Burdett & Co., c1901. 139 p. D. cl. .50 .45

This volume is made up of contributions secured by the members of the Boston Primary Teachers' Association. A committee was organized to collect and collate material. Contributions passed by this committee were edited by Sarah Louise Arnold, supervisor of Boston schools. The book is published for the Primary Teachers' Association and any profits from its sale will be used for the association's work among Boston teachers.

References: Kindergarten occupations, 3-7; Language, spelling and reading, 29-49; Library, 48-49; Phonetics, 50-72; Drawing, 109-33; Writing, 134-39.

	List price.	Price to districts.

753. [602.] **Point of contact in teaching.** Patterson Du Bois. N. Y., Dodd, Mead & Co., 1900. 131 p. S. cl. .... .75 .45

A small book on one of the most vital principles of teaching.

754. [606.] (715.) **Rifle Creek papers and other essays, together with a few little sermons for teachers.** S. Y. Gillan. Milwaukee, S. Y. Gillan & Co., 1899. 160 p. D. cl. .... .65 .56

Will prove most helpful to country school teachers.

755. **School sanitation and decoration.** Severance Burrage, *and* Henry Turner Bailey. Bost., D. C. Heath & Co., c1899. 224 p. il. D. cl........... 1.50 1.10

A study of health and beauty in their relations to the public schools. The illustrations include reproductions of great master pieces, plans and elevations of school buildings, specimens of artistic work by pupils, and many suggestive diagrams. The book contains much that will be helpful to teachers and school officers who have become interested in the subject of the sanitation and decoration of schools.

Contents: Location of schools, 1–7; Construction and requirements of school buildings, 8–32; Principles of ventilation, heating, and lighting, 33–59; Sanitary problems of the schoolhouse, 60–72; School furniture, 73–82; The schoolroom, 83–93; Schoolroom decoration, 94–121; Old country schoolroom, 122–127; School children, 127–145; Influence of school life upon the eye, 146–58; School authorities and patrons, 159–67; Beauty in school work, 168–84; Classified list of works of art for schoolroom decorations, 213–19.

756. [600.] (531.) **School management.** Emerson E. White. N. Y., American Book Company, 1894. 320 p. D. cl. .... 1.00 .85

One of the best books on school management.

References: The teacher as governor, 17–47; conditions of easy control, 48–79; seating of pupils, 80–85; daily program, 86–93; will training, 105–129; incentives, 130–189; punishment, 190–217; moral instruction, 218–294.

PEDAGOGICAL STORIES.

                                                                      List price.   Price to districts.

757. [615.] **Autobiography of a tomboy.** Jeannette L. Gilder. N. Y., Doubleday, Page & Co., 1900. 349 p. il. D. cl. .... 1.25   .75

    The life of an active girl.

758. [611.] (281.) **Being a boy.** Charles Dudley Warner. Bost., Houghton, Mifflin & Co., 1896. 244 p. il. D. cl. .... .60   .50

    An interesting portrayal of a boy's life on a farm in New England.

759. [608.] (601.) **Court of Boyville.** William Allen White. N. Y., McClure, Phillips & Co., 1899. 358 p. il. D. cl. .... 1.50   .90

    The teacher will find this one of the best books to read on the subject of child study. The preface will stand much study on the part of the teacher.

760. [616.] **Evolution of "Dodd;"** a pedagogical story. William Hawley Smith. Chic., Rand, McNally & Co., 1897. 245 p. D. cl. .... 1.00   .48

    School life of a boy.

761. [607.] **In a boy's town.** William Dean Howells. N. Y., Harper & Bros., 1890. il. D. cl. .... 1.25   .75

    Shows wonderful insight into a boy's world.

762. **Jean Mitchell's school.** Angelina W. Wray. Bloomington, Public School Pub. Co., 1902. 244 p. il. D. cl. .... 1.25   .83

    An ideal story of a school in its working order from month to month throughout a school year. It is a charming picture of what a sincere, ambitious teacher can do and will prove an inspiration to every teacher.

	List price.	Price to districts.

763. [609.] **Johnnie.** E. O. Laughlin. Indianapolis, Bowen-Merrill Co., 1899. 227 p. il. D. cl............. 1.25 .75

The story of a boy's life.

764. [617.] **Playground Toni.** Anna Chapin Ray. N. Y., Thomas Y. Crowell & Co., 1900. 136 p. il. D. bds. .... .50 .30

A bit of life in a vacation school in the slums.

765. [610.] **Sentimental Tommy.** James M. Barrie. N. Y., C: Scribner's Sons, 1896. 478 p. il. D. cl... 1.50 .90

The story of an imaginative child.

A LIST OF GOOD BOOKS FOR THE FARMER.

The children may be made interested in the work of their parents, and through the children the parents may become interested in the library. The teachers will find much in these books which she may use in nature studies and in interesting the children in what is going on around them. Through this interest better farmers and better methods of farming may result.

	List price.	Price to districts.

766. [619.] (535.) **Agriculture.** Charles C. James. N. Y., D. Appleton & Co., 1898. 200 p. il. D. cl...... .80 .65

One of the best books on this subject.

767. [488.] (684.) **Corn plants;** their uses and ways of life. Frederick Leroy Sargent. Bost., Houghton, Mifflin & Co., 1899. 106 p. il. D. cl.......... .75 .45

Trustworthy information regarding some of the most valuable plants in the world. Will be found of great value in the teaching of geography as well as science. The upper form will read and the teacher will find much valuable material for work in the lower forms.

References: Corn plants in general, 1-75, 102-106; wheat, 75-79; oats, 80-82; rye, 83-84; barley, 85-88; rice, 89-90; maize, 91-101.

768. [622.] (540.) **Feeds and Feeding:** a handbook for the student and stockman. W. A. Henry. Madison, W. A. Henry, 1898. 657 p. O. cl.............. 2.00 1.20

A book full of interest and of value to the farmer. The teacher can use many facts from it in her nature work with the children.

769. [624.] (712.) **Garden-making:** suggestions for the utilizing of home grounds. L. H. Bailey. N. Y., Macmillan Co., 1899. 417 p. il. S. (Garden craft ser.) cl. .... 1.00 .67

A very suggestive book on garden making. Sections I, II, and III will be especially helpful in improving the school grounds.

	List price.	Price to districts.

770. [621.] (714.) **Handbook for farmers and dairymen.** F. W. Woll. N. Y., John Wiley & Sons, 1900. 437 p. S. cl. 1.50 1.10

A compendium of useful information on farm and dairy topics, valuable for reference.

771. **Hand-book of tree-planting.** Nathaniel H. Egleston. N. Y., D. Appleton & Co., 1900. 126 p. D. cl.... .75 .50

An excellent book on forestry for the farmer answering the questions—Why to plant? Where to plant? What to plant? And how to plant?

772. [625.] (713.) **Landscape gardening as applied to home decoration.** Samuel T. Maynard. N. Y., John Wiley & Sons, 1899. 338 p. il. D. cl..... 1.50 1.10

A complete, practical, and helpful treatise on gardening, especially valuable for home and school decoration.

773. **Life on the farm: or, scientific agriculture simplified.** A reading book for grammar and high schools. Hiram H. Shepard. Chic., A Flanagan Co., c1901. 166 p. il. D. (Home and school ser.) cl....... .50 .36

A simple and interesting book which gives much practical information about farm life.

References: Soil, 9–40; Plants, 41–84; Trees, 85–103; Insects, 104–129; Birds, 130–50; Bacteria, 151–166.

774. [620.] (538.) **Principles of agriculture.** *Ed.* by L. H. Bailey. N. Y., Macmillan Co., 1898. 300 p. il. D. cl. .... 1.25 .85

References: The soil, 16–36; texture of the soil, 37–46; moisture in the soil, 47–63; tillage of the soil, 64–76; enriching the soil, 77–105; offices of the plant, 106–111; how the plant lives, 112–131; propagation of plants, 132–144; preparation of land for seed, 145–158; care of the plant, 159–178; pastures, meadows, 179–200; offices of the animal, 201–207; how the animal lives, 208–238; feeding, 239–257; management of stock, 258–278.

775. [623.] (539.) **Principles of plant culture.** E. S. Goff. *2d ed., rev.* Madison, E. S. Goff, 1899. 288 p. il. D. cl. .... 1.10 .85

This book is intended for students who have had little or no previous instruction in botany. The older children will find much of interest in it.

PERIODICALS.

Whenever any of the periodicals given below have been used in the schools they have given excellent satisfaction. Papers filled with trashy stories and vicious pictures are constantly being freely circulated among boys and girls. The most certain preventive against power for harm in bad periodicals is access to good ones. The papers, too, may be made very serviceable as aids in the preparation of lessons and in the recitation.

	List price.	Price to districts.
St. Nicholas	$3.00	$2.75
Week's Current	1.25	.90
Youth's Companion, Boston, Mass.	1.75	1.75
Our Dumb Animals	.50	.45
Birds and Nature	1.50	1.30
Bird Lore	1.00	.90
Little Chronicle, Chicago	1.50	1.30
By the Wayside (Audubon Society)	.20	.20
Country Life	3.00	1.75

AUTHOR AND TITLE INDEX.

260.	Aaron in the wildwoods	J. C. Harris
190.	Abbot, Alice Balch	Frigate's namesake
600.	About the weather	M. W. Harrington
488.	Abraham Lincoln	Noah Brooks
489.	Abraham Lincoln	C. C. Coffin
60.	Adventures of a brownie	Mrs. D. M. M. Craik
367.	Adventures of a freshman	J. L. Williams
166.	Adventures of Joel Pepper	Mrs. H. M. Lothrop
576.	Adventures of two youths in a journey to Japan and China	T. W. Knox
766.	Agriculture	C. C. James
660.	A-hunting of the deer	C. D. Warner
71.	Aiken, Dr. and others	Eyes and no eyes
386.	Alcott, Louisa May	Eight cousins
194.	Alcott, Louisa May	Jack and Jill
208.	Alcott, Louisa May	Little men
209.	Alcott, Louisa May	Little women
407.	Alcott, Louisa May	Old-fashioned girl
228.	Alcott, Louisa May	Under the lilacs
21.	Aldrich, George I. & Forbes, A.	First book: pictures, rhymes
16.	Aldrich, George I. & Forbes, A.	Second book: stories, verses
17.	Aldrich, George I. & Forbes, A.	Third book: stories, studies
570.	Aldrich, Herbert L.	Arctic Alaska and Siberia
224.	Aldrich, Thomas Bailey	Story of a bad boy
167.	Alice's adventures in Wonderland	Lewis Carroll
312.	Alice's visit to the Hawaiian islands	M. H. Krout
616.	Allen, Grant	Flashlights on nature
640.	Allen, Grant	Story of the plants
437.	Allen, Willis Boyd	Cleared for action
460.	Allen, Willis Boyd	Navy blue
368.	Almost as good as a boy	A. M. Douglas
595.	Alton, Edmund	Among the law-makers
448.	Altsheler, J. A.	In hostile red
705.	American big-game hunting	Theodore Roosevelt and G. B. Grinnell
272.	American boys' life of William McKinley	Edward Stratemeyer

594.	American citizen	C. F. Dole
706.	American girls' handy book	L. and A. B. Beard
707.	American girls' home book of work and play	Helen Campbell
290.	American Indians	Frederick Starr
291.	American inventions and inventors	W. A. and A. M. Mowry
292.	American leaders and heroes	W. F. Gordy
672.	American war ballads and lyrics	G. C. Eggleston, ed.
120.	America's story for America's children. Bk. 1	M. L. Pratt
121.	America's story for America's children. Bk. 2	M. L. Pratt
371.	Amicis, Edmondo de	Boy's life at school: Cuore
701.	Among flowers and trees with the poets	M. C. Wait and M. C. Leonard, Comps.
233.	Among the camps	T. N. Page
156.	Among the farmyard people	C. D. Pierson
157.	Among the forest people	C. D. Pierson
595.	Among the law-makers	Edmund Alton
158.	Among the meadow people	C. D. Pierson
159.	Among the pond people	C. D. Pierson
109.	Andersen, Hans Christian	Stories
153.	Andrews, Jane	Seven little sisters prove their sisterhood
152.	Andrews, Jane	Seven little sisters who live on the round ball that floats in the air
165.	Andrews, Jane	Stories of my four friends
138.	Andrews, Jane	Ten boys who lived on the road from long ago to now
338.	Animal story book	Andrew Lang, ed.
601.	Animals in action	E. S. Brooks, comp.
432.	Anneke	E. W. Champney
602.	Apes and monkeys	L. Garner
61.	April baby's book of tunes	(Anon)
62.	Arabella and Araminta stories	Gertrude Smith
264.	Arabian nights	M. Clarke, ed.
570.	Arctic Alaska and Siberia	H. L. Aldrich
567.	Arnold, Emma J.	Stories of ancient peoples
9.	Arnold primer	S. L. Arnold
9.	Arnold, Sarah Louise	Arnold primer
752.	Arnold, Sarah Louise, ed.	Plans for busy work
139.	Around the world. Bk. 1	S. W. Carroll
140.	Around the world. Bk. 2	S. W. Carroll
313.	Around the world. Bk. 3	S. W. Carroll and E. M. Hart.
251.	Asgard stories	M. H. Foster and M. H. Cummings
708.	Ashmore, Ruth	Business girl in every phase of her life
314.	Asia	F. G. Carpenter
70.	Aspinwall, Alicia	Echo-maid and other stories
92.	Aspinwall, Alicia	Short stories for short people

745.	As the twig is bent	Susan Chenery
656.	As you like it	William Shakespeare
615.	Atkinson, George Francis	First studies of plant life
252.	At the back of the north wind	George MacDonald
100.	Atwater, Emily Paret	Tommy's adventures
168.	Aunt Hannah and Seth	James Otis Kaler
	Austin, Isabella, *joint author*	*See* Gilman, Mary L.
593.	Australia and the islands of the sea	E. M. C. Kellogg
757.	Autobiography of a tomboy	J. L. Gilder
490.	Autobiography of Benjamin Franklin.	
614.	Avery, Elroy M. *and* Sinnott, Charles P........................ First lessons in physical science	
72.	Ayers, Raymond Fuller	Four-footed folk
316.	Ayrton, *Mrs.* M. Chaplin.............................Child-life in Japan and Japanese child stories	

604.	Babcock, Charles A	Bird day: how to prepare for it
582.	Bacon, Alice Mabel	Japanese girls and women
592.	Badlam, Anna B	Views in Africa
	Bailey, Edmund. *See* Alton, Edmund, *pseud.*	
	Bailey, Henry Turner, *joint author. See* Burrage, Severance.	
769.	Bailey, L. H	Garden-making
774.	Bailey, L. H., *ed.*	Principles of agriculture
610.	Baker, Ray Stannard	Boy's book of inventions
534.	Baldwin, James.................................... Conquest of the old Northwest and its settlement by Americans	
535.	Baldwin, James .... Discovery of the old Northwest and its settlement by French	
123.	Baldwin, James	Fifty famous stories retold
129.	Baldwin, James	Four great Americans
115.	Baldwin, James	Old Greek stories
131.	Baldwin, James	Old stories of the East
38.	Baldwin, James	School reading by grades: First year
39.	Baldwin, James	School reading by grades: Second year
40.	Baldwin, James	School reading by grades: Third year
484.	Baldwin, James	Story of Roland
485.	Baldwin, James	Story of Siegfried
486.	Baldwin, James	Story of the golden age
108.	Baldwin, James, *ed.*	Fairy stories and fables
10.	Baldwin primer	May Kirk
669.	Ballad book	K. L. Bates, *ed.*
369.	Barbara's heritage	D. L. Hoyt
375.	Barbour, Ralph Henry	Captain of the crew

389.	Barbour, Ralph Henry	For the honor of the school
392.	Barbour, Ralph Henry	Half-back
280.	Barnard, Mordaunt R., *trans. See* Bull, J. B.	Fridtjof Nansen
495.	Barnes, James	Commodore Bainbridge
439.	Barnes, James	Drake and his yeomen
440.	Barnes, James	For king or country
501.	Barnes, James	Hero of Erie
456.	Barnes, James	Loyal traitor
512.	Barnes, James	Midshipman Farragut
478.	Barnes, James	Yankee ships and Yankee sailors
765.	Barrie, James M.	Sentimental Tommy
445.	Barton, William E.	Hero in homespun
461.	Barton, William E.	Prairie schooner
639.	Baskett, James Newton	Story of the fishes
669.	Bates, Katherine Lee, *ed.*	Ballad book
114.	Baum, Lyman Frank	New Wonderland
254.	Bay, J. Christian, *ed.*	Danish fairy and folk tales
	Bayley, Abner, *joint author. See* Marden, Orison Swett.	
620.	Bayliss, Clara Kern	In brook and bayou
146.	Bayliss, Clara Kern	Lolami, the little cliff-dweller
199.	Baylor, Frances Courtenay	Juan and Juanita
635.	Beal, William J.	Seed dispersal
	Beard, Adelia B., *joint author. See* Beard, Lina.	
717.	Beard, D. C.	Jack of all trades
718.	Beard, D. C.. Outdoor handy book for playground, field and forest	
611.	Beard, J. C.	Curious homes and their tenants
706.	Beard, Lina *and* Adelia B.	
	How to amuse yourself and others; American girls' handy book	
169.	Bears of Blue River	Charles Major
340.	Beasts of the field	William J. Long
171.	Beautiful Joe	M. Saunders
746.	Beckonings from little hands	Patterson Du Bois
63.	Bed-time stories	L. C. Moulton
160.	Bee people	Margaret W. Morley
750.	Beebe, Katherine	First school year for primary workers
	Beebe, Katherine, *joint author. See* Perry, Frances M.	
127.	Beebe, Mabel Borton	Four American naval heroes
758.	Being a boy	C. D. Warner
722.	Bell, Hugh *Mrs*	Fairy tale plays and how to act them
	Bender, Ida C., *joint editor. See* Judson, Harry Pratt.	
345.	Bergen, Fanny D.	Glimpses at the plant world
170.	Bernardo and Laurette	Marguerite Bouvet

433.	Between Boer and Briton	Edward Stratemeyer
737.	Betz, Carl, *ed.*	Gems of school song
234.	Big brother	G. C. Eggleston
64.	Big outdoors	Clara G. Froelich
141.	Big people and little people of other lands	Edward R. Shaw
350.	Bignell, Effie	Mr. Chupes and Miss Jenny
747.	Biography of a baby	Milicent W. Shinn
603.	Biography of a grizzly	Ernest Seton-Thompson
604.	Bird day: how to prepare for it	Charles A. Babcock
609.	Bird studies with a camera	Frank M. Chapman
605.	Birds and bees	John Burroughs
65.	Birds' Christmas carol	K. D. Wiggin
606.	Birds of lakeside and prairie	E. B. Clark
607.	Birds of song and story	Elizabeth *and* Joseph Grinnell
608.	Birds of village and field	F. A. Merriam
172.	Black Beauty	Anna Sewell
	Black, S. W., *joint author.* *See* Jones, L. E.	
403.	Blackmore, R. D.	Lorna Doone
308.	Blaisdell, Albert F., *ed.*	Stories of the Civil war
11.	Blaisdell, E. A. *and* M. F.	Child life: a first reader
12.	Blaisdell, E. A. *and* M. F. ....Child life in tale and fable: second reader	
	Blaisdell, M. F., *joint author.* *See* Blaisdell, Etta Austin.	
	Blaisdell, S. Lilian, *joint author.* *See* Gilman, Mary L.	
438.	Blanchard, Amy E.	Daughter of freedom
678.	Blue poetry book	Andrew Lang, *ed.*
569.	Boden, G. H. *and* D'Almeida, W. B., *eds.* ....Wonder stories from Herodotus	
720.	Bok, Edward	Successward
498.	Bolton, *Mrs.* Sarah	Famous American statesmen
500.	Bolton, *Mrs.* Sarah	Girls who became famous
515.	Bolton, *Mrs.* Sarah	Poor boys who became famous
630.	Bolton, *Mrs.* Sarah	Our devoted friend, the dog
491.	Book of American explorers	T. W. Higginson
690.	Book of famous verse	Agnes Repplier, *comp.*
103.	Book of legends told over again	H. E. Scudder
45.	Book of nursery rhymes	Charles Welsh
1.	Book of ships.	
571.	Book of the ocean	Ernest Ingersoll
93.	Booth, Maud Ballington	Sleepy-time stories
524.	Border wars of New England	S. A. Drake
66.	Boston collection kindergarten stories.	
	Bostwick, Arthur E., *joint author.* *See* Champlin, John D.	
170.	Bouvet, Marguerite	Bernardo and Laurette

AUTHOR AND TITLE INDEX.   191

98.	Bouvet, Marguerite	Sweet William
469.	Bouvet, Marguerite	Tales of an old chateau
434.	Boy emigrant	Noah Brooks
273.	Boy general	E. B. Custer
173.	Boy I knew, four dogs, and some more dogs	Laurence Hutton
274.	Boy life of Napoleon	E. S. Brooks
436.	Boy of the first empire	E. S. Brooks
572.	Boy travellers in Central Europe	T. W. Knox
573.	Boy travellers in Northern Europe	T. W. Knox
574.	Boy travellers in South America	T. W. Knox
575.	Boy travellers in Southern Europe	T. W. Knox
576.	Boy travellers in the far East	T. W. Knox
370.	Boyesen, Hjalmar Hjorth	Boyhood in Norway
370.	Boyhood in Norway	H. H. Boyesen
51.	Boylan, Grace Duffie *and* Morgan, Ike	Kids of many colors
492.	Boys' and girls' Plutarch	J. S. White
673.	Boy's book of battle lyrics	T. D. English
525.	Boy's book of explorations	Tudor Jenks
610.	Boy's book of inventions	R. S. Baker
694.	Boy's book of rhyme	Clinton Scollard
709.	Boys' book of sports	Maurice Thompson, *ed.*
670.	Boy's Browning	Robert Browning
371.	Boy's life at school	Edmondo de Amicis
372.	Boys of Fairport	Noah Brooks
435.	Boys of old Monmouth	E. T. Tomlinson
141a.	Boys of other countries	Bayard Taylor
293.	Boys of '76	C. C. Coffin
710.	Boy's workshop	
263.	Bradish, Sarah Powers	Old Norse stories
155.	Bradish, Sarah Powers	Stories of country life
283.	Brady, Cyrus Townsend	Reuben James
526.	Brave little Holland	W. E. Griffis
436.	Brooks, Elbridge S.	Boy of the first empire
528.	Brooks, Elbridge S.	Century book for young Americans
494.	Brooks, Elbridge S.	Century book of famous Americans
529.	Brooks, Elbridge S.	Century book of the American colonies
294.	Brooks, Elbridge S.	Century book of the American Revolution
441.	Brooks, Elbridge S.	Godson of Lafayette
507.	Brooks, Elbridge S.	Historic Americans
508.	Brooks, Elbridge S.	Historic girls
466.	Brooks, Elbridge S.	Son of the Revolution
551.	Brooks, Elbridge S.	Story of our war with Spain
286.	Brooks, Elbridge S.	True story of Benjamin Franklin
287.	Brooks, Elbridge S.	True story of Christopher Columbus

288.	Brooks, Elbridge S...............	True story of U. S. Grant
601.	Brooks, Elbridge S., comp.........	Animals in action
274.	Brooks, Elbridge S., trans.	Boy life of Napoleon
488.	Brooks, Noah....................	Abraham Lincoln
434.	Brooks, Noah....................	Boy emigrants
372.	Brooks, Noah....................	Boys of Fairport
536.	Brooks, Noah....................	First across the continent
205.	Brooks, Noah..............	Lem: a New England village boy
516.	Brooks, Noah....................	Statesmen
518.	Brooks, Noah....................	Story of Marco Polo
81.	Brown, Abbie Farwell.............	Lonesomest doll
80.	Brown, Helen Dawes..............	Little Miss Phoebe Gay
413.	Brown, John.....................	Rab and his friends
119.	Browne, Frances..........	Wonderful chair and the tales it told
670.	Browning, Robert.................	Boy's Browning
268.	Brun, Samuel Jacques.............	Tales of Languedoc
671.	Bryant, William Cullen............	Poetical works
613.	Buckley, Arabella B...............	Fairy-land of science
527.	Building the nation...............	C. C. Coffin
280.	Bull, Jacob B.	Fridtjof Nansen
409.	Bunyan, John....................	Pilgrim's progress
47.	Burgess, Gelett...................	Goops and how to be them
755.	Burrage, Severance and Bailey, H. T............................
		School sanitation and decoration
605.	Burroughs, John..................	Birds and bees
631.	Burroughs, John..................	Pepacton
638.	Burroughs, John.............	Squirrels and other fur-bearers
642.	Burroughs, John..................	Wake-robin
186.	Burt, Mary E., ed.................	Eugene Field book
	Burt, Mary E., joint editor. See Cable, George W.	
262.	Burt, Mary E. and Ragozin, Z. A........	Odysseus
128.	Burton, Alma Holman..............	Four American patriots
281.	Burton, Alma Holman...Lafayette the friend of American liberty	
304.	Burton, Alma Holman.............	Story of our country
708.	Business girl in every phase of her life....	Ashmore, Ruth
395.	Butterworth, Hezekiah............	In the days of Audubon
341.	Buz.............................	Maurice Noel
161.	Buz-buz.........................	C. S. Pratt
315.	By land and sea.	
174.	Cable, George W..................	Cable story book
174.	Cable story book.................	George W. Cable
373.	Cadet days......................	Capt. Charles King
235.	Cadet Standish of the St. Louis......	William Drysdale

AUTHOR AND TITLE INDEX. 193

44. Calmerton, Gail *and* Wheeler, W. H............................
........................Wheeler's graded readers: a primer
175. Camp and trail............................Isabel Hornibrook
374. Camp Venture: story of the Virginia mountains..G. C. Eggleston
707. Campbell, Helen....American girl's home book of work and play
711. Camping and camp outfits........................G. O. Shields
67. Captain Fritz................................E. H. Miller
176. Captain January................................L. E. Richards
375. Captain of the crew............................R. H. Barbour
493. Captains of industry............................James Parton
712. Careers of danger and daring.................Cleveland Moffett
314. Carpenter, F. G...Asia
577. Carpenter, F. G...Europe
584. Carpenter, F. G.......................................North America
334. Carpenter, F. G.......................................South America
Carroll, Lewis, *pseud. See* Dodgson, C. L.
139. Carroll, Stella W......................Around the world. Bk. 1
140. Carroll, Stella W. *and* Jerome, H. L....Around the world. Bk. 2
313. Carroll, Stella W. *and* Hart, E. M......Around the world. Bk. 3
Carroll, Clarence F., *ed. See* Carroll, Stella W. *and* Hart, E. M.
Caskoden, Edwin, *pseud. See* Major, Charles.
506. Catherwood, Mary Hartwell..........Heroes of the middle west
376. Cattle ranch to college....................Russell Doubleday
528. Century book for young Americans................E. S. Brooks
494. Century book of famous Americans................E. S. Brooks
529. Century book of the American colonies............E. S. Brooks
294. Century book of the American Revolution..........E. S. Brooks
177. Cervantes, Saavedra, M. de.................Child's Don Quixote
Chaillu, Paul Belloni du. *See* Du Chaillu, Paul Belloni.
727. Champlin, John Denison, *jr*..
................Young folks' cyclopedia of common things
729. Champlin, John Denison, *jr*..
..............Young folks' cyclopedia of literature and art
730. Champlin, John Denison, *jr*..
..............Young folks' cyclopedia of persons and places
559. Champlin, John Denison, *jr*..
..............Young folks' history of the war for the Union
728. Champlin, John Denison, *and* Bostwick, A. E................
..............Young folks' cyclopedia of games and sports
432. Champney, Elizabeth W...........................Anneke
487. Chapin, Anna Alice....................Story of the Rhinegold
141. Chaplin, Fannie P. *and* Humphrey, *Mrs*. F. A..................
............................Little folks of other lands
609. Chapman, Frank M.................Bird studies with a camera

194 LIST OF BOOKS FOR TOWNSHIP LIBRARIES.

617.	Chapman, Frank M., ed.....Four-footed Americans and their kin	
745.	Chenery, Susan..........................As the twig is bent	
11.	Child life: a first reader...............E. A. *and* M. F. Blaisdell	
530.	Child life in colonial days....................Alice Morse Earle	
316.	Child-life in Japan and Japanese child stories.................	
	.....................................Mrs. M. Chaplin Ayrton	
12.	Child life in tale and fable: a second reader...................	
	...................................E. A. *and* M. F. Blaisdell	
122.	Child of Urbino: Raphael...................Louise de la Ramé	
691.	Child-rhymes...J. W. Riley	
68.	Child stories and rhymes for little people of the nursery and kindergarten............................ Emilie Poulsson	
104.	Child stories from the masters..................Maud Menefee	
692.	Child world...J. W. Riley	
236.	Childhood of Ji-Shib', the Ojibwa...................A. E. Jenks	
679.	Childhood songs.............................Lucy Larcom	
275.	Children's life of Abraham Lincoln...............M. L. Putnam	
698.	Child's garden of verses......................R. L. Stevenson	
560.	Child's history of Ireland.........................P. W. Joyce	
731.	Children's songs and how to sing them..........W. L. Tomlins	
295.	Children's stories of American progress...........H. C. Wright	
46.	Chinese mother goose rhymes...................I. T. Headland	
363.	Choice literature. Intermediate grades. Vol. 1...............	
	..................................Sherman Williams, *comp.*	
364.	Choice literature. Intermediate grades. Vol. 2...............	
	..................................Sherman Williams, *comp.*	
662.	Choice literature. Grammar grades. Vol. 1..................	
	..................................Sherman Williams, *comp.*	
663.	Choice literature. Grammar grades. Vol. 2..................	
	..................................Sherman Williams, *comp.*	
105.	Choice literature. Primary grades. Vol. 1...................	
	..................................Sherman Williams, *comp.*	
13.	Choice literature. Primary grades. Vol. 2...................	
	..................................Sherman Williams, *comp.*	
732.	Choice songs................................H. O. R. Siefert	
178.	Christmas angel............................Katherine Pyle	
377.	Christmas carol............................Charles Dickens	
179.	Christmas every day........................W. D. Howells	
378.	Chronicles of Sir John Froissart............Adam Singleton, *ed.*	
180.	Chuck Purdy.................................W. O. Stoddard	
482.	Church, Alfred J..........................Stories from Homer	
483.	Church, Alfred J..........................Stories from Virgil	
471.	Church, Alfred J.......................Three Greek children	
380.	Churchill, Winston................................... Crisis	

AUTHOR AND TITLE INDEX.

181.	Citizen Dan of the Junior Republic	I. T. Thurston
379.	City boys in the woods	H. P. Wells
596.	Civics for young Americans	W. M. Giffin
606.	Clark, Edward B.	Birds of lakeside and prairie
163.	Clark, Edward B.	Jingle book of birds
53.	Clark, G. Orr	Moon babies
231.	Clark, Imogen	Will Shakespeare's little lad
264.	Clarke, M., ed.	Stories from the Arabian nights
266.	Clarke, M., ed.	Story of Aeneas
302.	Clarke, M., ed.	Story of Caesar
267.	Clarke, M., ed.	Story of Troy
106.	Classic stories for little ones	Mrs. L. B. McMurry
437.	Cleared for action	W. B. Allen
462.	Clemens, Samuel Langhorne	Prince and the pauper
279.	Cody, Sherwin	Four American poets
589.	Coe, Fanny E.	
	..... Our American neighbors. *World and its people.* Bk. 4	
599.	Coe, Fanny E..... Modern Europe. *World and its people.* Bk. 5	
489.	Coffin, Charles Carleton	Abraham Lincoln
293.	Coffin, Charles Carleton	Boys of '76
527.	Coffin, Charles Carleton	Building the nation
545.	Coffin, Charles Carleton	Old times in the colonies
531.	Colonies, 1492-1750	R. G. Thwaites
495.	Commodore Bainbridge	James Barnes
680.	Complete poetical works	H. W. Longfellow
689.	Complete poetical works	J. R. Lowell
702.	Complete poetical works	J. G. Whittier
598.	Conner, E.	Uncle Sam abroad
534.	Conquest of the old Northwest	James Baldwin
117.	Cook, Agnes Spofford, ed.	Story of Ulysses
	Cook, Agnes Spofford, *joint comp. See* **McMurry, Lida Brown.**	
113.	Cooke, Flora J., ed..... Nature myths and stories for little children	
382.	Cooper, James Fenimore	Deerslayer
454.	Cooper, James Fenimore	Last of the Mohicans
410.	Cooper, James Fenimore	Pilot
767.	Corn plants	F. L. Sargent
654.	Correggio	E. M. Hurll
422.	Cotes, Mrs. Sara Jeanette Duncan	Story of Sonny Sahib
69.	Counterpane fairy	Katherine Pyle
759.	Court of Boyville	W. A. White
253.	Court of King Arthur	W. H. Frost
681.	Courtship of Miles Standish	H. W. Longfellow
385.	Craddock, Charles Egbert	Down the ravine
467.	Craddock, Charles Egbert	Story of old Fort Loudon

60.	Craik, *Mrs.* Dinah Maria	Adventures of a brownie
79.	Craik, *Mrs.* Dinah Maria	Little lame prince
136.	Cravens, Frances	Story of Lincoln
562.	Creighton, Louise	Stories from English history
377.	Cricket on the hearth	Charles Dickens
380.	Crisis	Winston Churchill
37a.	Crosby, W. E.	Our little book for little folks
	Cross, Mary Ann Lewes. *See* Eliot, George, *pseud.*	
381.	Crowded out o' Crofield	W. O. Stoddard
	Cummings, Mabel H., *joint author*. *See* Foster, Mary H.	
365.	Cumnock, Robert McLean, *comp.*	Cumnock's school speaker
365.	Cumnock's school speaker	R. L. Cumnock, *comp.*
371.	Cuore:	Edmondo de Amicis
611.	Curious homes and their tenants	J. C. Beard
273.	Custer, Elizabeth B.	Boy general
182.	Dab Kinzer	W. O. Stoddard
	D'Almeida, W. Barrington, *joint author*. *See* Boden, G. H.	
633.	Dana, *Mrs.* William Starr	Plants and their children
254.	Danish fairy and folk tales	J. C. Bay, *ed.*
438.	Daughter of freedom	A. E. Blanchard
416.	Davis, Richard Harding	Stories for boys
	De Amicis, Edmondo. *See* Amicis, Edmondo de	
73.	De Burgh, Beatrice	Hal o' the fells
	De La Ramé, Louise. *See* Ramé, Louise de la	
496.	De Soto and his men in the land of Florida	Grace King
276.	Decatur and Somers	M. E. Seawell
382.	Deerslayer	J. F. Cooper
206.	Defoe, Daniel	Life and adventures of Robinson Crusoe
33.	Demarest, A. J. *and* Van Sickle, Wm.	New education reader. Bk. 1
34.	Demarest, A. J. *and* Van Sickle, Wm.	New education reader. Bk. 2
35.	Demarest, A. J. *and* Van Sickle, Wm.	New education reader. Bk. 3
4.	Denslow, W. W., *ed.*	Mother Goose
497.	Diary of Anna Green Winslow	A. M. Earle, *ed.*
377.	Dickens, Charles	Christmas carol
420.	Dickens, Charles	Story of little Nell
277.	Discoverers and explorers	E. R. Shaw
535.	Discovery of the old Northwest	James Baldwin
183.	Divided skates	Evelyn Raymond
533.	Division and reunion, 1829-1889	Woodrow Wilson

446.	Dix, Beulah Marie	Hugh Gwyeth
465.	Dix, Beulah Marie	Soldier Rigdale
237.	Docas, the Indian boy of Santa Clara	G. S. Snedden
384.	Dodge, *Mrs.* Mary Mapes	Donald and Dorothy
191.	Dodge, *Mrs.* Mary Mapes	Hans Brinker
324.	Dodge, *Mrs.* Mary Mapes	Land of pluck
84.	Dodge, *Mrs.* Mary Mapes, *comp*	New baby world
58.	Dodge, *Mrs.* Mary Mapes	When life is young
634.	Dodge, Richard Elwood	
	Reader in physical geography for beginners	
167.	Dodgson, Charles L	Alice's adventures in Wonderland
383.	Dog-watches at sea	S. H. King
	Dole, Helen B., *trans. See* Spyri, Frau Johanna	Heidi
594.	Dole, Charles F	American citizen
177.	Don Quixote	Saavedra M. de Cervantes
384.	Donald and Dorothy	M. M. Dodge
376.	Doubleday, Russell	Cattle ranch to college
368.	Douglas, Amanda M	Almost as good as a boy
385.	Down the ravine	C. E. Craddock
247.	Doyle, A. Conan	Micah Clarke
184.	Dozen from Lakerim	Rupert Hughes
439.	Drake and his yeomen	James Barnes
524.	Drake, Samuel Adams	Border wars of New England
541.	Drake, Samuel Adams	Making of New England
542.	Drake, Samuel Adams	Making of the great West
543.	Drake, Samuel Adams	
	Making of Virginia and the middle colonies	
235.	Drysdale, William	Cadet Standish of the St. Louis
411.	Drysdale, William	Pine Ridge plantation
428.	Drysdale, William	Treasury club
430.	Drysdale, William	Young consul
431.	Drysdale, William	Young supercargo
746.	Du Bois, Patterson	Beckonings from little hands
753.	Du Bois, Patterson	Point of contact in teaching
583.	Du Chaillu, Paul	Land of the long night
328.	Du Chaillu, Paul	Lost in the jungle
335.	Du Chaillu, Paul	Wild life under the Equator
645.	Du Chaillu, Paul	World of the great forest
	Duncan, Sara Jeanette. *See* Cotes, *Mrs.* (Everard) S. J. D.	
	Dunton, Larkin, *ed. See* World *and its people series.*	
733.	Earth, sky and air in song. Bk. 1	W. H. Neidlinger
734.	Earth, sky and air in song. Bk. 2	W. H. Neidlinger
530.	Earle, Alice Morse	Child life in colonial days

497.	Earle, Alice Morse, ed.............	Diary of Anna Green Winslow
70.	Echo-maid and other stories.................	Alicia Aspinwall
362.	Eckstrom, Fannie Hardy..........................	Woodpeckers
185.	Ednah and her brothers...........................	E. O. White
124.	Eggleston, Edward..............	First book in American history
443.	Eggleston, Edward	Graysons
538.	Eggleston, Edward............	History of the U. S. and its people
193.	Eggleston, Edward...........................	Hoosier school boy
132.	Eggleston, Edward......	Stories of American life and adventures
133.	Eggleston, Edward	
	............Stories of great Americans for little Americans	
672.	Eggleston, George Cary, ed......	American war ballads and lyrics
234.	Eggleston, George Cary.............................	Big brother
374.	Eggleston, George Cary..........................	Camp Venture
399.	Eggleston, George Cary.....................	Last of the flatboats
771.	Egleston, Nathaniel H................	Hand-book of tree-planting
386.	Eight cousins...	L. M. Alcott
296.	Elementary history of the United States............	A. C. Thomas
748.	Elements of pedagogics...........................	J. N. Patrick
749.	Elements of pedagogy.............................	E. E. White
713.	Elements of the theory and practice of cookery.................	
	.... M. E. Williams and K. R. Fisher	
387.	Enchanted burro.................................	C. F. Lummis
561.	England's story.................................	E. M. Tappan
673.	English, Thomas Dunn...............	Boy's book of battle lyrics
397.	Ensign, Hermon Lee..........	Lady Lee and other animal stories
186.	Eugene Field book.............................	M. E. Burt, ed.
577.	Europe..	F. G. Carpenter
578.	Europe and other continents......	R. S. Tarr and F. M. McMurry
	Everett-Green, Evelyn. See Green, Evelyn-Everett..............	
342.	Everyday birds................................	Bradford Torrey
760.	Evolution of "Dodd".............................	W. H. Smith
612.	Eye spy..	W. H. Gibson
71.	Eyes and no eyes and other stories........	Dr. Aiken and others

107.	Fables and folk stories......................	H. E. Scudder, ed.
613.	Fairy-land of science............................	A. B. Buckley
108.	Fairy stories and fables.....................	James Baldwin, ed.
14.	Fairy tale and fable: second year......	J. G. and T. E. Thompson
722.	Fairy tale plays and how to act them.............	Mrs. Hugh Bell
498.	Famous American statesmen..................	Mrs. S. K. Bolton
187.	Fanciful tales................................	F. R. Stockton
735.	Favorite songs and hymns.................	J. P. McCaskey, ed.

123.	Fifty famous stories retold	James Baldwin
768.	Feeds and feeding	W. A. Henry
243.	Fenn, G. Manville	King Robert's page
74.	Fenn, G. Manville *and others*	In the chimney corner
401.	Field, Eugene	Little book of profitable tales
674.	Field, Eugene	Little book of western verse
676.	Field, Eugene	Love-songs of childhood
677.	Field, Eugene	Lullaby-land
675.	Field, Eugene	Second book of verse
714.	Fighting a fire	C. T. Hill
536.	First across the continent	Noah Brooks
124.	First book in American history	Edward Eggleston
343.	First book of birds	O. T. Miller
15.	First book: pictures, rhymes, stories	G. I. Aldrich *and* Alex. Forbes
614.	First lessons in physical science	E. M. Avery *and* C. P. Sinnott
18.	First reader	L. E. Jones *and* S. W. Black
750.	First school year	Katharine Beebe
125.	First steps in the history of our country	W. A. *and* A. M. Mowry
615.	First studies of plant life	G. F. Atkinson
751.	First years in handicraft	W. J. Kenyon
	Fisher, Katharine Rolston, *joint author. See* Williams, Mary E.	
558.	Fiske, John	War of Independence
188.	Five little Peppers, and how they grew	*Mrs.* H. M. Lothrop
388.	Five little Peppers grown up	*Mrs.* H. M. Lothrop
616.	Flashlights on nature	Grant Allen
82.	Fletcher, Robert Howe	Marjorie and her papa
544.	Flint, Grover	Marching with Gomez
228.	Flower of the Wilderness	A. G. Plympton
344.	Flowers and their friends	M. W. Morley
274.	Foa, *Mme.* Eugénie	Boy life of Napoleon
26.	Folk-lore stories and proverbs	S. E. Wiltse
440.	For king or country	James Barnes
389.	For the honor of the school	R. H. Barbour
	Forbes, Alexander, *joint author. See* Aldrich, G. I.	
532.	Formation of the Union	A. B. Hart
554.	Forsyth, George A.	Story of a soldier
557.	Forsyth, George A.	Thrilling days in army life
251.	Foster, Mary H. *and* Cummings, M. H.	Asgard stories
126.	Four American inventors	F. M. Perry
127.	Four American naval heroes	M. B. Beebe
128.	Four American patriots	A. H. Burton
278.	Four American pioneers	F. M. Perry *and* K. Beebe
279.	Four American poets	Sherwin Cody

LIST OF BOOKS FOR TOWNSHIP LIBRARIES.

617.	Four-footed Americans		M. O. Wright
72.	Four-footed folk		R. F. Ayers
129.	Four great Americans		James Baldwin
618.	Four-handed folk		O. T. Miller
189.	Four on a farm		M. P. W. Smith
339.	Fowls of the air		W. J. Long
490.	Franklin, Benjamin		Autobiography
736.	Franklin square song collection		J. P. McCaskey, *comp.*
202.	French, Allen		Junior cup
280.	Fridtjof Nansen		J. B. Bull
190.	Frigate's namesake		A. B. Abbot
64.	Froelich, Clara G.		Big outdoors
23.	From many lands: a third reader		
	Florence Holbrook *and* M. F. Hall		
253.	Frost, William Henry		Court of King Arthur
257.	Frost, William Henry		Knights of the Round Table
271.	Frost, William Henry		Wagner story book
738.	Gantvoort, A. J.		Music reader for rural and village schools
769.	Garden-making		L. H. Bailey
602.	Garner, L.		Apes and monkeys
666.	Garrett, Phineas, *ed.*		
	Speaker's garland and literary bouquet, vol. 7		
667.	Garrett, Phineas, *ed.*		
	Speaker's garland and literary bouquet, vol. 8		
668.	Garrett, Phineas, *ed.*		
	Speaker's garland and literary bouquet, vol. 9		
744.	Gaynor, Jessie L.		Songs of the child-world
737.	Gems of school song		Carl Betz, *ed.*
142.	Geographical nature studies		F. O. Payne
324.	George, Marian M.		Little journeys to Alaska and Canada
325.	George, Marian M.		Little journeys to Cuba and Puerto Rico
326.	George, Marian M.		
	Little journeys to Hawaii and the Philippine islands		
499.	George Washington		H. E. Scudder
255.	German household tales		J. L. *and* W. K. Grimm, *eds.*
612.	Gibson, William Hamilton		Eye spy
625.	Gibson, William Hamilton		My studio neighbors
637.	Gibson, William Hamilton		Sharp eyes
596.	Giffin, William M.		Civics for young Americans
757.	Gilder, Jeanette L.		Autobiography of a tomboy
754.	Gillan, S. Y.		Riffle creek papers and other essays
21.	Gilman, Mary L., Austin, I., *and* Blaisdell, S. L.		Little-folk tales

	Gilman, Mary L., *joint author*. *See* Hall, Mary F.	
500.	Girls who became famous	Mrs. S. K. Bolton
345.	Glimpses at the plant world	F. D. Bergen
441.	Godson of Lafayette	E. S. Brooks
775.	Goff, Emmett Stull	Principles of plant culture
442.	Golden arrow	Ruth Hall
390.	Gold-seeking on the Dalton trail	A. R. Thompson
47.	Goops and how to be them	Gelett Burgess
239.	Gordon highlander	E. Everett-Green
292.	Gordy, Wilbur F.	American leaders and heroes
	Gottschalck, Oscar Hunt. *See* Von Gottschalck, Oscar Hunt.	
351.	Gould, Allen Walton	Mother nature's children
723.	Gould, Elizabeth Lincoln	Little men play
724.	Gould, Elizabeth Lincoln	Little women play
24.	Grated literature readers. Bk. 1 H. P. Judson *and* I. C. Bender, *eds.*	
25.	Graded literature readers. Bk. 2 H. P. Judson *and* I. C. Bender, *eds.*	
130.	Grandfather's chair	Nathaniel Hawthorne
537.	Grandmother's story of Bunker Hill	O. W. Holmes
629.	Grant, John B.	Our common birds and how to know them
195.	Grant, Robert	Jack Hall
391.	Gray champion	Nathaniel Hawthorne
443.	Graysons	Edward Eggleston
319.	Great American industries: Manufactures	W. F. Rocheleau
317.	Great American industries: Minerals	W. F. Rocheleau
318.	Great American industries: Products of the soil W. F. Rocheleau	
579.	Greater America.	
653.	Greek sculpture	E. M. Hurll
239.	Green, E. Everett-	Gordon highlander
452.	Green, E. Everett-	In the Wars of the roses
256.	Grey fairy book	Andrew Lang, *ed.*
526.	Griffis, William Elliot	Brave little Holland
550.	Grigsby, Melvin	Smoked Yank
255.	Grimm, Jakob Ludwig *and* Wilhelm Karl, *eds.* German household tales	
607.	Grinnell, Elizabeth *and* Joseph	Birds of song and story
352.	Grinnell, Elizabeth *and* Joseph	Our feathered friends
396.	Grinnell, George Bird	Jack among the Indians
197.	Grinnell, George Bird	Jack, the young ranchman
553.	Grinnell, George Bird	Story of the Indian
	Grinnell, George B., *joint ed. See* Roosevelt, Theodore.	
	Grinnell, Joseph, *joint author*. *See* Grinnell, Elizabeth.	

LIST OF BOOKS FOR TOWNSHIP LIBRARIES.

627.	Grinnell, Morton	Neighbours of field, wood and stream
137.	Guerber, H. A.	Story of the chosen people
564.	Guerber, H. A.	Story of the English
552.	Guerber, H. A.	Story of the great Republic
309.	Guerber, H. A.	Story of the Greeks
568.	Guerber, H. A.	Story of the Romans
555.	Guerber, H. A.	Story of the thirteen colonies
320.	Guyot geographical reader	M. H. S. Pratt
514.	Habberton, John	Poor boy's chances
394.	Hale, Edward Everett	His level best
457.	Hale, Edward Everett	Man without a country
	Hale, Edward Everett, *ed.* See **Trimmer, Sarah.**	
	Hall, Mary F., *joint author.* See **Holbrook, Florence.**	
22.	Hall, Mary F. *and* Gilman, Mary L.	Story land: second reader
442.	Hall, Ruth	Golden arrow
242.	Hall, Ruth	In the brave days of old
505.	Hall, T. W.	Heroes of our Revolution
73.	Hal o' the fells	Beatrice De Burgh
392.	Half-back	R. H. Barbour
770.	Handbook for farmers and dairymen	F. W. Woll
771.	Handbook of tree-planting	N. H. Egleston
109.	Hans Andersen's stories.	
191.	Hans Brinker	M. M. Dodge
2.	Happy playtimes.	
303.	Harding, Caroline H. *and* Samuel B.	Stories of Greek gods, heroes and men
76.	Harrington, John W.	Jumping kangaroo and the apple butter cat
600.	Harrington, Mark W.	About the weather
260.	Harris, Joel Chandler	Aaron in the wildwoods
258.	Harris, Joel Chandler	Little Mr. Thimblefinger
259.	Harris, Joel Chandler	Mr. Rabbit at home
261.	Harris, Joel Chandler	Story of Aaron so named
118.	Harris, Joel Chandler	Uncle Remus
532.	Hart, Albert Bushnell	Formation of the Union
	Hart, Albert Bushnell, *ed.* See **Epochs of American history series.**	
	Hart, Estelle M., *joint author.* See **Carroll, Stella W.**	
240.	Havelok the Dane	C. W. Whistler
580.	Hawaii and its people	A. S. Twombly
130.	Hawthorne, Nathaniel	Grandfather's chair
391.	Hawthorne, Nathaniel	Gray champion

207.	Hawthorne, Nathaniel	Little Daffydowndilly
269.	Hawthorne, Nathaniel	Tanglewood tales
523.	Hayens, Herbert	Ye mariners of England
46.	Headland, Isaac Taylor	Chinese mother goose rhymes
48.	Heart of oak books. Vol. 1	C. E. Norton, *ed.*
110.	Heart of oak books. Vol. 2	C. E. Norton, *ed.*
393.	Heart of the ancient wood	C. G. D. Roberts
192.	Heidi	Frau Johanna Spyri
768.	Henry, William Arnold	Feeds and feeding
444.	Hereward the Wake	Charles Kingsley
445.	Hero in homespun	W. E. Barton
501.	Hero of Erie	James Barnes
502.	Hero of Manila	Rossiter Johnson
503.	Hero tales from American history	H. C. Lodge *and* Theodore Roosevelt
504.	Heroes and martyrs of invention	G. M. Towle
479.	Heroes of Asgard	A. *and* E. Keary
505.	Heroes of our Revolution	T. W. Hall
506.	Heroes of the middle west	M. H. Catherwood
26.	Hiawatha primer	Florence Holbrook
682.	Hiawatha, song of	H. W. Longfellow
491.	Higginson, Thomas Wentworth, *ed.*	Book of American explorers
714.	Hill, Charles T.	Fighting a fire
394.	His level best	E. E. Hale
507.	Historic Americans	E. S. Brooks
508.	Historic girls	E. S. Brooks
162.	History of the robins	Sarah Trimmer
538.	History of the U. S. and its people	Edward Eggleston
539.	History of the United States for junior classes	F. N. Thorpe
26.	Holbrook, Florence	Hiawatha primer
116.	Holbrook, Florence	'Round the year in myth and song
23.	Holbrook, Florence *and* Hall, M. F.	From many lands: third reader
546.	Holden, Edward S.	Our country's flag and the flags of foreign countries
622.	Holder, Charles Frederick	Ivory king
357.	Holder, Charles Frederick	Stories of animal life
298.	Holman, Alma	Massasoit
537.	Holmes, Oliver Wendell	Grandmother's story of Bunker Hill
27.	Holton, M. Adelaide	Holton primer
27.	Holton primer	M. A. Holton
143.	Home geography	C. C. Long
321.	Home geography and the earth as a whole	R. S. Tarr *and* F. M. McMurry

619.	Home studies in nature	Mary Treat
193.	Hoosier school boy	Edward Eggleston
175.	Hornibrook, Isabel.	Camp and trail
715.	Hour of opportunity	O. S. Marden *and* Abner Bayley
179.	Howells, William Dean	Christmas every day
761.	Howells, William Dean	In a boy's town
297.	How New England was made	Mrs. F. A. Humphrey
509.	How they succeeded	O. S. Marden
716.	How to make baskets	Mary White
269.	Hoyt, Deristhe L.	Barbara's heritage
184.	Hughes, Rupert	Dozen from Lakerim
203.	Hughes, Rupert	Lakerim athletic club
426.	Hughes, Thomas	Tom Brown's school days
446.	Hugh Gwyeth	B. M. Dix
447.	Hugh Wynne	S. W. Mitchell
297	Humphrey, Mrs. F. A.	How New England was made
	Humphrey, Mrs. F. A., *joint author. See* Chaplin, Fannie P.	
654.	Hurll, Estelle M.	Correggio
653.	Hurll, Estelle M.	Greek sculpture
648.	Hurll, Estelle M.	Jean Francois Millet
646.	Hurll, Estelle M.	Landseer
647.	Hurll, Estelle M.	Michelangelo
649.	Hurll, Estelle M.	Raphael
650.	Hurll, Estelle M.	Rembrandt
651.	Hurll, Estelle M.	Sir Joshua Reynolds
652.	Hurll, Estelle M.	Titian
134.	Husted, Mary Hall	Stories of Indian chieftains
135.	Husted, Mary Hall	Stories of Indian children
173.	Hutton, Laurence	Boy I knew, four dogs, and some more dogs
366.	Hyde, William DeWitt, *ed.*	School speaker and reader

761.	In a boy's town	W. D. Howells
581.	In and out of Central America	Frank Vincent
620.	In brook and bayou	C. K. Bayliss
241.	In colonial times	M. E. Wilkins
448.	In hostile red	J. A. Altsheler
621.	In nesting time	O. T. Miller
242.	In the brave days of old	Ruth Hall
74.	In the chimney corner	G. M. Fenn *and others*
449.	In the days of Alfred, the great	E. M. Tappan
395.	In the days of Audubon	Hezekiah Butterworth
450.	In the days of William the Conqueror	E. M. Tappan
451.	In the hands of the red coats	E. T. Tomlinson

452.	In the Wars of the Roses	E. E. Green
112.	Ingelow, Jean	Mopsa the fairy
571.	Ingersoll, Ernest	Book of the ocean
644.	Ingersoll, Ernest	Wild neighbors
346.	Insect world	C. M. Weed
661.	Irving, Washington	Sketch book
415.	Irving, Washington	Stories and legends
453.	Ivanhoe	*Sir* Walter Scott
622.	Ivory King	C. F. Holder
306.	Jack among the Indians	G. B. Grinnell
194.	Jack and Jill	L. M. Alcott
195.	Jack Hall	Robert Grant
196.	Jack Morgan	W. O. Stoddard
717.	Jack of all trades	D. C. Beard
197.	Jack, the young ranchman	G. B. Grinnell
77.	Jackson, *Mrs.* Helen Hunt	Letters from a cat
212.	Jackson, *Mrs.* Helen Hunt	Nelly's silver mine
766.	James, Charles C.	Agriculture
83.	James, Martha	My friend Jim
90.	Jamison, *Mrs.* C. V.	Seraph, the little violiniste
582.	Japanese girls and women	A. M. Bacon
648.	Jean Francois Millet	E. M. Hurll
762.	Jean Mitchell's school	A. W. Wray
236.	Jenks, Albert Ernest	Childhood of Ji-shib', the Ojibwa
525.	Jenks, Tudor	Boy's book of explorations
	Jerome, H. L., *joint author. See* Carroll, Stella.	
214.	Jewett, Sarah Orne	Play days
49.	Jingle book	Carolyn Wells
163.	Jingle book of birds	E. B. Clark
721a.	John Nagle's philosophy	S. T. Pratt, *comp.*
763.	Johnnie	E. O. Laughlin
513.	Johnson, Henry	New exploits of Myles Standish
502.	Johnson, Rossiter	Hero of Manila
522.	Johnson, William Henry	World's discoverers
402.	Johnston, Annie Fellows	Little Colonel's house party
75.	Jolly good times	M. P. W. Smith
18.	Jones, Lottie E. *and* Black, S. W.	First reader
19.	Jones, Lottie E. *and* Black, S. W.	Second reader
198.	Josey and the chipmunk	Sydney Reid
560.	Joyce, Patrick Weston	Child's history of Ireland
199.	Juan and Juanita	F. C. Baylor
311.	Judd, Mary Catherine, *comp.*	Wigwam stories

LIST OF BOOKS FOR TOWNSHIP LIBRARIES.

599. Judson, Harry Pratt..........................Young American
24. **Judson, Harry Pratt** *and* **Bender, Ida C**........................
..........................Graded literature readers. Bk. 1
25. **Judson, Harry Pratt** *and* **Bender, Ida C**........................
..........................Graded literature readers. Bk. 2
657. Julius Caesar......:..................William Shakespeare
50. Jumblies and other nonesense verse..............Edward Lear
76. Jumping kangaroo and the apple butter cat....J. W. Harrington
200. Jungle book................................. Rudyard Kipling
202. Junior cup..Allen French

168. Kaler, James Otis......................Aunt Hannah and Seth
398. Kaler, James Otis....................Larry Hudson's ambition
204. Kaler, James Otis.......................................Left behind
400. Kaler, James Otis...................................Life savers
211. Kaler, James Otis.......................Mr. Stubbs's brother
226. Kaler, James Otis................................Tim and Tip
227. Kaler, James Otis...................................Toby Tyler
289. Kaler, James Otis ....With Perry on Lake Erie
474. Kaler, James Otis....................With Porter in the Essex
475. Kaler, James Otis........................With Preble at Tripoli
628. Kearton, Richard............................Our bird friends
479. Keary, A. *and* E........................Heroes of Asgard
52. Keeler, D. B........................Memoirs of Simple Simon
593. Kellogg, Eva M. C...........................Australia
and the islands of the sea. *World and its people.* Bk. 8
356. Kelly, *Mrs.* M. A. B..........Short stories of our shy neighbors
751. Kenyon, Walter J.....................First years in handicraft
51. Kids of many colors..............G. D. Boylan *and* Ike Morgan
373. King, Charles, *Capt*..................................Cadet days
332. King, Charles F......................Land we live in. Vol. 1
333. King, Charles F......................Land we live in. Vol. 2
331. King, Charles F.......................This continent of ours
496. King, Grace........De Soto and his men in the land of Florida
111. King of the golden river........................John Ruskin
243. King Robert's page............................G. M. Fenn
383. King, Stanton H.......................Dog-watches at sea
257. Knights of the Round Table....................W. H. Frost
444. Kingsley, Charles........................Hereward the Wake
229. Kingsley, Charles..............................Water babies
284. Kingsley, Nellie F.....................................Story
of Captain Meriwether Lewis and Captain William Clark
Kingston, W. H. G., *trans. See* Wyss, Jean Rudolph. Swiss
Family Robinson.

200.	Kipling, Rudyard	Jungle book
201.	Kipling, Rudyard	Second jungle book
10.	Kirk, May	Baldwin primer
571.	Knox, Thomas Wallace	Boy travellers in Central Europe
573.	Knox, Thomas Wallace	Boy travellers in Northern Europe
574.	Knox, Thomas Wallace	Boy travellers in South America
575.	Knox, Thomas Wallace	Boy travellers in Southern Europe
576.	Knox, Thomas Wallace	Boy travellers in the far East
312.	Krout, Mary H	Alice's visit to the Hawaiian islands
265.	Kupfer, Grace H	Story of long ago
404	La Flesche, Francis	Middle five
	La Victoire, Florence E., *joint author*. See Perdue, H. A.	
397.	Lady Lee and other animal stories	H. L. Ensign
695.	Lady of the lake	*Sir* Walter Scott
281.	Lafayette	A. H. Burton
203.	Lakerim athletic club	Rupert Hughes
323.	Land of pluck	M. M. Dodge
583.	Land of the long night	Paul Du Chaillu
772.	Landscape gardening as applied to home decoration	S. T. Maynard
332.	Land we live in. Vol. 1	C. F. King
333.	Land we live in. Vol. 2	C. F. King
646.	Landseer	E. M. Hurll
398.	Larry Hudson's ambition	J. O. Kaler
30.	Lane, Abby E	Lights to literature by grades. Bk. 3
94.	Lane, *Mrs.* Charles A	Stories for children
36.	Lane, M. A. L.	Oriole stories
338.	Land, Andrew, *ed*	Animal story book
678.	Lang, Andrew, *ed*	Blue poetry book
256.	Lang, Andrew, *ed*	Grey fairy book
55.	Lang, Andrew, *ed*	Nursery rhyme book
548.	Lang, Andrew, *ed*	Red true story book
270.	Lang, Andrew, *ed*	Violet fairy book
679.	Larcom, Lucy	Childhood songs
399.	Last of the flatboats	G. C. Eggleston
454.	Last of the Mohicans	J. F. Cooper
763.	Laughlin, E. O	Johnnie
684.	Lays of ancient Rome	T. B. Macaulay
540.	Leading events of Wisconsin history	H. E. Legler
50.	Lear, Edward	Jumblies and other nonsense verse
56.	Lear, Edward	Pelican chorus and other nonsense verse
164.	Leaves and flowers	M. A. Spear

LIST OF BOOKS FOR TOWNSHIP LIBRARIES.

101.	Lee, Albert.................................Tommy Toddles
	Leete, C. H., *joint editor*. *See* Chisholm, George G.
204.	Left behind..J. O. Kaler
540.	Legler, Henry E..........Leading events of Wisconsin history
205.	Lem: a New England village boy.................Noah Brooks
221.	Leonard, Mary F...............................Spectacle man
	Leonard, Merton Channing, *joint comp*. *See* Wait, Minnie Curtis
77.	Letters from a cat..........................*Mrs*. H. H. Jackson
206.	Life and adventures of Robinson Crusoe..........Daniel De Foe
623.	Life histories of American insects..................C. M. Weed
591.	Life in Asia......................................M. C. Smith
773.	Life on the farm................................H. H. Shepard
400.	Life savers......................................J. O. Kaler
30.	Lights to literature. Bk 3.........................A. E. Lane
28.	Lights to literature. Bk. 1...H. A. Perdue *and* F. E. La Victoire
29.	Lights to literature. Bk. 2.....................S. E. Sprague
655.	Lillie, Lucy C....Story of music and musicians for young readers
510.	Lincoln in story.............................S. G. Pratt, *ed*.
664.	Lincoln literary collection..............J. P. McCaskey, *comp*.
700.	Listening child................................L. W. Thatcher
401.	Little book of profitable tales.....................Eugene Field
674.	Little book of western verse.......................Eugene Field
347.	Little brothers of the air..........................O. T. Miller
402.	Little Colonel's house party.....................A. F. Johnston
207.	Little Daffydowndilly.....................Nathaniel Hawthorne
697.	Little-folk lyrics.................................F. D. Sherman
348.	Little folks in feathers and fur.....................O. T. Miller
144.	Little folks of other lands..................................
	.................F. P. Chapin *and* Mrs. F. A. Humphrey
21.	Little-folk tales: first reader.................................
	...:............M. L. Gilman, I. Austin, *and* S. L. Blaisdell
244.	Little girl of long ago...........................E. O. White
78.	Little Jarvis...................................M. E. Seawell
324.	Little journeys to Alaska and Canada............M. M. George
325.	Little journeys to Cuba and Puerto Rico..........M. M. George
326.	Little journeys to Hawaii and Philippine islands...M. M. George
79.	Little lame prince......................*Mrs*. D. M. M. Craik
208.	Little men......................................L. M. Alcott
723.	Little men play..................................E. L. Gould
80.	Little Miss Phoebe Gay..........................H. D. Brown
258.	Little Mr. Thimblefinger.........................J. C. Harris
327.	Little people of Asia.............................O. T. Miller
145.	Little people of the snow........................Mary Muller
3.	Little people's scrap book

245.	Little Smoke	W. O. Stoddard
209.	Little women	L. M. Alcott
724.	Little women play	E. L. Gould
624.	Lives of the hunted	E. Seton-Thompson
349.	Lobo, Rag, and Vixen	E. Seton-Thompson
503.	Lodge, Henry Cabot *and* Roosevelt, Theodore......Hero tales from American history	
42.	Logie, Alfred E., Uecke, C., *and* Milner, S. A.	Story reader
146.	Lolami, the little cliff-dweller	C. K. Bayliss
81.	Lonesomest doll	A. F. Brown
143.	Long, C. C.	Home geography
340.	Long, William J.	Beasts of the field
339.	Long, William J.	Fowls of the air
355.	Long, William J.	Secrets of the woods
360.	Long, William J.	Ways of wood folk
361.	Long, William J.	Wilderness ways
680.	Longfellow, Henry Wadsworth	Complete poetical works
681.	Longfellow, Henry Wadsworth	Courtship of Miles Standish
682.	Longfellow, Henry Wadsworth	Song of Hiawatha
147.	Longmans' pictorial geographical readers. Bk. 1.	
403.	Lorna Doone	R. D. Blackmore
328.	Lost in the jungle	Paul Du Chaillu
166.	Lothrop, *Mrs.* H. M. S.	Adventures of Joel Pepper
188.	Lothrop, *Mrs.* H. M. S.	Five little Peppers
388.	Lothrop, *Mrs.* H. M. S.	Five little Peppers grown up
408.	Lothrop, *Mrs.* H. M. S.	Phronsie Pepper
223.	Lothrop, *Mrs.* H. M. S.	Stories Polly Pepper told
683.	Lovejoy, Mary I., *comp.*	Poetry of the seasons
676.	Love-songs of childhood	Eugene Field
689.	Lowell, James Russell	Complete poetical works
455.	Loyal hearts and true	Ruth Ogden
456.	Loyal traitor	James Barnes
677.	Lullaby-land	Eugene Field
387.	Lummis, Charles F.	Enchanted burro
405.	Lummis, Charles F.	New Mexico David

480.	Mabie, Hamilton Wright	Norse stories retold from the Eddas
684.	Macaulay, T. B.	Lays of ancient Rome
658.	Macbeth	William Shakespeare
735.	McCaskey, J. P., *ed.*	Favorite songs and hymns
736.	McCaskey, J. P., *comp.*	Franklin Square song collection
664.	McCaskey, J. P., *comp.*	Lincoln literary collection
252.	MacDonald, George	At the back of the north wind

LIST OF BOOKS FOR TOWNSHIP LIBRARIES.

300.	McMaster, John Bach	Primary history of the United States	
299.	McMurry, Charles	Pioneer history stories	
	McMurry, Frank M., *joint author.* See **Tarr, Ralph S.**		
106.	McMurry, *Mrs.* Lida Brown	Classic stories for little ones	
685.	McMurry, *Mrs.* Lida Brown *and* Cook, Agnes Spofford		
		Songs of the treetop and meadow	
210.	Maggie McLanehan	Gulielma Zollinger	
169.	Major, Charles	Bears of Blue River	
541.	Making of New England	S. A. Drake	
542.	Making of the great west	S. A. Drake	
543.	Making of Virginia	S. A. Drake	
	Mallon, *Mrs.* Isabel A. See **Ashmore, Ruth.**		
457.	Man without a country	E. E. Hale	
246.	Mann, Millicent E	Margot: the Court shoemaker's child	
544.	Marching with Gomez	Grover Flint	
509.	Marden, Orison Swett	How they succeeded	
715.	Marden, Orison Swett *and* Bayley, Abner	Hour of opportunity	
246.	Margot	M. E. Mann	
82.	Marjorie and her papa	R. H. Fletcher	
337.	Markwick, W. Fisher *and* Smith, W. A.		
		South American republics	
597.	Markwick, W. Fisher *and* Smith, W. A.	True citizen	
696.	Marmion	*Sir* Walter Scott	
298.	Massasoit	Alma Holman	
686.	Matthews, Brander, *comp.*	Poems of American patriotism	
742.	Matthews, W. S. B.	Songs of all lands	
772.	Maynard, Samuel T.		
		Landscape gardening as applied to home decoration	
97.	Meade, L. T. *and others*	Sunny days	
52.	Memoirs of Simple Simon	D. B. Keeler	
511.	Men of business	W. O. Stoddard	
458.	Men of iron	Howard Pyle	
104.	Menefee, Maud	Child stories from the masters	
659.	Merchant of Venice	William Shakespeare	
608.	Merriam, Florence A.	Birds of village and field	
459.	Merry adventures of Robin Hood	Howard Pyle	
247.	Micah Clarke	A. Conan Doyle	
647.	Michelangelo	E. M. Hurll	
404.	Middle five	Francis La Flesche	
512.	Midshipman Farragut	James Barnes	
67.	Miller, Emily Huntington	Captain Fritz	
	Miller, *Mrs.* Harriet Mann. See **Miller, Olive Thorne.**		
343.	Miller, Olive Thorne	First book of birds	
618.	Miller, Olive Thorn	Four-handed folk	

AUTHOR AND TITLE INDEX.

621.	Miller, Olive Thorne	In nesting time
347.	Miller, Olive Thorne	Little brothers of the air
348.	Miller, Olive Thorne	Little folks in feathers and fur
327.	Miller, Olive Thorne	Little people of Asia
354.	Miller, Olive Thorne	Second book of birds
641.	Miller, Olive Thorne	Upon the tree-tops
	Milner, Sarah A., *joint author. See* Logie, Alfred E.	
350.	Mr. Chupes and Miss Jenny	Effie Bignell
259.	Mr. Rabbit at home	J. C. Harris
211.	Mr. Stubbs's brother	J. O. Kaler
447.	Mitchell, S. Weir	Hugh Wynne
590.	Modern Europe	F. E. Coe
712.	Moffett, Cleveland	Careers of danger and daring
53.	Moon babies	G. O. Clark
112.	Mopsa the fairy	Jean Ingelow
	Morgan, Ike, *joint author. See* Boylan, Grace Duffie.	
665.	Morgan, Thomas J.	Patriotic citizenship
121.	Morley, Margaret Warner	Bee people
344.	Morley, Margaret Warner	Flowers and their friends
218.	Morse, Livingston B.	Road to nowhere
4.	Mother goose	W. W. Denslow, *ed.*
54.	Mother Goose jingles	
251.	Mother Nature's children	A. W. Gould
63.	Moulton, Louise Chandler	Bed-time stories
	Mowry, Arthur May, *joint author. See* Mowry, William A.	
291.	Mowry, William A. *and* A. M.	American inventions and inventors
125.	Mowry, William A. *and* A. M.	First steps in the history of our country
145.	Muller, Mary	Little people of the snow
	Murfree, Mary Noailles. *See* Craddock, Charles Egbert.	
738.	Music reader for rural and village schools	A. J. Gantvoort
83.	My friend Jim	Martha James
625.	My studio neighbors	W. H. Gibson

37.	Nageler, J. G., *joint author. See* Sell, W. T.	
626.	Nature biographies	C. M. Weed
113.	Nature myths	F. J. Cooke, *ed.*
460.	Navy blue	W. B. Allen
353.	Needham, James G.	Outdoor studies
693.	Neghborly poems	J. W. Riley
733.	Neidlinger, W. H.	Earth, sky and air in song. Bk. 1
734.	Neidlinger, W. H.	Earth, sky and air in song. Bk. 2

627.	Neighbours of field, wood and stream	Morton Grinnell
212.	Nelly's silver mine	H. H. Jackson
84.	New baby world	M. M. Dodge, *comp.*
31.	Century second reader	H. A. Perdue *and* F. E. La Victoire
32.	New century third reader	H. S. Tibbits
33.	New educational readers. Bk. 1	A. J. Demarest *and* W. M. Van Sickle
34.	New educational readers. Bk. 2	A. J. Demarest *and* W. M. Van Sickle
35.	New educational readers. Bk. 3	A. J. Demarest *and* W. M. Van Sickle
513.	New exploits of Myles Standish	Henry Johnson
405.	New Mexico David	C. F. Lummis
114.	New Wonderland	L. F. Baum
248.	Noank's log	W. O. Stoddard
341.	**Noel, Maurice**	Buz
480.	Norse stories retold from the Eddas	H. W. Mabie
584.	North America	F. G. Carpenter
322.	North America	R. S. Tarr *and* F. M. McMurry
48.	**Norton, Charles Eliot,** *ed.*	Heart of oak books. Vol. 1
110.	**Norton, Charles Eliot,** *ed.*	Heart of oak books. Vol. 2
406.	Nurnberg stove	Louise de la Ramé
55.	Nursery rhyme book	Andrew Lang, *ed.*

566.	**Ober, Frederick A.**	Storied West Indies
262.	Odysseus	M. E. Burt *and* Z. A. Ragozin
455.	**Ogden, Ruth**	Loyal hearts and true
213.	Old ballads in prose	E. M. Tappan
407.	Old-fashioned girl	L. M. Alcott
37.	Old friends in new dresses	W. F. Sell *and* J. G. Nageler
115.	Old Greek stories	James Baldwin
263.	Old Norse stories	S. P. Bradish
131.	Old stories of the east	James Baldwin
545.	Old times in the colonies	C. C. Coffin
703.	Once upon a time	M. E. Wilkins
36.	Oriole stories	M. A. L. Lane
	Otis, James, *pseud.* See **Kaler, J. O.**	
249.	Otto of the silver hand	Howard Pyle
589.	Our American neighbors	F. E. Coe
628.	Our bird friends	Richard Kearton
629.	Our common birds and how to know them	J. B. Grant
329.	**Our** country: East.	
330.	**Our** country: West.	

546.	Our country's flag	E. S. Holden
687.	Our country in poem and prose	E. A. Persons, *comp.*
630.	Our devoted friend, the dog	S. K. Bolton
5.	Our doggies.	
6.	Our farmyard.	
352.	Our feathered friends	E. *and* J. Grinnell
37a.	Our little book	W. E. Crosby
148.	Our little Brown cousin	M. H. Wade
149.	Our little Indian cousin	M. H. Wade
150.	Our little Japanese cousin	M. H. Wade
151.	Our little Russian cousin	M. H. Wade
547.	Our navy in the war with Spain	John Spears
336.	Our own country	M. C. Smith
718.	Outdoor handy book for playground, field and forest	D. C. Beard
353.	Outdoor studies	J. G. Needham

233.	Page, Thomas Nelson	Among the camps
414.	Page, Thomas Nelson	Santa Claus's partner
250.	Page, Thomas Nelson	Two little confederates
417.	Palmer, Bertha, *ed.*	
	Stories from the classic literature of many nations	
477.	Parton, James	Captains of industry. Vol. 1
493.	Parton, James	Captains of industry. Vol. 2
748.	Patrick, J. N.	Elements of pedagogics
665.	Patriotic citizenship	T. J. Morgan
216.	Patteson, S. Louise	Pussy meow
282.	Paul Jones	M. E. Seawell
142.	Payne, Frank Owen	Geographical nature studies
154.	Peary, Josephine Diebitsch	Snow baby
56.	Pelican chorus	Edward Lear
631.	Pepacton	John Burroughs
28.	Perdue, H. Avis *and* La Victoire, F. E.	
	Lights to literature: first reader. Bk. 1	
31.	Perdue, H. Avis *and* La Victoire, F. E.	
	New Century second reader	
126.	Perry, Francis M.	Four American inventors
278.	Perry, Frances M. *and* Beebe, Katherine	
	Four American pioneers	
585.	Personally conducted	F. R. Stockton
687.	Persons, Eleanor A., *comp.*	Our country in poem and prose
7.	Pets' picture farm.	
408.	Phronsie Pepper	*Mrs.* H. M. S. Lothrop
331.	Picturesque geographical reader. Bk. 2	C. F. King

332.	Picturesque geographical reader. Bk. 3	C. F. King
333.	Picturesque geographical reader. Bk. 4	C. F. King
8.	Pictures for little people.	
156.	Pierson, Clara Dillingham	Among the farmyard people
157.	Pierson, Clara Dillingham	Among the forest people
158.	Pierson, Clara Dillingham	Among the meadow people
159.	Pierson, Clara Dillingham	Among the pond people
409.	Pilgrim's progress	John Bunyan
410.	Pilot	J. F. Cooper
411.	Pine Ridge plantation	William Drysdale
299.	Pioneer history stories	Charles McMurry
752.	Plans for busy work	S. L. Arnold, *ed.*
632.	Plant world	Frank Vincent, *ed.*
633.	Plants and their children	*Mrs.* W. S. Dana
214.	Play days	S. O. Jewett
764.	Playground Toni	A. C. Ray
492.	Plutarch	Lives
238.	Plympton, Almira C.	Flower of the wilderness
686.	Poems of American patriotism	Brander Matthews, *comp.*
671.	Poetical works	William Cullen Bryant
699.	Poetic and dramatic works	Alfred Tennyson
683.	Poetry of the seasons	M. I. Lovejoy, *comp.*
753.	Point of contract in teaching	Patterson Du Bois
412.	Polly Oliver's problem	K. D. Wiggin
514.	Poor boys' chances	John Habberton
515.	Poor boys who became famous	*Mrs.* S. K. Bolton
68.	Poulsson, Emilie	Child stories and rhymes for little people of nursery and kindergarten
99.	Poulsson, Emilie	Through the farmyard gate
461.	Prairie schooner	W. E. Barton
161.	Pratt, Charles Stuart	Buz-buz
320.	Pratt, Mary Howe Smith	Guyot geographical reader
120.	Pratt, Mara L.	America's story for America's children. Bk. 1
121.	Pratt, Mara L.	America's story for America's children. Bk. 2
510.	Pratt, Silas G., *ed.*	Lincoln in story
721a.	Pratt, S. T., *comp.*	John Nagle's philosophy
739.	Pratt, Waldo S., *ed.*	St. Nicholas songs
300.	Primary history of the United States	J. B. McMaster
462.	Prince and the pauper	S. L. Clemens
86.	Prince Uno.	
774.	Principles of agriculture	L. H. Bailey, *ed.*
775.	Principles of plant culture	E. S. Goff
688.	Prose and verse for children	Katherine Pyle
215.	Purpose and success.	

216.	Pussy meow	S. Louise Patteson
275.	Putnam, M. Louise	Children's life of Abraham Lincoln
458.	Pyle, Howard	Men of iron
459.	Pyle, Howard	Merry adventures of Robin Hood
249.	Pyle, Howard	Otto of the silver hand
178.	Pyle, Katherine	Christmas angel
69.	Pyle, Katherine	Counterpane fairy
688.	Pyle, Katherine	Prose and verse for children
217.	Quartet	W. O. Stoddard
413.	Rab and his friends	John Brown
87.	Rabbit's ransome	Clara Vawter
481.	Ragozin, Zenaide A.	Siegfried
	Ragozin, Z. A., *joint author. See* Burt, Mary E.	
122.	Ramé, Louise de la	Child of Urbino: Raphael
406.	Ramé, Louise de la	Nürnberg stove
649.	Raphael	E. M. Hurll
764.	Ray, Anna Chapin	Playground Toni
183.	Raymond, Evelyn	Divided skates
634.	Reader in physical geography for beginners	R. E. Dodge
548.	Red true story book	Andrew Lang, *ed.*
198.	Reid, Sydney	Josey and the chipmunk
650.	Rembrandt	E. M. Hurll
690.	Repplier, Agnes, *comp.*	Book of famous verse
283.	Reuben James	C. T. Brady
89.	Reynolds, Cuyler	Rosamund tales
176.	Richards, Laura E.	Captain January
754.	Riffle creek papers	S. Y. Gillan
691.	Riley, James Whitcomb	Child-rhymes
692.	Riley, James Whitcomb	Child world
693.	Riley, James Whitcomb	Neghborly poems
740.	Ripley, Frederick H. *and* Tapper, Thos.	Short course in music. Bk. 1
741.	Ripley, Frederick H. *and* Tapper, Thos.	Short course in music. Bk. 2
218.	Road to nowhere	L. B. Morse
719.	Robert, Joseph Thomas	Robert's primer of parliamentary law
393.	Roberts, C. G. D.	Heart of the ancient wood
719.	Robert's primer of parliamentary law	J. T. Robert
206.	Robinson Crusoe	D. Defoe
317.	Rocheleau, W. F.	Great American industries. Vol. 1: Minerals

318.	Rocheleau, W. F.	
	....Great American industries. Vol. 2: Products of the soil	
319.	Rocheleau, W. F.	
	.........Great American industries. Vol. 3: Manufactures	
463.	Rock of the lion	M. E. Seawell
88.	Roggie and Reggie stories	Gertrude Smith
705.	Roosevelt, Theodore *and* Grinnell, G. B., *eds.*	
	..............................American big-game hunting	
	Roosevelt, Theodore, *joint author.* *See* Lodge, Henry C.	
89.	Rosamond tales	Cuyler Reynolds
116.	'Round the year in myth and song	Florence Holbrook
111.	Ruskin, John	King of the golden river

586.	Sailing alone around the world	*Captain* Joshua Slocum
725.	St. Nicholas book of plays and operettas.	
219.	St. Nicholas Christmas book.	
739.	St. Nicholas songs	W. S. Pratt, *ed.*
587.	Sanborn, Helen J.	Winter in Central America and Mexico
414.	Santa Claus's partner	T. N. Page
767.	Sargent, Frederick Leroy	Corn plants
171.	Saunders, Marshall	Beautiful Joe
756.	School management	E. E. White
38.	School reading by grades. Bk. 1	James Baldwin
39.	School reading by grades. Bk. 2	James Baldwin
40.	School reading by grades. Bk. 3	James Baldwin
755.	School sanitation and decoration	
	....................Severance Burrage *and* H. T. Bailey	
366.	School speaker and reader	W. D. Hyde, *ed.*
694.	Scollard, Clinton	Boy's book of rhymes
453.	Scott, *Sir* Walter	Ivanhoe
695.	Scott, *Sir* Walter	Lady of the lake
696.	Scott, *Sir* Walter	Marmion
103.	Scudder, Horace E.	Book of legends told over again
107.	Scudder, Horace E., *ed.*	Fables and folk stories
499.	Scudder, Horace E.	George Washington
91.	Scudder, Horace E.	Seven little people and their friends
301.	Scudder, Horace E.	Short history of the U. S.
57.	Scudder, Horace E.	Verse and prose for beginners
276.	Seawell, Molly Elliot	Decatur and Somers
78.	Seawell, Molly Elliot	Little Jarvis
282.	Seawell, Molly Elliot	Paul Jones
463.	Seawell, Molly Elliott	Rock of the lion
521.	Seawell, Molly Elliot	Twelve naval captains

16.	Second book: pictures, rhymes, stories............................	G. I. Aldrich *and* Alex. Forbes
354.	Second book of birds.............................	O. T. Miller
675.	Second book of verse.............................	Eugene Field
201.	Second jungle book...........................	Rudyard Kipling
19.	Second reader......................	L. E. Jones *and* S. W. Black
355.	Secrets of the woods...............................	W. J. Long
635.	Seed dispersal...	W. J. Beal
636.	Seed-travellers......................................	C. M. Weed
517.	Seelye, Elizabeth Eggleston.................	Story of Columbus
519.	Seelye, Elizabeth Eggleston................	Story of Washington
37.	Sell, W. T., *and* Nageler, J. G.........	Old friends in new dresses
765.	Sentimental Tommy................................	J. M. Barrie
90.	Seraph, the little violiniste..................	*Mrs.* C. V. Jamison
	Seton-Thompson, Ernest. *See* Thompson, Ernest Seton.	
91.	Seven little people..............................	H. E. Scudder
152.	Seven little sisters............................	Jane Andrews
153.	Seven little sisters prove their sisterhood..........	Jane Andrews
172.	Sewell, Anna.......................................	Black Beauty
656.	Shakespeare, William.............................	As you like it
657.	Shakespeare, William.............................	Julius Caesar
658.	Shakespeare, William...............................	Macbeth
659.	Shakespeare, William......................	Merchant of Venice
637.	Sharp eyes..	W. H. Gibson
605.	Sharp eyes......................................	John Burroughs
141.	Shaw, Edward R......	Big people and little people of other lands
277.	Shaw, Edward R.....................	Discoverers and explorers
773.	Shepard, Hiram H............................	Life on the farm
697.	Sherman, Frank Dempster.....................	Little-folk lyrics
711.	Shields, G. O.	Camping and camp outfits
747.	Shinn, Milicent W........................	Biography of a baby
740.	Short course in music. Bk. 1....	F. H. Ripley *and* Thos. Tapper
741.	Short course in music. Bk. 2....	F. H. Ripley *and* Thos. Tapper
549.	Short history of the American Revolution....	Everett Tomlinson
301.	Short history of U. S. of America................	H. E. Scudder
356.	Short stories of our shy neighbors..........	*Mrs.* M. A. B. Kelly
92.	Short stories for short people..................	Alicia Aspinwall
	Sidney, Margaret, *pseud. See* Lothrop, *Mrs.* H. M. (Stone)	
732.	Siefert, H. O. R.....................................	Choice songs
481.	Siegfried and Beowulf........................	Z. A. Ragozin
41.	Sight reader: primary teachers.	
378.	Singleton, Adam, *ed*............	Chronicles of Sir John Froissart
588.	Singleton, Esther, *ed*......................	Wonders of nature

Sinnott, Charles P., *joint author.* See **Avery, Elroy M.**
651. Sir Joshua Reynolds................................E. M. Hurll
661. Sketch book................................Washington Irving
93. Sleepy-time stories................................M. B. Booth
586. Slocum, Joshua *Capt.*............Sailing alone around the world
357a. Smith, C. W................................Summer of Saturdays
743. Smith, Eleanor.......................Songs of life and nature
62. Smith, Gertrude.................Arabella and Araminta stories
88. Smith, Gertrude....................Roggie and Reggie stories
591. Smith, Mary Cate ....Life in Asia
189. Smith, Mary P. Wells........................Four on a farm
75. Smith, Mary P. Wells........................Jolly good times
336. Smith, Minna C................................Our own country
429. Smith, Nora Archibald...................Under the cactus flag
     Smith, Nora Archibald, *joint author.* See **Wiggin, Kate Douglas**
     Smith, William, *joint author.* See **Markwick, W. Fisher**........
760. Smith, William Hawley....................Evolution of "Dodd"
550. Smoked Yank................................Melvin Grigsby
237. Snedden, Genevra Sisson...Docas, the Indian boy of Santa Clara
154. Snow baby..J. D. Peary
464. Soldier of Virginia...........................B. E. Stevenson
465. Soldier Rigdale........ ....B. M. Dix
220. Solomon Crow's Christmas pockets...............R. M. Stuart
466. Son of the Revolution............................E. S. Brooks
742. Songs of all lands.........................W. S. B. Matthews
743. Songs of life and nature.....................Eleanor Smith
744. Songs of the child-world....................Jessie L. Gaynor
685. Songs of the tree-top and meadow..........................
     ....L. B. McMurry *and* A. S. Cook, *comps.*
334. South America................................F. G. Carpenter
337. South American republics......W. F. Markwick *and* Wm. Smith
666. Speaker's garland and literary bouquet. Vol. 7...............
     ....Phineas Garrett, *ed.*
667. Speaker's garland and literary bouquet. Vol. 8...............
     ....Phineas Garrett, *ed.*
668. Speaker's garland and literary bouquet. Vol. 9...............
     ....Phineas Garrett, *ed.*
164. Spear, Mary A..........................Leaves and flowers
547. Spears, John................Our navy in the war with Spain
221. Spectacle man................................M. F. Leonard
29. Sprague, Sarah E..
     ....Lights to literature, second reader. Bk. 2
192. Spyri, Frau Johanna..Heidi
638. Squirrels and other fur-bearers................John Burroughs

290.	Starr, Frederick	American Indians
310.	Starr, Frederick	Strange peoples
516.	Statesmen	Noah Brooks
464.	Stevenson, Burton E.	Soldier of Virginia
698.	Stevenson, Robert Louis	Child's garden of verses
427.	Stevenson, Robert Louis	Treasure Island
187.	Stockton, Frank R.	Fanciful tales
585.	Stockton, Frank R.	Personally conducted
180.	Stoddard, William Osborn	Chuck Purdy
381.	Stoddard, William Osborn	Crowded out o' Crofield
182.	Stoddard, William Osborn	Dab Kinzer
196.	Stoddard, William Osborn	Jack Morgan
245.	Stoddard, William Osborn	Little Smoke
511.	Stoddard, William Osborn	Men of business
248.	Stoddard, William Osborn	Noank's log
217.	Stoddard, William Osborn	Quartet
225.	Stoddard, William Osborn	Success against odds
232.	Stoddard, William Osborn	Winter fun
359.	Stokes, Susan	Ten common trees
566.	Storied West Indies	F. A. Ober
415.	Stories and legends	Washington Irving
222.	Stories and poems for children	Celia Thaxter
416.	Stories for boys	R. H. Davis
94.	Stories for children	*Mrs.* C. A. Lane
95.	Stories for kindergartens	S. E. Wiltse
562.	Stories from English history	Louise Creighton
563.	Stories from English history	H. P. Warren, *ed.*
482.	Stories from Homer	A. J. Church
417.	Stories from the classic literature of many nations...Bertha Palmer, *ed.*	
483.	Stories from Virgil	A. J. Church
132.	Stories of American life and adventure	Edward Eggleston
567.	Stories of ancient peoples	E. J. Arnold
357.	Stories of animal life	C. F. Holder
155.	Stories of country life	S. P. Bradish
133.	Stories of great Americans	Edward Eggleston
303.	Stories of Greek gods, heroes and men	C. H. *and* S. B. Harding
134.	Stories of Indian chieftains	M. H. Husted
135.	Stories of Indian children	M. H. Husted
265.	Stories of long ago	G. H. Kupfer
165.	Stories of my four friends	Jane Andrews
305.	Stories of the American Revolution. Vol. 1	E. T. Tomlinson
306.	Stories of the American Revolution. Vol. 2	E. T. Tomlinson
307.	Stories of the Badger state	R. G. Thwaites

308.	Stories of the civil war	A. F. Blaisdell, *ed.*
223.	Stories Polly Pepper told	Mrs. H. M. S. Lothrop
96.	Story hour	K. D. Wiggin *and* N. A. Smith
22.	Story land: second reader	M. F. Hall *and* L. M. Gilman
224.	Story of a bad boy	T. B. Aldrich
261.	Story of Aaron	J. C. Harris
418.	Story of Ab	Stanley Waterloo
266.	Story of Aeneas	M. Clarke, *ed.*
419.	Story of Babette	R. M. Stuart
302.	Story of Caesar	M. Clarke
284.	Story of Captain Meriwether Lewis	N. F. Kingsley
517.	Story of Columbus	E. E. Seelye
565.	Story of Japan	R. Van Bergen
136.	Story of Lincoln	Frances Cravens
420.	Story of little Nell	Charles Dickens
518.	Story of Marco Polo	Noah Brooks
655.	Story of music and musicians for young readers	L. C. Lillie
467.	Story of old Fort Loudon	C. E. Craddock
304.	Story of our country	A. H. Burton
551.	Story of our war with Spain	E. S. Brooks
421.	Story of Patsy	K. D. Wiggin
484.	Story of Roland	James Baldwin
485.	Story of Siegfried	James Baldwin
422.	Story of Sonny Sahib	S. J. D. Cotes
468.	Story of the Cid for young people	C. D. Wilson
137.	Story of the chosen people	H. A. Guerber
564.	Story of the English	H. A. Guerber
639.	Story of the fishes	J. N. Baskett
486.	Story of the golden age	James Baldwin
552.	Story of the great Republic	H. A. Guerber
309.	Story of the Greeks	H. A. Guerber
553.	Story of the Indian	G. B. Grinnell
640.	Story of the plants	Grant Allen
487.	Story of the Rhinegold	A. A. Chapin
568.	Story of the Romans	H. A. Guerber
554.	Story of the soldier	G. A. Forsyth
555.	Story of the thirteen colonies	H. A. Guerber
42.	Story reader	A. E. Logie, C. Uecke, *and* S. A. Milner
267.	Story of Troy	M. Clarke, *ed.*
117.	Story of Ulysses	A. S. Cook, *ed.*
519.	Story of Washington	E. E. Seelye
556.	Story of Wisconsin	R. G. Thwaites
310.	Strange peoples	Frederick Starr
272.	**Stratemeyer, Edward**	American boys' life of William McKinley

AUTHOR AND TITLE INDEX.

433. Stratemeyer, Edward..................Between Boer and Briton
476. Stratemeyer, Edward.............With Washington in the West
220. Stuart, Ruth McEnery.......Solomon Crow's Christmas pockets
419. Stuart, Ruth McEnery......................Story of Babette
225. Success against odds........................W. O. Stoddard
720. Successward.................................... Edward Bok
424. Summer in cañon................................K. D. Wiggin
357a. Summer of Saturdays............................C. W. Smith
97. Sunny days........................L. T. Meade *and others*
98. Sweet William............................Marguerite Bouvet
423. Swiss family Robinson...........................J. R. Wyss

469. Tales of an old chateau....................Marguerite Bouvet
268. Tales of Languedoc...............................S. J. Brun
358. Talks about animals.
285. Talks about Authors and their work................E. R. Ware
269. Tanglewood tales....................... Nathaniel Hawthorne
561. Tappan, Eva March..........................England's story
449. Tappan, Eva March.............In the days of Alfred, the Great
450. Tappan, Eva March........In the days of William the Conqueror
213. Tappan, Eva March.......................Old ballads in prose
Tapper, Thomas, *joint author*. *See* Ripley, Frederick H.
578. Tarr, Ralph S. *and* McMurry, Frank M......................
...............................Europe and other continents
321. Tarr, Ralph S. *and* McMurry, Frank M.........Home geography
322. Tarr, Ralph S. *and* McMurry, Frank M..........North America
141a. Taylor, Bayard........................Boys of other countries
43. Taylor, Frances Lillian.......Taylor school readers: first reader
43. Taylor school readers: first reader...............F. L. Taylor
138. Ten boys.................................... Jane Andrews
359. Ten common trees...........................Susan Stokes
699. Tennyson, Alfred..................Poetic and dramatic works
700. Thatcher, Lucy W........................Listening child
222. Thaxter, Celia.................Stories and poems for children
520. Thayer, William M........Turning points in successful careers
17. Third book: stories, studies, rhymes, riddles..................
..........................G. I. Aldrich *and* Alex. Forbes
331. This continent of ours..........................C. F. King
296. Thomas, A. C.........Elementary history of the United States
390. Thompson, Arthur R...........Gold-seeking on the Dalton trail
603. Thompson, Ernest Seton-.................Biography of a grizzly
624. Thompson, Ernest Seton-....................Lives of the hunted
349. Thompson, Ernest Seton-..................Lobo, Rag, and Vixen

643.	Thompson, Ernest Seton-	Wild animals I have known
726.	Thompson, Ernest Seton-	Wild animal for children
14.	Thompson, J. G. and T. E.	Fairy tale and fable: second year
709.	Thompson, Maurice, ed.	Boy's book of sports
	Thompson, T. E., joint author. See Thompson, J. C.	
539.	Thorpe, Francis Newton	History of the U. S. for junior classes
470.	Three colonial boys	E. T. Tomlinson
471.	Three Greek children	A. J. Church
472.	Three young continentals	E. T. Tomlinson
557.	Thrilling days in army life	G. A. Forsyth
99.	Through the farmyard gate	Emilie Poulsson
704.	Through the year with birds and poets	Sarah Williams, comp.
181.	Thurston, Ida T.	Citizen Dan of the Junior Republic
531.	Thwaites, Reuben Gold	Colonies
307.	Thwaites, Reuben Gold	Stories of the Badger state
556.	Thwaites, Reuben Gold	Story of Wisconsin
32.	Tibbits, H. S.	New Century third reader
226.	Tim and Tip	J. O. Kaler
425.	Timothy's quest	K. D. Wiggin
652.	Titian	E. M. Hurll
227.	Toby Tyler	J. O. Kaler
426.	Tom Brown's school days	Thomas Hughes
731.	Tomlins, Wm. L.	Children's songs and how to sing them
435.	Tomlinson, Everett T.	Boys of old Monmouth
451.	Tomlinson, Everett T.	In the hands of the red coats
549.	Tomlinson, Everett T.	Short history of the American Revolution
305.	Tomlinson, Everett T.	Stories of the American Revolution. Bk. 1
306.	Tomlinson, Everett T.	Stories of the American Revolution. Bk. 2
470.	Tomlinson, Everett T.	Three colonial boys
472.	Tomlinson, Everett T.	Three young continentals
473.	Tomlinson, Everett T.	Washington's young aids
100.	Tommy's adventures	E. P. Atwater
101.	Tommy Toddles	A. Lee
342.	Torrey, Bradford	Everyday birds
504.	Towle, George M.	Heroes and martyrs of invention
427.	Treasure island	R. L. Stevenson
428.	Treasury club	William Drysdale
619.	Treat, Mary	Home studies in nature
162.	Trimmer, Sarah	History of the robins
597.	True citizen	W. F. Markwick and W. A. Smith

130.	True stories from New England history....	Nathaniel Hawthorne
286.	True story of Benjamin Franklin..................	E. S. Brooks
287.	True story of Christopher Columbus..............	E. S. Brooks
288.	True story of U. S. Grant.......................	E. S. Brooks
520.	Turning points in successful careers............	W. M. Thayer
	Twain, Mark, *pseud. See* Clemens, Samuel Langhorne.........	
521.	Twelve naval captains........................	M. E. Seawell
250.	Two little confederates...........................	T. N. Page
580.	**Twombly, Alexander S**.................	Hawaii and its people
	Uecke, Claire, *joint author. See* Logie, Alfred E.	
118.	Uncle Remus.......................................	J. C. Harris
598.	Uncle Sam abroad.................................	E. Conner
429.	Under the cactus flag............................	N. A. Smith
228.	Under the lilacs.................................	L. M. Alcott
641.	Upon the tree-tops...............................	O. T. Miller
565.	**Van Bergen, R.**.............................	Story of Japan
	Van Sickle, William, *joint author. See* A. J. Demarest	
87.	**Vawter, Clara**...............................	Rabbit's ransome
57.	Verse and prose for beginners in reading.....	H. E. Scudder, *ed.*
592.	Views in Africa...................................	A. B. Badlam
581.	**Vincent, Frank**.................	In and out of Central America
632.	**Vincent, Frank**, *ed.*.............................	Plant world
270.	Violet fairy book..........................	Andrew Lang, *ed.*
59.	**Von Gottschalck, Oscar Hunt**............	Yankee Doodle gander
148.	**Wade, Mary Hazelton**..................	Our little Brown cousin
149.	**Wade, Mary Hazelton**..................	Our little Indian cousin
150.	**Wade, Mary Hazelton**................	Our little Japanese cousin
151.	**Wade, Mary Hazelton**................	Our little Russian cousin
271.	Wagner story book.............................	W. H. Frost
701.	**Wait, Minnie Curtis**, *and* **Leonard, M. C.**, *comps.*...............	
	................Among flowers and trees with the poets	
642.	Wake-robin.................................	John Burroughs
558.	War of Independence...........................	John Fiske
285.	**Ware, Ella Reeve**..........	Talks about authors and their work
660.	**Warner, Charles Dudley**...............	A-hunting of the deer
758.	**Warner, Charles Dudley**.........................	Being a boy
563.	**Warren, Henry P.**, *ed.*..............	Stories from English history
473.	Washington's young aids......................	E. T. Tomlinson
418.	**Waterloo, Stanley**...............................	Story of Ab
229.	Water babies.................................	Charles Kingsley
360.	Ways of wood folk..............................	W. J. Long

346.	Weed, Clarence Moores	Insect world
623.	Weed, Clarence Moores	Life histories of American insects
626.	Weed, Clarence Moores	Nature biographies
636.	Weed, Clarence Moores	Seed-travellers
49.	Wells, Carolyn	Jingle book
379.	Wells, Henry P.	City boys in the woods
45.	Welsh, Charles	Book of nursery rhymes
721.	Wheeler, Charles G.	Woodworking for beginners
	Wheeler, William H., *joint author*. *See* Calmerton, Gail.	
44.	Wheeler's graded readers: a primer............Gail Calmerton *and* W. H. Wheeler	
58.	When life is young	M. M. Dodge
102.	When Molly was six	E. O. White
240.	Whistler, Charles W.	Havelok the Dane
749.	White, Emerson Elbridge	Elements of pedagogy
756.	White, Emerson Elbridge	School management
185.	White, Eliza Orne	Ednah and her brothers
244.	White, Eliza Orne	Little girl of long ago
102.	White, Eliza Orne	When Molly was six
492.	White, John S., *ed.*	Boys' and girls' Plutarch
716.	White, Mary	How to make baskets
759.	White, William Allen	Court of Boyville
702.	Whittier, John Greenleaf	Complete poetical works
230.	Widow O'Callaghan's boys	Gulielma Zollinger
65.	Wiggin, Kate Douglas	Birds' Christmas carol
412.	Wiggin, Kate Douglas	Polly Oliver's problem
421.	Wiggin, Kate Douglas	Story of Patsy
424.	Wiggin, Kate Douglas	Summer in a cañon
425.	Wiggin, Kate Douglas	Timothy's quest
96.	Wiggin, Kate Douglas *and* Smith, Nora A.	Story hour
311.	Wigwam stories	M. C. Judd, *comp.*
726.	Wild animal play for children	E. S. Thompson
643.	Wild animals I have known	E. S. Thompson
335.	Wild life under the equator	Paul Du Chaillu
644.	Wild neighbors	Ernest Ingersoll
361.	Wilderness ways	W. J. Long
241.	Wilkins, Mary E.	In colonial times
703.	Wilkins, Mary E.	Once upon a time
231.	Will Shakespeare's little lad	Imogen Clark
367.	Williams, Jesse Lynch	Adventures of a freshman
713.	Williams, Mary E., *and* Fisher, K. R.............Elements of the theory and practice of cookery	
704.	William, Sarah, *comp.*	Through the year with birds and poets
105.	Williams, Sherman, *comp.*............Choice literature for primary grades. Bk. 1	

13.	Williams, Sherman, *comp*...............................	
	...............Choice literature for primary grades. Bk. 2	
363.	Williams, Sherman, *comp*...............................	
	..........Choice literature for intermediate grades. Bk. 1	
364.	Williams, Sherman, *comp*...............................	
	..........Choice literature for intermediate grades. Bk. 2	
662.	Williams, Sherman, *comp*...............................	
	...............Choice literature for grammar grades. Bk. 1	
663.	Williams, Sherman, *comp*...............................	
	...............Choice literature for grammar grades. Bk. 2	
468.	Wilson, Calvin Dill............Story of the Cid for young people	
	Wilson, Calvin Dill. *See* Cervantes, Saavedra M. de, Don Quixote: retold by C. D. Wilson, 1901.	
533.	Wilson, Woodrow.......................Division and reunion	
20.	Wiltse, Sara E...................Folklore stories and proverbs	
95.	Wiltse, Sara E......................Stories for kindergartens	
232.	Winter fun...............................W. O. Stoddard	
587.	Winter in Central America and Mexico..........H. J. Sanborn	
289.	With Perry on Lake Erie..........................J. O. Kaler	
474.	With Porter in the Essex..........................J. O. Kaler	
475.	With Preble at Tripoli...........................J. O. Kaler	
476.	With Washington in the west............Edward Stratemeyer	
770.	Woll, Fritz W............Handbook for farmers and dairymen	
569.	Wonder stories from Herodotus.............................	
	..................G. H. Boden *and* W. B. D'Almeida, *eds*.	
119.	Wonderful chair and the tales it told..........Frances Browne	
588.	Wonders of nature.....................Esther Singleton, *ed*.	
362.	Woodpeckers................................F. H. Eckstorm	
721.	Woodworking for beginners....................C. G. Wheeler	
336.	World and its people. Bk. 3....................M. C. Smith	
589.	World and its people. Bk. 4.....................F. E. Coe	
590.	World and its people. Bk. 5.....................F. E. Coe	
591.	World and its people. Bk. 6....................M. C. Smith	
592.	World and its people. Bk. 7...................A. B. Badlam	
593.	World and its people. Bk. 8................E. M. C. Kellogg	
580.	World and its people. Bk. 9..................A. S. Twombly	
337.	World and its people. Bk. 10...W. F. Markwick *and* Wm. Smith	
645.	World of the great forest....................Paul Du Chaillu	
522.	World's discoverers..........................W. H. Johnson	
762.	Wray, Angelina W....................Jean Mitchell's school	
295.	Wright, Henrietta Christian.............................	
	................Children's stories of American progress	
617.	Wright, Mabel Osgood.....Four-footed Americans and their kin	
423.	Wyss, Jean Rudolph...................Swiss family Robinson	

59.	Yankee Doodle gander	O. H. Von Gottschalck
478.	Yankee ships and Yankee sailors	James Barnes
523.	Ye mariners of England	Herbert Hayens
599.	Young American	H. P. Judson
430.	Young consul	William Drysdale
431.	Young supercargo	William Drysdale
727.	Young folks' cyclopedia of common things	J. D. Champlin, *jr.*
728.	Young folks' cyclopedia of games and sports	J. D. Champlin *and* A. E. Bostwick
729.	Young folks' cyclopedia of literature and art	J. D. Champlin, *jr.*
730.	Young folks' cyclopedia of persons and places	J. D. Champlin, *jr.*
559.	Young folks' history of the War for the Union	J. D. Champlin, *jr.*
210.	Zollinger, Gulielma	Maggie McLanehan
230.	Zollinger, Gulielma	Widow O'Callaghan's boys

SUBJECT INDEX.

Acrobats.
    112. Moffett, Cleveland. *See his* Careers of danger and daring. 1901. p. 255-92.

Adams, John.
    507. Brooks, E. S. *See his* Historic Americans. 1899. p. 86-99.

Adams, John Quincy.
    507. Brooks, E. S. *See his* Historic Americans. 1899. p. 202-17.

Adams, John Quincy.
    503. Lodge, H. C. John Quincy Adams and the right of petition. *See* Lodge *and* Roosevelt's Hero tales from American history. 1898. p. 151-59.

Adams, Samuel.
    507. Brooks, E. S. *See his* Historic Americans. 1899. p. 60-72.
    292. Gordy, W. F. *See his* American leaders and heroes. 1901. p. 156-64.

Aerial navigation.
    610. Baker, R. S. *See his* Boy's book of inventions. 1899. p. 324-54.
    712. Moffett, Cleveland. Ballooning. *See his* Careers of danger and daring. 1901. p. 87-129.

Africa—*Description and travel.*
    152. Andrews, Jane. Little dark girl. *See her* Seven little sisters. 1890. p. 94-107.
    592. Badlam, A. B. Views in Africa. 1895. (*World and its people.* Bk. 7.)
    328. Du Chaillu, P. B. Lost in the jungle. 1869.
    335. Du Chaillu, P. P. Wild life under the equator. 1868.
    525. Jenks, Tudor. Boys' book of explorations. 1900.
    593. Kellogg, E. M. C. *See her* Australia and the islands of the sea. 1898. p. 225, 330. (*World and its people.* Bk. 8.)
    141. Shaw, E. R. Pygmies; Bangala. *See his* Big people. 1900. p. 98-102, 118-22.

Africa—*Description and travel.* (Cont.)
    578. Tarr, R. S. and McMurry, F. M. *See their* Europe and other continents. 1901. p. 415-60. (*Tarr & McMurry's geographies. Bk. 3.*)
    321. Tarr, R. S., and McMurry, F. M. *See their* Home geography. 1901. p. 242-48. (*Tarr & McMurry's geographies. Bk. 1.*)
    141a. Taylor, Bayard. Boys of other countries. 1901.

Africa—*History.*
    310. Starr, Frederick. African peoples. *See his* Strange peoples. 1901. p. 123-50.

Agassiz, Lewis.
    285. Ware, Ella R. *See her* Talks about Authors and their work. 1899. p. 62-70.

Agriculture.
    769. Bailey, L. H. Garden-making. 1899.
    774. Bailey, L. H., *ed.* Principles of agriculture. 1898.
    155. Bradish, S. P. Haying, Harvesting, Thrashing, Corn Husking. *See her* Stories of country life. 1901. p. 72-95.
    634. Dodge, R. E. *See his* Reader in physical geography. 1900. p. 36-40.
    768. Henry, W. A. Feeds and feeding. 1898.
    766. James, C. C. Agriculture. 1898.
    767. Sargent, F. L. Corn plants. 1899.
    773. Shepard, H. H. Life on the farm. 1901.
    322. Tarr, R. S. *and* McMurry, F. M. *See* Index to *their* North America. 1901. (*Tarr & McMurry's geographies. Bk. 2.*)
    770. Woll, F. W. Handbook for farmers and dairymen. 1900.
    See also **Bees, Botany, Cattle, Cotton, Fruit, Gardening, Grain, Horse, Maize, Milk, Sheep, Soils, Tobacco, Trees, Wheat, Wool.**

Air.
    331. King, C. F. Air and vapor. *See his* This continent of ours. 1891. p. 73-79. (*Picturesque geographical readers. Bk. 2.*)
    142. Payne, F. O. *See his* Geographical nature studies. c1898. p. 11-20.
    321. Tarr, R. S., *and* McMurry, F. M. *See their* Home geography. 1901. p. 71-80. (*Tarr & McMurry's geographies. Bk. 1.*)
    See also **Aerial navigation.**

Alaska—*Description and travel.*
    570. Aldrich, H. L. Arctic Alaska and Siberia. 1889.
    584. Carpenter, F. G. Alaska and the seal islands. *See his* North America. 1898. p. 298-306.

Alaska—*Description and travel.* (Cont.)
   313. Carroll, S. W. *and* Hart, E. M. *See their* Around the world. Book 3. 1901. p. 122–31. (*Carroll's geographical series.*)
   324. George, Marian M. Little Journeys to Alaska and Canada. 1901.
   321. Tarr, R. S. *and* McMurry, F. M. *See their* Home geography. 1901. p. 188–89. (*Tarr & McMurry's geographies. Bk. 1.*)
   593. Kellogg, E. M. C. Aleutian islands. *See her* Australia. 1898. p. 437. (*World and its people. Book 8.*)
   322. Tarr, R. S. *and* McMurry, F. M. *See their* North America. 1901. p. 323–30. (*Tarr & McMurry's geographies. Bk. 2.*)
   330. Young, Leigh, *and others. See* Our country: West: 1897. p. 3–64.

Alcibiades.
   492. Plutarch. *See his* Lives. 1893. p. 233–59.

Alcott, Louisa May.
   500. Bolton, S. K. Louisa M. Alcott. *See her* Lives of girls who became famous. 1886. p. 104–21.
   285. Ware, E. R. *See her* Talks about Authors and their work. 1899. p. 163–72.

Alden, Betty.
   120. Pratt, M. L. *See her* America's story for America's children. Bk. 1. 1901. p. 89–100.

Alexander the Great.
   492. Plutarch. *See his* Lives. 1893. p. 420–44.

Alfred, King.
   449. Tappan, E. M. In the days of Alfred, the great. 1900.
   563. Warren, H. P., *ed. See his* Stories from English history. 1901. p. 26–41.

Alligator.
   358. Munroe, K. Crocodiles and alligators. *See* Talks about animals. 1895. p. 211–16.

Alps.
   315. Byers, S. H. M. Alpine village life. *See* By land and sea. 1895. p. 42–46.
   588. Singleton, Esther, *ed. See her* Wonders of nature. 1900. p. 205–11.

Amateur drama.
  722. Bell, *Mrs.* Hugh. Fairy tale plays and how to act them. 1899.
  723. Gould, E. L. Lttle men play. 1900.
  724. Gould, E. L. Little women play. 1900.
  725. St. Nicholas book of plays and operettas. 1900.
  726. Thompson, E. S. Wild animal play for children. 1900.

Amateur operas.
  725. St. Nicholas book of plays and operettas. 1900.

American authors. *See* **Biography; Names of authors.**

Amusements. *See* **Games and sports.**

Anderson, Hans Christian.
  285. Ware, E. R. *See her* Talks-about Authors and their work. 1899. p. 41-51.

Andes mountains.
  331. Carpenter, F. G. *See his* South America. 1899. p. 67-86.

Andrews, Jane.
  152. Hopkins, L. P. Memorial of Miss Jane Andrews. *See* Jane Andrews' Seven little sisters. 1890. p. 7-26.

Angelus.
  104. Menefee, Maud. *See her* Child stories from the masters. 1901. p. 69-72.

Animal tamers.
  712. Moffett, Cleveland. *See his* Careers of danger and daring. 1901. p. 293-347.

Animals—*Legends and stories of.*
  72. Ayers, R. F. Four-footed folk. 1901.
  630. Bolton, S. K. Our devoted friend, the dog. 1902.
  601. Brooks, E. S., *comp.* Animals in action. 1901.
  413. Brown, John. Rab and his friends. n. d.
  645. Du Chaillu, Paul. World of the great forest. 1900.
  397. Ensign, H. L. Lady Lee and other animal stories. 1901.
  627. Grinnell, Morton. Neighbours of field, wood and stream. c1901.
  76. Harrington, J. W. Jumping kangaroo and the apple butter cat. 1900.
  357. Holder, C. F. Stories of animal life. 1899.
  173. Hutton, Laurence. Boy I knew, four dogs, and some more dogs. 1901.

Animals—*Legends and stories of.* (Cont.)
  200. Kipling, Rudyard. Jungle book. 1898.
  201. Kipling, Rudyard. Second jungle book. 1897.
  338. Lang, Andrew, *ed.* Animal story book. 1896.
  340. Long, W. J. Beasts of the field. 1901.
  361. Long, W. J. Wilderness ways. 1901.
  67. Miller, E. H. Catain Fritz. 1887.
  216. Patteson, S. L. Pussy meow. 1901.
  393. Roberts, C. G. D. Heart of the ancient wood. 1900.
  171. Saunders, Marshall. Beautiful Joe. 1898.
  603. Thompson-Seton, Ernest. Biography of a grizzly. 1900.
  624. Thompson-Seton, Ernest. Lives of the hunted. 1901.
  349. Thompson-Seton, Ernest. Lobo, Rag, and Vixen. 1899.
  643. Thompson-Seton, Ernest. Wild animals I have known. 1898.
  See also **Names of animals.**

Annapolis.
  460. Allen, W. B. Navy blue. 1899.

Ant-lion.
  353. Needham, J. G. Ant-lions. *See his* Outdoor studies. 1898. p. 81–85.

Ants.
  100. Atwater, E. P. *See her* Tommy's adventures. 1900. p. 7–33.
  356. Kelly, *Mrs. M. A. B.* Moving day. *See her* Short stories of our shy neighbors. 1896. p. 114–22.
  346. Weed, C. M. *See his* Insect world. 1899. p. 54–61.

Arabia—*Description and travel.*
  152. Andrews, Jane. Gemila, the child of the desert. *See her* Seven little sisters. 1890. p. 48–66.
  141. Shaw, E. R. Arabia. *See his* Big people. 1900. p. 25–36.

Arabs.
  310. Starr, Frederick. *See his* Strange peoples. 1901. p. 118–23.

Arbor-day. (*Poems.*)
  664. McCaskey, J. P., *comp.* Arbor-day. *See his* Lincoln literary collection. 1897. p. 242–58.
  701. Wait, M. C. *and* Leonard, M. C., *comps.* Among flowers and trees with poets. 1901.
  704. Williams, Sarah, *comp.* Through the year with birds and poets. 1900.
  See also **Forestry, Trees.**

Archimedes.
    492. Plutarch. *See his* Lives. 1893. p. 370–74.

Architecture.
    330. Kellogg, S. F. Adobe houses in New Mexico. *See* Our country: West. 1897. p. 189–92.

Arctic regions.
    570. Aldrich, H. L. Arctic Alaska and Siberia. 1889.
    280. Bull, J. B. Fridtjof Nansen. 1898.
    315. By land and sea. 1895.
    583. Du Chaillu, Paul. Land of the long night. 1899.
    571. Ingersoll, Ernest. Secrets won from the frozen north. *See his* Book on the ocean. 1898. p. 77–106.
    593. Kellogg, E. M. C. Pen pictures of Greenland and Iceland. *See* her Australia and the islands of the sea. 1898. p. 95–136, 150–60. (*World and its people series, Bk. 8.*)
    331. King, C. F. Frozen region. *See his* This continent of ours. 1891. p. 1–12. (*Picturesque geographical readers. Bk. 2.*)
    145. Muller, Mary. Little people of the snow. 1900.
    154. Peary, J. D. Snow baby. 1901.
    310. Starr, Frederick. See his Strange peoples. 1901. p. 6–12, 47–59.
    141a. Taylor, Bayard. Jon of Iceland. See his Boys of other countries. 1901. p. 32–90.
    See also Alaska; Esquimaux.

Aristides.
    492. Plutarch. *See his* Lives. 1893. p. 288–304.

Arizona—*Description and travel.*
    330. Uberroth, P. H. *and* Bates, H. F. Cave-dwellers of Arizona. *See* Our country: West. 1897. p. 167–77.

Armour, Philip D.
    509. Marden, O. S. *See his* How they succeeded. 1901. p. 65–86.

Arnold, Benedict.
    293. Coffin, C. C. *See his* Boys of '76. 1876. p. 71–81, 123–28, 303–33.
    519. Seelye, E. E. *See her* Story of Washington. 1893. p. 270–82.

Arthur, *King.*
    253. Frost, W. H. Court of King Arthur. 1898.
    257. Frost, W. H. Knights of the Round Table. 1898.

Arts, Fine.
- 729. Champlin, J. D. Young folks' cyclopedia of literature and art. 1901.
- 369. Hoyt, D. L. Barbara's heritage. 1899.
- 104. Menefee, Maud. Child stories from the masters. 1901.
  See also Architecture, Artists, Glass, Music, Sculpture.

Arts, Useful.
- 155. Bradish, S. P. Stories of country ife. 1901.
- 584. Carpenter, F. G. North America. c1898. (*Carpenter's geographical readers.*)
- 634. Dodge, R. E. See *his* Reader in physical geography. 1900. p. 28-58.
- 142. Payne, F. O. Geographical nature studies for primary work in home geography. c1898.
- 319. Rocheleau, W. F. Great American industries. Book 3. Manufactures. 1900.
- 317. Rocheleau, W. F. Great American industries. Book 1. Minerals. 1896.
- 318. Rocheleau, W. F. Great American industries. Book 2. Products of the soil. 1898.
  See also Agriculture, Architecture, Bridges, Commerce, Gardening, Glass, Inventions, Machinery, Manual training, Manufactures, Mines *and* mining, Photography, Printing, Telegraph.

Artists.
- 654. Hurll, E. M. Correggio. 1901·
- 648. Hurll, E. M. Jean Francois Millet. 1900.
- 646. Hurll, E. M. Landseer. 1901.
- 647. Hurll, E. M. Michelangelo. 1899.
- 649. Hurll, E. M. Raphael. 1899.
- 650. Hurll, E. M. Rembrandt. 1899.
- 651. Hurll, E. M. Sir Joshua Reynolds. 1900.
- 652. Hurll, E. M. Titian. 1901.
- 122. Ramé, Louisa de la. Child of Urbino: Raphael. 1900.
- 285. Ware, E. R. Wolfgang Mozart and Felix Mendelssohn. See *her* Talks about Authors and their work. 1899. p. 9-16.
  See also Musicians.

Asia—*Description and travel.*
- 314. Carpenter, F. G. Asia. 1897. *(Carpenter's geographical readers.)*
- 525. Jenks, Tudor. See *his* Boys' book of explorations. 1900. p. 333-90.
- 327. Miller, O. T. Little people of Asia. 1896.

Asia—*Description and travel.* (Cont.)
- 591. Smith, M. C. Life in Asia. 1898. *(World and its people, Bk. 6.)*
- 578. Tarr, R. S. and McMurry, F. M. *See their* Europe and other continents. 1901. p. 353–414. *(Tarr & McMurry's geographies. Bk. 3.)*
- 321. Tarr, R. S. and McMurry, F. M. *See their* Home geography. 1901. p. 230–41. *(Tarr & McMurry's geographies. Bk. 1.)*

Asia—*History.*
- 310. Starr, Frederick. Peoples of Asia. *See his* Strange peoples. 1901. p. 65–123.

See also **Arctic regions**; names of the countries of Asia.

Audubon, John James.
- 395. Butterworth, Hezekiah. In the days of Audubon. 1901.

Australia—*Description and travel.*
- 525. Jenks, Tudor. *See his* Boys' book of explorations. 1900. p. 393–430.
- 593. Kellogg, E. M. C. Pen pictures of Australia. *See her* Australia and the islands of the sea. 1898. p. 13–73. *(World and its people series. Bk. 8.)*
- 310. Starr, Frederick. *See his* Strange peoples. 1901. p. 163–80.
- 578. Tarr, R. S. and McMurry, F. M. *See their* Europe and other continents. 1901. p. 461–85. *(Tarr & McMurry's geographies. Bk. 3.)*
- 321. Tarr, R. S. and McMurry, F. M. *See their* Home geography. 1901. p. 249–55. *(Tarr & McMurry's geographies. Bk. 1.)*

Automobiles.
- 610. Baker, R. S. *See his* Boys' book of inventions. 1899. p. 121–69.

Bacon, Nathaniel.
- 292. Gordy, W. F. *See his* American leaders and heroes. 1901. p. 55–63.

Bacon's rebellion.
- 555. Guerber, H. A. *See his* Story of the Thirteen colonies. 1898. p. 157–60.

Bacteria.
- 773. Shepard, H. H. *See his* Life on the farm. 1901. p. 151–66.

SUBJECT INDEX.

Bainbridge, William.
- 495. Barnes, James. Commodore Bainbridge. 1897.
- 521. Seawell, M. E. *See her* Twelve naval captains. 1899. p. 53–82.

Ballads.
- 707. Campbell, Helen. *See her* American girl's home book of work and play. 1896. p. 102–12.
- 213. Tappan, E. M. Old ballads in prose. 1901.
- See also **Legends, Poetry, Songs.**

Balloons. *See* **Aerial navigation.**

Barbary.
- 295. Wright, H. C. Barbary pirates. *See her* Children's stories of American progress. 1898. p. 41–54.

Barley.
- 767. Sargent, F. L. *See his* Corn plants. 1899. p. 85–88.

Barr, Amelia.
- 509. Marden, O. S. *See his* How they succeeded. 1901. p. 304–13.

Base ball.
- 205. Brooks, Noah. *See his* Lem. 1901. p. 93–97.

Baskets.
- 716. White, Mary. How to make baskets. 1901.

Bat.
- 358. Cushman, S. E. My captive bats. See Talks about animals. 1895. p. 165–69.

Beaver.
- 358. Sandys, E. W. Little lumberman. *See Talks* about animals. 1895. p. 226–30.

Bees.
- 100. Atwater, E. P. *See her* Tommy's adventures. 1900. p. 34–55.
- 605. Burroughs, John. Birds and bees. 1897.
- 631. Burroughs, John. Idyl of the honey-bee. *See his* Pepacton. 1897. p. 53–77, 122–25.
- 707. Campbell, Helen. *See her* American girl's home book of work and play. 1896. p. 384–89.
- 356. Kelly, Mrs. M. A. B. Divided household. *See her* Short stories of our shy neighbors. 1896. p. 143–55.
- 121. Morley, M. W. Bee people. 1900.

Bees. (Cont.)
- 353. Needham, J. G. Butter and eggs and bumble-bees. *See his* Out-door studies. 1898. p. 7-12.
- 341. Noel, Maurice. Buz. 1892.
- 156. Pierson, C. D. Fussy queen bee. *See her* Among the farm-yard people. 1899. p. 47-63.
- 161. Pratt, C. S. Buz-buz. 1898.
- 358. Warren, Arthur. Bee-keeping. *See* Talks about animals. 1895. p. 137-43.
- 346. Weed, C. M. *See his* Insect world. 1899. p. 188-91, 200-207.

Beetle.
- 612. Gibson, W. H. *See his* Eye spy. 1898. p. 1-10, 83-90, 130-35.

Belgium—*Description and travel.*
- 315. Terrell, E. H. Walk and play in Belgium. *See* By land and sea. 1895. p. 16-21.

Bell, Alexander G.
- 509. Marden, O. S. *See his* How they succeeded. 1901. p. 30-43.

Benton, Thomas Hart.
- 516. Brooks, Noah. Thomas H. Benton. *See his* Statesmen. 1898. p. 91-118.

Bermudas—*Description and travel.*
- 593. Kellogg, E. M. C. Bermudas. *See her* Australia and the islands of the sea. 1898. p. 172-77. (*World and its people series. Bk. 8.*)
- 322. Tarr, R. S. and McMurry, F. M. *See their* North America. 1901. p. 399-400. (*Tarr & McMurry's geographies. Bk. 2.*)

Bessemer, *Sir* **Henry.**
- 515. Bolton, *Mrs.* S. K. Sir Henry Bessemer. *See her* Boys who became famous. 1885. p. 112-123.
- 477. Parton, James. Henry Bessemer. *See his* Captains of industry, Vol. 1. 1891. p. 206-211.

Bible.
- 131. Baldwin, James. Old stories of the East. 1896.
- 137. Guerber, H. A. Story of the chosen people. 1896.

Biography, *Collective.*
- 138. Andrews, Jane. Ten boys. 1886.
- 129. Baldwin, James. Four great Americans. 1896.
- 127. Beebe, M. B. Four American naval heroes. 1899.

Biography—*Collective.* (Cont.)
- 494. Brooks, E. S. Century book of famous Americans. 1896.
- 507. Brooks, E. S. Historic Americans. 1899.
- 508. Brooks, E. S. Historic girls. 1887.
- 128. Burton, A. H. Four American patriots. 1898.
- 730. Champlin, J. D., *jr.* Young folks' cyclopaedia of persons and places. Ed. 2. rev. 1880.
- 133. Eggleston, Edward. Stories of great Americans for little Americans. 1895.
- 505. Hall, T. W. Heroes of our Revolution. 1900.
- 523. Hayens, Herbert. Ye mariners of England. 1901.
- 509. Marden, O. S. How they succeeded. 1901.
- 477, 493. Parton, James. Captains of industry. 2 vol. 1884.
- 126. Perry, F. M. Four American inventors. 1901.
- 521. Seawall, M. E. Twelve naval captains. 1899.
- 511. Stoddard, W. O. Men of business. 1893.
- 520. Thayer, W. M. Turning points in successful careers. 1895.
- 285. Ware, E. R. Talks about Authors and their work. 1899.

See also **Artists; Explorers; History; Musicians; Naval biography; Soldiers; Statesmen.** (The life of any one person is entered under his name.)

Bird-day.
- 604. Babcock, C. A. Bird day: how to prepare for it. 1901.
- 664. McCaskey, J. P. *Comp.* Bird day. *See his* Lincoln literary collection. 1897. p. 278-287.

Birds.
- 616. Allen, Grant. Woodland tragedy. *See his* Flashlights on nature. 1898. p. 71-93.
- 604. Babcock, C. A. Bird day: how to prepare for it. 1901.
- 350. Bignell, Effie. Mr. Chupes and Miss Jenny. 1901.
- 358. Bits of bird life. *See* Talks about animals. 1895. p. 65-128.
- 155. Bradish, S. P. *See her* Stories of country life. 1901. p. 30-34, 65-67, 131-33.
- 605. Burroughs, John. Birds and bees; essays. 1879.
- 642. Burroughs, John. Wake-robin. 1871.
- 395. Butterworth, Hezekiah. In the days of Audubon. 1901.
- 609. Chapman, F. M. Bird studies with a camera. 1900.
- 606. Clarke, E. B. Birds of lakeside and prairie. 1901.
- 163. Clark, E. B. Jingle book of birds. 1901.
- 645. Du Chaillu, Paul. World of the great forest. 1900.
- 362. Eckstorm, F. H. Woodpeckers. 1901.
- 625. Gibson, W. H. Cuckoos and the outwitted cow-bird. *See his* My studio neighbors. 1898. p. 23-53.
- 637. Gibson, W. H. Sharp eyes. 1891.

Birds. (Cont.)
- 629. Grant, J. B. Our common birds and how to know them. 1901.
- 607. Grinnell, Elizabeth *and* Joseph. Birds of song and story. 1901.
- 352. Grinnell, E. *and* J. Our feathered friends. 1898.
- 627. Grinnell, Morton. Neighbours of field, wood and stream. c1901.
- 357. Holder, C. F. *See his* Stories of animal life. 1899. p. 21-33, 108-15, 247-55.
- 628. Kearton, Richard. Our bird friends. 1900.
- 356. Kelly, *Mrs.* M. A. B. Phoebe's family. *See her* Short stories of our shy neighbors. 1896. p. 22-198.
- 339. Long, W. J. Fowls of the air. 1901.
- 608. Merriam, F. A. Birds of village and field. 1898.
- 343. Miller, O. T. First book of birds. 1900.
- 621. Miller, O. T. In nesting time. 1898.
- 347. Miller, O. T. Little brothers of the air. 1892.
- 354. Miller, O. T. Second book of birds. 1901.
- 641. Miller, O. T. Upon the tree-tops. 1898.
- 156. Pierson, C. D. Story that the swallow didn't tell. *See her* Among the farmyard people. 1899. p. 1-11.
- 773. Shepard, H. H. *See his* Life on the farm. 1901. p. 130-50.
- 357a. Smith, C. W. Summer of Saturdays. c1900.
- 342. Torrey, Bradford. Everyday birds. 1901.
- 619. Treat, Mary. *See her* Home studies in nature. 1885. p. 15-76.
- 162. Trimmer, Sarah. History of the robins. 1901.

Birds, *Bibliography.*
- 608. Merriam, F. A. Books of reference. *See her* Birds of village and field. 1898. p. 390-94.

Birds, *Poems on.* See Reference list in *Arbor and Bird Day annual.* 1902.

Bjornsen, Bjornstjerne.
- 285. Ware, E. R. *See her* Talks about authors and their work. 1899. p. 159-62.

Black Hawk war.
- 461. Barton, W. E. Prairie schooner. 1900.
- 441. Brooks, E. S. *See his* Godson of Lafayette. 1900. p. 163-327.
- 540. Legler, H. E. *See his* Leading events of Wisconsin history. 1898. p. 172-80.
- 307. Thwaites, R. G. *See his* Stories of the Badger state. 1900. p. 134-45.
- 556. Thwaites, R. G. *See his* Story of Wisconsin. 1891. p. 180-9.

Blacksmithing.
155. Bradish, S. P. *See her* Stories of country life. 1901. p. 20-25.

Blaine, James Gillespie.
516. Brooks, Noah. James G. Blaine. *See his* Statesmen. 1898. p. 281-312.
520. Thayer, W. M. *See his* Turning points in successful careers. 1895. p. 140-47.

Boating.
707. Campbell, Helen. *See her* American girl's home book of work and play. 1896. p. 196-203.
See also Yachting.

Boats.
610. Baker, R. S. *See his* Boy's book of inventions. 1899. p. 1-39.

Bonheur, Rosa.
500. Bolton, *Mrs.* S. K. Rosa Bonheur. *See her* Lives of girls who became famous. 1886. p. 180-93.

Books.
319. Rocheleau, W. F. *See his* Great American industries. Vol. 3. Manufactures. 1900. p. 222-36.

Boone, Daniel.
292. Gordy, W. F. *See his* American leaders and heroes. 1901. p. 222-33.
555. Guerber, H. A. *See his* Story of the thirteen colonies. 1898. p. 288-93.
299. McMurry, Charles. Daniel Boone. *See his* Pioneer history stories. 1895. p. 91-102.
278. Perry, F. M. *and* Beebe, K. *See their* Four American pioneers. 1900. p. 11-68.
503. Roosevelt, Theodore. Daniel Boone and the founding of Kentucky. *See* Lodge and Roosevelt's Hero tales from American history. 1898. p. 19-28.
296. Thomas, A. C. *See his* Elementary history of the United States. 1901. p. 219-31.

Boston.
584. Carpenter, F. G. In Boston. *See his* North America. 1898. p. 91-99.

Boston tea party.
292. Gordy, W. F. *See his* American leaders and heroes. 1901. p. 156-64.
301. Scudder, H. E. *See his* Short history of the United States. 1890. p. 110-15.

Botany.
- 616. Allen, Grant. Plant that melts ice. *See his* Flashlights on nature. 1898. p. 25–283.
- 640. Allen, Grant. Story of the plants. 1898.
- 615. Atkinson, G. F. First studies of plant life. 1901.
- 345. Bergen, F. D. Glimpses at the plant world. 1891.
- 633. Dana, *Mrs.* S. W. Plants and their children. 1896.
- 768. Henry, W. A. The plant, how it grows and elaborates food for animals. *See his* Feeds and feeding. 1898. p. 1–11.
- 571. Ingersoll, Ernest. Plants of the sea and their uses. *See his* Book of the ocean. 1898. p. 249–258.
- 344. Morley, M. W. Flowers and their friends. 1901.
- 164. Spear, M. A. Leaves and flowers. 1900.
- 359. Stokes, Susan. Ten common trees. 1901.
- 632. Vincent, Frank. *ed* Plant world. 1897.

See also Agriculture; Bacteria; Buds; Fertilization of plants; Flowers; Fruit; Gardening; Leaves; Seeds; Trees.

Bowditch, Nathaniel.
- 520. Thayer, W. M. *See his* Turning points in successful careers. 1895. p. 83–91.

Boys.
- 515. Bolton, *Mrs.* S. K. Poor boys who became famous. 1885.

See also Children.

Brassey, Anne (Allnutt) *Lady*.
- 500. Bolton, *Mrs.* S. K. Lady Brassey. *See her* Lives of girls who became famous. 1886. p. 300–19.

Bridge builders.
- 515. Bolton, *Mrs.* S. K. *Capt.* J. B. Eads. *See her* Boys who became famous. 1885. p. 56–35.
- 712. Moffett, Cleveland. *See his* Careers of danger and daring. 1901. p. 173–208.
- 504. Towle, G. M. Robert Stephenson, the great bridge-builder. *See his* Heroes and martyrs of invention. 1890. p. 151–59.

Bridges.
- 329. Rideing, W. H. Brooklyn bridge. *See* Our Country: East. 1898. p. 183–186.

See also Cables.

Briggs, George N.
- 520. Thayer, W. M. *See his* Turning points in successful careers. 1895. p. 155–64.

Bright, John.
    477. Parton, James. John Bright. *See his* Captains of industry. 1891. Vol. 1, p. 212-23.

British America—*Description and travel.*
    584. Carpenter, F. G. British America. *See his* North America. 1898. p. 306-27.

Brown, John.
    494. Brooks, E. S. *See his* Century book of famous Americans. 1896. p. 216.
    527. Coffin, C. C. *See his* Building the nation. 1882. p. 460-67.
    See also **John Brown's raid.**

Browning, Elizabeth Barrett.
    500. Bolton, *Mrs.* S. K. Elizabeth Barrett Browning. *See her* Lives of girls who became famous. 1886. p. 194-212.

Bryant, William Cullen.
    279. Cody, Sherwin. *See his* Four American poets. 1899. p. 9-68.

Buds.
    633. Dana, *Mrs.* S. W. *See her* Plants and their children. 1896. p. 125-34.

Bull, Ole.
    515. Bolton, *Mrs.* S. K. Ole Bull. *See her* Boys who became famous. 1885. p. 284-302.

Bull-fight.
    357. Holder, C. F. *See his* Stories of animal life. 1899. p. 86-96.

Bunker Hill.
    294. Brooks, E. S. Bunker Hill. *See his* Century book of the American Revolution. 1897. p. 55-72.
    555. Guerber, H. A. *See his* Story of the thirteen colonies. 1898. p. 237-41.
    537. Holmes, O. W. Grandmother's story of Bunker Hill battle. 1891.
    301. Scudder, H. E. *See his* Short history of the United States. 1890. p. 120-25.

Buoys.
    315. Low, W. F. Buoys. *See* By land and sea. 1895. p. 225-30.

Burnett, Frances Hodgson.
    285. Ware, E. R. *See her* Talks about Authors and their work. 1899. p. 182-89.

Burns, Robert.
    285. Ware, E. R. *See her* Talks about Authors and their work. 1899. p. 17-25.

Burros.
    330. Lewis, H. *and others.* Rocky mountain burro. *See* Our country: West. 1897. p. 86-89, 236-43.

Burroughs, John.
    509. Marden, O. S. *See his* How they succeeded. 1901. p. 327-40.

Busy work.
    752. Arnold, S. L., *ed.* Plans for busy work. 1901.

Butterflies.
    100. Atwater, E. P. *See her* Tommy's adventures. 1900. p. 56-78.
    356. Kelly, *Mrs.* M. A. B. Birth of a young lord. *See her* Short stories of our shy neighbors. 1896. p. 15-21; 51-56.
    626. Weed, C. M. Nature biographies. 1901.

Cabeza de Vaca.
    491. Higginson, T. W., *ed.* Strange voyage of Cabeza de Vaca. *See his* Book of American explorers. 1877. p. 73-96.

Cables. (*Atlantic cable.*)
    552. Guerber, H. A. *See his* Story of the Great Republic. 1899. p. 257-62.
    291. Mowry, W. A. *and* A. M. *See their* American inventions and inventors. 1900. p. 278-85.
    See also Telegraph.

Cabot, John.
    491. Higginson, T. W. Cabot and Verrazzano. *See his* Book of American explorers. 1877. p. 55-69.

Caesar, Julius.
    302. Clarke, M. Story of Caesar. 1898.
    492. Plutarch. *See his* Lives. 1893. p. 446-48.

Calhoun, John C.
    494. Brooks, E. S. *See his* Century book of famous Americans. 1896. p. 140-44.
    507. Brooks, E. S. *See his* Historic Americans. 1899. p. 291-304.
    516. Brooks, Noah. John C. Calhoun. *See his* Statesmen. 1898. p. 69-90.

Carpenter's geographical readers series.
   314. Carpenter, F. G. Asia. c1897.
   584. Carpenter, F. G. North America. c1898.
   334. Carpenter, F. G. South America. 1899.
   577. Carpenter, F. G. Europe. 1902.

Carson, Kit.
   278. Perry, F. M. *and* Beebe, K. *See their* Four American pioneers. 1900. p. 197-255.

Cartier, Jacques.
   491. Higginson, T. W. French in Canada. *See his* Book of American explorers. 1877. p. 99-117.

Cattle ranching.
   330. Harger, C. M. *and* Horn, P. W. Great cattle trails. *See* Our country: West. 1897. p. 228-35.
   322. Tarr, R. S. *and* McMurry, F. M. *See* Index to their North America. 1901. (*Tarr & McMurry's geographies. Bk. 2.*)
   See also Milk.

Cats.
   216. Patteson, S. L. Pussy meow. 1901.

Cave and cliff dwellers.
   146. Bayliss, C. K. Lolami. 1901.
   313. Carroll, S. W. *and* Hart, E. M. *See their* Around the world. Bk. 3. 1901. p. 119-21. (*Carroll's geographical series.*)
   418. Waterloo, Stanley. Story of Ab: a tale of the time of the cave man. 1897.

Caves.
   329. Dexter, M. Luray cavern. *See* Our country: East. 1898. p. 144-48.
   329. Hovey, H. C. Mammoth cave. *See* Our country: East. 1898. p. 57-64.

Caxton, William.
   563. Warren, H. P., *ed. See his* Stories from English history. 1901. p. 156-65.

Central America—*Description and travel.*
   584. Carpenter, F. G. Central America. *See his* North America. 1898. p. 345-52.
   589. Coe, F. E. *See her* Our American neighbors, 1897. p. 197-213. (*World and its people series. Bk. 4.*)
   587. Sanborn, H. J. Winter in Central America and Mexico. 1887.
   322. Tarr, R. S. *and* McMurry, F. M. *See their* North America. 1901. p. 389-92. (*Tarr & McMurry's geographies. Bk. 2.*)
   581. Vincent, Frank. In and out of Central America. 1896.

Champlain, Samuel de. *See* **Explorers.**

Charades.
    707. Campbell, Helen. *See her* American girl's home book of work and play. 1896. p. 116-43.

Charter Oak.
    555. Guerber, H. A. *See his* Story of the thirteen colonies. 1898. p. 166-70.

Chase, Salmon Portland.
    516. Brooks, Noah. Salmon P. Chase. *See his* Statesmen. 1898. p. 143-74.
    520. Thayer, W. M. *See his* Turning points in successful careers. 1895. p. 9-16.

Cheese.
    313. Carroll, S. W. *and* Hart, E. M. Cheese factory. *See their* Around the world. Bk. 3, 1901. p. 201-3. (*Carroll's geographical series.*)

Chicago.
    584. Carpenter, F. G. Greatest lake port in the world. *See his* North America. 1898. p. 225-34.

Child-study.
    765. Barrie, J. M. Sentimental Tommy. 1896.
    205. Brooks, Noah: Lem: a New England village boy. 1901.
    745. Chenery, Susan. As the twig is bent. 1901.
    746. Du Bois, Patterson. Beckonings from little hands. 1898.
    757. Gilder, J. L. Autobiography of a tomboy. 1900.
    761. Howells, W. D. In a boy's town. 1890.
    173. Hutton, Laurence. Boy I knew, four dogs, and some more dogs. 1901.
    763. Laughlin, E. O. Johnnie. 1899.
    764. Ray, A. C. Playground Toni. 1900.
    747. Shinn, M. W. Biography of a baby. 1900.
    760. Smith, W. H. Evolution of "Dodd." 1897.
    759. White, W. A. Court of Boyville. 1899.
    See also **Kindergarten.**

Children's poetry.
    84. Dodge, M. M., *comp.* New baby world. 1897.
    58. Dodge, M. M. When life is young. 1894.
    676. Field, Eugene. Love-songs of childhood. 1901.
    677. Field, Eugene. Lullaby-land. 1894.
    116. Holbrook, Florence, *ed.* 'Round the year in myth and song. 1897.

LIST OF BOOKS FOR TOWNSHIP LIBRARIES.

Children's poetry. (Cont.)
   678. Lang, Andrew, *ed.* Blue poetry book. 1896.
        Lang, Andrew, *ed.* Nursery rhyme book. 1898.
        Larcom, Lucy. Childhood songs. 1898.
        Lear, Edward. Pelican chorus and other nonsense verses. 1900.
        Longfellow, H. W. Song of Hiawatha. 1898.
        McMurry, L. B. *and* Cook, A. S. Songs of the tree-top and meadow. 1899.
        Norton, C. E., *ed.* Heart of oak books. Vol. 1. 1897.
        Persons, E. A. Our country in poem and prose. 1899.
   633. Pyle, Katherine. Prose and verse for children. 1899.
        Repplier, Agnes, *comp.* Book of famous verse. 1894.
        Riley, James Whitcomb. Child-rhymes. 1899.
        Riley, J. W. Child world. 1897.
        Scollard, Clinton. Boy's book of rhyme. 1896.
   57. Scudder, H. E. *ed.* Verse and prose for beginners in reading. 1893.
   697. Sherman, F. D. Little-folk lyrics. 1897.
        Stevenson, R. L. Child's garden of verses. 1901.
        Thatcher, L. W. Listening child. 1900.
        Thaxter, Celia. Stories and poems for children. 1883.
   703. Wilkins, M. E. Once upon a time. 1897.

Childs, George William.
   515. Bolton, *Mrs.* S. K. George W. Childs. *See her* Boys who became famous. 1885. p. 313-22.
   520. Thayer, W. M. *See his* Turning points in successful careers. 1895. p. 69-76.

Chimneys.
   291. Mowry, W. A. *and* A. M. *See their* American inventions and inventors. 1900. p. 31-36.

China—*Description and travel.*
   152. Andrews, Jane. Story of Pense. *See her* Seven little sisters. 1890. p. 80-93.
   153. Andrews, Jane. New work for Pense and Lin. *See her* Seven little sisters prove their sisterhood. 1890.
   315. Huntington, A. O. *and others.* In Chinese streets. *See* By land and sea. 1895. 131-40
   576. Knox, T. W. Adventures of two youths in a journey to Japan and China. 1879.
   31. Perdue, H. A. *and* La Victoire, F. E. *See their* New Century second reader. 1899. p. 52-76.
   141. Shaw, E. R. China. *See his* Big people and little people of other lands. 1900. p. 5-14.

SUBJECT INDEX. 247

Chinese.
> 310. Starr, Frederick. *See his* Strange peoples. 1901. p. 69-75.

Chipmunk.
> 155. Bradish, S. P. See her Stories of country life. 1901. p. 18-19.
> 638. Burroughs, John. *See his* Squirrels and other fur-bearers. 1900. p. 15-31.
> 358. Burroughs, John. Chipmunk. *See* Talks about animals. 1895. p. 174-76.
> 356. Kelly, *Mrs.* M. A. B. Chipmunk. *See her* Short stories of our shy neighbors. 1896. p. 200-1.
> 353. Needham, J. G. Chipmunks. *See his* Outdoor studies. 1898. p. 13-17.

Chivalry.
> 458. Pyle, Howard. Men of iron.
> *See also* Crusades; Middle ages.

Christiana, *Queen of Sweden.*
> 508. Brooks, E. S. *See his* Historic girls. 1887. p. 192-207.

Christmas.
> 153. Andrews, Jane. Christmas time again for Louise. *See her* Seven little sisters prove their sisterhood. 1890.
> 152. Andrews, Jane. Louise, the child of the Rhine. *See her* Seven little sisters. 1894. p. 108-20.
> 717. Beard, D. C. *See his* Jack of all trades. 1900. p. 237-52.
> 700. Beard, Lina *and* Beard, A. B. *See their* American girls' handy book. 1890. p. 317-45.
> 707. Campbell, Helen. Fifty Christmas gifts for small fingers. *See her* American girl's home book of work and play. 1896. p. 248-75.
> 461. Field, Eugene. The first Christmas tree. *See his Little* book of profitable tales. 1901. p. 3-11.
> 179. Howells, W. D. Christmas every day and other stories. 1893.
> 214. Jewett, S. O. Patty's dull Christmas. *See her* Playdays. 1889. p. 180-200.
> 631. McCaskey, J. P., *comp.* Christmas songs. *See his* Lincoln literary collection. 1897. p. 414-16.
> 106. McMurry, *Mrs.* L. B. The fir-tree. *See her* Classic stories for little ones. 1897. p. 37-44.
> 63. Moulton, L. C. Just a little bit of Christmas. *See her* Bed-time stories. 1898. p. 153-66.
> 414. Page, T. N. Santa Claus's partner. 1899.
> 178. Pyle, Katherine. Christmas angel. 1900.

Christmas. (Cont.)
- 91. Scudder, H. E. Christmas stocking with a hole in it. *See his* Seven little people. 1891. p. 57-96.
- 187. Stockton, F. R. Christmas truants. *See his* Fanciful tales. 1899. p. 108-30.
- 220. Stuart, R. M. Solomon Crow's Christmas pockets. 1896.
- 219. St. Nicholas Christmas book. 1899.
- 195. Wiltse, S. E. Iddly Bung's first Christmas tree. *See her* Stories for kindergartens. 1890. p. 69-77.
- 102. White, E. O. Riley's Christmas tree. *See her* When Molly was six. 1898. p. 123-33.
- 65. Wiggin, K. D. Birds' Christmas carol. 1894.

Cicero.
- 492. Plutarch. *See his Lives.* 1893. p. 190-228.

Cincinnati, *Ohio.*
- 299. McMurry, Charles. Cincinnati and Marietta. *See his* Pioneer history stories. 1895. p. 127-35.

Citizenship.
- 597. Markwick, W. F. *and* Smith, W. A. True citizen. 1900.
- 665. Morgan, T. J. Patriotic citizenship. 1895.

Clark, George Rogers.
- 299. McMurry, Charles. *See his* Pioneer history stories. 1895. p. 33-49.
- 503. Roosevelt, Theodore. George Rogers Clark and the conquest of the Northwest. *See* Lodge and Roosevelt's Hero tales from American history. 1891. p. 29-41.

Clark, Captain William. *See* **Lewis and Clark.**

Clay, Henry.
- 498. Bolton, *Mrs.* S. K. *See her* Famous American Statesmen. 1888. p. 230-67.
- 494. Brooks, E. S. *See his* Century book of famous Americans. 1896. p. 145-55.
- 507. Brooks, E. S. See his Historic Americans. 1899. p. 277-90.
- 516. Brooks, Noah. *See his* Statesmen. 1898. p. 9-38.
- 520. Thayer, W. M. *See his* Turning points in successful careers. 1895. p. 52-58.

Clemens, Samuel.
- 285. Ware, E. R. *See her* Talks about Authors and their work. 1899. p. 173-81.

Cleopatra.
    492. Plutarch. *See his* Lives. 1893. p. 375–79.

Cleveland, Grover.
    516. Brooks, Noah. Grover Cleveland. *See his* Statesmen. 1898. p. 333–47.

Climate.
    331. King, C. F. *See his* This continent of ours. 1891. p. 120–28. (*Picturesque geographical readers. Bk. 2.*)
    See also **Weather.**

Clocks and watches.
    332. King, C. F. Time-keepers; Making watches. *See his* Land we live in. 1892. p. 118–41. (*Picturesque geographical readers. Bk. 3.*)

Clothing.
    291. Mowry, W. A. *and* A. M. *See their* American inventions and inventors. 1900. p. 143–84.
    142. Payne, F. O. Our clothing. *See his* Geographical nature studies. c1898. p. 95–97.

Clotilda (*France*).
    508. Brooks, E. S. *See his* Historic girls. 1887. p. 61–78.

Coal and coal mines.
    155. Bradish, S. P. *See her* Stories of country life. 1901. p. 96–130.
    139. Carroll, S. W. *and* Hart, E. M. *See their* Around the world. Bk. 3. 1901. p. 56–59.
    332. King, C. F. Coal mines. *See his* Land we live in. 1892. Vol. 2. p. 71–86. (*Picturesque geographical readers. Bk. 4.*)
    291. Mowry, W. A. *and* A. M. *See their* American inventions and inventors. 1900. p. 44–50.
    317. Rocheleau, W. F. *See his* Great American industries. Vol. 1. Minerals. 1896. p. 7–44.
    See also **Mines and mining.**

Cocoons.
    612. Gibson, W. H. *See his* Eye spy. 1898. p. 145–53.

College life.
    367. Williams, J. L. Adventures of a freshman. 1899.
    See also **School life.**

Colorado—*Life*.
    212. Jackson, H. H. Nelly's silver mine. 1900.

Columbus, Christopher.
    287. Brooks, E. S. True story of Christopher Columbus, called the Great Admiral. 1892.
    292. Gordy, W. F. *See his* American leaders and heroes. 1901. p. 1–21.
    555. Guerber, H. A. *See* his Story of the thirteen colonies. 1898. p. 36–59.
    491. Higginson, T. W. Book of American explorers. 1877.
    571. Ingersoll, Ernest. *See his* Book of the ocean. 1898. p. 59–62.
    522. Johnson, W. H. *See his* World's discoverers. 1900. p. 18–92.
    301. Scudder, H. E. *See his* Short history of the United States. 1890. p. 22–26.
    517. Seelye, E. E. Story of Columbus. 1892.
    296. Thomas, A. C. *See his* Elementary history of the United States. 1901. p. 7–25.

Comedy. *See* Drama.

Commerce.
    634. Dodge, R. E. *See his* Reader in physical geography. 1900. p. 33–36.
    571. Ingersoll, Ernest. Merchants of the sea. *See his* Book of the ocean. 1898. p. 155–70.
    321. Tarr, R. S. *and* McMurry, F. M. *See their* Home geography. 1901. p. 81–91. (*Tarr & McMurry's geographies. Bk. 1.*)
    See also Manufactures; Railroads; Transportation.

Compass.
    315. Parton, James. Mariner's compass. *See* By land and sea. 1895. p. 214–19.

Conquest of Peru.
    548. Lang, Andrew, *ed. See his* Red true story book. 1897. p. 133–65.

Consuls.
    598. Conner, E. Consular service of U. S. *See his* Uncle Sam abroad. 1900. p. 43–120.

Cookery.
    713. Williams, M. E. *and* Fisher, K. R. Elements of the theory and practice of cookery. 1901.
    See also Food.

per, Peter.
520. Thayer, W. M. *See his* Turning points in successful careers. 1895. p. 273-80.

)per.
313. Carroll, S. W., *and* Hart, E. M. Copper mines. *See their* Around the world. Bk. 3. 1901.

dova, *Spain.*
315. Moulton, L. C. Toledo and Cordova. *See* By land and sea. 1895. p. 27-32.

ea.
315. Carpenter, F. G. Corea and its army. *See* By land and sea. 1895. p. 141-45.

eans.
310. Starr, Frederick. *See his* Strange peoples. 1901. p. 76-81.

olanus.
492. Plutarch. *See his* Lives. 1893. p. 260-84.

nell, Ezra.
515. Bolton, *Mrs.* S. K. Ezra Cornell. *See her* Poor boys who became famous. 1885. p. 238-50.

ez, Hernando. *See* Explorers.

:er, Laurence.
504. Towle, G. M. Laurence Coster, the discoverer of type-writing. *See his* Heroes and martyrs of invention. 1892. p. 23-32.

on.
584. Carpenter, F. G. In the land of cotton. *See his* North America. 1898. p. 109-18.
313. Carroll, S. W. *and* Hart, E. M. *See their* Around the world. Bk. 3. 1901. p. 159-66.
332, 333. King, C. F. Pair of sheets; In a manufacturing town. *See his* Land we live in. vol. 1. 1892. p. 23-39; vol. 2. 1893. p. 17-30. (*Picturesque geographical readers.* Bks. 3, 4.)
291. Mowry, W. A. *and* A. M. *See their* American inventions and

Cotton-gin.
 552. Guerber, H. A. *See his* Story of the great Republic. 1899. p. 43–48.
 291. Mowry, W. A. *aid* A. M. *See their* American inventions and inventors. 1900. p. 148–52.

Cotton plantation.
 411. Drysdale, William. Pine Ridge plantation. 1901.

Country life.
 189. Smith, M. P. W. Four on a farm. 1901.
 See also Agriculture; Camping; Gardening; Hunting; Sports.

Coyote.
 330. Quest, I. N. Hated coyote. *See* Our country: West. 1897. p. 208–11.

Crayfish.
 356. Kelly, *Mrs.* M. A. B. Crusty fellow. *See her* Short stories of our shy neighbors. 1896. p. 67–71.

Crickets.
 100. Atwater, E. P. *See her* Tommy's adventures. 1900. p. 79–91.

Crimean war.
 563. Warren, H. P., *ed. See his* Stories from English history. 1901. p. 423–26.

Crockett, David.
 278. Perry, F. M. *and* Beebe, K. *See their* Four American pioneers. 1900. p. 135–94.

Crocodile.
 358. Munroe, Kirk. Crocodiles and alligators. *See* Talks about animals. 1895. p. 211–16.

Cromwell, Oliver.
 207. Hawthorne, Nathaniel. *See his* Little Daffydowndilly. 1887. p. 44–53.
 520. Thayer, W. M. *See his* Turning points in successful careers. 1895. p. 102–10.
 563. Warren, H. P., *ed. See his* Stories from English history. 1901. p. 280–91.

Crow.
 353. Needham, J. G. Not so black as he is painted. *See his* Outdoor studies. 1898. p. 47–53.

Crusades.
- 526. Griffis, W. E. Dutch crusades; What followed the crusades. *See his* Brave little Holland. 1894. p. 79-98.
- 563. Warren, H. P., ed. *See his* Stories from English history. 1901. p. 81-88.

See also Chivalry; Middle ages.

Cuba—*Description and travel.*
- 313. Carroll, S. W. *and* Hart, E. M. *See their* Around the world. Bk. 3. 1901. p. 215-22.
- 325. George, M. M. Little journeys to Cuba and Puerto Rico. 1900.
- 593. Kellogg, E. M. C. *See her* Australia and the islands of the sea. 1898. p. 190-206. (*World and its people series.* Bk. 8.)
- 322. Tarr, R. S. *and* McMurry, F. M. *See their* North America. 1901. p. 330-36. (*Tarr & McMurry's geographies.* Bk. 2.)

Cuba—*History.*
- 235. Drysdale, William. Cadet Standish of the St. Louis. 1899.

Cushing, *Lieut.* **W. B.**
- 503. Roosevelt, Theodore. *See* Lodge and Roosevelt's Hero tales from American history. 1898. p. 291-300.

Custer, *Gen.* **George A.**
- 273. Custer, E. B. Boy general. 1901.

Cyclone.
- 600. Harrington, M. W. *See his* About the weather. 1899. p. 110-35.

Cyclopedias.
- 727. Champlin, J. D., jr. Young folks' cyclopedia of common things. 1893.
- 728. Champlin, J. D. *and* Bostwick, A. E. Young folks' cyclopedia of games and sports. 1899.
- 729. Champlin, J. D. *jr.* Young folks' cyclopedia of Literature and Art. 1901.
- 730. Champlin, J. D. *jr.* Young folks' cyclopedia of persons and places. Ed. 2, rev. 1880.

Dale, Richard.
- 521. Seawell, M. E. *See her* Twelve naval captains. 1899. p. 28-41.

Dare, Virginia.
    120. Pratt, M. L. *See her* America's story for America's children. Bk. 1. 1901. p. 83-88.

Decatur, Stephen.
    521. Seawell, M. E. *See her* Twelve naval captains. 1899. p. 102-29.

Declaration of Independence.
    494. Brooks, E. S. *See his* Century book of famous Americans. 1896. p. 76-77.
    555. Guerber, H. A. *See his* Story of the thirteen colonies. 1898. p. 248-53.
    665. Morgan, T. J. *See his* Patriotic citizenship. 1895. p. 359-62.
    301. Scudder, H. E. *See his* Short history of the United States. 1890. p. 128-31.

Decoration day. *See* **Memorial day.**

Demosthenes.
    492. Plutarch. *See his* Lives. 1893. p. 168-89.

Deserts.
    334. Carpenter, F. G. Great South American desert. *See his* South America. 1899. p. 50-58.

De Soto, Hernando. *See* **Soto, Hernando de.**

Dewey, George.
    127. Beebe, M. B. Story of Admiral Dewey and the navy of 1898. *See her* Four American naval heroes. 1899. p. 195-254.
    502.. Johnson, Rossiter. Hero of Manila. 1899.

Dickens, Charles.
    285. Ware, E. R. *See her* Talks about Authors and their work. 1899. p. 101-15.

Diplomacy.
    598. Conner, E. Uncle Sam abroad. 1900.
    See also **Consuls.**

Diving.
    712. Moffett, Cleveland. *See his* Careers of danger and daring. 1901. p. 40-86.

Dogs.
    630. Bolton, S. K. Our devoted friend, the dog. 1902.
    173. Hutton, Laurence. Boy I knew, four dogs, and some more dogs. 1901.
    329. Keith, M. A. *and* Stevens, H. J. Dog-sledges in Michigan; The Ishpeming dog-race. *See* Our country: East. 1898. p. 20–27.

Douglas, S. A.
    488. Brooks, Noah. *See his* Abraham Lincoln. 1901. p. 72–147.

Dragon-fly.
    353. Needham, J. G. Dragon flies. *See his* Outdoor studies. 1898. p. 54–72.

Drake, *Sir* Francis.
    439. Barnes, James. Drake and his yeoman. 1899.
    See also Explorers.

Drama.
    656. Shakespeare, William. As you like it. 1897.
    657. Shakespeare, William. Julius Caesar. 1897.
    658. Shakespeare, William. Macbeth. 1900.
    659. Shakespeare, William. Merchant of Venice. 1897.
    See also Amateur drama.

Drawing.
    752. Arnold, S. L., *ed. See* her Plans for busy work. 1901. p. 101–33.

Dred Scott decision.
    488. Brooks, Noah. *See his* Abraham Lincoln. 1901. p. 108–9, 144.
    See also Indexes of United States histories on list.

Dynamite.
    712. Moffett, Cleveland. Dynamite worker. *See his* Careers of danger and daring. 1901. p. 348–76.

Eads, *Captain* James B.
    515. Bolton, *Mrs.* S. K. *See her* Boys who became famous. 1885. p. 26–32.

Earth.
    321. Tarr, R. S. *and* McMurry, F. M. *See their* Home geography. 1901. p. 111–36. (*Tarr & McMurry's geographies. Bk. 1.*)
    See also Arctic regions; Geography; Mines and mining; Vol-

East Indies.
    593. Kellogg, E. M. C. Borneo, Sumatra, Java. *See her* Australia, 1898. p. 350–74. (*World and its people. Bk. 8.*)

Edda.
    480. Mabie, H. W. Norse stories retold from the Eddas. 1900.

Edison, Thomas A.
    509. Marden, O. S. *See his* How the succeeded. 1901. p. 220–40.
    126. Perry, F. M. *See her* Four American inventors. 1901. p. 205–60.

Eggleston, Edward.
    285. Ware, E. R. *See her* Talks about Authors and their work. 1899. p. 132–39.

Egypt—*Description and travel.*
    315. Crosby, E. R. Some little Egyptians. *See* By land and sea. 1895. p. 183–87.
    141a. Taylor, Bayard. Pasha's son. *See his* Boys of other countries. 1901. p. 16–31.

Electric light.
    291. Mowry, W. A. *and* A. M. *See their* American inventions and inventors. 1900. p. 85–89.

Electricity.
    610. Baker, R. S. Motor vehicle; Phonograph; Wireless telegraphy; X-ray. *See his* Boys' book of inventions. 1899.

Elephant.
    622. Holder, C. F. Ivory king. 1897.
    357. Holder, C. F. *See his* Stories of animal life. 1899. p. 96–133.
    358. Van Someren, G. J. Tame elephants in India. *See* Talks about animals. 1895. p. 195–202.

Eliot, George. (*Pseud. of* Mrs. Lewes Cross.)
    500. Bolton, *Mrs.* S. K. George Eliot. *See her* Lives of girls who became famous. 1886. p. 213–39.

Elizabeth, *Queen.*
    508. Brooks, E. S. *See his* Historic girls. 1887. p. 174–91.
    563. Warren, H. P., *ed. See his* Stories from English history. 1901. p. 214–21.

Elk.
    330. Davis, Sherwood. Hunting elk on skees. *See* Our country: West. 1897. p. 73–77.

Emancipation proclamation.
    488. Brooks, Noah. *See his* Abraham Lincoln. 1901. p. 160, 162-64.

Encyclopedia. *See* **Cyclopedias.**

Engineers.
    712. Moffett, Cleveland. *See his* Careers of danger and daring. 1901. p. 377-419.

England—*Description and travel.*
    577. Carpenter, F. G. *See his* Europe. 1902. p. 48-84.
    590. Coe, F. E. *See her* Modern Europe. 1898. p. 18-59. (*World and its people. Bk. 5.*)
    593. Kellogg, E. M. C. *See her* Australia. 1898. p. 137, 266-73. (*World and its people. Bk. 8.*)
    585. Stockton, F. R. England. *See his* Personally conducted. 1889. p. 181-200.

England—*History.*
    462. Clemens, S. L. Prince and the pauper. 1898.
    562. Creighton, Louise. Stories from English history. 1898.
    564. Guerber, H. A. Story of the English. 1898.
    523. Hayens, Herbert. Ye mariners of England. 1901.
    561. Tappan, E. M. England's story. 1901.
    449. Tappan, E. M. In the days of Alfred, the great. 1900.
    450. Tappan, E. M. In the days of William the Conqueror. 1901.
    563. Warren, H. P., ed. Stories from English history. 1901.

England—*History.* (*Fiction.*)
    446. Dix, B. M. Hugh Gwyeth. 1899.
    247. Doyle, A. C. Micah Clarke. 1894.
    452. Green, E. Everett- In the wars of the Roses. 1897.
    242. Hall, Ruth. In the brave days of old. 1898.
    444. Kingsley, Charles. Hereward the Wake, the last of the English. 1893.
    458. Pyle, Howard. Men of iron. 1898.
    453. Scott, *Sir* Walter. Ivanhoe. 1892.
    240. Whistler, C. W. Havelok the Dane. 1900.

English authors. *See* **Biography; Names of authors.**

Epochs of American history series.
    Hart, A. B. *ed.*
    531. Thwaites, R. G. Colonies, 1492-1750. 1898.
    532. Hart, A. B. Formation of the Union, 1750-1829. 1898.
    533. Wilson, Woodrow. Division and reunion, 1829-1889. 1899.

Equator.
    334. Carpenter, F. G. Land of the equator. *See his* South America. 1899. p. 38–50.

Erie canal.
    552. Guerber, H. A. *See his* Story of the great Republic. 1899. p. 91–94.

Erosion.
    634. Dodge, R. E. *See his* Reader in physical geography. 1900. p. 65–127.
    143. Long, C. C. Work of flowing rivers. *See his* Home geography. c1894. p. 59–68.
    142. Payne, F. O. *See his* Geographical nature studies. c1898. p. 61–66.
    See also **Glaciers; Valleys.**

Eskimo. *See* **Esquimaux.**

Esquimaux.
    570. Aldrich, H. L. Arctic Alaska and Siberia. 1889.
    152. Andrews, Jane. Agoonack, the Esquimaux sister. *See her* Seven little sisters. 1890. p. 35–47.
    611. Beard, J. C. Homes of the Eskimos. *See his* Curious homes and their tenants. 1897. p. 167–73.
    145. Muller, Mary. Little people of the snow. 1900.
    330. Murdoch, John. Alaska Eskimo houses. *See* Our country: West. 1897. p. 26–30.
    154. Peary, J. D. Snow baby. 1901.
    31. Perdue, H. A. *and* La Victoire, F. E. *See their* New Century second reader. 1899. p. 38–51.
    141. Shaw, E. R. Greenland. *See his* Big people. 1900. p. 62–69.
    310. Starr, Frederick. *See his* Strange peoples. 1901. p. 6–12.
    322. Tarr, R. S. *and* McMurry, F. M. *See* Index to their North America. 1901. (*Tarr & McMurry's geographies. Bk. 2.*)
    See also **Alaska; Arctic regions.**

Essays.
    605. Burroughs, John. Birds and bees. 1887.
    631. Burroughs, John. Pepacton. 1897.
    642. Burroughs, John. Wake-robin. 1896.
    661. Irving, Washington. Sketch book. 1897.
    660. Warner, C. D. A-hunting of the deer. 1878.

Ethics.
    597. Markwick, W. F. *and* Smith, W. A. True citizen. 1900.
    See also **Amusements; Children; Patriotism; Slavery; Success.**

Ethnology.
    310. Starr, Frederick. List of books regarding Strange peoples. *See his* Strange peoples. 1901. p. 185–86.
    See also **Climate; Folk-lore; Language; Mound-builders; Mythology; Negroes.**

Europe—*Description and travel.*
    577. Carpenter, F. G. Europe. 1902.
    590. Coe, F. E. Modern Europe. 1896.
    571. Knox, T. W. Boy travellers in Central Europe. 1893.
    573. Knox, T. W. Boy travellers in Northern Europe. 1892.
    575. Knox, T. W. Boy travellers in Southern Europe. 1894.
    585. Stockton, F. R. Personally conducted. 1889.
    578. Tarr, R. S. *and* McMurry, F. M. *See their* Europe and other continents. 1901. p 149–352. (*Tarr & McMurry's geographies. Bk. 3.*)
    321. Tarr, R. S. *and* McMurry, F. M. *See their* Home geography. 1901. p. 207–29. (*Tarr & McMurry's geographies. Bk. 1.*)

Europe—*History.*
    310. Starr, Frederick. Peoples of Europe—fair whites; dark whites. *See his* Strange peoples. 1901. p. 33–43.

Expansion.
    598. Conner, E. *See his* Uncle Sam abroad. 1900. p. 159–96.

Explorers.
    536. Brooks, Noah. First across the continent. 1901.
    518. Brooks, Noah. Story of Marco Polo. 1898.
    491. Higginson, T. W. Book of American explorers. 1877.
    525. Jenks, Tudor. Boys' book of explorations. 1900.
    522. Johnson, W. H. World's discoverers. 1900.
    284. Kingsley, N. F. Story of Captain Meriwether Lewis and Captain William Clark. 1900.
    548. Lang, Andrew. *ed.* Burke and Wills exploring expedition. *See his* Red true story book. 1897. p. 80–102.
    299. McMurry, Charles. Pioneer history stories. Ed. 2. 1894.
    120. Pratt, M. L. America's story for America's children. Bk. 2. 1901.
    517. Seelye, E. E. Story of Columbus. 1892.
    277. Shaw, E. R. Discoverers and explorers. 1900.
    296. Thomas, A. C. *See his* Elementary history of the United States. 1901. p. 7–66.
    See also **Geography; Voyages.**

Eye.

755. Burrage, Severance *and* Bailey, H. T. Influence of school life upon the eye. *See their* School sanitation and decoration. 1899. p. 146–58.

Fahrenheit, Gabriel Daniel.

493. Parton, James. Gabriel Daniel Fahrenheit. *See his* Captains of industry. Vol. 2. 1896. p. 148–54.

Fairy tales.

109. Anderson, H. C. Stories. 1891.
108. Baldwin, James. *ed.* Fairy stories and fables. 1895.
114. Baum; L. F. New wonderland. 1900.
254. Bay, J. Christian. *ed.* Danish fairy and folk tales. 1899.
722. Bell, *Mrs.* Hugh. Fairy tale plays and how to act them. 1899.
119. Browne, Frances. Wonderful chair and the tales it told. 1900.
167. Carroll, Lewis. (*pseud.*) Alice's adventures in Wonderland. New ed. 1888.
60. Craik, *Mrs.* D. M. M. Adventures of a brownie. n. d.
79. Craik, *Mrs.* D. M. M. Little lame prince. n. d.
112. Ingelow, Jean. Mopsa the fairy. 1901.
229. Kingsley, Charles. Water babies. n. d.
338. Lang, Andrew. *ed.* Animal story book. 1896.
256. Lang, Andrew. *ed.* Grey fairy book. 1900.
270. Lang, Andrew. *ed.* Violet fairy book. 1901.
252. MacDonald, George. At the back of the north wind. n. d.
106. McMurry, *Mrs.* L. B. Classic stories for little ones. 1894.
86. Prince Uno: Uncle Frank's visit to fairy-land. 1899.
111. Ruskin, John. King of the Golden River. 1898.
91. Scudder, H. E. Seven little people and their friends. 1891.

See also **Folk-lore.**

Faneuil Hall.

494. Brooks, E. S. *See his* Century book of famous Americans. 1896. p. 3–5, 11.
292. Gordy, W. F. *See his* American leaders and heroes. 1901. p. 159–60.

Faraday, Michael.

515. Bolton, *Mrs.* S. K. Michael Faraday. *See her* Boys who became famous. 1885. p. 96–111.

Farming. *See* **Agriculture.**

Farragut, David Glasgow.
    127. Beebe, M. B. Story of Admiral Farragut. *See her* Four American naval heroes. 1899. p. 133-92.
    515. Bolton, Mrs. S. K. David G. Farragut. *See her* Boys who became famous. 1885. p. 219-37.
    503. Roosevelt, Theodore. Farragut at Mobile Bay. *See* Lodge and Roosevelt's Hero tales from American history. 1898. p. 303-22.
    520. Thayer, W. M. *See his* Turning points in successful careers. 1895. p. 1-8.

Fertilization of plants.
    640. Allen, Grant. *See his* Story of the plants. 1898. p. 73-149.

Feudal system.
    526. Griffis, W. E. Feudal system. *See his* Brave little Holland. 1894. p. 64-78.

Field, Cyrus West.
    520. Thayer, W. M. *See his* Turning points in successful careers. 1895. p. 77-82.

Field, Eugene.
    285. Ware, E. R. *See her* Talks about Authors and their work. 1899. p. 199-202.

Field, Marshall.
    509. Marden, O. S. *See his* How they succeeded. 1901. p. 19-29.

Finlanders.
    310. Starr, Frederick. *See his* Strange peoples. 1901. p. 47-53.

Fireman.
    714. Hill, C. T. Fighting a fire. 1897.
    712. Moffett, Cleveland. *See his* Careers of danger and daring. 1901. p. 209-54.
    See also **Chimneys.**

Fish.
    639. Baskett, J. N. Story of the fishes. 1899.
    357. Holder, C. F. *See his* Stories of animal life. 1899. p. 194-247.
    358. Life in the sea. *See* Talks about animals. 1895. p. 3-64.
    See also **Fish-culture; Fishing.**

Fish-culture.
    329. Hawkes, M. New Hampshire fish-farm. *See* Our country: East. 1898. p. 229-32.

262 LIST OF BOOKS FOR TOWNSHIP LIBRARIES.

Fishing.
- 329. Ellis, C. Winter fishing on Saginaw Bay; Maryland fishing-farms. *See* Our Country: East. 1898 p. 16–19, 170–73.
- 571. Ingersoll, Ernest. Fishing and other marine industries. *See his* Book of the ocean. 1898. p. 231–48.
- 322. Tarr, R. S. *and* McMurry, F. M. *See* Index to their North America. 1901. (*Tarr & McMurry's geographies. Bk. 2.*)

Flags.
- 546. Holden, E. S. Our country's flag. 1898.
- 665. Morgan, T. J. *See his* Patriotic citizenship. 1895. p. 37–50.

Flax.
- 155. Bradish, S. P. *See* her Stories of country life. 1901. p. 58–64.

Flies.
- 626. Weed, C. M. Nature biographies. 1901.

Florida—*Description and travel.*
- 584. Carpenter, F. G. Florida and its orange groves. *See his* North America. 1898. p. 130–35.

Florida—*History.*
- 295. Wright, H. C. Purchase of Florida. *See her* Children's stories of American progress. 1898. p. 145–58.

Flowers.
- 633. Dana, Mrs. S. W. Flowers. *See her* Plants and their children. 1896. p. 187–256.
- 612. Gibson, W. H. Eye spy. 1898.
- 637. Gibson, W. H. Sharp eyes. 1891.
- 625. Gibson, W. H. Welcomes of the flowers. *See his* My studio neighbors. 1898. p. 105–48.
- 344. Morley, M. W. Flowers and their friends. 1901.
- 164. Spear, M. A. Leaves and flowers. 1900.

See also **Botany; Buds; Fertilization of plants; Gardening; Plants.**

Flying machines. *See* **Aerial navigation.**

Folk-lore.
- 254. Bay, J. C. *ed.* Danish fairy and folk tales. 1899.
- 263. Bradish, S. P. Old Norse stories. 1900.
- 268. Brun, S. J. Tales of Languedoc. 1899.
- 255. Grimm, J. L. *and* W. K. *eds.* German household tales. 1897.
- 260. Harris, J. C. Aaron in the wildwoods. 1897.
- 258. Harris, J. C. Little Mr. Thimblefinger. 1895.

SUBJECT INDEX.

Folk-lore. (Cont.)
- 259. Harris, J. C. Mr. Rabbit at home. 1895.
- 261. Harris, J. C. Story of Aaron. 1897.
- 118. Harris, J. C. Uncle Remus. 1880.
- 20. Wiltse, S. E. Folklore stories and proverbs. 1901.

  See also **Fairy tales; Legends; Mythology.**

Food.
- 291. Mowry, W. A. *and* A. M. *See their* American inventions and inventors. 1900. p. 99-140.
- 142. Payne, F. O. *See his* Geographical nature studies. 1898. p. 90-93.
- 713. Williams, M. E. *and* Fisher, K. R. Elements of the theory and practice of cookery. 1901.

  See also **Fruit; Grain; Meat; Milk; Mushrooms; Oyster; Sugar.**

Forestry.
- 771. Egleston, N. H. Hand-book of tree-planting. 1900.
- 318. Rocheleau, W. F. Lumber. *See his* Great American industries. Vol. 2. Products of the soil. 1898. p. 36-50.
- 359. Stokes, Susan. Forests and their preservation. *See her* Ten common trees. 1901. p. 105-108.

Fox.
- 638. Burroughs, John. *See his* Squirrels and other fur-bearers. 1900. p. 53-71.

Fox fire.
- 612. Gibson, W. H. *See his* Eye spy. 1898. p. 7-23.

France—*Description and travel.*
- 577. Carpenter, F. G. *See his* Europe. 1902. p. 85-124.
- 571. Knox, T. W. *See his* Boy travellers in Central Europe. 1893. p. 1-257.
- 585. Stockton, F. R. Queen Paris. *See his* Personally conducted. 1889. p. 138-57.

France—*History.*
- 548. Lang, Andrew. *ed. See his* Red true story book. 1897. p. 21-80.

  See also **Napoleon I.**

France—*History.* (*Fiction.*)
- 484. Baldwin, James. Story of Roland. 1901.
- 98. Bouvet, Marguerite. Sweet William. 1895.
- 436. Brooks, E. S. Boy of the first empire. (Napoleon I). 1901.

  See also **French Revolution.** (*Fiction.*)

Franklin, Benjamin.
- 490. Autobiography. 1886.
- 129. Baldwin, James. *See his* Four great Americans. 1897. p. 70–122.
- 498. Bolton, *Mrs.* S. K. *See her* Famous American statesmen. 1888. p. 38–66.
- 494. Brooks, E. S. *See his* Century book of famous Americans. 1896. p. 68–76.
- 507. Brooks, E. S. *See his* Historic Americans. 1899. p. 18–33.
- 286. Brooks, E. S. True story of Benjamin Franklin. 1898.
- 292. Gordy, W. F. *See his* American leaders and heroes. 1901. p. 175–88.
- 555. Guerber, H. A. *See his* Story of the thirteen colonies. 1898. p. 199–205.
- 207. Hawthorne, Nathaniel. *See his* Little Daffydowndilly. 1887. p. 55–68.
- 301. Scudder, H. E. *See his* Short history of the United States. 1890. 89–102.
- 520. Thayer, W. M. *See his* Turning points in successful careers. 1895. p. 346–55.
- 296. Thomas, A. C. *See his* Elementary history of the United States. 1901. p. 150–67.

Free soilers.
- 488. Brooks, Noah. *See his* Abraham Lincoln. 1901. p. 75–6, 77.

Fremont, John Charles.
- 299. McMurry, Charles. *See his* Pioneer history stories. 1895. p. 149–62.

French and Indian war.
- 298. Holman, Alma. *See her* Massasoit. 1897. p. 253–61.
- 296. Thomas, A. C. *See his* Elementary history of the United States. 1901. p. 168–86.
- *See also* Indexes to United States histories on list.

French and Indian war. (*Fiction.*)
- 476. Stratemeyer, Edward. With Washington in the west. 1901.

French Revolution. (*Fiction.*)
- 469. Bouvet, Marguerite. Tales of an old chateau. 1899.

Frog.
- 356. Kelly, *Mrs.* M. A. B. Mr. Rana's dinner. *See her* Short stories of our shy neighbors. 1896. p. 41–51.

SUBJECT INDEX.

Froissart, *Sir* **John.**
    378. Singleton, Adam. *ed.* Chronicles of Sir John Froissart. 1900.

Fruit.
    633. Dana, *Mrs.* W. S. Fruits and seeds. *See her* Plants and their children. 1896. p. 9–74.
    329. Munroe, Kirk. Pineapples; Cape Cod cranberries. *See* Our country: East. 1898. p. 106–210.
    See also **Agriculture; Gardening.**

Fry, Elizabeth.
    500. Bolton, *Mrs.* S. K. *See her* Lives of girls who became famous. 1886. p. 240–60.
    493. Parton, James. *See his* Captains of industry. Vol. 2. 1896. p. 344–52.
    520. Thayer, W. M. *See his* Turning points in successful careers. 1895. p. 188–95.

Fuel.
    291. Mowry, W. A. *and* A. M. *See their* American inventions and inventors. 1900. p. 37–43.
    See also **Coal; Gas; Petroleum.**

Fulton, Robert.
    292. Gordy, W. F. *See his* American leaders and heroes. 1901. p. 246–52.
    126. Perry, F. M. *See her* Four American inventors. 1901. p. 11–69.
    504. Towle, G. M. Robert Fulton and the steamboat. *See his* Heroes and martyrs of invention. 1892. p. 160–69.
    295. Wright, H. C. First steamboat. *See her* Children's stories of American progress. 1898. p. 104–20.

Fur-traders.
    540. Legler, H. E. *See his* Leading events of Wisconsin history. 1898. p. 118–21, 152–56.
    556. Thwaites, R. G. Explorers and fur-traders of New France. *See his* Story of Wisconsin. 1891. p. 61–88.

Galls.
    353. Needham, J. G. Houses that grow. *See his* Outdoor studies. 1898. p. 18–28.

Gamo, Vasco da. *See* **Vasco da Gamo.**

Games *and* Sports.
- 718. Beard, D. C. Outdoor handy book for playground, field and forest. 1900.
- 717. Beard, D. C. Jack of all trades. 1900.
- 706. Beard, L. *and* A. B. How to amuse yourselves and others; the American girls' handy book. 1890.
- 707. Campbell, Helen. *See her* American girl's home book of work and play. 1896. p. 23–101.
- 728. Champlin, J. D. *and* Bostwick, A. E. Young folks' cyclopedia of games and sports. 1899.
- 709. Thompson, Maurice. *ed.* Boys' book of sports and outdoor life. 1886.

See also **Kindergarten; Bull fights; Camping; Hunting; Skating; Yachting; School life.**

Gardening.
- 775. Goff, E. S. Principles of plant culture. 1899.

See also **Agriculture; Botany; Fruit.**

Garfield, James Abram.
- 498. Bolton, *Mrs.* S. K. *See her* Famous American statesmen. 1888. p. 361–99.
- 516. Brooks, Noah. *See his* Statesmen. 1898. p. 313–32.
- 520. Thayer, W. M. *See his* Turning points in successful careers. 1895. p. 111–21.

Garibaldi, Guiseppe.
- 515. Bolton, *Mrs.* S. K. *See her* Poor boys who became famous. 1885. p. 172–86.

Garrison, William Lloyd.
- 515. Bolton, *Mrs.* S. K. *See her* Poor boys who became famous. 1885. p. 156–71.

Gas.
- 329. Munroe, Kirk. Natural gas. *See* Our country: East. 1898. p. 41–45.
- 317. Rocheleau, W. F. Natural gas. *See his* Great American industries. Vol. 1. Minerals. 1896. p. 69–74.
- 322. Tarr, R. S. *and* McMurry, F. M. *See their* North America. 1901. p. 173–74; 255–56; 413. (*Tarr and McMurry's geographies. Bk. 2.*)

Geography.
- 152. Andrews, Jane. Seven little sisters. 1894.
- 153. Andrews, Jane. Seven little sisters prove their sisterhood. 1890.

Geography (Cont.).
- 315. By land and sea. 1895.
- 314. Carpenter, F. G. Asia. 1897.
- 577. Carpenter, F. G. Europe. 1902.
- 584. Carpenter, F. G. North America. 1898.
- 334. Carpenter, F. G. South America. 1899.
- 139. Carroll, S. W. Around the world. Bk. 1. 1901.
- 140. Carroll, S. W. *and* Jerome, H. L. Around the world. Bk. 2. 1897.
- 313. Carroll, S. W. *and* Hart, E. M. Around the world. Bk. 3. 1901.
- Dunton, Larkin, ed. *See* World and its people series.
- 332. King, C. F. Land we live in. Vol. 1. 1892. (*Picturesque geographical readers. Bk. 3.*)
- 333. King, C. F. Land we live in. Vol. 2. 1893. (*Picturesque geographical readers. Bk. 4.*)
- 331. King, C. F. This continent of ours. 1891. (*Picturesque geographical readers. Bk. 2.*)
- 143. Long, C. C. Home geography. 1894.
- 147. Longmans' pictorial geographical readers. Bk. 1. 1901.
- 330. Our country: West. 1897.
- 329. Our country: East. 1898.
- 142. Payne, F. O. Geographical nature studies. 1898.
- 31. Perdue, H. A. *and* La Victoire, F. E. New Century second reader. 1899.
- 320. Pratt, M. H. S. Guyot geographical reader. 1882.
- 141. Shaw, E. R. Big people and little people of other lands. 1900.
- 578. Tarr, R. S. *and* McMurry, F. M. Europe and other continents. 1901. (*Tarr & McMurry's geographies. Bk. 3.*)
- 321. Tarr, R. S. *and* McMurry, F. M. Home geography. 1901. (*Tarr & McMurry's geographies. Bk. 1.*)
- 322. Tarr, R. S. *and* McMurry, F. M. North America. 1901. (*Tarr & McMurry's geographies. Bk. 2.*)
- 141a. Taylor, Bayard. Boys of other countries. 1901.
- 148. Wade, M. H. Our little Brown cousin. 1901. (*Little cousin series.*)
- 149. Wade, M. H. Our little Indian cousin. 1901. (*Little cousin series.*)
- 150. Wade, M. H. Our little Japanese cousin. 1901. (*Little cousin series.*)
- 151. Wade, M. H. Our little Russian cousin. 1901. (*Little cousin series.*)

See also **Arctic regions; Ethnology; Explorers; Voyages and travels.**

Geography—*Bibliography.*
    321. Tarr, R. S. *and* McMurry, F. M. *See their* Home geography. 1901. p. 256-61. (*Tarr & McMurry's geographies. Bk. 1.*)

German literature.
    271. Frost, W. H. Wagner story book. 1898.

Germany—*Description and travel.*
    152. Andrews, Jane. Louise, the child of the beautiful river Rhine. *See her* Seven little sisters. 1890. p. 108-136.
    577. Carpenter, F. G. *See his* Europe. 1902. p. 186-233.
    315. Dexter, M. Down the Moselle. See By land and sea. 1895. p. 47-52.
    31. Perdue, H. A. *and* La Victoire, F. E. *See their* New Century second reader. 1899. p. 138-46.
    141a. Taylor, Bayard. Boys of other countries. 1901.

Gettysburg.
    503. Lodge, H. C. *and* Roosevelt, Theodore. *See their* Hero tales from American history. 1898. p. 227-36.

Gibraltar, *siege of.* (*Fiction.*)
    463. Seawell, M. E. Rock of the lion. 1898.

Glaciers.
    634. Dodge, R. E. *See his* Reader in physical geography. 1900. p. 121-36.
    322. Tarr, R. S. *and* McMurry, F. M. *See their* North America. 1901. p. 12-19, 324-25, 375-76. (*Tarr & McMurry's geographies. Bk. 2.*)
    See also **Erosion; Ice.**

Glass.
    319. Rocheleau, W. F. *See his* Great American industries. Vol. 3, Manufactures. 1900. p. 37-74.

Glover, Joshua.
    540. Legler, H. E. Rescue of Joshua Glover, a runaway slave. *See his* Leading events of Wisconsin history. 1898. p. 226-29.

Gold.
    313. Carroll, S. W. *and* Hart, E. M. Gold mining. *See their* Around the world. Bk. 3. 1901. p. 133-39.
    317. Rocheleau, W. F. Gold and silver. *See his* Great American industries. Vol. 1, Minerals. 1896. p. 163-92.
    295. Wright, H. C. Discovery of gold. *See her* Children's stories of American progress. 1898. p. 279-98.
    See also **Mines and mining.**

Goldenrod.
    353. Needham, J. G. Goldenrod; its visitors and its tenants. *See his* Outdoor studies. 1898. p. 29-46.

Goldsmith, Oliver.
    515. Bolton, *Mrs.* S. K. Oliver Goldsmith. *See her* Boys who became famous. 1885. p. 90-95.

Gopher.
    358. Milvain, Edward. About gophers. *See* Talks about animals. 1895. p. 182-85.

Gould, Helen.
    509. Marden, O. S. *See his* How they succeeded. 1901. p. 44-64.

Government.
    321. Tarr, R. S. *and* McMurry, F. M. *See their* Home geography. 1901. p. 92-101. (*Tarr & McMurry's geographies. Bk. 1.*)

Grain.
    143. Long, C, C. Useful grains. *See his* Home geography. c1894. p. 88-92.
    318. Rocheleau, W. F. Cereals. *See his* Great American industries. Vol. 2. Products of the soil. 1898. p. 124-78.
    See also **Wheat.**

Grand cañon.
    330. Owens, J. G. Grand canon. *See* Our country: West. 1897. p. 161-66.

Granite.
    317. Rocheleau, W. F. Granite. *See his* Great American industries. Vol. 1. Minerals. 1896. p. 135-55.

Grant, Ulysses Simpson.
    498. Bolton, *Mrs.* S. K. *See her* Famous American statesmen. 1888. p. 307-60.
    494. Brooks, E. S. *See his* Century book of famous Americans. 1896. p. 180-91.
    507. Brooks, E. S. *See his* Historic Americans. 1899. p. 369-84.
    288. Brooks, E. S. True story of U. S. Grant. 1897.
    488. Brooks, Noah. *See his* Abraham Lincoln. 1901. p. 76, 79-81, 188-93.
    128. Burton, A. H. *See his* Four American patriots. 1898. p. 195-254.
    292. Gordy, W. F. *See his* American leaders and heroes. 1901. p. 302-13.

Grant, Ulysses Simpson. (Cont.)
    503. Lodge, H. C. General Grant and the Vicksburg campaign. *See* Lodge and Roosevelt's Hero tales from American history. 1898. p. 239-48.
    520. Thayer, W. M. *See his* Turning points in successful careers. 1895. p. 92-101.

Grasshoppers.
    626. Weed, C. M. Nature biographies. 1901.

Great Lakes.
    313. Carroll, S. W. *and* Hart, E. M. *See their* Around the world. Bk. 3. 1901. p. 63-73.

Great Salt Lake.
    313. Carroll, S. W. *and* Hart, E. M. *See their* Around the world. Bk. 3. 1901. p. 147-49.

Great Seal of U. S.
    430. Drysdale, William. *See his* Young consul. 1901. p. 53-70.

Greece—*Description and travel.*
    593. Kellogg, E. M. C. *See her* Australia and islands of the sea. 1898. p. 314, 319. (*World and its people. Bk. 8.*)

Greece—*History, Ancient.*
    267. Clarke, M. Story of Troy. 1898.
    309. Guerber, H. A. Story of the Greeks. 1896.
    303. Harding, C. H. *and* S. B. Stories from Greek history. *See their* Stories of Greek gods. 1897. p. 129-95.

Greece—*Literature.*
    486. Baldwin, James. Story of the golden age. 1901.
    482. Church, Alfred J. Stories from Homer. 1901.
    269. Hawthorne, Nathaniel. Tanglewood tales. 1883.

Greeley, Horace.
    515. Bolton, *Mrs.* S. K. *See her* Boys who became famous. 1885. p. 138-55.
    477. Parton, James. Horace Greeley's start. *See his* Captains of industry. Vol. 1. 1891. p. 254-63.

Greene, Nathaniel.
    292. Gordy, W. F. *See his* American leaders and heroes. 1901. p. 210-21.

Greenland—*Description and travel.*
 593. Kellogg, E. M. C. Pen pictures of Greenland. *See her* Australia and the islands of the sea. 1898. p. 95–102. (*World and its people series. Bk. 8.*)
 141. Shaw, E. R. Greenland. *See his* Big people. 1900. p. 62–69.
 See also **Arctic regions.**

Grenville, *Sir* **Richard.**
 548. Lang, Andrew. *ed. See his* Red true story book. 1897. p. 102–108.

Grimm, Jakob L. *and* **W. K.**
 285. Ware, E. R. Grimm Brothers. *See her* Talks about Authors and their work. 1899. p. 37–40.

Gulf stream.
 315. Pillsbury, J. E. *See* By land and sea. 1895. p. 201–206.

Gutenberg, John.
 504. Towle, G. M. John Gutenberg, the inventor of the printing-press. *See his* Heroes and martyrs of invention. 1892. p. 33–42.

Hale, Edward Everett.
 285. Ware, E. R. *See her* Talks about Authors and their work. 1899. p. 153–58.

Hale, Nathan.
 301. Scudder, H. E. *See his* Short history of the United States. 1890. p. 139–40.

Halloween.
 706. Beard, Lina *and* A. B. *See their* American girls' handy book. 1890. p. 180–200.
 707. Campbell, Helen. *See her* American girl's home book of work and play. 1896. p. 144–46.

Hamilton, Alexander.
 498. Bolton, *Mrs.* S. K. *See her* Famous American statesmen. 1888. p. 99–132.
 494. Brooks, E. S. *See his* Century book of famous Americans. 1896. p. 54–63.
 507. Brooks, E. S. *See his* Historic Americans. 1899. p. 115–29.
 128. Burton, A. H. *See his* Four American patriots. 1898. p. 71–130.

Harris, Joel Chandler.
    285. Ware, E. R. *See her* Talks about Authors and their work. 1899. p. 190-97.

Harvard college.
    541. Drake, S. A. *See his* Making of New England. 1900. p. 214-16.

Hawaiian islands—*Description and travel.*
    313. Carroll, S. W. *and* Hart, E. M. *See their* Around the world. Bk. 3. 1901. p. 228-40.
    326. George, M. M. Little journeys to Hawaii and the Philippine islands. 1900.
    579. Greater America. 1900. p. 131-89.
    552. Guerber, H. A. *See his* Story of the great Republic. 1899. p. 323-31.
    593. Kellogg, E. M. C. Hawaiian islands. *See her* Australia and the islands of the sea. 1898. (*World and its people series. Bk. 8.*)
    312. Krout, M. H. Alice's visit to the Hawaiian islands. 1900.
    322. Tarr, R. S. *and* McMurry, F. M. *See their* North America. 1901. p. 336-40. (*Tarr & McMurry's geographies. Bk. 2.*)
    580. Twombly, A. S. Hawaii and its people. 1900.

Hawthorne, Nathaniel.
    285. Ware, E. R. *See her* Talks about Authors and their work. 1899. p. 52-61.

Hawthorne readers series.
    21. Gilman, M. L. *and* Austin, I. *and* Blaisdell, S. L. Little-folk tales. 1901. Bk. 1.
    22. Hall, M. F. *and* Gilman, M. L. Story land. 1901. Bk. 2.
    23. Holbrook, Florence *and* Hall, M. F. From many lands. 1901. Bk. 3.

Heat.
    291. Mowry, W. A. *and* A. M. *See their* American inventions and inventors. 1900. p. 11-57.

Helena (*Constantine's mother*).
    508. Brooks, E. S. *See his* Historic girls. 1887. p. 22-44.

Hennepin, Louis.
    299. McMurry, Charles. Hennepin's trip up the Mississippi. *See his* Pioneer history stories. 1895. p. 69-77.

Henry, Patrick.
- 494. Brooks, E. S. *See his* Century book of famous Americans. 1896. p. 94–101.
- 507. Brooks, E. S. *See his* Historic Americans. 1899. p. 73–85.
- 128. Burton, A. H. *See his* Four American patriots. 1898. p. 9–68.
- 292. Gordy, W. F. *See his* American leaders and heroes. 1901. p. 146–55.
- 520. Thayer, W. M. *See his* Turning points in successful careers. 1895. p. 395–402.

Herodotus.
- 569. Boden, G. H. *and* D'Almeida, W. B. Wonder stories from Herodotus. 1900.

Herreshoff, John B.
- 509. Marden, O. S. *See his* How they succeeded. 1901. p. 276–303.

Hills.
- 321. Tarr, R. S. *and* McMurry, F. M. *See their* Home geography. 1901. p. 10–16. (*Tarr & McMurry's geographies. Bk. 1.*)

Hindus.
- 310. Starr, Frederick. *See his* Strange peoples. 1901. p. 101–107.

Historical fiction.
- 437. Allen, W. B. Cleared for action. 1900.
- 448. Altsheler, J. A. In hostile red. 1900.
- 484. Baldwin, James. Story of Roland. 1901.
- 495. Barnes, James. Commodore Bainbridge. 1897.
- 440. Barnes, James. For king or country. 1898.
- 501. Barnes, James. Hero of Erie, Oliver Hazard Perry. 1898.
- 456. Barnes, James. Loyal traitor. 1899.
- 512. Barnes, James. Midshipman Farragut. 1898.
- 478. Barnes, James. Yankee ships and Yankee sailors. 1898.
- 445. Barton, W. E. Hero in homespun. 1897.
- 461. Barton, W. E. Prairie schooner. 1900.
- 438. Blanchard, A. E. Daughter of freedom. 1900.
- 469. Bouvet, Marguerite. Tales of an old chateau. 1899.
- 436. Brooks, E. S. Boy of the first empire. 1901.
- 441. Brooks, E. S. Godson of Lafayette. 1900.
- 466. Brooks, E. S. Son of the Revolution. 1898.
- 432. Champney, E. W. Anneke. 1900.
- 471. Church, A. J. Three Greek children. 1895.
- 380. Churchill, Winston. Crisis. 1901.
- 454. Cooper, J. F. Last of the Mohicans. 1900.

Historical fiction (Cont.).

- 467. Craddock, C. E. Story of old Fort Loudon. 1899.
- 465. Dix, B. M. Soldier Rigdale. 1899.
- 247. Doyle, A. C. Micah Clarke. 1894.
- 235. Drysdale, William. Cadet Standish of the St. Louis. 1899.
- 443. Eggleston, Edward. Graysons. 1900.
- 452. Green, E. E. In the Wars of the Roses. 1897.
- 457. Hale, E. E. Man without a country. 1899. New ed.
- 442. Hall, Ruth. Golden arrow. 1901.
- 242. Hall, Ruth. In the brave days of old. 1898.
- 130. Hawthorne, Nathaniel. Grandfather's chair. 1883.
- 236. Jenks, A. E. Childhood of Ji-shib, the Ojibwa. 1900.
- 444. Kingsley, Charles. Hereward the Wake, the last of the English. 1893.
- 246. Mann, M. E. Margot: the Court shoemaker's child. 1901.
- 447. Mitchell, S. W. Hugh Wynne, free quaker. 1900.
- 455. Ogden, Ruth. Loyal hearts and true. 1899.
- 289. Otis, James. With Perry on Lake Erie. 1899.
- 474. Otis James. With Porter in the Essex. 1901.
- 475. Otis, James. With Preble at Tripoli. 1900.
- 233. Page, T. N. Among the camps. 1892.
- 250. Page, T. N. Two little confederates. 1891.
- 238. Plympton, A. G. Flower of the wilderness. 1899.
- 458. Pyle, Howard. Men of iron. 1898.
- 459. Pyle, Howard. Merry adventures of Robin Hood. 1883.
- 249. Pyle, Howard. Otto of the silver hand. 1901.
- 453. Scott, *Sir* Walter. Ivanhoe. 1892.
- 276. Seawell, M. E. Decatur and Somers. 1894.
- 463. Seawell, M. E. Rock of the lion. 1898.
- 464. Stevenson, B. E. Soldier of Virginia. 1901.
- 196. Stoddard, W. O. Jack Morgan. 1901.
- 245. Stoddard, W. O. Little Smoke. 1898.
- 248. Stoddard, W. O. Noank's log. 1900.
- 435. Tomlinson, E. T. Boys of Old Monmouth. 1898.
- 451. Tomlinson, E. T. In the hands of the red coats. 1900.
- 470. Tomlinson, E. T. Three colonial boys. 1895.
- 472. Tomlinson, E. T. Three young continentals. 1896.
- 473. Tomlinson, E. T. Washington's young aids. 1897.
- 462. Twain, Mark. Prince and the pauper. 1898.
- 240. Whistler, C. W. Havelok the Dane. 1900.
- 241. Wilkins, M. E. In colonial times. 1899.

History, *Ancient.*

- 567. Arnold, E. J. Stories of ancient peoples. 1901.

History. *See also* **Crusades; Ethnology; Geography; Historical fiction; History,** *Ancient***; Middle ages; Names of countries.**

Holland—*Description and travel.*
  577. Carpenter, F. G. *See his* Europe. 1902. p. 133–55.
  191. Dodge, M. M. Hans Brinker. 1901.
  324. Dodge, M. M. Land of pluck. 1894.
    31. Perdue, H. A. *and* La Victoire, F. E. *See their* New Century second reader. 1899. p. 118–38.
  315. Scenes in Holland. *See* By land and sea. 1895. p. 12–15.
  141. Shaw, E. R. *See his* Big people. 1900. p. 83–91.
  585. Stockton, F. R. *See his* Personally conducted. 1889. p. 201–8.

Holland—*History.*
  526. Griffis, W. E. Brave little Holland. 1894.

Holmes, Oliver Wendell.
  279. Cody, Sherwin. *See his* Four American poets. 1899. p. 195–254.

Homer.
  262. Burt, M. E. *and* Ragozin, Z. A. Odysseus: the hero of Ithaca. 1898.
  482. Church, A. J. Stories from Homer. 1901.
  267. Clarke, M., *ed.* Story of Troy. 1897.
  117. Cook, A. S., *ed.* Story of Ulysses. 1897.

Horse.
  397. Ensign, H. L. Lady Lee and other animal stories. 1901.
  156. Pierson, C. D. Bay colt learns to mind. *See her* Among the farmyard people. 1899. p. 64–81.

Hosmer, Harriet G.
  500. Bolton, *Mrs.* S. K. *See her* Lives of girls who became famous. 1886. p. 141–57.

Howe, (*Mrs.*) Julia Ward.
  509. Marden, O. S. *See his* How they succeeded. 1901. p. 209–19.

Howells, William Dean.
  509. Marden, O. S. *See his* How they succeeded. 1901. p. 171–84.
  285. Ware, E. R. *See her* Talks about Authors and their work. 1899. p. 141–47.

Hudson, Henry.
    491. Higginson, T.. W., *ed.* Henry Hudson and the New Netherlands. *See his* Book of American explorers. 1877. p. 281–307.

Hull, Isaac.
    521. Seawell, M. E. *See her* Twelve naval captains. 1899. p. 145–66.

Humming bird.
    357. Holder, C. F. *See his* Stories of animal life. 1899. p. 78–86.

Hundred years war.
    563. Warren, H. P., *ed. See his* Stories from English history. 1901. p. 121–37.

Hunting.
    313. Carroll, S. W. *and* Hart, E. M. Maine woods. *See their* Around the world. Bk. 3. 1901. p. 28–38.
    175. Hornibrook, Isabel. Camp and trail. 1897.
    705. Roosevelt, Theodore, *and* Grinnell, G. B. American big-game hunting. 1893.
    See also **Dogs; Fishing.**

Ice.
    313. Carroll, S. W. *and* Hart, E. M. Ice crop. *See their* Around the world. Bk. 3. 1901. p. 212–14.
    See also **Alps; Arctic regions; Glaciers; Skating.**

Icebergs.
    315. Harvey, M. About icebergs. *See* By land and sea. 1895. p. 195–99.

Iceland—*Description and travel.*
    141a. Taylor, Bayard. Boys of other countries. 1901.
    See also **Arctic regions.**

India—*Description and travel.*
    315. Duncan, S. J. *and others.* House keeping in East India. *See* By land and sea. 1895. p. 166–77.
    141. Shaw, E. R. India. *See his* Big people. 1900. p. 46–52.
    310. Starr, Frederick. *See his* Strange peoples. 1901. p. 101–17.

India—*Description and travel. (Fiction.)*
    422. Duncan, S. J. Story of Sonny Sahib. 1896.

Indian corn. *See* **Maize.**

Indians of North America.
- 536. Brooks, Noah. First across the continent. 1901.
- 584. Carpenter, F. G. Among the Indians. *See his* North America. 1898. p. 290–97.
- 313. Carroll, S. W. *and* Hart, E. M. *See their* Around the world. Bk. 3. 1901. p. 39–42, 150–52.
- 541. Drake, S. A. Indian traits. *See his* Making of New England. 1900. p. 142–48.
- 543. Drake, S. A. *See his* Making of Virginia and the middle colonies. 1893. p. 30–31, 40–42, 86–107.
- 553. Grinnell, G. B. Story of the Indian. 1898.
- 298. Holman, Alma. Massasoit. 1897.
- 134. Husted, M. H. Stories of Indian chieftains. 1900.
- 311. Judd, M. C. Wigwam stories told by North American Indians. 1901.
- 333. King, C. F. Indians. *See his* Land we live in. Vol. 2. 1893. p. 197–208. (*Picturesque Geog. readers. Bk. 4.*)
- 284. Kingsley, N. F. Story of Captain Meriwether Lewis and Captain William Clark. 1900.
- 548. Lang, Andrew, *ed.* Peter Williamson. *See his* Red true story book. 1897. p. 108–19.
- 540. Legler, H. E. Red men of Wisconsin. *See his* Leading events of Wisconsin history. 1898. p. 22–28.
- 291. Mowry, W. A. *and* A. M. Indian homes. *See their* American inventions and inventors. 1900. p. 17–23.
- 31. Perdue, H. A. *and* La Victoire, F. E. *See their* New Century second reader. 1899. p. 9–33.
- 301. Scudder, H. E. How the Indians lived. *See his* Short history of the United States. 1890. p. 14–21, 81–82.
- 141. Shaw, E. R. *See his* Big people. 1900. p. 103–9.
- 237. Snedden, G. S. Docas, the Indian boy of Santa Clara. 1899.
- 290. Starr, Frederick. American Indians. 1899.
- 310. Starr, Frederick. Wild Indians. *See his* Strange peoples. 1901. p. 13–16.
- 322. Tarr, R. S. *and* McMurry, F. M. *See* Index to their North America. 1901. (*Tarr & McMurry's geographies. Bk. 2.*)
- 330. Uberroth, P. H. Cave-dwellers of Arizona. *See* Our country: West. 1897. p. 167–72.
- 149. Wade, M. H. Our little Indian cousin. 1901.

See also Indexes to United States histories on list.

Indians of North America. (*Fiction.*)
- 454. Cooper, J. F. Last of the Mohicans. 1900.
- 467. Craddock, C. E. Story of old Fort Loudon. 1899.

Indians of North America (Cont.).
- 376. Doubleday, Russell. Cattle ranch to college. 1899.
- 234. Eggleston, G. C. Big brother: a story of Indian war. 1898.
- 396. Grinnell, G. B. Jack among the Indians. 1900.
- 135. Husted, M. H. Stories of Indian children, 1898.
- 236. Jenks, A. E. Childhood of Ji-shib, the Ojibwa. 1900.
- 404. La Flesche, Francis. Middle-five Indian boys at school. 1900.
- 245. Stoddard, W. O. Little Smoke. 1898.

See also **Mound-builders.**

Indians of North America—*Bibliography*.
- 682. Books relating to the Indians. *See* Longfellow's "Song of Hiawatha." 1898. p. 11–12.

Industrial arts. *See* **Arts, Useful; Manufactures.**

Ingelow, Jean.
- 500. Bolton, *Mrs.* S. K. *See her* Lives of girls who became famous. 1886. p. 331–47.

Insects.
- 616. Allen, Grant. *See his* Flashlights on nature. 1898. p. 1–24; 121–203; 232–57; 284–312.
- 645. Du Chaillu, Paul. World of the great forest. 1900.
- 612. Gibson, W. H. Eye spy. 1898.
- 625. Gibson, W. H. My studio neighbors. 1898.
- 637. Gibson, W. H. Sharp eyes. 1891.
- 356. Kelly, *Mrs.* M. A. B. *See her* Short stories of our shy neighbors. 1896. p. 72–75; 84–91; 98–108; 131–39; 155–58.
- 353. Needham, J. G. Bogus eyes. *See his* Outdoor studies. 1898. p. 73–80.
- 773. Shepard, H. H. *See his* Life on the farm. 1901. p. 104–29.
- 619. Treat, Mary. *See her* Home studies in nature. 1885. p. 79–136.
- 346. Weed, C. M. Insect world. 1899.
- 623. Weed, C. M. Life histories of American insects. 1897.
- 626. Weed, C. M. Nature biographies. 1901.

See also **Bees; Beetle; Butterflies; Moths.**

Inventions.
- 610. Baker, R. S. Boy's book of inventions. 1899.
- 552. Guerber, H. A. *See his* Story of the great Republic. 1899. p. 109–13.
- 291. Mowry, W. A. *and* A. M. *See their* American inventions and inventors. 1900.
- 504. Towle, G. M. Heroes and martyrs of invention. 1890.

See also **Edison; Franklin; Fulton; Morse; Whitney; Inventors.**

Inventors.

126. Perry, F. M. Four American inventors. 1901.
296. Thomas, A. C. John Fitch, Robert Fulton, Eli Whitney, and others. *See his* Elementary history of the United States. 1901. p. 253-64, 277-89.

See also **Names of Inventors.**

Ireland—*Description and travel.*

577. Carpenter, F. G. *See his* Europe. 1902. p. 15-31.

Ireland—*History.*

560. Joyce, P. W. Child's history of Ireland. 1897.

Iron.

155. Bradish, S. P. *See her* Stories of country life. 1901. p. 134-43.
584. Carpenter, F. G. Pittsburg and its iron works. *See his* North America. 1898. p. 218-25.
313. Carroll, S. W. *and* Hart, E. M. *See their* Around the world. Bk. 3. 1901. p. 53-56.
333. King, C. F. Iron furnaces. *See his* Land we live in. Vol. 2. 1893. p. 51-60. (*Picturesque geographical readers. Bk. 4.*)
317. Rocheleau, W. F. *See his* Great American industries. vol. 1. Minerals. 1896. p. 75-112.

See also **Mines and mining.**

Irrigation.

322. Tarr, R. S. *and* McMurry, F. M. *See their* North America. 1901. p. 297-302. (*Tarr & McMurry's geographies. Bk. 2.*)

See also **Canals.**

Irving, Washington.

507. Brooks, E. S. *See his* Historic Americans. 1899. p. 263-76.
285. Ware, E. R. *See her* Talks about Authors and their work. 1899. p. 26-36.

Islands.

593. Kellogg, E. M. C. Australia and the islands of the sea. 1898. (*World and its people series. Bk. 8.*)

Italy—*Description and travel.*

369. Hoyt, D. L. Barbara's heritage. 1899.
575. Knox, T. W. *See his* Boy travellers in Southern Europe. 1894. p. 1-349.

Jackson, Andrew.
- 498. Bolton, *Mrs.* S. K. *See her* Famous American statesmen. 1888. p. 133-76.
- 494. Brooks, E. S. *See his* Century book of famous Americans. 1896. p. 162-72.
- 507. Brooks, E. S. *See his* Historic Americans. 1899. p. 231-46.
- 128. Burton, A. H. *See her* Four American patriots. 1898. p. 133-92.
- 292. Gordy, W. F. *See his* American leaders and heroes. 1901. p. 253-63.
- 493. Parton, James. *See his* Captains of industry. vol. 2. 1896. p. 98-110.

Jackson, *Mrs.* Helen Hunt.
- 500. Bolton, *Mrs.* S. K. *See her* Lives of girls who became famous. 1886. p. 18-32.
- 520. Thayer, W. M. *See his* Turning points in successful careers. 1895. p. 329-37.

James, Reuben.
- 283. Brady, C. T. Reuben James. 1900.

Jamestown.
- 301. Scudder, H. E. First English colony. *See his* Short history of the United States. 1890. p. 36-39.

Japan—*Description and travel*.
- 316. Ayrton, *Mrs.* M. C. Child-life in Japan and Japanese child stories. 1901.
- 582. Bacon, A. M. Japanese girls and women. 1891.
- 315. Goodrich, J. K. *and others.* Japanese garden party. *See* By land and sea. 1895. p. 147-59.
- 576. Knox, T. W. Adventures of two youths in a journey to Japan and China. 1879.
- 31. Perdue, H. A. *and* La Victoire, F. E. *See their* New Century second reader. 1899. p. 77-96.
- 141. Shaw, E. R. Japan. *See his* Big people. 1900. p. 15-24.
- 150. Wade, M. H. Our little Japanese cousin. 1901.

Japan—*History*.
- 565. Van Bergen, R. Story of Japan. 1897.

Japanese.
- 310. Starr, Frederick. *See his* Strange peoples. 1901. p. 88-95.

SUBJECT INDEX.

Jay, John.
    507. Brooks, E. S. *See his* Historic Americans. 1899. p. 146-60.

Jefferson, Thomas.
    498. Bolton, *Mrs.* S. K. *See her* Famous American statesmen. 1888. p. 67-98.
    494. Brooks, E. S. *See his* Century book of famous Americans. 1896. p. 125-32.
    507. Brooks, E. S. *See his* Historic Americans. 1899. p. 100-14.
    292. Gordy, W. F. *See his* American leaders and heroes. 1901. p. 234-45.
    296. Thomas, A. C. *See his* Elementary history of the United States. 1901. p. 232-40.

Jelly fishes.
    357. Holder, C. F. *See his* Stories of animal life. 1899. p. 133-39.

Jesuits.
    540. Legler, H. E. Jesuits in Wisconsin. *See his* Leading events of Wisconsin history. 1898. p. 62-77.

Jewish history.
    137. Guerber, H. A. Story of the chosen people. 1896.

Joan of Arc.
    548. Lang, Andrew, *ed. See his* Red true story book. 1897. p. 21-80.
    563. Warren, H. P., *ed. See his* Stories from English history. 1901. p. 133-37.

John Brown's raid.
    552. Guerber, H. A. *See his* Story of the great Republic. 1899. p. 156-61.

Johnson, Samuel.
    515. Bolton, *Mrs.* S. K. *See her* Boys who became famous. 1885. p. 83-89.
    207. Hawthorne, Nathaniel. *See his* Little Daffydowndilly. 1887. p. 32-42.

Joliet, Louis.
    299. McMurry, Charles. Joliet and Marquette. *See his* Pioneer history stories. 1895. p. 60-68.
    See also **Explorers.**

Jones, John Paul.
  127. Beebe, M. B. *See her* Four American naval heroes. 1899. p. 17-68.
  282. Seawell, M. E. Paul Jones. 1893.
  521. Seawell, M. E. *See her* Twelve naval captains. 1899. p. 1-27.

Junior Republic.
  181. Thurston, I. T. Citizen Dan of the Junior Republic. 1901.

Kindergarten.
  752. Arnold, S. L., *ed.* Kindergarten occupations. *See her* Plans for busy work. 1901. p. 3-7.
  750. Beebe, Katharine. First school year. 1895.
  See also Child study; Nature study.

Kindergarten stories.
  66. Boston collection of kindergarten stories. 1898.
  104. Menefee, Maud. Child stories from the masters. 1901.
  68. Poulsson, Emilie. Child stories and rhymes. 1898.
  99. Poulsson, Emilie. Through the farmyard gate. 1896.

King Philip's war.
  298. Holman, Alma. *See her* Massasoit. 1897. p. 193-205.
  296. Thomas, A. C. *See his* Elementary history of the United States. 1901. p. 95-101.

Kingsley, Charles.
  285. Ware, E. R. *See her* Talks about Authors and their work. 1899. p. 126-31.

Kipling, Rudyard.
  285. Ware, E. R. *See her* Talks about Authors and their work. 1899. p. 219-30.

Kites.
  610. Baker, R. S. *See his* Boy's book of inventions. 1899. p. 207-47.

Klondike.
  390. Thompson, A. R. Gold-seeking on the Dalton trail. 1900.

Korea—*Description and travel.*
  141. Shaw, E. R. *See his* Big people. 1900. p. 37-45.

Lafayette, Marquis de.
  281. Burton, A. H. Lafayette, the friend of American liberty. 1898.

Lakes.
    331. King, C. F. Some of our lakes and a way to them. *See his* This continent of ours. 1891. p. 129-39. (*Picturesque geographical readers. Bk. 2.*)
    321. Tarr, R. S. *and* McMurry, F. M. *See their* Home geography. 1901. p. 53-61. (*Tarr & McMurry's geographies. Bk. 1.*)
    See also **Ponds.**

Landscape gardening.
    772. Maynard, S. T. Landscape gardening as applied to home decoration. 1899.

Language.
    752. Arnold, S. L., *ed.* *See her* Plans for busy work. 1901. p. 29-49.
    291. Mowry, W. A. *and* A. M. *See their* American inventions and inventors. 1900. p. 247-51.

Lapland—*Description and travel.*
    141. Shaw, E. R. *See his* Big people. p. 53-61.

Laplanders.
    583. Du Chaillu, Paul. *See his* Land of the long night. 1899. p. 31-240.
    310. Starr, Frederick. *See his* Strange peoples. 1901. p. 53-59.

Larcom, Lucy.
    520. Thayer, W. M. *See his* Turning points in successful careers. 1895. p. 59-68.

La Salle.
    292. Gordy, W. F. *See his* American leaders and heroes. 1901. p. 103-15.
    540. Legler, H. E. *See his* Leading events of Wisconsin history. 1898. p. 78-79.
    299. McMurry, Charles. La Salle's trip down the Mississippi. *See his* Pioneer history stories. 1895. p. 1-32.
    See also **Explorers.**

Latin literature.
    483. Church, A. J. Stories from Virgil. 1901.

Lawn tennis.
    707. Campbell, Helen. *See her* American girl's home book of work and play. 1896. p. 151-74.

Lawrence, James.
521. Seawell, M. E. *See her* Twelve naval captains. 1899. p. 208-33.

Leather.
291. Mowry, W. A. *and* A. M. *See their* American inventions and inventors. 1900. p. 164-71.
319. Rocheleau, W. F. *See his* Great American industries. vol. 3. Manufactures. 1900. p. 75-80.
See also Shoes.

Leaves.
640. Allen, Grant. How plants eat. *See his* Story of the plants. 1898. p. 33-53.
633. Dana, *Mrs.* S. W. *See her* Plants and their children. 1896. p. 135-86.

Lee, Robert E.
552. Guerber, H. A. *See his* Story of the great Republic. 1899. p. 247-52.

Legendary lore of Wisconsin Indians.
540. Legler, H. E. *See his* Leading events of Wisconsin history. 1898. p. 29-37.

Levees.
584. Carpenter, F. G. *See his* North America. 1898. p. 154-56.

Lewis, *Capt.* **Meriwether** *and* **Clark,** *Capt.* **William.**
536. Brooks, Noah. First across the continent. 1901.
284. Kingsley, N. F. Story of Captain Meriwether Lewis and Captain William Clark. 1900.
299. McMurry, Charles. *See his* Pioneer history stories. 1895. p. 136-48.
296. Thomas, A. C. *See his* Elementary history of the United States. 1901. p. 241-47.
295. Wright, H. C. Expedition of Lewis and Clarke to the Pacific ocean. *See her* Children's stories of American progress. 1898. p. 86-103.

Library.
752. Arnold, S. L., *ed. See her* Plans for busy work. 1901. p. 48-49.

Life-saving.
    714. Hill, C. T. Fighting a fire. 1897.
    571. Ingersoll, Ernest. Dangers of the deep. *See his* Book of the ocean. 1898. p. 201–32.
    400. Otis, James. Life savers. 1899.
    315. Ross, W. G. U. S. life-saving service. *See By* land and sea. 1895. p. 249–56.
    See also **Fires; Light-houses; Ship-wrecks.**

Light.
    291. Mowry, W. A. *and* A. M. *See their* American inventions and inventors. 1900. p. 60–96.

Lighthouses.
    315. Haynes, E. J. *and others.* Minot's ledge light. *See* By land and sea. 1895. p. 220–24; 237–43.
    571. Ingersoll, Ernest. Dangers of the deep. *See his* Book of the ocean. 1898. p. 211–20.
    333. King, C. F. Among the lighthouses. *See his* Land we live in. Vol. 2. 1893. p. 120–39. (*Picturesque geographical readers. Bk. 4.*)
    291. Mowry, W. A. *and* A. M. *See their* American inventions and inventors. 1900. p. 90–96.
    176. Richards, L. E. Captain January. 1898.
    504. Towle, G. M. Builders of the Eddystone. *See his* Heroes and martyrs of invention. 1892. p. 62–70.

Lincoln, Abraham.
    129. Baldwin, James. *See his* Four great Americans. 1897. p. 187–246.
    515. Bolton, *Mrs.* S. K. *See her* Boys who became famous. 1885. p. 342–67.
    494. Brooks, E. S. *See his* Century book of famous Americans. 1896. p. 193–210.
    507. Brooks, E. S. *See his* Historic Americans. 1899. p. 335–53.
    516. Brooks, Noah. Abraham Lincoln. *See his* Statesmen. 1898. p. 175–222.
    489. Coffin, C. C. Abraham Lincoln. 1892.
    136. Cravens, Frances. Story of Lincoln for children. 1898.
    292. Gordy, W. F. *See his* American leaders and heroes. 1901. p. 282–301.
    552. Guerber, H. A. *See his* Story of the great Republic. 1899. p. 161–67, 239–47.
    503. Lodge, H. C. Lincoln. *See* Lodge and Roosevelt's Hero tales from American history. 1898. p. 325–35.

Lincoln, Abraham. (Cont.)
 299. McMurry, Charles. *See his* Pioneer history stories. 1895. p. 50–59.
 510. Pratt, Silas G. Lincoln in story. 1901.
 275. Putnam, M. L. Children's life of Abraham Lincoln. Ed. 6. 1892.
 520. Thayer, W. M. *See his* Turning points in successful careers. 1895. p. 42–51.
 296. Thomas, A. C. *See his* Elementary history of the United States. 1901. p. 306–17.

Lincoln, Abraham. (*Fiction.*)
 380. Churchill, Winston. Crisis. 1901.
 443. Eggleston, Edward. Graysons. 1900.

Liquid air.
 610. Baker, R. S. *See his* Boy's book of inventions. 1899. p. 43–76.

Literature.
 729. Champlin, J. D. Young folks' cyclopedia of literature and art. 1901.
  See also Ballads; Drama; Essays; Folk-lore; Language; Legends; Poetry; Readers and speakers.

Little cousin series.
 150. Wade, M. H. Our little Japanese cousin. 1901. Bk. 1.
 149. Wade, M. H. Our little Indian cousin. 1901. Bk. 2.
 148. Wade, M. H. Our little Brown cousin. 1901. Bk. 3.
 151. Wade, M. H. Our little Russian cousin. 1901. Bk. 4.

Livingstone, David.
 525. Jenks, Tudor. *See his* Boy's book of explorations. 1900. p. 85–182.
 520. Thayer, W. M. *See his* Turning points in successful careers. 1895. p. 265–72.

Lizard.
 358. Milvain, Edward. Chameleon lizards. *See* Talks about animals. 1895. p. 155–59.

Livermore, Mary Ashton.
 500. Bolton, *Mrs.* S. K. *See her* Lives of girls who became famous. 1886. p. 50–67.

London.
 315. Rideing, W. H. *See* By land and sea. 1895. p. 3–5.

Longfellow, Henry Wadsworth.
    507. Brooks, E. S. *See his* Historic Americans. 1899. p. 354–68.
    279. Cody, Sherwin. *See his* Four American poets. 1899. p. 71–130.
    285. Ware, E. R. *See her* Talks about Authors and their work. 1899. p. 71–86.

Louisiana purchase.
    292. Gordy, W. F. *See his* American leaders and heroes. 1901. p. 241–44.
    295. Wright, H. C. *See her* Children's stories of American progress. 1898. p. 55–85.

Lucullus.
    492. Plutarch. *See his* Lives. 1893. p. 401–405.

Lumbering.
    155. Bradish, S. P. *See her* Stories of country life. 1901. p. 35–49.
    584. Carpenter, F. G. Life in the lumber regions. *See his* North America. 1898. p. 184–89.
    313. Carroll, S. W. *and* Hart, E. M. *See their* Around the world. Bk. 3. 1901. p. 20–22.
    634. Dodge, R. E. *See his* Reader in physical geography. 1900. p. 43–46.
    330. Rideing, W. H. Lumberman of the Sierras. *See* Our country: West. 1897. p. 135–38.
    318. Rocheleau, W. F. *See his* Great American industries. Vol. 2. Products of the soil. 1898. p. 7–50.
    322. Tarr, R. S. *and* McMurry, F. M. *See* Index to their North America. 1901. (*Tarr & McMurry's geographies. Bk. 2.*)
    See also **Forestry.**

Lycurgus.
    492. Plutarch. *See his* Lives. 1893. p. 49–72.

Lyon, Mary.
    500. Bolton, *Mrs.* S. K. *See her* Lives of girls who became famous. 1886. p. 122–40.
    520. Thayer, W. M. *See his* Turning points in successful careers. 1895. p. 296–304.

Macdonough, Thomas.
    521. Seawell, M. E. *See her* Twelve naval captains. 1899. p. 192–207.

Machinery.
   504. Towle, G. M. Inventors of cotton-machinery. *See his* Heroes and martyrs of invention. 1892. p. 71–102.
   See also Manufactures; Mines *and* Mining; Railroads.

McKinley, William.
   292. Gordy, W. F. *See his* American leaders and heroes. 1901. p. 317–19.
   272. Stratemeyer, Edward. American boys' life of William McKinley. 1901.

Madison, James.
   507. Brooks, E. S. *See his* Historic Americans. 1899. p. 175–87.

Magellan.
   522. Johnson, W. H. *See his* World's discoverers. 1900. p. 119–76.

Maize.
   584. Carpenter, F. G. Indian corn and the corn belt. *See his* North America. 1898. p. 159–64.
   767. Sargent, F. L. *See his* Corn plants. 1899. p. 91–101.

Malays.
   310. Starr, Frederick. *See his* Strange peoples. 1901. p. 150–56.

Mammoth cave.
   494. Brooks, E. S. *See his* Century book of famous Americans. 1896. p. 173–4.
   588. Singleton, Esther, *ed. See her* Wonders of nature. 1900. p. 283–94.

Manila—*Description and travel.*
   579. Greater America. 1900. p. 67–130.

Mann, Horace.
   507. Brooks, E. S. *See his* Historic Americans. 1899. p. 320–34.

Mantis.
   358. Miller, O. T. Little lady in green. *See* Talks about animals. 1895. p. 187–92.

Manual training.
   710. Boy's workshop. 1884.
   751. Kenyon, W. J. First years in handicraft. 1901.
   721. Wheeler, C. G. Woodworking for beginners. 1900.
   716. White, Mary. How to make baskets. 1901.

Manufactures.
    319. Rocheleau, W. F. Great American industries. Vol. 3. Manufactures. 1900.
    322. Tarr, R. S. *and* McMurry, F. M. *See* Index to their North America. 1901. (*Tarr & McMurry's geographies. Bk. 2.*)
    See also Arts, useful; Clocks *and* watches; Clothing; Commerce; Gas; Glass; Leather; Machinery; Paper; Shoes.

Maps.
    321. Tarr, R. S. *and* McMurry, F. M. *See their* Home geography. 1901. p. 102-10. (*Tarr & McMurry's geographies. Bk. 1.*)

Marble.
    317. Rocheleau, W. F. *See his* Great American industries. Vol. 1. Minerals. 1896. p. 113-34.

Mariette, *Ohio.*
    299. McMurry, Charles. *See his* Pioneer history stories. 1895. p. 122-27.

Marine zoology.
    620. Bayliss, C. K. In brook and bayou. 1897.
    571. Ingersoll, Ernest. Animal life in the sea. *See his* Book of the ocean. 1898. p. 259-74.

Marion, Francis.
    292. Gordy, W. F. *See his* American leaders and heroes. 1901. p. 217-21.

Marquette, Jacques. *See* **Explorers; Joliet, Louis.**

Marshall, John. (*Chief Justice.*)
    507. Brooks, E. S. *See his* Historic Americans. 1899. p. 161-74.

Mary, *Queen of Scots.*
    563. Warren, H. P., ed. *See his* Stories from English history. 1901. p. 222-28.

Mason & Slidell.
    488. Brooks, Noah. *See his* Abraham Lincoln. 1901. p. 152-55.

Massasoit.
    292. Gordy, W. F. *See his* American leaders and heroes. 1901. p. 75-76.

Matches.
    291. Mowry, W. A. *and* A. M. *See their* American inventions and inventors. 1900. p. 51-57.

Meat.
    319. Rocheleau, W. F. *See his* Great American industries. Vol. 3. Manufactures. 1900. p. 100–125.

Memorial Day.
    552. Guerber, H. A. *See his* Story of the great Republic. 1899. p. 236–39.
    664. McCaskey, J. P. *comp. See his* Lincoln literary collection. 1897. p. 366–71.

Mendelssohn, Felix.
    285. Ware, E. R. *See her* Talks about Authors and their work. 1899. p. 13–16.

Men of achievement series.
    516. Brooks, Noah. Statesmen. 1898.
    511. Stoddard, W. O. Men of business. 1893.

Mexicans.
    310. Starr, Frederick. *See his* Strange peoples. 1901. p. 17–25.

Mexican War.
    552. Guerber, H. A. *See his* Story of the great Republic. 1899. p. 125–29.

Mexico—*Description and travel.*
    584. Carpenter, F. G. Spanish North America–Mexico. *See his* North America. 1898. p. 327–45.
    589. Coe, F. E. *See her* Our American neighbors. 1897. p. 151–91. (*World and its people series. Bk. 4.*)
    331. King, C. F. Off to Mexico. *See his* This continent of ours. 1891. p. 252–85. (*Picturesque geographical readers. Bk. 2.*)
    315. Miller, J. and others. In the grand plaza of Mexico. *See* By land and sea. 1895. p. 102–12.
    587. Sanborn, H. J. Winter in Central America and Mexico. 1887.
    429. Smith, N. A. Under the cactus flag. 1899.
    322. Tarr, R. S. *and* McMurry, F. M. *See their* North America. 1901. p. 378–88. (*Tarr & McMurry's geographies. Bk. 2.*)

Mice.
    638. Burroughs, John. *See his* Squirrels and other fur-bearers. 1900. p. 111–24.

Michelangelo.
    647. Hurll, E. M. A collection of pictures and portrait of the painter, with introduction and interpretation. 1899.

Middle ages. (*Fiction.*)
    484. Baldwin, James. Story of Roland. 1888.
    249. Pyle, Howard. Otto of the silver hand. 1901.
    See also **Chivalry; Crusades.**

Milk.
    329. McIlvaine, C. How milk is marketed. *See* Our country: East. 1898. p. 174–78.

Millet, Jean Francois.
    648. Hurll, E. M. Collection of fifteen pictures and portrait of the painter with introduction and interpretation. 1900.

Milton, John.
    563. Warren, H. P, ed. *See his* Stories from English history. 1901. p. 297–301.

Mines and mining.
    584. Carpenter, F. G. Iron and copper mines of Lake Superior; Travels in coal regions; Visit to a gold mine; Silver mine. *See his* North America. 1898. p. 179–84; 211–18; 241–55.
    334. Carpenter, F. G. Mineral wealth of the Andes; Coal mines of Chile. *See his* South America. 1899. p. 95–100; 144–50.
    322. Tarr, R. S. *and* McMurry, F. M. *See* Index to their North America. 1901. (*Tarr & McMurry's geographies. Bk. 2.*)
    See also **Coal; Gold; Iron; Silver.**

Mink.
    638. Burroughs, John. *See his* Squirrels and other fur-bearers. 1900. p. 90–93.

Mint. *See* **U. S.,** *Mint.*

Missouri compromise.
    488 Brooks, Noah. *See his* Abraham Lincoln. 1901. p. 91–94. 108.

Mitchell, Maria.
    500. Bolton, *Mrs.* S. K. *See her* Lives of girls who became famous. 1886. p. 87–103.

Money.
    428. Drysdale, William. How money is made. *See his* Treasury club. 1900. p. 267–78.
    See also **Commerce; Gold.**

Monkeys.
    602. Garner, L. Apes and monkeys. 1900.
    358. Stevens, Thomas. Monkey life in British India. *See* Talks about animals. 1895. p. 231–39.

Monmouth's rebellion. (*Fiction.*)
    247. Doyle, A. C. Micah Clarke. 1894.

Monroe, James.
    507. Brooks, E. S. *See his* Historic Americans. 1899. p. 188–201.

Montezuma.
    121. Pratt, M. L. *See her* American's story for America's children. Bk. 1. 1901. p. 37–52.

Monuments.
    329. Stephens, C. A. Grant monument. *See* Our country: East. 1898. p. 187–89.

Moody, Dwight Lyman.
    515. Bolton, *Mrs.* S. K. *See her* Boys who became famous. 1885. p. 323–41.

Moonshiners.
    374. Eggleston, G. C. Camp Venture: story of the Virginia mountains. 1901.

More, *Sir* Thomas.
    563. Warren, H. P., *ed. See his* Stories from English history. 1901. p. 199–205.

Mormons.
    552. Guerber, H. A. *See his* Story of the great Republic. 1899. p. 117–21.

Morris, Gouverneur.
    503. Lodge, H. C. *See* Lodge and Roosevelt's Hero tales from American history. 1898. p. 93–99.

Morris, Robert.
    507. Brooks, E. S. *See his* Historic Americans. 1899. p. 132–45.

Morse, Samuel.
    507. Brooks, E. S. *See his* Historic Americans. 1899. p. 305–19.
    292. Gordy, W. F. *See his* American leaders and heroes. 1901. p. 273–81.
    126. Perry, F. M. *See her* Four American inventors. 1901. p. 133–201.
    520. Thayer, W. M. *See his* Turning points in successful careers. 1895. p. 257–64.

Morton, Thomas.
    298. Holman, Alma. Merrymount. *See her* Massasoit. 1897. p. 128–32.

Mother Goose rhymes.
    45. Welsh, Charles. Book of nursery rhymes. 1901.

Moths.
    356. Kelly, *Mrs.* M. A. B. *See her* Short stories of our shy neighbors. 1896. p. 7–14; 30–40; 61–67; 76–79.
    626. Weed, C. M. Nature biographies. 1901.

Motors.
    319. Rocheleau, W. F. *See his* Great American industries. Vol. 3. Manufactures. 1900. p. 7–36.
    See also **Machinery.**

Mott, Lucretia.
    500. Bolton, *Mrs.* S. K. *See her* Lives of girls who became famous. 1886. p. 33–49.
    520. Thayer, W. M. *See his* Turning points in successful careers. 1895. p. 122–30.

Mound-builders.
    555. Guerber, H. A. *See his* Story of the thirteen olonies. 1898. p. 20–23.
    329. Henshaw, H. W. *See* Our country: East. 1898. p. 50–56.
    540. Legler, H. E. Builders of the mounds in Wisconsin. *See his* Leading events of Wisconsin history. 1898. p. 14–17.
    556. Thwaites, R. G. Mound-builders in Wisconsin. *See his* Story of Wisconsin. 1891. p. 18–19.
    See also **Indians of North America.**

Mt. Vernon.
    528. Brooks, E. S. *See his* Century book for young Americans. 1894. p. 103–5.

Mountaineering.
    315. Rolfe, E. M. Climb up Mount Vesuvius. *See* By land and sea. 1895. p. 37–41.

Mountains.
    634. Dodge, R. E. *See his* Reader in physical geography. 1900. p. 144–53.
    331. King, C. F. Lofty mountains; White mountains. *See his* This continent of ours. 1891. p. 32–47; 80–89. (*Picturesque geographical readers. Bk. 2.*)
    321. Tarr, R. S. *and* McMurry, F. M. *See their* Home geography. 1901. p. 17–27. (*Tarr & McMurry's geographies. Bk. 1.*)
    See also **Mountaineering; Volcanoes.**

Mouse.
356. Kelly, *Mrs.* M. A. B. Four pink babies. *See her* Short stories of our shy neighbors. 1896. p. 92-98.

Mozart, Wolfgang.
515. Bolton, *Mrs.* S. K. *See her* Boys who became famous. 1885. p. 72-82.
285. Ware, E. R. *See her* Talks about Authors and their work. 1899. p. 9-12.

Mushrooms.
612. Gibson, W. H. *See his* Eye spy. 1898. p. 136-44.

Music and musicians.
655. Lillie, L. C. Story of music and musicians for young readers. 1899.
740, 741. Ripley, F. H. *and* Tapper, Thos. Short course in music. Bks. 1 and 2. 1898.
See also **Musicians.**

Muskrat.
638. Burroughs, John. *See his* Squirrels and other fur-bearers. 1900. p. 43-47.
358. Whittle, G. S. Queer little animal. *See* Talks about animals. 1895. p. 221-25.

Mythology.
115. Baldwin, James. Old Greek stories. 1895.
485. Baldwin, James. Story of Siegfried. 1901.
486. Baldwin, James. Story of the golden age. 1901.
262. Burt, E. M. *and* Ragozin, Z. A. Odysseus: the hero of Ithaca. 1898.
266. Clarke, M., *ed.* Story of Aeneas. 1898.
267. Clarke M., *ed.* Story of Troy. 1897.
117. Cook, A. S., *ed.* Story of Ulysses. 1897.
113. Cooke, F. J., *ed.* Nature myths and stories for little children. 1895.
251. Foster, M. H. *and* Cummings, M. H. Asgard stories. 1901.
303. Harding, C. H. *and* S. B. Stories of Greek gods, heroes and men. 1897.
269. Hawthorne, Nathaniel. Tanglewood tales. 1883.
116. Holbrook, Florence, *ed.* 'Round the year in myth and song. 1897.
479. Keary, A. *and* E. Heroes of Asgard. 1893.
265. Kupfer, G. H. Stories of long ago. 1897.
480. Mabie, H. W. Norse stories retold from the Eddas. 1900.
104. Menefee, Maud. Child stories from the masters. 1901.
See also **Animals,** *legends and stories of;* **Fairy tales; Folk-lore; Legends.**

Nails.
    155. Bradish, S. P. *See her* Stories of country life. 1901. p. 53-55.

Nansen, Fridtjof.
    280. Bull, J. B. Fridtjof Nansen. 1898.

Napoleon I.
    436. Brooks, E. S. Boy of the first empire. 1901.
    274. Foa, Mme. E. Boy life of Napoleon. 1895.

Natural gas. *See* **Gas.**

Nature poems.
    704. Williams, Sarah. *comp.* Through the year with birds and poets. 1900.

Nature stories.
    64. Froehlich, C. G. Big outdoors. 1899.
    See also **Nature study.**

Nature study.
    165. Andrews, Jane. Stories of my four friends. 1901.
    620. Bayliss, C. K. In brook and bayou. 1897.
    613. Buckley, A. B. Fairy-land of science. 1899.
    631. Burroughs, John. Pepacton. 1881.
    605. Burroughs, John. Sharp eyes and other papers. Bound with Birds and bees. 1887.
    633. Dana, *Mrs.* S. W. Learning to see. *See* her Plants and their children. 1896. p. 257-65.
    612. Gibson, W. H. Eye spy. 1898.
    625. Gibson, W. H. My studio neighbors. 1898.
    637. Gibson, W. H. Sharp eyes. 1891.
    351. Gould, A. W. Mother Nature's children. 1900.
    627. Grinnell, Morton. Neighbours of field, wood and stream. c1901.
    340. Long, W. J. Beasts of the field. 1901.
    339. Long, W. J. Fowls of the air. 1901.
    355. Long, W. J. Secrets of the woods. 1901.
    360. Long, W. J. Ways of wood folk. 1899.
    361. Long, W. J. Wilderness ways. 1901.
    353. Needham, J. G. Outdoor studies. 1898.
    156. Pierson, C. D. Among the farmyard people. 1899.
    157. Pierson, C. D. Among the forest people. 1898.
    158. Pierson, C. D. Among the meadow people. 1897.
    159. Pierson, C. D. Among the pond people. 1901.
    619. Treat, Mary. Home studies in nature. 1885.

Nature study. (*Poems.*)
- 685. McMurry, L. B. *and* Cook, A. S. Songs of the tree-top and meadow. 1899.
- 701. Wait, M. C. *and* Leonard, M. C. *comps.* Among flowers and trees with the poets. 1901.
- 704. Williams, Sarah. *comp.* Through the year with birds and poets. 1900.

Nature study. (*Fiction.*)
- 393. Roberts, C. G. D. Heart of the ancient wood. 1900.

Naval biography.
- 495. Barnes, James. Commodore Bainbridge. 1897.
- 501. Barnes, James. Hero of Erie. 1898.
- 512. Barnes, James. Midshipman Farragut. 1898.
- 127. Beebe, M. B. Four American naval heroes. 1899.
- 548. Lang, Andrew, *ed.* Sir Richard Grenville. *See his* Red true story book. 1897. p. 102-8.
- 521. Seawell, M. E. Twelve naval captains. 1899.

Naval history.
- 571. Ingersoll, Ernest. War-ships and naval battles. *See his* Book of the ocean. 1898. p. 107-54.

See also **Naval biography.**

Naval life. (*Fiction.*)
- 560. Allen, W. B. Navy blue. 1899.
- 373. King, Charles, *Capt.* Cadet days. 1894.

Needles.
- 291. Mowry, W. A. *and* A. M. *See their* American inventions and inventors. 1900. p. 172-77.
- 319. Rocheleau, W. F. *See his* Great American industries. Vol. 3. Manufactures. 1900. p. 129-32.

Negro life.
- 260. Harris, J. C. Aaron in the wildwoods. 1897.
- 258. Harris, J. C. Little Mr. Thimblefinger. 1895.
- 259. Harris, J. C. Mr. Rabbit at home. 1895.
- 261. Harris, J. C. Story of Aaron (so named): the son of Ben Ali. 1897.
- 233. Page, T. N. Among the camps. 1892.

Negroes.
- 310. Starr, Frederick. *See his* Strange peoples. 1901. p. 128-34.

Nevada—*Description and travel.*
    330. Mighels, P. V. *and* Moore, M. V. Queer surface of Nevada; Pyramid lake. *See* Our country: West. 1897. p. 153–60.

New England—*Description and travel.*
    313. Carroll, S. W. *and* Hart, E. M. *See their* Around the world. Bk. 3. 1901. p. 170–214.

New England—*History.*
    524. Drake, S. A. Border wars of New England. 1897.
    541. Drake, S. A. Making of New England, 1580–1643. 1900.
    130. Hawthorne, Nathaniel. Grandfather's chair. 1883.
    297. Humphrey, *Mrs.* F. A. How New England was made. 1890.

Newfoundland—*Description and travel.*
    593. Kellogg, E. M. C. Newfoundland, Cape Breton, and Prince Edward islands. *See her* Australia and the islands of the sea. 1898. p. 160–71. (*World and its people series. Bk. 8.*)
    331. King, C. F. *See his* This continent of ours. 1891. p. 207–21. (*Picturesque geographical readers. Bk. 2.*)
    322. Tarr, R. S. *and* McMurry, F. M. *See their* North America. 1901. p. 351–71. (*Tarr & McMurry's geographies. Bk. 2.*)

New Mexico—*Description and travel.*
    330. Jackson, 'H. H. *and others.* Oldest American houses; New Mexico; Adobe. *See* Our country: West. 1897. p. 178–92.
    387. Lummis, C. F. Enchanted burro: stories of New Mexico and South America. 1897.

New Orleans.
    584. Carpenter, F. G. Through the Mississippi jetties to New Orleans. *See his* North America. 1898. p. 135–43.

Newspapers.
    319. Rocheleau, W. F. *See his* Great American industries. Vol. 3. Manufactures. 1900. p. 193–221.

New York. (*City.*)
    584. Carpenter, F. G. New York and some of its wonders. *See his* North America. 1898. p. 57–75.

Newt.
    356. Kelly, *Mrs.* M. A. B. Rain frogs. *See her* Short stories of our shy neighbors. 1896. p. 108–13.
    358. Worstell, M. V. My little tenants. *See* Talks about animals. 1895. p. 160–64.

Newton, *Sir* **Isaac.**
- 207. Hawthorne, Nathaniel. *See his* Little Daffydowndilly. 1887. p. 23–30.
- 520. Thayer, W. M. *See his* Turning points in successful careers. 1895. p. 165–71.

Niagara Falls.
- 584. Carpenter, F. G. A visit to Niagara Falls. *See his* North America. 1898. p. 195–202.
- 313. Carroll, S. W. *and* Hart, F. M. *See their* Around the world. Bk. 3. 1901. p. 23–27.
- 588. Singleton, Esther, *ed. See her* Wonders of nature. 1900. p. 79–89.

Nibelungen Lied.
- 487. Chapin, A. A. Story of the Rhinegold. 1897.
- 481. Ragozin, Z. A. Siegfried, the hero of the North. 1898.

Nightingale, Florence.
- 500. Bolton, *Mrs.* S. K. *See her* Lives of girls who became famous. 1886. p. 278–99.

Nordica, Lillian.
- 509. Marden, O. S. *See his* How they succeeded. 1901. p. 149–70.

Norman conquest.
- 563. Warren, H. P., *ed. See his* Stories from English history. 1901. p. 47–61.

Norseland.
- 263. Bradish, S. P. Old Norse stories. 1900.
- 120. Pratt, M. L. *See her* America's story for America's children. Bk. 2. 1901. p. 1–10.

North America—*Description and travel.*
- 584. Carpenter, F. G. North America. 1898.
- 331. King, C. F. This continent of ours. 1891. (*Picturesque geographical readers. Bk. 2.*)
- 578. Tarr, R. S. *and* McMurry, F. M. *See their* Europe and other continents. 1901. p. 487–522. (*Tarr & McMurry's geographies. Bk. 3.*)
- 322. Tarr, R. S. *and* McMurry, F. M. *See their* North America. 1901. p. 1–120. (*Tarr & McMurry's geographies. Bk. 2.*)

See also **Alaska; Central America; Mexico; United States.**

North America—*Description and travel. Bibliography.*
    331. King, C. F. *See his* This continent of ours. 1891. p. 311–12. (*Picturesque geographical readers. Bk. 2.*)

North American Indians. *See* **Indians of North America.**

Northmen.
    555. Guerber, H. A. *See his* Story of the thirteen colonies. 1898. p. 24–30.
    491. Higginson, T. W. Legends of the Northmen, 985–1008. *See his* Book of American explorers. 1877. p. 3–15.

Northwest boundary of the U. S.
    295. Wright, H. C. Settlement of the Northwest boundary. *See her* Children's stories of American progress. 1898. p. 268–78.

Norway—*Description and travel.*
    370. Boyesen, H. H. Boyhood in Norway. Ed. 4. 1898.
    315. Cory, W. H. Life in Norway. *See* By land and sea. 1895. p. 61–64.
    31. Perdue, H. A. *and* La Victoire, F. E. *See their* New Century second reader. 1899. p. 102–17.

Nursery rhymes.
    4. Denslow, W. W., *ed.* Mother Goose. 1901.
    45. Welsh, Charles. Book of nursery rhymes. 1901.

Oats.
    767. Sargent, F. L. *See his* Corn plants. 1899. p. 80–82.

Ocean.
    315. Harvey, M. *and others.* Old ocean. *See* By land and sea. 1895. p. 195–256.
    571. Ingersoll, Ernest. Ocean and its origin. *See his* Book of the ocean. 1898. p. 1–26.
    321. Tarr, R. S. *and* McMurry, F. M. *See their* Home geography. 1901. p. 62–70. (*Tarr & McMurry's geographies. Bk. 1.*)
    See also **Commerce; Shipwrecks; Voyages and travels.**

Odysseus.
    486. Baldwin, James. Story of the golden age. 1901.

Oil.
    313. Carroll, S. W. *and* Hart, E. M. *See their* Around the world. Bk. 3. 1901. p. 60–62.

Oil. (Cont.)

329. Eaton, E. H. Oil-country crater. *See* Our country: East. 1898. p. 46–49.
333. King, C. F. Oil fields. *See his* Land we live in. Vol. 2. 1893. p. 61–70. (*Picturesque geographical readers. Bk. 4.*)
291. Mowry, W. A. *and* A. M. Whale oil; kerosene. *See their* American inventions and inventors. 1900. p. 72–84.

One hundred choice selections.

666. Garrett, Phineas, *ed.* Speaker's garland and literary bouquet. 1899. Vol 7.
667. Garrett, Phineas. *ed.* Speaker's garland and literary bouquet. 1899. Vol. 8.
668. Garrett, Phineas. *ed.* Speaker's garland and literary bouquet. 1899. Vol. 9.

Opera.

271. Frost, W. H. Wagner story book. 1898.

See also **Amateur opera.**

Opossum.

638. Burroughs, John. *See his* Squirrels and other fur-bearers. 1900. p. 106–10.

Orchids.

315. Hodgens, E. Oriental sweetmeats. *See* By land and sea. 1895. p. 189–92.

Ordinance of 1787.

488. Brooks, Noah. *See his* Abraham Lincoln. 1901.

See also **Indexes to United States histories on list.**

Orient.

315. Hodgens, E. Oriental sweetmeats. *See* By land and sea. 1895. p. 189–92.

Ossoli, Margaret Fuller.

500. Bolton, *Mrs.* S. K. Margaret Fuller Ossoli. *See her* Lives of girls who became famous. 1886. p. 68–86.

Ostrich.

313. Carroll, S. W. *and* Hart, E. M. *See their* Around the world. Bk. 3. 1901. p. 101–103.

Otis, James.

507. Brooks, E. S. *See his* Historic Americans. 1899. p. 34–45.

Oyster.
- 584. Carpenter, F. G. Baltimore and our oyster beds. *See his* North America. 1898. p. 45-49.
- 329. Knox, T. W. Chesapeake oysters. *See* Our country: East. 1898. p. 165-69.

Palissy, Bernard.
- 515. Bolton, *Mrs.* S. K. *See her* Boys who became famous. 1885. p. 54-64.
- 504. Towle, G. M. Palissy the potter. *See his* Heroes and martyrs of invention. 1892. p. 43-51.

Panama, Isthmus of.
- 334. Carpenter, F. G. *See his* South America. 1899. p. 16-29.

Paper.
- 319. Rocheleau, W. F. *See his* Great American industries. Vol. 3. Manufactures. 1900. p. 141-59.

Paris.
- 315. Blake, E. M. Boys and girls of Paris. *See* By land and sea. 1895. p. 22-26.

Parliamentary practice.
- 719. Robert, J. T. Robert's primer of parliamentary law. 1900.

Parkman, Francis.
- 503. Lodge, H. C. Francis Parkman. *See* Lodge and Roosevelt's Hero tales from American history. 1898. p. 163-70.

Patagonia—*Description and travel.*
- 141. Shaw, E. R. Patagonia. *See his* Big people. 1900. p. 92-97.

Patriotism.
- 457. Hale, E. E. Man without a country. 1899.
- 599. Judson, H. P. Young American, a civic reader. 1897.
- 686. Matthews, Brander. Poems of American patriotism. 1899.
- 665. Morgan, T. J. Patriotic citizenship. 1895.

Peabody, George.
- 515. Bolton, *Mrs.* S. K. *See her* Boys who became famous. 1885. p. 1-12.
- 493. Parton, James. *See his* Captains of Industry. vol. 2. 1896. p. 208-17.
- 520. Thayer, W. M. *See his* Turning points in successful careers. 1895. p. 131-39.

Peanuts.
 329. Spear, G. B. Peanuts. *See* Our country: East. 1898. p. 160-4.

Pedagogical stories.
 745. Chenery, Susan. As the twig is bent. 1901.
 764. Ray, A. C. Playground Toni. 1900.
 747. Shinn, M. W. Biography of a baby. 1900.
 760. Smith, W. H. Evolution of "Dodd." 1897.
 762. Wray, A. W. Jean Mitchell's school. 1902.
 230. Zollinger, Guilielma. Widow O'Callaghan's boys. 1898.

Pedagogy. *See* **Teaching.**

Pencils.
 319. Rocheleau, W. F. *See his* Great American industries. vol. 3. Manufactures. 1900. p. 132-36.

Penn, William.
 292. Gordy, W. F. *See his* American leaders and heroes. 1901. p. 92-102.
 555. Guerber, H. A. *See his* Story of the thirteen colonies. 1898. p. 147-52.
 301. Scudder, H. E. William Penn and the Indians. *See his* Short history of the United States. 1890. p. 61-66.
 296. Thomas, A. C. *See his* Elementary history of the United States. 1901. p. 123-32.

Pens.
 319. Rocheleau, W. F. *See his* Great American industries. vol. 3. Manufactures. 1900. p. 136-40.

Pequod war.
 541. Drake, S. A. *See his* Making of New England. 1900. p. 203-13.
 442. Hall, Ruth. *See her* Golden arrow. 1901. p. 32-81.
 298. Holman, Alma. *See her* Massasoit. 1897. p. 137-50.

Pericles.
 492. Plutarch. *See his* Lives. 1893. p. 137-67.

Perry, Oliver Hazard.
 501. Barnes, James. Hero of Erie, Oliver Hazard Prery. 1898.
 127. Beebe, M. B. *See her* Four American naval heroes. 1899. p. 71-130.
 289. Otis, James. With Perry on Lake Erie. 1899.
 521. Seawell, M. E. *See her* Twelve naval captains. 1899. p. 182-91.

Persia—*Description and travel.*
>315. Benjamin, S. G. W. Fire-worshippers. *See* By land and sea. 1895. p. 178-82.

Petroleum.
>584. Carpenter, F. G. Travels in the oil regions. *See his* North America. 1898. p. 203-10.
>317. Rocheleau, W. F. *See his* Great American industries. vol. I. Minerals. 1896. p. 45-74.
>322. Tarr, R. S. *and* McMurry, F. M. *See* Index to their North America. 1901. (*Tarr & McMurry's geographies. Bk. 2.*)

Philippine islands—*Description and travel.*
>140. Carroll, S. W. *and* Hart, E. M. *See their* Around the world. Bk. 3. 1901. p. 241-66.
>326. George, M. M. Little journeys to Hawaii and the Philippine islands. 1900.
>593. Kellogg, E. M. C. Philippine islands. *See her* Australia and the islands of the sea. 1898. p. 378-82. (*World and its people series. Bk. 8.*)
>141. Shaw, E. R. Philippine islands. *See his* Big people. 1900. p. 110-17.
>310. Starr, Frederick. People of Philippines. *See his* Strange peoples. 1901. p. 156-63.
>322. Tarr, R. S. *and* McMurry, F. M. *See their* North America. 1901. p. 341-49. (*Tarr & McMurry's geographies. Bk. 2.*)

Phonetics.
>752. Arnold, S. L.,*ed. See her* Plans for busy work. 1901. p. 50-72.

Phonograph.
>610. Baker, R. S. *See his* Boy's book of inventions. 1899. p. 251-80.

Photography. (*X-Ray.*)
>610. Baker, R. S. *See his* Boy's book of inventions. 1899. p. 174-203.

Physical geography.
>634. Dodge, R. E. Reader in physical geography for beginners. 1900.
>>*See also* Caves; Deserts; Climate; Erosion; Geography; Ice; Rivers; Valleys.

Physics.
- 614. Avery, E. M. and Sinnott, C. P. First lessons in physical science, for use in grammar schools. 1897.

   See also **Air; Heat; Light; Physical geography.**

Pictures—*animals.*
- 5. Our doggies.
- 7. Pets' picture farm.

Picturesque geographical readers series.
- 331. King, C. F. This continent of ours. Bk. 2. 1891.
- 332. King, C. F. Land we live in. Bk. 3. 1892.
- 333. King, C. F. Land we live in. Bk. 4. 1893.

Pike's Peak.
- 588. Singleton, Esther, ed. *See her* Wonders of nature. 1900. p. 263-67.
- 330. Smith, J. H. Signal station on Pike's Peak. *See* Our country: West. 1897. p. 121-28.

Pilgrims.
- 541. Drake, S. A. *See his* Making of New England. 1900. p. 67-103.
- 292. Gordy, W. F. *See his* American leaders and heroes. 1901. p. 64-80.
- 526. Griffis, W. E. Pilgrim fathers in Leyden; Pilgrims emigrate to America. *See his* Brave little Holland. 1894. p. 192-209.
- 491. Higginson, T. W. Pilgrims at Plymouth. *See his* Book of American explorers. 1877. p. 311-37.
- 298. Holman, Alma. *See her* Massasoit. 1897. p. 88-112.
- 301. Scudder, H. E. *See his* Short history of the United States. 1890. p. 42-44.
- 296. Thomas, A. C. *See his* Elementary history of the United States. 1901. p. 67-84.
- 563. Warren, H. P., ed. See his Stories from English history. 1901. p. 255-57.

   See also **New England**—*History;* **U. S.**—*History. Discovery and Colonial.*

Pilots.
- 315. Barker, W. E. Pilot-boat. *See* By land and sea. 1895. p. 231-36.
- 712. Moffett, Cleveland. *See his* Careers of danger and daring. 1901. p. 130-72.

Pins.
- 319. Rocheleau, W. F. *See his* Great American industries. vol. 3. Manufactures. 1900. p. 127-29.

Pirates.
    298. Holman, Alma. Pirates of New England. *See her* Massasoit. 1897. p. 244-52.
    571. Ingersoll, Ernest. Robbers of the sea. *See his* Book of the ocean. 1898. p. 171-86.

Pizarro, Francisco. *See* **Explorers.**

Plants.
    773. Shepard, H. H. *See his* Life on the farm. 1901. p. 41-84.
    619. Treat, Mary. *See her* Home studies in nature. 1885. p. 139-239.
    See also **Agriculture; Botany; Flowers; Gardening.**

Plays. *See* **Amateur drama; Drama; Games; Sports.**

Plymouth Rock.
    555. Guerber, H. A. *See his* Story of the thirteen colonies. 1898. p. 109-13.

Pocahontas.
    508. Brooks, E. S. *See his* Historic girls. 1887. p. 208-25.
    555. Guerber, H. A. *See his* Story of the thirteen colonies. 1898. p. 97-101.
    See also **Smith,** *Capt.* **John.**

Poetry.
    669. Bates, K. L., *ed.* Ballad book. 1890.
    670. Browning, Robert. Boy's Browning. 1899.
    671. Bryant, W. C. Poetical works. 1897.
    674. Field, Eugene. Little book of western verse. 1901.
    676. Field, Eugene. Love-songs of childhood. 1901.
    675. Field, Eugene. Second book of verse. 1901.
    680. Longfellow, H. W. Complete poetical works. 1893.
    683. Lovejoy, M. I., *comp.* Poetry of the seasons. 1898.
    689. Lowell, J. R. Complete poetical works. 1896.
    664. McCaskey, J. P., *comp.* Lincoln literary collection. 1897.
    693. Riley, J. W. Neghborly poems. 1899.
    696. Scott, *Sir* Walter. Marmion. 1892.
    699. Tennyson, Alfred. Poetic and dramatic works. 1898.
    701. Wait, M. C. *and* Leonard, M. C., *comps.* Among flowers and trees with the poets. 1901.
    702. Whittier, J. G. Complete poetical works. 1894.
    363, 364. Williams, Sherman, *comp. See his* Choice literature for intermediate grades. 1898. 2 vols.

Poetry. (Cont.)
    662, 663. Williams, Sherman, *comp.* *See his* Choice literature for grammar grades. 1898. 2 vols.
    704. Williams, Sarah, *comp.* Through the year with birds and poets. 1900.
    See also Children's poetry; Readers and speakers; Songs.

Poetry of places. *Bibliography.*
    332, 333. King, C. F. List of poems. *See his* Land we live in. vol. 1. 1892. p. 219-22; vol. 2. 1893. p. 229-30. (*Picturesque geographical readers. Bks. 3-4.*)

Polo, Marco.
    518. Brooks, Noah. Story of Marco Polo. 1898.
    522. Johnson, W. H. *See his* World's discoverers. 1900. p. 3-13.
    See also Explorers.

Pompey.
    492. Plutarch. *See his* Lives. 1893. p. 326-69.

Ponds.
    616. Allen, Grant. Frozen world. *See his* Flashlights on nature. 1898. p. 204-31.

Pontiac.
    506. Catherwood, M. H. *See her* Heroes of the Middle West. 1898. p. 117-41.
    134. Husted, M. H. *See her* Stories of Indian chieftains. 1900. p. 87-97.

Porcupine.
    638. Burroughs, John. *See his* Squirrels and other fur-bearers. 1900. p. 98-105.

Porter, *Capt.* **David.**
    512. Barnes, James. Midshipman Farragut. (Cruise of the "Essex."). 1898.
    474. Otis, James. With Porter in the Essex. 1901.

Porto Rico—*Description and travel.*
    313. Carroll, S. W. *and* Hart, E. M. *See their* Around the world. Bk. 3. 1901. p. 223-27.
    325. George, M. M. Little journeys to Cuba and Porto Rico. 1900.
    579. Greater America. 1900.
    322. Tarr, R. S. *and* McMurry, F. M. *See their* North America. 1901. p. 330-36. (*Tarr & McMurry's geographies. Bk. 2.*)

Postal system.
 291. Mowry, W. A. *and* A. M. See their American inventions and inventors. 1900. p. 258–64.

Prairie.
 330. Fullerton, J. *and* Garland, H. Prairie schooner; Prairie signs; Boy life on the prairie. *See* Our country: West. 1897. p. 195–202; 212–16.
 461. Barton, W. E. Prairie schooner. 1900.

Prairie-dog.
 358. Hornaday, W. T. *See* Talks about animals. 1895. p. 177–81.

Preble, Edward.
 521. Seawell, M. E. *See her* Twelve naval captains. 1899. p. 83–101.

Printing.
 526. Griffis, W. E. Discovery of printing. *See his* Brave little Holland. 1894. p. 122–26.
 332. King, C. F. Types and paper; How books are made. *See his* Land we live in. vol. 1. 1892. p. 78–94. (*Picturesque geog. readers. Bk. 3.*)
 319. Rocheleau, W. F. *See his* Great American industries. vol. 3; Manufactures. 1900. p. 160–92.
 504. Towle, G. M. Discovery of printing. *See his* Heroes and martyrs of invention. 1890. p. 23–32.
 See also **Paper.**

Printing press.
 541. Drake, S. A. *See his* Making of New England. 1900. p. 216–18.
 291. Mowry, W. A. *and* A. M. *See their* American inventions and inventors. 1900. p. 252–57.
 504. Towle, G. M. Gutenberg, the inventor of the printing-press. *See his* Heroes and martyrs of inventions. 1890. p. 33–42.

Proctor, Mary E.
 509. Marden, O. S. *See his* How they succeeded. 1901. p. 87–95.

Progressive course in reading series.
 21. Aldrich, G. I. *and* Forbes, A. First book: Pictures, rhymes, stories. 1899.
 16. Aldrich, G. I. *and* Forbes, A. Second book: Stories, verses, nature studies. 1899.
 17. Aldrich, G. I. *and* Forbes, A. Third book: Stories, studies, rhymes, riddles. 1900.

Pulcheria. (*Constantinople.*)
    508. Brooks, E. S. *See his* Historic girls. 1887. p. 45-60.

Puritans.
    541. Drake, S. A. *See his* Making of New England. 1900. p. 149-60.
    543. Drake, S. A. *See his* Making of Virginia and the middle colonies. 1893. p. 81-82.
    292. Gordy, W. F. *See his* American leaders and heroes. 1901. p. 81-91.
    298. Holman, Alma. *See her* Massasoit. 1897. p. 133-36.
    301. Scudder, H. E. *See his* Short history of the United States. 1890. p. 48-56.
    296. Thomas, A. C. *See his* Elementary history of the United States. 1901. p. 85-91.

Putnam, Israel.
    477. Parton, James. *See his* Captains of industry. Vol. 1. 1891. p. 96-103.

Pygmies.
    141. Shaw, E. R. *See his* Big people. 1900. p. 98-102.
    310. Starr, Frederick. *See his* Strange peoples. 1901. p. 138-42.

Quakers.
    292. Gordy, W. F. *See his* American leaders and heroes. 1901. p. 92-102.
    555. Guerber, H. A. *See his* Story of the thirteen colonies. 1898. p. 134-36.

Rabbit.
    638. Burroughs, John. *See his* Squirrels and other fur-bearers. 1900. p. 38-42.

Raccoon.
    638. Burroughs, John. *See his* Squirrels and other fur-bearers. 1900. p. 94-97.

Races of man. *See* **Ethnology.**

Railroads.
    552. Guerber, H. A. *See his* Story of the great Republic. 1899. p. 94-95.
    330. Harbour, J. L. Where railroads go. *See* Our country: West. 1897. p. 102-6.

Railroads. (Cont.)

    333. King, C. F. Our railroads. *See his* Land we live in. Vol. 2. 1893. p. 173-96. (*Picturesque geographical readers. Bk. 4.*)

    712. Moffett, Cleveland. Locomotive engineer. *See his* Careers of danger and daring. 1901. p. 377-419.

    291. Mowry, W. A. *and* A. M. *See their* American inventions and inventors. 1900. p. 223-28.

    329. Owen, M. Elevated railroads. *See* Our country: East 1898. p. 190-92.

    504. Towle, G. M. George Stephenson, the inventor of the railway locomotive. *See his* Heroes and martyrs of invention. 1890. p. 141-50.

    295. Wright, H. C. Story of the railroad. *See her* Children's stories of American progress. 1898. p. 179-98.

    See also **Bridges.**

Rain.

    331. King, C. F. Rain and wind. *See his* This continent of ours. 1891. p. 90-98. (*Picturesque geographical readers. Bk. 2.*)

    142. Payne, F. O. Where the rain comes from; What the rain does. *See his* Geographical nature studies. c1898. p. 31, 22-23.

Raleigh, *Sir* **Walter.**

    292. Gordy, W. F. *See his* American leaders and heroes. 1901. p. 31-41.

Ranching. *See* **Cattle ranching.**

Raphael.

    649. Hurll, E. M. A collection of fifteen pictures and portrait of the painter with introduction and interpretation. 1899.

    122. Ramé, Louise de la. Child of Urbino: Raphael. 1900.

Readers and speakers.

    21. Aldrich, G. I. *and* Forbes, A. First book: Pictures, rhymes, stories. 1899.

    16. Aldrich, G. I. *and* Forbes, A. Second book: Stories, verses, nature studies. 1899.

    17. Aldrich, G. I. *and* Forbes, A. Third book: Stories, studies, rhymes, riddles. 1900.

    9 Arnold, S. L. Arnold primer. 1901.

    38, 39, 40. Baldwin, James. School reading by grades. First, second and third years. 1897.

Readers and speakers. (Cont.)
- 11. Blaisdell, E. A. *and* M. F. Child life: a first reader. 1899.
- 12. Blaisdell, E. A. *and* M. F. Child life in tale and fable: a second reader. 1899.
- 308. Blaisdell, A. F., *ed.* Stories of the Civil war. 1890.
- 44. Calmerton, Gail *and* Wheeler, W. H. Wheeler's graded readers: a primer. 1900.
- 139. Carroll, S. W. Around the world. Bk. 1. 1897.
- 37a. Crosby, W. E. Our little book for little folks. 1896.
- 365. Cumnock, R. M., *comp.* Cumnock's school speaker. 1899.
- 33. Demarest, A. J. *and* Van Sickle, W. M. New Education readers: Bk. 1. 1900.
- 34. Demarest, A. J. *and* Van Sickle, W. M. New Education readers: Bk. 2. 1900.
- 35. Demarest, A. J. *and* Van Sickle, W. M. New Education readers: Bk. 3. 1901.
- 666. Garrett, Phineas, *ed.* Speaker's garland and literary bouquet. 1899. vol. 7.
- 667. Garrett, Phineas, *ed.* Speaker's garland and literary bouquet. 1899. vol. 8.
- 668. Garrett, Phineas, *ed.* Speaker's garland and literary bouquet. 1899. vol. 9.
- 21. Gilman, M. L., *and* Austin, I., *and* Blaisdell, S. L. Little-folk tales. 1901.
- 22. Hall, M. F., *and* Gilman, M. L. Story land. 1901.
- 23. Holbrook, Florence, *and* Hall, M. F. From many lands. 1901.
- 26. Holbrook, Florence. Hiawatha primer. 1898.
- 27. Holton, A. M. Holton primer. 1901.
- 366. Hyde, W. D., *ed.* School speaker and reader. 1901.
- 18. Jones, L. E. *and* Black, S. W. First reader. 1897.
- 19. Jones, L. E. *and* Black, S. W. Second reader. 1897.
- 24. Judson, H. P. *and* Bender, I. C. Graded literature readers: First book. 1899.
- 25. Judson, H. P. *and* Bender, I. C. Graded literature readers: Second book. 1900.
- 599. Judson, H. P. Young American, a civic reader. 1897.
- 10. Kirk, May. Baldwin primer. 1899.
- 36. Lane, M. A. L. Oriole stories. 1900.
- 94. Lane, *Mrs.* C. A. Stories for children. 1895.
- 30. Lane, A. E. Lights to literature: book three. 1898.
- 42. Logie, A. E., *and* Uecke, C., *and* Milner, S. A. Story reader. 1901.
- 48. Norton, C. E., *ed.* Heart of oak books. vol. 1. 1895.

SUBJECT INDEX. 311

Readers and speakers. (Cont.)
- 110. Norton, C. E., *ed.* Heart of oak books. vol. 2. 1897.
- 28. Perdue, H. A. *and* La Victoire, F. E. Lights to literature: book one: a first reader. 1898.
- 31. Perdue, H. A. *and* La Victoire, F. E. New Century second reader. 1899.
- 687. Persons, E. A. Our country in poem and prose. 1899.
- 37. Sell, W. F. *and* Nageler, J. G. Old friends in new dresses. 1900.
- 41. Sight reader: primary teachers. 1898.
- 29. Sprague, S. E. Lights to literature: book two: a second reader. 1898.
- 45. Taylor, F. L. Taylor school readers: first reader. 1900.
- 14. Thompson, J. G. *and* T. E. Fairy tale and fable: second year. 1899.
- 32. Tibbitts, H. C. New Century third reader. 1901.
- 105. Williams, Sherman, *comp.* Choice literature for primary grades. Bk. 1. 1898.
- 13. Williams, Sherman, *comp.* Choice literature for primary grades. Bk. 2. 1900.
- 363. Williams, Sherman, *comp.* Choice literature for intermediate grades. Bk. 1. 1898.
- 364. Williams, Sherman, *comp.* Choice literature for intermediate grades. Bk. 2. 1898.
- 662. Williams, Sherman, *comp.* Choice literature for grammar grades. Bk. 1. 1898.
- 663. Williams, Sherman, *comp.* Choice literature for grammar grades. Bk. 2. 1898.

See also **Poetry.**

Reading.
- 752. Arnold, S. L., *ed. See her* Plans for busy work. 1901. p. 29-49.

Recitations. *See* **Readers and speakers.**

Reformation.
- 563. Warren, H. P., *ed. See his* Stories from English history. 1901. p. 188-98.

Reindeer.
- 330. Adams, Charles. Reinder for Alaska. *See* Our country: West. 1897. p. 31-36.
- 583. Du Chaillu, Paul. *See his* Land of the long night. 1899. p. 92-98, 104-105, 138-40.

Rembrandt.
　　650. Hurll, E. M. A collection of pictures and portrait of the painter with introduction and interpretation. 1899.

Reptiles.
　　645. Du Chaillu, Paul. World of the great forest. 1900.

Revere, Paul.
　　292. Gordy, W. F. *See his* American leaders and heroes. 1901. p. 165–74.

Reynolds, *Sir Joshua.*
　　651. Hurll, E. M. A collection of fifteen pictures and portrait of the painter with introduction and interpretation. 1900.

Rhymes and jingles.
　　163. Clark, E. B. Jingle book of birds. 1901.
　　52. Keeler, D. B. Memoirs of Simple Simon. 1901.
　　50. Lear, Edward. Jumblies and other nonsense verses. n. d.
　　54. Mother Goose Jingles. n. d.
　　59. Von Gottschalck, O. H. Yankee Doodle gander. 1901.

Rice.
　　584. Carpenter, F. G. Among the rice fields. *See his* North America. 1898. p. 119–24.
　　767. Sargent, F. L. *See his* Corn plants. 1899. p. 89–90.

Riley, James Whitcomb.
　　509. Marden, O. S. *See his* How they succeeded. 1901. p. 357–65.
　　285. Ware, E. R. *See her* Talks about Authors and their work. 1899. p. 211–18.

Rivers.
　　331. King, C. F. Some noted rivers; Other rivers. *See his* This continent of ours. 1891. p. 98–119. (*Picturesque geographical readers.* Bk. 2.)
　　143. Long, C. C. How rivers are made: Work of rivers. *See his* Home geography. c1894. p. 50–62.
　　321. Tarr, R. S. *and* McMurry, F. M. *See their* Home geography. 1901. p. 39–52. (*Tarr & McMurry's geographies.* Bk. 1.)
　　See also Erosion; Valleys.

Rockefeller, John D.
　　509. Marden, O. S. *See his* How they succeeded. 1901. p. 185–208.

Rocky mountains.
    330. Brisbin, J. S. *and others.* Among the Rockies. *See* Our country: West. 1897. p. 67–128.
    584. Carpenter, F. G. Wonders and treasures of the Rock mountain region. *See his* North America. 1898. p. 235–41.

Roland.
    484. Baldwin, James. Story of Roland. 1883.

Rome—*Description and travel.*
    577. Carpenter, F. G. *See his* Europe. 1902. p. 411–16.
    575. Knox, T. W. *See his* Boy travellers in Southern Europe. 1894. p. 255–330.
    585. Stockton, F. R. *See his* Personally conducted. 1889. p. 45–80.

Rome—*History.*
    568. Guerber, H. A. Story of the Romans. 1896.
    492. Plutarch. Roman triumph. *See his* Lives. 1893. p. 388–92.

Romulus.
    492. Plutarch. Romulus. *See his* Lives. 1893. p. 28–48.

Roots.
    640. Allen, Grant. How plants drink. *See his* Story of the plants. 1898. p. 53–73.

Russia—*Description and travel.*
    577. Carpenter, F. G. *See his* Europe. 1902. p. 311–50.
    141. Shaw, E. R. Russia. *See his* Big people. 1900. p. 70–76.
    141a. Taylor, Bayard. Boys of other countries. 1901.
    151. Wade, M. H. Our little Russian cousin. 1901.

Rye.
    767. Sargent, F. L. *See his* Corn plants. 1899. p. 83–94.

Sahara, *Desert of.*
    588. Singleton, Esther, *ed. See her* Wonders of nature. 1900. p. 55–61.

St. Elias, *Mt.*
    330. Schwatka, F. Loneliest place in the U. S. *See* Our country: West. 1897. p. 21–25.

Salmon fisheries.
    313. Carroll, S. W. *and* Hart, E. M. *See their* Around the world. Bk. 3. 1901. p. 142–43.

Salt Lake city.
584. Carpenter, F. G. Across the Rockies to Salt Lake. *See his* North America. 1898. p. 256–64.

San Francisco.
584. Carpenter, F. G. San Francisco and the Chinese. *See his* North America. 1898. p. 274–78.

Sanitary science. *See* **Hygiene; School hygiene.**

Savonarola.
575. Knox, T. W. See his Boy travellers in Southern Europe. 1894. p. 198–201.

School buildings.
755. Burrage, Severance *and* Bailey, H. T. Construction and requirements of; ventilation, heating and lighting. *See their* School sanitation and decoration. 1889. p. 8–32.

School hygiene.
755. Burrage, Severance *and* Bailey, H. T. *See their* School sanitation and decoration. 1899. p. 60–72.

School life. (*Stories of.*)
371. Amicis, Edmondo de. Boy's life at school. 1901.
375. Barbour, R. H. Captain of the crew. 1901.
389. Barbour, R. H. For the honor of the school. 1900.
392. Barbour, R. H. Half-back. 1899.
193. Eggleston, Edward. Hoosier school-boy. 1899.
202. French, Allen. Junior cup. 1901.
195. Grant, Robert. Jack Hall. 1898.
184. Hughes, Rupert. Dozen from Lakerim. 1899.
426. Hughes, Thomas. Tom Brown's school days. 1895.
373. King, *Capt.* Charles. Cadet days. 1894.
404. La Flesche, Francis. Middle five: Indian boys at school. 1900.

School room decoration.
755. Burrage, Severance *and* Bailey, H. T. *See their* School sanitation and decoration. 1899. p. 94–121.

School songs.
737. Betz, Carl, *ed.* Gems of school songs. 1896.
738. Gantvoort, A. J. Music readers for rural and village schools. n. d.
744. Gaynor, J. L. Songs of child-world. 1897.
736. McCaskey, J. P., *comp.* Franklin Square song collection. 1897.

School songs. (Cont.)
>733. Neidlinger, W. H. Earth, sky and air in song. Bk. 1. 1900.
>734. Neidlinger, W. H. Earth, sky and air in song. Bk. 2. 1900.
>732. Siefert, H. O. R. Choice songs. 1899.
>743. Smith, Eleanor. Songs of life and nature. 1898.
>731. Tomlins, W. L. Children's songs and how to sing them. 1894.
>
>*See also* **Songs.**

Schools.
>333. King, C. F. American schools. *See his* Land we live in. vol. 2, 1893. p. 87–106. (*Picturesque geographical readers. Bk. 4.*)
>
>*See also* **Kindergarten.**

Schurman, Jacob Gould.
>509. Marden, O. S. *See his* How they succeeded. 1901. p. 96–104.

Scotland—*Description and travel.*
>577. Carpenter, F. G. *See his* Europe. 1902. p. 40–47.

Science.
>613. Buckley, A. B. Fairy-land of science. 1899.
>
>*See also* **Arts, Useful; Botany; Ethics; Ethnology; Geography; Inventions; Language; Nature study; Physical geography; Zoology.**

Sculpture.
>653. Hurll, E. M. Greek sculpture. 1901.
>329. Owen, M. Statue of liberty. *See* Our country: East. 1898. p. 179–81.
>
>*See also* **Arts, Fine.**

Sea.
>315. Harvey, M., *and others.* Old ocean. *See* By land and sea. 1895. p.195–248.
>571. Ingersoll, Ernest. Book of the ocean. 1898.

Seal *(animal).*
>357. Holder, C. F. *See his* Stories of animal life. 1899. p. 235–39.
>322. Tarr, R. S. *and* McMurry, F. M. *See their* North America. 1901. p. 327–28, 361. (*Tarr & McMurry's geographies. Bk. 2.*)

Seal fisheries.
>313. Carroll, S. W. *and* Hart, E. M. *See their* Around the world. Bk. 3. 1901. p. 131–32.

Sea-life.
　383. King, S. H. Dogwatches at sea. 1901.

Sea-lions.
　330. Putnam, G. B. *See* Our country: West. 1897. p. 53–56.

Sea-otter.
　330. Elliott, H. W. Hunting the sea-otter. *See* Our country: West. 1897. p. 57–64.

Seasons.
　142. Payne, F. O. *See his* Geographical nature studies. c1898. p. 25–26.

Seeds.
　635. Beal, W. J. Seed dispersal. 1898.
　633. Dana, *Mrs.* W. S. Fruits and seeds. *See her* Plants and their children. 1896. p. 9–74.
　636. Weed, C. M. Seed-travellers. 1898.

Serpents.
　358. Arnold, *Sir* E. Indian snakes and tigers. *See* Talks about animals. 1895. p. 240–48.

Sevier, John.
　299. McMurry, Charles. *See his* Pioneer history stories. 1895. p. 117–21.

Seward, William Henry.
　516. Brooks, Noah. *See his* Statesmen. 1898. p. 119–42.
　520. Thayer, W. M. *See his* Turning points in successful careers. 1895. p. 33–41.

Sewing.
　707. Campbell, Helen. *See her* American girl's home book of work and play. 1896. p. 234–47.

Shaftesbury. *Lord.*
　520. Thayer, W. M. *See his* Turning points in successful careers. 1895 p. 25–32.

Shakespeare, William.
　231. Clark, Imogen. Will Shakespeare's little lad. 1897.
　563. Warren, H. P., *ed. See his* Stories from English history. 1901. p. 248–54.

Sheep.
　156. Pierson, C. D. Lamb with the longest tail. Why the sheep ran away. *See her* Among the farmyard people. 1899. p. 12–19; 160–71.
　See also **Wool.**

SUBJECT INDEX. 317

Sheep raising.
    322. Tarr, R. S. *and* McMurry, F. M. *See* Index to their North America. 1901. (*Tarr & McMurry's geographies. Bk. 2.*)

Sheridan, Philip Henry.
    515. Bolton, *Mrs.* S. K. *See her* Boys who became famous. 1885. p. 251-69.
    503. Lodge, H. C. Sheridan at Cedar Creek. *See* Lodge and Roosevelt's Hero tales from American history. 1898. p. 281-90.

Ships.
    571. Ingersoll, Ernest. Building and rigging of ships; warships. *See his* Book of the ocean. 1898. 27-38; 139-54.
    See also **Commerce; Shipwrecks.**

Shipwrecks.
    571. Ingersoll, Ernest. Dangers of the deep. *See his* Book of the ocean. 1898. p. 201-32.
    329. Munroe, Kirk. Florida wreckers. *See* Our country: East. 1898. p. 91-95.
    See also **Life-saving.**

Shoes.
    332. King, C. F. Pair of shoes. *See his* Land we live in. vol. 1. 1892. p. 55-62.
    319. Rocheleau, W. F. Boots and shoes. *See his* Great American industries. vol. 3: Manufactures. 1900. p. 81-99.

Siam.
    315. Lee, S. Siam and its royal white elephant. *See By* land and sea. 1895. p. 161-65.

Siberia—*Description and travel.*
    570. Aldrich, H. L. Arctic Alaska and Siberia. 1889.

Sicily.
    593. Kellogg, E. M. C. Sicily. *See her* Australia and the islands of the sea. 1898. p. 299-308. (*World and its people series. Bk. 8.*)

Siegfried.
    485. Baldwin, James. Story of Siegfried. 1901.
    104. Menefee, Maud. Story of Siegfried. *See her* Child stories from the masters. 1901. p. 29-37.

Sierra Nevada mountains.
  330. Rideing, W. H. *and* Channing, G. E. Lumbermen of the Sierras; A road of the Sierras. *See* Our country: West. 1897. p. 135-42.

Signaling.
  291. Mowry, W. A. *and* A. M. *See their* American inventions and inventors. 1900. p. 265-69.

Signals.
  315. Gunnison, H. F. Ocean observatory. *See* By land and sea. 1895. p. 244-48.

Silk-worm.
  707. Campbell, Helen. *See her* American girl's home book of work and play. 1896. p. 390-93.
  358. Shepard, Naomi. Makers of silk. *See* Talks about animals. 1895. p. 145-49.

Silver.
  317. Rocheleau, W. F. Gold and silver. *See his* Great American industries. vol. 1. Minerals. 1896. p. 163-92.
  See also Mines *and* mining.

Skating.
  329. Whitney, A. W. Wisconsin skate-sail. *See* Our country: East. 1898. p. 28-30.

Skunk.
  638. Burroughs, John. *See his* Squirrels and other fur-bearers. 1900. p. 47-52.

Slate.
  317. Rocheleau, W. F. Slate. *See his* Great American industries. vol. 1. Minerals. 1896. p. 156-62.

Slavery.
  552. Guerber, H. A. *See his* Story of the great Republic. 1899. p. 130-32, 156-61.
  301. Scudder, H. E. *See his* Short history of the United States. 1890. p. 175-81, 204-26.
  295. Wright, H. C. Story of slavery. *See her* Children's stories of American progress. 1898. p. 159-78.
  See also Negroes; United States—*History.*

SUBJECT INDEX. 319

Smith, *Capt.* **John.**
    543. Drake, S. A. *See his* Making of Virginia and the middle colonies. 1893. p. 42-54.
    292. Gordy, W. F. *See his* American leaders and heroes. 1901. p. 42-54.
    555. Guerber, H. A. *See his* Story of the thirteen colonies. 1898. p. 87-97.
    491. Higginson, T. W. *See his* Book of American explorers. 1877. p. 231-65.
    301. Scudder, H. E. *See his* Short history of the United States. 1890. p. 39-41.
    See also **Pocahontas.**

Snail.
    356. Kelly, *Mrs.* M. A. B. Always at home. *See her* Short stories of our shy neighbors. 1896. p. 164-67.

Soil.
    634. Dodge, R. E. *See his* Reader in physical geography. 1900. p. 198-205.
    291. Mowry, W. A. *and* A. M. *See their* American inventions and inventors. 1900. p. 124-30.
    773. Shepard, H. H. *See his* Life on the farm. 1901. p. 9-40.
    321. Tarr, R. S. *and* McMurry, F. M. *See their* Home geography. 1901. p. 1-9. (*Tarr & McMurry's geographies. Bk. 1.*)

Soldiers.
    554. Forsyth, George. Story of the soldier. 1900.

Solon.
    492. Plutarch. Solon. *See his* Lives. 1893. p. 73-87.

Somers, Richard.
    521. Seawell, M. E. *See her* Twelve naval captains. 1899. p. 130-44.

Songs.
    735. McCaskey, J. P., *ed.* Favorite songs and hymns. 1899.
    712. Matthews, W. S. B. Songs of all lands. 1899.
    739. Pratt, W. S., *ed.* St. Nicholas songs. 1885.
    See also **School songs.**

Soto, Hernando de.
    292. Gordy, W. F. *See his* American leaders and heroes. 1901. p. 22-30.
    491. Higginson, T. W. *See his* Book of American explorers. 1877. p. 121-40.

Soto, Hernando de. (Cont.)
- 496. King, Grace. De Soto and his men in the land of Florida. 1898.
- 299. McMurry, Charles. *See his* Pioneer history stories. 1895. p. 163-73.

See also Explorers.

South Africa—*History.*
- 548. Lang, Andrew, ed. Wilson's last fight. *See his* Red true story book. 1897. p. 1-21.

South Africa—*History. (Fiction.)*
- 239. Green, E. E. Gordon highlander. (South African war.) 1901.
- 433. Stratemeyer, Edward. Between Boer and Briton. 1900.

South America—*Description and travel.*
- 334. Carpenter, F. G. South America. 1899.
- 589. Coe, F. E. *See her* Our American neighbors. 1897. p. 219-324. (*World and its people series. Bk. 4.*)
- 315. Curtis, W. E. *and others. See* By land and sea. 1895. p 67-96.
- 574. Knox, T. W. Boy travellers in South America. 1885.
- 387. Lummis, C. F. Enchanted burro. 1897.
- 337. Markwick, W. F. *and* Smith, Wm. South American republic. 1901. (*World and its people series. Bk. 10.*)
- 141. Shaw, E. R. Amazon valley. *See his* Big people. 1900. p. 123-28.
- 578. Tarr, R. S. *and* McMurry, F. M. *See their* Europe and other continents. 1901. p. 96-148. (*Tarr & McMurry's geographies. Bk. 3.*)
- 321. Tarr, R. S. *and* McMurry, F. M. *See their* Home geography. 1901. p. 199-206. (*Tarr & McMurry's geographies. Bk. 1.*)

South America—*History.*
- 310. Starr, Frederick. South American peoples. *See his* Strange peoples. 1901. p. 26-32.

Southern states of U. S.—*Life.*
- 445. Barton, W. E. Hero in homespun. 1897.
- 174. Cable, G. W. Cable story book. 1899.
- 313. Carroll, S. W. *and* Hart, E. M. *See their* Around the world. Bk. 3. 1901. p. 153-69.
- 385. Craddock, C. E. Down the ravine. 1897.
- 411. Drysdale, William. Pine Ridge plantation. 1901.
- 419. Stuart, R. M. Story of Babette: a little Creole girl. 1898.
- 295. Wright, H. C. South after the war. *See her* Children's stories of American progress. 1898. p. 328-33.

Spain—*Description and travel.*
   577. Carpenter, F. G. *See his* Europe. 1902. p. 428-44.
   575. Knox, T. W. *See his* Boy travellers in Southern Europe. 1894. p. 492-544.

Spain—*History.* (*Fiction.*)
   468. Wilson, C. D. Story of the Cid for young people. 1901.

Spanish Armada.
   563. Warren, H. P., ed. *See his* Stories from English history. 1901. p. 234-41.

Spelling.
   752. Arnold, S. L., ed. *See her* Plans for busy work. 1901. p. 29-49.

Spider.
   616. Allen, Grant. Beast of prey. *See his* Flashlights on nature. 1898. p. 47-70.
   100. Atwater, E. P. *See her* Tommy's adventures. 1900. 92-100.
   358. Dingee, L. A. Black sentinel. *See* Talks about animals. 1895. p. 131-36.
   612. Gibson, W. H. *See his* Eye spy. 1898. p. 104-21.
   356. Kelly, *Mrs.* M. A. B. Skillful spinner; A devoted mother; Lines to a spider. *See her* Short stories of our shy neighbors. 1896. p. 168-80.
   329. McCook, H. C. Purseweb spider. *See* Our country: East. 1898. p. 111-16.
   See **Games** *and* **sports.**

Springs.
   631. Burroughs, John. *See his* Pepacton. 1897. p. 35-51.

Squirrel.
   638. Burroughs, John. *See his* Squirrels and other fur-bearers. 1900. p. 1-14.
   356. Kelly, *Mrs.* M. A. B. *See her* Short stories of our shy neighbors. 1896. p. 202-5.
   358. M. M. Flying squirrel. *See* Talks about animals. 1895. p. 170-73.

Stael, Madame de.
   500. Bolton, *Mrs.* S. K. *See her* Lives of girls who became famous. 1886. p. 158-79.

Stage coaches.
   291. Mowry, W. A. *and* A. M. *See their* American inventions and inventors. 1900. p. 200-206.

Standish, Miles.
  465. Dix, B. M. Soldier Rigdale. 1899.
  292. Gordy, W. F. *See his* American leaders and heroes. 1901. p. 64–80.
  513. Johnson, Henry. New exploits of Myles Standish. 1897.

Stanford, Leland.
  511. Stoddard, W. O. *See his* Men of business. 1897. p. 295–317.
  520. Thayer, W. M. *See his* Turning points in successful careers. 1895. p. 288–95.

Stanley, Henry Morton.
  525. Jenks, Tudor. *See his* Boy's book of explorations. 1900. p. 247–303.

Statesmen.
  129. Baldwin, James. Four great Americans. 1896.
  516. Brooks, Noah. Statesmen. 1893.
  128. Burton, A. H. Four American patriots. 1898.

Steamboat.
  292. Gordy, W. F. Robert Fulton and the steamboat. *See his* American leaders and heroes. 1901. p. 246–52.
  552. Guerber, H. A. *See his* Story of the great Republic. 1899. p. 69–72.
  291. Mowry, W. A. *and* A. M. *See their* American inventions and inventors. 1900. p. 207–14.
  301. Scudder, H. E. *See his* Short history of the United States. 1890. 170–71.

Steam engine.
  291. Mowry, W. A. *and* A. M. *See their* American inventions and inventors. 1900. p. 178–84.
  See also **Machinery; Railroads.**

Steel.
  155. Bradish, S. P. *See her* Stories of country life. 1901. p. 144–46.

Steeple-climbing.
  712. Moffett, Cleveland. *See his* Careers of danger and daring. 1901. p. 3–39.

Stephenson, George.
  504. Towle, G. M. George Stephenson, the inventor of the railway locomotive. *See his* Heroes and martyrs of invention. 1892. p. 141–50.

Stevenson, Robert Louis.
    285. Ware, E. R. *See her* Talk about Authors and their work. 1899. p. 203-10.

Stewart, Charles.
    521. Seawell, M. E. *See her* Twelve naval captains. 1899. p. 167-81.

Stock yards.
    313. Carroll, S. W. *and* Hart, E. M. *See their* Around the world. Bk. 3. 1901. p. 81-85.

Story of the states series.
    556. Thwaites, R. G. Story of Wisconsin. 1891.

Stowe, Harriet Beecher.
    501. Bolton, *Mrs.* S. K. Harriet Beecher Stowe. *See her* Lives of girls who became famous. 1886. p. 1-17.
    285. Ware, E. R. *See her* Talks about Authors and their work. 1899. p. 117-25.

Success.
    720. Bok, Edward. Successward. 1899.
    411. Drysdale, William. Pine Ridge plantation. 1901.
    428. Drysdale, William. Treasury club. 1900.
    431. Drysdale, William. Young supercargo. 1898.
    514. Habberton, John. Poor boys' chances. 1900.
    398. Kaler, J. O. Larry Hudson's ambition. 1901.
    509. Marden, O. S. How they succeeded. 1901.
    493. Parton, James. Captains of industry. 2 vol. 1891-96.
    215. Purpose and success. 1900.
    511. Stoddard, W. O. Men of business. 1893.
    210. Zollinger, Gulielma. Maggie McLanehan. 1901.
    230. Zollinger, Gulielma. Widow O'Callaghan's boys. 1898.

Sugar.
    155. Bradish, S. P. *See her* Stories of country life. 1901. p. 5-13.
    584. Carpenter, F. G. Visit to a sugar plantation. *See his* North America. 1898. p. 143-50.
    313. Carroll, S. W. *and* Hart, E. M. Sugar making. *See their* Around the world. Bk. 3. 1901. p. 198-201.
    318. Rocheleau, W. F. *See his* Great American industries. vol. 2: Products of the soil. 1898. p.51-88.
    322. Tarr, R. S. *and* McMurry, F. M. *See* Index to their North America. 1901. (*Tarr & McMurry's geographies. Bk. 2.*)

Sumner, Charles.
 498. Bolton, *Mrs.* S. K. *See her* Famous American statesmen. 1888. p. 268-306.
 516. Brooks, Noah. *See his* Statesmen. 1898. p. 223-54.
 520. Thayer, W. M. *See his* Turning points in successful careers. 1895. p. 172-80.

Sweden.—*Description and travel.*
 141a. Taylor, Bayard. Boys of other countries. 1901.
 315. Thomas, W. W. *jr. See* By land and sea. 1895. p. 53-59.

Switzerland—*Description and travel.*
 152. Andrews, Jane. Little mountain maiden. *See her* Seven little sisters. 1890. p. 67-79.
 315. Byers, S. H. M. Alpine village life. *See* By land and sea. 1895. p. 42-46.
 577. Carpenter, F. G. *See his* Europe. 1902. p. 249-70.
 571. Knox, T. W. *See his* Boy travellers in Central Europe. 1893. p. 258-403.
 141. Shaw, E. R. *See his* Big people. 1900. p. 77-82.
 192. Spyri, *Frau* Johanna. Heidi. 1900.

Taylor, Bayard.
 515. Bolton, *Mrs.* S. K. Bayard Taylor. *See her* Boys who became famous. 1885. p. 13-25.

Teaching.
 752. Arnold, S. L., *ed.* Plans for busy work. 1901.
 753. Du Bois, Patterson. Point of contact in teaching. 1900.
 748. Patrick, J. N. Elements of pedagogics. 1894.
 749. White, E. E. Elements of pedagogy. 1886.
 756. White, E. E. School management. 1894.
 See also **Child study; Kindergarten; Nature study; Pedagogical stories.**

Telegraph.
 292. Gordy, W. F. Samuel Finley Breese Morse and the electric telegraph. *See his* American leaders and heroes. 1901. p. 273-81.
 552. Guerber, H. A. *See his* Story of the great Republic. 1899. p. 122-25.
 291. Mowry, W. A. *and* A. M. *See their* American inventions and inventors. 1900. p. 270-77.
 295. Wright, H. C. Story of the telegraph. *See her* Children's stories of American progress. 1898. p. 209-28.

Telephone.
  291. Mowry, W. A. *and* A. M. *See their* American inventions and inventors. 1900. p. 286-91.

Texas—*History.*
  488. Brooks, Noah. *See his* Abraham Lincoln. 1901. p. 69-78.
  295. Wright, H. C. Annexation of Texas. *See her* Children's stories of American progress. 1898. p. 229-47.

Thanksgiving.
  401. Field, Eugene. Ezra's Thanksgivin' out West. *See his* Little book of profitable tales. 1901. p. 167-81.
  555. Guerber. H. A. *See his* Story of the thirteen colonies. 1898. p. 113-17.
  298. Holman, Alma. *See her* Massasoit. 1897. p. 107-12.
  96. Smith, N. A. First Thanksgiving day. *See* Wiggin and Smith's Story hour. 1896. p. 103-14.

Themistocles.
  492. Plutarch. See his Lives. 1893. p. 88-105.

Thomas, Theodore.
  509. Marden; O. S. *See his* How they succeeded. 1901. p. 314-26.

Tides.
  634. Dodge, R. E. *See his* Reader in physical geography. 1900. p. 111-13.
  See also Ocean.

Tilden, Samuel Jones.
  516. Brooks, Noah. *See his* Statesmen. 1898. p. 255-80.

Tobacco.
  584. Carpenter, F. G. Raising tobacco. *See his* North America. 1898. p. 104-8.
  292. Gordy, W. F. *See his* American leaders and heroes. 1901. p. 56-58.
  322. Tarr, R. S. *and* McMurry, F. M. *See* Index to their North America. 1901. (*Tarr & McMurry's geographies. Bk. 2.*)

Toledo, *Spain.*
  315. Moulton, L. C. Toledo and Cordova. *See* By land and sea. 1895. p. 27-32.

Trade winds.
    322. Tarr, R. S. *and* McMurry, F. M. *See their* North America. 1901. p. 42-50. (*Tarr & McMurry's geographies. Bk. 2.*)

Transportation.
    330. Fullerton, J. Prairie schooner. *See* Our country: West. 1897.
    291. Mowry, W. A. *and* A. M. *See their* American inventions and inventors. 1900. p. 187-244.
    142. Payne, F. O. Transportation by land and water. *See his* Geographical nature studies. c1898. p. 125-29.
    See also **Commerce; Railroads.**

Trapping.
    379. Wells, H. P. City boys in the woods. 1889.
    See also **Hunting.**

Trees.
    329. Chamberlin, J. E. Great arboretum. *See* Our country: East. 1898. p. 214-18.
    771. Egleston, N. H. Hand-book of tree-planting. 1900.
    330. Lakes, A. *and* Moore, M. V. Petrified big tree; the big trees of California. *See* Our country: West. 1897. p. 112-16; 131-33.
    113. Long, C. C. Forest trees. *See his* Home geography. c1894. p. 99-103.
    773. Shepard, H. H. *See his* Life on the farm. 1901. p. 85-103.
    329. Simpson, C. T. Tree that builds islands. *See* Our country: East. 1898. p. 101-5.
    359. Stokes, Susan. Ten common trees. 1901.
    See also **Arbor-day; Botany; Fruit; Lumbering.**

Trent affair.
    488. Brooks, Noah. *See his* Abraham Lincoln. 1901.

Tripolitan war. (*Fiction.*)
    475. Otis, James. With Preble at Tripoli. 1900.
    276. Seawell, M. E. Decatur and Somers. 1894.

Trojan war.
    486. Baldwin, James. Story of the golden age. 1901.

Troy.
    262. Burt, M. E. *and* Ragozin, Z. A. Odysseus: the hero of Ithaca. 1898.
    267. Clarke, M., *ed.* Story of Troy. 1897.

Truxtun, Thomas.
    521. Seawell, M. E. *See her* Twelve naval captains. 1899. p. 42-52.

Tunnels.
    329. Prout, H. G. St. Clair tunnel. *See* Our country: East. 1898. p. 9-15.

Turpentine.
    584. Carpenter, F. G. Visit to a turpentine farm. *See his* North America. 1898. p. 125-30.
    313. Carroll, S. W. *and* Hart, E. M. *See their* Around the world. Bk. 3. 1901. p. 156-59.

Turks.
    310. Starr, Frederick. *See his* Strange peoples. 1901. p. 60-65.

U. S.—*Commerce.*
    584. Carpenter, F. G. Our foreign commerce. *See his* North America. 1898. p. 65-84.

U. S.—*Constitution.*
    552. Guerber, H. A. *See his* Story of the great Republic. 1899. p. 25-31.

U. S.—*Department of State.*
    598. Conner, E. *See his* Uncle Sam abroad. 1900. p. 11-42.
    430. Drysdale, William. Young consul. 1901.

U. S.—*Treasury, department of.*
    428. Drysdale, William. Treasury club. 1900.

U. S.—*Description and travel.*
    313. Carroll, S. W. *and* Hart, E. M. Around the world. Bk. 3. 1901.
    332. King, C. F. Land we live in. vol. 1. 1892. (*Picturesque geog. readers. Bk. 3.*)
    333. King, C. F. Land we live in. vol. 2. 1893. (*Picturesque geog. readers. Bk. 4.*)
    331. King, C. F. This continent of ours. 1891. (*Picturesque geog. readers. Bk. 2.*)
    329. Our country: East. 1898.
    330. Our country: West. 1897.
    336. Smith, M. C. Our own country. 1898. (*World and its people ser. Bk. 3.*)
    578. Tarr, R. S. *and* McMurry, F. M. *See their* Europe and other continents. 1901. p. 487-516, 523-41. (*Tarr & McMurry's geographies. Bk. 3*)

LIST OF BOOKS FOR TOWNSHIP LIBRARIES.

U. S.—*Description and travel.* (Cont.)

321. Tarr, R. S. *and* McMurry, F. M. See their Home geography. 1901. p. 141-87. (*Tarr & McMurry's geographies. Bk. 1.*)
322. Tarr, R. S. *and* McMurry, F. M. See their North America. 1901. p. 121-349. (*Tarr & McMurry's geographies. Bk. 2.*)
    See also Southern states—*Life;* Western states—*Life;* Names of states.

U. S.—*Description and travel. Bibliography.*

332. King, C. F. See his Land we live in. Vol. 1. 1892. p. 223. (*Picturesque geog. readers. Bk. 3.*)
333. King C. F. See his Land we live in. Vol. 2. 1893. p. 231. (*Picturesque geog. readers. Bk. 4*).

U. S.—*History. General.*

494. Brooks, E. S. Century book of famous Americans. 1896.
507. Brooks, E. S. Historic Americans. 1899.
304. Burton, A. H. Story of our country. 1896.
124. Eggleston, Edward. First book in American history. 1889.
538. Eggleston, Edward. History of the U. S. and its people. 1888.
132. Eggleston, Edward. Stories of American life and adventure. 1895.
133. Eggleston, Edward. Stories of Great Americans for little Americans. 1895.
292. Gordy, W. F. American leaders and heroes. 1901.
552. Guerber, H. A. Story of the great Republic. 1899.
532. Hart, A. B. Formation of the Union. 1898.
503. Lodge, H. C. *and* Roosevelt, Theodore. Hero tales from American history. 1895.
300. McMaster, J. B. Primary history of the United States. 1901.
125. Mowry, W. A. *and* A. M. First steps in the history of our country. 1899.
276. Seawell, M. E. Decatur and Somers. 1894.
301. Scudder, H. E. Short history of the United States. 1890.
272. Stratemeyer, Edward. American boy's life of William McKinley. 1901.
296. Thomas, A. C. Elementary history of the United States. 1901.
539. Thorpe, F. N. History of the United States for junior classes. 1901.
531. Thwaites, R. G. Colonies, 1492-1750. 1898.
533. Wilson, Woodrow. Division and reunion. 1899.
    See also **U. S.,** *Constitution;* **U. S.,** *Politics and government.*

U. S.—*History. Discovery and colonial.*

- 534. Baldwin, James. Conquest of the old Northwest and its settlement by Americans. 1901.
- 535. Baldwin, James. Discovery of the old Northwest and its settlement by the French. 1901.
- 529. Brooks, E. S. Century book of the American colonies. 1900.
- 536. Brooks, Noah. First across the continent. 1901.
- 506. Catherwood, M. H. Heroes of the middle west; the French. 1898.
- 545. Coffin, C. C. Old times in the colonies. 1898.
- 524. Drake, S. A. Border wars of England. 1897.
- 541. Drake, S. A. Making of New England. 1900.
- 542. Drake, S. A. Making of the great west. 1896.
- 543. Drake, S. A. Making of Virginia and the middle colonies. 1893.
- 530. Earle, A. M. Child life in colonial days. 1899.
- 497. Earle, A. M. *ed.* Diary of Anna Green Winslow. 1896.
- 526. Griffis, W. E. Dutch in America. *See his* Brave little Holland. 1894. p. 210–19.
- 555. Guerber, H. A. Story of the thirteen colonies. 1898.
- 130. Hawthorne, Nathaniel. True stories from New England history. 1893. *In* Grandfather's chair.
- 491. Higginson, T. W. Book of American explorers. 1877.
- 298. Holman, Alma. Massasoit. 1897.
- 571. Ingersoll, Ernest. Early voyages and explorations. *See his* Book of the ocean. 1898. p. 39–76.
- 513. Johnson, Henry. New exploits of Myles Standish. 1897.
- 522. Johnson, W. H. World's discoverers. 1900.
- 299. McMurry, Charles. Pioneer history stories of the Mississippi valley. 1894.
- 291. Mowry, W. A. *and* A. M. Colonial homes; Colonial clothing; Transportation. *See their* American inventions and inventors. 1900. p. 24–30; 143–47; 187–99.
- 120. Pratt, M. L. America's story for America's children. Bk. 1. 1901.
- 121. Pratt, M. L. America's story for America's children. Bk. 2. 1901.
- 277. Shaw, E. R. Discoverers and explorers. 1900.
- 531. Thwaites, R. G. Colonies. 1898.
- 563. Warren, H. P., *ed. See his* Stories from English history. 1901. p. 171–87.

See also **Indians of North America.**

U. S.—*History. Discovery and colonial, Bibliography.*
   120. Pratt, M. L. America's story for America's children. Bk. 2.

U. S.—*History. Discovery and colonial. (Fiction.)*
   432. Champney, E. W. Anneke. 1900.
   467. Craddock, C. E. Story of old Fort Loudon. 1899.
   465. Dix, B. M. Soldier Rigdale. 1899.
   442. Hall, Ruth. Golden arrow. 1901.
   238. Plympton, A. G. Flower of the wilderness. 1899.
   241. Wilkins, M. E. In colonial times. 1899.

U. S.—*History. French and Indian war.* See **French and Indian war.**

U. S.—*History. Revolution.*
   294. Brooks, E. S. Century book of the American Revolution. 1897.
   293. Coffin, C. C. Boys of '76. 1876.
   526. Griffis, W. E. Nederland and the American Revolution. *See his* Brave little Holland. 1894. p. 226-34.
   555. Guerber, H. A. *See his* Story of the thirteen colonies. 1898. p. 214-323.
   505. Hall, T. W. Heroes of our Revolution. 1900.
   282. Seawell, M. E. Paul Jones. 1893.
   519. Seelye, E. E. *See her* Story of Washington. 1893. p. 101-326.
   296. Thomas, A. C. *See his* Elementary history of the United States. 1901. p. 187-218.
   549. Tomlinson, E. T. Short history of the American Revolution. 1901.
   305. Tomlinson, E. T. Stories of the American Revolution. Vol. 1. 1897.
   306. Tomlinson, E. T. Stories of the American Revolution. Vol. 2. 1898.
   See also **John Adams; John Quincy Adams; Samuel Adams; Ethan Allen; Benjamin Franklin; Alexander Hamilton; Thomas Jefferson; Lafayette; Gouverneur Morris; Israel Putnam; George Washington.**

U. S.—*History. Revolution. (Fiction.)*
   448. Altsheler, J. A. In hostile red. 1900.
   440. Barnes, James. For king or country. 1898.
   438. Blanchard, A. E. Daughter of freedom. 1900.
   447. Mitchell, S. W. Hugh Wynne, free quaker. 1900.
   464. Stevenson, B. E. Soldier of Virginia. 1901.

U. S.—*History. Revolution. (Fiction.)* (Cont.)
    248. Stoddard, W. O. Noank's log. 1900.
    435. Tomlinson, E. T. Boys of old Monmouth. 1898.
    470. Tomlinson, E. T. Three colonial boys. 1895.
    451. Tomlinson, E. T. In the hands of the red coats. 1900.
    472. Tomlinson, E. T. Three young continentals. 1896.
    473. Tomlinson, E. T. Washington's young aids. 1897.

U. S.—*History. Middle period.*
    527. Coffin, C. C. Building of the nation. 1882.
    542. Drake, S. A. Making of the Great West. 1887.
    532. Hart, A. B. Formation of the Union. 1898.
    307. Thwaites, R. G. Stories of the Badger state. 1900.
    556. Thwaites, R. G. Story of Wisconsin. 1891.
    533. Wilson, Woodrow. Division and reunion. 1899.
    295. Wright, H. C. Children's stories of American progress. 1898.

U. S.—*History. Middle period. (Fiction.)*
    434. Brooks, Noah. Boy emigrants. 1898.
    395. Butterworth, Hezekiah. In the days of Audubon. 1901.
    78. Seawell, M. E. Little Jarvis. 1894.

U. S.—*History. War of 1812.*
    552. Guerber, H. A. *See his* Story of the great Republic. 1899. p. 75–91.
    474. Otis, James. With Porter in the Essex. 1901.
    296. Thomas, A. C. *See his* Elementary history of the United States. 1901. p. 265–76.
    295. Wright, H. C. *See her* Children's stories of American progress. 1898. p. 130–44.

U. S.—*History. War of 1812. (Fiction.)*
    456. Barnes, James. Loyal traitor. 1899.
    478. Barnes, James. Yankee ships and Yankee sailors. 1898.
    289. Otis, James. With Perry on Lake Erie. 1899.
    196. Stoddard, W. O. Jack Morgan: a boy of 1812. 1901.

U. S.—*History. Civil war.*
    308. Blaisdell, A. F., *ed.* Stories of the Civil war. 1890.
    488. Brooks, Noah. *See his* Abraam Lincoln. 1901. p. 90–200.
    559. Champlin, J. D., *jr.* Young folks' history of the war for the Union. 1881.
    558. Fiske, J. War of Independence. 1889.
    557. Forsythe, George. Thrilling days in army life. 1900.
    550. Grigsby, Melvin. Smoked Yank. 1888.

U. S.—*History. Civil war.* (Cont.)
- 552. Guerber, H. A. *See his* Story of the great Republic. 1899. p. 167–236.
- 540. Legler, H. E. *See his* Leading events of Wisconsin history. 1898. p. 244–79.
- 296. Thomas, A. C. *See his* Elementary history of the United States. 1901. p. 318–28.
- 556. Thwaites, R. G. *See his* Story of Wisconsin. 1901. p. 270–329.
- 295. Wright, H. C. *See her* Children's stories of American progress. 1898. p. 299–327.

See also Slavery; David Glasgow Farragut; Ulysses S. Grant; Abraham Lincoln; William Henry Seward; Philip H. Sheridan.

U. S.—*History. Civil war.* (*Fiction.*)
- 445. Barton, W. E. Hero in homespun. 1897.
- 380. Churchill, Winston. Crisis. 1901.
- 233. Page, T. N. Among the camps. 1892.
- 250. Page, T. N. Two little confederates. 1891.

U. S.—*History. Spanish-American war.*
- 551. Brooks, E. S. Story of our war with Spain. 1899.
- 544. Flint, Grover. Marching with Gomez. 1899.
- 292. Gordy, W. F. *See his* American leaders and heroes. 1901. p. 314–26.
- 552. Guerber, H. A. *See his* Story of the great Republic. 1899. p. 304–23.
- 301. Scudder, H. E. *See his* Short history of the United States. 1890. p. 274a–274d.
- 547. Spears, John. Our navy in the war with Spain. 1898.

U. S.—*History. Spanish-American war.* (*Fiction.*)
- 437. Allen, W. B. Cleared for action. 1900.
- 235. Drysdale, William. Cadet Standish of the St. Louis. 1899.

U. S.—*History. Mexican war.*
- 542. Drake, S. A. *See his* Making of the Great West. 1887. p. 241–64.
- 295. Wright, H. C. Mexican war. *See her* Children's stories of American progress. 1898. p. 248–67.

U. S.—*History. Naval.*
    283. Brady, C. T. Reuben, James. 1900.
    502. Johnson, Rossiter. Hero of Manila. 1899.
    289. Otis, James. With Perry on Lake Erie. 1899.
    474. Otis, James. With Porter in the Essex. 1901.
    282. Seawell, M. E. Paul Jones. 1893.
    521. Seawell, M. E. Twelve naval captains. 1899.
    547. Spears, John. Our navy in the war with Spain. 1898.

U. S.—*History. Naval. (Fiction.)*
    437. Allen, W. B. Cleared for action. 1900.

U. S.—*Manufactures.*
    584. Carpenter, F. G. New England—commerce and manufactures. *See his* North America. 1898. p. 76–84.

U. S.—*Mint.*
    584. Carpenter, F. G. Philadelphia—a visit to the mint. *See his* North America. 1898. p. 50–57.
    428. Drysdale, William. Philadelphia mint. *See his* Treasury Club. 1900. p. 248–66.

U. S.—*Navy. (Fiction.)*
    460. Allen, W. B. Navy blue. 1899.
    455. Ogden, Ruth. Loyal hearts and true. 1899.

U. S.—*Politics and government.*
    595. Alton, E. *pseud.* Among the law-makers. 1896.
    528. Brooks, E. S. Century book for young Americans. 1894.
    584. Carpenter, F. G. Visit to the president and to the halls of Congress; Department of the government. *See his* North America. 1898. p. 25–45.
    598. Conner, E. Uncle Sam abroad. 1900.
    594. Dole, C. F. American citizen. 1891.
    596. Giffin, W. M. Civics for young Americans. 1888.
    599. Judson, H. P. Young American. 1897.
    332. King, C. F. Our government; another day in Washington. *See his* Land we live in. Vol. 1. 1892. p. 200–12. (*Picturesque geog. readers. Bk. 3.*)

U. S.—*Politics and government. Bibliography.*
    594. Dole, C. F. Books for reference. *See his* American citizen. 1891. p. 317–20.

Valleys.
    142. Payne, F. O. Valleys. *See his* Geographical nature studies. c1898. p. 36–47.
    321. Tarr, R. S. *and* McMurry, F. M. *See their* Home geography 1901. p. 28–38. (*Tarr & McMurry's geographies. Bk. 1.*)
    See also Erosion; Rivers.

Vasco da Gama.
    522. Johnson, W. H. *See his* World's discoverers. 1900. p. 93–118.

Venice.
    315. Bacon, H. Venetian gondola. *See* By land and sea. 1895. p. 33–36.

Verrazano.
    522. Johnson, W. H. *See his* World's discoverers. 1900. p. 177–88.

Vesuvius, *Mount.*
    588. Singleton, Esther, *ed. See her* Wonders of nature. 1900. p. 25–38.

Vicksburg.
    503. Lodge, H. C. *and* Roosevelt, Theodore. Vicksburg campaign. *See their* Hero tales from American history. 1898. p. 239–48.

Victoria, *Queen.*
    563. Warren, H. P., *ed. See his* Stories from English history. 1901. p. 455–63.

Virgil.
    266. Clarke, M., *ed.* Story of Aeneas. 1898.

Virginia—*History.*
    543. Drake, S. A. Making of Virginia and the middle colonies. 1893.

Volcanoes.
    315. Curtis, W. E. Young and growing mountain. *See* By land and sea. 1895. p. 97–101.
    634. Dodge, R. E. *See his* Reader in physical geography. 1900. p. 154–64.
    322. Tarr, R. S. *and* McMurry, F. M. *See* Index to their North America. 1901. (*Tarr & McMurry's geographies. Bk. 2.*)

Voyages and travels.
   315. By land and sea. 1895.
   139. Carroll, S. W. Around the world. 1897. Bk. 1.
   144. Chaplin, F. P. *and* Humphrey, *Mrs.* F. A. Little folks of other lands. 1882.
   431. Drysdale, William. Young supercargo. 1898.
   588. Singleton, Esther, *ed.* Wonders of nature as seen and described by famous writers. 1900.
   586. Slocum, Joshua. Sailing alone around the world. 1900.
   See also **Arctic regions; Explorers; Geography.**

Vreeland, Herbert H.
   509. Marden, O. S. *See his* How they succeeded. 1901. p. 341-56.

Wallace, *Gen.* **Lew.**
   509. Marden, O. S. *See his* How they succeeded. 1901. p. 241-52.

Walking.
   537. Holmes, O. W. Physiology of walking. 1891. *In* Grandmother's story of Bunker Hill battle.

Wanamaker, John.
   509. Marden, O. S. *See his* How they succeeded. 1901. p. 105-28.

War poetry.
   672. Eggleston, G. C., *ed.* American war ballads and lyrics. 1889.
   673. English, T. D. Boy's book of battle lyrics. 1885.
   537. Holmes, O. W. Grandmother's story of Bunker Hill battle. 1891.
   686. Matthews, Brander. Poems of American patriotism. 1899.

Wars of the Roses.
   563. Warren, H. P., *ed. See his* Stories from English history. 1901. p. 147-55.

Washington, George.
   129. Baldwin, James. *See his* Four great Americans. 1897. p. 9-68.
   498. Bolton, *Mrs.* S. K. *See her* Famous American statesmen. 1888. p. 1-37.
   507. Brooks, E. S. *See his* Historic Americans. 1899. p. 46-59.
   292. Gordy, W. F. *See his* American leaders and heroes. 1901. p. 117-35, 189-210.
   555. Guerber, H. A. *See his* Story of the thirteen colonies. 1898. p. 191-99.
   503. Lodge, H. C. George Washington. *See* Lodge and Roosevelt's Hero tales from American history. 1898. p. 1-15.

Washington, George. (Cont.)
- 519. Seelye, E. E. Story of Washington. 1893.
- 499. Scudder, H. E. George Washington; an historical biography. 1889.
- 301. Scudder, H. E. *See his* Short history of the United States. 1890. p. 149–53.
- 476. Stratemeyer, Edward. With Washington in the west. 1901.
- 520. Thayer, W. M. *See his* Turning points in successful careers. 1895. p. 196–204.
- 296. Thomas, A. C. *See his* Elementary history of the United States. 1901. p. 168–86.

Washington (*City*).
- 528. Brooks, E. S. *See his* Century book for young Americans. 1894. p. 219–34.
- 584. Carpenter, F. G. In our national capital. *See his* North America. 1898. p. 14–24.
- 313. Carroll, S. W. *and* Hart, E. M. *See their* Around the world. Bk. 3. 1901. p. 47–53.

Wasps.
- 612. Gibson, W. H. *See his* Eye spy. 1898. p. 91–103.

Waterfalls.
- 329. Brown, C. Harnessing Niagara. *See* Our country: East. 1898. p. 3–8.

Watt, James.
- 515. Bolton, *Mrs.* S. K. *See her* Boys who became famous. 1885. p. 33–45.
- 504. Towle, G. M. James Watt, the inventor of the steam-engine. *See his* Heroes and martyrs of invention. 1892. p. 103–12.

Weasel.
- 638. Burroughs, John. *See his* Squirrels and other fur-bearers. 1900. p. 72–89.
- 356. Kelly, *Mrs.* M. A. B. Weasels. *See her* Short stories of our shy neighbors. 1896. p. 205–7.

Weather.
- 634. Dodge, R. E. *See his* Reader in physical geography. 1900. p. 171–75.
- 600. Harrington, M. W. About the weather. 1899.

See also **Climate; Winds.**

Weather maps.
- 322. Tarr, R. S. *and* McMurry, F. M. *See their* North America. 1901. p. 56–57. (*Tarr & McMurry's geographies.* Bk. 2.)

Webster, Daniel.
    129. Baldwin, James. *See his* Four great Americans. 1897. p. 125-84.
    498. Bolton, *Mrs.* S. K. *See her* Famous American statesmen. 1888. p. 177-229.
    507. Brooks, E. S. *See his* Historic Americans. 1899. p. 247-62.
    516. Brooks, Noah. *See his* Statesmen. 1898. p. 39-68.
    292. Gordy, W. F. *See his* American leaders and heroes. 1901. p. 265-72.
    552. Guerber, H. A. *See his* Story of the great Republic. 1899. p. 132-39.
    520. Thayer, W. M. *See his* Turning points in successful careers. 1895. p. 17-24.

West, Benjamin.
    207. Hawthorne, Nathaniel. *See his* Little Daffydowndilly. 1887. p. 10-20.

West Indies—*Description and travel.*
    315. Butterworth, Hezekiah *and others*. Sea of the discovery. *See* By land and sea. 1895. p. 113-28.
    593. Kellogg, E. M. C. West Indies-Cuba. *See her* Australia and the islands of the sea. 1898. p. 187-233. (*World and its people series. Bk. 8.*)
    331. King, C. F. West Indies. *See his* This continent of ours. 1891. p. 288-303. (*Picturesque geog. readers. Bk. 2.*)
    566. Ober, F. A. Storied West Indies. 1900.
    322. Tarr, R. S. *and* McMurry, F. M. *See their* North America. 1901. p. 393-98. (*Tarr & McMurry's geographies. Bk. 2.*)

West Indies—*History.*
    566. Ober, F. A. Storied West Indies. 1900.

Western states of U. S.—*Life.*
    376. Doubleday, Russell. Cattle ranch to college. 1899.
    396. Grinnell, G. B. Jack among the Indians. 1900.
    197. Grinnell, G. B. Jack, the young ranchman. 1899.

Western states—*Description and travel.*
    330. Moore, M. V. *and others*. In the southwest; On the plains. *See* Our country: West. 1897. p. 131-256.

Western states—*History.*
    542. Drake, S. A. Making of the great west. 1887.
    295. Wright, H. C. Beginning of western settlement. *See her* Children's stories of American progress. 1898. p. 1-40.

Western states—*History.* (*Fiction.*)
    434. Brooks, Noah. Boy emigrants. 1898.
    See also Indians; Rocky mountains.

Westminster Abbey.
    315. Farrar, F. W. In Westminster Abbey. *See* By land and sea. 1895. p. 6-11.

West Point (*Fiction*).
    373. King, Charles, *Capt.* Cadet days. 1894.

Whales.
    357. Holder, C. F. *See his* Stories of animal life. 1899. p. 73-77.
    291. Mowry, W. A. *and* A. M. Whale oil. *See their* American inventions and inventors. 1900. p. 72-76.

Whaling.
    570. Aldrich, H. L. *See his* Arctic Alaska and Siberia. 1889. p. 90-113.
    331. King, C. F. Whaling. *See his* This continent of ours. 1891. p. 14-20. (*Picturesque geog. readers. Bk. 2.*)

Wheat.
    155. Bradish, S. P. *See her* Stories of country life. 1901. p. 14-17, 147-70.
    584. Carpenter, F. G. Visit to a great wheat farm. *See his* North America. 1898. p. 164-71.
    313. Carroll, S. W. *and* Hart, E. M. Wheat fields. *See their* Around the world. Bk. 3, 1901. p. 76-81.
    142. Payne, F. O. Study of a food grain-wheat. *See his* Geographical nature studies. c1898. p. 104.
    767. Sargent, F. L. *See his* Corn plants. 1899. p. 75-79.
    See also Grain.

Whitney, Eli.
    507. Brooks, E. S. *See his* Historic Americans. 1899. p. 218-30.
    126. Perry, F. M. *See her* Four American inventors. 1901. p. 73-130.
    520. Thayer, W. M. *See his* Turning points in successful careers. 1895. p. 403-10.

Whittier, John Greenleaf.
    279. Cody, Sherwin. *See his* Four great American poets. 1899. p. 133-92.
    285. Ware, E. R. *See her* Talks about Authors and their work. 1899. p. 87-99.

Wilberforce, William.
    520. Thayer, W. M. *See his* Turning points in successful careers. 1895. p. 181–87.

Willard, Frances.
    285. Ware, E. R. *See her* Talks about Authors and their work. 1899. p. 149–51.

William the Conqueror.
    450. Tappan, E. M. In the days of William the Conqueror. 1901.

Williams, Eleazer.
    441. Brooks, E. S. Godson of Lafayette. 1900.
    540. Legler, H. E. Strange story of a spurious prince. *See his* Leading events of Wisconsin history. 1898. p. 235–41.

Williams, Roger.
    541. Drake, S. A. *See his* Making of New England. 1900. p. 194–99.
    292. Gordy, W. F. *See his* American leaders and heroes. 1901. p. 81–91.
    555. Guerber, H. A. *See his* Story of the thirteen colonies. 1898. p. 127–34.
    442. Hall, Ruth. Golden arrow. 1901.

Williamson, Peter.
    548. Lang, Andrew, *ed. See his* Red true story book. 1897. p. 108–19.

Wilson, Henry.
    520. Thayer, W. M. *See his* Turning points in successful careers. 1895. p. 247–56.

Winds.
    600. Harrington, M. W. *See his* About the weather. 1899. p. 48–59.
    331. King, C. F. Rain and wind. *See his* This continent of ours. 1891. p. 90–98. (*Picturesque geog. readers. Bk. 2.*)
    315. Underwood, E. B. Trade wind. *See* By land and sea. 1895. p. 210–13.

Winthrop, John.
    507. Brooks, E. S. *See his* Historic Americans. 1899. p. 1–17.

Wireless telegraphy.
    610. Baker, R. S. *See his* Boy's book of inventions. 1899. p. 79–117.

Wisconsin—*History.*
    540. Legler, H. E. Leading events of Wisconsin history: the story of the state. 1898.
    307. Thwaites, R. G. Stories of the Badger State. 1900.
    556. Thwaites, R. G. Story of Wisconsin. 1891.

Witchcraft.
    555. Guerber, H. A. *See his* Story of the thirteen colonies. 1898. p. 170–73.

Wolfe, James.
    292. Gordy, W. F. *See his* American leaders and heroes. 1901. p. 136–45.

Wolverine.
    358. Schwatka, Frederick. Arctic wolverine. *See* Talks about animals. 1895. p. 249–56.

Wood-chuck.
    638. Burroughs, John. *See his* Squirrels and other fur-bearers. 1900. p. 32–37.

Wool.
    332. King, C. F. Suit of clothes. *See his* Land we live in. Vol. 1. 1892. p. 189–94. (*Picturesque geog. readers. Bk. 3.*)
    291. Mowry, W. A. *and* A. M. *See their* American inventions and inventors. 1900. p. 158–63.
    See also **Sheep.**

World and its people series. Dunton, Larkin, *ed.*
    336. Smith, Minna C. Our own country. 1898. Bk. 3.
    589. Coe, Fannie E. Our American neighbors. 1897. Bk. 4.
    590. Coe, F. E. Modern Europe. 1898. Bk. 5.
    591. Smith, Mary Cate. Life in Asia. 1898. Bk. 6.
    592. Badlam, Anna B. Views in Africa. 1898. Bk. 7.
    593. Kellogg, E. M. C. Australia and the islands of the sea. 1898. Bk. 8.
    580. Twombly, A. S. Hawaii and its people. 1900. Bk. 9.
    337. Markwick, W. F. *and* Smith, Wm. South American republics. 1901 Bk. 10.

World's Fairs.
    552. Guerber, H. A. *See his* Story of the great Republic. 1899. p. 151–56, 300–304.

Writing.
    752. Arnold, S. L., *ed*. *See her* Plans for busy work. 1901. p. 134-39.
    See also **Paper.**

Yachting.
    571. Ingersoll, Ernest. Yachting and pleasure boating. *See his* Book of the ocean. 1899. p. 187-201.
    See also **Boating.**

Yellowstone park.
    330. Anderson, G. S. *and* Stephens, C. A. Visiting the Yellowstone park. *See* Our country: West. 1897. p. 78-85.
    584. Carpenter, F. G. Yellowstone national park. *See his* North America. 1898. p. 284-90.
    313. Carroll, S. W. *and* Hart, E. M. *See their* Around the world. Bk. 3. 1901. p. 144-46.
    331. King, C. F. Wonderland. *See his* This continent of ours. 1891. p. 47-57. (*Picturesque geog. readers. Bk. 2.*)
    588. Singleton, Esther, *ed*. *See her* Wonders of nature. 1900. p. 352-66.

Zenobia.
    508. Brooks, E. S. *See his* Historic girls. 1887. p. 1-20.

Zinc.
    313. Carroll, S. W. *and* Hart, E. M. Zinc mining, Missouri. *See their* Around the world. Bk. 3. 1901. p. 86-88.

Zoology.
    611. Beard, J. C. Curious homes and their tenants. 1897.
    645. Du Chaillu, Paul. World of the great forest. 1900.
    602. Garner, L. Apes and monkeys. 1900.
    627. Grinnell, Morton. Neighbours of field, wood and stream. c1901.
    768. Henry, W. A. Mastication, digestion, etc. *See his* Feeds and feeding. 1898. p. 11-118.
    644. Ingersoll, Ernest. Wild neighbors; out-door studies in the U. S. 1897.
    356. Kelly, *Mrs*. M. A. B. Short studies of our shy neighbors. 1896.
    330. Lakes, A. Some Rocky Mt. animals. *See* Our country: West. 1897. p. 96-101.
    355. Long, W. J. Secrets of the woods. 1901.
    360. Long, W. J. Ways of the wood folk. 1899.

Zoology. (Cont.)
- 361. Long, W. J. Wilderness ways. 1901.
- 618. Miller, O. T. Four handed folk. 1897.
- 348. Miller, O. T. Little folks in feathers and furs. 1891.
- 156. Pierson, C. D. Among the farmyard people. 1899.
- 157. Pierson, C. D. Among the forest people. 1898.
- 158. Pierson, C. D. Among the meadow people. 1897.
- 159. Pierson, C. D. Among the pond people. 1901.
- 626. Weed, C. M. Nature biographies. 1901.
- 617. Wright, M. O. Four-footed Americans and their kin. 1898.
- 358. Talks about animals. 1895.

See also **Birds; Fish; Insects; Reptiles.**

GENERAL INDEX.

	Page
Abbreviations	14
Author Index	186
Books	
Agriculture	183
Amateur plays	174
Amusement, games, and sports	171
Arts, Fine	157
Biography, Middle Form	70
Biography, Primary Form	35
Biography, Upper Form	119
Civics, Upper Form	144
Collections, Literature: Middle Form	94
Collections, Literature: Upper Form	160
Cookery	172
Drama, Upper Form	159
Encyclopaedias	175
Essays, Upper Form	159
Fairy Stories, Folk-stories, Myths, and Legends: Middle Form	63
Fairy Stories, Folk-stories, Myths, and Legends: Primary Form	31
Fiction, Middle Form	47
Fiction, (Historical) Middle Form	59
Fiction, Primary Form	23
Fiction, Upper Form	96
Fiction, (Historical) Upper Form	109
First books for children's reading	16
Geography, Middle Form	79
Geography, Primary Form	40
Geography, Upper Form	137
History, Middle Form	74
History, Primary Form	35
History, Upper Form	127
Middle Form	47
Miscellaneous	171
Myths and Legends, Upper Form	117

	Page
Books (Continued)	
New books added in 1902	12
Nursery rhymes and jingles	20
Ordering of	12
Pedagogical stories	181
Picture books	15
Poetry	162
Primary Form	15
Rates to school officers and teachers	15
Science, Middle Form	87
Science, Primary Form	44
Science, Upper Form	146
Selection of	9
Song books	176
Teachers, books for	178
Travel, See Geography	137
Upper Form	96
Library Law	3
Periodicals	185
Subject Index	227
Title Index	186